Lecture Notes in Computer Science 9905

Commenced Publication in 1973
Founding and Former Series Editors:
Gerhard Goos, Juris Hartmanis, and Jan van Leeuwen

T0189107

More information about this series at http://www.springer.com/series/7412

Bastian Leibe · Jiri Matas
Nicu Sebe · Max Welling (Eds.)

Computer Vision – ECCV 2016

14th European Conference
Amsterdam, The Netherlands, October 11–14, 2016
Proceedings, Part I

 Springer

Editors
Bastian Leibe
RWTH Aachen
Aachen
Germany

Jiri Matas
Czech Technical University
Prague 2
Czech Republic

Nicu Sebe
University of Trento
Povo - Trento
Italy

Max Welling
University of Amsterdam
Amsterdam
The Netherlands

ISSN 0302-9743   ISSN 1611-3349   (electronic)
Lecture Notes in Computer Science
ISBN 978-3-319-46447-3   ISBN 978-3-319-46448-0   (eBook)
DOI 10.1007/978-3-319-46448-0

Library of Congress Control Number: 2016951693

LNCS Sublibrary: SL6 – Image Processing, Computer Vision, Pattern Recognition, and Graphics

Printed on acid-free paper

This Springer imprint is published by Springer Nature
The registered company is Springer International Publishing AG
The registered company address is: Gewerbestrasse 11, 6330 Cham, Switzerland

Foreword

Welcome to the proceedings of the 2016 edition of the European Conference on Computer Vision held in Amsterdam! It is safe to say that the European Conference on Computer Vision is one of the top conferences in computer vision. It is good to reiterate the history of the conference to see the broad base the conference has built in its 13 editions. First held in 1990 in Antibes (France), it was followed by subsequent conferences in Santa Margherita Ligure (Italy) in 1992, Stockholm (Sweden) in 1994, Cambridge (UK) in 1996, Freiburg (Germany) in 1998, Dublin (Ireland) in 2000, Copenhagen (Denmark) in 2002, Prague (Czech Republic) in 2004, Graz (Austria) in 2006, Marseille (France) in 2008, Heraklion (Greece) in 2010, Florence (Italy) in 2012, and Zürich (Switzerland) in 2014.

For the 14th edition, many people worked hard to provide attendees with a most warm welcome while enjoying the best science. The Program Committee, Bastian Leibe, Jiri Matas, Nicu Sebe, and Max Welling, did an excellent job. Apart from the scientific program, the workshops were selected and handled by Hervé Jégou and Gang Hua, and the tutorials by Jacob Verbeek and Rita Cucchiara. Thanks for the great job. The coordination with the subsequent ACM Multimedia offered an opportunity to expand the tutorials with an additional invited session, offered by the University of Amsterdam and organized together with the help of ACM Multimedia.

Of the many people who worked hard as local organizers, we would like to single out Martine de Wit of the UvA Conference Office, who delicately and efficiently organized the main body. Also the local organizers Hamdi Dibeklioglu, Efstratios Gavves, Jan van Gemert, Thomas Mensink, and Mihir Jain had their hands full. As a venue, we chose the Royal Theatre Carré located on the canals of the Amstel River in downtown Amsterdam. Space in Amsterdam is sparse, so it was a little tighter than usual. The university lent us their downtown campuses for the tutorials and the workshops. A relatively new thing was the industry and the sponsors for which Ronald Poppe and Peter de With did a great job, while Andy Bagdanov and John Schavemaker arranged the demos. Michael Wilkinson took care to make Yom Kippur as comfortable as possible for those for whom it is an important day. We thank Marc Pollefeys, Alberto del Bimbo, and Virginie Mes for their advice and help behind the scenes. We thank all the anonymous volunteers for their hard and precise work. We also thank our generous sponsors. Their support is an essential part of the program. It is good to see such a level of industrial interest in what our community is doing!

Amsterdam does not need any introduction. Please emerge yourself but do not drown in it, have a nice time.

October 2016

Theo Gevers
Arnold Smeulders

Preface

Welcome to the proceedings of the 2016 European Conference on Computer Vision (ECCV 2016) held in Amsterdam, The Netherlands. We are delighted to present this volume reflecting a strong and exciting program, the result of an extensive review process. In total, we received 1,561 paper submissions. Of these, 81 violated the ECCV submission guidelines or did not pass the plagiarism test and were rejected without review. We employed the iThenticate software (www.ithenticate.com) for plagiarism detection. Of the remaining papers, 415 were accepted (26.6 %): 342 as posters (22.6 %), 45 as spotlights (2.9 %), and 28 as oral presentations (1.8 %). The spotlights – short, five-minute podium presentations – are novel to ECCV and were introduced after their success at the CVPR 2016 conference. All orals and spotlights are presented as posters as well. The selection process was a combined effort of four program co-chairs (PCs), 74 area chairs (ACs), 1,086 Program Committee members, and 77 additional reviewers.

As PCs, we were primarily responsible for the design and execution of the review process. Beyond administrative rejections, we were involved in acceptance decisions only in the very few cases where the ACs were not able to agree on a decision. PCs, as is customary in the field, were not allowed to co-author a submission. General co-chairs and other co-organizers played no role in the review process, were permitted to submit papers, and were treated as any other author.

Acceptance decisions were made by two independent ACs. There were 74 ACs, selected by the PCs according to their technical expertise, experience, and geographical diversity (41 from European, five from Asian, two from Australian, and 26 from North American institutions). The ACs were aided by 1,086 Program Committee members to whom papers were assigned for reviewing. There were 77 additional reviewers, each supervised by a Program Committee member. The Program Committee was selected from committees of previous ECCV, ICCV, and CVPR conferences and was extended on the basis of suggestions from the ACs and the PCs. Having a large pool of Program Committee members for reviewing allowed us to match expertise while bounding reviewer loads. Typically five papers, but never more than eight, were assigned to a Program Committee member. Graduate students had a maximum of four papers to review.

The ECCV 2016 review process was in principle double-blind. Authors did not know reviewer identities, nor the ACs handling their paper(s). However, anonymity becomes difficult to maintain as more and more submissions appear concurrently on arXiv.org. This was not against the ECCV 2016 double submission rules, which followed the practice of other major computer vision conferences in the recent past. The existence of arXiv publications, mostly not peer-reviewed, raises difficult problems with the assessment of unpublished, concurrent, and prior art, content overlap, plagiarism, and self-plagiarism. Moreover, it undermines the anonymity of submissions. We found that not all cases can be covered by a simple set of rules. Almost all controversies during the review process were related to the arXiv issue. Most of the reviewer inquiries were resolved by giving the benefit of the doubt to ECCV authors. However, the problem will have to be discussed by the community so that consensus is found on how to handle the issues brought by publishing on arXiv.

Particular attention was paid to handling conflicts of interest. Conflicts of interest between ACs, Program Committee members, and papers were identified based on the authorship of ECCV 2016 submissions, on the home institutions, and on previous collaborations of all researchers involved. To find institutional conflicts, all authors, Program Committee members, and ACs were asked to list the Internet domains of their current institutions. To find collaborators, the Researcher.cc database (http://researcher.cc/), funded by the Computer Vision Foundation, was used to find any co-authored papers in the period 2012–2016. We pre-assigned approximately 100 papers to each AC, based on affinity scores from the Toronto Paper Matching System. ACs then bid on these, indicating their level of expertise. Based on these bids, and conflicts of interest, approximately 40 papers were assigned to each AC. The ACs then suggested seven reviewers from the pool of Program Committee members for each paper, in ranked order, from which three were chosen automatically by CMT (Microsofts Academic Conference Management Service), taking load balancing and conflicts of interest into account.

The initial reviewing period was five weeks long, after which reviewers provided reviews with preliminary recommendations. With the generous help of several last-minute reviewers, each paper received three reviews. Submissions with all three reviews suggesting rejection were independently checked by two ACs and if they agreed, the manuscript was rejected at this stage ("early rejects"). In total, 334 manuscripts (22.5 %) were early-rejected, reducing the average AC load to about 30.

Authors of the remaining submissions were then given the opportunity to rebut the reviews, primarily to identify factual errors. Following this, reviewers and ACs discussed papers at length, after which reviewers finalized their reviews and gave a final recommendation to the ACs. Each manuscript was evaluated independently by two ACs who were not aware of each others, identities. In most of the cases, after extensive discussions, the two ACs arrived at a common decision, which was always adhered to by the PCs. In the very few borderline cases where an agreement was not reached, the PCs acted as tie-breakers. Owing to the rapid expansion of the field, which led to an unexpectedly large increase in the number of submissions, the size of the venue became a limiting factor and a hard upper bound on the number of accepted papers had to be imposed. We were able to increase the limit by replacing one oral session by a poster session. Nevertheless, this forced the PCs to reject some borderline papers that could otherwise have been accepted.

We want to thank everyone involved in making the ECCV 2016 possible. First and foremost, the success of ECCV 2016 depended on the quality of papers submitted by the authors, and on the very hard work of the ACs, the Program Committee members, and the additional reviewers. We are particularly grateful to Rene Vidal for his continuous support and sharing experience from organizing ICCV 2015, to Laurent Charlin for the use of the Toronto Paper Matching System, to Ari Kobren for the use of the Researcher.cc tools, to the Computer Vision Foundation (CVF) for facilitating the use of the iThenticate plagiarism detection software, and to Gloria Zen and Radu-Laurentiu Vieriu for setting up CMT and managing the various tools involved. We also owe a debt of gratitude for the support of the Amsterdam local organizers, especially Hamdi Dibeklioglu for keeping the website always up to date. Finally, the preparation of these proceedings would not have been possible without the diligent effort of the publication chairs, Albert Ali Salah and Robby Tan, and of Anna Kramer from Springer.

October 2016

Bastian Leibe
Jiri Matas
Nicu Sebe
Max Welling

Organization

General Chairs

Theo Gevers — University of Amsterdam, The Netherlands
Arnold Smeulders — University of Amsterdam, The Netherlands

Program Committee Co-chairs

Bastian Leibe — RWTH Aachen, Germany
Jiri Matas — Czech Technical University, Czech Republic
Nicu Sebe — University of Trento, Italy
Max Welling — University of Amsterdam, The Netherlands

Honorary Chair

Jan Koenderink — Delft University of Technology, The Netherlands
and KU Leuven, Belgium

Advisory Program Chair

Luc van Gool — ETH Zurich, Switzerland

Advisory Workshop Chair

Josef Kittler — University of Surrey, UK

Advisory Conference Chair

Alberto del Bimbo — University of Florence, Italy

Local Arrangements Chairs

Hamdi Dibeklioglu — Delft University of Technology, The Netherlands
Efstratios Gavves — University of Amsterdam, The Netherlands
Jan van Gemert — Delft University of Technology, The Netherlands
Thomas Mensink — University of Amsterdam, The Netherlands
Michael Wilkinson — University of Groningen, The Netherlands

Workshop Chairs

Hervé Jégou   Facebook AI Research, USA
Gang Hua   Microsoft Research Asia, China

Tutorial Chairs

Jacob Verbeek   Inria Grenoble, France
Rita Cucchiara   University of Modena and Reggio Emilia, Italy

Poster Chairs

Jasper Uijlings   University of Edinburgh, UK
Roberto Valenti   Sightcorp, The Netherlands

Publication Chairs

Albert Ali Salah   Boğaziçi University, Turkey
Robby T. Tan   Yale-NUS College and National University
                               of Singapore, Singapore

Video Chair

Mihir Jain   University of Amsterdam, The Netherlands

Demo Chairs

John Schavemaker   Twnkls, The Netherlands
Andy Bagdanov   University of Florence, Italy

Social Media Chair

Efstratios Gavves   University of Amsterdam, The Netherlands

Industrial Liaison Chairs

Ronald Poppe   Utrecht University, The Netherlands
Peter de With   Eindhoven University of Technology, The Netherlands

Conference Coordinator, Accommodation, and Finance

Conference Office
Martine de Wit   University of Amsterdam, The Netherlands
Melanie Venverloo   University of Amsterdam, The Netherlands
Niels Klein   University of Amsterdam, The Netherlands

Area Chairs

Radhakrishna Achanta	Ecole Polytechnique Fédérale de Lausanne, Switzerland
Antonis Argyros	FORTH and University of Crete, Greece
Michael Bronstein	Universitá della Svizzera Italiana, Switzerland
Gabriel Brostow	University College London, UK
Thomas Brox	University of Freiburg, Germany
Barbara Caputo	Sapienza University of Rome, Italy
Miguel Carreira-Perpinan	University of California, Merced, USA
Ondra Chum	Czech Technical University, Czech Republic
Daniel Cremers	Technical University of Munich, Germany
Rita Cucchiara	University of Modena and Reggio Emilia, Italy
Trevor Darrell	University of California, Berkeley, USA
Andrew Davison	Imperial College London, UK
Fernando de la Torre	Carnegie Mellon University, USA
Piotr Dollar	Facebook AI Research, USA
Vittorio Ferrari	University of Edinburgh, UK
Charless Fowlkes	University of California, Irvine, USA
Jan-Michael Frahm	University of North Carolina at Chapel Hill, USA
Mario Fritz	Max Planck Institute, Germany
Pascal Fua	Ecole Polytechnique Fédérale de Lausanne, Switzerland
Juergen Gall	University of Bonn, Germany
Peter Gehler	University of Tübingen — Max Planck Institute, Germany
Andreas Geiger	Max Planck Institute, Germany
Ross Girshick	Facebook AI Research, USA
Kristen Grauman	University of Texas at Austin, USA
Abhinav Gupta	Carnegie Mellon University, USA
Hervé Jégou	Facebook AI Research, USA
Fredrik Kahl	Lund University, Sweden
Iasonas Kokkinos	Ecole Centrale Paris, France
Philipp Krähenbühl	University of California, Berkeley, USA
Pawan Kumar	University of Oxford, UK
Christoph Lampert	Institute of Science and Technology Austria, Austria
Hugo Larochelle	Université de Sherbrooke, Canada
Neil Lawrence	University of Sheffield, UK
Svetlana Lazebnik	University of Illinois at Urbana-Champaign, USA
Honglak Lee	Stanford University, USA
Kyoung Mu Lee	Seoul National University, Republic of Korea
Vincent Lepetit	Graz University of Technology, Austria
Hongdong Li	Australian National University, Australia
Julien Mairal	Inria, France
Yasuyuki Matsushita	Osaka University, Japan
Nassir Navab	Technical University of Munich, Germany

Sebastian Nowozin	Microsoft Research, Cambridge, UK
Tomas Pajdla	Czech Technical University, Czech Republic
Maja Pantic	Imperial College London, UK
Devi Parikh	Virginia Tech, USA
Thomas Pock	Graz University of Technology, Austria
Elisa Ricci	FBK Technologies of Vision, Italy
Bodo Rosenhahn	Leibniz-University of Hannover, Germany
Stefan Roth	Technical University of Darmstadt, Germany
Carsten Rother	Technical University of Dresden, Germany
Silvio Savarese	Stanford University, USA
Bernt Schiele	Max Planck Institute, Germany
Konrad Schindler	ETH Zürich, Switzerland
Cordelia Schmid	Inria, France
Cristian Sminchisescu	Lund University, Sweden
Noah Snavely	Cornell University, USA
Sabine Süsstrunk	Ecole Polytechnique Fédérale de Lausanne, Switzerland
Qi Tian	University of Texas at San Antonio, USA
Antonio Torralba	Massachusetts Institute of Technology, USA
Zhuowen Tu	University of California, San Diego, USA
Raquel Urtasun	University of Toronto, Canada
Joost van de Weijer	Universitat Autònoma de Barcelona, Spain
Laurens van der Maaten	Facebook AI Research, USA
Nuno Vasconcelos	University of California, San Diego, USA
Andrea Vedaldi	University of Oxford, UK
Xiaogang Wang	Chinese University of Hong Kong, Hong Kong, SAR China
Jingdong Wang	Microsoft Research Asia, China
Lior Wolf	Tel Aviv University, Israel
Ying Wu	Northwestern University, USA
Dong Xu	University of Sydney, Australia
Shuicheng Yan	National University of Singapore, Singapore
MingHsuan Yang	University of California, Merced, USA
Ramin Zabih	Cornell NYC Tech, USA
Larry Zitnick	Facebook AI Research, USA

Technical Program Committee

Austin Abrams	Pulkit Agrawal	Andrea Albarelli
Supreeth Achar	Jorgen Ahlberg	Alexandra Albu
Tameem Adel	Haizhou Ai	Saad Ali
Khurrum Aftab	Zeynep Akata	Daniel Aliaga
Lourdes Agapito	Ijaz Akhter	Marina Alterman
Sameer Agarwal	Karteek Alahari	Hani Altwaijry
Aishwarya Agrawal	Xavier Alameda-Pineda	Jose M. Alvarez

Mitsuru Ambai
Mohamed Amer
Senjian An
Cosmin Ancuti
Juan Andrade-Cetto
Marco Andreetto
Elli Angelopoulou
Relja Arandjelovic
Helder Araujo
Pablo Arbelaez
Chetan Arora
Carlos Arteta
Kalle Astroem
Nikolay Atanasov
Vassilis Athitsos
Mathieu Aubry
Yannis Avrithis
Hossein Azizpour
Artem Babenko
Andrew Bagdanov
Yuval Bahat
Xiang Bai
Lamberto Ballan
Arunava Banerjee
Adrian Barbu
Nick Barnes
Peter Barnum
Jonathan Barron
Adrien Bartoli
Dhruv Batra
Eduardo
    Bayro-Corrochano
Jean-Charles Bazin
Paul Beardsley
Vasileios Belagiannis
Ismail Ben Ayed
Boulbaba Benamor
Abhijit Bendale
Rodrigo Benenson
Fabian Benitez-Quiroz
Ohad Ben-Shahar
Dana Berman
Lucas Beyer
Subhabrata Bhattacharya
Binod Bhattarai
Arnav Bhavsar

Simone Bianco
Hakan Bilen
Horst Bischof
Tom Bishop
Arijit Biswas
Soma Biswas
Marten Bjoerkman
Volker Blanz
Federica Bogo
Xavier Boix
Piotr Bojanowski
Terrance Boult
Katie Bouman
Thierry Bouwmans
Edmond Boyer
Yuri Boykov
Hakan Boyraz
Steven Branson
Mathieu Bredif
Francois Bremond
Stefan Breuers
Michael Brown
Marcus Brubaker
Luc Brun
Andrei Bursuc
Zoya Bylinskii
Daniel Cabrini Hauagge
Deng Cai
Jianfei Cai
Simone Calderara
Neill Campbell
Octavia Camps
Liangliang Cao
Xiaochun Cao
Xun Cao
Gustavo Carneiro
Dan Casas
Tom Cashman
Umberto Castellani
Carlos Castillo
Andrea Cavallaro
Jan Cech
Ayan Chakrabarti
Rudrasis Chakraborty
Krzysztof Chalupka
Tat-Jen Cham

Antoni Chan
Manmohan Chandraker
Sharat Chandran
Hong Chang
Hyun Sung Chang
Jason Chang
Ju Yong Chang
Xiaojun Chang
Yu-Wei Chao
Visesh Chari
Rizwan Chaudhry
Rama Chellappa
Bo Chen
Chao Chen
Chao-Yeh Chen
Chu-Song Chen
Hwann-Tzong Chen
Lin Chen
Mei Chen
Terrence Chen
Xilin Chen
Yunjin Chen
Guang Chen
Qifeng Chen
Xinlei Chen
Jian Cheng
Ming-Ming Cheng
Anoop Cherian
Guilhem Cheron
Dmitry Chetverikov
Liang-Tien Chia
Naoki Chiba
Tat-Jun Chin
Margarita Chli
Minsu Cho
Sunghyun Cho
TaeEun Choe
Jongmoo Choi
Seungjin Choi
Wongun Choi
Wen-Sheng Chu
Yung-Yu Chuang
Albert Chung
Gokberk Cinbis
Arridhana Ciptadi
Javier Civera

James Clark
Brian Clipp
Michael Cogswell
Taco Cohen
Toby Collins
John Collomosse
Camille Couprie
David Crandall
Marco Cristani
James Crowley
Jinshi Cui
Yin Cui
Jifeng Dai
Qieyun Dai
Shengyang Dai
Yuchao Dai
Zhenwen Dai
Dima Damen
Kristin Dana
Kostas Danilidiis
Mohamed Daoudi
Larry Davis
Teofilo de Campos
Marleen de Bruijne
Koichiro Deguchi
Alessio Del Bue
Luca del Pero
Antoine Deleforge
Hervé Delingette
David Demirdjian
Jia Deng
Joachim Denzler
Konstantinos Derpanis
Frederic Devernay
Hamdi Dibeklioglu
Santosh Kumar Divvala
Carl Doersch
Weisheng Dong
Jian Dong
Gianfranco Doretto
Alexey Dosovitskiy
Matthijs Douze
Bruce Draper
Tom Drummond
Shichuan Du
Jean-Luc Dugelay

Enrique Dunn
Zoran Duric
Pinar Duygulu
Alexei Efros
Carl Henrik Ek
Jan-Olof Eklundh
Jayan Eledath
Ehsan Elhamifar
Ian Endres
Aykut Erdem
Anders Eriksson
Sergio Escalera
Victor Escorcia
Francisco Estrada
Bin Fan
Quanfu Fan
Chen Fang
Tian Fang
Masoud Faraki
Ali Farhadi
Giovanni Farinella
Ryan Farrell
Raanan Fattal
Michael Felsberg
Jiashi Feng
Michele Fenzi
Andras Ferencz
Basura Fernando
Sanja Fidler
Mario Figueiredo
Michael Firman
Robert Fisher
John Fisher III
Alexander Fix
Boris Flach
Matt Flagg
Francois Fleuret
Wolfgang Foerstner
David Fofi
Gianluca Foresti
Per-Erik Forssen
David Fouhey
Jean-Sebastien Franco
Friedrich Fraundorfer
Oren Freifeld
Simone Frintrop

Huazhu Fu
Yun Fu
Jan Funke
Brian Funt
Ryo Furukawa
Yasutaka Furukawa
Andrea Fusiello
David Gallup
Chuang Gan
Junbin Gao
Jochen Gast
Stratis Gavves
Xin Geng
Bogdan Georgescu
David Geronimo
Bernard Ghanem
Riccardo Gherardi
Golnaz Ghiasi
Soumya Ghosh
Andrew Gilbert
Ioannis Gkioulekas
Georgia Gkioxari
Guy Godin
Roland Goecke
Boqing Gong
Shaogang Gong
Yunchao Gong
German Gonzalez
Jordi Gonzalez
Paulo Gotardo
Stephen Gould
Venu M. Govindu
Helmut Grabner
Etienne Grossmann
Chunhui Gu
David Gu
Sergio Guadarrama
Li Guan
Matthieu Guillaumin
Jean-Yves Guillemaut
Guodong Guo
Ruiqi Guo
Yanwen Guo
Saurabh Gupta
Pierre Gurdjos
Diego Gutierrez

Abner Guzman Rivera
Christian Haene
Niels Haering
Ralf Haeusler
David Hall
Peter Hall
Onur Hamsici
Dongfeng Han
Mei Han
Xufeng Han
Yahong Han
Ankur Handa
Kenji Hara
Tatsuya Harada
Mehrtash Harandi
Bharath Hariharan
Tal Hassner
Soren Hauberg
Michal Havlena
Tamir Hazan
Junfeng He
Kaiming He
Lei He
Ran He
Xuming He
Zhihai He
Felix Heide
Janne Heikkila
Jared Heinly
Mattias Heinrich
Pierre Hellier
Stephane Herbin
Isabelle Herlin
Alexander Hermans
Anders Heyden
Adrian Hilton
Vaclav Hlavac
Minh Hoai
Judy Hoffman
Steven Hoi
Derek Hoiem
Seunghoon Hong
Byung-Woo Hong
Anthony Hoogs
Yedid Hoshen
Winston Hsu

Changbo Hu
Wenze Hu
Zhe Hu
Gang Hua
Dong Huang
Gary Huang
Heng Huang
Jia-Bin Huang
Kaiqi Huang
Qingming Huang
Rui Huang
Xinyu Huang
Weilin Huang
Zhiwu Huang
Ahmad Humayun
Mohamed Hussein
Wonjun Hwang
Juan Iglesias
Nazli Ikizler-Cinbis
Evren Imre
Eldar Insafutdinov
Catalin Ionescu
Go Irie
Hossam Isack
Phillip Isola
Hamid Izadinia
Nathan Jacobs
Varadarajan Jagannadan
Aastha Jain
Suyog Jain
Varun Jampani
Jeremy Jancsary
C.V. Jawahar
Dinesh Jayaraman
Ian Jermyn
Hueihan Jhuang
Hui Ji
Qiang Ji
Jiaya Jia
Kui Jia
Yangqing Jia
Hao Jiang
Tingting Jiang
Yu-Gang Jiang
Zhuolin Jiang
Alexis Joly

Shantanu Joshi
Frederic Jurie
Achuta Kadambi
Samuel Kadoury
Yannis Kalantidis
Amit Kale
Sebastian Kaltwang
Joni-Kristian Kamarainen
George Kamberov
Chandra Kambhamettu
Martin Kampel
Kenichi Kanatani
Atul Kanaujia
Melih Kandemir
Zhuoliang Kang
Mohan Kankanhalli
Abhishek Kar
Leonid Karlinsky
Andrej Karpathy
Zoltan Kato
Rei Kawakami
Kristian Kersting
Margret Keuper
Nima Khademi Kalantari
Sameh Khamis
Fahad Khan
Aditya Khosla
Hadi Kiapour
Edward Kim
Gunhee Kim
Hansung Kim
Jae-Hak Kim
Kihwan Kim
Seon Joo Kim
Tae Hyun Kim
Tae-Kyun Kim
Vladimir Kim
Benjamin Kimia
Akisato Kimura
Durk Kingma
Thomas Kipf
Kris Kitani
Martin Kleinsteuber
Laurent Kneip
Kevin Koeser
Effrosyni Kokiopoulou

Piotr Koniusz
Theodora Kontogianni
Sanjeev Koppal
Dimitrios Kosmopoulos
Adriana Kovashka
Adarsh Kowdle
Michael Kramp
Josip Krapac
Jonathan Krause
Pavel Krsek
Hilde Kuehne
Shiro Kumano
Avinash Kumar
Sebastian Kurtek
Kyros Kutulakos
Suha Kwak
In So Kweon
Roland Kwitt
Junghyun Kwon
Junseok Kwon
Jan Kybic
Jorma Laaksonen
Alexander Ladikos
Florent Lafarge
Pierre-Yves Laffont
Wei-Sheng Lai
Jean-Francois Lalonde
Michael Langer
Oswald Lanz
Agata Lapedriza
Ivan Laptev
Diane Larlus
Christoph Lassner
Olivier Le Meur
Laura Leal-Taixé
Joon-Young Lee
Seungkyu Lee
Chen-Yu Lee
Andreas Lehrmann
Ido Leichter
Frank Lenzen
Matt Leotta
Stefan Leutenegger
Baoxin Li
Chunming Li
Dingzeyu Li

Fuxin Li
Hao Li
Houqiang Li
Qi Li
Stan Li
Wu-Jun Li
Xirong Li
Xuelong Li
Yi Li
Yongjie Li
Wei Li
Wen Li
Yeqing Li
Yujia Li
Wang Liang
Shengcai Liao
Jongwoo Lim
Joseph Lim
Di Lin
Weiyao Lin
Yen-Yu Lin
Min Lin
Liang Lin
Haibin Ling
Jim Little
Buyu Liu
Miaomiao Liu
Risheng Liu
Si Liu
Wanquan Liu
Yebin Liu
Ziwei Liu
Zhen Liu
Sifei Liu
Marcus Liwicki
Roberto Lopez-Sastre
Javier Lorenzo
Christos Louizos
Manolis Lourakis
Brian Lovell
Chen-Change Loy
Cewu Lu
Huchuan Lu
Jiwen Lu
Le Lu
Yijuan Lu

Canyi Lu
Jiebo Luo
Ping Luo
Siwei Lyu
Zhigang Ma
Chao Ma
Oisin Mac Aodha
John MacCormick
Vijay Mahadevan
Dhruv Mahajan
Aravindh Mahendran
Mohammed Mahoor
Michael Maire
Subhransu Maji
Aditi Majumder
Atsuto Maki
Yasushi Makihara
Alexandros Makris
Mateusz Malinowski
Clement Mallet
Arun Mallya
Dixit Mandar
Junhua Mao
Dmitrii Marin
Elisabeta Marinoiu
Renaud Marlet
Ricardo Martin
Aleix Martinez
Jonathan Masci
David Masip
Diana Mateus
Markus Mathias
Iain Matthews
Kevin Matzen
Bruce Maxwell
Stephen Maybank
Scott McCloskey
Ted Meeds
Christopher Mei
Tao Mei
Xue Mei
Jason Meltzer
Heydi Mendez
Thomas Mensink
Michele Merler
Domingo Mery

Ajmal Mian
Tomer Michaeli
Ondrej Miksik
Anton Milan
Erik Miller
Gregor Miller
Majid Mirmehdi
Ishan Misra
Anurag Mittal
Daisuke Miyazaki
Hossein Mobahi
Pascal Monasse
Sandino Morales
Vlad Morariu
Philippos Mordohai
Francesc Moreno-Noguer
Greg Mori
Bryan Morse
Roozbeh Mottaghi
Yadong Mu
Yasuhiro Mukaigawa
Lopamudra Mukherjee
Joseph Mundy
Mario Munich
Ana Murillo
Vittorio Murino
Naila Murray
Damien Muselet
Sobhan Naderi Parizi
Hajime Nagahara
Nikhil Naik
P.J. Narayanan
Fabian Nater
Jan Neumann
Ram Nevatia
Shawn Newsam
Bingbing Ni
Juan Carlos Niebles
Jifeng Ning
Ko Nishino
Masashi Nishiyama
Shohei Nobuhara
Ifeoma Nwogu
Peter Ochs
Jean-Marc Odobez
Francesca Odone

Iason Oikonomidis
Takeshi Oishi
Takahiro Okabe
Takayuki Okatani
Carl Olsson
Vicente Ordonez
Ivan Oseledets
Magnus Oskarsson
Martin R. Oswald
Matthew O'Toole
Wanli Ouyang
Andrew Owens
Mustafa Ozuysal
Jason Pacheco
Manohar Paluri
Gang Pan
Jinshan Pan
Yannis Panagakis
Sharath Pankanti
George Papandreou
Hyun Soo Park
In Kyu Park
Jaesik Park
Seyoung Park
Omkar Parkhi
Ioannis Patras
Viorica Patraucean
Genevieve Patterson
Vladimir Pavlovic
Kim Pedersen
Robert Peharz
Shmuel Peleg
Marcello Pelillo
Otavio Penatti
Xavier Pennec
Federico Pernici
Adrian Peter
Stavros Petridis
Vladimir Petrovic
Tomas Pfister
Justus Piater
Pedro Pinheiro
Bernardo Pires
Fiora Pirri
Leonid Pishchulin
Daniel Pizarro

Robert Pless
Tobias Pltz
Yair Poleg
Gerard Pons-Moll
Jordi Pont-Tuset
Ronald Poppe
Andrea Prati
Jan Prokaj
Daniel Prusa
Nicolas Pugeault
Guido Pusiol
Guo-Jun Qi
Gang Qian
Yu Qiao
Novi Quadrianto
Julian Quiroga
Andrew Rabinovich
Rahul Raguram
Srikumar Ramalingam
Deva Ramanan
Narayanan Ramanathan
Vignesh Ramanathan
Sebastian Ramos
Rene Ranftl
Anand Rangarajan
Avinash Ravichandran
Ramin Raziperchikolaei
Carlo Regazzoni
Christian Reinbacher
Michal Reinstein
Emonet Remi
Fabio Remondino
Shaoqing Ren
Zhile Ren
Jerome Revaud
Hayko Riemenschneider
Tobias Ritschel
Mariano Rivera
Patrick Rives
Antonio Robles-Kelly
Jason Rock
Erik Rodner
Emanuele Rodola
Mikel Rodriguez
Antonio
   Rodriguez Sanchez

Ganesh Sundaramoorthi
Jinli Suo
Supasorn Suwajanakorn
Tomas Svoboda
Chris Sweeney
Paul Swoboda
Raza Syed Hussain
Christian Szegedy
Yuichi Taguchi
Yu-Wing Tai
Hugues Talbot
Toru Tamaki
Mingkui Tan
Robby Tan
Xiaoyang Tan
Masayuki Tanaka
Meng Tang
Siyu Tang
Ran Tao
Dacheng Tao
Makarand Tapaswi
Jean-Philippe Tarel
Camillo Taylor
Christian Theobalt
Diego Thomas
Rajat Thomas
Xinmei Tian
Yonglong Tian
YingLi Tian
Yonghong Tian
Kinh Tieu
Joseph Tighe
Radu Timofte
Massimo Tistarelli
Sinisa Todorovic
Giorgos Tolias
Federico Tombari
Akihiko Torii
Andrea Torsello
Du Tran
Quoc-Huy Tran
Rudolph Triebel
Roberto Tron
Leonardo Trujillo
Eduard Trulls
Tomasz Trzcinski

Yi-Hsuan Tsai
Gavriil Tsechpenakis
Chourmouzios Tsiotsios
Stavros Tsogkas
Kewei Tu
Shubham Tulsiani
Tony Tung
Pavan Turaga
Matthew Turk
Tinne Tuytelaars
Oncel Tuzel
Georgios Tzimiropoulos
Norimichi Ukita
Osman Ulusoy
Martin Urschler
Arash Vahdat
Michel Valstar
Ernest Valveny
Jan van Gemert
Kiran Varanasi
Mayank Vatsa
Javier Vazquez-Corral
Ramakrishna Vedantam
Ashok Veeraraghavan
Olga Veksler
Jakob Verbeek
Francisco Vicente
Rene Vidal
Jordi Vitria
Max Vladymyrov
Christoph Vogel
Carl Vondrick
Sven Wachsmuth
Toshikazu Wada
Catherine Wah
Jacob Walker
Xiaolong Wang
Wei Wang
Limin Wang
Liang Wang
Hua Wang
Lijun Wang
Naiyan Wang
Xinggang Wang
Yining Wang
Baoyuan Wang

Chaohui Wang
Gang Wang
Heng Wang
Lei Wang
Linwei Wang
Liwei Wang
Ping Wang
Qi Wang
Qian Wang
Shenlong Wang
Song Wang
Tao Wang
Yang Wang
Yu-Chiang Frank Wang
Zhaowen Wang
Simon Warfield
Yichen Wei
Philippe Weinzaepfel
Longyin Wen
Tomas Werner
Aaron Wetzler
Yonatan Wexler
Michael Wilber
Kyle Wilson
Thomas Windheuser
David Wipf
Paul Wohlhart
Christian Wolf
Kwan-Yee Kenneth Wong
John Wright
Jiajun Wu
Jianxin Wu
Tianfu Wu
Yang Wu
Yi Wu
Zheng Wu
Stefanie Wuhrer
Jonas Wulff
Rolf Wurtz
Lu Xia
Tao Xiang
Yu Xiang
Lei Xiao
Yang Xiao
Tong Xiao
Wenxuan Xie

Lingxi Xie
Pengtao Xie
Saining Xie
Yuchen Xie
Junliang Xing
Bo Xiong
Fei Xiong
Jia Xu
Yong Xu
Tianfan Xue
Toshihiko Yamasaki
Takayoshi Yamashita
Junjie Yan
Rong Yan
Yan Yan
Keiji Yanai
Jian Yang
Jianchao Yang
Jiaolong Yang
Jie Yang
Jimei Yang
Michael Ying Yang
Ming Yang
Ruiduo Yang
Yi Yang
Angela Yao
Cong Yao
Jian Yao
Jianhua Yao
Jinwei Ye
Shuai Yi
Alper Yilmaz
Lijun Yin
Zhaozheng Yin

Xianghua Ying
Kuk-Jin Yoon
Chong You
Aron Yu
Felix Yu
Fisher Yu
Lap-Fai Yu
Stella Yu
Jing Yuan
Junsong Yuan
Lu Yuan
Xiao-Tong Yuan
Alan Yuille
Xenophon Zabulis
Stefanos Zafeiriou
Sergey Zagoruyko
Amir Zamir
Andrei Zanfir
Mihai Zanfir
Lihi Zelnik-Manor
Xingyu Zeng
Josiane Zerubia
Changshui Zhang
Cheng Zhang
Guofeng Zhang
Jianguo Zhang
Junping Zhang
Ning Zhang
Quanshi Zhang
Shaoting Zhang
Tianzhu Zhang
Xiaoqun Zhang
Yinda Zhang
Yu Zhang

Shiliang Zhang
Lei Zhang
Xiaoqin Zhang
Shanshan Zhang
Ting Zhang
Bin Zhao
Rui Zhao
Yibiao Zhao
Enliang Zheng
Wenming Zheng
Yinqiang Zheng
Yuanjie Zheng
Yin Zheng
Wei-Shi Zheng
Liang Zheng
Dingfu Zhou
Wengang Zhou
Tinghui Zhou
Bolei Zhou
Feng Zhou
Huiyu Zhou
Jun Zhou
Kevin Zhou
Kun Zhou
Xiaowei Zhou
Zihan Zhou
Jun Zhu
Jun-Yan Zhu
Zhenyao Zhu
Zeeshan Zia
Henning Zimmer
Karel Zimmermann
Wangmeng Zuo

Additional Reviewers

Felix Achilles
Sarah Adel Bargal
Hessam Bagherinezhad
Qinxun Bai
Gedas Bertasius
Michal Busta
Erik Bylow
Marinella Cadoni

Dan Andrei Calian
Lilian Calvet
Federico Camposeco
Olivier Canevet
Anirban Chakraborty
Yu-Wei Chao
Sotirios Chatzis
Tatjana Chavdarova

Jimmy Chen
Melissa Cote
Berkan Demirel
Zhiwei Deng
Guy Gilboa
Albert Gordo
Daniel Gordon
Ankur Gupta

Kun He
Yang He
Daniel Holtmann-Rice
Xun Huang
Liang Hui
Drew Jaegle
Cijo Jose
Marco Karrer
Mehran Khodabandeh
Anna Khoreva
Hyo-Jin Kim
Theodora Kontogianni
Pengpeng Liang
Shugao Ma
Ludovic Magerand
Francesco Malapelle
Julio Marco
Vlad Morariu

Rajitha Navarathna
Junhyuk Oh
Federico Perazzi
Marcel Piotraschke
Srivignesh Rajendran
Joe Redmon
Helge Rhodin
Anna Rohrbach
Beatrice Rossi
Wolfgang Roth
Pietro Salvagnini
Hosnieh Sattar
Ana Serrano
Zhixin Shu
Sven Sickert
Jakub Simanek
Ramprakash Srinivasan
Oren Tadmor

Xin Tao
Lucas Teixeira
Mårten Wädenback
Qing Wang
Yaser Yacoob
Takayoshi Yamashita
Huiyuan Yang
Ryo Yonetani
Sejong Yoon
Shaodi You
Xu Zhan
Jianming Zhang
Richard Zhang
Xiaoqun Zhang
Xu Zhang
Zheng Zhang

Contents – Part I

Scene Understanding

Detection, Recognition and Retrieval

CNN Image Retrieval Learns from BoW: Unsupervised Fine-Tuning with Hard Examples

Filip Radenović[(✉)], Giorgos Tolias, and Ondřej Chum

CMP, Faculty of Electrical Engineering, Czech Technical University in Prague,
Prague, Czech Republic
{filip.radenovic,giorgos.tolias,chum}@cmp.felk.cvut.cz

Abstract. Convolutional Neural Networks (CNNs) achieve state-of-the-art performance in many computer vision tasks. However, this achievement is preceded by extreme manual annotation in order to perform either training from scratch or fine-tuning for the target task. In this work, we propose to fine-tune CNN for image retrieval from a large collection of unordered images in a fully automated manner. We employ state-of-the-art retrieval and Structure-from-Motion (SfM) methods to obtain 3D models, which are used to guide the selection of the training data for CNN fine-tuning. We show that both hard positive and hard negative examples enhance the final performance in particular object retrieval with compact codes.

Keywords: CNN fine-tuning · Unsupervised learning · Image retrieval

1 Introduction

Image retrieval has received a lot of attention since the advent of invariant local features, such as SIFT [1], and since the seminal work of Sivic and Zisserman [2] based on Bag-of-Words (BoW). Retrieval systems have reached a higher level of maturity by incorporating large visual codebooks [3,4], spatial verification [3,5] and query expansion [6–8]. These ingredients constitute the state of the art on particular object retrieval. Another line of research focuses on compact image representations in order to decrease memory requirements and increase the search efficiency. Representative approaches are Fisher vectors [9], VLAD [10] and alternatives [11–13]. Recent advances [14,15] show that Convolutional Neural Networks (CNN) offer an attractive alternative for image search representations with small memory footprint.

CNNs attracted a lot of attention after the work of Krizhevsky *et al.* [16]. Their success is mainly due to the computational power of GPUs and the use of very large annotated datasets [17]. Generation of the latter comes at the expense of costly manual annotation. Using CNN layer activations as off-the-shelf image descriptors [18,19] appears very effective and is adopted in many tasks [20–22]. In particular for image retrieval, Babenko *et al.* [14] and Gong *et al.* [22] concurrently propose the use of Fully Connected (FC) layer

© Springer International Publishing AG 2016
B. Leibe et al. (Eds.): ECCV 2016, Part I, LNCS 9905, pp. 3–20, 2016.
DOI: 10.1007/978-3-319-46448-0_1

activations as descriptors, while convolutional layer activations are later shown to have superior performance [15, 23–25].

Generalization to other tasks [26] is attained by CNN activations, at least up to some extent. However, initialization by a pre-trained network and re-training for another task, a process called *fine-tuning*, significantly improves the adaptation ability [27, 28]. Fine-tuning by training with classes of particular objects, *e.g.* building classes in the work of Babenko *et al.* [14], is known to improve retrieval accuracy. This formulation is much closer to classification than to the desired properties of instance retrieval. Typical architectures for metric learning, such as siamese [29–31] or triplet networks [32–34] employ *matching* and *non-matching* pairs to perform the training and better suit to this task. In this fashion, Arandjelovic *et al.* [35] perform fine-tuning based on geo-tagged databases and, similar to our work, they directly optimize the similarity measure to be used in the final task. In contrast to them, we dispense with the need of annotated data or any assumptions on the training dataset. A concurrent work [36] bears resemblance to ours but their focus is on boosting performance through end-to-end learning of a more sophisticated representation, while we target to reveal the importance of hard examples and of training data variation.

A number of image clustering methods based on local features have been introduced [37–39]. Due to the spatial verification, the *clusters* discovered by these methods are reliable. In fact, the methods provide not only clusters, but also a matching graph or sub-graph on the cluster images. These graphs are further used as an input to a Structure-from-Motion (SfM) pipeline to build a 3D model [40]. The SfM filters out virtually all mismatched images, and also provides camera positions for all matched images in the cluster. The whole process from unordered collection of images to 3D reconstructions is fully automatic.

In this paper, we address an unsupervised fine-tuning of CNN for image retrieval. We propose to exploit 3D reconstructions to select the training data for CNN. We show that compared to previous supervised approaches, the variability in the training data from 3D reconstructions delivers superior performance in the image retrieval task. During the training process the CNN is trained to learn what a state-of-the-art retrieval system based on local features and spatial verification would match. Such a system has large memory requirements and high query times, while our goal is to mimic this via CNN-based representation. We derive a short image representation and achieve similar performance to such state-of-the-art systems.

In particular we make the following contributions. (1) We exploit SfM information and enforce not only hard non-matching (*negative*) but also hard matching (*positive*) examples to be learned by the CNN. This is shown to enhance the derived image representation. (2) We show that the whitening traditionally performed on short representations [41] is, in some cases, unstable and we rather propose to learn the whitening through the same training data. Its effect is complementary to fine-tuning and it further boosts performance. (3) Finally, we set a new state-of-the-art based on compact representations for Oxford Buildings and Paris datasets by re-training well known CNNs, such as AlexNet [16] and VGG [42]. Remarkably, we are on par with existing 256D compact representations even by using 32D image vectors.

2   Related Work

A variety of previous methods apply CNN activations on the task of image retrieval [15,22–25,43]. The achieved accuracy on retrieval is evidence for the generalization properties of CNNs. The employed networks were trained for image classification using ImageNet dataset, optimizing classification error. Babenko *et al.* [14] go one step further and re-train such networks with a dataset that is closer to the target task. They perform training with object classes that correspond to particular landmarks/buildings. Performance is improved on standard retrieval benchmarks. Despite the achievement, still, the final metric and utilized layers are different to the ones actually optimized during learning.

Constructing such training datasets requires manual effort. The same stands for attempts on different tasks [19,25] that perform fine-tuning and achieve increase of performance. In a recent work, geo-tagged datasets with timestamps offer the ground for weakly supervised fine-tuning of a triplet network [35]. Two images taken far from each other can be easily considered as non-matching, while matching examples are picked by the most similar nearby images. In the latter case, similarity is defined by the current representation of the CNN. This is the first approach that performs end-to-end fine-tuning for image retrieval and in particular for the task of geo-localization. The employed training data are now much closer to the final task. We differentiate by discovering matching and non-matching image pairs in an unsupervised way. Moreover, we derive matching examples based on 3D reconstruction which allows for harder examples, compared to the ones that the current network identifies. Even though hard negative mining is a standard process [20,35], this is not the case with hard positive examples. Large intra-class variation in classification tasks requires the positive pairs to be sampled carefully; forcing the model to learn extremely hard positives may result in over-fitting. Another exception is the work Simo-Serra *et al.* [44] where they mine hard positive patches for descriptor learning. They are also guided by 3D reconstruction but only at patch level.

Despite the fact that one of the recent advances is the triplet loss [32–34], note that also Arandjelovic *et al.* [35] use it, there are no extensive and direct comparisons to siamese networks and the contrastive loss. One exception is the work of Hoffer and Ailon [34], where triplet loss is shown to be marginally better only on MNIST dataset. We rather employ a siamese architecture with the contrastive loss and find it to generalize better and to converge at higher performance than the triplet loss.

3   Network Architecture and Image Representation

In this section we describe the derived image representation that is based on CNN and we present the network architecture used to perform the end-to-end learning in a siamese fashion. Finally, we describe how, after fine-tuning, we use the same training data to learn projections that appear to be an effective post-processing step.

3.1   Image Representation

We adopt a compact representation that is derived from activations of convolutional layers and is shown to be effective for particular object retrieval [25, 26]. We assume that a network is fully convolutional [45] or that all fully connected layers are discarded. Now, given an input image, the output is a 3D tensor $\mathcal{X}$ of $W \times H \times K$ dimensions, where K is the number of feature maps in the last layer. Let $\mathcal{X}_k$ be the set of all $W \times H$ activations for feature map $k \in \{1 \dots K\}$. The network output consists of K such sets of activations. The image representation, called Maximum Activations of Convolutions (MAC) [15, 25], is simply constructed by max-pooling over all dimensions per feature map and is given by

$$\mathbf{f} = [\mathrm{f}_1 \dots \mathrm{f}_k \dots \mathrm{f}_K]^\top, \text{ with } \mathrm{f}_k = \max_{x \in \mathcal{X}_k} x \cdot \mathbb{1}(x > 0). \tag{1}$$

The indicator function $\mathbb{1}$ takes care that the feature vector $\mathbf{f}$ is non-negative, as if the last network layer was a Rectified Linear Unit (ReLU). The feature vector finally consists of the maximum activation per feature map and its dimensionality is equal to K. For many popular networks this is equal to 256 or 512, which makes it a compact image representation. MAC vectors are subsequently ℓ_2-normalized and similarity between two images is evaluated with inner product. The contribution of a feature map to the image similarity is measured by the product of the corresponding MAC vector components. In Fig. 1 we show the image patches in correspondence that contribute most to the similarity. Such implicit correspondences are improved after fine-tuning. Moreover, the CNN fires less to ImageNet classes, e.g. cars and bicycles.

3.2   Network and Siamese Learning

The proposed approach is applicable to any CNN that consists of only convolutional layers. In this paper, we focus on re-training (i.e. fine-tuning) state-of-the-art CNNs for classification, in particular AlexNet and VGG. Fully connected layers are discarded and the pre-trained networks constitute the initialization for our convolutional layers. Now, the last convolutional layer is followed by a MAC layer that performs MAC vector computation (1). The input of a MAC layer is a 3D tensor of activation and the output is a non-negative vector. Then, an ℓ_2-normalization block takes care that output vectors are normalized. In the rest of the paper, MAC corresponds to the ℓ_2-normalized vector $\bar{\mathbf{f}}$.

We adopt a siamese architecture and train a two branch network. Each branch is a clone of the other, meaning that they share the same parameters. Training input consists of image pairs (i, j) and labels $Y(i, j) \in \{0, 1\}$ declaring whether a pair is non-matching (label 0) or matching (label 1). We employ the contrastive loss [29] that acts on the (non-)matching pairs and is defined as

$$\mathcal{L}(i, j) = \frac{1}{2} \left(Y(i, j) \|\bar{\mathbf{f}}(i) - \bar{\mathbf{f}}(j)\|^2 + (1 - Y(i, j)) \left(\max\{0, \tau - \|\bar{\mathbf{f}}(i) - \bar{\mathbf{f}}(j)\|\} \right)^2 \right), \tag{2}$$

where $\bar{\mathbf{f}}(i)$ is the ℓ_2-normalized MAC vector of image i, and τ is a parameter defining when non-matching pairs have large enough distance in order not to be

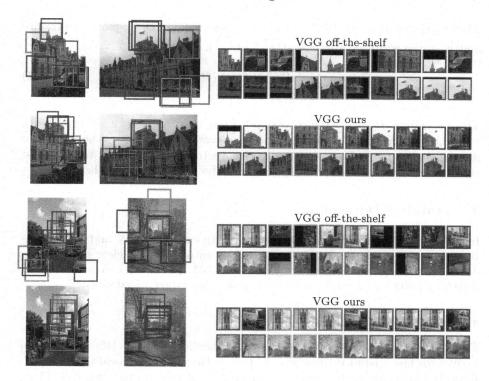

Fig. 1. Visualization of patches corresponding to the MAC vector components that have the highest contribution to the pairwise image similarity. Examples shown use CNN before (top) and after (bottom) fine-tuning of VGG. The same color corresponds to the same vector component (feature map) per image pair. The patch size is equal to the receptive field of the last pooling layer.

taken into account in the loss. We train the network using Stochastic Gradient Descent (SGD) and a large training set created automatically (see Sect. 4).

3.3 Whitening and Dimensionality Reduction

In this section, the post-processing of fine-tuned MAC vectors is considered. Previous methods [23,25] use PCA of an independent set for whitening and dimensionality reduction, that is the covariance matrix of all descriptors is analyzed. We propose to take advantage of the label data provided by the 3D models and use linear discriminant projections originally proposed by Mikolajczyk and Matas [46]. The projection is decomposed into two parts, whitening and rotation. The whitening part is the inverse of the square-root of the intraclass (matching pairs) covariance matrix $C_S^{-\frac{1}{2}}$, where

$$C_S = \sum_{Y(i,j)=1} \left(\bar{\mathbf{f}}(i) - \bar{\mathbf{f}}(j)\right)\left(\bar{\mathbf{f}}(i) - \bar{\mathbf{f}}(j)\right)^\top . \tag{3}$$

The rotation part is the PCA of the interclass (non-matching pairs) covariance matrix in the whitened space $\text{eig}(C_S^{-\frac{1}{2}} C_D C_S^{-\frac{1}{2}})$, where

$$C_D = \sum_{Y(i,j)=0} \left(\bar{\mathbf{f}}(i) - \bar{\mathbf{f}}(j)\right) \left(\bar{\mathbf{f}}(i) - \bar{\mathbf{f}}(j)\right)^\top. \tag{4}$$

The projection $P = C_S^{-\frac{1}{2}} \text{eig}(C_S^{-\frac{1}{2}} C_D C_S^{-\frac{1}{2}})$ is then applied as $P^\top(\bar{\mathbf{f}}(i) - \mu)$, where μ is the mean MAC vector to perform centering. To reduce the descriptor dimensionality to D dimensions, only eigenvectors corresponding to D largest eigenvalues are used. Projected vectors are subsequently ℓ_2-normalized.

4   Training Dataset

In this section we briefly summarize the tightly-coupled BoW and SfM reconstruction system [40,47] that is employed to automatically select our training data. Then, we describe how we exploit the 3D information to select harder matching pairs and hard non-matching pairs with larger variability.

4.1   BoW and 3D Reconstruction

The retrieval engine used in the work of Schonberger *et al.* [40] builds upon BoW with fast spatial verification [3]. It uses Hessian affine local features [48], RootSIFT descriptors [49], and a fine vocabulary of 16M visual words [50]. Then, query images are chosen via min-hash and spatial verification, as in [37]. Image retrieval based on BoW is used to collect images of the objects/landmarks. These images serve as the initial matching graph for the succeeding SfM reconstruction, which is performed using state-of-the-art SfM [51,52]. Different mining techniques, *e.g.* zoom in, zoom out [53,54], sideways crawl [40], help to build larger and complete model.

In this work, we exploit the outcome of such a system. Given a large unannotated image collection, images are clustered and a 3D model is constructed per cluster. We use the terms *3D model*, *model* and *cluster* interchangeably. For each image, the estimated camera position is known, as well as the local features registered on the 3D model. We drop redundant (overlapping) 3D models, that might have been constructed from different seeds. Models reconstructing the same landmark but from different and disjoint viewpoints are considered as non-overlapping.

4.2   Selection of Training Image Pairs

A 3D model is described as a bipartite visibility graph $\mathbb{G} = (\mathcal{I} \cup \mathcal{P}, \mathcal{E})$ [55], where images $\mathcal{I}$ and points $\mathcal{P}$ are the vertices of the graph. Edges of this graph are defined by visibility relations between cameras and points, *i.e.* if a point $p \in \mathcal{P}$ is visible in an image $i \in \mathcal{I}$, then there exists an edge $(i,p) \in \mathcal{E}$. The set of points observed by an image i is given by

$$\mathcal{P}(i) = \{p \in \mathcal{P} : (i, p) \in \mathcal{E}\}. \tag{5}$$

We create a dataset of tuples $(q, m(q), \mathcal{N}(q))$, where q represents a query image, $m(q)$ is a positive image that matches the query, and $\mathcal{N}(q)$ is a set of negative images that do not match the query. These tuples are used to form training image pairs, where each tuple corresponds to $|\mathcal{N}(q)| + 1$ pairs. For a query image q, a pool $\mathcal{M}(q)$ of candidate positive images is constructed based on the camera positions in the cluster of q. It consists of the k images with closest camera centers to the query. Due to the wide range of camera orientations, these do not necessarily depict the same object. We therefore propose three different ways to sample the positive image. The positives examples are fixed during the whole training process for all three strategies.

Positive images: MAC distance. The image that has the lowest MAC distance to the query is chosen as positive, formally

$$m_1(q) = \underset{i \in \mathcal{M}(q)}{\operatorname{argmin}} ||\bar{\mathbf{f}}(q) - \bar{\mathbf{f}}(i)||. \tag{6}$$

This strategy is similar to the one followed by Arandjelovic $et\ al.$ [35]. They adopt this choice since only GPS coordinates are available and not camera orientations. Downside of this approach is that the chosen matching examples already have low distance, thus not forcing network to learn much out of the positive samples.

Positive images: maximum inliers. In this approach, the 3D information is exploited to choose the positive image, independently of the CNN descriptor. In particular, the image that has the highest number of co-observed 3D points with the query is chosen. That is,

$$m_2(q) = \underset{i \in \mathcal{M}(q)}{\operatorname{argmax}} |\mathcal{P}(q) \cap \mathcal{P}(i)|. \tag{7}$$

This measure corresponds to the number of spatially verified features between two images, a measure commonly used for ranking in BoW-based retrieval. As this choice is independent of the CNN representation, it delivers more challenging positive examples.

Positive images: relaxed inliers. Even though both previous methods choose positive images depicting the same object as the query, the variance of viewpoints is limited. Instead of using a pool of images with similar camera position, the positive example is selected at random from a set of images that co-observe enough points with the query, but do not exhibit too extreme scale change. The positive example in this case is

$$m_3(q) = \mathtt{random}\left\{i \in \mathcal{M}(q) : \frac{|\mathcal{P}(i) \cap \mathcal{P}(q)|}{|\mathcal{P}(q)|} \geq t_i,\ \mathtt{scale}(i, q) \leq t_s\right\}, \tag{8}$$

where $\mathtt{scale}(i, q)$ is the scale change between the two images. This method results in selecting harder matching examples which are still guaranteed to depict

Fig. 2. Examples of training query images (green border) and matching images selected as positive examples by methods (from left to right) $m_1(q)$, $m_2(q)$, and $m_3(q)$. (Color figure online)

the same object. Method m_3 chooses different image than m_1 on 86.5 % of the queries. In Fig. 2 we present examples of query images and the corresponding positives selected with the three different methods. The relaxed method increases the variability of viewpoints.

Negative images. Negative examples are selected from clusters different than the cluster of the query image, as the clusters are non-overlapping. Following a well-known procedure, we choose hard negatives [20,44], that is, non-matching images with the most similar descriptor. Two different strategies are proposed. In the first, $\mathcal{N}_1(q)$, k-nearest neighbors from all non-matching images are selected. In the other, $\mathcal{N}_2(q)$, the same criterion is used, but at most one image per cluster is allowed. While $\mathcal{N}_1(q)$ often leads to multiple, and very similar, instances of

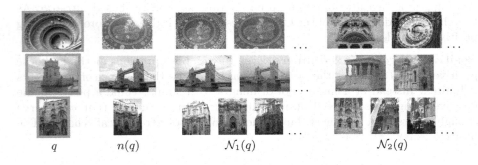

$$q \qquad n(q) \qquad \mathcal{N}_1(q) \qquad \mathcal{N}_2(q)$$

Fig. 3. Examples of training query images q (green border), hardest non-matching images $n(q)$ that are always selected as negative examples, and additional non-matching images selected as negative examples by $\mathcal{N}_1(q)$ and $\mathcal{N}_2(q)$ methods respectively. (Color figure online)

the same object, $\mathcal{N}_2(q)$ provides higher variability of the negative examples, see Fig. 3. While positives examples are fixed during the whole training process, hard negatives depend on the current CNN parameters and are re-mined multiple times per epoch.

5 Experiments

In this section we discuss implementation details of our training, evaluate different components of our method, and compare to the state of the art.

5.1 Training Setup and Implementation Details

Our training samples are derived from the dataset used in the work of Schonberger *et al.* [40], which consists of 7.4 million images downloaded from Flickr using keywords of popular landmarks, cities and countries across the world. The clustering procedure [37] gives 19,546 images to serve as query seeds. The extensive retrieval-SfM reconstruction [47] of the whole dataset results in 1,474 reconstructed 3D models. Removing overlapping models leaves us with 713 3D models containing 163,671 unique images from the initial dataset. The initial dataset contained on purpose all images of Oxford5k and Paris6k datasets. In this way, we are able to exclude 98 clusters that contain any image (or their near duplicates) from these test datasets.

The largest model has 11,042 images, while the smallest has 25. We randomly select 551 models (133,659 images) for training and 162 (30,012) for validation. The number of training queries per cluster is 10% of the cluster size for clusters of 300 or less images, or 30 images for larger clusters. A total number of 5,974 images is selected for training queries, and 1,691 for validation queries.

Each training and validation tuple contains 1 query, 1 positive and 5 negative images. The pool of candidate positives consists of $k = 100$ images with closest camera centers to the query. In particular, for method m_3, the inliers overlap threshold is $t_i = 0.2$, and the scale change threshold $t_s = 1.5$. Hard negatives are re-mined 3 times per epoch, *i.e.* roughly every 2,000 training queries. Given the chosen queries and the chosen positives, we further add 20 images per cluster to serve as candidate negatives during re-mining. This constitutes a training set of 22,156 images and it corresponds to the case that all 3D models are included for training.

To perform the fine-tuning as described in Sect. 3, we initialize by the convolutional layers of AlexNet [16] or VGG [42]. We use learning rate equal to 0.001, which is divided by 5 every 10 epochs, momentum 0.9, weight decay 0.0005, parameter τ for contrastive loss 0.7, and batch size of 5 training tuples. All training images are resized to a maximum 362×362 dimensionality, while keeping the original aspect ratio. Training is done for at most 30 epochs and the best network is selected based on performance, measured via mean Average Precision (mAP) [3], on validation tuples.

5.2 Test Datasets and Evaluation Protocol

We evaluate our approach on Oxford buildings [3], Paris [56] and Holidays[1] [57] datasets. First two are closer to our training data, while the last differentiates by containing similar scenes and not only man made objects or buildings. These are also combined with 100k distractors from Oxford100k to allow for evaluation at larger scale. The performance is measured via mAP. We follow the standard evaluation protocol for Oxford and Paris and crop the query images with the provided bounding box. The cropped image is fed as input to the CNN. However, to deliver a direct comparison with other methods, we also evaluate queries generated by keeping all activations that fall into this bounding box [23,35] when the full query image is used as input to the network. We refer to the cropped images approach as $Crop_{\mathcal{I}}$ and the cropped activations [23,35] as $Crop_{\mathcal{X}}$. The dimensionality of the images fed into the CNN is limited to 1024×1024 pixels. In our experiments, no vector post-processing is applied if not otherwise stated.

5.3 Results on Image Retrieval

Learning. We evaluate the off-the-shelf CNN and our fine-tuned ones after different number of training epochs. Our different methods for positive and negative selection are evaluated independently in order to decompose the benefit of each ingredient. Finally, we also perform a comparison with the triplet loss [35], trained on exactly the same training data as the ones used for our architecture with the contrastive loss. Results are presented in Fig. 4. The results show that positive examples with larger view point variability, and negative examples with higher content variability, both acquire a consistent increase in the performance. The triplet loss[2] appears to be inferior in our context; we observe oscillation of the error in the validation set from early epochs, which implies over-fitting. In the rest of the paper, we adopt the $m_3, \mathcal{N}_2$ approach.

Dataset variability. We perform fine-tuning by using a subset of the available 3D models. Results are presented in Fig. 5 with 10, 100 and 551 (all available) clusters, while keeping the amount of training data, *i.e.* training queries, fixed. In the case of 10 and 100 models we use the largest ones, *i.e.* ones with the highest number of images. It is better to train with all 3D models due to the higher variability in the training set. Remarkably, significant increase in performance is achieved even with 10 or 100 models. However, the network is able to over-fit in the case of few clusters. All models are utilized in all other experiments.

Learned projections. The PCA-whitening [41] (PCA_w) is shown to be essential in some cases of CNN-based descriptors [14,23,25]. On the other hand, it is shown that on some of the datasets, the performance after PCA_w substantially drops compared with the raw descriptors (max pooling on Oxford5k [23]).

---

[1] We use the up-right version of Holidays dataset (rotated).
[2] The margin parameter for the triplet loss is set equal to 0.1 [35].

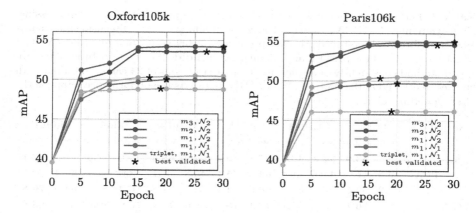

Fig. 4. Performance comparison of methods for positive and negative example selection. Evaluation is performed on AlexNet MAC on Oxford105k and Paris106k datasets. The plot shows the evolution of mAP with the number of training epochs. Epoch 0 corresponds to the off-the-shelf network. All approaches use contrastive loss, except if otherwise stated. The network with the best performance on the validation set is marked with $\star$.

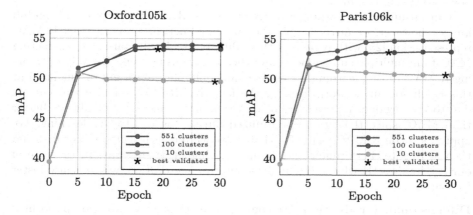

Fig. 5. Influence of the number of 3D models used for CNN fine-tuning. Performance is evaluated on AlexNet MAC on Oxford105k and Paris106k datasets using 10, 100 and 551 (all available) 3D models. The network with the best performance on the validation set is marked with $\star$.

We perform comparison of this traditional way of whitening and our learned whitening (L_w), described in Sect. 3.3. Table 1 shows results without post-processing and with the two different methods of whitening. Our experiments confirm, that PCA_w often reduces the performance. In contrast to that, the proposed L_w achieves the best performance in most cases and is never the worst performing method. Compared to no post-processing baseline, L_w reduces the

Table 1. Performance comparison of CNN vector post-processing: no post-processing, PCA-whitening [41] (PCA$_w$) and our learned whitening (L$_w$). No dimensionality reduction is performed. Fine-tuned AlexNet produces a 256D vector and fine-tuned VGG a 512D vector. The best performance highlighted in **bold**, the worst in blue. The proposed method consistently performs either the best (18 out of 24 cases) or on par with the best method. On the contrary, PCA$_w$ [41] often hurts the performance significantly. Best viewed in color.

Net	Post	Oxf5k		Oxf105k		Par6k		Par106k		Hol		Hol101k	
		MAC	R-MAC	MAC	R-MAC	MAC	R-MAC	MAC	R-MAC	MAC	R-MAC	MAC	R-MAC
Alex	–	**60.2**	**53.9**	**54.2**	**46.4**	67.5	**70.2**	**54.9**	**58.4**	73.1	**77.3**	61.6	**67.1**
	PCA$_w$	56.9	60.0	44.1	48.4	64.3	75.1	46.8	61.7	**73.0**	81.7	59.4	70.4
	L$_w$	**62.2**	**62.5**	52.8	**53.2**	**68.9**	74.4	54.7	**61.8**	**76.2**	81.5	**63.8**	70.8
VGG	–	78.7	70.1	72.7	63.1	77.1	78.1	69.6	70.4	76.9	80.0	65.3	**68.8**
	PCA$_w$	76.1	76.3	**68.9**	68.5	79.0	**84.5**	**69.1**	**77.1**	77.1	82.3	**63.6**	71.0
	L$_w$	**79.7**	**77.0**	**73.9**	69.2	**82.4**	83.8	**74.6**	76.4	**79.5**	**82.5**	67.0	71.5

performance twice for AlexNet, but the drop is negligible compared to the drop observed for PCA$_w$. For the VGG, the proposed L$_w$ *always* outperforms the no post-processing baseline.

Our unsupervised learning directly optimizes MAC when extracted from full images, however, we further apply the fine-tuned networks to construct R-MAC representation [25] with regions of three different scales. It consists of extracting MAC from multiple sub-windows and then aggregating them. Directly optimizing R-MAC during learning is possible and could offer extra improvements, but this is left for future work. Despite the fact that R-MAC offers improvements due to the regional representation, in our experiments it is not always better than MAC, since the latter is optimized during the end-to-end learning. We apply PCA$_w$ on R-MAC as in [25], that is, we whiten each region vector first and then aggregate. Performance is significantly higher in this way. In the case of our L$_w$, we directly whiten the final vector after aggregation, which is also faster to compute.

Dimensionality reduction. We compare dimensionality reduction performed with PCA$_w$ [41] and with our L$_w$. The performance for varying descriptor dimensionality is plotted in Fig. 6. The plots suggest that L$_w$ works better in higher dimensionalities, while PCA$_w$ works slightly better for the lower ones. Remarkably, MAC reduced down to 16D outperforms state-of-the-art on BoW-based 128D compact codes [11] on Oxford105k (45.5 vs 41.4). Further results on very short codes can be found in Table 2.

Over-fitting and generalization. In all experiments, all clusters including any image (not only query landmarks) from Oxford5k or Paris6k datasets are removed. To evaluate whether the network tends to over-fit to the training data

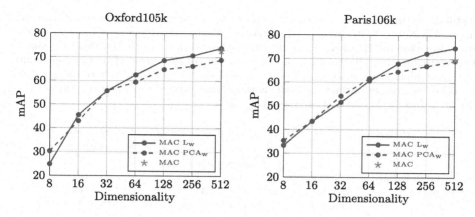

Fig. 6. Performance comparison of the dimensionality reduction performed by PCA_w and our L_w on fine-tuned VGG MAC on Oxford105k and Paris106k datasets.

or to generalize, we repeat the training, this time using all 3D reconstructions, including those of Oxford and Paris landmarks. The same amount of training queries is used for a fair comparison. We observe negligible difference in the performance of the network on Oxford and Paris evaluation results, *i.e.* the difference in mAP was on average +0.3 over all testing datasets. We conclude that the network generalizes well and is relatively insensitive to over-fitting.

Comparison with the state of the art. We extensively compare our results with the state-of-the-art performance on compact image representations and extremely short codes. The results for MAC and R-MAC with the fine-tuned networks are summarized together with previously published results in Table 2. The proposed methods outperform the state of the art on Paris and Oxford datasets, with and without distractors with all 16D, 32D, 128D, 256D, and 512D descriptors. On Holidays dataset, the Neural codes [14] win the extreme short code category, while off-the-shelf NetVlad performs the best on 256D and higher.

We additionally combine MAC and R-MAC with recent localization method for re-ranking [25] to further boost the performance. Our scores compete with state-of-the-art systems based on local features and query expansion. These have much higher memory needs and larger query times.

Observations on the recently published NetVLAD [35]: (1) After fine-tuning, NetVLAD performance drops on Holidays, while our training improves off-the-shelf results on all datasets. (2) Our 32D MAC descriptor has comparable performance to 256D NetVLAD on Oxford5k (ours 69.2 vs NetVLAD 63.5), and on Paris6k (ours 69.5 vs NetVLAD 73.5).

Table 2. Performance comparison with the state of the art. Results reported with the use of AlexNet or VGG are marked by (**A**) or (**V**), respectively. Use of fine-tuned network is marked by (**f**), otherwise the off-the-shelf network is implied. D: Dimensionality. Our methods are marked with ⋆ and they are always accompanied by L_w. New state of the art highlighted in **red**, surpassed state of the art in **bold**, state of the art that retained the title in outline, and our methods that outperform previous state of the art on a gray background. Best viewed in color.

Method		D	Oxf5k		Oxf105k		Par6k		Par106k		Hol	Hol 101k
			Crop$_I$	Crop$_X$	Crop$_I$	Crop$_X$	Crop$_I$	Crop$_X$	Crop$_I$	Crop$_X$		
Compact representations												
mVoc/BoW [11]		128	48.8	–	41.4	–	–	–	–	–	65.6	–
Neural codes[a] [14]	(fA)	128	–	55.7	–	52.3	–	–	–	–	78.9	–
MAC[b]	(V)	128	53.5	55.7	43.8	45.6	69.5	70.6	53.4	55.4	72.6	56.7
CroW [24]	(V)	128	59.2	–	51.6	–	74.6	–	63.2	–	–	–
⋆ MAC	(fV)	128	75.8	76.8	68.6	70.8	77.6	78.8	68.0	69.0	73.2	58.8
⋆ R-MAC	(fV)	128	72.5	76.7	64.3	69.7	78.5	80.3	69.3	71.2	79.3	65.2
MAC[b]	(V)	256	54.7	56.9	45.6	47.8	71.5	72.4	55.7	57.3	76.5	61.3
SPoC [23]	(V)	256	–	53.1	–	50.1	–	–	–	–	80.2	–
R-MAC [25]	(A)	256	56.1	–	47.0	–	72.9	–	60.1	–	–	–
CroW [24]	(V)	256	65.4	–	59.3	–	77.9	–	67.8	–	83.1	–
NetVlad [35]	(V)	256	–	55.5	–	–	–	67.7	–	–	86.0	–
NetVlad [35]	(fV)	256	–	63.5	–	–	–	73.5	–	–	84.3	–
⋆ MAC	(fA)	256	62.2	65.4	52.8	58.0	68.9	72.2	54.7	58.5	76.2	63.8
⋆ R-MAC	(fA)	256	62.5	68.9	53.2	61.2	74.4	76.6	61.8	64.8	81.5	70.8
⋆ MAC	(fV)	256	77.4	78.2	70.7	72.6	80.8	81.9	72.2	73.4	77.3	62.9
⋆ R-MAC	(fV)	256	74.9	78.2	67.5	72.1	82.3	83.5	74.1	75.6	81.4	69.4
MAC[b]	(V)	512	56.4	58.3	47.8	49.2	72.3	72.6	58.0	59.1	76.7	62.7
R-MAC [25]	(V)	512	66.9	–	61.6	–	83.0	–	75.7	–	–	–
CroW [24]	(V)	512	68.2	–	63.2	–	79.6	–	71.0	–	84.9	–
⋆ MAC	(fV)	512	79.7	80.0	73.9	75.1	82.4	82.9	74.6	75.3	79.5	67.0
⋆ R-MAC	(fV)	512	77.0	80.1	69.2	74.1	83.8	85.0	76.4	77.9	82.5	71.5
Extreme short codes												
Neural codes[a] [14]	(fA)	16	–	41.8	–	35.4	–	–	–	–	60.9	–
⋆ MAC	(fV)	16	56.2	57.4	45.5	47.6	57.3	62.9	43.4	48.5	51.3	25.6
⋆ R-MAC	(fV)	16	46.9	52.1	37.9	41.6	58.8	63.2	45.6	49.6	54.4	31.7
Neural codes[a] [14]	(fA)	32	–	51.5	–	46.7	–	–	–	–	72.9	–
⋆ MAC	(fV)	32	65.3	69.2	55.6	59.5	63.9	69.5	51.6	56.3	62.4	41.8
⋆ R-MAC	(fV)	32	58.4	64.2	50.1	55.1	63.9	67.4	52.7	55.8	68.0	49.6
Re-ranking (R) and query expansion (QE)												
BoW(1M)+QE [6]		–	82.7	–	76.7	–	80.5	–	71.0	–	–	–
BoW(16M)+QE [50]		–	84.9	–	79.5	–	82.4	–	77.3	–	–	–
HQE(65k) [8]		–	88.0	–	84.0	–	82.8	–	–	–	–	–
R-MAC+R+QE [25]	(V)	512	77.3	–	73.2	–	86.5	–	79.8	–	–	–
CroW+QE [24]	(V)	512	72.2	–	67.8	–	85.5	–	79.7	–	–	–
⋆ MAC+R+QE	(fV)	512	85.0	85.4	81.8	82.3	86.5	87.0	78.8	79.6	–	–
⋆ R-MAC+R+QE	(fV)	512	82.9	84.5	77.9	80.4	85.6	86.4	78.3	79.7	–	–

[a]: Full images are used as queries making the results not directly comparable on Oxford and Paris.
[b]: Our evaluation of MAC with PCA$_w$ as in [25] with the off-the-shelf network.

6   Conclusions

We addressed fine-tuning of CNN for image retrieval. The training data are selected from an automated 3D reconstruction system applied on a large unordered photo collection. The proposed method does not require any manual annotation and yet outperforms the state of the art on a number of standard benchmarks for wide range (16 to 512) of descriptor dimensionality. The achieved results are reaching the level of the best systems based on local features with spatial matching and query expansion, while being faster and requiring less memory. Training data, fine-tuned networks and evaluation code are publicly available[3].

Acknowledgment. Work was supported by the MSMT LL1303 ERC-CZ grant.

References

1. Lowe, D.: Distinctive image features from scale-invariant keypoints. IJCV **60**, 91–110 (2004)
2. Sivic, J., Zisserman, A.: Video Google: A text retrieval approach to object matching in videos. In: ICCV (2003)
3. Philbin, J., Chum, O., Isard, M., Sivic, J., Zisserman, A.: Object retrieval with large vocabularies and fast spatial matching. In: CVPR (2007)
4. Avrithis, Y., Kalantidis, Y.: Approximate Gaussian mixtures for large scale vocabularies. In: Fitzgibbon, A., Lazebnik, S., Perona, P., Sato, Y., Schmid, C. (eds.) ECCV 2012. LNCS, vol. 7574, pp. 15–28. Springer, Heidelberg (2012). doi:10.1007/978-3-642-33712-3_2
5. Shen, X., Lin, Z., Brandt, J., Wu, Y.: Spatially-constrained similarity measure for large-scale object retrieval. PAMI **36**, 1229–1241 (2014)
6. Chum, O., Mikulik, A., Perdoch, M., Matas, J.: Total recall II: query expansion revisited. In: CVPR (2011)
7. Danfeng, Q., Gammeter, S., Bossard, L., Quack, T., Gool, L.V.: Hello neighbor: accurate object retrieval with k-reciprocal nearest neighbors. In: CVPR (2011)
8. Tolias, G., Jégou, H.: Visual query expansion with or without geometry: refining local descriptors by feature aggregation. Pattern Recogn. **47**, 3466–3476 (2014)
9. Perronnin, F., Liu, Y., Sanchez, J., Poirier, H.: Large-scale image retrieval with compressed Fisher vectors. In: CVPR (2010)
10. Jégou, H., Perronnin, F., Douze, M., Sánchez, J., Pérez, P., Schmid, C.: Aggregating local descriptors into compact codes. PAMI **34**, 1704–1716 (2012)
11. Radenović, F., Jegou, H., Chum, O.: Multiple measurements and joint dimensionality reduction for large scale image search with short vectors. In: ICMR (2015)
12. Arandjelovic, R., Zisserman, A.: All about VLAD. In: CVPR (2013)
13. Tolias, G., Furon, T., Jégou, H.: Orientation covariant aggregation of local descriptors with embeddings. In: Fleet, D., Pajdla, T., Schiele, B., Tuytelaars, T. (eds.) ECCV 2014. LNCS, vol. 8694, pp. 382–397. Springer, Heidelberg (2014). doi:10.1007/978-3-319-10599-4_25
14. Babenko, A., Slesarev, A., Chigorin, A., Lempitsky, V.: Neural codes for image retrieval. In: Fleet, D., Pajdla, T., Schiele, B., Tuytelaars, T. (eds.) ECCV 2014. LNCS, vol. 8689, pp. 584–599. Springer, Heidelberg (2014). doi:10.1007/978-3-319-10590-1_38

---

[3] http://cmp.felk.cvut.cz/~radenfil/projects/siamac.html

15. Razavian, A.S., Sullivan, J., Maki, A., Carlsson, S.: A baseline for visual instance retrieval with deep convolutional networks. arXiv:1412.6574 (2014)
16. Krizhevsky, A., Sutskever, I., Hinton, G.E.: Imagenet classification with deep convolutional neural networks. In: NIPS (2012)
17. Russakovsky, O., Deng, J., Su, H., Krause, J., Satheesh, S., Ma, S., Huang, Z., Karpathy, A., Khosla, A., Bernstein, M., et al.: Imagenet large scale visual recognition challenge. IJCV **115**, 211–252 (2015)
18. Donahue, J., Jia, Y., Vinyals, O., Hoffman, J., Zhang, N., Tzeng, E., Darrell, T.: DeCAF: a deep convolutional activation feature for generic visual recognition. arXiv:1310.1531 (2013)
19. Razavian, A.S., Azizpour, H., Sullivan, J., Carlsson, S.: CNN features off-the-shelf: an astounding baseline for recognition. In: CVPRW (2014)
20. Girshick, R., Donahue, J., Darrell, T., Malik, J.: Rich feature hierarchies for accurate object detection and semantic segmentation. In: CVPR (2014)
21. Iandola, F., Moskewicz, M., Karayev, S., Girshick, R., Darrell, T., Keutzer, K.: DenseNet: implementing efficient ConvNet descriptor pyramids. arXiv:1404.1869 (2014)
22. Gong, Y., Wang, L., Guo, R., Lazebnik, S.: Multi-scale orderless pooling of deep convolutional activation features. In: Fleet, D., Pajdla, T., Schiele, B., Tuytelaars, T. (eds.) ECCV 2014. LNCS, vol. 8695, pp. 392–407. Springer, Heidelberg (2014). doi:10.1007/978-3-319-10584-0_26
23. Babenko, A., Lempitsky, V.: Aggregating deep convolutional features for image retrieval. In: ICCV (2015)
24. Kalantidis, Y., Mellina, C., Osindero, S.: Cross-dimensional weighting for aggregated deep convolutional features. arXiv:1512.04065 (2015)
25. Tolias, G., Sicre, R., Jégou, H.: Particular object retrieval with integral max-pooling of CNN activations. In: ICLR (2016)
26. Azizpour, H., Razavian, A.S., Sullivan, J., Maki, A., Carlsson, S.: From generic to specific deep representations for visual recognition. In: CVPRW (2015)
27. Zhang, N., Donahue, J., Girshick, R., Darrell, T.: Part-based R-CNNs for fine-grained category detection. In: Fleet, D., Pajdla, T., Schiele, B., Tuytelaars, T. (eds.) ECCV 2014. LNCS, vol. 8689, pp. 834–849. Springer, Heidelberg (2014). doi:10.1007/978-3-319-10590-1_54
28. Oquab, M., Bottou, L., Laptev, I., Sivic, J.: Learning and transferring mid-level image representations using convolutional neural networks. In: CVPR (2014)
29. Chopra, S., Hadsell, R., LeCun, Y.: Learning a similarity metric discriminatively, with application to face verification. In: CVPR (2005)
30. Hadsell, R., Chopra, S., LeCun, Y.: Dimensionality reduction by learning an invariant mapping. In: CVPR (2006)
31. Hu, J., Lu, J., Tan, Y.P.: Discriminative deep metric learning for face verification in the wild. In: CVPR (2014)
32. Wang, J., Song, Y., Leung, T., Rosenberg, C., Wang, J., Philbin, J., Chen, B., Wu, Y.: Learning fine-grained image similarity with deep ranking. In: CVPR (2014)
33. Schroff, F., Kalenichenko, D., Philbin, J.: FaceNet: a unified embedding for face recognition and clustering. In: CVPR (2015)
34. Hoffer, E., Ailon, N.: Deep metric learning using triplet network. In: ICLR Workshop (2015)
35. Arandjelovic, R., Gronat, P., Torii, A., Pajdla, T., Sivic, J.: NetVLAD: CNN architecture for weakly supervised place recognition. In: CVPR (2016)

36. Gordo, A., Almazan, J., Revaud, J., Larlus, D.: Deep image retrieval: learning global representations for image search. In: Leibe, B., Mata, J., Sebe, N., Welling, M. (eds.) ECCV 2016. LNCS, vol. 9910, pp. 241–257. Springer, Switzerland (2016)
37. Chum, O., Matas, J.: Large-scale discovery of spatially related images. PAMI **32**, 371–377 (2010)
38. Weyand, T., Leibe, B.: Discovering details and scene structure with hierarchical iconoid shift. In: ICCV (2013)
39. Philbin, J., Sivic, J., Zisserman, A.: Geometric latent Dirichlet allocation on a matching graph for large-scale image datasets. IJCV **95**, 138–153 (2011)
40. Schönberger, J.L., Radenović, F., Chum, O., Frahm, J.M.: From single image query to detailed 3D reconstruction. In: CVPR (2015)
41. Jégou, H., Chum, O.: Negative evidences and co-occurences in image retrieval: the benefit of PCA and whitening. In: Fitzgibbon, A., Lazebnik, S., Perona, P., Sato, Y., Schmid, C. (eds.) ECCV 2012. LNCS, vol. 7573, pp. 774–787. Springer, Heidelberg (2012). doi:10.1007/978-3-642-33709-3_55
42. Simonyan, K., Zisserman, A.: Very deep convolutional networks for large-scale image recognition. arXiv:1409.1556 (2014)
43. Zheng, L., Zhao, Y., Wang, S., Wang, J., Tian, Q.: Good practice in CNN feature transfer. arXiv:1604.00133 (2016)
44. Simo-Serra, E., Trulls, E., Ferraz, L., Kokkinos, I., Moreno-Noguer, F.: Fracking deep convolutional image descriptors. arxiv:1412.6537 (2014)
45. Papandreou, G., Kokkinos, I., Savalle, P.A.: Modeling local and global deformations in deep learning: epitomic convolution, multiple instance learning, and sliding window detection. In: CVPR (2015)
46. Mikolajczyk, K., Matas, J.: Improving descriptors for fast tree matching by optimal linear projection. In: ICCV (2007)
47. Radenović, F., Schönberger, J.L., Ji, D., Frahm, J.M., Chum, O., Matas, J.: From dusk till dawn: modeling in the dark. In: CVPR (2016)
48. Mikolajczyk, K., Tuytelaars, T., Schmid, C., Zisserman, A., Matas, J., Schaffalitzky, F., Kadir, T., Gool, L.V.: A comparison of affine region detectors. IJCV 65, 43-72 (2005)
49. Arandjelovic, R., Zisserman, A.: Three things everyone should know to improve object retrieval. In: CVPR (2012)
50. Mikulik, A., Perdoch, M., Chum, O., Matas, J.: Learning vocabularies over a fine quantization. IJCV **13**, 163–175 (2013)
51. Frahm, J.-M., et al.: Building Rome on a cloudless day. In: Daniilidis, K., Maragos, P., Paragios, N. (eds.) ECCV 2010. LNCS, vol. 6314, pp. 368–381. Springer, Heidelberg (2010). doi:10.1007/978-3-642-15561-1_27
52. Agarwal, S., Furukawa, Y., Snavely, N., Simon, I., Curless, B., Seitz, S.M., Szeliski, R.: Building Rome in a day. Commun. ACM **54**, 105–112 (2011)
53. Mikulik, A., Chum, O., Matas, J.: Image retrieval for online browsing in large image collections. In: Brisaboa, N., Pedreira, O., Zezula, P. (eds.) SISAP 2013. LNCS, vol. 8199, pp. 3–15. Springer, Heidelberg (2013). doi:10.1007/978-3-642-41062-8_2
54. Mikulík, A., Radenović, F., Chum, O., Matas, J.: Efficient image detail mining. In: Cremers, D., Reid, I., Saito, H., Yang, M.-H. (eds.) ACCV 2014. LNCS, vol. 9004, pp. 118–132. Springer, Heidelberg (2015). doi:10.1007/978-3-319-16808-1_9
55. Li, Y., Snavely, N., Huttenlocher, D.P.: Location recognition using prioritized feature matching. In: Daniilidis, K., Maragos, P., Paragios, N. (eds.) ECCV 2010. LNCS, vol. 6312, pp. 791–804. Springer, Heidelberg (2010). doi:10.1007/978-3-642-15552-9_57

56. Philbin, J., Chum, O., Isard, M., Sivic, J., Zisserman, A.: Lost in quantization: improving particular object retrieval in large scale image databases. In: CVPR (2008)
57. Jegou, H., Douze, M., Schmid, C.: Hamming embedding and weak geometric consistency for large scale image search. In: Forsyth, D., Torr, P., Zisserman, A. (eds.) ECCV 2008. LNCS, vol. 5302, pp. 304–317. Springer, Heidelberg (2008). doi:10.1007/978-3-540-88682-2_24

SSD: Single Shot MultiBox Detector

Wei Liu[1]($\boxtimes$), Dragomir Anguelov[2], Dumitru Erhan[3], Christian Szegedy[3],
Scott Reed[4], Cheng-Yang Fu[1], and Alexander C. Berg[1]

[1] UNC Chapel Hill, Chapel Hill, USA
{wliu,cyfu,aberg}@cs.unc.edu
[2] Zoox Inc., Palo Alto, USA
drago@zoox.com
[3] Google Inc., Mountain View, USA
{dumitru,szegedy}@google.com
[4] University of Michigan, Ann-Arbor, USA
reedscot@umich.edu

Abstract. We present a method for detecting objects in images using a single deep neural network. Our approach, named SSD, discretizes the output space of bounding boxes into a set of default boxes over different aspect ratios and scales per feature map location. At prediction time, the network generates scores for the presence of each object category in each default box and produces adjustments to the box to better match the object shape. Additionally, the network combines predictions from multiple feature maps with different resolutions to naturally handle objects of various sizes. SSD is simple relative to methods that require object proposals because it completely eliminates proposal generation and subsequent pixel or feature resampling stages and encapsulates all computation in a single network. This makes SSD easy to train and straightforward to integrate into systems that require a detection component. Experimental results on the PASCAL VOC, COCO, and ILSVRC datasets confirm that SSD has competitive accuracy to methods that utilize an additional object proposal step and is much faster, while providing a unified framework for both training and inference. For 300×300 input, SSD achieves 74.3 % mAP on VOC2007 test at 59 FPS on a Nvidia Titan X and for 512×512 input, SSD achieves 76.9 % mAP, outperforming a comparable state of the art Faster R-CNN model. Compared to other single stage methods, SSD has much better accuracy even with a smaller input image size. Code is available at https://github.com/weiliu89/caffe/tree/ssd.

Keywords: Real-time object detection · Convolutional neural network

1 Introduction

Current state-of-the-art object detection systems are variants of the following approach: hypothesize bounding boxes, resample pixels or features for each box, and

© Springer International Publishing AG 2016
B. Leibe et al. (Eds.): ECCV 2016, Part I, LNCS 9905, pp. 21–37, 2016.
DOI: 10.1007/978-3-319-46448-0_2

apply a high-quality classifier. This pipeline has prevailed on detection benchmarks since the Selective Search work [1] through the current leading results on PASCAL VOC, COCO, and ILSVRC detection all based on Faster R-CNN [2] albeit with deeper features such as [3]. While accurate, these approaches have been too computationally intensive for embedded systems and, even with high-end hardware, too slow for real-time applications. Often detection speed for these approaches is measured in frames per second, and even the fastest high-accuracy detector, Faster R-CNN, operates at only 7 frames per second (FPS). There have been many attempts to build faster detectors by attacking each stage of the detection pipeline (see related work in Sect. 4), but so far, significantly increased speed comes only at the cost of significantly decreased detection accuracy.

This paper presents the first deep network based object detector that does not resample pixels or features for bounding box hypotheses and is as accurate as approaches that do. This results in a significant improvement in speed for high-accuracy detection (59 FPS with mAP 74.3 % on VOC2007 test, vs Faster R-CNN 7 FPS with mAP 73.2 % or YOLO 45 FPS with mAP 63.4 %). The fundamental improvement in speed comes from eliminating bounding box proposals and the subsequent pixel or feature resampling stage. We are not the first to do this (cf. [4,5]), but by adding a series of improvements, we manage to increase the accuracy significantly over previous attempts. Our improvements include using a small convolutional filter to predict object categories and offsets in bounding box locations, using separate predictors (filters) for different aspect ratio detections, and applying these filters to multiple feature maps from the later stages of a network in order to perform detection at multiple scales. With these modifications—especially using multiple layers for prediction at different scales—we can achieve high-accuracy using relatively low resolution input, further increasing detection speed. While these contributions may seem small independently, we note that the resulting system improves accuracy on real-time detection for PASCAL VOC from 63.4 % mAP for YOLO to 74.3 % mAP for our SSD. This is a larger relative improvement in detection accuracy than that from the recent, very high-profile work on residual networks [3]. Furthermore, significantly improving the speed of high-quality detection can broaden the range of settings where computer vision is useful.

We summarize our contributions as follows:

- We introduce SSD, a single-shot detector for multiple categories that is faster than the previous state-of-the-art for single shot detectors (YOLO), and significantly more accurate, in fact as accurate as slower techniques that perform explicit region proposals and pooling (including Faster R-CNN).
- The core of SSD is predicting category scores and box offsets for a fixed set of default bounding boxes using small convolutional filters applied to feature maps.
- To achieve high detection accuracy we produce predictions of different scales from feature maps of different scales, and explicitly separate predictions by aspect ratio.

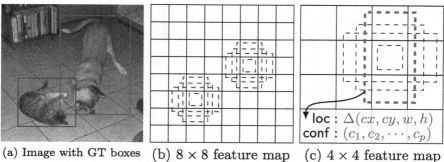

(a) Image with GT boxes   (b) 8 × 8 feature map   (c) 4 × 4 feature map

Fig. 1. SSD framework. (a) SSD only needs an input image and ground truth boxes for each object during training. In a convolutional fashion, we evaluate a small set (e.g. 4) of default boxes of different aspect ratios at each location in several feature maps with different scales (e.g. 8 × 8 and 4 × 4 in (b) and (c)). For each default box, we predict both the shape offsets and the confidences for all object categories $((c_1, c_2, \cdots, c_p))$. At training time, we first match these default boxes to the ground truth boxes. For example, we have matched two default boxes with the cat and one with the dog, which are treated as positives and the rest as negatives. The model loss is a weighted sum between localization loss (e.g. Smooth L1 [6]) and confidence loss (e.g. Softmax).

– These design features lead to simple end-to-end training and high accuracy, even on low resolution input images, further improving the speed vs accuracy trade-off.
– Experiments include timing and accuracy analysis on models with varying input size evaluated on PASCAL VOC, COCO, and ILSVRC and are compared to a range of recent state-of-the-art approaches.

2 The Single Shot Detector (SSD)

This section describes our proposed SSD framework for detection (Sect. 2.1) and the associated training methodology (Sect. 2.2). Afterwards, Sect. 3 presents dataset-specific model details and experimental results.

2.1 Model

The SSD approach is based on a feed-forward convolutional network that produces a fixed-size collection of bounding boxes and scores for the presence of object class instances in those boxes, followed by a non-maximum suppression step to produce the final detections. The early network layers are based on a standard architecture used for high quality image classification (truncated before any classification layers), which we will call the base network[1]. We then add auxiliary structure to the network to produce detections with the following key features:

---

[1] We use the VGG-16 network as a base, but other networks should also produce good results.

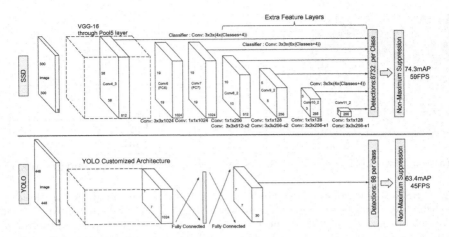

Fig. 2. A comparison between two single shot detection models: SSD and YOLO [5]. Our SSD model adds several feature layers to the end of a base network, which predict the offsets to default boxes of different scales and aspect ratios and their associated confidences. SSD with a 300 × 300 input size significantly outperforms its 448 × 448 YOLO counterpart in accuracy on VOC2007 test while also improving the speed.

Multi-scale feature maps for detection. We add convolutional feature layers to the end of the truncated base network. These layers decrease in size progressively and allow predictions of detections at multiple scales. The convolutional model for predicting detections is different for each feature layer (*cf* Overfeat [4] and YOLO [5] that operate on a single scale feature map).

Convolutional predictors for detection. Each added feature layer (or optionally an existing feature layer from the base network) can produce a fixed set of detection predictions using a set of convolutional filters. These are indicated on top of the SSD network architecture in Fig. 2. For a feature layer of size $m \times n$ with p channels, the basic element for predicting parameters of a potential detection is a $3 \times 3 \times p$ *small kernel* that produces either a score for a category, or a shape offset relative to the default box coordinates. At each of the $m \times n$ locations where the kernel is applied, it produces an output value. The bounding box offset output values are measured relative to a default box position relative to each feature map location (*cf* the architecture of YOLO [5] that uses an intermediate fully connected layer instead of a convolutional filter for this step).

Default boxes and aspect ratios. We associate a set of default bounding boxes with each feature map cell, for multiple feature maps at the top of the network. The default boxes tile the feature map in a convolutional manner, so that the position of each box relative to its corresponding cell is fixed. At each feature map cell, we predict the offsets relative to the default box shapes in the cell, as well as the per-class scores that indicate the presence of a class instance in each of those boxes. Specifically, for each box out of k at a given location, we compute c class scores and the 4 offsets relative to the original default box shape. This results in a total of $(c+4)k$ filters that are applied around each location in the feature map, yielding $(c+4)kmn$ outputs for a $m \times n$ feature map. For an illustration of default boxes, please refer to Fig. 1. Our default boxes are similar to the *anchor boxes* used in Faster R-CNN [2], however we apply them to several feature maps of different resolutions. Allowing different default box shapes in several feature maps let us efficiently discretize the space of possible output box shapes.

2.2   Training

The key difference between training SSD and training a typical detector that uses region proposals, is that ground truth information needs to be assigned to specific outputs in the fixed set of detector outputs. Some version of this is also required for training in YOLO [5] and for the region proposal stage of Faster R-CNN [2] and MultiBox [7]. Once this assignment is determined, the loss function and back propagation are applied end-to-end. Training also involves choosing the set of default boxes and scales for detection as well as the hard negative mining and data augmentation strategies.

Matching Strategy. During training we need to determine which default boxes correspond to a ground truth detection and train the network accordingly. For each ground truth box we are selecting from default boxes that vary over location, aspect ratio, and scale. We begin by matching each ground truth box to the default box with the best Jaccard overlap (as in MultiBox [7]). Unlike MultiBox, we then match default boxes to any ground truth with Jaccard overlap higher than a threshold (0.5). This simplifies the learning problem, allowing the network to predict high scores for multiple overlapping default boxes rather than requiring it to pick only the one with maximum overlap.

Training Objective. The SSD training objective is derived from the MultiBox objective [7,8] but is extended to handle multiple object categories. Let $x_{ij}^p = \{1, 0\}$ be an indicator for matching the i-th default box to the j-th ground truth box of category p. In the matching strategy above, we can have $\sum_i x_{ij}^p \geq 1$. The overall objective loss function is a weighted sum of the localization loss (loc) and the confidence loss (conf):

$$L(x, c, l, g) = \frac{1}{N}(L_{conf}(x, c) + \alpha L_{loc}(x, l, g)) \qquad (1)$$

where N is the number of matched default boxes, and the localization loss is the Smooth L1 loss [6] between the predicted box (l) and the ground truth box (g) parameters. Similar to Faster R-CNN [2], we regress to offsets for the center of the bounding box and for its width and height. Our confidence loss is the softmax loss over multiple classes confidences (c) and the weight term α is set to 1 by cross validation.

Choosing Scales and Aspect Ratios for Default Boxes. To handle different object scales, some methods [4,9] suggest processing the image at different sizes and combining the results afterwards. However, by utilizing feature maps from several different layers in a single network for prediction we can mimic the same effect, while also sharing parameters across all object scales. Previous works [10,11] have shown that using feature maps from the lower layers can improve semantic segmentation quality because the lower layers capture more fine details of the input objects. Similarly, [12] showed that adding global context pooled from a feature map can help smooth the segmentation results. Motivated by these methods, we use both the lower and upper feature maps for detection. Figure 1 shows two exemplar feature maps (8×8 and 4×4) which are used in the framework. In practice, we can use many more with small computational overhead.

We design the tiling of default boxes so that specific feature maps learn to be responsive to particular scales of the objects. Suppose we want to use m feature maps for prediction. The scale of the default boxes for each feature map is computed as:

$$s_k = s_{\min} + \frac{s_{\max} - s_{\min}}{m - 1}(k - 1), \quad k \in [1, m] \tag{2}$$

where $s_{\min}$ is 0.2 and $s_{\max}$ is 0.9, meaning the lowest layer has a scale of 0.2 and the highest layer has a scale of 0.9, and all layers in between are regularly spaced. We impose different aspect ratios for the default boxes, and denote them as $a_r \in \{1, 2, 3, \frac{1}{2}, \frac{1}{3}\}$. We can compute the width ($w_k^a = s_k \sqrt{a_r}$) and height ($h_k^a = s_k / \sqrt{a_r}$) for each default box. For the aspect ratio of 1, we also add a default box whose scale is $s'_k = \sqrt{s_k s_{k+1}}$, resulting in 6 default boxes per feature map location. We set the center of each default box to ($\frac{i+0.5}{|f_k|}, \frac{j+0.5}{|f_k|}$), where $|f_k|$ is the size of the k-th square feature map, $i, j \in [0, |f_k|)$. In practice, one can also design a distribution of default boxes to best fit a specific dataset.

By combining predictions for all default boxes with different scales and aspect ratios from all locations of many feature maps, we have a diverse set of predictions, covering various input object sizes and shapes. For example, in Fig. 1, the dog is matched to a default box in the 4×4 feature map, but not to any default boxes in the 8×8 feature map. This is because those boxes have different scales and do not match the dog box, and therefore are considered as negatives during training.

Hard Negative Mining. After the matching step, most of the default boxes are negatives, especially when the number of possible default boxes is large. This introduces a significant imbalance between the positive and negative training examples. Instead of using all the negative examples, we sort them using the highest confidence loss for each default box and pick the top ones so that the ratio between the negatives and positives is at most 3:1. We found that this leads to faster optimization and a more stable training.

Data Augmentation. To make the model more robust to various input object sizes and shapes, each training image is randomly sampled by one of the following options:

- Use the entire original input image.
- Sample a patch so that the *minimum* Jaccard overlap with the objects is 0.1, 0.3, 0.5, 0.7, or 0.9.
- Randomly sample a patch.

The size of each sampled patch is $[0.1, 1]$ of the original image size, and the aspect ratio is between $\frac{1}{2}$ and 2. We keep the overlapped part of the ground truth box if the center of it is in the sampled patch. After the aforementioned sampling step, each sampled patch is resized to fixed size and is horizontally flipped with probability of 0.5, in addition to applying some photo-metric distortions similar to those described in [13].

3   Experimental Results

Base Network. Our experiments are all based on VGG16 [14], which is pre-trained on the ILSVRC CLS-LOC dataset [15]. Similar to DeepLab-LargeFOV [16], we convert fc6 and fc7 to convolutional layers, subsample parameters from fc6 and fc7, change pool5 from $2 \times 2 - s2$ to $3 \times 3 - s1$, and use the atrous algorithm to fill the "holes". We remove all the dropout layers and the fc8 layer. We fine-tune the resulting model using SGD with initial learning rate 10^{-3}, 0.9 momentum, 0.0005 weight decay, and batch size 32. The learning rate decay policy is slightly different for each dataset, and we will describe details later. The full training and testing code is built on Caffe [17] and is open source at https://github.com/weiliu89/caffe/tree/ssd.

3.1   PASCAL VOC2007

On this dataset, we compare against Fast R-CNN [6] and Faster R-CNN [2] on VOC2007 `test` (4952 images). All methods use the same pre-trained VGG16 network.

Figure 2 shows the architecture details of the SSD300 model. We use conv4_3, conv7 (fc7), conv8_2, conv9_2, conv10_2, and conv11_2 to predict both location and confidences[2]. We initialize the parameters for all the newly added convolutional layers with the "xavier" method [18]. For conv4_3, conv10_2 and conv11_2, we only associate 4 default boxes at each feature map location – omitting aspect ratios of $\frac{1}{3}$ and 3. For all other layers, we put 6 default boxes as described in Sect. 2.2. Since, as pointed out in [12], conv4_3 has a different feature scale compared to the other layers, we use the L2 normalization technique introduced in [12] to scale the feature norm at each location in the feature map to 20 and learn the scale during back propagation. We use the 10^{-3} learning rate for 40k

---

[2] For SSD512 model, we add extra conv12_2 for prediction.

Table 1. PASCAL VOC2007 test detection results. Both Fast and Faster R-CNN use input images whose minimum dimension is 600. The two SSD models have exactly the same settings except that they have different input sizes (300 × 300 vs. 512 × 512). It is obvious that larger input size leads to better results, and more data always helps. Data: "07": VOC2007 trainval, "07+12": union of VOC2007 and VOC2012 trainval. "07+12+COCO": first train on COCO trainval35k then fine-tune on 07+12.

Method	data	mAP	aero	bike	bird	boat	bottle	bus	car	cat	chair	cow	table	dog	horse	mbike	person	plant	sheep	sofa	train	tv
Fast [6]	07	66.9	74.5	78.3	69.2	53.2	36.6	77.3	78.2	82.0	40.7	72.7	67.9	79.6	79.2	73.0	69.0	30.1	65.4	70.2	75.8	65.8
Fast [6]	07+12	70.0	77.0	78.1	69.3	59.4	38.3	81.6	78.6	86.7	42.8	78.8	68.9	84.7	82.0	76.6	69.9	31.8	70.1	74.8	80.4	70.4
Faster [2]	07	69.9	70.0	80.6	70.1	57.3	49.9	78.2	80.4	82.0	52.2	75.3	67.2	80.3	79.8	75.0	76.3	39.1	68.3	67.3	81.1	67.6
Faster [2]	07+12	73.2	76.5	79.0	70.9	65.5	52.1	83.1	84.7	86.4	52.0	81.9	65.7	84.8	84.6	77.5	76.7	38.8	73.6	73.9	83.0	72.6
Faster [2]	07+12+COCO	78.8	84.3	82.0	77.7	68.9	65.7	88.1	88.4	88.9	63.6	86.3	70.8	85.9	87.6	80.1	82.3	53.6	80.4	75.8	86.6	78.9
SSD300	07	68.0	73.4	77.5	64.1	59.0	38.9	75.2	80.8	78.5	46.0	67.8	69.2	76.6	82.1	77.0	72.5	41.2	64.2	69.1	78.0	68.5
SSD300	07+12	74.1	74.6	80.2	72.2	66.2	47.1	82.9	83.4	86.1	54.4	78.5	73.9	84.4	84.5	82.4	76.1	48.6	74.3	75.0	84.3	74.0
SSD300	07+12+COCO	79.6	80.9	86.3	79.0	76.2	57.6	87.3	88.2	88.6	60.5	85.4	76.7	87.5	89.2	84.5	81.4	55.0	81.9	81.5	85.9	78.9
SSD512	07	71.6	75.1	81.4	69.8	60.8	46.3	82.6	84.7	84.1	48.5	75.0	67.4	82.3	83.9	79.4	76.6	44.9	69.9	69.1	78.1	71.8
SSD512	07+12	76.8	82.4	84.7	78.4	73.8	53.2	86.2	87.5	86.0	57.8	83.1	70.2	84.9	85.2	83.9	79.7	50.3	77.9	73.9	82.5	75.3
SSD512	07+12+COCO	81.5	86.9	87.5	82.0	75.5	66.4	88.2	88.7	89.3	65.2	88.3	74.4	87.1	88.9	85.9	84.5	57.6	84.6	80.7	87.1	81.7

iterations, then we continue training for 10k iterations with 10^{-4} and 10^{-5}. When training on VOC2007 trainval, Table 1 shows that our low resolution SSD300 model is already more accurate than Fast R-CNN. When we train SSD on a larger 512 × 512 input image it is even more accurate, surpassing Faster R-CNN by 1.7 % mAP. If we train SSD with more (i.e. 07 + 12) data, we observe that SSD300 is already better than Faster R-CNN by 0.9 % and that SSD512 is 3.6 % better. If we take models trained on COCO trainval35k as described in Sect. 3.4 and fine-tuning them on the 07 + 12 dataset with SSD512, we achieve the best results: 81.5 % mAP.

To understand the performance of our two SSD models in more details, we used the detection analysis tool from [19]. Figure 3 shows that SSD can detect various object categories with high quality (large white area). The majority of its confident detections are correct. The recall is around 85–90 %, and is much higher with "weak" (0.1 Jaccard overlap) criteria. Compared to R-CNN [20], SSD has less localization error, indicating that SSD can localize objects better because it directly learns to regress the object shape and classify object categories instead of using two decoupled steps. However, SSD has more confusions with similar object categories (especially for animals), partly because we share locations for multiple categories. Figure 4 shows that SSD is very sensitive to the bounding box size. In other words, it has much worse performance on smaller objects than bigger objects. This is not surprising because those small objects may not even have any information at the very top layers. Increasing the input size (e.g. from 300 × 300 to 512 × 512) can help improve detecting small objects, but there is still a lot of room to improve. On the positive side, we can clearly see that SSD performs really well on large objects. And it is very robust to different object aspect ratios because we use default boxes of various aspect ratios per feature map location.

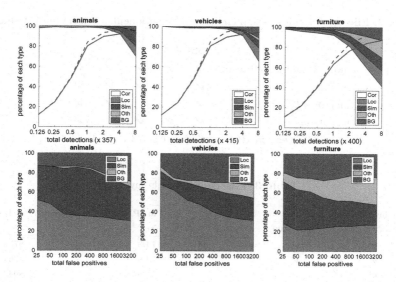

Fig. 3. Visualization of performance for SSD 512 on animals, vehicles, and furniture from VOC2007 test using [19]. The top row shows the cumulative fraction of detections that are correct (Cor) or false positive due to poor localization (Loc), confusion with similar categories (Sim), with others (Oth), or with background (BG). The bottom row shows the distribution of top-ranked false positive types.

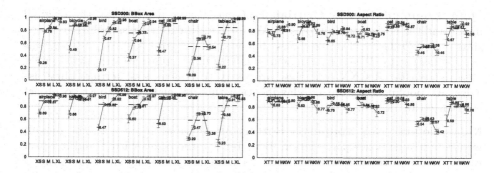

Fig. 4. Sensitivity and impact of different object characteristics on VOC2007 test set using [19]. The plot on the left shows the effects of BBox Area per category, and the right plot shows the effect of Aspect Ratio.

3.2 Model Analysis

To understand SSD better, we carried out controlled experiments to examine how each component affects performance. For all the experiments, we use the same settings and input size (300 × 300), except for specified changes to the settings or component(s).

Table 2. Effects of various design choices and components on SSD performance.

	SSD300				
more data augmentation?		✔	✔	✔	✔
include $\{\frac{1}{2}, 2\}$ box?	✔		✔	✔	✔
include $\{\frac{1}{3}, 3\}$ box?	✔			✔	✔
use atrous?	✔	✔	✔		✔
VOC2007 test mAP	65.5	71.6	73.7	74.4	74.3

Table 3. Effects of multiple layers.

Source layers from:						mAP use boundary boxes?		# Boxes
conv4_3	conv7	conv8_2	conv9_2	conv10_2	conv11_2	Yes	No	
✔	✔	✔	✔	✔	✔	74.3	63.4	8732
✔	✔	✔	✔	✔		74.6	63.1	8764
✔	✔	✔	✔			73.8	68.4	8942
✔	✔	✔				70.7	69.2	9864
✔	✔					64.2	64.4	9025
	✔					62.4	64.0	8664

Data Augmentation is Crucial. Fast and Faster R-CNN use the original image and the horizontal flip to train. We use a more extensive sampling strategy, similar to YOLO [5]. Table 2 shows that we can improve 8.8 % mAP with this sampling strategy. We do not know how much our sampling strategy will benefit Fast and Faster R-CNN, but they are likely to benefit less because they use a feature pooling step during classification that is relatively robust to object translation by design.

More Default Box Shapes is Better. As described in Sect. 2.2, by default we use 6 default boxes per location. If we remove the boxes with $\frac{1}{3}$ and 3 aspect ratios, the performance drops by 0.6 %. By further removing the boxes with $\frac{1}{2}$ and 2 aspect ratios, the performance drops another 2.1 %. Using a variety of default box shapes seems to make the task of predicting boxes easier for the network.

Atrous is Faster. As described in Sect. 3, we used the atrous version of a sub-sampled VGG16, following DeepLab-LargeFOV [16]. If we use the full VGG16, keeping pool5 with $2 \times 2 - s2$ and not subsampling parameters from fc6 and fc7, and add conv5_3 for prediction, the result is about the same while the speed is about 20 % slower.

Multiple Output Layers at Different Resolutions is Better. A major contribution of SSD is using default boxes of different scales on different output layers. To measure the advantage gained, we progressively remove layers and compare results. For a fair comparison, every time we remove a layer, we adjust the default box tiling to keep the total number of boxes similar to the original (8732). This is done by stacking more scales of boxes on remaining layers and adjusting scales of boxes if needed. We do not exhaustively optimize the tiling for each setting. Table 3 shows a decrease in accuracy with fewer layers, dropping monotonically from 74.3 to 62.4. When we stack boxes of multiple scales on a layer, many are on the image boundary and need to be handled carefully. We tried the strategy used in Faster R-CNN [2], ignoring boxes which are on the boundary. We observe some interesting trends. For example, it hurts the performance by a large margin if we use very coarse feature maps (e.g. conv11_2 (1×1) or conv10_2 (3×3)). The reason might be that we do not have enough large boxes to cover large objects after the pruning. When we use primarily finer resolution maps, the performance starts increasing again because even after pruning a sufficient number of large boxes remains. If we only use conv7 for prediction, the performance is the worst, reinforcing the message that it is critical to spread boxes of different scales over different layers.

3.3 PASCAL VOC2012

We use the same settings as those used for our basic VOC2007 experiments above, except that we use VOC2012 `trainval` and VOC2007 `trainval` and `test` (21503 images) for training, and test on VOC2012 `test` (10991 images). We train the models with 10^{-3} learning rate for 60k iterations, then 10^{-4} for 20k iterations. Table 4 shows the results of our SSD300 and SSD512[3] model. We see the same performance trend as we observed on VOC2007 test. Our SSD300 improves accuracy over Fast/Faster R-CNN. By increasing the training and testing image size to 512×512, we are 4.5 % more accurate than Faster R-CNN. Compared to YOLO, SSD is significantly more accurate, likely due to the use of convolutional default boxes from multiple feature maps and our matching strategy during training. When fine-tuned from models trained on COCO, our SSD512 achieves 80.0 % mAP, which is 4.1 % higher than Faster R-CNN.

3.4 COCO

To further validate the SSD framework, we trained our SSD300 and SSD512 architectures on the COCO dataset. Since objects in COCO tend to be smaller than PASCAL VOC, we use smaller default boxes for all layers. We follow the strategy mentioned in Sect. 2.2, but now our smallest default box has a scale of 0.15 instead of 0.2, and the scale of the default box on conv4_3 is 0.07 (e.g. 21 pixels for a 300×300 image).

We use the `trainval35k` [21] for training. We first train the model with 10^{-3} learning rate for 160k iterations, and then continue training for 40k iterations with 10^{-4} and 40k iterations with 10^{-5}. Table 5 shows the results on

---

[3] http://host.robots.ox.ac.uk:8080/leaderboard/displaylb.php?cls= mean&challengeid=11&compid=4.

Table 4. PASCAL VOC2012 test detection results. Fast and Faster R-CNN use images with minimum dimension 600, while the image size for YOLO is 448 × 448. data: "07++12": union of VOC2007 trainval and test and VOC2012 trainval. "07++12+COCO": first train on COCO trainval35k then fine-tune on 07++12.

Method	data	mAP	aero	bike	bird	boat	bottle	bus	car	cat	chair	cow	table	dog	horse	mbike	person	plant	sheep	sofa	train	tv
Fast[6]	07++12	68.4	82.3	78.4	70.8	52.3	38.7	77.8	71.6	89.3	44.2	73.0	55.0	87.5	80.5	80.8	72.0	35.1	68.3	65.7	80.4	64.2
Faster[2]	07++12	70.4	84.9	79.8	74.3	53.9	49.8	77.5	75.9	88.5	45.6	77.1	55.3	86.9	81.7	80.9	79.6	40.1	72.6	60.9	81.2	61.5
Faster[2]	07++12+COCO	75.9	87.4	83.6	76.8	62.9	59.6	81.9	82.0	91.3	54.9	82.6	59.0	89.0	85.5	84.7	84.1	52.2	78.9	65.5	85.4	70.2
YOLO[5]	07++12	57.9	77.0	67.2	57.7	38.3	22.7	68.3	55.9	81.4	36.2	60.8	48.5	77.2	72.3	71.3	63.5	28.9	52.2	54.8	73.9	50.8
SSD300	07++12	72.4	85.6	80.1	70.5	57.6	46.2	79.4	76.1	89.2	53.0	77.0	60.8	87.0	83.1	82.3	79.4	45.9	75.9	69.5	81.9	67.5
SSD300	07++12+COCO	77.5	90.2	83.3	76.3	63.0	53.6	83.8	82.8	92.0	59.7	82.7	63.5	89.3	87.6	85.9	84.3	52.6	82.5	**74.1**	88.4	74.2
SSD512	07++12	74.9	87.4	82.3	75.8	59.0	52.6	81.7	81.5	90.0	55.4	79.0	59.8	88.4	84.3	84.7	83.3	50.2	78.0	66.3	86.3	72.0
SSD512	07++12+COCO	**80.0**	**90.7**	**86.8**	**80.5**	**67.8**	**60.8**	**86.3**	**85.5**	**93.5**	**63.2**	**85.7**	**64.4**	**90.9**	**89.0**	**88.9**	**86.8**	**57.2**	**85.1**	72.8	**88.4**	**75.9**

Table 5. COCO test-dev2015 detection results.

Method	Data	Mean average precision		
		0.5	0.75	0.5:0.95
Fast R-CNN [6]	train	35.9	-	19.7
Fast R-CNN [21]	train	39.9	20.5	19.4
Faster R-CNN [2]	train	42.1	-	21.5
Faster R-CNN [2]	trainval	42.7	-	21.9
Faster R-CNN [22]	trainval	45.3	24.2	23.5
ION [21]	train	42.0	23.0	23.0
SSD300	trainval35k	41.2	23.2	23.4
SSD512	trainval35k	**46.4**	**26.7**	**27.7**

test-dev2015. Similar to what we observed on the PASCAL VOC dataset, SSD300 is better than Fast R-CNN in both mAP@0.5 and mAP@[0.5:0.95]. SSD300 has a similar mAP@[0.5:0.95] to Faster R-CNN [22]. However, the mAP@0.5 is worse and we conjecture that it is because the image size is too small, which prevents the model from detecting many small objects. But overall, SSD can localize objects more accurately. By increasing the image size to 512×512, our SSD512 is better than Faster R-CNN in both criteria. In addition, our SSD512 model is also better than ION [21], a multi-scale version of Fast R-CNN with explicit modeling of context using a recurrent network. In Fig. 5, we show some detection examples on COCO test-dev with the SSD512 model.

3.5   Preliminary ILSVRC Results

We applied the same network architecture we used for COCO to the ILSVRC DET dataset [15]. We train a SSD300 model using the ILSVRC2014 DET train and val1 as used in [20]. We first train the model with 10^{-3} learning rate for 320k iterations, and then continue training for 80k iterations with 10^{-4} and 40k iterations with 10^{-5}. We can achieve 43.2 mAP on the val2 set [20]. Again, it validates that SSD is a general framework for high quality real-time detection.

3.6 Inference Time

Considering the large number of boxes generated from our method, it is essential to perform non-maximum suppression (nms) efficiently during inference. By using a confidence threshold of 0.01, we can filter out most boxes. We then apply nms with Jaccard overlap of 0.45 per class and keep the top 200 detections per image. This step costs about 1.7 ms per image for SSD300 and 20 VOC classes, which is close to the total time (2.4 ms) spent on all newly added layers.

Table 6 shows the comparison between SSD, Faster R-CNN [2], and YOLO [5]. Both our SSD300 and SSD512 method outperforms Faster R-CNN in both speed and accuracy. Although Fast YOLO [5] can run at 155 FPS, it has lower accuracy by almost 22 % mAP. To the best of our knowledge, SSD300 is the first real-time method to achieve above 70 % mAP. Note that about 80 % of the forward time is spent on the base network (VGG16 in our case). Therefore, using a faster base network could further improve the speed, making the SSD512 model real-time as well.

Table 6. Results on Pascal VOC2007 test. SSD300 is the only real-time detection method that can achieve above 70 % mAP. By using a larger input image, SSD512 outperforms all methods on accuracy while maintaining a close to real-time speed. Using a test batch size of 8 improves the speed further.

Method	mAP	FPS	Test batch size	# Boxes
Faster R-CNN [2] (VGG16)	73.2	7	1	300
Faster R-CNN [2] (ZF)	62.1	17	1	300
YOLO [5]	63.4	45	1	98
Fast YOLO [5]	52.7	155	1	98
SSD300	74.3	46	1	8732
SSD512	76.8	19	1	24564
SSD300	74.3	59	8	8732
SSD512	76.8	22	8	24564

4 Related Work

There are two established classes of methods for object detection in images, one based on sliding windows and the other based on region proposal classification. Before the advent of convolutional neural networks, the state of the art for those two approaches – Deformable Part Model (DPM) [23] and Selective Search [1] – had comparable performance. However, after the dramatic improvement brought on by R-CNN [20], which combines selective search region proposals and convolutional network based post-classification, region proposal object detection methods became prevalent.

The original R-CNN approach has been improved in a variety of ways. The first set of approaches improve the quality and speed of post-classification, since it requires the classification of thousands of image crops, which is expensive and time-consuming. SPPnet [9] speeds up the original R-CNN approach significantly. It introduces a spatial pyramid pooling layer that is more robust to region size and scale and allows the classification layers to reuse features computed over feature maps generated at several image resolutions. Fast R-CNN [6] extends SPPnet so that it can fine-tune all layers end-to-end by minimizing a loss for both confidences and bounding box regression, which was first introduced in MultiBox [7] for learning objectness.

The second set of approaches improve the quality of proposal generation using deep neural networks. In the most recent works like MultiBox [7,8], the Selective Search region proposals, which are based on low-level image features, are replaced by proposals generated directly from a separate deep neural network. This further improves the detection accuracy but results in a somewhat complex setup, requiring the training of two neural networks with a dependency between them. Faster R-CNN [2] replaces selective search proposals by ones learned from a region proposal network (RPN), and introduces a method to integrate the RPN with Fast R-CNN by alternating between fine-tuning shared convolutional layers and prediction layers for these two networks. This way region proposals are used to pool mid-level features and the final classification step is less expensive. Our SSD is very similar to the region proposal network (RPN) in Faster R-CNN in that we also use a fixed set of (default) boxes for prediction, similar to the achor boxes in the RPN. But instead of using these to pool features and evaluate another classifier, we simultaneously produce a score for each object category in each box. Thus, our approach avoids the complication of merging RPN with Fast R-CNN and is easier to train, faster, and straightforward to integrate in other tasks.

Another set of methods, which are directly related to our approach, skip the proposal step altogether and predict bounding boxes and confidences for multiple categories directly. OverFeat [4], a deep version of the sliding window method, predicts a bounding box directly from each location of the topmost feature map after knowing the confidences of the underlying object categories. YOLO [5] uses the whole topmost feature map to predict both confidences for multiple categories and bounding boxes (which are shared for these categories). Our SSD method falls in this category because we do not have the proposal step but use the default boxes. However, our approach is more flexible than the existing methods because we can use default boxes of different aspect ratios on each feature location from multiple feature maps at different scales. If we only use one default box per location from the topmost feature map, our SSD would have similar architecture to OverFeat [4]; if we use the whole topmost feature map and add a fully connected layer for predictions instead of our convolutional

Fig. 5. Detection examples on COCO test-dev with SSD512 model. We show detections with scores higher than 0.6. Each color corresponds to an object category.

predictors, and do not explicitly consider multiple aspect ratios, we can approximately reproduce YOLO [5].

5 Conclusions

This paper introduces SSD, a fast single-shot object detector for multiple categories. A key feature of our model is the use of multi-scale convolutional bounding box outputs attached to multiple feature maps at the top of the network. This representation allows us to efficiently model the space of possible box shapes. We experimentally validate that given appropriate training strategies, a larger number of carefully chosen default bounding boxes results in improved performance. We build SSD models with at least an order of magnitude more box predictions sampling location, scale, and aspect ratio, than existing methods [5,7].

We demonstrate that given the same VGG-16 base architecture, SSD compares favorably to its state-of-the-art object detector counterparts in terms of both accuracy and speed. Our SSD512 model significantly outperforms the state-of-the-art Faster R-CNN [2] in terms of accuracy on PASCAL VOC and COCO, while being 3× faster. Our real time SSD300 model runs at 59 FPS, which is faster than the current real time YOLO [5] alternative, while producing markedly superior detection accuracy.

Apart from its standalone utility, we believe that our monolithic and relatively simple SSD model provides a useful building block for larger systems that employ an object detection component. A promising future direction is to explore its use as part of a system using recurrent neural networks to detect and track objects in video simultaneously.

Acknowledgment. This work was started as an internship project at Google and continued at UNC. We would like to thank Alex Toshev for helpful discussions and are indebted to the Image Understanding and DistBelief teams at Google. We also thank Philip Ammirato and Patrick Poirson for helpful comments. We thank NVIDIA for providing GPUs and acknowledge support from NSF 1452851, 1446631, 1526367, 1533771.

References

1. Uijlings, J.R., van de Sande, K.E., Gevers, T., Smeulders, A.W.: Selective search for object recognition. IJCV **104**, 154 (2013)
2. Ren, S., He, K., Girshick, R., Sun, J.: Faster R-CNN: towards real-time object detection with region proposal networks. In: NIPS (2015)
3. He, K., Zhang, X., Ren, S., Sun, J.: Deep residual learning for image recognition. In: CVPR (2016)
4. Sermanet, P., Eigen, D., Zhang, X., Mathieu, M., Fergus, R., LeCun, Y.: Overfeat: integrated recognition, localization and detection using convolutional networks. In: ICLR (2014)
5. Redmon, J., Divvala, S., Girshick, R., Farhadi, A.: You only look once: unified, real-time object detection. In: CVPR (2016)
6. Girshick, R.: Fast R-CNN. In: ICCV (2015)
7. Erhan, D., Szegedy, C., Toshev, A., Anguelov, D.: Scalable object detection using deep neural networks. In: CVPR (2014)
8. Szegedy, C., Reed, S., Erhan, D., Anguelov, D.: Scalable, high-quality object detection. arXiv preprint v3 (2015). arXiv:1412.1441
9. He, K., Zhang, X., Ren, S., Sun, J.: Spatial pyramid pooling in deep convolutional networks for visual recognition. In: Fleet, D., Pajdla, T., Schiele, B., Tuytelaars, T. (eds.) ECCV 2014. LNCS, vol. 8691, pp. 346–361. Springer, Heidelberg (2014). doi:10.1007/978-3-319-10578-9_23
10. Long, J., Shelhamer, E., Darrell, T.: Fully convolutional networks for semantic segmentation. In: CVPR (2015)
11. Hariharan, B., Arbeláez, P., Girshick, R., Malik, J.: Hypercolumns for object segmentation and fine-grained localization. In: CVPR (2015)
12. Liu, W., Rabinovich, A., Berg, A.C.: ParseNet: looking wider to see better. In: ILCR (2016)
13. Howard, A.G.: Some improvements on deep convolutional neural network based image classification. arXiv preprint (2013). arXiv:1312.5402
14. Simonyan, K., Zisserman, A.: Very deep convolutional networks for large-scale image recognition. In: NIPS (2015)

15. Russakovsky, O., Deng, J., Su, H., Krause, J., Satheesh, S., Ma, S., Huang, Z., Karpathy, A., Khosla, A., Bernstein, M., Berg, A.C., Fei-Fei, L.: Imagenet large scale visual recognition challenge. IJCV **115**, 211 (2015)
16. Chen, L.C., Papandreou, G., Kokkinos, I., Murphy, K., Yuille, A.L.: Semantic image segmentation with deep convolutional nets and fully connected CRFs. In: ICLR (2015)
17. Jia, Y., Shelhamer, E., Donahue, J., Karayev, S., Long, J., Girshick, R., Guadarrama, S., Darrell, T.: Caffe: convolutional architecture for fast feature embedding. In: MM. ACM (2014)
18. Glorot, X., Bengio, Y.: Understanding the difficulty of training deep feedforward neural networks. In: AISTATS (2010)
19. Hoiem, D., Chodpathumwan, Y., Dai, Q.: Diagnosing error in object detectors. In: Fitzgibbon, A., Lazebnik, S., Perona, P., Sato, Y., Schmid, C. (eds.) ECCV 2012. LNCS, vol. 7574, pp. 340–353. Springer, Heidelberg (2012). doi:10.1007/978-3-642-33712-3_25
20. Girshick, R., Donahue, J., Darrell, T., Malik, J.: Rich feature hierarchies for accurate object detection and semantic segmentation. In: CVPR (2014)
21. Bell, S., Zitnick, C.L., Bala, K., Girshick, R.: Inside-outside net: detecting objects in context with skip pooling and recurrent neural networks. In: CVPR (2016)
22. COCO:Common Objects in Context (2016). http://mscoco.org/dataset/#detections-leaderboard. Accessed 25 July 2016
23. Felzenszwalb, P., McAllester, D., Ramanan, D.: A discriminatively trained, multi-scale, deformable part model. In: CVPR (2008)

A Recurrent Encoder-Decoder Network
for Sequential Face Alignment

Xi Peng[1]([✉]), Rogerio S. Feris[2], Xiaoyu Wang[3], and Dimitris N. Metaxas[1]

[1] Rutgers University, Piscataway, USA
{xipeng.cs,dnm}@rutgers.edu
[2] IBM T. J. Watson Research Center, Yorktown Heights, USA
rsferis@us.ibm.com
[3] Snapchat Research, Venice, CA, USA
xiaoyu.wang@snapchat.com

Abstract. We propose a novel recurrent encoder-decoder network model for real-time video-based face alignment. Our proposed model predicts 2D facial point maps regularized by a regression loss, while uniquely exploiting recurrent learning at both spatial and temporal dimensions. At the spatial level, we add a feedback loop connection between the combined output response map and the input, in order to enable iterative coarse-to-fine face alignment using a *single network model*. At the temporal level, we first decouple the features in the bottleneck of the network into *temporal-variant factors*, such as pose and expression, and *temporal-invariant factors*, such as identity information. Temporal recurrent learning is then applied to the decoupled temporal-variant features, yielding better generalization and significantly more accurate results at test time. We perform a comprehensive experimental analysis, showing the importance of each component of our proposed model, as well as superior results over the state-of-the-art in standard datasets.

Keywords: Recurrent learning · Encoder-decoder · Face alignment

1 Introduction

Face landmark detection plays a fundamental role in many computer vision tasks, such as face recognition, expression analysis, and 3D face modeling. In the past few years, many methods have been proposed to address this problem, with significant progress being made towards systems that work in real-world conditions ("in the wild").

Regression-based approaches [6,50] have achieved impressive results by cascading discriminative regression functions that directly map facial appearance to landmark coordinates. In this framework, deep convolutional neural networks have proven effective as a choice for feature extraction and non-linear regression modeling [21,54,55]. Although these methods can achieve very reliable results in

ⓒ Springer International Publishing AG 2016
B. Leibe et al. (Eds.): ECCV 2016, Part I, LNCS 9905, pp. 38–56, 2016.
DOI: 10.1007/978-3-319-46448-0_3

standard benchmark datasets, they still suffer from limited performance in challenging scenarios, e.g., involving large face pose variations and heavy occlusions.

A promising direction to address these challenges is to consider video-based face alignment (i.e., sequential face landmark detection) [39], leveraging temporal information as an additional constraint [47]. Despite the long history of research in rigid and non-rigid face tracking [5,10,32,33], current efforts have mostly focused on face alignment in still images [37,45,54,57]. In fact, most methods often perform video-based landmark detection by independently applying models trained on still images in each frame in a tracking-by-detection manner [48], with notable exceptions such as [1,36], which explore incremental learning based on previous frames. How to effectively model long-term temporal constraints while handling large face pose variations and occlusions is an open research problem for video-based face alignment.

In this work, we address this problem by proposing a novel recurrent encoder-decoder deep neural network model (see Fig. 1). The encoding module projects image pixels into a low-dimensional feature space, whereas the decoding module maps features in this space to 2D facial point maps, which are further regularized by a regression loss. In order to handle large face pose variations, we introduce a feedback loop connection between the aggregated 2D facial point maps and the input. The intuition is similar to cascading multiple regression functions [50,54] for iterative course-to-fine face alignment, but in our approach the iterations are modeled jointly with shared parameters, using a single network model.

For more effective temporal modeling, we first decouple the features in the bottleneck of the network into temporal-variant factors, such as pose and expression, and temporal-invariant factors, such as identity. More specifically, we split the features into two components, where one component is used to learn face recognition using identity labels, and recurrent temporal learning is applied to the other component, which encodes temporal-variant factors only. We show in our experiments that recurrent learning in both spatial and temporal dimensions is crucial to improve performance of sequential face landmark detection.

In summary, our work makes the following **contributions**:

- We propose a novel recurrent encoder-decoder network model for real-time sequential face landmark detection. To the best of our knowledge, this is the first time a recurrent model is investigated to perform video-based facial landmark detection.
- Our proposed *spatial recurrent learning* enables a novel iterative coarse-to-fine face alignment using a single network model. This is critical to handle large face pose changes and a more effective alternative than cascading multiple network models in terms of accuracy and memory footprint.
- Different from traditional methods, we apply *temporal recurrent learning* to temporal-variant features which are decoupled from temporal-invariant features in the bottleneck of the network, achieving better generalization and more accurate results.

– We provide a detailed experimental analysis of each component of our model, as well as insights about key contributing factors to achieve superior performance over the state-of-the-art. The project page is public available.[1]

2   Related Work

Face alignment has been advanced in last decades. Remarkably, regression based methods [1,2,6,17,41,45,49,50,54,57,58] significantly boost the generalization performance of face landmark detection, compared to algorithms based on statistical models such as Active shape models [9,29] and Active appearance models [12]. A regression-based approach directly regresses landmark locations where features extracted from face images serve as regressors. Landmark models are learned either in an independent manner, or in a joint fashion [6]. This paper performs landmark detection via both a classification model and a regression model. Different from most of the previous methods, this work deals with face alignment in a video. It jointly optimizes detection output by utilizing multiple observations from the same person.

Learning cascade-like regression models show superior performance on the face alignment task [41,50,54]. Supervised descent method [50] learns cascades of regression models based on SIFT feature. Sun et al. [41] proposed to use three levels of neural networks to predict landmark locations. Zhang et al. [54] studied the problem via cascades of stacked auto-encoders which gradually refine the landmark position with higher resolution inputs. Compared to these efforts which explicitly define cascade structures, our method learns a spatial recurrent model which implicitly incorporates the cascade structure with shared parameters. It is also more "end-to-end" compared to previous works that handcraftly divide the learning process into multiple stages.

Recurrent neural networks (RNNs) are widely employed in the literature of speech recognition [28] and natural language processing [27]. They are also recently used in computer vision. For example, in the task of image captioning [18] and video captioning [52], RNNs are employed for text generation. Veeriah et al. [46] use RNNs to learn complex time-series representations via high-order derivatives of states for action recognition. Benefiting from the deep architecture, RNNs are naturally good alternatives to Conditional Random Fields (CRFs) [56] which are popular in image segmentation.

Encoder and decoder networks are well studied in machine translation [7] where the encoder learns the intermediate representation and the decoder generates the translation from the representation. It is also investigated in speech recognition [26] and computer vision [3,14]. Yang et al. [51] proposed to decouple identity units and pose units in the bottleneck of the network for 3D view synthesis. However, how to fully utilize the decoupled units for correspondence regularization [25] is still unexplored. In this work, we employ the encoder to learn a joint representation for identity, pose, expression as well as landmarks.

---

[1] https://sites.google.com/site/xipengcshomepage/project/face-alignment.

The decoder translates the representation to landmark heatmaps. Our spatial recurrent model loops the whole encoder-decoder framework.

3 Recurrent Encoder-Decoder Network

In this section, we first give an overview of our approach. Then we describe the novelty of our work in detail: spatial and temporal recurrent learning, supervised identity disentangling, and constrained shape prediction.

3.1 Method Overview

Our task is to locate L landmarks in sequential images using an end-to-end deep neural network. Figure 1 shows the overview of our approach. We consider $f_{\star}$ as potential nonlinear and multi-layered functions. The input of the network are the image $\mathbf{x} \in \mathbb{R}^{w \times h \times 3}$ and the landmark label map $\mathbf{z} \in \mathbb{R}^{w \times h \times 1}$. Each pixel in $\mathbf{z}$ is a discrete label $\{0, \cdots, L\}$ that marks the presence of the corresponding landmark, where 0 denotes a non-landmark area.

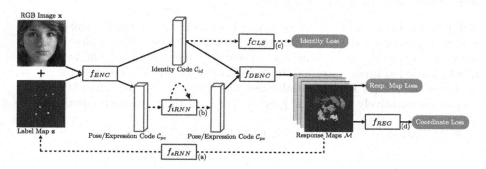

Fig. 1. Overview of the recurrent encoder-decoder network: **(a)** spatial recurrent learning (Sect. 3.2); **(b)** temporal recurrent learning (Sect. 3.3); **(c)** supervised identity disentangling (Sect. 3.4); and **(d)** constrained shape prediction (Sect. 3.5). $f_{ENC}, f_{DENC}, f_{sRNN}, f_{tRNN}, f_{CLS}, f_{REG}$ are potentially nonlinear and multi-layered mappings.

The *encoder* (f_{ENC}) performs a sequence of convolution, pooling and batch normalization [15] to extract a representation code from inputs:

$$\mathcal{C} = f_{ENC}(\mathbf{x}, \mathbf{z}; \theta_{ENC}), \ \mathcal{C} \in \mathbb{R}^{w_c \times h_c \times d_c}, \tag{1}$$

where $\mathcal{C}$ represents the encoded features. θ_{ENC} denotes encoder parameters. Symmetrically, the *decoder* (f_{DENC}) performs a sequence of unpooling, convolution and batch normalization to upsample the representation codes to a multi-channel response map:

$$\mathcal{M} = f_{DENC}(\mathcal{C}; \theta_{DENC}), \ \mathcal{M} \in \mathbb{R}^{w \times h \times (L+1)}, \tag{2}$$

where θ_{DENC} denotes the decoder parameters. The first channel of $\mathcal{M}$ represents the background, while the rest L channels of $\mathcal{M}$ present pixel-wise confidence of the corresponding landmarks. The $(L+1)$-channel response map is crucial to preserve the landmark unity, compared with a 2-channel setup (landmark *v.s.* non-landmark).

The encoder-decoder framework plays an important role in our task. **First**, it is convenient to perform *spatial recurrent learning* (f_{sRNN}) since $\mathcal{M}$ has the same dimension (but different number of channels) as $\mathbf{x}$. The output of the decoder can be directly fed back into the encoder to provide pixel-wise spatial cues for the next recurrent step. **Second**, we can decouple $\mathcal{C}$ in the bottleneck of the network into temporal-variant and -invariant factors. The former is further exploited in *temporal recurrent learning* (f_{tRNN}) for robust alignment, while the latter is used in *supervised identity disentangling* (f_{CLS}) to facilitate the network training. **Third**, $\mathcal{M}$ can be further regularized in *constrained shape prediction* (f_{REG}) to directly output landmark coordinates. The details of each module are explained in following subsections.

3.2 Spatial Recurrent Learning

The purpose of spatial recurrent learning is to pinpoint landmark locations in a coarse-to-fine manner. Unlike existing approaches [41,54] that employ multiple networks in cascade, we accomplish the coarse-to-fine search in a single network in which the parameters are jointly learned in successive recurrent steps.

Given an image $\mathbf{x}$ and initial guess of the shape $\mathbf{z}_0$, we refine the shape prediction iteratively $\{\mathbf{z}^1, \cdots, \mathbf{z}^k\}$ by feeding back the previous prediction:

$$\mathbf{z}^k = f_{sRNN}(\mathcal{M}^{k-1}) = f_{sRNN}(f_{DENC}(f_{ENC}(\mathbf{x}, \mathbf{z}^{k-1}))), \ k = 1, \cdots, K, \quad (3)$$

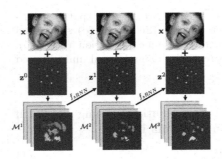

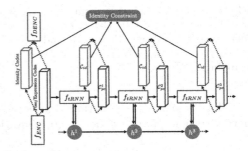

Fig. 2. An unrolled illustration of *spatial recurrent learning*. The response map is pretty coarse when the initial guess is far away from the ground truth if large pose and expression exist. It eventually gets refined in the successive recurrent steps.

Fig. 3. An unrolled illustration of *temporal recurrent learning*. $\mathcal{C}_{id}$ encodes temporal-invariant factor which subjects to the same identity constraint. $\mathcal{C}_{pe}$ encodes temporal-variant factors which is further modeled in f_{tRNN}.

where we omit network parameters θ_{ENC} and θ_{DENC} for concise expression. The network parameters are learned by recurrently minimizing the classification loss between the annotation and the response map output by the encoder-decoder:

$$\underset{\theta_{ENC},\theta_{DENC}}{\operatorname{argmin}} \sum_{k=1}^{K}\sum_{l=0}^{L} \ell(\mathcal{M}_l^*, f_{DENC}(f_{ENC}(\mathbf{x},\mathbf{z}^k))_l), \qquad (4)$$

where k counts iterations and l counts landmarks. $\mathcal{M}_l^* \in \mathbb{R}^{w \times h \times 1}$ is the ground truth of the response map for the l-th landmark. As shown in Fig. 2, our recurrent model progressively improves the prediction accuracy when a face exhibits challenging pose or expression. The whole process is learned end-to-end during training.

3.3 Temporal Recurrent Learning

The recurrent learning is performed at both the spatial and temporal dimensions. Given T successive frames $\{\mathbf{x}^t; t = 1, \cdots, T\}$, the encoder extracts a sequence of representation codes $\{\mathcal{C}^t; t = 1, \cdots, T\}$. We can decouple $\mathcal{C}$ as: identity code $\mathcal{C}_{id}$ that is *temporal-invariant* since all frames are subject to the same identity constraint; and pose/expression code $\mathcal{C}_{pe}$ that is *temporal-variant* since pose and expression changes over time [34]. We exploit the temporal consistence of $\mathcal{C}_{pe}$ via the proposed temporal recurrent learning.

Figure 3 shows the unrolled illustration of the proposed temporal recurrent learning. More specifically, we aim to achieve a nonlinear mapping f_{tRNN}, which simultaneously tracks the latent state $\{h^t; t = 1, \cdots, T\}$ and updates $\mathcal{C}_{pe}$ at time t:

$$h^t = p(\mathcal{C}_{pe}^t, h^{t-1}; \theta_{tRNN}), \ \mathcal{C}_{pe}^{t\,\prime} = q(h^t; \theta_{tRNN}), \ t = 1, \cdots, T \qquad (5)$$

where $p(\cdot)$ and $q(\cdot)$ are functions of f_{tRNN}. $\mathcal{C}_{pe}^{t\,\prime}$ is the update of $\mathcal{C}_{pe}^t$. θ_{tRNN} corresponds to mapping parameters which are learned in the end-to-end task using the same classification loss as Eq. 4 but unrolled at the temporal dimension:

$$\underset{\theta_{ENC},\theta_{DENC},\theta_{tRNN}}{\operatorname{argmin}} \sum_{t=1}^{T}\sum_{l=0}^{L} \ell_{tRNN}(\mathcal{M}_l^{t*}, f_{DENC}(\mathcal{C}_{id}^t, \mathcal{C}_{pe}^t)_l), \qquad (6)$$

where t counts time steps and l counts landmarks. Note that both spatial and temporal recurrent learning are performed to jointly learn θ_{ENC}, θ_{DENC} and θ_{tRNN} in the same task according to Eqs. 4 and 6.

The temporal recurrent learning memorize the motion patterns of pose and expression variations from offline training data. It can significantly improve the fitting accuracy and robustness when large variations and partial occlusions exist.

3.4 Supervised Identity Disentangling

There is no guarantee that temporal-invariant and -variant factors can be completely decoupled in the bottleneck by simply splitting the representation codes into two parts. More supervised information is required to achieve the decoupling. To address this issue, we propose to apply a face recognition task on the identity code, in addition to the temporal recurrent learning applied on pose/expression code.

The supervised identity disentangling is formulated as an N-way classification problem. N is the number of unique individuals present in the training sequences. In general, the classification network f_{CLS} associates the identity code $\mathcal{C}_{id}$ with a vector indicating the score of each identity. Classification loss is used to learn the mapping parameters:

$$\underset{\theta_{CLS}}{\mathrm{argmin}} \sum_{m=1}^{M} \ell_{CLS}(\mathbf{e}^*, f_{CLS}(\mathcal{C}_{id}; \theta_{CLS})), \tag{7}$$

where m counts the number of training images in a mini batch. $\mathbf{e}^*$ is the one-hot identity annotation vector with a 1 for the correct identity and all 0s for others.

It has been shown in [55] that learning the face alignment task together with correlated tasks, *e.g.* head pose, can improve the fitting performance. We have the similar observation when adding face recognition task to the alignment task. More specifically, we found that supervised identity disentangling can significantly improve the generalization as well as fitting accuracy at test time. In this case, the factors are better decoupled, which facilitates f_{tRNN} to better handle temporal variations.

3.5 Constrained Shape Prediction

The response map output by the encoder-decoder may have a few false high responses when distractions exist in the background. Although this issue is significantly alleviated by spatial recurrent learning, it still impairs the fitting accuracy in challenging conditions. Besides, the response map uses separate channels to depict each landmark. The spatial dependencies among landmarks are not well explored. To overcome these limitations, we append nonlinear mappings after the encoder-decoder to learn the shape constraint for shape prediction.

f_{REG} takes the response map as the input and outputs landmark coordinates $\mathbf{y} \in \mathbb{R}^{2L \times 1}$. Regression loss is used to learn the mapping parameters:

$$\underset{\theta_{REG}}{\mathrm{argmin}} \sum_{n=1}^{N} \ell_{REG}(\mathbf{y}^*, f_{REG}(\mathcal{M}; \theta_{REG})), \tag{8}$$

where $\mathbf{y}^*$ is the ground truth of landmark coordinates. All coordinates are normalized by subtracting a mean shape calculated from training images. The summation accumulates loss within a mini batch to avoid gradient jiggling.

4 Network Architecture and Implementation Details

All modules are embedded in a unified framework that can be trained end-to-end. Next we provide more details about how we guarantee efficient training convergence and robust performance at test time.

4.1 f_{ENC} and f_{DENC}

Figure 4 illustrates the detailed configuration of the encoder-decoder. The encoder is designed based on a variant of the VGG-16 network [19,40]. It has 13 convolutional layers with constant 3×3 filters which correspond to the first 13 convolutional layers in VGG-16. We can therefore initialize the training process from weights trained on large datasets for object classification. We remove all fully connected layers in favor of *fully convolutional networks* (FCNs) [24] and output two $4 \times 4 \times 256$ feature maps in the bottleneck. This strategy not only reduces the number of parameters from 117 M to 14.8 M [3], but also preserves spatial information in high-resolution feature maps instead of fully-connected feature vectors, which is crucial for our landmark localization task.

There are 5 max-pooling layers with 2×2 pooling windows and a constant stride of 2 in the encoder to halve the resolution of feature maps after each convolutional stage. Although max-pooling can help to achieve translation invariance, it inevitably results in a considerable loss of spatial information especially when several max-pooling layers are applied in succession. To solve this issue, we use a 2-bit code to record the index of the maximum activation selected in a 2×2 pooling window [53]. As illustrated in Fig. 4, the memorized index is then used in the corresponding unpooling layer to place each activation back to its original location. This strategy is particularly useful for the decoder to recover the input

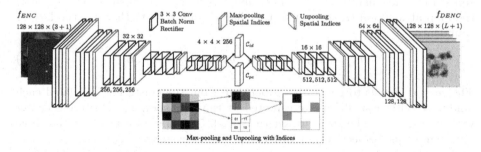

Fig. 4. Architecture of f_{ENC} and f_{DENC}. The input of the encoder is the concatenation of 3-channel image and 1-channel label map. The decoder is exactly symmetrical to the encoder except the output is a $(L+1)$-channel response map. The representation code is split into $\mathcal{C}_{id}$ and $\mathcal{C}_{pe}$ in the bottleneck, where each one is a $4 \times 4 \times 256$ feature map. 3×3 kernels are used in all convolutional layers. 2×2 max-pooling or unpooling windows are applied in all pooling layers. The corresponding max-pooling and unpooling share pooling indices with a 2-bit switch for each 2×2 pooling window.

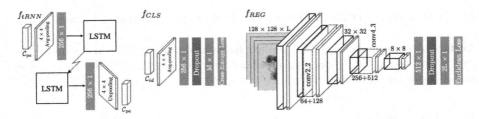

Fig. 5. Architecture of f_{tRNN}, f_{CLS} and f_{REG}. In f_{tRNN}, pooling and unpooling with spatial indices are applied to cut down the input and output complexity of LSTM module. In f_{REG}, intermediate feature maps from the encoder, *i.e.* conv2_2 and conv4_3, are concatenated to incorporate both global and local features.

structure from the highly compressed feature map. Besides, it is much more efficient to store the spatial indices than to memorize the entire feature map in float precision as proposed in FCNs [24].

The decoder is symmetrical to the encoder with a mirrored configuration but replacing all max-pooling layers with corresponding unpooling layers. The final output of the decoder is a $(L+1)$-channel response map which is fed to a softmax classifier to predict pixel-wise confidence. We find that batch normalization [15] can significantly boost the training speed as it can effectively reduce internal shift within a mini batch. Therefore, batch normalization and rectified linear unit (ReLU) [30] are applied after each convolutional layer.

4.2 f_{sRNN} and f_{tRNN}

As shown in Figs. 1 and 2, f_{sRNN} maps the $(L+1)$-channel response map $\mathcal{M}$ to a single-channel label map **z**. This mapping can be achieved efficiently in two steps. First, we merge $\mathcal{M}$ to a single map with $(L+1)$ clusters. The value of the map at location (i,j) is set to the channel index of $\mathcal{M}$ that has the largest confidence:

$$m_{ij} = \underset{l}{\mathrm{argmax}}(\mathcal{M}_{ij})_l, \ where \ l = 0, \cdots, L. \tag{9}$$

The second step is to generate a label map from the clustering. We label each landmark with a small square centered at the corresponding clustering center with varied sizes. The sizes are set to 7-pixel, 5-pixel, and 3-pixel for the three recurrent steps, respectively, in order to provide the spatial feedback in a coarse-to-fine manner.

We employ Long Short-Term Memory (LSTM) [13,31] networks to model f_{tRNN}. 256 hidden units are used in the LSTM layer we empirically set $T = 10$. The prediction loss is calculated at each time step and then accumulated after T steps for backpropagation. Directly feeding $\mathcal{C}_{pe}^t$ into the LSTM layer leads to a low training rate as it needs $4 \times 4 \times 256 = 4096$ neurons for both the input and output. We apply 4×4 pooling and unpooling to compress $\mathcal{C}_{pe}$ to a 256×1 vector as illustrated in Fig. 5.

4.3 f_{CLS} and f_{REG}

To facilitate the decoupling in the bottleneck, we use a classification network to predict identity labels from C_{id}. f_{CLS} takes C_{id} as input and applies 4×4 average pooling to obtain a $256d$ feature vector for identity representation. Instead of using a very long feature vector in former face recognition network [43], *e.g.* $4096d$, we use a more compact vector, *e.g.* $256d$, to reduce the computational cost without losing recognition accuracy [38,42]. To avoid overfitting, 0.4 dropout is applied, followed with a fully connected layer with M neurons to predict the entity using the cross-entropy loss.

The regression network takes $128 \times 128 \times (L + 1)$ response map as input to directly predict $2L \times 1$ normalized landmark coordinates. The network architecture is similar to the encoder but using fewer feature maps in each convolutional layer: 64-64-256-256-512. The dimension of feature maps is halved after each 2×2 max-pooling layer except the last 8×8 pooling layer to achieve a $512d$ feature vector. Similar to the classification network, 0.4 dropout is applied. A fully connected layer with $2L \times 1$ neurons is used to output landmark coordinates, which is used to compute the Euclidean loss.

We experienced suboptimal performance with the designed f_{REG} at the beginning. The reason is the response map is highly abstract and missing detailed information of the input image. To address this issue, we incorporate feature maps from the encoder to boost the regression accuracy. More specifically, we concatenate feature maps from both shallow layer (*conv2_2*) and deep layer (*conv4_3*) to the corresponding layers in f_{REG} to utilize both global and local features. Figure 5 illustrates the idea. Both *conv2_2* and *conv4_3* are learned in the encoder-decoder and remain unchanged in f_{REG}.

5 Experiments

In this section, we first demonstrate the effectiveness of each component in our framework, followed with performance comparison against the state-of-the-arts on both controlled and unconstrained datasets.

5.1 Datasets and Settings

Datasets. We conduct our experiments on widely used benchmark datasets as listed in Table 1. These datasets present challenges in multiple aspects such as large pose, extensive expression variation, severe occlusion and dynamic illumination.

We generated 7-landmark annotation for all datasets to locate eye corners, nose tip and mouth corners. Besides, we followed [37] for unified 68-landmark annotation for Helen, LFPW, Talking Face (TF), Face Movie (FM) and 300-VW. Moreover, we manually labeled the identity for each video in TF, FM and 300-VW. The landmark annotation of LFW is given by [23].

AFLW and 300-VW have the largest number of labeled images. They are also more challenging than others due to the extensive variations. Therefore,

Table 1. The *image* and *video datasets* used in training and evaluation. LFW, TF, FM and 300-VW have both landmark and identity annotation. AFLW and 300-VW are split into two sets for both training and evaluation.

	AFLW [20]	LFW [23]	Helen [22]	LFPW [4]	TF [11]	FM [36]	300-VW [39]
In-the-wild	Y	Y	Y	Y	N	Y	Y
Image	21,080	12,007	2,330	1,035	500	2,150	114,000
Video	-	-	-	-	5	6	114
Landmark	21	7	194	68	68	68	68
Identity	-	5,371	-	-	1	6	105
Training	16,864	12,007	2,330	1,035	0	0	90,000
Evaluation	4,216	0	0	0	500	2150	24,000

we used them for both training and evaluation. More specifically, 80 % of the images in AFLW and 90 out of 114 videos in 300-VW were used for training, and the rest were used for evaluation. We sampled videos to roughly cover the three different scenarios defined in [8], *i.e.* "Scenario 1", "Scenario 2" and "Scenario 3", corresponding to well-lit, mild unconstrained and completely unconstrained conditions, respectively.

We performed data augmentation by sampling ten variations from each image in the image training datasets. The sampling was achieved by random perturbation of scale (0.9 to 1.1), rotation (±15°), translation (7 pixels), as well as horizontal flip. To generate sequential training data, we randomly sampled 100 clips from each training video, where each clip has 10 frames. It is worthy mentioning that no augmentation is applied on video training data to preserve the temporal consistency in the successive frames.

Training. Our approach is capable of end-to-end training on the video datasets. However, there are only 105 different identities in 300-VW. To make full use of all annotated datasets, we conducted the training through three steps. In each step, we optimized the network parameters by using *stochastic gradient descent* (SGD) with 0.9 momentum. The learning rate started at 0.01 and decayed 20 % after every 10 epochs.

In the first step, we trained the network without f_{CLS} and f_{tRNN} using AFLW, Helen and LFPW. We initialized f_{ENC} using pre-trained weights in VGG-16 [40], and left other modules with Gaussian initialization [16]. The training was performed for 30 epochs. In the second step, we added f_{CLS} and fine-tuned other modules using LFW. The training was performed for 20 epochs. In the third step, we added f_{tRNN} and fine-tuned the entire network using 300-VW. The mini-batch size was set to 5 clips that had no identity overlap to avoid oscillations of the identity loss. For each training clip, we performed temporal recurrent learning for another 50 epochs in both forward and backward direction to double the training data.

Evaluation. To avoid overfitting, we ensure that the training and testing videos do not have identity overlap on the 300-VW (16 videos share 7 identities).

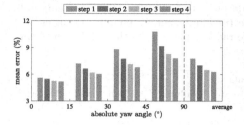

Fig. 6. Mean errors after each spatial recurrent step on the validation set of AFLW [20]. The fitting improvement is more significant on faces with large head poses (45°–90°) than near frontal faces (0°–15°). Three-step recurrent learning achieve a good trade-off between fitting accuracy and efficiency, as the fourth step has very limited improvement.

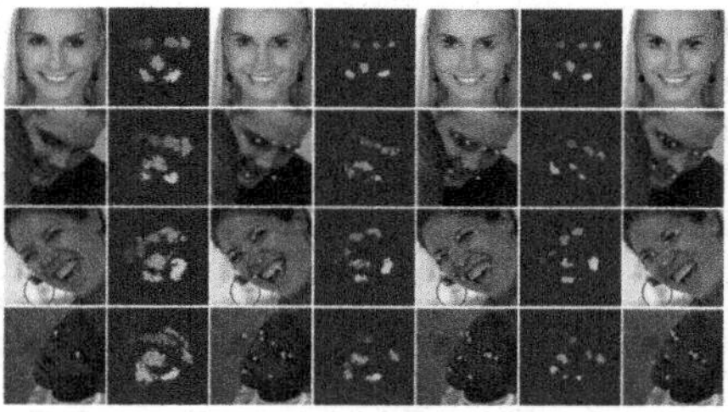

Fig. 7. Examples of three-step spatial recurrent learning. Successive recurrent steps are not necessary in easy cases (first row), but is crucial in challenging cases such as large pose and intense expression (rest of rows). The response clusters shrink and converge in successive recurrent steps, which moves landmarks toward ground truth step by step.

Table 2. Mean error comparison between the proposed spatial recurrent learning and the widely used cascade learning on large pose (> 30°) set of AFLW. Each network in cascade has exactly the same architecture as the recurrent version but not sharing weight among cascades. The recurrent learning beats the cascade variant in terms of fitting accuracy and efficiency.

	Left eye (%)	Right eye (%)	Nose (%)	Mouth (%)	Mean (%)	Std (%)	Failure (%)	Time (ms)	Memory (MB)
Cascade	8.32	7.37	9.60	7.52	8.07	6.36	25.5	31.7	88.9
Recurrent	7.59	7.21	8.76	6.45	7.33	3.94	17.3	28.5	29.6

We used normalized *root mean square error* (RMSE) [37] for fitting accuracy evaluation. A prediction with larger than 10% mean error was reported as a failure [39,44].

5.2 Validation of Spatial Recurrent Learning

We validate the proposed spatial recurrent learning on the validation set of AFLW. To better investigate the benefits of spatial recurrent learning, we partitioned the validation set into four image groups according to the absolute value of yaw angle [35]: 0°–15°, 15°–30°, 30°–45° and 45°–90°.

First, we trained a 4-step recurrent model and reported the mean error after each step in Fig. 6. From which, we had the following observations: **(1)** The fitting errors decrease in the successive recurrent steps. **(2)** The improvement of fitting accuracy is much more significant on faces with large head poses than

Table 3. Mean error comparison between the proposed temporal recurrent learning and the variant without f_{tRNN} on the validation set of 300-VW [37]. The temporal recurrent learning significantly improves the tracking accuracy (smaller mean error) and robustness (smaller std and lower failure rate), especially on the validation set in challenging settings.

	Common			Challenging			Full		
	Mean (%)	Std (%)	Failure (%)	Mean (%)	Std (%)	Failure (%)	Mean (%)	Std (%)	Failure (%)
w/o f_{tRNN}	4.52	2.24	3.48	6.27	5.33	13.3	5.83	3.42	6.43
f_{tRNN}	4.21	1.85	1.71	5.64	3.28	5.40	5.25	2.15	2.82

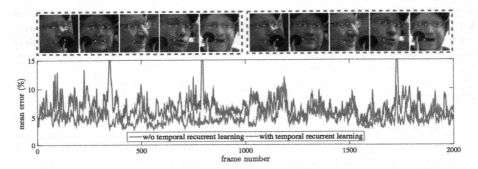

Fig. 8. Examples of validation results in challenging settings. The tracked subject undergoes intensive pose and expression variations as well as severe partial occlusions. The proposed temporal recurrent learning has substantial improvement in terms of tracking accuracy and robustness, especially for landmarks on nose tips and mouth corners.

near frontal faces, *e.g.* 23.3 % improvement on 45 °–90 ° set and 6.10 % improvement on 0 °–15 ° pose set. **(3)** The improvement is saturated after the first three recurrent steps as the fourth step has very limited improvement. These observations validate the proposed spatial recurrent learning to improve the fitting accuracy especially in challenging cases such as large pose. Besides, we set the number of recurrent steps to 3 in the following experiments, as it achieves a good trade-off between fitting accuracy and efficiency. Figure 7 shows examples of recurrent learning. The response clusters shrink and converge in successive recurrent steps, which moves landmarks from initial to ground truth step by step.

Second, it is reasonable to compare the proposed spatial recurrent learning with the widely used cascade learning such as [41,54]. For a fair comparison, we implemented a three-step cascade variant of our approach. Each network in the cascade has exactly the same architecture as the spatial recurrent version but there is no weight sharing among cascades. We fully trained the cascade networks

using the same training set and validated the performance on the large pose
($> 30°$) set of AFLW. The comparison is presented in Table 2. We can see that
the spatial recurrent learning can significantly improve the fitting performance.
The underlying reason is the recurrent network learns the tep-by-step fitting
strategy jointly, while the cascade networks learn each step independently. It can
better handle the challenging case where the initial guess is usually far away from
the ground truth. Moreover, a single network with shared weights can instantly
reduce the memory usage to one third of the cascaded implementation.

5.3 Validation of Temporal Recurrent Learning

In this section, we validate the proposed temporal recurrent learning on the validation set of 300-VW. To better study the performance under different settings,
we split the validation set into two groups: 9 videos in common settings that
roughly match "Scenario 1", and 15 videos in challenging settings that roughly
match "Scenario 2" and "Scenario 3". The common, challenging and full sets
were used in the following evaluation.

We implemented a variant of our approach that turns off the temporal recurrent learning f_{tRNN}. It was also pre-trained on the image training set and fine-
tuned on the video training set. Since there was no temporal recurrent learning,
we used frames instead of clips to conduct the fine-tuning which was performed
for the same 50 epochs. We showed the result with and without temporal recurrent learning in Table 3.

For videos in common settings, the temporal recurrent learning achieves 6.8 %
and 17.4 % improvement in terms of mean error and standard deviation respectively, while the failure rate is remarkably reduced by 50.8 %. Temporal modeling produces better prediction by taking consideration of history observations.

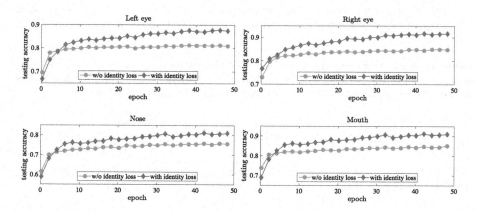

Fig. 9. Testing accuracy of different facial components with respect to the number
of training epochs. The proposed supervised identity disentangling helps to achieve a
more complete factor decoupling in the bottleneck of the encoder-decoder, which yields
better generalization capability and more accurate testing results.

It may implicitly learn to model the motion dynamics in the hidden units from the training clips.

For videos in challenging settings, the temporal recurrent learning won with even bigger margin. Without f_{tRNN}, it is hard to capture the drastic motion or changes in consecutive frames, which inevitably results in higher mean error, std and failure rate. Figure 8 shows an example where the subject exhibits intensive pose and expression variations as well as severe partial occlusions. The curve showed our recurrent model obviously reduced landmark errors, especially for landmarks on nose tip and mouth corners. The less oscillating error also suggests that f_{tRNN} significantly improves the prediction stability over frames.

5.4   Benefits of Supervised Identity Disentangling

The supervised identity disentangling is proposed to better decouple the temporal-invariant and temporal-variant factors in the bottleneck of the encoder-decoder. This facilitates the temporal recurrent training, yielding better generalization and more accurate fittings at test time.

To study the effectiveness of the identity network, we removed f_{CLS} and follow the exact training steps. The testing accuracy comparison on the 300-VW dataset is shown in Fig. 9. The accuracy was calculated as the ratio of pixels that were correctly classified in the corresponding channel(s) of the response map.

The validation results of different facial components show similar trends: (**1**) The network demonstrates better generalization capability by using additional identity cues, which results in a more efficient training. For instance, after only 10 training epochs, the validation accuracy for landmarks located at the left eye reaches 0.84 with identity loss compared to 0.8 without identity loss. (**2**) The supervised identity information can substantially boost the testing accuracy. There is an approximately 9 % improvement by using the additional identity loss. It worth mentioning that, at the very beginning of the training (< 5 epochs), the network has inferior testing accuracy with supervised identity disentangling.

Table 4. Mean error comparison with state-of-the-art methods on multiple video validation sets. The top performance in each dataset is highlighted. Our approach achieves the best fitting accuracy on both controlled and unconstrained datasets.

	7 landmarks				68 landmarks		
	TF [11]	FM [36]	300-VW [39]		TF [11]	FM [36]	300VW [39]
	%	%	Challenging		%	%	Challenging
DRMF [2]	4.43	8.53	9.16	ESR [6]	3.49	6.74	7.09
ESR [6]	3.81	7.58	7.83	SDM [50]	3.80	7.38	7.25
SDM [50]	4.01	7.49	7.65	CFAN [54]	3.31	6.47	6.64
IFA [1]	3.45	6.39	6.78	TCDCN [55]	3.45	6.92	7.59
DCNC [41]	3.67	6.16	6.43	PIEFA [36]	3.24	**6.07**	6.37
OURS	**3.32**	**5.43**	**5.64**	OURS	**3.17**	6.18	**6.25**

It is because the suddenly added identity loss perturbs the backpropagation process. However, the testing accuracy with identity loss increases rapidly and outperforms the one without identity loss after only a few more training epochs.

5.5 Comparison with State-of-the-Art Methods

We compared our framework with both traditional approaches and deep learning based approaches. The methods with hand-crafted features include: **(1)** DRMF [2], **(2)** ESR [6], **(3)** SDM [50], **(4)** IFA [1], and **(5)** PIEFA [36]. The deep learning based methods include: **(1)** DCNC [41], **(2)** CFAN [54], and **(3)** TCDCN [55]. All these methods were recently proposed and reported state-of-the-art performance. For fair comparison, we evaluated these methods in a tracking protocol: fitting result of current frame was used as the initial shape (DRMF, SDM and IFA) or the bounding box (ESR and PIEFA) in the next frame. The comparison was performed on both controlled, *e.g.* Talking Face (TF) [11], and in-the-wild datasets, *e.g.* Face Movie (FM) [36] and 300-VW [39].

We report the evaluation results for both 7 and 68 landmark setups in Table 4. Our approach achieves state-of-the-art performance under both settings. It outperforms others with a substantial margin on all datasets under 7-landmark evaluation. The performance gain is more significant on the challenging datasets (FM and 300-VW) than controlled dataset (TF). The performance of our approach degrades slightly under 68-landmark evaluation. It is a reasonable degradation considering training images (3k) that have 68-landmark annotation are much less than the ones that have 7-landmark annotation (30k). Although the training set of 300-VW contains 90k frames, the variations are limited as only 105 different identities are present. Our alignment model runs fairly fast, it takes around 30ms to process an image using a Tesla K40 GPU accelerator.

6 Future Work

In this paper, we proposed a novel recurrent encoder-decoder network for real-time sequential face alignment. Intensive experiments demonstrated the effectiveness of our framework and its superior performance. It decouples temporal-invariant and -variant factors in the bottleneck of the network, and exploits recurrent learning at both spatial and temporal dimensions.

The proposed method provides a general framework that can be further applied to other localization-sensitive tasks, such as human pose estimation, object detection, scene classification, etc. In the future, we plan to further exploit the proposed recurrent encoder-decoder network for boarder impact.

References

1. Asthana, A., Zafeiriou, S., Cheng, S., Pantic, M.: Incremental face alignment in the wild. In: CVPR (2014)
2. Asthana, A., Zafeiriou, S., Cheng, S., Pantic, M.: Robust discriminative response map fitting with constrained local models. In: CVPR, pp. 3444–3451 (2013)

3. Badrinarayanan, V., Kendall, A., Cipolla, R.: Segnet: a deep convolutional encoder-decoder architecture for image segmentation. CoRR (2015)
4. Belhumeur, P.N., Jacobs, D.W., Kriegman, D.J., Kumar, N.: Localizing parts of faces using a consensus of exemplars. In: CVPR (2011)
5. Black, M., Yacoob, Y.: Tracking and recognizing rigid and non-rigid facial motions using local parametric models of image motion. In: CVPR, pp. 374–381 (1995)
6. Cao, X., Wei, Y., Wen, F., Sun, J.: Face alignment by explicit shape regression. IJCV **107**(2), 177–190 (2014)
7. Cho, K., van Merrienboer, B., Bahdanau, D., Bengio, Y.: On the properties of neural machine translation: encoder-decoder approaches. CoRR abs/1409.1259 (2014)
8. Chrysos, G.G., Antonakos, E., Zafeiriou, S., Snape, P.: Offline deformable face tracking in arbitrary videos. In: ICCVW, pp. 954–962 (2015)
9. Cootes, T.F., Taylor, C.J.: Active shape models-smart snakes. In: BMVC (1992)
10. Decarlo, D., Metaxas, D.: Optical flow constraints on deformable models with applications to face tracking. IJCV **38**(2), 99–127 (2000)
11. FGNet: talking face video. Technical report (2004). http://www-prima.inrialpes.fr/FGnet/data/01-TalkingFace/talking_face.html
12. Gao, X., Su, Y., Li, X., Tao, D.: A review of active appearance models. IEEE Trans. Syst. Man Cybern. **40**(2), 145–158 (2010)
13. Hochreiter, S., Schmidhuber, J.: Long short-term memory. Neural Comput. **9**(8), 1735–1780 (1997)
14. Hong, S., Noh, H., Han, B.: Decoupled deep neural network for semi-supervised semantic segmentation. CoRR abs/1506.04924 (2015)
15. Ioffe, S., Szegedy, C.: Batch normalization: accelerating deep network training by reducing internal covariate shift. CoRR abs/1502.03167 (2015)
16. Jia, Y., Shelhamer, E., Donahue, J., Karayev, S., Long, J., Girshick, R., Guadarrama, S., Darrell, T.: Caffe: convolutional architecture for fast feature embedding. In: ACMM, pp. 675–678 (2014)
17. Jourabloo, A., Liu, X.: Large-pose face alignment via cnn-based dense 3D model fitting. In: CVPR (2016)
18. Karpathy, A., Fei-Fei, L.: Deep visual-semantic alignments for generating image descriptions. In: CVPR, June 2015
19. Kendall, A., Badrinarayanan, V., Cipolla, R.: Bayesian segnet: model uncertainty in deep convolutional encoder-decoder architectures for scene understanding. CoRR abs/1511.02680 (2015)
20. Koestinger, M., Wohlhart, P., Roth, P.M., Bischof, H.: Annotated facial landmarks in the wild: a large-scale, real-world database for facial landmark localization. In: Workshop on Benchmarking Facial Image Analysis Technologies (2011)
21. Lai, H., Xiao, S., Cui, Z., Pan, Y., Xu, C., Yan, S.: Deep cascaded regression for face alignment (2015). arXiv:1510.09083v2
22. Le, V., Brandt, J., Lin, Z., Bourdev, L., Huang, T.S.: Interactive facial feature localization. In: Fitzgibbon, A., Lazebnik, S., Perona, P., Sato, Y., Schmid, C. (eds.) ECCV 2012. LNCS, vol. 7574, pp. 679–692. Springer, Heidelberg (2012). doi:10.1007/978-3-642-33712-3_49
23. Learned-Miller, G.: Labeled faces in the wild: updates and new reporting procedures. Technical report. UM-CS-2014-003, University of Massachusetts, Amherst (2014)
24. Long, J., Shelhamer, E., Darrell, T.: Fully convolutional networks for semantic segmentation. CoRR abs/1411.4038 (2014)

25. Long, J.L., Zhang, N., Darrell, T.: Do convnets learn correspondence? In: NIPS, pp. 1601–1609 (2014)
26. Lu, L., Zhang, X., Cho, K., Renals, S.: A study of the recurrent neural network encoder-decoder for lar ge vocabulary speech recognition. In: INTERSPEECH (2015)
27. Mikolov, T., Joulin, A., Chopra, S., Mathieu, M., Ranzato, M.: Learning longer memory in recurrent neural networks. CoRR abs/1412.7753 (2014)
28. Mikolov, T., Karafiát, M., Burget, L., Cernocký, J., Khudanpur, S.: Recurrent neural network based language model. In: INTERSPEECH, pp. 1045–1048 (2010)
29. Milborrow, S., Nicolls, F.: Locating facial features with an extended active shape model. In: Forsyth, D., Torr, P., Zisserman, A. (eds.) ECCV 2008. LNCS, vol. 5305, pp. 504–513. Springer, Heidelberg (2008). doi:10.1007/978-3-540-88693-8_37
30. Nair, V., Hinton, G.E.: Rectified linear units improve restricted Boltzmann machines. In: ICML, pp. 807–814 (2010)
31. Oh, J., Guo, X., Lee, H., Lewis, R.L., Singh, S.: Action-conditional video prediction using deep networks in atari games. In: NIPS, pp. 2845–2853 (2015)
32. Oliver, N., Pentland, A., Berard, F.: Lafter: lips and face real time tracker. In: CVPR, pp. 123–129 (1997)
33. Patras, I., Pantic, M.: Particle filtering with factorized likelihoods for tracking facial features. In: Proceedings of Automatic Face and Gesture Recognition, pp. 97–102 (2004)
34. Peng, X., Huang, J., Hu, Q., Zhang, S., Elgammal, A., Metaxas, D.: From circle to 3-sphere: head pose estimation by instance parameterization. CVIU **136**, 92–102 (2015)
35. Peng, X., Huang, J., Hu, Q., Zhang, S., Metaxas, D.N.: Three-dimensional head pose estimation in-the-wild. In: FG, vol. 1, pp. 1–6 (2015)
36. Peng, X., Zhang, S., Yang, Y., Metaxas, D.N.: Piefa: personalized incremental and ensemble face alignment. In: ICCV (2015)
37. Sagonas, C., Tzimiropoulos, G., Zafeiriou, S., Pantic, M.: 300 faces in-the-wild challenge: the first facial landmark localization challenge. In: ICCVW (2013)
38. Schroff, F., Kalenichenko, D., Philbin, J.: Facenet: a unified embedding for face recognition and clustering. In: CVPR, pp. 815–823 (2015)
39. Shen, J., Zafeiriou, S., Chrysos, G., Kossaifi, J., Tzimiropoulos, G., Pantic, M.: The first facial landmark tracking in-the-wild challenge: benchmark and results. In: ICCVW (2015)
40. Simonyan, K., Zisserman, A.: Very deep convolutional networks for large-scale image recognition. CoRR abs/1409.1556 (2014)
41. Sun, Y., Wang, X., Tang, X.: Deep convolutional network cascade for facial point detection. In: CVPR, pp. 3476–3483 (2013)
42. Sun, Y., Wang, X., Tang, X.: Deeply learned face representations are sparse, selective, and robust. In: CVPR, pp. 2892–2900 (2015)
43. Taigman, Y., Yang, M., Ranzato, M., Wolf, L.: Deepface: closing the gap to human-level performance in face verification. In: CVPR (2014)
44. Tang, M., Peng, X.: Robust tracking with discriminative ranking lists. TIP **21**(7), 3273–3281 (2012)
45. Tzimiropoulos, G.: Project-out cascaded regression with an application to face alignment. In: CVPR, pp. 3659–3667 (2015)
46. Veeriah, V., Zhuang, N., Qi, G.J.: Differential recurrent neural networks for action recognition. In: ICCV, December 2015
47. Wang, J., Cheng, Y., Feris, R.S.: Walk and learn: facial attribute representation learning from egocentric video and contextual data. In: CVPR (2016)

48. Wang, X., Yang, M., Zhu, S., Lin, Y.: Regionlets for generic object detection. TPAMI **37**(10), 2071–2084 (2015)
49. Wu, Y., Ji, Q.: Constrained joint cascade regression framework for simultaneous facial action unit recognition and facial landmark detection. In: CVPR (2016)
50. Xuehan-Xiong, D., la Torre, F.: Supervised descent method and its application to face alignment. In: CVPR (2013)
51. Yang, J., Reed, S., Yang, M.H., Lee, H.: Weakly-supervised disentangling with recurrent transformations for 3D view synthesis. In: NIPS (2015)
52. Yao, L., Torabi, A., Cho, K., Ballas, N., Pal, C., Larochelle, H., Courville, A.: Describing videos by exploiting temporal structure. In: ICCV, December 2015
53. Zeiler, M.D., Fergus, R.: Visualizing and understanding convolutional networks. In: Fleet, D., Pajdla, T., Schiele, B., Tuytelaars, T. (eds.) ECCV 2014. LNCS, vol. 8689, pp. 818–833. Springer, Heidelberg (2014). doi:10.1007/978-3-319-10590-1_53
54. Zhang, J., Shan, S., Kan, M., Chen, X.: Coarse-to-Fine Auto-Encoder Networks (CFAN) for real-time face alignment. In: Fleet, D., Pajdla, T., Schiele, B., Tuytelaars, T. (eds.) ECCV 2014. LNCS, vol. 8690, pp. 1–16. Springer, Heidelberg (2014). doi:10.1007/978-3-319-10605-2_1
55. Zhang, Z., Luo, P., Loy, C.C., Tang, X.: Facial landmark detection by deep multi-task learning. In: Fleet, D., Pajdla, T., Schiele, B., Tuytelaars, T. (eds.) ECCV 2014. LNCS, vol. 8694, pp. 94–108. Springer, Heidelberg (2014). doi:10.1007/978-3-319-10599-4_7
56. Zheng, S., Jayasumana, S., Romera-Paredes, B., Vineet, V., Su, Z., Du, D., Huang, C., Torr, P.H.S.: Conditional random fields as recurrent neural networks. In: ICCV, December 2015
57. Zhu, S., Li, C., Loy, C.C., Tang, X.: Face alignment by coarse-to-fine shape searching. In: CVPR, pp. 4998–5006 (2015)
58. Zhu, X., Lei, Z., Liu, X., Shi, H., Li, S.Z.: Face alignment across large poses: a 3D solution. In: CVPR (2016)

Robust Facial Landmark Detection via Recurrent Attentive-Refinement Networks

Shengtao Xiao[1]([⊠]), Jiashi Feng[1], Junliang Xing[3], Hanjiang Lai[1], Shuicheng Yan[1,2], and Ashraf Kassim[1]

[1] Department of Electrical and Computer Engineering,
National University of Singapore, Singapore, Singapore
xiao_shengtao@u.nus.edu, {elefjia,eleyans,ashraf}@nus.edu.sg,
laihanj3@mail.sysu.edu.cn
[2] Artificial Intelligence Institute, 360, Beijing, China
[3] Institute of Automation, Chinese Academy of Sciences, Beijing, China
jlxing@nlpr.ia.ac.cn

Abstract. In this work, we introduce a novel **R**ecurrent **A**ttentive-**R**efinement (RAR) network for facial landmark detection under unconstrained conditions, suffering from challenges like facial occlusions and/or pose variations. RAR follows the pipeline of cascaded regressions that refines landmark locations progressively. However, instead of updating all the landmark locations together, RAR refines the landmark locations sequentially at each recurrent stage. In this way, more reliable landmark points are refined earlier and help to infer locations of other challenging landmarks that may stay with occlusions and/or extreme poses. RAR can thus effectively control detection errors from those challenging landmarks and improve overall performance even in presence of heavy occlusions and/or extreme conditions. To determine the sequence of landmarks, RAR employs an attentive-refinement mechanism. The attention LSTM (A-LSTM) and refinement LSTM (R-LSTM) models are introduced in RAR. At each recurrent stage, A-LSTM implicitly identifies a reliable landmark as the attention center. Following the sequence of attention centers, R-LSTM sequentially refines the landmarks near or correlated with the attention centers and provides ultimate detection results finally. To further enhance algorithmic robustness, instead of using mean shape for initialization, RAR adaptively determines the initialization by selecting from a pool of shape centers clustered from all training shapes. As an end-to-end trainable model, RAR demonstrates superior performance in detecting challenging landmarks in comprehensive experiments and it also establishes new state-of-the-arts on the 300-W, COFW and AFLW benchmark datasets.

Keywords: Facial landmark detection · Occlusion · Face alignment · Recurrent neural network

© Springer International Publishing AG 2016
B. Leibe et al. (Eds.): ECCV 2016, Part I, LNCS 9905, pp. 57–72, 2016.
DOI: 10.1007/978-3-319-46448-0_4

1   Introduction

In facial landmark detection, a set of pre-defined key points on a human face are automatically localized to solve various face analysis problems from face recognition [1] and face morphing [2,3] to 3D face modelling [4]. Among recent research efforts to develop more accurate models for localizing facial landmark points under *unconstrained* conditions [5–12], cascaded regression based approaches [8–12] have demonstrated state-of-the-art performance in both efficiency and accuracy, even in challenging scenarios.

Cascaded regression methods progressively refine landmark detections through multiple cascading stages beginning with the extraction of visual features from current predicted landmarks that are used to update estimates of the face shape[1], which gives rise to new landmarks that are fed into the next stage as inputs. In this way, landmark detection is progressively refined until convergence. As the performance of these cascaded regression methods heavily depends on the quality of the initial locations of landmarks as well as the visual features, recent efforts have focused on enhancing robustness of detection methods e.g., smart restarts [13] and coarse-to-fine searching [12,14].

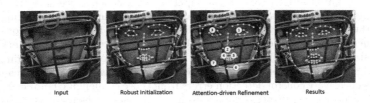

Input   Robust Initialization   Attention-driven Refinement   Results

Fig. 1. Illustration of our proposed Recurrent Attention-Refinement (RAR) network. Given an input face image, our model first produces a robust initial estimate of the face shape specified by landmarks. RAR identifies a proper sequence of attention centers which steer the refinement process and make the result robust to challenging conditions.

Recently, deep learning methods [15–18] have been successfully applied to learn discriminative features for face analysis and demonstrated good performance in detecting landmarks under moderate conditions. However, their performance is still "fragile" under extreme scenarios such as severe occlusion or large pose variations.

In this work, we propose a novel recurrent neural network-based facial landmark detection model, called recurrent Attentive-Refinement network (RAR), to work under unconstrained conditions. RAR follows a pipeline similar to cascaded regression methods that refines landmark detection results progressively via multi-stage predictions. However, while existing cascading methods update

---

[1] The face shape depicts global spatial configuration of all the landmark points for a face. Throughout the paper, we use shape to denote the collection of all the landmarks.

all landmark locations concurrently and globally, RAR refines landmark locations in a sequential manner at each recurrent stage as illustrated in Fig. 1.

Given an input face image, to obtain a good initial estimate for landmark locations, RAR employs a robust initialization strategy that refines a preliminary landmark detection result by fitting it to a population prior on human face shapes. Then, at each recurrent stage, RAR adopts a sequential decision making policy to update the landmark points. Reliable information is collected from earlier landmarks in the sequence which is then used to help detect other challenging landmarks selected later. To automatically identify the sequence of landmarks and refine them progressively, RAR employs two LSTM based components – an attention LSTM (A-LSTM) and a refinement LSTM (R-LSTM) – that work collaboratively. At each recurrent stage, A-LSTM selects one landmark point with highest reliability as an *attention center*[2] and R-LSTM refines those landmarks that are close to the attention center. In this way, reliable information from the attention center is communicated to other landmarks to better refine their locations. Landmark points that are occluded or noisy will be selected by A-LSTM very late, and so their impact is effectively alleviated. Finally, context information provided by other landmarks enables the challenging landmarks to be also detected accurately. Therefore, RAR can provide accurate landmark detection results even in presence of heavy occlusion or other extreme conditions. This sequential detection procedure adopted by RAR is similar to the process how people annotate landmarks of a face image: "easy" landmarks with strong discriminative visual features are usually annotated first and "difficult" landmarks are annotated later with the reference from earlier annotated landmarks.

The main contributions of this paper can be summarized as follows:

– We propose to reform the regression-based face landmark detection in a sequential manner which is more robust to extreme face conditions;
– We present a recurrent attentive-refinement network to realize our sequential formulation which seamlessly incorporates an attention LSTM and a refinement LSTM to perform robust face landmark detection;
– We also develop a robust method to estimate the initial facial shapes which works well even under very challenging conditions;
– Our framework provides new state-of-the-art performance on 300-W, COFW and AFLW sets and significantly outperforms all existing methods.

2 Related Work

2.1 Regression Based Face Feature Points Detection

Regression based face landmark detection models [9,12,19,20] directly learn a mapping function from the feature space to the shape space. To improve accuracy, the shape indexed features are often employed [10] and the regression

---

[2] This name is inspired by the process how humans annotate facial landmarks manually: one prefers to annotate the most clear and reliable landmark points first and then infer the position of other landmark points according to overall face shape.

process is often implemented in a cascade manner that learns a series of projection functions to iteratively update the positions. The face shape output at convergence is then regarded as the landmark detection result. Denote the face shape represented by L landmarks as the $S \in \mathbb{R}^{L \times 2}$, and the regression process can generally be formulated as

$$\hat{S} = \lim_{\Delta S_t \to 0} S_t = \lim_{\Delta S_t \to 0} \{S_{t-1} + \Delta S_t\} = \lim_{\Delta S_t \to 0} \{S_{t-1} + f(\varPhi(I, S_{t-1}))\}, \quad (1)$$

where $\varPhi(I, S_t)$ is the shape indexed feature extractor and f is the regression function, which is usually modelled through a linear projection process, $i.e.$, $\Delta S_t = f(\varPhi(I, S_t)) = W_t \varPhi(I, S_t)$. Here W_t is the projection matrix which needs to be learned as the model parameters. Given a training set $\{I_n, S_n^{\star}\}_{n=1}^{N}$ with N samples, each of which consists of a face image I_n and an annotated true face shape $S_n^{\star}$, the optimal projection matrix can be obtained by minimizing the following objective function:

$$\min_{W_t} \sum_{n=1}^{N} \|S_n^{\star} - \hat{S}_{t,n} - W_t \varPhi(I_n, \hat{S}_{t,n})\|_2^2. \quad (2)$$

To improve the effectiveness of the learned model, some regularizations can be imposed on the model parameters to avoid over-fitting [12,19] and more complex non-linear mapping functions have also been employed [21].

2.2   Recurrent Neural Network

Recurrent neural network (RNN) has drawn great interests from researchers in the field of computer vision recently. Long short term memory (LSTM) [22] is a typical neural network which has achieved great success in many sequential data analysis applications, [23,24]. The computation within an LSTM can be described as follows:

$$f_{t+1} = \sigma(W_f \cdot [C_t, h_t, \varPhi_t] + b_f), \quad (3)$$

$$i_{t+1} = \sigma(W_i \cdot [C_t, h_t, \varPhi_t] + b_i), \quad (4)$$

$$o_{t+1} = \sigma(W_o \cdot [C_t, h_t, \varPhi_t] + b_o), \quad (5)$$

$$\tilde{C}_{t+1} = \tanh(W_C \cdot [h_t, \varPhi_t] + b_C), \quad (6)$$

where C_t, h_t and $\varPhi_t$ are the inputs to the LSTM. Ws and bs are model parameters. σ is the sigmoid activation function. f, i, o are the forgetting, input and output gates of a standard LSTM unit [22] which control the contribution of historical information to current decision. The outputs of an LTSM are

$$C_{t+1} = f_{t+1}C_t + i_{t+1}\tilde{C}_{t+1}, \quad (7)$$

$$h_{t+1} = o_{t+1}\tanh(C_{t+1}). \quad (8)$$

For clarity, we denote the output of LSTM by $h_{t+1} = \mathrm{LSTM}(\varPhi_t)$ with $\varPhi_t$ being the only external signal that is passed into the LSTM.

3 Recurrent Attentive-Refinement Network for Landmark Detection

3.1 Overview of RAR Network

We first provide an overview on the framework of our proposed RAR network in Fig. 2, before introducing each of its components in details. As shown in the figure, our proposed model first directly predicts the locations of all landmarks via a convolutional neural network (CNN). We develop a robust initialization module to alleviate the interference of noisy detection from conv8 and ensures a good starting face shape for the following regression task.

We then extract shape-indexed features [17] from convolutional layers. After that, these features along with the initial landmark estimation are fed into the recurrent attentive-refinement network for progressively updating the landmarks. At each recurrent step, two LSTM units are employed. The first one is an Attention LSTM (A-LSTM) that determines which region to be updated first by selecting an attention center among existing feature points, according to the current global features and memory information. Then, starting with the selected attention center, landmarks around the center will be refined with high priority by an Refinement LSTM (R-LSTM). Other landmarks can also be fine tuned once an attention center close to them is selected. Repeating the attentive-refinement

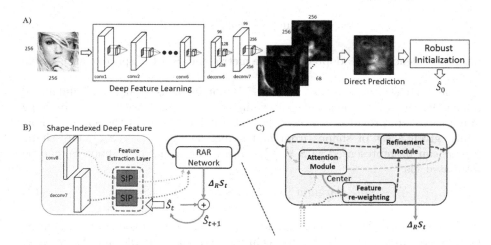

Fig. 2. The proposed framework for facial landmarks detection. (A) Deep convolutional neural network is employed to perform softmax regression to the landmark locations. A robust initialization module is introduced to select a good initial shape for further refinement. (B) Recurrent attentive-refinement network (RAR) takes shape-indexed deep features and past information as inputs and recurrently revises the landmark locations. (C) Within the RAR unit, an attention module generates an attention center at each step and re-weights regression features to encourage landmarks around the attention center to be primarily refined.

process for several times until convergence gives the final landmark detection results. We now proceed to explain each component in details.

3.2 Robust Initialization

The quality of initial landmark estimation is critical for final performance of the cascaded regression methods. Most of previous methods use an average face shape learned from the training set as the initial estimation. This may fail the regression model when processing faces with large pose and expression variations.

To get a good initial estimation of the face shape, we first design a deep CNN model inspired by [16,17] to generate detection results of all landmarks. However, detection of these landmark is often very sensitive to occlusion and it will contaminate the following shape regression steps. We therefore propose a more robust face shape initialization based on the detection results.

Intuitively, the initialized face shape should meet the following two considerations: (1) the shape should be like a human face, or in other words, the shape should satisfy a global configuration constraint on the landmarks; and (2) the initial shape should not be far away from the one detected by CNN on the raw face image, which is denoted as S_d for ease of illustration. Denote the face shape vector encoded by L landmark locations as $S = [x_1, y_1; \ldots; x_L, y_L] \in \mathbb{R}^{L \times 2}$. Based on the above two criteria, the process of looking for a good initial shape S_0 can be formulated as

$$S_0 = \underset{S}{\mathrm{argmin}} \, \|S - S_d\|, \text{ s.t. } S \in \mathcal{F}, \tag{9}$$

where $\| \cdot \|$ denotes the adopted distance metric and $\mathcal{F}$ is the space of all possible face shapes.

Searching for the solution within $\mathcal{F}$ is not easy, as $\mathcal{F}$ itself is difficult to model. Fortunately, when sufficient training face images with accurate shape annotations are provided, we can take them as basis to span the space $\mathcal{F}$. Formally, given a set of shapes from m training faces, $\{S_1, \ldots, S_m\}$, any shape $S \in \mathcal{F}$ can be represented as $S = \sum_{i=1}^{m} \beta_i S_i$. The initial face shape S_0 can be estimated via

$$S_0 = \underset{S, c_i}{\mathrm{argmin}} \, \|S - S_d\|, \text{ s.t. } S = \sum_{i=1}^{m} c_i S_i. \tag{10}$$

In the above formulation, both S_d and S_i could be noisy. Some landmarks in S_d may be corrupted severely due to occlusion and some sample may be wrongly labelled. We therefore further enhance the above objective by introducing the ℓ_0-induced distance metric and regularization:

$$S_0 = \underset{S, \mathbf{c} \doteq [c_i]}{\mathrm{argmin}} \, \|S - S_d\|_0 + \lambda \|\mathbf{c}\|_0, \text{ s.t. } S = \sum_{i=1}^{m} c_i S_i. \tag{11}$$

The above function is our final objective for robust face shape initialization. Finding its global optimum is very time consuming due to the involved ℓ_0 norm.

Fig. 3. This figure depicts how an attention center steers refinement of landmarks at different stages. A-LSTM selects a suitable landmark as the attention center at a recurrent step. Landmarks close (connected with red solid lines) to the attention center will be to refined significantly. Those landmarks distant (connected with green dot lines) from the attention center will be slightly refined. (Color figure online)

To ease optimization, we introduce following two simple yet effective heuristics. First, reduce the size of the problem. When m is large, the problem is extremely hard to optimize. Therefore, we first apply K-means clustering on the shapes $S_1, \ldots, S_m$ to get K representative shapes $\{\bar{S}_1, \ldots, \bar{S}_K\}$ and use these K shapes as the basis of $\mathcal{F}$. Thus the problem size is reduced from m to K. Secondly, we adopt a RANSAC flavor method to filter out significant outliers in S_d and sample some basis to evaluate the objective to find better initial shapes. The obtained face shape with the best objective value is used as the initial face shape in the following regression process.

3.3 Attention LSTM for Sequential Attention-Center Selection

Ideally, A-LSTM selects the most reliable landmark point as an attention center first. Then it proceeds to find less reliable landmarks and finally addresses the noisy landmarks (*e.g.*, occluded ones or the ones lying in the face regions with extreme illumination condition). As shown in Fig. 3, at each recurrent stage, A-LSTM selects an attention center. Locations of landmarks close to the attention center will be primarily updated at the current recurrent step and those far away from the center are slightly refined. Compared with updating all the landmark points simultaneously, treating different landmarks separately in a proper sequence can effectively alleviate the contamination from noisy landmark points and reduce the accumulative errors in the recurrent process.

A-LSTM determines which landmark points to be selected for the current step using a confidence driven strategy. By taking the features of all the landmark points and history of selections as inputs, A-LSTM estimates the confidence scores (or reliability) of all the landmark points first. The landmark having the maximal confidence score at the current step is then selected as the current attention center, $c^* \in \{1, \ldots, L\}$. This process is formally written as

$$c^* = \underset{c \in \{1, \ldots, L\}}{\arg\max} \; \text{A–LSTM}\left(\varPhi(I_t, \hat{S}_t); W_a, c\right), \tag{12}$$

where the operator $\Phi(\cdot, \cdot)$ extracts shape-indexed features according to current predicted shape $\hat{S}_t$ and A-LSTM outputs L confidence scores for the landmark points, based on its input feature and parameter W_a.

Training of A-LSTM. A-LSTM aims to find a suitable selection sequence of landmarks such that the following long term attention center selection reward can be maximized:

$$\mathcal{R}_a = \sum_{t=1}^{\infty} \eta^{t-1} R(\hat{S}_{t-1}, \hat{S}_t), \tag{13}$$

where $\eta < 1$ is the discount factor and t indexes the recurrent steps. Here $R(\hat{S}_{t-1}, \hat{S}_t)$ is the intermediate reward measuring how much improvement brought by updating the shape estimate from the $\hat{S}_{t-1}$ to $\hat{S}_t$ and it is defined as

$$R(\hat{S}_{t-1}, \hat{S}_t) = \|\Gamma_t \Delta S_{t-1}\|_2^2 - \|\Gamma_t \Delta S_t\|_2^2, \tag{14}$$

with $\Delta S_t = S^\star - \hat{S}_t$ as the offset of current shape estimate from the ground truth $S^\star$. $\Gamma_t \in \mathbb{R}^L$ is the distance-based coefficient vector which re-weights each landmark point in the offset calculation in proportion to their distance from the attention center landmark $\hat{S}_t^{c^*}$ (recall c^* is attention center landmark index):

$$\Gamma_t = [\gamma_t^1, \gamma_t^2, \dots, \gamma_t^L] \text{ with } \gamma_t^l = \kappa \exp(-\|\hat{S}_t^l - \hat{S}_t^{c^*}\|_{\ell_2}^2 / (2D_t)^2), \tag{15}$$

where D_t is the inter-ocular distance based on the shape estimate $\hat{S}_t$ and $\kappa = 1/\sum_{l=1}^{L} \gamma_t^l$ is a normalization factor. Here $2D_t$ gives an estimation of the width of the face bounding box.

Training A-LSTM to maximize the long-term award $\mathcal{R}_a$ encourages the A-LSTM to make a sequence of decisions on the landmark selection such that the selected attention center would have positive impact on the overall landmark detection in the future. Here for light notations, we hide the sample index $n \in \{1 \dots N\}$ and this notation is used throughout the entire section.

3.4   R-LSTM for Attention-Center-Driven Shape Refinement

Once A-LSTM selects one attention center landmark, the refinement component will focus on refining landmarks around the attention center. We adopt a second LSTM model to perform refinement, which is called Refinement LSTM (R-LSTM). R-LSTM will suppress refinement of landmarks far away from the attention center as their correlation to attention center is small. Thus, at each recurrent step, only a limited number of landmarks are updated significantly and the rest are slightly updated. Given the attention center from A-LSTM, we first extract attention-center aware global feature for current shape $\hat{S}_t$:

$$\Phi(I_t, \hat{S}_t) = [\gamma_t^1 \phi_t^1, \gamma_t^2 \phi_t^2, \dots, \gamma_t^L \phi_t^L], \tag{16}$$

where γ_t^l for $l = 1, \dots, L$ is the distance-based weighting coefficient for the l-th landmark whose computation is given in Eq. (15). The ϕ_t^l represents a shape-indexed feature extracted around the l-th landmark from the shape $\hat{S}_t$. R-LSTM takes the features and generates offset shape for update.

Training of R-LSTM. The parameters of R-LSTM are optimized through minimizing the following loss:

$$\mathcal{L}_R^t = \|\Gamma_t(\Delta_R S_t - \Delta S_t)\|_{\ell_2}^2, \text{ with } \Delta_R S_t = \alpha\Gamma_t \text{R–LSTM}\left(\Phi(\hat{S}_t)\right) \qquad (17)$$

where $\Delta S_t = S_t^\star - \hat{S}_t$ is the offset from the ground truth. R-LSTM predicts an offset $\Delta_R S_t$ specifying where the shape should be updated towards. We use a fixed scaling factor $\alpha = 128$ to rectify the outputs of R-LSTM, considering the dimension of images is 256×256 and the magnitude of R-LSTM falls in a small range of $(-1, 1)$. Without scaling, R-LSTM only provides negligible shape update at each step. We observe that the scaling factor can significantly accelerate the convergence rate for training R-LSTM. In the loss, Γ_t further ensures that RAR to focus on refining landmarks around the attention center at a certain step.

3.5   Training and Testing Strategies

Considering costs from both attention center selection and refinement, the overall cost to be optimized for training RAR is

$$\sum_{t=1}^{T}\sum_{n=1}^{N} -\gamma^{t-1}\mathcal{R}_a(\hat{S}_{t-1,n}, \hat{S}_{t,n}) + \mathcal{L}_{R,n}^t, \qquad (18)$$

where T is a pre-defined number of recurrent steps which also serves as an early-stop regularization and N is the number of training samples.

This overall objective function can be optimized in an end-to-end manner by applying the standard error back propagation method. Filters of the convolutional layers are tuned not only by the softmax regression loss from conv8 when performing direct landmark prediction but also the overall shape regression loss in Eq. (18). This ensures the learned features are much more informative for landmark detection compared with hand-crafted features, e.g. SIFT and HOG.

At the testing stage, a face image is first passed through the CNN for feature extraction. Landmark locations estimated via conv8 in the CNN, S_d, are then used to search for a good initial shape $\hat{S}_0$ as described in Sect. 3.2. After that, $\hat{S}_0$ is fed into the RAR and updated recurrently as follows:

$$\hat{S}_{t+1} = \hat{S}_t + \Gamma_t \Delta_R S_t \qquad (19)$$

where $\Delta_R S_t$ and Γ_t are the predicted offset and the distance-based weighting vector as given in Sect. 3.3.

4   Experiments

4.1   Implementation Details

Configuration. Our model is developed with the open source platform Caffe [25]. All the images including both training and testing ones are cropped according to provided bounding boxes and scaled to 256 × 256 pixels. Note that in testing, before evaluation we project the detected landmark locations on the 256 × 256 image back to the images of the original size, in order to avoid the possible truncation error due to image scaling. We empirically set the number of recurrent regression stages as $T = 15$ as we do not observe any substantial performance enhancement by further increasing the number of recurrent steps. Our model is trained via standard stochastic gradient descent method with a momentum of 0.9, a mini-batch of 2 images and a weight decay parameter of 0.0001. The weights of LSTM are randomly initialized with a uniform distribution of $[-0.1, 0.1]$. Relevant layers in our model are initialized using the pretrained VGG-19 model provided in [26]. All experiments are conducted using one Nvidia Titan-Z GPU. During test, it takes about 250 ms for our model to process a 256 × 256 face image.

Data Augmentation. Our RAR is trained on 300-W [27] training set which consists of 3,148 face images. We also generate training samples with occlusions incurred by natural objects, *e.g.*, sunglasses, medical masks, phones, hands, and cups, on the original 300-W images to introduce more occluded samples. Training samples are further augmented by rotation, scaling and mirroring. Note that in all the baselines we compare with data augmentation is also performed in different ways. In [9,19], augmentation is performed by introducing bounding box disturbances and random scaling/rotatoin to the original face images. In [28], the authors generate occluded face images with synthesized plausible coherent occlusion patterns to train an occlusion-aware model.

4.2 Benchmark Datasets

We evaluate our model on 300-W [27], Caltech Occluded Face in the Wild (COFW) [13] and Annotated Facial Landmarks in the Wild (AFLW) [29]. 300-W is a standard benchmark for facial landmark detection. The COFW consists of a large number of occluded face images. AFLW is another benchmark which contains face images with large pose variations and heavy partial occlusion.

300-W, COFW and AFLW are annotated with 68, 29 and 21 landmarks respectively. To evaluate our model on COFW, we follow the steps mentioned in [28]. We also evaluate our model for detecting five key landmark points, *i.e.* eye centers, mouth corners and nose tip, on the AFLW benchmark. This follows exactly the same settings as stated in [18]. Common evaluation metric is used, *i.e.* mean error normalized by inter-ocular distance [13,19,20].

We compare performance of our model with results from recent publications. For 300-W and AFLW, cascaded regression-based models ESR [8], SDM [9], RCPR [13], LBF [19], CFSS [12] showed great performance improvement on the benchmark over the past years. Deep learning-based methods CFAN [14] and TCDCN [18] showed slightly better performance as compared to those regression-based methods. We compare our performance on COFW with recently published algorithms RCPR, HPM [28], and RPP [30] which are designed to handle occlusion. We further compare our results with those mentioned methods on AFLW.

4.3 Results

Results on 300-W. We report the landmark detection results of our proposed model as well as results of current state-of-the-art methods on the 300-W testing set. The results are listed in Table 1. From the table, one can observe that our proposed model significantly outperforms the state-of-the-art, TCDCN [18]. Our model has improved on it for more than 10 % on the full set and 14 % on the common set. Note that TCDCN pre-trained their facial landmark detection model on the Multi-Attribute Facial Landmark database (MAFL) [18] which consists of 19,000 different face images with multiple facial attributes information and tuned their model on 300-W. On the other hand, our model is trained only on about 3,148 original face images from 300-W training set. Compared with the best ever reported regression-based method, *i.e.* CFSS [12], our model brings error reduction up to 16.3 % and 12.9 % on the challenging and common set.

Table 1. Landmark detection results on different subsets of the 300-W dataset.

Methods	Helen	LFPW	Common set	Challenging set	Full set
RCPR [13]	5.67	5.93	6.18	17.26	8.35
SDM [9]	–	–	5.57	15.40	7.50
CFAN [14]	5.44	5.53	5.50	–	–
LBF [19]	–	–	4.95	11.98	6.32
CFSS [12]	4.87	4.63	4.73	9.98	5.76
TCDCN [18]	–	–	4.8	8.6	5.54
RAR	**4.30**	**3.99**	**4.12**	**8.35**	**4.94**

Results on COFW. Table 2 shows the results of our model and baselines on the COFW dataset. It can be seen that our model outperforms all reported results on this dataset. In particular, one model gives 19.2 % performance improvement over the state-of-the-art [28]. We also report failure rates of the compared methods on this dataset in Table 2. One can observe that our model reduces the failure rate dramatically. For example, compared with the best baseline HPM, our model reduces the failure rate from 13.24 % to 4.14 %. Small failure rate also indicates the robustness of our framework to various occlusions from the dataset.

We also visualize some example detection results on COFW in top row of Fig. 4. From the examples, one can observe that our model can accurately detect the landmark points even for faces with heavy occlusion. The results clearly demonstrate the strong robustness of our model to occlusion and other extreme conditions, benefiting from the built-in attention and sequential selection model.

Results on AFLW. Table 3 shows the results of our model and baselines on the AFLW dataset. The proposed model outperformed all existing methods for at least 5 % which further verifies our model's robustness on datasets with large poses and occlusion.

Table 2. Mean error on COFW

Methods	Normalized ME	Failure rate
RCPR [13]	8.50	20.00 %
HPM [28]	7.46	13.24 %
RPP [30]	7.52	16.2 %
TCDCN [18]	8.05	-
RAR	**6.03**	4.14 %

Table 3. Mean error on AFLW

Methods	Normalized ME
RCPR [13]	11.6
SDM [9]	8.5
CFAN [14]	10.94
TCDCN [18]	7.6
RAR	**7.23**

4.4 Discussion

Attention Selection and Shape Updating. It is interesting to look into how the proposed A-LSTM selects attention centers at different stages for different faces. Table 4 visualizes the frequency of different landmarks being selected as the attention center. From the results, one can observe that at the early recurrent stages, *i.e.*, S1 to S5, the A-LSTM tends to more often select landmarks from the face centers with strong discriminative features, *e.g.*, the ones on eyebrow, mouth and nose tip. Indeed, this policy — localizing central landmarks first — is essentially useful when the initial shape is not good. Global shape refinement at early stages can significantly improve the detection performance and selecting attention centers around the center of a face can help refine all the landmarks. In contrast, as shown in Table 4, the A-LSTM usually selects landmarks on the face contour at very late stages such as S11 to S15. This is reasonable as landmarks on the face contour are difficult to annotate due to their weak discriminative features and should be inferred with help from other points.

We also perform ablation studies on the effectiveness of attention LSTM and sequential selection on landmarks. In the experiments, we set the parameter γ_t^l in Eq. (16) to be 1 for all possible attention centers. By doing so, the impact of selecting attention center via A-LSTM is actually disabled as the features and training objectives are independent of the selected center now. Then we train the "attentionless" model under the same setting as above and its normalized mean error on 300-W and COFW is 5.02 and 6.11 respectively. The results are worse than the ones given by the RAR. This verifies the essential role of the attention center in the landmark prediction process. Sample images from last two columns of Fig. 4 also indicate that our model can perform better in detecting fine-grained landmarks. Since the RAR explicitly selects region of interest to refine at each step, an occluded area can be focused at certain time step and landmarks within the area will be carefully refined. However, without the attention mechanism, refinement is performed globally at every step and landmarks heavily occluded can hardly be explicitly refined.

Approaches for Estimating the Initial Shapes. Recent regression-based methods usually use mean shape [9,19] or multiple random shapes [8,13] as an initial estimate of the shapes. However, those methods hardly prevent the

Table 4. Attention center selection frequency at different stages. Y-axis represents the mean regional error of all 300-W samples calculated by taking average of weighted errors by Γ_t. The area of the red circle indicates the frequency of that landmark being selected as an attention center. Landmarks with top-10 frequencies are shown.

Stages	Center Selection Frequency VS Regional Error
S1-S5	
S6-S10	
S11-S15	

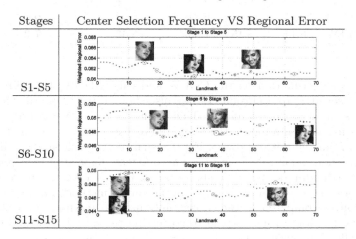

regressed shape from being trapped at a local optimum if the face pose is large. In contrast, our model directly estimates the initial shape with a softmax regression layer (*i.e.*, the Conv8 layer) and selects a good initial shape based on proposed robust initialization scheme (Sect. 3.2). This approach provides a good initial shape closer to the ground truth compared with conventional shape initialization methods, which offers a solid foundation for further shape refinement. This part investigates how the robust initialization strategy contributes to the final performance. Table 5 shows the results of four different initialization strategies including directly applying regression on the output of the conv8 layer (denoted as "direct" in the table), using mean shape and random shape as well as our proposed robust one. We also compare them with the "baseline" results that are directly output by the conv8 layer, From the results, one can observe the conv8

Fig. 4. Testing results on selected samples from the COFW testing set. Images from the top row show results of our full model. Images from the bottom row show results of other models, *i.e.* mean shape initialization(1,2), random initialization(3,4) and direct regression(5,6) and "attentionless" model(7,8).

Table 5. Mean error of RAR with different initial shape estimation approaches.

Dataset	Baseline	Direct	Mean shape	Random shape	Robust
300-W	6.24	6.66	5.26	5.22	**4.94**
COFW	30.14	11.52	6.24	6.12	**6.03**
AFLW	8.14	8.15	7.36	7.42	**7.23**

offers very bad estimation on the COFW and this indicates that direct detection is very sensitive to occlusion. Table 5 also shows directly initializing the face shape gives the worst performance. This verifies our earlier concern that noisy landmarks indeed contaminate the training process and hurt the final results.

Images from the bottom row of Fig. 4 visualize the performance differences. Direct regression can hardly guarantee a normal face shape after recurrent regression. Outlier landmarks from S_d shows direct impact over the final predicted shape. Mean shape and random shape initialization methods are more sensitive to occlusion as compared to the robust initialization method. This is possibly because too much attention is paid to correcting the initial error and occlusion is not specifically considered by the A-LSTM's under this situation (Fig. 5).

Comparison with Canonical Regression Methods. Canonical regression based methods try to optimize the shape regression objective independently at different stages [9, 19]. Lacking information shared across consecutive regression stages makes those methods easy to be trapped at a bad local optimum. In contrast, the RAR employs LSTM to memorize all benefiting information from previous stages for both attention center selection and landmark refinement. This leads to superior performance of our model as shown in Tables 1 to 3.

Fig. 5. RAR shows superior results on samples from 300-W challenge set.

5   Conclusion

In this paper, we developed a facial landmark detection framework which is shown to be robust to challenging conditions via the developed recurrent attentive-refinement network. The framework first directly detects landmarks using a CNN model. The detected landmarks are then used to initialize a good starting shape by alleviating the negative impact of noisy landmarks. Deep shape indexed features are extracted at each regression stage and passed to the A-LSTM module to select attention center at each stage. R-LSTM module then refines landmarks close to the center with high priority. This framework was extensively evaluated on the 300-W, COFW and AFLW datasets and showed significant performance improvements over the state-of-the-arts.

Acknowledgement. The work of Jiashi Feng was partially supported by National University of Singapore startup grant R-263-000-C08-133 and Ministry of Education of Singapore AcRF Tier One grant R-263-000-C21-112 and the work of Junliang Xing was partially supported by NSFC (Grant No. 61303178).

References

1. Zhao, W., Chellappa, R., Phillips, P.J., Rosenfeld, A.: Face recognition: a literature survey. ACM Comput. Surv. **35**(4), 399–458 (2003)
2. Liu, L., Xing, J., Liu, S., Xu, H., Zhou, X., Yan, S.: Wow! you are so beautiful today!. ACM Trans. Multimedia Comput. Commun. Appl. **11**(1s), 20 (2014)
3. Kemelmacher-Shlizerman, I., Suwajanakorn, S., Seitz, S.M.: Illumination-aware age progression. In: Proceedings of IEEE International Conference on Computer Vision and Pattern Recognition, pp. 3334–3341. IEEE (2014)
4. Cao, C., Hou, Q., Zhou, K.: Displaced dynamic expression regression for real-time facial tracking and animation. ACM Trans. Graph. **33**(4), 43 (2014)
5. Saragih, J.M., Lucey, S., Cohn, J.F.: Deformable model fitting by regularized landmark mean-shift. Int. J. Comput. Vis. **91**(2), 200–215 (2011)
6. Zhu, X., Ramanan, D.: Face detection, pose estimation, and landmark localization in the wild. In: Proceedings of IEEE International Conference on Computer Vision and Pattern Recognition, pp. 2879–2886. IEEE (2012)
7. Martins, P., Caseiro, R., Batista, J.: Generative face alignment through 2.5 d active appearance models. Comput. Vis. Image Underst. **117**(3), 250–268 (2013)
8. Cao, X., Wei, Y., Wen, F., Sun, J.: Face alignment by explicit shape regression. Int. J. Comput. Vis. **107**(2), 177–190 (2014)
9. Xiong, X., De la Torre, F.: Supervised descent method and its applications to face alignment. In: Proceedings of IEEE International Conference on Computer Vision and Pattern Recognition, pp. 532–539. IEEE (2013)
10. Dollár, P., Welinder, P., Perona, P.: Cascaded pose regression. In: Proceedings of IEEE International Conference on Computer Vision and Pattern Recognition, pp. 1078–1085. IEEE (2010)
11. Lee, D., Park, H., Yoo, C.D.: Face alignment using cascade gaussian process regression trees. In: Proceedings of IEEE International Conference on Computer Vision and Pattern Recognition, pp. 4204–4212. IEEE (2015)
12. Zhu, S., Li, C., Loy, C.C., Tang, X.: Face alignment by coarse-to-fine shape searching. In: CVPR, pp. 4998–5006. IEEE (2015)
13. Burgos-Artizzu, X.P., Perona, P., Dollár, P.: Robust face landmark estimation under occlusion. In: Proceedings of IEEE International Conference on Computer Vision, pp. 1513–1520. IEEE (2013)

14. Zhang, J., Shan, S., Kan, M., Chen, X.: Coarse-to-fine auto-encoder networks (cfan) for real-time face alignment. In: Proceedings of European Conference on Computer Vision, pp. 1–16 (2014)
15. Luo, P., Wang, X., Tang, X.: Hierarchical face parsing via deep learning. In: Proceedings of IEEE International Conference on Computer Vision and Pattern Recognition, pp. 2480–2487. IEEE (2012)
16. Sun, Y., Wang, X., Tang, X.: Deep convolutional network cascade for facial point detection. In: Proceedings of IEEE International Conference on Computer Vision and Pattern Recognition, pp. 3476–3483. IEEE (2013)
17. Lai, H., Xiao, S., Cui, Z., Pan, Y., Xu, C., Yan, S.: Deep Cascaded Regression for Face Alignment. ArXiv e-prints, October 2015
18. Zhang, Z., Luo, P., Loy, C.C., Tang, X.: Learning deep representation for face alignment with auxiliary attributes. IEEE Trans. Pattern Anal. Mach. Intell. **PP**(99), 1 (2015)
19. Ren, S., Cao, X., Wei, Y., Sun, J.: Face alignment at 3000 fps via regressing local binary features. In: Proceedings of IEEE International Conference on Computer Vision and Pattern Recognition, pp. 1685–1692. IEEE (2014)
20. Xing, J., Niu, Z., Huang, J., Hu, W., Yan, S.: Towards multi-view and partially-occluded face alignment. In: Proceedings of the IEEE Conference on Computer Vision and Pattern Recognition, pp. 1829–1836. IEEE (2014)
21. Sauer, P., Cootes, T.F., Taylor, C.J.: Accurate regression procedures for active appearance models. In: Proceedings of British Machine Vision Conference, pp. 1–11(2011)
22. Hochreiter, S., Schmidhuber, J.: Long short-term memory. Neural Comput. **9**(8), 1735–1780 (1997)
23. Graves, A., Mohamed, A.r., Hinton, G.: Speech recognition with deep recurrent neural networks. In: 2013 IEEE International Conference on Acoustics, Speech and Signal Processing (ICASSP), pp. 6645–6649. IEEE (2013)
24. Sutskever, I., Vinyals, O., Le, Q.V.: Sequence to sequence learning with neural networks. In: Advances in Neural Information Processing Systems, pp. 3104–3112 (2014)
25. Jia, Y., Shelhamer, E., Donahue, J., Karayev, S., Long, J., Girshick, R., Guadarrama, S., Darrell, T.: Caffe: Convolutional architecture for fast feature embedding. arXiv preprint arXiv:1408.5093 (2014)
26. Simonyan, K., Zisserman, A.: Very deep convolutional networks for large-scale image recognition. arXiv preprint arXiv:1409.1556 (2014)
27. Sagonas, C., Tzimiropoulos, G., Zafeiriou, S., Pantic, M.: 300 faces in-the-wild challenge: the first facial landmark localization challenge. In: Proceedings of IEEE International Conference on Computer Vision Workshops. IEEE (2013)
28. Ghiasi, G., Fowlkes, C.C.: Occlusion coherence: Localizing occluded faces with a hierarchical deformable part model. In: Proceedings of IEEE International Conference on Computer Vision and Pattern Recognition, pp. 1899–1906. IEEE (2014)
29. Köstinger, M., Wohlhart, P., Roth, P.M., Bischof, H.: Annotated facial landmarks in the wild: a large-scale, real-world database for facial landmark localization. In: 2011 IEEE International Conference on Computer Vision Workshops (ICCV Workshops), pp. 2144–2151. IEEE (2011)
30. Yang, H., He, X., Jia, X., Patras, I.: Robust face alignment under occlusion via regional predictive power estimation. IEEE Trans. Image Process. **24**(8), 2393–2403 (2015)

Poster Session 1

Learning to Refine Object Segments

Pedro O. Pinheiro[1,2(✉)], Tsung-Yi Lin[1,3], Ronan Collobert[1], and Piotr Dollár[1]

[1] Facebook AI Research, Menlo Park, USA
pedro@opinheiro.com
[2] Idiap Research Institute and Ecole Polytechnique Fédérale de Lausanne,
Lausanne, Switzerland
[3] Cornell Tech, Cornell University, New York, USA

Abstract. Object segmentation requires both object-level information and low-level pixel data. This presents a challenge for feedforward networks: lower layers in convolutional nets capture rich spatial information, while upper layers encode object-level knowledge but are invariant to factors such as pose and appearance. In this work we propose to augment feedforward nets for object segmentation with a novel top-down refinement approach. The resulting bottom-up/top-down architecture is capable of efficiently generating high-fidelity object masks. Similarly to skip connections, our approach leverages features at all layers of the net. Unlike skip connections, our approach does not attempt to output independent predictions at each layer. Instead, we first output a coarse 'mask encoding' in a feedforward pass, then refine this mask encoding in a top-down pass utilizing features at successively lower layers. The approach is simple, fast, and effective. Building on the recent DeepMask network for generating object proposals, we show accuracy improvements of 10–20% in average recall for various setups. Additionally, by optimizing the overall network architecture, our approach, which we call SharpMask, is 50% faster than the original DeepMask network (under .8 s per image).

1 Introduction

As object detection [1–8] has rapidly progressed, there has been a renewed interest in object instance segmentation [9]. As the name implies, the goal is to both detect and segment each individual object. The task is related to both object detection with bounding boxes [9–11] and semantic segmentation [10,12–19]. It involves challenges from both domains, requiring accurate pixel-level object segmentation coupled with identification of each individual object instance.

A number of recent papers have explored the use convolutional neural networks (CNNs) [20] for object instance segmentation [21–24]. Standard feedforward CNNs [25–28] interleave convolutional layers (with pointwise nonlinearities) and pooling layers. Pooling controls model capacity and increases receptive field size, resulting in a coarse, highly-semantic feature representation. While effective

---

P.O. Pinheiro and T.-Y. Lin—Authors contributed equally to this work while doing internships at FAIR.

B. Leibe et al. (Eds.): ECCV 2016, Part I, LNCS 9905, pp. 75–91, 2016.
DOI: 10.1007/978-3-319-46448-0_5

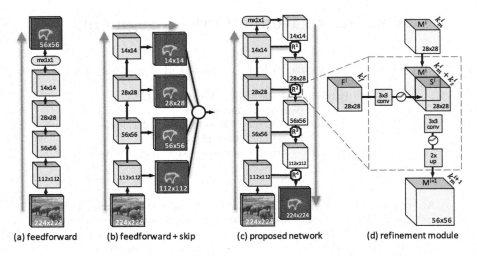

(a) feedforward   (b) feedforward + skip   (c) proposed network   (d) refinement module

Fig. 1. Architectures for object instance segmentation. (a) Feedforward nets, such as DeepMask [22], predict masks using only upper-layer CNN features, resulting in coarse pixel masks. (b) Common 'skip' architectures are equivalent to making independent predictions from each layer and averaging the results [24,29,30], such an approach is not well suited for object instance segmentation. (c,d) In this work we propose to augment feedforward nets with a novel top-down refinement approach. The resulting bottom-up/top-down architecture is capable of efficiently generating high-fidelity object masks.

and necessary for extracting object-level information, this general architecture results in low resolution features that are invariant to pixel-level variations. This is beneficial for classification and identifying object instances but poses challenge for pixel-labeling tasks. Hence, CNNs that utilize only upper network layers for object instance segmentation [21–23], as in Fig. 1a, can effectively generate coarse object masks but have difficulty generating pixel-accurate segmentations.

For pixel-labeling tasks such as semantic segmentation and edge detection, 'skip' connections [24,29–31], as shown in Fig. 1b, are popular. In practice, common skip architectures are equivalent to making independent predictions from each network layer and upsampling and averaging the results (see Fig. 2 in [24], Fig. 3 in [29], and Fig. 3 in [30]). This is effective for semantic segmentation as local receptive fields in early layers can provide sufficient data for pixel labeling. For object segmentation, however, it is necessary to differentiate between object instances, for which local receptive fields are insufficient (e.g. local patches of sheep fur can be labeled as such but without object-level information it can be difficult to determine if they belong to the same animal).

In this paper, we propose a novel CNN which efficiently merges the spatially rich information from low-level features with the high-level object knowledge encoded in upper network layers. Rather than generating independent outputs from multiple network layers, our approach first generates a coarse *mask encoding* in a feedforward manner, which is simply a semantically meaningful feature map with multiple channels, then refines it by successively integrating information from earlier layers. Specifically, we introduce a *refinement module* and stack successive such modules together into a top-down refinement process. See Figs. 1c and d. Each refinement module is responsible for 'inverting' the effect of pooling by taking a mask encoding generated in the top-down pass, along with the matching features from the bottom-up pass, and merging the information in both to generate a new mask encoding with double the spatial resolution. The process continues until full resolution is restored and the final output encodes the object mask. The refinement module is efficient and fully backpropable.

We apply our approach in the context of object proposal generation [32–38]. The seminal object detection work on R-CNN [5] follows a two-phase approach: first, an object proposal algorithm is used to find regions in images that may contain objects; second, a CNN assigns each proposal a category label. While originally object proposals were constructed from low-level grouping and saliency cues [38], recently CNNs have been adopted for this task [3,7,22], leading to massive improvements in detection accuracy. In particular, Pinheiro et al. [22] demonstrated how to adopt a CNN to generate rich object instance segmentations in an image. The proposed model, called DeepMask, predicts how likely an image patch is to fully contain a centered object and also outputs an associated segmentation mask for the object, if present. The model is run convolutionally to generate a dense set of object proposals for an image. DeepMask outperforms previous object segment proposal methods by a substantial margin [22].

In this work we utilize the DeepMask architecture as our starting point for object instance segmentation due to its simplicity and effectiveness. We augment the basic DeepMask architecture with our refinement module (see Fig. 1) and refer to the resulting approach as *SharpMask* to emphasize its ability to produce sharper, higher-fidelity object segmentation masks. In addition to the top-down refinement, we also revisit the basic bottom-up architecture of the DeepMask network and likewise optimize it for the segmentation task.

SharpMask improves segmentation mask quality relative to DeepMask. For object proposal generation, average recall on the COCO dataset [9] improves 10–20% and establishes the new state-of-the-art on this task. Moreover, we optimize our core architecture and improve speed by 50 % with respect to DeepMask, with an average of .76 s per image. Our fast model, which still outperforms previous results, runs at .46 s, or, by using additional image scales, we can boost small object recall by ∼2×. Finally we show SharpMask proposals substantially improve object detection results when coupled with the Fast R-CNN detector [6].

The paper is organized as follows: Sect. 2 presents related work, Sect. 3 introduces our novel top-down refinement network, Sect. 4 describes optimizations to the network architecture, and finally Sect. 5 validates our approach experimentally.

All source code for reproducing the methods in this paper will be released.

2   Related Work

Following their success in image classification [25–28], CNNs have been adopted with great effect to pixel-labeling tasks such as depth estimation [15], optical

flow [39], and semantic segmentation [13]. Below we describe architectural innovations for such tasks, and discuss how they relate to our approach. Aside from
skip connections [24,29–31], which were discussed in Sect. 1, these techniques
can be roughly classified as multiscale architectures, deconvolutional networks,
and graphical model networks. We discuss each in turn next. We emphasize,
however, that most of these approaches are not applicable to our domain due
to severe computational constraints: we must refine hundreds of proposals per
image implying the marginal time per proposal must be minimal.

Multiscale architectures: [13–15] compute features over multiple rescaled versions of an image. Features can be computed independently at each scale [13], or
the output from one scale can be used as additional input to the next finer scale
[14,15]. Our approach relies on similar intuition but does not require recomputing features at each image scale. This allows us to apply refinement efficiently
to hundreds of locations per image as necessary for object proposal generation.

Deconvolutional networks: [40] proposed to invert the pooling process in a
CNN to generate progressively higher resolution input images by storing the
'switch' variables from the pooling operation. Deconv networks have recently
been applied successfully to semantic segmentation [19]. Deconv layers share
similarities with our refinement module, however, 'switches' are communicated
instead of the feature values, which limits the information that can be transferred. Finally, [39] proposed to progressively increase the resolution of an optical
flow map. This can be seen as a special case of our refinement approach where:
(1) the 'features' for refinement are set to be the flow field itself, (2) no feature
transform is applied to the bottom-up features, and (3) the approach is applied
monolithically to the entire image. Restricting our method in any of these ways
would cause it to fail in our setting as discussed in Sect. 5.

Graphical model networks: a number of recent papers have proposed integrating graphical models into CNNs by demonstrating they can be formulated as
recurrent nets [16–18]. Good results were demonstrated on semantic segmentation. While too slow to apply to multiple proposals per image, these approaches
likewise attempt to sharpen a coarse segmentation mask.

3   Learning Mask Refinement

We apply our proposed bottom-up/top-down refinement architecture to object
instance segmentation. Specifically, we focus on object proposal generation [38],
which forms the cornerstone of modern object detection [5]. We note that
although we test the proposed refinement architecture on the task of object
segmentation, it could potentially be applied to other pixel-labeling tasks.

Object proposal algorithms aim to find diverse regions in an image which
are likely to contain objects; both proposal recall and quality correlate strongly
with detector performance [38]. We adopt the DeepMask network [22] as the
starting point for proposal generation. DeepMask is trained to jointly generate
a class-agnostic object mask and an associated 'objectness' score for each input

(a) DeepMask Output   (b) SharpMask Output

Fig. 2. Qualitative comparison of DeepMask versus SharpMask segmentations. Proposals with highest IoU to the ground truth are shown for each method. Both DeepMask and SharpMask generate object masks that capture the general shape of the objects. However, SharpMask improves the masks near object boundaries.

image patch. At inference time, the model is run convolutionally to generate a dense set of scored segmentation proposals. We refer readers to [22] for full details.

A simplified diagram of the segmentation branch of DeepMask is illustrated in Fig. 1a. The network is trained to infer the mask for the object located in the center of the input patch. It contains a series of convolutional layers interleaved with pooling stages that reduce the spatial dimensions of the feature maps, followed by a fully connected layer to generate the object mask. Hence, each pixel prediction is based on a complete view of the object, however, its input feature resolution is low due to the multiple pooling stages.

As a result, DeepMask generates masks that are accurate on the object level but only coarsely align with object boundaries, see Fig. 2a. In order to obtain higher-quality masks, we augment the basic DeepMask architecture with our refinement approach. We refer to the resulting method as *SharpMask* to emphasize its ability to produce sharper, pixel-accurate object masks, see Fig. 2b. We begin with a high-level overview of our approach followed by further details.

3.1   Refinement Overview

Our goal is to efficiently merge the spatially rich information from low-level features with the high-level semantic information encoded in upper network layers. Three principles guide our approach: (1) object-level information is often necessary to segment an object, (2) given object-level information, segmentation should proceed in a top-down fashion, successively integrating information from earlier layers, and (3) the approach should invert the loss of resolution from pooling (with the final output matching the resolution of the input).

To satisfy these principles, we augment standard feedforward nets with a top-down refinement process. An overview of our approach is shown in Fig. 1c. We introduce a 'refinement module' R that is responsible for inverting the effect of pooling and doubling the resolution of the input mask encoding. Each module R^i takes as input a mask encoding M^i generated in the top-down pass, along with matching features F^i generated in the bottom-up pass, and learns to merge the information to generate a new upsampled object encoding M^{i+1}. In other words: $M^{i+1} = R^i(M^i, F^i)$, see Fig. 1d. Multiple such modules are stacked (one module per pooling layer). The final output of our network is a pixel labeling of the same resolution as the input image. We present full details next.

3.2 Refinement Details

The feedforward pathway of our network outputs a 'mask encoding' M^1, or simply, a low-resolution but semantically meaningful feature map with k_m^1 channels. M^1 serves as the input to the top-down refinement module, which is responsible for progressively increasing the mask encoding's resolution. Note that using $k_m^1 > 1$ allows the mask encoding to capture more information than a simple segmentation mask, which proves to be key for obtaining good accuracy.

Each refinement module R^i aggregates information from a coarse mask encoding M^i and features F^i from the corresponding layer of the bottom-up computation (we always use the last convolutional layer prior to pooling). By construction, M^i and F^i have the same spatial dimensions; the goal of R^i is to generate a new mask encoding M^{i+1} with double spatial resolution based on inputs M^i and F^i. We denote this via $M^{i+1} = R^i(M^i, F^i)$. This process is applied iteratively n times (where n is the number of pooling stages) until the feature map has the same dimensions as the input image patch. Each module R^i has separate parameters, allowing the network to learn stage-specific refinements.

The refinement module aims to enhance the mask encoding M^i using features F^i. As M^i and F^i have the same spatial dimensions, one option is to first simply concatenate M^i and F^i. However, directly concatenating F^i with M^i poses two challenges. Let k_m^i and k_f^i be the number of channels in M^i and F^i respectively. Typically, k_f^i can be quite large in modern CNNs, so using F^i directly would be computationally expensive. Second, typically $k_f^i \gg k_m^i$, so directly concatenating the features maps risks drowning out the signal in M^i.

Instead, we opt to first reduce the number of channels k_f^i (but preserving the spatial dimensions) of these features through a 3×3 convolutional module (plus ReLU), generating 'skip' features S^i, with $k_s^i \ll k_f^i$ channels. This substantially reduces computational requirements, moreover, it allows the network to transform F^i into a form S^i more suitable for use in refinement. An important but subtle point is that during full image inference, as with the features F^i, skip features are shared by overlapping image patches, making them highly efficient to compute. In contrast, the remaining computations of R^i are patch dependent as they depend on the local mask M^i and hence cannot be shared across locations.

The refinement module concatenates mask encoding M^i with skip features S^i resulting in a feature map with $k_m^i + k_s^i$ channels, and applies another 3×3

convolution (plus ReLU) to the result. Finally, the output is upsampled using bilinear upsampling by a factor of 2, resulting in a new mask encoding M^{i+1} with k_m^{i+1} channels (k_m^{i+1} is determined by the number of 3×3 kernels used for the convolution). As with the convolution for generating the skip features, this transformation is used to simultaneously learn a nonlinear mask encoding from the concatenated features and to control the capacity of the model. Please see Fig. 1d for a complete overview of the refinement module R. Further optimizations to R are possible, for details see the extended arXiv version.

Note that the refinement module uses only convolution, ReLU, bilinear upsampling, and concatenation, hence it is fully backpropable and highly efficient. In Sect. 5.2, we analyze different architecture choices for the refinement module in terms of performance and speed. As a general design principle, we aim to keep k_s^i and k_m^i large enough to capture rich information but small enough to keep computation low. In particular, we can start with a fairly large number of channels but as spatial resolution is increased the number of channels should decrease. This reverses the typical design of feedforward networks where spatial resolution decreases while the number of channels increases with increasing depth.

3.3   Training and Inference

We train SharpMask with an identical data definition and loss function as the original DeepMask model. Each training sample is a triplet containing an input patch, a label specifying if the input patch contains a centered object at the correct scale, and for positive samples a binary object mask. The network trunk parameters are initialized with a network that was pre-trained on ImageNet [11]. All the other layers are initialized randomly from a uniform distribution.

Training proceeds in two stages: first, the model is trained to jointly infer a coarse pixel-wise segmentation mask and an object score, second, the feedforward path is 'frozen' and the refinement modules trained. The first training stage is identical to [22]. Once learning of the first stage converges, the final mask prediction layer of the feedforward network is removed and replaced with a linear layer that generates a mask encoding M^1 in place of the actual mask output. We then add the refinement modules to the network and train using standard stochastic gradient descent, backpropagating the error only on the horizontal and vertical convolution layers on each of the n refinement modules.

This two-stage training procedure was selected for three reasons. First, we found it led to faster convergence. Second, at inference time, a *single* network trained in this manner can be used to generate either a coarse mask using the forward path only or a sharp mask using our bottom-up/top-down approach. Third, we found the gains of fine-tuning through the entire network to be minimal once the forward branch had converged.

During full-image inference, similarly to [22], most computation for neighboring windows is shared through use of convolution, including for skip layers S^i. However, as discussed, the refinement modules receive a unique input M^1 at each spatial location, hence, computation proceeds independently at each location for this stage. Rather than refine every proposal, we simply refine only the most promising locations. Specifically, we select the top N scoring proposal windows and apply the refinement in a batch mode to these top N locations.

To further clarify all implementation details, full source code will be released.

4   Feedforward Architecture

While the focus of our work is on top-down mask refinement, to obtain a better understanding of object segmentation we also explore factors that effect a feedforward network's ability to generate accurate object masks. In the next two subsections we carefully examine the design of the network 'trunk' and 'head'.

4.1   Trunk Architecture

We begin by identifying model bottlenecks. DeepMask spends 40 % of its time for feature extraction, 40 % for mask prediction, and 20 % for score prediction. Given the time of feature extraction, increasing model depth or breadth can incur a non-trivial computational cost. Simply upgrading the 11-layer VGG-A model [26] used in [22] to the 16-layer VGG-D model can double run time. Recently He et al. [28] introduced Residual Networks (ResNet) and showed excellent results. In this work, we use the 50-layer ResNet model pre-trained on ImageNet, which achieves the accuracy of VGG-D but with the inference time of VGG-A.

We explore models with varying input size **W**, number of pooling layers **P**, stride density **S**, model depth **D**, and final number of features channels **F**. These factors are intertwined but we can achieve significant insight by a targeted study.

Input size W: Given a minimum object size O, the input image needs to be upsampled by W/O to detect small objects. Hence, reducing W improves speed of both mask prediction and inference for small objects. However, smaller W reduces the input resolution which in turn lowers the accuracy of mask prediction. Moreover, reducing W decreases stride density S which further harms accuracy.

Pooling layers P: Assuming 2×2 pooling, the final kernel width is $W/2^P$. During inference, this necessitates convolving with a large $W/2^P$ kernel in order to aggregate information (e.g., 14×14 for DeepMask). However, while more pooling P results in faster computation, it also results in loss of feature resolution.

Stride density S: We define the stride density to be S=W/stride (where typically stride is 2^P). The smaller the stride, the denser the overlap with ground truth locations. We found that the stride density is key for mask prediction. Doubling the stride while keeping W constant greatly reduces performance as the model must be more spatially invariant relative to a fixed object size.

Depth D: For typical networks [25–28], spatial resolution decreases with increasing D while the number of features channels F increases. In the context of instance segmentation, reducing spatial resolution hurts performance.

Table 1. Model performance (upper bound on AR) for varying input size W, number of pooling layers P, stride density S, depth D, and features channels F. See Sects. 4.1 and 5.1 for details. Timing is for multiscale inference excluding the time for score prediction. Total time for DeepMask & SharpMask is 1.59 s & .76 s.

	W	P	D	S	kernel	F	AR	AR^S	AR^M	AR^L	Time
DeepMask	224	4	8	14	$512 \times 14 \times 14$	512	36.6	18.2	48.7	50.6	1.32 s
W160-P4-D8-VGG	160	4	8	10	$1024 \times 10 \times 10$	512	35.5	15.1	47.5	53.2	.58 s
W160-P4-D39	160	4	39	10	$1024 \times 10 \times 10$	512	37.0	15.9	50.5	53.9	.58 s
W160-P4-D39-F128	160	4	39	10	$1024 \times 10 \times 10$	128	36.9	15.6	49.9	54.8	.45 s
W112-P4-D39	112	4	39	7	$1024 \times 7 \times 7$	512	30.8	11.2	42.3	47.8	.31 s
W112-P3-D21	112	3	21	14	$512 \times 14 \times 14$	512	36.7	16.7	49.1	53.1	.75 s
W112-P3-D21-F128	112	3	21	14	$512 \times 14 \times 14$	128	36.1	16.3	48.4	52.2	.33 s
SharpMask	160	4	39	10	$1024 \times 10 \times 10$	128	39.3	18.1	52.1	57.1	.75 s

One possible direction is to start with lower layers that have less pooling and increase the depth of the model without reducing spatial resolution or increasing F. This would require training networks from scratch which we leave to future work.

Feature channels F: The high dimensional features at the top layer introduce a bottleneck for feature aggregation. An efficient approach is to first apply dimensionality reduction before feature aggregation. We adopt 1×1 convolution to reduce F and show that we can achieve large speedups in this manner.

In Sect. 5.1 and Table 1 we examine various choices for W, P, S, D, and F.

4.2   Head Architecture

We also examine the 'head' of the DeepMask model, focusing on score prediction. Our goal is to simplify the head and further improve inference speed.

In DeepMask, the mask and scoring heads branch after the final $512 \times 14 \times 14$ feature map (see Fig. 3a). Both mask and score prediction require a large convolution, and in addition, the score branch requires an extra pooling step and hence interleaving to match the stride of the mask network during inference. Overall, this leads to a fairly inelegant and slow inference procedure.

We propose a sequence of simplified network structures that have identical mask branches but that share progressively more computation. A series of model heads A-C is detailed in Fig. 3. Head A removes the need for interleaving in DeepMask by removing max pooling and replacing the $512 \times 7 \times 7$ convolutions by $128 \times 10 \times 10$ convolutions; overall this network is much faster. Head B simplifies this by having the $128 \times 10 \times 10$ features shared by both the mask and score branch. Finally, model C further reduces computation by having the score prediction utilize the same low rank $512 \times 1 \times 1$ features used for the mask.

In Sect. 5.1 we evaluate these variants in terms of performance and speed.

84   P.O. Pinheiro et al.

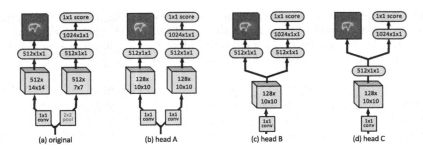

Fig. 3. Network head architecture. (a) The original DeepMask head. (b–d) Various head options with increasing simplicity and speed. The heads share identical pathways for mask prediction but have progressively simplified score branches.

Fig. 4. SharpMask proposals with highest IoU to the ground truth on selected COCO images. Missed objects (no matching proposals with IoU >0.5) are marked in red. The last row shows a number of failure cases.

5   Experiments

We train our model on the training set of the COCO dataset [9], which contains 80 k training images and 500k instance annotations. For most of our experiments, results are reported on the first 5 k COCO validation images. Mask accuracy is measured by Intersection over Union (IoU) which is the ratio of the intersection of the predicted mask and ground truth annotation to their union. A common method for summarizing object proposal accuracy is using the average recall (AR) between IoU 0.5 and .95 for a fixed number of proposals. Hosang et al. [38] show that AR correlates well with object detector performance.

Our results are measured in terms of AR at 10, 100, and 1000 proposals and averaged across all counts (AUC). As the COCO dataset contains objects in a wide range of scales, it is also common practice to divide objects into roughly equally sized sets according to object pixel area a: small ($a < 32^2$), medium ($32^2 \leq a \leq 96^2$), and large ($a > 96^2$) objects, and report accuracy at each scale.

We use a different subset of the COCO validation set to decide architecture choices and hyper-parameter selection. We use a learning rate of 1e-3 for training the refinement stage, which takes about 2 days to train on an Nvidia Tesla K40m GPU. To mitigate the mismatch of per-patch training with convolutional inference, we found that training deeper model such as ResNet requires adding extra image content (32 pixels) surrounding the training patches and using reflective-padding instead of 0-padding at every convolutional layer. Finally, following [22], we binarize our continuous mask prediction using a threshold of 0.2.

5.1   Architecture Optimization

We begin by reporting our optimizations of the feedforward model. For our initial results, we measure AR for densely computed masks ($\sim 10^4$ proposals per image). This allows us to factor out the effect of objectness score prediction and focus exclusively on evaluating mask quality. In our experiments, AR across all proposals is highly correlated, hence this upper bound on AR is predictive of performance at more realistic settings (e.g. at AR^{100}).

Trunk Architecture: We begin by investigating effect of the network trunk parameters described in Sect. 4.1 with the goal of optimizing both speed and accuracy. Performance of a number of representative models is shown in Table 1. First, replacing the 224×224 DeepMask VGG-A model with a 160×160 version is much faster (over $2\times$). Surprisingly, accuracy loss for this model, W160-P4-D8-VGG, is only minor, partially due to an improved learning schedule. Upgrading to a ResNet trunk, W160-P4-D39, restores accuracy and keeps speed identical. We found that reducing the feature dimension to 128 (-F128) shows almost no loss, but improves speed. Finally, as input size is a bottleneck, we also tested a number of W112 models. Nevertheless, overall, W160-P4-D39-F128 gave the best tradeoff between speed and accuracy.

Head Architecture: In Table 2 we evaluate the performance of the various network heads in Fig. 3 (using standard AR, not upper-bound AR as in Table 1).

Table 2. All model variants of the head have similar performance. Head C is a win in terms of both simplicity and speed. See Fig. 3 for head definitions.

	AR^{10}	AR^{100}	AR^{1K}	AUC^S	AUC^M	AUC^L	AUC	Mask	Score	Total
DeepMask	12.6	24.5	33.1	2.3	26.6	33.6	18.3	1.32 s	.27 s	1.59 s
Head A	14.0	25.8	33.4	2.2	27.3	36.6	19.3	.45 s	.06 s	.51 s
Head B	14.0	25.4	33.0	2.0	27.0	36.9	19.1	.45 s	.05 s	.50 s
Head C	14.4	25.8	33.1	2.2	27.3	37.4	19.4	.45 s	.01 s	.46 s

Head A is already substantially faster than DeepMask. All heads achieve similar accuracy with a decreasing inference time as the score branch shares progressively more computation with the mask. Interestingly, head C is able to predict both the score and mask from a single compact 512 dimensional vector. We chose this variant due to its simplicity and speed.

DeepMask-ours: Based on all of these observations, we combine the W160-P4-D39-F128 trunk with the C head. We refer to the resulting architecture as *DeepMask-ours*. DeepMask-ours is over 3× faster than the original DeepMask (.46 s per image versus 1.59 s) and also more accurate. Moreover, model parameter count is reduced from ~75 M to ~17 M. For all SharpMask experiments, we adopt DeepMask-ours as the base feedforward architecture.

5.2   SharpMask Analysis

We now analyze different parameter settings for our top-down refinement network. As described in Sect. 3, each of the four refinement modules R^i in Sharp-Mask is controlled by two parameters k_m^i and k_s^i, which denote the size of the mask encoding M^i and skip encoding S^i, respectively. These parameters control network capacity and effect inference speed. We experiment with two different schedules for these parameters: (a) $k_m^i = k_s^i = k$ and (b) $k_m^i = k_s^i = \frac{k}{2^{i-1}}$ for each $i \leq 4$.

Figure 5(a–b) shows performance for the two schedules for different k both in terms of AUC and inference time (measured when refining the top 500 proposals per image, at which point object detection performance saturates, see Fig. 5c). We consistently observe higher performance as we increase the capacity, with no sign of overfitting. Parameter schedule b, in particular with $k = 32$, has the best trade-off between performance and speed, so we chose this as our final model.

We note that we were unable to obtain good results with schedule a for $k \leq 2$, indicating the importance of using sufficiently large k. Also, we observed that a single 3×3 convolution encounters learning difficulties when ($k_s^i \ll k_f^i$). Therefore, in all experiments we used a sequence of two 3×3 convolutions (followed by ReLUs) to generate S^i from F^i, reducing F^i to 64 channels first followed by a further reduction to k_s^i channels.

Finally, we performed two additional ablation studies. First, we removed all downward convs, set $k_m^i = k_s^i = 1$, and averaged the output of all layers. Second,

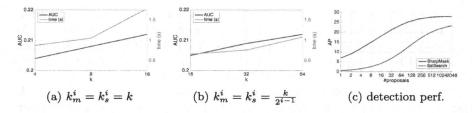

(a) $k_m^i = k_s^i = k$ (b) $k_m^i = k_s^i = \frac{k}{2^{i-1}}$ (c) detection perf.

Fig. 5. (a–b) Performance and inference time for multiple SharpMask variants. (c) Fast R-CNN detection performance versus number and type of proposals.

we kept the vertical convs but removed all horizontal convs. These two variants are related to 'skip' and 'deconv' networks, respectively. Neither setup showed meaningful improvement over the baseline feedforward network. In short, we found that both horizontal and vertical connections were necessary for this task.

5.3 Comparison with State of the Art

Table 3 compares the performance of our model, SharpMask, to other existing methods on the COCO dataset. We compare results both on box and segmentation proposals (for box proposals we extract tight bounding boxes surrounding our segmentation masks). SharpMask achieves the state of the art in all metrics for both speed and accuracy by a large margin. Additionally, because Sharp-Mask has a smaller input size, it can be applied to an additional one to two scales (*SharpMaskZoom*) and achieves a large boost in AR for small objects.

Our feedforward architecture improvements, *DeepMask-ours*, alone, improve over the original DeepMask, in particular for bounding box proposals. Not only is

Table 3. Results on the COCO validation set on box and segmentation proposals. AR at different proposals counts is reported and also AUC (AR averaged across all proposal counts). For segmentation proposals, we also report AUC at multiple scales. SharpMask has largest for segmentation proposals and large objects.

	Box proposals				Segmentation proposals						
	AR^{10}	AR^{100}	AR^{1K}	AUC	AR^{10}	AR^{100}	AR^{1K}	AUC^S	AUC^M	AUC^L	AUC
EdgeBoxes [34]	7.4	17.8	33.8	13.9	—	—	—	—	—	—	—
Geodesic [36]	4.0	18.0	35.9	12.6	2.3	12.3	25.3	1.3	8.6	20.5	8.5
Rigor [37]	—	13.3	33.7	10.1	—	9.4	25.3	2.2	6.0	17.8	7.4
SelectiveSearch [33]	5.2	16.3	35.7	12.6	2.5	9.5	23.0	0.6	5.5	21.4	7.4
MCG [35]	10.1	24.6	39.8	18.0	7.7	18.6	29.9	3.1	12.9	32.4	13.7
RPN [7,8]	12.8	29.2	42.6	21.4	—	—	—	—	—	—	—
DeepMask [22]	15.3	31.3	44.6	23.3	12.6	24.5	33.1	2.3	26.6	33.6	18.3
DeepMaskZoom [22]	15.0	32.6	48.2	24.2	12.7	26.1	36.6	6.8	26.3	30.8	19.4
DeepMask-ours	18.7	34.9	46.5	26.2	14.4	25.8	33.1	2.2	27.3	37.4	19.4
SharpMask	19.7	36.4	48.2	27.4	15.6	27.6	35.5	2.5	29.1	40.4	20.9
SharpMaskZoom	20.1	39.4	52.8	29.1	16.1	30.3	39.2	6.9	29.7	38.4	22.4
SharpMaskZoom^2	19.2	39.9	55.0	29.2	15.4	30.7	40.8	10.6	27.3	36.0	22.5

the new baseline more accurate, with our architecture optimization to the trunk and head of the network (see Sect. 4), speed is improved to .46 s per image. We emphasize that DeepMask was the previous state-of-the-art on this task, outperforming all bottom-up proposal methods as well as Region Proposal Networks (RPN) [7] (we obtained improved RPN proposals from the authors of [8]).

We train SharpMask using DeepMask-ours as the feedforward network. As the two networks have an identical score branch, we can disentangle the performance improvements achieved by our top-down refinement approach. Once again, we observe a considerable boost in performance on AR due to the top-down refinement. We note that improvement for segmentation predictions is bigger than box predictions, which is not surprising, as sharpening masks might not change the tight box around the objects in many examples. Inference for SharpMask is .76 s per image, over 2× faster than DeepMask; moreover, the refinement modules require fewer than 3 M additional parameters.

In Fig. 2, we show direct comparison between SharpMask and DeepMask and we can see SharpMask generates higher-fidelity masks that more accurately delineate object boundaries. In Fig. 4, we show more qualitative results. Additional results and plots are reported in an extended arXiv version of this work.

5.4 Object Detection

In this section, we use SharpMask in the Fast R-CNN pipeline [6] and analyze the improvements of using our proposals for object detection. In the following experiments we coupled SharpMask proposals with two classifiers: VGG [26] and MultiPathNet (MPN) [41], which introduces a number of improvements to the VGG classifier. In future work we will also test our proposals with ResNets [28].

First, Fig. 5c shows the comparison of bounding box detection results for SharpMask and SelSearch [33] on the COCO val set with the MPN classifier

Table 4. Top: COCO bounding box results of various baselines without bells and whistles, trained on the train set only, and reported on test-dev (results for [6,7] obtained from original papers). We denote methods using 'proposal+classifier' notation for clarity. SharpMask achieves top results, outperforming both RPN and SelSearch proposals. **Middle**: Winners of the 2015 COCO segmentation challenge. **Bottom**: Winners of the 2015 COCO bounding box challenge.

	AP	AP^{50}	AP^{75}	AP^S	AP^M	AP^L	AR^1	AR^{10}	AR^{100}	AR^S	AR^M	AR^L
SelSearch + VGG [6]	19.3	39.3	—	—	—	—	—	—	—	—	—	—
RPN + VGG [7]	21.9	42.7	—	—	—	—	—	—	—	—	—	—
SharpMask + VGG	25.2	43.4	—	—	—	—	—	—	—	—	—	—
ResNet++ [28]	28.2	51.5	27.9	9.3	30.6	45.2	25.7	37.4	38.2	16.8	43.9	57.6
SharpMask+MPN [41]	25.1	45.8	24.8	7.4	29.2	39.1	24.1	36.8	38.7	17.3	46.9	53.9
ResNet++ [28]	37.3	58.9	39.9	18.3	41.9	52.4	32.1	47.7	49.1	27.3	55.6	67.9
SharpMask+MPN [41]	33.5	52.6	36.6	13.9	37.8	47.7	30.2	46.2	48.5	24.1	56.1	66.4
ION [8]	31.0	53.3	31.8	12.3	33.2	44.7	27.9	43.1	45.7	23.8	50.4	62.8

applied to both. SharpMask achieves 28 AP, which is 5 AP higher than SelSearch. Also, performance converges using only ∼500 SharpMask proposals per image.

Next, Table 4 top shows results of various baselines without bells and whistles, trained on the train set only. SharpMask achieves top results with the VGG classifier, outperforming both RPN [7] and SelSearch [33].

Finally, Table 4 middle/bottom shows results from the 2015 COCO detection challenges. The performance is reported with model ensembling and the MPN classifier. The ensemble model achieve 33.5 AP for boxes and 25.1 AP for segments, and achieved second place in the challenges. Note that for the challenges, both SharpMask and MPN used the VGG trunk (ResNets were concurrent work, and won the competitions). We have not re-run our model with ensembling and additional bells and whistles after integrating ResNets into SharpMask.

6   Conclusion

In this paper, we introduce a novel architecture for object instance segmentation, based on an augmentation of feedforward networks with top-down refinement modules. Our model achieves a new state of the art for object proposals generation, both in terms of performance and speed. The proposed refinement approach is general and could be applied to other pixel-labeling tasks.

References

1. Felzenszwalb, P.F., Girshick, R.B., McAllester, D., Ramanan, D.: Object detection with discriminatively trained part-based models. PAMI **32**, 1627–1645 (2010)
2. Sermanet, P., Eigen, D., Zhang, X., Mathieu, M., Fergus, R., LeCun, Y.: Overfeat: integrated recognition, localization and detection using conv nets. In: ICLR (2014)
3. Szegedy, C., Reed, S., Erhan, D., Anguelov, D.: Scalable, high-quality object detection. arXiv:1412.1441 (2014)
4. He, K., Zhang, X., Ren, S., Sun, J.: Spatial pyramid pooling in deep convolutional networks for visual recognition. In: Fleet, D., Pajdla, T., Schiele, B., Tuytelaars, T. (eds.) ECCV 2014. LNCS, vol. 8691, pp. 346–361. Springer, Heidelberg (2014). doi:10.1007/978-3-319-10578-9_23
5. Girshick, R., Donahue, J., Darrell, T., Malik, J.: Rich feature hierarchies for accurate object detection and semantic segmentation. In: CVPR (2014)
6. Girshick, R.: Fast R-CNN. In: ICCV (2015)
7. Ren, S., He, K., Girshick, R., Sun, J.: Faster R-CNN: towards real-time object detection with region proposal networks. In: NIPS (2015)
8. Bell, S., Zitnick, C.L., Bala, K., Girshick, R.: Inside-outside net: detecting objects in context with skip pooling and recurrent neural nets. In: CVPR (2016)
9. Lin, T.Y., Maire, M., Belongie, S., Bourdev, L., Girshick, R., Hays, J., Perona, P., Ramanan, D., Zitnick, C.L., Dollár, P.: Microsoft COCO: common objects in context. arXiv:1405.0312 (2015)
10. Everingham, M., Gool, L.V., Williams, C.K.I., Winn, J., Zisserman, A.: The PASCAL visual object classes (VOC) challenge. IJCV **88**, 303–338 (2010)
11. Deng, J., Dong, W., Socher, R., Li, L., Li, K., Fei-Fei, L.: Imagenet: a large-scale hierarchical image database. In: CVPR (2009)

12. Shotton, J., Johnson, M., Cipolla, R.: Semantic texton forests for image categorization and segmentation. In: CVPR (2008)
13. Farabet, C., Couprie, C., Najman, L., LeCun, Y.: Learning hierarchical features for scene labeling. PAMI 35, 1915–1929 (2013)
14. Pinheiro, P.O., Collobert, R.: Recurrent conv. neural networks for scene labeling. In: ICML (2014)
15. Eigen, D., Fergus, R.: Predicting depth, surface normals and semantic labels with a common multi-scale convolutional architecture. In: ICCV (2015)
16. Zheng, S., Jayasumana, S., Romera-Paredes, B., Vineet, B., Su, Z., Du, D., Huang, C., Torr, P.: Conditional random fields as recurrent neural nets. In: ICCV (2015)
17. Chen, L., Papandreou, G., Kokkinos, I., Murphy, K., Yuille, A.L.: Semantic image segmentation with deep conv. nets and fully connected CRFs. In: ICLR (2015)
18. Schwing, A.G., Urtasun, R.: Fully connected deep structured networks. arXiv:1503.02351 (2015)
19. Noh, H., Hong, S., Han, B.: Learning deconvolution network for semantic segmentation. In: ICCV (2015)
20. LeCun, Y., Bottou, L., Bengio, Y., Haffner, P.: Gradient-based learning applied to document recognition. In: Proceedings of the IEEE (1998)
21. Hariharan, B., Arbeláez, P., Girshick, R., Malik, J.: Simultaneous detection and segmentation. In: Fleet, D., Pajdla, T., Schiele, B., Tuytelaars, T. (eds.) ECCV 2014. LNCS, vol. 8695, pp. 297–312. Springer, Heidelberg (2014). doi:10.1007/978-3-319-10584-0_20
22. Pinheiro, P.O., Collobert, R., Dollár, P.: Learning to segment object candidates. In: NIPS (2015)
23. Dai, J., He, K., Sun, J.: Instance-aware semantic segmentation via multi-task network cascades. In: CVPR (2016)
24. Hariharan, B., Arbeláez, P., Girshick, R., Malik, J.: Hypercolumns for object segmentation and fine-grained localization. In: CVPR (2015)
25. Krizhevsky, A., Sutskever, I., Hinton, G.: Imagenet classification with deep convolutional neural networks. In: NIPS (2012)
26. Simonyan, K., Zisserman, A.: Very deep convolutional networks for large-scale image recognition. In: ICLR (2015)
27. Szegedy, C., Liu, W., Jia, Y., Sermanet, P., Reed, S., Anguelov, D., Erhan, D., Vanhoucke, V., Rabinovich, A.: Going deeper with convolutions. In: CVPR (2015)
28. He, K., Zhang, X., Ren, S., Sun, J.: Deep residual learning for image recognition. In: CVPR (2016)
29. Long, J., Shelhamer, E., Darrell, T.: Fully convolutional networks for semantic segmentation. In: CVPR (2015)
30. Xie, S., Tu, Z.: Holistically-nested edge detection. In: ICCV (2015)
31. Sermanet, P., Kavukcuoglu, K., Chintala, S., LeCun, Y.: Pedestrian detection with unsupervised multi-stage feature learning. In: CVPR (2013)
32. Alexe, B., Deselaers, T., Ferrari, V.: Measuring the objectness of image windows. PAMI 34, 2189–2202 (2012)
33. Uijlings, J., van de Sande, K., Gevers, T., Smeulders, A.: Selective search for object recog. IJCV 104, 154 (2013)
34. Zitnick, C.L., Dollár, P.: Edge boxes: locating object proposals from edges. In: Fleet, D., Pajdla, T., Schiele, B., Tuytelaars, T. (eds.) ECCV 2014. LNCS, vol. 8693, pp. 391–405. Springer, Heidelberg (2014). doi:10.1007/978-3-319-10602-1_26
35. Pont-Tuset, J., Arbeláez, P., Barron, J., Marques, F., Malik, J.: Multiscale combinatorial grouping for image segmentation and object proposal gen. PAMI PP(99), 1 (2015)

36. Krähenbühl, P., Koltun, V.: Geodesic object proposals. In: Fleet, D., Pajdla, T., Schiele, B., Tuytelaars, T. (eds.) ECCV 2014. LNCS, vol. 8693, pp. 725–739. Springer, Heidelberg (2014). doi:10.1007/978-3-319-10602-1_47

37. Humayun, A., Li, F., Rehg, J.M.: RIGOR: reusing inference in graph cuts for generating object regions. In: CVPR (2014)

38. Hosang, J., Benenson, R., Dollár, P., Schiele, B.: What makes for effective detection proposals? PAMI **38**(4), 814–830 (2015)

39. Dosovitskiy, A., Fischer, P., Ilg, E., Hausser, P., Hazirbas, C., Golkov, V., v.d. Smagt, P., Cremers, D., Brox, T.: Flownet: learning optical flow with convolutional networks. In: ICCV (2015)

40. Zeiler, M.D., Krishnan, D., Taylor, G.W., Fergus, R.: Deconvolutional networks. In: CVPR (2010)

41. Zagoruyko, S., Lerer, A., Lin, T.Y., Pinheiro, P.O., Gross, S., Chintala, S., Dollár, P.: A multipath network for object detection. In: BMVC (2016)

Deep Automatic Portrait Matting

Xiaoyong Shen[(✉)], Xin Tao, Hongyun Gao, Chao Zhou, and Jiaya Jia

The Chinese University of Hong Kong, Sha Tin, Hong Kong
xyshen@cse.cuhk.edu.hk
http://www.cse.cuhk.edu.hk/leojia/projects/automatting

Abstract. We propose an automatic image matting method for portrait images. This method does not need user interaction, which was however essential in most previous approaches. In order to accomplish this goal, a new end-to-end convolutional neural network (CNN) based framework is proposed taking the input of a portrait image. It outputs the matte result. Our method considers not only image semantic prediction but also pixel-level image matte optimization. A new portrait image dataset is constructed with our labeled matting ground truth. Our automatic method achieves comparable results with state-of-the-art methods that require specified foreground and background regions or pixels. Many applications are enabled given the automatic nature of our system.

Keywords: Portrait · Matting · Automatic method · Neural network

1 Introduction

Prevalence of smart phones makes self-portrait photography, i.e., selfie, possible whenever wanted. Accordingly image enhancement software gets popular for portrait beatification, image stylization, etc. to meet various aesthetic requirements. Interaction is a key component in many of these algorithms to draw strokes and select necessary areas. One important technique that is generally not automatic is image matting, which is widely employed in image composition and object extraction. Interaction is involved in existing systems to select foreground and background color samples using either strokes or regions.

Image matting takes a color image I as input and decomposes it into background B and foreground F assuming that I is blended linearly by F and B. Such composite can be expressed as

$$I = (1 - \alpha)B + \alpha F, \tag{1}$$

where α is the alpha matte for each pixel with range in $[0, 1]$. Since F, B and α are unknown, seven variables are to be estimated for each pixel, which makes the original matting problem ill-posed. Image matting techniques [1,2] require users specify foreground and background color samples with strokes or trimaps as shown in Fig. 1.

© Springer International Publishing AG 2016
B. Leibe et al. (Eds.): ECCV 2016, Part I, LNCS 9905, pp. 92–107, 2016.
DOI: 10.1007/978-3-319-46448-0_6

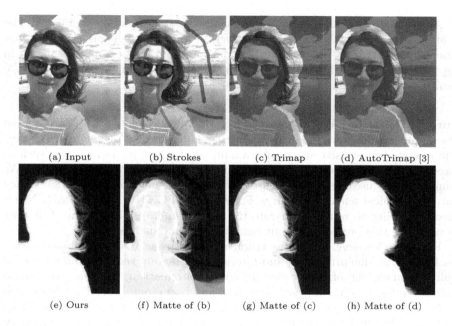

(a) Input   (b) Strokes   (c) Trimap   (d) AutoTrimap [3]

(e) Ours   (f) Matte of (b)   (g) Matte of (c)   (h) Matte of (d)

Fig. 1. Existing image matting methods need to specify background and foreground color samples. (b) and (c) show carefully created strokes and trimap. (f) and (g) show the corresponding closed-form matting results [1]. (d) is the trimap generated by automatic segmentation [3] followed by eroding the boundary for 50 pixels and (h) shows the corresponding closed-form matting result. (e) is our automatic matting result.

Problems of Interaction. Such interaction could be difficult for nonprofessional users without image matting knowledge. A more serious problem is that even with user-drawn strokes or regions, it is still not easy to know whether the color samples are enough or not before system optimization. As shown in Fig. 1(b) and (c), the human created strokes and trimap are already complicated, but the matting results by the powerful method [1] shown in (f) and (g) indicate the collected color samples are still insufficient. We note this is a very common problem even for professionals.

Statistically, 83.4 % chance is yielded to edit an image again after seeing the matting results in the first pass. On average 3.4 passes are needed to produce reasonable results on natural portrait images. Also the maximum number of passes to carefully edit a portrait image for color sample collection by us is 29. It shows a lot of effort has to be put to produce a reasonable alpha matte.

Importance and Difficulty of Automatic Matting. The above statistics lift the veil – automatic portrait image matting is essential for large-scale editing systems. It can relieve the burden for users to understand properties of color samples and the necessity to evaluate if they are enough for every local region.

Albeit fundamental, making an automatic matting system is difficult. The solution to compute the trimap intuitively from body segmentation may not generate good trimap with simple boundary erosion. One example is shown in Fig. 1(d), where the trimap by the automatic portrait segmentation method [3] results in the matte shown in (h).

Our Contribution. We propose a convolutional neural networks (CNNs) based system incorporating newly defined matting components. Although CNNs have demonstrated impressive success for a number of computer vision tasks such as detection [4–6], classification [7,8], recognition [9], and segmentation [10,11]. We cannot directly use existing structures for solving the matting problem since they learn hierarchical semantic features. For example, FCN [10] and CRFasRNN [11] have the ability to roughly separate the background and foreground. But they do not solve this problem without handling matting details.

For other low-level computer vision methods using CNNs for image super-resolution [12], deblurring [13] and filtering [14], mainly the powerful regression ability is made use of. They also do not fit our matting problem because no semantic information, such as human face and background scene, is considered.

Our network structure is novel on integrating two powerful functions. First, pixels are classified into background, foreground and unknown labels based on fully convolutional networks with several new components. For the second part, we propose the novel matting layer with forward and backward image matting formation. These two functions are incorporated in the unified end-to-end system without user interaction. Our method achieves decent performance for portrait image matting and benefits many tasks.

Further, we create a dateset including 2,000 portrait images, each with a full matte that involves all necessary details for training and testing.

2   Previous Work

We review natural image matting, as well as CNNs for pixel prediction related to our method.

2.1   Natural Image Matting

Natural image matting is originally ill-posed. To make the problem tractable, user specified strokes or trimap are used to sample foreground and background colors. There are quite a few matting methods, categorized according to color sampling and propagation. A survey is given in [15]. Quantitative benchmark is provided by Rhemann et al. [16].

Color Sampling Methods. Alpha values for two pixels can be close if the corresponding colors are similar. This rule motivates color sampling methods. Chuang et al. [17] proposed Bayesian matting by modeling background and foreground color samples as Gaussian mixtures. Alpha values are solved for by using alternative optimization. Following methods include global color strategy [18], sample optimization [19], global sampling method [20], etc. Most color sampling methods need a high quality trimap, which is not easy to draw or refine.

Propagation Approaches. Another line is to propagate user-drawn information to unknown pixels according to pixel affinities. Levin et al. [1] developed closed-form matting by defining matting Laplacian under the color-line model. It updates to cluster-based spectral matting in [21]. To accelerate matting Laplacian computation, He et al. [22] computed the large-kernel Laplacian. Assuming intensity change locally smooth, Sun et al. [23] proposed Poisson image matting. The Laplacian affinities matrix can be constructed using nonlocal pixels. Following this principle, Chen et al. [2] developed the KNN matting. Since only sparse strokes are input to these systems, specifying them needs algorithm-level knowledge and the methods involve iterative update.

2.2 CNNs for Pixel Prediction

Semantic segmentation [24] has demonstrated the capability for predicting image pixel information. CNNs for segmentation are applied mainly in two ways. One is to learn image features and apply classification schemes to infer labels [25–27]. The other line is end-to-end learning from the image to the label map. Long et al. [10] designed a fully convolutional networks (FCN) for this task.

Directly regressing labels may lose edge accuracy. Recent work combines input image information to guide segmentation refinement, such as DeepLab [28], CRFasRNN [11], and deep parsing network [24]. Dai et al. [29] proposed box suppression. These CNNs for pixel prediction generate piece-wise constant label maps, which cannot be used for natural image matting.

3 Problem Understanding

Difficulties of automatic portrait image matting can be summarized in the following, facilitated by the illustrations in Fig. 2.

- **Rich Matte Details.** Portrait matting needs alpha values for all pixels and the matte is with rich details as shown in (d). These details often include hair with only several-pixel width, leading to difficult value prediction.
- **Ambiguous Semantic Prediction.** Portrait images have semantically meaningful structures in the foreground layer, such as eyes, hair, clothes, and mouth as shown in (e). Features are important to describe them.
- **Discrepant Matte Value.** There are only 5 % fractional values in the alpha matte, as shown in (c), with nearly 50 % of foreground semantic pixels that also create edges and boundaries. Such discrepancy often leads to inherent difficulty to estimate the small number of fractional alpha values.

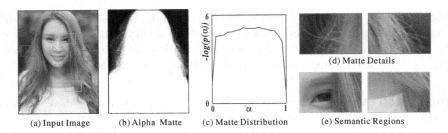

(a) Input Image   (b) Alpha Matte   (c) Matte Distribution   (d) Matte Details   (e) Semantic Regions

Fig. 2. An example to illustrate challenges. (a) and (b) are the input image and labeled alpha matte respectively. (c) is the alpha value distribution of (b) after negative-log transform. (d) are patches with matte details and (e) are semantic patches.

These issues make learning the alpha matte nontrivial. The CNNs for detection, classification and recognition are not concerned with image details. Segmentation CNNs [10] are with limited labels. Low-level task networks generally perform regression where the input and output are in the same domain of intensity or gradient. Crossing-domain inference from intensity to alpha matte is however considered in this paper.

4   Our Approach

We show the pipeline of our system in Fig. 3. The input is a portrait image I and the output is the alpha matte $\mathcal{A}$. Our network includes the trimap labeling and image matting modules.

4.1   Trimap Labeling

Each trimap includes foreground, background and unknown pixels. Our trimap labeling aims to predict the probability that each pixel belongs to these classes. As shown in Fig. 3, this part takes the input image and generates three channels F^s, B^s and U^s. Each value of a pixel stores the score for one channel. A large score indicates high probability in the corresponding class.

We model it as a pixel classification problem. We follow the FCN-8s setting [10] and incorporate special components for matting. The output is on the 3 aforementioned channels and one extra channel of *shape mask* for further performance improvement.

Shape Mask. The shape mask channel is shown in Fig. 3(a). It is based on the fact that a typical portrait includes head and part of shoulder, arm, and upper body. We thus include a channel, in which a subject region is aligned with the actual portrait. This is particularly useful since we explicitly provide feature to the network for reasonable initialization of the alpha matte.

To generate this channel, we compute an aligned average mask from our training data. For each training portrait-matte pair $\{P^i, M^i\}$ where P^i is the

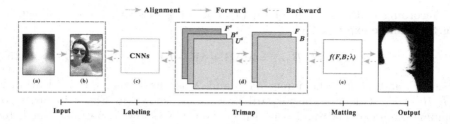

Fig. 3. Pipeline of our end-to-end portrait image matting network. It includes trimap labeling (c) and image matting (e). They are linked with forward and backward propagation functions.

feature point computing by face alignment [30] and M^i is the labeled alpha matte, we transform M^i using homography $\mathcal{T}_i$, estimated from the facial feature points of P^i and a face template. We compute the mean of these transformed mattes as

$$M = \frac{\sum_i m_i \cdot \mathcal{T}_i(M^i)}{\sum_i m_i}, \qquad (2)$$

where m_i is a matrix with the same size as M^i, indicating whether the pixel in M^i is outside the image or not after transform $\mathcal{T}_i$. The value is 1 if the pixel is inside the image, otherwise it is 0. The operator $\cdot$ denotes element-wise multiplication. This shape mask M, which has been aligned to a portrait template, can then be similarly transformed for alignment with the facial feature points of the input portrait. The added shape mask helps reduce prediction errors. We will discuss its performance in our experiment section.

4.2 Image Matting Layer

With the output score channels F^s, B^s and U^s, we get the probability maps F and B for foreground and background respectively by a softmax function. The formulation for F is written as

$$F = \frac{\exp(F^s)}{\exp(F^s) + \exp(B^s) + \exp(U^s)}. \qquad (3)$$

Similarly, we obtain the probability map B for background pixels. For convenience, F and B are expressed as vectors. Then the alpha matte can be computed through propagation as

$$\min \quad \lambda \mathcal{A}^T \mathbf{B} \mathcal{A} + \lambda (\mathcal{A} - \mathbf{1})^T \mathbf{F} (\mathcal{A} - \mathbf{1}) + \mathcal{A}^T \mathcal{L} \mathcal{A}, \qquad (4)$$

where $\mathcal{A}$ is the alpha matte vector and $\mathbf{1}$ is an all-1 vector. $\mathbf{B} = \mathrm{diag}(B)$ and $\mathbf{F} = \mathrm{diag}(F)$. $\mathcal{L}$ is the matting Laplacian matrix [1] with respect to the input image I. λ is a parameter to balance the data term and the matting Laplacian.

According to the solution of Eq. (4), our image matting layer as shown in Fig. 3(e) can be expressed as

$$f(F, B; \lambda) = \lambda(\lambda\mathbf{B} + \lambda\mathbf{F} + \mathcal{L})^{-1}F, \tag{5}$$

where F and B are the input data and λ is the parameter for learning. $f(F, B; \lambda) = \mathcal{A}$ defines the forward process. As shown in Fig. 3, in order to combine the image matting layer with previous CNNs, one important issue is to back propagate errors. Each layer should provide the derivatives $\frac{\partial f}{\partial F}$, $\frac{\partial f}{\partial B}$ and $\frac{\partial f}{\partial \lambda}$ with respect to the input and parameters.

Claim. Partial derivatives of Eq. (5) with respect to B, F and λ are with the closed-form expression as

$$\frac{\partial f}{\partial B} = -\lambda^2 \mathbf{D}^{-1}\text{diag}(\mathbf{D}^{-1}F), \tag{6}$$

$$\frac{\partial f}{\partial F} = \frac{\partial f}{\partial B} + \lambda\mathbf{D}^{-1}, \tag{7}$$

$$\frac{\partial f}{\partial \lambda} = -\lambda\mathbf{D}^{-1}\text{diag}(F + B)\mathbf{D}^{-1}F + \mathbf{D}^{-1}F, \tag{8}$$

where $\mathbf{D} = \lambda\mathbf{B} + \lambda\mathbf{F} + \mathcal{L}$. $\frac{\partial f}{\partial B}$, $\frac{\partial f}{\partial F}$ and $\frac{\partial f}{\partial \lambda}$ vector-form derivatives. They can be efficiently computed by solving sparse linear systems.

Proof. Given $\partial(AB) = (\partial A)B + A(\partial B)$ and $\partial(A^{-1}) = -A^{-1}(\partial A)A^{-1}$, we get

$$\frac{\partial f}{\partial B} = -\lambda\mathbf{D}^{-1}\frac{\partial \mathbf{D}}{\partial B}\mathbf{D}^{-1}F + \lambda\mathbf{D}^{-1}\frac{\partial F}{\partial B}. \tag{9}$$

Now, since $\frac{\partial \mathbf{D}}{\partial B_i} = \text{diag}(\frac{\partial(\lambda B + \lambda F)}{\partial B_i})$, a matrix is formed with its ith diagonal element being λ and all others being zeros. Since the second term of Eq. (9) gives a zero matrix, this directly yields Eq. (6). With similar derivation, we produce Eqs. (7) and (8). Because $\mathbf{D}$ is a sparse 25 diagonal matrix [1] and $\mathbf{D}^{-1}F$ can be computed by solving the linear system $\mathbf{D}X = F$, all derivatives can be updated by solving sparse linear systems.

With these derivatives, the image matting layer can be added to the CNNs as shown in Fig. 3 for optimization using the forward and backward propagation strategy. The parameter λ, which balances the data term and matting Laplacian, is also adjusted during the training process. Note that it is manually tuned in previous work.

4.3   Loss Function

The loss function measures the error between the predicted alpha matte and ground truth. Generally, the errors are calculated as the L_2- or L_1-norm distance. But in our task, most pixels have 0 or 1 alpha values because solid foreground and background pixels are the majority as shown in Fig. 2.

Therefore, directly applying L_2- or L_1-norm measure will be biased to absolute background and foreground pixels, which is not what we want. We find that setting different weights to alpha values make the system more reliable. It leads to our final loss function as

$$L(\mathcal{A}, \mathcal{A}^{gt}) = \sum_i w(\mathcal{A}_i^{gt}) \|\mathcal{A}_i - \mathcal{A}_i^{gt}\|, \tag{10}$$

where $\mathcal{A}$ is the alpha matte to be measured and $\mathcal{A}^{gt}$ is the corresponding ground truth. i indexes pixel position. $w(\mathcal{A}_i^{gt})$ is the weight function, which we define according to the value distribution of ground truth mattes, written as

$$w(\mathcal{A}_i^{gt}) = -\log(p(A = \mathcal{A}_i^{gt})), \tag{11}$$

where A is the random variable for the alpha matte and $p(A)$ models its probability distribution. We compute $p(A)$ from our ground truth mattes, which will be detailed later. Note that such a loss function is essential for our framework because there are only 5 % pixels in the image with alpha values not 0 or 1.

4.4 Analysis

Our end-to-end network for portrait image matting directly learns the alpha matte from the input image. We incorporate the trimap channel as a layer before image matting, as shown in Fig. 3. This setting is better than straightforward learning the trimap. We analyze it from our back-propagation process. We denote the total loss from F and B to the ground truth $\mathcal{A}^{gt}$ as $L^*(F, B, \lambda; \mathcal{A}^{gt})$. With the back-propagation formula, its derivative according to B is expressed as

$$\frac{\partial L^*(F, B, \lambda; \mathcal{A}^{gt})}{\partial B} = \frac{\partial L(\mathcal{A}, \mathcal{A}^{gt})}{\partial \mathcal{A}} \frac{\partial f(F, B; \lambda)}{\partial B}, \tag{12}$$

where $L(\mathcal{A}, \mathcal{A}^{gt})$ and $f(F, B; \lambda)$ are the loss function and matting function defined in Eqs. (10) and (5) respectively. $\mathcal{A}$ is the output value of $f(F, B; \lambda)$. Since

(a) Input Image   (b) Directly Learning   (c) Ours

Fig. 4. Trimap comparison between directly learning and learning in our end-to-end framework.

$\frac{\partial f(F,B;\lambda)}{\partial B}$ (defined in Eq. (6)) is related to the matting Laplacian $\mathcal{L}$, the loss $L^*(F, B, \lambda; \mathcal{A}^{gt})$ is related to not only the alpha matte loss $L(\mathcal{A}, \mathcal{A}^{gt})$ but also the matting function $f(F, B; \lambda)$. This indicates that the predicted trimap is optimized according to the matting scheme, and explains why such setting outperforms direct trimap learning.

To demonstrate it, we conduct experiments based on the model that only includes the trimap labeling part. In the training process, the ground truth trimap is obtained according to the alpha matte, where we set pixels with values between 0 and 1 as unknown ones. We compare the trimap results of this naive system with our complete ones. As shown in Fig. 4(b), directly learning the trimap makes hair predicted as background. Our complete system, as shown in (c), addresses this problem.

5   Data Preparation and Training

We provide new training data to appropriately learn the model for portrait image matting.

Dataset. We collected portrait images from Flickr. They are then selected to make sure portraits are with a good variety of age, color, clothing, accessories, hair style, head position, background scene, etc. The matting regions are mainly around hair and soft edges caused by depth-of-field. All images are cropped such that the face rectangles are with similar sizes. Several examples are shown in Fig. 5.

With the selected portrait images, we create alpha mattes with intensive user interaction to make sure they are with high quality. First, we label the

Fig. 5. Images in our dataset. They are with large structure variation for both foreground and background regions.

trimap of each image by zoom-in into local areas. Then we compute mattes using closed-form matting [1] and KNN matting [2]. The two computed mattes for each image overlay a background image for manually inspecting the quality. We choose the better one for our dataset. The result is discarded if both mattes cannot meet our high standard. When necessary, small errors are remedied by Photoshop [31]. After this labeling process, we collect 2,000 images with high-quality mattes. These images are randomly split into the training and testing sets with 1,700 and 300 images respectively.

Model Training. We augment the number of images by perturbing them with rotation and scaling. Four rotation angles $\{-45°, -22°, 22°, 45°\}$ and four scales $\{0.6, 0.8, 1.2, 1.5\}$ are used. We also apply four different Gamma transforms to increase color variation. The Gamma values are $\{0.5, 0.8, 1.2, 1.5\}$. After these transforms, we have 16K+ training images. The variation we introduce greatly improves the performance of our system to handle new images with possibly different scale, rotation and tone.

We set our model training and testing on the Caffe platform [32]. With the model illustrated in Fig. 3, we implement the image matting layer and loss layer as new components in the system. To efficiently solve the sparse linear system defined in the forward and back-propagation phases, we apply Intel MKL Parallel Direct Sparse Solver (PARDISO). The widely used SGD solver is adopted to optimize our model during training.

We initialize parameters using the FCN-8s model. Since our network only outputs three channels, we randomly select their parameters from the original 21 channels for initialization. For the matting layer, we set the initial λ to 100. We tune the learning rates in range $[1e - 3, 1e - 6]$. For each learning rate, we analyze the loss change and test the performance.

Running Time. We conduct training and testing on a single NVIDIA Titan X graphics card. Our model training phase requires about 20 epochs. The training time is about one day. For the testing phase, the running time on a 600×800 color image is 0.6 second. Our testing conducted on CPU takes about 6 seconds using the Intel MKL-optimized Caffe.

6   Experiments and Results

We show the performance of our system and perform comparison. Applications related to our automatic portrait image matting are also presented.

6.1   Performance Evaluation

We first evaluate our method using the testing dataset. Comparison with baselines is analyzed below.

Accuracy Measure. We follow the matte perceptual error [16] to measure matting quality. The two types of errors are *gradient* and *connectivity* ones expressed as

$$G(\mathcal{A}, \mathcal{A}^{gt}) = \frac{1}{K} \sum_i \|\nabla \mathcal{A}_i - \nabla \mathcal{A}_i^{gt}\|, \tag{13}$$

$$C(\mathcal{A}, \mathcal{A}^{gt}) = \frac{1}{K} \sum_i \|\varphi(\mathcal{A}_i, \Omega) - \varphi(\mathcal{A}_i^{gt}, \Omega)\|, \tag{14}$$

where $\mathcal{A}$ is the matte and $\mathcal{A}^{gt}$ is the corresponding ground truth. K is the number of pixels in $\mathcal{A}$. ∇ is the operator to compute gradients. $\varphi(\mathcal{A}_i, \Omega)$ measures connectivity of the matte in pixel i regarding neighborhood Ω [16].

Methods Comparison. We compare several automatic schemes as baselines for matting. The first one is automatic trimap generation based on segmentation from graph cuts [33]. To collect seeds, the face tracker [30] is employed to produce face feature points; then color samples around these points are set as foreground seeds. The background seeds are randomly sampled. Finally, the trimap is computed by eroding segmentation result and the final alpha matte is optimized by closed-form matting. We test different eroding widths and parameters in matting and choose the best result for comparison. Similar to graph-cut segmentation, we also generate trimap from the automatic portrait segmentation method [3] and compute the closed-form matting result.

The other three baselines are achieved by learning the trimap via semantic segmentation FCN [10], DeepLab [28] and CRFasRNN [11]. To adapt these frameworks to the matting problem, we modify the output channel number to three for background, foreground and unknown pixels. The trimap ground truth is computed from our training dataset by setting the alpha matte values between 0 and 1 as unknown. After getting the trimap, parameter-tuned closed-form matting is conducted to compute the final alpha matte. Parameters for learning are also adjusted according to the matting performance.

We report the performance of these automatic matting methods in Table 1. Several examples are shown in Fig. 6. The results indicate that the graph-cut

Table 1. Accuracy of our method and four other automatic matting baselines on our testing dataset. Usefulness of the shape mask is also verified.

Methods	Grad. Error ($\times 10^{-3}$)	Conn. Error ($\times 10^{-4}$)
Graph-cut trimap	4.93	7.73
Trimap by [3]	4.61	7.63
Trimap by FCN [10]	4.14	7.61
Trimap by DeepLab [28]	3.91	7.52
Trimap by CRFasRNN [11]	3.56	7.39
Ours without shape mask	3.11	6.99
Ours	**3.03**	**6.90**

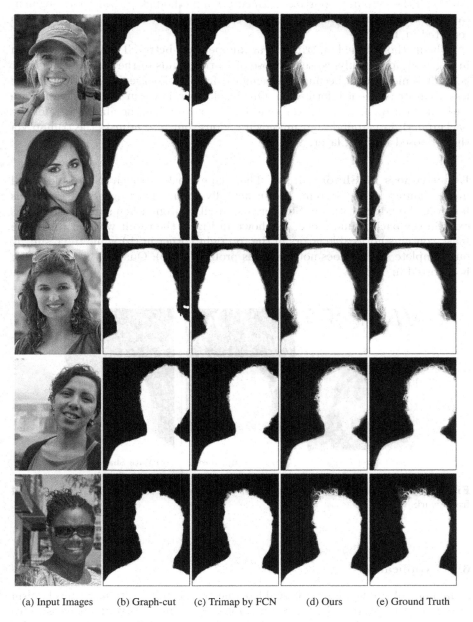

(a) Input Images   (b) Graph-cut   (c) Trimap by FCN   (d) Ours   (e) Ground Truth

Fig. 6. Visual comparison. (a) Input images. (b) Graph-cut trimap baseline results. (c) Trimaps by FCN baseline. (d) Our results. (e) Ground truth mattes.

based baseline does not work well because the segmentation is with large errors. Although the automatic portrait segmentation method [3] provides nice segmentation results, simple boundary erosion cannot generate high-quality matting as reported in Table 1.

The methods based on trimap learning perform better. The errors, as shown in Fig. 6(c), are mainly caused by lose of matte details in the learned trimap. It is, as aforementioned, because the semantic frameworks are designed to produce less accurate segment information. Our results are shown in Fig. 6(d), which are with the best quality. Our end-to-end CNN not only has the ability to infer the background, foreground, and unknown regions, but also adjusts the trimap via the proposed matting layer.

Effectiveness of Shape Mask. The shape mask is taken as an additional input channel in our system. It can actually reduce matting errors for pixels far from the portrait region. Such errors are ubiquitous when similar structures exist in the background scene. As shown in Fig. 7, the result without the shape mask contains noticeable errors in the top right corner in (b) while the result by our complete system does not have this problem in (c). Quantitative evaluation is reported in Table 1.

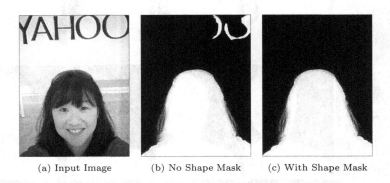

(a) Input Image   (b) No Shape Mask   (c) With Shape Mask

Fig. 7. Trimap comparison between directly learning and learning in our end-to-end framework.

6.2   Applications

A number of applications are enabled due to the fully automatic mechanism of our matting system. In Fig. 8, the alpha matte in a portrait image is automatically generated by our method. They are ready for fast stylization, color transform, depth-of-field and background editing. Respective effects are shown from (c)–(h). More results are provided in our supplementary material.

(a) Input Image	(b) Our Matting	(c) Stylization	(c) Stylization
(d) Color Transform	(e) Depth-of-field	(f) Background Edit	(f) Background Edit

Fig. 8. Applications of our automatic portrait matting. (a) and (b) are the input image and our automatic matting result. (c)–(h) show different editing effects.

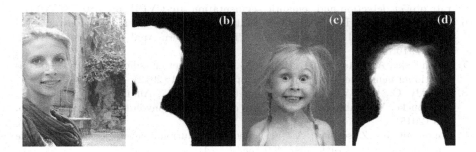

Fig. 9. Failure cases. The first example in (a) shows very low contrast between the foreground and background. The second image in (c) is with complicated hair structure. (b) and (d) are our results respectively.

7 Conclusion and Limitations

We have proposed a fully automatic matting system for portrait photos. It is based on end-to-end CNNs with several new components, including trimap labeling, shape mask incorporation, and matting layer design. A new portrait dataset containing images and their corresponding high quality alpha mattes is constructed for system training and testing. Our method achieves decent performance without any user interaction.

There are inevitable limitations. First, when contrast between background and foreground is rather low or the unknown region is quite large, our method may not work well. One example is shown in Fig. 9(a), which the color of hair is very similar to background. Second, complicated structure on foreground hair or background scene that is not common in images could also adversely influence our method. One example is given in Fig. 9(c).

Acknowledgements. This work is supported by a grant from the Research Grants Council of the Hong Kong SAR (project No. 2150760) and by the National Science Foundation China, under Grant 61133009.

References

1. Levin, A., Lischinski, D., Weiss, Y.: A closed-form solution to natural image matting. IEEE Trans. Pattern Anal. Mach. Intell. **30**(2), 228–242 (2008)
2. Chen, Q., Li, D., Tang, C.: KNN matting. IEEE Trans. Pattern Anal. Mach. Intell. **35**(9), 2175–2188 (2013)
3. Shen, X., Hertzmann, A., Jia, J., Paris, S., Price, B., Shechtman, E., Sachs, I.: Automatic portrait segmentation for image stylization. In: Eurographcis (2016)
4. Sermanet, P., Eigen, D., Zhang, X., Mathieu, M., Fergus, R., LeCun, Y.: Overfeat: Integrated recognition, localization and detection using convolutional networks. CoRR abs/1312.6229 (2013)
5. Girshick, R.B., Donahue, J., Darrell, T., Malik, J.: Rich feature hierarchies for accurate object detection and semantic segmentation. In: CVPR, pp. 580–587(2014)
6. He, K., Zhang, X., Ren, S., Sun, J.: Spatial pyramid pooling in deep convolutional networks for visual recognition. IEEE Trans. Pattern Anal. Mach. Intell. **37**(9), 1904–1916 (2015)
7. Krizhevsky, A., Sutskever, I., Hinton, G.E.: Imagenet classification with deep convolutional neural networks. In: NIPS, pp. 1106–1114 (2012)
8. Szegedy, C., Liu, W., Jia, Y., Sermanet, P., Reed, S., Anguelov, D., Erhan, D., Vanhoucke, V., Rabinovich, A.: Going deeper with convolutions. In: CVPR, pp. 1–9 (2015)
9. Simonyan, K., Zisserman, A.: Very deep convolutional networks for large-scale image recognition. CoRR abs/1409.1556 (2014)
10. Long, J., Shelhamer, E., Darrell, T.: Fully convolutional networks for semantic segmentation. In: CVPR (2014)
11. Zheng, S., Jayasumana, S., Romera-Paredes, B., Vineet, V., Su, Z., Du, D., Huang, C., Torr, P.H.S.: Conditional random fields as recurrent neural networks. In: ICCV (2015)
12. Dong, C., Loy, C.C., He, K., Tang, X.: Image super-resolution using deep convolutional networks. In: ECCV (2014)
13. Xu, L., Ren, J.S.J., Liu, C., Jia, J.: Deep convolutional neural network for image deconvolution. In: NIPS, pp. 1790–1798 (2014)
14. Xu, L., Ren, J., Yan, Q., Liao, R., Jia, J.: Deep edge-aware filters. In: ICML, pp. 1669–1678 (2015)
15. Wang, J., Cohen, M.F.: Image and video matting: a survey. Found. Trends Comput. Graph. Vis. **3**(2), 97–175 (2007)

16. Rhemann, C., Rother, C., Wang, J., Gelautz, M., Kohli, P., Rott, P.: A perceptually motivated online benchmark for image matting. In: CVPR, pp. 1826–1833 (2009)
17. Chuang, Y., Curless, B., Salesin, D., Szeliski, R.: A bayesian approach to digital matting. In: CVPR, pp. 264–271 (2001)
18. Wang, J., Cohen, M.F.: An iterative optimization approach for unified image segmentation and matting. In: CVPR, pp. 936–943 (2005)
19. Wang, J., Cohen, M.F.: Optimized color sampling for robust matting. In: CVPR (2007)
20. He, K., Rhemann, C., Rother, C., Tang, X., Sun, J.: A global sampling method for alpha matting. In: CVPR, pp. 2049–2056 (2011)
21. Levin, A., Rav-Acha, A., Lischinski, D.: Spectral matting. IEEE Trans. Pattern Anal. Mach. Intell. 30(10), 1699–1712 (2008)
22. He, K., Sun, J., Tang, X.: Fast matting using large kernel matting laplacian matrices. In: CVPR, pp. 2165–2172 (2010)
23. Sun, J., Jia, J., Tang, C., Shum, H.: Poisson matting. ACM Trans. Graph. 23(3), 315–321 (2004)
24. Liu, Z., Li, X., Luo, P., Loy, C.C., Tang, X.: Semantic image segmentation via deep parsing network. In: ICCV (2015)
25. Arbelaez, P., Hariharan, B., Gu, C., Gupta, S., Bourdev, L.D., Malik, J.: Semantic segmentation using regions and parts. In: CVPR, pp. 3378–3385 (2012)
26. Mostajabi, M., Yadollahpour, P., Shakhnarovich, G.: Feedforward semantic segmentation with zoom-out features. In: CVPR (2014)
27. Farabet, C., Couprie, C., Najman, L., LeCun, Y.: Learning hierarchical features for scene labeling. IEEE Trans. Pattern Anal. Mach. Intell. 35(8), 1915–1929 (2013)
28. Chen, L., Papandreou, G., Kokkinos, I., Murphy, K., Yuille, A.L.: Semantic image segmentation with deep convolutional nets and fully connected crfs. In: ICLR (2014)
29. Dai, J., He, K., Sun, J.: Boxsup: Exploiting bounding boxes to supervise convolutional networks for semantic segmentation. In: CVPR (2015)
30. Saragih, J.M., Lucey, S., Cohn, J.F.: Face alignment through subspace constrained mean-shifts. In: ICCV, pp. 1034–1041 (2009)
31. Systems, A.: Adobe photoshop cc 2015 tutorial
32. Jia, Y., Shelhamer, E., Donahue, J., Karayev, S., Long, J., Girshick, R., Guadarrama, S., Darrell, T.: Caffe: Convolutional architecture for fast feature embedding. arXiv preprint arXiv:1408.5093 (2014)
33. Boykov, Y.Y., Jolly, M.P.: Interactive graph cuts for optimal boundary & region segmentation of objects in nd images. In: ICCV, vol. 1, pp. 105–112 (2001)

Segmentation from Natural Language Expressions

Ronghang Hu[1(✉)], Marcus Rohrbach[1,2], and Trevor Darrell[1]

[1] UC Berkeley EECS, Berkeley, CA, USA
{ronghang,rohrbach,trevor}@eecs.berkeley.edu
[2] ICSI, Berkeley, CA, USA

Abstract. In this paper we approach the novel problem of segmenting an image based on a natural language expression. This is different from traditional semantic segmentation over a predefined set of semantic classes, as e.g., the phrase *"two men sitting on the right bench"* requires segmenting only the two people on the right bench and no one standing or sitting on another bench. Previous approaches suitable for this task were limited to a fixed set of categories and/or rectangular regions. To produce pixelwise segmentation for the language expression, we propose an end-to-end trainable recurrent and convolutional network model that jointly learns to process visual and linguistic information. In our model, a recurrent neural network is used to encode the referential expression into a vector representation, and a fully convolutional network is used to a extract a spatial feature map from the image and output a spatial response map for the target object. We demonstrate on a benchmark dataset that our model can produce quality segmentation output from the natural language expression, and outperforms baseline methods by a large margin.

Keywords: Natural language · Segmentation · Recurrent neural network · Fully convolutional network

1 Introduction

Semantic image segmentation is a core problem in computer vision and significant progress has been made using large visual datasets and rich representations based on convolution neural networks [4,6,17,21,32,33]. Although these existing segmentation methods can predict precise pixelwise masks for query categories like "train" or "cat", they are not capable of predicting segmentation for more complicated queries such as the natural language expression "the two people on the right side of the car wearing black shirts".

Electronic supplementary material The online version of this chapter (doi:10.1007/978-3-319-46448-0_7) contains supplementary material, which is available to authorized users.

© Springer International Publishing AG 2016
B. Leibe et al. (Eds.): ECCV 2016, Part I, LNCS 9905, pp. 108–124, 2016.
DOI: 10.1007/978-3-319-46448-0_7

(a) input image   (b) object class   (c) object instance   (d) segmentation
                   segmentation of   segmentation of   from expression
                   class **people**   class **people**   *"people in blue coat"*

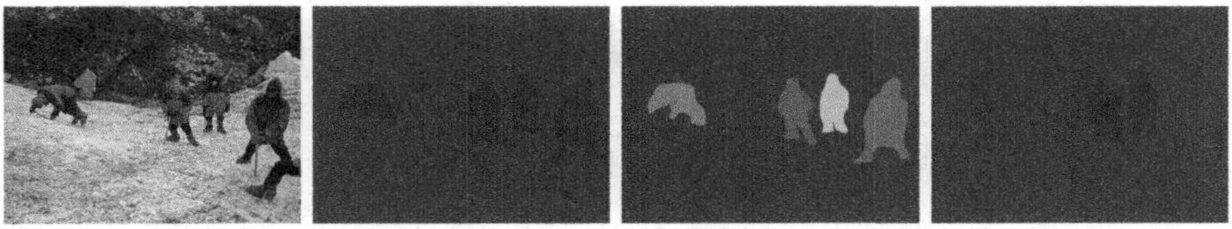

Fig. 1. In this work we approach the novel problem of *segmentation from natural language expressions*, which is different from traditional semantic image segmentation and object instance segmentation, as visualized in this figure. (Color figure online)

In this paper we address the following problem: given an image and a natural language expression that describes a certain part of the image, we want to segment the corresponding region(s) that covers the visual entities described by the expression. For example, as shown in Fig. 1(d), for the phrase e.g. *"people in blue coat"* we want to predict a segmentation that covers the two people in the middle wearing blue coat, but not the other two people. This problem is related to but different from the core computer vision problems of *semantic segmentation* (e.g. PASCAL VOC segmentation challenge on 20 object classes [10]), which is concerned with predicting the pixelwise label for a predefined set of object or stuff categories (Fig. 1b), and *instance segmentation* (e.g. [12]), which additionally distinguishes different instances of an object class (Fig. 1c). It also differs from language-independent foreground segmentation (e.g. [24]), where the goal is to generate a mask over the foreground (or the most salient) object. Instead of assigning a semantic label to every pixel in the image as in semantic image segmentation, the goal in this paper is to produce a segmentation mask for the visual entities of interest based on the given expression. Rather than being fixed on a set of object and stuff categories, natural language descriptions may involve also attributes such as *"black"* and *"smooth"*, actions such as *"running"*, spatial relationships such as *"on the right"* and interactions between different visual entities such as *"the person who is riding a horse"*.

The task of segmenting an image from natural language expressions has a wide range of applications, such as building language-based human-robot interface to give instructions like *"pick up the jar on the table next to the apples"*. Here, it is important to be able to use multi-word referential expressions to distinguish between different object instances but also important to get a precise segmentation in contrast to just a bounding box, especially for non-grid-aligned objects (see e.g. Fig. 2). This could also be interesting for interactive photo editing where one could refer with natural language to certain parts or objects of the image to be manipulated, e.g. *"blur the person with a red shirt"*, or referring to parts of your meal to estimate their nutrition, *"two large pieces of bacon"*, to decide better if one should eat it rather than the full meal as in [20].

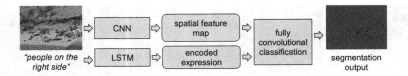

Fig. 2. Overview of our method for segmentation from natural language expressions.

As described in more details in Sect. 2, prior methods suitable for this task were limited to resolving only a bounding box in the image [15,18,23], and/or were limited to a fixed set of categories determined *a priori* [6,17,32,33]. In this paper, we propose an end-to-end trainable recurrent convolutional network model that jointly learns to process visual and linguistic information, and produces segmentation output for the target image region described by the natural language expression, as illustrated in Fig. 2. We encode the expression into a fixed-length vector representation through a recurrent Long short-term memory network (LSTM), and use a convolutional neural network (CNN) to extract a spatial feature map from the image. The encoded expression and the feature map are then processed by a multi-layer classifier network in a fully convolutional manner to produce a coarse response map, which is upsampled with deconvolution [17,21] to obtain a pixel-level segmentation mask of the target image region. Experimental results demonstrate that our model can generate quality segmentation predictions from natural language expressions, and outperforms baseline methods significantly. Our model is trained using standard back-propagation, and is much more efficient at test time than previous approaches relying on scoring each bounding box.

2   Related Work

Localizing Objects with Natural Language. Our work is related to recent work on object localization with natural language, where the task is to localize a target object in a scene from its natural language description (by drawing a bounding box over it). The methods reported in [15,18] build upon image captioning frameworks such as LRCN [8] or mRNN [19], and localize objects by selecting the bounding box where the expression has the highest probability. Our model differs from [15,18] in that we do not have to learn to generate expressions from image regions. Rohrbach *et al.* [23] propose a model to localize a textual phrase by attending to a region on which the phrase can be best reconstructed. In [22], Canonical Correlation Analysis (CCA) is used to learn a joint embedding space of visual features and words, and given a natural language query, the corresponding target object is localized by finding the closest region to the text sequence in the joint embedding space. Also, the concept of visual phrases [26] is related to our work as it captures compositions of multiple words or objects. However, [26] only deals with 17 manually chosen object compositions, whereas our method captures much richer queries represented by natural language.

To the best of our knowledge, all previous localization methods can only return a bounding box of the target object, and no prior work has learned to directly output a segmentation mask of an object given a natural language description as query. As a comparison, in Sect. 4.1 we also evaluate using foreground segmentation over the bounding box prediction from [15, 23].

Fully Convolutional Networks for Segmentation. Fully convolutional networks are convolutional neural networks consisting of only convolutional (and pooling) layers, which are the state-of-the-art method for semantic segmentation over a pre-defined set of semantic categories [6, 17, 32, 33]. A nice property of fully convolutional networks is that spatial information is preserved in the output, which makes these networks suitable for segmentation tasks that require spatial grid output. In our model, both feature extraction and segmentation output are performed through fully convolutional networks. We also use a fully convolution network for per-word segmentation as a baseline in Sect. 4.1.

Attention and Visual Question Answering. Recently, attention models have been used in several areas including image recognition, image captioning and visual question answering. In [30], image captions are generated through focusing on a specific image region for each word. In recent visual question answering models [29, 31], the answer is determined through attending to one or multiple image regions. Andreas *et al.* [2] propose a visual question answering method that answers object reference questions like *"Where is the black cat?"* by parsing the sentence and generating individual attention maps for *"black"* and *"cat"* and then combining them. This mechanism has some similarity to our per-word baselines.

These attention models are related to our work as they also learn to generate spatial grid "attention maps" which often cover the objects of interest. However, these attention models differ from our work as they only learn to generate coarse spatial outputs and the purpose of the attention map is to facilitate other tasks such as image captioning, rather than a precise segmentation of the object.

3 Our Model

Given an image and a natural language expression as query, the goal is to output a segmentation mask for the visual entities described by the expression. This problem requires both visual and linguistic understanding of the image and the expression. To accomplish this goal, we propose a model with three main components: a natural language expression encoder based on a recurrent LSTM network, a fully convolutional network to extract local image descriptors and generate a spatial feature map, and a fully convolutional classification and upsampling network that takes as input the encoded expression and the spatial feature map and outputs a pixelwise segmentation mask. Figure 3 shows the outline of our method; we introduce the details of these components in Sects. 3.1, 3.2 and 3.3. The network architecture for feature map extraction and classification is similar to the FCN model [17], which has been shown effective for semantic image segmentation.

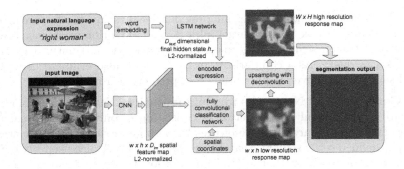

Fig. 3. Our model for segmentation from natural language expressions consists of three main components: an expression encoder based upon a recurrent LSTM network, a fully convolutional network to generate a spatial feature map, and a fully convolutional classification and upsampling network to predict pixelwise segmentation.

Compared with related work [15,18], we do not explicitly produce a word sequence corresponding to object descriptions given a visual representation, since we are interested in predicting image segmentation from an expression rather than predicting the expression. In this way, our model has less parameters compared with [15,18] as it does not have to learn to predict the next word.

3.1   Spatial Feature Map Extraction

Given an image of a scene, we want to obtain a discriminative feature representation of it while preserving the spatial information in the representation so that it is easier to predict a spatial segmentation mask. This is accomplished through a fully convolutional network model similar to FCN-32s [17], where the image is fed through a series of convolutional (and pooling) layers to obtain a spatial map output as feature representation. Given an input image of size $W \times H$, we obtain a $w \times h$ spatial feature map, with each position on the feature map containing D_{im} channels (D_{im} dimensional local descriptors).

For each spatial location on the feature map, we apply L2-normalization to the D_{im} dimensional local descriptor at that position in order to obtain a more robust feature representation. In this way, we can extract a $w \times h \times D_{im}$ spatial feature map as the representation for each image.

Also, to allow the model to reason about spatial relationships such as "right woman" in Fig. 3, two extra channels are added to the feature maps: the x and y coordinate of each spatial location. We use relative coordinates, where the upper left corner and the lower right corner of the feature map are represented as $(-1, -1)$ and $(+1, +1)$, respectively. In this way, we obtain a $w \times h \times (D_{im}+2)$ representation containing local image descriptors and spatial coordinates.

In our implementation, we adopt the VGG-16 architecture [27] as our fully convolutional network by treating fc6, fc7 and fc8 as convolutional layers, which outputs $D_{im} = 1000$ dimensional local descriptors. The resulting feature map size is $w = W/s$ and $h = H/s$, where $s = 32$ is the pixel stride on fc8 layer output. The units on the spatial feature map have a very large receptive field of 384 pixels, so our method has the potential to aggregate contextual information from nearby regions, which can help to reason about interaction between visual entities, such as "the man next to the table".

3.2   Encoding Expressions with LSTM Network

For the input natural language expression that describes an image region, we would like to represent the text sequence as a vector since it is easier to process fixed-length vectors than variable-length sequences. To achieve this goal, we take the encoder approach in sequence to sequence learning methods [7,28]. In our encoder for the natural language expression, we first embed each word into a vector through a word embedding matrix, and then use a recurrent Long-Short Term Memory (LSTM) [13] network with D_{text} dimensional hidden state to scan through the embedded word sequence. For a text sequence $S = (w_1, ..., w_T)$ with T words (where w_t is the vector embedding for the t-th word), at each time step t, the LSTM network takes as input the embedded word vector w_t from the word embedding matrix. At the final time step $t = T$ after the LSTM network has seen the whole text sequence, we use the hidden state h_T of the LSTM network as the encoded vector representation of the expression. Similar to Sect. 3.1, we also L2-normalize the D_{text} dimensions in h_T. We use an LSTM network with a $D_{text} = 1000$ dimensional hidden state in our implementation.

3.3   Spatial Classification and Upsampling

After extracting the spatial feature map from the image in Sect. 3.1 and the encoded expression h_T in Sect. 3.2, we want to determine whether or not each spatial location on the feature map belongs the foreground (the visual entities described by the natural language expression). In our model, this is done by a fully convolutional classifier over the local image descriptor and the encoded expression. We first tile and concatenate h_T to the local descriptor at each spatial location in the spatial grid to obtain a $w \times h \times D^*$ (where $D^* = D_{im} + D_{text} + 2$) spatial map containing both visual and linguistic features. Then, we train a two-layer classification network, with a $D_{cls} = 500$ dimensional hidden layer, which takes as input the D^* dimensional representation and output a score to indicate whether a spatial location belong to the target image region or not.

This classification network is applied in a fully convolutional way over the underlying $w \times h$ feature map as two 1×1 convolutional layers (with ReLU nonlinearity between them). The fully convolutional classification network outputs a $w \times h$ coarse *low-resolution response map* containing classification scores, which can be seen as a low-resolution segmentation of the referential expression, as shown in Fig. 3.

In order obtain a segmentation mask with higher resolution, we further perform upsampling through deconvolution (swapping the forward and backward pass of convolution operation) [17,21]. Here we use a $2s \times 2s$ deconvolution filter with stride s (where $s = 32$ for the VGG-16 network architecture we use), which is similar to the FCN-32s model [17]. The deconvolution operation produces a $W \times H$ *high resolution response map* that has the same size as the input image, and the values on the high resolution response map represent the confidence of whether a pixel belongs to the target object. We use the pixelwise classification results (i.e. whether a pixel score is above 0) as the final segmentation prediction.

At training time, each training instance in our training set is a tuple (I, S, M), where I is an image, S is a natural language expression describing a region within that image, and M is a binary segmentation mask of that region. The loss function during training is defined as the average over pixelwise loss

$$Loss = \frac{1}{WH} \sum_{i=1}^{W} \sum_{j=1}^{H} L(v_{ij}, M_{ij}) \tag{1}$$

where W and H are image width and height, v_{ij} is the response value (score) on the high resolution response map and M_{ij} is the binary ground-truth label at pixel (i, j). L is the per-pixel weighed logistic regression loss as follows

$$L(v_{ij}, M_{ij}) = \begin{cases} \alpha_f \log(1 + \exp(-v_{ij})) & \text{if } M_{ij} = 1 \\ \alpha_b \log(1 + \exp(v_{ij})) & \text{if } M_{ij} = 0 \end{cases} \tag{2}$$

where α_f and α_b are loss weights for foreground and background pixels. In practice, we find that training converges faster using higher loss weights for foreground pixels, and we use $\alpha_f = 3$ and $\alpha_b = 1$ in $L(v_{ij}, M_{ij})$.

The parameters in the feature map extraction network are initialized from a VGG-16 network [27] pretrained on the 1000-class ILSVRC classification task [25], the deconvolution filter for upsampling is initialized from bilinear interpolation. All other parameters in our model, including the word embedding matrix, the LSTM parameters and the classifier parameters, are randomly initialized. The whole network is trained with standard back-propagation using SGD with momentum. Our model is implemented using TensorFlow [1], and our code and data are available at http://ronghanghu.com/text_objseg.

4   Experiments

Compared with the widely used datasets in image segmentation such as PASCAL VOC [10], there are only a few publicly available datasets with natural language annotations over segmented image regions. In our experiments, we train and test our method on the ReferIt dataset [16] with natural language descriptions of visual entities and their segmentation masks. The ReferIt dataset [16] is built upon the IAPR TC-12 dataset [11] and has 20,000 images. There are 130,525 expressions annotated on 96,654 segmented image regions (some regions are annotated with multiple expressions). In this dataset, the ground-truth segmentation comes from the SAIAPR-12 dataset [9]. The expressions in the ReferIt dataset are discriminative for the regions, as they were collected in a two-player game whose goal was to make the target region easily distinguishable through the expression from the rest of the image. At the time of writing, the ReferIt dataset [16] is the biggest publicly available dataset that contains natural language expressions annotated on segmented image regions.

On this dataset, we use the same trainval and test split as in [15,23]. There are 10,000 images for training and validation, and 10,000 images for testing. The annotated regions in the ReferIt dataset contains both "object" regions such as car, person and bottle and "stuff" regions such as sky, river and mountain.

Since there has not been prior work that directly learns to predict segmentation based on natural language expressions as far as we know, to evaluate our method, we construct several strong baseline methods as described in Sect. 4.1, and compare our approach with these methods. All the baselines and our method are trained on the ReferIt dataset for comparison.

4.1 Baseline Methods

Combination of Per-word Segmentation. In this baseline method, instead of first encoding the whole expression with a recurrent LSTM network, each word in the expression is segmented individually, and the per-word segmentation results are then combined to obtain the final prediction. This method can be seen as using a "bag-of-word" representation of the expression. We take the N most frequently appearing words in ReferIt dataset (after manually removing some stop words like "the" and "towards"), and train a FCN model [17] to segment each word. Similar to the PASCAL VOC segmentation challenge [10], in this method, each word is treated as an independent semantic category. However, unlike in PASCAL VOC segmentation, here a pixel can belong to multiple categories (words) simultaneously and thus have multiple labels. During training, we generate a per-word pixelwise label map for each training sample (an image and an expression) in the training set. For a given expression, the corresponding foreground pixels are labeled with a N-dimensional binary vector l, where $l_i = 1$ if and only if word i is present in the expression, and background pixels are labeled with l equal to all zeros. In our experiments, we use $N = 500$ and initialize the network from a FCN-32s network pretrained on PASCAL VOC 2011 segmentation task [17], and train the whole network with a multi-label logistic regression loss over the words.

At test time, given an image and a natural language expression as input, the network outputs pixelwise score maps for the N words, and the per-word scores are further combined to obtain the segmentation for the input expression. In our implementation, we experiment with three different approaches to combine the per-word segmentation: for those words (among the N-word list) that appear in the expression, we (a) take the average of their scores or (b) take the intersection of their prediction or (c) take the union of their prediction. In some rare cases (2.83 % of the test samples), none of the words in the expression are among the N most frequent words, and we do not output any segmentation for this expression, i.e. all pixels are predicted as background.

Foreground Segmentation from Bounding Boxes. In this baseline method, we first use a localization method based on natural language input [15,23] to obtain a bounding box localization of the given expression, and then extract the foreground segmentation from the bounding box using GrabCut [24]. Given an image and a natural language expression, we use two recently proposed methods SCRC [15] and GroundeR [23] to obtain a bounding box prediction from the image and the expression. SCRC uses a model adapted from image captioning and localizes a referential expression by finding the candidate bounding box where the expression receives the highest probability. GroundeR relies on an attention model over candidate bounding boxes to ground (localize) a referential expression, either in an unsupervised manner by finding the region that can best reconstruct the expression, or in a supervised manner to directly train the model to attend to the best bounding box. In this work we use a re-implementation of the fully-supervised GroundeR. Following [15,23], we use 100 top-scoring Edge-Box [34] proposals as a set of candidate bounding boxes for each image. At test time, given an input expression, we compute the scores of the 100 Edge-Box proposals using SCRC [15] or GroundeR [23], and evaluate two approaches: either using the entire rectangular region of the highest scoring bounding box, or the foreground segmentation from it using GrabCut [24]. We use the supervised version of [23] in our experiments.

Classification over Segmentation Proposals. Inspired by text-based bounding box localization method [23], in this baseline we replace the bounding box proposals in [23] with segmentation proposals (e.g. CPMC [5] and MCG [3]) to output segmentation for the input expression. We use a similar pipeline in this baseline as in the supervised version of [23]. First, visual features are extracted from each proposal and concatenated with the encoded sentence. Then, a classification network is trained on concatenated features to classify a segmentation proposal into either foreground or background. We use 100 top-scoring segmentation proposals from MCG [3], and extract visual features from each proposal by resizing the segmentation proposal regions to 224×224 (i.e. filling pixels outside the proposal region with channel mean and resizing the enclosing bounding box of the proposal) and extracting visual feature from the resized proposal regions with a VGG-16 network pretrained on ILSVRC classification task. The whole network is then trained end-to-end. The main difference between this baseline and our method is that our method performs pixelwise classification through a fully convolutional network, while this baseline requires another proposal method to obtain candidate regions.

Whole Image. As an additional trivial baseline, we also evaluate using the whole image as a segmentation for every expression.

4.2   Evaluation on ReferIt Dataset

We train our model and the baseline methods in Sect. 4.1 on the 10,000 trainval images in the ReferIt dataset [16] (leaving out a small proportion for validation), following the same split as in [15]. In our implementation, we resize and pad all

Table 1. The performance (in %) of our model and baselines on the ReferIt dataset.

Method	prec@0.5	prec@0.6	prec@0.7	prec@0.8	prec@0.9	overall IoU
whole image	5.07	2.85	1.58	0.81	0.41	15.12
per-word average	10.97	5.94	2.35	0.45	0.00	27.23
per-word intersection	9.58	5.35	2.20	0.43	0.00	26.69
per-word union	10.46	5.65	2.28	0.44	0.00	19.37
SCRC [15] bbox	9.73	4.43	1.51	0.27	0.03	21.72
SCRC [15] grabcut	11.91	7.71	4.33	1.78	0.36	17.84
GroundeR [23] bbox	11.08	6.20	2.74	0.78	0.20	20.50
GroundeR [23] grabcut	14.09	9.62	5.78	2.65	0.62	20.09
MCG classification	12.72	9.88	7.38	4.73	1.88	18.08
Ours (low resolution)	29.54	21.61	13.69	5.94	0.75	45.57
Ours (high resolution)	**34.02**	**26.71**	**19.32**	**11.63**	**3.92**	**48.03**

images and ground-truth segmentation to a fixed size $W \times H$ (where we set $W = H = 512$), keeping their aspect ratio and padding the outside regions with zero, and map the segmentation output back to the original image size to obtain the final segmentation.

In our experiments, we use a two-stage training strategy: we first train a low resolution version of our model, and then fine-tune from it to obtain the final high resolution model (i.e. our full model in Fig. 3). In our low resolution version, we do not add the deconvolution filter in Sect. 3.3, so the model only outputs a $w \times h = 16 \times 16$ coarse response map in Fig. 3. We also downsample the ground-truth label to $w \times h$ and directly train on the coarse response map to match the downsampled label. After training the low resolution model, we construct our final high resolution model by adding a $2s \times 2s$ deconvolution filter with stride $s = 32$, as described in Sect. 3.3, and initialize the filter weights from bilinear interpolation (all other parameters are initialized from low resolution model). The high resolution model is then fine-tuned on the training set using $W \times H$ ground-truth segmentation mask labels. We empirically find this two stage training converges faster than directly training our full model to predict $W \times H$ high resolution segmentation.

We evaluate the performance of our model and the baselines method in Sect. 4.1 on the 10,000 images in the test set. The following two metrics are used for evaluation: the *overall intersection-over-union* (overall IoU) metric and the *precision* metric. The overall IoU is the total intersection area divided by the total union area, where both intersection area and union area are accumulated over all test samples (each test sample is an image and a referential expression). Although the overall IoU metric is the standard metric used in PASCAL VOC segmentation [15], our evaluation is slighly different as we would like to measure how accurate the model can segment the foreground region described by the input expression against the background, and the overall IoU metric favors large regions like sky and ground. So we also evaluate with the precision metric at 5

query expression= *"person"*

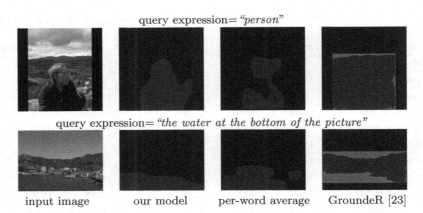

query expression= *"the water at the bottom of the picture"*

input image   our model   per-word average   GroundeR [23]

Fig. 4. Segmentation examples using our model and baseline methods. For GroundeR [23], the bounding box prediction is in orange and GrabCut segmentation is in red. (Color figure online)

different IoU thresholds from easy to hard: 0.5, 0.6, 0.7, 0.8, 0.9. The precision metric is the percentage of test samples where the IoU between prediction and ground-truth passes the threshold. For example, precision@0.5 is the percentage of expressions where the predicted segmentation overlaps with the ground-truth region by at least 50 % IoU.

Results. The main results for our evaluation are summarized in Table 1. By simply returning the whole image, one already gets 15 % overall IoU. This is partially due to the fact that the ReferIt dataset contains some large regions such as "sky" and "city" and the overall IoU metric put more weights on large regions. However, as expected, the whole image baseline has the lowest precision.

It can be seen from Table 1 that one can get a reasonable overall IoU through per-word segmentation and combining the results from each word. Among the three different ways to combine the per-word results in Sect. 4.1, it works best to average the scores from each word. Using the whole bounding box prediction from SCRC [15] ("SCRC bbox") or GroundeR [23] ("GroundeR bbox") achieves comparable precision to averaging per-word segmentation, while they are worse in terms of overall IoU, and using classification over segmentation proposals from MCG ("MCG classification") leads to slightly higher precision than these two methods. Also, it can be seen that using GrabCut [24] to segment the foreground from bounding boxes ("SCRC grabcut" and "GroundeR grabcut")

Table 2. Average time consumption to segmentation an input (a given image and a natural language expression) using different methods.

Method	per-word	SCRC [15] grabcut	GroundeR [23] grabcut	MCG classification	Ours (high resolution)
time (sec)	0.169	4.319	3.753	9.375	0.325

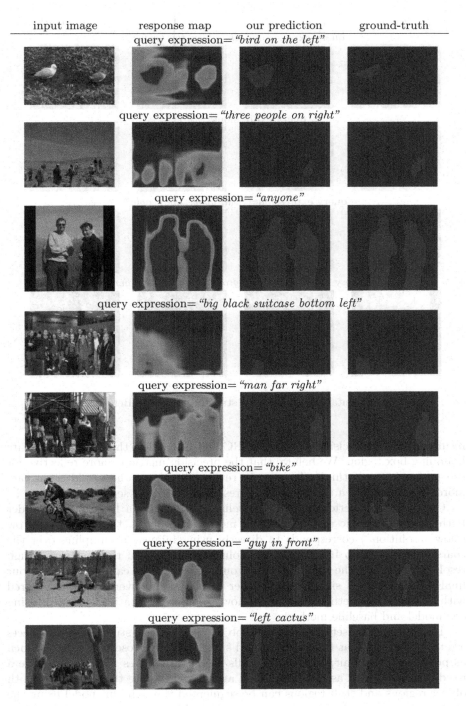

Fig. 5. Segmentation examples on object regions in the ReferIt dataset.

input image	response map	our prediction	ground-truth

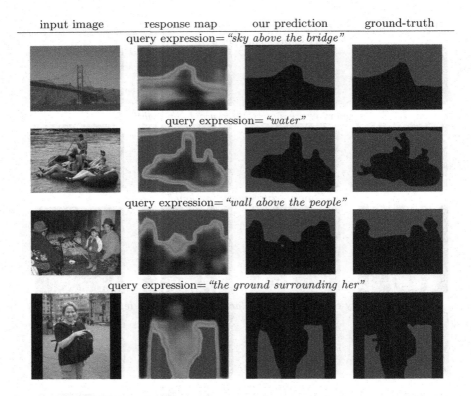

query expression= *"sky above the bridge"*

query expression= *"water"*

query expression= *"wall above the people"*

query expression= *"the ground surrounding her"*

Fig. 6. Segmentation examples on stuff regions in the ReferIt dataset.

results in higher precision for both SCRC and GroundeR than using the entire bounding box region. We believe that the precision metric is more reflective for the performance of this task, since in real applications, one would often care more about how often a referential expression is correctly segmented.

Our model outperforms all the baseline methods by a large margin under both precision metric and overall IoU metric. In Table 1, the second last row ("low resolution") corresponds to directly using bilinear upsampling over the coarse response map from our low resolution model, and the last row ("high resolution") shows the performance of our full model. It can be seen that our final model achieves significantly higher precision and overall IoU, compared with the baseline methods. Figure 4 shows some segmentation examples using our model and baseline methods.

The ReferIt dataset contains both object regions and stuff regions. Objects are those entities that have well-defined structures and closed boundaries, such as person, dog and airplane, while stuffs are those entities that do not have a fixed structure, such as sky, river, road and snow. Despite this difference, both object regions and stuff regions can be segmented through our model using the same approach. Figure 5 shows some segmentation examples on object regions

input image	response map	our prediction	ground-truth

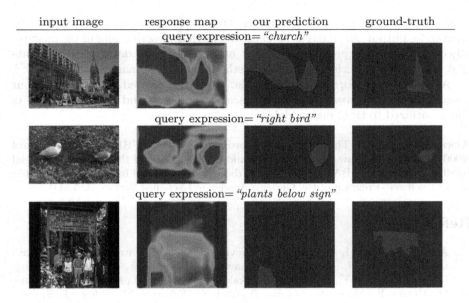

query expression= *"church"*

query expression= *"right bird"*

query expression= *"plants below sign"*

Fig. 7. Some failure cases where IoU < 50 % between prediction and ground-truth.

from our model, and Fig. 6 shows examples on stuff regions. It can be seen that our model can predict reasonable segmentation for both object expressions like "bird on the left" and stuff expressions like "sky above the bridge".

Figure 7 shows some failure cases on the ReferIt dataset, where the IoU between prediction and ground-truth segmentation is less than 50 %. In some failure cases (e.g. Fig. 7, middle), our model produces reasonable response maps that cover the target regions of the natural language referential expressions, but fails to precisely segment out the boundary of objects or stuffs.

Speed. We also compare the speed of our method and baseline methods. Table 2 shows the average time consumption for different models to predict a segmentation at test time, on a single machine with NVIDIA Tesla K40 GPU. It can be seen that although our method is slower than the per-word segmentation baseline, it is significantly faster than proposal-based methods such as "SCRC grabcut" or "MCG classification".

5   Conclusion

In this paper, we address the challenging problem of segmenting natural language expressions, to generate a pixelwise segmentation output for the image region described by the referential expression. To solve this problem, we propose an end-to-end trainable recurrent convolutional neural network model to encode the expression into a vector representation, extract a spatial feature map representation from the image, and output pixelwise segmentation based on fully convolutional classifier and upsampling. Our model can efficiently predict segmentation output for referential expressions that describe single or multiple objects or stuffs. Experimental results on a benchmark dataset demonstrate that our model outperforms baseline methods by a large margin.

As the datasets for learning this task directly is limited, we explore in our on-going work [14] how existing large scale vision-only and text-only datasets can be utilized to train our model.

Acknowledgments. This work was supported by DARPA, AFRL, DoD MURI award N000141110688, NSF awards IIS-1427425 and IIS-1212798, and the Berkeley Artificial Intelligence Research (BAIR) Lab. M. Rohrbach was supported by a fellowship within the FITweltweit-Program of the German Academic Exchange Service (DAAD).

References

1. Abadi, M., Agarwal, A., Barham, P., Brevdo, E., Chen, Z., Citro, C., Corrado, G.S., Davis, A., Dean, J., Devin, M., Ghemawat, S., Goodfellow, I., Harp, A., Irving, G., Isard, M., Jia, Y., Jozefowicz, R., Kaiser, L., Kudlur, M., Levenberg, J., Mané, D., Monga, R., Moore, S., Murray, D., Olah, C., Schuster, M., Shlens, J., Steiner, B., Sutskever, I., Talwar, K., Tucker, P., Vanhoucke, V., Vasudevan, V., Viégas, F., Vinyals, O., Warden, P., Wattenberg, M., Wicke, M., Yu, Y., Zheng, X.: TensorFlow: large-scale machine learning on heterogeneous systems. arXiv:1603.04467 (2016)
2. Andreas, J., Rohrbach, M., Darrell, T., Klein, D.: Neural module networks. In: Proceedings of the IEEE International Conference on Computer Vision (2016)
3. Arbeláez, P., Pont-Tuset, J., Barron, J., Marques, F., Malik, J.: Multiscale combinatorial grouping. In: Proceedings of the IEEE Conference on Computer Vision and Pattern Recognition, pp. 328–335 (2014)
4. Carreira, J., Caseiro, R., Batista, J., Sminchisescu, C.: Semantic segmentation with second-order pooling. In: Fitzgibbon, A., Lazebnik, S., Perona, P., Sato, Y., Schmid, C. (eds.) ECCV 2012. LNCS, vol. 7578, pp. 430–443. Springer, Heidelberg (2012). doi:10.1007/978-3-642-33786-4_32
5. Carreira, J., Sminchisescu, C.: CPMC: automatic object segmentation using constrained parametric min-cuts. IEEE Trans. Pattern Anal. Mach. Intell. **34**(7), 1312–1328 (2012)
6. Chen, L.C., Papandreou, G., Kokkinos, I., Murphy, K., Yuille, A.L.: Semantic image segmentation with deep convolutional nets and fully connected CRFs. In: Proceedings of the International Conference on Learning Representations (2015)
7. Cho, K., van Merriënboer, B., Bahdanau, D., Bengio, Y.: On the properties of neural machine translation: encoder-decoder approaches. In: Syntax, Semantics and Structure in Statistical Translation (2014)
8. Donahue, J., Anne Hendricks, L., Guadarrama, S., Rohrbach, M., Venugopalan, S., Saenko, K., Darrell, T.: Long-term recurrent convolutional networks for visual recognition and description. In: Proceedings of the IEEE Conference on Computer Vision and Pattern Recognition, pp. 2625–2634 (2015)
9. Escalante, H.J., Hernández, C.A., Gonzalez, J.A., López-López, A., Montes, M., Morales, E.F., Sucar, L.E., Villaseñor, L., Grubinger, M.: The segmented and annotated IAPR TC-12 benchmark. Comput. Vis. Image Underst. **114**(4), 419–428 (2010)

10. Everingham, M., Van Gool, L., Williams, C.K.I., Winn, J., Zisserman, A.: The PASCAL Visual Object Classes Challenge 2012 (VOC 2012) Results (2012). http://www.pascal-network.org/challenges/VOC/voc2012/workshop/index.html
11. Grubinger, M., Clough, P., Müller, H., Deselaers, T.: The IAPR TC-12 benchmark: a new evaluation resource for visual information systems. In: International Workshop OntoImage, pp. 13–23 (2006)
12. Hariharan, B., Arbeláez, P., Girshick, R., Malik, J.: Simultaneous detection and segmentation. In: Fleet, D., Pajdla, T., Schiele, B., Tuytelaars, T. (eds.) ECCV 2014. LNCS, vol. 8695, pp. 297–312. Springer, Heidelberg (2014). doi:10.1007/978-3-319-10584-0_20
13. Hochreiter, S., Schmidhuber, J.: Long short-term memory. Neural Comput. **9**(8), 1735–1780 (1997)
14. Hu, R., Rohrbach, M., Venugopalan, S., Darrell, T.: Utilizing large scale vision and text datasets for image segmentation from referring expressions. arXiv preprint (2016)
15. Hu, R., Xu, H., Rohrbach, M., Feng, J., Saenko, K., Darrell, T.: Natural language object retrieval. In: Proceedings of the IEEE Conference on Computer Vision and Pattern Recognition (CVPR) (2016)
16. Kazemzadeh, S., Ordonez, V., Matten, M., Berg, T.L.: ReferitGame: referring to objects in photographs of natural scenes. In: Proceedings of the 2014 Conference on Empirical Methods in Natural Language Processing (EMNLP), pp. 787–798 (2014)
17. Long, J., Shelhamer, E., Darrell, T.: Fully convolutional networks for semantic segmentation. In: Proceedings of the IEEE Conference on Computer Vision and Pattern Recognition (2015)
18. Mao, J., Huang, J., Toshev, A., Camburu, O., Yuille, A., Murphy, K.: Generation and comprehension of unambiguous object descriptions. In: Proceedings of the IEEE Conference on Computer Vision and Pattern Recognition (CVPR) (2016)
19. Mao, J., Xu, W., Yang, Y., Wang, J., Huang, Z., Yuille, A.: Deep captioning with multimodal recurrent neural networks (m-RNN). In: Proceedings of the International Conference on Learning Representations (2015)
20. Meyers, A., Johnston, N., Rathod, V., Korattikara, A., Gorban, A., Silberman, N., Guadarrama, S., Papandreou, G., Huang, J., Murphy, K.P.: Im2Calories: towards an automated mobile vision food diary. In: Proceedings of the IEEE International Conference on Computer Vision, pp. 1233–1241 (2015)
21. Noh, H., Hong, S., Han, B.: Learning deconvolution network for semantic segmentation. In: Proceedings of the IEEE International Conference on Computer Vision, pp. 1520–1528 (2015)
22. Plummer, B., Wang, L., Cervantes, C., Caicedo, J., Hockenmaier, J., Lazebnik, S.: Flickr30k entities: collecting region-to-phrase correspondences for richer image-to-sentence models. In: Proceedings of the IEEE International Conference on Computer Vision (ICCV) (2015)
23. Rohrbach, A., Rohrbach, M., Hu, R., Darrell, T., Schiele, B.: Grounding of textual phrases in images by reconstruction. In: Leibe, B., Matas, J., Sebe, N., Welling, M. (eds.) ECCV 2016. LNCS, vol. 9905, pp. 817–834. Springer, Heidelberg (2016)
24. Rother, C., Kolmogorov, V., Blake, A.: GrabCut: interactive foreground extraction using iterated graph cuts. ACM Trans. Graph. (TOG) **23**, 309–314 (2004). ACM
25. Russakovsky, O., Deng, J., Su, H., Krause, J., Satheesh, S., Ma, S., Huang, Z., Karpathy, A., Khosla, A., Bernstein, M., et al.: Imagenet large scale visual recognition challenge. Int. J. Comput. Vis. **115**(3), 211–252 (2015)

26. Sadeghi, M.A., Farhadi, A.: Recognition using visual phrases. In: 2011 IEEE Conference on Computer Vision and Pattern Recognition (CVPR), pp. 1745–1752. IEEE (2011)
27. Simonyan, K., Zisserman, A.: Very deep convolutional networks for large-scale image recognition. In: Proceedings of the International Conference on Learning Representations (2015)
28. Sutskever, I., Vinyals, O., Le, Q.V.: Sequence to sequence learning with neural networks. In: Advances in Neural Information Processing Systems, pp. 3104–3112 (2014)
29. Xu, H., Saenko, K.: Ask, attend and answer: exploring question-guided spatial attention for visual question answering. arXiv preprint arXiv:1511.05234 (2015)
30. Xu, K., Ba, J., Kiros, R., Courville, A., Salakhutdinov, R., Zemel, R., Bengio, Y.: Show, attend and tell: neural image caption generation with visual attention. In: Proceedings of the International Conference on Machine Learning (ICML) (2015)
31. Yang, Z., He, X., Gao, J., Deng, L., Smola, A.: Stacked attention networks for image question answering. In: Proceedings of the IEEE International Conference on Computer Vision (2016)
32. Yu, F., Koltun, V.: Multi-scale context aggregation by dilated convolutions. In: Proceedings of the International Conference on Learning Representations (2016)
33. Zheng, S., Jayasumana, S., Romera-Paredes, B., Vineet, V., Su, Z., Du, D., Huang, C., Torr, P.H.: Conditional random fields as recurrent neural networks. In: Proceedings of the IEEE International Conference on Computer Vision (2015)
34. Zitnick, C.L., Dollár, P.: Edge boxes: locating object proposals from edges. In: Fleet, D., Pajdla, T., Schiele, B., Tuytelaars, T. (eds.) ECCV 2014. LNCS, vol. 8693, pp. 391–405. Springer, Heidelberg (2014). doi:10.1007/978-3-319-10602-1_26

Semantic Object Parsing with Graph LSTM

Xiaodan Liang[1], Xiaohui Shen[4], Jiashi Feng[3], Liang Lin[1(✉)],
and Shuicheng Yan[2,3]

[1] Sun Yat-sen University, Guangzhou, China
xdliang328@gmail.com, linliang@ieee.org
[2] 360 AI Instiue, Singapore, Singapore
eleyans@nus.edu.sg
[3] National University of Singapore, Singapore, Singapore
elefjia@nus.edu.sg
[4] Adobe Research, San Jose, USA
xshen@adobe.com

Abstract. By taking the semantic object parsing task as an exemplar application scenario, we propose the Graph Long Short-Term Memory (Graph LSTM) network, which is the generalization of LSTM from sequential data or multi-dimensional data to general graph-structured data. Particularly, instead of evenly and fixedly dividing an image to pixels or patches in existing multi-dimensional LSTM structures (e.g., Row, Grid and Diagonal LSTMs), we take each arbitrary-shaped superpixel as a semantically consistent node, and adaptively construct an undirected graph for each image, where the spatial relations of the superpixels are naturally used as edges. Constructed on such an adaptive graph topology, the Graph LSTM is more naturally aligned with the visual patterns in the image (e.g., object boundaries or appearance similarities) and provides a more economical information propagation route. Furthermore, for each optimization step over Graph LSTM, we propose to use a confidence-driven scheme to update the hidden and memory states of nodes progressively till all nodes are updated. In addition, for each node, the forgets gates are adaptively learned to capture different degrees of semantic correlation with neighboring nodes. Comprehensive evaluations on four diverse semantic object parsing datasets well demonstrate the significant superiority of our Graph LSTM over other state-of-the-art solutions.

Keywords: Object parsing · Graph LSTM · Recurrent neural networks

1 Introduction

Beyond traditional image semantic segmentation, semantic object parsing aims to segment an object within an image into multiple parts with more fine-grained semantics and provide full understanding of image contents, as shown in Fig. 1. Many higher-level computer vision applications [1,2] can benefit from a powerful

B. Leibe et al. (Eds.): ECCV 2016, Part I, LNCS 9905, pp. 125–143, 2016.
DOI: 10.1007/978-3-319-46448-0_8

Fig. 1. Examples of semantic object parsing results by the proposed Graph LSTM model. It parses an object into multiple parts with different semantic meanings. Best viewed in color.

semantic object parser, including person re-identification [3], human behavior analysis [4–7].

Recently, Convolutional Neural Networks (CNNs) have demonstrated exciting success in various pixel-wise prediction tasks such as semantic segmentation and detection [8,9], semantic part segmentation [10,11] and depth prediction [12]. However, the pure convolutional filters can only capture limited local context while the precise inference for semantic part layouts and their interactions requires a global perspective of the image. To consider the global structural context, previous works thus use dense pairwise connections (Conditional Random Fields (CRFs)) upon pure pixel-wise CNN classifiers [8,13–15]. However, most of them try to model the structure information based on the predicted confidence maps, and do not explicitly enhance the feature representations in capturing global contextual information, leading to suboptimal segmentation results under complex scenarios.

An alternative strategy is to exploit long-range dependencies by directly augmenting the intermediate features. The multi-dimensional Long Short-Term Memory (LSTM) networks have produced very promising results in modeling 2D images [16–19], where long-range dependencies, which are essential to object and scene understanding, can be well memorized by sequentially functioning on all pixels. However, in terms of the information propagation route in each LSTM unit, most of existing LSTMs [19–21] have only explored pre-defined fixed topologies. As illustrated in the top row of Fig. 2, for each individual image, the prediction for each pixel by those methods is influenced by the predictions of fixed neighbors (e.g., 2 or 8 adjacent pixels or diagonal neighbors) in each timestep. The natural properties of images (e.g., local boundaries and semantically consistent groups of pixels) have not be fully utilized to enable more meaningful and economical inference in such fixed locally factorized LSTMs. In addition, much computation with the fixed topology is redundant and inefficient as it has to consider all the pixels, even for the ones in a simple plain region.

In this paper, we propose a novel Graph LSTM model that extends the traditional LSTMs from sequential and multi-dimensional data to general graph-structured data, and demonstrate its superiority on the semantic object parsing task. Instead of evenly and fixedly dividing an image into pixels or patches as previous LSTMs did, Graph LSTM takes each arbitrary-shaped superpixel as a semantically consistent node of a graph, while the spatial neighborhood relations

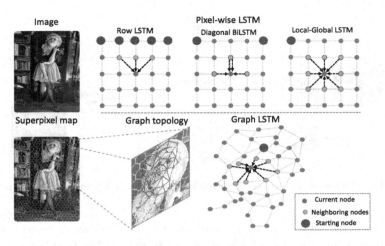

Fig. 2. The proposed Graph LSTM structure. (1) The top row shows the traditional pixel-wise LSTM structures, including Row LSTM [21], Diagonal BiLSTM [20,21] and Local-Global LSTM [19]. (2) The bottom row illustrates the proposed Graph LSTM that is built upon the superpixel over-segmentation map for each image.

are naturally used to construct the undirected graph edges. The adaptive graph topology can thus be constructed where different nodes are connected with different numbers of neighbors, depending on the local structures in the image. As shown in the bottom row of Fig. 2, instead of broadcasting information to a fixed local neighborhood following a fixed updating sequence as in the previous LSTMs, Graph LSTM proposes to effectively propagate information from one adaptive starting superpixel node to all superpixel nodes along the adaptive graph topology for each image. It can effectively reduce redundant computational costs while better preserving object/part boundaries to facilitate global reasoning.

Together with the adaptively constructed graph topology of an image, we propose a confidence-driven scheme to subsequently update the features of all nodes, which is inspired by the recent visual attention models [22,23]. Previous LSTMs [20,21] often simply start at pre-defined pixel or patch locations and then proceed toward other pixels or patches following a fixed updating route for different images. In contrast, we assume that starting from a proper superpixel node and updating the nodes following a certain content-adaptive path can lead to a more flexible and reliable inference for global context modelling, where the visual characteristics of each image can be better captured. As shown in Fig. 3, the Graph LSTM, as an independent layer, can be easily appended to the intermediate convolutional layers in a Fully Convolutional Neural Network [24] to strengthen visual feature learning by incorporating long-range contextual information. The hidden states represent the reinforced features, and the memory states recurrently encode the global structures.

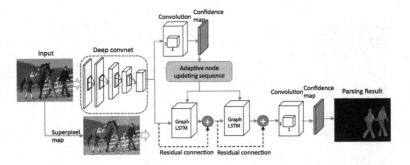

Fig. 3. Illustration of the proposed network architecture for semantic object parsing.

Our contributions can be summarized in the following four aspects. (1) We propose a novel Graph LSTM structure to extend the traditional LSTMs from sequential and multi-dimensional data to general graph-structured data, which effectively exploits global context by following an adaptive graph topology derived from the content of each image. (2) We propose a confidence-driven scheme to select the starting node and sequentially update all nodes, which facilitates the flexible inference while preserving the visual characteristics of each image. (3) In each Graph LSTM unit, different forget gates for the neighboring nodes are learned to dynamically incorporate the local contextual interactions in accordance with their semantic relations. (4) We apply the proposed Graph LSTM in semantic object parsing, and demonstrate its superiority through comprehensive comparisons on four challenging semantic object parsing datasets (i.e., PASCAL-Person-Part dataset [25], Horse-Cow parsing dataset [26], ATR dataset [27] and Fashionista dataset [28]).

2   Related Work

LSTM on Image Processing: Recurrent neural networks have been first introduced to address the sequential prediction tasks [29–31], and then extended to multi-dimensional image processing tasks [16,17]. Benefiting from the long-range memorization of LSTM networks, they can obtain considerably larger dependency fields by sequentially performing LSTM units on all pixels, compared to the local convolutional filters. Nevertheless, in each LSTM unit, the prediction of each pixel is affected by a fixed factorization (e.g., 2 or 8 neighboring pixels [19,20,32,33] or diagonal neighborhood [17,21]), where diverse natural visual correlations (e.g., local boundaries and homogeneous regions) have not been considered. Meanwhile, the computation is very costly and redundant due to the sequential computation on all pixels. Tree-LSTM [34] introduces the structure with tree-structured topologies for predicting semantic representations of sentences. Compared to Tree-LSTM, Graph LSTM is more natural and general for 2D image processing with arbitrary graph topologies and adaptive updating schemes.

Semantic Object Parsing: There has been increasing research interest on the semantic object parsing problem including the general object parsing [14,25,26, 35,36], person part segmentation [10,11] and human parsing [28,37–42]. To capture the rich structure information based on the advanced CNN architecture, one common way is the combination of CNNs and CRFs [8,13,14,43], where the CNN outputs are treated as unary potentials while CRF further incorporates pairwise or higher order factors. Instead of learning features only from local convolutional kernels as in these previous methods, we incorporate the global context by the novel Graph LSTM structure to capture long-distance dependencies on the superpixels. The dependency field of Graph LSTM can effectively cover the entire image context.

3   The Proposed Graph LSTM

We take semantic object parsing as its application scenario, which aims to generate pixel-wise semantic part segmentation for each image. Figure 3 illustrates the designed network architecture based on Graph LSTM. The input image first passes through a stack of convolutional layers to generate the convolutional feature maps. The proposed Graph LSTM takes the convolutional features and the adaptively specified node updating sequence for each image as the input, and then efficiently propagates the aggregated contextual information towards all nodes, leading to enhanced visual features and better parsing results. To both increase convergence speed and propagate signals more directly through the network, we deploy residual connections [44] after one Graph LSTM layer to generate the input features of the next Graph LSTM layer. Note that residual connections are performed to generate the element-wise input features for each layer, which would not destroy the computed graph topology. After that, several 1×1 convolution filters are employed to produce the final parsing results. The following subsections will describe the main innovations inside Graph LSTM, including the graph construction and the Graph LSTM structure.

3.1   Graph Construction

The graph is constructed on superpixels that are obtained through image over-segmentation using SLIC [45][1]. Note that, after several convolutional layers, the feature maps of each image have been down-sampled. Therefore, in order to use the superpixel map for graph construction in each Graph LSTM layer, one needs to upsample the feature maps into the original size of the input image.

   The superpixel graph $\mathcal{G}$ for each image is then constructed by connecting a set of graph nodes $\{v_i\}_{i=1}^N$ via the graph edges $\{\mathcal{E}_{ij}\}$. Each graph node v_i represents a superpixel and each graph edge $\mathcal{E}_{ij}$ only connects two spatially neighboring superpixel nodes. The input features of each graph node v_i are

---

[1] Other over-segmentation methods such as entropy rate-based approach [41] could also be used, and we did not observe much difference in the final results in our experiments.

denoted as $\mathbf{f}_i \in \mathbb{R}^d$, where d is the feature dimension. The feature $\mathbf{f}_i$ is computed by averaging the features of all the pixels belonging to the same superpixel node v_i. As shown in Fig. 3, the input states of the first Graph LSTM layer come from the previous convolutional feature maps. For the subsequent Graph LSTM layers, the input states are generated after the residual connections [44] for the input features and the updated hidden states by the previous Graph LSTM layer. To make sure that the number of the input states for the first Graph LSTM layer is compatible with that of the following layers and that the residual connections can be applied, the dimensions of hidden and memory states in all Graph LSTM layers are set the same as the feature dimension of the last convolutional layer before the first Graph LSTM layer.

3.2 Graph LSTM

Confidence-driven Scheme. The node updating scheme is more important yet more challenging in Graph LSTM than the ones in traditional LSTMs [20,21] due to its adaptive graph topology. To enable better global reasoning, Graph LSTM specifies the adaptive starting node and node updating sequence for the information propagation of each image. Given the constructed undirected graph $\mathcal{G}$, we extensively tried several schemes to update all nodes in a graph in the experiments, including the Breadth-First Search (BFS), Depth-First Search (DFS) and Confidence-Driven Search (CDS). We find that the CDS achieves better performance. Specifically, as illustrated in Fig. 3, given the top convolutional feature maps, the 1×1 convolutional filters can be used to generate the initial confidence maps with regard to each semantic label. Then the confidence of each superpixel for each label is computed by averaging the confidences of its contained pixels, and the label with highest confidence could be assigned to the superpixel. Among all the foreground superpixels (i.e., assigned to any semantic part label), the node updating sequence can be determined by ranking all the superpixel nodes according to the confidences of their assigned labels.

During updating, the $(t + 1)$-th Graph LSTM layer determines the current states of each node v_i that comprises the hidden states $\mathbf{h}_{i,t+1} \in \mathbb{R}^d$ and memory states $\mathbf{m}_{i,t+1} \in \mathbb{R}^d$ of each node. Each node is influenced by its previous states and the states of neighboring graph nodes as well in order to propagate information to the whole image. Thus the inputs to Graph LSTM units consist of the input states $\mathbf{f}_{i,t+1}$ of the node v_i, its previous hidden states $\mathbf{h}_{i,t}$ and memory states $\mathbf{m}_{i,t}$, and the hidden and memory states of its neighboring nodes $v_j, j \in \mathcal{N}_{\mathcal{G}}(i)$.

Averaged Hidden States for Neighboring Nodes. Note that with an adaptive updating scheme, when operating on a specific node in each Graph LSTM layer, some of its neighboring nodes have already been updated while others may have not. We therefore use a visit flag q_j to indicate whether the graph node v_j has been updated, where q_j is set as 1 if updated, and otherwise 0. We then use the updated hidden states $\mathbf{h}_{j,t+1}$ for the visited nodes, i.e., $q_j = 1$ and the previous states $\mathbf{h}_{j,t}$ for the unvisited nodes. The $\mathbb{1}(\cdot)$ is an indicator function.

Note that the nodes in the graph may have an arbitrary number of neighboring nodes. Let $|\mathcal{N}_{\mathcal{G}}(i)|$ denote the number of neighboring graph nodes. To obtain a fixed feature dimension for the inputs of the Graph LSTM unit during network training, the hidden states $\bar{\mathbf{h}}_{i,t}$ used for computing the LSTM gates of the node v_i are obtained by averaging the hidden states of neighboring nodes, computed as:

$$\bar{\mathbf{h}}_{i,t} = \frac{\sum_{j\in\mathcal{N}_{\mathcal{G}}(i)}(\mathbb{1}(q_j = 1)\mathbf{h}_{j,t+1} + \mathbb{1}(q_j = 0)\mathbf{h}_{j,t})}{|\mathcal{N}_{\mathcal{G}}(i)|}. \tag{1}$$

Adaptive Forget Gates. Note that unlike the traditional LSTMs [20,46], the Graph LSTM specifies different forget gates for different neighboring nodes by functioning the input states of the current node with their hidden states, defined as $\bar{g}_{ij}^f, j \in \mathcal{N}_{\mathcal{G}}(i)$. It results in the different influences of neighboring nodes on the updated memory states $\mathbf{m}_{i,t+1}$ and hidden states $\mathbf{h}_{i,t+1}$. The memory states of each neighboring node are also utilized to update the memory states $\mathbf{m}_{i,t+1}$ of the current node. The shared weight metrics U^{fn} for all nodes are learned to guarantee the spatial transformation invariance and enable the learning with various neighbors. The intuition is that each pair of neighboring superpixels may be endowed with distinguished semantic correlations compared to other pairs.

Graph LSTM Unit. The Graph LSTM consists of four gates: the input gate g^u, the forget gate g^f, the adaptive forget gate $\bar{g}^f$, the memory gate g^c and the output gate g^o. The W^u, W^f, W^c, W^o are the recurrent gate weight matrices specified for input features while U^u, U^f, U^c, U^o are those for hidden states of each node. $U^{un}, U^{fn}, U^{cn}, U^{on}$ are the weight parameters specified for states of neighboring nodes. The hidden and memory states by the Graph LSTM can be updated as follows:

$$
\begin{aligned}
g_i^u &= \delta(W^u\mathbf{f}_{i,t+1} + U^u\mathbf{h}_{i,t} + U^{un}\bar{\mathbf{h}}_{i,t} + b^u),\\
\bar{g}_{ij}^f &= \delta(W^f\mathbf{f}_{i,t+1} + U^{fn}\mathbf{h}_{j,t} + b^f),\\
g_i^f &= \delta(W^f\mathbf{f}_{i,t+1} + U^f\mathbf{h}_{i,t} + b^f),\\
g_i^o &= \delta(W^o\mathbf{f}_{i,t+1} + U^o\mathbf{h}_{i,t} + U^{on}\bar{\mathbf{h}}_{i,t} + b^o),\\
g_i^c &= \tanh(W^c\mathbf{f}_{i,t+1} + U^c\mathbf{h}_{i,t} + U^{cn}\bar{\mathbf{h}}_{i,t} + b^c),\\
\mathbf{m}_{i,t+1} &= \frac{\sum_{j\in\mathcal{N}_{\mathcal{G}}(i)}(\mathbb{1}(q_j = 1)\bar{g}_{ij}^f \odot \mathbf{m}_{j,t+1} + \mathbb{1}(q_j = 0)\bar{g}_{ij}^f \odot \mathbf{m}_{j,t})}{|\mathcal{N}_{\mathcal{G}}(i)|}\\
&\quad + g_i^f \odot \mathbf{m}_{i,t} + g_i^u \odot g_i^c,\\
\mathbf{h}_{i,t+1} &= \tanh(g_i^o \odot \mathbf{m}_{i,t+1}).
\end{aligned}
\tag{2}
$$

Here δ is the logistic sigmoid function, and $\odot$ indicates a point-wise product. The memory states $\mathbf{m}_{i,t+1}$ of the node v_i are updated by combining the memory states of visited nodes and those of unvisited nodes by using the adaptive forget gates. Let $\mathbf{W}, \mathbf{U}$ denote the concatenation of all weight matrices and $\{\mathbf{Z}_{j,t}\}_{j\in\mathcal{N}_{\mathcal{G}}(i)}$ represent all related information of neighboring nodes. We can thus use G-LSTM($\cdot$) to shorten Eq. (2) as

$$(\mathbf{h}_{i,t+1}, \mathbf{m}_{i,t+1}) = \text{G-LSTM}(\mathbf{f}_{i,t+1}, \mathbf{h}_{i,t}, \mathbf{m}_{i,t}, \{\mathbf{Z}_{j,t}\}_{j \in \mathcal{N}_\mathcal{G}(i)}, \mathbf{W}, \mathbf{U}, \mathcal{G}). \qquad (3)$$

The mechanism acts as a memory system, where the information can be written into the memory states and sequentially recorded by each graph node, which is then used to communicate with the hidden states of subsequent graph nodes and previous Graph LSTM layer. The back propagation is used to train all the weight metrics.

4 Experiments

Dataset: We evaluate the performance of the proposed Graph LSTM structure on semantic object parsing on four challenging datasets.

PASCAL-Person-Part Dataset [25]. The public PASCAL-Person-part dataset concentrates on the human part segmentation annotated by Chen et al. [25] from PASCAL VOC 2010 dataset. The dataset contains detailed part annotations for every person. Following [10,11], the annotations are merged to be Head, Torso, Upper/Lower Arms and Upper/Lower Legs, resulting in six person part classes and one background class. $1,716$ images are used for training and $1,817$ for testing.

Horse-Cow Parsing Dataset [26]. The Horse-Cow parsing dataset is a part segmentation benchmark introduced in [26]. For each class, most observable instances from PASCAL VOC 2010 benchmark [47] are manually selected, including 294 training images and 227 testing images. Each image pixel is elaborately labeled as one of the four part classes, including head, leg, tail and body.

ATR Dataset [27] **and Fashionista dataset** [28]. Human parsing aims to predict every pixel of each image with 18 labels: face, sunglass, hat, scarf, hair, upper-clothes, left-arm, right-arm, belt, pants, left-leg, right-leg, skirt, left-shoe, right-shoe, bag, dress and null. Originally, 7,700 images are included in the ATR dataset [27], with 6,000 for training, 1,000 for testing and 700 for validation. 10,000 real-world human pictures are further collected by [42] to cover images with more challenging poses, occlusion and clothes variations. We follow the training and testing settings used in [42].

Evaluation Metric: The standard intersection over union (IOU) criterion and pixel-wise accuracy are adopted for evaluation on PASCAL-Person-Part dataset and Horse-Cow parsing dataset, following [11,26,36]. We use the same evaluation metrics as in [27,37,42] for evaluation on two human parsing datasets, including accuracy, average precision, average recall, and average F-1 score.

Network Architecture: For fair comparison with [10,11,14], our network is based on the publicly available model, "DeepLab-CRF-LargeFOV" [13] for the PASCAL-Person-Part and Horse-Cow parsing dataset, which slightly modifies VGG-16 net [48] to FCN [24]. For fair comparing with [19,42] on two human parsing datasets, the basic "Co-CNN" structure proposed in [42] is utilized due

Table 1. Comparison of object parsing performance with four state-of-the-art methods over the PASCAL-Person-Part dataset [26].

Method	head	torso	u-arms	l-arms	u-legs	l-legs	Bkg	Avg
DeepLab-LargeFOV [13]	78.09	54.02	37.29	36.85	33.73	29.61	92.85	51.78
HAZN [10]	80.79	59.11	43.05	42.76	38.99	34.46	93.59	56.11
Attention [11]	-	-	-	-	-	-	-	56.39
LG-LSTM [19]	**82.72**	60.99	45.40	**47.76**	42.33	37.96	88.63	57.97
Graph LSTM	82.69	**62.68**	**46.88**	47.71	**45.66**	**40.93**	**94.59**	**60.16**

to its leading accuracy. Our networks based on "Co-CNN" are trained from the scratch following the same setting in [42].

Training: We use the same data augmentation techniques for the object part segmentation and human parsing as in [14,42], respectively. The scale of the input image is fixed as 321 × 321 for training networks based on "DeepLab-CRF-LargeFOV". Based on "Co-CNN", the input image is rescaled to 150 × 100 as in [42]. We use the SLIC over-segmentation method [45] to generate averagely 1,000 superpixels for each image. Two training steps are employed to train the networks. First, we train the convolutional layer with 1 × 1 filters to generate initial confidence maps that are used to produce the starting node and the update sequence for all nodes in Graph LSTM. Then, the whole network is fine-tuned based on the pretrained model to produce final parsing results. In each step, the learning rate of the newly added layers, including Graph LSTM layers and convolutional layers is initialized as 0.001 and that of other previously learned layers, is initialized as 0.0001. All weight matrices used in the Graph LSTM units are randomly initialized from a uniform distribution of [−0.1, 0.1]. The Graph LSTM predicts the hidden and memory states with the same dimension as in the previous convolutional layers. We only use two Graph LSTM layers for all models since only slight improvements are observed by using more Graph LSTM layers, which also consumes more computation resources. We fine-tune the networks on "DeepLab-CRF-LargeFOV" for roughly 60 epochs and it takes about 1 day. For training based on "Co-CNN" from scratch, it takes about 4–5 days. In the testing stage, one image takes 0.5 s on average except for the superpixel extraction step.

4.1 Results and Comparisons

We compare the proposed Graph LSTM structure with several state-of-the-art methods on four public datasets.

PASCAL-Person-Part dataset [26]: We report the results and the comparisons with four recent state-of-the-art methods [10,11,13,19] in Table 1. The results of "DeepLab-LargeFOV" were originally reported in [10]. The proposed Graph LSTM structure substantially outperforms these baselines in terms of average IoU metric. In particular, for the semantic parts with more likely confusions such as upper-arms and lower-arms, the Graph LSTM provides

Table 2. Comparison of object parsing performance with five state-of-the-art methods over the Horse-Cow object parsing dataset [26].

Horse

Method	Bkg	head	body	leg	tail	Fg	IOU	Pix.Acc
SPS [26]	79.14	47.64	69.74	38.85	-	68.63	-	81.45
HC [36]	85.71	57.30	77.88	51.93	37.10	78.84	61.98	87.18
Joint [14]	87.34	60.02	77.52	58.35	51.88	80.70	65.02	88.49
LG-LSTM [19]	89.64	66.89	84.20	60.88	42.06	82.50	68.73	90.92
HAZN [10]	90.87	70.73	84.45	63.59	51.16	-	72.16	-
Graph LSTM	**91.73**	**72.89**	**86.34**	**69.04**	**53.76**	**87.51**	**74.75**	**92.76**

Cow

Method	Bkg	head	body	leg	tail	Fg	IOU	Pix.Acc
SPS [26]	78.00	40.55	61.65	36.32	-	71.98	-	78.97
HC [36]	81.86	55.18	72.75	42.03	11.04	77.04	52.57	84.43
Joint [14]	85.68	58.04	76.04	51.12	15.00	82.63	57.18	87.00
LG-LSTM [19]	89.71	68.43	82.47	53.93	19.41	85.41	62.79	90.43
HAZN [10]	90.66	**75.10**	83.30	57.17	28.46	-	66.94	-
Graph LSTM	**91.54**	73.88	**85.92**	**63.67**	**35.22**	**88.42**	**70.05**	**92.43**

Table 3. Comparison of human parsing performance with seven state-of-the-art methods when evaluating on ATR dataset [27].

Method	Acc.	F.g. acc.	Avg. prec.	Avg. recall	Avg. F-1 score
Yamaguchi et al. [28]	84.38	55.59	37.54	51.05	41.80
PaperDoll [37]	88.96	62.18	52.75	49.43	44.76
M-CNN [41]	89.57	73.98	64.56	65.17	62.81
ATR [27]	91.11	71.04	71.69	60.25	64.38
Co-CNN [42]	95.23	80.90	81.55	74.42	76.95
Co-CNN (more) [42]	96.02	83.57	84.95	77.66	80.14
LG-LSTM [19]	96.18	84.79	84.64	79.43	80.97
LG-LSTM (more) [19]	96.85	87.35	85.94	82.79	84.12
CRFasRNN (more) [8]	96.34	85.10	84.00	80.70	82.08
Graph LSTM	97.60	91.42	84.74	83.28	83.76
Graph LSTM (more)	**97.99**	**93.06**	**88.81**	**87.80**	**88.20**

considerably better prediction than baselines, e.g., 4.95 % and 6.67 % higher over [10] for lower-arms and upper-legs, respectively. This superior performance achieved by Graph LSTM demonstrates the effectiveness of exploiting global context to boost local prediction.

Horse-Cow Parsing Dataset [26]: Table 2 shows the comparison results with five state-of-the-art methods on the overall metrics. The proposed Graph LSTM gives a huge boost in average IOU. For example, Graph LSTM achieves 70.05 %, 7.26 % better than LG-LSTM [19] and 3.11 % better than HAZN [10] for the cow class. Large improvement, i.e. 2.59 % increase by Graph LSTM in IOU over the best performing state-of-the-art method, can also be observed from the comparisons on horse class.

Table 4. Comparison of human parsing performance with five state-of-the-art methods on the test images of Fashionista [28].

Method	Acc.	F.g. acc.	Avg. prec.	Avg. recall	Avg. F-1 score
Yamaguchi et al. [28]	87.87	58.85	51.04	48.05	42.87
PaperDoll [37]	89.98	65.66	54.87	51.16	46.80
ATR [27]	92.33	76.54	73.93	66.49	69.30
Co-CNN [42]	96.08	84.71	82.98	77.78	79.37
Co-CNN (more) [42]	97.06	89.15	87.83	81.73	83.78
LG-LSTM [19]	96.85	87.71	87.05	82.14	83.67
LG-LSTM (more) [19]	97.66	91.35	89.54	85.54	86.94
Graph LSTM	97.93	92.78	88.24	87.13	87.57
Graph LSTM (more)	**98.14**	**93.75**	**90.15**	**89.46**	**89.75**

ATR Dataset [27]: Table 3 and Table 5 report the comparison performance with seven state-of-the-arts on overall metrics and F-1 scores of individual semantic labels, respectively. The proposed Graph LSTM can significantly outperform these baselines, particularly, 83.76 % vs 76.95 % of Co-CNN [42] and 80.97 % of LG-LSTM [19] in terms of average F-1 score. Following [42], we also take the additional 10,000 images in [42] as extra training images and report the results as "Graph LSTM (more)". The "Graph LSTM (more)" can also improve the average F-1 score by 4.08 % over "LG-LSTM (more)". We show the F-1 score for each label in Table 5. Generally, our Graph LSTM shows much higher performance than other baselines. In addition, our "Graph LSTM (more)" significantly outperforms "CRFasRNN (more)" [8], verifying the superiority of Graph LSTM over the pair-wise terms in CRF in capturing global context. The results of "CRFasRNN (more)" [8] are obtained by training the network using their public code.

Table 5. Per-Class Comparison of F-1 scores with six state-of-the-art methods on ATR [27].

Method	Hat	Hair	S-gls	U-cloth	Skirt	Pants	Dress	Belt	L-shoe	R-shoe	Face	L-leg	R-leg	L-arm	R-arm	Bag	Scarf
Yamaguchi et al. [28]	8.44	59.96	12.09	56.07	17.57	55.42	40.94	14.68	38.24	38.33	72.10	58.52	57.03	45.33	46.65	24.53	11.43
PaperDoll [37]	1.72	63.58	0.23	71.87	40.20	69.35	59.49	16.94	45.79	44.47	61.63	52.19	55.60	45.23	46.75	30.52	2.95
M-CNN [41]	80.77	65.31	35.55	72.58	77.86	70.71	81.44	38.45	53.87	48.57	72.78	63.25	68.24	57.40	51.12	57.87	43.38
ATR [27]	77.97	68.18	29.20	79.39	80.36	79.77	82.02	22.88	53.51	50.26	74.71	69.07	71.69	53.79	58.57	53.66	57.07
Co-CNN [42]	72.07	86.33	72.81	85.72	70.82	83.05	69.95	37.66	76.48	76.80	89.02	85.49	85.23	84.16	84.04	81.51	44.94
Co-CNN more [42]	75.88	89.97	81.26	87.38	71.94	84.89	71.03	40.14	81.43	81.49	92.73	88.77	88.48	89.00	88.71	83.81	46.24
LG-LSTM (more) [19]	81.13	90.94	81.07	88.97	80.91	91.47	77.18	60.32	83.40	83.65	93.67	92.27	92.41	90.20	90.13	85.78	51.09
Graph LSTM (more)	**85.30**	90.47	72.77	**95.11**	**97.31**	**96.58**	**96.43**	**68.55**	**85.27**	**84.35**	92.70	91.13	**93.17**	**91.20**	81.00	**90.83**	**66.09**

Fashionista Dataset [28]: Table 4 gives the comparison results on the Fashionista dataset. Following [27], we only report the performance by training on the same large ATR dataset [27] and then testing on the 229 images of the Fashionista dataset. Our Graph LSTM architecture can substantially outperform the baselines by a large gain.

4.2 Discussions

Graph LSTM vs locally fixed factorized LSTM. To show the superiority of the Graph LSTM compared to previous locally fixed factorized LSTM [19–21], Table 6 gives the performance comparison among different LSTM structures. These variants use the same network architecture and only replace the Graph LSTM layer with the traditional fixedly factorized LSTM layer, including

Table 6. Performance comparisons of using different LSTM structures and taking the superpixel smoothing as the post-processing step when evaluating on PASCAL-Person-Part dataset.

Method	head	torso	u-arms	l-arms	u-legs	l-legs	Bkg	Avg
Grid LSTM [20]	81.85	58.85	43.10	46.87	40.07	34.59	85.97	55.90
Row LSTM [21]	82.60	60.13	44.29	47.22	40.83	35.51	87.07	56.80
Diagonal BiLSTM [21]	82.67	60.64	45.02	47.59	41.95	37.32	88.16	57.62
LG-LSTM [19]	82.72	60.99	45.40	47.76	42.33	37.96	88.63	57.97
Diagonal BiLSTM [21] + superpixel smoothing	82.91	61.34	46.01	48.07	42.56	37.91	89.21	58.29
LG-LSTM [19] + superpixel smoothing	**82.98**	61.58	46.27	**48.08**	42.94	38.55	89.66	58.58
Graph LSTM	82.69	**62.68**	**46.88**	47.71	**45.66**	**40.93**	**94.59**	**60.16**

Row LSTM [21], Diagonal BiLSTM [21], LG-LSTM [19] and Grid LSTM [20]. The experimented Grid LSTM [20] is a simplified version of Diagnocal BiL-STM [21] where only the top and left pixels are considered. Their basic structures are presented in Fig. 2. It can be observed that using richer local contexts (i.e., number of neighbors) to update the states of each pixel can lead to better parsing performance. In average, there are six neighboring nodes for each super-pixel node in the constructed graph topologies in Graph LSTM. Although the LG-LSTM [19] has employed eight neighboring pixels to guide local prediction, its performance is still worse than our Graph LSTM.

Graph LSTM vs Superpixel Smoothing. In Table 6, we further demonstrate that the performance gain by Graph LSTM is not just from using more accurate boundary information provided by superpixels. The superpixel smoothing can be used as a post-processing step to refine confidence maps by previous LSTMs. By comparing "Diagonal BiLSTM [21] + superpixel smoothing" and "LG-LSTM [19] + superpixel smoothing" with our "Graph LSTM", we can find that the Graph LSTM can still bring more performance gain benefiting from its advanced information propagation based on the graph-structured representation.

Node Updating Scheme. Different node updating schemes to update the states of all nodes are further investigated in Table 7. The Breadth-first search (BFS) and Depth-first search (DFS) are the traditional algorithms to search graph data structures. For one parent node, selecting different children nodes to first update may lead to different updated hidden states for all nodes. Two ways of selecting first children nodes for updating are thus evaluated: "BFS (location)" and "DFS (location)" choose the spatially left-most node among all children nodes to update first while "BFS (confidence)" and "DFS (confidence)" select the child node with maximal confidence on all foreground classes. We find that

Table 7. Performance comparisons with different node updating schemes when evaluating on PASCAL-Person-Part dataset.

Method	head	torso	u-arms	l-arms	u-legs	l-legs	Bkg	Avg
BFS (location)	**83.00**	61.63	46.18	**48.01**	44.09	38.71	93.82	58.63
BFS (confidence)	82.97	62.20	46.70	48.00	44.02	39.00	90.86	59.11
DFS (location)	82.85	61.25	45.89	48.02	42.50	38.10	89.04	58.23
DFS (confidence)	82.89	62.31	46.76	48.04	44.24	39.07	91.18	59.21
Graph LSTM (confidence-driven)	82.69	**62.68**	**46.88**	47.71	**45.66**	40.93	**94.59**	**60.16**

Table 8. Performance comparisons of using the confidence-drive scheme based on confidences on different foreground labels when evaluating on PASCAL-Person-Part dataset.

Foreground label	head	torso	u-arms	l-arms	u-legs	l-legs	Avg
Avg IoU	61.03	61.45	60.03	59.23	60.49	59.89	60.35

using our confidence-driven scheme can achieve better performance than other alternative ones. The possible reason may be that the features of superpixel nodes with higher foreground confidences embed more accurate semantic meanings and thus lead to more reliable global reasoning.

Note that we use the ranking of confidences on all foreground classes to generate the node updating scheme. In Table 8, we extensively test the performance of using the initial confidence maps of different foreground labels to produce the node updating sequence. In average, only slight performance differences are observed when using the confidences of different foreground labels. In particular, using the confidences of "head" and "torso" leads to improved performance over using those of all foreground classes, i.e., 61.03 % and 61.45 % vs 60.16 %. It is possible because the segmentation of head/torso are more reliable in the person parsing case, which further verifies that the reliability of nodes in the updating order is important. It is difficult to determine the best semantic label for each task, hence we just use the one over all the foreground labels for simplicity and efficiency in implementation.

Adaptive Forget Gates. In Graph LSTM, adaptive forget gates are adopted to treat the local contexts from different neighbors differently. The superiority of using adaptive forget gates can be verified in Table 9. "Identical forget gates" shows the results of learning identical forget gates for all neighbors and simultaneously ignoring the memory states of neighboring nodes. Thus in "Identical forget gates", the g_i^f and $\mathbf{m}_{i,t+1}$ in Eq. (2) can be simply computed as

$$
\begin{aligned}
g_i^f &= \delta(W^f \mathbf{f}_{i,t+1} + U^f \mathbf{h}_{i,t} + U^{fn} \bar{\mathbf{h}}_{i,t} + b^f), \\
\mathbf{m}_{i,t+1} &= g_i^f \odot \mathbf{m}_{i,t} + g_i^u \odot g_i^c.
\end{aligned}
\tag{4}
$$

It can be observed that learning adaptive forgets gates in Graph LSTM shows better performance over learning identical forget gates for all neighbors on the object parsing task, as diverse semantic correlations with local context can be considered and treated differently during the node updating. Compared to Eq. (4), no extra parameters is brought to specify adaptive forget gates due to the usage of the shared parameters U^{fn} in Eq. (2).

Superpixel number. The drawback of using superpixels is that superpixels may introduce quantization errors whenever pixels within one superpixel have different ground truth labels. We thus evaluate the performance of using different

Table 9. Comparisons of parsing performance by the version with or without learning adaptive forget gates for different neighboring nodes when evaluating on PASCAL-Person-Part dataset.

Method	head	torso	u-arms	l-arms	u-legs	l-legs	Bkg	Avg
Identical forget gates	**82.89**	62.31	46.76	**48.04**	44.24	39.07	91.18	59.21
Graph LSTM (dynamic forget gates)	82.69	**62.68**	**46.88**	47.71	**45.66**	**40.93**	**94.59**	**60.16**

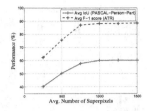

Fig. 4. Performance comparisons with six averaged numbers of superpixels when evaluating on PASCAL-Person-Part and ATR datasets, including 250, 500, 750, 1000, 1250, 1500.

average numbers of superpixels to construct the graph structure. As shown in Fig. 4, there are slight improvements when using over 1,000 superpixels. We thus use averagely 1,000 superpixels for each image in all our experiments.

Residual connections. Residual connections were first proposed in [44] to better train very deep convolutional layers. The version in which the residual connections are eliminated achieves 59.12 % in terms of Avg IoU on PASCAL-Person-Part dataset. It demonstrates that residual connections between Graph LSTM layers can also help boost the performance, i.e., 60.16 % vs 59.12 %. Note that our Graph LSTM version without using residual connections is still significantly better than all baselines in Table 1.

4.3 More Visual Comparison and Failure Cases

The qualitative comparisons of parsing results on PASCAL-Person-Part and ATR dataset are visualized in Figs. 5 and 6, respectively. In general, our Graph-LSTM outputs more reasonable results for confusing labels by effectively exploiting global context to assist the local prediction. We also show some failure cases on each dataset.

Fig. 5. Comparison of parsing results of our Graph LSTM and the baseline "DeepLab-LargeFov" and some failure cases by our Graph LSTM on PASCAL-Person-Part.

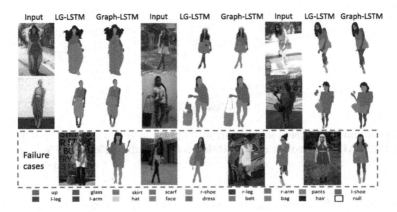

Fig. 6. Parsing result comparisons of our Graph LSTM and the LG-LSTM [19] and some failure cases by our Graph LSTM on ATR dataset.

5   Conclusion and Future Work

In this work, we proposed a novel Graph LSTM network to address the fundamental semantic object parsing task. Our Graph LSTM generalizes the existing LSTMs into the graph-structured data. The adaptive graph topology for each image is constructed by connecting the arbitrary-shaped superpixels nodes via their spatial neighborhood connections. The confidence-driven scheme is used to adaptively select the starting node and determine the node updating sequence. The Graph LSTM can thus sequentially update the states of all nodes. Comprehensive evaluations on four public semantic object parsing datasets well demonstrate the significant superiority of our graph LSTM. In future, we will explore how to dynamically adjust the graph structure to directly produce the semantic masks according to the connected superpixel nodes.

Acknowledgement. This work was supported in part by State Key Development Program under Grant 2016YFB1001000 and Special Program for Applied Research on Super Computation of the NSFC-Guangdong Joint Fund (the second phase). The work of Jiashi Feng was partially supported by National University of Singapore startup grant R-263-000-C08-133 and Ministry of Education of Singapore AcRF Tier One grant R-263-000-C21-112.

References

1. Zhang, H., Kim, G., Xing, E.P.: Dynamic topic modeling for monitoring market competition from online text and image data. In: ACM SIGKDD, pp. 1425–1434. ACM (2015)
2. Zhang, H., Hu, Z., Wei, J., Xie, P., Kim, G., Ho, Q., Xing, E.: Poseidon: a system architecture for efficient GPU-based deep learning on multiple machines. arXiv preprint arXiv:1512.06216 (2015)

3. Zhao, R., Ouyang, W., Wang, X.: Unsupervised salience learning for person re-identification. In: CVPR, pp. 3586–3593 (2013)
4. Wang, Y., Tran, D., Liao, Z., Forsyth, D.: Discriminative hierarchical part-based models for human parsing and action recognition. JMLR **13**(1), 3075–3102 (2012)
5. Gan, C., Wang, N., Yang, Y., Yeung, D.Y., Hauptmann, A.G.: DevNet: a deep event network for multimedia event detection and evidence recounting. In: CVPR, pp. 2568–2577 (2015)
6. Gan, C., Lin, M., Yang, Y., de Melo, G., Hauptmann, A.G.: Concepts not alone: exploring pairwise relationships for zero-shot video activity recognition. In: AAAI (2016)
7. Liang, X., Wei, Y., Shen, X., Yang, J., Lin, L., Yan, S.: Proposal-free network for instance-level object segmentation. arXiv preprint arXiv:1509.02636 (2015)
8. Zheng, S., Jayasumana, S., Romera-Paredes, B., Vineet, V., Su, Z., Du, D., Huang, C., Torr, P.: Conditional random fields as recurrent neural networks. In: ICCV (2015)
9. Liang, X., Liu, S., Wei, Y., Liu, L., Lin, L., Yan, S.: Towards computational baby learning: a weakly-supervised approach for object detection. In: ICCV, pp. 999–1007 (2015)
10. Xia, F., Wang, P., Chen, L.C., Yuille, A.L.: Zoom better to see clearer: human part segmentation with auto zoom net. In: Leibe, B., Matas, J., Sebe, N., Welling, M. (eds.) ECCV 2016. LNCS, vol. 9909, pp. 648–663. Springer, Switzerland (2016)
11. Chen, L.C., Yang, Y., Wang, J., Xu, W., Yuille, A.L.: Attention to scale: scale-aware semantic image segmentation. In: CVPR (2016)
12. Eigen, D., Fergus, R.: Predicting depth, surface normals and semantic labels with a common multi-scale convolutional architecture. In: ICCV (2015)
13. Chen, L.C., Papandreou, G., Kokkinos, I., Murphy, K., Yuille, A.L.: Semantic image segmentation with deep convolutional nets and fully connected CRFs. In: ICLR (2015)
14. Wang, P., Shen, X., Lin, Z., Cohen, S., Price, B., Yuille, A.: Joint object and part segmentation using deep learned potentials. In: ICCV (2015)
15. Gadde, R., Jampani, V., Kiefel, M., Gehler, P.V.: Superpixel convolutional networks using bilateral inceptions. In: ICLR (2016)
16. Byeon, W., Liwicki, M., Breuel, T.M.: Texture classification using 2D LSTM networks. In: ICPR, pp. 1144–1149 (2014)
17. Theis, L., Bethge, M.: Generative image modeling using spatial LSTMs. In: NIPS (2015)
18. Byeon, W., Breuel, T.M., Raue, F., Liwicki, M.: Scene labeling with LSTM recurrent neural networks. In: CVPR, pp. 3547–3555 (2015)
19. Liang, X., Shen, X., Xiang, D., Feng, J., Lin, L., Yan, S.: Semantic object parsing with local-global long short-term memory. In: CVPR (2016)
20. Kalchbrenner, N., Danihelka, I., Graves, A.: Grid long short-term memory. In: ICLR (2016)
21. van den Oord, A., Kalchbrenner, N., Kavukcuoglu, K.: Pixel recurrent neural networks. In: ICML (2016)
22. Sharma, S., Kiros, R., Salakhutdinov, R.: Action recognition using visual attention. arXiv preprint arXiv:1511.04119 (2015)
23. Mnih, V., Heess, N., Graves, A., et al.: Recurrent models of visual attention. In: Advances in Neural Information Processing Systems, pp. 2204–2212 (2014)
24. Long, J., Shelhamer, E., Darrell, T.: Fully convolutional networks for semantic segmentation. In: CVPR (2015)

25. Chen, X., Mottaghi, R., Liu, X., Fidler, S., Urtasun, R., et al.: Detect what you can: detecting and representing objects using holistic models and body parts. In: CVPR, pp. 1979–1986 (2014)
26. Wang, J., Yuille, A.: Semantic part segmentation using compositional model combining shape and appearance. In: CVPR (2015)
27. Liang, X., Liu, S., Shen, X., Yang, J., Liu, L., Dong, J., Lin, L., Yan, S.: Deep human parsing with active template regression. TPAMI **37**, 2402–2414 (2015)
28. Yamaguchi, K., Kiapour, M., Ortiz, L., Berg, T.: Parsing clothing in fashion photographs. In: CVPR (2012)
29. Graves, A., Schmidhuber, J.: Offline handwriting recognition with multidimensional recurrent neural networks. In: NIPS, pp. 545–552 (2009)
30. Sutskever, I., Vinyals, O., Le, Q.V.: Sequence to sequence learning with neural networks. In: NIPS, pp. 3104–3112 (2014)
31. Xu, K., Ba, J., Kiros, R., Cho, K., Courville, A.C., Salakhutdinov, R., Zemel, R.S., Bengio, Y.: Show, attend and tell: neural image caption generation with visual attention. In: ICML, pp. 2048–2057 (2015)
32. Graves, A., Fernández, S., Schmidhuber, J.: Multi-dimensional recurrent neural networks. In: de Sá, J.M., Alexandre, L.A., Duch, W., Mandic, D. (eds.) ICANN 2007. LNCS, vol. 4668, pp. 549–558. Springer, Heidelberg (2007). doi:10.1007/978-3-540-74690-4_56
33. Stollenga, M.F., Byeon, W., Liwicki, M., Schmidhuber, J.: Parallel multidimensional LSTM, with application to fast biomedical volumetric image segmentation. arXiv preprint arXiv:1506.07452 (2015)
34. Tai, K.S., Socher, R., Manning, C.D.: Improved semantic representations from tree-structured long short-term memory networks. arXiv preprint arXiv:1503.00075 (2015)
35. Lu, W., Lian, X., Yuille, A.: Parsing semantic parts of cars using graphical models and segment appearance consistency. In: BMVC (2014)
36. Hariharan, B., Arbeláez, P., Girshick, R., Malik, J.: Hypercolumns for object segmentation and fine-grained localization. In: CVPR, pp. 447–456
37. Yamaguchi, K., Kiapour, M., Berg, T.: Paper doll parsing: retrieving similar styles to parse clothing items. In: ICCV (2013)
38. Dong, J., Chen, Q., Xia, W., Huang, Z., Yan, S.: A deformable mixture parsing model with parselets. In: ICCV (2013)
39. Wang, N., Ai, H.: Who blocks who: simultaneous clothing segmentation for grouping images. In: ICCV (2011)
40. Simo-Serra, E., Fidler, S., Moreno-Noguer, F., Urtasun, R.: A high performance CRF model for clothes parsing. In: Cremers, D., Reid, I., Saito, H., Yang, M.-H. (eds.) ACCV 2014. LNCS, vol. 9005, pp. 64–81. Springer, Heidelberg (2015). doi:10.1007/978-3-319-16811-1_5
41. Liu, S., Liang, X., Liu, L., Shen, X., Yang, J., Xu, C., Lin, L., Cao, X., Yan, S.: Matching-CNN meets KNN: quasi-parametric human parsing. In: CVPR (2015)
42. Liang, X., Xu, C., Shen, X., Yang, J., Liu, S., Tang, J., Lin, L., Yan, S.: Human parsing with contextualized convolutional neural network. In: ICCV (2015)
43. Schwing, A.G., Urtasun, R.: Fully connected deep structured networks. arXiv preprint arXiv:1503.02351 (2015)
44. He, K., Zhang, X., Ren, S., Sun, J.: Deep residual learning for image recognition. In: CVPR (2016)
45. Achanta, R., Shaji, A., Smith, K., Lucchi, A., Fua, P., Süsstrunk, S.: Slic superpixels. Technical report (2010)

46. Hochreiter, S., Schmidhuber, J.: Long short-term memory. Neural Comput. **9**(8), 1735–1780 (1997)
47. Everingham, M., Van Gool, L., Williams, C.K., Winn, J., Zisserman, A.: The Pascal visual object classes challenge 2010 (VOC2010) results (2010)
48. Simonyan, K., Zisserman, A.: Very deep convolutional networks for large-scale image recognition. arXiv preprint arXiv:1409.1556 (2014)

SSHMT: Semi-supervised Hierarchical Merge Tree for Electron Microscopy Image Segmentation

Ting Liu[1][(✉)], Miaomiao Zhang[2], Mehran Javanmardi[1], Nisha Ramesh[1], and Tolga Tasdizen[1]

[1] Scientific Computing and Imaging Institute,
University of Utah, Salt Lake City, UT, USA
{ting,mehran,nshramesh,tolga}@sci.utah.edu
[2] CSAIL, Massachusetts Institute of Technology, Cambridge, MA, USA
miao86@mit.edu

Abstract. Region-based methods have proven necessary for improving segmentation accuracy of neuronal structures in electron microscopy (EM) images. Most region-based segmentation methods use a scoring function to determine region merging. Such functions are usually learned with supervised algorithms that demand considerable ground truth data, which are costly to collect. We propose a semi-supervised approach that reduces this demand. Based on a merge tree structure, we develop a differentiable unsupervised loss term that enforces consistent predictions from the learned function. We then propose a Bayesian model that combines the supervised and the unsupervised information for probabilistic learning. The experimental results on three EM data sets demonstrate that by using a subset of only 3 % to 7 % of the entire ground truth data, our approach consistently performs close to the state-of-the-art supervised method with the full labeled data set, and significantly outperforms the supervised method with the same labeled subset.

Keywords: Image segmentation · Electron microscopy · Semi-supervised learning · Hierarchical segmentation · Connectomics

1 Introduction

Connectomics researchers study structures of nervous systems to understand their function [1]. Electron microscopy (EM) is the only modality capable of imaging substantial tissue volumes at sufficient resolution and has been used for the reconstruction of neural circuitry [2–4]. The high resolution leads to image data sets at enormous scale, for which manual analysis is extremely laborious and can take decades to complete [5]. Therefore, reliable automatic connectome

Electronic supplementary material The online version of this chapter (doi:10. 1007/978-3-319-46448-0_9) contains supplementary material, which is available to authorized users.

© Springer International Publishing AG 2016
B. Leibe et al. (Eds.): ECCV 2016, Part I, LNCS 9905, pp. 144–159, 2016.
DOI: 10.1007/978-3-319-46448-0_9

reconstruction from EM images, and as the first step, automatic segmentation of neuronal structures is crucial. However, due to the anisotropic nature, deformation, complex cellular structures and semantic ambiguity of the image data, automatic segmentation still remains challenging after years of active research.

Similar to the boundary detection/region segmentation pipeline for natural image segmentation [6–9], most recent EM image segmentation methods use a membrane detection/cell segmentation pipeline. First, a membrane detector generates pixel-wise confidence maps of membrane predictions using local image cues [10–12]. Next, region-based methods are applied to transforming the membrane confidence maps into cell segments. It has been shown that region-based methods are necessary for improving the segmentation accuracy from membrane detections for EM images [13]. A common approach to region-based segmentation is to transform a membrane confidence map into over-segmenting superpixels and use them as "building blocks" for final segmentation. To correctly combine superpixels, greedy region agglomeration based on certain boundary saliency has been shown to work [14]. Meanwhile, structures, such as loopy graphs [15,16] or trees [17–19], are more often imposed to represent the region merging hierarchy and help transform the superpixel combination search into graph labeling problems. To this end, local [16,17] or structured [18,19] learning based methods are developed.

Most current region-based segmentation methods use a scoring function to determine how likely two adjacent regions should be combined. Such scoring functions are usually learned in a supervised manner that demands considerable amount of high-quality ground truth data. Obtaining such ground truth data, however, involves manual labeling of image pixels and is very labor intensive, especially given the large scale and complex structures of EM images. To alleviate this demand, Parag et al. recently propose an active learning framework [20,21] that starts with small sets of labeled samples and constantly measures the disagreement between a supervised classifier and a semi-supervised label propagation algorithm on unlabeled samples. Only the most disagreed samples are pushed to users for interactive labeling. The authors demonstrate that by using 15 % to 20 % of all labeled samples, the method can perform similar to the underlying fully supervised method with full training set. One disadvantage of this framework is that it does not directly explore the unsupervised information while searching for the optimal classification function. Also, retraining is required for the supervised algorithm at each iteration, which can be time consuming especially when more iterations with fewer samples per iteration are used to maximize the utilization of supervised information and minimize human effort. Moreover, repeated human interactions may lead to extra cost overhead in practice.

In this paper, we propose a semi-supervised learning framework for region-based neuron segmentation that seeks to reduce the demand for labeled data by exploiting the underlying correlation between unsupervised data samples. Based on the merge tree structure [17–19], we redefine the labeling constraint and formulate it into a differentiable loss function that can be effectively used to guide the unsupervised search in the function hypothesis space. We then develop a Bayesian model that incorporates both unsupervised and supervised information for probabilistic learning. The parameters that are essential to balancing the learning can be estimated from the data automatically. Our method works with very small amount of supervised data and requires no further human interaction. We show that by using only 3 % to 7 % of the labeled data, our method performs stably close to the state-of-the-art fully supervised algorithm with the entire supervised data set (Sect. 4). Also, our method can be conveniently adopted to replace the supervised algorithm in the active learning framework [20,21] and further improve the overall segmentation performance.

2   Hierarchical Merge Tree

Starting with an initial superpixel segmentation S_o of an image, a merge tree $T = (\mathcal{V}, \mathcal{E})$ is a graphical representation of superpixel merging order. Each node $v_i \in \mathcal{V}$ corresponds to an image region s_i. Each leaf node aligns with an initial superpixel in S_o. A non-leaf node corresponds to an image region combined by multiple superpixels, and the root node represents the whole image as a single region. An edge $e_{i,c} \in \mathcal{E}$ between v_i and one of its child v_c indicates $s_c \subset s_i$. Assuming only two regions are merged each time, we have T as a full binary tree. A clique $p_i = (\{v_i, v_{c_1}, v_{c_2}\}, \{e_{i,c_1}, e_{i,c_2}\})$ represents $s_i = s_{c_1} \cup s_{c_2}$. In this paper, we call clique p_i is at node v_i. We call the cliques p_{c_1} and p_{c_2} at v_{c_1} and v_{c_2} the child cliques of p_i, and p_i the parent clique of p_{c_1} and p_{c_2}. If v_i is a leaf node, $p_i = (\{v_i\}, \varnothing)$ is called a leaf clique. We call p_i a non-leaf/root/non-root clique if v_i is a non-leaf/root/non-root node. An example merge tree, as shown in Fig. 1c, represents the merging of superpixels in Fig. 1a. The red box in Fig. 1c shows a non-leaf clique $p_7 = (\{v_7, v_1, v_2\}, \{e_{7,1}, e_{7,2}\})$ as the child clique of $p_9 = (\{v_9, v_7, v_3\}, \{e_{9,7}, e_{9,3}\})$. A common approach to building a merge tree is to greedily merge regions based on certain boundary saliency measurement in an iterative fashion [17–19].

Given the merge tree, the problem of finding a final segmentation is equivalent to finding a complete label assignment $\mathbf{z} = \{z_i\}_{i=1}^{|\mathcal{V}|}$ for every node being a final segment ($z = 1$) or not ($z = 0$). Let $\rho(i)$ be a query function that returns the index of the parent node of v_i. The k-th ($k = 1, \ldots d_i$) ancestor of v_i is denoted as $\rho^k(i)$ with d_i being the depth of v_i in the tree, and $\rho^0(i) = i$. For every leaf-to-root path, we enforce the *region consistency constraint* that requires $\sum_{k=0}^{d_i} z_{\rho^k(i)} = 1$ for any leaf node v_i. As an example shown in Fig. 1c, the red nodes (v_6, v_8, and v_9) are labeled $z = 1$ and correspond to the final segmentation in Fig. 1b. The rest black nodes are labeled $z = 0$. Supervised algorithms are proposed to learn scoring functions in a local [9,17] or a structured [18,19] fashion, followed by greedy [17] or global [9,18,19] inference techniques for finding the optimal label assignment under the constraint. We refer to the local learning and greedy search inference framework in [17] as the hierarchical merge tree (HMT) method and follow its settings in the rest of this paper, as it has been shown to achieve state-of-the-art results in the public challenges [13,22].

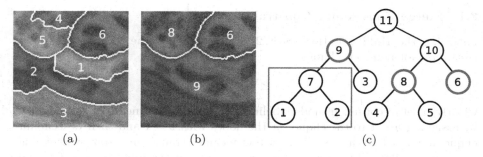

Fig. 1. Example of (a) an initial superpixel segmentation, (b) a consistent final segmentation, and (c) the corresponding merge tree. The red nodes are selected ($z = 1$) for the final segmentation, and the black nodes are not ($z = 0$). The red box shows a clique. (Color figure online)

A binary label y_i is used to denote whether the region merging at clique p_i occurs ("merge", $y_i = 1$) or not ("split", $y_i = 0$). For a leaf clique, $y = 1$. At training time, $\mathbf{y} = \{y_i\}_{i=1}^{|\mathcal{V}|}$ is generated by comparing both the "merge" and "split" cases for non-leaf cliques against the ground truth segmentation under certain error metric (e.g. adapted Rand error [13]). The one that causes the lower error is adopted. A binary classification function called the boundary classifier is trained with $(\mathbf{X}, \mathbf{y})$, where $\mathbf{X} = \{\mathbf{x}_i\}_{i=1}^{|\mathcal{V}|}$ is a collection of feature vectors. Shape and image appearance features are commonly used.

At testing time, each non-leaf clique p_i is assigned a likelihood score $P(y_i|\mathbf{x}_i)$ by the classifier. A potential for each node v_i is defined as

$$u_i = P(y_i = 1|\mathbf{x}_i) \cdot P(y_{\rho(i)} = 0|\mathbf{x}_{\rho(i)}). \tag{1}$$

The greedy inference algorithm iteratively assigns $z = 1$ to an unlabeled node with the highest potential and $z = 0$ to its ancestor and descendant nodes until every node in the merge tree receives a label. The nodes with $z = 1$ forms a final segmentation.

Note that HMT is not limited to segmenting images of any specific dimensionality. In practice, it has been successfully applied to both 2D [13,17] and 3D segmentation [22] of EM images.

3   SSHMT: Semi-supervised Hierarchical Merge Tree

The performance of HMT largely depends on accurate boundary predictions given fixed initial superpixels and tree structures. In this section, we propose a semi-supervised learning based HMT framework, named SSHMT, to learn accurate boundary classifiers with limited supervised data.

3.1 Merge Consistency Constraint

Following the HMT notation (Sect. 2), we first define the *merge consistency constraint* for non-root cliques:

$$y_i \geq y_{\rho(i)}, \forall i. \tag{2}$$

Clearly, a set of consistent node labeling $\mathbf{z}$ can be transformed to a consistent $\mathbf{y}$ by assigning $y = 1$ to the cliques at the nodes with $z = 1$ and their descendant cliques and $y = 0$ to the rest. A consistent $\mathbf{y}$ can be transformed to $\mathbf{z}$ by assigning $z = 1$ to the nodes in $\{v_i \in \mathcal{V} | \forall i, \text{s.t. } y_i = 1 \wedge (v_i \text{ is the root} \vee y_{\rho(i)} = 0)\}$ and $z = 0$ to the rest, vice versa.

Define a clique path of length L that starts at p_i as an ordered set $\boldsymbol{\pi}_i^L = \{p_{\rho^l(i)}\}_{l=0}^{L-1}$. We then have

Theorem 1. *Any consistent label sequence* $\mathbf{y}_i^L = \{y_{\rho^l(i)}\}_{l=0}^{L-1}$ *for* $\boldsymbol{\pi}_i^L$ *under the merge consistency constraint is monotonically non-increasing.*

Proof. Assume there exists a label sequence $\mathbf{y}_i^L$ subject to the merge consistency constraint that is not monotonically non-increasing. By definition, there must exist $k \geq 0$, s.t. $y_{\rho^k(i)} < y_{\rho^{k+1}(i)}$. Let $j = \rho^k(i)$, then $\rho^{k+1}(i) = \rho(j)$, and thus $y_j < y_{\rho(j)}$. This violates the merge consistency constraint (2), which contradicts the initial assumption that $\mathbf{y}_i^L$ is subject to the merge consistency constraint. Therefore, the initial assumption must be false, and all label sequences that are subject to the merge consistency constraint must be monotonically non-increasing. □

Intuitively, Theorem 1 states that while moving up in a merge tree, once a split occurs, no merge shall occur again among the ancestor cliques in that path. As an example, a consistent label sequence for the clique path $\{p_7, p_9, p_{11}\}$ in Fig. 1c can only be $\{y_7, y_9, y_{11}\} = \{0,0,0\}, \{1,0,0\}, \{1,1,0\}$, or $\{1,1,1\}$. Any other label sequence, such as $\{1,0,1\}$, is not consistent. In contrast to the region consistency constraint, the merge consistency constraint is a local constraint that holds for the entire leaf-to-root clique paths as well as any of their subparts. This allows certain computations to be decomposed as shown later in Sect. 4.

Let f_i be a predicate that denotes whether $y_i = 1$. We can express the non-increasing monotonicity of any consistent label sequence for $\boldsymbol{\pi}_i^L$ in disjunctive normal form (DNF) as

$$F_i^L = \bigvee_{j=0}^{L} \left(\bigwedge_{k=0}^{j-1} f_{\rho^k(i)} \wedge \bigwedge_{k=j}^{L-1} \neg f_{\rho^k(i)} \right), \tag{3}$$

which always holds *true* by Theorem 1. We approximate F_i^L with real-valued variables and operators by replacing *true* with 1, *false* with 0, and f with real-valued $\tilde{f}$. A negation $\neg f$ is replaced by $1 - \tilde{f}$; conjunctions are replaced by multiplications; disjunctions are transformed into negations of conjunctions using De Morgan's laws and then replaced. The real-valued DNF approximation is

$$\tilde{F}_i^L = 1 - \prod_{j=0}^{L} \left(1 - \prod_{k=0}^{j-1} \tilde{f}_{\rho^k(i)} \cdot \prod_{k=j}^{L-1} \left(1 - \tilde{f}_{\rho^k(i)} \right) \right), \tag{4}$$

which is valued 1 for any consistent label assignments. Observing $\tilde{f}$ is exactly a binary boundary classifier in HMT, we further relax it to be a classification function that predicts $P(y = 1|\mathbf{x}) \in [0, 1]$. The choice of $\tilde{f}$ can be arbitrary as long as it is (piecewise) differentiable (Sect. 3.2). In this paper, we use a logistic sigmoid function with a linear discriminant

$$\tilde{f}(\mathbf{x}; \boldsymbol{w}) = \frac{1}{1 + \exp(-\boldsymbol{w}^\top \mathbf{x})}, \tag{5}$$

which is parameterized by $\boldsymbol{w}$.

We would like to find an $\tilde{f}$ so that its predictions satisfy the DNF (4) for any path in a merge tree. We will introduce the learning of such $\tilde{f}$ in a semi-supervised manner in Sect. 3.2.

3.2   Bayesian Semi-supervised Learning

To learn the boundary classification function $\tilde{f}$, we use both supervised and unsupervised data. Supervised data are the clique samples with labels that are generated from ground truth segmentations. Unsupervised samples are those we do not have labels for. They can be from the images that we do not have the ground truth for or wish to segment. We use $\mathbf{X}_s$ to denote the collection of supervised sample feature vectors and $\mathbf{y}_s$ for their true labels. $\mathbf{X}$ is the collection of all supervised and unsupervised samples.

Let $\tilde{\boldsymbol{f}}_{\boldsymbol{w}} = [\tilde{f}_{j_1}, \ldots, \tilde{f}_{j_{N_s}}]^\top$ be the predictions about the supervised samples in $\mathbf{X}_s$, and $\tilde{\boldsymbol{F}}_{\boldsymbol{w}} = [\tilde{F}_{i_1}^L, \ldots, \tilde{F}_{i_{N_u}}^L]^\top$ be the DNF values (4) for all paths from $\mathbf{X}$. We are now ready to build a probabilistic model that includes a regularization prior, an unsupervised likelihood, and a supervised likelihood.

The prior is an i.i.d. Gaussian $\mathcal{N}(0, 1)$ that regularizes $\boldsymbol{w}$ to prevent overfitting. The unsupervised likelihood is an i.i.d. Gaussian $\mathcal{N}(0, \sigma_u)$ on the differences between each element of $\tilde{\boldsymbol{F}}_{\boldsymbol{w}}$ and 1. It requires the predictions of $\tilde{f}$ to conform the merge consistency constraint for every path. Maximizing the unsupervised likelihood allows us to narrow down the potential solutions to a subset in the classifier hypothesis space without label information by exploring the sample feature representation commonality. The supervised likelihood is an i.i.d. Gaussian $\mathcal{N}(0, \sigma_s)$ on the prediction errors for supervised samples to enforce accurate predictions. It helps avoid consistent but trivial solutions of $\tilde{f}$, such as the ones that always predict $y = 1$ or $y = 0$, and guides the search towards the correct solution. The standard deviation parameters σ_u and σ_s control the contributions of the three terms. They can be preset to reflect our prior knowledge about the model distributions, tuned using a holdout set, or estimated from data.

By applying Bayes' rule, we have the posterior distribution of w as

$$P(w \mid \mathbf{X}, \mathbf{X}_s, \mathbf{y}_s, \sigma_u, \sigma_s) \propto P(w) \cdot P(1 \mid \mathbf{X}, w, \sigma_u) \cdot P(\mathbf{y}_s \mid \mathbf{X}_s, w, \sigma_s)$$

$$\propto \exp\left(-\frac{\|w\|_2^2}{2}\right)$$

$$\cdot \frac{1}{\left(\sqrt{2\pi}\sigma_u\right)^{N_u}} \exp\left(-\frac{\|1 - \tilde{F}_w\|_2^2}{2\sigma_u^2}\right) \tag{6}$$

$$\cdot \frac{1}{\left(\sqrt{2\pi}\sigma_s\right)^{N_s}} \exp\left(-\frac{\|\mathbf{y}_s - \tilde{f}_w\|_2^2}{2\sigma_s^2}\right),$$

where N_u and N_s are the number of elements in $\tilde{F}_w$ and $\tilde{f}_w$, respectively; 1 is a N_u-dimensional vector of ones.

Inference. We infer the model parameters w, σ_u, and σ_s using maximum a posteriori estimation. We effectively minimize the negative logarithm of the posterior

$$J(w, \sigma_u, \sigma_s) = \frac{1}{2}\|w\|_2^2 + \frac{1}{2\sigma_u^2}\|1 - \tilde{F}_w\|_2^2 + N_u \log \sigma_u$$

$$+ \frac{1}{2\sigma_s^2}\|\mathbf{y}_s - \tilde{f}_w\|_2^2 + N_s \log \sigma_s. \tag{7}$$

Observe that the DNF formula in (4) is differentiable. With any (piecewise) differentiable choice of $\tilde{f}_w$, we can minimize (7) using (sub-) gradient descent. The gradient of (7) with respect to the classifier parameter w is

$$\nabla_w J = w^\top - \frac{1}{\sigma_u^2}\left(1 - \tilde{F}_w\right)^\top \nabla_w \tilde{F}_w - \frac{1}{\sigma_s^2}\left(\mathbf{y}_s - \tilde{f}_w\right)^\top \nabla_w \tilde{f}_w, \tag{8}$$

Since we choose $\tilde{f}$ to be a logistic sigmoid function with a linear discriminant (5), the j-th ($j = 1, \ldots, N_s$) row of $\nabla_w \tilde{f}_w$ is

$$\nabla_w \tilde{f}_j = \tilde{f}_j(1 - \tilde{f}_j) \cdot \mathbf{x}_j^\top. \tag{9}$$

where $\mathbf{x}_j$ is the j-th element in $\mathbf{X}_s$.

Define $g_j = \prod_{k=0}^{j-1} \tilde{f}_{\rho^k(i)} \cdot \prod_{k=j}^{L-1}(1 - \tilde{f}_{\rho^k(i)})$, $j = 0, \ldots, L$, we write (4) as $\tilde{F}_i^L = 1 - \prod_{j=0}^{L}(1 - g_j)$ as the i-th ($i = 1, \ldots, N_u$) element of $\tilde{F}_w$. Then the i-th row of $\nabla_w \tilde{F}_w$ is

$$\nabla_w \tilde{F}_i^L = \sum_{j=0}^{L} \left(g_j \prod_{\substack{k=0 \\ k \neq j}}^{L}(1 - g_k) \right) \left(\sum_{k=0}^{j-1} \frac{\nabla_w \tilde{f}_{\rho^k(i)}}{\tilde{f}_{\rho^k(i)}} - \sum_{k=j}^{L-1} \frac{\nabla_w \tilde{f}_{\rho^k(i)}}{1 - \tilde{f}_{\rho^k(i)}} \right), \tag{10}$$

where $\nabla_w \tilde{f}_{\rho^k(i)}$ can be computed using (9).

We also alternately estimate σ_u and σ_s along with $\boldsymbol{w}$. Setting $\nabla_{\sigma_u} J = 0$ and $\nabla_{\sigma_s} J = 0$, we update σ_u and σ_s using the closed-form solutions

$$\sigma_u = \frac{\|\mathbf{1} - \tilde{\boldsymbol{F}}_{\boldsymbol{w}}\|_2}{\sqrt{N_u}} \tag{11}$$

$$\sigma_s = \frac{\|\mathbf{y}_s - \tilde{\boldsymbol{f}}_{\boldsymbol{w}}\|_2}{\sqrt{N_s}}. \tag{12}$$

At testing time, we apply the learned $\tilde{f}$ to testing samples to predict their merging likelihood. Eventually, we compute the node potentials with (1) and apply the greedy inference algorithm to acquire the final node label assignment (Sect. 2).

4 Results

We validate the proposed algorithm for 2D and 3D segmentation of neurons in three EM image data sets. For each data set, we apply SSHMT to the same segmentation tasks using different amounts of randomly selected subsets of ground truth data as the supervised sets.

4.1 Data Sets

Mouse Neuropil Data Set. [23] consists of 70 2D SBFSEM images of size $700 \times 700 \times 700$ at $10 \times 10 \times 50$ nm/pixel resolution. A random selection of 14 images are considered as the whole supervised set, and the rest 56 images are used for testing. We test our algorithm using 14 (100 %), 7 (50 %), 3 (21.42 %), 2 (14.29 %), 1 (7.143 %), and half (3.571 %) ground truth image(s) as the supervised data. We use all the 70 images as the unsupervised data for training. We target at 2D segmentation for this data set.

Mouse Cortex Data Set. [22] is the original training set for the ISBI SNEMI3D Challenge [22]. It is a $1024 \times 1024 \times 100$ SSSEM image stack at $6 \times 6 \times 30$ nm/pixel resolution. We use the first $1024 \times 1024 \times 50$ substack as the supervised set and the second $1024 \times 1024 \times 50$ substack for testing. There are 327 ground truth neuron segments that are larger than 1000 pixels in the supervised substack, which we consider as all the available supervised data. We test the performance of our algorithm by using 327 (100 %), 163 (49.85 %), 81 (24.77 %), 40 (12.23 %), 20 (6.116 %), 10 (3.058 %), and 5 (1.529 %) true segments. Both the supervised and the testing substack are used for the unsupervised term. Due to the unavailability of the ground truth data, we did not experiment with the original testing image stack from the challenge. We target at 3D segmentation for this data set.

***Drosophila Melanogaster* Larval Neuropil Data Set.** [24] is a $500 \times 500 \times 500$ FIBSEM image volume at $10 \times 10 \times 10$ nm/pixel resolution. We divide the whole volume evenly into eight $250 \times 250 \times 250$ subvolumes and do eight-fold cross validation using one subvolume each time as the supervised set and the whole volume as the testing data. Each subvolume has from 204 to 260 ground truth neuron segments that are larger than 100 pixels. Following the setting in the mouse cortex data set experiment, we use subsets of 100 %, 50 %, 25 %, 12.5 %, 6.25 %, and 3.125 % of all true neuron segments from the respective supervised subvolume in each fold of the cross validation as the supervised data to generate boundary classification labels. We use the entire volume to generate unsupervised samples. We target at 3D segmentation for this data set.

4.2 Experiments

We use fully trained Cascaded Hierarchical Models [12] to generate membrane detection confidence maps and keep them fixed for the HMT and SSHMT experiments on each data set, respectively. To generate initial superpixels, we use the watershed algorithm [25] over the membrane confidence maps. For the boundary classification, we use features including shape information (region size, perimeter, bounding box, boundary length, etc.) and image intensity statistics (mean, standard deviation, minimum, maximum, etc.) of region interior and boundary pixels from both the original EM images and membrane detection confidence maps.

We use the adapted Rand error metric [13] to generate boundary classification labels using whole ground truth images (Sect. 2) for the 2D mouse neuropil data set. For the 3D mouse cortex and *Drosophila melanogaster* larval neuropil data sets, we determine the labels using individual ground truth segments instead. We use this setting in order to match the actual process of analyzing EM images by neuroscientists. Details about label generation using individual ground truth segments are provided in Appendix A.

We can see in (4) and (10) that computing $\tilde{F}_i^L$ and its gradient involves multiplications of L floating point numbers, which can cause underflow problems for leaf-to-root clique paths in a merge tree of even moderate height. To avoid this problem, we exploit the local property of the merge consistency constraint and compute $\tilde{F}_i^L$ for every path subpart of small length L. In this paper, we use $L = 3$ for all experiments. For inference, we initialize $\boldsymbol{w}$ by running gradient descent on (7) with only the supervised term and the regularizer before adding the unsupervised term for the whole optimization. We update σ_u and σ_s in between every 100 gradient descent steps on $\boldsymbol{w}$.

We compare SSHMT with the fully supervised HMT [17] as the baseline method. To make the comparison fair, we use the same logistic sigmoid function as the boundary classifier for both HMT and SSHMT. The fully supervised training uses the same Bayesian framework only without the unsupervised term in (7) and alternately estimates σ_s to balance the regularization term and the supervised term. All the hyperparameters are kept identical for HMT and SSHMT and fixed for all experiments. We use the adapted Rand error [13] following the public EM image segmentation challenges [13,22]. Due to the randomness in the selection of supervised data, we repeat each experiment 50 times, except in the cases that there are fewer possible combinations. We report the mean and standard deviation of errors for each set of repeats on the three data sets in Table 1. For the 2D mouse neuropil data set, we also threshold the membrane detection confidence maps at the optimal level, and the adapted Rand error is 0.2023. Since the membrane detection confidence maps are generated in 2D, we do not measure the thresholding errors of the other 3D data sets. In addition, we report the results from using the globally optimal tree inference [9] in the supplementary materials for comparison.

Examples of 2D segmentation testing results from the mouse neuropil data set using fully supervised HMT and SSHMT with 1 (7.143 %) ground truth image as supervised data are shown in Fig. 2. Examples of 3D individual neuron segmentation testing results from the *Drosophila melanogaster* larval neuropil data set using fully supervised HMT and SSHMT with 12 (6.25 %) true neuron segments as supervised data are shown in Fig. 3.

From Table 1, we can see that with abundant supervised data, the performance of SSHMT is similar to HMT in terms of segmentation accuracy, and both of them significantly improve from optimally thresholding (Table 1a). When the amount of supervised data becomes smaller, SSHMT significantly outperforms the fully supervised method with the accuracy close to the HMT results using the full supervised sets. Moreover, the introduction of the unsupervised term stabilizes the learning of the classification function and results in much more consistent segmentation performance, even when only very limited (3 % to 7 %) label data are available. Increases in errors and large variations are observed in the SSHMT results when the supervised data become too scarce. This is because the few supervised samples are incapable of providing sufficient guidance to balance the unsupervised term, and the boundary classifiers are biased to give trivial predictions.

Figure 2 shows that SSHMT is capable of fixing both over- and under-segmentation errors that occur in the HMT results. Figure 3 also shows that SSHMT can fix over-segmentation errors and generate highly accurate neuron segmentations. Note that in our experiments, we always randomly select the supervised data subsets. For realistic uses, we expect supervised samples of better representativeness to be provided with expertise and the performance of SSHMT to be further improved.

We also conducted an experiment with the mouse neuropil data set in which we use only 1 ground truth image to train the membrane detector, HMT, and SSHMT to test a fully semi-supervised EM segmentation pipeline. We repeat 14 times for every ground truth image in the supervised set. The optimal thresholding gives adapted Rand error 0.3603 ± 0.06827. The error of the HMT results is 0.2904 ± 0.09303, and the error of the SSHMT results is 0.2373 ± 0.06827. Despite the increase of error, which is mainly due to the fully supervised nature of the membrane detection algorithm, SSHMT again improves the region accuracy from optimal thresholding and has a clear advantage over HMT.

We have open-sourced our code at https://github.com/tingliu/glia. It takes approximately 80 seconds for our SSHMT implementation to train and test on the whole mouse neuropil data set using 50 2.5 GHz Intel Xeon CPUs and about 150 MB memory.

Table 1. Means and standard deviations of the adapted Rand errors of HMT and SSHMT segmentations for the three EM data sets. The left table columns show the amount of used ground truth data, in terms of (a) the number of images, (b) the number of segments, and (c) the percentage of all segments. Bold numbers in the tables show the results of the higher accuracy under comparison. The figures on the right visualize the means (dashed lines) and the standard deviations (solid bars) of the errors of HMT (red) and SSHMT (blue) results for each data set.

(a) Mouse neuropil

#GT	HMT Mean	HMT Std.	SSHMT Mean	SSHMT Std.
14	**0.1135**	–	0.1196	–
7	0.1382	0.03238	**0.1208**	0.004033
3	0.1492	0.04851	**0.1205**	0.001383
2	0.1811	0.07346	**0.1217**	0.004116
1	0.2035	0.1029	**0.1210**	0.002206
0.5	0.2505	0.1062	**0.1365**	0.1079
Optimal thresholding: 0.2023				

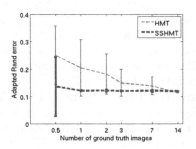

(b) Mouse cortex

#GT	HMT Mean	HMT Std.	SSHMT Mean	SSHMT Std.
327	**0.1101**	–	0.1104	–
163	0.1344	0.03660	**0.1189**	0.01506
81	0.1583	0.06909	**0.1215**	0.01661
40	0.1844	0.1019	**0.1198**	0.01690
20	0.2205	0.1226	**0.1238**	0.01466
10	0.2503	0.1561	**0.1219**	0.01273
5	0.4389	0.2769	**0.2008**	0.2285

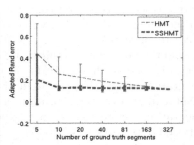

(c) *Drosophila melanogaster* larval neuropil

%GT	HMT Mean	HMT Std.	SSHMT Mean	SSHMT Std.
100%	0.06044	–	**0.05504**	–
50%	0.09004	0.04476	**0.05602**	0.005550
25%	0.1240	0.07491	**0.05803**	0.007703
12.5%	0.1418	0.1055	**0.05835**	0.007797
6.25%	0.1748	0.1389	**0.05756**	0.008933
3.125%	0.2017	0.1871	**0.06213**	0.03660

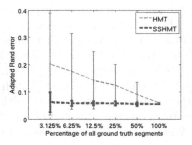

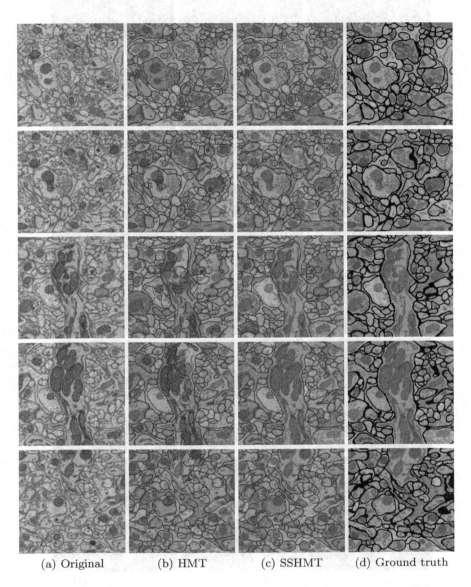

(a) Original   (b) HMT   (c) SSHMT   (d) Ground truth

Fig. 2. Examples of the 2D segmentation testing results for the mouse neuropil data set, including (a) original EM images, (b) HMT and (c) SSHMT results using 1 ground truth image as supervised data, and (d) the corresponding ground truth images. Different colors indicate different individual segments.

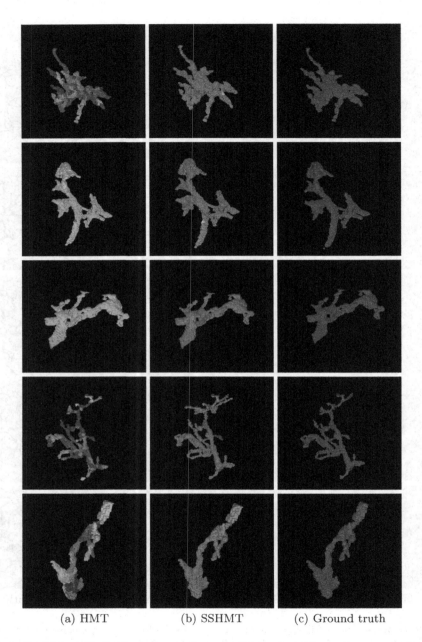

(a) HMT   (b) SSHMT   (c) Ground truth

Fig. 3. Examples of individual neurons from the 3D segmentation testing results for the *Drosophila melanogaster* larval neuropil data set, including (a) HMT and (b) SSHMT results using 12 (6.25 %) 3D ground truth segments as supervised data, and (c) the corresponding ground truth segments. Different colors indicate different individual segments. The 3D visualizations are generated using Fiji [26].

5   Conclusion

In this paper, we proposed a semi-supervised method that can consistently learn boundary classifiers with very limited amount of supervised data for region-based image segmentation. This dramatically reduces the high demands for ground truth data by fully supervised algorithms. We applied our method to neuron segmentation in EM images from three data sets and demonstrated that by using only a small amount of ground truth data, our method performed close to the state-of-the-art fully supervised method with full labeled data sets. In our future work, we will explore the integration of the proposed constraint based unsupervised loss in structural learning settings to further exploit the structured information for learning the boundary classification function. Also, we may replace the current logistic sigmoid function with more complex classifiers and combine our method with active learning frameworks to improve segmentation accuracy.

Acknowledgment. This work was supported by NSF IIS-1149299 and NIH 1R01NS075314-01. We thank the National Center for Microscopy and Imaging Research at the University of California, San Diego, for providing the mouse neuropil data set. We also thank Mehdi Sajjadi at the University of Utah for the constructive discussions.

A   Appendix: Generating Boundary Classification Labels Using Individual Ground Truth Segments

Assume we only have individual annotated image segments instead of entire image volumes as ground truth. Given a merge tree, we generate the best-effort ground truth classification labels for a subset of cliques as follows:

1. For every region represented by a tree node, compute the Jaccard indices of this region against all the annotated ground truth segments. Use the highest Jaccard index of each node as its eligible score.
2. Mark every node in the tree as "eligible" if its eligible score is above certain threshold (0.75 in practice) or "ineligible" otherwise.
3. Iteratively select a currently "eligible" node with the highest eligible score; mark it and its ancestors and descendants as "ineligible", until every node is "ineligible". This procedure generates a set of selected nodes.
4. For every selected node, label the cliques at itself and its descendants as $y = 1$ ("merge") and the cliques at its ancestors as $y = 0$ ("split").

Eventually, the clique samples that receive merge/split labels are considered as the supervised data.

References

1. Sporns, O., Tononi, G., Kötter, R.: The human connectome: a structural description of the human brain. PLoS Comput. Biol. **1**(4), e42 (2005)
2. Famiglietti, E.V.: Synaptic organization of starburst amacrine cells in rabbit retina: analysis of serial thin sections by electron microscopy and graphic reconstruction. J. Comp. Neurol. **309**(1), 40–70 (1991)
3. Briggman, K.L., Helmstaedter, M., Denk, W.: Wiring specificity in the direction-selectivity circuit of the retina. Nature **471**(7337), 183–188 (2011)
4. Helmstaedter, M.: Cellular-resolution connectomics: challenges of dense neural circuit reconstruction. Nat. Methods **10**(6), 501–507 (2013)
5. Briggman, K.L., Denk, W.: Towards neural circuit reconstruction with volume electron microscopy techniques. Current Opin. Neurobiol. **16**(5), 562–570 (2006)
6. Arbelaez, P., Maire, M., Fowlkes, C., Malik, J.: Contour detection and hierarchical image segmentation. IEEE Trans. Patt. Anal. Mach. Intell. **33**(5), 898–916 (2011)
7. Ren, Z., Shakhnarovich, G.: Image segmentation by cascaded region agglomeration. In: Proceedings of the IEEE Conference on Computer Vision and Pattern Recognition, pp. 2011–2018 (2013)
8. Arbeláez, P., Pont-Tuset, J., Barron, J., Marques, F., Malik, J.: Multiscale combinatorial grouping. In: Proceedings of the IEEE Conference on Computer Vision and Pattern Recognition, pp. 328–335 (2014)
9. Liu, T., Seyedhosseini, M., Tasdizen, T.: Image segmentation using hierarchical merge tree. IEEE Trans. Image Process. **25**(10), 4596–4607 (2016). doi:10.1109/TIP.2016.2592704
10. Sommer, C., Straehle, C., Koethe, U., Hamprecht, F.A.: ilastik: Interactive learning and segmentation toolkit. In: 2011 IEEE International Symposium on Biomedical Imaging: From Nano to Macro, pp. 230–233. IEEE (2011)
11. Ciresan, D., Giusti, A., Gambardella, L.M., Schmidhuber, J.: Deep neural networks segment neuronal membranes in electron microscopy images. Adv. Neural Inf. Process. Syst. **25**, 2852–2860 (2012)
12. Seyedhosseini, M., Sajjadi, M., Tasdizen, T.: Image segmentation with cascaded hierarchical models and logistic disjunctive normal networks. In: Proceedings of the IEEE International Conference on Computer Vision, pp. 2168–2175 (2013)
13. Arganda-Carreras, I., Turaga, S.C., Berger, D.R., Cireşan, D.: Crowdsourcing the creation of image segmentation algorithms for connectomics. Front. Neuroanat. **9**, 142 (2015)
14. Nunez-Iglesias, J., Kennedy, R., Parag, T., Shi, J., Chklovskii, D.B.: Machine learning of hierarchical clustering to segment 2D and 3D images. PLoS ONE **8**(8), e71715 (2013)
15. Kaynig, V., Vazquez-Reina, A., Knowles-Barley, S., Roberts, M., Jones, T.R., Kasthuri, N., Miller, E., Lichtman, J., Pfister, H.: Large-scale automatic reconstruction of neuronal processes from electron microscopy images. Med. Image Anal. **22**(1), 77–88 (2015)
16. Krasowski, N., Beier, T., Knott, G., Koethe, U., Hamprecht, F., Kreshuk, A.: Improving 3D EM data segmentation by joint optimization over boundary evidence and biological priors. In: 2015 IEEE 12th International Symposium on Biomedical Imaging (ISBI), pp. 536–539. IEEE (2015)
17. Liu, T., Jones, C., Seyedhosseini, M., Tasdizen, T.: A modular hierarchical approach to 3D electron microscopy image segmentation. J. Neurosci. Methods **226**, 88–102 (2014)

18. Funke, J., Hamprecht, F.A., Zhang, C.: Learning to segment: training hierarchical segmentation under a topological loss. In: Navab, N., Hornegger, J., Wells, W.M., Frangi, A.F. (eds.) MICCAI 2015. LNCS, vol. 9351, pp. 268–275. Springer, Heidelberg (2015). doi:10.1007/978-3-319-24574-4_32

19. Uzunbas, M.G., Chen, C., Metaxas, D.: An efficient conditional random field approach for automatic and interactive neuron segmentation. Med. Image Anal. **27**, 31–44 (2016)

20. Parag, T., Plaza, S., Scheffer, L.: Small sample learning of superpixel classifiers for EM segmentation. In: Golland, P., Hata, N., Barillot, C., Hornegger, J., Howe, R. (eds.) MICCAI 2014. LNCS, vol. 8673, pp. 389–397. Springer, Heidelberg (2014). doi:10.1007/978-3-319-10404-1_49

21. Parag, T., Ciresan, D.C., Giusti, A.: Efficient classifier training to minimize false merges in electron microscopy segmentation. In: Proceedings of the IEEE International Conference on Computer Vision, pp. 657–665 (2015)

22. Arganda-Carreras, I., Seung, H.S., Vishwanathan, A., Berger, D.: 3D segmentation of neurites in EM images challenge - ISBI 2013 (2013). http://brainiac2.mit.edu/SNEMI3D/. Accessed 16 Feb 2016

23. Deerinck, T.J., Bushong, E.A., Lev-Ram, V., Shu, X., Tsien, R.Y., Ellisman, M.H.: Enhancing serial block-face scanning electron microscopy to enable high resolution 3-D nanohistology of cells and tissues. Microsc. Microanal. **16**(S2), 1138–1139 (2010)

24. Knott, G., Marchman, H., Wall, D., Lich, B.: Serial section scanning electron microscopy of adult brain tissue using focused ion beam milling. J. Neurosci. **28**(12), 2959–2964 (2008)

25. Beucher, S., Meyer, F.: The morphological approach to segmentation: the watershed transformation. Math. Morphol. Image Process. **34**, 433–481 (1993). Marcel Dekker AG

26. Schindelin, J., Arganda-Carreras, I., Frise, E., Kaynig, V., Longair, M., Pietzsch, T., Preibisch, S., Rueden, C., Saalfeld, S., Schmid, B., et al.: Fiji: an open-source platform for biological-image analysis. Nat. Methods **9**(7), 676–682 (2012)

Towards Viewpoint Invariant 3D Human Pose Estimation

Albert Haque$^{(\boxtimes)}$, Boya Peng, Zelun Luo, Alexandre Alahi, Serena Yeung, and Li Fei-Fei

Stanford University, Stanford, CA, USA
ahaque@cs.stanford.edu

Abstract. We propose a viewpoint invariant model for 3D human pose estimation from a single depth image. To achieve this, our discriminative model embeds local regions into a learned viewpoint invariant feature space. Formulated as a multi-task learning problem, our model is able to selectively predict partial poses in the presence of noise and occlusion. Our approach leverages a convolutional and recurrent network architecture with a top-down error feedback mechanism to self-correct previous pose estimates in an end-to-end manner. We evaluate our model on a previously published depth dataset and a newly collected human pose dataset containing 100 K annotated depth images from extreme viewpoints. Experiments show that our model achieves competitive performance on frontal views while achieving state-of-the-art performance on alternate viewpoints.

1 Introduction

Depth sensors are becoming ubiquitous in applications ranging from security to robotics and from entertainment to smart spaces [5]. While recent advances in pose estimation have improved performance on front and side views, most real-world settings present challenging viewpoints such as top or angled views in retail stores, hospital environments, or airport settings. These viewpoints introduce high levels of self-occlusion making human pose estimation difficult for existing algorithms.

Humans are remarkably robust at predicting full rigid-body and articulated poses in these challenging scenarios. However, most work in the human pose estimation literature has addressed relatively constrained settings. There has been a long line of work on generative pose models, where a pose is estimated by constructing a skeleton using templates or priors in a top-down manner [12,16,18,19]. In contrast, discriminative methods directly identify individual body parts, labels, or positions and construct the skeleton in a bottom-up approach [14,15,51,52,54]. However, recent research in both classes primarily focus

---

Electronic supplementary material The online version of this chapter (doi:10.1007/978-3-319-46448-0_10) contains supplementary material, which is available to authorized users.

B. Leibe et al. (Eds.): ECCV 2016, Part I, LNCS 9905, pp. 160–177, 2016.
DOI: 10.1007/978-3-319-46448-0_10

on frontal views with few occlusions despite the abundance of occlusion and partial-pose research in object detection [2–4,7,9,22,23,32,53,61]. Even modern representation learning techniques address human pose estimation from frontal or side views [10,17,34,41,42,59,60]. While the above methods improve human pose estimation, they fail to address viewpoint variances.

In this work we address the problem of viewpoint invariant pose estimation from single depth images. There are two challenges towards this goal. The first challenge is designing a model that is not only rich enough to reason about 3D spatial information but also robust to viewpoint changes. The model must understand both local and global human pose structure. That is, it must fuse techniques from local part-based discriminative models and global skeleton-driven generative models. Additionally, it must be able to reason about 3D volumes, geometric, and viewpoint transformations. The second challenge is that existing real-world depth datasets are often small in size, both in terms of number of frames and number of classes [20,21]. As a result, the use of representation learning methods and viewpoint transfer techniques has been limited.

To address these challenges, our contributions are as follows: First, on the technical side, we embed local pose information into a learned, viewpoint invariant feature space. Furthermore, we extend the iterative error feedback model [10] to model higher-order temporal dependencies (Fig. 1). To handle occlusions, we formulate our model with a multi-task learning objective. Second, we introduce a new dataset of 100 K depth images with pixel-wise body part labels and 3D human joint locations. The dataset consists of extreme cases of viewpoint variance with front, top, and side views of people performing 15 actions with occluded body parts. We evaluate our model on an existing public dataset [21] and our newly collected dataset demonstrating state-of-the-art performance on viewpoint invariant pose estimation.

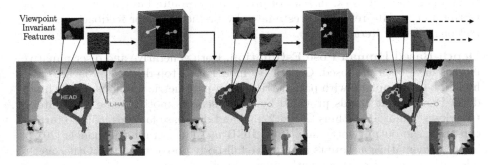

Fig. 1. From a single depth image, our model uses learned viewpoint invariant feature representations to perform 3D human pose estimation with iterative refinement. To provide additional three-dimensional context to the reader, a front view is shown in the lower right of each frame.

2   Related Work

RGB-Based Human Pose Estimation. Several methods have been proposed for human pose estimation, including edge-based histograms of the human-body [48] and silhouette contours [25]. More general techniques using pictorial structures [12,16,19] and deformable part models [18], continued to build appearance models for each local body part independently. Subsequently, higher-level part-based models were developed to capture more complex body part relationships and obtain more discriminative templates [14,15,51,52,54].

These models continued to evolve, attempting to capture even higher-level part features. Convolutional networks [39,40], a class of representation learning methods [8], began to exhibit performance gains not only in human pose estimation, but various areas of computer vision [37]. Since valid human poses represent a much lower-dimensional manifold in the high-dimensional input space, it is difficult to directly regress from input image to output poses with a convolutional network. As a solution to this, researchers framed the problem as a multi-task learning problem where human joints must be first detected then precisely localized [17,41,42]. Jain et al. [34] enforce global pose consistency with a Markov random field representing human anatomical constraints. Follow up work by Tompson et al. [59] combines a convolutional network part-detector with a part-based spatial model into a unified framework.

Because human pose estimation is ultimately a structured prediction task, it is difficult for convolutional networks to correctly regress the full pose in a single pass. Recently, iterative refinement techniques have been proposed to address this issue. In [58], Sun et al. proposed a multi-stage system of convolutional networks for predicting facial point locations. Each stage refines the output from the previous stage given a local region of the input. Building on this work, Deep-Pose [60] uses a cascade of convolutional networks for full-body pose estimation. In another body of work, instead of predicting absolute human joint locations, Carreira et al. [10] refine pose estimates by predicting error feedback (i.e. corrections) at each iteration.

Depth-Based Human Pose Estimation. Both generative and discriminative models have been proposed. Generative models (i.e. top-down approaches) fit a human body template, with parametric or non-parametric methods, to the input data. Dense point clouds provided by depth sensors motivate the use of iterative closest point algorithms [21,26,27,36] and database lookups [65]. To further constrain the output space similar to RGB methods, graphical models [20,29] impose kinematic constraints to improve full-body pose estimation. Other methods such as kernel methods with kinematic chain structures [13] and template fitting with Gaussian mixture models [66] have been proposed.

Discriminative methods (i.e. bottom-up approaches) detect instances of body parts instead of fitting a skeleton template. In [56], Shotton et al. trained a random forest classifier for body part segmentation from a single depth image and used mean shift to estimate joint locations. This work inspired an entire line of depth-based pose estimation research exploring regression tree methods:

Hough forests [24], random ferns [30], and random tree walks [67] have been proposed in recent years.

Occlusion Handling and Viewpoint Invariance. One popular approach to model occlusions is to treat visibility as a binary mask and jointly reason on this mask with the input images [53,61]. Other approaches such as [7,23], include templates for occluded versions of each part. More sophisticated models introduce occlusion priors [9,32] or semantic information [22].

For rigid body pose estimation and 3D object analysis, several descriptors have been proposed. Given the success of SIFT [44], there have been several attempts at embedding rotational and translational invariance [2,55,62]. Other features such as viewpoint invariant 3D feature maps [43], histograms of 3D joint locations [63], multifractal spectrum [64], volumetric attention models [28], and volumetric convolutional filters [45,46] have been proposed for 3D modeling. Instead of proposing invariant features, Ozuysal et al. [50] trained a classifier for each viewpoint. Building on the success of representation learning from RGB, discriminative pose estimation from the depth domain, viewpoint invariant features, and occlusion modeling, we design a model which achieves viewpoint invariant 3D human pose estimation.

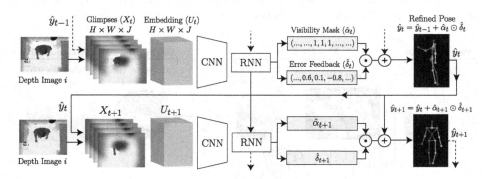

Fig. 2. Model overview. The input to our model is a single depth image. We perform several iterations on this image. At iteration t, the input to our convolutional network is (i) a set of retina-like patches X_t extracted from the input depth image and (ii) the current pose estimate $\hat{y}_{t-1}$. Our model predicts offsets $\hat{\delta}_t$ and selectively applies them to the previous pose estimate based on a predicted visibility mask $\hat{\alpha}_t$. The refined pose at the end of iteration t is denoted by $\hat{y}_t$. Element-wise product is denoted by $\odot$.

3   Model

Overview. The goal of our model is to achieve viewpoint invariant pose estimation. The iterative error feedback mechanism proposed by [10] demonstrates promising results on front and side view RGB images. However, a fundamental challenge remains unsolved: how can a model learn to be viewpoint invariant?

Our core contribution is as follows: we leverage depth data to embed local patches into a learned viewpoint invariant feature space. As a result, we can train a body part detector to be invariant to viewpoint changes. To provide richer context, we also introduce recurrent connections to enable our model to reason on past actions and guide downstream global pose estimation (see Fig. 2).

3.1   Model Architecture

Local Input Representation. One of our goals is to use local body part context to guide downstream global pose prediction. To achieve this, we propose a two-step process. First, we extract a set of patches from the input depth image where each patch is centered around each predicted body part. By feeding these patches into our model, it can reason on low-level, local part information. We transform these patches into patches called *glimpses* [38,47]. A glimpse is a retina-like encoding of the original input that encodes pixels further from the center with a progressively lower resolution. As a result, the model must focus on specific input regions with high resolution while maintaining some, but not all spatial information. These glimpses are stacked and denoted by $X \in \mathbb{R}^{H \times W \times J}$ where J is the number of joints, H is the glimpse height, and W is the glimpse and width. Glimpses for iteration t are generated using the predicted pose $\hat{y}_{t-1}$ from the previous iteration $t-1$. When $t = 0$, we use the average pose $\hat{y}_0$.

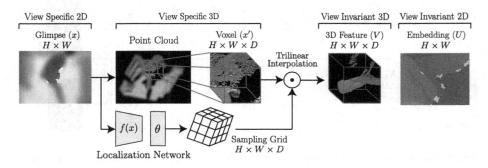

Fig. 3. Learned viewpoint invariant embedding for a single glimpse. A single glimpse x is converted into a voxel x'. A localization network $f(x)$ regresses 3D transformation parameters θ which are applied to x' with a trilinear sampler. The resulting feature map V is projected onto 2D which gives the embedding U.

Learned Viewpoint Invariant Embedding. We embed the input into a learned, viewpoint invariant feature space (see Fig. 3). Since each glimpse x is a real world depth map, we can convert each glimpse into a voxel $x' \in \mathbb{R}^{H \times W \times D}$ where D is the depth of the voxel. We refer to *voxel* as a volumetric representation of the depth map and not a full 3D model. This representation allows us to transform the glimpse in 3D thereby simulating occlusions and geometric variations which may be present from other viewpoints.

Given the voxel x', we now transform it into a viewpoint invariant feature map $V \in \mathbb{R}^{H \times W \times D}$. We follow [33] in a two-step process: First, we use a *localization network* $f(\cdot)$ to estimate a set of 3D transformation parameters θ which will be applied to the voxel x'. Second, we compute a *sampling grid* defined as $G \in \mathbb{R}^{H \times W \times D}$. Each coordinate of the sampling grid, i.e. $G_{ijk} = (x_{ijk}^{(G)}, y_{ijk}^{(G)}, z_{ijk}^{(G)})$, defines where we must apply a sampling kernel in voxel x' to compute V_{ijk} of the output feature map. However, since $x_{ijk}^{(G)}, y_{ijk}^{(G)}$ and $z_{ijk}^{(G)}$ are real-valued, we convolve x' with a sampling kernel, $\mathrm{ker}(\cdot)$, and define the output feature map V:

$$V_{ijk} = \sum_{a=1}^{H} \sum_{b=1}^{W} \sum_{c=1}^{D} x'_{abc} \, \mathrm{ker}\left(\frac{a - x_{ijk}^{(G)}}{H}\right) \mathrm{ker}\left(\frac{b - y_{ijk}^{(G)}}{W}\right) \mathrm{ker}\left(\frac{c - z_{ijk}^{(G)}}{D}\right) \quad (1)$$

where the kernel $\mathrm{ker}(\cdot) = \max(0, 1 - |\cdot|)$ is the trilinear sampling kernel. As a final step, we project the viewpoint invariant 3D feature map V into a viewpoint invariant 2D feature map U:

$$U_{ij} = \sum_{c=1}^{D} V_{ijc} \quad \text{such that} \quad U \in \mathbb{R}^{H \times W} \quad (2)$$

Notice that Eqs. (1) and (2) are linear functions applied to the voxel x'. As a result, upstream gradients can flow smoothly through these mathematical units. The resulting U now represents two-dimensional viewpoint invariant representation of the input glimpse. At this point, U is used as input into a convolutional network for human body part detection and error feedback prediction.

Convolutional and Recurrent Networks. As previously mentioned, our goal is to use local input patches to guide downstream global pose predictions. We stack the viewpoint invariant feature maps U for each joint to form a $H \times W \times J$ tensor. This tensor is fed to a convolutional network. Through the hierarchical receptive fields of the convolutional network, the network's output is a global representation of the human pose. Directly regressing body part positions from the dense activation layers[1] has proven to be difficult due to the highly non-linear mapping present in traditional human pose estimation [59].

Inspired by [10]'s work in the RGB domain, we adopt an iterative refinement technique which uses multiple steps to fine-tune the pose by correcting previous pose estimates. In [10], each refinement step is only indirectly influenced by previous iterations through the accumulation of error feedback. We claim that these refinement iterations should have a more direct and shared temporal representation. To remedy this, we introduce recurrent connections between each iteration; specifically a long short term memory (LSTM) module [31]. This enables our model to directly access the underlying hidden network state which generated prior feedback and model higher-order temporal dependencies.

---

[1] This is referred to as *direct prediction* in our experiments in Table 3.

3.2   Multi-task Loss

Our primary goal is to achieve viewpoint invariance. In extreme cases such as top views, many human joints are occluded. To be robust to such occlusions, we want our model to reason on the visibility of joints. We formulate the optimization procedure as a multi-task problem consisting of two objectives: (i) a body-part detection task, where the goal is to determine whether a body part is visible or occluded in the input and (ii) a pose regression task, where we predict the offsets to the correct real world 3D position of visible human body joints.

Body-Part Detection. For body part detection, the goal is to determine whether a particular body part is visible or occluded in the input. This is denoted by the predicted visibility mask $\hat{\alpha}$ which is a $1 \times J$ binary vector, where J is the total number of body joints. The ground truth visibility mask is denoted by α. If a body part is predicted to be visible, then $\hat{\alpha}_j = 1$, otherwise $\hat{\alpha}_j = 0$ denotes occlusion. The visibility mask $\hat{\alpha}$ is computed using a softmax over the unnormalized log probabilities p generated by the LSTM. Hence, our objective is to minimize the cross-entropy. The visibility loss for a single example is:

$$\mathcal{L}_\alpha = -\sum_{j=1}^{J} \alpha_j \log(p_j) + (1 - \alpha_j) \log(1 - p_j) \tag{3}$$

Regardless of the ground truth and the predicted visibility mask, the above formulation forces our model to improve its part detection. Additionally, it allows for occluded body part recovery if the ground truth visibility is fixed to $\alpha = 1$.

Partial Error Feedback. Ultimately, our goal is to predict the location of the joint corresponding to each visible human body part. To achieve this, we refine our previous pose prediction by learning correction offsets (i.e. feedback) denoted by δ. Furthermore, we only learn correction offsets for joints that are visible. At each time step, a regression predicts offsets $\hat{\delta}$ which are used to update the current pose estimate $\hat{y}$. Specifically: $\hat{\delta}, \delta, \hat{y}, y \in \mathbb{R}^{J \times 3}$ denote real-world (x, y, z) positions of each joint.

$$\mathcal{L}_\delta = \sum_{j=1}^{J} \mathbb{1}\{\alpha_j = 1\} ||\hat{\delta}_j - \delta_j||_2^2 \tag{4}$$

The loss shown in (4) is motivated by our goal of predicting partial poses. Consider the case of when the right knee is not visible in the input. If our model successfully labels the right knee as occluded, we wish to prevent the error feedback loss from backpropagating through our network. To achieve this, we include the indicator term $\mathbb{1}\{\alpha_j = 1\}$ which only backpropagates pose error feedback if a particular joint is visible in the original image. A secondary benefit is that we do not force the regressor to output dummy real values (if a joint is occluded) which may skew the model's understanding of output magnitude.

Global Loss. The resulting objective is the linear combination of the error feedback cost function for all joints and the detection cost function for all body parts: $\mathcal{L} = \lambda_\alpha \mathcal{L}_\alpha + \lambda_\delta \mathcal{L}_\delta$. The mixing parameters λ_α and λ_δ define the relative weight of each sub-objective.

3.3 Training and Optimization

We train the full model end-to-end in a single step of optimization. We train the convolutional and recurrent network from scratch with all weights initialized from a Gaussian with $\mu = 0, \sigma = 0.001$. Gradients are computed using $\mathcal{L}$ and flow through the recurrent and convolutional networks. We use the Adam [35] optimizer with an initial learning rate of 1×10^{-5}, $\beta_1 = 0.9$, and $\beta_2 = 0.999$. An exponential learning rate decay schedule is applied with a decay rate of 0.99 every 1,000 iterations.

4 Datasets

We evaluate our model on a publicly available dataset that has been used by recent state-of-the-art human pose methods. To more rigorously evaluate our model, we also collected a new dataset consisting of varied camera viewpoints. See Fig. 4 for samples.

Previous Depth Datasets. We use the Stanford EVAL dataset [21] which consists of 9 K front-facing depth images. The dataset contains 3 people performing 8 action sequences each. The EVAL dataset was recorded using the Microsoft Kinect camera at 30 fps. Similar to leave-one-out cross validation, we adopt a leave-one-out train-test procedure. One person is selected as the test set and the other two people are designated as the training set. This is performed three times such that each person is the test set once.

(a) EVAL [21]   (b) ITOP (Front)   (c) ITOP (Top)

Fig. 4. Examples images from each of the datasets. Our newly collected ITOP dataset contains challenging front and top view images.

Invariant-Top View Dataset (ITOP). Existing depth datasets for pose estimation are often small in size, both in the number of people and number of frames per person [20,21]. To address these issues, we collected a new dataset consisting of 100 K real-world depth images from multiple camera viewpoints. Named ITOP, the dataset consists of 20 people performing 15 action sequences each. Each depth image is labeled with real-world 3D joint locations from the point of view of the respective camera. The dataset consists of two "views," namely the front/side view and the top view. The frontal view contains 360° views of each person, although not necessarily uniformly distributed. The top view contains images captured solely from the top (i.e. camera on the ceiling pointed down to the floor).

Data Collection. Two Asus Xtion PRO cameras were used. One camera was placed on the ceiling facing down while another camera was from a traditional front-facing viewpoint. To annotate each frame, we used a series of steps that progressively involved more human supervision if necessary. First, 3D joints were estimated using [56] from the front-facing camera. These coordinates were then transformed into the respective world coordinate system of each camera in the system. Second, we used an iterative ground truth error correction technique based on per-pixel labeling using k-nearest neighbors and center of mass convergence. Finally, humans manually validated, corrected, and discarded noisy frames. On average, the human labeling procedure took one second per frame.

5   Experiments

5.1   Evaluation Metrics

We evaluate our model using two metrics. As introduced in [6], we use the percentage of correct keypoints (PCKh) with a variable threshold. This metric defines a successful human joint localization if the predicted joint is within 50 % of the head segment length to the ground truth joint.

For summary tables and figures, we use the mean average precision (mAP) which is the average precision for all human body parts. Precision is reported for individual body parts. A successful detection occurs when the predicted joint is less than 10 cm from the ground truth in 3D space.

5.2   Implementation Details

Our model is implemented in TensorFlow [1]. We use mini-batches of size 10 and 10 refinement steps per batch. We use the VGG-16 [57] architecture for our convolutional network but instead modify the first layer to accommodate the increased number of input channels. Additionally, we reduce the number of neurons in the dense layers to 2048. We remove the final softmax layer and use the second dense layer activations as input into a recurrent network. For the recurrent network, we use a long short term memory (LSTM) module [31] consisting of 2048 hidden units. The LSTM hidden state is duplicated and passed to a softmax layer and a regression layer for loss computation and pose-error computation. The model is trained from scratch.

The grid generator is a convolutional network with four layers. Each layer contains: (i) a convolutional layer with 32 filters of size 3×3 with stride 1 and padding 1, (ii) a rectified linear unit [49], (iii) a max-pooling over a 2×2 region

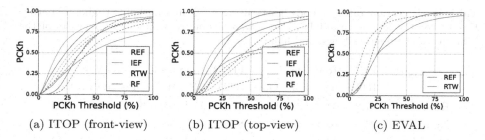

(a) ITOP (front-view)   (b) ITOP (top-view)   (c) EVAL

Fig. 5. Percentage of correct keypoints based on the head (PCKh). Colors indicate different methods. Solid lines indicate full body performance. Dashed lines indicate upper body performance. Higher is better. (Color figure online)

with stride 2. The fourth layer's output is $10 \times 10 \times 32$ and is connected to a dense layer consisting of 12 output nodes which defines θ. The specific 3D transformation parameters are defined in [33].

To generate glimpses for the first refinement iteration, the mean 3D pose from the training set is used. Glimpses are 160 pixels in height and width and centered at each joint location (in the image plane). Each glimpse consists of 4 patches where each patch is quadratically downsampled according to the patch number (i.e. its distance from the glimpse center). The input to our convolutional network is $160 \times 160 \times J$ where J is the number of body part joints.

5.3   Comparison with State-of-the-Art

We compare our model to three state-of-the-art methods: random forests [56], random tree walks (RTW) [67], and iterative error feedback (IEF) [10]. One of our primary goals is to achieve viewpoint invariance. To evaluate this, we perform three sets of experiments, progressing in level of difficulty. First, we train and test all models on front view images. This is the classical human pose estimation task. Second, we train and test all models on top view images. This is similar to the classical pose estimation task but from a different viewpoint. Third, we train on front view images and test on top view images. This is the most difficult experiment and truly tests a model's ability to learn viewpoint transfer.

Baselines. We give a brief overview of the baseline algorithms:

1. The random forest model [56] consists of multiple decision trees that traverse each pixel to find the body part labels for that pixel. Once pixels are classified into body parts, joint positions are found with mean shift [11].
2. Random tree walk (RTW) [67] trains a regression tree to estimate the probability distribution to the direction toward the particular joint, relative to the current position. At test time, the direction for the random walk is randomly chosen from a set of representative directions.
3. Iterative error feedback (IEF) [10] is a self-correcting model used to progressively make changes to an initial pose estimation by using *error feedback*.

Table 1. Detection rates of body parts using a 10 cm threshold. Higher is better. Results for the left and right body part were averaged. Upper body consists of the head, neck, shoulders, elbows, and hands.

Body part	ITOP (front-view)				ITOP (top-view)				EVAL	
	RTW	RF	IEF	Ours	RTW	RF	IEF	Ours	RTW	Ours
Head	97.8	63.8	96.2	98.1	98.4	95.4	83.8	98.1	90.9	93.9
Neck	95.8	86.4	85.2	97.5	82.2	98.5	50.0	97.6	87.4	94.7
Shoulders	94.1	83.3	77.2	96.5	91.8	89.0	67.3	96.1	87.8	87.0
Elbows	77.9	73.2	45.4	73.3	80.1	57.4	40.2	86.2	27.5	45.5
Hands	70.5	51.3	30.9	68.7	76.9	49.1	39.0	85.5	32.3	39.6
Torso	93.8	65.0	84.7	85.6	68.2	80.5	30.5	72.9	—	—
Hips	80.3	50.8	83.5	72.0	55.7	20.0	38.9	61.2	—	—
Knees	68.8	65.7	81.8	69.0	53.9	2.6	54.0	51.6	83.4	86.0
Feet	68.4	61.3	80.9	60.8	28.7	0.0	62.4	51.5	90.0	92.3
Upper body	84.8	70.7	61.0	84.0	84.8	73.1	51.7	91.4	59.2	73.8
Lower body	72.5	59.3	82.1	67.3	46.1	7.5	53.3	54.7	86.7	89.2
Full body	80.5	65.8	71.0	77.4	68.2	47.4	51.2	75.5	68.3	74.1

Train on Front Views, Test on Front Views. Table 1 shows the average precision for each joint using a 10 cm threshold and the overall mean average precision (mAP) while Fig. 5 shows the PCKh for all models. IEF and the random forest methods were not evaluated on the EVAL dataset. Random forest depends on a per-pixel body part labeling, which is not provided by EVAL. IEF was unable to converge to comparable results on the EVAL dataset. We discuss the ITOP results below. For frontal views, RTW achieves a mAP of 84.8 and 80.5 for the upper and full body, respectively. Our recurrent error feedback (REF) model performs similarly to RTW, achieving a mAP of 2 to 3 points less. The random forest algorithm achieves the lowest full body mAP of 65.8. This could be attributed to the limited amount of training data. The original algorithm [56] was trained on 900 K synthetic depth images.

We show qualitative results in Fig. 6. The front-view ITOP dataset is shown in columns (c) and (d). Both our model and IEF make similar mistakes: both models sometimes fail to learn sufficient feedback to converge to the correct body part location. Since we do not impose joint position constraints or enforce skeleton priors, our method incorrectly predicts the elbow location.

Train on Top View, Test on Top View. Figure 6 shows examples of qualitative results from frontal and top down views for Shotton et al. [56] and random tree walk (RTW) [67]. For the top-down view, we show only 8 joints on the upper body (i.e. head, neck, left shoulder, right shoulder, left elbow, right elbow, left hand, and right hand) as the lower body joints are almost always occluded. RF and RTW give reasonable results when all joints are visible (see Fig. 6a and c)

Fig. 6. Qualitative results without viewpoint transfer

but do not perform well in the case of occlusion (Fig. 6b and d). For the random forest method, we can see from Fig. 6b that the prediction for the occluded right elbow is topologically invalid though both right shoulder and hand are visible and correctly predicted. This is because the model doesn't take into account the topological information among joints, so it is not able to modify its prediction for one joint base on the predicted positions of neighboring joints. For RTW, Fig. 6b shows that the predicted position for right hand goes to the right leg. Though legs and hands possess very different depth information, the model mistook the right leg for right hand when the hand is occluded and the leg appears in the common spatial location of a hand.

Table 2. Detection rate for the viewpoint transfer task

Body part	RTW	RF	IEF	Our model
Head	1.5	48.1	47.9	55.6
Neck	8.1	5.9	39.0	40.9
Torso	3.9	4.7	41.9	35.0
Upper body	2.2	19.7	23.9	29.4
Full body	2.0	10.8	17.4	20.4

Train on Frontal Views, Test on Top Views. This is the most difficult task for 3D pose estimation algorithms since the test set contains significant scale and shape differences from the training data. Results are shown in Table 2. RTW gives the lowest performance as the model relies heavily on topological information. If the prediction for an initial joint fails, error will accumulate onto subsequent joints. Both deep learning methods are able to localize joints despite the viewpoint change. IEF achieves a 47.9 detection rate for the head while our model achieves a 55.6 detection rate. This can be attributed to the proximity of upper body joints in both viewpoints. The head, neck, and torso locations are similarly positioned across viewpoints.

Runtime Analysis. Methods which employ deep learning techniques often require more computation for forward propagation compared to non deep learning approaches. Our model requires 1.7 s per frame (10 iterations, forward-pass only) while the random tree walk requires 0.1 s per frame. While this is dependent on implementation details, it does illustrate the tradeoff between speed and performance.

5.4   Ablation Studies

To further gauge the effectiveness of our model, we analyze each component of our model and provide both quantitative and qualitative analyses. Specifically, we evaluate the effect of error feedback and discuss the relevance of the input glimpse representation.

Effect of Recurrent Connections. We analyze the effect of recurrent connections compared to regular iterative error feedback and direct prediction. To evaluate iterative feedback, we use our final model but remove the LSTM module and regress the visibility mask $\hat{\alpha}$ and error feedback $\hat{\delta}$ using the dense layer activations. Note that we still use a multi-task loss and glimpse inputs. Direct prediction does not involve feedback but instead attempts to directly regress correct pose locations in a single pass.

Table 3. Detection rate of our model with different feedback mechanisms on the ITOP front dataset. Rows denote a different body parts. Model is trained without viewpoint transfer and the detection threshold is 10 cm.

Body part	Direct prediction		Iterative feedback		Recurrent feedback	
	Front	Top	Front	Top	Front	Top
Head	27.8	32.1	96.2	83.8	98.1	98.1
Hands	1.3	1.8	30.9	39.0	68.7	85.5
Upper body	15.0	17.8	61.0	51.7	84.0	91.4
Full body	21.8	23.8	71.0	51.2	77.4	75.5

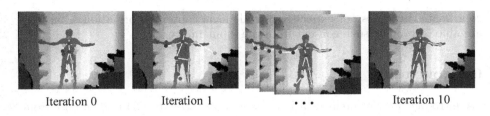

| Iteration 0 | Iteration 1 | ⋯ | Iteration 10 |

Fig. 7. Our model's estimated pose at different iterations of the refinement process. Initialized with the average pose, it converges to the correct pose over time.

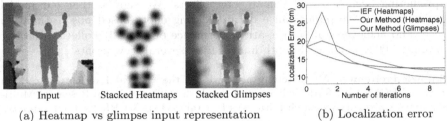

| Input | Stacked Heatmaps | Stacked Glimpses |

(a) Heatmap vs glimpse input representation   (b) Localization error

Fig. 8. Comparison of heatmap and glimpse input representations. (a) Multi-channel heatmap and glimpse input projected onto a 2D image. (b) Localization error as a function of refinement iterations. Lower error is better.

Quantitative results are shown in Table 3. Direct prediction, as expected, performs poorly as it is very difficult to regress exact 3D joint locations in a single pass. Iterative-based approaches significantly improve performance by 30 points. It is clear that recurrent connections improve performance, especially in the top-view case where recurrent feedback achieves 91.4 upper body mAP while iterative feedback achieves 51.7 upper body mAP.

Figure 7 shows how our model updates the pose over time. Consistent across all images, the first iteration always involves a large, seemingly random transformation of the pose. This can be thought of as the model is "looking around" the initial pose estimate. Once the model understands the initial surrounding area, it returns to the human body and begins to fine-tune the pose prediction, as shown in iteration 10. Figure 8b quantitatively illustrates this result.

Effect of Glimpses. Our motivation for glimpses is to provide additional local context to our model to guide downstream, global pose estimation. In Fig. 8 we evaluate the performance of glimpses vs indicator masks (i.e. heatmaps). Figure 8b shows that glimpses do provide more context for the global pose prediction task. As the number of refinement iterations increases, using glimpses, the localization error for each joint is less than the error with heatmaps. By looking at Fig. 8a, it becomes apparent that heatmaps provide limited spatial information. The indicator mask is a way of encoding two-dimensional body part coordinates but does not explicitly provide local context information. Glimpses are able to provide such context from the input image.

6   Conclusion

We introduced a viewpoint invariant model that estimates 3D human pose from a single depth image. Our model is formulated as a deep discriminative model that attends to glimpses in the input. Using a multi-task optimization objective, our model is able to selectively predict partial poses by using a predicted visibility mask. This enables our model to iteratively improve its pose estimates by predicting occlusion and human joint offsets. We showed that our model achieves competitive performance on an existing depth-based pose estimation dataset and achieves state-of-the-art performance on a newly collected dataset containing 100 K annotated depth images from several view points.

Acknowledgements. We gratefully acknowledge the Clinical Excellence Research Center (CERC) at Stanford Medicine and thank the Office of Naval Research, Multidisciplinary University Research Initiatives Program (ONR MURI) for their support.

References

1. Abadi, M., Agarwal, A., Barham, P., Brevdo, E., Chen, Z., Citro, C., Corrado, G.S., Davis, A., Dean, J., Devin, M., et al.: Tensorflow: large-scale machine learning on heterogeneous systems (2015). Software available from tensorflow.org
2. Alahi, A., Bierlaire, M., Kunt, M.: Object detection and matching with mobile cameras collaborating with fixed cameras (2008)
3. Alahi, A., Bierlaire, M., Vandergheynst, P.: Robust real-time pedestrians detection in urban environments with low-resolution cameras (2014)
4. Alahi, A., Boursier, Y., Jacques, L., Vandergheynst, P.: A sparsity constrained inverse problem to locate people in a network of cameras. In: Digital Signal Processing. IEEE (2009)
5. Alahi, A., Ramanathan, V., Fei-Fei, L.: Socially-aware large-scale crowd forecasting. In: CVPR (2014)
6. Andriluka, M., Pishchulin, L., Gehler, P., Schiele, B.: 2d human pose estimation: new benchmark and state of the art analysis. In: CVPR (2014)
7. Azizpour, H., Laptev, I.: Object detection using strongly-supervised deformable part models. In: Fitzgibbon, A., Lazebnik, S., Perona, P., Sato, Y., Schmid, C. (eds.) ECCV 2012. LNCS, vol. 7572, pp. 836–849. Springer, Heidelberg (2012). doi:10.1007/978-3-642-33718-5_60
8. Bengio, Y., Courville, A., Vincent, P.: Representation learning: a review and new perspectives. In: PAMI (2013)
9. Bonde, U., Badrinarayanan, V., Cipolla, R.: Robust instance recognition in presence of occlusion and clutter. In: Fleet, D., Pajdla, T., Schiele, B., Tuytelaars, T. (eds.) ECCV 2014. LNCS, vol. 8690, pp. 520–535. Springer, Heidelberg (2014). doi:10.1007/978-3-319-10605-2_34
10. Carreira, J., Agrawal, P., Fragkiadaki, K., Malik, J.: Human pose estimation with iterative error feedback. In: CVPR (2016)

11. Comaniciu, D., Meer, P.: Mean shift: a robust approach toward feature space analysis. In: PAMI (2002)
12. Dantone, M., Gall, J., Leistner, C., Gool, L.: Human pose estimation using body parts dependent joint regressors. In: CVPR (2013)
13. Ding, M., Fan, G.: Articulated gaussian kernel correlation for human pose estimation. In: CVPR Workshops (2015)
14. Eichner, M., Ferrari, V.: Appearance sharing for collective human pose estimation. In: Lee, K.M., Matsushita, Y., Rehg, J.M., Hu, Z. (eds.) ACCV 2012. LNCS, vol. 7724, pp. 138–151. Springer, Heidelberg (2013). doi:10.1007/978-3-642-37331-2_11
15. Eichner, M., Ferrari, V., Zurich, S.: Better appearance models for pictorial structures. In: BMVC (2009)
16. Eichner, M., Marin-Jimenez, M., Zisserman, A., Ferrari, V.: 2d articulated human pose estimation and retrieval in (almost) unconstrained still images. IJCV **99**(2), 190–2014 (2012)
17. Fan, X., Zheng, K., Lin, Y., Wang, S.: Combining local appearance and holistic view: dual-source deep neural networks for human pose estimation. In: CVPR (2015)
18. Felzenszwalb, P.F., Girshick, R.B., McAllester, D., Ramanan, D.: Object detection with discriminatively trained part-based models. In: PAMI (2010)
19. Felzenszwalb, P.F., Huttenlocher, D.P.: Pictorial structures for object recognition. IJCV **61**(1), 55–79 (2005). Springer
20. Ganapathi, V., Plagemann, C., Koller, D., Thrun, S.: Real time motion capture using a single time-of-flight camera. In: CVPR (2010)
21. Ganapathi, V., Plagemann, C., Koller, D., Thrun, S.: Real-time human pose tracking from range data. In: Fitzgibbon, A., Lazebnik, S., Perona, P., Sato, Y., Schmid, C. (eds.) ECCV 2012. LNCS, vol. 7577, pp. 738–751. Springer, Heidelberg (2012). doi:10.1007/978-3-642-33783-3_53
22. Gao, T., Packer, B., Koller, D.: A segmentation-aware object detection model with occlusion handling. In: CVPR (2011)
23. Ghiasi, G., Yang, Y., Ramanan, D., Fowlkes, C.: Parsing occluded people. In: CVPR (2014)
24. Girshick, R., Shotton, J., Kohli, P., Criminisi, A., Fitzgibbon, A.: Efficient regression of general-activity human poses from depth images. In: ICCV (2011)
25. Grauman, K., Shakhnarovich, G., Darrell, T.: Inferring 3d structure with a statistical image-based shape model. In: ICCV (2003)
26. Grest, D., Woetzel, J., Koch, R.: Nonlinear body pose estimation from depth images. In: Kropatsch, W.G., Sablatnig, R., Hanbury, A. (eds.) DAGM 2005. LNCS, vol. 3663, pp. 285–292. Springer, Heidelberg (2005). doi:10.1007/11550518_36
27. Haehnel, D., Thrun, S., Burgard, W.: An extension of the ICP algorithm for modeling nonrigid objects with mobile robots. In: IJCAI (2003)
28. Haque, A., Alahi, A., Fei-Fei, L.: Recurrent attention models for depth-based person identification. In: CVPR (2016)
29. He, L., Wang, G., Liao, Q., Xue, J.H.: Depth-images-based pose estimation using regression forests and graphical models. Neurocomputing **164**, 210–219 (2015). Elsevier
30. Hesse, N., Stachowiak, G., Breuer, T., Arens, M.: Estimating body pose of infants in depth images using random ferns. In: CVPR Workshops (2015)
31. Hochreiter, S., Schmidhuber, J.: Long short-term memory. Neural Comput. **9**, 1735–1780 (1997). MIT Press

32. Hsiao, E., Hebert, M.: Occlusion reasoning for object detectionunder arbitrary viewpoint. In: PAMI (2014)
33. Jaderberg, M., Simonyan, K., Zisserman, A., et al.: Spatial transformer networks. In: NIPS (2015)
34. Jain, A., Tompson, J., Andriluka, M., Taylor, G.W., Bregler, C.: Learning human pose estimation features with convolutional networks. In: ICLR (2013)
35. Kingma, D., Ba, J.: Adam: a method for stochastic optimization. In: ICLR (2014)
36. Knoop, S., Vacek, S., Dillmann, R.: Sensor fusion for 3d human body tracking with an articulated 3d body model. In: ICRA (2006)
37. Krizhevsky, A., Sutskever, I., Hinton, G.E.: Imagenet classification with deep convolutional neural networks. In: NIPS (2012)
38. Larochelle, H., Hinton, G.E.: Learning to combine foveal glimpses with a third-order boltzmann machine. In: NIPS (2010)
39. LeCun, Y., Bengio, Y.: Convolutional networks for images, speech, and time series. In: Arbib, M.A. (ed.) The Handbook of Brain Theory and Neural Networks. MIT Press, Cambridge (1995)
40. LeCun, Y., Boser, B., Denker, J., Henderson, D., Howard, R.E., Hubbard, W., Jackel, L.: Handwritten digit recognition with a back-propagation network. In: NIPS (1990)
41. Li, S., Liu, Z.Q., Chan, A.: Heterogeneous multi-task learning for human pose estimation with deep convolutional neural network. IJCV **113**, 19–36 (2015)
42. Li, S., Zhang, W., Chan, A.B.: Maximum-margin structured learning with deep networks for 3d human pose estimation. In: ICCV (2015)
43. Liebelt, J., Schmid, C., Schertler, K.: Viewpoint-independent object class detection using 3d feature maps. In: CVPR (2008)
44. Lowe, D.G.: Object recognition from local scale-invariant features. In: ICCV (1999)
45. Maturana, D., Scherer, S.: 3d convolutional neural networks for landing zone detection from lidar. In: ICRA (2015)
46. Maturana, D., Scherer, S.: Voxnet: a 3d convolutional neural network for real-time object recognition. In: Intelligent Robots and Systems (2015)
47. Mnih, V., Heess, N., Graves, A., et al.: Recurrent models of visual attention. In: NIPS (2014)
48. Mori, G., Malik, J.: Estimating human body configurations using shape context matching. In: Heyden, A., Sparr, G., Nielsen, M., Johansen, P. (eds.) ECCV 2002. LNCS, vol. 2352, pp. 666–680. Springer, Heidelberg (2002). doi:10.1007/3-540-47977-5_44
49. Nair, V., Hinton, G.E.: Rectified linear units improve restricted boltzmann machines. In: ICML (2010)
50. Ozuysal, M., Lepetit, V., Fua, P.: Pose estimation for category specific multiview object localization. In: CVPR (2009)
51. Pishchulin, L., Andriluka, M., Gehler, P., Schiele, B.: Poselet conditioned pictorial structures. In: CVPR (2013)
52. Pishchulin, L., Andriluka, M., Gehler, P., Schiele, B.: Strong appearance and expressive spatial models for human pose estimation. In: ICCV (2013)
53. Rafi, U., Gall, J., Leibe, B.: A semantic occlusion model for human pose estimation from a single depth image. In: CVPR Workshops (2015)
54. Sapp, B., Taskar, B.: Modec: multimodal decomposable models for human pose estimation. In: CVPR (2013)
55. Savarese, S., Fei-Fei, L.: 3d generic object categorization, localization and pose estimation. In: ICCV (2007)

56. Shotton, J., Sharp, T., Kipman, A., Fitzgibbon, A., Finocchio, M., Blake, A., Cook, M., Moore, R.: Real-time human pose recognition in parts from single depth images. In: CVPR (2011)
57. Simonyan, K., Zisserman, A.: Very deep convolutional networks for large-scale image recognition. In: ICLR (2015)
58. Sun, Y., Wang, X., Tang, X.: Deep convolutional network cascade for facial point detection. In: CVPR (2013)
59. Tompson, J.J., Jain, A., LeCun, Y., Bregler, C.: Joint training of a convolutional network and a graphical model for human pose estimation. In: NIPS (2014)
60. Toshev, A., Szegedy, C.: Deeppose: human pose estimation via deep neural networks. In: CVPR (2014)
61. Wang, T., He, X., Barnes, N.: Learning structured hough voting for joint object detection and occlusion reasoning. In: CVPR (2013)
62. Wu, C., Clipp, B., Li, X., Frahm, J.M., Pollefeys, M.: 3d model matching with viewpoint-invariant patches. In: CVPR (2008)
63. Xia, L., Chen, C.C., Aggarwal, J.: View invariant human action recognition using histograms of 3d joints. In: CVPR Workshops (2012)
64. Xu, Y., Ji, H., Fermüller, C.: Viewpoint invariant texture description using fractal analysis. IJCV **83**, 85–100 (2009)
65. Ye, M., Wang, X., Yang, R., Ren, L., Pollefeys, M.: Accurate 3d pose estimation from a single depth image. In: ICCV (2011)
66. Ye, M., Yang, R.: Real-time simultaneous pose and shape estimation for articulated objects using a single depth camera. In: CVPR (2014)
67. Yub Jung, H., Lee, S., Seok Heo, Y., Dong Yun, I.: Random tree walk toward instantaneous 3d human pose estimation. In: CVPR (2015)

Person Re-Identification by Unsupervised ℓ_1 Graph Learning

Elyor Kodirov$^{(\boxtimes)}$, Tao Xiang, Zhenyong Fu, and Shaogang Gong

School of EECS, Queen Mary University of London, London, UK
{e.kodirov,t.xiang,z.fu,s.gong}@qmul.ac.uk

Abstract. Most existing person re-identification (Re-ID) methods are based on supervised learning of a discriminative distance metric. They thus require a large amount of labelled training image pairs which severely limits their scalability. In this work, we propose a novel unsupervised Re-ID approach which requires no labelled training data yet is able to capture discriminative information for cross-view identity matching. Our model is based on a new graph regularised dictionary learning algorithm. By introducing a ℓ_1-norm graph Laplacian term, instead of the conventional squared ℓ_2-norm, our model is robust against outliers caused by dramatic changes in background, pose, and occlusion typical in a Re-ID scenario. Importantly we propose to learn jointly the graph and representation resulting in further alleviation of the effects of data outliers. Experiments on four benchmark datasets demonstrate that the proposed model significantly outperforms the state-of-the-art unsupervised learning based alternatives whilst being extremely efficient to compute.

Keywords: Unsupervised person Re-ID · Dictionary learning · Robust graph regularisation · Graph learning

1 Introduction

The problem of matching people across non-overlapping cameras, known as person re-identification (Re-ID), has drawn a great deal of attention recently [20,53]. It remains an unsolved problem due to two reasons: (1) A person's appearance often changes dramatically across cameras views due to occlusion, lighting, illumination and pose changes; (2) Many people in public spaces wear similar clothes (e.g. dark coats, jeans) thus having similar visual appearance.

Most recent Re-ID methods are based on supervised learning. Given a set of labelled training data consisting of images of people paired across camera views according to identity, a distance metric is learned either using hand-crafted features [9,14,19,25,31,37,38,46,48,49,55,56,58,60], or end-to-end using deep

Electronic supplementary material The online version of this chapter (doi:10. 1007/978-3-319-46448-0_11) contains supplementary material, which is available to authorized users.

© Springer International Publishing AG 2016
B. Leibe et al. (Eds.): ECCV 2016, Part I, LNCS 9905, pp. 178–195, 2016.
DOI: 10.1007/978-3-319-46448-0_11

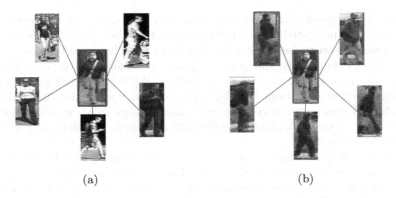

(a)   (b)

Fig. 1. An illustration of graph learning for person re-id. (a) A graph constructed in the original low-level feature space; (b) A graph learned using the proposed model in this work. One graph node and its five connected neighbours are shown, with the neighbour capturing the same person highlighted in red. (Color figure online)

neural networks [2,36]. However, they require images of hundreds or more people to be paired across each pair of camera views which is both tedious and sometimes not possible – some people do not reappear in other camera views. This severely limits the scalability of the existing methods making them unsuitable for practical large scale Re-ID tasks. To overcome this problem, a number of unsupervised Re-ID methods have been proposed [30,41,54,57]. However, without labelled training data, they can only focus on learning salient and view invariant representations. Their performance is thus much weaker compared to the supervised methods. This is because they are unable to learn the cross-view discriminative information effectively, critical for matching the same person whilst separating the person from imposters of similar appearance. Due to their uncompetitiveness in published benchmarking metrics, these unsupervised learning models have received little attention when practicality and scalability are not considered in current benchmarking.

In this work, we propose to learn a low-dimensional feature representation from a set of unlabelled data that can be easily collected. To learn a feature representation that is both view-invariant and discriminative, we exploit dictionary learning models that are shared across camera views. It is easy to understand how a representation obtained by dictionary learning can be view-invariant and low-dimensional – dictionary learning is widely used as an unsupervised model for dimensionality reduction [1,28,43]; and by sharing the same dictionary across camera views, it intrinsically requires that the learned representation to be view-invariant. It is the discriminative part that is non-trivial: How can we enforce that the learned representation is good for matching people across camera views, without the discriminative information from a set of paired training data?

Our solution is to relax the definition of discriminativity. Consider each dictionary word as a new feature dimension, a learned dictionary defines a subspace, into which the original data points represented by high-dimensional low-level feature vectors are projected. Instead of enforcing that data points corresponding to the *same* person to be as close as possible whilst being further away from other people in the learned subspace as in supervised learning, we constrain the visually *similar* people to be close to each other. Without identity labels, this is obviously a weaker constraint but the best available. Specifically, discriminativity is achieved unsupervised via a visual similarity constraint, which is enforced by introducing a graph Laplacian regularisation term in the dictionary learning objective function [44].

However, two problems remain when the conventional graph Laplacian constraint is used in our problem context: (1) The conventional term has a squared ℓ_2-norm, which makes the term susceptible to data outliers. This is particularly unsuitable for the Re-ID problem as there are plenty of data outliers in Re-ID, caused by various reasons such as the person detection boxes being imperfect and severe (self-)occlusions. (2) The visual similarity is encoded in a graph whose topology and edge weights are all determined by distances computed using the original high-dimensional low-level features. However, these features are not ideal for people matching, hence learning a new representation in the first place. As illustrated in Fig. 1(a), a graph constructed using the low-level features connects many visually dissimilar neighbours to each node. This diminishes the power of the graph regularisation term as a visual similarity constraint.

To overcome these two problems, we introduce a robust graph regularisation term and propose to learn the new representation and the optimal graph jointly. Specifically, a ℓ_1-norm is introduced in our graph regularisation term to make it robust against outliers. With this ℓ_1-norm and joint graph and dictionary learning, our learning objective function is both non-smooth and non-convex. Solving this optimisation problem is thus non-trivial. An efficient iterative optimisation algorithm is formulated in this work to solve it. Once learned, our model can be used to compute a representation for each image much more efficiently than any existing unsupervised Re-ID method. The final matching is done by computing a simple cosine distance between a pair of the representation vectors.

1.1 Related Work

Most existing person Re-ID techniques are based on supervised learning: After hand-crafted features are extracted from each image, the optimal cross-view matching function is learned by either distance metric learning [14,31], learning to rank [7,46], or discriminant subspace learning [19,24,25,47,56,58]. Recently representation and metric learning are combined end-to-end based on deep neural networks [2,36] achieving state-of-the-art results when a large number of labelled training images are available. As mentioned early, all of them rely on hundreds of labelled data per camera pair. Considering that a modest-sized surveillance video network can easily have hundreds of cameras, these supervised learning Re-ID models are of very limited practical use. Our model is related to the discriminant subspace learning methods [19,24,25,47,56,58]. However, none of them can be employed under the unsupervised setting. In addition, kernelisation is critical to make them work [55]. In contrast, no kernelisation is required for our model resulting in small memory footprint.

The existing models for unsupervised learning of either features or representations for Re-ID fall into three categories. (1) Many focus on designing hand-crafted appearance features [10,16,37,39,40,42]. However, it is very challenging to design a set of view-invariant features which are suitable for all camera view conditions. (2) Several methods exploit localised saliency statistics [54,57]. Without being able to utilise cross-view identity-discriminative information, their performance is typically weak. Also, they are patch based methods and separate models are learned for every patch which makes them computational expensive. (3) There are also dictionary learning based methods which can intrinsically be used in an unsupervised setting [30,41]. The key difference in this work is the use of robust graph Laplacian regularisation and joint graph and dictionary learning. We show experimentally that the proposed method is clearly superior to the existing unsupervised alternatives in both matching accuracy and running cost.

Beyond person Re-ID, dictionary learning [1,28,43] and graph regularisation [12,18,61] have been exploited in many different fields including unsupervised clustering [34], supervised face verification/recognition [21] and semi-supervised learning [5,8,33]. Graph learning has also been considered for subspace clustering [22,45]. However, none of the existing models is directly applicable to the unsupervised cross-view person matching problem. Importantly none of them exploits both graph learning and robust graph regularisation. We show experimentally that both properties are critical for dictionary learning to be effective for solving the unsupervised Re-ID problem.

1.2 Contributions

Our contributions are two-fold: (1) We formulate a novel graph regularised dictionary learning model for unsupervised Re-ID with a new robust ℓ_1-norm graph regularisation term and joint graph and dictionary learning. The model only requires unlabelled training data, which makes it suitable for large-scale Re-ID problems. (2) We develop an efficient iterative optimisation algorithm for the non-smooth and non-convex objective function of our model. During test time, the model is linear and has a closed-form solution for inference; it is thus extremely efficient. Extensive experiments are conducted on four large benchmark datasets, and the results show that our method significantly outperforms existing unsupervised methods in terms of both matching accuracy and running cost.

2 Methodology

2.1 Problem Definition

Suppose we have a set of *unlabelled* training data collected from two camera views[1]. They are denoted as $\mathbf{X} = [\mathbf{X}^a, \mathbf{X}^b] \in \mathbb{R}^{n \times m}$, where $\mathbf{X}^a = [\mathbf{x}_1^a, \ldots, \mathbf{x}_{m_1}^a] \in$

---

[1] In practice our model is not restricted by the number of camera views. We use two here purely for notational simplicity.

$\mathbb{R}^{n \times m_1}$ contains n-dimensional feature vectors of m_1 images in view A, and $\mathbf{X}^b = [\mathbf{x}_1^b, \ldots, \mathbf{x}_{m_2}^b] \in \mathbb{R}^{n \times m_2}$ of m_2 images in view B. We thus have $m = m_1 + m_2$ data points in total. The objective of unsupervised person Re-ID is to learn a matching function f from $\mathbf{X}$, so that given $\mathbf{x}^a$ and $\mathbf{x}^b$ as two test person images from A and B respectively, $f(\mathbf{x}^a, \mathbf{x}^b)$ can match their identities.

2.2   Robust Graph Regularised Dictionary Learning

We solve the problem defined above by learning a dictionary $\mathbf{D} \in \mathbb{R}^{k \times n}$ shared by the two camera views using $\mathbf{X}$. Every atom of the learned dictionary (column of $\mathbf{D}$) can be considered as a latent appearance attribute that is invariant to camera view condition changes. Therefore, with this dictionary, each n-dimensional low-level feature vector, regardless which view it comes from, is represented by the coefficients of the k dictionary atoms. This is equivalent to projecting the original n-dimensional low-level feature vectors to a lower-dimensional ($k < n$) latent attribute space. The matching is done by computing a simple cosine distance between two coefficient vectors in the space. Formally, we aim to learn the optimal dictionary $\mathbf{D}$, such that the latent attribute representation of $\mathbf{X}$, denoted as $\mathbf{Y} = [\mathbf{Y}^a, \mathbf{Y}^b] \in \mathbb{R}^{k \times m}$, where $\mathbf{Y}^a = [\mathbf{y}_1^a, \ldots, \mathbf{y}_{m_1}^a] \in \mathbb{R}^{k \times m_1}$ and $\mathbf{Y}^b = [\mathbf{y}_1^b, \ldots, \mathbf{y}_{m_2}^b] \in \mathbb{R}^{k \times m_2}$, are optimised for matching the training data. We expect the same $\mathbf{D}$ can be generalised to match unseen test data across camera views.

Conventional dictionary learning methods estimate the dicitionary $\mathbf{D}$ and the representation $\mathbf{Y}$ simultaneously by solving the following optimisation problem:

$$(\mathbf{D}^*, \mathbf{Y}^*) = \min_{\mathbf{D}, \mathbf{Y}} \|\mathbf{X} - \mathbf{D}\mathbf{Y}\|_F^2 + \lambda_1 \Omega(\mathbf{Y}) \quad s.t. \quad \|\mathbf{d}_i\|_2^2 \leq 1, \qquad (1)$$

where $\|\mathbf{X} - \mathbf{D}\mathbf{Y}\|_F^2$ is the reconstruction error evaluating how well a linear combination of the learned atoms can approximate the input data, and $\|.\|_F$ denotes the matrix Frobenious norm. $\Omega(\mathbf{Y})$ is a regularisation term that is weighted by λ_1. Different models differ mainly in the choice of the regularisation term on $\mathbf{Y}$. The sparsity term, $\Omega(\mathbf{Y}) = \|\mathbf{Y}\|_1$ is widely used which favours a small number of atoms for reconstruction. The constraint $\|\mathbf{d}_i\|^2 \leq 1$ ($\mathbf{d}_i$ is a column of $\mathbf{D}$, $i = 1, ..., k$) enforces the learned dictionary atoms to be compact. It is clear from this formulation that a conventional dictionary learning model only cares about how to best reconstruct $\mathbf{X}$ using $\mathbf{D}$ and $\mathbf{Y}$, without taking into account whether the representation $\mathbf{Y}$ is discriminative. For learning a discriminative dictionary for cross-view Re-ID, one must exploit cross-view identity discriminative information.

A learned dictionary can be made discriminative by using a graph regularisation term which dictates that visually similar people will be close to each other in the learned latent attribute space [11]. Let $\mathbf{G} = (\mathbf{V}, \mathbf{E})$ be an undirected graph connecting between the data points where $\mathbf{V}$ and $\mathbf{E}$ are a set of graph vertices representing the data points and an edge set, respectively. This graph can be encoded by an affinity matrix $\mathbf{W} \in \mathbb{R}^{m \times m}$ for m data points where $\mathbf{W}_{i,j} \neq 0$ if the two vertices are connected, i.e. the corresponding data points are in a local neighbourhood. Note: (1) In the context of person Re-ID, we focus on the cross-view discriminative dictionary learning, thus restricting the graph edges to connecting cross-view nodes only. (2) We use the graph regularisation term to replace the commonly used sparsity constraint $\|\mathbf{Y}\|_1$, for reasons to be explained later.

A standard graph regularisation term $\Omega(\mathbf{Y})$ is defined as:

$$\Omega(\mathbf{Y}) = \sum_{ij}^{m} \mathbf{W}_{ij} \|\mathbf{y}_i - \mathbf{y}_j\|_2^2. \tag{2}$$

This regularisation essentially requires that the projected data points in the learned latent attribute space to be smooth with regards to the graph, that is, their distances need to conform to the visual similarity relationship embedded in the graph. However, we find that Eq. (2) has two critical limitations that make it unsuitable for the unsupervised Re-ID problem. First, the distance between two projected data points is calculated with a *squared ℓ_2-norm*. It is well-known that a square-based regularisation function can be easily dominated by outlying data samples. Unfortunately outlying samples are commonplace in Re-ID because of background in person detection bounding boxes, detector errors, and (self-)occlusions. Another limitation arises from how the graph is constructed. Most existing methods build the graph in the original high dimensional low-level feature space using $\mathbf{X}$. This is suboptimal – if the low-level feature space is good for measuring cross-camera visual similarity, we would have already solved the Re-ID problem. Learning a discriminative latent attribute space is precisely due to the fact that measuring visual similarity in the original space is unreliable and error-prone, as illustrated in Fig. 1. To tackle both limitations simultaneously, we introduce a robust graph regularisation formulation and a joint graph and dictionary learning method.

Robust Graph Regularisation. This new term is designed to alleviate the effect of outlying samples during model learning. To derive our robust graph regularisation, let us first rewrite Eq. (2) in a matrix form with trace notation:

$$\Omega(\mathbf{Y}) = \sum_{ij}^{m} \mathbf{W}_{ij} \|\mathbf{y}_i - \mathbf{y}_j\|_2^2 = tr(\mathbf{Y}\mathbf{L}_\mathbf{W}\mathbf{Y}^\mathbf{T}), \tag{3}$$

where $\mathbf{L}_\mathbf{W} = \mathbf{D} - \mathbf{W}$ is the Laplacian matrix, $\mathbf{D}_{ii} = \sum_j \mathbf{W}_{ij}$ is a degree matrix. Let $\mathbf{L}_\mathbf{W} = \mathbf{U}_\mathbf{W}\mathbf{S}_\mathbf{W}\mathbf{U}_\mathbf{W}^\mathbf{T}$ using the eigen decomposition technique, and after some matrix manipulation, we have

$$tr(\mathbf{Y}\mathbf{L}_\mathbf{W}\mathbf{Y}^\mathbf{T}) = tr(\mathbf{Y}\mathbf{U}_\mathbf{W}\mathbf{S}_\mathbf{W}\mathbf{U}_\mathbf{W}^\mathbf{T}\mathbf{Y}^\mathbf{T}) =$$
$$tr(\mathbf{Y}\mathbf{U}_\mathbf{W}\mathbf{S}_\mathbf{W}^{\frac{1}{2}}\mathbf{S}_\mathbf{W}^{\frac{1}{2}}\mathbf{U}_\mathbf{W}^\mathbf{T}\mathbf{Y}^\mathbf{T}) = \|\mathbf{Y}\mathbf{A}_\mathbf{W}\|_F^2, \tag{4}$$

where $\mathbf{A}_\mathbf{W} = \mathbf{U}_\mathbf{W}\mathbf{S}_\mathbf{W}^{\frac{1}{2}}$. Equation (4) above is quadratic. To promote sparsity and suppress effects of outlying samples, we adopt a ℓ_1-norm instead of the Frobenius norm. This gives the proposed graph weighted ℓ_1-norm regularisation term

$$\Omega_{R1}(\mathbf{Y}) = \|\mathbf{YA_W}\|_1. \tag{5}$$

Replacing $\Omega(\mathbf{Y})$ with $\Omega_{R1}(\mathbf{Y})$ in Eq. (1), we have a robust graph regularised dictionary learning model:

$$\min_{\mathbf{D},\mathbf{Y}} \quad \frac{1}{2}\|\mathbf{X} - \mathbf{DY}\|_F^2 + \lambda_1\|\mathbf{YA_W}\|_1 \quad s.t. \quad \|\mathbf{d}_i\|^2 \le 1 \tag{6}$$

The key advantages of the proposed robust graph regularisation in this work over the conventional regularisation formulation, including the existing dictionary learning based Re-ID model DLLAP [30], are as follows:

1. *Non-linearity.* Robust graph regularisation introduces non-linearity into the objective, i.e. $\mathbf{Y}$ is non-linear with respect to the original data $\mathbf{X}$, whilst the conventional graph regularisation is linear.
2. *Sparsity.* It is well-known that ℓ_1-norm has a shrinkage property thus promotes sparsity [27,29]. Intuitively, in the presence of noise and outliers, the magnitude of $\|\mathbf{YA}_W\|_F^2$ of the regularisation becomes very big for those outlying data points, and as a result the whole objective function could be dominated by the noise and outliers. In contrast, $\|\mathbf{YA}_W\|_1$ becomes sparse due to the use of ℓ_1-norm, consequently suppressing the impact of outliers and noises. Moreover, in the proposed robust regularisation model, explicit sparsity constraint such as $\|\mathbf{Y}\|_1$ is no longer needed[2].

Joint graph and dictionary learning. Instead of computing $\mathbf{W}$ using $\mathbf{X}$ and fixing it during model learning, we assume that $\mathbf{W}$ (hence the graph $\mathbf{G}$ as $\mathbf{W}$ depends on the topology of $\mathbf{G}$) is unknown and has to be learned together with $\mathbf{D}$ and $\mathbf{Y}$. Our objective function thus becomes:

$$\min_{\mathbf{D},\mathbf{W},\mathbf{Y}} \frac{1}{2}\|\mathbf{X} - \mathbf{DY}\|_F^2 + \lambda_1\|\mathbf{YA_W}\|_1 + \lambda_2\|\mathbf{W}\|_F^2$$
$$s.t. \quad \|\mathbf{d}_i\|_2^2 \le 1, \ \mathbf{W}_i^T\mathbf{1} = 1, \ \mathbf{W}_i \ge 0. \tag{7}$$

where $\lambda_2\|\mathbf{W}\|_F^2$ is a regularisation term on $\mathbf{W}$ weighted by λ_2 to prevent trivial solutions. The constraints, $\mathbf{W^T1} = 1$ and $\mathbf{W} \ge 0$, ensure the validity of the learned graph. We show in our experiments (Sect. 3.2) that this novel joint learning of graph and dictionary has significant advantage over the existing dictionary learning based Re-ID model DLLAP [30].

2.3   Optimisation

The optimisation problem in (7) is non-convex and non-smooth. Solving it is thus more difficult than (1) due to the ℓ_1-norm used in $\Omega_{R1}(\mathbf{Y})$ and the additional

---

[2] Empirically we found that adding an extra $\|\mathbf{Y}\|_1$ term makes little difference to the Re-ID performance, but results in more complex solver and higher computational cost.

unknown variable $\mathbf{W}$. Next, we develop an efficient solver for (7) based on the Alternating Direction Method of Multipliers (ADMM) [6].

First, we transform (7) by letting $\mathbf{U} = \mathbf{YA_W}$, then the Augmented Lagrangian function of (7) with the introduced constraint is:

$$
\begin{aligned}
\mathcal{L}_{(\mathbf{D},\mathbf{Y},\mathbf{U},\mathbf{W})} = &\frac{1}{2}\|\mathbf{X} - \mathbf{DY}\|_F^2 + \lambda_1\|\mathbf{U}\|_1 + \langle \mathbf{F}, \mathbf{U} - \mathbf{YA_W}\rangle \\
&+ \frac{\gamma}{2}\|\mathbf{U} - \mathbf{YA_W}\|_F^2 + \lambda_2\|\mathbf{W}\|_F^2
\end{aligned}
\tag{8}
$$

$$
s.t. \qquad \|\mathbf{d}_i\|^2 \leq 1,\ \mathbf{W^T 1} = 1,\ \mathbf{W} \geq 0.
$$

where $\mathbf{F}$ is Lagrangian multiplier, and γ is a penalty parameter. Now, we can solve it alternatingly with the following five steps with respect to $\mathbf{D}$, $\mathbf{Y}$, $\mathbf{U}$, and $\mathbf{W}$, respectively.

(1) Solving for D: To learn $\mathbf{D}$ for a given $\mathbf{Y}$, the objective function reduces to:

$$
\min_{\mathbf{D}} \frac{1}{2}\|\mathbf{X} - \mathbf{DY}\|_F^2 \quad s.t.\ \|\mathbf{d}_i\|_2^2 \leq 1
\tag{9}
$$

To solve this, we use the Lagrange dual method as in [32]. The analytical solution of $\mathbf{D}$ can be computed as: $\mathbf{D}^* = \mathbf{XY^T}(\mathbf{YY^T} + \mathbf{\Lambda}^*)^{-1}$, where $\mathbf{\Lambda}^*$ is a diagonal matrix constructed from all the optimal dual variables.

(2) Solving for Y: For a given $\mathbf{D}$, solve the following objective to estimate $\mathbf{Y}$:

$$
\min_{\mathbf{Y}} \frac{1}{2}\|\mathbf{X} - \mathbf{DY}\|_F^2 + \frac{\gamma}{2}\|\mathbf{U} - (\mathbf{YA_W} - \frac{\mathbf{F}}{\gamma})\|_F^2.
$$

Since each term in this objective is quadratic, we can take its derivative and set it to zero which gives

$$
(\mathbf{D^T DY} + \gamma \mathbf{YA_W A_W^T}) = \mathbf{D^T X} + \gamma \mathbf{U A_W^T} + \mathbf{F A_W^T}.
$$

This is a standard Sylvester equation, which is solved using the Bartels-Stewart algorithm [4].

(3) Solving for U: For a given $\mathbf{Y}$, solve the following objective to estimate $\mathbf{U}$:

$$
\min_{\mathbf{U}} \lambda_1\|\mathbf{U}\|_1 + \frac{\gamma}{2}\|\mathbf{U} - (\mathbf{YA_W} - \frac{\mathbf{F}}{\gamma})\|_F^2.
$$

We can use the soft-thresholding operator to get $\mathbf{U}$:

$$
\mathbf{U} = \text{sign}\left(\mathbf{YA_W} - \frac{\mathbf{F}}{\gamma}\right) \max(\left|\mathbf{YA_W} - \frac{\mathbf{F}}{\gamma}\right| - \frac{\lambda_1}{\gamma}).
\tag{10}
$$

(4) Solving for W: Given $\mathbf{Y}$, the objective function with respect to $\mathbf{W}$ is:

$$
\min_{\mathbf{W}} \lambda_1 \sum_{ij}^{m} \mathbf{W}_{ij}\|\mathbf{y}_i - \mathbf{y}_j\|_1 + \lambda_2\|\mathbf{W}\|_F^2 \quad s.t.\ \mathbf{W}_i^T 1 = 1, \mathbf{W}_i \geq 0.
$$

We set $\lambda_1 = 1$ for easiness, and denote $\mathbf{d}_{ij} = \frac{\|\mathbf{y}_i - \mathbf{y}_j\|_1}{2\lambda_2}$ and $\|\mathbf{W}\|_F^2 = \sum_{ij} \mathbf{W}_{ij}^2$, then

$$\min_{\mathbf{W}} \sum_{ij}^{m} \mathbf{W}_{ij} \mathbf{d}_{ij} + \sum_{ij}^{m} \mathbf{W}_{ij}^2 \quad s.t. \quad \mathbf{W}_i^{\mathbf{T}} \mathbf{1} = 1, \mathbf{W}_i \geq 0.$$

The above optimisation problem is composed of independent problems with respect to i, and therefore can be rewritten in a vector form:

$$\min_{\mathbf{W}_i} \|\mathbf{W}_i + \mathbf{d}_i\|_2^2 \quad s.t. \quad \mathbf{W}_i \mathbf{1} = 1, \mathbf{W}_i \geq 0.$$

There is a closed-form solution using Lagrange multipliers [22,45] for this problem:

$$\mathbf{W}_i = \left(\frac{1 + \sum_{j=1}^{K} \tilde{\mathbf{d}}_j}{K} \mathbf{1} - \mathbf{d}_i \right)_+ \tag{11}$$

where the operator $(\mathbf{q})_+$ projects negative elements in $\mathbf{q}$ to 0. K is the parameter that controls the number of neighbours. $\tilde{\mathbf{d}}_i$ is $\mathbf{d}_i$ but with ascending order. After obtaining $\mathbf{W}$, we symmetrise it, and do eigen-decomposition to get $\mathbf{U_W}$ and $\mathbf{S_W}$. Then we set $\mathbf{A_W} = \mathbf{U_W} \mathbf{S_W^{\frac{1}{2}}}$. Note that the regularisation parameter λ_2 can be determined by [45]:

$$\lambda_2 = \frac{1}{m} \sum_{i=1}^{m} \left(\frac{K}{2} \mathbf{d}_{i,K+1} - \frac{1}{2} \sum_{j=1}^{K} \mathbf{d}_{i,j} \right). \tag{12}$$

(5) Updating multipliers: $\mathbf{F}, \gamma$,

$$\mathbf{F} = \mathbf{F}^{old} + \gamma(\mathbf{U} - \mathbf{Y}\mathbf{A_W}), \quad \gamma = \rho\gamma^{old}$$

In this work, we set ρ to 1.1 and initialise γ to 0.1. Typically the value for ρ is set between 1.0 and 1.8 [6].

We continue to alternate solving for $\mathbf{D}, \mathbf{Y}, \mathbf{U}, \mathbf{W}$ until a maximum number of iterations is reached or a predefined threshold (10^{-3}) is satisfied.

Convergence Analysis. The theoretical convergence proof of ADMM does not exist. However, in practice it is guaranteed that the objective function converges to at least a stable point [6]. This is validated by our experiments (see Sect. 3). In particular, it is observed that the proposed algorithm has a stable convergence behaviour, always converging after 10–25 iterations.

Remark on Computational Complexity and Scalability. Due to space limit we leave the computational complexity analysis and scalability with respect to the number of samples in the supplementary material.

2.4 Cross-View Matching

After learning the dictionary $\mathbf{D}$ using the unlabelled training data $\mathbf{X}$, given a pair of test samples $\mathbf{x}_i^a$ and $\mathbf{x}_i^b$, we first compute their collaborative representations $\mathbf{y}_i^a$ and $\mathbf{y}_i^b$ by solving the following problems:

$$\mathbf{y}_i^{a*} = \arg min_{\mathbf{y}_i^a} \|\mathbf{x}_i^a - \mathbf{D}\mathbf{y}_i^a\|_F^2 + \lambda\|\mathbf{y}_i^a\|_2^2 \tag{13}$$

$$\mathbf{y}_i^{b*} = \arg min_{\mathbf{y}_i^b} \|\mathbf{x}_i^b - \mathbf{D}\mathbf{y}_i^b\|_F^2 + \lambda\|\mathbf{y}_i^b\|_2^2 \tag{14}$$

These are standard ℓ_2-norm regularised least squares problems with closed-form solutions: $\mathbf{y}_i^{a*} = \mathbf{P}\mathbf{x}_i^a$ and $\mathbf{y}_i^{b*} = \mathbf{P}\mathbf{x}_i^b$, where $\mathbf{P} = (\mathbf{D}^{\mathbf{T}}\mathbf{D} + \lambda\mathbf{I})^{-1}\mathbf{D}^{\mathbf{T}}$. Then, after obtaining $\mathbf{y}_i^{a*}$ and $\mathbf{y}_i^{b*}$ their cosine distance is used to measure the visual similarity for Re-ID. Hence, our model is very efficient in testing.

2.5 Extension to Supervised Re-ID

Although our model is designed for unsupervised Re-ID, it can be easily extended if labelled cross-view pairs become available. More specifically, the label information can be encoded in the graph $\mathbf{W}$. That is, instead of learning $\mathbf{W}$, it is now fixed so that if the corresponding cross-view pair (i, j) is labelled as containing the same person, we set $\mathbf{W}_{i,j}$ to 1, otherwise it is set as 0. This essentially gives thus the ideal graph and the relaxed visual similarity constraint becomes a more stringent identity constraint which requires that people of the same identity to be close in the learned attribute space and vice versa.

3 Experiments

3.1 Datasets and Settings

Datasets. Four widely used benchmark datasets are used for the experiments. *VIPeR* [15] contains 632 image pairs of people captured outdoor from two non-overlapping camera views. Following the standard setting which is single-shot i.e., one image per person per view, the dataset is randomly split into two sets of 316 image pairs, one for training and the other for testing. For the test set, all images from one view is used as the gallery set and the others probe set. The results for all evaluations were obtained by averaging over 10 splits. *PRID* [23] is different from the other available datasets in that the gallery and probe sets have different numbers of people. In our experiments, we use the single-shot version of the dataset as in [19,26,46]. Specifically, out of the 749 people captured in two camera views, only 200 people appear in both views. In each data split, 100 out of that 200 people are chosen randomly for training, while the remaining 100 of one view are used as the probe set, and the remaining 649 people's images of the other view are used as gallery, which thus includes the 100 people in the probe set. Experiments are carried out on the same 10 splits as in [19,26] with the average results reported. *CUHK01* [35] consists of 971 people with two images per person per camera view i.e. multi-shot. We follow the standard setting [35]:

486 persons for training, while 485 persons for test. *CUHK03* [36] contains 13,164 images of 1,467 people. Two versions exist which differs in whether the images were obtained by manual cropping or automatically by applying the DPM person detector [17]. The detector-generated images are used as they reflect better the real-world application scenarios for testing the robustness of our model against outliers. There are in total six camera views but each person is observed in only two out of the six views, and has 4.8 images on average for each view. We used the same setting and random splits as in [36] with a single-shot setting: for the probe set we randomly select 100 people with two images each, whilst images of the remaining people are used for training. Note that out of the four datasets, CHUK03 is much bigger than the other three in terms of both the number of identities and the number of images in the training set.

Settings. *Features*: The features introduced in [19] are adopted. Each image is scaled to 128×48 in all datasets, and then histogram-based image descriptors are computed consisting of three types: (1) Colour histogram using HS, RGB, and Lab colour spaces (2880-D colour vector), (2) HOG (1040-D) [13], and (3) LBP (1218-D) [3]. The final image feature vector, 5138-D, is obtained as the concatenation of these three types of features. *Evaluation metrics*: We obtain the Cumulative Matching Characteristics (CMC) curves. Due to space constraint, we only report matching accuracies at Rank 1 here and leave the full CMC curves in the supplementary material. *Parameter settings*: There are a number of parameters in our model. As an unsupervised learning method, there are no other means but setting them manually. For the dictionary size k, we do not tune it carefully and set it to 256 for the two small datasets VIPeR and PRID, and 512 for the larger CUHK01 and CUHK03 dataset. Its effects on the performance will be discussed later. In the objective function (Eq. (7)), there are two weights λ_1 and λ_2 for the two regularisation terms respectively. As explained in Sect. 2.3, λ_2 is set automatically using Eq. (12) in the ADMM algorithm, whilst for λ_1 we simply set it to 1 throughout, as we found that the algorithm is insensitive to its value. Similarly for the initial construction of graph $\mathbf{G}$, we use a KNN graph with cosine distance and $K = 5$ for all datasets.

3.2 Evaluation of Unsupervised Learning Based Re-ID

Compared methods. Under this setting, we compared our approach with state-of-the-art unsupervised alternatives which fall into four categories: (1) The hand-crafted feature-based methods including SDALF [16] and CPS [10]. (2) The saliency learning-based eSDC [57] and GTS [54]; (3) The dictionary learning (DLLAP) [30] which uses the same 5138-D features for fair comparison. (4) The codebook learning method (BGG) [59].

Results. Table 1 compares the results of the proposed method against the six alternatives and a non-learning ℓ_1 distance based baseline. From Table 1, the following observations can be made: (1) Our robust graph regularised dictionary learning model outperforms all existing unsupervised methods on all four datasets, and often by a big margin. (2) The margin is in general bigger on the

Table 1. Unsupervised Re-ID results measured in Rank-1 matching accuracy (%) on VIPeR, PRID, CUHK01, CUHK03, where '-' denotes no reported result.

Datasets	VIPeR	PRID	CUHK01	CUHK03
ℓ_1	15.6	13.9	10.9	12.5
SDALF [16]	19.9	16.3	9.9	4.9
DLLAP [30]	29.6	21.1	28.4	22.3
eSDC [57]	26.7	-	26.6	7.7
CPS [10]	22.0	-	-	-
GTS [54]	25.2	-	-	-
BGG [59]	21.7	-	-	18.9
Ours	**33.5**	**25.0**	**41.0**	**30.4**

two larger datasets CUHK01 and CUHK03, which indicates that our model can benefit more from larger unlabelled training data. (3) Among the alternatives, the dictionary learning based method (DLLAP) [30] is the most competitive. However, the gap is still significant due to the introduced two novel components: robust graph regularisation and joint graph and dictionary learning. This result also suggests that learning a low-dimensional latent attribute representation is more suited for unsupervised Re-ID than the alternative models. In particular, the difference between Ours and ℓ_1 is large which means that matching people is made much easier in this learned discriminative subspace with less than one tenth of the original dimensions. The advantage of our method's computational efficiency over other methods will be discussed later.

3.3 Evaluation of Supervised Learning Based Re-ID

Compared methods. Since the performance of different existing methods on different datasets often vary drastically[3], we choose the best methods for each dataset separately to better reflect the state-of-the-art. All methods are published in the last two years. Note that multi-feature fusion based methods are separated from single feature or deep models as typically any method can benefit from multi-feature fusion. As mentioned in Sect. 2.5, our model can also operate in the supervised mode; denoted as Ours_sup, this can be considered as the upper bound of our model's performance under the unsupervised setting when the graph is learned perfectly.

Results. We have the following key findings from Table 2: (1) The gap between Ours_un and Our_sup is moderate. This indicates that our graph learning method is very effective and the performance of the unsupervised model is not far off from its upper bound. (2) On the two smaller datasets, VIPeR and PRID, our

---

[3] For example, deep learning based methods often perform stronger on the large datasets than the small ones due to the need for large training data.

Table 2. Comparison state-of-the-art supervised methods

Datasets	VIPeR		PRID		CUHK01		CUHK03	
	Ref	Rank 1	Ref	Rank 1	Ref	Rank 1	Ref	Rank 1
Single-feature Methods	[37]	40.0	[19]	14.5	[58]	34.3	[37]	46.4
	[2]	34.8	[55]	19.7	[2]	47.5	[2]	44.9
	[38]	40.7	[30]	25.2	[36]	29.4	[38]	51.2
	[9]	36.1	[48]	16.0	[36]	27.8	[36]	19.9
	[50]	40.9	[51]	18.0	[37]	63.5	[50]	52.1
	[60]	30.2	[38]	12.3	[38]	**64.2**	[52]	**59.2**
Multi-feature Fusion	[46]	**45.9**	[46]	17.9	[46]	53.4	–	–
Ours_un		33.5		25.0		41.0		30.4
Ours_sup		41.5		**30.1**		50.1		39.0

model is very competitive under the supervised setting: on VIPeR it beats all single feature-based methods and on PRID, it outperforms all existing supervised methods, often significantly. Even our unsupervised model outperforms some very recent supervised models. Note that this is without any kernalisation which could further improve our model's performance. (3) On the two larger datasets CUHK01 and CUHK03 (with detected person images), the gap between our method and the state-of-the-art begins to appear[4]. Our model (both supervised and unsupervised) remains competitive on CUHK01, but on CUHK03, the gap is big, in particular to our unsupervised model. This is expected: with over 10,000 labelled training images from 1,367 people, an unsupervised model cannot compete with a supervised one, especially those based on deep learning. However, we would like to point out that in practice collecting hundreds of labelled training samples is very difficult and collecting thousands would be near impossible across even just a handful of camera views.

3.4   Further Analysis

The contributions of individual components. Our proposed method has two key components and to see the impact of each we compare our full model with various striped-down versions of the model under the unsupervised setting: (1) Ours_DL – without graph regularisation which is the same as conventional dictionary learning; (2) Ours_ℓ_2 – the graph is fixed and ℓ_2-norm is used for graph regularisation; (3) Ours_ℓ_2_graph – the graph is learned and ℓ_2-norm is used for graph regularisation; (4) Ours_ℓ_1 – the graph is fixed and ℓ_1-norm is used for graph regularisation; (5) Ours_full – our full proposed model in which the graph is learned and ℓ_1-norm is used for graph regularisation. Table 3 shows

---

[4] The gap is much smaller if more powerful features are used - see supplementary material for details.

Table 3. The contributions of individual model components

Methods	Ours_DL	Ours_ℓ_2	Ours_ℓ_2-graph	Ours_ℓ_1	Ours_full
VIPeR	19.6	29.4	30.1	32.0	33.5
CUHK01	17.4	36.9	37.5	38.7	41.0

 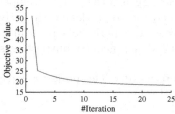

Fig. 2. (Left) Rank 1 accuracies with different dictionary sizes on VIPeR dataset; (Right) Objective function value with respect to the number of iterations on CUHK01.

Table 4. Average testing time of different methods on VIPeR

Stage	SDALF	eSDC	BGG	Ours
Feature extraction (s)	2.92	0.76	0.62	0.03
Matching (s)	550.80	9.7	0.44	0.01

that both using robust ℓ_1-norm graph regularisation and joint graph and dictionary learning contribute positively toward the final performance. The result (comparing Ours_DL with the other models) also shows that adding a graph regularisation term to learn cross-view discriminative information in general is critical for dictionary-learning-based Re-ID.

Effect of dictionary size and convergence analysis. The only parameter we tuned for each dataset is the dictionary size. Figure 2(Left) shows that when the size is over 100, its effect is small. Furthermore, Fig. 2(Right) shows the proposed method converges rapidly. Although there is no theoretically proof, convergence is observed in all our experiments within 25 iterations.

Running cost. Our experiments were conducted in MATLAB on a PC with two 3.40 GHz CPUs and 16 G RAM. The training of the model on VIPeR takes 178.3 s but during test it is very efficient: once the 5138-D features are extracted, it takes only 0.01 s to match one probe image against 316 images from the gallery. Table 4 compares the running time of feature extraction and matching during test time against a number of alternative unsupervised methods. It is clear that our method is often a few magnitudes faster than its competitors.

4 Conclusion

We have proposed a novel unsupervised Re-ID model based on dictionary learning. The key contributions are the introduction of a robust ℓ_1-norm graph regularisation term in the dictionary learning formulation so that cross-view discriminative information can be learned. In addition, a joint graph and dictionary learning algorithm is developed which further improves the ability of the proposed model to deal with outlying samples abundant in person Re-ID data. Extensive experiments on four benchmark datasets show that the proposed method significantly outperforms existing unsupervised methods.

Acknowledgments. This project was partly funded by the EU FP7 Project SUNNY (grant no. 313243).

References

1. Aharon, M., Elad, M., Bruckstein, A.: K-svd: An algorithm for designing over-complete dictionaries for sparse representation. IEEE Trans. Sig. Process. **54**(11), 4311–4322 (2006)
2. Ahmed, E., Jones, M., Marks, T.K.: An improved deep learning architecture for person re-identification. In: The IEEE Conference on Computer Vision and Pattern Recognition (CVPR), June 2015
3. Ahonen, T., Hadid, A., Pietikainen, M.: Face description with local binary patterns: application to face recognition. IEEE Trans. Pattern Anal. Mach, Intell (2006)
4. Bartels, R.H., Stewart, G.W.: Solution of the matrix equation ax + xb = c [f4]. Commun. ACM **15**(9), 820–826 (1972). http://doi.acm.org/10.1145/361573. 361582
5. Belkin, M., Niyogi, P., Sindhwani, V.: Manifold regularization: a geometric framework for learning from labeled and unlabeled examples. J. Mach. Learn. Res. **7**, 2399–2434 (2006)
6. Boyd, S., Parikh, N., Chu, E., Peleato, B., Eckstein, J.: Distributed optimization and statistical learning via the alternating direction method of multipliers. Found. Trends Mach. Learn. **3**(1), 1–122 (2011)
7. Bryan, P., Wei-Shi, Z., Gong, S., Xiang, T.: Person re-identification by support vector ranking. In: Proceedings of BMVC (2010)
8. Cai, D., He, X., Han, J.: Semi-supervised discriminant analysis. In: IEEE 11th International Conference on Computer Vision, ICCV 2007, pp. 1–7. IEEE (2007)
9. Chen, D., Yuan, Z., Hua, G., Zheng, N., Wang, J.: Similarity learning on an explicit polynomial kernel feature map for person re-identification. In: The IEEE Conference on Computer Vision and Pattern Recognition (CVPR), June 2015
10. Cheng, D.S., Cristani, M., Bazzani, L., Murino, V.: Custom pictorial structures for re-identification. In: Proceedings of BMVC (2011)
11. Chung, F.R.: Spectral Graph Theory, vol. 92. American Mathematical Soc., Providence (1997)
12. Daitch, S.I., Kelner, J.A., Spielman, D.A.: Fitting a graph to vector data. In: Proceedings of the 26th Annual International Conference on Machine Learning, pp. 201–208. ACM (2009)
13. Dalal, N., Triggs, B.: Histograms of oriented gradients for human detection. In: Proceedings of CVPR (2005)

14. Dikmen, M., Akbas, E., Huang, T.S., Ahuja, N.: Pedestrian recognition with a learned metric. In: Proceedings of ACCV (2011)
15. Douglas, G., Shane, B., Hai, T.: Evaluating appearance models for recognition, reacquisition and tracking. In: PETS (2007)
16. Farenzena, M., Bazzani, L., Perina, A., Murino, V., Cristani, M.: Person re-identification by symmetry-driven accumulation of local features. In: Proceedings of CVPR (2010)
17. Felzenszwalb, P.F., Girshick, R.B., McAllester, D., Ramanan, D.: Object detection with discriminatively trained part-based models. IEEE Trans. Pattern Anal. Mach. Intell. **32**(9), 1627–1645 (2010)
18. Gao, S., Tsang, I., Chia, L., Zhao, P.: Local features are not lonely laplacian sparse coding for image classification. In: Proceedings of CVPR (2010)
19. Giuseppe, L., Iacopo, M., Alberto, D.B.: Matching people across camera views using kernel canonical correlation analysis. In: Proceedings of ICDSC (2014)
20. Gong, S., Cristani, M., Yan, S., Loy, C.C.: Person Re-Identification, vol. 1. Springer, London (2014)
21. Guo, H., Jiang, Z., Davis, L.S.: Discriminative dictionary learning with pairwise constraints. In: Proceedings of ACCV (2014)
22. Guo, X.: Robust subspace segmentation by simultaneously learning data representations and their affinity matrix. In: Proceedings of the 25th International Joint Conference on Artificial Intelligence (IJCAI) (2015)
23. Hirzer, M., Beleznai, C., Roth, M., Bischof, H.: Person re-identification by descriptive and discriminative classification. In: Proceedings of SCIA (2011)
24. Hirzer, M., Roth, M., Bischof, H.: Person re-identification by efficient impostor-based metric learning. In: Proceedings of AVSS (2012)
25. Hirzer, M., Roth, M., Koestinger, M., Bischof, H.: Relaxed pairwise learned metric for person re-identification. In: Proceedings of ECCV (2012)
26. Hirzer, M., Roth, P.M., Köstinger, M., Bischof, H.: Relaxed pairwise learned metric for person re-identification. In: Fitzgibbon, A., Lazebnik, S., Perona, P., Sato, Y., Schmid, C. (eds.) ECCV 2012. LNCS, vol. 7577, pp. 780–793. Springer, Heidelberg (2012). doi:10.1007/978-3-642-33783-3_56
27. James, G., Witten, D., Hastie, T., Tibshirani, R.: An Introduction to Statistical Learning, vol. 112. Springer, New York (2013)
28. Kenneth, K., Joseph, M., Bhaskar, R., Kjersti, E., Te-Won, L., Terrence, S.: Dictionary learning algorithms for sparse representation. Neural Comput. **15**(2), 349–396 (2003)
29. Kim, S.J., Koh, K., Boyd, S., Gorinevsky, D.: \ell_1 trend filtering. SIAM Rev. **51**(2), 339–360 (2009)
30. Kodirov, E., Xiang, T., Gong, S.: Dictionary learning with iterative laplacian regularisation for unsupervised person re-identification. In: Xianghua Xie, M.W.J., Tam, G.K.L. (eds.) Proceedings of the British Machine Vision Conference (BMVC), pp. 44.1–44.12. BMVA Press. https://dx.doi.org/10.5244/C.29.44
31. Layne, R., Hospedales, T., Gong, S.: Re-id: hunting attributes in the wild. In: Proceedings of BMVC (2014)
32. Lee, H., Battle, A., Raina, R., Ng, A.Y.: Efficient sparse coding algorithms. In: Advances in Neural Information Processing Systems, pp. 801–808 (2006)
33. Li, C.G., Lin, Z., Zhang, H., Guo, J.: Learning semi-supervised representation towards a unified optimization framework for semi-supervised learning. In: The IEEE International Conference on Computer Vision (ICCV), December 2015

34. Li, C.G., Vidal, R.: Structured sparse subspace clustering: a unified optimization framework. In: The IEEE Conference on Computer Vision and Pattern Recognition (CVPR), June 2015
35. Li, W., Zhao, R., Wang, X.: Human reidentification with transferred metric learning. In: Lee, K.M., Matsushita, Y., Rehg, J.M., Hu, Z. (eds.) ACCV 2012. LNCS, vol. 7724, pp. 31–44. Springer, Heidelberg (2013). doi:10.1007/978-3-642-37331-2_3
36. Li, W., Zhao, R., Xiao, T., Wang, X.: Deepreid: deep filter pairing neural network for person re-identification. In: Proceedings of the IEEE Conference on Computer Vision and Pattern Recognition, pp. 152–159 (2014)
37. Liao, S., Hu, Y., Zhu, X., Li, S.Z.: Person re-identification by local maximal occurrence representation and metric learning. In: The IEEE Conference on Computer Vision and Pattern Recognition (CVPR), June 2015
38. Liao, S., Li, S.Z.: Efficient psd constrained asymmetric metric learning for person re-identification. In: The IEEE International Conference on Computer Vision (ICCV), December 2015
39. Lisanti, G., Masi, I., Bagdanov, A.D., Bimbo, A.D.: Person re-identification by iterative re-weighted sparse ranking. IEEE Trans. Pattern Anal. Mach. Intell. **37**(8), 1629–1642 (2013)
40. Liu, C., Gong, S., Loy, C.C.: On-the-fly feature importance mining for person re-identification. Pattern Recogn. **47**(4), 1602–1615 (2014)
41. Liu, X., Song, M., Tao, D., Zhou, X., Chen, C., Bu, J.: Semi-supervised coupled dictionary learning for person re-identification. In: Proceedings of CVPR (2014)
42. Ma, B., Su, Y., Jurie, F.: Bicov: a novel image representation for person re-identification and face verification. In: Proceedings of BMVC (2012)
43. Mairal, J., Bach, F., Ponce, J., Sapiro, G.: Online learning for matrix factorization and sparse coding. J. Mach. Learn. Res. **11**, 19–60 (2010)
44. Nie, F., Wang, H., Huang, H., Ding, C.: Unsupervised and semi-supervised learning via l_1-norm graph. In: ICCV (2011)
45. Nie, F., Wang, X., Huang, H.: Clustering and projected clustering with adaptive neighbors. In: Proceedings of the 20th ACM SIGKDD International Conference On Knowledge Discovery and Data Mining, pp. 977–986. ACM (2014)
46. Paisitkriangkrai, S., Shen, C., van den Hengel, A.: Learning to rank in person re-identification with metric ensembles. In: The IEEE Conference on Computer Vision and Pattern Recognition (CVPR), June 2015
47. Pedagadi, S., Orwell, J., Velastin, S., Boghossian, B.: Local fisher discriminant analysis for pedestrian re-identification. In: Proceedings of CVPR (2013)
48. Roth, P.M., Hirzer, M., Köstinger, M., Beleznai, C., Bischof, H.: Mahalanobis distance learning for person re-identification. In: Gong, S., Cristani, M., Yan, S., Loy, C.C. (eds.) Person Re-Identification, pp. 247–267. Springer, London (2014)
49. Shen, Y., Lin, W., Yan, J., Xu, M., Wu, J., Wang, J.: Person re-identification with correspondence structure learning. In: Proceedings of the IEEE International Conference on Computer Vision, pp. 3200–3208 (2015)
50. Shi, H., Zhu, X., Liao, S., Lei, Z., Yang, Y., Li, S.Z.: Constrained deep metric learning for person re-identification. CoRR abs/1511.07545 (2015). http://arxiv.org/abs/1511.07545
51. Su, C., Yang, F., Zhang, S., Tian, Q., Davis, L.S., Gao, W.: Multi-task learning with low rank attribute embedding for person re-identification. In: The IEEE International Conference on Computer Vision (ICCV), December 2015
52. Ustinova, E., Ganin, Y., Lempitsky, V.S.: Multiregion bilinear convolutional neural networks for person re-identification. CoRR abs/1512.05300 (2015). http://arxiv.org/abs/1512.05300

53. Vezzani, R., Baltieri, D., Cucchiara, R.: People reidentification in surveillance and forensics: a survey. ACM Comput. Surv. (CSUR) **46**(2), 29 (2013)
54. Wang, H., Gong, S., Xiang, T.: Unsupervised learning of generative topic saliency for person re-identification. In: Proceedings of BMVC (2014)
55. Xiong, F., Gou, M., Camps, O., Sznaier, M.: Person re-identification using kernel-based metric learning methods. In: Proceedings of ECCV (2014)
56. Yang, Y., Yang, J., Yan, J., Liao, S., Yi, D., Li, S.Z.: Salient color names for person re-identification. In: Fleet, D., Pajdla, T., Schiele, B., Tuytelaars, T. (eds.) ECCV 2014. LNCS, vol. 8689, pp. 536–551. Springer, Heidelberg (2014). doi:10.1007/978-3-319-10590-1_35
57. Zhao, R., Ouyang, W., Wang, X.: Unsupervised salience learning for person re-identification. In: Proceedings of CVPR (2013)
58. Zhao, R., Ouyang, W., Wang, X.: Learning mid-level filters for person re-identification. In: Proceedings of CVPR (2014)
59. Zheng, L., Shen, L., Tian, L., Wang, S., Wang, J., Tian, Q.: Scalable person re-identification: a benchmark. In: Proceedings of the IEEE International Conference on Computer Vision, pp. 1116–1124 (2015)
60. Zheng, L., Wang, S., Tian, L., He, F., Liu, Z., Tian, Q.: Query-adaptive late fusion for image search and person re-identification. In: The IEEE Conference on Computer Vision and Pattern Recognition (CVPR), June 2015
61. Zheng, M., Bu, J., Chen, C., Wang, C., Zhang, L., Qiu, G., Cai, D.: Graph regularized sparse coding for image representation. IEEE Trans. Image Process. **20**(5), 1327–1336 (2011)

Deep Learning the City:
Quantifying Urban Perception at a Global Scale

Abhimanyu Dubey[1], Nikhil Naik[3(✉)], Devi Parikh[2], Ramesh Raskar[3],
and César A. Hidalgo[3]

[1] Indian Institute of Technology, Delhi, India
abhimanyu1401@gmail.com
[2] Virginia Tech, Blacksburg, USA
parikh@vt.edu
[3] MIT Media Lab, Cambridge, USA
{naik,raskar,hidalgo}@mit.edu

Abstract. Computer vision methods that quantify the perception of
urban environment are increasingly being used to study the relationship
between a city's physical appearance and the behavior and health of its
residents. Yet, the throughput of current methods is too limited to quantify the perception of cities across the world. To tackle this challenge, we
introduce a new crowdsourced dataset containing 110,988 images from
56 cities, and 1,170,000 pairwise comparisons provided by 81,630 online
volunteers along six perceptual attributes: safe, lively, boring, wealthy,
depressing, and beautiful. Using this data, we train a Siamese-like convolutional neural architecture, which learns from a joint classification and
ranking loss, to predict human judgments of pairwise image comparisons.
Our results show that crowdsourcing combined with neural networks can
produce urban perception data at the global scale.

Keywords: Perception · Attributes · Street view · Crowdsourcing

1 Introduction

We shape our buildings, and thereafter our buildings shape us. – Winston
Churchill.

These famous remarks reflect the widely-held belief among policymakers, urban
planners and social scientists that the physical appearance of cities, and it's
perception, impacts the behavior and health of their residents. Based on this idea,
major policy initiatives—such as the New York City "Quality of Life Program"—
have been launched across the world to improve the appearance of cities. Social
scientists have either predicted or found evidence for the impact of the perceived
unsafety and disorderliness of cities on criminal behavior [1,2], education [3],

Electronic supplementary material The online version of this chapter (doi:10.
1007/978-3-319-46448-0_12) contains supplementary material, which is available to
authorized users.

© Springer International Publishing AG 2016
B. Leibe et al. (Eds.): ECCV 2016, Part I, LNCS 9905, pp. 196–212, 2016.
DOI: 10.1007/978-3-319-46448-0_12

health [4], and mobility [5], among others. However, these studies have been limited to a few neighborhoods, or a handful of cities at most, due to a lack of quantified data on the perception of cities. Historically, social scientists have collected this data using field surveys [6]. In the past decade, a new source of data on urban appearance has emerged, in the form of "Street View" imagery. Street View has enabled researchers to conduct virtual audits of urban appearance, with the help of trained experts [7, 8] or crowdsourcing [9, 10].

However, field surveys, virtual audits and crowdsourced studies lack both the resolution and the scale to fully utilize the global corpus of Street View imagery. For instance, New York City alone has roughly one million street blocks, which makes generating an exhaustive city-wide dataset of urban appearance a daunting task. Naturally, generating urban appearance data through human efforts for hundreds of cities across the world, at several time points, and across different attributes (e.g., cleanliness, safety, beauty), remains impractical. The solution to this problem is to develop computer vision algorithms—trained with human-labeled data—that conduct automated surveys of the built environment at street-level resolution and global scale.

A notable example of this approach is Streetscore by Naik et al. [11]—a computer vision algorithm trained using Place Pulse 1.0 [9], a crowdsourced game. In Place Pulse 1.0, users are asked to select one of the two Street View images in response to question "Which place looks safer?", "Which place looks more unique?", and "Which places looks more upper class?". This survey collected a total of 200,000 pairwise comparisons across the three attributes for 4,109 images from New York, Boston, Linz, and Saltzburg. Naik et al. converted the pairwise comparisons for perceived safety to ranked scores and trained a regression algorithm using generic image features to predict the ranked score for perceived safety (also see the work by Ordonez and Berg [12] and Porzi et al. [13]). Streetscore was employed to automatically generate a dataset of urban appearance covering 21 U.S. cities [14], which has been used to identify the impact of historic preservation districts on urban appearance [15], for quantifying urban change using time-series street-level imagery [16], and to determine the effects of urban design on perceived safety [17].

Yet the Streetscore algorithm is not unboundedly scalable. Streetscore was trained using a dataset containing a few thousand images from New York and Boston, so it cannot accurately measure the perceived safety of images from cities outside of the Northeast and Midwest of United States, which may have different architecture styles and urban planning constructs. This limits our ability to generate a truly **global dataset of urban appearance**. Streetscore was also trained using a dataset with a relatively dense set of preferences (each image was involved in roughly 30 pairwise comparisons). But collecting such a dense set of preferences with crowdsourcing is challenging for a study that involves hundreds of thousands of images from several cities, and multiple attributes. So scaling up the computational methods to map urban appearance from the regional scale, to the global scale, requires methods that can be trained on larger and sparser datasets—which contain a large, visually diverse set of images with relatively few comparisons among them.

With the motivation of developing a global dataset of urban appearance, in this paper, we introduce a new crowdsourced dataset of urban appearance and a computer vision technique to rank street-level images for urban appearance in this paper. Our dataset, which we call the **Place Pulse 2.0** dataset, contains 1.17 million pairwise comparisons for 110,988 images from 56 cities from 28 countries across 6 continents, scored by 81,630 online volunteers, along six perceptual dimensions: safe, lively, boring, wealthy, depressing, and beautiful. We use the Place Pulse 2.0 (PP 2.0) dataset to train convolutional neural network models which are able to predict the pairwise comparisons for perceptual attributes by taking an image pair as input. We propose two related network architectures: (i) the Streetscore-CNN (**SS-CNN** for short) and (ii) the Ranking SS-CNN (**RSS-CNN**). The SS-CNN consists of two disjoint identical sets of layers with tied weights, followed by a fusion sub-network, which minimizes the classification loss on pairwise comparison prediction. The RSS-CNN includes an additional ranking sub-network, which tries to simultaneously minimize the loss on both pairwise classification and ordinal ranking over the dataset. The SS-CNN architecture—fine-tuned with the PP 2.0 dataset—significantly outperforms the same network architecture with pre-trained AlexNet [18], PlacesNet [19], or VGGNet [20] weights. RSS-CNN shows better prediction performance than SS-CNN, owing to end-to-end learning based on both classification and ranking loss. Moreover, our CNN architecture obtains much better performance over a geographically disparate test set when trained with PP 2.0, in comparison to PP 1.0, due to the larger size and visual diversity (110,988 images from 56 cities, versus 4,109 images from 4 cities).

We find that networks trained to predict one visual attribute (e.g., *Safe*), are fairly accurate in the prediction of other visual attributes (e.g., *Lively, Beautiful*, etc.). We also use a trained network to predict the perceived safety of streetscapes from 6 new cities from 6 continents, that were not part of the training set. Finally, we hope that this work and our publicly released dataset will enable further progress on global studies of the social and economic effects of architectural and urban planning choices.

2   Related Work

Our paper speaks to four different strands of the academic literature: (1) predicting perceptual responses to images, (2) using urban imagery to understand cities, (3) understanding the connection between urban appearance and socioeconomic outcomes, and (4) generating image rankings and comparisons.

There is a growing body of literature on **predicting the perceptual responses to images**, such as aesthetics [21], memorability [22], interestingness [23], and virality [24]. In particular, our work is related to the literature on predicting the perception of street-level imagery. Naik et al. [11] use generic image features and support vector regression to develop Streetscore, an algorithm that predicts the perceived safety of street-level images from United States, using training data from the Place Pulse 1.0 dataset [9]. Ordonez and Berg [12] use the Place Pulse 1.0 dataset and report similar results for prediction of perceived safety, wealth, and uniqueness using Fisher vectors and DeCAF features [25]. Porzi et al. [13] identify the mid-level visual elements [26] that contribute to the perception of safety in the Place Pulse 1.0 dataset.

This new body of literature that utilizes **urban imagery to understand cities** has been enabled by new sources of data from both commercial providers (e.g., Google Street View) and photo-sharing websites (e.g., Flickr). These data sources have enabled applications for computer vision techniques in the fields of architecture, urban planning, urban economics and sociology. Doersch et al. [26] identify geographically distinctive visual elements from Street View data. Lee et al. [27] extend this work in the temporal domain by identifying architectural elements which are distinctive to specific historic periods. Arietta et al. [28] and Glaeser et al. [29] develop regression models based on Street View imagery to predict socioeconomic indicators. Zhou et al. [30] develop a unique city identity based on a high-level set of attributes derived from Flickr images. Khosla et al. [31] use Street View data and crowdsourcing to demonstrate that both humans and computers can navigate an unknown urban environment to locate businesses.

Our research also speaks to the more traditional stream of literature studying the connection between **urban appearance and socioeconomic outcomes** of urban residents, especially health and criminal behavioral. Researchers have studied the connection between the perception of unsafety and alcoholism [32], obesity [33], and the spread of STDs [4]. The influential "Broken Windows Theory (BWT)" [1] hypothesizes that criminal activity is more likely to occur in places that appear disorderly and visually unsafe. There has been a vigorous debate among scholars on BWT, who have found evidence in support [2,34] and against the theory [35,36]. Once again, this is another area where methods to quantify urban appearance may illuminate important questions.

Finally, our work is related to literature on **ranking and comparing images** based on both semantic and subjective attributes, or generating metrics for image comparisons. The concept of "relative attributes" [37]—ranking object/scene types according to different attributes—has been shown to be useful for applications such as image classification [38] and guided image search [39]. Kiapour et al. [40] rank images based on clothing styles using annotations collected from an online game, and generic image features. Zhu et al. [41] rank facial images for attractiveness, for generating better portrait images. Wang et al. [42] introduce a deep ranking method for image similarity metric computation. Zagoruyko and Komodakis [43] develop a Siamese architecture for computing image patch similarity for applications like wide-baseline stereo. Work on image perception summarized earlier [11–13] also ranks street-level images based on perceptual metrics.

In this paper, we contribute to these literatures by introducing a CNN-based technique to predict human judgments on urban appearance, using a global crowdsourced dataset.

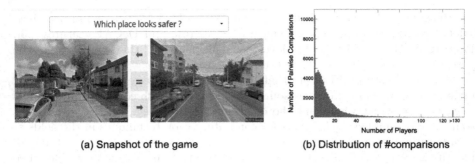

(a) Snapshot of the game   (b) Distribution of #comparisons

Fig. 1. Using a crowdsourced online game (a), we collect 1.1 million pairwise comparisons on urban appearance from 81,630 volunteers. The distribution of number of pairwise comparisons contributed by players is shown in (b).

3   The Place Pulse 2.0 Dataset

Our first goal is to collect a crowdsourced dataset of perceptual attributes for street-level images. To create this dataset, we chose Google Street View images from 56 major cities from 28 countries spread across all six inhabited continents. We obtained the latitude-longitude values for locations in these cities using a uniform grid [44] of points calculated on top of polygons of city boundaries. We queried the Google Street View Image API[1] using the latitude-longitude values, and obtained a total of 110,988 images captured between years 2007 and 2012.

Following Salesses et al. [9], we created a web-interface (Fig. 1-(a)) for collecting pairwise comparisons from users. Studies have shown that gathering relative comparisons is a more efficient and accurate way of obtaining human rankings as compared to obtaining numerical scores from each user [45,46]. In our implementation, we showed users a randomly-chosen pair of images side by side, and asked them to choose one in response to one of the six questions, preselected by the user. The questions were: "Which place looks safer?", "Which place looks livelier?", "Which place looks more boring?", "Which place looks wealthier?", "Which place looks more depressing?", and "Which place looks more beautiful?".

We generated traffic on our website primarily from organic media sources and by using Facebook advertisements targeted to English-speaking users who are interested in online games, architecture, cities, sociology, and urban planning. We collected a total of 1,169,078 pairwise comparisons from 81,630 online users between May 2013 and February 2016. The online users provided 16.6 comparisons on average. 6,118 users provided a single comparison each, while 30 users provided more than 1,000 comparisons (Fig. 1-(b)). The maximum number of comparisons provided by a single user was 7,168. We obtained the highest responses (370,134) for the question "Which place looks safer?", and the lowest responses (111,184) for the question "Which place looks more boring?". We attracted users from 162 countries (based on data from web analytics).

---

[1] https://developers.google.com/maps/documentation/streetview/.

Our user base contained a good mix of residents of both developed and developing countries. The top five countries of origin for these users were United States (31.4 %), India (22.4 %), United Kingdom (5.8 %), Brazil (4.6 %), and Canada (3.6 %). It is worth noting that the Place Pulse 1.0 study found that individual preferences for urban appearance were not driven by participants' age, gender, or location [9], indicating that there is no significant cultural bias in the dataset. Place Pulse 1.0 also found high inter-user reproducibility and high transitivity in people's perception of urban appearance, which is indicative of consistency in data collected for this task. With that established, we did not collect demographic information from users for our much larger PP 2.0 dataset, but we did use the exact same data collection interface and user recruitment strategy as PP 1.0. Table 1 summarizes the key facts about the Global Perception dataset.

Table 1. The place pulse 2.0 dataset at a glance

(a) Statistics on Images

Continent	#Cities	#Images
Asia	7	11,342
Africa	3	5,069
Australia	2	6,082
Europe	22	38,636
North America	15	33,691
South America	7	16,168
Total	56	110,988

(b) Statistics on Pairwise Comparisons (PC)

Question	#PC	#Per-image PC
Safe	370,134	7.67
Lively	268,494	5.52
Beautiful	166,823	3.46
Wealthy	137,688	2.87
Depressing	114,755	2.47
Boring	111,184	2.40
Total	1,169,078	16.73

4   Learning from the Place Pulse 2.0 Dataset

We now describe how we use the Place Pulse 2.0 dataset to train a neural network model to predict pairwise comparisons. Collecting pairwise comparisons has been the method of choice for learning subjective visual attributes such as style, perception, and taste. Examples include learning clothing styles [40], urban appearance [11], emotive responses to GIFs [47], or affective responses to paintings [48]. All these efforts use a two-step process for learning these subjective visual attributes—image ranking, followed by image classification/regression based on the visual attribute. In the first step, these methods [11,40,47,48] convert the pairwise comparisons to ranked scores for images using the Microsoft TrueSkill [49] algorithm. TrueSkill is a Bayesian ranking method, which generates a ranked score for a player (in this case, an image) in a two-player game by iteratively updating the ranked score of players after every contest (in this case, a human-contributed pairwise comparison). Note that this approach for producing image rankings does not take image features into account. In the next step, the ranked scores, along with image features are used to train classification or regression algorithms, to predict the score of a previously unseen image.

However, this two-step process has a few limitations. First, for larger datasets, the number of crowdsourced pairwise comparisons required becomes quite large. TrueSkill needs 24 to 36 comparisons per image for obtaining stable rankings [49]. Therefore, we would require ~**1.2 to 1.9 million comparisons** per question, to obtain stable TrueSkill scores for 110,988 images in the Place Pulse 2.0 dataset. This number is hard to achieve, even with the impressive number of users attracted by the Place Pulse game. Indeed, we are able to collect only 3.35 comparisons per image per question on average, after 33 months of data collection. Second, this two-step process ignores the visual content of images in the ranking process. We believe it is better to use visual content in the image ranking stage itself by learning to predict pairwise comparisons directly, which is similar in spirit to learning ranking functions for semantic attributes from image data [37] (also see Porzi et al. [13] for additional discussion on ranking versus regression). To address both problems, we propose to predict pairwise comparisons by training a neural network directly from image pairs and their crowdsourced comparisons from the Global Perception dataset. We describe the problem formulation and our neural network model next.

Problem Formulation: The Place Pulse 2.0 dataset consists of a set of m images $I = \{x_i\}_{i=1}^{m} \in \mathbb{R}^n$ in pixel-space and a set of N image comparison triplets $P = \{(i_k, j_k, y_k)\}_{k=1}^{N}$, $i, j \in \{1, ..., m\}, y \in \{+1, -1\}$, which specify a pairwise comparison between the ith and the jth image in the set. $y = +1$ denotes a win for image i, and $y = -1$ denotes a win for image j. Our goal is to learn a ranking function $f_r(x)$ on the raw image pixels such that we satisfy the maximum number of constraints

$$y \cdot (f_r(x_i) - f_r(x_j)) > 0 \ \ \forall \ (i, j, y) \in P \tag{1}$$

over the dataset. We aim to approximate a solution for this NP-hard problem [50] using a ranking approach, motivated by the direct adaptation of the RankSVM [50] formulation by Parikh and Grauman [37].

As the first step towards solving this problem, we transform the ranking task to a classification task. Specifically, our goal is to design a function which given an image pair, extracts low-level and mid-level features for each image as well as higher-level features discriminating the pair of images, and then predicts a winner. We next describe a convolutional neural network architecture which learns such a function.

4.1 Streetscore-CNN

We design the Streetscore-CNN (**SS-CNN**) for predicting the winner in a pairwise comparison task, by taking an image pair as input (Fig. 2). SS-CNN consists of two disjoint identical sets of layers with tied weights for feature extraction (similar to a Siamese network [51]). These feature extractor layers are concatenated and followed by a *fusion* sub-network, which consists of a set of convolutional layers culminating in a fully-connected layer with softmax loss used to

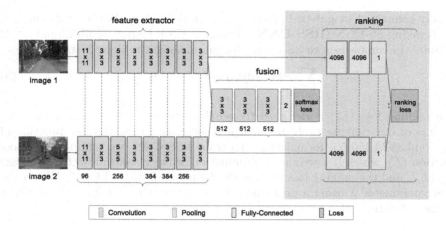

Fig. 2. We introduce two networks architectures, based on the Siamese model, for predicting pairwise comparisons of urban appearance. The basic model (SS-CNN) is trained with softmax loss in the fusion layer. We also introduce ranking loss layers to train the Ranking SS-CNN (additional layers shown in light blue background). While we experiment with AlexNet, PlacesNet, and VGGNet, this figure shows the AlexNet configuration. (Color figure online)

train the network. The fusion sub-network was inspired by the *temporal fusion* architecture [52] used to learn temporal features from video frames. The temporal fusion architecture learns convolutional filters by combining information from different activations in time. We employ a similar tactic to learn discriminative filters from pairwise image comparisons. We train SS-CNN for binary classification using the standard softmax or classification loss (L_c) with stochastic gradient descent. Since we perform classification between two categories (left image, right image), the softmax loss is specified as

$$L_c = \sum_{(i,j,y) \in P} \sum_{k}^{K} -\mathbb{1}[y = k] \log(g_k(\mathrm{x}_i, \mathrm{x}_j)) \qquad (2)$$

where $K = 2$ and g is the softmax of final layer activations.

4.2 Ranking Streetscore-CNN

While the SS-CNN architecture learns to predict pairwise comparisons from two images, training with logistic loss does not account for the ordinal ranking over all the images in the dataset. Moreover, training for only binary classification may not be sufficient to train such complex networks to understand the fine-grained differences between image pairs [42]. Therefore, we explicitly incorporate the ranking function $f_r(\mathrm{x})$ (Eq. 1) in the end-to-end learning process, we modify this basic SS-CNN architecture by attaching a ranking sub-network, consisting of fully-connected weight-tied layers (Fig. 2, in light blue). We call this network the Ranking SS-CNN (**RSS-CNN**). The RSS-CNN learns an additional set of weights—in comparison to SS-CNN—for minimizing a ranking loss,

$$L_r = \sum_{(i,j,y) \in P} \left(\max(0, y \cdot (f_r(\mathrm{x}_j) - f_r(\mathrm{x}_i))) \right)^2. \tag{3}$$

The ranking loss (L_r) is designed to penalize the network to satisfy the constraints of our ranking problem—which is identical to the the loss function of the RankSVM [50,53] formulation. To train RSS-CNN, we minimize the loss function (L), which is a weighted combination of the classification (or softmax) loss (L_c), and the ranking loss (L_r), in the form $L = L_c(P) + \lambda L_r(P)$. We set the hyper-parameter λ using a grid-search to maximize the classification accuracy on the validation set.

5   Experiments and Results

After defining SS-CNN and RSS-CNN, we evaluate their performance in Sects. 5.1 and 5.2, using the 370, 134 pairwise comparisons collected for the question "Which place looks safer?", since this question has the highest number of responses. Results for other attributes are described in Sect. 5.3.

Implementation Details. For all experiments, we split the set of triplets (P) for a given question randomly in the ratio 65–5–30 for training, validation and testing. We conducted experiments using the latest stable implementation of the Caffe library [54]. For both SS-CNN and RSS-CNN, we initialized the feature extractor layers using the pre-trained model weights of the following networks using their publicly available Caffe models[2] (one at a time): (i) the **AlexNet** image classification model [18], (ii) the **VGGNet** [20] 19-layer image classification model, and (iii) the **PlacesNet** [19] scene classification model. The weights for layers in fusion and ranking sub-networks were initialized from a zero-mean Gaussian distribution with standard deviation 0.01, following [18].

We trained the models on a single NVIDIA GeForce Titan X GPU. The momentum was set to 0.9. The initial learning rate was set to 0.001. When the validation error stopped improving with current learning rate, we reduced it by a factor of 10, repeating this process a maximum of four times (following [18]). The networks were trained to 100,000–150,000 iterations, stopping when the validation error stopped improving even after decreasing the learning rate. We will publicly release the models and the dataset upon acceptance.

5.1   Predicting Pairwise Comparisons

SS-CNN: We experiment with SS-CNN initialized using AlexNet, PlacesNet, and VGGNet, and evaluated their performance using three methods described below.

---

[2] https://github.com/BVLC/caffe/wiki/Model-Zoo.

Table 2. Pairwise comparison prediction accuracy

(a) SS-CNN

Network	Ranking Method		
	Softmax	TrueSkill	RankSVM
AlexNet	53.0%	55.7%	58.4%
SS-CNN (AlexNet)	60.3%	62.6%	65.5%
PlacesNet	56.4%	58.8%	61.6%
SS-CNN (PlacesNet)	62.2%	64.7%	68.1%
VGGNet	60.9%	62.7%	63.5%
SS-CNN (VGGNet)	65.3%	67.8%	**72.4%**

(b) RSS-CNN

Model	Prediction Acc.
AlexNet	64.1%
PlacesNet	68.8%
VGGNet	**73.5%**

1. **Softmax:** We calculate the binary prediction accuracy of the softmax output for prediction of pairwise comparisons.
2. **TrueSkill:** We generate 30 "synthetic" pairwise comparisons per image using the network, by feeding random image pairs, and calculate the TrueSkill score for each image with these comparisons. We compare TrueSkill scores of the two images in a pair, to predict the winning image for each pair in the test set, and measure the binary prediction accuracy. We use this method since TrueSkill is able to generate stable scores for images, which allows us to reduce the noise in independent binary predictions on image pairs.
3. **RankSVM:** We feed a combined feature representation of the image pair obtained from the final convolution layer of SS-CNN to a RankSVM [50] (using the LIBLINEAR [55] implementation), and learn a ranking function. We then use the ranking scores for images in the test set to decide the winner from test image pairs, and calculate the binary prediction accuracy.

We evaluate the accuracy for all three networks with (i) original (pre-trained) weights, and (ii) weights fine-tuned with the Place Pulse 2.0 dataset. Table 2-(a) shows that, in all cases, the binary prediction accuracy increases significantly— 6.5 % on average—across all experiments. The gain in performance can be attributed to both, end-to-end learning of the pairwise classification task and the size and diversity of the Place Pulse 2.0 dataset. SS-CNN (VGGNet), the deepest architecture, obtains the best performance over all three methods. We also observe that RankSVM consistently outperforms TrueSkill, which in turn, outperforms softmax. This makes sense, since TrueSkill is not designed to maximize prediction accuracy for pairwise comparisons, but rather to generate stable ranked scores from pairwise comparisons. In contrast, the RankSVM loss function explicitly tries to minimize misclassification in pairwise comparisons.

RSS-CNN: We test the performance of the RSS-CNN architecture with AlexNet, PlacesNet, and VGGNet. Since we explicitly learn a ranking function $f_r(x)$ in the case of RSS-CNN, we compare the ranking function outputs for both images in a test pair to decide which image wins, and calculate the binary prediction accuracy. Table 2-(b) summarizes the results for the three models.

Table 3. Comparing place pulse 1.0 and place pulse 2.0 datasets

Ranking SS-CNN	AlexNet	PlacesNet	VGGNet
Place Pulse 1.0 (PP 1.0)	59.8 %	60.9 %	64.1 %
Place Pulse 2.0 (same #comparisons as PP 1.0)	61.9 %	66.2 %	64.2 %
Place Pulse 2.0 (all comparisons)	64.1 %	68.8 %	73.5 %

The Ranking SS-CNN (VGGNet) obtains the highest accuracy for pairwise comparison prediction (73.5 %). Since the RSS-CNN performs end-to-end learning based on both the classification and ranking loss, it significantly outperforms the SS-CNN trained with only classification loss (Table 2-(a), column 1). The RSS-CNN also does better than the combination of SS-CNN and RankSVM (Table 2-(a), column 3) in most cases. We also find that RSS-CNN learns better with more data, and continues to do so, whereas the SS-CNN architecture plateaus after encountering approximately 60 % of the training data. See supplementary material for additional analysis on data size and performance.

5.2   Comparing Place Pulse 1.0 and Place Pulse 2.0 Datasets

The Place Pulse 2.0 (PP 2.0) dataset has significantly higher visual diversity (56 cities from 28 countries) as compared to the Place Pulse 1.0 (PP 1.0) dataset (4 cities from 2 countries). It also contains significantly more training data. For the visual attribute of *Safety*, the PP 2.0 dataset contains 370,134 comparisons for 110,988 images, while the PP 1.0 dataset contains 73,806 comparisons for 4,109 images. We are interested in studying the gain in performance obtained by this increased visual diversity and size. So we compare the binary prediction accuracy on PP 2.0 data, of an RSS-CNN trained with the three network architectures using (i) all 73,806 comparisons from PP 1.0, (ii) 73,806 comparisons randomly chosen from PP 2.0 (the same amount of data as PP 1.0, but an increase in visual diversity), and (iii) 240,587 comparisons from PP 2.0 (the entire training set) (an increase in both the amount and the visual diversity of data). Comparing experiments (i) and (ii) (Table 3), we find that increasing visual diversity improves the accuracy for all three networks, for the same amount of data. The gain in performance is least for VGGNet, which is the deepest network, and hence needs larger amount of data to train. Finally, training with the entire PP 2.0 dataset (experiment (iii)) improves accuracy by an average of 7.2 % as compared to training with the PP 1.0.

   We also conduct the reverse experiment to measure the performance of the PP 2.0 dataset on PP 1.0. We calculate the five-fold cross-validation accuracy (following [13]) for pairwise comparison prediction for the *Safety* attribute using a RankSVM trained with features of image pairs from the PP 1.0 dataset. We experiment with two different features, extracted, respectively, from (i) the SS-CNN (VGGNet) trained with PP 2.0 data and (ii) the SS-CNN (VGGNet) trained with PP 2.0 data and fine-tuned further with PP 1.0 data. Experiments

Table 4. Prediction performance across attributes

Train	Test					
	Safe	Lively	Beautiful	Wealthy	Boring	Depressing
Safe	**73.5 %**	67.7 %	66.3 %	60.3 %	47.2 %	42.3 %
Lively	63.8 %	**70.3 %**	65.8 %	61.3 %	58.9 %	53.7 %
Beautiful	61.2 %	67.1 %	**70.2 %**	53.5 %	50.2 %	51.4 %
Wealthy	60.7 %	54.6 %	52.7 %	**65.7 %**	52.8 %	55.9 %
Boring	48.6 %	55.6 %	52.3 %	53.1 %	**66.1 %**	59.8 %
Depressing	54.5 %	54.2 %	43.2 %	49.7 %	57.2 %	**62.8 %**

(i) and (ii) yield an accuracy of 81.6 % and 81.1 % respectively. The previous best result reported for the pairwise comparison prediction task [13] on the PP 1.0 dataset is 70.2 %, albeit from a model trained with PP 1.0 data alone. Note that our models are too deep to be trained with only PP 1.0 data.

Comparison with Generic Image Features: Prior work [11–13] has found that generic image features do well on the Place Pulse 1.0 dataset, for predicting both ranked scores and pairwise comparisons. Based on this literature, we extract three best performing features—GIST [56], Texton Histograms [57], and CIELab Color Histograms [58]—from images in the PP 2.0 dataset. We find that the pairwise prediction accuracy of a RankSVM trained with feature vector consisting of these features is 56.7 % on the PP 2.0 dataset, significantly lower than all variations of SS-CNN. Our best performing model RSS-CNN (VGGNet) has an accuracy of 73.5 %.

5.3 Predicting Different Perceptual Attributes

Our dataset contains a total of six perceptual attributes—*Safe, Lively, Beautiful, Wealthy, Boring,* and *Depressing.* We now evaluate the prediction performance of RSS-CNN on these six attributes. Specifically, we train the RSS-CNN (VGGNet) network for each attribute, and measure it's performance using binary prediction accuracy. Table 4 shows that the *in-attribute* prediction performance is roughly proportional to the number of comparisons available for training, with the best prediction performance for *Safe,* and the worst performance for *Depressing.* We also evaluate the performance of the network trained to predict one perceptual attribute in predicting the pairwise comparisons for the other three attributes (*cross-attribute* prediction). The *Safe* network shows strong performance in prediction of *Lively, Beautiful,* and *Wealthy* attributes, which is indicative of the high correlation between different perceptual attributes.

A model trained to predict pairwise comparisons can be used to generate "synthetic" comparisons by taking random image pairs as input. A large number of comparisons can be then fed to ranking algorithms (like TrueSkill) to

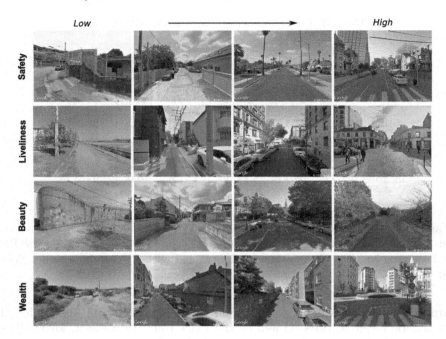

Fig. 3. Example results from the Place Pulse 2.0 dataset, containing images ranked based on pairwise comparisons generated by the RSS-CNN.

obtain stable ranked scores. We use this trick to generate TrueSkill scores for four attributes using pairwise comparisons predicted by a trained RSS-CNN (VGGNet) (30 per image). Figure 3 shows examples from the dataset, and Fig. 4 shows failure cases. We find that, for instance, highway images with forest cover are predicted to be highly safe, and overcast images as highly boring. Quantitatively, the correlation coefficient (R^2) of *Safe* with *Lively*, *Beautiful*, and *Wealthy* is 0.80, 0.83, and 0.65 respectively. This indicates that there is relatively large orthogonality ($(1 - R^2)$) between attributes. See supplement for details.

5.4 Predicting Urban Appearance Across Countries

Our hope is that the Place Pulse 2.0 dataset will enable algorithms to conduct automated audits of urban appearance for cities all across the world. The Streetscore [11] algorithm was able to successfully generalize to the Northeast and Midwest of the U.S., based on training data from just two cities, New York and Boston. This indicates that models trained with the PP 2.0 dataset containing images from 28 countries should be able to generalize to large regions in these countries, and beyond. For a qualitative experiment to test generalization, we download 22,282 Street View images from six cities from six continents—Vancouver, Buenos Aires, St. Petersburg, Durban, Seoul, and Brisbane—that were not a part of the PP 2.0 dataset. We map the perceived safety for these

Safety = 7.11/10   Liveliness = 8.02/10   Beauty = 1.66/10   Wealth = 7.97/10

Fig. 4. Example failure cases from the prediction results, containing images and their TrueSkill scores for attributes computed from pairwise comparisons generated by the RSS-CNN.

cities using TrueSkill scores for images computed from 30 "synthetic" pairwise comparisons generated with RSS-CNN (VGGNet). While the prediction performance of the network on these images cannot be quantified due to a lack of human-labeled ground truth, visual inspection shows that the scores assigned to streetscapes conform with visual intuition (see supplement for map visualizations and example images).

6 Discussion and Concluding Remarks

In this paper, we introduced a new crowdsourced dataset of global urban appearance containing pairwise image comparisons and proposed a neural network architecture for predicting the human-labeled comparisons. Since we focussed on predicting pairwise win/loss decisions to aid image ranking, we ignored the image pairs where the users perceive the images to be *equal* for the given perceptual attribute. However, 13.2 % pairwise comparisons in our dataset are *equal*, and incorporating the prediction of equality in comparisons should be a part of future work. Future work can also explore the determinants of perceptual attributes of urban appearance (e.g., what makes an image appear safe? or lively?) Such studies would allow better visual designs that optimize attributes of urban appearance. From a computer vision perspective, understanding the geographical range over which models trained on street-level imagery from different regions of the world are able to generalize would be an interesting future direction, since the architectural similarities between cities are determined by a complex interaction of history, culture, and economics.

Our technique can be generalized for computer vision tasks of studying the style, perception, or visual attributes of images, objects, or scene categories. Our trained networks can be used to generate a global dataset of urban appearance, which will enable the study a variety of research questions: How does urban appearance affect the behavior and health of residents, and how do these effects vary across countries? How are different architectural styles perceived? How similar/different are different cities across the world in terms of perception? Can visual appearance be used as a proxy for inequality within cities? A global dataset of urban appearance will thus aid computational studies in architecture, art history, sociology, and economics. These datasets can also help policymakers and city governments make data-driven decisions on allocation of resources to different cities or neighborhoods for improving urban appearance.

References

1. Wilson, J.Q., Kelling, G.L.: Broken windows. Atlantic Monthly **249**(3), 29–38 (1982)
2. Keizer, K., Lindenberg, S., Steg, L.: The spreading of disorder. Science **322**(5908), 1681–1685 (2008)
3. Milam, A., Furr-Holden, C., Leaf, P.: Perceived school and neighborhood safety, neighborhood violence and academic achievement in urban school children. Urban Rev. **42**(5), 458–467 (2010)
4. Cohen, D.A., Mason, K., Bedimo, A., Scribner, R., Basolo, V., Farley, T.A.: Neighborhood physical conditions and health. Am. J. Public Health **93**(3), 467–471 (2003)
5. Piro, F.N., Nœss, Ø., Claussen, B.: Physical activity among elderly people in a city population: the influence of neighbourhood level violence and self perceived safety. J. Epidemiol. Commun. Health **60**(7), 626–632 (2006)
6. Sampson, R.J.: Great American City: Chicago and the enduring neighborhood effect. University of Chicago Press, Chicago (2012)
7. Miller, D.K.: Using google street view to audit the built environment: inter-rater reliability results. Ann. Behav. Med. **45**(1), 108–112 (2013)
8. Hwang, J., Sampson, R.J.: Divergent pathways of gentrification racial inequality and the social order of renewal in chicago neighborhoods. Am. Sociol. Rev. **79**(4), 726–751 (2014)
9. Salesses, P., Schechtner, K., Hidalgo, C.A.: The collaborative image of the city: mapping the inequality of urban perception. PloS One **8**(7), e68–400 (2013)
10. Quercia, D., O'Hare, N.K., Cramer, H.: Aesthetic capital: what makes London look beautiful, quiet, and happy? In: ACM Conference on Computer Supported Cooperative Work & Social Computing, pp. 945–955 (2014)
11. Naik, N., Philipoom, J., Raskar, R., Hidalgo, C.: Streetscore-Predicting the perceived safety of one million streetscapes. In: IEEE CVPR Workshops, pp. 793–799 (2014)
12. Ordonez, V., Berg, T.L.: Learning high-level judgments of urban perception. In: Fleet, D., Pajdla, T., Schiele, B., Tuytelaars, T. (eds.) ECCV 2014. LNCS, vol. 8694, pp. 494–510. Springer, Heidelberg (2014). doi:10.1007/978-3-319-10599-4_32
13. Porzi, L., Rota Bulò, S., Lepri, B., Ricci, E.: Predicting and understanding urban perception with convolutional neural networks. In: ACM Conference on Multimedia, pp. 139–148 (2015)
14. Naik, N., Raskar, R., Hidalgo, C.A.: Cities are physical too: using computer vision to measure the quality and impact of urban appearance. Am. Econ. Rev. **106**(5), 128–132 (2016)
15. Been, V., Ellen, I.G., Gedal, M., Glaeser, E., McCabe, B.J.: Preserving history or restricting development? the heterogeneous effects of historic districts on local housing markets in new york city. J. Urban Econ. **92**, 16–30 (2015)
16. Naik, N., Kominers, S.D., Raskar, R., Glaeser, E.L., Hidalgo, C.A.: Do people shape cities, or do cities shape people? the co-evolution of physical, social, and economic change in five major U.S. cities. Working Paper 21620, National Bureau of Economic Research (2015)
17. Harvey, C., Aultman-Hall, L., Hurley, S.E., Troy, A.: Effects of skeletal streetscape design on perceived safety. Landscape Urban Plann. **142**, 18–28 (2015)
18. Krizhevsky, A., Sutskever, I., Hinton, G.E.: Imagenet classification with deep convolutional neural networks. In: Advances in Neural Information Processing Systems, pp. 1097–1105(2012)

19. Zhou, B., Lapedriza, A., Xiao, J., Torralba, A., Oliva, A.: Learning deep features for scene recognition using places database. In: Advances in Neural Information Processing Systems, pp. 487–495 (2014)
20. Simonyan, K., Zisserman, A.: Very deep convolutional networks for large-scale image recognition (2014). arXiv preprint arXiv:1409.1556
21. Joshi, D., Datta, R., Fedorovskaya, E., Luong, Q.T., Wang, J.Z., Li, J., Luo, J.: Aesthetics and emotions in images. IEEE Sig. Process. Mag. 28(5), 94–115 (2011)
22. Isola, P., Xiao, J., Torralba, A., Oliva, A.: What makes an image memorable? In: IEEE CVPR, pp. 145–152 (2011)
23. Dhar, S., Ordonez, V.: Berg, T.L.: High level describable attributes for predicting aesthetics and interestingness. In: IEEE CVPR, pp. 1657–1664 (2011)
24. Deza, A., Parikh, D.: Understanding image virality. In: IEEE CVPR, pp. 1818–1826 (2015)
25. Donahue, J., Jia, Y., Vinyals, O., Hoffman, J., Zhang, N., Tzeng, E., Darrell, T.: Decaf: a deep convolutional activation feature for generic visual recognition (2013). arXiv preprint arXiv:1310.1531
26. Doersch, C., Singh, S., Gupta, A., Sivic, J., Efros, A.A.: What makes paris look like paris? ACM Trans. Graph. 31(4), 101 (2012)
27. Lee, S., Maisonneuve, N., Crandall, D., Efros, A., Sivic, J.: Linking past to present: discovering style in two centuries of architecture. In: IEEE International Conference on Computational Photography (2015)
28. Arietta, S.M., Efros, A.A., Ramamoorthi, R., Agrawala, M.: City forensics: using visual elements to predict non-visual city attributes. IEEE Trans. Visual. Comput. Graph. 20(12), 2624–2633 (2014)
29. Glaeser, E.L., Kominers, S.D., Luca, M., Naik, N.: Big data and big cities: the promises and limitations of improved measures of urban life. Working Paper 21778, National Bureau of Economic Research (2015)
30. Zhou, B., Liu, L., Oliva, A., Torralba, A.: Recognizing city identity via attribute analysis of geo-tagged images. In: Fleet, D., Pajdla, T., Schiele, B., Tuytelaars, T. (eds.) ECCV 2014. LNCS, vol. 8691, pp. 519–534. Springer, Heidelberg (2014). doi:10.1007/978-3-319-10578-9_34
31. Khosla, A., An, B., Lim, J.J., Torralba, A.: Looking beyond the visible scene. In: IEEE CVPR, pp. 3710–3717 (2014)
32. Kuipers, M.A., van Poppel, M.N., van den Brink, W., Wingen, M., Kunst, A.E.: The association between neighborhood disorder, social cohesion and hazardous alcohol use: a national multilevel study. Drug Alcohol Depend. 126(1), 27–34 (2012)
33. Dulin-Keita, A., Thind, H.K., Affuso, O., Baskin, M.L.: The associations of perceived neighborhood disorder and physical activity with obesity among african american adolescents. BMC Pub. Health 13(1), 440 (2013)
34. Kelling, G.L., Coles, C.M.: Fixing Broken Windows: Restoring Order and Reducing Crime in Our Communities. Simon and Schuster, New York (1997)
35. Sampson, R.J., Raudenbush, S.W.: Disorder in urban neighborhoods: Does it lead to crime. National Institute of Justice (2001)
36. Harcourt, B.E.: Reflecting on the subject: a critique of the social influence conception of deterrence, the broken windows theory, and order-maintenance policing New York style. Mich. Law Rev. 97(2), 291–389 (1998)
37. Parikh, D., Grauman, K.: Relative attributes. In: IEEE ICCV, pp. 503–510 (2011)
38. Parkash, A., Parikh, D.: Attributes for classifier feedback. In: Fitzgibbon, A., Lazebnik, S., Perona, P., Sato, Y., Schmid, C. (eds.) ECCV 2012. LNCS, vol. 7574, pp. 354–368. Springer, Heidelberg (2012). doi:10.1007/978-3-642-33712-3_26

39. Kovashka, A., Parikh, D., Grauman, K.: Whittlesearch: Image search with relative attribute feedback. In: IEEE CVPR, pp. 2973–2980 (2012)
40. Kiapour, M.H., Yamaguchi, K., Berg, A.C., Berg, T.L.: Hipster wars: discovering elements of fashion styles. In: Fleet, D., Pajdla, T., Schiele, B., Tuytelaars, T. (eds.) ECCV 2014. LNCS, vol. 8689, pp. 472–488. Springer, Heidelberg (2014). doi:10.1007/978-3-319-10590-1_31
41. Zhu, J.Y., Agarwala, A., Efros, A.A., Shechtman, E., Wang, J.: Mirror mirror: crowdsourcing better portraits. ACM Trans. Graph. $33(6)$, 234 (2014)
42. Wang, J., Song, Y., Leung, T., Rosenberg, C., Wang, J., Philbin, J., Chen, B., Wu, Y.: Learning fine-grained image similarity with deep ranking. In: IEEE CVPR, pp. 1386–1393 (2014)
43. Zagoruyko, S., Komodakis, N.: Learning to compare image patches via convolutional neural networks. In: IEEE CVPR, pp. 4353–4361 (2015)
44. Persson, P.O., Strang, G.: A simple mesh generator in MATLAB. SIAM Rev. $46(2)$, 329–345 (2004)
45. Stewart, N., Brown, G.D., Chater, N.: Absolute identification by relative judgment. Psychol. Rev. $112(4)$, 881 (2005)
46. Bijmolt, T.H., Wedel, M.: The effects of alternative methods of collecting similarity data for multidimensional scaling. Int. J. Res. Mark. $12(4)$, 363–371 (1995)
47. Jou, B., Bhattacharya, S., Chang, S.F.: Predicting viewer perceived emotions in animated GIFs. In: ACM International Conference on Multimedia, pp. 213–216 (2014)
48. Sartori, A., Yanulevskaya, V., Salah, A.A., Uijlings, J., Bruni, E., Sebe, N.: Affective analysis of professional and amateur abstract paintings using statistical analysis and art theory. ACM Trans. Interact. Intell. Syst. $5(2)$, 8 (2015)
49. Herbrich, R., Minka, T., Graepel, T.: TrueSkill: a bayesian skill rating system. In: Advances in Neural Information Processing Systems, pp. 569–576 (2006)
50. Joachims, T.: Optimizing search engines using clickthrough data. In: ACM International Conference on Knowledge Discovery and Data Mining, pp. 133–142 (2002)
51. Chopra, S., Hadsell, R., LeCun, Y.: Learning a similarity metric discriminatively, with application to face verification. In: IEEE CVPR, vol. 1, pp. 539–546 (2005)
52. Karpathy, A., Toderici, G., Shetty, S., Leung, T., Sukthankar, R., Fei-Fei, L.: Large-scale video classification with convolutional neural networks. In: IEEE CVPR, pp. 1725–1732 (2014)
53. Chapelle, O., Keerthi, S.S.: Efficient algorithms for ranking with SVMs. Inf. Retrieval $13(3)$, 201–215 (2010)
54. Jia, Y., Shelhamer, E., Donahue, J., Karayev, S., Long, J., Girshick, R., Guadarrama, S., Darrell, T.: Caffe: convolutional architecture for fast feature embedding. In: ACM International Conference on Multimedia, pp. 675–678 (2014)
55. Fan, R.E., Chang, K.W., Hsieh, C.J., Wang, X.R., Lin, C.J.: Liblinear: a library for large linear classification. J. Mach. Learn. Res. 9, 1871–1874 (2008)
56. Oliva, A., Torralba, A.: Modeling the shape of the scene: a holistic representation of the spatial envelope. Int. J. Comput. Vis. $42(3)$, 145–175 (2001)
57. Malik, J., Belongie, S., Leung, T., Shi, J.: Contour and texture analysis for image segmentation. Int. J. Comput. Vis. $43(1)$, 7–27 (2001)
58. Xiao, J., Hays, J., Ehinger, K.A., Oliva, A., Torralba, A.: Sun database: large-scale scene recognition from abbey to zoo. In: IEEE CVPR, pp. 3485–3492 (2010)

4D Match Trees for Non-rigid Surface Alignment

Armin Mustafa$^{(\boxtimes)}$, Hansung Kim, and Adrian Hilton

CVSSP, University of Surrey, Guildford, UK
{a.mustafa,h.kim,a.hilton}@surrey.ac.uk

Abstract. This paper presents a method for dense 4D temporal alignment of partial reconstructions of non-rigid surfaces observed from single or multiple moving cameras of complex scenes. *4D Match Trees* are introduced for robust global alignment of non-rigid shape based on the similarity between images across sequences and views. Wide-timeframe sparse correspondence between arbitrary pairs of images is established using a segmentation-based feature detector (SFD) which is demonstrated to give improved matching of non-rigid shape. Sparse SFD correspondence allows the similarity between any pair of image frames to be estimated for moving cameras and multiple views. This enables the 4D Match Tree to be constructed which minimises the observed change in non-rigid shape for global alignment across all images. Dense 4D temporal correspondence across all frames is then estimated by traversing the 4D Match tree using optical flow initialised from the sparse feature matches. The approach is evaluated on single and multiple view images sequences for alignment of partial surface reconstructions of dynamic objects in complex indoor and outdoor scenes to obtain a temporally consistent 4D representation. Comparison to previous 2D and 3D scene flow demonstrates that 4D Match Trees achieve reduced errors due to drift and improved robustness to large non-rigid deformations.

Keywords: Non-sequential tracking · Surface alignment · Temporal coherence · Dynamic scene reconstruction · 4D modeling

1 Introduction

Recent advances in computer vision have demonstrated reconstruction of complex dynamic real-world scenes from multiple view video or single view depth acquisition. These approaches typically produce an independent 3D scene model at each time instant with partial and erroneous surface reconstruction for moving objects due to occlusion and inherent visual ambiguity [1–4]. For non-rigid objects, such as people with loose clothing or animals, producing a temporally coherent 4D representation from partial surface reconstructions remains a challenging problem.

Electronic supplementary material The online version of this chapter (doi:10.1007/978-3-319-46448-0_13) contains supplementary material, which is available to authorized users.

© Springer International Publishing AG 2016
B. Leibe et al. (Eds.): ECCV 2016, Part I, LNCS 9905, pp. 213–229, 2016.
DOI: 10.1007/978-3-319-46448-0_13

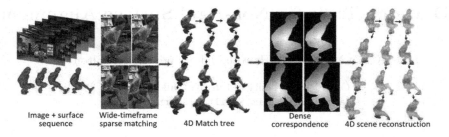

Image + surface   Wide-timeframe   Dense
sequence   sparse matching   4D Match tree   correspondence   4D scene reconstruction

Fig. 1. 4D Match Tree framework for global alignment of partial surface reconstructions

In this paper we introduce a framework for global alignment of non-rigid shape observed in one or more views with a moving camera assuming that a partial surface reconstruction or depth image is available at each frame. The objective is to estimate the dense surface correspondence across all observations from single or multiple view acquisition. An overview of the approach is presented in Fig. 1. The input is the sequence of frames $\{F_i\}_{i=1}^{N}$ where N is the number of frames. Each frame F_i consists of a set of images from multiple viewpoints $\{V_c\}_{c=1}^{M}$, where M is the number of viewpoints for each time instant $(M \geq 1)$. Robust sparse feature matching between arbitrary pairs of image observations of the non-rigid shape at different times is used to evaluate similarity. This allows a *4D Match Tree* to be constructed which represents the optimal alignment path for all observations across multiple sequences and views that minimises the total dissimilarity between frames or non-rigid shape deformation. 4D alignment is then achieved by traversing the 4D match tree using dense optical flow initialised from the sparse inter-frame non-rigid shape correspondence. This approach allows global alignment of partial surface reconstructions for complex dynamic scenes with multiple interacting people and loose clothing.

Previous work on 4D modelling of complex dynamic objects has primarily focused on acquisition under controlled conditions such as a multiple camera studio environment to reliably reconstruct the complete object surface at each frame using shape-from-silhouette and multiple view stereo [5–7]. Robust techniques have been introduced for temporal alignment of the reconstructed non-rigid shape to obtain a 4D model based on tracking the complete surface shape or volume with impressive results for complex motion. However, these approaches assume a reconstruction of the full non-rigid object surface at each time frame and do not easily extend to 4D alignment of partial surface reconstructions or depth maps.

The wide-spread availability of low-cost depth sensors has motivated the development of methods for temporal correspondence or alignment and 4D modelling from partial dynamic surface observations [8–11]. Scene flow techniques [12,13] typically estimate the pairwise surface or volume correspondence between reconstructions at successive frames but do not extend to 4D alignment or correspondence across complete sequences due to drift and failure for rapid and complex motion. Existing feature matching techniques either work in 2D [14] or 3D [15] or for sparse [16,17] or dense [18] points. However these methods fail in the case of occlusion, large motions, background clutter, deformation, moving cameras and appearance of new parts of objects. Recent work has introduced approaches, such as DynamicFusion [8], for 4D modelling from depth image sequences integrating temporal observations of non-rigid shape to resolve fine detail. Approaches to 4D modelling from partial surface observations are currently limited to relatively simple isolated objects such as the human face or upper-body and do not handle large non-rigid deformations such as loose clothing.

In this paper we introduce the *4D Match Tree* for robust global alignment of partial reconstructions of complex dynamic scenes. This enables the estimation of temporal surface correspondence for non-rigid shape across all frames and views from moving cameras to obtain a temporally coherent 4D representation of the scene. Contributions of this work include:

– Robust global 4D alignment of partial reconstructions of non-rigid shape from single or multiple-view sequences with moving cameras
– Sparse matching between wide-timeframe image pairs of non-rigid shape using a segmentation-based feature descriptor
– 4D Match Trees to represent the optimal non-sequential alignment path which minimises change in the observed shape
– Dense 4D surface correspondence for large non-rigid shape deformations using optic-flow guided by sparse matching

1.1 Related Work

Temporal alignment for reconstructions of dynamic scenes is an area of extensive research in computer vision. Consistent mesh sequences finds application in performance capture, animation and motion analysis. A number of approaches for surface reconstruction [19,20] do not produce temporally coherent models for an entire sequence rather they align pairs of frames sequentially. Other methods proposed for 4D alignment of surface reconstructions assume that a complete mesh of the dynamic object is available for the entire sequence [21–25]. Partial surface tracking methods for single view [26] and RGBD data [8,27] perform sequential alignment of the reconstructions using frame-to-frame tracking. Sequential methods suffer from drift due to accumulation of errors in alignment between successive frames and failure is observed due to large non-rigid motion. Non-sequential approaches address these issues but existing methods require complete surface reconstruction [24,25]. In this paper we propose a non-sequential method to align partial surface reconstructions of dynamic objects for general dynamic outdoor and indoor scenes with large non-rigid motions across sequences and views.

Alignment across a sequence can be established using correspondence information between frames. Methods have been proposed to obtain sparse [14,16,17] and dense [13,15,18] correspondence between consecutive frames for entire sequence. Existing sparse correspondence methods work sequentially on a frame-to-frame basis for single view [14] or multi-view [16] and require a strong prior initialization [17]. Existing dense matching or scene flow methods [12,13] require a strong prior which fails in the case of large motion and moving cameras. Other methods are limited to RGBD data [18] or narrow timeframe [15,28] for dynamic scenes. In this paper we aim to establish robust sparse wide-timeframe correspondence to construct 4D Match Trees. Dense matching is performed on the 4D Match Tree non-sequentially using the sparse matches as an initialization for optical flow to handle large non-rigid motion and deformation across the sequence.

2   Methodology

The aim of this work is to obtain 4D temporally coherent models from partial surface reconstructions of dynamic scenes. Our approach is motivated by previous non-sequential approaches to surface alignment [24,29,30] which have been shown to achieve robust 4D alignment of complete surface reconstructions over multiple sequences with large non-rigid deformations. These approaches use an intermediate tree structure to represent the unaligned data based on a measure of shape similarity. This defines an optimal alignment path which minimises the total shape deformation. In this paper we introduce the 4D Match Tree to represent the similarity between unaligned partial surface reconstructions. In contrast to previous work the similarity between any pair of frames is estimated from wide-timeframe sparse feature matching between the images of the non-rigid shape. Sparse correspondence gives a similarity measure which approximates the overlap and amount of non-rigid deformation between images of the partial surface reconstructions at different time instants. This enables robust non-sequential alignment and initialisation of dense 4D correspondence across all frames.

2.1   Overview

An overview of the 4D Match Tree framework is presented in Fig. 1. The input is a partial surface reconstruction or depth map of a general dynamic scenes at each frame together with single or multiple view images. Cameras may be static or moving and camera calibration is assumed to be known or estimated together with the scene reconstruction [3,20,31,32]. The first step is to estimate sparse wide-timeframe feature correspondence. Robust feature matching between frames is achieved using a robust segmentation-based feature detector (SFD) previously proposed for wide-baseline stereo correspondence [33]. The 4D Match Tree is constructed as the minimum spanning tree based on the surface overlap and non-rigid shape similarity between pairs of frames estimated from the sparse feature correspondence. This tree defines an optimal path for alignment across all frames which minimises the total dissimilarity or shape deformation. Traversal of the 4D Match Tree from the root to leaf nodes is performed to estimate dense 4D surface correspondence and obtain a temporally coherent representation. Dense surface correspondence is estimated by performing optical flow between each image pair initialised by the sparse feature correspondence. The 2D optical flow correspondence is back-projected to the 3D partial surface reconstruction to obtain a 4D temporally coherent representation. The approach is evaluated on publicly available benchmark datasets for partial reconstructions of indoor and outdoor dynamic scenes from static and moving cameras: Dance1 [34]; Dance2, Cathedral, Odzemok, [35]; Magician and Juggler [36].

2.2 Robust Wide-Timeframe Sparse Correspondence

Sparse feature matching is performed between any pair of frames to obtain an initial estimate of the surface correspondence. This is used to estimate the similarity between observations of the non-rigid shape at different frames for construction of the 4D Match Tree and subsequently to initialize dense correspondence between adjacent pairs of frames on the tree branches. For partial reconstruction of non-rigid shape in general scenes we require feature matching which is robust to both large shape deformation, change in viewpoint, occlusion and errors in the reconstruction due to visual ambiguity. To overcome these challenges sparse feature matching is performed in the 2D domain between image pairs and projected onto the reconstructed 3D surface to obtain 3D matches. In the case of multiple view images consistency is enforced across views at each time frame.

Segmentation-Based Feature Detection: Several feature detection and matching approaches previously used in wide-baseline matching of rigid scenes have been evaluated for wide-timeframe matching between images of non-rigid shape. Figure 2 and Table 1 present results for SIFT [37], FAST [38] and SFD [33] feature detection. This comparison shows that segmentation-based feature detector (SFD) [33] gives a relatively high number of correct matches. SFD detects keypoints at the triple points between segmented regions which correspond to local maxima of the image gradient. Previous work showed that these keypoints are stable to change in viewpoint and give an increased number of accurate matches compared to other widely used feature detectors. Results indicate that SFD can successfully establish sparse correspondence for large non-rigid deformations as well as changes in viewpoint with improved coverage and number of features. SFD features are detected on the segmented dynamic object for each view c and the set of initial keypoints are defined as: $X^c = \{x^c_{F_0}, x^c_{F_1}, ..., x^c_{F_N}\}$. The SIFT descriptor [37] for each detected SFD keypoint is used for feature matching.

Table 1. Number of sparse wide-timeframe correspondences for all datasets.

No. of matches	Dance1	Dance2	Odzemok	Cathedral	Magician	Juggler
SFD	**416**	**1233**	**916**	**665**	**392**	**547**
SIFT	124	493	366	301	141	273
FAST	57	96	82	77	53	68

Fig. 2. Comparison of feature detectors for wide-timeframe matching on 3 datasets.

Fig. 3. Sparse feature matching and dense correspondence for the Odzemok dataset: (a)Color coding scheme, (b) Dense matching with and without the sparse match initialization and, (c) Sparse and dense correspondence example

Wide-Timeframe Matching: Once we have extracted keypoints and their descriptors from two or more images, the next step is to establish some preliminary feature matches between these images. As the time between the initial frame and the current frame can become arbitrarily large, robust matching technique are used to establish correspondences. A match $s^c_{F_i,F_j}$ is a feature correspondence $s^c_{F_i,F_j} = (x^c_{F_i}, x^c_{F_j})$, between $x^c_{F_i}$ and $x^c_{F_j}$ in view c at frames i and j respectively. Nearest neighbor matching is used to establish matches between keypoints $x^c_{F_i}$ from the ith frame to candidate interest points $x^c_{F_j}$ in the jth frame. The ratio of the first to second nearest neighbor descriptor matching score is used to eliminate ambiguous matches ($ratio < 0.85$). This is followed by a symmetry test which employs the principal of forward and backward match consistency to remove the erroneous correspondences. Two-way matching is performed and inconsistent correspondences are eliminated. To further refine the sparse matching and eliminate outliers we enforce local spatial coherence in the matching. For matches in an $m \times m$ ($m = 11$) neighborhood of each feature we find the average Euclidean distance and constrain the match to be within a threshold ($\pm\eta < 2 *$ Average Euclidean distance).

Multiple-View Consistency: In the case of multiple views ($M > 1$) consistency of matching across views is also enforced. Each match must satisfying the constraint: $\left\| s^{c,c}_{F_i,F_j} - (s^{c,k}_{F_j,F_j} + s^{k,k}_{F_i,F_j} + s^{c,k}_{F_i,F_i}) \right\| < \epsilon$ ($\epsilon = 0.25$). The multi-view consistency check ensures that correspondences between any two views remain

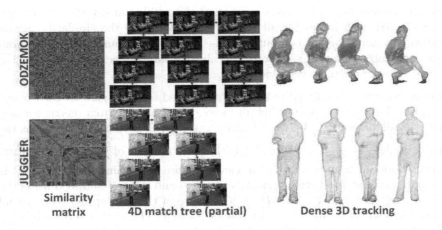

Fig. 4. The similarity matrix, partial 4D Match Tree and 4D alignment for Odzemok and Juggler datasets

consistent for successive frames and views. This gives a final set of sparse matches of the non-rigid shape between frames for the same view which is used to calculate the similarity metric for the non-sequential alignment of frames and initialise dense correspondence.

An example of sparse matching is shown in Fig. 3(c). For visualization features are color coded in one frame according to the colour map as illustrated in Fig. 3(a) and this color is propagated to feature matches at other frames.

2.3 4D Match Trees for Non-sequential Alignment

Our aim is to estimate dense correspondence for partial non-rigid surface reconstructions across complete sequences to obtain a temporally coherent 4D representation. Previous research has employed a tree structure to represent nonrigid shape of complete surfaces to achieve robust non-sequential alignment for sequences with large non-rigid deformations [24,29,30]. Inspired by the success of these approaches we propose the *4D Match Tree* as an intermediate representation for alignment of partial non-rigid surface reconstructions. An important difference of this approach is the use of an image-based metric to estimate the similarity in non-rigid shape between frames. Similarity between any pair of frames is estimated from the sparse wide-timeframe feature matching. The 4D Match Tree represents the optimal traversal path for global alignment of all frames as a minimum spanning tree according to the similarity metric.

The space of all possible pairwise transitions between frames of the sequence is represented by a dissimilarity matrix D of size $N \times N$ where both rows and columns correspond to individual frames. The elements $D(i,j) = d(F_i, F_j)$ are proportional to the cost of dissimilarity between frames i and j. The matrix is symmetrical $(d(F_i, F_j) = d(F_j, F_i))$ and has zero diagonal $(d(F_i, F_i) = 0)$.

For each dynamic object in a scene a graph Ω of possible frame-to-frame matches is constructed with nodes for all frames F_i. $d(F_i, F_j)$ is the similarity metric between two nodes and is computed using information from sparse correspondences and intersection of silhouettes obtained from the back-projection of the surface reconstructions in each view.

Feature Match Metric: SFD keypoints detected for each view at each frame are matched between frames using all views. The feature match metric for non sequential alignment $M_{i,j}^c$ between frame i and j for each view c is defined as the inlier ratio $M_{i,j}^c = \frac{|s_{F_i,F_j}^c|}{R_{i,j}^c}$, where $R_{i,j}^c$ is the total number of preliminary feature matches between frames i and j for view c before constraining, and $|s_{F_i,F_j}^c|$ is the number of matches between view c of frame i and frame j obtained using the method explained in Sect. 2.2. $M_{i,j}^c$ is a measure of the overlap between partial surface reconstruction for view c at frames i and j. The visible surface overlap is a measure of their suitability for pairwise dense alignment.

Silhouette Match Metric: The partial surface reconstruction at each frame is back-projected in all views to obtain silhouettes of the dynamic object. Silhouettes between two frames for the same camera view c are aligned by an affine warp [39]. The aligned silhouette intersection area $h_{i,j}^c$ between frames i and j for view c is evaluated. A silhouette match metric $I_{i,j}^c$ is defined as: $I_{i,j}^c = \frac{h_{i,j}^c}{A_{i,j}^c}$, where $A_{i,}^c$ is the union of the area under the silhouette at frame i and j for view c. This gives a measure of the shape similarity between observations of the non-rigid shape between pairs of frames.

Similarity Metric: The two metrics $I_{i,j}^c$ and $M_{i,j}^c$ are combined to calculate the dissimilarity between frames used as graph edge-weights. The edge-weight $d(F_i, F_j)$ for Ω is defined as:

$$d(F_i, F_j) = \begin{cases} 0 & \text{, if } |s_{F_i,F_j}^c| < 0.006 * max(\text{W}, \text{H}) \\ \frac{1}{\sum_{c=1}^{M} M_{i,j}^c \times I_{i,j}^c} & \text{, otherwise} \end{cases} \qquad (1)$$

where W and H are the width and height of the input image. Note small values of $d()$ indicates a high similarity in feature matches between frames. Figure 4 presents the dissimilarity matrix D between all pairs of frames for two sequences (red indicates similar frames, blue dissimilar). The matrix off diagonal red areas indicate frames with similar views of the non-rigid shape suitable for non-sequential alignment. A minimum spanning tree is constructed over this graph to obtain the 4D Match Tree.

4D Match Tree: A fully connected graph is constructed using the dissimilarity metric as edge-weights and the minimum spanning tree is evaluated [40,41]. Optimal paths through the sequence to every frame can be jointly optimised based on $d()$. The paths are represented by a traversal tree $T = (\mathbb{N}; E)$ with the nodes $\mathbb{N} = \{F_i\}_{i=1}^N$. The edges E are undirected and weighted by the dissimilarity

$e_{i,j} = d(F_i, F_j)$ for $e_{i,j} \in E$. The optimal tree T_o is defined as the minimum spanning tree (MST) which minimises the total cost of pairwise matching given by d:

$$T_o = \arg\min_{\forall T \in \Omega} \left(\sum_{\forall i,j \in T} d(F_i, F_j) \right) \qquad (2)$$

This results in the 4D Match Tree T_o which minimises the total dissimilarity
between frames due to non-rigid deformation and changes in surface visibility.
Given T_o for a dynamic object we estimate the dense correspondence for the
entire sequence to obtain a temporally coherent 4D surface. The tree root node
M_{root} is defined as the node with minimum path length to all nodes in T_o. The
minimum spanning tree can be efficiently evaluated using established algorithms
with order $O(N \log N)$ complexity where N is the number of nodes in the graph
Ω. The mesh at the root node is subsequently tracked to other frames by traversing through the branches of the tree T towards the leaves. Examples of partial
4D Match Trees for two datasets are shown in Fig. 4.

2.4 Dense Non-rigid Aligment

Given the 4D Match Tree global alignment is performed by traversing the tree
to estimate dense correspondence between each pair of frames connected by
an edge. Sparse SFD feature matches are used to initialise the pairwise dense
correspondence which is estimated using optical flow [42]. The sparse feature
correspondences provides a robust initialisation of the optical flow for large non-
rigid shape deformation. The estimated dense correspondence is back projected
to the 3D visible surface to establish dense 4D correspondence between frames.
In the case of multiple views dense 4D correspondence is combined across views
to obtain a consistent estimate and increase surface coverage. Dense temporal
correspondence is propagated to new surface regions as they appear using the
sparse feature matching and dense optical flow. An example of the propagated
mask with and without sparse initialization for a single view is shown in Fig. 3(b).
The large motion in the leg of the actor is correctly estimated with sparse match
initialization but fails without (shown by the red region indicating no correspondence). Pairwise 4D dense surface correspondences are combined across the tree
to obtain a temporally coherent 4D alignment across all frames. An example is
shown for the Odzemok dataset in Fig. 3(c) with optical flow information for
each frame. Figure 4 presents two examples of 4D aligned meshes resulting from
the global alignment with the 4D match tree.

3 Results and Performance Evaluation

The proposed approach is tested on various datasets introduced in Sect. 2.1 and
the properties of datasets are described in Table 2. Algorithm parameters set
empirically are constant for all results.

Table 2. Properties of all datasets and their 4D Match Trees.

Datasets	Number of views	Sequence length	Resolution	Tree depth (frames)	Tree depth (%)
Dance1	8 static	200	780 × 582	65	33
Dance2	7 static, 1 moving	244	1920 × 1080	73	29
Odzemok	6 static, 2 moving	232	1920 × 1080	82	35
Cathedral	8 static	217	1920 × 1080	92	42
Magician	6 moving	400	960 × 544	127	32
Juggler	6 moving	400	960 × 544	104	26

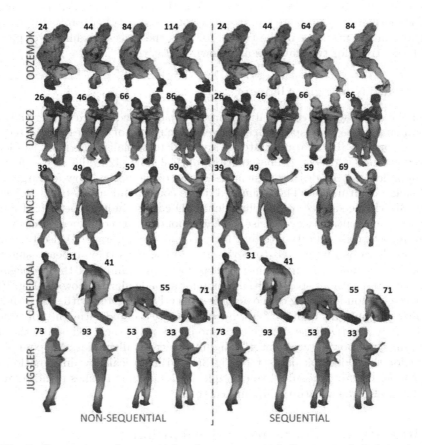

Fig. 5. Comparison of sequential and non-sequential alignment of all datasets.

3.1   Sequential vs. Non-sequential Alignment

4D Match Trees are constructed for all datasets using the method described in Sect. 2.3. The maximum length of branches in the 4D Match Tree for global alignment of each dataset is described in Table 2. The longest alignment path for all sequences is < 50 % of the total sequence length leading to a significant reduction in the accumulation of errors due to drift in the sequential alignment process. Non-rigid alignment is performed over the branches of the tree to obtain temporally consistent 4D representation for all datasets. Comparison of 4D aligned surfaces obtained from the proposed non-sequential approach against sequential tracking without the 4D Match tree is shown in Fig. 5. Sequential tracking fails to estimate the correct 4D alignment (Odzemok-64, Dance2-66, Cathedral-55) whereas the non-sequential approach obtains consistent correspondence for all frames for sequences with large non-rigid deformations. To illustrate the surface alignment a color map is applied to the root mesh of the 4D Match tree and propagated to all frames based on the estimated dense correspondence. The color map is consistently aligned across all frames for large non-rigid motions of dynamic shapes in each dataset demonstrating qualitatively that the global alignment achieves reliable correspondence compared to sequential tracking.

3.2   Sparse Wide-Timeframe Correspondence

Sparse correspondences are obtained for the entire sequence using the traversal path in the 4D Match tree from the root node towards the leaves. Results of the sparse and dense 4D correspondence are shown in 6. Sparse matches obtained using SFD are evaluated against a state-of-the-art method for sparse correspondence Nebehay [43]. For fair comparison Nebehay is initialized with SFD keypoints instead of FAST (which produces a low number of matches). Qualitative results are shown in Fig. 7 and quantitative results are shown in Table 3. Matches obtained using the proposed approach are approx 50 % higher and consistent across frames compared to Nebehay [43] demonstrating the robustness of the proposed wide-timeframe matching using SFD keypoints.

Table 3. Quantitative evaluation for sparse and dense correspondence for all the datasets; Prop. represents proposed non-sequential approach and Matches depicts the number of sparse matches between frames averaged over the entire sequence.

Datasets	Silhouette overlap error								Matches	
	Seq	Prop.	Deepflow	SIFT	Nebehay	1 view	2 views	4 views	Prop.	Nebehay
Dance1	0.42	**0.35**	0.97	0.92	0.96	1.53	1.30	0.99	**416**	249
Dance2	0.83	**0.63**	1.36	1.43	1.38	2.13	1.78	1.47	**1233**	863
Odzemok	0.98	**0.89**	2.82	2.59	2.69	4.35	3.66	2.76	**916**	687
Cathedral	0.83	**0.69**	1.14	1.10	1.29	1.92	1.65	1.09	**665**	465
Magician	1.07	**0.86**	3.43	3.22	3.77	5.46	4.67	3.18	**392**	293
Juggler	0.78	**0.65**	1.24	1.19	1.31	2.12	1.76	1.44	**547**	437

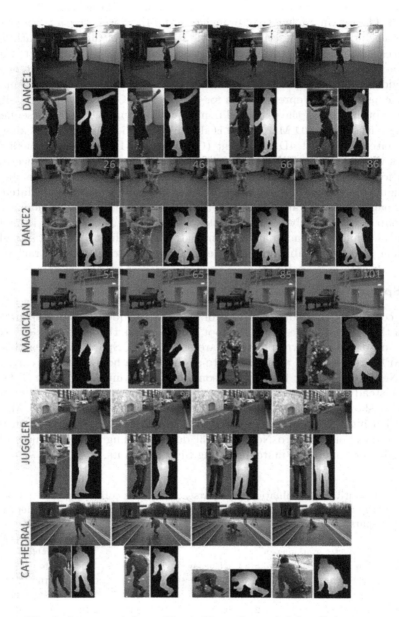

Fig. 6. Sparse and dense 2D tracking color coded for all datasets

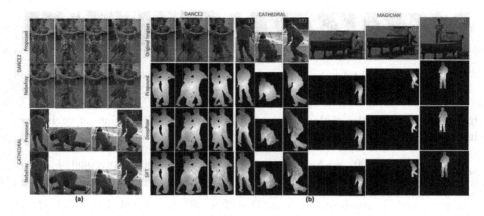

Fig. 7. Qualitative comparison: (a) Sparse tracking comparison for one indoor and one outdoor dataset and (b) Dense tracking comparison for two indoor and one outdoor datasets.

3.3   Dense 4D Correspondence

Dense correspondence are obtained on the 4D match tree and the color coded results are shown in Fig. 6 for all datasets. To illustrate the dense alignment the color coding scheme shown in Fig. 3 is applied to the silhouette of the dense mesh on the root node for each view and propagated using the 4D Match Tree. The proposed approach is qualitatively shown to propagate the correspondences reliably over the entire sequence for complex dynamic scenes.

For comparative evaluation of dense matching we use: (a) SIFT features with the proposed method in Sect. 2 to obtain dense correspondence; (b) Sparse correspondence obtained using Nebehay [43] with the proposed dense matching; and (c) state-of-the-art dense flow algorithm Deepflow [44] over the 4D Match Tree for each dataset. Qualitative results against SIFT and Deepflow are shown in Fig. 7. The propagated color map using deep flow and SIFT based alignment does not remain consistent across the sequence as compared to the proposed method (red regions indicate correspondence failure).

For quantitative evaluation we compare the silhouette overlap error (SOE). Dense correspondence over time is used to create propagated mask for each image. The propagated mask is overlapped with the silhouette of the projected partial surface reconstruction at each frame to evaluate the accuracy of the dense propagation. The error is defined as:

$$SOE = \frac{1}{M * N} \sum_{i=1}^{N} \sum_{c=1}^{M} \frac{\text{Area of intersection}}{\text{Area of back-projected mask}}$$

Evaluation against sequential and non-sequential Deepflow, SIFT and Nebehay are shown in Table 3 for all datasets. As observed the silhouette overlap error is lowest for the proposed SFD based non-sequential approach showing relatively

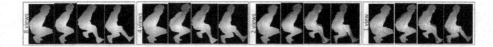

Fig. 8. Single and Multi-view alignment comparison results for Odzemok dataset

high accuracy. We also evaluate the completeness of the 3D points at each time instant as observed in Table 4:

$$completeness = \frac{100}{M * N} \sum_{i=1}^{N} \sum_{c=1}^{M} \frac{\text{Number of 3D points propagated}}{\text{Number of surface points visible from 'c' [45]}}$$

The proposed approach outperforms Deepflow, SIFT and Nebehay all of which result in errors as observed in Fig. 7 and Table 4.

Table 4. Evaluation of completeness of dense 3D correspondence averaged over the entire sequence in %.

Completeness(%)	Deepflow	SIFT	Nebehay	Sequential	Proposed (Non-sequential)			
				All views	1 view	2 views	4 views	All views
Dance1	81.56	83.28	82.55	91.52	60.78	71.65	81.30	**98.22**
Dance2	83.26	85.80	83.96	92.76	61.98	72.30	82.87	**99.36**
Odzemok	81.46	79.83	80.91	90.51	62.73	70.87	77.64	**98.19**
Cathedral	79.54	81.53	81.78	89.21	59.77	69.05	76.98	**97.40**
Magician	82.58	82.92	80.65	89.58	61.29	71.23	75.56	**97.53**
Juggler	79.09	80.11	81.33	91.89	59.54	68.40	78.81	**97.89**

3.4   Single vs Multi-view

The proposed 4D Match Tree global alignment method can be applied to single or multi-view image sequence with partial surface reconstruction. Dense correspondence for the Odzemok dataset using different numbers of views are compared in Fig. 8. Quantitative evaluation using *SOE* and *completeness* obtained from single, 2, 4 and all views for all datasets are presented in Tables 3 and 4 respectively. This shows that even with a single view the 4D Match Tree achieves 60 % completeness due to the restricted surface visibility. Completeness increases with the number of views to > 97 % for all views which is significantly higher than other approaches.

4   Conclusions

A framework has been presented for dense 4D global alignment of partial surface reconstructions of complex dynamic scenes using 4D Match trees. 4D Match Trees represent the similarity in the observed non-rigid surface shape across the sequence. This enables non-sequential alignment to obtain dense surface correspondence across all frames. Robust wide-timeframe correspondence between pairs of frames is estimated using a segmentation-based feature detector (SFD). This sparse correspondence is used to estimate the similarity in non-rigid shape and overlap between frames. Dense 4D temporal correspondence is estimated from the 4D Match tree across all frames using guided optical flow. This is shown to provide improved robustness to large non-rigid deformation compared to sequential and other state-of-the-art sparse and dense correspondence methods. The proposed approach is evaluated on single and multi-view sequences of complex dynamic scenes with large non-rigid deformations to obtain a temporally consistent 4D representation. Results demonstrate completeness and accuracy of the resulting global 4D alignment.

Limitations: The proposed method fails in case of objects with large deformations (high ambiguity), fast spinning (failure of optical flow), and uniform appearance or highly crowded dynamic environments where no reliable sparse matches can be obtained or surface reconstruction fails due to occlusion.

References

1. Zhang, G., Jia, J., Hua, W., Bao, H.: Robust bilayer segmentation and motion/depth estimation with a handheld camera. PAMI **33**, 603–617 (2011)
2. Jiang, H., Liu, H., Tan, P., Zhang, G., Bao, H.: 3D reconstruction of dynamic scenes with multiple handheld cameras. In: Fitzgibbon, A., Lazebnik, S., Perona, P., Sato, Y., Schmid, C. (eds.) ECCV 2012. LNCS, pp. 601–615. Springer, Heidelberg (2012). doi:10.1007/978-3-642-33709-3_43
3. Taneja, A., Ballan, L., Pollefeys, M.: Modeling dynamic scenes recorded with freely moving cameras. In: Kimmel, R., Klette, R., Sugimoto, A. (eds.) ACCV 2010. LNCS, vol. 6494, pp. 613–626. Springer, Heidelberg (2011). doi:10.1007/978-3-642-19318-7_48
4. Mustafa, A., Kim, H., Guillemaut, J., Hilton, A.: General dynamic scene reconstruction from wide-baseline views. In: ICCV (2015)
5. Kanade, T., Rander, P., Narayanan, P.J.: Virtualized reality: constructing virtual worlds from real scenes. IEEE MultiMedia **4**, 34–47 (1997)
6. Franco, J.S., Boyer, E.: Exact polyhedral visual hulls. In: Proceedings of BMVC, pp. 32:1–32:10 (2003)
7. Starck, J., Hilton, A.: Model-based multiple view reconstruction of people. In: ICCV, pp. 915–922 (2003)
8. Newcombe, R., Fox, D., Seitz, S.: DynamicFusion: reconstruction and tracking of non-rigid scenes in real-time. In: CVPR (2015)
9. Tevs, A., Berner, A., Wand, M., Ihrke, I., Bokeloh, M., Kerber, J., Seidel, H.P.: Animation cartography: intrinsic reconstruction of shape and motion. ACM Trans. Graph. **31**, 12:1–12:15 (2012)
10. Wei, L., Huang, Q., Ceylan, D., Vouga, E., Li, H.: Dense human body correspondences using convolutional networks (2015). CoRR abs/1511.05904
11. Malleson, C., Klaudiny, M., Guillemaut, J.Y., Hilton, A.: Structured representation of non-rigid surfaces from single view 3D point tracks. In: 3DV (2014)
12. Wedel, A., Brox, T., Vaudrey, T., Rabe, C., Franke, U., Cremers, D.: Stereoscopic scene flow computation for 3d motion understanding. IJCV **95**, 29–51 (2011)

13. Basha, T., Moses, Y., Kiryati, N.: Multi-view scene flow estimation: a view centered variational approach. In: CVPR, pp. 1506–1513 (2010)
14. Sundaram, N., Brox, T., Keutzer, K.: Dense point trajectories by GPU-accelerated large displacement optical flow. In: Daniilidis, K., Maragos, P., Paragios, N. (eds.) ECCV 2010. LNCS, vol. 6311, pp. 438–451. Springer, Heidelberg (2010). doi:10.1007/978-3-642-15549-9_32
15. Menze, M., Geiger, A.: Object scene flow for autonomous vehicles. In: CVPR (2015)
16. Joo, H., Liu, H., Tan, L., Gui, L., Nabbe, B., Matthews, I., Kanade, T., Nobuhara, S., Sheikh, Y.: Panoptic studio: a massively multiview system for social motion capture. In: ICCV (2015)
17. Zheng, E., Ji, D., Dunn, E., Frahm, J.M.: Sparse dynamic 3D reconstruction from unsynchronized videos. In: ICCV (2015)
18. Zanfir, A., Sminchisescu, C.: Large displacement 3D scene flow with occlusion reasoning. In: ICCV (2015)
19. Lei, C., Chen, X.D., Yang, Y.H.: A new multiview spacetime-consistent depth recovery framework for free viewpoint video rendering. In: ICCV, pp. 1570–1577 (2009)
20. Mustafa, A., Kim, H., Guillemaut, J.Y., Hilton, A.: Temporally coherent 4D reconstruction of complex dynamic scenes. In: CVPR (2016)
21. Vlasic, D., Baran, I., Matusik, W., Popović, J.: Articulated mesh animation from multi-view silhouettes. ACM Trans. Graph. **27**, 97:1–97:9 (2008)
22. Tung, T., Nobuhara, S., Matsuyama, T.: Complete multi-view reconstruction of dynamic scenes from probabilistic fusion of narrow and wide baseline stereo. In: ICCV, pp. 1709–1716 (2009)
23. Cagniart, C., Boyer, E., Ilic, S.: Probabilistic deformable surface tracking from multiple videos. In: Daniilidis, K., Maragos, P., Paragios, N. (eds.) ECCV 2010. LNCS, vol. 6314, pp. 326–339. Springer, Heidelberg (2010). doi:10.1007/978-3-642-15561-1_24
24. Budd, C., Huang, P., Klaudiny, M., Hilton, A.: Global non-rigid alignment of surface sequences. Int. J. Comput. Vis. **102**, 256–270 (2013)
25. Huang, C., Cagniart, C., Boyer, E., Ilic, S.: A Bayesian approach to multi-view 4D modeling. Int. J. Comput. Vis. **116**, 115–135 (2016)
26. Russell, C., Yu, R., Agapito, L.: Video pop-up: monocular 3D reconstruction of dynamic scenes. In: Fleet, D., Pajdla, T., Schiele, B., Tuytelaars, T. (eds.) ECCV 2014. LNCS, vol. 8695, pp. 583–598. Springer, Heidelberg (2014). doi:10.1007/978-3-319-10584-0_38
27. Guo, K., Xu, F., Wang, Y., Liu, Y., Dai, Q.: Robust non-rigid motion tracking and surface reconstruction using l0 regularization. In: ICCV (2015)
28. Bailer, C., Taetz, B., Stricker, D.: Flow fields: dense correspondence fields for highly accurate large displacement optical flow estimation. In: ICCV (2015)
29. Cao, X., Wei, Y., Wen, F., Sun, J.: Face alignment by explicit shape regression. In: CVPR (2012)
30. Collet, A., Chuang, M., Sweeney, P., Gillett, D., Evseev, D., Calabrese, D., Hoppe, H., Kirk, A., Sullivan, S.: High-quality streamable free-viewpoint video. ACM Trans. Graph. **34**(4), 69:1–69:13 (2015)
31. Ji, D., Dunn, E., Frahm, J.-M.: 3D reconstruction of dynamic textures in crowd sourced data. In: Fleet, D., Pajdla, T., Schiele, B., Tuytelaars, T. (eds.) ECCV 2014. LNCS, vol. 8689, pp. 143–158. Springer, Heidelberg (2014). doi:10.1007/978-3-319-10590-1_10

32. Oswald, M.R., Stühmer, J., Cremers, D.: Generalized connectivity constraints for spatio-temporal 3D reconstruction. In: Fleet, D., Pajdla, T., Schiele, B., Tuytelaars, T. (eds.) ECCV 2014. LNCS, vol. 8692, pp. 32–46. Springer, Heidelberg (2014). doi:10.1007/978-3-319-10593-2_3

33. Mustafa, A., Kim, H., Imre, E., Hilton, A.: Segmentation based features for wide-baseline multi-view reconstruction. In: 3DV (2015)

34. 4D repository. In: Institut national de recherche en informatique et en automatique (INRIA) Rhone Alpes. http://4drepository.inrialpes.fr/

35. 4D and multiview video repository. In: Centre for Vision Speech and Signal Processing, University of Surrey, UK

36. Ballan, L., Brostow, G.J., Puwein, J., Pollefeys, M.: Unstructured video-based rendering: interactive exploration of casually captured videos. ACM Trans. Graph. **29**, 1–11 (2010)

37. Lowe, D.G.: Distinctive image features from scale-invariant keypoints. IJCV **60**, 91–110 (2004)

38. Rosten, E., Porter, R., Drummond, T.: Faster and better: a machine learning approach to corner detection. PAMI **32**, 105–119 (2010)

39. Evangelidis, G.D., Psarakis, E.Z.: Parametric image alignment using enhanced correlation coefficient maximization. IEEE Trans. Pattern Anal. Mach. Intell. **30**, 1858–1865 (2008)

40. Kruskal, J.B.: On the shortest spanning subtree of a graph and the traveling salesman problem. Proc. Am. Math. Soc. **7**, 48–50 (1956)

41. Prim, R.C.: Shortest connection networks and some generalizations. Bell Syst. Tech. J. **36**, 1389–1401 (1957)

42. Farnebäck, G.: Two-frame motion estimation based on polynomial expansion. In: Bigun, J., Gustavsson, T. (eds.) SCIA 2003. LNCS, vol. 2749, pp. 363–370. Springer, Heidelberg (2003). doi:10.1007/3-540-45103-X_50

43. Nebehay, G., Pflugfelder, R.: Clustering of static-adaptive correspondences for deformable object tracking. In: CVPR (2015)

44. Weinzaepfel, P., Revaud, J., Harchaoui, Z., Schmid, C.: Deepflow: large displacement optical flow with deep matching. In: ICCV, pp. 1385–1392(2013)

45. Joo, H., Soo Park, H., Sheikh, Y.: Map visibility estimation for large-scale dynamic 3D reconstruction. In: CVPR (2014)

Eigen Appearance Maps of Dynamic Shapes

Adnane Boukhayma$^{(\boxtimes)}$, Vagia Tsiminaki, Jean-Sébastien Franco,
and Edmond Boyer

LJK, Université Grenoble Alpes, Inria Grenoble Rhône-Alpes, Grenoble, France
{adnane.boukhayma,vagia.tsiminaki,jean-sebastien.franco,
edmond.boyer}@inria.fr

Abstract. We address the problem of building efficient appearance representations of shapes observed from multiple viewpoints and in several movements. Multi-view systems now allow the acquisition of spatio-temporal models of such moving objects. While efficient geometric representations for these models have been widely studied, appearance information, as provided by the observed images, is mainly considered on a per frame basis, and no global strategy yet addresses the case where several temporal sequences of a shape are available. We propose a per subject representation that builds on PCA to identify the underlying manifold structure of the appearance information relative to a shape. The resulting eigen representation encodes shape appearance variabilities due to viewpoint and motion, with Eigen textures, and due to local inaccuracies in the geometric model, with Eigen warps. In addition to providing compact representations, such decompositions also allow for appearance interpolation and appearance completion. We evaluate their performances over different characters and with respect to their ability to reproduce compelling appearances in a compact way.

1   Introduction

The last decade has seen the emergence of 3D dynamic shape models of moving objects, in particular humans, acquired from multiple videos. These spatio-temporal models comprise geometric and appearance information extracted from images, and they allow for subject motions to be recorded and reused. This is of interest for applications that require real 3D contents for analysis, free viewpoint and animation purposes and also for interactive experiences made possible with new virtual reality devices. This ability to now record datasets of subject motions bolsters the need for shape and appearance representations that make optimal use of the massive amount of image information usually produced. While dynamic shape representations have been extensively studied, from temporally coherent representations over a single sequence, to shape spaces that can encode

---

Electronic supplementary material The online version of this chapter (doi:10.1007/978-3-319-46448-0_14) contains supplementary material, which is available to authorized users.

B. Leibe et al. (Eds.): ECCV 2016, Part I, LNCS 9905, pp. 230–245, 2016.
DOI: 10.1007/978-3-319-46448-0_14

both pose and subject variabilities over multiple sequences and multiple subjects, appearance representations have received less attention in this context. In this paper, we investigate this issue.

Currently, appearance information is still most often estimated and stored once per frame, e.g. a texture map associated to a 3D model [1], and the leap to an efficient temporal appearance representation is still a largely open problem. This is despite the obvious redundancy with which the appearance of subjects is observed, across temporal frames, different viewpoints of the same scene, and often several sequences of the same subject performing different actions or motions. At the opposite of the spectrum, and given registered geometries, one can store only one texture for a sequence or even for a subject in several sequences, hence dramatically reducing sizes, but in so doing would drop the ability to represent desirable appearance variations, such as change in lighting or personal expression of the subject.

In this paper, we advance this aspect by providing a view-independent appearance representation and estimation algorithm, to encode the appearance variability of a dynamic subject, observed over one or several temporal sequences. Compactly representing image data from all frames and viewpoints of the subject can be seen as a non-linear dimensionality reduction problem in image space, where the main non-linearities are due to the underlying scene geometry. Our strategy is to remove these non-linearities with state-of-the-art geometric and image-space alignment techniques, so as to reduce the problem to a single texture space, where the remaining image variabilities can be straightforwardly identified with PCA and thus encoded as Eigen texture combinations. To this goal, we identify two geometric alignment steps (Fig. 1). First, we coarsely register geometric shape models of all time frames to a single shape template, for which we pre-computed a single reference surface-to-texture unwrapping. Second, to cope with remaining fine-scale misalignments due to registration errors, we estimate realignment warps in the texture domain. Because they encode low-magnitude, residual geometric variations, they are also advantageously decomposed using PCA, yielding Eigen warps. The full appearance information of all subject sequences can then be compactly stored as linear combinations of Eigen textures and Eigen warps. Our strategy can be seen as a generalization of the popular work of Nishino et al. [2], which introduces Eigen textures to encode appearance variations of a static object under varying viewing conditions, to the case of fully dynamic subjects with several viewpoints and motions.

The pipeline is shown to yield effective estimation performance. In addition, the learned texture and warp manifolds allow for efficient generalizations, such as texture interpolations to generate new unobserved content from blended input sequences, or completions to cope with missing observations due to e.g. occlusions. To summarize our main contribution is to propose and evaluate a new appearance model that specifically addresses dynamic scene modeling by accounting for both appearance changes and local geometric inaccuracies.

2   Related Work

Obtaining appearance of 3D models from images was first tackled from static images for inanimate objects, e.g. [2,3], a case largely explored since e.g. [4,5]. The task also gained interest for the case of subjects in motion, e.g. for human faces [6]. With the advent of full body capture and 3D interaction systems [1,7] the task of recovering appearance has become a key issue, as the appearance vastly enhances the quality of restitution of acquired 3D models.

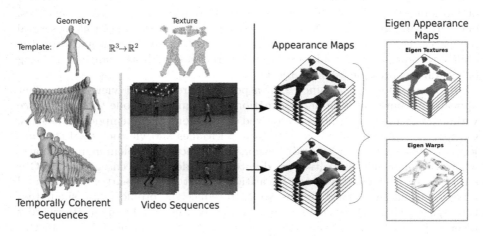

Fig. 1. Overview: Time consistent shape modeling provides datasets of appearance maps. Our proposed method exploits the manifold structure of these appearance information through PCA decomposition to generate the Eigen appearance maps relative to a shape.

A central aspect of the problem is how to represent appearance, while achieving a proper trade-off between storage size and quality. 3D capture traditionally generates full 3D reconstructions, albeit of inconsistent topology across time. In this context the natural solution is to build a representation per time frame which uses or maps to that instant's 3D model. Such per instant representations come in two main forms. View-dependent texturing stores and resamples from each initial video frame [8], eventually with additional alignments to avoid ghosting effects [9]. This strategy creates high quality restitutions managing visibility issues on the fly, but is memory costly as it requires storing all images from all viewpoints. On the other hand, one can compute a single appearance texture map from the input views in an offline process [1], reducing storage but potentially introducing sampling artifacts. These involve evaluating camera visibility and surface viewing angles to patch and blend the view contributions in a single common mapping space. To overcome the resolution and sampling limitations, 3D superresolution techniques have been devised that leverage the viewpoint multiplicity to build such maps with enhanced density and quality [10–12].

In recent years, a leap has been made in the representation of 3D surfaces captured, as they can now be estimated as a deformed surface of time-coherent topology [13,14]. This in turns allows any surface unwrapping and mapping to be consistently propagated in time, however in practice existing methods have only started leveraging this aspect. Tsiminaki *et al.* [11] examines small temporal segments for single texture resolution enhancement. Volino *et al.* [15] uses a view-based multi-layer texture map representation to favour view-dependant dynamic appearance, using some adjacent neighbouring frames. Collet *et al.* [1] use tracked surfaces over small segments to improve compression rates of mesh and texture sequences. Methods are intrinsically limited in considering longer segments because significant temporal variability then appears due to light change and movement. While global geometry consistency has been studied [16–18], most such works were primarily aimed at animation synthesis using mesh data, and do not propose a global appearance model for sequences. In contrast, we propose an analysis and representation spanning full sequences and multiples sequences of a subject.

For this purpose, we build an Eigen texture and appearance representation that extends concepts initially explored for faces and static objects [2,6,19,20]. Eigenfaces [19] were initially used to represent the face variability of a population for recognition purposes. The concept was broadened to built a 3D generative model of human faces both in the geometry and texture domains, using the fact that the appearance and geometry of faces are well suited to learning their variability as linear subspaces [6]. Cootes *et al.* [20] perform the linear PCA analysis of appearance and geometry landmarks jointly in their active appearance model. Nishino *et al.* [2] instead use such linear subspaces to encode the appearance variability of static objects under light and viewpoint changes at the polygon level. We use linear subspaces for full body appearance and over multiple sequences. Because the linear assumption doesn't hold for whole body pose variation, we use state of the art tracking techniques [21] to remove the non-linear pose component by aligning a single subject-specific template to all the subject's sequence. This in turn allows to model the appearance in a single mapping space associated to the subject template, where small geometric variations and appearances changes can then be linearly modeled.

3   Method

To eliminate the main geometric non-linearity, we first align sequence geometries to a single template shape and extract the texture maps of a subject over different motion sequences in a common texture space using a state-of-the-art method [11]. Other per-frame texture extractions may be considered. From these subject specific textures, Eigen textures and Eigen warps that span the appearance space are estimated. The main steps of the method below are depicted in Fig. 2 and detailed in the following sections.

1. Texture deformation fields that map input textures to, and from, their aligned versions are estimated using optical flows. Given the deformation fields, Poisson reconstruction is used to warp textures.

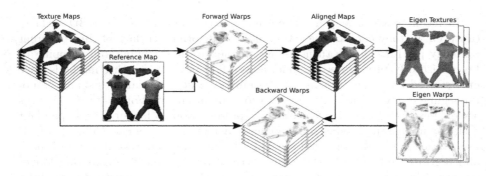

Fig. 2. Method pipeline from input textures (left) to eigen maps (right).

2. PCA is applied to the aligned maps and to the texture warps to generate the Eigen textures and the Eigen warps that encode the appearance variations due to, respectively, viewpoint, illumination, and geometric inaccuracies in the reference model.

Hence, The main modes of variation of aligned textures and deformation fields, namely Eigen textures and Eigen warps respectively, span the appearance space in our representation. The main steps of this method are depicted in Fig. 2 and detailed in the following sections.

Note that due to texture space discretization, the warps between textures are not one-to-one and, in practice, two separate sets of warps are estimated. Forward warps map the original texture maps to the reference map. Backward warps map the aligned texture maps back to the corresponding input textures (see Fig. 2).

3.1   Aligning Texture Maps

Appearance variations that are due to viewpoint and illumination changes are captured through PCA under linearity assumption for these variations. To this purpose, textures are first aligned in order to reduce geometric errors resulting from calibration, reconstruction and tracking imprecisions. Such alignment is performed using optical flow, as described below, and with respect to a reference map taken from the input textures. An exhaustive search of the best reference map with the least total alignment error over all input textures is prohibitive since it requires N^2 alignments given N input textures. We follow instead a medoid shift strategy over the alignment errors.

The alignment algorithm (see Algorithm 1) first initializes the reference map as one texture from the input set. All texture maps are then aligned to this reference map, and the alignment error is computed as the cumulative sum of squared pixel differences between the reference and the aligned texture maps. The medoid over the aligned texture maps, with respect to alignment error, then identifies the new reference map. These two steps, alignment and medoid shift, are iterated until the total alignment error stops decreasing.

Data: Texture maps $\{I_k\}_{k \in [\![1..N]\!]}$
Result: Reference map A_{ref}, aligned textures A_k
A_{ref}, e_0 initializations;
while $e_i < e_{i-1}$ **do**

> Compute alignment warps: $\{w_k\}_{k \in [\![1..N]\!]}$ s.t. $A_{ref} \approx I_k(x + w_k)$;
> Align texture maps: $A_k = I_k(x + w_k)$;
> Update alignment error: $e_i = \sum_k \|A_k - A_{ref}\|^2$;
> Set A_{ref} as the texture that gives the medoid of the aligned textures:
> $A_{ref} = I_{k_0}$ s.t. $k_0 = arg \min_k \sum_l \|A_k - A_l\|^2$;

end
Algorithm 1. Texture alignment with iterative reference map selection.

Dense Texture Correspondence with Optical Flow. The warps $\{w_k\}$ in the alignment algorithm, both forward and backward in practice, are estimated as dense pixel correspondences with an optical flow method [22]. We mention here that the optical flow assumptions: brightness consistency, spatial coherency and temporal persistence, are not necessarily verified by the input textures. In particular, the brightness consistency does not hold if we assume appearance variations with respect to viewpoint and illumination changes. To cope with this in the flow estimation, we use histogram equalization as a preprocessing step, which presents the benefit of enhancing contrast and edges within images. Additionally, local changes in intensities are reduced using bilateral filtering, which smooths low spatial-frequency details while preserving edges.

Texture Warping. Optical flows give dense correspondences $\{w\}$ between the reference map and the input textures. To estimate the aligned textures $\{A\}$, we cast the problem as an optimization that seeks the texture map which, once moved according to w, best aligns with the considered input texture both in the color and gradient domains. Our experiments show that solving over both color and gradient domains significantly improves results as it tends to better preserve edges than with colors only. This is also demonstrated in works that use the Poisson editing for image composition, e.g. [23,24] or interpolation, e.g. [25,26]. We follow here a similar strategy.

We are given an input texture map I, a dense flow w from A_{ref} to I, and the gradient image ∇I. The aligned texture A of I with respect to A_{ref} is then the map that minimizes the following term:

$$E(A) = \Sigma_x \|\nabla^2 A(x) - \overrightarrow{\nabla}.\nabla I(x + w)\|^2 + \lambda \|A(x) - I(x + w)\|^2, \qquad (1)$$

where ∇^2 is the Laplacian operator, $\overrightarrow{\nabla}.$ the divergence operator, and x denotes pixel locations in texture maps. The weight λ balances the influence of color and gradient information. In our experiments, we found that the value 0.02 gives the best results with our datasets.

Original Textrue   Direct Warping   Poisson Warping

Fig. 3. Poisson versus direct texture warping.

Using a vector image representation, the above energy can be minimized by solving, in the least-squares sense, the overdetermined $2N \times N$ system below, where N is the active region size of texture maps:

$$\begin{pmatrix} L \\ \Lambda \end{pmatrix} A = \begin{pmatrix} \overrightarrow{\nabla}.\nabla I(x+w) \\ \Lambda I(x+w) \end{pmatrix}, \tag{2}$$

where L is the linear Laplacian operator and $\Lambda = diag_N(\lambda)$. A solution for A is easily found by solving the associated normal equations:

$$\left(L^T L + \Lambda^2\right) A = L^T \overrightarrow{\nabla}.\nabla I(x+w) + \Lambda^2 I(x+w). \tag{3}$$

Figure 3 shows an example where a texture map is warped, given a warp field, using both direct pixel remapping and Poisson warping. The latter strategy achieves visually more compelling and edge preserving results.

3.2 Eigen Textures and Eigen Warps

Once the aligned textures and the warps are estimated, we can proceed with the statistical analysis of appearances. Given the true geometry of shapes and their motions, texture map pixels could be considered as shape appearance samples over time and PCA applied directly to the textures would then capture appearance variability. In practice, incorrect geometry causes distortions in the texture space and textures must be first aligned before any statistical analysis. In turn, de-alignment must be also estimated to map the aligned textures back to their associated input textures (see Fig. 2). And these backward warps must be part of the appearance model to enable appearance reconstruction. In the following, warps denote the backward warps. Also, we consider vector representations of the aligned texture maps and of the warps. These representations include only pixels that fall inside active regions within texture maps. We perform Principal Component Analysis on the textures and on the warp data separately to find the orthonormal bases that encode the main modes of variation in the texture space and in the warp space independently. We refer to vectors spanning the texture space as Eigen textures, and to vectors spanning the warp space as Eigen warps.

Let us consider first texture maps. Assume N is the dimension of the vectorized representation of active texture elements, and F the total number of frames available for the subject under consideration. To give orders of magnitude for our datasets, $N = 22438995$ and $F = 207$ for the TOMAS dataset, and $N = 25966476$

and $F = 290$ for the CATY dataset that will be presented in the next section. We start by computing the mean image $\bar{A}$ and the centered data matrix M from aligned texture maps $\{A_i\}_{i \in [1..F]}$:

$$\bar{A} = \frac{1}{F} \sum_k A_k, \quad M = \begin{bmatrix} | & & | \\ A_1 - \bar{A} & ... & A_F - \bar{A} \\ | & & | \end{bmatrix}. \tag{4}$$

Traditionally, the PCA basis for this data is formed by the Eigen vectors of the covariance matrix MM^T, of size $N \times N$, but finding such vectors can easily become prohibitive as a consequence of the texture dimensions. However, it appears that the non zero eigen values of MM^T are equal to the non zero Eigen values of $M^T M$, of size $(F \times F)$ this time, and that they are at most: $\min(F, N) - 1$. Based on this observation, and since $F << N$ in our experiments, we solve the characteristic equation $\det(MM^T - \alpha I_N) = 0$ by performing Singular Value Decomposition on the matrix $M^T M$, as explained in [19]:

$$M^T M = D \Sigma D^T, \quad D = \begin{bmatrix} | & & | \\ V_1 & ... & V_F \\ | & & | \end{bmatrix} \tag{5}$$

where D contains the $(F - 1)$ orthonormal Eigen vectors $\{V_i\}$ of $M^T M$, and $\Sigma = diag(\alpha_i)_{1 \leq i \leq F}$ contains the eigen values $\{\alpha_i\}_{1 \leq i \leq F-1}$. We can then write:

$$M^T M V_i = \alpha_i V_i, \quad i \in [1..F - 1], \tag{6}$$

and hence:

$$MM^T \underbrace{MV_i}_{T_i} = \alpha_i \underbrace{MV_i}_{T_i}, \quad i \in [1..F - 1], \tag{7}$$

where T_i are the Eigen vectors of MM^T and therefore form the orthonormal basis of the aligned texture space after normalization, namely the Eigen textures.

In a similar way, we obtain the mean warp $\bar{w}$ and the orthonormal basis of the warp space $\{W_i\}_{1 \leq i \leq F-1}$, the Eigen warps.

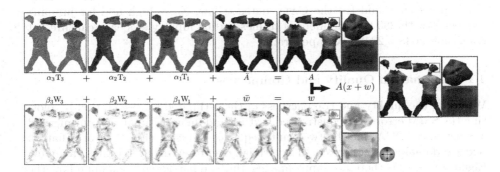

Fig. 4. Texture map generation by linear combination.

3.3   Texture Generation

Given the Eigen textures and the Eigen warps, and as shown in Fig. 4, a texture can be generated by first creating an aligned texture by linearly combining Eigen textures and second de-aligning this new texture using another linear combination of the Eigen warps.

4   Performance Evaluation

To validate the estimation quality of our method, we apply our estimation pipeline to several datasets, project and warp input data using the built eigenspaces, then evaluate the reconstruction error. To distinguish the different error sources, we evaluate this error both in texture space before projection, and in image domain by projecting into the input views, as compared to the original views of the object and the texture before any reconstruction in texture space, estimated in our pipeline using [11]. For the image error measurement, we use the 3D model that was fitted to the sequence, as tracked to fit the test frames selected [21], and render the model as textured with our reconstructed appearance map, using a standard graphics pipeline. In both cases, we use the structural similarity index (SSIM) [27] as metric to compare to the original. All of our SSIM estimates are computed in the active regions of the texture and image domains, that is on the set of texels actually mapped to the 3D model in the texture domain, and only among actual silhouette pixels in the image domain.

We study in particular the compactness and generalization abilities of our method, by examining the error response as a function of the number of eigen components kept after constructing the linear subspaces, and the number of training images selected. For all these evaluations, we also provide the results for a naive PCA strategy, where only a set of eigen appearance maps are built in texture space and use to project and reconstruct textures, to show the performance contribution of including the Eigen warps.

For validation, we used two multi-sequence datasets: (1) the TOMAS dataset which consists of 4 different sequences left, right, run and walk with 207 total number of frames and 68 input views each captured at resolution 2048 × 2048 pixels per frame; and (2) the CATY dataset: low, close, high and far jumping sequences with 290 total number of frames and 68 input views each captured at resolution 2048 × 2048 pixels per frame.

4.1   Estimation Quality and Compactness

We study the quality and compactness of the estimated representation by plotting the SSIM errors of reconstructed texture and image estimates of our method against naive PCA, for the two multi-sequence datasets (Fig. 5). Note that all texture domain variability could be trivially represented by retaining as many Eigen textures as there are input images, thus we particularly examine how the quality degrades with the fraction of Eigen components kept. In the case of image

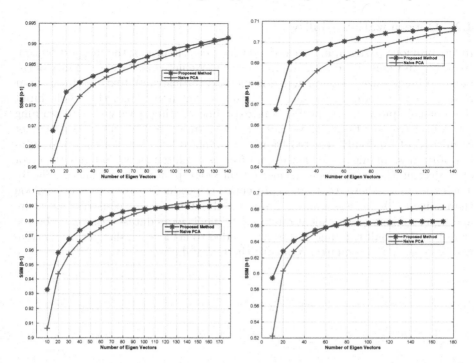

Fig. 5. Reconstruction Error for TOMAS and CATY Dataset from top to down in Texture and Image Domain from left to right.

domain evaluations, we plot the average SSIM among all viewpoints. Our method outperforms naive PCA in image and texture domains on both datasets, achieving higher quality with a lower number of Eigen components, and only marginally lower quality as the number of components grows, where the method would be anyway less useful. Higher number of Eigen components marginally favors naive PCA, because naive PCA converges to input textures when increasing the Eigen textures retained by construction, whereas our method hits a quality plateau due to small errors introduced by texture warp estimation and decomposition. For both datasets, virtually no error (0.98 SSIM) is introduced by our method in the texture domain with as low as 50 components, a substantially low fraction compared to the number of input frames (207 and 290). This illustrates the validity of the linear variability hypothesis in texture domain. The error is quite higher in the image domain (bounded by 0.7) for both our method and naive PCA, because measurements are then subject to fixed upstream errors due to geometric alignments, projections and image discretizations. Nevertheless, visually indistinguishable results are achieved with 50 Eigen components (images and warps), with a significant compactness gain.

4.2   Generalization Ability

In the previous paragraph, we examined the performance of the method by constructing an Eigen space with all input frames. We here evaluate the ability of the model to generalize, *i.e.* how well the method reconstructs textures from input frames under a reduced number of examples that don't span the whole input set. For this purpose, we perform an experiment using a varying size training set, and a test set from frames not in the training set. We use a training set comprised of randomly selected frames spanning 0 % to 60 % of the total number of frames, among all sequences and frames of all datasets, and plot the error of projecting the complement frames on the corresponding Eigen space (Fig. 6). The experiment shows that our representation produces a better generalization than naive PCA, *i.e.* less training frames need to be used to reconstruct a texture and reprojections of equivalent quality. For the TOMAS dataset, one can observe than less than half training images are needed to achieve similar performance in texture space, and a quarter less with the CATY dataset.

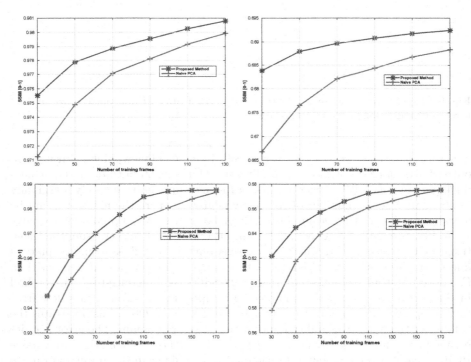

Fig. 6. Generalization Error for THOMAS and CATY Dataset from top to down in Texture and Image Domain from left to right.

5   Applications

We investigate below two applications of the appearance representation we propose. First, the interpolation between frames at different time instants and second, the completion of appearance maps at frames where some appearance information is lacking due to occlusions or missing observations during the acquisition. Results are shown in the following section and the supplementary video.

5.1   Interpolation

In our framework, appearance interpolation benefits from the pre-computed warps and the low dimensionality of our representation to efficiently synthesize compelling new appearances with reduced ghosting-artefacts. It also easily enables extension of appearance interpolation from pairwise to multiple frames. Assume that shapes between two given frames are interpolated using a standard non-linear shape interpolation, for instance [28]. Consider then the associated aligned textures and associated warps at the given frames. We perform a linear interpolation in the Eigen texture and Eigen warp spaces respectively by blending the projection coefficients of the input appearance maps. Poisson warping, as introduced in Sect. 3.1 is used to build de-aligned interpolated texture with the interpolated backward warp. Figure 7 compares interpolation using our pipeline to a standard linear interpolation for 4 examples with the CATY and TOMAS datasets. Note that our method is also linear but benefits from the alignment performed in the texture space to reduce interpolation artefacts, as well as from the simplified computational aspects since interpolation applies to projection coefficients only.

5.2   Completion

As mentioned earlier, appearance maps can be incomplete due to acquisition issues. For instance, as shown in Fig. 8, during the running sequence the actor TOMAS bends his knees in such a way that the upper parts of his left and right shins become momentarily hidden to the acquisition system. This results in missing information for those body parts in the texture maps and over a few frames. Such an issue can be solved with our texture representation by omitting the incomplete frames when building our appearance representations, and then projecting these incomplete appearance maps in the Eigen spaces and reconstructing them using the projection coefficients and Poisson texture warping. Figure 8 shows two examples of this principle with occluded regions. Note however, that while effectively filling gaps in the appearance map, this completion might yet loose appearance details in regions of the incomplete map where information is not duplicated in the training set.

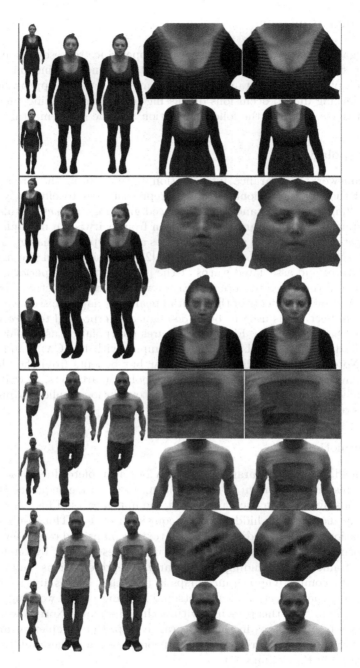

Fig. 7. Interpolation examples using linear interpolation (left) and our pipeline (right). From left to right: Input frames, Interpolated models, and a close-up on the texture maps (top) and the rendered images (bottom).

Fig. 8. Completion examples. From left to right: Input and completed models, close-up on input and completed texture maps (top) and rendered images (bottom).

6   Conclusion

We have presented a novel framework to efficiently represent the appearance of a subject observed from multiple viewpoints and in different motions. We propose a straightforward representation which builds on PCA and decomposes into Eigen textures and Eigen warps that encode, respectively, the appearance variations due to viewpoint and illumination changes and due to geometric modeling imprecisions. The framework was evaluated on 2 datasets and with respect to: (i) its ability to accurately reproduce appearances with compact representations; (ii) its ability to resolve appearance interpolation and completion tasks. In both cases, the interest of a global appearance model for a given subject was demonstrated. Among the limitations, the representation performances are dependent on the underlying geometries. Future strategies that combine both shape and appearance information would thus be of particular interest. The proposed model could also be extended to global representations over populations of subjects.

References

1. Collet, A., Chuang, M., Sweeney, P., Gillett, D., Evseev, D., Calabrese, D., Hoppe, H., Kirk, A., Sullivan, S.: High-quality streamable free-viewpoint video. ACM Trans. Graph. **34**, 69:1–69:13 (2015)
2. Nishino, K., Sato, Y., Ikeuchi, K.: Eigen-texture method: appearance compression and synthesis based on a 3D model. IEEE Trans. Pattern Anal. Mach. Intell. **23**, 1257–1265 (2001)
3. Debevec, P.E., Taylor, C.J., Malik, J.: Modeling and rendering architecture from photographs: a hybrid geometry- and image-based approach. In: ACM SIGGRAPH 1996 (1996)
4. Lempitsky, V.S., Ivanov, D.V.: Seamless mosaicing of image-based texture maps. In: CVPR (2007)
5. Waechter, M., Moehrle, N., Goesele, M.: Let there be color! Large-scale texturing of 3D reconstructions. In: Fleet, D., Pajdla, T., Schiele, B., Tuytelaars, T. (eds.) ECCV 2014. LNCS, vol. 8693, pp. 836–850. Springer, Heidelberg (2014). doi:10.1007/978-3-319-10602-1_54
6. Blanz, V., Vetter, T.: A morphable model for the synthesis of 3D faces. In: ACM SIGGRAPH 1996 (1999)
7. Carranza, J., Theobalt, C., Magnor, M.A., Seidel, H.P.: Free-viewpoint video of human actors. ACM Trans. Graph. **22**, 569–577 (2003)
8. Zitnick, C., Kang, S., Uyttendaele, M., Winder, S., Szeliski, R.: High-quality video view interpolation using a layered representation. In: ACM SIGGRAPH 2004 (2004)
9. Eisemann, M., De Decker, B., Magnor, M., Bekaert, P., de Aguiar, E., Ahmed, N., Theobalt, C., Sellent, A.: Floating textures. Comput. Graph Forum (Proc. of Eurographics) **27**, 409–418 (2008)
10. Tung, T.: Simultaneous super-resolution and 3D video using graph-cuts (2008)
11. Tsiminaki, V., Franco, J.S., Boyer, E.: High resolution 3D shape texture from multiple videos. In: CVPR (2014)
12. Goldlücke, B., Aubry, M., Kolev, K., Cremers, D.: A super-resolution framework for high-accuracy multiview reconstruction. Int. J. Comput. Vis. **106**, 172–191 (2014)
13. de Aguiar, E., Stoll, C., Theobalt, C., Ahmed, N., Seidel, H.P., Thrun, S.: Performance capture from sparse multi-view video. ACM Trans. Graph. **27**, 98:1–98:10 (2008)
14. Cagniart, C., Boyer, E., Ilic, S.: Free-from mesh tracking: a patch-based approach. In: CVPR (2010)
15. Volino, M., Casas, D., Collomosse, J., Hilton, A.: Optimal representation of multiple view video. In: BMVC (2014)
16. Boukhayma, A., Boyer, E.: Video based animation synthesis with the essential graph. In: 3DV (2015)
17. Casas, D., Tejera, M., Guillemaut, J.Y., Hilton, A.: 4D parametric motion graphs for interactive animation. In: ACM SIGGRAPH Symposium on Interactive 3D Graphics and Games (2012)
18. Casas, D., Volino, M., Collomosse, J., Hilton, A.: 4D video textures for interactive character appearance. Comput. Graph. Forum (Proc. of Eurographics) **33**, 371–380 (2014)
19. Turk, M., Pentland, A.: Eigenfaces for recognition. J. Cogn. Neurosci. **3**, 71–86 (1991)

20. Cootes, T.F., Edwards, G.J., Taylor, C.J.: Active appearance models. IEEE Trans. Pattern Anal. Mach. Intell. **23**(6), 681–685 (2001)
21. Allain, B., Franco, J.S., Boyer, E.: An efficient volumetric framework for shape tracking. In: CVPR (2015)
22. Sanchez Prez, J., Meinhardt-Llopis, E., Facciolo, G.: TV-L1 optical flow estimation. Image Process. On Line **3**, 137–150 (2013)
23. Pérez, P., Gangnet, M., Blake, A.: Poisson image editing. ACM Trans. Graph. **22**(3), 313–318 (2003)
24. Chen, T., Zhu, J.Y., Shamir, A., Hu, S.M.: Motion-aware gradient domain video composition. IEEE Trans. Image Process. **22**(7), 2532–2544 (2013)
25. Linz, C., Lipski, C., Magnor, M.: Multi-image interpolation based on graph-cuts and symmetric optical flow (2010)
26. Mahajan, D., Huang, F.C., Matusik, W., Ramamoorthi, R., Belhumeur, P.N.: Moving gradients: a path-based method for plausible image interpolation. ACM Trans. Graph. **28**(3), 1–11 (2009)
27. Wang, Z., Bovik, A.C., Sheikh, H.R., Simoncelli, E.P.: Image quality assessment: from error visibility to structural similarity. IEEE Trans. Image Process. **13**, 600–612 (2004)
28. Xu, D., Zhang, H., Wang, Q., Bao, H.: Poisson shape interpolation. In: ACM Symposium on Solid and Physical Modeling (2005)

Learnable Histogram: Statistical Context Features for Deep Neural Networks

Zhe Wang, Hongsheng Li$^{(\boxtimes)}$, Wanli Ouyang, and Xiaogang Wang$^{(\boxtimes)}$

Department of Electronic Engineering, The Chinese University of Hong Kong,
Sha Tin, Hong Kong
{zwang,hsli,wlouyang,xgwang}@ee.cuhk.edu.hk

Abstract. Statistical features, such as histogram, Bag-of-Words (BoW) and Fisher Vector, were commonly used with hand-crafted features in conventional classification methods, but attract less attention since the popularity of deep learning methods. In this paper, we propose a learnable histogram layer, which learns histogram features within deep neural networks in end-to-end training. Such a layer is able to back-propagate (BP) errors, learn optimal bin centers and bin widths, and be jointly optimized with other layers in deep networks during training. Two vision problems, semantic segmentation and object detection, are explored by integrating the learnable histogram layer into deep networks, which show that the proposed layer could be well generalized to different applications. In-depth investigations are conducted to provide insights on the newly introduced layer.

Keywords: Histogram · Deep learning · Semantic segmentation · Object detection

1 Introduction

Context features play a crucial role in many vision classification problems, such as semantic segmentation [1–6], object detection [7,8] and pose estimation [9,10]. As illustrated by the toy example in Fig. 1, when performing classification on the blurry white objects with similar appearance, if the semantic histogram from the whole image has a higher bin on the class "sea", then the object is more likely to be classified as a "boat"; if the histogram has a higher bin on the class "sky", then it is more likely to be classified as a "bird". The semantic context thus acts as an important indicator for this classification task.

Context features could be mainly categorized into statistical and non-statistical ones depending on whether they abandon the spatial orders of the context information. On the one hand, for most deep learning methods that gain increasing attention in recent years, non-statistical context features dominate. Some examples include [11] for object detection and [12] for semantic segmentation.

On the other hand, statistical context features were mostly used in conventional classification methods with hand-crafted features. Commonly used statistical features include histogram, Bag-of-Words (BoW) [13], Fisher vector [14],

© Springer International Publishing AG 2016
B. Leibe et al. (Eds.): ECCV 2016, Part I, LNCS 9905, pp. 246–262, 2016.
DOI: 10.1007/978-3-319-46448-0_15

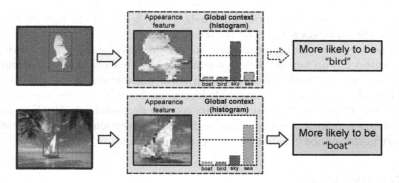

Fig. 1. A toy example showing that the global context (histogram) of a whole image is helpful for classifying image patches. The image patch is more likely to be a "bird" if the histogram has higher bin counts on the class "sky", or a "boat" if the histogram has higher bin counts on the class "sea".

Second-order pooling [15], etc. Such global context features performed successfully with hand-crafted low-level features at their times. However, they were much less studied since the popularity of deep learning. There are a limited number of deep learning methods that tried to incorporate statistical features into deep neural networks. Such examples include the deep Fisher network [16] that incorporate Fisher vector and orderless pooling [17] that combines with Vector of Locally Aggregated Descriptors (VLAD). Both methods aim to improve the image classification performance. However, when calculating the statistical features, both methods fix the network parameters and simply treat features by deep networks as off-the-shelf features. In such a way, the deep networks and the statistical operations are not jointly optimized, which is one of the key factors for the success of deep networks. In this work, we introduce a learnable histogram layer for deep neural networks.

Unlike existing deep learning methods that treat statistical operations as a separate module, our proposed histogram layer is able to back-propagate (BP) errors and learn optimal bin centers and bin width during training. Such properties make it possible to be integrated into neural networks and end-to-end trained. In this way, the appearance and statistical features in a neural network could effectively adapt each other and thus lead to better classification accuracy.

The proposed learnable histogram layer could be used for various applications. We propose the HistNet-SS network for semantic segmentation and the HistNet-OD network for object detection. Both networks are built based on state-of-the-art deep neural networks with the learnable histogram layer. Jointly training the HistNets in an end-to-end manner helps convolution layers learn more discriminative feature representations and boosts the final accuracy. Thus our contributions of this paper can be summarized as three-fold:

– We propose the learnable histogram layer for deep neural networks, which is able to BP errors, calculate histogram features, and learn optimal bin centers and widths. To the best of our knowledge, such learnable histogram features are introduced to deep learning for the first time.

- We conduct thorough investigations on the proposed statistical feature with comparison to the non-statistical counterparts. We show that statistical features help achieve better accuracy with fewer parameters in certain cases.
- We show that the proposed learnable histogram layer is easy to generalize and could be utilized for different applications. We proposed two HistNet models for solving semantic segmentation and object detection problems. State-of-the-art performance is achieved for both applications.

2   Related Work

Semantic Segmentation by Deep Learning. The goal of semantic segmentation is to densely classify pixels in a given image into one of the predefined categories. Recently, deep learning based methods have dramatically improved the performance of semantic segmentation. Farabet et al. [12] proposed a multi-scale convolution neural network for semantic segmentation. Their model takes a large image patch as input to cover more context around the center pixel, and applies post-processing techniques such as superpixel voting and Conditional Random Field (CRF) to improve the consistency of the labeling map. Pinheiro et al. [18] used a Recurrent Neural Network (RNN) to recursively correct its own mistakes by taking the raw image together with the predictions of the previous stage as input. Long et al. [19] proposed the Fully Convolution Network (FCN) which takes the whole image as input and is trained in an end-to-end manner. Following [19], many works have been proposed to incorporate more semantic context information into deep learning model. Chen et al. [20] combined the output of the FCN with a fully connected CRF. However, the two components are treated as two separate parts and greedily trained. Zheng et al. [21] showed that the mean-field algorithm for solving a fully connected CRF is equivalent to a RNN, which can be jointly trained with the FCN in an end-to-end manner. Liu et al. [22] designed layers to model pairwise terms in a MRF, which approximate the mean-field by only one iteration, and thus makes inference much faster. Our work differ with these methods in the way that we model context as statistical features while they model context with graphical models. These methods and our proposed method are complementary, and can be utilized in a unified framework to further improve the performance.

Object Detection by Deep Learning. The object detection aims at locating the objects of predefined categories in a given image. RCNN [11] is a famous pipeline based on CNN. It first pre-trains the CNN on the image classification task, and then uses the learned weights as the initial point for training the detection task with region proposals. Many works have been proposed to improve RCNN. The faster-RCNN [23] simultaneously predicts the region proposals and outputs the detection scores in a given image, while the two parts share the same convolution layers. Although their model takes the whole image as input, the global context information is ignored. Ouyang et al. [8] used the image classification scores from another CNN as the semantic context information to refine the detection scores of the bounding boxes produced by the RCNN pipeline. Szegedy et al. [7] concatenated the topmost features of image classification to those of all the detection bounding boxes. However, both methods require extra training data and labels on the image classification task. In comparison, our work calculates the likelihood histogram of the base model's own prediction as global context, which does not require any extra annotation.

Statistical Features in Deep Learning. Some other works have been proposed to incorporate statistical models into a deep learning framework. Simonyan et al. [16] proposed a Fisher Vector Layer, which is the generalization of a standard Fisher Vector, and a Fisher Vector network, which consists of a stack of Fisher Vector Layers. However, they still use conventional hand-crafted features as input of the network. Gong [17] presented a multi-scale orderless pooling scheme to extract global context features for image classification and image retrieval tasks. They adopted the Vector of Local Aggregated Descriptors (VLAD) for encoding activations from a convolution neural network. However, unlike our learnable histogram layer layer, their model is not differentiable thus unable to BP errors.

Differentiable Histograms. Chiu et al. [24] exploited the pipeline of Histogram of Oriented Gradient (HOG) descriptor and showed it is piecewise differentiable. The key differences between our proposed layers and the differentiable HOG are three-fold. (1) Our learnable histogram layer does not only BP errors but also learns optimal bin centers and bin widths during training, while the differentiable HOG has fixed bin centers and widths. (2) We for the first time introduce the learnable histogram layer into deep neural networks for end-to-end training. All the learnable layers in a neural network could effectively adapt each other for learning better feature representations. (3) We also show that such a learnable histogram layer could be formulated by a stack of existing CNN layers and thus significantly lowers the implementation difficulty.

3 Methods

3.1 The Overall Frameworks

Global semantic context has been shown of great effectiveness in various classification problems including semantic segmentation [1–6], object detection [7,8] and pose estimation [9,10]. Histogram is one of the most-commonly-used conventional statistical features for describing context. However, such statistical features are little investigated by existing deep learning methods.

We propose two deep neural networks, the HistNet-SS for semantic segmentation and the HistNet-OD for object detection. Both include a learnable histogram layer that calculates histogram features for a likelihood map or vector.

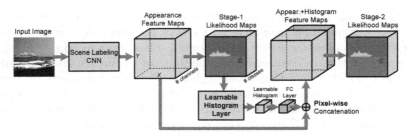

(a) HistNet-SS: the proposed network for semantic segmentation.

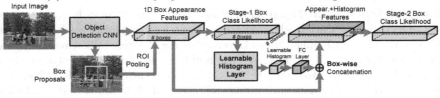

(b) HistNet-OD: the proposed network for object detection.

Fig. 2. The pipelines of the proposed HistNet-SS for semantic segmentation and HistNet-OD for object detection. A learnable histogram layer is included to incorperate the global semantic context information.

The learnable histogram layer can BP errors to bottom layers, and automatically learns the optimal bin centers and bin widths. Such properties make it possible to be trained in a deep neural network in an end-to-end manner.

The semantic segmentation task requires labeling each pixel of an input image with a given class. Our HistNet-SS is based on the FCN-VGG network [19], which takes a whole image as input and outputs all pixels' class likelihood simultaneously. As shown in Fig. 2(a), our proposed HistNet-SS model adds a learnable histogram layer following the initial class likelihood map (stage-1 likelihood map) by the FCN-VGG to obtain the histogram features of the likelihood map of the whole image. Such histogram features are then forwarded through a Fully Connected (FC) layer and pixel-wisely concatenated with the topmost feature maps of the FCN-VGG. A new 1×1 convolution layer is added as the stage-2 classifier to generate the stage-2 likelihood map for each pixel of the input image. In this way, the global semantic context could provide vital information when classifying each pixel. For instance, for an image in the SIFTFlow dataset [25], if the histogram shows that the "sea" class has very large counts of high likelihoods, then the probability of classifying the pixels as "street light" should be diminished to some extent. The likelihood maps as output of stage-2 classifier can form a new histogram, which can be concatenated with the appearance features again to refine prediction in stage-3 and so on. The final class likelihood map is calculated as the average of the likelihood maps at all stages. During training, the supervision signals are applied to all the likelihood maps.

For the object detection task, each object of interest in an input image is required to be annotated by a bounding box with a confidence score.

Our HistNet-OD is based on the faster-RCNN model [23], which includes a Region Proposal Network (RPN) and a fast-RCNN detector. For each input image, the RPN generates region proposals and the fast-RCNN detector extracts features for each region from the topmost feature map via ROI pooling and predicts the likelihoods of each box proposal belonging to pre-defined classes. Similar to our HistNet-SS model, our network feeds the initial box class likelihood (stage-1 box class likelihood) to our learnable histogram layer. The output histogram features encode statistics of the prediction class likelihood for the input image and then go through a FC layer. The resulting context features are then box-wisely concatenated with each box proposal's appearance features and classified by a fully connected layer to generate the stage-2 box class likelihood. The supervision signals are applied to all likelihood vectors, and the final likelihood are obtained by averaging those of the multiple stages.

3.2   The Learnable Histogram Layer

Conventional Histograms. For the semantic segmentation or the object detection task, each sample (either a pixel or a box proposal) is labeled with K scores by a neural network to denote its confidences on the K pre-defined classes. For calculating a conventional histogram on the samples' class scores, we divide each class score into B bins, and the histogram is therefore of size $K \times B$. Each of the sample's K class likelihoods casts a vote to its corresponding bin, and all bins' votes are then normalized to obtain the conventional histogram. The voting process for each bin of the conventional histogram could be treated as an indication function, which either votes 1 (belonging to the bin) or 0 (not belonging to the bin) for a specific sample. Those functions are not differentiable and cannot be utilized in a deep neural network for end-to-end training.

Learnable Histograms. Inspired by the differentiable Histogram of Oriented Gradient (HOG) in [24], we design the learnable histogram layer for deep neural networks, which is piecewise differentiable and is able to BP errors. The differences between our work and [24] are summarized in Sect. 2.

The bth bin of class k in the learnable histogram is modeled by a piecewise linear basis function $\psi_{k,b}(x_k)$, (Fig. 3(a))

$$\psi_{k,b}(x_k) = \max\left\{0, 1 - |x_k - \mu_{k,b}| \times w_{k,b}\right\}, \qquad (1)$$

where $\mu_{k,b}$ is its bth bin center for class k, $w_{k,b}$ is the bin width, and $\max\{\cdot, \cdot\}$ takes the maximum of the two values. Both the bin centers $\mu_{k,b}$ and bin widths $w_{k,b}$ could be learned during training. If a sample's class-k score x_k falls into the bth bin, i.e., the interval of $[\mu_b - w_{k,b}, \mu_b + w_{k,b}]$, this sample votes for the bth bin with a positive weight $\psi_{k,b}(x_k)$. Note that each sample generally votes for multiple bins with different non-negative weights. The histogram of the class k can then be calculated by normalizing all the votes with the number of samples. Such a process repeats for all classes to create the $K \times B$-dimensional histogram features for a likelihood map or vector. Figures 3(b) and (c) show an example of

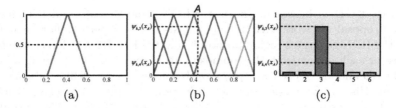

Fig. 3. (a) An example of the histogram basis function $\psi_{k,b}$. It corresponds to bin 3 of the histogram functions in (b). (b) The histogram basis functions for class k with $B = 6$ bins. The sample A with likelihood x_A would vote for bin 3, 4 with non-negative weights $\psi_{k,3}(x_A)$ and $\psi_{k,4}(x_A)$. (c) The histogram of sample A's class-k likelihoods.

the histogram basis functions for class k with $B = 6$ bins. The sample A with the class score x_A would vote for two neighboring bins with non-negative weights $\psi_{k,3}(x_A)$ and $\psi_{k,3}(x_A)$ respectively.

Unlike the indication functions of the conventional histogram, the linear basis functions for our histogram layer are piecewise differentiable. They can BP errors to lower neural layers, and can calculate the gradients of bin centers and bin widths according to the errors E from its following layers,

$$\frac{\partial E}{\partial w_{k,b}} = \begin{cases} |x_k - \mu_{k,b}|, & \psi_{k,b}(x_k) > 0, \\ 0, & \text{otherwise.} \end{cases} \tag{2}$$

$$\frac{\partial E}{\partial u_{k,b}} = \begin{cases} w_{k,b}, & \psi_{k,b}(x_k) > 0 \text{ and } x_k - \mu_{k,b} > 0, \\ -w_{k,b}, & \psi_{k,b}(x_k) > 0 \text{ and } x_k - \mu_{k,b} < 0, \\ 0, & \text{otherwise.} \end{cases} \tag{3}$$

$\mu_{k,b}$ and $w_{k,b}$ could then be updated by Stochastic Gradient Descent (SGD). Note that the bin centers and bin widths for different classes are independently learned to capture different data statistics of the classes.

Learnable Histogram Layer as Existing CNN Layers. One nice property of our proposed learnable histogram layer is that it can be modeled by stacking existing CNN layers, which significantly lowers the implementation difficulty. Such implementation is illustrated in Fig. 4. The input of the histogram layer is a likelihood map or vector from the classification layer, and the output is a $K \times B$-dimensional histogram feature vector. In this subsection, an input likelihood vector is treated as a likelihood map with one spatial dimension equalling 1.

The operation $x_k - \mu_{k,b}$ for class k and a bin centered at $\mu_{k,b}$ is equivalent to convolving the input likelihood map by a fixed 1×1 kernel $H_{k,b}^{\mathrm{I}} \in \mathbf{R}^K$ and a learnable bias term $-\mu_{k,b}$ ("Convolution I" in Fig. 4). Each 1×1 kernel $H_{k,b}^{\mathrm{I}}$ is a fixed unit vector,

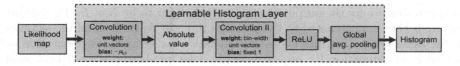

Fig. 4. Modeling the learnable histogram layer as a stack of existing CNN layers.

$$H_{k,b}^{I}(c) = \begin{cases} 1, & c = k, \\ 0, & \text{otherwise}, \end{cases} \tag{4}$$

where $H_{k,b}^{I}(c)$ denotes the cth entry of the kernel $H_{k,b}^{I}$. For class k, by convolving the likelihood maps with B such filters we can obtain B new score maps $x_k - \mu_{k,b}$. Since we build a histogram for all B classes, the similar convolutions with different unit-vector kernels and learnable biases would be applied to the input likelihood map for B times. We obtain $K \times B$ new score maps in total, each of which records the results for one bin of a class, and their spatial sizes remain the same. After taking the absolute value of the new score maps, we apply another set of convolutions ("Convolution II" in Fig. 4) with a total of $K \times B$ learnable 1×1 kernels $H_{k,b}^{II} \in \mathbf{R}^{K \cdot B}$ and fixed bias terms 1 modeling the operation of $1 - |x_k - \mu_{k,b}| \times w_{k,b}$. $|x_k - \mu_{k,b}|$ is the output feature map by the absolute value layer. Each convolution kernel $H_{k,b}^{II}$ is a scaled unit vector that models the learnable bin width $w_{k,b}$ for the bth bin of class k of the histogram as

$$H_{k,b}^{II}(c) = \begin{cases} w_{k,b}, & c = (k-1)B + k, \\ 0, & \text{otherwise}. \end{cases} \tag{5}$$

The $\max\{0, \cdot\}$ function in Eq. (1) is equivalent to the Rectifier Linear Unit (ReLU) non-linearity layer, which takes the feature maps by the "Convolution II" as input. The final learnable histogram feature is then obtained by conducting a channel-wise global average pooling on the resulting feature maps.

When training the learnable histogram layer, we "lock" the filters for $H_{k,b}^{I}$ and $H_{k,b}^{II}$ so that only the non-zero entries of them are updated. In this way, we keep the physical meaning of the histogram. These non-zero entries of the filters and the bias terms are not shared across channels, which makes learning bin centers and bin widths for each category independent. We tested abandoning the physical meaning of histograms and allowing the network to freely update all parameters of both convolution filters, which results in inferior performance than our "locked" filters (see investigations in Sect. 4.4).

3.3 Concatenating the Histogram Features

Features from our learnable histogram layer capture the global semantic context of the stage-1 likelihood maps or vectors. However, it might not be linearly separable compared with the features by the previous topmost convolution layer. Therefore, we feed the histogram feature into another fully connected layer.

In this paper, we fix the output channels of this layer to be $K \times B$. The output feature is then concatenated to the previous topmost features of all the samples in the same image (i.e., pixel-wise concatenation for semantic segmentation or box-wise concatenation for object detection.) for predicting stage-2 likelihood map or vector (see Fig. 2 for illustration).

3.4   Training Schemes

Our two HistNet models are finetuned based on pre-trained base models (i.e., the VGG-FCN for semantic segmentation and faster-RCNN for object detection) in an incremental manner with 2 phases. In the first phase, only the newly added FC layers are finetuned, with the base models and the learnable histogram layer fixed. The bin centers and widths for each class are initially set as $w_{k,b} = 0.2$ and $\mu_k = \{0, 0.2, 0.4, 0.6, 0.8, 1\}$. In the second phase, we jointly finetune all the layers, with the exception of the above mentioned convolution layers in the learnable histogram layer, which update only their non-zero entries.

4   Experiments on Semantic Segmentation

4.1   Experimental Setup

We evaluated the proposed HistNet-SS on the semantic segmentation task. The HistNet-SS adopted the VGG-FCN model in [19] as the base model for generating stage-1 likelihood maps. The base model is initialized by the weights from a VGG-19 model pretrained on ImageNet [26] classification dataset. Following [19], we first train the coarse FCN-32s version and use its weights to initialize the final FCN-16s version. All the upsampling deconvolution layers were initialized as bilinear interpolation and allowed adaptation during training. All the new convolutional layers for classification were initialized by Gaussians with zero mean and a standard deviation of 0.01 and constant biases of 0.

During training, we adopted the mini-batch Stochastic Gradient Descent (SGD) to optimize the CNN models and used a mini-batch of 10 images for the semantic segmentation task and 2 images for the object detection task, respectively. We used a gradually decreasing learning rate starting from 10^{-2} with a stepsize of 20,000 and a momentum of 0.9.

4.2   Datasets and Evaluation Metrics

We evaluate the proposed HistNet-SS on the SIFTFlow [25], Stanford background [2] and PASCAL VOC 2012 [27] segmentation datasets. The SIFTFLow dataset consists of 2488 training images and 200 test images. All the images are of size 256×256 and contain 33 semantic labels. The Stanford background dataset contains 715 images of outdoor scenes composed of 8 classes. Following the train/test split in [28,29], 572 images are selected as the training set and the rest 143 images as the test set. PASCAL VOC datasets consists of 1464, 1449, and 1456 images for training, validation, and testing, respectively. The dataset is augmented by the extra annotations provided by [30], resulting in 10582 training images. For the first two dataset, we augmented the training set by randomly scaling, rotating and horizontally flipping each training image for 5 times. The scaling factors and the rotation angles were randomly chosen in the ranges of [0.9, 1.1] and [−8°, 8°]. For PASCAL VOC dataset, we did not conduct data augmentation. No class balancing is performed on any dataset.

Following the common practice, we evaluate the compared methods by the per-pixel and per-class accuracies on SIFTFlow and Stanford background datasets. For PASCAL VOC 2012 segmentation dataset, The performance is measured in terms of intersection-over-union (IOU) averaged across the 21 classes.

4.3 Overall Performance

SIFTFlow Dataset. For the SIFTFlow dataset, we compared our method with state-of-the-art methods, which include both deep-learning-based [12,18, 19,29,31], and non-deep-learning-based methods [1,25,32]. The accuracies by different methods are reported in Table 1(a). The HistNet-SS achieves state-of-the-art performance. Note that here the HistNet-SS is based on the FCN model implemented by ourselves. This FCN baseline achieves a higher per-pixel (0.86 v.s. 0.851) accuracy but a lower per-class accuracy (0.457 v.s. 0.517) compared to the results reported in [19], which might result from different data distribution caused by our data augmentation. The HistNet-SS is initialized by our implemented FCN model. Some qualitative results are shown in Fig. 5.

As shown in Table 1(a), with the learnable histogram layer, HistNet outperformed its VGG-FCN base model by 1.9 % and 5 % for per-pixel and per-class accuracies, respectively. The base model of HistNet (denoted as HistNet-SS stage-1) has exactly the same net structure with the VGG-FCN but is jointly fine-tuned within the HistNet-SS. It is interesting to see that the prediction by the base

Table 1. Per-pixel and per-class accuracies on (a) the SIFTFlow dataset and (b) the Stanford background dataset by different methods. Best accuracies are marked in bold.

Methods	Per-pixel	Per-class
Tighe et al. [32]	0.769	0.294
Liu et al. [25]	0.748	n/a
Farabet et al. [12]	0.785	0.296
Pinheiho et al. [18]	0.777	0.298
Sharma et al. [29]	0.796	0.336
Yang et al. [1]	0.798	0.487
Eigen et al. [31]	0.868	0.464
FCN [19]	0.851	**0.517**
FCN (our implement)	0.860	0.457
FCN+FC-CRF	0.865	0.468
HistNet-SS stage-1	0.876	0.505
HistNet-SS	**0.879**	0.5
HistNet-SS+FC-CRF	**0.879**	0.512

(a) SIFTFlow dataset

Method	Per-pixel	Per-class
Gould et al. [2]	0.764	n/a
Tighe et al. [32]	0.775	n/a
Socher et al. [28]	0.781	n/a
Lempitzky et al. [33]	0.819	0.724
Farabet et al. [12]	0.814	0.76
Pinheiho et al. [18]	0.802	0.699
Sharma et al. [29]	0.823	0.791
FCN (our implement)	0.851	0.811
FCN+FC-CRF	0.862	0.82
FCN+MOPCNN [17]	0.863	0.811
HistNet-SS stage-1	0.871	**0.838**
HistNet-SS	0.871	0.837
HistNet-SS+FC-CRF	**0.881**	0.837

(b) Stanford background dataset

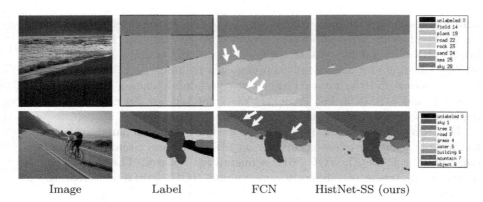

Image   Label   FCN   HistNet-SS (ours)

Fig. 5. Example results on scene labeling by our HistNet-SS. (Row 1) HistNet-SS successfully predicts most erroneous "plant" and "road" pixels by FCN to "sea" and "sand", which are more likely to appear at sea shore. (Row 2) HistNet-SS labels most "mountain" pixels correctly and discovers some "water" pixels not found by FCN.

model also benefited from the joint finetuning. This demonstrates that the bottom convolution layers now learn better feature representations, while keeping the same model complexity and without extra training data or supervision.

Stanford Background Dataset. The results on the Stanford background dataset are reported in Table 1(b). Since FCN [19] did not report their results on this dataset, here we only report the results of FCN implemented by ourselves, which surpasses state-of-the-art methods. Our proposed HistNet-SS achieves the best performance with both evaluation metrics, which shows the effectiveness of incorporating the global histogram layer into the network. We also evaluated the performance of the HistNet-SS stage-1, i.e., the base model after jointly fine-tuning with the proposed learnable histogram layer. Its performance is slightly better than the final combined result. This may be an evidence that the HistNet-SS does not simply improve its performance by adding more parameters to fit the dataset. On the contrary, it helps bottom convolution layers learn more discriminative features with statistical context features.

We also compared HistNet-SS with Gong et al. [17], which also used global features in a CNN framework. We used their code to extract image-level features by an ImageNet-pretrained AlexNet model [34]. Then the off-the-shelf feature is repeatedly concatenated to the original feature maps at each location, followed by a newly trained classifier. As shown in Table 1, the result FCN + MOPCNN is inferior than HistNet-SS, since it cannot be trained in an end-to-end manner.

In addition, we also tried to utilize the fully-connected CRF algorithm [35] to regularize the output likelihood map by our HistNet-SS following [20]. The accuracies on both SIFTFlow and Stanford background datasets could be further improved, which demonstrate that our histogram context features are complementary to the semantic context modeled by graphical models.

PASCAL VOC 2012 Segmentation Dataset. We also trained HistNet-SS based on the publicly-available DeepLab model (multi-scale features and large field-of-view) [20] with the augmented "train" set. DeepLab [20] achieves a 64.2 % mean IOU, while our method HistNet-SS improves it to 67.5 %. It shows that the HistNet-SS benefits from the learned histogram of foreground objects categories.

4.4 Investigation on the HistNet-SS

To further verify the effectiveness of the HistNet-SS, we designed multiple baseline networks to analyse each component of our learnable histogram layer.

Learnable Histogram v.s. Fix-Bin Histogram v.s. "unlocked Histogram". In order to find out whether we can benefit from learning histogram bin centers and bin widths, and whether keeping the physical meaning of the histogram helps training, we designed two baselines, FCN-fix-hist and FCN-free-all. They were both initialized in the same way as HistNet-SS. For FCN-fix-hist, we fixed its bin centers and widths during training. Recall that for HistNet-SS, we "locked" the 1×1 kernels to make it only update the non-zero entries. For FCN-free-all, we "unlocked" all the convolution kernels and biases in the learnable histogram layer so that they could adapt freely. It no longer holds the physical meaning of a histogram. As shown in Table 2, FCN-fix-hist is not as good as our HistNet-SS, which confirms our assumption that a learnable histogram is critical to better describe the context. FCN-free-all performs inferiorly to HistNet-SS by a small margin. It may suggest that keeping the physical meaning of the histogram acts as a regularizer which has fewer learnable parameters to avoid overfitting.

Statistical Context v.s. Non-statistical Context. To verify whether statistical context is better than non-statistical context, we trained two different

Table 2. Performance of different baseline models of the HistNet-SS and their corresponding numbers of extra parameters.

Methods	SIFTFlow		Stanford background		# Extra parameters (SIFTFlow/Stanford)
	Per-pixel	Per-class	Per-pixel	Per-class	
FCN baseline	0.860	0.450	0.851	0.811	0
FCN-fix-hist	0.872	0.481	0.860	0.829	$\sim 190,000$ / $36,000$
FCN-free-all	0.870	0.489	0.862	0.824	$\sim 190,000$ / $36,000$
FCN-fc7-global	0.870	0.462	-	-	$\sim 960,000$ / $23,000$
FCN-score-global	0.873	0.480	0.863	0.825	$\sim 150,000$ / $35,000$
R-HistNet-SS	**0.880**	0.486	**0.872**	**0.845**	$\sim 380,000$ / $72,000$
HistNet-SS (ours)	0.879	**0.5**	0.871	0.837	$\sim 190,000$ / $36,000$

baseline networks. FCN-fc7-global feeds the VGG-FCN fc7 layer's output, i.e., the topmost feature maps, to a 1×1 convolution layer with $K \times B$ output feature maps to match the HistNet-SS. It applies global average pooling first and then concatenates the same vector at each location of the topmost feature maps, followed by a fully connected classification layer. FCN-score-global is similar to FCN-fc7-global, except it takes the likelihood maps as input. The numbers of extra parameters are recorded in Table 2. The HistNet-SS has the fewest extra parameters among the settings. In Table 2 it can be seen that FCN-score-global and FCN-fc7-global perform comparably. However, they are inferior to the HistNet-SS. We also tried adding another learnable histogram layer to the stage-2 likelihood maps to form a recurrent HistNet (denoted as R-HistNet-SS), which is initialized by HistNet-SS and its prediction is based on the average of three likelihood maps. However, no significant improvement is observed.

5   Experiments on Object Detection

5.1   Experimental Setting

We adopted the faster-RCNN [23] pipeline to build the proposed HistNet-OD model and evaluated it on the PASCAL VOC 2007 detection benchmark [37]. This dataset consists of about 5k trainval images and 5k test images over 20 categories. The standard evaluation metric is the mean Average Precision (mAP). We utilized the faster-RCNN model trained by its python interface, which is provided by the authors of [23]. It has a slightly lower mAP than the MATLAB version one reported in their paper (0.695 v.s. 0.699). HistNet-OD stage-1 is initialized by this model. The histogram layer parameters are initialized as mentioned in Sect. 3.2. The new fully connected layers were initialized by zero-mean Gaussian with a standard deviation of 0.01. We finetuned the HistNet-OD with the VOC07 trainval set and tested it with the VOC07 test set.

5.2   Overall Performance

We report the overall performance of the HistNet-OD on the VOC 2007 test dataset. As shown in Table 3, the HistNet-OD outperforms the faster-RCNN by 1.9 %. This result shows that the learnable histogram layer has good generalization ability and can also be applied to the object detection task. Similar to the semantic segmentation task, our base model HistNet-OD stage-1 was also improved by jointly finetuning with the learnable histogram layer, which indicates that the feature representations learned by the base model are also improved.

5.3   Investigation on the HistNet-OD

Similar to the experiments in semantic segmentation (Sect. 4.4), we also designed a baseline models, faster-RCNN-fc7-global, to study the influence of statistical

Table 3. Results of object detection (mAP %) on the VOC 2007 test dataset. RCNN and fast RCNN results are from [36].

Methods	Aero	Bike	Bird	Boat	Bottle	Bus	Car	Cat	Chair	Cow	
RCNN [11]	73.4	77.0	63.4	45.4	44.6	75.1	78.1	79.8	40.5	73.7	
fast RCNN [36]	74.5	78.3	69.2	53.2	36.6	77.3	78.2	82.0	40.7	72.7	
faster RCNN [23]	69.1	78.3	68.9	55.7	49.8	77.6	79.7	85.0	51.0	76.1	
HistNet-OD stage-1	68	80.3	74.1	55.7	53.3	83.6	80.2	85.1	53.7	74.2	
HistNet-OD	67.6	80.3	74.1	55.6	53.2	83.4	80.2	85.1	53.6	74	
	Table	Dog	Horse	Mbike	Person	Plant	Sheep	Sofa	Train	Tv	**mAP**
RCNN [11]	62.2	79.4	78.1	73.1	64.2	35.6	66.8	67.2	70.4	71.1	66.0
fast RCNN [36]	67.9	79.6	79.2	73.0	69.0	30.1	65.4	70.2	75.8	65.8	66.9
faster RCNN [23]	64.2	82.0	80.5	76.2	75.8	38.5	71.4	65.4	77.8	66.1	69.5
HistNet-OD stage-1	69.3	82.5	84.9	76.5	77.7	44.2	71.7	66.6	75.5	71.8	71.4
HistNet-OD	69.3	82.5	84.8	76.3	77.6	44.1	71.9	66.8	75.4	71.9	71.4

context and non-statistical context features. The features of the faster-RCNN's fc7 layer go through a new FC layer, and are concatenated back to the previous topmost features after global average pooling. A new FC layer acting as the classifier is trained on top of the new concatenated features.

The mAP result of faster-RCNN-fc7-global is 0.704, with 170k extra parameters, compared to 0.714 by HistNet-OD, with only 91k extra parameters. This confirms that the learnable statistical feature outperforms the non-statistical one with fewer parameters. If the histogram parameters of HistNet-OD are fixed, the mAP is 0.707. It shows that HistNet-OD can benefit from tuning the parameters.

6 Conclusions

One interesting observation is that by training with the learnable histogram layer, the base network is also improved by jointly finetuning. Previous works [38–40] mostly focus on designing deeper networks to have stronger expressive power. However, this work shows that after finetuning with a deeper network, the original base model can also be improved, which may suggest a new way for model training: we can train a deep neural network with learnable histogram layers and multiple loss functions at different layers, and only use the base network for deployment.

In this work, we proposed a learnable histogram layer for deep neural networks, which does not only back-propagate errors, but also learns optimal bin centers and bin widths. Based on this learnable histogram layer, two models are designed for semantic segmentation and object detection, respectively. Both models show state-of-the-art performance, which demonstrates that the proposed learnable histogram layer is able to learn effective statistical features and is easy to generalize to different domains. In-depth investigations were conducted to analyse the effectiveness of different components of the learnable histogram layer.

Acknowledgements. This work is supported by SenseTime Group Limited, the General Research Fund sponsored by the Research Grants Council of Hong Kong (Project Nos. CUHK14206114, CUHK14205615, CUHK417011, CUHK419 412, CUHK14203015, and CUHK14207814), the Hong Kong Innovation and Technology Support Programme (No. ITS/221/13FP), National Natural Science Foundation of China (Nos. 61371192, 61301269), and PhD programs foundation of China (No. 20130185120039). Both Hongsheng Li and Xiaogang Wang are corresponding authors.

References

1. Yang, J., Price, B., Cohen, S., Yang, M.H.: Context driven scene parsing with attention to rare classes. In: Proceedings of CVPR (2014)
2. Gould, S., Fulton, R., Koller, D.: Decomposing a scene into geometric and semantically consistent regions. In: Proceedings of ICCV (2009)
3. Barinova, O., Lempitsky, V., Tretiak, E., Kohli, P.: Geometric image parsing in man-made environments. In: Daniilidis, K., Maragos, P., Paragios, N. (eds.) ECCV 2010. LNCS, vol. 6312, pp. 57–70. Springer, Heidelberg (2010). doi:10.1007/978-3-642-15552-9_5
4. Ladicky, L., Russell, C., Kohli, P., Torr, P.H.S.: Graph cut based inference with co-occurrence statistics. In: Daniilidis, K., Maragos, P., Paragios, N. (eds.) ECCV 2010. LNCS, vol. 6315, pp. 239–253. Springer, Heidelberg (2010). doi:10.1007/978-3-642-15555-0_18
5. Shotton, J., Winn, J., Rother, C., Criminisi, A.: *TextonBoost*: joint appearance, shape and context modeling for multi-class object recognition and segmentation. In: Leonardis, A., Bischof, H., Pinz, A. (eds.) ECCV 2006. LNCS, vol. 3951, pp. 1–15. Springer, Heidelberg (2006). doi:10.1007/11744023_1
6. Yao, J., Fidler, S., Urtasun, R.: Describing the scene as a whole: joint object detection. In: Proceedings of CVPR (2012)
7. Szegedy, C., Reed, S., Erhan, D., Anguelov, D.: Scalable, high-quality object detection (2014). arXiv preprint arXiv:1412.1441
8. Ouyang, W., Wang, X., Zeng, X., Qiu, S., Luo, P., Tian, Y., Li, H., Yang, S., Wang, Z., Loy, C.C., et al.: Deepid-net: deformable deep convolutional neural networks for object detection. In: Proceedings of CVPR (2015)
9. Fan, X., Zheng, K., Lin, Y., Wang, S.: Combining local appearance and holistic view: dual-source deep neural networks for human pose estimation. In: Proceedings of CVPR (2015)
10. Carreira, J., Agrawal, P., Fragkiadaki, K., Malik, J.: Human pose estimation with iterative error feedback (2015). arXiv preprint arXiv:1507.06550
11. Girshick, R., Donahue, J., Darrell, T., Malik, J.: Rich feature hierarchies for accurate object detection and semantic segmentation. In: Proceedings of CVPR (2014)
12. Farabet, C., Couprie, C., Najman, L., LeCun, Y.: Learning hierarchical features for scene labeling. TPAMI **35**(8), 1915–1929 (2013)
13. Lazebnik, S., Schmid, C., Ponce, J.: Beyond bags of features: spatial pyramid matching for recognizing natural scene categories. In: Proceedings of CVPR (2006)
14. Perronnin, F., Sánchez, J., Mensink, T.: Improving the Fisher kernel for large-scale image classification. In: Daniilidis, K., Maragos, P., Paragios, N. (eds.) ECCV 2010. LNCS, vol. 6314, pp. 143–156. Springer, Heidelberg (2010). doi:10.1007/978-3-642-15561-1_11

15. Carreira, J., Caseiro, R., Batista, J., Sminchisescu, C.: Semantic segmentation with second-order pooling. In: Fitzgibbon, A., Lazebnik, S., Perona, P., Sato, Y., Schmid, C. (eds.) ECCV 2012. LNCS, vol. 7578, pp. 430–443. Springer, Heidelberg (2012). doi:10.1007/978-3-642-33786-4_32

16. Simonyan, K., Vedaldi, A., Zisserman, A.: Deep Fisher networks for large-scale image classification. In: Proceedings of NIPS (2013)

17. Gong, Y., Wang, L., Guo, R., Lazebnik, S.: Multi-scale orderless pooling of deep convolutional activation features. In: Fleet, D., Pajdla, T., Schiele, B., Tuytelaars, T. (eds.) ECCV 2014. LNCS, vol. 8695, pp. 392–407. Springer, Heidelberg (2014). doi:10.1007/978-3-319-10584-0_26

18. Pinheiro, P.H.O., Collobert, R.: Recurrent convolutional neural networks for scene labeling. In: Proceedings of ICML (2014)

19. Long, J., Shelhamer, E., Darrell, T.: Fully convolutional networks for semantic segmentation. In: Proceedings of CVPR (2014)

20. Chen, L.C., Papandreou, G., Kokkinos, I., Murphy, K., Yuille, A.L.: Semantic image segmentation with deep convolutional nets and fully connected CRFs. In: Proceedings of ICLR (2015)

21. Zheng, S., Jayasumana, S., Romera-Paredes, B., Vineet, V., Su, Z., Du, D., Huang, C., Torr, P.: Conditional random fields as recurrent neural networks. In: Proceedings of ICCV (2015)

22. Liu, Z., Li, X., Luo, P., Loy, C.C., Tang, X.: Semantic image segmentation via deep parsing network. In: Proceedings of ICCV (2015)

23. Ren, S., He, K., Girshick, R., Sun, J.: Faster R-CNN: towards real-time object detection with region proposal networks. In: Proceedings of NIPS (2015)

24. Chiu, W.C., Fritz, M.: See the difference: direct pre-image reconstruction and pose estimation by differentiating HOG. In: Proceedings of ICCV, pp. 468–476 (2015)

25. Liu, C., Yuen, J., Torralba, A., Sivic, J., Freeman, W.T.: SIFT flow: dense correspondence across different scenes. In: Forsyth, D., Torr, P., Zisserman, A. (eds.) ECCV 2008. LNCS, vol. 5304, pp. 28–42. Springer, Heidelberg (2008). doi:10.1007/978-3-540-88690-7_3

26. Russakovsky, O., Deng, J., Su, H., Krause, J., Satheesh, S., Ma, S., Huang, Z., Karpathy, A., Khosla, A., Bernstein, M., Berg, A.C., Fei-Fei, L.: ImageNet large scale visual recognition challenge. IJCV **115**(3), 211–252 (2015)

27. Everingham, M., Van Gool, L., Williams, C.K.I., Winn, J., Zisserman, A.: The PASCAL visual object classes challenge 2012 (VOC2012) results. http://www.pascal-network.org/challenges/VOC/voc2012/workshop/index.html

28. Socher, R., Lin, C.C., Manning, C., Ng, A.Y.: Parsing natural scenes and natural language with recursive neural networks. In: Proceedings of ICML (2011)

29. Sharma, A., Tuzel, O., Jacobs, D.W.: Deep hierarchical parsing for semantic segmentation. In: Proceedings of CVPR (2015)

30. Hariharan, B., Arbeláez, P., Bourdev, L., Maji, S., Malik, J.: Semantic contours from inverse detectors. In: Proceedings of ICCV (2011)

31. Eigen, D., Fergus, R.: Predicting depth, surface normals and semantic labels with a common multi-scale convolutional architecture. In: Proceedings of ICCV (2015)

32. Tighe, J., Lazebnik, S.: SuperParsing: scalable nonparametric image parsing with superpixels. In: Daniilidis, K., Maragos, P., Paragios, N. (eds.) ECCV 2010. LNCS, vol. 6315, pp. 352–365. Springer, Heidelberg (2010). doi:10.1007/978-3-642-15555-0_26

33. Lempitsky, V., Vedaldi, A., Zisserman, A.: Pylon model for semantic segmentation. In: Proceedings of NIPS (2011)

34. Krizhevsky, A., Sutskever, I., Hinton, G.E.: Imagenet classification with deep convolutional neural networks. In: Proceedings of NIPS (2012)
35. Koltun, V.: Efficient inference in fully connected crfs with Gaussian edge potentials. In: Proceedings of NIPS (2011)
36. Girshick, R.: Fast R-CNN. In: Proceedings of ICCV (2015)
37. Everingham, M., Winn, J.: The PASCAL visual object classes challenge 2007 (VOC2007) development kit. University of Leeds, Technical report (2007)
38. Chatfield, K., Simonyan, K., Vedaldi, A., Zisserman, A.: Return of the devil in the details: delving deep into convolutional nets (2014)
39. Szegedy, C., Liu, W., Jia, Y., Sermanet, P., Reed, S., Anguelov, D., Erhan, D., Vanhoucke, V., Rabinovich, A.: Going deeper with convolutions. In: Proceedings of CVPR (2015)
40. He, K., Zhang, X., Ren, S., Sun, J.: Deep residual learning for image recognition (2015). arXiv:1512.03385

Pedestrian Behavior Understanding and Prediction with Deep Neural Networks

Shuai Yi[1,2], Hongsheng Li[1(✉)], and Xiaogang Wang[1(✉)]

[1] Department of Electronic Engineering,
Chinese University of Hong Kong, Hong Kong, China
{syi,hsli,xgwang}@ee.cuhk.edu.hk
[2] Sensetime Group Limited, Hong Kong, China
yishuai@sensetime.com

Abstract. In this paper, a deep neural network (Behavior-CNN) is proposed to model pedestrian behaviors in crowded scenes, which has many applications in surveillance. A pedestrian behavior encoding scheme is designed to provide a general representation of walking paths, which can be used as the input and output of CNN. The proposed Behavior-CNN is trained with real-scene crowd data and then thoroughly investigated from multiple aspects, including the location map and location awareness property, semantic meanings of learned filters, and the influence of receptive fields on behavior modeling. Multiple applications, including walking path prediction, destination prediction, and tracking, demonstrate the effectiveness of Behavior-CNN on pedestrian behavior modeling.

1 Introduction

Pedestrian behavior modeling is gaining increasing attention and can be used for various applications including behavior prediction [1–4], pedestrian detection and tracking [5–7], crowd motion analysis [8–11], and abnormal detection [12–14].

Modeling pedestrian behaviors is challenging. Pedestrian decision making is complex and can be influenced by various factors. The decision making process of individuals [15], the interactions among moving and stationary pedestrians [4,16], and historical motion statistics of a scene provide information for predicting future behaviors of pedestrians. While existing works focused some of these aspects with simplified rules or energy functions [15,17], our proposed model takes all these factors into account through a complex deep convolution neural network (Behavior-CNN) and makes more reliable predictions.

When using deep neural networks to model pedestrian behaviors, the main difficulty is how to make good use of pedestrian walking information as the input of networks. A straightforward way was to use dense optical flow maps to describe motions of a whole frame. However, it introduces ambiguities when merging and splitting events happen frequently in crowded scenes. As shown in Fig. 1(c), two separate pedestrians A and B at time $t-1$ move to occlude each other at location C at time t. The two flow vectors $(A \rightarrow C)$ and $(B \rightarrow C)$ describe the associations between $t-1$ and t. If the two pedestrians move to locations D and E

© Springer International Publishing AG 2016
B. Leibe et al. (Eds.): ECCV 2016, Part I, LNCS 9905, pp. 263–279, 2016.
DOI: 10.1007/978-3-319-46448-0_16

Fig. 1. Prediction results by the proposed Behavior-CNN (a) and the Social Force Model [15] (b). The input, predicted and ground-truth walking paths are shown as blue, red, and green dots, respectively. Only some pedestrians' prediction results are shown in the figure. (c) Illustration of association ambiguity in dense flow maps. (Color figure online)

at $t+1$ with flow vectors $(C \rightarrow D)$ and $(C \rightarrow E)$, it is obvious that the association ambiguities between (A, B) and (D, E) cannot be clarified by the flow vectors. It implies important information loss by using flow maps as the representation of input. A motion encoding scheme is proposed. The displacement volumes are used as the input/output of Behavior-CNN to address association ambiguity across multiple frames and avoid cumulative errors during prediction. As shown in Fig. 1(a), the input to our system is encoded from previous walking paths of all the pedestrians in the scene (blue dots) while the output of Behavior-CNN can recover future walking paths of all these pedestrians (red dots).

The contribution of this paper can be summarized into three-folds. (1) Long-term pedestrian behaviors is modeled with deep CNN. In-depth investigations on the proposed Behavior-CNN is conducted on the learned location map and the location awareness property, semantic meaning of learned filters, and the influence of receptive fields on behavior modeling. (2) A pedestrian behavior encoding scheme is proposed to encode pedestrian walking paths into sparse displacement volumes, which can be directly used as input/output for deep networks without association ambiguities. (3) The effectiveness of Behavior-CNN is demonstrated through applications on path prediction, destination prediction, and tracking.

2   Related Work

2.1   Pedestrian Walking Behavior Modeling

There have been a large number of works on modeling motion patterns. Topic models [18–21] were widely used for modeling crowd flows based on spatio-temporal dependency. Trajectory clustering was another way of learning motion patterns [22,23]. These methods only learned general historical motion statistics of a scene, without modeling the decision making process of each individual.

Katani's work [24] focus on path planning of a single target based on static scene structures. It does not model person-to-person interactions and cannot quickly adapt to varying scene dynamics.

Agent-based models [12,15,17,25,26] could model the decision making process of individuals and their interactions, and were used for simulation, prediction, and abnormal detection. However, historical motion statistics of scenes were not well utilized. Moreover, most agent-based methods used predefined rules. How to design the rules and whether the rules were proper to describe the complex pedestrian behaviors in a particular scene could not be guaranteed.

2.2 Deep Learning

Deep CNNs have shown impressive performance on various vision tasks [27], such as image classification [28], object detection [21,29,30], object tracking [31], and image segmentation [32,33]. However, no deep model has been specially designed for pedestrian behavior modeling. The main difficulty arises from how to design the network input and output, which properly encode pedestrian behavior information and are also suitable for the CNN.

The motion patterns of a whole frame were represented by dense optical flow maps for tasks such as motion segmentation [34], action recognition [35], and crowd scene understanding [36]. As discussed in Sect. 1, ambiguity exists when associating dense optical flows across multiple frames. Someone tried to learn motions directly from video input for human action recognition [37] and video classification [38]. It is not an efficient way of describing pedestrian walking behaviors from raw videos. Some methods used dynamic texture to model video motion [39,40]. They could only capture incremental motion information cross frames, but not long-term motion of pedestrian behaviors. Trajectories were most widely used for pedestrian behavior understanding in non-deep-learning approaches. However, it is not clear how to make them suitable as the input and output of CNN, as they are of variable lengths and observed in different periods.

3 Pedestrian Behavior Modeling and Prediction

The overall framework is shown in Fig. 2. The input to our system is pedestrian walking paths in previous frames (colored curves in Fig. 2(a)). They could be obtained by simple trackers such as KLT [41]. They are then encoded into a displacement volume (Fig. 2(b)) with the proposed walking behavior encoding scheme. Behavior-CNN in Fig. 2(c) takes the encoded displacement volume as

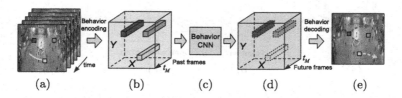

(a)   (b)   (c)   (d)   (e)

Fig. 2. System flowchart. (a) Pedestrian walking paths in previous frames. Three examples are shown in different colors. Rectangles indicate current locations of pedestrians. (b) The displacement volume encoded from pedestrians' past walking paths in (a). (c) Behavior-CNN. (d) The predicted displacement volume by Behavior-CNN. (e) Predicted future pedestrian walking paths decoded from (d).

input and predict an output displacement volume (Fig. 2(d)) for all the pedestrians simultaneously. A behavior decoding scheme then translates the output displacement volume to future walking paths of all individuals (Fig. 2(e)).

The pedestrian walking behavior encoding scheme is introduced in Sect. 3.1, and Behavior-CNN is discussed in Sect. 3.2. The walking behavior decoding is the inverse process of the encoding. The loss function and training schemes are introduced in Sect. 3.3.

3.1   Pedestrian Walking Behavior Encoding

The walking paths are encoded as displacement volumes and used as input/output for Behavior-CNN. The gap between walking path information and feature representations can be bridged without ambiguity by the proposed encoding scheme.

The encoding process is illustrated in Fig. 3. Let $p_1, ..., p_N$ be N pedestrians in a scene, $t_1, ..., t_M$ be M uniformly sampled time points to be used as input for behavior encoding, and t_M be the current time point. The normalized spatial location of p_i ($i \in [1, N]$) at time point t_m ($m \in [1, M]$) is denoted as $\mathbf{l}_i^m = [x_i^m/X, y_i^m/Y]$, where $x_i^m \in [1, X]$, $y_i^m \in [1, Y]$ are the spatial coordinates of p_i at time t_m, and $[X, Y]$ is the spatial size of the input frames. The locations are grid based and thus discrete. A $2M$-dimensional displacement vector $\mathbf{d}_i = [\mathbf{l}_i^M - \mathbf{l}_i^1, \mathbf{l}_i^M - \mathbf{l}_i^2, ..., \mathbf{l}_i^M - \mathbf{l}_i^{M-1}, \mathbf{l}_i^M - \mathbf{l}_i^M]^T \in \mathbb{R}^{2M}$ is used to describe pedestrian p_i's walking path in the past M frames with respect to t_M (Fig. 3(b)).

The input of CNN is constructed as a 3D displacement volume $\mathcal{D} \in \mathbb{R}^{X \times Y \times 2M}$ based on $\mathbf{d}_i$. For each pedestrian p_i, all the $2M$ channels of $\mathcal{D}$ at p_i's current location (x_i^M, y_i^M) are assigned with the displacement vector $\mathbf{d}_i$. $\mathcal{D}(x_i^M, y_i^M, :) = \mathbf{d}_i + \mathbf{1}^T$, where $\mathbf{1}^T$ represents an all-one vector. All the remaining entries of $\mathcal{D}$ are set as zeros. The elements in $\mathbf{d}_i$ is within the range of $(-1, 1)$. By adding 1, $\mathbf{d}_i$ is transformed to be in the range of $(0, 2)$ before being assigned

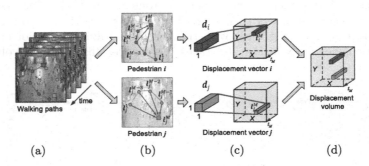

(a)   (b)   (c)   (d)

Fig. 3. Illustration of the pedestrian walking behavior encoding scheme. (a) Pedestrian walking paths in the previous M time points, $t_1, ..., t_M$. Two pedestrians, i (red) and j (green) are shown as examples. (b) Spatial locations of each person at these time points, $\mathbf{l}_i^m$ and $\mathbf{l}_j^m$ for $m \in [1, M]$. (c) Computed $2M$-dimensional displacement vector $\mathbf{d}_i$ and $\mathbf{d}_j$ for pedestrians i and j. (d) Encoded displacement volume $\mathcal{D}$ combined from displacement vectors of all pedestrians in the scene. (Color figure online)

to $\mathcal{D}$ so that pedestrians with no movements (1 displacement value in $\mathcal{D}$) can now be distinguished from background locations (0 displacement value in $\mathcal{D}$).

With the proposed encoding process, pedestrian walking path information are well aligned to the current location of this pedestrian ($\mathbf{1}_i^M$ in Fig. 3(c)). All the pedestrians in the scene and their spatial relationships are preserved in $\mathcal{D}$. Importantly, such encoding and its inverse decoding schemes avoid association ambiguity when describing pedestrian walking paths.

3.2 Behavior-CNN

Behavior-CNN takes the displacement volume $\mathcal{D} \in \mathbb{R}^{X \times Y \times 2M}$ as input, and predict future displacement volume ($\mathcal{D}^* \in \mathbb{R}^{X \times Y \times 2M^*}$) as output. $t_1, ..., t_M$ are M previous time points, and $t_{M+1}, ..., t_{M+M^*}$ are M^* future time points to predict. As shown in Fig. 4, Behavior-CNN contains three bottom convolution layers (Fig. 4(b)), one max-pooling layer and an element-wise addition layer (Fig. 4(c)), three top convolution layers (Fig. 4(d)), and one deconvolution layer (Fig. 4(e)). conv1-5 are followed by ReLU nonlinearity layers.

Three bottom convolution layers, conv1, conv2, and conv3, are to be convolved with input data of size $X \times Y \times 2M$. conv1 contains 64 filters of size $3 \times 3 \times 2M$, while both conv2 and conv3 contain 64 filters of size $3 \times 3 \times 64$. Zeros are padded to each convolution input in order to guarantee feature maps of these layers be of the same spatial size with the input. The three bottom convolution layers are followed by max pooling layers max-pool with stride 2. The output size of max-pool is $X/2 \times Y/2 \times 64$. In this way, the receptive field of the network can be doubled. Large receptive field is necessary for the task of pedestrian walking behavior modeling because each individual's behavior are significantly influenced by his/her neighbors. A learnable location bias map of size $X/2 \times Y/2$ is channel-wisely added to each of the pooled feature maps. Every spatial location has one independent bias value shared across channels. With the location bias map, location information of the scene can be automatically learned by the proposed Behavior-CNN. As for the three top convolution layers, conv4 and conv5 contain 64 filters of size $3 \times 3 \times 64$, while conv6 contains $2M^*$ filters of size $3 \times 3 \times 64$ to output the predicted displacement volume. Zeros are also

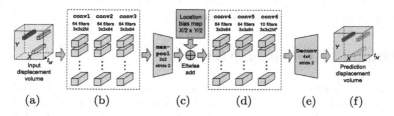

Fig. 4. Behavior-CNN architecture. (a) An input displacement volume $\mathcal{D}$. (b) Three bottom convolution layers. (c) A max-pooling layer and an element-wise addition layer that adds a learnable bias to each location of the feature maps. (d) Three top convolution layers. (e) A deconvolution layer. (f) An output displacement volume $\mathcal{D}^*$.

padded to each convolution input to keep the output spatial size unchanged. Some high-level walking path information and complex walking behaviors of pedestrians are expected to be encoded in the output volume of conv6. Finally, a deconvolution layer is used to upsample the output prediction of conv6 to the same spatial size as the input displacement volume, $i.e.$ $\mathcal{D}^* \in \mathbb{R}^{X \times Y \times 2M^*}$.

3.3   Loss Function and Training Schemes

During the training stage, the loss function of Behavior-CNN is defined as the averaged squared L_2 distance between the predicted displacement volume $\widehat{\mathcal{D}^*}$ and the ground truth output displacement volume $\mathcal{D}^*$ on all the valid (non-zero) entries of $\mathcal{D}^*$.

$$\text{Loss} = \frac{1}{\sum \mathcal{M}} ||(\widehat{\mathcal{D}^*} - \mathcal{D}^*) \circ \mathcal{M}||_2^2, \tag{1}$$

where $\circ$ is the Hadamard product operator, and $\mathcal{M}$ is a binary mask. $\mathcal{M}$ is 1 for the entries where $\mathcal{D}^*$ is non-zero, while $\mathcal{M}$ is 0 for the entries where $\mathcal{D}^*$ is zero. $\sum \mathcal{M}$ counts the total number of non-zeros entries of $\mathcal{M}$ for normalization.

The training samples of pedestrian walking paths can be obtained in multiple possible ways. Two strategies are tested in this paper. The annotated pedestrian locations are first used for both model training and evaluation to investigate the properties of the learned Behavior-CNN. Moreover, in order to handle real-world scenarios, our model is also trained with keypoint tracking results by the KLT tracker [41] while the human annotations are only used for evaluation.

Due to the high sparsity of input data, the network may converge to a bad local minimum if all the parameters are trained together from random initialization. Thus a layer-by-layer training strategy is adopted. A simpler network with three convolution layers is first randomly initialized and trained until convergence. Afterwards, the trained convolution layers are used as the bottom layers of Behavior-CNN (conv1-3). The following layers (max-pool, eltwise-add, conv4-6, deconv) are then appended and parameters of the newly added layers are trained from random initialization. Lastly, all the layers are jointly fine-tuned.

Stochastic gradient descent is adopted for training and the model converged at around 10k iterations. Optimal model is chosen based on a validation set which is a subset of the training samples.

4   Data and Evaluation Metric

Behavior-CNN is evaluated mainly on two datasets. Dataset I is the Pedestrian Walking Route Dataset proposed in [1]. It is 4,000 s in length and 12,684 pedestrians are annotated. Dataset II is collected and annotated by us. We follow the same annotation strategy on Dataset II as in [1]. The complete trajectories of 797 pedestrians from the time point he/she enters the scene to the time he/she leaves are annotated every 20 frames.

To prepare training and testing samples, $M + M^*$ frames at time $t_1, ..., t_M$, $t_{M+1}, ..., t_{M+M^*}$ are uniformly sampled from input videos, and resized to the size of 256×256 ($X = Y = 256$). The first M frames at time $t_1, ..., t_M$ are encoded to the input displacement volumes $\mathcal{D}$ as introduced in Sect. 3.1, which are the input of the Behavior-CNN. The following M^* frames at time $t_{M+1}, ..., t_{M+M^*}$ are encoded to the output displacement volume $\mathcal{D}^*$ as the ground truth.

The encoding of $\mathcal{D}^*$ is similar to that of $\mathcal{D}$. A $2M^*$-dimensional displacement vector $\mathbf{d}_i^* \in \mathbb{R}^{2M^*}$ is used to capture the future path of pedestrian p_i with respect to the current time point t_M, $\mathbf{d}_i^* = [\mathbf{l}_i^M - \mathbf{l}_i^{M+1}, \mathbf{l}_i^M - \mathbf{l}_i^{M+2}, ..., \mathbf{l}_i^M - \mathbf{l}_i^{M+M^*}]$, where $\mathbf{l}_i^m$ is the normalized spatial location of pedestrian p_i at time t_m ($m \in [M + 1, M + M^*]$). $\mathcal{D}^* \in \mathbb{R}^{X \times Y \times 2M^*}$ are constructed by assigning $\mathbf{d}_i^*$ to $\mathcal{D}^*$, $\mathcal{D}^*(x_i^M, y_i^M, :) = \mathbf{d}_i^* + \mathbf{1}^T$. With such encoding, future walking path information of each individual is also aligned to the pedestrian current location at time t_M.

By setting different M and M^*, Behavior-CNN can make prediction at different time scales. In our current implementation, M and M^* are both set to 5, i.e. five time points are uniformly sampled as input and five future locations of each pedestrian are predicted. The sample interval is 20 frames (0.8 s) for both input and output. That is to say, based on the output result, our model predicts the pedestrian paths in the coming 4 s. Longer-term behaviors can be predicted by recurrently using output again as new input of Behavior-CNN (detailed in Sect. 6.2). With larger M values and more computation cost, performance should be slightly improved because more information is given.

4990 short clips are uniformly segmented from Dataset I and one sample can be obtained from each clip. For Dataset II, 550 samples are generated. The first 90 % samples are used for training while the remaining for test on both datasets.

Mean squared error (MSE) is adopted as the evaluation metric for the task of pedestrian walking path prediction. The average L_2 distance between normalized predicted pedestrian locations and normalized ground-truth pedestrian locations of all the N pedestrians at all the M^* predicted time points are computed.

$$\text{MSE} = \frac{1}{NM^*} \sum_{i=1}^{N} \sum_{m=1}^{M^*} ||\mathbf{l}_i^{M+m} - \widehat{\mathbf{l}}_i^{M+m}||_2 \times 100\,\%, \qquad (2)$$

where $\widehat{\mathbf{l}}_i^{M+m} = [x_i^{M+m}/X, y_i^{M+m}/Y]$ is the normalized location of p_i at time t_{M+m} with respect to the size of the scene.

5   Investigations on Behavior-CNN

In-depth investigations are conducted on Behavior-CNN. It reveals underlying properties of the proposed deep behavior model. Human annotated pedestrian walking paths are used to train the models in this section.

5.1   Bias Map and Location Awareness Property of Behavior-CNN

For a specific scene, different locations generally have different traffic patterns because of scene structures. The proposed bias map helps capture such information. Experiments are conducted to investigate the effect of the location

Table 1. (a) Prediction results with/without the location bias map. (b) Prediction results of different flipping strategies.

Investigations on	MSE	Dataset I	Dataset II
(a) Location bias map	With	2.421 %	2.348 %
	Without	2.703 %	2.628 %
(b) Flipping strategies	No flipping	2.421 %	2.348 %
	Horizontal flipping	2.470 %	2.592 %
	Vertical flipping	2.468 %	2.585 %
	Horizontal and vertical flipping	2.502 %	2.668 %

bias map. The errors of the proposed method with/without the bias map are listed in Table 1(a). Without the bias map, prediction errors increase for both datasets.

One more experiment is conducted to validate the location awareness of Behavior-CNN. Given the trained model (with location bias map) fixed, testing samples are flipped horizontally and/or vertically, and the results of different flipping strategies are reported in Table 1(b). If the prediction of our model has location invariance, flipping all the pedestrian paths at all the locations in the same way will not make difference on prediction errors. However, Table 1(b) shows that prediction error increases if testing samples are flipped, which indicates different locations have different dependence on moving directions.

With the learned location bias map, our Behavior-CNN can distinguish different locations of the scene based on the motion patterns of small regions (receptive field size of the Behavior-CNN). In Fig. 5(b), the scene is segmented into 8 by 8 grids. For each grid, the distributions of the walking directions of all the training samples, together with the distributions of the walking directions of all the predicted paths by Behavior-CNN are computed. Two example grids are shown in Fig. 5(a) and (c). Three types of walking patterns, moving up, down, and left, are observed frequently for the "crossing" grid (Fig. 5(a)). Two types of walking patterns, moving up and moving down, are common patterns in the "corridor" grid (Fig. 5(c)). Strong correlations are observed between the predicted walking pattern and the training walking pattern. The correlation for the crossing grid (Fig. 5(a)) is 0.88 while the correlation for the corridor grid (Fig. 5(c)) is 0.91. With the location bias map, our learned model is able to capture the location information and scene layout from the input pedestrian walking paths, such as the patterns shown in Fig. 5(a) and (c).

Based on location awareness, our model can successfully infer scene structures from local motion patterns in input and the learned location bias map. The pedestrian spatial distributions of training samples, which reflect scene layout, and our model's predictions are shown in Fig. 5(d). Strong correlations are observed between them, which demonstrates that our model can capture the scene layout information. From the prediction distribution, some impossible locations such as scene obstacles can be automatically distinguished by Behavior-CNN.

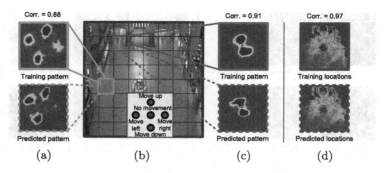

Fig. 5. Investigation on location awareness of Behavior-CNN. (a–c) Behavior-CNN can capture different motion patterns for different regions of the scene. The scene is segmented into 8 by 8 grids in (b). The motion patterns of training samples and prediction results of the "crossing" grid (green) is shown in (a) and those of the "corridor" grid (red) are shown in (c). Warmer color indicates higher frequency of corresponding motion as indicated in (b). (d) Strong correlation can also be observed between the spatial distributions of the training samples, which reflect scene structures and the existence of obstacles, and the spatial distributions of predictions. (Color figure online)

5.2   Learned Feature Filters of Behavior-CNN

From feature maps generated by filters in different layers, strong correlations between specific walking patterns and filter response maps can be well observed. Generally speaking, the three bottom convolution layers (`conv1-3`) take all the pedestrian behaviors as input and gradually classify them into finer and finer categories according to various criteria. In top layers, the influences of all different categories are combined together to generate the prediction.

For bottom convolution layers, different pedestrians are roughly classified by filters based on their walking behaviors. Examples are shown in Fig. 6(a–c). Two feature maps generated from filter #33 and filter #59 of `conv1` are shown in Fig. 6(a). The high-response pedestrians in the two feature maps are visualized in Fig. 6(b). It is observed that most pedestrians with high response to filter #33 move down-leftwards, while pedestrians with high response to filter #59 move upwards. In this way, the input pedestrian paths can be classified into some rough categories by the filters in `conv1`. We computed the correlations between the feature maps by the two filters (Fig. 6(a)) and the locations of all moving down-leftwards/upwards pedestrians at different training iterations. As shown by the correlation curves in Fig. 6(c), the two filters gradually learned to capture these specific motion patterns during training.

Some high-response pedestrians by filters of `conv2` and `conv3` are shown in Fig. 6(d–e). These filters generally classify pedestrians into finer and more specific categories compared with those of `conv1`. In Fig. 6(d), down-leftward/upward pedestrians in Fig. 6(a) are further classified based on spatial locations, such as the left-bottom corner and the left-up corner. In Fig. 6(e), pedestrians are more meticulously classified based on precise moving directions.

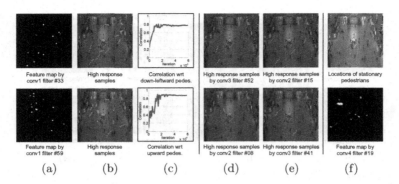

Fig. 6. Investigations on learned filters. (a) Two feature maps generated by filter #33 and filter #59 of conv1. (b) Input pedestrian walking paths with high responses on the feature maps in (a). Red dots indicate current locations. Filter #33 corresponds to moving down-leftwards while filter #59 corresponds to moving upwards. (c) Correlation values between the feature maps in (a) and the location maps of all down-leftwards/upward pedestrians in the scene at different training iterations. (d–e) Some high response pedestrians by filters of conv2-3. (f) Stationary pedestrians captured by the feature map of filter #19 in conv4. (Color figure online)

For filters in higher-level layers, they generally encode more complex behaviors. As shown by one example in Fig. 6(f), stationary pedestrians are assigned with high-responses by the filter #19 of conv4, which demonstrates that stationary crowds could influence other pedestrians' walking patterns.

5.3   Receptive Fields

We observe that pedestrian walking behaviors are significantly influenced by nearby pedestrians. By increasing the size of the receptive field, the sensing range of the network can be increased and the predictions are more reliable. The current receptive field size is around 10 % of the scene, which is large enough to capture the pedestrians and activities within their nearby regions.

Two alternative net structures are designed to decrease the receptive field size. (a) The filter size of all layers is changed from 3×3 to 1×1. In order to keep the same parameter size, the numbers of filters are all increased by 9 times in the meanwhile. (b) The proposed net structure (3conv+pool+3conv+deconv) is simplified to 3conv+pool+3conv and 3conv+3conv by removing some layers. The alternatives are used to demonstrate the power of large receptive field size when predicting future pedestrian walking behaviors.

The results of different net structures are shown in Table 2. With the same model complexity, the prediction error increases for the 1×1 filters compared with the 3×3 filters. Moreover, the better performance of the 3conv+pool+3conv structure compared with the 3conv+3conv structure also demonstrates the effectiveness of large receptive field introduced by the pooling layer.

Table 2. Prediction results (MSE) of different net structures on Dataset I.

	3×3 (ours)	1×1
3conv+pool+3conv+deconv (ours)	2.421 %	2.555 %
3conv+pool+3conv	2.431 %	2.571 %
3conv+3conv	2.468 %	2.858 %

6   Experiments

6.1   Pedestrian Walking Path Prediction

The prediction results of the proposed Behavior-CNN are evaluated quantitatively and qualitatively for both Dataset I and Dataset II. For each of the dataset, two trained models were evaluated. One was trained with the human annotated pedestrian locations and the other one was trained with KLT trajectories. The trajectories are not verified and may contain mistakes. All the models are evaluated using the annotated ground truth pedestrian walking paths. Due to the insufficient training samples of Dataset II, the models trained on Dataset I were used as the initial points to train the models for Dataset II.[1]

Three baselines and three state-of-the-art methods [2,15,17] on pedestrian behavior prediction were compared. The constant velocity and constant acceleration regressors were used as the first two baselines to predict future walking path of each pedestrian. Moreover, the same displacement vectors were used as features and a second-order SVM regressor was used for prediction. Existing computer vision methods in comparison include the Social Force Model (SFM) [15] where pedestrian walking paths were predicted as its simulation results, the Linear Trajectory Avoidance model (LTA) [17] where pedestrian walking paths were predicted based on energy minimization, and Temporal Information Model (TIM) [2] where pedestrian walking paths were predicted as the minimal paths.

MSE introduced in Sect. 4 was evaluated and the results are reported in Table 3. Behavior-CNN achieves the best performance among all the comparisons. This is because the learned feature representations of Behavior-CNN are much more powerful and can capture complex pedestrian behaviors. The model trained with annotations (2.421 %) performs only slightly better than that trained with KLT (2.517 %) on Dataset I, which also demonstrates the robustness of the proposed method to KLT errors.

Several examples of prediction results are visualized in Fig. 7. Behavior-CNN can successfully predict some complex walking patterns, such as change of walking directions, slowing down, speeding up (Pedestrian A in Fig. 7(a)). It also learns the scene layout, which cannot be learned by the other two methods from

---

[1] The model trained solely with annotations on Dataset I generates a 4.18 % error if directly testing on Dataset II, which is still better than the comparisons. However, with bias map removed, the error decreases to 3.42 %. It indicates that the bias map hinders model transfer ability to a certain degree.

Table 3. Prediction results (MSE) of different methods trained on the annotated pedestrian walking paths or the KLT trajectories on Dataset I and Dataset II.

	Dataset I (Annotation)	Dataset II (Annotation)	Dataset I (KLT)	Dataset II (KLT)
Behavior-CNN	2.421 %	2.348 %	2.517 %	3.816 %
Constant velocity	6.091 %	6.468 %	5.864 %	5.635 %
Constant acceleration	9.899 %	9.428 %	6.619 %	7.656 %
SVM regression	4.639 %	4.276 %	5.053 %	5.327 %
SFM [15]	4.280 %	5.921 %	4.447 %	5.044 %
LTA [17]	4.723 %	4.571 %	4.346 %	4.639 %
TIM [2]	4.075 %	4.141 %	4.790 %	4.790 %

(a) Behavior-CNN   (b) Constant velocity   (c) LTA [17]

Fig. 7. Prediction results by (a) Behavior-CNN, (b) the constant-velocity model, and (c) the LTA model, with KLT trajectories as input on both datasets. The KLT trajectories are used to train the model. Input previous locations, ground truth future locations, and predicted future locations are marked by blue, green and red dots, respectively. (Color figure online)

training samples. Taking Pedestrian B in Fig. 7 as an example, our prediction avoids scene obstacles while the predictions by the other two methods indicate the pedestrian walking into a concrete wall.

In order to validate prediction robustness, the proposed method is also evaluated on five more datasets, *i.e.* ETH [17], Hotel [17], ZARA01 [42], ZARA02 [42], and UCY [42]. Following the same experimental setup and evaluation criteria as [43], leave-one-out validation is adopted and average displacement errors of our proposed method on the five datasets are 0.35, 0.18, 0.20, 0.23, and 0.25, while [43] achieves 0.50, 0.11, 0.22, 0.25, and 0.27.

6.2   Application I: Pedestrian Destination Prediction

Behavior-CNN is able to predict the walking paths of all the pedestrians in the scene for in the next 4 s ($M^* = 5$). However, by decoding the output displacement

(a) Behavior-CNN   (b) SFM [15]   (c) Entrance/exit regions

Fig. 8. (a–b) Long-term path prediction results in Dataset I using Behavior-CNN and Social Force Model [15]. Behavior-CNN is recurrently forward-propagated three times and locations at 15 future time points are predicted. Input previous locations, ground-truth future locations, and predicted future locations are marked by blue, green, and red dots. (c) Ten entrance/exit regions labeled in Dataset I [1]. (Color figure online)

Table 4. *Top-N* accuracies of destination prediction on Dataset I.

	Top 1	Top2	Top3
Behavior-CNN	53 %	72 %	84 %
EMM [1]	48 %	69 %	83 %
MDA [8]	43 %	-	-
UVP [44]	45 %	-	-

volume and re-encoding the prediction results, the predicted walking paths can be fed back into Behavior-CNN as input. In this way, long-term walking paths can be recurrently predicted. The prediction results of several pedestrians by Behavior-CNN and the Social Force Model [15] are shown in Fig. 8(a) and (b). Behavior-CNN can predict reasonable long-term walking paths.

The long-term prediction results can be used for destination prediction. The destination is determined as the nearest exit to the predicted future walking path. Prediction performance was evaluated on Dataset I, where ten entrance/exit regions are labeled [1] as shown in Fig. 8(c). The *top-N* accuracy (ground truth is within the top-N predictions) was adopted for evaluation.

Three existing methods were used as comparisons, *i.e.*, the energy map modeling approach (EMM) [1] where destinations were predicted by minimizing energy function, MDA [8] where predictions were made based on trajectory properties, and an unsupervised visual prediction approach (UVP) [44] where destinations were predicted as the nearest exit to the predicted trajectories. In order to make fair comparisons, all the methods use previous 5 frames (4 s in length) as input. Estimation results are reported in Table 4. Our method performs better as it can better predict long-term motion patterns.

6.3   Application II: Predictions as Tracking Prior

Based on predicted pedestrian walking paths, Behavior-CNN can provide prior information to improve tracking. The KLT tracker, whose trajectories are often fragmented or early terminated, is used as a baseline tracking algorithm to

276   S. Yi et al.

Table 5. Results of pedestrian tracking on Dataset I

Methods	KLT+Behavior-CNN	KLT+RFT [45]	KLT
Error (L_2 distance)	83.79	228.33	411.71

Fig. 9. Improved pedestrian tracking results by Behavior-CNN (red dots) and RFT [45] (blue dots). Ground truth trajectories are shown as green dots. Successfully tracked pedestrians of the proposed method and mis-tracked pedestrians by the RFT method are marked by the red and blue rectangles. (Color figure online)

be improved. A tracking association strategy is adopted when a key point fails to be tracked. Given successfully tracked locations (up to the failing time) as input, $M^* = 5$ future locations (4 s) can be predicted by Behavior-CNN. Then the tracklet that best matches prediction is selected to be connected with the fragmented tracklet. In this way, long-term trajectories could be formed by connecting fragmented ones and tracking performance can be improved. Another association strategy in [45] was also used for comparison (RFT). Trajectories are connected based on the local location and speed information when tracking fails.

The average L_2 distance between ground truth walking paths and tracking results of 1000 pedestrians in Dataset I were used for evaluation. The results of both strategies, together with the results of the baseline KLT tracking are listed in Table 5. The proposed association strategy significantly decreases the tracking error compared with RFT [45]. From the examples in Fig. 9, our method could successfully generate correct and complete trajectories, while the association by the RFT method made wrong associations and lost the tracking targets.

7   Conclusion

Behavior-CNN is proposed to model pedestrian behaviors. A behavior encoding scheme is adopted to encode pedestrian behavior into sparse displacement volumes which can be directly used as network input. Behavior-CNN is thoroughly investigated in terms of the learned location map and the location awareness property, semantic meanings of learned filters, and influence of receptive fields. The effectiveness is demonstrated through multiple applications, including walking path prediction, destination prediction, and improving tracking.

Acknowledgment. This work was supported in part by the Ph.D. Programs Foundation of China under Grant 20130185120039, in part by the Hong Kong Innovation and Technology Support Programme under Grant ITS/221/13FP, in part by the National Natural Science Foundation of China under Grant 61371192 and Grant 61301269, and in part by the General Research Fund through the Research Grants Council, Hong Kong, under Grant CUHK14206114, Grant CUHK14205615, Grant CUHK419412, and Grant CUHK14203015.

References

1. Yi, S., Li, H., Wang, X.: Understanding pedestrian behaviors from stationary crowd groups. In: Proceedings of CVPR (2015)
2. Cancela, B., Iglesias, A., Ortega, M., Penedo, M.: Unsupervised trajectory modelling using temporal information via minimal paths. In: Proceedings of CVPR (2014)
3. Alahi, A., Ramanathan, V., Fei-Fei, L.: Socially-aware large-scale crowd forecasting. In: Proceedings of CVPR (2014)
4. Yi, S., Li, H., Wang, X.: Pedestrian behavior modeling from stationary crowds with applications to intelligent surveillance. TIP **25**(9), 4354–4368 (2016)
5. Tang, S., Andriluka, M., Milan, A., Schindler, K., Roth, S., Schiele, B.: Learning people detectors for tracking in crowded scenes. In: Proceedings of ICCV (2013)
6. Shu, G., Dehghan, A., Oreifej, O., Hand, E., Shah, M.: Part-based multiple-person tracking with partial occlusion handling. In: Proceedings of CVPR (2012)
7. Leal-Taixé, L., Fenzi, M., Kuznetsova, A., Rosenhahn, B., Savarese, S.: Learning an image-based motion context for multiple people tracking. In: Proceedings of CVPR (2014)
8. Zhou, B., Wang, X., Tang, X.: Understanding collective crowd behaviors: learning a mixture model of dynamic pedestrian-agents. In: Proceedings of CVPR (2012)
9. Nascimento, J.C., Marques, J.S., Lemos, J.M.: Modeling and classifying human activities from trajectories using a class of space-varying parametric motion fields. TIP **22**(5), 2066–2080 (2013)
10. Kim, K., Lee, D., Essa, I.: Gaussian process regression flow for analysis of motion trajectories. In: Proceedings of ICCV (2011)
11. Chang, M.C., Krahnstoever, N., Ge, W.: Probabilistic group-level motion analysis and scenario recognition. In: Proceedings of ICCV (2011)
12. Mehran, R., Oyama, A., Shah, M.: Abnormal crowd behavior detection using social force model. In: Proceedings of CVPR (2009)
13. Lu, C., Shi, J., Jia, J.: Abnormal event detection at 150 FPS in matlab. In: Proceedings of ICCV (2013)
14. Mahadevan, V., Li, W., Bhalodia, V., Vasconcelos, N.: Anomaly detection in crowded scenes. In: Proceedings of CVPR (2010)
15. Helbing, D., Molnar, P.: Social force model for pedestrian dynamics. Phys. Rev. E **51**(5), 4282 (1995)
16. Yi, S., Wang, X., Lu, C., Jia, J., Li, H.: L0 regularized stationary-time estimation for crowd analysis. TPAMI **PP**(99), 1 (2016). doi:10.1109/TPAMI.2016.2560807
17. Pellegrini, S., Ess, A., Schindler, K., Van Gool, L.: You'll never walk alone: modeling social behavior for multi-target tracking. In: Proceedings of ICCV (2009)
18. Kuettel, D., Breitenstein, M.D., Van Gool, L., Ferrari, V.: What's going on? Discovering spatio-temporal dependencies in dynamic scenes. In: Proceedings of CVPR (2010)
19. Wang, X., Ma, X., Grimson, W.E.L.: Unsupervised activity perception in crowded and complicated scenes using hierarchical Bayesian models. TPAMI **31**(3), 539–555 (2009)

20. Hospedales, T.M., Li, J., Gong, S., Xiang, T.: Identifying rare and subtle behaviors: a weakly supervised joint topic model. TPAMI **33**(12), 2451–2464 (2011)
21. Basharat, A., Gritai, A., Shah, M.: Learning object motion patterns for anomaly detection and improved object detection. In: Proceedings of CVPR (2008)
22. Morris, B.T., Trivedi, M.M.: Trajectory learning for activity understanding: unsupervised, multilevel, and long-term adaptive approach. TPAMI **33**(11), 2287–2301 (2011)
23. Wang, X., Ma, K.T., Ng, G.W., Grimson, W.E.L.: Trajectory analysis and semantic region modeling using nonparametric hierarchical Bayesian models. IJCV **95**(3), 287–312 (2011)
24. Kitani, K.M., Ziebart, B.D., Bagnell, J.A., Hebert, M.: Activity forecasting. In: Fitzgibbon, A., Lazebnik, S., Perona, P., Sato, Y., Schmid, C. (eds.) ECCV 2012. LNCS, vol. 7575, pp. 201–214. Springer, Heidelberg (2012). doi:10.1007/978-3-642-33765-9_15
25. Bonabeau, E.: Agent-based modeling: methods and techniques for simulating human systems. PNAS **99**(Suppl 3), 7280–7287 (2002)
26. Helbing, D., Farkas, I., Vicsek, T.: Simulating dynamical features of escape panic. Nature **407**(6803), 487–490 (2000)
27. Bengio, Y.: Learning deep architectures for AI. Found. Trends® Mach. Learn. **2**(1), 1–127 (2009)
28. Krizhevsky, A., Sutskever, I., Hinton, G.E.: Imagenet classification with deep convolutional neural networks. In: Proceedings of NIPS (2012)
29. Girshick, R.: Fast R-CNN. In: Proceedings of ICCV (2015)
30. Ren, S., He, K., Girshick, R., Sun, J.: Faster R-CNN: towards real-time object detection with region proposal networks. In: Proceedings of NIPS (2015)
31. Wang, N., Yeung, D.Y.: Learning a deep compact image representation for visual tracking. In: Proceedings of NIPS (2013)
32. Farabet, C., Couprie, C., Najman, L., LeCun, Y.: Learning hierarchical features for scene labeling. TPAMI **35**(8), 1915–1929 (2013)
33. Long, J., Shelhamer, E., Darrell, T.: Fully convolutional networks for semantic segmentation. In: Proceedings of CVPR (2015)
34. Reddy, N.D., Singhal, P., Krishna, K.M.: Semantic motion segmentation using dense CRF formulation. In: Proceedings of ICVGIP (2014)
35. Simonyan, K., Zisserman, A.: Two-stream convolutional networks for action recognition in videos. In: Proceedings of NIPS (2014)
36. Shao, J., Kang, K., Loy, C.C., Wang, X.: Deeply learned attributes for crowded scene understanding. In: Proceedings of CVPR (2015)
37. Ji, S., Xu, W., Yang, M., Yu, K.: 3D convolutional neural networks for human action recognition. TPAMI **35**(1), 221–231 (2013)
38. Karpathy, A., Toderici, G., Shetty, S., Leung, T., Sukthankar, R., Fei-Fei, L.: Large-scale video classification with convolutional neural networks. In: Proceedings of CVPR (2014)
39. Yan, X., Chang, H., Shan, S., Chen, X.: Modeling video dynamics with deep dynencoder. In: Fleet, D., Pajdla, T., Schiele, B., Tuytelaars, T. (eds.) ECCV 2014. LNCS, vol. 8692, pp. 215–230. Springer, Heidelberg (2014). doi:10.1007/978-3-319-10593-2_15
40. Srivastava, N., Mansimov, E., Salakhutdinov, R.: Unsupervised learning of video representations using lstms (2015). arXiv preprint arXiv:1502.04681
41. Tomasi, C., Kanade, T.: Detection and tracking of point features. School of Computer Science, Carnegie Mellon Univ. Pittsburgh (1991)

42. Lerner, A., Chrysanthou, Y., Lischinski, D.: Crowds by example. In: Computer Graphics Forum, vol. 26, pp. 655–664. Wiley Online Library (2007)
43. Alahi, A., Goel, K., Ramanathan, V., Robicquet, A., Fei-Fei, L., Savarese, S.: Social lstm: human trajectory prediction in crowded spaces. In: Proceedings of CVPR (2016)
44. Walker, J., Gupta, A., Hebert, M.: Patch to the future: unsupervised visual prediction. In: Proceedings of CVPR (2014)
45. Zhou, B., Wang, X., Tang, X.: Random field topic model for semantic region analysis in crowded scenes from tracklets. In: Proceedings of CVPR (2011)

Real-Time RGB-D Activity Prediction by Soft Regression

Jian-Fang Hu[2,3,4], Wei-Shi Zheng[2,3(✉)], Lianyang Ma[4], Gang Wang[4], and Jianhuang Lai[1,3]

[1] Guangdong Key Laboratory of Information Security Technology,
Guangzhou, China
[2] Key Laboratory of Machine Intelligence and Advanced Computing,
MOE, Guangzhou, China
wszheng@ieee.org
[3] Sun Yat-sen University, Guangzhou, China
hujianf@mail2.sysu.edu.cn, stsljh@mail.sysu.edu.cn
[4] Nanyang Technological University, Singapore, Singapore
wanggang@ntu.edu.sg, lianyangma2012@gmail.com

Abstract. In this paper, we propose a novel approach for predicting ongoing activities captured by a low-cost depth camera. Our approach avoids a usual assumption in existing activity prediction systems that the progress level of ongoing sequence is given. We overcome this limitation by learning a soft label for each subsequence and develop a soft regression framework for activity prediction to learn both predictor and soft labels jointly. In order to make activity prediction work in a real-time manner, we introduce a new RGB-D feature called "local accumulative frame feature (LAFF)", which can be computed efficiently by constructing an integral feature map. Our experiments on two RGB-D benchmark datasets demonstrate that the proposed regression-based activity prediction model outperforms existing models significantly and also show that the activity prediction on RGB-D sequence is more accurate than that on RGB channel.

Keywords: Activity prediction · RGB-D · Soft regression

1 Introduction

Recognizing activities before they are fully executed is very important for some real-world applications like visual surveillance, robot designing [1,2], and clinical monitoring [3]. Activity prediction is to predict ongoing activities using the observed subsequences that only contain partial activity execution.

Existing action/activity prediction model [4] requires manual labeling of a large amount of video segments, which however record mostly low level actions shared among activities, and thus it is too expensive and sometimes is difficult to label. Although an alternative way is to simply label a subsequence[1] as the

---

[1] In this work, the subsequence of an activity means the accumulation of consecutive segments from the start of the activity.

© Springer International Publishing AG 2016
B. Leibe et al. (Eds.): ECCV 2016, Part I, LNCS 9905, pp. 280–296, 2016.
DOI: 10.1007/978-3-319-46448-0_17

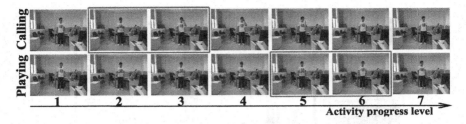

Fig. 1. Snapshots from activities *calling with a cell-phone* and *playing with a cell-phone*. As presented in the first row, it is hard to recognize the activity when its progress level is less than 3. However, if the segment with temporal interval [3, 4] (marked with red box) are provided, it becomes clear that the subject is performing the activity *calling with a cell-phone*. We also observe that the subsequences at progress level 2 (temporal interval [1, 2]) in the two activities contain the same action "taking out a cell-phone". (Color figure online)

label of the full sequence [5], sometimes, this naive labeling would make ambiguity for predicting ongoing activity. It is because an activity sequence consists of several segments, and segments from different activities could be similar so that each segment could be ambiguous when used to predict the label of the full activity. Taking Fig. 1 as an example, the action *"taking out a cell-phone"* appears in both the activity sequences *"calling with a cell-phone"* and *"playing with a cell-phone"*, so it will mislead the predictor learning if we directly treat the subsequence of taking out phone in the first row as *"calling with phone"* while define the similar subsequence in the second row as *"playing with a cell-phone"*.

To address the above problem, we learn a soft label for the subsequences of each progress level. The soft label tells how likely the subsequence is performing the activity depicted in the corresponding full sequence. Introducing the soft labels for subsequences can alleviate the confusion caused by the fact that subsequences from different activities could contain similar activity contents. A regression-based activity prediction model is therefore developed to regress these soft labels. A characteristic of our regression-based prediction model is to learn the activity predictor and the soft labels jointly without any prior knowledge set for soft labels. In this way, our modeling avoids overfitting caused by the ambiguity of subsequence on prediction and meanwhile makes the prediction model work in a discriminant way on partially observed activity sequences. And more importantly, by learning soft labels, the usual assumption on given the progress level of subsequence [6, 7] is not necessary for our model.

In addition, most of activity prediction works in literatures focus on predicting human activities from RGB sequences by matching visual appearance and human motion among the activities executed at different progress levels [3, 4, 6, 8, 9]. However, RGB sequences are intrinsically limited in capturing highly articulated motions due to the inherent visual ambiguity caused by clothing similarity among people, appearance changes from view point difference, illumination variation, cluttered background and occlusions [10, 11]. The recently introduced

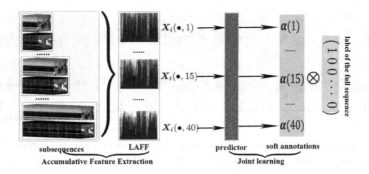

Fig. 2. A graphic illustration of our soft regression model. $\otimes$ is Kronecker product.

low-cost depth cameras can alleviate the ambiguity due to the availability of more modal data describing activity such as depth of scene and 3D joint positions of human skeleton. Hence, in this work, we explore real-time activity prediction with the assistance of depth sensors.

Towards making our prediction model work on RGB-D sequence in real-time, we design "local accumulative frame feature (LAFF)" to characterize the activity context of RGB-D sequence with arbitrary activity progress levels. The RGB-D context will include the appearance, shapes and skeletons of human body parts, manipulated objects and even scene (background). By employing the popularly used integral map computing technique, we demonstrate that the formulated LAFF can be efficiently computed in a recursive manner and thus be suitable for real-time prediction. The flowchart of our method is illustrated in Fig. 2.

In summary, the main contributions are: (1) A soft regression-based activity prediction model is formulated for overcoming the usual assumption that the progress level of ongoing activity is given; and (2) A local accumulative frame feature (LAFF) is developed for real-time activity prediction on RGB-D sequences. We claim that the prediction on RGB-D sequences works much better than that on RGB videos only. To verify our claim, we have tested our method on two RGB-D activity sets. The proposed method can obtain more reliable performances for predicting activities at varied progress levels. It can process more than 40 frames per second on a normal PC using MATLAB without elaborate optimization of programming, which can be used for real-time activity prediction.

2   Related Work

Activity prediction. In many real-world scenarios like surveillance, it would be more important to correctly predict an activity before it is fully executed. Many efforts are on developing early activity detectors or future activity prediction systems [7–9, 12–14]. For example, [12, 15] explored the application of max-margin learning in early event recognition and detection. [8] developed an early activity prediction system according to the change of feature distribution as more and more video streams were observed. Lan et al. proposed to represent human movements in a hierarchical manner and employ a max-margin learning framework to select the most discriminative features for prediction [3]. [4] proposed to mine some sequential patterns that frequently appear in the training samples for prediction. Recently, [7] extended the max-margin event detector for activity prediction and obtained the state-of-the-art results on several benchmark sets. However, it is assumed in [7] that the progress level of ongoing activity is provided along with the observed sequence even in the test phase, which renders their method unrealistic in the real-world applications as it is hard to obtain the progress level of ongoing activity until it has been fully executed and observed.

Recent researches on human activity prediction is mainly focusing on predicting activities from ongoing RGB sequences, while less work has been reported on RGB-D sequences captured by low-cost depth cameras. In this paper, we consider the prediction of RGB-D activity sequence and develop a real-time system for predicting human activities without any additional prior information about the progress level of ongoing activity. The most closest to our approach is the online RGB-D activity prediction system in [5]. However, the system in [5] is based on frame-level prediction and the long-term motions are discarded in their model. Moreover, the subsequences with partial activity executions are not exploited for prediction, which renders their method less accurate for activity prediction.

Activity recognition with monocular video sensor. Human activity recognition is a long-term research topic and it has attracted a lot of attentions in the past decades. A large number of considerable progresses have been made for developing robust spatiotemporal features (Cuboids [16], interest point clouds [17], HOG3D [18], dense trajectory [19], and two-stream CNN [20] etc.) and feature learning techniques (sparse coding [21], max-margin learning [22–24], Fisher vector [19] etc.). Activity recognition aims at developing algorithms and systems for after-of-the-fact prediction of human activity, where activity sequence is entirely observed. Consequently, the activity recognition methods cannot be directly used for activity prediction task, which needs to work on ongoing sequences.

Activity recognition with depth cameras. The emergence of Kinect device has lit up the research of human activity recognition with depth cameras in these years. In the literatures, how to acquire a robust feature representation for the depth sequences is one of the most fundamental research topics. A lot of RGB video descriptors have been extended in order to characterize 3D geometries depicted in depth sequences [25–29]. For example, [25,26] developed their depth descriptors by extending the idea of constructing histogram of oriented gradient [27]. Considering the close relationship between human pose(skeleton [30]) and activity, some researchers sought to represent human activities using positional dynamics of each skeleton joint [31–33] or joint pairs [34–39]. Human activity may contain complex interactions between the actor and objects, using depth and skeleton channels is not sufficient for describing the interactions. RGB channel is also utilized for feature representation [10,11,40]. In this paper, we construct a

RGB-D sequence feature by combining the local descriptors extracted from color patterns, depth patterns and skeletons. Different from the previous work that extracts features for off-line computation [10,11,40], we formulate our feature modeling in a recursive manner so that it can be computed in real-time.

It is worth noting that the conception of soft label has also been recently explored in [41] for improving RGB-D activity recognition, where the authors allow the human annotators to assign a soft label for the video segment with ambiguity. However, it requires manual setting on labeling.

3   Our Approach

3.1   Problem Statement

We concern a real-time prediction system for identifying ongoing activity sequence. In activity prediction, the activity depicted in the observed sequence is always uncompleted before it has been fully executed. In this work, we consider a more realistic setting for this problem. Unlike the activity prediction considered in [6,7], we do not assume that the progress level of ongoing activity is known in the test phase, as it is hard (if not impossible) to have a surveillance system obtain the progress level of ongoing activity until it has been fully executed. In this work, we propose a predictor that can be generally used for predicting an (ongoing) activity sequence at any progress level.

Notation. Throughout this paper, we use bold uppercase characters to denote matrices and bold lowercase characters (or Greek letters) to denote vectors. For any matrix A, we use $A(i,\cdot)$, $A(\cdot,j)$ and $A(i,j)$ to denote the $i-th$ row, the $j-th$ column and the (i,j)-element of A, respectively. A^T denotes the transpose matrix of A. In this work, we consider the Frobenius norm $||A||_F$ and $L_{1,2}$-norm $||A||_{1,2}$ of a matrix and the l_2 norm $||a||_2$ of a vector. The $L_{1,2}$-norm for matrix $A \in \mathbb{R}^{m \times n}$ is defined as:

$$||A||_{1,2} = \sum_{j=1}^{n} \sqrt{\sum_{i=1}^{m} A(i,j)^2} = \sum_{j=1}^{n} r(j). \qquad (1)$$

Here, $r(j)$ represents the l_2 norm of the $j-th$ column $A(\cdot,j)$. Then we can obtain the generalized gradient[2] $\frac{\partial ||A||_{1,2}}{\partial A(i,j)} = \frac{\partial r(j)}{\partial A(i,j)} = \frac{A(i,j)}{r(j)}$. This equation indicates that the gradient of $||A||_{1,2}$ with respect to A can be easily obtained by performing a column-wise normalization on the matrix A. Here we denote this column-wise normalization operator as $\pounds$ for convenience.

3.2   Local Accumulative Frame Feature (LAFF)

Since existing RGB-D sequence features [10,11,40] are not for online feature extraction, they are less applicable for online activity prediction. To overcome

---

[2] We would add a small positive constant ϵ to $r(j)$ when it is zero.

this problem, we propose an effective RGB-D sequence feature representation by employing the popularly used integral map computing technique. In details, we extract local HOG descriptors from RGB and depth patches around each body part and extract relative skeleton features for each frame in order to capture activity contexts including human motions, appearance, shapes of human body parts, the manipulated objects and even the scene. In order to further capture temporal structure, a $3 - level$ temporal pyramid is constructed by repeatedly partitioning the observed sequence into increasingly finer sub-segments along temporal dimension. The features of the frames found in each sub-segment are accumulated together using a mean pooling method. The concatenation of all accumulative features forms our local accumulative frame feature (LAFF).

In the following, we show that LAFF can be calculated efficiently by constructing an integral feature map $\boldsymbol{I}$:

$$\boldsymbol{I}(\cdot, T) = \sum_{t=1}^{T} \boldsymbol{F}(\cdot, t). \tag{2}$$

where $\boldsymbol{F} \in \mathbb{R}^{d \times T}$ is the local features extracted from frames in the sequence, d denotes the feature dimension and T is the number of total frames. We can compute the accumulative feature $\boldsymbol{x}$ between frames t_1 and t_2 $(t_2 > t_1)$ as follows:

$$\boldsymbol{x} = \frac{\boldsymbol{I}(\cdot, t_2) - \boldsymbol{I}(\cdot, t_1 - 1)}{t_2 - t_1 + 1}. \tag{3}$$

Therefore, the LAFF features with 7 temporal intervals $(1 + 2 + 4$ sub-segments in the 3-level pyramid) can be efficiently computed from the formulated integral feature map using Eq. (3). This enables online and real-time computation.

3.3 Model Formulation

We assume that training activity sequences contain complete activity executions. To train an activity predictor, similar to existing works [7,8], we uniformly divide the fully observed training sequences into N segments. Let $V(\cdot, \cdot, \cdot)$ be the full sequence, and we use a vector $\boldsymbol{\pi}^3 \in \mathbb{R}^{N+1}$ to indicate the temporal locations of the segments. For example, $V(\cdot, \cdot, \boldsymbol{\pi}(1) : \boldsymbol{\pi}(2))$ represents the sequence of the first segment. Always, we call $V(:, \boldsymbol{\pi}(1), \boldsymbol{\pi}(n + 1))$ an activity's subsequence of progress level n. And correspondingly, its *observation ratio* can be defined as $\frac{n}{N}$.

Let $\{(\boldsymbol{X}_1, \boldsymbol{y}_1), (\boldsymbol{X}_2, \boldsymbol{y}_2), ..., (\boldsymbol{X}_I, \boldsymbol{y}_I)\}$ be the training data that consist of I examples from L classes, where $\boldsymbol{y}_i \in \mathbb{R}^N$ is a label vector of $\boldsymbol{X}_i$, each $\boldsymbol{X}_i \in \mathbb{R}^{d \times N}$ has N instances, and each instance $\boldsymbol{X}_i(\cdot, n)$ is represented by the LAFF feature of the subsequence of progress level n. The label vector $\boldsymbol{y}_i$ is a binary vector, having its $j - th$ entry set to 1 if it is from the $j - th$ class and 0 otherwise.

Indeed, the unfinished subsequences are quite different from the full sequences because the contents contained in the unobserved duration may include some important conception for the complete activity definition.

---

[3] Intuitively, we need the vector to satisfy the boundary constraint $\boldsymbol{\pi}(1) = 1$, $\boldsymbol{\pi}(N + 1) = T$ and the monotonicity constraint $\boldsymbol{\pi}(t_1) \leq \boldsymbol{\pi}(t_2)$ for any $t_1 \leq t_2$.

Since a subsequence is ambiguous, labeling it as the label of its full sequence could make confusing. To overcome this problem, we learn a soft label for each subsequence and define the label of the subsequence with a progress level n as $\boldsymbol{\alpha}(n)\boldsymbol{y}_i$ where $0 \leq \boldsymbol{\alpha}(n) \leq 1$. $\boldsymbol{\alpha}(n)\boldsymbol{y}_i$ can be conceived as how likely the subsequence is from the activity class $\boldsymbol{y}_i$. Using and learning soft labels can alleviate the confusion caused by the fact that subsequences from different activities could contain similar activity content (See Fig. 1 for example). In addition, it also enables the prediction of ongoing activity at any progress level in our modeling.

To learn the soft labels rather than setting them empirically, we form a soft regression model for learning them and activity predictor jointly as follows:

$$\min_{\boldsymbol{W},\boldsymbol{\alpha}} \sum_{i=1}^{I}\sum_{n=1}^{N} \overbrace{\boldsymbol{s}(n)||\boldsymbol{W}^T\boldsymbol{X}_i(\cdot,n) - \boldsymbol{y}_i\boldsymbol{\alpha}(n)||_{1,2}}^{Prediction\ loss\ term} + \frac{\xi_2}{2} \overbrace{||\boldsymbol{W}||_F^2}^{Regularization\ term}$$
$$s.t. \quad \boldsymbol{\alpha}^T\boldsymbol{e}_N = 1, 0 \leqslant \boldsymbol{\alpha} \leqslant 1, \xi_2 \geq 0. \tag{4}$$

where $\boldsymbol{W} \in \mathbb{R}^{d \times C}$ is the transformation matrix of the multi-class discriminative linear predictor and it is constrained by a conventional ridge regularization. Since the prediction loss of subsequences at different progress levels should contribute differently to the prediction, we introduce a $\boldsymbol{s}(n)$ to weight each regression loss. By denoting S as the diagonal matrix generated by $\boldsymbol{s}$, the prediction loss can be expressed in a matrix form as $||(\boldsymbol{W}^T\boldsymbol{X}_i - \boldsymbol{y}_i\boldsymbol{\alpha}^T)\boldsymbol{S}||_{1,2}$. The $L_{1,2}$ norm is used to measure the regression loss because it is robust to noise and outliers [42].

In the above formulation, we constrain $\boldsymbol{\alpha}(N) = \boldsymbol{\alpha}^T\boldsymbol{e}_N = 1$ to ensure that a strong label can be derived if the entire sequence is observed, where $\boldsymbol{e}_N$ is a binary vector with only the $N-th$ entry being 1. In addition, we also restrict all entries in $\boldsymbol{\alpha}$ within $[0,1]$.

In order to make sure the variation of soft label is smooth, we further impose a consistency constraint on $\boldsymbol{\alpha}$ as follows:

$$\min_{\boldsymbol{W},\boldsymbol{\alpha}} \sum_{i=1}^{I}\sum_{n=1}^{N} \overbrace{||(\boldsymbol{W}^T\boldsymbol{X}_i - \boldsymbol{y}_i\boldsymbol{\alpha}^T)\boldsymbol{S}||_{1,2}}^{Prediction\ loss\ term} + \frac{\xi_1}{2}\overbrace{||\nabla\boldsymbol{\alpha}||_2^2}^{Consistency\ term} + \frac{\xi_2}{2}\overbrace{||\boldsymbol{W}||_F^2}^{Regularization\ term}$$
$$s.t. \quad \boldsymbol{\alpha}^T\boldsymbol{e}_N = 1, 0 \leqslant \boldsymbol{\alpha} \leqslant 1.\xi_1, \xi_2 \geq 0. \tag{5}$$

Consistency term $||\nabla\boldsymbol{\alpha}||_2^2$. This constraint is to enforce the label consistency between subsequences. We compute the gradient of soft labels and measure its norm in order to control the variations of soft labels between subsequences. The effect of the consistency term is controlled by ξ_1. As the gradient operator $\nabla\boldsymbol{\alpha}$ is a linear operator, the consistency term can be rewritten in a matrix form $\boldsymbol{G}\boldsymbol{\alpha}$ equivalently, where we set $\boldsymbol{G}$ as $\begin{pmatrix} 1 & -1 & 0 & 0 \\ 0 & \ddots & \ddots & 0 \\ 0 & 0 & 1 & -1 \end{pmatrix} \in \mathbb{R}^{N-1 \times N}$. In this way, we can rewrite our soft regression model as follows:

$$\min_{\boldsymbol{W}, \boldsymbol{\alpha}} \sum_{i=1}^{I} ||(\boldsymbol{W}^T \boldsymbol{X}_i - \boldsymbol{y}_i \boldsymbol{\alpha}^T) \boldsymbol{S}||_{1,2} + \frac{\xi_1}{2} ||\boldsymbol{G}\boldsymbol{\alpha}||_2^2 + \frac{\xi_2}{2} ||\boldsymbol{W}||_F^2$$

$$s.t. \quad \boldsymbol{\alpha}^T \boldsymbol{e}_N = 1, 0 \leqslant \boldsymbol{\alpha} \leqslant 1, \xi_1, \xi_2 \geq 0. \tag{6}$$

3.4   Model Optimization

We solve our soft regression model (6) using a coordinate descent algorithm which would optimize over one parameter at each step while holding the others fixed. The optimization is achieved by iterating over the following two steps. At step 1, we optimize the predictor $\boldsymbol{W}$ with $\boldsymbol{\alpha}$ fixed. At step 2, we optimize it over $\boldsymbol{\alpha}$ with $\boldsymbol{W}$ fixed. The objective function (6) can be monotonically decreased with a guaranteed convergence. We provide some details in the following.

STEP 1. For fixed soft labels $\boldsymbol{\alpha}$, optimize the predictor $\boldsymbol{W}$:

$$\min_{\boldsymbol{W}} \sum_{i=1}^{I} ||(\boldsymbol{W}^T \boldsymbol{X}_i - \boldsymbol{y}_i \boldsymbol{\alpha}^T) \boldsymbol{S}||_{1,2} + \frac{\xi_2}{2} ||\boldsymbol{W}||_F^2. \tag{7}$$

This is an unconstrained optimization problem and we can solve it with a standard gradient descent method. Let us denote the matrix $(\boldsymbol{W}^T \boldsymbol{X}_i - \boldsymbol{y}_i \boldsymbol{\alpha}^T) \boldsymbol{S}$ as $\boldsymbol{M}_i$. Then the gradient of the objective function with respect to $\boldsymbol{W}$ can be given by $\boldsymbol{G} = \sum_{i=1}^{i=I} \boldsymbol{X}_i \boldsymbol{S} \mathcal{L}(\boldsymbol{M}_i) + \xi_2 \boldsymbol{W}$, where $\mathcal{L}$ is the column-wise normalization operator defined previously.

STEP 2. For fixed predictor $\boldsymbol{W}$, optimize the soft labels $\boldsymbol{\alpha}$:

$$\min_{\boldsymbol{\alpha}} \sum_{i=1}^{I} ||(\boldsymbol{W}^T \boldsymbol{X}_i - \boldsymbol{y}_i \boldsymbol{\alpha}^T) \boldsymbol{S}||_{1,2} + \frac{\xi_1}{2} ||\boldsymbol{G}\boldsymbol{\alpha}||_2^2 \tag{8}$$

$$s.t. \quad \boldsymbol{\alpha}^T \boldsymbol{e}_N = 1, 0 \leqslant \boldsymbol{\alpha} \leqslant 1. \tag{9}$$

It is hard to directly solve the above problem because the existence of the sparse constraint in the prediction term and the bounded constraints in Eq. (9). Here, we introduce a method to find an approximate solution based on the popularly used projected gradient descent method. Firstly, we optimize the following problem without any constraint

$$\min_{\boldsymbol{\alpha}} \sum_{i=1}^{I} ||(\boldsymbol{W}^T \boldsymbol{X}_i - \boldsymbol{y}_i \boldsymbol{\alpha}^T) \boldsymbol{S}||_{1,2} + \frac{\xi_1}{2} ||\boldsymbol{G}\boldsymbol{\alpha}||_2^2. \tag{10}$$

The above unconstrained problem can be optimized using a gradient descent based method. Specially, given the t-th step estimator $\boldsymbol{\alpha}_t$, the new updated point can be obtained by projecting $\boldsymbol{\alpha}_t - \tau \boldsymbol{g}_t$ into the feasible solution space $\{\boldsymbol{\alpha} \in \mathbb{R}^N | 0 \leq \boldsymbol{\alpha} \leq 1, \boldsymbol{\alpha}^T \boldsymbol{e}_N = 1\}$. The gradient $\boldsymbol{g}_t$ is given by $\sum_{i=1}^{i=I} \boldsymbol{y}_i^T \mathcal{L}(\boldsymbol{W}^T \boldsymbol{X}_i \boldsymbol{S} - \boldsymbol{y}_i \boldsymbol{\alpha}_t \boldsymbol{S}) \boldsymbol{S} + \xi_1 \boldsymbol{G} \boldsymbol{\alpha}_t$. Here τ is the iteration step size and an optimal step size is determined by a line search method within each iteration in order to monotonically decrease the objective function (10).

3.5   Prediction

Given a probe ongoing activity sequence (the progress level is unknown), we first extracted the corresponding LAFF feature x using the online constructed integral map I. Then the prediction was made by finding the label that has the maximum score in $W^T x$. Our method can predict ongoing activity without given the progress level.

4   Experiments

We evaluated our methods on two benchmark 3D activity datasets: *Online RGB-D Action* dataset [5] and *SYSU 3DHOI* dataset [11].

4.1   Compared Methods and Implementation

We have implemented the following approaches using the same proposed features (i.e. LAFF) for comparison:

SVM on the Finished Activities (SVM-FA). As the simplest baseline, it trains a generic activity classifier on the completely executed sequences and the partial activity subsequences were not used for the training. During the test phase, all the ongoing subsequences were predicted using the learnt activity classifier. Comparison to this baseline is to demonstrate that the subsequences containing partial activity executions are important for the predictor learning.

Brute-force Prediction using SVM (BPSVM). It learns an activity predictor from all the available subsequences. In this baseline, we assigned the label of each subsequence with the label of its full sequence. That means these labels were not soft labels as described in our methods. This baseline is introduced in order to show the benefits of using soft labels. We denote it as "BPSVM".

Multiple Stages SVM (MSSVM). We trained a SVM predictor on the sequences obtained at each progress level separately. While in the test phase, we followed the same assumption in [7] that the progress level of ongoing activity is known and thus we can directly make the prediction using the predictor specifically trained for that progress level. Although practical system is hard to have a chance to obtain the progress level of ongoing activity sequence until the activity has been completely executed, it still serves as a good reference for evaluating activity prediction models. We denote this baseline as "MSSVM".

Other related activity prediction methods. In addition to the above comparison, we also compared the state-of-the-art activity prediction systems developed for RGB-D sequences [5] and RGB video clips [6,8].

For implementation of our proposed model, the regularization parameters ξ_1 and ξ_2 were set as 5000 and 1 throughout all the experiments, respectively. The total subsequence number N was set as 40. The weight $s(n)$ can be understood as prior weighting on the regression loss of the $n - th$ subsequence in Eq. (5). In general the loss of the subsequence at the end of the sequence is more important as the type of action becomes more clear. Hence, we increased $s(n)$ in Eq. (5) from 0.25 to 1 uniformly. Its influence will be studied in Sect. 4.4.

4.2   Results on Online RGB-D Action Dataset

The Online RGB-D Action Dataset (ORGBD) was collected for online activity recognition and activity prediction [5]. Some activity examples are shown in Fig. 3. For evaluation, we used the same-environment evaluation protocol detailed in [5], where half of the subjects were used for training a predictor and the rest were used for testing. In this setting, there are totally 224 RGB-D sequences of sixteen subjects, including seven human-object interaction activities (*drinking, eating, using laptop, reading cell phone, making phone call, reading book* and *using remote*). The mean accuracies were computed via a 2-fold validation.

Fig. 3. Some examples from the ORGBD and SYSU 3DHOI sets. The first and last two rows present samples from ORGBD and SYSU 3DHOI set, respectively.

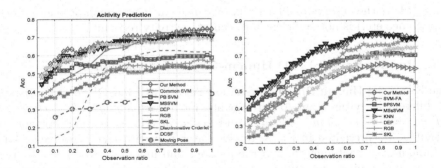

Fig. 4. Comparison results on ORGBD (left) and SYSU 3DHOI (right) sets.

We compared with the baselines and other related prediction methods as described in Sect. 4.1. The results are presented in Fig. 4 and Table 1. As shown, our method can produce better prediction results at most of the observation ratios than the competitors. We also find that the performance gap became larger if fewer activity frames were observed. This is as expected because our soft regression model explicitly makes use of the subsequences that contains partial

Table 1. Prediction (%) on ORGBD set. The last row provides the mean accuracies over all the observation ratios. "Ob. ratio", "MP", "DCSF", and "DO" denote observation ratio, "Moving Pose [5,43]", "DSTIP+DCSF [5,44]", and "Discriminative Order-let [5]".

Ob. ratio	RGB	DEP	SKL	MSSVM	BPSVM	SVM-FA	MP	DCSF	DO	Our Method
10 %	43.3	**54.5**	36.6	53.1	54.5	53.6	25.9	14.3	43.8	**57.1**
60 %	54.5	**67.4**	50.5	**67.4**	64.7	**67.4**	33.9	55.4	63.4	**70.1**
100 %	56.7	68.3	53.1	70.1	66.1	70.1	38.4	61.6	**71.4**	**74.1**
Mean	51.3	63.9	47.8	64.7	61.8	**64.9**	34.3	49.5	63.0	**67.2**

activity executions for obtaining a reliable predictor. By carefully examining the comparisons of our method and the baselines BPSVM and SVM-FA, we find that the introduced soft label learning mechanism can significantly improve prediction performance, and it also outperformed MSSVM which predicts ongoing activities with known progress level using multiple pre-trained predictors.

In addition, we also compared the state-of-the-art prediction algorithms reported on this set [5,44]. The proposed method outperformed the state-of-the-art method (discriminative order-let model) [5] by a large margin (more than 10 percent) when only 10 % of the sequence were used. If full sequence was provided, our predictor still performed better and obtained an accuracy of 74.1 %, which is 2.7 % higher than the discriminative order-let model. This suggests that the long-duration motion information ignored by the frame-level prediction model [5] is very important for identifying human activities, especially at early activity stages where the observed still activity evidence (such as human pose and object appearance etc.) is not sufficient for accurate activity recognition.

4.3   Results on SYSU 3D Human-Object Interaction Set

The SYSU 3D Human-Object Interaction Set (SYSU 3DHOI Set)[4] consists of 12 different activities from 40 participants, including *playing with a cell-phone*, *calling with a cell-phone*, *mopping* and *sweeping* etc. Some snapshots of the activities are presented in Fig. 3. In this dataset, each activity involves a kind of human-object interaction, and the motions and manipulated objects by participant performing are similar among some activities [11]. For evaluation, we employed the cross-subject setting popularly used in RGB-D activity recognition. In particular, we trained our predictor and all compared methods using the samples performed by the first 20 subjects and then tested on the rest subjects.

The prediction comparison results are presented in the second column of Fig. 4 and Table 2. As shown, our predictor can obtain a good performance at most of the progress levels and it significantly outperformed BPSVM and SVM-FA. Since activities at the same progress level often contain more similar activity

---

[4] It can be downloaded from http://isee.sysu.edu.cn/~hujianfang/.

Table 2. Prediction (%) on SYSU 3DHOI set. "Ob. ratio" denotes the observation ratio. The last row provides the mean accuracies over all the observation ratios.

Ob. ratio	RGB	DEP	SKL	kNN	MSSVM	BPSVM	SVM-FA	Our Method
10 %	38.3	28.3	26.7	35.8	**50.8**	45.0	33.8	**45.8**
60 %	67.5	62.9	53.3	61.3	**78.8**	68.3	72.9	**76.3**
100 %	70.8	74.2	54.2	62.1	**79.2**	70.0	**79.2**	**80.0**
Mean	59.5	54.4	44.5	54.7	**71.1**	61.9	61.0	**69.6**

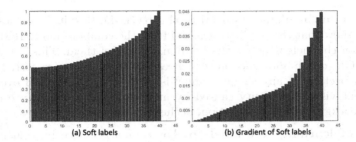

(a) Soft labels   (b) Gradient of Soft labels

Fig. 5. Example soft labels learned on SYSU 3DHOI set. The vertical axis indicates the values for the soft labels and the horizontal axis is the index of subsequence.

context in this set, additionally using the progress level of an activity to train predictors is beneficial. So, MSSVM performs slightly better than our method at the early stages, but both perform comparably after that, and our method performs better when complete activity sequences were observed (i.e., the conventional activity recognition task). It again demonstrates that the generated large amount of unfinished subsequences can be used to benefit the task of activity recognition.

The learnt soft labels are presented in Fig. 5. We can observe that the soft labels starts around 0.5. This is as expected because some activities can be easily recognized at early stages by activity context (e.g., shapes and textures of objects). In general, the soft labels increase as more about the action is observed.

4.4 More Evaluations

RGB vs. RGB-D prediction. Intuitively, the RGB-D activity prediction can be casted as a RGB activity prediction problem by discarding the depth and skeleton modalities and RGB activity prediction methods can be easily implemented. Here, we tabulated the results on the SYSU 3DHOI set obtained by methods (DBOW [8], SC, and MSSC [6]) developed in [6][5] as well as our method in Table 3. As shown, our soft regression model have a significant advantage over these methods even using the same input data (RGB data). From the results, we can conclude that a RGB-D based prediction system has its unique benefit.

---

[5] The original codes are downloaded from http://www.visioncao.com/index.html.

Table 3. Comparisons of our method with RGB activity prediction methods.

Observation ratio	10 %	20 %	30 %	40 %	50 %	60 %	70 %	80 %	90 %	100 %	Mean
DBOW [8]	31.7	40.0	43.8	46.7	52.1	54.2	58.8	59.6	62.1	62.5	51.1
SC [6]	30.4	41.3	50.8	53.3	57.1	57.9	57.9	58.8	60.4	61.3	52.9
MSSC [6]	30.4	40.8	47.1	55.0	56.7	59.6	57.5	60.8	62.1	62.9	53.3
Our Method (RGB)	38.3	45.8	52.9	60.8	63.3	67.5	69.6	70.4	70.4	70.8	61.0
Our Method(RGB-D)	45.8	55.0	64.6	71.3	73.8	76.3	80.8	81.3	80.8	80.0	70.9

Evaluation on the elements used in the RGB-D. Results in Tables 1 and 2 and Fig. 4 show that the predictor learned from the combination of RGB, depth and skeleton channels is better than only using one of them. This is reasonable because RGB, depth and skeleton sequences indeed characterize activities from different aspects, and any single channel is intrinsically limited in overcoming the inherent visual ambiguity caused by human (object) appearance changes, cluttered background, view variation, occlusions and etc.

Benefits of learning soft labels α. For comparison, we implemented two baselines, where different strategies were employed to manually determine the soft labels: (1) we set all the elements of α as 1; and (2) we randomly generated a set of soft labels for our regression model with 20 replicates. As shown in Fig. 6(a), the prediction accuracy decreased a lot if the soft labels were simply defined as the label of the whole sequence or randomly generated.

The influence of consistency constraint. We studied the influence of the parameter ξ_1, which is employed to control the effect of the consistency term in our model (5). Figure 6(b) shows the performances of setting ξ_1 as 0, 500, 5000, 50000 and 500000, respectively. As shown, our method can obtain a promising result with $\xi_1 = 5000$. In general, a small or large ξ_1 would lead to a lower prediction accuracy. Especially, when ξ_1 is larger than a certain number (e.g. 500000), the soft labels learnt by our method became useless as all of its entries will be the same and thus an unreliable prediction result was obtained.

Impact of the s. In our regression model (5), we use a vector s to control the contribution of the regression losses caused by the subsequences of different progress levels. Here, we tested its influence. In the evaluation, we considered five different settings for s, which were presented in the Fig. 6(c). The prediction performance obtained by each setting was presented in Fig. 6(d) with the same color. As shown, an s with incremental items performed better than the constant or even diminishing ones. This is desirable, because the subsequences in the latter progress levels should contain more activity execution and thus can provide more strong information for our predictor learning.

The convergence of the model. Our method converged to a minimum after a limited number of iterations. We empirically observed that 400 iterations were sufficient for obtaining a reliable solution in our experiments.

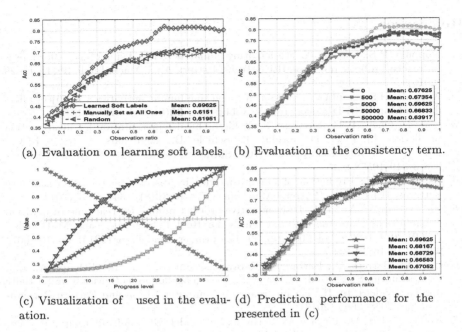

(a) Evaluation on learning soft labels. (b) Evaluation on the consistency term.

(c) Visualization of   used in the evalu- (d) Prediction performance for the
ation.   presented in (c)

Fig. 6. More evaluations on the system performance.

The speed of prediction. We report the average speed (in fps) of the developed
human activity prediction system. Our system can identify an activity of ongoing
RGB-D sequences in real-time. Especially, it processed more than 40 frames per
second using MATLAB on a normal desktop PC (CPU i5-4570), which is about
15 fps faster than the prediction system developed in [5].

5   Conclusions

We have developed a real-time RGB-D activity prediction system to identify
ongoing activities under a regression framework. In such a regression framework,
we learn soft labels for regression on subsequences containing partial activity executions so that it is not necessary to assume that the progress level of each subsequence is given. We learn both the soft labels and predictor jointly. In addition, a
new RGB-D sequence feature called "local accumulative frame feature (LAFF)",
which can be computed efficiently by constructing an integral feature map, is
designed to characterize activity contexts. We demonstrate the effectiveness of
our approach on RGB-D activity prediction and show that depth information is
important for achieving much more robust prediction performance.

Acknowledgment. This work was supported partially by the NSFC (No.61573387,
61472456, 61522115, 61661130157), the GuangDong Program (No.2015B010105005),
the Guangdong Science and Technology Planning Project (No.2016A010102012),
and Guangdong Program for Support of Top-notch Young Professionals (No.2014T
Q01X779).

References

1. Koppula, H.S., Saxena, A.: Anticipating human activities using object affordances for reactive robotic response. IEEE Trans. Pattern Anal. Mach. Intell. **38**(1), 14–29 (2016)
2. Koppula, H.S., Gupta, R., Saxena, A.: Learning human activities and object affordances from RGB-D videos. Int. J. Robot. Res. **32**(8), 951–970 (2013)
3. Lan, T., Chen, T.-C., Savarese, S.: A hierarchical representation for future action prediction. In: Fleet, D., Pajdla, T., Schiele, B., Tuytelaars, T. (eds.) ECCV 2014. LNCS, vol. 8691, pp. 689–704. Springer, Heidelberg (2014). doi:10.1007/978-3-319-10578-9_45
4. Li, K., Fu, Y.: Prediction of human activity by discovering temporal sequence patterns. IEEE Trans. Pattern Anal. Mach. Intell. **36**(8), 1644–1657 (2014)
5. Yu, G., Liu, Z., Yuan, J.: Discriminative orderlet mining for real-time recognition of human-object interaction. In: Cremers, D., Reid, I., Saito, H., Yang, M.-H. (eds.) ACCV 2014. LNCS, vol. 9007, pp. 50–65. Springer, Heidelberg (2015). doi:10.1007/978-3-319-16814-2_4
6. Cao, Y., Barrett, D., Barbu, A., Narayanaswamy, S., Yu, H., Michaux, A., Lin, Y., Dickinson, S., Siskind, J., Wang, S.: Recognize human activities from partially observed videos. In: IEEE Conference on Computer Vision and Pattern Recognition, pp. 2658–2665 (2013)
7. Kong, Y., Kit, D., Fu, Y.: A discriminative model with multiple temporal scales for action prediction. In: Fleet, D., Pajdla, T., Schiele, B., Tuytelaars, T. (eds.) ECCV 2014. LNCS, vol. 8693, pp. 596–611. Springer, Heidelberg (2014). doi:10.1007/978-3-319-10602-1_39
8. Ryoo, M.: Human activity prediction: Early recognition of ongoing activities from streaming videos. In: International Conference on Computer Vision, pp. 1036–1043 (2011)
9. Xu, Z., Qing, L., Miao, J.: Activity auto-completion: predicting human activities from partial videos. In: IEEE International Conference on Computer Vision, pp. 3191–3199 (2015)
10. Wang, J., Liu, Z., Wu, Y., Yuan, J.: Learning actionlet ensemble for 3D human action recognition. IEEE Trans. Pattern Anal. Mach. Intell. **20**(11), 914 (2013)
11. Hu, J.F., Zheng, W.S., Lai, J., Zhang, J.: Jointly learning heterogeneous features for RGB-D activity recognition. In: IEEE International Conference on Computer Vision and Pattern Recognition, pp. 5344–5352 (2015)
12. Hoai, M., De la Torre, F.: Max-margin early event detectors. Int. J. Comput. Vis. **107**(2), 191–202 (2014)
13. Kitani, K.M., Ziebart, B.D., Bagnell, J.A., Hebert, M.: Activity forecasting. In: Fitzgibbon, A., Lazebnik, S., Perona, P., Sato, Y., Schmid, C. (eds.) ECCV 2012. LNCS, vol. 7575, pp. 201–214. Springer, Heidelberg (2012). doi:10.1007/978-3-642-33765-9_15
14. Vondrick, C., Pirsiavash, H., Torralba, A.: Anticipating the future by watching unlabeled video (2015). arXiv preprint arXiv:1504.08023
15. Huang, D., Yao, S., Wang, Y., Torre, F.: Sequential max-margin event detectors. In: Fleet, D., Pajdla, T., Schiele, B., Tuytelaars, T. (eds.) ECCV 2014. LNCS, vol. 8691, pp. 410–424. Springer, Heidelberg (2014). doi:10.1007/978-3-319-10578-9_27
16. Dollár, P., Rabaud, V., Cottrell, G., Belongie, S.: Behavior recognition via sparse spatio-temporal features. In: IEEE International Workshop on Visual Surveillance and Performance Evaluation of Tracking and Surveillance, pp. 65–72 (2005)

17. Bregonzio, M., Gong, S., Xiang, T.: Recognising action as clouds of space-time interest points. In: IEEE Conference on Computer Vision and Pattern Recognition 2009, pp. 1948–1955 (2009)

18. Klaser, A., Marszałek, M., Schmid, C.: A spatio-temporal descriptor based on 3D-gradients. In: British Machine Vision Conference, pp. 275–281. British Machine Vision Association (2008)

19. Wang, H., Schmid, C.: Action recognition with improved trajectories. In: IEEE International Conference on Computer Vision, pp. 3551–3558 (2013)

20. Simonyan, K., Zisserman, A.: Two-stream convolutional networks for action recognition in videos. In: Proceedings of Advances in Neural Information Processing Systems, pp. 568–576 (2014)

21. Yang, X., Tian, Y.L.: Action recognition using super sparse coding vector with spatio-temporal awareness. In: Fleet, D., Pajdla, T., Schiele, B., Tuytelaars, T. (eds.) ECCV 2014. LNCS, vol. 8690, pp. 727–741. Springer, Heidelberg (2014). doi:10.1007/978-3-319-10605-2_47

22. Zhu, J., Wang, B., Yang, X., Zhang, W., Tu, Z.: Action recognition with actons. In: Proceedings of the IEEE International Conference on Computer Vision, pp. 3559–3566 (2013)

23. Hu, J.F., Zheng, W.S., Lai, J., Gong, S., Xiang, T.: Exemplar-based recognition of human-object interactions. IEEE Trans. Circ. Syst. Video Technol. 26(4), 647–660 (2016)

24. Hu, J.F., Zheng, W.S., Lai, J., Gong, S., Xiang, T.: Recognising human-object interaction via exemplar based modelling. In: International Conference on Computer Vision (2013)

25. Oreifej, O., Liu, Z.: Hon4d: histogram of oriented 4D normals for activity recognition from depth sequences. In: IEEE International Conference on Computer Vision and Pattern Recognition, pp. 716–723 (2013)

26. Yang, X., Tian, Y.: Super normal vector for activity recognition using depth sequences. In: IEEE International Conference on Computer Vision and Pattern Recognition, pp. 804–811 (2014)

27. Dalal, N., Triggs, B.: Histograms of oriented gradients for human detection. In: IEEE International Conference on Computer Vision and Pattern Recognition, vol. 1, pp. 886–893 (2005)

28. Lu, C., Jia, J., Tang, C.K.: Range-sample depth feature for action recognition. In: IEEE International Conference on Computer Vision and Pattern Recognition, pp. 772–779 (2014)

29. Wang, J., Liu, Z., Chorowski, J., Chen, Z., Wu, Y.: Robust 3D action recognition with random occupancy patterns. In: Fitzgibbon, A., Lazebnik, S., Perona, P., Sato, Y., Schmid, C. (eds.) ECCV 2012. LNCS, vol. 7573, pp. 872–885. Springer, Heidelberg (2012)

30. Shotton, J., Sharp, T., Kipman, A., Fitzgibbon, A., Finocchio, M., Blake, A., Cook, M., Moore, R.: Real-time human pose recognition in parts from single depth images. Commun. ACM 56(1), 116–124 (2013)

31. Hussein, M.E., Torki, M., Gowayyed, M.A., El-Saban, M.: Human action recognition using a temporal hierarchy of covariance descriptors on 3D joint locations. IJCAI 13, 2466–2472 (2013)

32. Xia, L., Chen, C.C., Aggarwal, J.: View invariant human action recognition using histograms of 3D joints. In: IEEE International Conference on Computer Vision and Pattern RecognitionW, pp. 20–27 (2012)

33. Du, Y., Wang, W., Wang, L.: Hierarchical recurrent neural network for skeleton based action recognition. In: IEEE International Conference on Computer Vision and Pattern Recognition, pp. 1110–1118 (2015)
34. Yang, X., Tian, Y.: Eigenjoints-based action recognition using naive-bayes-nearest-neighbor. In: IEEE International Conference on Computer Vision and Pattern RecognitionW, pp. 14–19 (2012)
35. Ofli, F., Chaudhry, R., Kurillo, G., Vidal, R., Bajcsy, R.: Sequence of the most informative joints (SMIJ): a new representation for human skeletal action recognition. JVCIR **25**(1), 24–38 (2014)
36. Lillo, I., Soto, A., Niebles, J.C.: Discriminative hierarchical modeling of spatio-temporally composable human activities. In: IEEE International Conference on Computer Vision and Pattern Recognition, pp. 812–819 (2014)
37. Zanfir, M., Leordeanu, M., Sminchisescu, C.: The moving pose: An efficient 3D kinematics descriptor for low-latency action recognition and detection. In: IEEE International Conference on Computer Vision, pp. 2752–2759 (2013)
38. Shahroudy, A., Ng, T.T., Yang, Q., Wang, G.: Multimodal multipart learning for action recognition in depth videos. IEEE Trans. Pattern Anal. Mach. Intell
39. Liu, J., Shahroudy, A., Xu, D., Wang, G.: Spatio-temporal lstm with trust gates for 3D human action recognition. In: European Conference on Computer Vision (2016)
40. Wei, P., Zhao, Y., Zheng, N., Zhu, S.C.: Modeling 4D human-object interactions for event and object recognition. In: International Conference on Computer Vision, pp. 3272–3279 (2013)
41. Hu, N., Lou, Z., Englebienne, G., Kröse, B.: Learning to recognize human activities from soft labeled data. In: Proceedings of Robotics Science and Systems, Berkeley, USA (2014)
42. Li, Z., Liu, J., Tang, J., Lu, H.: Robust structured subspace learning for data representation. IEEE Trans. Pattern Anal. Mach. Intell. **37**(10), 2085–2098 (2015)
43. Gupta, A., Davis, L.S.: Objects in action: an approach for combining action understanding and object perception. In: IEEE Conference on Computer Vision and Pattern Recognition, pp. 1–8 (2007)
44. Xia, L., Aggarwal, J.: Spatio-temporal depth cuboid similarity feature for activity recognition using depth camera. In: IEEE International Conference on Computer Vision and Pattern Recognition, pp. 2834–2841 (2013)

A 3D Morphable Eye Region Model
for Gaze Estimation

Erroll Wood[1(✉)], Tadas Baltrušaitis[2], Louis-Philippe Morency[2],
Peter Robinson[1], and Andreas Bulling[3]

[1] University of Cambridge, Cambridge, UK
{eww23,pr10}@cl.cam.ac.uk
[2] Carnegie Mellon University, Pittsburgh, USA
{tbaltrus,morency}@cs.cmu.edu
[3] Max Planck Institute for Informatics, Saarbrücken, Germany
bulling@mpi-inf.mpg.de

Abstract. Morphable face models are a powerful tool, but have previously failed to model the eye accurately due to complexities in its material and motion. We present a new multi-part model of the eye that includes a morphable model of the facial eye region, as well as an anatomy-based eyeball model. It is the first morphable model that accurately captures eye region shape, since it was built from high-quality head scans. It is also the first to allow independent eyeball movement, since we treat it as a separate part. To showcase our model we present a new method for illumination- and head-pose–invariant gaze estimation from a single RGB image. We fit our model to an image through analysis-by-synthesis, solving for eye region shape, texture, eyeball pose, and illumination simultaneously. The fitted eyeball pose parameters are then used to estimate gaze direction. Through evaluation on two standard datasets we show that our method generalizes to both webcam and high-quality camera images, and outperforms a state-of-the-art CNN method achieving a gaze estimation accuracy of $9.44°$ in a challenging user-independent scenario.

Keywords: Morphable model · Gaze estimation · Analysis-by-synthesis

1 Introduction

The eyes and their movements convey our attention, indicate our interests, and play a key role in communicating social and emotional information [1]. Estimating eye gaze is therefore an important problem for computer vision, with applications ranging from facial analysis [2] to gaze-based interfaces [3,4]. However, estimating gaze remotely under unconstrained lighting conditions and significant head-pose is a yet-outstanding challenge. Appearance-based methods

Electronic supplementary material The online version of this chapter (doi:10.1007/978-3-319-46448-0_18) contains supplementary material, which is available to authorized users.

© Springer International Publishing AG 2016
B. Leibe et al. (Eds.): ECCV 2016, Part I, LNCS 9905, pp. 297–313, 2016.
DOI: 10.1007/978-3-319-46448-0_18

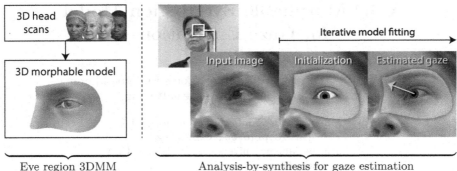

Fig. 1. Our generic gaze estimator is enabled by two contributions. First, a novel 3DMM of the eye built from high quality head scans. Second, a new method for gaze estimation – we fit our 3DMM to an image using analysis-by-synthesis, and estimate gaze from fitted parameters.

that directly estimate gaze from an eye image have recently improved upon person- and device-independent gaze estimation by learning invariances from large amounts of labelled training data. In particular, Zhang et al. trained a multi-modal convolutional neural network with 200,000 images collected during everyday laptop use [5], and Wood et al. rendered over one million synthetic training images with artificial illumination variation [6]. It has been shown that the performance of such methods heavily depends on the head pose and gaze range that the training data covers – results are best when the training data closely matches the desired test condition [7]. This means a gaze estimator trained in one scenario does not perform well in another. Instead, we would prefer a generic gaze estimator that performs well in all conditions.

3D morphable models (3DMM) are a powerful tool as they combine a model of face variation with a model of image formation, allowing pose and illumination invariance. Since their introduction [8], they have become an established method for many tasks including inverse rendering [9,10], face recognition [11,12], and expression re-targeting [13]. Given a face image, such systems use model fitting to discover the most likely shape, texture, expression, pose, and illumination parameters that generated it. However, previous work has failed to accurately model the eyes, portraying them as a static geometry [8,11], or removing them from the face entirely [13,14]. This is a result of two complexities that are not handled by current methods: (1) The eyeball's materials make it difficult to reconstruct in 3D, leading to poor correspondence and loss of detail in the 3DMM, (2) Previous work uses blendshapes to model facial expression – a technique not compatible with independent eyeball movement. We make two specific contributions:

An Eye Region 3DMM. Our first contribution is a novel multi-part 3DMM that includes the eyeball, allowing us to accurately model variation in eye

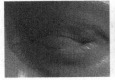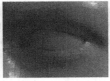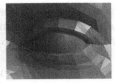

Fig. 2. A comparison between the Basel Face Model (BFM, left) [11], and our own (right). Note the BFM's lack of caruncle and unrealistic eyeball proxy geometry. Our model has well-defined correspondences for these difficult regions.

appearance and eyeball pose (see Fig. 1 left). Recent work presented a morphable shape model of the eye region, but did not capture texture variation [6]. We constructed a 3DMM of the facial eye region by carefully registering a set of high-quality 3D head scans, and extracting modes of shape and texture variation using PCA. We combined this with an anatomy-based eyeball model that can be posed separately to simulate changes in eye gaze.

Analysis-by-Synthesis for Gaze Estimation. Our second contribution is a novel method for gaze estimation: fitting our 3DMM to an input image using analysis-by-synthesis (see Fig. 1 right). We solve for shape, texture, pose, and illumination simultaneously, so our fitted model parameters provide us with a robust estimate of where someone is looking in a 3D scene. Previous approaches for remote RGB gaze estimation can be categorized as either appearance-based, feature-based, or model-based [3]. Our method is first to combine the benefits of all three: (1) We minimize the appearance difference between synthesized and observed images using a dense image-error term. (2) We use sparse facial features localized with a face tracker [15] for initialization and regularization. (3) We use our morphable model to capture variation between people and eye motion itself. We iteratively fit our model using gradient descent with numerical derivatives efficiently calculated with a tailored GPU rasterizer.

2   Related Work

2.1   3D Morphable Models

A 3D morphable model is a statistically-derived generative model, parameterized by shape and texture coefficients. They are closely related to their 2D analogue, active appearance models [16]. 3DMMs have been successfully applied to various face-related computer vision problems ranging from reconstruction [8,10] to recognition [11,12], and have also been extended to other body parts, such as the hand [17] as well as the entire body itself [18,19].

Blanz and Vetter built the first 3DMM from a set of 200 laser scans of faces with neutral expression [8]. They first computed a dense correspondences between the scans, then used PCA to extract modes of variation. Subsequent work with 3DMMs has followed the same approach, building similar models with higher quality scans [11], or more training samples [12,20]. However, despite advances in scanning technology, the eye remains problematic for 3D reconstruction, leading to poor correspondences and loss of quality in the 3DMM (see Fig. 2).

3DMMs represent a face with neutral expression, so they are often combined with a model of facial motion. Vlasic et al. used a multi-linear model to separately encode identity and expression, and demonstrated its use in facial transfer [21]. More recent works have instead used blend shapes – an animation technique that stores a different version of a mesh for each expression, and interpolates between them [14]. However, while blend shapes work well for skin, they cannot represent the independent motion of the eyeball. For these reasons, previous work either replaced the scanned eyeball with a proxy mesh [11] or completely removed the eye from the 3DMM mesh [13,22]. Bérard et al. recently presented a 3D morphable eyeball model [23] built from a database of eyeball scans [24], showing impressive results for high-quality semi-automatic eyeball reconstruction. Our work uses a simpler model that is sufficient for low-quality input data, and our fitting procedure is fully automatic.

2.2   Remote Gaze Estimation

Gaze estimation is a well established topic in computer vision (see [3,25] for reviews). Methods can be categorized as (1) *appearance-based* – map directly from image pixels to a gaze direction [5,26,27], (2) *feature-based* – localize facial feature points (e.g. pupil centre, eye corner) and map these to gaze [28,29], or (3) *model-based* – estimate gaze using a geometric model of the eye [30–32]. Some systems combine these techniques, e.g. using facial features for image alignment [26,33], mapping appearance to a 2D generative model [34], or combining head pose with image pixels in a multi-modal neural network [5]. To the best of our knowledge, no work so far has combined appearance, facial features, and a generative model into a single method, solving for shape, texture, eyeball pose, and illumination simultaneously.

The current outstanding challenge for remote RGB gaze estimation is achieving person- and device- independence under unconstrained conditions [5]. The state-of-the-art methods for this are appearance-based, attempting to learn invariances from large amounts of training data. However, such systems are still limited by their training data with respect to appearance, gaze, and head pose variation [5,27]. To address this, recent work used graphics to synthesize large amounts of training images. These learning-by-synthesis methods cover a larger range of head pose, gaze, appearance, and illumination variation without additional costs for data collection or ground truth annotation. Specifically, Wood et al. rendered 10 K images and used them to pre-train a multi-modal CNN, significantly improving upon state-of-the-art gaze estimation accuracy [7]. They later rendered 1M images with improved appearance variation for training a k-Nearest-Neighbour classifier, again improving over state-of-the-art CNN results [6].

While previous work used 3D models to synthesise training data [6], ours is first to use analysis-by-synthesis – a technique where synthesis is used for gaze estimation itself. This approach is not constrained by a limited variation in training images but instead can, in theory, generalise to arbitrary settings. Additionally, while previous work strove for realism [7], our forward synthesis method focuses on speed in order to make analysis-by-synthesis tractable.

3 Overview

At the heart of our generic gaze estimator are two core contributions. In Sect. 4 we present our first contribution: a novel multi-part eye region 3DMM. We constructed this from 22 high-resolution face scans acquired from an online store[1], combined with an anatomy-based eyeball model. Our model is described by a set of parameters Φ that cover both geometric (shape, texture, and pose) and photometric (illumination and camera projection) variation.

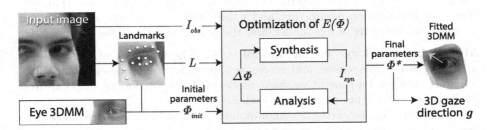

Fig. 3. An overview our fitting process: We localize landmarks L in an image, and use them to initialze our 3DMM. We then use analysis-by-synthesis to render an I_{syn} that best matches I_{obs}. We finally extract gaze g from fitted paramters Φ^*.

In Sect. 5 we present our second contribution: analysis-by-synthesis for gaze estimation (see Fig. 3). The core idea is to fit our 3DMM to an image using *analysis-by-synthesis* – given an observed image I_{obs}, we wish to produce a synthesized image I_{syn} that matches it. We then estimate gaze from the fitted eyeball pose parameters. Key in this process is our objective function $E(\Phi)$, which considers both a local dense measure of appearance similarity, as well as a holistic sparse measure of facial feature-point similarity (see Eq. 10).

4 3D Eye Region Model

Our goal is to use a 3D eye region model to synthesize an image which matches an input RGB eye image. To render synthetic views, we used a multi-part model consisting of the facial eye region and the eyeball. These were posed in a scene,

---

[1] Ten24 3D Scan Store – http://3dscanstore.com/.

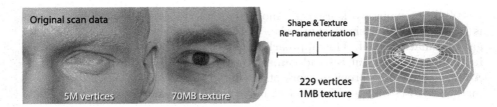

Fig. 4. We re-parameterize high-resolution 3D head scan data (left) into a more efficient lower resolution form (right). We use a carefully designed generic eye region topology [6] for consistent correspondences and realistic animation.

illuminated, and then rendered using a model of camera projection. Our total set of model and scene parameters Φ are:

$$\Phi = \{\beta, \tau, \theta, \iota, \kappa\}, \tag{1}$$

where β are the shape parameters, τ the texture parameters, θ the pose parameters, ι the illumination parameters, and κ the camera parameters. In this section we describe each part of our model, and the parameters that affect it.

Morphable facial eye region model $-\ \beta, \tau$ The first part of our model is a 3DMM of the eye region, and serves as a prior for facial appearance. While previous work used a generative shape model of the eye region [6], ours captures both shape and texture variation, allowing.

We started by acquiring 22 high-quality head scans as source data. The first stage of constructing a morphable model is bringing scan data into correspondence, so a point in one face mesh is semantically equivalent to a point in another. While previous work computed a dense point-to-point correspondence from original scan data [8,11], we compute sparse correspondences that describe 3D shape more efficiently. We manually re-parameterised each original high-resolution scamn into a low resolution topology containing the eye region only (see Fig. 4). This topology does not include the eyeball, as we wish to pose that separately to simulate its independent movement. Additionally, we maintain correspondences for detailed parts, e.g. the interior eyelid margins, which are poorly defined for previous models [11]. We uv-unwrap the mesh and represent color as a texture map, coupling our low-resolution mesh with a high-resolution texture.

Following this registration, the facial eye regions are represented as a combination of 3D shape s (n vertices) and 2D texture t (m texels), encoded as $3n$ and $3m$ dimensional vectors respectively,

$$s = [x_1, y_1, z_1, x_2, ...y_n, z_n]^T \in \mathbb{R}^{3n} \tag{2}$$

$$t = [r_1, g_1, b_1, r_2, ...g_m, b_m]^T \in \mathbb{R}^{3m} \tag{3}$$

where x_i, y_i, z_i is the 3D position of the ith vertex, and r_j, b_j, g_j is the color of the jth texel. We then performed *Principal Component Analysis* (PCA) on our set

Mean shape
$\boldsymbol{\mu}_s$

Modes of shape variation

$\boldsymbol{\mu}_s \pm 2\boldsymbol{\sigma}\boldsymbol{U}_1$ $\boldsymbol{\mu}_s \pm 2\boldsymbol{\sigma}\boldsymbol{U}_2$ $\boldsymbol{\mu}_s \pm 2\boldsymbol{\sigma}\boldsymbol{U}_3$ $\boldsymbol{\mu}_s \pm 2\boldsymbol{\sigma}\boldsymbol{U}_4$

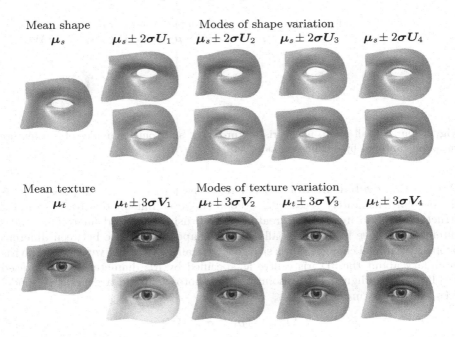

Mean texture
$\boldsymbol{\mu}_t$

Modes of texture variation

$\boldsymbol{\mu}_t \pm 3\boldsymbol{\sigma}\boldsymbol{V}_1$ $\boldsymbol{\mu}_t \pm 3\boldsymbol{\sigma}\boldsymbol{V}_2$ $\boldsymbol{\mu}_t \pm 3\boldsymbol{\sigma}\boldsymbol{V}_3$ $\boldsymbol{\mu}_t \pm 3\boldsymbol{\sigma}\boldsymbol{V}_4$

Fig. 5. The mean shape $\boldsymbol{\mu}_s$ and texture $\boldsymbol{\mu}_t$ along with the first four modes of variation. The first shape mode $\boldsymbol{U}_1$ varies between hooded and protruding eyes, and the first texture mode $\boldsymbol{V}_1$ varies between dark and light skin.

of c ordered scans to extract orthogonal shape and texture basis functions: $\boldsymbol{U} \in \mathbb{R}^{3n \times c}$ and $\boldsymbol{V} \in \mathbb{R}^{3m \times c}$. For each of the $2m$ shape and texture basis functions, we fit a Gaussian distribution to the original data. Using this we can construct linear models that describe variation in both shape $\mathcal{M}_s$ and texture $\mathcal{M}_t$,

$$\mathcal{M}_s = (\boldsymbol{\mu}_s, \boldsymbol{\sigma}_s, \boldsymbol{U}) \qquad \mathcal{M}_t = (\boldsymbol{\mu}_t, \boldsymbol{\sigma}_t, \boldsymbol{V}) \tag{4}$$

where $\boldsymbol{\mu}_s \in \mathbb{R}^{3n}$ and $\boldsymbol{\mu}_t \in \mathbb{R}^{3m}$ are the average 3D shape and 2D texture, and $\boldsymbol{\sigma}_s = [\sigma_{s1}...\sigma_{sc}]$ and $\boldsymbol{\sigma}_t = [\sigma_{t1}...\sigma_{tc}]$ describe the Gaussian distributions of each shape and texture basis function. Figure 5 shows the mean shape and texture, along with the four most important modes of variation. Facial eye region shapes $\boldsymbol{s}$ and textures $\boldsymbol{t}$ can then be generated from shape ($\beta_{face} \subset \beta$) and texture coefficients ($\tau_{face} \subset \tau$) as follows:

$$\boldsymbol{s}(\beta_{face}) = \boldsymbol{\mu}_s + \boldsymbol{U} \operatorname{diag}(\boldsymbol{\sigma}_s)\, \beta_{face} \tag{5}$$

$$\boldsymbol{t}(\tau_{face}) = \boldsymbol{\mu}_t + \boldsymbol{V} \operatorname{diag}(\boldsymbol{\sigma}_t)\, \tau_{face} \tag{6}$$

From our set of $c = 22$ scans, 90 % of shape and texture variation can be encoded in 8 shape and 7 texture coefficients. This reduction in dimensionality is important for fitting our model efficiently. Additionally, as eyelashes can provide a visual cue to gaze direction, we model them model them using a semi-transparent mesh controlled by a simple hair simulation [6].

Eyeball   Mean texture   Examples of iris variation
3D mesh $\boldsymbol{\mu}_{iris}$ $\boldsymbol{\mu}_{iris}+2\boldsymbol{\sigma}\boldsymbol{W}_1$ $\boldsymbol{\mu}_{iris}-2\boldsymbol{\sigma}\boldsymbol{W}_1$ $\boldsymbol{\mu}_{iris}+2\boldsymbol{\sigma}\boldsymbol{W}_2$

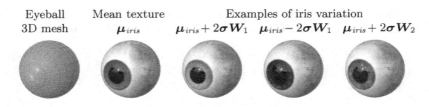

Fig. 6. Our eyeball mesh, mean iris texture $\boldsymbol{\mu}_{iris}$, and some examples of iris texture variation captured by our linear model $\mathcal{M}_{iris}$.

Parametric eyeball model $-\beta,\tau$ The second part of our multi-part model is the eyeball. Accurately recovering eyeball shape is difficult due to its complex structure [24], so instead we created a mesh using standard anatomical measurements [6] (see Fig. 6). Eyeballs vary in shape and texture between different people. We model changes in iris size geometrically, by scaling vertices on the iris boundary about the 3D iris centre as specified by iris diameter β_{iris}. We used a collection of aligned high-resolution iris photos to build a generative model $\mathcal{M}_{iris}$ of iris texture using PCA,

$$\mathcal{M}_{iris} = (\boldsymbol{\mu}_{iris}, \boldsymbol{\sigma}_{iris}, \boldsymbol{W}) \tag{7}$$

This can be used to generate new iris textures $\boldsymbol{t}_{iris}$. As the "white" of the eye is not purely white, we model variations in sclera color by multiplying the eyeball texture with a tint color $\tau_{tint} \in \mathbb{R}^3$. In reality, the eyeball has a complex layered structure with a transparent cornea covering the iris. We avoid explicitly modelling this by computing refraction effects in texture-space [6,35].

Posing our multi-part model $-\theta$ Global and local pose information is encoded by θ. Our model's parts are defined in a local coordinate system with origin at the eyeball centre, so we use model-to-world transforms $\boldsymbol{M}_{face}$ and $\boldsymbol{M}_{eye}$ to position them in a scene. The facial eye region part has degrees of freedom in translation and rotation. These are encoded as 4×4 homogenous transformation matrices $\boldsymbol{T}$ and $\boldsymbol{R}$, so model-to-world transform $\boldsymbol{M}_{face} = \boldsymbol{T}\boldsymbol{R}$. The eyball's position is anchored to the face model, but it can rotate separately through local pitch and yaw transforms $\boldsymbol{R}_x(\theta_p)$ and $\boldsymbol{R}_y(\theta_y)$, giving $\boldsymbol{M}_{eye} = \boldsymbol{T}\boldsymbol{R}_x\boldsymbol{R}_y$.

When the eye looks up or down, the eyelid follows it. Eyelid motion is modelled using procedural animation [6] – each eyelid vertex is rotated about the inter-eye-corner axis, with rotational amounts chosen to match measurements from an anatomical study [36]. As our multi-part model contains disjoint parts, we also "shrinkrwap" the eyelid skin to the eyeball, projecting eyelid vertices onto the eyeball mesh to avoid gaps and clipping issues.

Scene illumination $-\iota$ As we focus on a small region of the face, we assume a simple illumination model where lighting is distant and surface materials are purely Lambertian. Our illumination model consists of an ambient light with color $\boldsymbol{l}_{amb} \in \mathbb{R}^3$, and a directional light with color $\boldsymbol{l}_{dir} \in \mathbb{R}^3$ and 3D direction vector $\boldsymbol{L}$. We do not consider specular effects, global illumination, or self-shadowing,

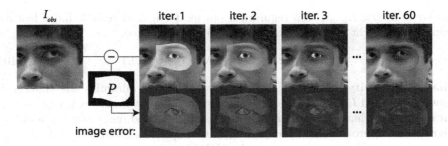

Fig. 7. We measure dense image-similarity as the mean absolute error between I_{obs} and I_{syn}, over a mask of rendered foreground pixels P (white). We ignore error for background pixels (black).

so illumination depends only on surface normal and albedo. Radiant illumination $\mathcal{L}$ at a point on the surface with normal N and albedo c is calculated as:

$$\mathcal{L}(n, c) = c\, l_{amb} + c\, l_{dir}(N \cdot L) \tag{8}$$

While this model is simple, we found it to be sufficient. If we considered a larger facial region, or fit models to both eyes at once, we would explore more advanced material or illumination models, as seen in previous work [13].

Camera projection $- \kappa$ For a complete model of image formation, we also consider camera projection. We fix our axis-aligned camera at world origin, allowing us to set our world-to-view transform as the identity I_4. We assume knowledge of intrinsic camera calibration parameters κ, and use these to build a full projection transform P. A local point in our model can then be transformed into image space using the model-view-projection transform $PM_{\{face|eye\}}$.

5 Analysis-by-synthesis for Gaze Estimation

Given an observed image I_{obs}, we wish to produce a synthesized image $I_{syn}(\Phi^*)$ that best matches it. 3D gaze direction g can then be extracted from eyeball pose parameters. We search for optimal model parameters Φ^* using *analysis-by-synthesis*. To do this, we iteratively render a synthetic image $I_{syn}(\Phi)$, compare it to I_{obs} using our energy function, and update Φ accordingly. We cast this as an unconstrained energy minimization problem for unknown Φ.

$$\Phi^* = \underset{\Phi}{\operatorname{argmin}}\ E(\Phi) \tag{9}$$

5.1 Objective Function

Our energy is formulated as a combination of a dense *image similarity metric* E_{image} that minimizes difference in image appearance, and a sparse *landmark similarity metric* E_{ldmks} that regularizes our model against reliable facial feature points, and weight λ controlling their relative importance.

$$E(\Phi) = E_{image}(\Phi) + \lambda \cdot E_{ldmks}(\Phi, L) \tag{10}$$

Image similarity metric. Our primary goal is to minimise the difference between I_{syn} and I_{obs}. This can be seen as an ideal energy function: if $I_{syn} = I_{obs}$, our model must have perfectly fit the data, so virtual and real eyeballs should be aligned. We approach this by including a dense photo-consistency term E_{image} in our energy function. However, as the 3DMM in I_{syn} does not cover the entire of I_{obs}, we split our image into two regions: a set of rendered foreground pixels P that we compute error over, and a set of background pixels that we ignore (see Fig. 7). Image similarity is then computed as the mean absolute difference between I_{syn} and I_{obs} for foreground pixels $p \in P$.

$$E_{image}(\Phi) = \frac{1}{|P|} \sum_{p \in P} |I_{syn}(\Phi, p) - I_{obs}(p)| \tag{11}$$

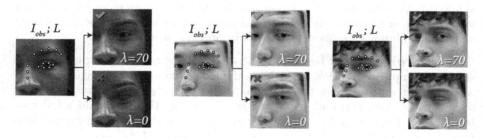

Fig. 8. I_{obs} with landmarks L (white dots), and model fits with our landmark similarity term (top), and without (bottom). Note how it prevents erroneous drift in global pose, eye region shape, and local eyelid pose.

Landmark similarity metric. The face contains important *landmark* feature points that can be localized reliably [13]. These can be used to efficiently consider the appearance of the whole face, as well as the local appearance of the eye region. We use a state-of-the-art face tracker [15] to localize 14 landmarks L around the eye region in image-space (see Fig. 8). For each landmark $l \in L$ we compute a corresponding synthesized landmark l' using our 3DMM. The sparse landmark-similarity term is calculated as the distance between both sets of landmarks, normalized by the foreground area to avoid bias from image or eye region size. This acts as a regularizer to prevent our pose θ from drifting too far from a reliable estimate.

$$E_{ldmks}(\Phi, L) = \frac{1}{|L|} \sum_{i=0}^{|L|} \|l_i - l_i'\| \tag{12}$$

5.2   Optimization Procedure

We fit our model to the subject's left eye. This is a challenging non-convex, high-dimensional optimization problem. To approach it we use gradient descent (GD) with an annealing step size. Calculating analytic derivatives for a scene as complex as our eye region is challenging due to occlusions. We therefore use numeric central derivatives ∇E to guide our optimization procedure:

$$\Phi_{i+1} = \Phi_i - \boldsymbol{t} \cdot r^i \, \nabla E(\Phi_i) \qquad \text{where} \qquad (13)$$

$$\nabla E(\Phi_i) = \left(\frac{\partial E}{\phi_1} \dots \frac{\partial E}{\phi_{|\Phi|}} \right) \quad \text{and} \quad \frac{\partial E}{\phi_j} = \frac{E(\Phi_i + h_j) - E(\Phi_i - h_j)}{2h_j} \qquad (14)$$

where $\boldsymbol{t} = [t_1 ... t_{|\Phi|}]$ are per-parameter step-sizes, $\boldsymbol{h} = [h_1 ... h_{|\Phi|}]$ are per-parameter numerical values, and r the annealing rate. $\boldsymbol{t}$ and $\boldsymbol{h}$ were calibrated through experimentation. We explored alternate optimization techniques including LBFGS [37], and rprop [38] and momentum variants of GD, but we found these to be less stable, perhaps due to our use of numerical rather than analytical derivatives. Computing our gradients is expensive, requiring rendering and differencing two images per parameter. Their efficient computation is possible with our tailored GPU DirectX rasterizer that can render I_{syn} at over 5000fps.

Initialization. As we perform local optimization, we require an initial model configuration to start from. We use 3D eye corner landmarks and head rotation from the face tracker [15] to initialize $\boldsymbol{T}$ and $\boldsymbol{R}$. We then use 2D iris landmarks

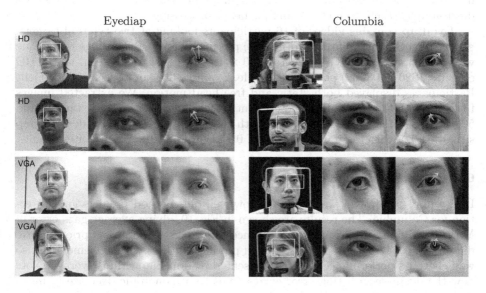

Fig. 9. Example model fits on gaze datasets Eyediap [39] (HD and VGA) and Columbia [40], showing estimated gaze (yellow) and labelled gaze (blue).

and a single sphere eyeball model to initialize gaze [2]. β and τ are initialized to **0**, and illumination l_{amb} and l_{dir} are set to $[0.8, 0.8, 0.8]$.

Runtime. Figure 7 shows convergence for a typical input image, with I_{obs} size 800×533px, and I_{syn} size 125×87px. We converge after 60 iterations for 39 parameters, taking 3.69 s on a typical PC (3.3Ghz CPU, GTX 660 GPU).

5.3   Extracting Gaze Direction

Our task is estimating 3D gaze direction g in camera-space. Once our fitting procedure has converged, g can be extracted by applying the eyeball model transform to a vector pointing along the optical axis in model-space: $g = M_{eye} [0, 0, -1]^T$.

6   Experiments

We evaluated our approach on two publicly available eye gaze datasets: Columbia [40] and Eyediap [39]. We chose these datasets as they show the full face, as required for our facial-landmark based initialization.

Columbia contains of images of 56 people looking at a target grid on the wall. The participants were constrained by a head-clamp device, and images were taken from five different head orientations (from $-30°$ to $30°$). Example fits can be seen in Fig. 9 right. In our experiments we used a subset of 34 people (excluding those with eyeglasses) with 20 images per person, resulting in 680 images. As the images were taken by a high quality camera (5184×3456px), we downsampled them to 800×533px for faster processing.

Eyediap contains videos of 16 participants looking at two types of targets: *screen* targets on a monitor; and *floating* physical targets. Recordings were made with two cameras: a VGA camera (640×480px) below the screen, and a HD camera (1920×1080px) placed to the side. Example fits can be seen in Fig. 9 left. Participants displayed both static and free head motion. We extracted images from the VGA videos for our experiment – 622 images with screen targets and 500 images with floating targets. In both cases we used a gradient descent step size of 0.0025 with an annealing rate of 0.95 that started after 10th iteration.

6.1   Gaze Estimation

In the first experiment we evaluated how well our method predicts gaze direction for Columbia. The results are shown in Fig. 10, giving average gaze error of $M = 8.87°, Mdn = 7.54°$ after convergence. As we do not impose a prior on predicted gaze distribution, our system can produce outliers with extreme error, so we believe its performance is best represented by a median (Mdn) average. Note how the decrease in fitting error corresponds to a monotonic decrease in mean and median gaze errors. Furthermore, our approach outperformes the geometric approach used to initialize it [2], a recently proposed k-Nearest-Neighbour

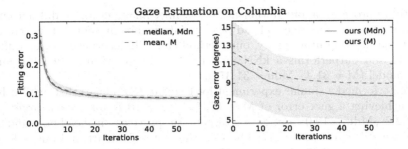

Fig. 10. Fitting error (left) and gaze estimation error (right). Note how gaze error improves from the initial estimate. Filled regions show inter-quartile range.

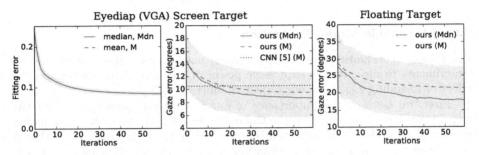

Fig. 11. Fitting (blue) and gaze estimation (red) error on Eyediap (VGA). We outperform a state-of-the-art CNN [5]. Additionally, the CNN was not able to generalize to the floating target condition, while ours can. (Color figure online)

approach [6] ($M = 19.9°, Mdn = 19.5°$) and a naïve model that always predicts forwards gaze ($M = 12.00°, Mdn = 11.17°$).

The results for Eyediap VGA images can be seen in Fig. 11. As before the decrease in pixel error corresponds in the decrease in gaze errors. Furthermore, our final gaze estimation error on the Eyediap *screen* condition ($M = 9.44°, Mdn = 8.63°$) outperfoms that reported in literature previously ($p < .0001$, independent t-test) – $10.5°$ using a Convolutional Neural Network [5]. See Table 1 for other comparisons. We also outperform the initialization model, a kNN model ($M = 21.49°, Mdn = 20.93°$), and a naïve model ($M = 12.62°, Mdn = 12.79°$). The results for floating targets are less accurate

Table 1. We outperform state-of-the-art cross-dataset methods trained on UT [27] and synthetic data [6]: CNN [5], Random Forests (RF) [27], kNN [5], Adaptive Linear Regression (ALR) [33], and Support Vector Regression (SVR) [26].

	ours	CNN	RF	kNN	ALR	SVR	synth
Gaze error ($M°$)	**9.44**	10.5	12.0	12.2	12.7	15.1	19.9

but still improve upon our initialisation baseline. Zhang et al. [5] did not evaluate on floating targets due to head pose variations not present in their training set. Despite a drop in accuracy, our method can still generalize to this difficult scenario and outperforms a kNN model (M = 30.85°, Mdn = 28.92°), and a naïve model (M = 31.4°, Mdn = 31.37°).

We performed a similar experiment for Eyediap HD images that exhibit head pose, achieving a gaze error of M = 11.0°, Mdn = 10.4° for screen targets and M = 22.2°, Mdn = 19.0° for floating targets. Despite extreme head pose and gaze range, we still perform comparably with the state-of-the-art and outperform a kNN model (M = 29.39°, Mdn = 28.62° for screen, and M = 34.6°, Mdn = 33.19° for floating target), and a naïve model (M = 22.67°, Mdn = 22.06° for screen, and M = 35.08°, Mdn = 34.35° for floating target).

6.2   Morphable Model Evaluation

In addition to evaluating our system's gaze estimation capabilities, we performed experiments to measure the expressive power of our morphable model and the effect of including E_{ldmks} in our objective function.

First, we assessed the importance of our facial point similarity weight (λ) to gaze estimation accuracy on the Columbia dataset. We used the same fitting strategy, but varied λ. Results can be seen in Fig. 12 (right). It is clear that λ has a positive impact on gaze estimation accuracy, by not allowing fits to drift too far from the reliable estimates and by reducing the variance of the error.

Second, we wanted to see if modelling more degrees of shape and appearance variation led to better image fitting and gaze estimation. We therefore varied the number of shape (β) and texture (τ) principal components (PCs) that our model was allowed to use during fitting on Columbia. We varied both the texture and shape PCs together, using the same number for both. As seen in Fig. 12 (left), more PCs lead to better image fitting error, as I_{syn} matches I_{obs} better when allowed more variation. A similar downward trend can be seen for gaze error,

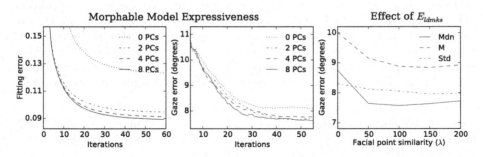

Fig. 12. As we include more shape and texture and shape principal components (PCs) in the facial morphable model, both fitting and gaze error decrease. Also note the effect of our landmark regularization term λ which decreases the error (and its standard deviation) by not allowing the fit to drift.

suggesting better modelling of nearby facial shape and texture is important for correctly aligning the eyeball model, and thus determining gaze direction.

7 Conclusion

We presented the first multi-part 3D morphable model of the eye region. It includes a separate eyeball model, allowing us to capture gaze – a facial expression not captured by previous systems [13,14]. We then presented a novel approach for gaze estimation: fitting our model to an image with analysis-by-synthesis, and extracting the gaze direction from fitted parameters. Our method is the first to jointly optimize a dense image metric, a sparse feature metric, and a generative 3D model together for gaze estimation. It generalizes to different quality images and wide gaze ranges, and out-performs a state-of-the-art CNN method [5].

Limitations still remain. While other gaze estimation systems can operate in real time [2,5], ours takes several seconds per image. However, previous analysis-by-synthesis systems have been made real time through careful engineering [41]; we believe this is possible for our method too. Our method can also become trapped in local minima (see Fig. 8). To avoid this and improve robustness, we plan to fit both eyes simultaneously in future work.

References

1. Kleinke, C.L.: Gaze and eye contact: a research review. Psychol. Bull. **100**(1), 78–100 (1986)
2. Baltrušaitis, T., Robinson, P., Morency, L.P.: Openface: an open source facial behavior analysis toolkit. In: IEEE WACV (2016)
3. Hansen, D.W., Ji, Q.: In the eye of the beholder: a survey of models for eyes and gaze. IEEE TPAMI **32**, 478–500 (2010)
4. Majaranta, P., Bulling, A.: Eye tracking and eye-based human-computer interaction. In: Fairclough, S.H., Gilleade, K. (eds.) Advances in Physiological Computing, pp. 39–65. Springer, New York (2014)
5. Zhang, X., Sugano, Y., Fritz, M., Bulling, A.: Appearance-based gaze estimation in the wild. In: Proceedings of the IEEE Conference on Computer Vision and Pattern Recognition, pp. 4511–4520 (2015)
6. Wood, E., Baltrušaitis, T., Morency, L.P., Robinson, P., Bulling, A.: Learning an appearance-based gaze estimator from one million synthesised images. In: Proceedings of the ETRA (2016)
7. Wood, E., Baltrušaitis, T., Zhang, X., Sugano, Y., Robinson, P., Bulling, A.: Rendering of eyes for eye-shape registration and gaze estimation. In: ICCV (2015)
8. Blanz, V., Vetter, T.: A morphable model for the synthesis of 3d faces. In: Conference on Computer Graphics and Interactive Techniques, ACM (1999)
9. Romdhani, S., Vetter, T.: Estimating 3d shape and texture using pixel intensity, edges, specular highlights, texture constraints and a prior. In: Proceedings CVPR 2005, vol. 2, pp. 986–993. IEEE (2005)
10. Aldrian, O., Smith, W.A.: Inverse rendering of faces with a 3d morphable model. IEEE Trans. Pattern Anal. Mach. Intell. **35**(5), 1080–1093 (2013)

11. Paysan, P., Knothe, R., Amberg, B., Romdhani, S., Vetter, T.: A 3d face model for pose and illumination invariant face recognition. In: Proceedings of the AVSS (2009)
12. Yi, D., Lei, Z., Li, S.: Towards pose robust face recognition. In: Proceedings of the IEEE Conference on Computer Vision and Pattern Recognition, pp. 13539–3545 (2013)
13. Thies, J., Zollhöfer, M., Nießner, M., Valgaerts, L., Stamminger, M., Theobalt, C.: Real-time expression transfer for facial reenactment. ACM TOG **32**, 40 (2015)
14. Cao, C., Weng, Y., Lin, S., Zhou, K.: 3d shape regression for real-time facial animation. ACM TOG (2013)
15. Baltrušaitis, T., Morency, L.P., Robinson, P.: Constrained local neural fields for robust facial landmark detection in the wild. In: IEEE ICCVW (2013)
16. Cootes, T.F., Edwards, G.J., Taylor, C.J., et al.: Active appearance models. IEEE Trans. Pattern Anal. Mach. Intell. **23**(6), 681–685 (2001)
17. Khamis, S., Taylor, J., Shotton, J., Keskin, C., Izadi, S., Fitzgibbon, A.: Learning an efficient model of hand shape variation from depth images. In: Proceedings of the IEEE Conference on Computer Vision and Pattern Recognition, pp. 2540–2548 (2015)
18. Anguelov, D., Srinivasan, P., Koller, D., Thrun, S., Rodgers, J., Davis, J.: Scape: shape completion and animation of people. ACM Trans. Graph. (TOG) **24**, 408–416 (2005). ACM
19. Hasler, N., Stoll, C., Sunkel, M., Rosenhahn, B., Seidel, H.P.: A statistical model of human pose and body shape. In: Computer Graphics Forum, vol. 28, pp. 337–346. Wiley Online Library (2009)
20. Booth, J., Roussos, A., Zafeiriou, S., Ponniah, A., Dunaway, D.: A 3d morphable model learnt from 10,000 faces. In: Proceedings of the CVPR 2016 (2016)
21. Vlasic, D., Brand, M., Pfister, H., Popović, J.: Face transfer with multilinear models. ACM Trans. Graph. (TOG) **24**, 426–433 (2005). ACM
22. Cao, C., Weng, Y., Zhou, S., Tong, Y., Zhou, K.: Facewarehouse: a 3d facial expression database for visual computing. TVGC **20**(3), 413–425 (2014)
23. Bérard, P., Bradley, D., Gross, M., Beeler, T.: Lightweight eye capture using a parametric model. ACM Trans. Graph. (TOG) **35**(4), 117 (2016)
24. Bérard, P., Bradley, D., Nitti, M., Beeler, T., Gross, M.: Highquality capture of eyes. ACM Trans. Graph. **33**, 1–12 (2014)
25. Ferhat, O., Vilarino, F.: Low cost eye tracking: the current panorama. J. Comput. Intell. Neurosci. **22**(23), 24
26. Schneider, T., Schauerte, B., Stiefelhagen, R.: Manifold alignment for person independent appearance-based gaze estimation. In: 2014 22nd International Conference on Pattern Recognition (ICPR), pp. 1167–1172. IEEE (2014)
27. Sugano, Y., Matsushita, Y., Sato, Y.: Learning-by-synthesis for appearance-based 3d gaze estimation. In: Proceedings of the IEEE Conference on Computer Vision and Pattern Recognition, pp. 1821–1828 (2014)
28. Sesma, L., Villanueva, A., Cabeza, R.: Evaluation of pupil center-eye corner vector for gaze estimation using a web cam. In: Proceedings of the Symposium on Eye Tracking Research and Applications, pp. 217–220. ACM (2012)
29. Torricelli, D., Conforto, S., Schmid, M., DAlessio, A.: A neural-based remote eye-gaze tracker under natural head motion. Comput. Methods Programs Inbiomed. **92**(1), 66–78 (2008)
30. Wood, E., Bulling, A.: Eyetab: Model-based gaze estimation on unmodified tablet computers. In: Proceedings of the Symposium on Eye Tracking Research and Applications, pp. 207–210. ACM (2014)

31. Wang, J., Sung, E., Venkateswarlu, R.: Eye gaze estimation from a single image of one eye. In: Ninth IEEE International Conference on Computer Vision, 2003, Proceedings, pp. 136–143. IEEE (2003)

32. Wu, H., Chen, Q., Wada, T.: Conic-based algorithm for visual line estimation from one image. In: Sixth IEEE International Conference on Automatic Face and Gesture Recognition, 2004, Proceedings, pp. 260–265. IEEE (2004)

33. Lu, F., Sugano, Y., Okabe, T., Sato, Y.: Adaptive linear regression for appearance-based gaze estimation. IEEE Trans. Pattern Anal. Mach. Intell. **36**(10), 2033–2046 (2014)

34. Mora, K., Odobez, J.M.: Geometric generative gaze estimation (g3e) for remote rgb-d cameras. In: Proceedings of the IEEE Conference on Computer Vision and Pattern Recognition, pp. 1773–1780 (2014)

35. Jimenez, J., Danvoye, E., von der Pahlen, J.: Photorealistic eyes rendering. In: SIGGRAPH Talks, Advances in Real-Time Rendering, ACM (2012)

36. Malbouisson, J.M., e Cruz, A.A.V., Messias, A., Leite, L.V., Rios, G.D.: Upper and lower eyelid saccades describe a harmonic oscillator function. Invest. Ophthalmol. Vis. Sci. **46**(3), 857–862 (2005)

37. Liu, D.C., Nocedal, J.: On the limited memory bfgs method for large scale optimization. Math. Program. **45**(1–3), 503–528 (1989)

38. Riedmiller, M., Braun, H.: Rprop-a fast adaptive learning algorithm. In: Proceedings of ISCIS VII), Universitat, Citeseer (1992)

39. Funes Mora, K.A., Monay, F., Odobez, J.M.: EYEDIAP: a database for the development and evaluation of gaze estimation algorithms from RGB and RGB-D cameras. In: Proceedings of the ETRA (2014)

40. Smith, B., Yin, Q., Feiner, S., Nayar, S.: Gaze locking: passive eye contactdetection for humanobject interaction. In: ACM Symposium on User InterfaceSoftware and Technology (UIST), pp. 271–280, Oct 2013

41. Thies, J., Zollhöfer, M., Stamminger, M., Theobalt, C., Nießner, M.: Face2face: real-time face capture and reenactment of rgb videos. In: Proceedings of the Computer Vision and Pattern Recognition (CVPR), p. 1. IEEE (2016)

Foreground Segmentation via Dynamic Tree-Structured Sparse RPCA

Salehe Erfanian Ebadi[✉] and Ebroul Izquierdo

School of Electronic Engineering and Computer Science,
Queen Mary University of London, London, UK
{s.erfanianebadi,e.izquierdo}@qmul.ac.uk

Abstract. Video analysis often begins with background subtraction which consists of creation of a background model, followed by a regularization scheme. Recent evaluation of representative background subtraction techniques demonstrated that there are still considerable challenges facing these methods. We present a new method in which we regard the image sequence as being made up of the sum of a low-rank background matrix and a dynamic tree-structured sparse outlier matrix and solve the decomposition using our approximated Robust Principal Component Analysis method extended to handle camera motion. Our contribution lies in dynamically estimating the support of the foreground regions via a superpixel generation step, so as to impose spatial coherence on these regions, and to obtain crisp and meaningful foreground regions. These advantages enable our method to outperform state-of-the-art alternatives in three benchmark datasets.

1 Introduction

Foreground segmentation plays a critical role in applications such as automated surveillance, action recognition, and motion analysis. Despite the efforts in this field, recent evaluation of state-of-the-art techniques [1,2] showed that there are still shortcomings in addressing all challenges in foreground segmentation. Addressing these challenges, leads to a number of considerations in designing a background model, as well as expected behavior from foreground objects, which in complex real-life applications remains an open problem. The background model can undergo sudden or gradual *illumination changes*, as well as *background motions* such as trees swaying or water rippling in a lake. In addition, *global motion* caused by camera movement or jitter can affect detection of genuine foreground objects. *Noise* is another problematic factor which is interleaved with challenges of *camouflage*. In most cases noise can increase the range of values considered to belong to the background, allowing camouflaged objects to remain undetected. A desirable background model must be able to learn a variety of modes from the video feed, such that it handles variations in the background, *moved objects*, and noise without compromising its ability to detect camouflaged regions.

© Springer International Publishing AG 2016
B. Leibe et al. (Eds.): ECCV 2016, Part I, LNCS 9905, pp. 314–329, 2016.
DOI: 10.1007/978-3-319-46448-0_19

In this paper, we handle all these challenges using an approximated *Robust Principal Component Analysis* (RPCA) based method for background modeling. Given a data matrix containing the frames of a video sequence stacked as its columns, $A \in \mathbb{R}^{m \times n}$, RPCA [3] solves the matrix decomposition problem

$$\min_{L,S} \|L\|_* + \lambda \|S\|_1 \quad s.t. \quad A = L + S, \tag{1}$$

as a surrogate for the actual problem

$$\min_{L,S} rank(L) + \lambda \|S\|_0 \quad s.t. \quad A = L + S, \tag{2}$$

where L is the low-rank component corresponding to the background and S is the sparse component containing the foreground outliers. We are interested in a case where we can decompose the matrix A into three components, namely a low-rank part L that can describe the background of the sequence, along with adaptivity to changes introduced to it, a sparse component S containing only the genuine deforming foreground regions, and a noise component E that collectively contains residual error, noise, and ambiguous pixels:

$$A = L + S + E, \tag{3}$$

meaning that the model does not seek the exact solution of decomposing a scene into background and foreground, but rather the approximate solution $A \approx L + S$ [4–7] whereby the residual error E will have the desired properties described above. λ is a tuning parameter ensuring no genuine foreground regions will be missed. This formulation is still inadequate and we need to introduce some necessary steps to lead to substantially better results.

Background modeling by the low-rank approximation has a number of benefits: firstly, that a robust estimation of the mostly static regions of the image is guaranteed; secondly, that this approximation can in part handle the variations in illumination in the background, such as a tree swaying backwards and forward, or water rippling in a lake, traffic light changes that can be modeled by a few modes, or billboards in a street displaying a few images on repeat during a day. Thirdly, a low-rank approximation of the background can help distinguish between general motion in the scene – which can be due to camera movement – and local varying motions caused by moving objects even in the case of large objects such as a huge truck moving across the scene; since the background regions obey a single highly correlated motion pattern.

Despite the promising effects of using a low-rank approximation for obtaining the background model, a sparse constraint for foreground objects, is far too limited. The foreground regions are usually spatially coherent clusters. Thus, we prefer to detect contiguous regions of various sizes, and then lots of zero entries (regions) in the sparse matrix. With this objective in mind, we propose structured-sparsity inducing norms in the context of a novel dynamic group structure, by which the natural structure of foreground objects in the sparse matrix is preserved. The dynamicity of group structures is derived from the natural shape of objects in the scene, by selecting clusters of pixels via the SLIC superpixels [8], and dynamically refining the size of these clusters in an iterative process. This proposition, has been proven to be successful in reducing the *foreground aperture* and *camouflage* problems in our experiments.

Because we solve an approximated RPCA problem, it is important to drive the algorithm by means of a knowledge of salient regions and the distribution of outliers, so that the algorithm converges to the correct solution. However, knowledge of the object of interest before even segmenting it seems to make the problem as one of the many chicken-egg problems in computer vision, as we usually need to segment the scene to recognize the objects in it. So, to identify an object and its probable size and location even before segmenting it, we use an intuitive *tandem* initialization step by which the background is encouraged to lean towards the best low-rank approximation of the static parts in the scene, and the sparse part is initialized to take on high probability values for regions of the scene where they exhibit highest statistical *leverage* scores.

In a nutshell contributions of this paper are: inducing structured-sparsity in a novel group structure, namely a dynamic superpixel structure; insensitivity to foreground object size, as a result of using within-patch normalized regularization; assumption of a noise part for discarding false positive pixels (false alarms); low-rank approximation of background to accommodate illumination and small scene changes; a *tandem* algorithm for removal of unwanted ghosting effects that persist in most background subtraction techniques, and targets the unascertained prior knowledge of distribution of outliers; and an exhaustive evaluation using three datasets [9–11] demonstrates top performance in comparison with the state-of-the-art alternatives.

2   Related Work

In the recent years, global models such as principal component analysis (PCA) [3], have gained some popularity due to their computational simplicity and effectiveness in camera shake. However, in those early models the spatial distribution of outliers was not considered. In an effort to incorporate such prior an MRF-based solution [12] has been proposed. But the result of imposing such smoothness constraint is that the foreground regions tend to be over-smoothed; as an example, the details in the silhouette of hands and legs of a moving person is sacrificed in favor of a more compact blob. Our idea is established in the so-called structured-sparsity or group-sparsity measures to incorporate the spatial prior. Structural information about nonzero patterns of variables have been developed and used in sparse signal recovery, and many approaches have been applied to these problems successfully [13]. However, the majority of related methods such as [14] typically assume that the block structure and its location is known or will suffer in *regularization, bootstrapping*, or *foreground aperture*. To lift up some of the difficulties the sparsity structure is estimated automatically in [13], however parameter tuning is required to control the balance between the sparsity prior and the group clustering prior for different cases. The authors of [14] used a two-pass RPCA framework, in which the first pass generates a saliency map that corresponds to locations of the outliers, and then the second pass uses pre-defined salient blocks in the image, to favor spatially contiguous outliers. In another effort [15] used a group sparse structure, in which overlapping pre-defined groups of pixels in a region of an image are used in conjunction with a maximum norm regularization to take into account the spatial connection of foreground regions. In a recent work [16] a superpixel-based max-norm matrix decomposition approach has been proposed, in which homogeneous static or dynamic regions of image are classified as a graph partitioning problem, via Generalized Fused Lasso. In contrast to all the above, our method does not assume a prior size or location or structure for sparsity, and dynamically updates these to best fit the natural object shape in the scene, without a separate training phase or the need for a clean background for background training. In the next section, we introduce our dynamic tree-structured sparsity-inducing norms that leads to substantially better results than other RPCA based methods [4–7] and other state-of-the-art alternatives.

3   Our Algorithm

3.1   Approximated RPCA via Structured-Sparsity Inducing Norms

We propose sparsity-inducing norms that can incorporate prior structures on the support of the errors such as spatial continuity. We essentially consider a special case to the following problem

$$\min_{rank(L)\leq r,S,\tau} \|A \circ \tau - L - S\|_F + \lambda\psi(S) \quad s.t. \quad A \circ \tau = L + S + E, \quad (4)$$

where $\|L\|_F$ is the Frobenius norm of matrix L, defined as $\|L\|_F = \sqrt{\sum_{i,j} L_{ij}^2}$, and λ set at a value that ensures no genuine foreground regions will be missed. We strictly have $rank(L) \leq r < rank(A)$. E is a matrix containing the residual error of the approximation of A by $L + S$. The entries of this matrix can be very large in magnitude, but random and scattered, exhibiting noise-like behavior, and showing no structured shape in the sparsity domain. Therefore, they should neither remain in the foreground as they will trigger many false positives and pollute the foreground model, nor be able to get absorbed into the background model; and the robust low-rank approximation will already ensure the latter case. Most background subtraction methods suffer from this kind of contamination polluting their foreground model, and consequently resort to a final thresholding step or post-processing once the foreground support is calculated. The choice of λ is justified by observations in our experiments, where λ controls a good trade-off between the sparsity of $S + E$ and structured-sparsity of S. We have assumed that the images in matrix $A \circ \tau$ are well aligned, where τ stands for some transformation in the image domain (e.g., 2D affine transformation for correcting misalignment, or 2D projective transformation for handling some perspective change).

The regularizer $\psi(\cdot)$ on S is chosen to be $\|S\|_{2,1}$. $\ell_{2,1}$-norm is a group sparsity inducing norm defined as the ℓ_1-norm of the vector formed by taking the ℓ_2-norm of a matrix. Clearly, the ℓ_1-norm regularization treats each entry (pixel) in S independently. It does not take into account any specific structures or possible relations among subsets of the entries. While in background subtraction scenarios, outliers (objects in the scene) normally have the structural properties of spatial contiguity and locality. Hence, our choice of $\ell_{2,1}$-norm assures selecting the discriminative input features shared across multiple binary predictors.

To induce more diverse and sophisticated sparse error patterns, we consider structured sparsity-inducing norms that involve overlapping groups of variables, motivated by recent advances in structured sparsity [17]. Although it still assumes pre-defined group structures, the overlapping patterns of groups and norms associated with the groups of variables allow to encode much richer classes of structured sparsity. In this work, we consider a tree-structured sparsity-inducing norm. It involves a hierarchical partition of the m variables in S into groups, as shown in Fig. 1(a). The tree is defined in a way that leaf nodes are singleton groups corresponding to individual pixels, and internal nodes/groups correspond to local patches of varying size. Thus each parent node contains a hierarchy of child nodes that are spatially adjacent to each other and constitute a local part in the sparse image S. As illustrated in Fig. 1(a) in the grayed-out regions, when a parent node goes to zero all its descendants in the tree must go to zero. Consequently, the nonzero or support patterns are formed by removing those nodes forced to zero. This is exactly the desired effect of structured error patterns of spatial locality and contiguity.

We can represent a scene using a tree structure by subdivision. In such a tree structure each child node is a subset of its parent node and the nodes of the same depth level do not overlap. Denote $\mathcal{G}$ as a set of groups from the power set of the index set $\{1, \ldots, m\}$, with each group $G \in \mathcal{G}$ containing a subset of these indices. The aforementioned tree-structured groups used in this paper are formally defined as follows: A set of groups $\mathcal{G}$ is said to be *tree-structured* in $\{1, \ldots, m\}$ if $\mathcal{G} = \{\ldots, G_1^i, G_2^i, \ldots, G_{b_i}^i, \ldots\}$ where $i = 0, 1, 2, \ldots, d$, d is the depth of the tree, $b_0 = 1$ and $G_1^0 = \{1, 2, \ldots, m\}$, $b_d = m$ and correspondingly $\{G_j^d\}_{j=1}^m$ are singleton groups. Let G_j^i be the parent node of a node $G_{j'}^{i+1}$ in the tree, we have $G_{j'}^{i+1} \subseteq G_j^i$. We also have $G_j^i \cap G_k^i = \emptyset, \forall i = 1, \ldots, d, j \neq k, 1 \leq j, k \leq b_i$. Similar group structures are also considered in [17]. With the above notation, a general tree-structured sparsity-inducing norm can be written as

$$\psi(S) = \sum_{i=0}^{d} \sum_{j=1}^{b_i} w_j^i \|S_{G_j^i}\|_{2,1}, \tag{5}$$

where $S_{G_j^i}$ is a vector with entries equal to those of S for the indices in G_j^i and 0 otherwise. w_j^i are positive weights for groups G_j^i. It is chosen as $w_j^i = 1/max(A_{G_j^i})$ to overcome sensitivity of the regularization scheme to illumination variance across patches. This within patch normalized regularization is crucial. As we will explain later, using the same regularizing parameter for all the patches

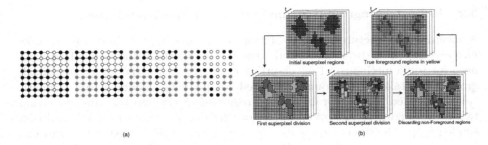

Fig. 1. (a) Tree-structured groups in sparsity induction, division, and discarding procedure. (b) same procedure in superpixel regions where the size and location of groups are not known and change from one frame to next. Grayed-out regions in (a) and (b) are the result of discarding process that is immediately performed on groups that are foreground-absent; thus, saving computation time as they are not processed ever after.

in the scene will usually favor the most prominent features (in this case the illumination variations with largest magnitude). By normalizing each patch with a weight associated with the highest color variation in that patch, this issue is largely subsided; and as such the *camouflaged* objects will have a higher chance of being detected. For the $\ell_{2,1}$-norm, it is the maximum value of pixels in a group that decides if the group is set to nonzero or not, and it does encourage the rest of the pixels to take arbitrary (hence close to maximum) values. Thus, the objective function in the optimization program (3) is modified to the following

$$\min_{rank(L)\leq r,S,\tau} \|A \circ \tau - L - S\|_F + \lambda \sum_{i=0}^{d} \sum_{j=1}^{b_i} w_j^i \|S_{G_j^i}\|_{2,1} \quad s.t. \quad A \circ \tau = L + S + E$$

$$(6)$$

To solve (6) we use an alternating minimization procedure. This kind of iterative linearization has a long history in gradient algorithms. We first find a good initialization for τ by pre-aligning all frames in the sequences to the middle frame, before the main loops of minimization. Then the linearization of τ is done by the robust multiresolution method proposed in [6,7]. We then proceed by minimizing the function for two parameters L and S one at a time until the solution reaches convergence; that means solving two reduced problems, each being minimized independently form one another

$$L^t = \arg\min_{rank(L)\leq r} \|A \circ \tau - L - S^{t-1}\|_F^2$$

$$(7)$$

$$S^t = \arg\min_{S} \|A \circ \tau - L^t - S\|_F^2 + \lambda \sum_{i=0}^{d} \sum_{j=1}^{b_i} w_j^i \|S_{G_j^i}\|_{2,1}$$

$$(8)$$

3.2   Robust Foreground Segmentation via Structured Sparsity

A meaningful structured-sparse solution, is the one that is best able to take into account the natural shape and structure of objects in the scene. There is a need for some mechanism that describes each tree-structured group $\psi(\cdot)$. Each group must take into account connected components belonging to a semantically connected region. For example, a region of pixels with the same color and texture belonging to part of an object (a wheel of a car) must be assigned to a single group. The structured sparse inducing framework defined in the previous section can then be used within the group class to decide whether it belongs to foreground or must be classified as background.

As mentioned before, most block-structured sparse solutions have two limitations. Firstly, the size and location of the blocks need to be set in advance. Secondly, it is hard to see how each block is adapting its shape to the natural structure of objects in the scene. Motivated by these limitations, we propose a new group structure, in which the structure of sparse part is the same as the natural object structure in the scene. In a test image, the scene can be classified into multiple *superpixels*. A good superpixel must obtain perceptually meaningful atomic regions, which can be used to replace the rigid structure of the pixel grid. Moreover, as these results will be used as a pre-processing step in our foreground detection framework, they should be fast to compute, memory efficient, and simple to use. Also, in our segmentation scenario, superpixels should both increase the speed and improve the quality of the results.

We therefore, adopt the *simple linear iterative clustering* (SLIC) algorithm based on the empirical comparison of six state-of-the-art superpixel methods [8]. SLIC adapts k-means clustering to generate superpixels, and is freely available[1]. By default, the only parameters of the algorithm are the desired number of approximately equally-sized superpixels ξ and compactness factor φ controlling adherence of each superpixel region to object boundaries. For our test images, $\xi = 800$ and $\varphi = 20$ are sufficient to adhere well to all object boundaries.

Once the superpixels are obtained, the structured sparsity inducing norms are applied to groups, that are now each superpixel region in the test image. Figure 1(b) shows an example of this procedure. We have adapted SLIC to be able to dynamically divide each superpixel region into approximately equal-sized smaller superpixels that best adhere to object boundaries. If a small superpixel region does not contain any foreground, it is discarded as background immediately and no further processing is performed for this region. If otherwise a region hints presence of foreground, it is divided into several smaller superpixels again. The same process is performed for these smaller regions, and the resulting regions containing foreground are once again divided and put to test. Our experiments have shown that at this depth the classification can be performed without having to perform any further divisions, as the regions are both small enough to safely discard non-foreground regions, and large enough to crisply classify all foreground objects in the scene with fine details correctly. We denote this procedure as sparsity *induction, division* and *discarding*. Thus, in the

---

[1] http://ivrl.epfl.ch/research/superpixels.

general tree-structured sparsity-inducing norm (5) depth of each tree is $d = 3$ and $m = \mathcal{M}$ is dynamically decided by SLIC, since it depends on the natural shape of the objects in the scene. Therefore $\mathcal{G} = \{\ldots, G_1^i, G_2^i, \ldots, G_{b_i}^i, \ldots\}$ where $i = \{0, 1, 2, 3\}$, $b_0 = 1$ and $G_1^0 = \{1, 2, \ldots, \mathcal{M}\}$, $b_d = \mathcal{M}$ and correspondingly $\{G_j^d\}_{j=1}^{\mathcal{M}}$ are the smallest superpixel groups.

3.3   Tandem Initialization for Removing Ghosting Effects

In this section we propose the *tandem* approximated RPCA where just like a tandem bicycle the front drive is supported by the back pedaling power. This proposition involves an initialization step before the actual optimization takes place. It is different from algorithms that require a two-pass optimization [14], where the optimization is twice performed to refine results. This is rather expensive in an RPCA framework; instead, we strategically initialize the variables such that we gain even better results. This modification will introduce a prior knowledge of the spatial distribution of the outliers to the model. The direct impact of this modification to the RPCA algorithm is faster convergence. The indirect impact is how it alleviates a persisting problem in background subtraction algorithms, called *"ghosting"* effect. The *ghosts* are either parts of the foreground object that remain in the background model, or parts of the background that leak into the foreground. The main reasons causing these artifacts are: an object moving slowly, or remaining inactive for some period of time, and when the foreground object obscures part of the background during the training period. With current RPCA-based optimizations the ghosts usually persist during the iterative process; this can be seen in Fig. 2. The optimization problems described in Sects. 3.1 and 3.2 are solved by iterative procedures that need to be initialized using starting values of the matrices L, S, and τ. The iterative process is started with a standard (naïve) initialization of $L^0 = A$, $S^0 = 0$, and $\tau^0 = 0$. The rank-r matrix that is the nearest to the matrix A is a low-rank matrix that gives a good first approximation for the static part of the sequence but some parts of the moving objects remain in this rank-r matrix. Hence we propose to construct a matrix S^0 whose columns contain only the more salient part of the difference between A and L^0, where L^0 is the rank-r matrix approximation of the matrix A. This difference matrix $S = A - L^0$ will contain a sketch of the moving objects in the scene, and therefore is a good initial approximation that contributes to the nonuniformity of the structure of the matrix. We adopt the statistical *leverage* scores to measure the importance of the columns of the difference matrix. These scores can be regarded as a pseudo-motion saliency map.

Let the i-th column of the matrix to be a linear combination of the orthonormal basis given by the left singular vectors of the matrix $\mathcal{S}^i = \sum_{r=1}^{rank} \sigma_r U_r V_r^i$, $i = 1, \ldots, \eta$ where U_r is the r-th left singular vector, V_r^i is the i-th coordinate of the r-th right singular vector, and $rank$ is the rank of the matrix S. As the matrices $\mathcal{S}_j$ are approximations of the frames containing the moving objects, they can be considered as approximations to low-rank matrices. One can assume

$$\mathcal{S}_j^i \approx \sum_{r=1}^{\rho} \sigma_r U_r V_r^i, \quad \rho \ll rank \tag{9}$$

Note that any two columns i_1 and i_2 differ only by $\sum_{r=1}^{\rho} V_r^{i_1}$ and $\sum_{r=1}^{\rho} V_r^{i_2}$. Then these terms can be used to measure the importance or contribution of each column to the matrix. The normalized statistical leverage scores [18] of the i-th column of matrix $\mathcal{S}_j$ is defined as

$$\ell_i = \frac{1}{\rho} \sum_{r=1}^{\rho} V_r^i, \quad i = 1, \dots, \eta, \tag{10}$$

where η is the number of columns of each frame of the sequence. The sub-index j is removed to help understanding this expression. Leverages have been used historically for outlier detection in statistical regression but recently they have been used to give column (or row) order of the amount of motion saliency in a specific part of the image. The vector ℓ_i is a probability vector, i.e. $\sum_{i=1}^{\eta} \ell_i = 1$. Therefore, the columns of each matrix $\mathcal{S}_j$ with leverages greater than $\frac{1}{\eta}$ are the more important columns. So the columns of the initial approximation S^0 contain only the more important columns of the matrices $\mathcal{S}_j$, $j = 1, \dots, n$. Consequently, the less salient parts of the image are not included in the initialization of the sparse part, making the iterative process faster to converge, yielding more stable results, and increasing the segmentation accuracy.

$$S_j^{0^i} = \begin{cases} \mathcal{S}_j^i, & \ell(\mathcal{S}_j^i) \geq \frac{1}{\eta} \\ 0, & otherwise \end{cases} \tag{11}$$

In Fig. 2 we have shown the effect of the tandem initialization in our model, with comparison to other RPCA-based algorithms. The ghost effects are visible in foreground parts in the forth to sixth columns of this figure, which in turn contaminate the background model in the eighth to tenth columns. Algorithm 1 shows the pseudo-code for our model with tandem initialization and motion parameter estimation.

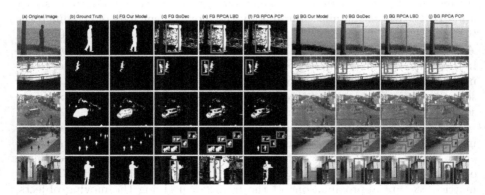

Fig. 2. *Ghosting effects* that persist in RPCA-based methods [19–21]. A contaminated background model in red regions affects the foreground segmentation in green regions. Our tandem model is able to eliminate these artifacts, without post-processing.

Algorithm 1. Pseudo-code with background motion parameter estimation and Tandem initialization

1: **Input:** A, $rank$, λ, ϵ, $maxIter$
2: **Output:** S, L, E, τ
3: *Calculate* $\mathcal{S} \approx \sum_{r=1}^{\rho} \sigma_r U_r V_r$, $\quad \rho \ll rank$
4: *Tandem initialization:* $\tau^0 = \tau_{pre-align}$, $L^0 = A$, $S^0 = \begin{cases} \mathcal{S}, & \ell(\mathcal{S}) \geq \frac{1}{\eta} \\ 0, & otherwise \end{cases}$
5: **while** $\|A \circ \tau^t - L^t - S^t\|_F^2 / \|A\|_F^2 > \epsilon$ $\quad$ or $\quad t < maxIter$ **do**
  1) Form the matrix $A \circ \tau$ calculating the parameters τ_i^t that infer the mapping that transforms the column vector A_i to the i-th column vector of the matrix $L^{t-1} + S^{t-1}$.
  2) Calculate $L^t = \sum_{i=1}^{rank} \sigma_i U_i V_i^T$ where $svd(A \circ \tau^t - S^{t-1}) = U\Sigma V^T$.
  3) Calculate $S^t = \mathcal{P}_\lambda(\psi(A \circ \tau^t - L^t))$ where $\mathcal{P}_\lambda(x) = sign(x)\max(|x| - \lambda, 0)$.
  4) Calculate the residual noise $E = A - L - S$.
6: **end while**

4 Experiments and Analysis

Our algorithm is implemented and tested in MATLAB on a desktop machine, single core on an Intel Core i7-4770 CPU and 32 GB of RAM. The average processing time on a sequence of 100 RGB frames with resolution 600×800 with image alignment and background motion estimation and superpixel generation step is about 1674 seconds. We perform extensive tests using three datasets [9–11] comprised of a total of 49 videos, allowing us to compare our method to a large number of alternative methods. For all the tests these same set of parameters are used: regularizing parameter $\lambda = 3/\sqrt{\max(m, n)}$, depth of each tree $d = 3$, number of singleton groups $\mathcal{M}$ dynamically chosen by SLIC, number of superpixels per image $\xi = 800$, and compactness factor $\varphi = 20$. All the tests were conducted on the *temporal region of interest* of the sequences, meaning no training stage with clean background was used to obtain the background model. All our results have been reported without refinement or post-processing. We refer to our method as DSPSS short for Dynamic Superpixel Structured-Sparse.

4.1 Qualitative Results

In Fig. 2 we have shown the effect of the tandem initialization in our model, with comparison to other RPCA-based algorithms that suffer from ghosting effects. A contaminated background model visible in red regions, would in turn affect the foreground segmentation in green regions, resulting in high false positive rate. Our algorithm is capable of adapting to slow-moving foreground objects in these sequences, all the while being able to discard non-genuine false-alarm foreground pixels with the robust foreground segmentation via our tree structured sparsity-inducing norms; notice the eliminated water rippling pixels in the foreground segmentation of the first row. Our model is robust to variations in foreground object size; this can be seen in the third row results, where a

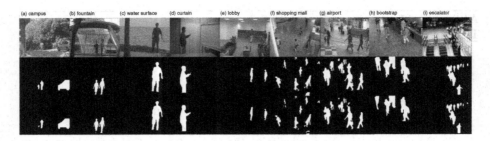

Fig. 3. *i2R* results: top row is the original image, second row is the ground truth, and the last row is our unrefined results without post-processing. We used the same frames as [15,16,22–25], for qualitative comparison.

large foreground object is well-segmented simultaneously with small pedestrians in the scene. Our sparsity-inducing norms defined in superpixel regions prove to be effective in obtaining accurate silhouette of foreground regions in all the examples of Fig. 2, specially in the case of first row where the legs of the person walking are *camouflaged* due to similar intensity with the background.

Figure 3 shows segmentation results for the i2R dataset. The top row is the original image, second row is the ground truth, and the last row is our results. We have used the same frames as [15,16,22–25], for qualitative comparison. Figure 3(a) is a scene with pedestrians and cars passing in front of a very dynamic background with trees swaying back and forth and illumination changing rapidly. Our method has been able to crisply detect genuine foreground regions while discarding the dynamic pixels in background. The same scenario applies to Fig. 3(b) and (c), where the fountain and water rippling in the lake make it hard to distinguish genuine foreground regions. The sparsity-inducing norms defined in superpixel regions manifest their effectiveness in adhering well to coherent foreground segmentation, while the tree-structure successfully discards the non-rigid and random foreground alarms caused by the fountain and water turbulence. In (d) a person appears in front of a curtain that moves with wind, and remains there for a period of time, and again walks out of the scene. Our background model has adapted itself to the variations in the scene such that the inactive foreground does not get absorbed into the background. The column (e) is an indoor scene with sudden illumination change; our method suffers a bit from this sudden change, but quickly adapts itself so that the foreground objects would not go undetected. (f) and (g) are simpler to process, except for some camouflage in (f) due to color similarity between some foreground objects and the background, but again good performance is obtained in these scenes. For (h) no training period for background is available; i.e., no foreground-absent frame is seen, but our model is able to obtain a robust background model nonetheless. (i) is a scene with a very fast moving escalator, and people appearing from the end of a hallway that is poorly-lit. Evidently, background modeling with low-rank approximation best proves itself here by adapting well to the repetitive motion of the escalator, by a few modes, and the sparsity-inducing norms are well able to detect the people moving in the darkness at the back of the scene. Also, the within-patch normalized regularization guarantees insensitivity to foreground object size and illumination invariant performance in all cases.

4.2 Quantitative Results

For quantitative comparison we present the F-measure scores, defined as the harmonic mean of the recall and precision:

$$\text{recall} = \frac{tp}{tp+fn}, \quad \text{precision} = \frac{tp}{tp+fp}, \quad \text{F-measure} = 2\frac{\text{recall}\cdot\text{precision}}{\text{recall}+\text{precision}},$$

where fp is the number of false positives, tn the number of true negatives, etc. The change detection dataset [10] is the largest dataset in our evaluation, and includes a dense ground truth. It also limits parameter tuning, such that a single parameter must be used for all the 31 videos. Video resolution is not great however, often with a low quality de-interlacing algorithm that creates ghosts. The dataset is comprised of six categories, 31 real-world videos (including thermal sequences), totaling over 80,000 frames, to include diverse motion and change detection challenges. The results for these sequences can be seen in Table 1. For the reason of space limit, in each category we compare our model with the top performing methods that have submitted results for that category (readers are referred to [10] and its website for complete list of references and the corresponding performance figures). In addition to this list, we have included the DP-GMM [23] and five RPCA-based methods PCP [21], DECOLOR [12], and very recent 2-pass RPCA [14]. For LSD-GSRPCA [15] and SPGFL [16] only a fraction of the results were reported in their papers, therefore they are included where results are reported. For PCP we use our pre-alignment step for the *camera jitter* sequences and as such we denote it as PCP+Alignment.

The most challenging categories are *intermittent motion* and *thermal*. We advantage at *intermittent motion* category thanks to the tandem initialization to remove the ghosting problem, and the robust low-rank approximation of the background, that can learn multiple modes for the background of a sequence. However, in *thermal* since we do not have a mechanism for handling thermal images our algorithm suffers from artifacts such as heat stamps (e.g., bright spots left on a seat after a person gets up and leaves), heat reflection on floors and windows, and camouflage effects when a moving object has the same temperature as the surrounding regions. In all other categories, our method achieves top performance, thanks to the robust low-rank approximation of the background, that can learn multiple modes for the background of a sequence, to the tandem initialization to remove the ghosting problem, and the pre-alignment step and motion parameter estimation simultaneously with decomposition. Overall, we win on average for the CDnet dataset. This is because our model can handle backgrounds that are complex and dynamic. This ability, in combination with the tree-structured sparsity inducing mechanisms allows it to effectively segment genuine well-outlined foreground regions.

Table 1. *CDNet* [10] dataset: F-measure results for all the categories for the most competitive methods. Table accurate as of March 2016, with results from CDnet http://changedetection.net/. The online chart keeps updating.

Method	Baseline	Camera jitter	Dynamic background	Intermittent motion	Shadow	Thermal	Mean
LSD-GSRPCA [15]	.7173 (9)	-	-	-	-	-	-
SPGFL [16]	.9469 (3)	-	.8519 (3)	.6988 (3)	-	.8156 (3)	-
PCP+Alignment [21]	.9109 (8)	.7218 (7)	.6941 (8)	.5371 (8)	.7885 (7)	.7192 (7)	.7286 (7)
DECOLOR [12]	.9215 (7)	.7776 (5)	.7084 (7)	.5945 (6)	.8317 (4)	.7081 (8)	.7570 (6)
DP-GMM [23]	.9286 (5)	.7477 (6)	.8137 (5)	.5418 (7)	.8127 (5)	.8134 (4)	.7763 (5)
2-pass RPCA [14]	.9281 (6)	.8152 (2)	.7818 (6)	.6826 (4)	.8063 (6)	.7597 (5)	.7956 (4)
SuBSENSE [26]	.9500 (2)	.8150 (3)	.8180 (4)	.6570 (5)	.8990 (2)	.8170 (2)	.8260 (3)
PAWCS [27]	.9397 (4)	.8137 (4)	.8938 (2)	.7764 (2)	.8710 (3)	**.8324 (1)**	.8545 (2)
DSPSS	**.9664 (1)**	**.8662 (1)**	**.9057 (1)**	**.7870 (1)**	**.9177 (1)**	.7328 (6)	**.8626 (1)**

Table 2. *SABS* [9] dataset: F-measure results for nine challenges; only the most competitive algorithms were included.

Method	Basic	Dynamic background	Bootstrap	Darkening	Light switch	Noisy night	Camouflage	No camouflage	H264, 40 kbps	Mean
Barnich [28]	.761 (4)	.711 (3)	.685 (3)	.678 (3)	.268 (4)	.271 (4)	.741 (4)	.799 (4)	.774 (3)	.632 (4)
Zivkovic [29]	.768 (3)	.704 (4)	.632 (4)	.620 (4)	.300 (3)	.321 (3)	.820 (3)	.829 (3)	.748 (4)	.638 (3)
DP-GMM [23]	.853 (2)	.853 (2)	.796 (2)	.861 (2)	**.603 (1)**	.788 (2)	.864 (2)	.867 (2)	.827 (2)	.812 (2)
DSPSS	**.867 (1)**	**.871 (1)**	**.822 (1)**	**.907 (1)**	.570 (2)	**.897 (1)**	**.894 (1)**	**.913 (1)**	**.841 (1)**	**.842 (1)**

Table 3. *i2R* [11] dataset F-measure results. We report our results without parameter tuning, although the dataset allows this.

Method	cam	ft	ws	mc	lb	sm	ap	br	ss	Mean
DECOLOR [12]	.3416 (6)	.2075 (6)	.9022 (5)	.8700 (4)	.646 (6)	.6822 (5)	.8169 (2)	.6589 (4)	.7480 (3)	.6525 (6)
DP-GMM [23]	.7876 (3)	.7424 (5)	.9298 (3)	.8411 (5)	.6665 (5)	.6733 (6)	.5675 (6)	.6496 (5)	.5522 (6)	.7122 (5)
PCP [21]	.5226 (5)	.8650 (3)	.6082 (6)	.9014 (3)	.7245 (4)	.7785 (3)	.5879 (5)	.8322 (3)	.7374 (4)	.7286 (4)
LSD-GSRPCA [15]	.7613 (4)	.8371 (4)	.9050 (4)	.8357 (6)	.7313 (3)	.7362 (4)	.7222 (4)	.5842 (6)	.7214 (5)	.7594 (3)
SPGFL [16]	.8574 (2)	**.9322 (1)**	**.9856 (1)**	**.9744 (1)**	**.8840 (1)**	.8265 (2)	.7739 (3)	.8394 (2)	.8029 (2)	.8751 (2)
DSPSS	**.8993 (1)**	.9105 (2)	.9674 (2)	.9228 (2)	.7680 (2)	**.8499 (1)**	**.8593 (1)**	**.8922 (1)**	**.9163 (1)**	**.8873 (1)**

The SABS dataset [9] presents synthetic image sequences divided into nine categories. As can be seen in the results in Table 2, our algorithm takes the first place in all the scenarios except for *light switch*, since our background model has slowly adapted to changes in this scene.

The i2R dataset [11] dataset results can be seen in Table 3. We achieve top performance again overall for this dataset. We have reported our results without parameter tuning, although the dataset allows this.

5   Conclusion

We have presented a new background subtraction method and validated its efficacy and effectiveness with extensive testing. The method is based on an existing model, namely RPCA, but with new sparsity-inducing norms and group-structured sparsity constraints. Our model surpasses state-of-the-art performance by taking advantage of the natural shape and structure of objects in the scene, where our sparsity model dynamically evolves to best describe genuine foreground objects in the scene; this gives us a significant advantage when it comes to handling dynamic backgrounds, foreground aperture, and camouflage. Moreover, a novel tandem initialization method is proposed to speed up convergence and remove ghosting effects persisting in RPCA-based methods. Specifically, our model is able to learn a robust background model that can change over time, to cope with a variety of scene changes, in comparison with the existing more heuristic RPCA-based methods. It proves itself to have excellent performance in dealing with heavy noise, thanks to the approximated RPCA model where the residual error is discarded into a third matrix in the decomposition as noise. In addition, estimation of background motion induced by a jittering or moving camera is performed simultaneously with low-rank approximation, that results in excellent performance in shaky videos. Certain improvements can be considered. Our model is yet another batch method, as the frames need to be stored for obtaining a background model. Sudden illumination changes are slowly adapted by the background model, and hence it fails to handle some indoor lighting changes. Furthermore, a more sophisticated model should be able to handle shadows, that are not interesting for later processing. Solutions to these problems could be adapted to our method.

Acknowledgments. The research leading to this paper was fully supported by the LASIE project (http://www.lasie-project.eu/) with funding from the European Unions Seventh Framework Program for research and technological development, grant agreement 607480.

References

1. Bloisi, D.D.: Background Modeling and Foreground Detection for Video Surveillance. CRC Press, Taylor and Francis Group, July 2014
2. Bouwmans, T., Zahzah, E.: Robust PCA via principal component pursuit: a review for a comparative evaluation in video surveillance. Special Isssue on Background Models Challenge, Computer Vision and Image Understanding (2014)
3. Candès, E.J., Li, X., Ma, Y., Wright, J.: Robust principal component analysis? J. ACM **58**(3), 11:1–11:37 (2011)
4. Erfanian Ebadi, S., Guerra Ones, V., Izquierdo, E.: Dynamic tree structured sparse RPCA via column subset selection for background modeling and foreground detection. In: 2016 IEEE International Conference on Image Processing (ICIP) (2016)
5. Erfanian Ebadi, S., Guerra Ones, V., Izquierdo, E.: Approximated robust principal component analysis for improved general scene background subtraction. CoRR abs/1603.05875 (2016)
6. Erfanian Ebadi, S., Guerra Ones, V., Izquierdo, E.: Efficient background subtraction with low-rank and sparse matrix decomposition. In: 2015 IEEE International Conference on Image Processing (ICIP), pp. 4863–4867, September 2015
7. Erfanian Ebadi, S., Izquierdo, E.: Approximated RPCA for fast and efficient recovery of corrupted and linearly correlated images and video frames. In: 2015 International Conference on Systems, Signals and Image Processing (IWSSIP), pp. 49–52, September 2015

8. Achanta, R., Shaji, A., Smith, K., Lucchi, A., Fua, P., Susstrunk, S.: SLIC super-pixels compared to state-of-the-art superpixel methods. IEEE Trans. Pattern Anal. Mach. Intell. **34**(11), 2274–2282 (2012)

9. Brutzer, S., Höferlin, B., Heidemann, G.: Evaluation of background subtraction techniques for video surveillance. In: Computer Vision and Pattern Recognition (CVPR), pp. 1937–1944. IEEE (2011)

10. Wang, Y., Jodoin, P.M., Porikli, F., Konrad, J., Benezeth, Y., Ishwar, P.: CDnet 2014: An Expanded Change Detection Benchmark Dataset. In: IEEE CVPR Change Detection workshop, United States 8 p., June 2014. https://hal-univ-bourgogne.archives-ouvertes.fr/hal-01018757

11. Li, L., Huang, W., Gu, I.Y.H., Tian, Q.: Statistical modeling of complex back-grounds for foreground object detection. IEEE Trans. Image Process. **13**(11), 1459–1472 (2004)

12. Zhou, X., Yang, C., Yu, W.: DECOLOR: moving object detection by detecting contiguous outliers in the low-rank representation. IEEE Trans. Pattern Anal. Mach. Intell. **35**(3), 597–610 (2013)

13. Huang, J., Huang, X., Metaxas, D.: Learning with dynamic group sparsity. In: 2009 IEEE 12th International Conference on Computer Vision, pp. 64–71. IEEE (2009)

14. Gao, Z., Cheong, L.F., Wang, Y.X.: Block-sparse rpca for salient motion detection. IEEE Trans. Pattern Anal. Mach. Intell. **36**(10), 1975–1987 (2014)

15. Liu, X., Zhao, G., Yao, J., Qi, C.: Background subtraction based on low-rank and structured sparse decomposition (2015)

16. Javed, S., Oh, S., Sobral, A., Bouwmans, T., Jung, S.: Background subtraction via superpixel-based online matrix decomposition with structured foreground con-straints. In: Workshop on Robust Subspace Learning and Computer Vision, ICCV 2015 (2015)

17. Jia, K., Chan, T.-H., Ma, Y.: Robust and practical face recognition via structured sparsity. In: Fitzgibbon, A., Lazebnik, S., Perona, P., Sato, Y., Schmid, C. (eds.) ECCV 2012. LNCS, vol. 7575, pp. 331–344. Springer, Heidelberg (2012). doi:10.1007/978-3-642-33765-9_24

18. Mahoney, M.W., Drineas, P.: CUR matrix decompositions for improved data analy-sis. Proc. Nat. Acad. Sci. **106**(3), 697–702 (2009)

19. Zhou, T., Tao, D.: GoDec: Randomized low-rank and sparse matrix decomposition in noisy case. In: Getoor, L., Scheffer, T. (eds.) Proceedings of the 28th Interna-tional Conference on Machine Learning (ICML-11), ICML 2011, pp. 33–40. ACM, June 2011

20. Guyon, C., Bouwmans, T., Zahzah, E.: Foreground detection based on low-rank and block-sparse matrix decomposition. In: International Conference on Image Processing, ICIP 2012 (2012)

21. Zhou, Z., Li, X., Wright, J., Candès, E.J., Ma, Y.: Stable principal component pursuit. CoRR abs/1001.2363 (2010)

22. Xin, B., Tian, Y., Wang, Y., Gao, W.: Background subtraction via generalized fused Lasso foreground modeling. arXiv preprint arXiv:1504.03707 (2015)

23. Haines, T., Xiang, T.: Background subtraction with dirichletprocess mixture mod-els. IEEE Trans. Pattern Anal. Mach. Intell. **36**(4), 670–683 (2014)

24. Culibrk, D., Marques, O., Socek, D., Kalva, H., Furht, B.: Neural network approach to background modeling for video object segmentation. IEEE Trans. Neural Netw. **18**(6), 1614–1627 (2007)

25. Maddalena, L., Petrosino, A.: A self-organizing approach to background subtraction for visual surveillance applications. IEEE Trans. Image Process. **17**(7), 1168–1177 (2008)
26. St-Charles, P.L., Bilodeau, G.A., Bergevin, R.: Subsense: a universal change detection method with local adaptive sensitivity. IEEE Trans. Image Process. **24**(1), 359–373 (2015)
27. St-Charles, P.L., Bilodeau, G.A., Bergevin, R.: A self-adjusting approach to change detection based on background word consensus. In: 2015 IEEE Winter Conference on Applications of Computer Vision (WACV), pp. 990–997. IEEE (2015)
28. Barnich, O., Van Droogenbroeck, M.: Vibe: a powerful random technique to estimate the background in video sequences. In: IEEE International Conference on Acoustics, Speech and Signal Processing, ICASSP 2009, pp. 945–948. IEEE (2009)
29. Zivkovic, Z., van der Heijden, F.: Efficient adaptive density estimation per image pixel for the task of background subtraction. Pattern Recogn. Lett. **27**(7), 773–780 (2006)

Contextual Priming and Feedback
for Faster R-CNN

Abhinav Shrivastava[✉] and Abhinav Gupta

Carnegie Mellon University, Pittsburgh, USA
ashrivas@cs.cmu.edu

Abstract. The field of object detection has seen dramatic performance improvements in the last few years. Most of these gains are attributed to bottom-up, feedforward ConvNet frameworks. However, in case of humans, top-down information, context and feedback play an important role in doing object detection. This paper investigates how we can incorporate top-down information and feedback in the state-of-the-art Faster R-CNN framework. Specifically, we propose to: (a) augment Faster R-CNN with a semantic segmentation network; (b) use segmentation for top-down contextual priming; (c) use segmentation to provide top-down iterative feedback using two stage training. Our results indicate that all three contributions improve the performance on object detection, semantic segmentation and region proposal generation.

1 Introduction

The field of object detection has changed drastically over the past few years. We have moved from manually designed features [13,22] to learned ConvNet features [29,37,44,68]; from the original sliding window approaches [22,77] to region proposals [28,29,32,63,78]; and from pipeline based frameworks such as Region-based CNN (R-CNN) [29] to more end-to-end learning frameworks such as Fast [28] and Faster R-CNN [63]. The performance has continued to soar higher, and things have never looked better. There seems to be a growing consensus – powerful representations learned by ConvNets are well suited for this task, and designing and learning deeper networks lead to better performance.

Most recent gains in the field have come from bottom-up, feedforward framework of ConvNets. On the other hand, in the case of human visual system, the number of feedback connections significantly outnumber the feedforward connections. In fact, many behavioral studies have shown the importance of context and top-down information for the task of object detection. This raises a few important questions – Are we on the right path as we try to develop deeper and deeper, but only feedforward networks? Is there a way we can bridge the gap between empirical results and theory, when it comes to incorporating top-down information, feedback and/or contextual reasoning in object detection?

This paper investigates how we can break the feedforward mold in current detection pipelines and incorporate context, feedback and top-down information. Current detection frameworks have two components: the first component

© Springer International Publishing AG 2016
B. Leibe et al. (Eds.): ECCV 2016, Part I, LNCS 9905, pp. 330–348, 2016.
DOI: 10.1007/978-3-319-46448-0_20

generates region proposals and the second classifies them as an object category or background. These region proposals seem to be beneficial because (a) they reduce the search space; and (b) they reduce false positives by focusing the 'attention' in right areas. In fact, this is in line with the psychological experiments that support the idea of priming (although note that while region proposals mostly use bottom-up segmentation [3,32], top-down context provides the priming in humans [53,75,79]). So, as a first attempt, we propose to use top-down information in generating region proposals. Specifically, we add segmentation as a complementary task and use it to provide top-down information to guide region proposal generation and object detection. The intuition is that semantic segmentation captures contextual relationships between objects (e.g., support, likelihood, size etc. [6]), and will essentially guide the region proposal module to focus attention in the right areas and learn detectors from them.

But contextual priming using top-down attention mechanism is only part of the story. In case of humans, the top-down information provides feedback to the whole visual pathway (as early as V1 [41,43]). Therefore, we further explore providing top-down feedback to the entire network in order to modulate feature extraction in all layers. This is accomplished by providing the semantic segmentation output as input to different parts of the network and training another stage of our model. The hypothesis is that equipping the network with this top-down semantic feedback would guide the visual attention of feature extractors to the regions relevant for the task at hand.

To summarize, we propose to revisit the architecture of a current state-of-the-art detector (Faster R-CNN [63]) to incorporate top-down information, feedback and contextual information. Our new architecture includes:

- **Semantic Segmentation Network:** We augment Faster R-CNN with a semantic segmentation network. We believe this segmentation can be used to provide top-down feedback to Faster R-CNN (as discussed below).
- **Contextual Priming via Semantic Segmentation:** In Faster R-CNN, both region proposal and object detection modules are feedforward. We propose to use semantic segmentation to provide top-down feedback to these modules. This is analogous to contextual priming; in this case top-down semantic feedback helps propose better regions and learn better detectors.
- **Iterative Top-Down Feedback:** We also propose to use semantic segmentation to provide top-down feedback to low-level filters, so that they become better suited for the detection problem. In particular, we use segmentation as an additional input to lower layers of a second round of Faster R-CNN.

2   Related Work

Object detection was once dominated by the sliding window search paradigm [22,77]. Soon after the resurgence of ConvNets for image classification [15,44,47], there were attempts at using this sliding window machinery with ConvNets [19,66,70]; but a key limitation was the computational complexity of brute-force search.

As a consequence, there was major paradigm shift in detection which completely bypassed the exhaustive search in favor of region-based methods and object proposals [1–3,8,18,32,76,84]. By reducing the search space, it allowed us to use sophisticated (both manually designed [12,23,78] and learned ConvNet [5,29,35,36,38,52,63]) features. Moreover, this also helped focus the attention of detectors to regions well supported by perceptual structures in the image. However, recently, Faster R-CNN [63] showed that even these region proposals can be generated by using ConvNet features. It removed segmentation from proposal pipeline by training a small network on top of ConvNet features that proposes a few object candidates. This raises an important question: Do ConvNet features already capture the structure that was earlier given by segmentation or does segmentation provide complementary information?

To answer this, we study the impact of using semantic segmentation in the region proposal and object detection modules of Faster R-CNN [63]. In fact, there has been a lot of interest in using segmentation in tandem with detection [10,12,17,23]; e.g., Fidler et al. [23] proposed to use segmentation proposals as additional features for DPM detection hypothesis. In contrast, we propose to use semantic segmentation to guide/prime the region proposal generation itself. There is ample evidence of the importance of similar top-down contextual priming in the human visual system [14,53], and its utility in reducing areas to focus our attention on for recognizing objects [75,79].

This prevalence and success of region proposals is only part of the story. Another key ingredient is the powerful ConvNet features [37,44,68]. ConvNets are multi-layered hierarchical feature extractors, inspired by visual pathways in humans [21,43]. But so far, our focus has been on designing deeper [37,68] feedforward architectures, even when there is a broad agreement on the importance of feedback connections [11,27,41] and limitations of purely feedforward recognition [46,80] in human visual systems. Inspired by this, we investigate how can we start incorporating top-down feedback in our current object detection architectures. There have been attempts earlier at exploiting feedback mechanisms; some well known examples are auto-context [74] and inference machines [64]. These iteratively use predictions from a previous iteration to provide contextual features to the next round of processing; however they do not trivially extend to ConvNet architectures. Closest to our goal are the contemporary works on using feedback to learn selective attention [55,69] and using top-down iterative feedback to improve at a task at hand [7,25,48]. In this work, we additionally explore using top-down feedback from one task to another.

The discussion on using global top-down feedback to contextually prime object recognition is incomplete without relating it to 'context' in general, which has a long history in cognitive neuroscience [6,39,40,53,59,60,75,79] and computer vision [16,24,58,62,71–73,81]. It is widely accepted that human visual inference of objects is heavily influenced by 'context', be it contextual relationships [6,39], priming for focusing attention [53,75,79] or importance of scene context [14,40,59,60]. These ideas have inspired lot of computer vision research (see [16,24] for survey). However, these approaches seldom lead to strong empirical gains. Moreover, they are mostly confined to weaker visual features (e.g., [13]) and have not been explored much in ConvNet-based object detectors.

For region-based ConvNet object detectors, simple contextual features are slowly becoming popular; e.g., computing local context features by expanding the region [26,56,57,83], using other objects (e.g., people) as context [33] and using other regions [30]. In comparison, the use of context has been much more popular for semantic segmentation. E.g., CRFs are commonly used to incorporate context and post-process segmentation outputs [9,65,82] or to jointly reason about regions, segmentation and detection [45,83]. More recently, RNNs have also been employed to either integrate intuitions from CRFs [49,61,82] in end-to-end learning systems or to capture context outside the region [5]. But empirically, at least for detection, such uses of context have mostly given feeble gains.

3   Preliminaries: Faster R-CNN

We first describe the two core modules of the Faster R-CNN [63] framework (Fig. 1). The first module takes an image as input and proposes rectangular regions of interest (RoIs). The second module is the Fast R-CNN [28] (FRCN) detector that classifies these proposed regions. In this paper, both modules use the VGG16 [68] network, which has 13 convolutional (conv) and 2 fully connected (fc) layers. Both modules share all conv layers and branch out at conv5_3. Given an arbitrary sized image, the last conv feature map (conv5_3) is used as input to both the modules as described below.

Region Proposal Network (RPN). The region proposal module (Fig. 1(left) in green) is a small fully convolutional network that operates on the last feature map and outputs a set of rectangular object proposals, each with a score. RPN is composed of a conv layer and 2 sibling fc layers. The conv layer operates on the input feature map to produce a D-dim. output at every spatial location; which is then fed to two fc layers – classification (cls) and box-regression (breg). At each spatial location, RPN considers k candidate boxes (anchors) and learns to classify them as either foreground or background based on their IOU overlap with the ground-truth boxes. For foreground boxes, breg layer learns to regress to the closest ground-truth box. A typical setting is $D = 512$ and $k = 9$ (3 scales, 3 aspect-ratios) (see [63] for details).

Using RPN regions in FRCN. For training the Fast R-CNN (FRCN) module, a mini-batch is constructed using the regions from RPN. Each region in the mini-batch is projected onto the last conv feature map and a fixed-length feature vector is extracted using RoI-pooling [28,38]. Each feature is then fed to two fc layers, which finally give two outputs: (1) a probability distribution over object classes and background; and (2) regressed coordinates for box re-localization. An illustration is shown in Fig. 1(left) in blue.

Training Faster R-CNN. Both RPN and FRCN modules of Faster R-CNN are trained by minimizing the multi-task loss (for classification and box-regression)

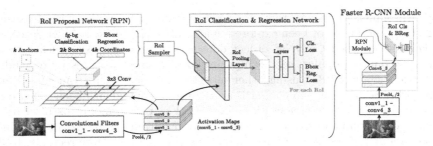

Fig. 1. Faster R-CNN. (left) Overview of Region Proposal Network (RPN) and RoI classification and box regression. (right) Shorthand diagram of Faster R-CNN. (Color figure online)

from [28,63] using mini-batch SGD. To construct a mini-batch for RPN, 256 anchors are randomly sampled with 1 : 1 foreground to background ratio; and for FRCN, 128 proposals are sampled with 1 : 3 ratio. We train both modules jointly using the 'approximate joint training'. For more details, refer to [28,29,63,67].

Given an image during training, a forward pass through all the conv layers produces conv5_3 feature map. RPN operates on this feature to propose two sets of regions, one each for training RPN and FRCN. Independent forward-backward passes are computed for RPN and FRCN using their region sets, gradients are accumulated at conv5_3 and back-propagated through the conv layers.

Why Faster R-CNN? Apart from being the current state-of-the-art object detector, Faster R-CNN is also the first framework that *learns* where to guide the 'attention' of an object detector along with the detector itself. This end-to-end learning of proposal generation and object detection provides a principled testbed for studying the proposed top-down contextual feedback mechanisms.

In the following sections, we first describe how we add a segmentation module to Faster R-CNN (Sect. 4.1) and then present how we use segmentation for top-down contextual priming (Sect. 4.2) and iterative feedback (Sect. 4.3).

4   Our Approach

We propose to use semantic segmentation as a top-down feedback signal to the RPN and FRCN modules in Faster R-CNN, and iteratively to the entire network. We argue that a raw semantic segmentation output is a compact signal that captures the desired contextual information such as relationships between objects (Sect. 2) along with global structures in the image, and hence is a good representation for top-down feedback.

4.1   Augmenting Faster R-CNN with Segmentation

The first step is to augment Faster R-CNN framework with an additional segmentation module. This module should ideally: (1) be fast, so that we do not give

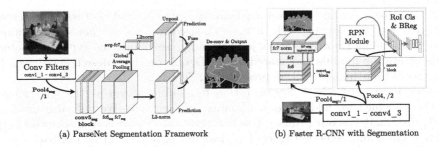

(a) ParseNet Segmentation Framework   (b) Faster R-CNN with Segmentation

Fig. 2. (a) Overview of ParseNet. (b) Shorthand diagram of our multi-task setup (Faster R-CNN + Segmentation). Refer to Sects. 4.1 and 5.2 for details.

up the speed advantages of [28,63]; (2) closely follow the network used by Faster R-CNN (VGG16 in this paper), for easy integration; and (3) use minimal (preferably no) post-processing, so that we can train it jointly with Faster R-CNN. Out of several possible architectures [4,9,51,52,82], we choose the ParseNet architecture [51] because of the simplicity.

ParseNet [51] is a fully convolutional network [52] for segmentation. It is fast because it uses filter rarefication technique (a-trous algorithm) from [9]. Its architecture is similar to VGG16. Moreover, it uses no post-processing; and instead adds an average pooling layer to incorporate global context; which is shown to have similar benefits to using CRFs [9,49].

Architecture Details. An overview is shown in Fig. 2(a). The key difference from standard VGG16 is that the pooling after `conv4_3` (`pool4`$_{seg}$) does no downsampling, as opposed to the standard `pool4` which down-samples by a factor of 2. After the `conv5` block, it has two 1×1 `conv` layers with 1024 channels applied with a filter stride [9,51]. Finally, it has a global average pooling step which given the feature map of after any layer ($H \times W \times D$) computes its spatial average ($1 \times 1 \times D$) and 'unpools' the features. Both source and its average feature maps are normalized and used to predict per-pixel labels. These outputs are then fused and a $8 \times$ `deconv` layer is used to produce the final output.

Faster R-CNN with Segmentation – A Multi-task Setup. In the joint network (Fig. 2(b)), both the Faster R-CNN modules and the segmentation module share the first 10 `conv` layers (`conv1_1` - `conv4_3`) and differ `pool4` onwards. For the segmentation module, we branch out `pool4`$_{seg}$ layer with stride of 1 and add the remaining ParseNet layers (`conv5_1` to `deconv`) (Fig. 2). The final architecture is a multi-task setup [54], which produces both semantic segmentation and object detection outputs simultaneously.

Training Details. Now that we have a joint architecture, we can train segmentation, RPN and detection modules by minimizing a multi-task loss. However, there are some key issues: (1) Faster R-CNN can operate on an arbitrary sized input image, whereas ParseNet requires a fixed 500×500 image. In this joint framework, our segmentation module is adapted to handle arbitrary sized images;

(2) Faster R-CNN and ParseNet are trained using very different set of hyperparameters (e.g., learning rate schedule, batch-size etc.); and neither set of parameters is optimal for the other. So for joint training, we modify the hyperparameters of segmentation module and shared layers. Details on these design decisions and analysis of their impact will be presented in Sect. 5.2.

This Faster R-CNN + Segmentation framework serves as the base model on top of which we add top-down contextual feedback. We will also use this multi-task model as our primary baseline (Base-MT) as it is trained using both segmentation and detection labels but does not have contextual feedback.

4.2   Contextual Priming via Segmentation

We propose to use semantic segmentation as top-down feedback to the region proposal and object detection modules of our base model. We argue that segmentation captures contextual information which will 'prime' the region proposal and object detection modules to propose better regions and learn better detectors.

In our base multi-task model, the Faster R-CNN modules operate on the conv feature map from the shared network. To contextually prime these modules, their input is modified to be a combination of aforementioned conv features and the segmentation output. Both modules can now learn to guide their operations based on the semantic segmentation of an image – it can learn to ignore background regions, find smaller objects or find large occluded objects (e.g., tables) etc.. Specifically, we take the raw segmentation output and append it to the conv4_3 feature. The conv5 block of filters operate on this new input ('seg + conv4_3') and their output is input to the individual Faster R-CNN modules. Hence, a top-down feedback signal from segmentation 'primes' both Faster R-CNN modules. However, because of the RoI-pooling operation, the detection module only sees the segmentation signal local to a particular region. To provide a global context to each region, we also append segmentation to the fixed-length feature vector ('seg + pool5') before feeding it to fc6. Overview in Fig. 3(a).

This entire system (three modules with connections between them) is trained jointly. After a forward pass through the shared conv layers and the segmentation module, their outputs are used as input to both Faster R-CNN modules. A forward-backward pass is performed for both RPN and FRCN. Next, the segmentation module does a backward pass using the gradients from its loss and from the other modules. Finally, gradients are accumulated at conv4_3 from all three modules and backward pass is performed for the shared conv layers.

Architecture Details. Given an $(H_I \times W_I \times 3)$ input, the conv4_3 produces a $(H_c \times W_c \times 512)$ feature map, where $(H_c, W_c) \approx (H_I/8, W_I/8)$. Using this feature map, the segmentation module produces a $(H_I \times W_I \times (K+1))$ output, which is a pixel-wise probability distribution over $K+1$ classes. We ignore the background class and only use $(H_I \times W_I \times K)$ output, which we refer to as S. Now, S needs to be combined with conv4_3 feature for the Faster R-CNN modules and each region's $(7 \times 7 \times K)$-dim. pool5 feature map for FRCN, but there are 2 issues: (1) spatial dimensions of S does not match either, and (2) feature values from

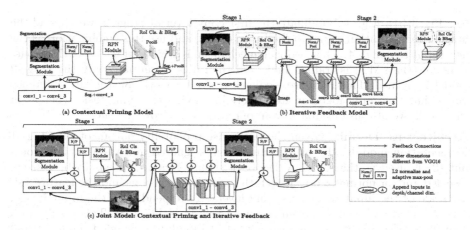

Fig. 3. Overview of the proposed models for top-down feedback. (a) **Contextual Priming via Segmentation** (Sect. 4.2) uses segmentation as top-down feedback signal to guide the RPN and FRCN modules of Faster R-CNN. (b) **Iterative Feedback** (Sect. 4.3) is a 2-unit model, where the Stage-1 provides top-down feedback for Stage-2 filters. (c) **Joint Model** (Sect. 4.4) uses (a) as the base unit in (b).

different layers are at drastically different scales [51]. To deal with the spatial dimension mis-match, we utilize the RoI/spatial-pooling layer from [28,38]: We `maxpool S` using an adaptive grid to produce two outputs S_c and S_p, which have the same spatial dimensions as `conv4_3` and `pool5` respectively. Now, we normalize and scale S_c to S_{cN} and S_p to S_{pN}, such that their L2-norm [51] is of the same scale as the per-channel L2-norm of their corresponding features (`conv4_3` and `pool5` respectively). Now, we append S_{cN} to `conv4_3` and the resulting $(H_c \times W_c \times (512 + K))$ feature is the input for Faster R-CNN. Finally, we append S_{pN} with each region's `pool5` and the resulting $(7 \times 7 \times (512 + K))$ feature is the input for `fc6` of FRCN. This network architecture is trained from a VGG16 initialized base model; and the additional K channels in `conv5_3` and `fc6` are initialized randomly using [31,68]. Refer to Fig. 3(a) for an overview.

4.3 Iterative Feedback via Segmentation

The architecture proposed in the previous section provides top-down semantic feedback and modulates only the Faster R-CNN module. We also propose to provide top-down information to the whole network, especially the shared `conv` layers, to modulate low-level filters. The hypothesis is that this feedback will help the earlier `conv` layers to focus on areas likely to have objects. We again build from the Base-MT model (Sect. 4.1).

This top-down feedback is iterative in nature and will pass from one instantiation of our base model to another. To provide this top-down feedback, we take the raw segmentation output of our base model (Stage-1) and append it to the input of the `conv` layer to be modulated in the second model instance (Stage-2) (see Fig. 3(b)). E.g., to modulate the first conv layer of Stage-2, we append the Stage-1 segmentation signal to the input image, and use this combination as the new input to conv1_1. This feedback mechanism is trained stage-wise: the Stage-1 model (Base-MT) is trained first; and then it is frozen and only the Stage-2 model is trained. This iterative feedback is similar to [7,48]; the key difference being that they only focus on iteratively improving the same task, whereas in this work, we also use feedback from one task to improve another.

Architecture Details. Given the pixel-wise probability output of the Stage-1 segmentation module, the background class is ignored and the remaining output (S) is used as the semantic feedback signal. Again, S needs to be resized, rescaled and/or normalized to match the spatial dimensions and the feature values scale of the input to various conv layers. To append with the input image, S is re-scaled and centered element-wise to lie in $[-127, 128]$. This results in a new $(H_I \times W_I \times (3 + K))$ input for conv1_1. To modulate conv2_1, conv3_1 and conv4_1, we maxpool and L2-normalize S to match the spatial dimensions and the feature value scales of pool1, pool2 and pool3 features respectively (similar to Sect. 4.2). The filters corresponding to additional K channels in conv1_1, conv2_1, conv3_1 and conv4_1 are initialized using [31].

4.4   Joint Model

So far, given our multi-task base model, we have proposed a top-down feedback for contextual priming of region proposal and object detection modules and an iterative top-down feedback mechanism to the entire architecture. Next, we put these two pieces together in a single joint framework. Our final model is a 2-unit model: each individual unit being the contextual priming model (from Sect. 4.2), and both units being connected for iterative top-down feedback (Sect. 4.3). We train this 2-unit model stage-wise (Sect. 4.3). Architecture details of the joint model follow from Sects. 4.2 and 4.3 (see Fig. 3(c)).

Through extensive evaluation, presented in the following sections, we show that: (1) individually, both contextual priming and iterative feedback models are effective and improve performance; and (2) the joint model is better than both individual models, indicating their complementary nature. We would like to highlight that our method is fairly general – both segmentation and detection modules can easily utilize newer network architectures (e.g., [4,37]).

5   Experiments

We conduct experiments to better understand the impact of contextual priming and iterative feedback; and provide ablation analysis of various design decisions. Our implementation uses the Caffe [42] library.

5.1   Experimental Setup

For ablation studies, we use the multi-task setup from Sect. 4.1 as our baseline (Base-MT). We also compare our method to Faster R-CNN [63] and

Table 1. Ablation analysis of modifying ParseNet training methodology (Sect. 5.2).

Notes	Input dim.	Learning Rates (LR) Base LR	Layer LR	LR Policy	Batch-size	#iter	Normalize Loss?	mIOU (12S val)
(1) [51] (Original ParseNet)	500×500	10^{-8}	1	poly	8	20k	N	69.6
(2) Reproducing [51][b] (ParseNet)	500×500	10^{-8}	1	poly	8	20k	N	68.2
(3) Faster R-CNN LR-policy, Norm. Loss	500×500	10^{-3}	1	step	8	20k	Y	68.5
(4) Faster R-CNN batch-size, new LR	500×500	$2.5×10^{-4}$	1	step	2	80k	Y	67.8
(5) Faster R-CNN Base-LR	500×500	10^{-3}	0.25	step	2	80k	Y	67.8
(6) Faster R-CNN input dim. (ParseNet*)	[600×1000][†]	10^{-3}	0.25	step	2	80k	Y	66

[a] min dim. is 600, max dim. capped at 1000.

[b] https://github.com/weiliu89/caffe/tree/fcn

ParseNet [51] frameworks. For quantitative evaluation, we use the standard mean average precision (mAP) [20] metric for object detection and mean intersection-over-union metric (mIOU) [20,28] for segmentation.

Datasets. All models in this section are trained on the PASCAL VOC12 [20] segmentation set (12S), augmented with the extra annotations (A) from [34] as is standard practice. Results are analyzed on VOC12 segmentation val set. For analysis, we chose the segmentation set, and not detection, because *all* images have *both* segmentation *and* bounding-box annotations; this helps us isolate the effects of using segmentation as top-down semantic feedback without worrying about missing segmentation labels in the standard detection split. Results on the standard splits will be presented in Sect. 6.

5.2 Base Model – Augmenting Faster R-CNN with Segmentation

Faster R-CNN and ParseNet both use mini-batch SGD for training, however, they follow different training methodologies. We first describe the implementation details and design decisions adopted to augment the segmentation module to Faster R-CNN and report baseline performances.

ParseNet Optimization. ParseNet is trained for 20 k SGD iterations using an effective mini-batch of 8 images, an initial learning rate (LR) of 10^{-8} and polynomial LR decay policy. Compare this to Faster R-CNN, which is trained for 70 k SGD iterations with a mini-batch size of 2, 10^{-3} initial LR and step LR decay policy (step at 50 k). Since we are augmenting Faster R-CNN, we try to adapt ParseNet's optimization. On the 12 S val set, [51] reports 69.6 % (we achieved 68.2 % using the released code, Table 1(1–2)). We will refer to the latter as ParseNet throughout. Similar to [52], ParseNet does not normalize the Softmax loss by number of valid pixels. But to train with Faster R-CNN in a multi-task setup, all losses need to have similar magnitude; so, we normalize the loss of ParseNet and modify the LR accordingly. Next, we change the LR decay policy from polynomial to step (step at 12.5 k) to match that of Faster R-CNN. These changes result in similar performance (+0.3 points, Table 1(2–3)). We now reduce the batch size to 2 and adjust the LR appropriately (Table 1(4)). To keep the base LR of Faster R-CNN and ParseNet same, we change it to 10^{-3} and modify the LR associated with each ParseNet layer to 0.25, thus keeping the same effective LR for ParseNet (Table 1(4–5)).

Training Data. ParseNet re-scales the input images and their segmentation labels to a fixed size (500 × 500), thus ignoring the aspect-ratio. On the other hand, Faster R-CNN maintains the aspect-ratio and re-scales the input images such that their shorter side is 600 pixels (and the max dim. is capped at 1000). We found that ignoring the aspect-ratio drops Faster R-CNN performance and maintaining it drops the performance of ParseNet (−1.8 points, Table 1(5–6)). Because our main task is detection, we opted to use Faster R-CNN strategy, and treat the new ParseNet (ParseNet*) as the baseline for our base model.

Base Model Optimization. Following the changes mentioned above, our base model uses these standardized parameters: batch size of 2, 10^{-3} base LR, step decay policy (step at 50 k), LR of 0.25 for segmentation and shared `conv` layers, and 80k SGD iterations. This model serves as our multi-task baseline (Base-MT).

Baselines. For comparison, re-train Fast [28] and Faster R-CNN [63] on VOC 12S+A training set. Results of the Base-MT model for detection and segmentation are reported in Tables 2 and 3 respectively. Performance increases by 0.3 mAP on detection and drops by 0.1 mIOU on segmentation. This will serve as our primary baseline.

Table 2. Detection results on VOC 2012 segmentation val set. All methods use VOC12S+A training set (Sect. 5.1). Legend: **S**: uses segmentation labels (Sect. 4.1), **P**: contextual priming (Sect. 4.2), **F**: iterative feedback (Sect. 4.3)

method	S	P	F	mAP	aero	bike	bird	boat	bottle	bus	car	cat	chair	cow	table	dog	horse	mbike	persn	plant	sheep	sofa	train	tv
Fast R-CNN [29]				71.6	88.2	79.7	83.6	62.8	42.3	84.0	69.4	87.5	41.5	73.7	57.4	84.7	77.7	85.8	75.8	35.3	73.1	67.7	85.0	76.3
Faster R-CNN [64]				75.3	92.3	80.9	86.7	65.4	49.3	87.1	78.2	89.7	42.7	79.8	61.4	87.4	82.8	89.4	82.2	46.1	78.2	64.6	86.8	75.6
Base-MT (sec. 4.1)	✓			75.6	93.0	82.5	88.1	70.2	47.2	86.5	76.5	89.3	47.7	78.3	56.4	88.0	80.2	88.9	80.7	43.6	81.5	87.9	89.4	75.2
Ours (priming, sec. 4.2)	✓	✓		77.0	91.1	82.3	85.3	70.8	47.5	90.3	75.2	90.9	46.0	82.3	65.6	88.0	83.3	91.2	81.0	49.6	81.0	69.8	92.1	76.0
Ours (feedback, sec. 4.3)	✓		✓	77.3	90.7	82.9	90.4	70.3	51.2	89.7	77.0	91.7	49.9	81.4	66.9	87.8	81.1	90.3	82.2	50.4	79.2	70.2	85.9	76.9
Ours (joint, sec. 4.4)	✓	✓	✓	**77.8**	89.8	83.8	84.0	72.1	54.2	92.0	75.5	91.2	53.6	82.1	69.8	85.7	81.7	92.4	82.5	49.9	76.2	72.5	89.3	78.4

5.3 Contextual Priming

We evaluate the effects of using segmentation as top-down semantic feedback to the region proposal generation and object detection modules. We follow the same optimization hyperparameters as the Base-MT model, and report the results in Tables 2 and 3. Table 2 shows that providing top-down feedback via priming to the Faster R-CNN modules improves its detection performance by **1.4** points over the Base-MT model and **1.7** points over Faster R-CNN. Results in Table 3 show that performance of segmentation drops slightly when it is used for priming.

Design Evaluation. In Table 4(a), we report the impact of providing segmentation signal to different modules. We see that just priming `conv5_1` gives a 1 point boost over Bast-MT and adding the segmentation signal to each individual region ('`seg+pool5`' to `fc6`) gives another 0.4 points boost. It is interesting

Table 3. Segmentation results on VOC 2012 segmentation val set. All methods use VOC12S+A training set (Sect. 5.1). Legend: **S**: uses segmentation labels, **P**: contextual priming, **F**: iterative feedback

method	S	P	F	mIOU	bg	aero	bike	bird	boat	bottle	bus	car	cat	chair	cow	table	dog	horse	mbike	persn	plant	sheep	sofa	train	tv
ParseNet (Table 1(2))	✓			68.2	92.3	86.9	38.4	77.1	66.4	66.5	83.0	80.9	82.5	31.0	72.9	49.5	71.4	73.9	76.7	79.3	47.9	73.3	40.3	78.3	63.6
ParseNet* (Table 1(6))	✓			66.0	91.7	85.2	36.8	73.2	64.0	60.8	82.4	76.9	81.8	30.4	65.4	51.3	69.6	73.5	75.4	78.2	43.9	71.3	38.9	79.3	56.2
Base-MT (sec. 4.1)	✓			65.8	91.6	84.3	37.1	71.5	63.8	60.8	82.3	74.8	80.3	30.8	68.7	48.8	71.4	75.7	73.8	77.7	42.8	70.1	39.1	79.9	56.4
Ours (priming, sec. 4.2)	✓	✓		65.3	91.5	85.1	36.4	73.3	64.0	60.4	81.4	75.1	81.8	31.7	64.8	48.8	69.0	73.7	73.4	77.1	41.6	69.9	38.4	78.1	55.5
Ours (feedback, sec. 4.3)	✓		✓	69.5	92.8	87.3	39.4	76.9	66.7	68.1	86.9	80.6	86.4	33.4	68.1	50.9	71.8	80.1	77.3	81.3	48.6	73.3	42.0	82.8	65.5
Ours (joint, sec. 4.4)	✓	✓	✓	**69.6**	92.9	88.5	39.4	78.1	66.9	69.1	84.5	79.8	84.9	37.8	69.2	50.5	71.4	79.7	77.5	81.3	47.1	74.2	43.4	80.1	65.0

Table 4. Analation analysis of Contextual Priming and Iterative Feedback on VOC 12S val set. All methods use VOC 12S+A train set for training

(a) Evaluating Priming different layers

	mAP	mIOU
Base-MT	75.6	**65.8**
Priming conv5_1	76.6	**65.8**
Priming conv5_1, each fc6	**77.0**	65.3

(b) Evaluating Iterative Feedback design decisions

	Stage-2 Init.	mAP	mIOU
Base-MT	-	75.6	65.8
Iterative Feedback to conv1_1	ImageNet	76.5	69.3
	Stage-1	76.3	69.3
Iterative Feedback to conv{1,2,3,4}_1	ImageNet	76.3	69.1
	Stage-1	**77.3**	**69.5**

that the segmentation performance is not affected when priming conv5_1, but it drops by 0.5 mIOU when we prime each region. Our hypothesis is that gradients accumulated from all regions in the mini-batch start overpowering the gradients from segmentation. To deal with this, methods like [54] can be used in the future.

5.4 Iterative Feedback

Next we study the impact of giving iterative top-down semantic feedback to the entire network. In this 2-unit setup, the first unit (Stage-1) is a trained Base-MT model and the second unit (Stage-2) is a Stage-1 initialized Base-MT model. During inference, we have the option of using the outputs from both units or just the Stage-2 unit. Given that segmentation is used as feedback, it is supposed to self-improve across units, therefore we use the Stage-2 output as our final output (similar to [7,48]). For detection, we combine the outputs from both units; because the Stage-2 unit is modulated by segmentation, and the first unit is not, hence both might focus on different regions.

This iterative feedback improves the segmentation performance (Table 3) by **3.7** points over Base-MT (**3.5** points over ParseNet*). For detection, it improves over the Base-MT model by **1.7** points (**2** points over Faster R-CNN) (Table 2).

Design Evaluation. We study the impact of: (1) varying the degree of feedback to the Stage-2 unit, and (2) different Stage-2 initializations. In Table 4(b), we see that when initializing the Stage-2 unit with an ImageNet trained network, varying iterative feedback does not have much impact; however, when initializing with a Stage-1 model, providing more feedback leads to better performance.

Specifically, iterative feedback to all shared `conv` layers improves both detection and segmentation by 1.7 mAP and 3.7 mIOU respectively, as opposed to feedback to just `conv1_1` (as in [7,48]) which results in lower gains (Table 4(b)). Our hypothesis is that iterative feedback to a Stage-1 initialized unit allows the network to correct its mistakes and/or refine its predictions; therefore, providing more feedback leads to better performance.

5.5 Joint Model

Finally, we evaluate our joint 2-unit model, where each unit is a model with contextual priming, and both units are connected via segmentation feedback. In this setup, a trained contextual priming model is used as the Stage-1 unit as well as the initialization for the Stage-2 unit. We remove the dropout layers from Stage-2 unit. Inference follows the procedure described in Sect. 5.4.

As shown in Table 2, for detection, the joint model achieves **77.8 %** mAP (**+2.2** points over Base-MT and **+2.5** points over Faster R-CNN), which is better than both priming only and feedback only models. This suggests that both forms of top-down feedback are complementary for object detection. The segmentation performance (Table 3) is similar to the feedback only model, which is expected since in both cases, the segmentation module receives similar feedback.

6 Results

We now report results on the PASCAL VOC and MS COCO [50] datasets. We also evaluate the region proposal generation on the proxy metric of average recall.

Experimental Setup. When training on the VOC datasets with extra data (Tables 5, 6 and 7), we use 100 k SGD iterations (other hyperparameters follow Sect. 5); and for MS COCO, we use 490 k SGD iterations with an initial LR of 10^{-3} and decay step size of 200 k, owing to a larger epoch size.

VOC07 and VOC12 Results. Table 5 shows that on VOC07, our joint priming and feedback model improves the detection mAP by **1.7** points over Base-MT and **3.2** points over Faster R-CNN. Similarly, on VOC12 (Table 6), priming and feedback lead to **1.5** points boost over Bast-MT (**2.2** over Faster R-CNN). For segmentation on VOC12 (Table 7), we see a huge **5** point boost in mIOU over Base-MT. We would like highlight that both Base-MT and our joint model use exactly the same annotations and hyperparameters; therefore the performance boosts are because of contextual priming and iterative feedback in our model.

Recall-to-IOU. Since our hypothesis is that priming and feedback lead to better proposal generation, we also evaluate the recall of region proposals by the RPN module from various models, at different IOU thresholds. In Fig. 4, we show the results of using 2000 proposal per RPN module. Since feedback models have 2 units, we report their number with both 4000 and top 2000 proposals (sorted by `cls` score). As can be seen priming, feedback and joint models all lead to higher average recall (shown in legend) over the baseline RPN module.

Table 5. Detection results on VOC 2007 detection test set. All methods are trained on union of VOC07 trainval and VOC12 trainval

method	S	mAP	aero	bike	bird	boat	bottle	bus	car	cat	chair	cow	table	dog	horse	mbike	persn	plant	sheep	sofa	train	tv
Fast R-CNN [29]		70.0	77.0	78.1	69.3	59.4	38.3	81.6	78.6	86.7	42.8	78.8	68.9	84.7	82.0	76.6	69.9	31.8	70.1	74.8	80.4	70.4
Faster R-CNN [64]		73.2	76.5	79.0	70.9	65.5	52.1	83.1	84.7	86.4	52.0	81.9	65.7	84.8	84.6	77.5	76.7	38.8	73.6	73.9	83.0	72.6
Base-MT	✓	74.7	78.4	79.3	75.9	63.2	56.8	85.9	85.4	88.4	54.9	83.9	68.6	84.6	85.6	78.5	78.1	41.3	74.6	74.8	84.0	72.4
Ours (joint)	✓	**76.4**	79.3	80.5	76.8	72.0	58.2	85.1	86.5	89.3	60.6	82.2	69.2	87.0	87.2	81.6	78.2	44.6	77.9	76.7	82.4	71.9

Table 6. Detection results on VOC 2012 detection test set. All methods are trained on union of VOC07 trainval, VOC07 test and VOC12 trainval

method	S	mAP	aero	bike	bird	boat	bottle	bus	car	cat	chair	cow	table	dog	horse	mbike	persn	plant	sheep	sofa	train	tv
Fast R-CNN [29]		68.4	82.3	78.4	70.8	52.3	38.7	77.8	71.6	89.3	44.2	73.0	55.0	87.5	80.5	80.8	72.0	35.1	68.3	65.7	80.4	64.2
Faster R-CNN [64]		70.4	84.9	79.8	74.3	53.9	49.8	77.5	75.9	88.5	45.6	77.1	55.3	86.9	81.7	80.9	79.6	40.1	72.6	60.9	81.2	61.5
Base MT	✓	71.1^	84.2	80.9	73.1	55.1	50.6	78.2	75.6	89.0	48.6	76.7	54.8	87.6	82.5	83.0	80.0	41.7	74.2	60.7	81.4	63.1
Ours (joint)	✓	**72.6**◊	84.0	81.2	75.9	60.4	51.8	81.2	77.4	90.9	50.2	77.6	58.7	88.4	83.6	82.0	80.4	41.5	75.0	64.2	82.9	65.1

^http://host.robots.ox.ac.uk:8080/anonymous/RUZFQC.html, ◊http://host.robots.ox.ac.uk:8080/anonymous/YFSUQA.html

Table 7. Segmentation results on VOC 2012 segmentation test set. All methods are trained on union of VOC07 trainval, VOC07 test and VOC12 trainval

method	S	mIOU	bg	aero	bike	bird	boat	bottle	bus	car	cat	chair	cow	table	dog	horse	mbike	persn	plant	sheep	sofa	train	tv
Base MT	✓	66.4^	91.3	82.0	37.7	77.6	58.8	58.8	84.0	75.6	83.1	25.1	70.9	57.8	74.0	74.6	76.4	75.0	48.8	73.7	45.6	72.3	52.0
Ours (joint)	✓	**71.4**◊	93.0	89.3	41.4	84.1	63.8	65.2	88.1	80.9	88.6	28.4	75.4	60.6	80.3	80.9	83.1	79.7	55.4	77.9	48.2	75.8	58.8

^http://host.robots.ox.ac.uk:8080/anonymous/RUZFQC.html, ◊http://host.robots.ox.ac.uk:8080/anonymous/YFSUQA.html

MS COCO Results.

We also perform additional analysis of contextual priming on the COCO [50] dataset. Our priming model results in +**1.2** AP points (+2.1 AP50) over Faster R-CNN and +**0.8** AP points (+1.1 AP50) over Base-MT on the COCO minival5k set [5, 28]. On further analysis, we notice that the most performance gains are for objects where context should intuitively help; e.g., +12.4 for 'parking-meter', +8.7 for 'suitcase', +8.3 for 'umbrella' etc. on AP50 wrt. to Faster R-CNN. In fact, we consistently see >3 points improvement over Base-MT (>5 points over Faster R-CNN) in AP50 for top-20 improved objects (Table 8).

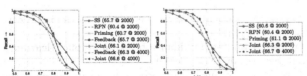

Fig. 4. Recall-to-IoU on VOC12 Segmentation val set (left) and VOC07 test set (right) (best viewed digitally).

Table 8. Detection results on COCO minival5k set.

Method	S	AP	AP50	AP75
[63]		24.5	45.7	23.8
Base-MT	✓	24.9	46.7	24.2
Ours (priming)	✓	25.7	47.8	25.2

7   Conclusion

We presented and investigated how we can incorporate top-down semantic feedback in the state-of-the-art Faster R-CNN framework. We proposed to augment a segmentation network to Faster R-CNN, which is then used to provide top-down contextual feedback to the region proposal generation and object detection modules. We also use this segmentation network to provide top-down feedback to the entire Faster R-CNN network iteratively. Our results demonstrate the effectiveness of these top-down feedback mechanisms for the tasks of region proposal generation, object detection and semantic segmentation.

Acknowledgments. We thank Ross Girshick, Ishan Misra and Sean Bell for helpful discussions. AS was supported by the Microsoft Research PhD Fellowship. This work was also partially supported by ONR MURI N000141612007. We thank NVIDIA for donating GPUs.

References

1. Alexe, B., Deselaers, T., Ferrari, V.: What is an object? In: CVPR (2010)
2. Alexe, B., Deselaers, T., Ferrari, V.: Measuring the objectness of image windows. TPAMI **34**, 2189–2202 (2012)
3. Arbeláez, P., Pont-Tuset, J., Barron, J.T., Marques, F., Malik, J.: Multiscale combinatorial grouping. In: CVPR (2014)
4. Badrinarayanan, V., Kendall, A., Cipolla, R.: Segnet: A deep convolutional encoder-decoder architecture for image segmentation. arXiv preprint arXiv:1511.00561 (2015)
5. Bell, S., Zitnick, C.L., Bala, K., Girshick, R.: Inside-outside net: detecting objects in context with skip pooling and recurrent neural networks. arXiv preprint arXiv:1512.04143 (2015)
6. Biederman, I.: On the semantics of a glance at a scene (1981)
7. Carreira, J., Agrawal, P., Fragkiadaki, K., Malik, J.: Human pose estimation with iterative error feedback. arXiv preprint arXiv:1507.06550 (2015)
8. Carreira, J., Sminchisescu, C.: Constrained parametric min-cuts for automatic object segmentation. In: CVPR (2010)
9. Chen, L.C., Papandreou, G., Kokkinos, I., Murphy, K., Yuille, A.L.: Semantic image segmentation with deep convolutional nets and fully connected crfs. In: ICLR (2015)
10. Chen, X., Shrivastava, A., Gupta, A.: Enriching visual knowledge bases via object discovery and segmentation. In: CVPR (2014)
11. Chun, M.M., Jiang, Y.: Top-down attentional guidance based on implicit learning of visual covariation. Psychol. Sci. **10**, 360–365 (1999)
12. Cinbis, R.G., Verbeek, J., Schmid, C.: Segmentation driven object detection with Fisher vectors. In: ICCV (2013)
13. Dalal, N., Triggs, B.: Histograms of oriented gradients for human detection. In: CVPR (2005)
14. Davenport, J.L., Potter, M.C.: Scene consistency in object and background perception. Psychol. Sci. **15**, 559–664 (2004)
15. Deng, J., Dong, W., Socher, R., Li, L.J., Li, K., Fei-Fei., L.: Imagenet: A large-scale hierarchical image database. In: CVPR (2009)

16. Divvala, S.K., Hoiem, D., Hays, J.H., Efros, A.A., Hebert, M.: An empirical study of context in object detection. In: CVPR (2009)
17. Dong, J., Chen, Q., Yan, S., Yuille, A.: Towards unified object detection and semantic segmentation. In: Fleet, D., Pajdla, T., Schiele, B., Tuytelaars, T. (eds.) ECCV 2014. LNCS, vol. 8693, pp. 299–314. Springer, Heidelberg (2014). doi:10.1007/978-3-319-10602-1_20
18. Endres, I., Hoiem, D.: Category independent object proposals. In: Daniilidis, K., Maragos, P., Paragios, N. (eds.) ECCV 2010. LNCS, vol. 6315, pp. 575–588. Springer, Heidelberg (2010). doi:10.1007/978-3-642-15555-0_42
19. Erhan, D., Szegedy, C., Toshev, A., Anguelov, D.: Scalable object detection using deep neural networks. In: CVPR (2014)
20. Everingham, M., Van Gool, L., Williams, C.K.I., Winn, J., Zisserman, A.: The pascal visual object classes (voc) challenge. IJCV 88, 303–338 (2010)
21. Felleman, D.J., Van Essen, D.C.: Distributed hierarchical processing in the primate cerebral cortex. Cereb. Cortex 1, 1–47 (1991)
22. Felzenszwalb, P., Girshick, R., McAllester, D., Ramanan, D.: Object detection with discriminatively trained part-based models. PAMI 32, 1627–1645 (2010)
23. Fidler, S., Mottaghi, R., Yuille, A., Urtasun, R.: Bottom-up segmentation for top-down detection. In: CVPR (2013)
24. Galleguillos, C., Belongie, S.: Context based object categorization: a critical survey. CVIU 114, 712–722 (2010)
25. Gatta, C., Romero, A., van de Veijer, J.: Unrolling loopy top-down semantic feedback in convolutional deep networks. In: CVPR Workshops (2014)
26. Gidaris, S., Komodakis, N.: Object detection via a multi-region & semantic segmentation-aware cnn model. arXiv preprint arXiv:1505.01749 (2015)
27. Gilbert, C.D., Sigman, M.: Brain states: top-down influences in sensory processing. Neuron 54, 677–696 (2007)
28. Girshick, R.: Fast R-CNN. In: ICCV (2015)
29. Girshick, R., Donahue, J., Darrell, T., Malik, J.: Rich feature hierarchies for accurate object detection and semantic segmentation. In: CVPR (2014)
30. Gkioxari, G., Girshick, R., Malik, J.: Contextual action recognition with RCNN. In: ICCV (2015)
31. Glorot, X., Bengio, Y.: Understanding the difficulty of training deep feedforward neural networks. In: AISTATS (2010)
32. Gu, C., Lim, J.J., Arbeláez, P., Malik, J.: Recognition using regions. In: CVPR (2009)
33. Gupta, S., Hariharan, B., Malik, J.: Exploring person context and local scene context for object detection. arXiv preprint arXiv:1511.08177 (2015)
34. Hariharan, B., Arbeláez, P., Bourdev, L., Maji, S., Malik, J.: Semantic contours from inverse detectors. In: ICCV (2011)
35. Hariharan, B., Arbeláez, P., Girshick, R., Malik, J.: Simultaneous detection and segmentation. In: Fleet, D., Pajdla, T., Schiele, B., Tuytelaars, T. (eds.) ECCV 2014. LNCS, vol. 8695, pp. 297–312. Springer, Heidelberg (2014). doi:10.1007/978-3-319-10584-0_20
36. Hariharan, B., Arbeláez, P., Girshick, R., Malik, J.: Hypercolumns for object segmentation and fine-grained localization. In: CVPR (2015)
37. He, K., Zhang, X., Ren, S., Sun, J.: Deep residual learning for image recognition. arXiv preprint arXiv:1512.03385 (2015)
38. He, K., Zhang, X., Ren, S., Sun, J.: Spatial pyramid pooling in deep convolutional networks for visual recognition. PAMI (2015)

39. Hock, H.S., Gordon, G.P., Whitehurst, R.: Contextual relations: the influence of familiarity, physical plausibility, and belongingness. Percept. Psychophys. **16**, 4–8 (1974)
40. Hollingworth, A.: Does consistent scene context facilitate object perception? J. Exp. Psychol. Gen. **127**, 398–415 (1998)
41. Hupe, J., James, A., Payne, B., Lomber, S., Girard, P., Bullier, J.: Cortical feedback improves discrimination between figure and background by v1, v2 and v3 neurons. Nature **394**, 784–787 (1998)
42. Jia, Y., Shelhamer, E., Donahue, J., Karayev, S., Long, J., Girshick, R., Guadarrama, S., Darrell, T.: Caffe: Convolutional architecture for fast feature embedding. arXiv preprint arXiv:1408.5093 (2014)
43. Kravitz, D.J., Saleem, K.S., Baker, C.I., Ungerleider, L.G., Mishkin, M.: The ventral visual pathway: an expanded neural framework for the processing of object quality. Trends Cogn. Sci. **17**, 26–49 (2013)
44. Krizhevsky, A., Sutskever, I., Hinton, G.E.: Imagenet classification with deep convolutional neural networks. In: NIPS (2012)
45. Ladický, Ľ., Sturgess, P., Alahari, K., Russell, C., Torr, P.H.S.: What, Where and How many? Combining object detectors and CRFs. In: Daniilidis, K., Maragos, P., Paragios, N. (eds.) ECCV 2010. LNCS, vol. 6314, pp. 424–437. Springer, Heidelberg (2010). doi:10.1007/978-3-642-15561-1_31
46. Lamme, V.A., Roelfsema, P.R.: The distinct modes of vision offered by feedforward and recurrent processing. Trends Neurosci. **23**, 571–579 (2000)
47. LeCun, Y., Bottou, L., Bengio, Y., Haffner, P.: Gradient-based learning applied to document recognition. Proc. IEEE **86**, 2278–2324 (1998)
48. Li, K., Hariharan, B., Malik, J.: Iterative instance segmentation. arXiv preprint arXiv:1511.08498 (2015)
49. Lin, G., Shen, C., Reid, I., et al.: Efficient piecewise training of deep structured models for semantic segmentation. arXiv preprint arXiv:1504.01013 (2015)
50. Lin, T.-Y., Maire, M., Belongie, S., Hays, J., Perona, P., Ramanan, D., Dollár, P., Zitnick, C.L.: Microsoft COCO: common objects in context. In: Fleet, D., Pajdla, T., Schiele, B., Tuytelaars, T. (eds.) ECCV 2014. LNCS, vol. 8693, pp. 740–755. Springer, Heidelberg (2014). doi:10.1007/978-3-319-10602-1_48
51. Liu, W., Rabinovich, A., Berg, A.C.: Parsenet: looking wider to see better. arXiv preprint arXiv:1506.04579 (2015)
52. Long, J., Shelhamer, E., Darrell, T.: Fully convolutional networks for semantic segmentation. In: CVPR (2015)
53. Meng, Y., Ye, X., Gonsalves, B.D.: Neural processing of recollection, familiarity and priming at encoding: evidence from a forced-choice recognition paradigm. Brain Res. **1585**, 72–82 (2014)
54. Misra, I., Shrivastava, A., Gupta, A., Hebert, M.: Cross-stitch networks for multi-task learning. In: CVPR (2016)
55. Mnih, V., Heess, N., Graves, A., et al.: Recurrent models of visual attention. In: NIPS (2014)
56. Mostajabi, M., Yadollahpour, P., Shakhnarovich, G.: Feedforward semantic segmentation with zoom-out features. In: CVPR (2015)
57. Mottaghi, R., Chen, X., Liu, X., Cho, N.G., Lee, S.W., Fidler, S., Urtasun, R., Yuille, A.: The role of context for object detection and semantic segmentation in the wild. In: CVPR (2014)
58. Murphy, K., Torralba, A., Freeman, W., et al.: Using the forest to see the trees: a graphical model relating features, objects and scenes. In: NIPS (2003)

59. Oliva, A., Torralba, A.: The role of context in object recognition. Trends Cogn. Sci. **11**, 520–527 (2007)
60. Palmer, T.E.: The effects of contextual scenes on the identification of objects. Memory Cogn. **3**, 519–526 (1975)
61. Pinheiro, P.O., Collobert, R., Dollar, P.: Learning to segment object candidates. In: NIPS (2015)
62. Rabinovich, A., Vedaldi, A., Galleguillos, C., Wiewiora, E., Belongie, S.: Objects in context. In: ICCV (2007)
63. Ren, S., He, K., Girshick, R., Sun, J.: Faster R-CNN: towards real-time object detection with region proposal networks. arXiv preprint arXiv:1506.01497 (2015)
64. Ross, S., Munoz, D., Hebert, M., Bagnell, J.A.: Learning message-passing inference machines for structured prediction. In: CVPR (2011)
65. Schwing, A.G., Urtasun, R.: Fully connected deep structured networks. arXiv preprint arXiv:1503.02351 (2015)
66. Sermanet, P., Eigen, D., Zhang, X., Mathieu, M., Fergus, R., LeCun, Y.: Overfeat: integrated recognition, localization and detection using convolutional networks. In: ICLR (2015)
67. Shrivastava, A., Gupta, A., Girshick, R.: Training region-based object detectors with online hard example mining. In: CVPR (2016)
68. Simonyan, K., Zisserman, A.: Very deep convolutional networks for large-scale image recognition. In: ICLR (2015)
69. Stollenga, M.F., Masci, J., Gomez, F., Schmidhuber, J.: Deep networks with internal selective attention through feedback connections. In: NIPS (2014)
70. Szegedy, C., Toshev, A., Erhan, D.: Deep neural networks for object detection. In: NIPS (2013)
71. Torralba, A.: Contextual priming for object detection. IJCV **53**, 169–191 (2003)
72. Torralba, A., Murphy, K.P., Freeman, W.T., Rubin, M.A.: Context-based vision system for place and object recognition. In: ICCV (2003)
73. Torralba, A., Sinha, P.: Statistical context priming for object detection. In: ICCV (2001)
74. Tu, Z., Bai, X.: Auto-context and its application to high-level vision tasks and 3d brain image segmentation. PAMI **32**, 1744–1757 (2010)
75. Tulving, E., Schacter, D.L.: Priming and human memory systems. Science **247**, 301–306 (1990)
76. Uijlings, J., van de Sande, K., Gevers, T., Smeulders, A.: Selective search for object recognition. IJCV **104**, 154–171 (2013)
77. Viola, P., Jones, M.: Robust real-time object detection. IJCV **57**, 137–154 (2001)
78. Wang, X., Yang, M., Zhu, S., Lin, Y.: Regionlets for generic object detection. In: ICCV (2013)
79. Wig, G.S., Grafton, S.T., Demos, K.E., Kelley, W.M.: Reductions in neural activity underlie behavioral components of repetition priming. Nature Neurosci. **8**, 1228–1233 (2005)
80. Wyatte, D., Curran, T., O'Reilly, R.: The limits of feedforward vision: recurrent processing promotes robust object recognition when objects are degraded. J. Cogn. Neurosci. **24**, 2248–2261 (2012)
81. Yao, J., Fidler, S., Urtasun, R.: Describing the scene as a whole: joint object detection, scene classification and semantic segmentation. In: CVPR (2012)
82. Zheng, S., Jayasumana, S., Romera-Paredes, B., Vineet, V., Su, Z., Du, D., Huang, C., Torr, P.H.: Conditional random fields as recurrent neural networks. In: ICCV (2015)

83. Zhu, Y., Urtasun, R., Salakhutdinov, R., Fidler, S.: segdeepm: Exploiting segmentation and context in deep neural networks for object detection. In: CVPR (2015)
84. Zitnick, C.L., Dollár, P.: Edge boxes: locating object proposals from edges. In: Fleet, D., Pajdla, T., Schiele, B., Tuytelaars, T. (eds.) ECCV 2014. LNCS, vol. 8693, pp. 391–405. Springer, Heidelberg (2014). doi:10.1007/978-3-319-10602-1_26

Efficient Multi-view Surface Refinement with Adaptive Resolution Control

Shiwei Li, Sing Yu Siu, Tian Fang$^{(\boxtimes)}$, and Long Quan

Hong Kong University of Science and Technology, Kowloon, Hong Kong
{slibc,sysiuaa,tianft,quan}@cse.ust.hk

Abstract. The existing stereo refinement methods optimize a surface representation using a multi-view photo-consistency functional. Such optimization is iterative and requires repeated computation of gradients over all surface regions, which is the bottleneck affecting adversely the computational efficiency of the refinement. In this paper, we present a flexible and efficient framework for mesh surface refinement in multi-view stereo. The newly proposed Adaptive Resolution Control (ARC) evaluates an optimal trade-off between the geometry accuracy and the performance via curve analysis. Then, it classifies the regions into the significant and insignificant ones using a graph-cut optimization. After that, each region is subdivided and simplified accordingly in the remaining refinement process, producing a triangular mesh in adaptive resolutions. Consequently, the ARC accelerates the stereo refinement by severalfold by culling out most insignificant regions, while still maintaining a similar level of geometry details that the state-of-the-art methods could achieve. We have implemented the ARC and demonstrated intensively on both public benchmarks and private datasets, which all confirm the effectiveness and the robustness of the ARC.

1 Introduction

Recovering a realistic 3D model from images is the ultimate goal of Multiple View Stereo (MVS) methods. Boosted by the public MVS benchmarks [7,15,16], the accuracy of stereovision has dramatically increased in last decade. It is believed the key factor to high accuracy is the final surface refinement step. With a triangular mesh representing the surface, refinement is a process of iterative adjustment of vertex locations by optimizing multi-view photo-consistency.

Such iterative refinement is of heavy computation. The primary reason is the repeated computation of refinement gradient over all visible surface areas. Another reason is that *mesh subdivision* used in the refinement will dramatically increase the *#vertices* to be optimized. The higher density of mesh vertex also leads to slower mesh-related operations, *e.g.*, mesh smoothing, visibility testing.

Electronic supplementary material The online version of this chapter (doi:10. 1007/978-3-319-46448-0_21) contains supplementary material, which is available to authorized users.

B. Leibe et al. (Eds.): ECCV 2016, Part I, LNCS 9905, pp. 349–364, 2016.
DOI: 10.1007/978-3-319-46448-0_21

| (a) Initial noisy mesh | (b) ARC labeling | (c) Adaptive mesh density | (d) Final refined mesh |

Fig. 1. With a noisy mesh as input (a), the ARC labels the mesh into two regions (b). Refinement applies only on the significant regions (orange), while the other insignificant regions (purple) will be culled out and simplified (c). This method greatly reduces the surface area to be optimized, but it is still able to produce valuable details (d). (Color figure online)

According to our observation, not all regions of refinement contribute equally to the geometry improvement. For example, most planar or low-textured regions barely have valuable refinement gradient, probably due to early convergence or lack of gradient on those regions. Refinement virtually produces no geometry improvement to them. Besides, mesh subdivision on such regions creates over-dense triangles, bringing extra computation and memory burden. In fact, these regions sometimes occupy quite a large proportion of the mesh surface (Fig. 4). Giving up their refinement can exchange for a decent performance speedup.

Unlike previous methods that target only at optimal photo-consistency, we also take the running time performance as our objective. To be specific, we quantify the performance and accuracy, and find an optimal trade-off in between which enables maximal performance speedup with minimal accuracy loss. Below, we demonstrate twofold contributions of our work.

Firstly, we present a mesh surface refinement framework with improvements to the baseline method [19]. Our refinement algorithm is divided into an *image registration* problem and a *gradient aggregation* problem. We employ a more efficient and direct approach to solve for the gradient of image similarity, which gives the steepest orientation for refinement. Besides, we identify the silhouette problem and handle it by explicitly culling out the problematic areas. The refinement framework is the fundamental that ensures a high accuracy reconstruction.

Secondly, we propose the novel *Adaptive Resolution Control* (ARC). The ARC labels the mesh into two regions (Fig. 1(b)), where the *active* regions are most contributive to geometry improvement, and the *inactive* regions are unimportant ones (usually planar or non-textured regions). To keep the labeling piecewise smooth, a graph cut optimization is employed. Only the *active* regions will be refined and subdivided, while the *inactive* regions will be discarded and simplified into fewer triangles. This leads to a mesh in adaptive resolution: the *active* regions have denser triangles while the *inactive* regions are sparser (Fig. 1(c)). Our method achieves a severalfold speedup thanks to the dramatic reduction of the refinement area and #vertex of the mesh. As shown in Fig. 1(d), our method is still able to preserve the fine details.

1.1   Related Work

MVS starts with known camera parameters, aiming to reconstruct the dense representation of the target object. A huge volume of work has been conducted on MVS [15,16]. Here, we only survey the works regarding surface refinement.

Surface Refinement is the last step in MVS and the key factor to the final accuracy. Given a rough initial surface, it aims to refine the details by optimizing photo-consistency (usually minimizing the reprojection error).

Pons *et al.* [14] proposed a variational method [8] of surface refinement and scene-flow estimation for level set framework. Their formulation minimizes the global image reprojection error functional. Vu *et al.* [19] further extended their work to apply on discrete triangular meshes. Their method iteratively refines and subdivides the input triangular mesh, producing highly detailed results. Delaunoy *et al.* [4,5] rigorously modeled the mesh refinement problem with the consideration of visibility change. Their formulation is further extended for the bundle adjustment problem [3]. Other than surface, patch-based methods [10, 12] apply the refinement to the patch representation (*i.e.*, normal and depth). Some earlier methods [6,9,18] estimated the refinement gradient using object silhouette information, but these methods are limited to conditioned scenarios.

Most refinement methods employ an iterative scheme to optimize the surface shape. Our refinement framework is closest to Vu's method [19], which can be seen as the baseline of our method. In the rest of the paper, we first present an improved surface refinement framework in Sect. 2. Then we propose the novel *Adaptive Resolution Control* in Sect. 3. Intensive experiments have been conducted in Sect. 4.1 to support the effectiveness of the proposed method.

2   Mesh Surface Refinement

Previous refinement methods for triangular meshes produce impressive results [3, 19]. Our method sticks to this main rule, but we view it as a combination of two sub-problems (image registration and gradient aggregation). We also propose the fast photo-consistency (NCC) gradient computation (Sect. 2.2) and the silhouette culling (Sect. 2.3) as improvements to previous method.

2.1   The Formulation

Denote a pair of images $\mathbf{I}_i$, $\mathbf{I}_j$ and surface $\mathbf{S}$. As introduced by [14], the standard formulation minimizing their reprojection error is formulated as:

$$E_{i,j}(\mathbf{S}) = \int_{x_i \in \mathbf{I}_i \cap \mathbf{I}_j^{\mathbf{S},i}} -\mathcal{M}(\mathbf{I}_i(x_i), \mathbf{I}_j^{\mathbf{S},i}(x_i)) dx_i, \qquad (1)$$

where $\mathbf{I}_j^{\mathbf{S},i}$ is the reprojection of image j in view i via surface $\mathbf{S}$, and $\mathcal{M}$ is the image similarity measurement. $E_{i,j}(\mathbf{S})$ integrates the error over commonly visible area for image pair i and j. Then the error summing up all image pairs

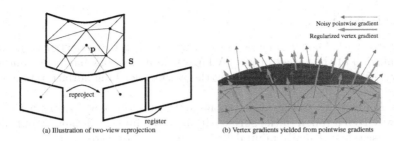

(a) Illustration of two-view reprojection   (b) Vertex gradients yielded from pointwise gradients

Fig. 2. (a) The two-view refinement problem is formulated as an image registration problem and a gradient aggregation problem. (b) The discrete vertex gradient is solved by a least square of pointwise gradient with regularization enforcement.

$E(\mathbf{S}) = \sum_{i,j} E_{i,j}(\mathbf{S})$ is minimized. Assuming camera parameters are correct and objects are Lambertian, the difference between $\mathbf{I}_i$ and $\mathbf{I}_j^{\mathbf{S},i}$ is due to the inaccurate surface $\mathbf{S}$. Here, we separate the minimization into two sub-problems.

Image Registration. The original formulation Eq. 1 measures the photo-consistency between $\mathbf{I}_i$ and $\mathbf{I}_j^{\mathbf{S},i}$. Instead, we switch the measurement space to x_j coordinate, *i.e.*, measuring $\mathbf{I}_i^{\mathbf{S},j}$ and $\mathbf{I}_j$. This particular choice enables two sub-problems to be recombined via the proxy x_j. To maximize the image similarity $\mathcal{M}$, we take the partial derivative of $-\mathcal{M}$ to the coordinate x_j of its first argument:

$$\nabla(-\mathcal{M})[x_j] = -\frac{\partial_1 \mathcal{M}(\mathbf{I}_i^{\mathbf{S},j}, \mathbf{I}_j)(x_j)}{\partial x_j} = \mathbf{G}_{\mathbf{I}_i^{\mathbf{S},j}}(x_j) \in \mathbb{R}^2. \qquad (2)$$

The 2D gradient field $\mathbf{G}_{\mathbf{I}_i^{\mathbf{S},j}}$ can be viewed as the optical-flow that registers $\mathbf{I}_i^{\mathbf{S},j}$ onto $\mathbf{I}_j$. We will show its fast computation in Sect. 2.2.

Gradient Aggregation. We consider a two-view scenario (Fig. 2(a)): a surface point $\mathbf{p}$ has two projected coordinates $x_i = \mathbf{\Pi}_i(\mathbf{p})$, $x_j = \mathbf{\Pi}_j(\mathbf{p})$. The image reprojection $\mathbf{I}_i^{\mathbf{S},j}$ deforms as surface $\mathbf{S}$ deforms. As $\mathbf{G}_{\mathbf{I}_i^{\mathbf{S},j}}$ is the gradient optimizes $\mathcal{M}$, we solve for the surface gradient $\mathbf{G}_{\mathbf{S}}$ which induces the desired $\mathbf{G}_{\mathbf{I}_i^{\mathbf{S},j}}$. To bridge them, we replace Eq. 2 with the derivative to a surface variation $\delta \mathbf{S}$:

$$\begin{aligned} \nabla(-\mathcal{M})[\delta \mathbf{S}](x_i) &= -\frac{\partial \mathcal{M}(\mathbf{I}_i^{\mathbf{S},j}(x_i \circ \mathbf{\Pi}_{i,\mathbf{S}+\epsilon\delta\mathbf{S}}^{-1} \circ \mathbf{\Pi}_j), \mathbf{I}_j)}{\partial \epsilon}\bigg|_{\epsilon=0} \\ &= \left(-\frac{\partial_1 \mathcal{M}(\mathbf{I}_i^{\mathbf{S},j}, \mathbf{I}_j)(x_j)}{\partial x_j}\right)\left(\frac{dx_j}{d\mathbf{p}}\right)\left(\frac{\partial \mathbf{\Pi}_{i,\mathbf{S}+\epsilon\delta\mathbf{S}}^{-1}(x_i)}{\partial \epsilon}\bigg|_{\epsilon=0}\right) \\ &= \left[\mathbf{G}_{\mathbf{I}_i^{\mathbf{S},j}}(x_j) \cdot \mathbf{J}_j \cdot \frac{\mathbf{d}_i}{\mathbf{N}^{\mathrm{T}}\mathbf{d}_i}\right] \mathbf{N}^{\mathrm{T}} \delta \mathbf{S}. \end{aligned}$$

Note that in line two, the first term $-\frac{\partial_1 \mathcal{M}(\mathbf{I}_i^{\mathbf{S},j},\mathbf{I}_j)(x_j)}{\partial x_j} = \mathbf{G}_{\mathbf{I}_i^{\mathbf{S},j}}(x_j)$ is pre-computed. The second term $\frac{dx_j}{d\mathbf{p}} = \mathbf{J}_j$ is the Jacobian of projection matrix $\mathbf{\Pi}_j$. The third term, assuming the surface movement is along its normal direction [14], can convert to $\left.\frac{\partial \mathbf{\Pi}_{i,\mathbf{S}+\epsilon\delta\mathbf{S}}^{-1}(x_i)}{\partial \epsilon}\right|_{\epsilon=0} = \frac{\mathbf{N}^T \delta\mathbf{S}(\mathbf{p})}{\mathbf{N}^T \mathbf{d}_i}\mathbf{d}_i$, where $\mathbf{N}$ is the normal of $\mathbf{p}$, and $\mathbf{d}_i$ is the joining vector from the camera center i to $\mathbf{p}$. Then, the gradient for a surface point $\mathbf{p}$ is:

$$\mathbf{G}_{\mathbf{S}}(\mathbf{p}) = \left[\mathbf{G}_{\mathbf{I}_i^{\mathbf{S},j}}(x_j) \cdot \mathbf{J}_j \cdot \frac{\mathbf{d}_i}{\mathbf{N}^T \mathbf{d}_i}\right] \mathbf{N}. \tag{3}$$

Regularized Discretization. Here, an optimize-then-discretize strategy is employed. The surface is represented by triangular mesh $\mathbf{M} = \{\mathbf{v}_0, \mathbf{v}_1, ...\mathbf{v}_n\}$, and the vertex refinement gradient is denoted as $\mathbf{G_M}$. An arbitrary surface point $\mathbf{p}$ can be written as the barycentric coordinate of the enclosing triangle vertices $\mathbf{p} = \sum_k \phi_k \mathbf{v_k}$, where $\sum_k \phi_k = 1$. This relation also holds for their gradient $\mathbf{G_S}(\mathbf{p}) = \sum_k \phi_k \mathbf{G_M}(\mathbf{v}_k)$. To solve for $\mathbf{G_M}$, we formulate it as a linear least square problem $\mathbf{A}_{[m*n]}\mathbf{G_M} = \mathbf{G_S}$, where matrix $\mathbf{A}$ fills with corresponding barycentric weights ϕ, and $m = \#surface\ points$, $n = \#vertices$ ($m \gg n$). As illustrated in Fig. 2(b), a pointwise gradient $\mathbf{G_S}(\mathbf{p})$ is sensitive to noise. However, the least-squared discrete gradient $\mathbf{G_M}(\mathbf{v})$ is much more regularized.

An additional regularization is applied to the data-term: the gradient of a vertex is expected to be smooth to its neighborhood: $\mathbf{G_M}(\mathbf{v}_i) = \frac{1}{N}\sum_{j\in N(i)}\mathbf{G_M}(\mathbf{v}_j)$. This relation for all the vertices can be written as $\beta\mathbf{B}_{[n*n]}\mathbf{G_M} = 0$, where β is a weight adjusting the smoothness. Stacking up matrix $\mathbf{A}$ and $\beta\mathbf{B}$ forms a massive sparse matrix, and the $\mathbf{G_M}$ can be solved via bi-conjugate gradient method. The $\mathbf{G_M}$ is applied to the mesh in each iteration: $\mathbf{M_{i+1}} = \mathbf{M_i} + \epsilon\mathbf{G_M}$.

Note that in previous method [19], the gradient of a vertex is the sum over its one-ring triangles from all pairs. Although it is faithful to its formulation, the gradient magnitude would be biased when the surface visibility is not balanced. *e.g.*, Regions viewed by more image pairs have larger magnitude. Our discretization based on a least square can prevent from the visibility bias problem.

Coarse-to-Fine. To alleviate the local optimal problem, we adopt a coarse-to-fine strategy. Multiple scales of images are set up beforehand. The input mesh is first smoothed and simplified to a certain level, followed by the refinement by images from low-res to high-res gradually over the iterations. A triangle would be subdivided if its projection area covers more than 9 pixels in any image pair. The step size ϵ is globally adjusted according to the edge length of the mesh.

2.2 Fast NCC Gradient

The image similarity gradient essentially drives the surface refinement. It is also the biggest performance bottleneck of the whole algorithm. Here, we provide a fast gradient computation on NCC similarity measurement.

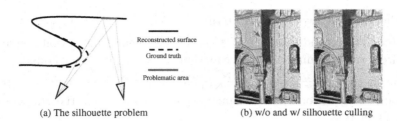

(a) The silhouette problem   (b) w/o and w/ silhouette culling

Fig. 3. Inaccurate surface induces image reprojection onto a wrong layer (a), and leads to a wrong refinement gradient ((b) left). With silhouette culling, this problem is avoided ((b) right).

In [5], the similarity metric is simply the rooted squared difference of pixel intensity $\|\mathbf{I}_i - \mathbf{I}_j\|_2$, which is fragile to inconsistent illumination. In [14,19], they employ ZNCC as similarity metric, but the gradient $\frac{\partial_1 \mathcal{M}}{\partial x}$ is separated into $\frac{\partial_1 \mathcal{M}}{\partial \mathbf{I}(x)} \frac{d\mathbf{I}(x)}{dx}$ using chain rules, where $\frac{d\mathbf{I}(x)}{dx} = \nabla \mathbf{I}(x)$ is simply the image gradient. We argue that it slows down the convergence due to two reasons: (1) as $\frac{\partial_1 \mathcal{M}}{\partial \mathbf{I}(x)}$ is a scalar, it implicitly constraints the refinement gradient $\frac{\partial_1 \mathcal{M}}{\partial x}$ to be on the image gradient orientation $\nabla \mathbf{I}(x)$, but in fact it may not be the steepest orientation; (2) a single pixel intensity $\mathbf{I}(x)$ is used to connect the chain rule, but the real computation of ZNCC is over a neighborhood of x.

To improve, we resort to a more efficient and direct way to solve for $\frac{\partial_1 \mathcal{M}}{\partial x}$. Concretely, we use Normalized Cross Correlation (NCC) instead of the zero-mean version, which reduces the chance of zero denominator. Consider Eq. 2 as the computation for gradient that registers a dynamic image $\mathbf{I}_d$ to a static image $\mathbf{I}_s$. We denote the scalar product $\mathrm{S}(d,s,x) = \sum_{x_k \in N(x)} (\mathbf{I}_d(x_k)\mathbf{I}_s(x_k))$, and then $\mathbf{NCC}(\mathbf{I}_d, \mathbf{I}_s)(x) = \frac{\mathrm{S}(d,s,x)}{[\mathrm{S}(d,d,x)\mathrm{S}(s,s,x)]^{1/2}} = \frac{A}{B}$. The gradient is computed by taking the derivative to the coordinate x of dynamic image $\mathbf{I}_d$:

$$\mathbf{G_I}(x) = \frac{\partial_1 \mathbf{NCC}(\mathbf{I}_d, \mathbf{I}_s)(x)}{\partial x} = \frac{\partial}{\partial x}\left(\frac{A}{B}\right) = \frac{B\frac{\partial A}{\partial x} - A\frac{\partial B}{\partial x}}{B^2},$$

where

$$\frac{\partial A}{\partial x} = \frac{\partial \mathrm{S}(d,s,x)}{\partial x} = \sum_N (\mathbf{D}_d(x)\mathbf{I}_s(x)) = \mathrm{S}(d',s,x),$$

$$\frac{\partial B}{\partial x} = \frac{\partial [\mathrm{S}(d,d,x)\mathrm{S}(s,s,x)]^{1/2}}{\partial x} = \left[\frac{\mathrm{S}(s,s,x)}{\mathrm{S}(d,d,x)}\right]^{\frac{1}{2}} \mathrm{S}(d',d,x).$$

$\mathbf{D}$ denotes the image gradient. The final formulation simplifies to:

$$\mathbf{G_I}(x) = \frac{\mathrm{S}(d',s,x) - \mathrm{S}(d',d,x)\frac{\mathrm{S}(d,s,x)}{\mathrm{S}(d,d,x)}}{\sqrt{\mathrm{S}(d,d,x)\mathrm{S}(s,s,x)}}.$$

The computation of $\mathbf{G_I}(x)$ is independent for every pixel x, making it perfectly suitable for GPU parallelism.

2.3 Silhouette Culling

Due to the inaccurate initial mesh, the image i is potentially reprojected to a wrong depth layer. This often happens along the silhouettes of the object, as shown in Fig. 3(a). While this problem is unsolved in the previous method, we handle it by explicitly detecting the silhouettes during the rendering for reprojection, and culling out problematic silhouette areas. A mesh edge $\mathbf{E}$ is a silhouette edge w.r.t. view i if and only if its two incident triangles $t_{0/1}$ are front face and back face. *i.e.*, silhouette edges $\mathbf{SE} = \{\mathbf{E}|\langle \mathbf{N}_{t_0}, \mathbf{N}_{view} \rangle \oplus \langle \mathbf{N}_{t_1}, \mathbf{N}_{view} \rangle, t_0, t_1 \in N(\mathbf{E})\}$. Pixels on $\mathbf{SE}$ are discarded in the refinement.

3 Adaptive Resolution Control

Motivated by the observation in Fig. 4, the ARC relaxes the original full refinement to partial refinement on selected regions. Specifically, the ARC segments the surface into two regions namely, *active* and *inactive*. *Active* represents those significant ones that will apply refinement. *Inactive* means those insignificant ones and would be discarded from refinement in exchange of performance gain.

Let f be a function that assigns each surface region R a label $f(R) \in \{active, inactive\}$. The trade-off can be formulated as an utility maximization:

$$u(f) = u_{accuracy}(f) + u_{time\_reduction}(f). \tag{4}$$

$u_{accuracy}(f)$ measures the utility derived from accuracy of ARC refinement. This can be measured as the *geometry improvement* achieved by refining only *active* regions. $u_{time\_reduction}(f)$ measures the utility derived from *time reduction* achieved by culling out *inactive* regions in refinement.

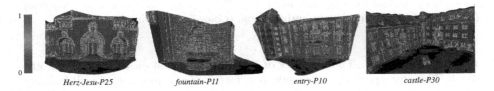

Herz-Jesu-P25   fountain-P11   entry-P10   castle-P30

Fig. 4. The magnitude of refinement gradient for four EPFL dataset [16] in early iteration. Most regions such as flat walls or grounds have very small gradient values (blue). They have very little geometry changes before and after refinement. (Color figure online)

3.1   Quantification on Triangular Meshes

In the context of meshes, triangle is the smallest unit of surface region. We define two metrics on triangle to concretely formulate the trade-off problem on meshes.

Geometry Improvement. As illustrated earlier, refinement on each vertex contributes differently to geometry improvement. To quantify the improvement, we borrow the *quadric error metric* used in mesh simplification [11], to capture the amount of geometry difference a vertex displacement can bring. This is a better alternative than vertex gradient magnitude alone because refinement has opposite goal[1] to simplification and hence should use the same set of metric. Let $\mathbf{v}$ and $\mathbf{v}'$ be the same vertex before and after a refinement iteration. As shown in Fig. 5(a), we define *geometry improvement (gi)* for a vertex $\mathbf{v}$ as the maximum of squared distances between $\mathbf{v}$ and one-ring neighbor planes of $\mathbf{v}'$, referred as $planes(\mathbf{v}')$, and gi for a triangle as the average of its three vertices:

$$gi_{\mathbf{v}} = max_{\mathbf{p} \in planes(\mathbf{v}')}\{(\mathbf{p}^t\mathbf{v})^2\}$$

$$gi_t = \frac{1}{3}\sum_i^3 gi_{\mathbf{v}_i},$$

where $\mathbf{v} = [v_x \ v_y \ v_z \ 1]^t$, $\mathbf{p} = [a \ b \ c \ d]^t$ represents a plane in standard form.

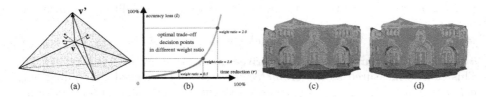

(a)   (b)   (c)   (d)

Fig. 5. (a) The *geometry improvement* of vertex is the maximum squared distance from $\mathbf{v}$ to $planes(\mathbf{v}')$. (b) Trade-off curve between time reduction and accuracy loss. (c) Labeling by *optimal trade-off decision* $f^{optimality}$. (orange – *active*, purple – *inactive*). (d) Final labeling by graph-cut optimization. (Color figure online)

Running Time Cost. The majority of computation spent on the refinement gradient. The cost spent on a triangle is a factor of the number of visible image pairs times its area. Then, the *time cost (tc)* for a triangle t is formulated as:

$$tc_t = \frac{1}{2}|(\mathbf{v_2} - \mathbf{v_0}) \times (\mathbf{v_1} - \mathbf{v_0})| \cdot (\#visible \ image \ pair(t)),$$

where $\mathbf{v_0}, \mathbf{v_1}, \mathbf{v_2}$ are three vertices of t.

---

[1] Simplification minimizes the geometry changes while refinement maximizes it.

3.2   Optimal Trade-Off Decision

Given the metrics introduced previously, we define the *cost effectiveness* (ce_t) of a triangle t as the ratio of its *geometry improvement* over its *time cost*, *i.e.*, $ce_t = gi_t/tc_t$. A higher *ce* means more accuracy can be achieved over the same unit of *time cost* by labeling it as *active*. Therefore we should always label triangles as *inactive* from the lowest *ce* to the highest *ce*.

To better illustrate the effect of this labeling principle, we compute the ce_t for all triangles and sort them in ascending order. Then we obtain an accumulation curve by incremental summation of tc_t on x-axis, and gi_t on y-axis in this sorted order. Every point on this curve represents a labeling configuration based on the principle, which will label all triangles below and above that particular point as *inactive* and *active*. Then we normalize both axes to $[0,1]$, and the x, y-axis can be interpreted as the *time reduction* $(r) = \sum_{inactive} tc_{t_i} / \sum_{total} tc_{t_i}$ and *accuracy loss* $(l) = \sum_{inactive} gi_{t_i} / \sum_{total} gi_{t_i}$ (as shown in Fig. 5(b)).

This curve gives us flexibility to control the amount of trade-off. We can fix a threshold or range on either *time reduction* or *accuracy loss* according to our application needs. More importantly, we can transform the problem space from label assignment function f to 2D space $(r, l) \in curve$. We rewrite Eq. 4 as:

$$u(r, l) = u_{accuracy}(l) + u_{time\_reduction}(r)$$
$$= w_l \cdot (1 - l) + w_r \cdot r,$$

where w_l and w_r are the weights for *accuracy loss* and *time reduction*. The *optimal trade-off decision point* (r_o, l_o) is on the curve such that

$$u(r_o, l_o) = max_{(r,l) \in curve} u(r, l),$$

which can be solved by taking derivative on $u(r, l)$. It can be deduced the optimal point (r_o, l_o) on curve has slope equal to $\frac{w_r}{w_l}$. This point represents the optimal labeling, *i.e.*, $f^{optimality}$ and it is unique because the slope of the curve is strictly increasing since it is already sorted. Note that *full refinement* can be seen as a special case represented by the point $(0, 0)$ on curve. The weight ratio $\frac{w_r}{w_l}$ is representing the relative importance of *time reduction* over *accuracy loss*. By default and in the following experiments, we use weight ratio $= 1$, which means putting equal weights on *accuracy loss* and *time reduction*.

3.3   Graph Optimization

Labeling the mesh by the *optimal trade-off decision* alone maximizes our utility function, but it also makes the labeling fragmented into a lot of small regions. An example is given in Fig. 5(c). A desired labeling should be consistent with the data-term labeling while being piecewise smooth over the mesh. Therefore graph cut optimization [1] is employed to cope with this problem.

Let f be a labeling configuration that assigns each triangle t a label $f_t \in \{active, inactive\}$. The energy function of f formulates as the sum of three terms:

$$\mathbf{E}(f) = \mathbf{E}_{optimality}(f) + \mathbf{E}_{smoothness}(f) + \mathbf{E}_{prior}(f). \tag{5}$$

Optimality. It is desirable that the final labeling keeps as much fidelity as possible to the data-term label given by *optimal trade-off decision*, $f^{optimality}$. So $\mathbf{E}_{optimality}(f)$ accumulates the penalty for all the triangle labels that violate the optimality labels, *i.e.*, $\mathbf{E}_{optimality}(f) = \sum_i 1[f_{t_i}^{optimality} \neq f_{t_i}]$.

Smoothness. As a nature prior, the labeling should be piecewise smooth. More importantly, a smooth labeling enables an effective simplification applied to a larger pieces of the mesh. We simply use the Potts model $\mathbf{E}_{smoothness}(f) = \sum_{i,j \in e_{ij}} 1[f_{t_i} \neq f_{t_j}]$ to enforce the labeling smoothness between neighboring triangles t_i and t_j. From our experiences, we omit using a weighting scheme such as edge length $||e_{i,j}||$, because a further normalization will easily be affected by the longest edge. Instead, we use uniform weighting to achieve a reasonable balance with $\mathbf{E}_{optimality}(f)$.

Textureness Prior. It is optional to add the textureness prior to the graph optimization. A sharp gradient change in 2D image does not always mean the real detail in 3D scene (*e.g.*, textured pattern on a flat wall), but it is true that, in most cases, a real 3D geometry detail will generate sharp gradient on its projected 2D image. We employ a prior energy to encourage the textured regions to be labeled as *active*. Specifically, we compute the average image gradient magnitude $||\nabla \mathbf{I}(t)||_2$ (normalized to $[0,1]$) over the pixels on the image which has the largest projection area of the triangle t. *i.e.*, $\mathbf{E}_{prior}(f) = \sum_t ||\nabla \mathbf{I}(t)||_2 \cdot [f_t = inactive]$.

Graph-cut optimization above yields a piecewise smooth labeling (as shown in Fig. 5(d)). Worth-mentioning, the labeling is naturally adapted to the scene. For example, the more non-textured regions the model has, the higher proportion will be labeled as *inactive*, and thus gives higher performance gain.

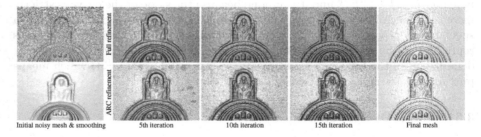

Initial noisy mesh & smoothing   5th iteration   10th iteration   15th iteration   Final mesh

Fig. 6. Left: the noisy mesh is smoothed before refinement. Right: comparison between *full refinement* and *ARC refinement* over iterations. The *full refinement* generates an evenly dense mesh, while the *ARC refinement* produces a mesh in adaptive resolution: the valuable (*e.g.*, edges) region has much denser triangles than unimportant regions (*e.g.*, planes), but the final quality is very similar to the fully refined one.

3.4 Combining with Refinement

Recall that the refinement employs a coarse-to-fine strategy. By default an image pyramid of three levels and 20 iterations of refinement are used. The ARC labeling recomputes once the image level changes, so ARC only executes three times in the whole refinement, which is of trivial cost. The *active* triangles go through the refinement algorithm, and would be subdivided if necessary. The *inactive* ones undergo a QEM [11] simplification with a certain simplifying ratio. This ratio is set to 0.2 in our experiments. The dramatic drop on #*triangle* effectively accelerates the rendering and mesh operations as well. Then, these triangles are fixed in later iterations. Except for the visibility testing, all computations regarding to them are culled out.

Figure 6 shows an evolutionary comparison between the baseline *full refinement* and our *ARC refinement*. The input noisy mesh will be smoothed before refinement. Overall, the *full refinement* produces much denser mesh, while the *ARC* method generates a very compact mesh in adaptive resolution. The final quality of both mesh surfaces are very close, and hardly be distinguished visually.

4 Experiment

The proposed method is implemented and evaluated on a machine with 8-core Intel i7-4770K and 32 GB of memory. The image reprojection and the refinement gradient is computed using OpenGL with a NVIDIA GTX980 graphic card.

In below experiments, two configurations of our method are compared. The *full refinement* refers to the highest accuracy refinement. The *ARC refinement* is with our *ARC* described in Sect. 3 using the default parameters.

4.1 Benchmarking

Our results are evaluated on two public MVS benchmarks [13,15].

Table 1. Quantitative comparison on selected datasets of DTU benchmark [13]. The term "our full" – *full refinement*, and "our ARC" – *ARC refinement*. Smaller is better.

	scan 36				scan 63				scan 106			
	Accuracy		Completeness		Accuracy		Completeness		Accuracy		Completeness	
	Mean	Med.	Mean	Med.	Mean	Med.	Mean	Med.	Mean	Med.	Mean	Med.
our full	**0.2644**	**0.1677**	0.9565	0.2319	**0.8433**	0.2267	0.6645	0.2663	**0.2855**	**0.1822**	0.9719	0.3083
our ARC	0.2646	0.1693	0.9602	0.2325	0.8516	0.2295	0.6687	0.2686	0.2865	0.1853	0.9744	0.3097
Vu [19]	**0.2641**	0.1683	0.9840	0.2337	0.8576	**0.2266**	0.6720	**0.2567**	0.2864	0.1850	0.9741	0.3040
tola [17]	0.3125	0.2007	1.0331	0.2856	0.9082	0.2711	0.7189	0.2985	0.3028	0.1902	0.9950	0.3256
furu [10]	0.6270	0.2778	0.6101	0.2930	2.3992	1.1192	0.6401	0.3849	0.7881	0.3028	0.7004	0.3244
camp [2]	0.5972	0.2317	**0.4622**	**0.2317**	2.4241	0.2782	**0.4730**	0.2782	0.5918	0.2793	**0.6902**	**0.2793**

DTU Benchmark. [13] covers a wide range of objects and each consists of 49 or 64 different views of images at 1600 × 1200 resolution. The high accuracy camera calibration is provided along with the dataset. To test our refinement algorithm, we borrow the initial surface generated by the method *tola* [17], and evaluate the *accuracy* and *completeness* of our final refined mesh by following the author's guideline. Note that the *accuracy* is defined as the distance from generated surface to the ground truth, and *completeness* the other way around.

We have tested the *full refinement* and the *ARC refinement* comparing to the baseline refinement method *Vu* [19] and three referencing methods provided in the benchmark, namely *tola* [17], *furu* [10] and *camp* [2]. Table 1 shows the statistics of three selected datasets (*scan 36, 63, 106*) each from a different category in the benchmark. All three refinement algorithms consistently improve the accuracy and completeness comparing to the initial mesh [17], and accuracy of our *full refinement* is the most competitive among all three datasets. Worth mentioning, our *ARC refinement* can achieve very close *accuracy* and *completeness* to *full refinement* by only refining partial regions.

Middlebury Benchmark is the very first MVS benchmark developed by Seitz *et al.* [15]. Although the image resolution is relatively low (640 × 480) by today's standard, it provides a fair platform for quantitative comparison (completeness and accuracy) with many other competing methods. Our method is not designed for such explicit fore/back-ground objects, but we still submit our *full refinement* results to the benchmark challenge. As shown in Fig. 7, our results produce no less than 99.5 % completeness on all full and ring datasets, and all items of the *temple* data rank within top 8th, which is very competitive among all methods. Overall, our *accuracy* is less competitive as our initial mesh tends to generate extra surface than the ground truth (*e.g.*, the bottom of the object).

Sort By	Temple Full 312 views		Temple Ring 47 views		Temple Sparse 16 views		Dino Full 363 views		Dino Ring 48 views		Dino Sparse 16 views	
	Acc [mm]	Comp [%]	Acc [mm]	Comp [%]	Acc [mm]	Comp [%]	Acc [mm]	Comp [%]	Acc [mm]	Comp [%]	Acc [mm]	Comp [%]
Furukawa 3	0.49	99.6	0.47	99.6	0.63	99.3	0.33	99.8	0.28	99.8	0.37	99.2
Furukawa 2	0.54	99.3	0.55	99.1	0.62	99.2	0.32	99.9	0.33	99.6	0.42	99.2
Campbell	0.41	99.9	0.48	99.4	0.53	98.6						
ECCV2016_104	0.41	99.6	0.49	99.5	0.57	98.1	0.44	99.8	0.46	99.7	0.42	98.0
CVPR2016_466	0.41	99.7	0.5	99.5	0.59	97.8	0.26	99.8	0.25	99.9	0.34	99.7
DCV			0.73	98.2	0.86	97.3			0.28	100	0.3	100
Galliani	0.39	99.2	0.48	99.1	0.53	97.0	0.31	99.9	0.3	99.4	0.38	98.6
Vogiatzis2	0.5	98.4	0.64	99.2	0.69	96.9						
Liu2					0.65	96.9					0.51	98.7
SurfEvolution			0.56	98.9	0.78	96.8			0.56	97.7	0.66	97.6
Depth Fusion			0.53	99.5	0.72	96.8			0.46	99.5	0.42	97.8
CVPR2014_1287			0.51	99.1	0.7	96.6			0.51	98.7		

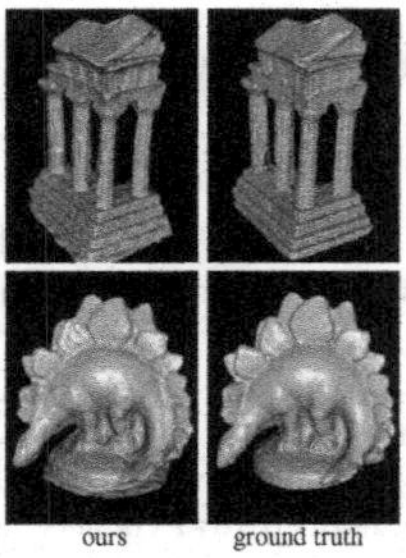

Fig. 7. Our results in Middlebury benchmark (highlighted in yellow). (Color figure online)

4.2   Performance Gain

We conducted experiments on public EPFL [16] and our private datasets to quantify the actual accuracy loss and performance gain of the *ARC refinement*.

To quantify the accuracy loss, we employ the *Hausdorff distance* to measure the difference between two meshes. The $accuracy\_loss = \frac{d_H(\mathbf{M}_{ARC},\mathbf{M}_{full})}{d_H(\mathbf{M}_{initial},\mathbf{M}_{full})}$, where $\mathbf{M}_{full}$ is the fully refined mesh, $\mathbf{M}_{ARC}$ the mesh by ARC refinement and $\mathbf{M}_{initial}$ the smoothed initial mesh, $d_H(\mathbf{M}_A,\mathbf{M}_B)$ means the distance from $\mathbf{M}_A$ to $\mathbf{M}_B$. The measured processing time excludes irrelevant common operations such as I/O. The performance gain is simply the ratio of processing time.

As shown in Table 2, the ARC achieves a 3-6x performance gain among all eight datasets. The actual performance gain varies on each individual dataset. For example, the *castle-P30* enjoys the highest performance gain and the second lowest accuracy loss because of the large area of plain walls and grounds in that dataset. However, the *campus* dataset has the highest accuracy loss and worst performance gain. We believe this is caused by the large area of vegetation in the dataset, which is deformable and thus not suitable for refinement. Vertices at such area usually have large but incorrect gradient. After all, the accuracy loss is less than 10 % for all datasets, which is tolerable for some applications.

We also record the *#vertex* at every refinement iteration for four EPFL datasets, shown in Fig. 8. The increase of the *#vertex* is caused by the subdi-

Table 2. The statistics of the performance comparison between *full refinement* and *ARC refinement*. Four EPFL datasets [16] and four large-scale datasets are evaluated.

Dataset name	Resolution	#image	Full refinement		ARC refinement		Accuracy loss	Performance gain
			#vertex	Time (sec)	#vertex	Time (sec)		
Herz-Jesu-P25	3072 x 2048	25	2438K	318	663K	56	3.86 %	5.68x
entry-P10	3072 x 2048	10	1564K	234	442K	43	7.28 %	5.44x
castle-P30	3072 x 2048	30	2901K	327	687K	54	2.87 %	6.06x
fountain-11	3072 x 2048	11	1455K	192	615K	49	3.74 %	3.92x
Santa_Prisca	4000 x 3000	129	5819K	1534	2160K	407	6.40 %	3.76x
memorial_hall	4000 x 3000	155	6928K	2395	2479K	438	2.17 %	5.47x
Swanstone	4000 x 3000	217	9233K	2408	3536K	554	4.82 %	4.35x
campus	6000 x 3376	276	35233K	7321	16513K	2420	9.68 %	3.02x

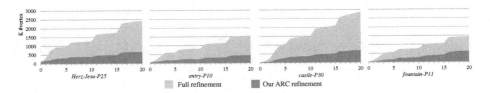

Fig. 8. Comparison of the *#vertex* throughout the iterations of refinement.

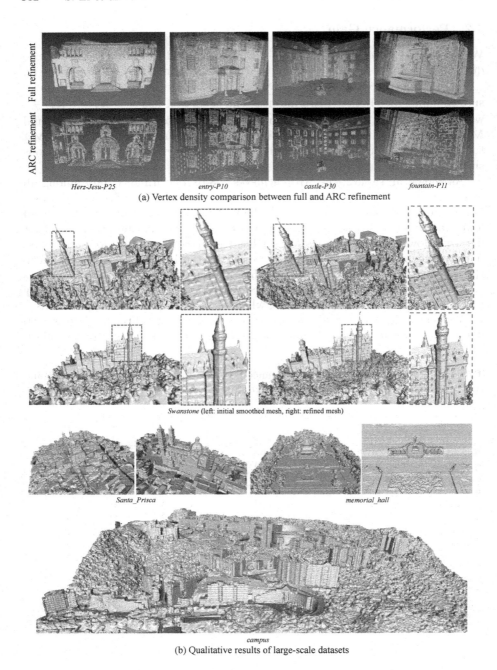

(a) Vertex density comparison between full and ARC refinement

Herz-Jesu-P25   *entry-P10*   *castle-P30*   *fountain-P11*

Swanstone (left: initial smoothed mesh, right: refined mesh)

Santa_Prisca   *memorial_hall*

campus

(b) Qualitative results of large-scale datasets

Fig. 9. Qualitative evaluation of our ARC refinement. The upper four (EPFL benchmark [16]) compare the vertex density. The lower four are samples of the refined mesh surface of several large-scale projects. **Best viewed on screen.**

vision on the mesh. The #vertex of ARC refinement keeps about one third of the #vertex of full refinement. The huge reduction in #vertex lowers the peak memory as well.

4.3 Qualitative Evaluation

We show the qualitative comparison using EPFL dataset [16] in Fig. 9(a). Our ARC refinement produces adaptive vertex density over the triangular mesh, and overall, much lower number of vertices and triangles than the full refinement.

The proposed method can handle large-scale projects by employing a divide-and-conquer strategy. The huge mesh will be divided into a few pieces such that each single piece with its visible images can fit in the memory. As shown in Fig. 9(b), four private datasets below are all captured by UAV. The Swanstone dataset composes 217 images at 4 K resolution. With a rough mesh surface as input, the ARC refinement is able to recover the fine details of the castle, such as the windows, or the crisp structures of the tower.

5 Conclusion

We have proposed the ARC refinement in this paper. The ARC estimates the most important regions to refinement and discard the other insignificant part in exchange for performance gain. The weight ratio controlling the trade-off between accuracy and performance is exposed and adjustable, which gives more flexibility to application demand. Our experiments demonstrate that ARC with default setting can achieve a dramatic speedup of 3-6x consistently with less than 10 % accuracy loss comparing to baseline full refinement, which conveys the fact that refinement in most regions is indeed almost futile. This confirms the effectiveness and robustness of our ARC design.

Acknowledgements. This work is supported by Hong Kong RGC 16208614, T22-603/15N, Hong Kong ITC PSKL12EG02, and China 973 program, 2012CB316300. We thank Ximin Lyu, Lidong Ma and Hector Duran for the private dataset.

References

1. Boykov, Y., Veksler, O., Zabih, R.: Fast approximate energy minimization via graph cuts. IEEE Trans. Pattern Anal. Mach. Intell. **23**(11), 1222–1239 (2001)
2. Campbell, N.D.F., Vogiatzis, G., Hernández, C., Cipolla, R.: Using multiple hypotheses to improve depth-maps for multi-view stereo. In: Forsyth, D., Torr, P., Zisserman, A. (eds.) ECCV 2008. LNCS, vol. 5302, pp. 766–779. Springer, Heidelberg (2008). doi:10.1007/978-3-540-88682-2_58
3. Delaunoy, A., Pollefeys, M.: Photometric bundle adjustment for dense multi-view 3d modeling. In: 2014 IEEE Conference on Computer Vision and Pattern Recognition (CVPR), pp. 1486–1493. IEEE (2014)

4. Delaunoy, A., Prados, E.: Gradient flows for optimizing triangular mesh-based surfaces: applications to 3d reconstruction problems dealing with visibility. Int. J. Comput. Vis. **95**(2), 100–123 (2011)
5. Delaunoy, A., Prados, E., Piracés, P.G.I., Pons, J.P., Sturm, P.: Minimizing the multi-view stereo reprojection error for triangular surface meshes. In: BMVC 2008-British Machine Vision Conference, pp. 1–10. BMVA (2008)
6. Esteban, C.H., Schmitt, F.: Silhouette and stereo fusion for 3d object modeling. Comput. Vis. Image Underst. **96**(3), 367–392 (2004)
7. Fabri, A., Pion, S.: Cgal: the computational geometry algorithms library. In: Proceedings of the 17th ACM SIGSPATIAL International Conference on Advances in Geographic Information Systems, pp. 538–539. ACM (2009)
8. Faugeras, O., Keriven, R.: Variational principles, surface evolution, PDE's, level set methods and the stereo problem. Technical report RR-3021, INRIA, October 1996
9. Furukawa, Y., Ponce, J.: Carved visual hulls for image-based modeling. In: Leonardis, A., Bischof, H., Pinz, A. (eds.) ECCV 2006. LNCS, vol. 3951, pp. 564–577. Springer, Heidelberg (2006). doi:10.1007/11744023_44
10. Furukawa, Y., Ponce, J.: Accurate, dense, and robust multiview stereopsis. IEEE Trans. Pattern Anal. Mach. Intell. **32**(8), 1362–1376 (2010)
11. Garland, M., Heckbert, P.S.: Surface simplification using quadric error metrics. In: Proceedings of the 24th Annual Conference on Computer Graphics And Interactive Techniques, pp. 209–216. ACM Press/Addison-Wesley Publishing Co. (1997)
12. Heise, P., Jensen, B., Klose, S., Knoll, A.: Variational patchmatch multiview reconstruction and refinement. In: Proceedings of the IEEE International Conference on Computer Vision, pp. 882–890 (2015)
13. Jensen, R., Dahl, A., Vogiatzis, G., Tola, E., Aanæs, H.: Large scale multi-view stereopsis evaluation. In: 2014 IEEE Conference on Computer Vision and Pattern Recognition (CVPR), pp. 406–413. IEEE (2014)
14. Pons, J.P., Keriven, R., Faugeras, O.: Multi-view stereo reconstruction and scene flow estimation with a global image-based matching score. Int. J. Comput. Vis. **72**(2), 179–193 (2007)
15. Seitz, S.M., Curless, B., Diebel, J., Scharstein, D., Szeliski, R.: A comparison and evaluation of multi-view stereo reconstruction algorithms. In: 2006 IEEE Computer Society Conference on Computer vision and pattern recognition, vol. 1, pp. 519–528. IEEE (2006)
16. Strecha, C., von Hansen, W., Gool, L.V., Fua, P., Thoennessen, U.: On benchmarking camera calibration and multi-view stereo for high resolution imagery. In: IEEE Conference on Computer Vision and Pattern Recognition, CVPR 2008, pp. 1–8. IEEE (2008)
17. Tola, E., Lepetit, V., Fua, P.: Daisy: an efficient dense descriptor applied to wide-baseline stereo. IEEE Trans. Pattern Anal. Mach. Intell. **32**(5), 815–830 (2010)
18. Tylecek, R., Sara, R.: Refinement of surface mesh for accurate multi-view reconstruction. Int. J. Virtual Reality **9**(1), 45–54 (2010)
19. Vu, H.H., Labatut, P., Pons, J.P., Keriven, R.: High accuracy and visibility-consistent dense multiview stereo. IEEE Trans. Pattern Anal. Mach. Intell. **34**(5), 889–901 (2012)

Gaussian Process Density Counting
from Weak Supervision

Matthias von Borstel[1], Melih Kandemir[1(✉)], Philip Schmidt[1],
Madhavi K. Rao[2], Kumar Rajamani[2], and Fred A. Hamprecht[1]

[1] HCI, Heidelberg University, Heidelberg, Germany
melih.kandemir@iwr.uni-heidelberg.de
[2] Robert Bosch Engineering, Bangalore, India

Abstract. As a novel learning setup, we introduce learning to count objects within an image from only region-level count information. This level of supervision is weaker than earlier approaches that require segmenting, drawing bounding boxes, or putting dots on centroids of all objects within training images. We devise a weakly supervised kernel learner that achieves higher count accuracies than previous counting models. We achieve this by placing a Gaussian process prior on a latent function the square of which is the count density. We impose non-negativeness and smooth the GP response as an intermediary step in model inference. We illustrate the effectiveness of our model on two benchmark applications: (i) synthetic cell and (ii) pedestrian counting, and one novel application: (iii) erythrocyte counting on blood samples of malaria patients.

1 Introduction

Counting objects of interest within an image is a fundamental requirement of many applications. Biologists gain insights on cell population dynamics from such counts, pedestrian counting helps urban planners, and counting cars is crucial for detecting or foreseeing traffic jams.

Traditional approaches to counting proceed by first detecting all targets and then counting them. The transductive principle [1], instead, suggests never to solve a harder problem than the target application necessitates. As a consequence, recent models [2–4] exploit the fact that estimating the object count does not necessarily require accurate detection of individual objects, let alone their segmentation. They focus exclusively on the easier task of assigning each pixel a density in such a way that when the densities within any image region are integrated, a good prediction of the true object count in that region is obtained. This approach is called *density counting* [2].

The main disadvantage of density counting is that it requires a sufficiently large number of per-object annotations. For instance, a common practice in cell counting is to densely annotate a few tens of images by marking the centroids of *all* cells with a dot. This task demands a considerable effort from the annotator. Given the dots, the ground-truth density counts of individual pixels are approximated by placing a Gaussian kernel on top of each dot within an image.

© Springer International Publishing AG 2016
B. Leibe et al. (Eds.): ECCV 2016, Part I, LNCS 9905, pp. 365–380, 2016.
DOI: 10.1007/978-3-319-46448-0_22

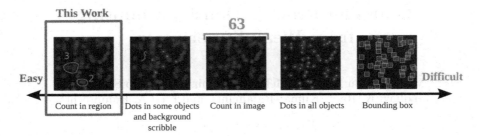

Fig. 1. Comparison of different annotation methods with respect to their difficulty for the annotator. Bounding box annotation is used by [5], dots in *all* objects by [2], dots in some objects by [3,4], and image-level annotations by [6,7].

We propose an object counting model that reconciles the density counting approach with weaker supervision. Our model *learns to predict density counts from a set of image regions for each of which only the number of contained objects is known*. Differently from earlier approaches, our model does not require the user to mark where the target objects are within these regions. Figure 1 gives a visual comparison of annotation requirements of our approach and previous work.

As the learner, we devise a Bayesian model that places a Gaussian process (GP) prior [8] on a latent function whose square is the count density. We impose a smoothness prior on this latent function and assume a Gaussian likelihood that relates the integral over the squared smoothed latent function over a region with the ground-truth count. In addition to facilitating intuitive modeling, the GP prior enables us to employ non-linear kernels on image features, resulting in a model with enhanced expressive power. A welcome feature of our Bayesian approach is that our model produces uncertainty estimates. Finally, we achieve fast and scalable training by sparsify the GP prior and applying stochastic variational inference [9]. Thanks to this scalability, our model is able to operate on individual pixels, rather than superpixels, keeping the model depend loosely on preprocessing.

We evaluate our model on two benchmark data sets: (i) cell counting in synthetic fluorescence microscopy images, and (ii) pedestrian counting from outdoor video sequences. Additionally, we introduce a novel application for density counting: counting of erythrocytes in blood samples of malaria patients which is useful for diagnostic purposes. In all of these experiments, we observe that the proposed model achieves higher counting accuracies than a large selection of models that are also trained with weak annotations. Our contributions can be summarized as follows. We introduce:

– A new learning setup: Density counting from weak supervision (i.e. region-level counts).
– A novel Bayesian model for weakly supervised density counting with a GP prior on a latent function the square of which is the count density.

- A fast inference algorithm that makes our model usable for pixel-level processing of the input image.
- The first application of density counting to malaria blood cell images.

2 Background

Counting. Approaches to object counting from images can be grouped into two categories: (i) counting by detection, and (ii) counting by regression. Counting by detection works by first detecting each individual object in an image and then counting the number of detections. In some cases this method is combined with a foregoing segmentation step where each segment is expected to contain one object. This method relies heavily on a good object detector or some other heuristic that identifies regions containing a individual object. These methods work best when the individual objects are clearly distinguishable [10–13].

Counting with regression skips the detection step and infers the count of objects in the image by regression over features associated with individual pixels, an entire image or regions found by a foregoing segmentation step. Segmented regions are allowed to contain multiple objects in this case. This approach is very suitable for cases where the objects are partly occluded or hard to detect individually [6,7,14–16]. Lempitsky and Zisserman [2] introduced a third alternative approach for counting objects in images: *density counting*. This method predicts not only an object count for the whole image but a count density for each pixel. Integrating over these pixel count densities in an arbitrary region yields the count of the region. This method has later on been adapted to sparse annotations [3] and has also been used within an interactive model where users could annotate according to feedbacks from the model [4], and finally, has been adapted to deep learning by [17]. These methods have in common that the regression model needs pixel-level density annotations. Providing pixel-level annotations is a tedious task and these methods circumvent this task by applying a density shape assumption around the center of each object specified by the user.

MIR. Our method does not need pixel-level annotations. Instead, it builds on a Multiple Instance Regression (MIR) formulation.[1] In MIR, several regions in the image are annotated with their corresponding counts. The model learns how to assign the pixel-level count densities to obtain the right region counts. The MIR formulation has different modes depending on fundamental assumptions about the structure of the data [18–22]. It either seeks for a prime instance (pixel) in each bag (region) that is responsible for the bag label (region count) or assumes that all instances (pixels) contribute to the bag label (region count). These two modes are called the *prime instance* assumption and the *instance relevance* assumption, respectively. In this work, we adopt the instance relevance assumption, hence, allow each instance label to contribute to the bag label. We then treat the sum of all instance labels as the bag label.

---

[1] Our definition of MIR differs from that put forward in [18], where a single instance in a bag determines the entire count for the bag.

GP. Gaussian processes are probabilistic kernel learners [23] which apply a prior on the space of functions mapping an input to a continuous output. This prior follows a multivariate normal distribution with a mean $\mu(\mathbf{x})$ and a covariance $k(\mathbf{x}, \mathbf{x}')$ function. It is customary to assume $\mu(\mathbf{x}) = 0$. As for $k(\mathbf{x}, \mathbf{x}')$, any positive definite function can be used. For a data matrix $\mathbf{X} = [\mathbf{x}_1, \cdots, \mathbf{x}_N]$ with N data points in rows and the corresponding noise-free outputs $\mathbf{f}$, a GP imposes an N-variate normal prior on the mapping function: $\mathbf{f}|\mathbf{X} \sim \mathcal{N}(\mathbf{0}, \mathbf{K_{XX}})$, where $\mathbf{K_{XX}}$ is a covariance matrix with entries is $\mathbf{K_{XX}}[ij] = k(\mathbf{x}_i, \mathbf{x}_j)$ calculated by a positive definite kernel function $k(\cdot, \cdot)$ applied on each pair of feature vectors $\mathbf{x}_i$ and $\mathbf{x}_j$.

GPs have been proven useful in many learning setups. GPLVM [28,33], the generative extension of GPs, attracted widespread attention as an effective non-linear dimensionality reduction tool. Its inference scheme has inspired techniques to scale GPs up to millions of data points [31] and to build alternative deep learning approaches that contain GPs as perceptrons [29]. Finally, GPs improved the state-of-the-art in binary classification from weak labels [24,25]. We show in this paper that they can be trained by weak supervision for density counting as well. We achieve this by placing a sparse approximation of the GP [26] as a prior on a latent value, the square of which gives the count density of a pixel.

3   Density Counting Setup and Notation

Following the seminal work by Lempitsky and Zisserman [2], we build on the density counting setup, which can formally be defined as follows. Let $\mathbf{I} \in \mathbb{R}^{N_x \times N_y \times N_c}$ be an image of $N_x \times N_y = N$ pixels and N_c channels. We look for a function $g : \mathbf{I} \to \boldsymbol{\rho}$ that maps this image onto its density map $\boldsymbol{\rho} \in \mathbb{R}_+^N$, such that the sum taken over any region b inside $\boldsymbol{\rho}$ gives the count c_b of target objects in that region: $\sum_{i \in \mathcal{B}_b} \rho_i = c_b$. The task here is to learn a function g that predicts density maps that lead to accurate object counts on all regions. For each pixel i in image $\mathbf{I}$, we extract a feature vector $\mathbf{x}_i \in \mathbb{R}^D$ from the neighbourhood of i and store it as a row in matrix $\mathbf{X} \in \mathbb{R}^{N \times D}$. We use B arbitrarly shaped regions in the image for annotations. One annotation b consists of the set of pixels $\mathcal{B}_b$ that belong to the region b and the count of target objects c_b that reside within that region. The feature vectors of all pixels i that belong to region b are stored as rows in matrix $\mathbf{X}_b \in \mathbb{R}^{N_b \times D}$ and the corresponding object count is element c_b of count vector $\mathbf{c} \in \mathbb{R}_+^B$.

4   Baseline: Counting with Linear Models

A simple model for function g that maps an image $\mathbf{I}$ to its density map $\boldsymbol{\rho}$ would be the linear mapping where the count c_b for each region b is given by

$$c_b = \sum_{i \in \mathcal{B}_b} \rho_i = \sum_{i \in \mathcal{B}_b} \boldsymbol{\omega}^T \mathbf{x}_i = \boldsymbol{\omega}^T \mathbf{X}_b^T \mathbf{1},$$

where $\mathbf{1} = [1, \ldots, 1]^T$ and $\boldsymbol{\omega} \in \mathbb{R}^D$. Several methods exist for learning a para-meter vector $\boldsymbol{\omega}$. In [4], a L-2 regularizer with the following objective function is minimized

$$L(\boldsymbol{\omega}; \theta, \varepsilon) = \frac{1}{2}\boldsymbol{\omega}^T\boldsymbol{\omega} + \theta \sum_b \max(0, |\boldsymbol{\omega}^T\mathbf{X}_b^T\mathbf{1} - c_b| - \varepsilon)^2$$

where ε is the allowed divergence from the true count and θ is a regulariza-tion parameter. We enhance this model by an additional regularization term to encourage smooth density maps and use as a baseline to motivate the core model proposed in the next section. The resultant objective function is

$$L(\boldsymbol{\omega}, \xi_b; \theta, \varepsilon) = \min_{\boldsymbol{\omega}, \xi_b} \left(\frac{1}{2}\boldsymbol{\omega}^T(\mathbf{X}^T\mathbf{D}^T\mathbf{D}\mathbf{X})\boldsymbol{\omega} + \theta \sum_b \xi_b \right)$$

subject to:

$$\boldsymbol{\omega}^T\mathbf{X}_b^T\mathbf{1} - c_b - \varepsilon \leq \xi_b, \qquad \boldsymbol{\omega}^T\mathbf{X}_b^T\mathbf{1} - c_b + \varepsilon \geq \xi_b, \qquad \xi_b \geq 0,$$

where $\mathbf{D}\mathbf{X}\boldsymbol{\omega} = \mathbf{D}\boldsymbol{\rho}$ is the first spatial derivative of the density map, and ξ_b are slack variables. The slack variables prevent the model from overfitting to data by allowing a small error on individual data points. This model gives a family of linear count regressors and includes the ridge regression model of [2] as a special case. Furthermore, it improves that model with large margin regulariza-tion and density smoothing. As there does not exist any earlier work tailored specifically for weakly supervised density counting, we take as a baseline the weakly-supervised version of a state-of-the-art global count regressor with an added smoothing term.

5   Gaussian Process Multiple Instance Counting

In this section, we describe the proposed GP-based weakly supervised density counting model.

5.1   Core Model

We introduce a novel probabilistic and non-linear model for object counting to address some severe limitations of linear models such as limited flexibility and the possibility of obtaining negative densities in some pixels. Our main contribution is that we place a Gaussian process prior on the latent function $\mathbf{f} \in \mathbb{R}^N$ whose square is the count density $\boldsymbol{\rho}$: $\mathbf{f}|\mathbf{X} \sim \mathcal{N}(\mathbf{f}|\mathbf{0}, \mathbf{K_{XX}})$. We impose the fact that a count is non-negative by assigning a region not the sum of $\mathbf{f}$ but the sum of its element-wise square $c_b = \sum_{i \in \mathcal{B}_b} \rho_i = \sum_{i \in \mathcal{B}_b} f_i^2 = \mathbf{f}_b^T\mathbf{f}_b$, where the index b indicates the part of latent vector $\mathbf{f}$ that belongs to bag b. We make the central assumption that *we only know the counts for image regions* (i.e. a group of pixels).

Following the multiple instance learning terminology, we denote each annotated pixel group as a *bag*. Hence, during training, we are given a group of observations partitioned into bags $\mathbf{X} = \{\mathbf{X}_1 \cup \mathbf{X}_2 \cup \cdots \cup \mathbf{X}_B\}$ with the corresponding bag labels $\mathbf{c} = \{c_1, \cdots, c_B\}$. Note that a bag $\mathcal{B}_b$ is a set of pixels from one or multiple image regions. Put together, the GP prior and the c_b formula above lead to the generative process

$$p(\mathbf{f}|\mathbf{X}) = \mathcal{N}(\mathbf{f}|\mathbf{0}, \mathbf{K}_{\mathbf{XX}}), \quad p(\mathbf{c}|\boldsymbol{\rho}) = \prod_{b=1}^{N_b} \mathcal{N}(c_b|\mathbf{f}_b^T \mathbf{f}_b, \beta^{-1}).$$

The first density is a GP prior on the latent function whose square is the count density map, and the latter performs density counting on the squared latent function $\mathbf{f}$ subject to a small additive measurement noise with precision β. We refer to this novel model as *Gaussian Process Multiple Instance Counting (GPMIC)*.

5.2 Sparsifying the GP

While the GP prior brings the model high expressive power by kernelizing the input patterns, it suffers from the fact that both storage and time complexities of the covariance matrix $\mathbf{K}$ grow quadratically with the total number of unique pixels in the annotated bags. Furthermore, the probability density function of the normal distribution requires inversion of this potentially large matrix. This prevents the above model from generalizing to even modest data set sizes (e.g. a few tens of thousands of instances). We overcome this problem using *Fully Independent Training Conditional (FITC)* [26], a well-known technique to approximate the full GP on vector $\mathbf{f}$ by

$$p(\mathbf{u}|\mathbf{Z}) = \mathcal{N}(\mathbf{u}|\mathbf{0}, \mathbf{K}_{\mathbf{ZZ}}), \qquad p(\mathbf{f}|\mathbf{u}, \mathbf{X}, \mathbf{Z}) = \mathcal{N}(\mathbf{f}|\mathbf{Au}, \mathbf{B}), \qquad (1)$$

where $\mathbf{A} = \mathbf{K}_{\mathbf{ZX}}^T \mathbf{K}_{\mathbf{ZZ}}^{-1}$ and $\mathbf{B} = diag(\mathbf{K}_{\mathbf{XX}} - \mathbf{K}_{\mathbf{ZX}}^T \mathbf{K}_{\mathbf{ZZ}}^{-1} \mathbf{K}_{\mathbf{ZX}})$. Note here that we no longer have to invert the full $\mathbf{K}_{\mathbf{XX}}$ matrix as it never determines the covariance of a normal distribution. Instead, we define a so-called *inducing point set* $\mathbf{Z} \in \mathbb{R}^{P \times D}$ with a much smaller number of data points than $\mathbf{X}$ (so that $P << N$). Then we assign a GP prior from $\mathbf{Z}$ to its so-called *inducing responses* $\mathbf{u}$. We assume that the responses $\mathbf{f}$ (i.e. the vector of latent values whose square gives the count densities of pixels) of our real data set $\mathbf{X}$ are generated as predictions from the GP on this small pseudo data set. The operator $diag(\cdot)$ returns the diagonal elements of the matrix in its argument as a diagonal matrix. Note that this matrix can easily be inverted by taking the reciprocal of its diagonal entries. The resultant model in Eq. 1 converts the non-parametric GP into a parametric model that can express the training set only by $\mathbf{u}$ and $\mathbf{Z}$, regardless of its size. This approximation has close ties to the well-known Nyström approximation of kernel matrices [27].

5.3 Smoothing the Density Map

Mapping the pixel (neighborhood) features onto density counts is very prone to produce uninterpretable density maps, since edges, image acquisition artifacts, and tiny fluctuations in appearances may lead to larger changes in feature descriptions of pixels than intended. Furthermore, in some cases such as cell counting, the objects of interest may have easily-encodable characteristic shapes. Providing the model with prior knowledge about how the density counts of the neighboring pixels should affect each other would be very desirable. Such information can be plugged into our model very easily.

Given an image $\mathbf{I}$ and its latent function whose square is the count density map $\mathbf{f}$, we are interested in smoothing the GP response, rather than the input. Hence, we convolve $\mathbf{f}$ by a $J \times J$-pixel-sized linear filter $\mathbf{W} \in \mathbb{R}^{J \times J}$. For this we can simply generate a matrix $\mathbf{R}_w$ such that $\mathbf{R}_w \mathbf{f} = \mathbf{F} * \mathbf{W}$, where $\mathbf{F} \in \mathbb{R}^{N_x \times N_y}$ is $\mathbf{f}$ expressed on the input image coordinates and $*$ is the convolution operator that convolves the filter in its right argument on the matrix in its left argument. We define a new latent random vector $\mathbf{g}$, which encodes the smoothed version of $\mathbf{f}$. Remember that $\mathbf{f}$ follows a GP prior, hence we have

$$p(\mathbf{f}|\mathbf{X}) = \mathcal{N}(\mathbf{f}|\mathbf{0}, \mathbf{K_{XX}}), \qquad p(\mathbf{g}|\mathbf{f}) = \mathcal{N}(\mathbf{g}|\mathbf{R}_w\mathbf{f}, \beta^{-1}\mathbb{I}),$$

where $\mathbb{I}$ is the identity matrix with size determined by the context. To see the effect of smoothing on the GP prior, let us integrate out $\mathbf{f}$:

$$p(\mathbf{g}|\mathbf{X}) = \int p(\mathbf{g}|\mathbf{f})p(\mathbf{f}|\mathbf{X})d\mathbf{f} = \int \mathcal{N}(\mathbf{g}|\mathbf{R}_w\mathbf{f}, \beta^{-1}\mathbb{I})\mathcal{N}(\mathbf{f}|\mathbf{0}, \mathbf{K_{XX}})d\mathbf{f}$$
$$= \mathcal{N}(\mathbf{g}|\mathbf{0}, \beta^{-1}\mathbb{I} + \mathbf{R}_w\mathbf{K_{XX}}\mathbf{R}_w^T). \tag{2}$$

Since $\mathbf{K}$ is a positive semi-definite matrix governed by a proper kernel function, we have $k(\mathbf{x}, \mathbf{x}') = \phi(\mathbf{x})^T\phi(\mathbf{x}')$. Hence, the kernel function projects our input observation $\mathbf{x}$ onto a higher-dimensional Hilbert space with $\phi(\cdot)$. Repeating the same on every data point by the capitalized argument $\mathbf{X}$, we can essentially express the entire $\mathbf{K_{XX}}$ on the Hilbert space as $\phi(\mathbf{X})^T\phi(\mathbf{X})$. Placing this into the covariance matrix in Eq. 2 leads to

$$\mathbf{K'_{XX}} = \beta^{-1}\mathbb{I} + \mathbf{R}_w\phi(\mathbf{X})^T\phi(\mathbf{X})\mathbf{R}_w^T.$$

This eventually gives a GP on $\mathbf{g}$ with a new kernel function

$$k'(\mathbf{x}_i, \mathbf{x}_j) = \phi'(\mathbf{x}_i)^T\phi'(\mathbf{x}_j) + \delta_{ij}\beta^{-1}$$

such that $\phi'(\mathbf{X}) = \phi(\mathbf{X}) * \mathbf{W}$. Here, δ_{ij} denotes the Kronecker delta function. Hence, the response of the former $\phi(\cdot)$ is convolved *on the Hilbert space* by the filter $\mathbf{W}$. As we will show in Sect. 6, smoothing the kernel *response* on the image space leads to more interpretable density counts.

5.4 Final Model

Putting together everything above, our model reads

$$p(\mathbf{u}|\mathbf{Z}) = \mathcal{N}(\mathbf{u}|\mathbf{0}, \mathbf{K_{ZZ}}), \qquad p(\mathbf{f}|\mathbf{u}, \mathbf{X}, \mathbf{Z}) = \mathcal{N}(\mathbf{f}|\mathbf{Au}, \mathbf{B}),$$

$$p(\mathbf{g}|\mathbf{f}) = \mathcal{N}(\mathbf{g}|\mathbf{R}_w\mathbf{f}, \beta^{-1}\mathbb{I}), \qquad p(\mathbf{c}|\mathbf{g}) = \prod_{b=1}^{B} \mathcal{N}\left(c_b\Big|\mathbf{g}_b^T\mathbf{g}_b, \alpha^{-1}\right),$$

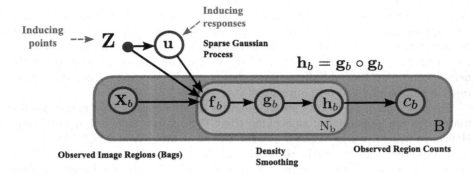

Fig. 2. Plate diagram of the proposed model. For simplicity, the diagram pretends that the annotated regions do not overlap, $\mathcal{B}_b \cap \mathcal{B}'_b = \emptyset$ for $b \neq b'$. Our actual model is not limited by this assumption.

where $\mathbf{g}_b$ denotes the subset of the smoothed pixel latent function whose square is the count density belonging to region b. Figure 2 depicts the plate diagram of the proposed model. Note here that the inner product $\mathbf{g}_b^T \mathbf{g}_b$ equals to the sum of the element-wise square of $\mathbf{g}_b$. With the former, the model performs density counting and with the latter non-negative counts are imposed. Principles of Bayesian statistics suggest integrating out all nuisance variables [30]. In this case, it is possible to integrate out $\mathbf{f}$, which leads to

$$p(\mathbf{g}|\mathbf{u}) = \int p(\mathbf{g}|\mathbf{f})p(\mathbf{f}|\mathbf{u})\mathrm{d}\mathbf{f} = \mathcal{N}(\mathbf{g}|\mathbf{R}_w\mathbf{A}\mathbf{u}, \beta^{-1}\mathbb{I} + \mathbf{R}_w\mathbf{B}\mathbf{R}_w^T).$$

Although integrating out $\mathbf{u}$ is possible [26], this would end up with a non-parametric model, preventing scalable inference. Following [31], we avoid this and keep $\mathbf{u}$ as a global parameter which paves our way towards stochastic variational inference [32].

5.5 Inference

In learning, our goal is to infer the posterior distribution

$$p(\mathbf{g}, \mathbf{u}|\mathbf{X}, \mathbf{c}) = \frac{p(\mathbf{c}, \mathbf{g}, \mathbf{u}|\mathbf{X})}{\int\int p(\mathbf{c}|\mathbf{g})p(\mathbf{g}|\mathbf{u}, \mathbf{X})p(\mathbf{u})d\mathbf{g}d\mathbf{u}} = \frac{p(\mathbf{c}|\mathbf{g})p(\mathbf{g}|\mathbf{u}, \mathbf{X})p(\mathbf{u})}{\int\int p(\mathbf{c}|\mathbf{g})p(\mathbf{g}|\mathbf{u}, \mathbf{X})p(\mathbf{u})d\mathbf{g}d\mathbf{u}}.$$

Since the integral in the denominator is not tractable, this posterior density needs to approximated. As shown in recent studies [31], FITC approximation leads to scalable variational Bayesian inference, which we also adopt in this work. As [33], we assume the variational distribution $Q = p(\mathbf{g}|\mathbf{u}, \mathbf{X}, \mathbf{Z})q(\mathbf{u})$ where $q(\mathbf{u}) = \mathcal{N}(\mathbf{u}|\mathbf{m}, \mathbf{L}^T\mathbf{L})$ and $\mathbf{L} \in \mathbb{R}^{P \times P}$. The decomposition $\mathbf{L}^T\mathbf{L}$ is made to guarantee a positive-semi definite covariance matrix. It is possible to decompose the marginal likelihood as:

$$\log\,p(\mathbf{c}|\mathbf{X},\mathbf{Z}) = \underbrace{\mathbb{E}_Q[\log p(\mathbf{c}|\mathbf{g})] - \mathbb{KL}(Q||p(\mathbf{u}|\mathbf{Z}))}_{ELBO(\mathcal{L})} + \mathbb{KL}(Q||p(\mathbf{g},\mathbf{u})),$$

where $\mathbb{KL}(\cdot||\cdot)$ denotes Kullback-Leibler (KL) divergence between the two densities in its arguments. The first two terms in this decomposition constitute the *Evidence Lower Bound (ELBO)*. During training, our goal is to maximize the ELBO, or in other words, minimize the KL divergence in the third term by updating the free parameters $\{\mathbf{m},\mathbf{L}\}$ of our approximate distribution Q. Note that the third term vanishes only when we reach the real posterior. This only provides an asymptotical guarantee. In practice, this term is never exactly zero. After computing all expectations, our ELBO reads

$$\mathcal{L}(\mathbf{m},\mathbf{L},\boldsymbol{\theta},\mathbf{Z}) = \frac{B}{2}\log\alpha + \sum_b \left(-\frac{\alpha}{2}c_b{}^2 - \frac{\alpha}{2}\mathbb{E}_Q[(\mathbf{g_b}^T\mathbf{g_b})^2] + \alpha c_b\mathbb{E}_Q[\mathbf{g_b}^T\mathbf{g_b}]\right)$$

$$+ \mathbb{E}_{q(\mathbf{u})}[\log p(\mathbf{u}|\mathbf{Z})] + \mathbb{H}[q(\mathbf{u})] - \frac{1}{2}\log\left(\frac{|\mathbf{K_{ZZ}^{-1}}|}{|\mathbf{L}^T\mathbf{L}|}\right) + \frac{dim(\mathbf{m})}{2}$$

$$= \alpha\sum_b\left[-\frac{1}{2}c_b^2 + c_b\left(\mathrm{Tr}\,[\mathbf{G}] + \mathbf{h}^T\mathbf{h}\right) - \left(2\mathrm{Tr}\,[\mathbf{G}^2] + 4\mathbf{h}^T\mathbf{Gh} + \left(\mathrm{Tr}\,[\mathbf{G}] + \mathbf{h}^T\mathbf{h}\right)^2\right)\right]$$

$$\frac{B}{2}\log\alpha - \frac{1}{2}\left[tr\left[\mathbf{K_{ZZ}^{-1}}\mathbf{L}^T\mathbf{L}\right] + \mathbf{m}^T\mathbf{K_{ZZ}^{-1}}\mathbf{m}\right],$$

where $\mathbf{G} = \beta^{-1}\mathbb{I} + \mathbf{R}_{wb}\mathbf{B}_b\mathbf{R}_{wb}^T + \mathbf{R}_{wb}\mathbf{A}_b\mathbf{L}^T\mathbf{L}\mathbf{A}_b^T\mathbf{R}_{wb}^T$ and $\mathbf{h} = \mathbf{R}_{wb}\mathbf{A}_b\mathbf{m}$ and $\mathbf{G}^2$ is the element-wise square of $\mathbf{G}$. The subscript b of the variables $\mathbf{g}_b$, $\mathbf{A}_b$ $\mathbf{B}_b$ and $\mathbf{R}_{wb}$ indicates a subset of these vectors or matrices corresponding to the pixels of bag b. Using these region-level values speeds up inference significantly, as the dimensionality of the kernels is now reduced to the size of each individual region. Above, $\mathbb{E}_Q[\cdot]$ denotes the expected value of the argument with respect to the distribution Q, $dim(\cdot)$ returns the dimension of the vector in the argument, and $\mathrm{Tr}[\cdot]$ is the Trace operator. Here, $\mathcal{L}$ depends on the kernel hyperparameters $\boldsymbol{\theta}$, variational parameters $\mathbf{m}$, $\mathbf{L}$, and the inducing points $\mathbf{Z}$, all of which can be learned by gradient updates. To this end, we use stochastic gradient descent updates where we randomly chose one bag during each iteration. This approach is known as stochastic variational inference [32].

5.6   Prediction

Given a new region $\mathbf{X}^*$, the predictive distribution on the density maps is

$$p(\mathbf{g}^*|\mathbf{X}^*) = \int p(\mathbf{c}^*|\mathbf{g}^*)p(\mathbf{g}^*|\mathbf{u},\mathbf{X},\mathbf{Z})p(\mathbf{u},\mathbf{g}|\mathbf{X},\mathbf{c})d\mathbf{u}d\mathbf{g}.$$

We approximate the posterior $p(\mathbf{u},\mathbf{g}|\mathbf{X},\mathbf{c})$ by the distribution learned during training $Q = p(\mathbf{g}|\mathbf{u},\mathbf{X},\mathbf{Z}) \times q(\mathbf{u})$. Both of the integrals here are tractable in closed form, leading to

$$p(\mathbf{g}^*|\mathbf{X}^*) = \mathcal{N}(\mathbf{g}^*|\mathbf{R}_w\mathbf{Am},\beta^{-1}\mathbb{I} + \mathbf{R}_w\mathbf{BR}_w^T).$$

6   Results

6.1   Baselines

Since no method exists that performs density counting from weak and sparse region annotations we adapted some existing methods to this new learning setup and treat as baselines. We also perform a lesion study on major components of our GPMIC. Consequently, we compare against the following models:

- **Linear Model:** This is the model introduced in Sect. 4, where the density of each pixel is a linear mapping of the feature vector of the pixel x_i with the parameter vector ω. The count c_b of region b is then given by the sum over the pixel densities. This is, in effect, a multiple instance regression model based on the instance relevance assumption: $c_b = \omega^T \sum_b x_b$.

- **MIR Cluster Bags:** This model is a variant of the above linear model and the one proposed in [21]. The key assumption of this model is that the bags have an internal structure. Hence, the individual instances in each bag belong to different abstract classes that correspond to clusters in the feature space. The model considers only the instances of one prime class to predict the count. This means the sum over the feature vectors x_{b_i} that belong to the prime cluster i of bag b is mapped to the count c_b of bag b using the parameter vector ω: $c_b = \omega^T \sum_{b_i} x_{b_i}$.

- **GPMIC No Square:** This is a simplified version of the proposed GPMIC with the difference that the GP prior is placed on the count density of each pixel instead of a latent value whose square is the count density. The probabilistic process if this baseline reads

$$p(\mathbf{u}|\mathbf{Z}) = \mathcal{N}(\mathbf{u}|\mathbf{0}, \mathbf{K}_{\mathbf{ZZ}}), \qquad p(\mathbf{f}|\mathbf{u}, \mathbf{X}, \mathbf{Z}) = \mathcal{N}(\mathbf{f}|\mathbf{Au}, \mathbf{B}),$$

$$p(\mathbf{g}|\mathbf{f}) = \mathcal{N}(\mathbf{g}|\mathbf{R}_w\mathbf{f}, \beta^{-1}\mathbb{I}), \qquad p(\mathbf{c}|\mathbf{g}) = \prod_{b=1}^{B} \mathcal{N}\left(c_b \Big| \mathbf{1}^T\mathbf{g}_b, \alpha^{-1}\right).$$

- **GPMIC Unsmoothed:** This is another variant of GPMIC where the smoothing step introduced to enforce spatial smoothness of the density map is omitted. We introduce this baseline to demonstrate the benefit of smoothing. The resultant model is

$$p(\mathbf{u}|\mathbf{Z}) = \mathcal{N}(\mathbf{u}|\mathbf{0}, \mathbf{K}_{\mathbf{ZZ}}), \qquad p(\mathbf{g}|\mathbf{u}, \mathbf{X}, \mathbf{Z}) = \mathcal{N}(\mathbf{g}|\mathbf{Au}, \mathbf{B}),$$

$$p(\mathbf{c}|\mathbf{g}) = \prod_{b=1}^{B} \mathcal{N}\left(c_b \Big| \mathbf{g}_b^T\mathbf{g}_b, \alpha^{-1}\right).$$

- **Bag level histogram:** This method, introduced as a baseline in [2], does not perform *density* counting, as it does not predict pixel-level count densities but instead directly predicts the count of whole images or regions of an image from a histogram that describes the image or the region. The count c_b of region b is given by a linear map of the histogram vector $\mathbf{h}_b$ with weight vector $\boldsymbol{\omega}$: $c_b = \boldsymbol{\omega}^T \mathbf{h}_b$.

- **Random Forest:** This baseline [3] is an application of random forests to density counting. The model in its vanilla form is trained with strong supervision at the pixel level. These labels are obtained by clicking on the center of an object and then placing a normal distribution with unit norm on this object center pixel to infer the count density for all the neighbouring pixels. To label background regions, users are asked to give a stroke to the background of an image and then all pixels that belong to that stroke are labeled with count density zero. We labeled the same parts of the training images with this method as we annotated for our weakly supervised methods.

- **Convolutional Neural Net (CNN):** This baseline uses the CNN architecture proposed in [17] for cell counting. We trained the CNN on 50 regions of 40×40-pixels that are strongly annotated using the same Gaussian density prior as the random forest. We use elastic transformations to augment the annotated data. We train the model for 15 epochs with gradually decreasing learning rate. We evaluate this model only on the synthetic cell data set, as the CNN architecture has been specifically tailored for this kind of data.

6.2   Experiments

We evaluate our proposed GP-based weakly supervised density counting model and the baselines described in Sect. 6.1 on two benchmark tasks: (i) synthetic cell counting, (ii) pedestrian counting from [2], and one novel task: (iii) erythrocyte counting in blood sample slides of malaria patients. The synthetic cell data set consists of a set of simulated fluorescence microscopy images containing round-shaped synthetic cells. The pedestrian counting application is based on a surveillance video of a street where pedestrians walk in two opposite directions. Finally, the Malaria data set consists of microscopy images of erythrocytes that are partly infected by Malaria and partly healthy. For all data sets, the position of the center pixel of each object is provided as ground truth. The general properties of the data sets are show in Table 1 and example images from the data sets are shown in the first column of Fig. 3.

Table 1. General properties of the data sets.

Name	# Images	Average count
Pedestrian	2000	29 ± 9
Synthetic cells	200	171 ± 64
Malaria	78	90 ± 84

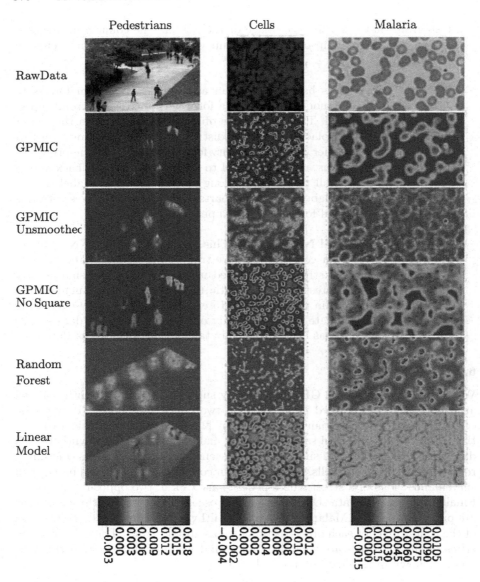

Fig. 3. Example densities for each dataset and all density counting methods. To illustrate the differences better, the Random Forest densities for the Pedestrian and Malaria data set were scaled by a factor of 0.35 and 0.47 respectively.

For the results reported in Table 2, we use regions annotated by humans. For the pedestrian and the synthetic cells data sets, we use the same features and identical pre- and post-processing procedures as described in [3]. We characterized each pixel by the feature set consisting of Gaussian and Laplacian of

Table 2. Mean Average Errors (MAE) of the models in comparison. The "Dense" column indicates whether a method provides a density map or not. GPMIC (Unsmoothed) and GPMIC (No Square) are more basic versions of the main GPMIC model. As the CNN of Xie et al. [17] is tailored specifically for the synthetic cell data set, we do not use it as a baseline in the remaining two applications.

Regression model	Pedestrians	Cells	Malaria	Dense
Linear model (Baseline Sect. 4)	21.3	22.1	23.7	Yes
MIR cluster bags [21]	4.8	15.5	19.6	No
Bag-level histogram linear [2]	10.7	17.4	23.7	No
Random forest [3]	3.6	10.0	21.1	Yes
Convolutional neural net [17]	–	7.8	-	Yes
GPMIC (Unsmoothed)	15.8	21.2	26.2	Yes
GPMIC (No square)	20.3	8.6	29.9	Yes
GPMIC (This work)	**3.5**	**6.7**	**18.0**	Yes

Gaussian filters, Gaussian gradient magnitude, and the eigenvalues of structure tensors at scales 0.8, 1.6, and 3.2. Also for the Malaria data set we use the same features as for the synthetic cells data set described in [3] but this time for all three color channels of the RGB images. As the density smoothing kernel $\mathbf{W}$, we use a 11×11-pixels sized Gaussian density normalized to unity on that patch with a variance of four for all three experiments. We use stochastic variational inference to maximize the ELBO with respect to $\mathbf{m}$ and $\mathbf{L}$. To achieve faster convergence we initialize

$$\mathbf{m} \to \arg \min_{m} \sum_{b} \left(\|\mathbf{A}_b \mathbf{m}\| - c_b r_1 \right),$$

$$\mathbf{L} \leftarrow \mathbb{I} \cdot 1/r_2,$$

where r_1 and r_2 are scaling parameters that further improve the initialization. We have observed that $r_1 = \bar{P}_b/10$ and $r_2 = 1000$, where $\bar{P}_b$ is the average number of pixels per bag, is a suitable choice.

For the experiment on the synthetic cells data set we take the same approach as described by [2] and use the first 100 images as training set and the last 100 images as test set. We then annotate 5 images from the training set with 14 weak annotations each. On the Pedestrian data set we use five out of the 2000 frames, sparsely annotate ten regions on each frame, and leave the rest for evaluation. On the Malaria data set we use five images with ten weak annotations on each image as training set and the rest of the 78 images as test set. We train the baseline models on the same annotated regions. In Fig. 3, we show the density maps obtained by our model and the baselines described in Sect. 6.1. Table 2 reports the mean average count prediction errors of the models in comparison, averaged over ten runs. GPMIC always gives the best performance in all three data sets, while it is tightly followed on the pedestrian data set by the random forest based density counting baseline. The results also reveal that the Malaria data set is harder than the other two benchmarks. This is understandable since the erythrocytes highly vary in shape when they are infected by malaria and they also overlap heavily no matter if they are healthy or diseased. Figure 3 clearly shows qualitative differences between the different methods. The smoothing step in GPMIC leads to a count density map that better reflects the real shape of the objects. A model without smoothing tends to learn a pronounced edge density in such cases as the Malaria data set. Note that GPMIC No Square allows negative count densities which also occur, as one can see in Fig. 3, and lead to worse performance compared to the original GPMIC model as shown in Table 2.

Once strong annotations are provided, it is possible to achieve marginally better results on the synthetic cells and pedestrian data sets as reported in various earlier work [2–4,7,14,17]. However, these models need considerably more annotation effort. Our model trains in 114, 32, and 341 s on pedestrian, cells, and malaria data sets, respectively on a machine with 8 GB RAM and 2.3 GHz CPU. The training times for the closest competitor, Random Forest [3], for the same data sets are in the sub-second range. The CNN of [17] designed specifically for the Cells data set trains in 5478 s. Consequently, our model achieves better prediction performance than the baselines within reasonable training time in all three applications.

7   Conclusion

We propose a novel machine learning setup, weakly supervised density counting, and introduce a novel model that gives state-of-the-art performance on this setup. For the first time, we show the usability of GPs as effective prior functions on pixel count densities. This is made possible by building on the recent advances on scalable variational inference, which enables the GP prior to operate at the pixel level. Secondly, we propose an intermediary density smoothing scheme, which proves effective to regularize the count densities and achieve interpretable estimates. Lastly, we show that density counting can be successfully performed on a new medical application: counting blood cells of malaria patients. We believe this outcome to evoke new ideas for a number of clinical use cases.

An alternative way to enforce smooth density maps would be to introduce a normal distributed latent variable $\mathbf{g}$ with the regularized Laplacian precision matrix $\mathbf{Q}$: $p(\mathbf{g}|\mathbf{f}) = \mathcal{N}(\mathbf{g}|\mathbf{f}, \mathbf{Q}^{-1})$. The disadvantage of this formulation is that the inverse of the regularized Laplacian matrix is needed during inference, which is computationally very demanding.

The Bayesian nature of GPMIC allows closed-form calculation of the posterior predictive density, which provides a second-order uncertainty measure (variance) for predictions. This measure can easily be used to build effective interactive learning interfaces using information-theoretic active learning criteria, such as *Bayesian Active Learning by Disagreement (BALD)* [34]. We are encouraged to address such interesting implications of the proposed model in future work.

References

1. Vapnik, V.: Statistical Learning Theory. Springer, New York (1998)
2. Lempitsky, V., Zisserman, A.: Learning to count objects in images. In: NIPS (2010)
3. Fiaschi, L., Nair, R., Koethe, U., Hamprecht, F., et al.: Learning to count with regression forest and structured labels. In: ICPR (2012)
4. Arteta, C., Lempitsky, V., Noble, J., Zisserman, A.: Interactive object counting. In: ECCV (2014)
5. Ryan, D., Denman, S., Fookes, C., Sridharan, S.: Crowd counting using group tracking and local features. In: AVSS (2010)
6. Cho, S.Y., Chow, T., Leung, C.T.: A neural-based crowd estimation by hybrid global learning algorithm. IEEE Trans. Syst. Man Cybern. Part B Cybern. $29(4)$, 535–541 (1999)
7. Kong, D., Gray, D., Tao, H.: A viewpoint invariant approach for crowd counting. In: ICPR (2006)
8. Williams, C., Rasmussen, C.: Gaussian Processes For Machine Learning, vol. $2(3)$, p. 4. The MIT Press, Cambridge (2006)
9. Hensman, J., Rattray, M., Lawrence, N.: Fast variational inference in the conjugate exponential family. In: NIPS (2012)
10. Bernardis, E., Stella, X.: Pop out many small structures from a very large microscopic image. Med. Image Anal. $15(5)$, 690–707 (2011)
11. Mualla, F., Schöll, S., Sommerfeldt, B., Maier, A., Steidl, S., Buchholz, R., Hornegger, J.: Unsupervised unstained cell detection by sift keypoint clustering andself-labeling algorithm. In: MICCAI (2014)
12. Arteta, C., Lempitsky, V., Noble, J., Zisserman, A.: Learning to detect cells usingnon-overlapping extremal regions. In: MICCAI (2012)
13. Kainz, P., Urschler, M., Schulter, S., Wohlhart, P., Lepetit, V.: You should use regression to detect cells. In: Navab, N., Hornegger, J., Wells, W.M., Frangi, A.F. (eds.) MICCAI 2015. LNCS, vol. 9351, pp. 276–283. Springer, Heidelberg (2015). doi:10.1007/978-3-319-24574-4_33
14. Ryan, D., Denman, S., Fookes, C., Sridharan, S.: Crowd counting using multiple local features. In: DICTA (2009)
15. Chan, A., Liang, Z.S., Vasconcelos, N.: Privacy preserving crowd monitoring: counting people without people models or tracking. In: CVPR (2008)
16. Chan, A., Vasconcelos, N.: Counting people with low-level features and Bayesian regression. IEEE Trans. Image Process. $21(4)$, 2160–2177 (2012)
17. Xie, W., Noble, J., Zisserman, A.: Microscopy cell counting with fully convolutional regression networks. In: MICCAI (2015)
18. Wang, Z., Lan, L., Vucetic, S.: Mixture model for multiple instance regression and applications in remote sensing. IEEE Trans. Geosci. Remote Sens. $50(6)$, 2226–2237 (2012)
19. Ray, S., Page, D.: Multiple instance regression. In: ICML (2001)
20. Wagstaff, K., Lane, T.: Salience assignment for multiple-instance regression. Jet Propulsion Laboratory, National Aeronautics and Space Administration, Pasadena, CA (2007)
21. Wagstaff, K., Lane, T., Roper, A.: Multiple-instance regression with structured data. In: ICDMW (2008)
22. Pappas, N., Marconi, R., Popescu-Belis, A.: Explaining the stars: weighted multiple-instance learning for aspect-based sentiment analysis. In: EMNLP (2014)

23. Rasmussen, C., Williams, C.: Gaussian Processes For Machine Learning. MIT Press, Cambridge (2006)
24. Kim, M., de la Torre, F.: Gaussian processes multiple instance learning. In: ICML (2010)
25. Kandemir, M., Zhang, C., Hamprecht, F.: Empowering multiple instance-histopathology cancer diagnosis by cell graphs. In: MICCAI (2014)
26. Snelson, E., Ghahramani, Z.: Local and global sparse Gaussian process approximations. In: AISTATS (2007)
27. Williams, C., Seeger, M.: Using the Nyström method to speed up kernel machines. In: NIPS (2001)
28. Lawrence, N.D. Gaussian process latent variable models for visualisation of high dimensional data. In: NIPS (2004)
29. Lawrence, N.D. Deep Gaussian processes. In: AISTATS (2013)
30. Gelman, A., Carlin, J., Stern, H., Rubin, D.: Bayesian Data Analysis, vol. 2. Chapman & Hall/CRC, Boca Raton (2014)
31. Hensman, J., Fusi, N., Lawrence, N.: Gaussian processes for big data (2013). arXiv preprint arXiv:1309.6835
32. Hoffman, M., Blei, D., Wang, C., Paisley, J.: Stochastic variational inference. J. Mach. Learn. Res. **14**(1), 1303–1347 (2013)
33. Titsias, M.K., Lawrence, N.D.: Bayesian Gaussian process latent variable model. In: AISTATS (2010)
34. Houlsby, N., Huszar, F., Ghahramani, Z., Hernández-Lobato, J.: Collaborative Gaussian processes for preference learning. In: NIPS (2012)

Region-Based Semantic Segmentation with End-to-End Training

Holger Caesar$^{(\boxtimes)}$, Jasper Uijlings, and Vittorio Ferrari

University of Edinburgh, Edinburgh, Scotland
holger.caesar@ed.ac.uk

Abstract. We propose a novel method for semantic segmentation, the task of labeling each pixel in an image with a semantic class. Our method combines the advantages of the two main competing paradigms. Methods based on region classification offer proper spatial support for appearance measurements, but typically operate in two separate stages, none of which targets pixel labeling performance at the end of the pipeline. More recent fully convolutional methods are capable of end-to-end training for the final pixel labeling, but resort to fixed patches as spatial support. We show how to modify modern region-based approaches to enable end-to-end training for semantic segmentation. This is achieved via a differentiable region-to-pixel layer and a differentiable free-form Region-of-Interest pooling layer. Our method improves the state-of-the-art in terms of class-average accuracy with 64.0 % on SIFT Flow and 49.9 % on PASCAL Context, and is particularly accurate at object boundaries.

1 Introduction

We address the task of semantic segmentation, labeling each pixel in an image with a semantic class. Currently, there are two main paradigms: classical region-based approaches [1–17] and, inspired by the Convolutional Neural Network (CNN) revolution, fully convolutional approaches [18–26].

In the fully convolutional approach the idea is to directly learn a mapping from image pixels to class labels using a CNN. This results in a single model, directly optimized end-to-end for the task at hand, including the intermediate image representations (i.e. the hidden layers in the network). However, the spatial support on which predictions are based are fixed-size square patches of the input image. Intuitively, this is suboptimal since: (I) Objects are free-form rather than square, so ideally the intermediate representations should take this into account. (II) Objects do not have a fixed size, but occur at various scales. Hence many patches either cover pieces of multiple objects and mix their representations, or cover a piece of an object, which is sometimes difficult to recognize in isolation (e.g. a patch on the belly of a cow). An additional problem is that fully convolutional methods typically make predictions at a coarse resolution, which often results in inaccurate object boundaries [18,20–22,24,26]. Figure 1 illustrates this on example outputs of [20].

© Springer International Publishing AG 2016
B. Leibe et al. (Eds.): ECCV 2016, Part I, LNCS 9905, pp. 381–397, 2016.
DOI: 10.1007/978-3-319-46448-0_23

Image   GT   Eigen [20]   Image   GT   Eigen [20]

Fig. 1. Fully convolutional methods typically produce fuzzy object boundaries, as illustrated here by examples from Eigen and Fergus [20].

In the region-based approach, the image is first segmented into coherent regions, which are described by image features [1–16]. Typically many regions are extracted at multiple scales [2–4,6–8,10–12], capturing complete objects and canonical object parts (e.g. faces) which in turn facilitates recognition. Furthermore, the segmentation process delivers regions which follow object boundaries quite well. However, these methods generally first extract region features and then train a classifier optimized for classifying regions rather than for the final semantic segmentation criterion (i.e. pixel-level labeling) [2–4,6–8,10]. Hence, while these methods benefit from the power of multi-scale, overlapping regions, they cannot be trained end-to-end for semantic segmentation.

In this paper we want the best of both worlds. We propose a region-based semantic segmentation model with an accompanying end-to-end training scheme based on a CNN architecture (Fig. 2c). To enable this we introduce a novel, differentiable region-to-pixel layer which maps from regions to image pixels. We insert this layer before the final classification layer, enabling the use of a pixel-level loss which allows us to directly optimize for semantic segmentation. Conceptually, our region-to-pixel layer ignores regions which have low activations for all classes and which therefore do not impact the final labeling. This is in contrast to all multi-scale region-based methods where such regions incorrectly affect training [2–4,6–8,10]. Additionally, we introduce a differentiable Region-of-Interest pooling layer which operates on the final convolutional layer in the spirit of Fast R-CNN [27], but which is adapted for free-form regions like [4,11,12]. Note how we use region proposals from a separate pre-processing stage. By end-to-end we mean training all parameters for the final pixel-level loss, rather than for region classification.

To summarize, our contributions are: (1) We introduce a region-to-pixel layer which enables full end-to-end training of semantic segmentation models based on multi-scale overlapping regions. (2) We introduce a Region-of-Interest pooling layer specialized for free-form regions. (3) We obtain state-of-the-art results on the SIFT Flow and the PASCAL Context datasets, in terms of class-average accuracy. Our approach delivers crisp object boundaries, as demonstrated in Fig. 5 and Sect. 4.3. We release the source code of our method at https://github.com/nightrome/matconvnet-calvin.

2 Related Work

2.1 Region-Based Semantic Segmentation

Region-based semantic segmentation methods first extract free-form regions [28–31] from an image and describe them with features. Afterwards a region classifier is trained. At test time, region-based predictions are mapped to pixels, usually by labeling a pixel according to the highest scoring region that contains it. Region-based methods generally yield crisp object boundaries [1–17]. Figure 2b shows a prototypical architecture for such an approach (which we modernized by basing it on Fast R-CNN [27]). We discuss several aspects below.

Multi-scale vs Single-Scale Regions. Several region-based methods use an oversegmentation to create small, non-overlapping regions [1,5,9,13–16]. Intuitively however, objects are more easily recognized as a whole than by looking at small object parts individually. The inherent multi-scale aspect of recognition is adequately captured in many recent works using multi-scale, overlapping regions [2–4,6–8,10–12].

Training Criterion. The final criterion is pixel-level prediction of class labels. However, we use overlapping regions whose predictions are in competition with each other on the pixel level. Typically, many methods initially ignore this by simply training a classifier to predict region labels [2–4,6–8,10], which is *different* from semantic segmentation (Sect. 3.1). At test time one labels a pixel by simply taking the maximum over all regions containing it [2–4,6,7]. A few works partially addressed the mismatch between training and test time through a post-processing stage using graphical models [8,10] or by joint calibration [2]. However, none of them does full end-to-end training.

Region Representations. Most older works use hand-crafted region-based features [1,3,5,8,10,13–16] often based on [3,13]. More recent works instead use the top convolutional layers of a pre-trained CNN (e.g. [32,33]) as feature representations [2,4,6,7,9,11,12]. These representations can be free-form respecting the shape of the region [4,6,7,9,11,12] or simply represent the bounding box around the region [2,6]. Furthermore regions can be cropped out from the image before being fed to the network [6,7,9] or one can create region representations from a convolutional layer [4,11,12], termed Region-of-Interest (ROI) pooling [27] or Convolutional Feature Masking [4]. CNN representations become more powerful when further trained for the task. In [2,6,7] they train CNNs, but for the task of region classification, not for semantic segmentation.

2.2 Fully Convolutional Semantic Segmentation

Fully convolutional methods learn a direct mapping from pixels to pixels, which was pioneered by [34] in the pre-CNN era. Early CNN-based approaches train relatively shallow end-to-end networks [21,25], whereas more recent works use much deeper networks whose weights are initialized by pre-training on the ILSVRC [35] image classification task [18–20, 22–24, 26]. The main insight to adapt these networks for semantic segmentation was to re-interpret the classification layer as 1×1 convolutions [23, 36]. A prototypical model is illustrated in Fig. 2a.

Square Receptive Fields. All fully convolutional methods have receptive fields of fixed shape (square) [18–26]. However, since objects are free-form this may be suboptimal.

Multi-scale. Recognition is a multi-scale problem, which is addressed by using two strategies: *(I) Multi-scale representations.* Using skip-layer connections [37, 38], representations from different convolutional layers can be combined [20, 22, 23, 25]. This leads to multi-scale representations of a predetermined size. *(II) Multi-scale application.* In [22, 24] they train and apply their method on multi-scale, rectangular image crops. However, this results in a mismatch between training time, where each crop is considered separately, and test time, where predictions of multiple crops are combined before evaluation.

Fuzzy Object Boundaries. It is widely acknowledged that fully convolutional approaches yield rather fuzzy object boundaries [18, 20–22, 24, 26]. A variety of strategies address this. *(I) Multi-scale.* The multi-scale methods discussed above [20, 22–25] include a fine scale resulting in improved object boundaries. *(II) Conditional Random Fields (CRFs).* CRFs are a classical tool to refine pixel-wise labelings and are used as post-processing step by [18, 21, 24, 26]. Notably, [26] reformulate the CRF as a recurrent neural network enabling them to train the whole network including convolutional layers in an end-to-end fashion. *(III) Post-processing by region proposals.* Finally, [21] averages pixel-wise network outputs over regions from an oversegmentation.

2.3 This Paper

We propose a model based on free-form, multi-scale, overlapping regions. We design a partially differentiable region-to-pixel layer enabling end-to-end training for semantic segmentation. Additionally we introduce a ROI pooling layer which is free-form [4, 11, 12] yet also differentiable [27].

3 Method

Section 3.1 presents a baseline model that is representative for modern region-based semantic segmentation [2, 4, 6, 7] (Fig. 2b), and explains its shortcomings. Sections 3.2, 3.3, 3.4 and 3.5 present our framework, which addresses these issues (Fig. 2c).

3.1 Region-Based Semantic Segmentation

Model. Figure 2b presents a typical region-based semantic segmentation architecture. It modernizes [2, 4, 6, 7] by using the Region-of-Interest pooling layer of [27]. We use this model as a baseline in our experiments (Sect. 4).

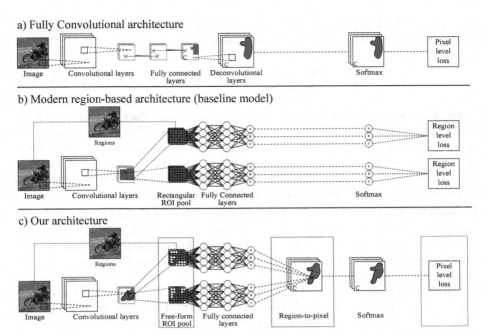

Fig. 2. Overview of three semantic segmentation architectures. We show only layers with trainable parameters, softmax and loss layers. We omit all pre- and post-processing steps. (a) shows the class of fully convolutional architectures that are end-to-end trainable, but do not have regions. (b) shows the baseline model, representative for modern region-based architectures. It is not end-to-end trainable for the desired pixel labeling criterion. (c) shows our suggested architecture, which pools activations of each region in a free-form manner, maps the region-level predictions to pixels and computes a loss at the pixel level. Hence our method combines regions and end-to-end training. Our main contributions are highlighted by orange boxes. (Color figure online)

The input to the network are images and free-form regions [29]. The image is fed through several convolutional layers. A Region-of-Interest pooling layer [27] creates a feature representation of the tight bounding boxes around each region. These region features are then fed through several fully connected layers and a classification layer, followed by a softmax, resulting in region-level predictions. At test time, these predictions are mapped from regions to pixels: each pixel p is assigned the label o_p with the highest probability over all classes and all regions containing p:

$$o_p = \operatorname*{argmax}_c \; \max_{r \ni p} \; \operatorname{softmax}_c S_{r,c} \tag{1}$$

Here $S_{r,c}$ denotes the classifier scores for region r and class c (i.e. activations of the classification layer).

Training. The training procedure searches for the network parameters that minimize a cross-entropy log-loss $\mathcal{L}$ over regions:

$$\mathcal{L} = -\sum_c \frac{1}{R} \sum_{r=1}^{R} y_{r,c} \log \operatorname*{softmax}_c S_{r,c} \qquad (2)$$

Here R indicates the number of regions in the training set and $y_{r,c} \in \{0, 1\}$ is a ground truth label indicating whether region r has label c. The network is trained with Stochastic Gradient Descent (SGD) with momentum. To update the network weights, one needs to compute the partial derivatives of the loss with respect to the weights. These derivatives depend on the partial derivatives of the loss with respect to the outputs of the respective layer.

Problems. A first problem arises because the softmax is applied before pixel assignment in Eq. (1): (I) regions with low but highly varying activation scores are unsure about the class, but can still yield high probabilities due to the softmax. Intuitively, this means that such non-discriminative regions can wrongly affect the final prediction.

More importantly, since $\max_{r \ni p}$ occurs at test time (Eq. (1)), but not at training time (Eq. (2)), the pixel-wise evaluation criterion at test time is *different* from the region-level optimization criterion at training time. This has several consequences: (II) While during training *all* regions affect the network, at test time most regions are ignored. (III) It is unclear what are good region training examples for achieving good performance at test time: Are positive examples only ground truth regions? Or should we use also region proposals which partially overlap with the ground truth? And with what threshold? What overlap are negative proposals allowed to have to count as negative examples? Hence one has to select overlap thresholds for positive and negative examples empirically using test time evaluations. (IV) Regions with different size have the same weight. (V) The network is not trained end-to-end for semantic segmentation, but for the intermediate task of region classification instead. Hence both the classification layer and the representation layers will be suboptimal for the actual semantic segmentation task.

3.2 End-to-End Training for Region-Based Semantic Segmentation

Model. To combine the paradigms of region-based semantic segmentation and end-to-end training, we map from regions to pixels as in Eq. (1), but *before* the softmax and loss computation on a pixel-level:

$$o_p = \operatorname*{argmax}_c \operatorname*{softmax}_c \operatorname*{max}_{r \ni p} S_{r,c} \qquad (3)$$

This region-to-pixel layer is shown in Fig. 2c. It brings two benefits. At training time, having the region-to-pixel layer before the loss enables optimizing a pixel-level loss. Furthermore, having the region-to-pixel layer before the softmax ensures that the class score for each pixel is taken from the region with the highest activation score, hence each class can be recognized at its appropriate scale.

Training. In Eq. (2) the baseline model computes a cross-entropy log-loss on the region-level. Here instead we compute a log-loss on the pixel-level:

$$\mathcal{L} = - \sum_c \frac{1}{P} \sum_{p=1}^{P} y_{p,c} \, \log \operatorname*{softmax}_c S_{p,c} \qquad (4)$$

Here P indicates the number of pixels in the training set, $y_{p,c} \in \{0,1\}$ indicates whether pixel p has ground truth label c, and $S_{p,c} = \max_{r \ni p} S_{r,c}$ is the pixel-level score for class c. As in Sect. 3.1 we train the network using SGD. To determine the partial derivatives of our region-to-pixel layer, we observe that it does not have any weights and we only need to compute the subgradients of the loss with respect to the region-level scores $S_{r,c}$:

$$\frac{\partial \mathcal{L}}{\partial S_{r,c}} = \sum_{p \, \in \, r \; | \; r \, = \, \operatorname{argmax}_{r' \ni p} \, S_{r',c}} \frac{\partial \mathcal{L}}{\partial S_{p,c}} \qquad (5)$$

This means that for each class we map each pixel-level gradient to the region with the highest score among all regions that include the pixel. If multiple pixels per class map to the same region, their gradient contributions are summed.

Advantages. Our model addresses all problems raised in Sect. 3.1: (I) Pixels are always labeled according to the relevant region with the highest activation score for that class. (II) Regions which do not affect the pixel-level prediction are ignored during training. (III) Since we evaluate pixels there is no need to assign class labels to regions for training. (IV) The pixel-level loss is agnostic to different sizes of region proposals. (V) We train our method end-to-end for the actual semantic segmentation criterion, resulting in properly optimized classifiers and region representations.

3.3   Pooling on Free-Form Regions

Model. While the baseline model classifies free-form regions, their feature representations are computed on the bounding box. This is suboptimal as the regions can take highly irregular shapes. We propose here a free-form Region-of-Interest (ROI) pooling layer which computes representations taking into account only pixels actually in the region (Fig. 2c):

$$S_{i,d,r}^{R} = \max_{j \; | \; \phi(j) \, = \, i, \, \delta_{j,r} \, = \, 1} S_{j,d}^{C} \qquad (6)$$

Here $S_{i,d,r}^{R}$ is the ROI pooling activation for ROI coordinate i, channel d and region r. For each ROI coordinate and channel we maximize over the corresponding coordinate j in the convolutional map $S_{j,d}^{C}$, considering only points inside the region, i.e. $\delta_{j,r} = 1$. The mapping ϕ from convolutional map coordinates to ROI ones is done as in [27,39], but operates on a free-form region rather than a bounding box.

Training. During the forward pass the highest scoring convolutional map coordinate $\pi(i,d,r)$ for each ROI coordinate and channel is computed as:

$$\pi(i,d,r) = \underset{j \mid \phi(j)=i,\, \delta_{j,r}=1}{\operatorname{argmax}} S_{j,d}^{C} \tag{7}$$

We use the technique of [27] to backpropagate through the pooling layer, computing the subgradients of the loss with respect to each coordinate in the last convolutional feature map. For each coordinate and channel in the ROI pooling output of a region, the gradients are passed to the convolutional feature map coordinate with the highest activations during the forward pass:

$$\frac{\partial \mathcal{L}}{\partial S_{j,d}^{C}} = \sum_{r} \sum_{i \mid \pi(i,d,r)=j} \frac{\partial \mathcal{L}}{\partial S_{i,d,r}^{R}} \tag{8}$$

Advantages. Our free-form region representations focus better on the region of interest, leading to purer representations. Additionally, they solve a common problem with bounding boxes: when objects of two classes occur in a part-container relationship (i.e. a bird in the sky), their free-form region proposals degenerate to the same bounding box. Hence higher network layers will receive two identical feature vectors for two different regions covering different classes. This leads to confusion between the two classes, both at training and test time.

Incorporating Region Context. Several works have shown that including local region context improves semantic segmentation [4,6,22], as many object classes appear in a characteristic context (e.g. a lion is more likely to occur in the savanna than indoors). We take into account region context by performing ROI pooling also on their bounding boxes using [27]. Hence we combine the advantages of using context with the advantages of free-form region representations.

As shown in Fig. 3, we combine region and bounding box representations using one of two strategies: *(I) Tied weights.* We use the same fully connected layers with the same weights for both region and bounding box representations and add the corresponding activations scores after the classification layers. Hence the number of network parameters stays the same and the region and its context are handled identically. *(II) Separate weights.* We concatenate the representations of region and bounding box before applying the consecutive fully connected layers. This strategy roughly doubles the total number of weights of our overall network architecture, but can develop separate classifiers for each representation.

Since ROI pooling on bounding boxes and free-form regions are both differentiable, the combined representations are also differentiable and allow for end-to-end training. We compare all representations experimentally (Table 4).

Relation to [4,6,27]. Girshick et al. [27] use a differentiable ROI pooling layer in Fast R-CNN for bounding boxes only. Girshick et al. [6] use free-form regions in R-CNN for semantic segmentation. For each region proposal they set the color values of the background pixels to zero. In our scheme we do not alter the image pixels of the input but pool exclusively over pixels inside the region. Dai et al. [4] perform Convolutional Feature Masking on the last convolutional feature map,

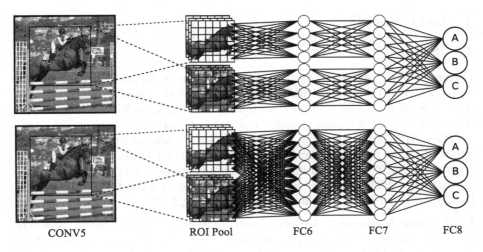

Fig. 3. We combine free-form region representations, which focus on the appearance of the region itself, with bounding box based representations, which also capture context. We combine them using tied weights (above) and separate weights (below).

followed by a Spatial Pyramid Pooling layer [39], but did not backpropagate through this layer. Both [4,6] combined free-form and bounding box representations. Only [4] took representations after the convolutional layers, but their model was not able to perform backpropagation. Both [4,6] optimized for region classification instead of semantic segmentation.

3.4 Attention to Rare Classes

Pixel-level class frequencies are often unbalanced [2,9,11,12,14,16,20,21,40–42]. This is typically addressed by using an inverse class frequency weighting $\frac{1}{P_c}$ [9,11,20,21]. Since we have a pixel-level loss, we can simply plug this into Eq. (4). However, we found that rare classes lead to large weight updates resulting in exploding gradients and numerical problems. To avoid these issues, we re-normalize the inverse frequency weights by a factor Z so that the total sum of weights for each training image is 1: $\frac{1}{Z} \sum_c \frac{1}{P_c} \sum_{p=1}^{P} y_{p,c} = 1$.

3.5 Efficient Evaluation of the Pixel-Level Loss

Evaluating the loss for each pixel separately is computationally expensive and redundant, because different pixels belonging to the same highest scoring region for a class are assigned the same score $S_{r,c}$. Hence we partition the set of region proposals for a training image into a set of non-overlapping, single-class regions using the ground truth. We then reformulate Eq. (4) into an equivalent loss in terms of these regions. This reduces the cost of loss evaluation by a factor 1000.

4   Experiments

4.1   Setup

Datasets. We evaluate our method on two challenging datasets: SIFT Flow [43] and PASCAL Context [17]. SIFT Flow contains 33 classes in 2688 images. The dataset is known for its extreme class imbalance [20, 21, 43]. We use the provided fixed split into 2488 training images and 200 test images.

PASCAL Context provides complete pixel-level annotations for both things and stuff classes in the popular PASCAL VOC 2010 [44] dataset. It contains 4998 training and 5105 validation images. As there is no dedicated test set available, we use the validation images exclusively for testing. We use the 59 classes plus background commonly used in the literature [4, 19, 23, 26].

Evaluation Measures. Semantic segmentation methods typically measure global accuracy and class-average accuracy. Global accuracy is the percentage of correctly labeled pixels in the dataset. But since class frequencies typically follow a power-law distribution, it is mostly influenced by a few common classes. Class-average accuracy instead takes all classes into account equally and it is generally considered a better measure. It first computes the accuracy for each class separately, and then averages over classes. Both measures are standard for SIFT Flow. The most common evaluation measure on PASCAL Context is mean Intersection-over-Union (IOU) [44]. For each class one divides the number of pixels of the intersection of the predicted and ground truth class by their union. Then the average is taken over classes.

Network. We use the state-of-the-art classification network VGG-16 [33] pre-trained for image classification on ILSVRC 2012 [35]. We use the layers up to CONV5, discarding all higher layers, as the basis of our network. We then append a free-form ROI pooling layer (Sect. 3.3), a region-to-pixel layer, a softmax layer and pixel-level loss (Sect. 3.2, Fig. 2c). To include local context, we combine region and entire bounding box using separate weights (Sect. 3.3).

Regions. We use Selective Search [29], which delivers three sets of region proposals, one per color space (RGB, HSV, LAB). During training we change the set of region proposals in each mini-batch to have a more diverse set of proposals without the additional overhead of having three times as many regions. We use region proposals with a minimum size of 100 pixels for SIFT Flow, and 400 pixels for PASCAL Context. This results in an average of 370 proposals for SIFT Flow and 150 proposals for PASCAL Context, for each of the three color spaces. Additionally we use all ground truth regions at training time. This is especially important for very small objects that are not tightly covered by region proposals.

Training. The network is trained using Stochastic Gradient Descent (SGD) with momentum. For 20 epochs we use a learning rate of 1e-3, followed by 10 epochs using learning rate 1e-4. All other SGD hyperparameters are taken from Fast R-CNN [27]. We use either an inverse-class frequency weighted loss (referred to as *balanced* below) or a natural frequency weighted loss (*unbalanced*).

4.2 Main Results

SIFT Flow. We compare our method to other works on SIFT Flow test in Table 1. We first compare in the balanced setting, which takes rare classes into account. Hence we train our model for the loss described in Sect. 3.4 and compare to methods using class-average accuracy. We achieve 64.0 %, which substantially outperforms the previous state-of-the-art, including the fully convolutional method [20] by +8.3 % and the region-based method [2] by +8.4 %.

We also compare in the unbalanced setting using global accuracy, which mainly measures performance on common classes. Hence we train our model for the loss in Eq. (4). This yields a competitive 84.3 % global accuracy, outperforming most previous methods, and coming close to the state-of-the-art [20] (86.8 %).

Table 1. Evaluation on SIFT Flow test. We show results for our model trained for either a balanced or an unbalanced loss. We also show results of previous works, where we report the maximum result for each metric if multiple results are given.

Method	Year	Class Acc.	Global Acc.	Method	Year	Class Acc.	Global Acc.
Byeon [41]	2015	22.6	68.7	Sharma [11]	2014	48.0	79.6
Gould [45]	2014	25.7	78.4	Yang [16]	2014	48.7	79.8
Tighe [13]	2010	29.4	76.9	George [5]	2015	50.1	81.7
Pinheiro [25]	2014	30.0	76.5	Farabet [21]	2013	50.8	78.5
Gatta [46]	2014	32.1	78.7	Long [23]	2015	51.7	**85.2**
Singh [47]	2013	33.8	79.2	Sharma [12]	2015	52.8	80.9
Shuai [42]	2015	39.7	80.1	Caesar [2]	2015	55.6	-
Tighe [14]	2013	41.1	78.6	Eigen [20]	2015	55.7	**86.8**
Kekeç [40]	2014	45.8	70.4	Ours	2016	**64.0**	84.3

PASCAL Context. We also evaluate our method on the recent PASCAL Context dataset [17]. In Table 2 we show the results using either a balanced or an unbalanced loss. Our balanced model achieves 49.9 % class-average accuracy, outperforming the only work that reports results for that measure [23] by +3.4 %. Our unbalanced model achieves competitive results on global accuracy (62.4 %) and reasonable results on mean IOU (32.5 %).

Qualitative Analysis. Figures 4 and 5 show example labelings generated by our method on SIFT Flow test and PASCAL Context validation. Notice how our method accurately adheres to object boundaries, such as buildings (Fig. 4e, and h), birds (Fig. 5a, and c) and boat (Fig. 5i). This is one of the advantages of using a region-based approach. Furthermore, our method correctly identifies small objects like pole (Fig. 4a) and the streetlight (Fig. 4d). This is facilitated by our method's ability to adaptively select the scale on which to do recognition. Finally, notice that our method sometimes even correctly labels parts of the image missing in the ground truth, such as fence (Fig. 4d) and cat whiskers (Fig. 5d).

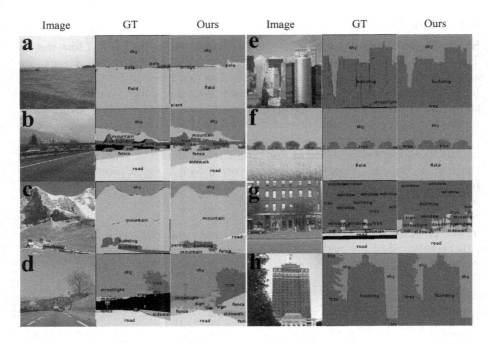

Fig. 4. Example labelings on SIFT Flow test. We show an image, the ground truth labeling and the output of our balanced model.

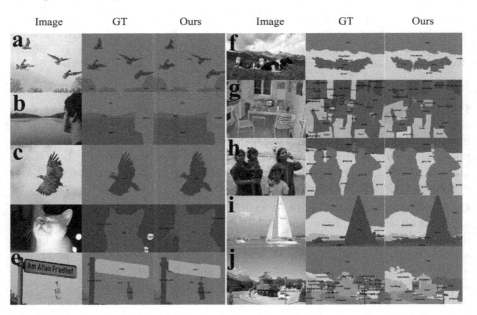

Fig. 5. Example labelings on PASCAL Context validation. We show an image, the ground truth labeling and the output of our unbalanced model.

Table 2. Evaluation on PASCAL Context validation. We show results using a balanced and an unbalanced version of our method, as well as the current state-of-the art, where we always report the maximum result for each metric. O2P results are from the errata of Mottaghi et al. [17]. Dai et al. [19] train using additional bounding box annotations.

Method	Year	Class Acc.	Global Acc.	Mean IOU
O2P [3]	2012	-	-	18.1
Dai et al. [4]	2015	-	-	34.4
Long et al. [23]	2015	46.5	**65.9**	35.1
Dai et al. [19]	2015	-	-	35.7
Zheng et al. [26]	2015	-	-	**39.3**
Dai et al. (add. boxes) [19]	2015	-	-	40.5
Ours	2016	**49.9**	62.4	32.5

4.3 Extra Analysis

Accuracy at Object Boundaries. Following [48,49], we evaluate the performance on image pixels that are within 4 pixels of a ground truth object boundary. We compare our method to the MatConvNet [50] reimplementation of Fully Convolutional Networks (FCN) [23] in Table 3. On SIFT Flow test, FCN-16s obtains 37.9 % class-average accuracy on boundaries, while our method gets to 57.3 %. When evaluated on all pixels in the image, FCN-16s brings 49.3 %, vs 64.0 % by our method. Hence, our method is +19.4 % better on boundaries and +14.7 % on complete images. Analogously, on PASCAL Context we get +4.9 % on boundaries and +1.8 % on complete images. Since our improvements are consistently larger on object boundaries, we conclude that our method is especially good at capturing them, compared to the basic FCN architecture (Fig. 2a).

End-to-End Training. Our region-to-pixel layer enables end-to-end training of region-based semantic segmentation models. We analyze how this end-to-end training influences performance, by comparing the baseline model (Fig. 2b) to our model (Fig. 2c). To isolate the effect of end-to-end training, in both models we perform ROI pooling on the bounding box only. Hence all components of the two models are identical, apart from the region-to-pixel layer and the loss they are trained for. On SIFT Flow test the baseline model achieves a global accuracy of 60.9 %, compared to our 83.7 %. We conclude that end-to-end training yields considerable accuracy gains over the baseline architecture in Fig. 2b.

Softmax Before Max. Our application of the max before the softmax (Eq. 3) enables us to recognize each object at its appropriate scale (Sect. 3.2). However, using the softmax before the max (Eq. 1) yields an alternative model. Interestingly, on SIFT Flow test our proposed order outperforms the alternative by +8.7 % class-average accuracy.

Importance of Multi-scale Regions. We argue that overlapping, multi-scale regions are important to unleash the full potential of region-based methods. To show this, we train and test our model with non-overlapping regions [51]. This

Table 3. Class-average accuracy at object boundaries on SIFT Flow test (top) and PASCAL Context validation (bottom). Improvements on boundaries are consistently larger than on full images.

	Boundaries	Full image
FCN-16s	37.9	49.3
Ours	57.3	64.0
difference	*+19.4*	*+14.7*
FCN-16s	34.0	48.1
Ours	38.9	49.9
difference	*+4.9*	*+1.8*

Table 4. Results on SIFT Flow test using free-form pooling, bounding box pooling or both. We also report results when regions are rectangular even in the region-to-pixel layer (purely rectangular).

ROI pooling		Class Acc.
Bounding box		62.3
Region		62.8
Region + box	tied weights	63.4
Region + box	separate weights	64.0
Bounding box	purely rect	59.3

yields 60.0 % class-average accuracy on SIFT Flow test, which is below the results when using multi-scale overlapping regions (64.0 % class-average accuracy).

Free-form versus Bounding Box Representations. We analyze the influence of the different representations resulting from different ROI pooling methods (Sect. 3.3). Keeping all else constant, we compare (I) free-form ROI pooling, (II) bounding box ROI pooling, (III) their combination with tied weights and (IV) their combination with separate weights. Results are shown in Table 4.

Free-form representations perform +0.5 % better than bounding box representations, demonstrating that focusing accurately on the object is better. Their combination does even better, yielding another +0.6 % gain with tied weights (same number of model parameters) and +0.6 % with separate weights. Hence both representations are complementary and best treated separately.

In all above experiments the region-to-pixel layer operates on free-form regions. To verify the importance of the free-form regions themselves, we perform an extra experiment using purely rectangular regions (both in the region-to-pixel layer and during ROI pooling). This lowers class-average accuracy by −4.7 %, demonstrating the value of free-form regions.

5   Conclusion

We propose a region-based semantic segmentation model with an accompanying end-to-end training scheme based on a CNN architecture. This architecture combines the advantages of crisp object boundaries and adaptive, multi-scale representations found in region-based methods with end-to-end training directly optimized for semantic segmentation found in fully convolutional methods. We achieve this by introducing a differentiable region-to-pixel layer and a differentiable free-form ROI pooling layer. In terms of class-average pixel accuracy, our method outperforms the state-of-the-art on two datasets, achieving 49.9 % on PASCAL Context and 64.0 % on SIFT Flow.

Acknowledgements. Work supported by the ERC Starting Grant VisCul.

References

1. Boix, X., Gonfaus, J., van de Weijer, J., Bagdanov, A.D., Serrat, J., Gonzàlez, J.: Harmony potentials: fusing global and local scale for semantic image segmentation. IJCV **96**(1), 83–102 (2012)
2. Caesar, H., Uijlings, J., Ferrari, V.: Joint calibration for semantic segmentation. In: BMVC (2015)
3. Carreira, J., Caseiro, R., Batista, J., Sminchisescu, C.: Semantic segmentation with second-order pooling. In: Fitzgibbon, A., Lazebnik, S., Perona, P., Sato, Y., Schmid, C. (eds.) ECCV 2012. LNCS, vol. 7578, pp. 430–443. Springer, Heidelberg (2012). doi:10.1007/978-3-642-33786-4_32
4. Dai, J., He, K., Sun, J.: Convolutional feature masking for joint object and stuff segmentation. In: CVPR (2015)
5. George, M.: Image parsing with a wide range of classes and scene-level context. In: CVPR (2015)
6. Girshick, R., Donahue, J., Darrell, T., Malik, J.: Rich feature hierarchies for accurate object detection and semantic segmentation. In: CVPR (2014)
7. Hariharan, B., Arbeláez, P., Girshick, R., Malik, J.: Simultaneous detection and segmentation. In: Fleet, D., Pajdla, T., Schiele, B., Tuytelaars, T. (eds.) ECCV 2014. LNCS, vol. 8695, pp. 297–312. Springer, Heidelberg (2014). doi:10.1007/978-3-319-10584-0_20
8. Li, F., Carreira, J., Lebanon, G., Sminchisescu, C.: Composite statistical inference for semantic segmentation. In: CVPR (2013)
9. Mostajabi, M., Yadollahpour, P., Shakhnarovich, G.: Feedforward semantic segmentation with zoom-out features. In: CVPR (2015)
10. Plath, N., Toussaint, M., Nakajima, S.: Multi-class image segmentation using conditional random fields and global classification. In: ICML (2009)
11. Sharma, A., Tuzel, O., Liu, M.Y.: Recursive context propagation network for semantic scene labeling. In: NIPS (2014)
12. Sharma, A., Tuzel, O., Jacobs, D.W.: Deep hierarchical parsing for semantic segmentation. In: CVPR (2015)
13. Tighe, J., Lazebnik, S.: SuperParsing: scalable nonparametric image parsing with superpixels. In: Daniilidis, K., Maragos, P., Paragios, N. (eds.) ECCV 2010. LNCS, vol. 6315, pp. 352–365. Springer, Heidelberg (2010). doi:10.1007/978-3-642-15555-0_26
14. Tighe, J., Lazebnik, S.: Finding things: Image parsing with regions and per-exemplar detectors. In: CVPR (2013)
15. Tighe, J., Niethammer, M., Lazebnik, S.: Scene parsing with object instances and occlusion ordering. In: CVPR (2014)
16. Yang, J., Price, B., Cohen, S., Yang, M.H.: Context driven scene parsing with attention to rare classes. In: CVPR (2014)
17. Mottaghi, R., Chen, X., Liu, X., Cho, N.G., Lee, S.W., Fidler, S., Urtasun, R., Yuille, A.: The role of context for object detection and semantic segmentation in the wild. In: CVPR (2014)
18. Chen, L.C., Papandreou, G., Kokkinos, I., Murphy, K., Yuille, A.L.: Semantic image segmentation with deep convolutional nets and fully connected CRFs. In: ICLR (2015)
19. Dai, J., He, K., Sun, J.: Boxsup: Exploiting bounding boxes to supervise convolutional networks for semantic segmentation. In: ICCV (2015)

20. Eigen, D., Fergus, R.: Predicting depth, surface normals and semantic labels with a common multi-scale convolutional architecture. In: ICCV (2015)
21. Farabet, C., Couprie, C., Najman, L., LeCun, Y.: Learning hierarchical features for scene labeling. IEEE Trans. PAMI **35**(8), 1915–1929 (2013)
22. Hariharan, B., Arbeláez, P., Girshick, R., Malik, J.: Hypercolumns for object segmentation and fine-grained localization. In: CVPR (2015)
23. Long, J., Shelhamer, E., Darrell, T.: Fully convolutional networks for semantic segmentation. In: CVPR (2015)
24. Noh, H., Hong, S., Han, B.: Learning deconvolution network for semantic segmentation. In: ICCV (2015)
25. Pinheiro, P., Collobert, R.: Recurrent convolutional neural networks for scene parsing. In: ICML (2014)
26. Zheng, S., Jayasumana, S., Romera-Paredes, B., Vineet, V., Su, Z., Du, D., Huang, C., Torr, P.: Conditional random fields as recurrent neural networks. In: ICCV (2015)
27. Girshick, R.: Fast R-CNN. In: ICCV (2015)
28. Carreira, J., Sminchisescu, C.: Constrained parametric min-cuts for automatic object segmentation. In: CVPR (2010)
29. Uijlings, J.R.R., van de Sande, K.E.A., Gevers, T., Smeulders, A.W.M.: Selective search for object recognition. IJCV **104**(2), 154–171 (2013)
30. Endres, I., Hoiem, D.: Category-independent object proposals with diverse ranking. IEEE Trans. PAMI **36**(2), 222–234 (2014)
31. Arbeláez, P., Pont-Tuset, J., Barron, J.T., Marques, F., Malik, J.: Multiscale combinatorial grouping. In: CVPR (2014)
32. Krizhevsky, A., Sutskever, I., Hinton, G.E.: Imagenet classification with deep convolutional neural networks. In: NIPS (2012)
33. Simonyan, K., Zisserman, A.: Very deep convolutional networks for large-scale image recognition. In: ICLR (2015)
34. Shotton, J., Winn, J., Rother, C., Criminisi, A.: TextonBoost for image understanding: multi-class object recognition and segmentation by jointly modeling appearance, shape and context. IJCV **81**(1), 2–23 (2009)
35. Russakovsky, O., Deng, J., Su, H., Krause, J., Satheesh, S., Ma, S., Huang, Z., Karpathy, A., Khosla, A., Bernstein, M., Berg, A., Fei-Fei, L.: ImageNet large scale visual recognition challenge. IJCV **115**(3), 211–252 (2015)
36. Sermanet, P., Eigen, D., Zhang, X., Mathieu, M., Fergus, R., LeCun, Y.: Overfeat: Integrated recognition, localization and detection using convolutional networks. In: ICLR (2014)
37. Bishop, C.: Neural Networks for Pattern Recognition. Oxford University Press, New York (1995)
38. Ripley, B.: Pattern Recognition and Neural Networks. Cambridge University Press, New York (1996)
39. He, K., Zhang, X., Ren, S., Sun, J.: Spatial pyramid pooling in deep convolutional networks for visual recognition. In: Fleet, D., Pajdla, T., Schiele, B., Tuytelaars, T. (eds.) ECCV 2014. LNCS, vol. 8691, pp. 346–361. Springer, Heidelberg (2014). doi:10.1007/978-3-319-10578-9_23
40. Kekeç, T., Emonet, R., Fromont, E., Trémeau, A., Wolf, C.: Contextually constrained deep networks for scene labeling. In: BMVC (2014)
41. Byeon, W., Breuel, T.M., Raue, F., Liwicki, M.: Scene labeling with LSTM recurrent neural networks. In: CVPR (2015)
42. Shuai, B., Wang, G., Zuo, Z., Wang, B., Zhao, L.: Integrating parametric and non-parametric models for scene labeling. In: CVPR (2015)

43. Liu, C., Yuen, J., Torralba, A.: Nonparametric scene parsing via label transfer. IEEE Trans. PAMI **33**(12), 2368–2382 (2011)
44. Everingham, M., Eslami, S., van Gool, L., Williams, C., Winn, J., Zisserman, A.: The PASCAL visual object classes challenge: a retrospective. IJCV **111**(1), 98–136 (2015)
45. Gould, S., Zhao, J., He, X., Zhang, Y.: Superpixel graph label transfer with learned distance metric. In: Fleet, D., Pajdla, T., Schiele, B., Tuytelaars, T. (eds.) ECCV 2014. LNCS, vol. 8689, pp. 632–647. Springer, Heidelberg (2014). doi:10.1007/978-3-319-10590-1_41
46. Gatta, C., Romero, A., van de Veijer, J.: Unrolling loopy top-down semantic feedback in convolutional deep networks. In: Workshop at CVPR (2014)
47. Singh, G., Kosecka, J.: Nonparametric scene parsing with adaptive feature relevance and semantic context. In: CVPR (2013)
48. Kohli, P., Ladicky, L., Torr, P.: Robust higher order potentials for enforcing label consistency. IJCV **82**(3), 302–324 (2009)
49. Krähenbühl, P., Koltun, V.: Efficient inference in fully connected CRFs with gaussian edge potentials. In: NIPS (2011)
50. Vedaldi, A., Lenc, K.: Matconvnet - convolutional neural networks for MATLAB. In: ACM Multimedia (2015)
51. Felzenszwalb, P.F., Huttenlocher, D.P.: Efficient graph-based image segmentation. IJCV **59**(2), 167–181 (2004)

Fast 6D Pose Estimation from a Monocular Image Using Hierarchical Pose Trees

Yoshinori Konishi[1]([⊠]), Yuki Hanzawa[1], Masato Kawade[1],
and Manabu Hashimoto[2]

[1] OMRON Corporation, Kyoto, Japan
{ykoni,hanzawa,kawade}@ari.ncl.omron.co.jp
[2] Chukyo University, Nagoya, Japan
mana@isl.sist.chukyo-u.ac.jp

Abstract. It has been shown that the template based approaches could quickly estimate 6D pose of texture-less objects from a monocular image. However, they tend to be slow when the number of templates amounts to tens of thousands for handling a wider range of 3D object pose. To alleviate this problem, we propose a novel image feature and a tree-structured model. Our proposed perspectively cumulated orientation feature (PCOF) is based on the orientation histograms extracted from randomly generated 2D projection images using 3D CAD data, and the template using PCOF explicitly handle a certain range of 3D object pose. The hierarchical pose trees (HPT) is built by clustering 3D object pose and reducing the resolutions of templates, and HPT accelerates 6D pose estimation based on a coarse-to-fine strategy with an image pyramid. In the experimental evaluation on our texture-less object dataset, the combination of PCOF and HPT showed higher accuracy and faster speed in comparison with state-of-the-art techniques.

Keywords: 6D pose estimation · Texture-less objects · Template matching

1 Introduction

Fast and accurate 6D pose estimation of object instances is one of the most important computer vision technologies for various robotic applications both for industrial and consumer robots. In recent years, low-cost 3D sensors such as Microsoft Kinect became popular and they have often been used for object detection and recognition in academic research. However, much more reliability and durability are required for sensors in industrial applications than in consumer applications. Thus the 3D sensors for industry are often far more expensive,

Electronic supplementary material The online version of this chapter (doi:10. 1007/978-3-319-46448-0_24) contains supplementary material, which is available to authorized users.

© Springer International Publishing AG 2016
B. Leibe et al. (Eds.): ECCV 2016, Part I, LNCS 9905, pp. 398–413, 2016.
DOI: 10.1007/978-3-319-46448-0_24

Fig. 1. Our new template based algorithm can estimate 6D pose of texture-less and shiny objects from a monocular image which contains cluttered backgrounds and partial occlusions. It takes an average of approximately 150 ms on a single CPU core.

larger in size and heavier than the consumer ones. Additionaly, most of 3D sensors even for industry cannot handle objects with specular surfaces, are sensitive to illumination conditions and require cumbersome 3D calibrations. For those reasons, monocular cameras are mainly used in the current industrial applications, and fast and accurate 6D pose estimation from a monocular image is still an important technique.

Many of industrial parts and products have little texture on their surfaces, and they are so-called texture-less objects. Object detection methods based on keypoints and local descriptors such as SIFT [1] and SURF [2] cannot handle texture-less objects because they require rich textures on the regions of target objects. It has been shown that template based approaches [3–9] which use whole 2D projection images from various viewpoints as their model templates successfully dealt with texture-less objects. However, they suffer from the speed degradation when the numbers of templates are increased for covering a wider range of 3D object pose.

We propose a novel image feature and a tree-structured model for fast template based 6D pose estimation (Fig. 1). Our main contributions are as follows:

- We introduce perspectively cumulated orientation feature (PCOF) extracted using 3D CAD data of target objects. PCOF is robust to the appearance changes caused by the changes in 3D object pose, and the number of templates are greatly reduced without loss of pose estimation accuracy.
- Hierarchical pose trees (HPT) is also introduced for efficient 6D pose search. HPT consists of hierarchically clustered templates whose resolutions are different at each level, and it accelerates the subwindow search by a coarse-to-fine strategy with an image pyramid.
- We make available a dataset of nine texture-less objects (some of them have specular surfaces) with the ground truth of 6D object pose. The dataset includes approximately 500 images per object taken from various viewpoints, and contains cluttered backgrounds and partial occlusions. 3D CAD data for training are also included.[1]

---

[1] http://isl.sist.chukyo-u.ac.jp/Archives/archives.html.

The remaining contents of the paper are organized as follows: Sect. 2 presented related work on 6D pose estimation, image features for texture-less objects and search data structures. Section 3 introduces our proposed PCOF, HPT and 6D pose estimation algorithm based on them. Section 4 evaluates the proposed method and compare it with state-of-the-art methods. Section 5 concludes the paper.

2   Related Work

6D Pose Estimation. 6D pose estimation has been extensively studied since 1980s and in the early days the template based approaches using a monocular image [3–5] were the mainstream. Since the early 2000s, keypoint detections and descriptor matchings became popular for detection and pose estimation of 2D/3D objects due to their scalability to the increasing search space and robustness to the changes in object pose. Though they can handle texture-less objects when using line features as the descriptors for matching [10,11], they were fragile to cluttered backgrounds because the line features were too simple to suffer from many false correspondences in the backgrounds.

Voting based approaches as well as template based approaches have a long history, and they have also been applied to detection and pose estimation of 2D/3D objects. Various voting based approaches were proposed for 6D pose estimation such as voting by dense point pair features [12], random ferns [13], Hough forests [14], and coordinate regressions [15]. Though they are scalable to increasing image resolutions and the number of object classes, the dimensionaliy of search space is too high to estimate precise object pose (excessive quantizations of 3D pose space are required). Thus they need post-processings for pose refinements, which spend additional time.

CNN based approaches [16–18] recently showed impressive results on 6D pose estimations. However, they take a few seconds even when using GPU and they are not suitable for robotic applications where near real-time processing is required on poor computational resources.

Template based approaches have been shown to be practical both in accuracy and speed for 6D pose estimation of texture-less objects [6,7,19]. Hinterstoisser et al. [8,9] showed their LINE-2D/LINE-MOD which is based on the quantized orientations and the optimally arranged memory quickly estimated 6D pose of texture-less objects against cluttered backgrounds. LINE-2D/LINE-MOD was further improved by discriminative training [20] and by hashing [21,22]. However, the discriminative trainig required additional negative samples and the hashing led to suboptimal performance in the estimation accuracy.

Image Features for Handling Texture-less Objects. Image features used in template matching heavily influence the performance of pose estimation from a monocular image. Though edges based template matchings have been applied to detection and pose estimation of texture-less objects, they often required the additional algorithm such as segmentation [19] or the additional hardware like a multi-flash camera [6] to suppress cluttered edges in the backgrounds.

It has been shown that the gradient direction vectors [23] and the quantized gradient orientations [24] were robust to cluttered backgrounds and illumination changes. However, it was pointed out that the similarity scores based on these features rapidly declined even if only slight changes in object pose occurred. To overcome this problem, dominant orientations within a grid of pixels (DOT) [25] and spread orientation which allowed some shifting in matching [8] were proposed. DOT and spread orientation are robust to the pose changes and slight deformations of target objects. However, they relax matching conditions both in foregrounds and backgrounds, and this possibly degrade the robustness to cluttered backgrounds. Konishi et al. [26] introduced cumulative orientation feature (COF) which was robust to the apperance changes caused by the changes in 2D object pose. However, COF did not explicitly handle appearance changes caused by the changes in 3D object pose.

Tree-Structured Models for Efficient Search. Search strategies and data structures are also important for template based approaches. The tree-structured models are popular in the nearest neighbor search for image classification [27–29] and for joint object class and pose recognition [30]. These tree-structured models were also used in joint 2D detection and 2D pose recognition [31] and joint 2D detection and 3D pose estimation [32]. Though they offered efficient search in 2D/3D object pose space but not in 2D image space (x-y translations). The well-known efficient search in 2D image space is the coarse-to-fine search [33]. Ulrich et al. [7] proposed the hierarchical model which combined the coarse-to-fine search and the viewpoint clustering based on similarity scores between templates. However, their model is not fully optimized for the search in 3D pose space when 2D projection images from separate viewpoints are similar, as is often the case with texture-less objects.

3   Proposed Method

Our proposed method consists of a image feature for dealing with the appearance changes caused by the changes in 3D object pose (Sect. 3.1) and a hierarchical model for the efficient search (Sect. 3.2). The template based 6D pose estimation algorithm using both PCOF and HPT is described in Sect. 3.3.

3.1   PCOF: Perspectively Cumulated Orientation Feature

In this subsection, the way how to extract PCOF is explained using L-Holder shown in Fig. 2(a) which is a typical texture-less object. Our PCOF is developed from COF [26] and the main difference is two-fold: One is that PCOF explicitly handle appearance changes caused by the changes in 3D object pose, whereas COF can handle appearance changes only by 2D pose changes. Another is that PCOF is based on a probabilistic representation of quantized orientations at each pixel, whereas COF uses all the orientations observed at each pixel.

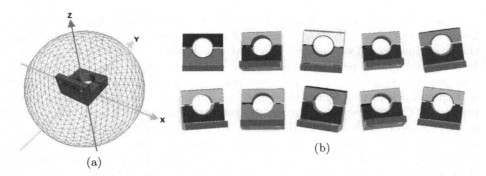

(b)

(a)

Fig. 2. (a) 3D CAD data of L-Holder, its coordinate axes and a sphere for viewpoint sampling. (b) Examples of the generated projection images from randomized viewpoints around the viewpoint on z-axis (upper-left image). Surfaces of objects are drawn by randomly selected colors in order to extract distinct image gradients.

Firstly many 2D projection images are generated using 3D CAD data from randomized viewpoints (Fig. 2(a)). The viewpoints are determined by four parameters those are rotation angles around x-y axes, a distance from the center of the object and a rotation angle around a optical axis. The range of randomized parameters should be limited so as to a single template can handle the appearance changes caused by the randomized parameters. In our research, the range of randomization were experimentally determined and those were ±12° around x-y axes, ±40 mm in the distance and ±7.5° around the optical axis. Figure 2(b) shows examples of generated projection images. The upper-left image of Fig. 2(b) is the projection image from the viewpoint where all rotation angles are zero and the distance from the object is 680 mm, and this viewpoint is at the center of these randomized examples. In generation of projection images, the neighboring meshes where the angle between them is larger than a threshold value are drawn by different color in order to extract distinct image gradients. In this study the threshold was 30°.

Secondly image gradients of all the generated images are computed using Sobel operators (the maximum gradients among RGB channels are used). We use only the gradient directions discarding gradient magnitudes because the magnitudes depend on the randomly selected mesh colors. The colored gradient directions of the central image (the upper-left in Fig. 2(b)) are shown in Fig. 3(a). Then the gradient direction is quantized into eight orientations disregarding its polarities (Fig. 3(b)), and the quantized orientation is used for voting to the orientation histogram at each pixel. The quantized orientations of all the generated images are voted to the orientation histograms at the corresponding pixels. Lastly the dominant orientations at each pixel are extracted by thresholding the histograms and they are represented by 8-bit binary strings [25]. The maximum frequencies of the histograms are used as weights in calculating a similarity score.

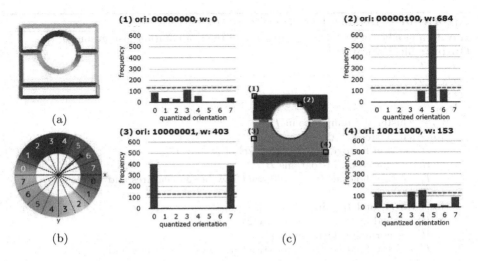

Fig. 3. (a) Colored gradient directions of the upper-left image in Fig. 2(b). (b) Quantization of gradient directions disregarding their polarities. (c) Examples of the orientation histograms, binary features (ori) and their weights (w) on arbitrarily selected four pixels. Red dotted lines show the threshold for feature extraction. (Color figure online)

The template T with n PCOF represented as follows:

$$T : \{x_i, y_i, ori_i, w_i | i = 1, ..., n\},\tag{1}$$

and the similarity score is given by following equation,

$$score(x,y) = \frac{\sum_{i=1}^{n} \delta_k(ori^I_{(x+x_i, y+y_i)} \in ori^T_i)}{\sum_{i=1}^{n} w_i}.\tag{2}$$

If the quantized orientation of the test image (ori^I) is included in the PCOF template (ori^T), the weight (w) is added to the score. The delta function in Eq. (2) is calculated quickly by a bitwise AND operation (the symbol $\wedge$). Additionally, this calculation can be accelerated using SIMD instructions where multiple binary features are matched by a single instruction.

$$\delta_i(ori^I \in ori^T) = \begin{cases} w_i & \text{if } ori^I \wedge ori^T > 0, \\ 0 & \text{otherwise.} \end{cases}\tag{3}$$

The orientation histograms, extracted binary features and their weights on arbitrarily selected four pixels are shown in Fig. 3(c). In our study, the number of generated images was 1,000 and the threshold value was 120. The votes were concentrated on a few orientations at the pixels along lines or arcs such as pixel (2) and (3). At these pixels the important features with large weights were extracted. On the contrary, the votes were scattered among many orientations at the pixels on corners and complicated structures such as pixel (1) and (4). At these pixels the features with small or zero weihts were extracted. Features with zero weights are not used for matching in pose estimation.

Algorithm 1. Building hierarchical pose trees

Input: a number of PCOF templates T and their orientation histograms H
Output: hierarchical pose trees

   $T'_0 \leftarrow T$
   $H'_0 \leftarrow H$
   $i \leftarrow 1$
   loop
      $C_i \leftarrow$ cluster the templates in T'_{i-1}
      for each cluster C_{ij} **do**
         $H_{ij} \leftarrow$ add histograms at each pixel of $H'_{i-1} \in C_{ij}$
         $H_{ij} \leftarrow$ normalize histograms H_{ij}
         $T_{ij} \leftarrow$ thresholding H_{ij} and extract new binary features and weights
      end for
      for each T_{ij} and H_{ij} **do**
         $H'_{ij} \leftarrow$ add histograms of nearby 2×2 pixels
         $H'_{ij} \leftarrow$ normalize histograms H'_{ij}
         $T'_{ij} \leftarrow$ thresholding H'_{ij} and extract new binary features and weights
      end for
      $N'_i \leftarrow$ minimum number of feature points in T'_i
      if $N'_i < N_{min}$ **then**
         break
      else
         $i \leftarrow i + 1$
      end if
   end loop

3.2   HPT: Hierarchical Pose Trees

A single PCOF template can handle the apparance changes caused by 3D pose changes generated in training ($\pm 12°$ around x-y axes, ± 40 mm in the distance and $\pm 7.5°$ around the optical axis). To cover a wider range of 3D object pose, additional templates are made at every vertices of the viewpoint sphere in Fig. 2(a) which contains 642 vertices as a whole and two adjacent vertices are approximately $8°$ apart. Additionally, the templates are made in every 30 mm in the distance to the object and in every $5°$ around the optical axes. These PCOF templates can redundantly cover the whole 3D pose space.

Our proposed hierarchical pose trees (HPT) are built in a bottom-up way starting from a lot of PCOF templates and their orientation histograms. The algorithm is shown in Algorithm 1 and it consists of three steps: clustering, integration and reduction of resolutions. Firstly all the templates are clustered based on the similarity scores (Eq. 2) between templates using X-means algorithms [34]. In X-means clustering, the optimum number of clusters are estimated based on Bayesian information criteria (BIC). Secondly the orientation histograms which belong to a same cluster are added and normalized at each pixel. Then the clustered templates are integrated to new templates by extracting the binary features and the weights from these integrated orientation histograms. Lastly the resolutions of the histograms are reduced to half by adding and normalizing

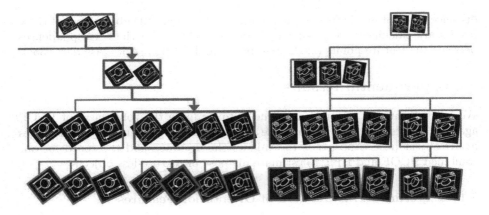

Fig. 4. Part of hierarchical pose trees are shown. Green and red rectangles represent templates used for matching. The bottom templates are originally created PCOF templates and the tree structures are built in a bottom-up way by clustering similar templates, integrating them into new templates and decreasing the resolutions of the templates. In estimation of object pose, HPT is traced from top to bottom along the red line, and the most promising template which contains the pose parameters is determined. (Color figure online)

histograms of neighboring 2×2 pixels. Then the low-resolution features and weights are extracted from these histograms. These procedures are iterated until the minimum number of feature points contained in low resolution templates is less than a threshold value (N_{min}). In our study N_{min} was 50.

Part of HPT are shown in Fig. 4. When the range of 3D pose was as same as the settings of experiment2 ($\pm 60°$ around x-y axes, 660 mm – 800 mm in the distance from the object and $\pm 180°$ around the optical axis), the total number of PCOF templates amounted to 73,800 (205 viewpoints $\times$ 5 distances $\times$ 72 angles around the optical axis). These initial templates were clustered and integrated into 23,115 templates at the end of first round in Algorithm 1, and the number of templates was further reduced to 4,269 at second round and to 233 at third round. In this experimental settings, the iteration of hierarchization stopped at third round.

3.3   6D Pose Estimation

In 6D pose estimation, firstly the image pyramid of a test image is built and the quantized orientations are calculated on each pyramid level. Then the top level of the pyramid is scanned using the root nodes of HPT (e.g. the number of root nodes was 233 in experiment2). The similarity scores are calculated based on Eq. 2. The promising candidates whose scores are higher than a search threshold are matched with the templates at the lower levels, and they trace HPT down to the bottom. Finally the estimated results of 2D positions on a test image and the matched templates which have four pose parameters (three rotation angles and a distance) are obtained after non-maximum suppressions. 6D object pose of these results are calculated by solving PnP problems based on the correspondences between 2D feature points on the test image and 3D points of CAD data [35].

4   Experimental Results

We carried out two experiments. One is to evaluate the robustness of PCOF against cluttered backgrounds and the appearance changes caused by the changes in 3D object pose. Another is to evaluate the accuracy and the speed for our combined PCOF and HPT to estimate 6D pose of texture-less objects.

4.1   Experiment1: Evaluation of Orientation Features

Experimental Settings. In experiment1, we evaluated four kinds of orientation features on two test image sets ("vertical" and "perspective") shown in Fig. 5. A vertical image (a) was captured from the viewpoint on z-axis distanced by 680 mm from the center of the object. The upper-left image in Fig. 2(b) is the 2D projection image of 3D CAD from the same viewpoint. Perspective images (b) were captured from the same viewpoint as the vertical image with L-Holder slightly rotated around x-y axes (approximately 8°, please see Fig. 2(b) as references). The number of the perspective images was eight (the combination of $+/0/-$ rotation around x-y axes) and these images contain almost the same cluttered backgrounds. Our proposed PCOF was compared with three existing orientation features: normalized gradient vector [23], spread orientation [8] and cumulative orientation feature (COF) [26]. Existing methods used the upper-left image in Fig. 2(b) as a model image.

Similarity scores based on four kinds of orientation features were calculated at every pixel on the vertical and perspective images. We show the differences between the maximum scores at the target object (FG: foreground) and at the backgrounds (BG) in Table 1. This difference represents how discriminative each feature is against cluttered backgrounds on the vertical image and is both against cluttered backgrounds and changes in 3D object pose on the perspective images. The larger the score difference is, the more discriminative the feature is. Regarding the differences on the perspective images, mean values are presented in Table 1.

(a)   (b)

Fig. 5. (a) Vertical image and (b) three examples of perspective images for evaluation of the orientation features in experiment1. These images are almost identical except for the 3D pose of the target object (L-Holder at the center of the images).

Table 1. Differences between a maximum score at the target object and at the backgrounds on the vertical and perspective images in experiment1.

	Steger [23]	Spread [8]	COF [26]	**PCOF(Ours)**
Vertical	0.332	0.465	0.477	**0.485**
Perspective	0.214	0.421	0.403	**0.483**

Normalized Gradient Vector. Steger et al. [23] showed that the sum of inner products of normalized gradient vectors was occlusion, clutter and illumination invariant. Our experimental results in Table 1 showed that the differences between FG - BG scores both on the vertical and perspective images were much lower than other three features. This demonstrated that Steger's similarity score was fragile both to the background clutters and to the changes in 3D object pose.

Spread Orientation. Hinterstoisser et al. [8] introduced the spread orientation in order to make their similarity score robust to small shifts and deformations. They efficiently spread the quantized orientations of test images by shifting the orientation features over the range of $\pm 4 \times \pm 4$ pixels and merging them with bitwise OR operations. In our experimental results in Table 1, the difference between FG - BG scores on the perspective images decreased from that on the vertical image. This indicated that the spread orientation was robust to cluttered backgrounds but not to the changes in 3D object pose.

Cumulative Orientation Feature (COF). Konishi et al. [26] introduced COF, which was robust both to cluttered backgrounds and the appearance changes caused by the changes in 2D object pose. Followoing their paper, we generated many images by transformimg the model image using randomized geometric transformation parameters (within the range of ± 1 pixel in x-y translations, $\pm 7.5°$ of in-plane rotation and $\pm 5\%$ of scale). Then COF was calculated at each pixel by merging all the quantized orientations observed on generated images. The COF template was matched with the test images and the results were shown in Table 1. As with the spread orientation, the difference between FG - BG scores on the perspective images was decreased and COF was robust to cluttered backgrounds but not to the change in 3D object pose.

Perspectively Cumulated Orientation Feature (PCOF). PCOF was calculated as described in Sect. 3.1 and matched with the quantized orientations extracted on the test images. The difference between FG - BG scores in Table 1 were higher than other three features both on the vertical and perspective images, and the score difference was not decreased on the perspective images compared to that on the vertical image. This shows that PCOF was robust both to cluttered backgrounds and the changes in 3D object pose. Due to this robustness, the template which consist of PCOF can handle a certain range of

3D object pose (approximately 8° in out-of-plane rotation angles) without loss of the robustness to cluttered backgrounds. This advantage enables PCOF templates to handle a wider range of 3D object pose with fewer number of templates than other image features.

4.2   Experiment2: 6D Pose Estimation

Experimental Settings. In experiment2, we evaluated the accuracy and the speed of our 6D pose estimation algorithm on our texture-less object dataset. The dataset consists of nine mechanical parts which are texture-less and some of them have specular surfaces. These objects were captured from various viewpoints within the range of ±60° around x-y axes, ±180° around the optical axis and 660 mm – 800 mm in distance from the center of the object. The resolution of the camera was VGA (640 × 480) and approximately 500 images were taken per object where cluttered backgrounds and partial occlusions were contained. The ground truth of 6D object pose were estimated based on the surrounding AR

Fig. 6. The example images of our dataset are presented. The dataset consists of nine texture-less objects and contains cluttered backgrounds and partial occlusions. Top: Connector, SideClamp and Stopper. Middle: L-Holder, T-Holder and Flange. Bottom: HingeBase, Bracket and PoleClamp. The edges of the objects extracted from 3D CAD data (green lines) and the coordinate axes (three colored arrows) are drawn on the images based on the estimated 6D pose by our proposed method. (Color figure online)

markers printed on the board where the target objects were placed on. The AR markers were recognized using ArUco library [36]. We counted the estimated 6D pose as correct if the errors of the result were within 10 mm along x-y axes, 40 mm along z axis, 10° around x-y axes and 7.5° around z axis. The exmaple images of our dataset are shown in Fig. 6. The estimated results by our proposed method are drawn on the images.

The existing 6D pose estimation algorithms by Ulrich et al. [7], Hinterstoisser et al. (LINE-2D) [8] and Konishi et al. (COF) [26] were also evaluated on the dataset. We used the function "find_shape_model_3d" in the machine vision library "HALCON 11" (MvTEC in Germany) as an implementation of [7], LINE-2D implemented in OpenCV 2.4.11 and the source code of COF which was provided by the authors. We prepared 2D projection images from the same viewpoints as PCOF (total of 205 images per object) and used them for the training of LINE-2D and COF. All the programs were run on a PC (CPU: Core i7 3.4 GHz, OS: Windows7 64 bit) using a single CPU core.

Estimation Accuracy. Figure 7 shows the curves representing the relation between the success rate of correctly estimated 6D pose (vertical axis) and false positives per image (FPPI, horizontal axis). The estimation results with various search thresholds are plotted on the graphs. When the threshold is low and FPPI is high, the success rate for each object is less than 1. This is because 6D pose estimation requires not only correct positions but also correct rotation angles around x-y-z axes, and the estimated rotation angles do not depend on the search thresholds. All the graphs indicate that our proposed method achieves higher accuracy in comparison with other existing methods.

As shown in experiment1 (Sect. 4.1), COF and spread orientation of LINE-2D are not robust to the appearance changes caused by the out-of-plane rotations of the object. The numbers of viewpoints for making the templates are same in COF, LINE-2D and PCOF. Thus the differences in the success rate between these three methods are mainly due to the different image features.

In the algorithm of Ulrich et al. [7], the templates using normalized gradint vectors of Steger et al. [23] are made at the viewpoints sampled more densely than other three methods. Then the viewpoints are clustered to some aspects based on the similarity scores between the templates. Thus the viewpoint sphere is divided into some aspects which are optimized for a single template to keep its similarity score higher than a certain threshold. This viewpoint sampling is better than the regularly spaced sampling as in COF and LINE-2D, and the success rate of Ulrich et al. is higher than those of COF and LINE-2D. However, a single template represented each aspect and the similarity score should be degraded at the edges of the aspect. This is because our method surpass Ulrich et al. in the success rate of correctly estimated 6D object pose.

Processing Time. The processing times (ms) for 6D pose estimation when FPPI is 0.5 are shown in Table 2. Our proposed method achieved faster speed

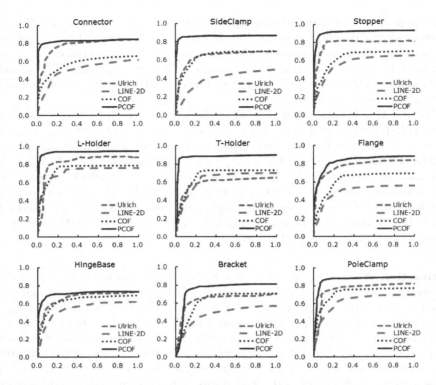

Fig. 7. The graphs showing the relation between the success rate of correctly estimated 6D pose (vertical axis) and false positives per image (FPPI, horizontal axis) are presented. There are nine graphs for each object in the dataset and the curves by four methods (Ulrich et al. [7], LINE-2D [8], COF [26] and PCOF (ours)) are drawn on each graph.

Table 2. The processing times (ms) for 6D pose estimation in experiment2 when FPPI is 0.5 are presented. The mean value is also shown at the bottom.

	Ulrich [7]	LINE-2D [8]	COF [26]	**PCOF (ours)**
Connector	964.1	375.8	1258.5	**167.1**
SideClamp	2724.4	383.2	1387.5	**220.4**
Stopper	2703.0	345.7	1149.9	**129.9**
L-Holder	963.8	357.1	1015.8	**122.6**
T-Holder	912.2	376.3	1140.1	**137.5**
Flange	973.0	390.5	1238.1	**137.4**
HingeBase	1137.1	348.9	1124.6	**226.1**
Bracket	792.4	358.5	961.4	**127.1**
PoleClamp	1439.0	375.9	1320.1	**137.4**
Mean	1401.0	368.0	1177.3	**156.2**

compared with the existing methods. PCOF and COF [26] use the same similarity scores calculated by bitwise ADD operations of binary features, and the main difference between them influencing the processing time is their search data structures. In COF the 2D object pose is estimated at each viewpoint independently, and the search strategy is optimized only in 2D pose space and not in 3D pose space. This is why the speed of COF was slower by approximately ten times than PCOF. The search model of LINE-2D [8] is also not efficient for search in 3D pose space. However, the similarity score of LINE-2D is calculated just by summing up the precomputed responce maps where the memory is linearized for reducing a cache miss, and this is much faster than the scores calculated by bitwise operations. Thus LINE-2D is much faster than COF.

Ulrich et al. [7] uses the normalized gradient vectors [23] which is not robust to the changes in 3D object pose, and their method requires more templates than PCOF in order to handle the same range of 3D object pose. Add to this, their search model is constructed by merging the neighboring viewpoints, and this is not fully efficient in the case that 2D views from separate viewpoints are similar, as is often the case with texture-less objects. Their similarity score which is based on floating-point arithmetic possibly lead to a slow matching of templates. From these reasons, 6D pose estimation of Ulrich et al. is slower by five to ten times than PCOF.

5 Conclusion

In this paper, we proposed PCOF and HPT for template based 6D pose estimation of texture-less objects from a monocular image. PCOF is extracted from randomly generated 2D projection images using 3D CAD data to explicitly handle a certain range of 3D object pose. HPT is built by clustering 3D object pose based on the similarities between 2D views and reducing the resolutions of PCOF features to accelerate 6D pose estimation using a coarse-to-fine search. The experimental evaluation demonstrated that PCOF was robust both to cluttered backgrounds and the appearance changes caused by the changes in 3D object pose. Another experimental result showed that our 6D pose estimation algorithm based on PCOF and HPT achieved higher success rate of correctly estimated 6D pose and faster speed in comparison with state-of-the-art methods on our challenging dataset.

References

1. Lowe, D.G.: Distinctive image features from scale-invariant keypoints. Int. J. Comput. Vis. **60**(2), 91–110 (2004)
2. Bay, H., Ess, A., Tuytelaars, T., Van Gool, L.: Speeded-up robust features (SURF). Comput. Vis. Image Underst. **110**(3), 346–359 (2008)
3. Grimson, W., Huttenlocher, D.: On the verification of hypothesized matches in model-based recognition. IEEE Trans. Pattern Anal. Mach. Intell. **13**(12), 1201–1213 (1991)

4. Lanser, S., Munkelt, O., Zierl, C.: Robust video-based object recognition using CAD models. In: Intelligent Autonomous Systems IAS-4, pp. 529–536 (1995)
5. Cyr, C.M., Kimia, B.B.: A similarity-based aspect-graph approach to 3D object recognition. Int. J. Comput. Vis. **57**(1), 5–22 (2004)
6. Liu, M.Y., Tuzel, O., Veeraraghavan, A., Taguchi, Y., Marks, T., Chellappa, R.: Fast object localization and pose estimation in heavy clutter for robotic bin picking. Int. J. Rob. Res. **31**(8), 951–973 (2012)
7. Ulrich, M., Wiedemann, C., Steger, C.: Combining scale-space and similarity-based aspect graphs for fast 3D object recognition. IEEE Trans. Pattern Anal. Mach. Intell. **34**(10), 1902–1914 (2012)
8. Hinterstoisser, S., Cagniart, C., Ilic, S., Sturm, P., Navab, N., Fua, P., Lepetit, V.: Gradient response maps for real-time detection of textureless objects. IEEE Trans. Pattern Anal. Mach. Intell. **34**(5), 876–888 (2012)
9. Hinterstoisser, S., Lepetit, V., Ilic, S., Holzer, S., Bradski, G., Konolige, K., Navab, N.: Model based training, detection and pose estimation of texture-less 3D objects in heavily cluttered scenes. In: Lee, K.M., Matsushita, Y., Rehg, J.M., Hu, Z. (eds.) ACCV 2012. LNCS, vol. 7724, pp. 548–562. Springer, Heidelberg (2013). doi:10.1007/978-3-642-37331-2_42
10. David, P., DeMenthon, D.: Object recognition in high clutter images using line features. In: CVPR, pp. 1581–1588 (2005)
11. Damen, D., Bunnun, P., Calway, A., Mayol-Cuevas, W.: Real-time learning and detection of 3D texture-less objects: a scalable approach. In: BMVC (2012)
12. Drost, B., Ulrich, M., Navab, N., Ilic, S.: Model globally, match locally: efficient and robust 3D object recognition. In: CVPR, pp. 998–1005 (2010)
13. Rodrigues, J., Kim, J.S., Furukawa, M., Xavier, J., Aguiar, P., Kanade, T.: 6D pose estimation of textureless shiny objects using random ferns for bin-picking. In: IROS, pp. 3334–3341 (2012)
14. Tejani, A., Tang, D., Kouskouridas, R., Kim, T.-K.: Latent-class hough forests for 3D object detection and pose estimation. In: Fleet, D., Pajdla, T., Schiele, B., Tuytelaars, T. (eds.) ECCV 2014. LNCS, vol. 8694, pp. 462–477. Springer, Heidelberg (2014). doi:10.1007/978-3-319-10599-4_30
15. Brachmann, E., Krull, A., Michel, F., Gumhold, S., Shotton, J., Rother, C.: Learning 6D object pose estimation using 3D object coordinates. In: Fleet, D., Pajdla, T., Schiele, B., Tuytelaars, T. (eds.) ECCV 2014. LNCS, vol. 8690, pp. 536–551. Springer, Heidelberg (2014). doi:10.1007/978-3-319-10605-2_35
16. Wohlhart, P., Lepetit, V.: Learning descriptors for object recognition and 3D pose estimation. In: CVPR, pp. 3109–3118 (2015)
17. Crivellaro, A., Rad, M., Verdie, Y., Yi, K.M., Fua, P., Lepetit, V.: A novel representation of parts for accurate 3D object detection and tracking in monocular images. In: ICCV, pp. 4391–4399 (2015)
18. Krull, A., Brachmann, E., Michel, F., Yang, M.Y., Gumhold, S., Rother, C.: Learning analysis-by-synthesis for 6D pose estimation in RGB-D images. In: ICCV, pp. 954–962 (2015)
19. Zhu, M., Derpanis, K., Yang, Y., Brahmbhatt, S., Zhang, M., Phillips, C., Lecce, M., Daniilidis, K.: Single image 3D object detection and pose estimation for grasping. In: ICRA, pp. 3936–3943 (2014)
20. Rios-Cabrera, R., Tuytelaars, T.: Discriminatively trained templates for 3D object detection: a real time scalable approach. In: ICCV, pp. 2048–2055 (2013)
21. Kehl, W., Tombari, F., Navab, N., Ilic, S., Lepetit, V.: Hashmod: a hashing method for scalable 3D object detection. In: BMVC (2015)

22. Hodan, T., Zabulis, X., Lourakis, M., Obdrzalek, S., Matas, J.: Detection and fine 3D pose estimation of texture-less objects in RGB-D images. In: IROS, pp. 4421–4428 (2015)
23. Steger, C.: Occlusion, clutter, and illumination invariant object recognition. In: International Archives of Photogrammetry and Remote Sensing, vol. XXXIV, Part 3A, pp. 345–350 (2002)
24. Ullah, F., Kaneko, S.: Using orientation codes for rotation-invariant template matching. Pattern Recogn. **37**(2), 201–209 (2004)
25. Hinterstoisser, S., Lepetit, V., Ilic, S., Fua, P., Navab, N.: Dominant orientation templates for real-time detection of texture-less objects. In: CVPR, pp. 2257–2264 (2010)
26. Konishi, Y., Ijiri, Y., Suwa, M., Kawade, M.: Textureless object detection using cumulative orientation feature. In: ICIP, pp. 1310–1313 (2015)
27. Nister, D., Stewenius, H.: Scalable recognition with a vocabulary tree. In: CVPR, pp. 2161–2168 (2006)
28. Silpa-Anan, C., Hartley, R.: Optimised KD-trees for fast image descriptor matching. In: CVPR, pp. 1–8 (2008)
29. Muja, M., Lowe, D.: Scalable nearest neighbor algorithms for high dimensional data. IEEE Trans. Pattern Anal. Mach. Intell. **36**(11), 2227–2240 (2014)
30. Lai, K., Bo, L., Ren, X., Fox, D.: A scalable tree-based approach for joint object and pose recognition. In: AAAI, pp. 1474–1480 (2011)
31. Gavrila, D.M.: A Bayesian, exemplar-based approach to hierarchical shape matching. IEEE Trans. Pattern Anal. Mach. Intell. **29**(8), 1408–1421 (2007)
32. Stenger, B., Thayananthan, A., Torr, P.H.S., Cipolla, R.: Hand pose estimation using hierarchical detection. In: Sebe, N., Lew, M., Huang, T.S. (eds.) CVHCI 2004. LNCS, vol. 3058, pp. 105–116. Springer, Heidelberg (2004). doi:10.1007/978-3-540-24837-8_11
33. Borgefors, G.: Hierarchical chamfer matching: a parametric edge matching algorithm. IEEE Trans. Pattern Anal. Mach. Intell. **10**(6), 849–865 (1988)
34. Pelleg, D., Moore, A.: X-means: extending k-means with efficient estimation of the number of clusters. In: ICML, pp. 727–734 (2000)
35. Hartley, R.I., Zisserman, A.: Multiple View Geometry in Computer Vision, 2nd edn. Cambridge University Press, Cambridge (2004). ISBN: 0521540518
36. Garrido-Jurado, S., Muñoz Salinas, R., Madrid-Cuevas, F.J., Marín-Jiménez, M.J.: Automatic generation and detection of highly reliable fiducial markers under occlusion. Pattern Recogn. **47**(6), 2280–2292 (2014)

Learning Models for Actions and Person-Object Interactions with Transfer to Question Answering

Arun Mallya[✉] and Svetlana Lazebnik

University of Illinois at Urbana-Champaign, Champaign, USA
{amallya2,slazebni}@illinois.edu

Abstract. This paper proposes deep convolutional network models that utilize local and global context to make human activity label predictions in still images, achieving state-of-the-art performance on two recent datasets with hundreds of labels each. We use multiple instance learning to handle the lack of supervision on the level of individual person instances, and weighted loss to handle unbalanced training data. Further, we show how specialized features trained on these datasets can be used to improve accuracy on the Visual Question Answering (VQA) task, in the form of multiple choice fill-in-the-blank questions (Visual Madlibs). Specifically, we tackle two types of questions on person activity and person-object relationship and show improvements over generic features trained on the ImageNet classification task

Keywords: Activity prediction · Deep networks · Visual Question Answering

1 Introduction

The task of Visual Question Answering (VQA) has recently garnered a lot of interest with multiple datasets [1–3] and systems [4–10] being proposed. Many of these systems rely on features extracted from deep convolutional neural networks (CNNs) pre-trained on the ImageNet classification task [11], with or without fine-tuning on the VQA dataset at hand. However, questions in VQA datasets tend to cover a wide variety of concepts such as the presence or absence of objects, counting, brand name recognition, emotion, activity, scene recognition and more. Generic ImageNet-trained networks are insufficiently well tailored for such open-ended tasks, and the VQA datasets themselves are currently too small to provide adequate training data for all types of visual content that are covered in their questions.

Fortunately, we are also seeing the release of valuable datasets targeting specific tasks such as scene recognition [12], age, gender, and emotion classification [13,14], human action recognition [15–17], etc. To better understand and answer questions about an image, we should draw on the knowledge from these specialized datasets. Given a specific question type, we should be able to choose

© Springer International Publishing AG 2016
B. Leibe et al. (Eds.): ECCV 2016, Part I, LNCS 9905, pp. 414–428, 2016.
DOI: 10.1007/978-3-319-46448-0_25

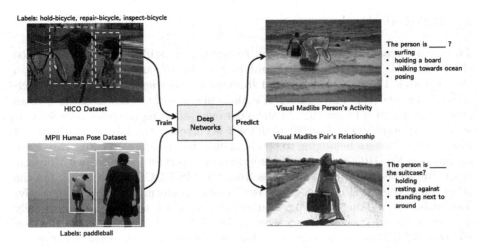

Fig. 1. We train CNNs on the HICO and MPII datasets to predict human activity labels. Our networks fuse features from the full image and the person bounding boxes, which are provided in the MPII dataset and detected in the HICO dataset. We then use these networks to answer two types of multiple choice questions from the MadLibs dataset – about a person's activity, and the relationship between a person and an object.

features from appropriate expert models or networks. In this paper, we show that transferring expert knowledge from a network trained on human activity prediction can not only improve question answering performance, but also help interpret the model's decisions. We train deep networks on the HICO [16] and MPII [17] datasets to predict human activity labels and apply these networks to answer two types of multiple choice fill-in-the-blank questions from the Madlibs dataset [3] on person activity and person-object relationships (Fig. 1). Our contributions are as follows:

1. We propose simple CNN models for predicting human activity labels by fusing features from a person bounding box and global context from the whole image. At training time, the person boxes are provided in the MPII dataset and must be automatically detected in HICO. Our CNN architecture is described in Sect. 3.
2. At training time, we use Multiple Instance Learning (MIL) to handle the lack of full person instance-label supervision and weighted loss to handle the unbalanced training data. The resulting models beat the previous state-of-the-art on the respective datasets, as shown in Sect. 4.
3. We transfer our models to VQA with the help of a standard image-text embedding (canonical correlation analysis or CCA) and show improved accuracy on MadLibs activity and person-object interaction questions in Sect. 5.

2   Related Work

There exist many datasets for action recognition in still images, including the older PASCAL VOC [18] and Stanford 40 Actions [19], and newer MPII Human Pose Dataset [17], COCO-A [20] and *Humans Interacting with Common Objects* (HICO) dataset [16]. The number of actions in some of the newer datasets is an order of magnitude larger than in the older ones, allowing us to learn vocabularies fit for general VQA. The HICO dataset is currently the largest, consisting of nearly 50000 images belonging to 600 human-object interaction categories. Each category in the HICO dataset is composed of a verb-object pair, with objects belonging to the 80 object categories from the MS COCO dataset [21]. On the other hand, the MPII dataset comprises humans performing 393 different activities including walking, running, skating, etc. in which they do not necessarily interact with objects. In this work, we train CNNs with simple architectures on HICO and MPII datasets, and show that they outperform the previous state-of-the-art models.

One limitation of the HICO dataset is that it provides labels for the image as a whole, instead of associating them with specific ground truth person instances. We disambiguate activity label assignment over the people in the image with the help of *Multiple Instance Learning* (MIL) [22], which has been widely used for recognition problems with weakly or incompletely labeled training data [23–26]. In the MIL framework, instead of receiving a set of individually labeled 'instances', the learner receives a set of 'bags,' each of which is labeled negative if all the instances inside it are negative, and labeled positive if it contains at least one positive instance. In this work, we treat each person bounding box as an 'instance' and the image, which contains one or more people in it, as a 'bag'. The exact formulation of our learning procedure is explained in Sect. 3.2.

To recognize a person's activity, we want to use not only the evidence from that person's bounding box, but also some kind of broader contextual information from the image. Previous work suggests the use of latent context boxes [27], multiresolution or zoom-out features [28,29] and complex 2-D recurrent structures [28]. In particular, Gkioxari *et al.* [27] have recently proposed an R*CNN network that chooses a second latent box that overlaps the bounding box of the person and provides the strongest evidence of a particular action being performed. They also proposed a simpler model, the Scene-RCNN, that uses the entire image instead of a chosen box. We explored using latent boxes but found their performance to be lacking on datasets with hundreds of labels, possibly due to overfitting and the infeasibility of thoroughly sampling latent boxes during training. Similarly, we could not obtain good results with multiresolution features owing to overfitting. Instead, we get surprisingly good results with a simpler architecture combining features from the entire image and the bounding box of the person under consideration, outperforming both R*CNN and Scene-RCNN.

3   Action Recognition Method

3.1   Network Architecture

Our network is based on the *Fast RCNN* [30] architecture with VGG-16 [31]. Fast RCNN includes a new adaptive max pooling layer, referred to as the ROI pooling layer, that replaces the standard max pooling layer (*pool5*) after the set of the first five convolutional layers. This layer takes in a list of bounding boxes, referred to as Regions Of Interest (ROI) and outputs a set of fixed-size feature maps for each input ROI that are then fed to the fully connected layers. During the forward pass of our network, we use two ROIs for each person instance in the image: the tight bounding box of the person, and the full image (we also experimented with using an expanded person bounding box instead of the full image, but found the full image to always work better). The ROI Pooling layer produces a feature of 512 channels and spatial size 7×7 for each ROI. The *fc6* layer of the VGG-16 network expects a feature of size $512 \times 7 \times 7$.

We explore two ways of combining the two ROI features: through stacking and dimensionality reduction (Fig. 2). In the first, referred to as Fusion-1, we stack features from the bounding box and the entire image along the channel dimension and obtain a feature of size $1024 \times 7 \times 7$. A convolutional layer of filter size 1×1 is used to perform dimensionality reduction of channels from 1024 to 512, while keeping the spatial size the same. In the second, referred to as Fusion-2, we first perform dimensionality reduction on the two ROI features individually to reduce the number of channels from 512 to 256 each, and then stack the outputs to obtain an input of size $512 \times 7 \times 7$ for the *fc6* layer.

Our architecture differs from R*CNN and Scene-RCNN [27] in two major ways. First, unlike R*CNN, we do not explicitly try to find a box or set of boxes that provide support for a particular label. Second, while R*CNN and Scene-RCNN independently perform prediction using the two features and then average them, we combine features before prediction. The results presented in Sect. 4 confirm that our "early" fusion strategy gives better performance. Further, our architecture is faster than R*CNN because it does not need to sample boxes during training and testing.

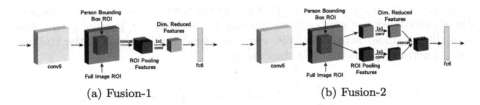

(a) Fusion-1   (b) Fusion-2

Fig. 2. Our networks extract ROI features [30] of dimension $512 \times 7 \times 7$ from both the person bounding box and the full image. The resulting feature is fed into the *fc6* layer of the VGG-16 network. (a) Fusion-1: The two ROI features are stacked and a 1×1 convolution is used for dimensionality reduction. (b) Fusion-2: Each ROI feature is separately reduced using 1×1 convolutions, and the outputs are then stacked.

3.2   Multiple Instance Learning for Label Prediction

In the HICO dataset, if at least one of the people in the image is performing an action, the label is marked as positive for the image. As our architecture makes predictions with respect to a person bounding box, we treat the assignment of labels to different people as latent variables and try to infer the assignment during end-to-end training of the network. For an image I, let B be the set of all person bounding boxes in the image. Using our network described above which takes as input an image I and a person bounding box $b \in B$, we obtain the score of an action a for the image as follows:

$$\text{score}(a; I) = \max_{b \in B} \ \text{score}(a; b, I) \tag{1}$$

where $\text{score}(a; b, I)$ is the score of action a for the person b in image I. The predicted label for the action can be obtained by passing the score through a logistic sigmoid or softmax unit as required. The max operator enforces the constraint that if a particular action label is active for a given image, then at least one person in the image is performing that action, and when a particular action label is inactive for a given image, then no person in the image is performing the action. During the forward pass, the score and thus the label for the image are predicted using the above relationship. The predicted label is compared to the groundtruth label in order to compute the loss and gradients for backpropagation.

3.3   Weighted Loss Function

Mostajabi et $al.$ [29] showed that use of an asymmetric weighted loss helps greatly in the case of an unbalanced dataset. For the HICO dataset, we have to learn 600 independent classifiers per image and this makes for a highly unbalanced scenario, with the number of negative examples greatly outnumbering the positive examples, even for the most populous categories (an average negative to positive ratio of 6000:1, worst case of 38116:1). We thus compute a weighted cross-entropy loss in which positive examples are weighted by a factor of w_p and negative examples by a factor of w_n. Given a training sample (I, B, y) consisting of an image I, set of person bounding boxes or detections B, and ground truth action label vector $y \in \{0, 1\}^C$ for C independent classes, the network produces probabilities of actions being present in the image by passing predictions through a sigmoid activation unit. For any given training sample, the training loss on network prediction $\hat{y}$ is thus given by

$$\text{loss}(I, B, y) = \sum_{i=1}^{C} w_p^i \cdot y^i \cdot \log(\hat{y}^i) + w_n^i \cdot (1 - y^i) \cdot \log(1 - \hat{y}^i) \tag{2}$$

In our experiments, we set $w_p = 10$ and $w_n = 1$ for all classes for simplicity.

4   Activity Prediction Experiments

Datasets. We train and test our system on two different activity classification datasets: HICO [16] and the MPII Human Pose Dataset [17]. The HICO dataset contains labels for 600 human-object interaction activities, any number of which might be simultaneously active for a given image. Labels are provided at the image level even though each image might contain multiple person instances, each performing the same or different activities. The labels can thus be thought of as an aggregate over labels of each person instance in the image. As the person bounding boxes are not provided with the HICO dataset, we run the Faster-RCNN detector [32] with the default confidence threshold of 0.8 on all the train and test images. The obtained person bounding boxes are thus not perfect and might have wrong or missing annotations. The HICO training set contains 38,116 images and the test set contains 9,658 images. The training set is highly unbalanced with 51 out of 600 categories having just 1 positive example.

The MPII dataset contains labels for 393 actions. Unlike in HICO, each image only has a single label together with one or more annotated person instances. All person instances inside an image are assumed to be performing the same task. Ground truth bounding boxes are available for each instance in the training set, so we do not need to use MIL can take advantage of the extra training data available by training on each person instance separately. On the test set, however, only a single point inside the bounding box is provided for each instance, so we run the Faster-RCNN detector to detect people. The training set consists of 15,200 images and 22,900 person instances and the test set has 5,709 images. Similar to HICO, the training set is unbalanced and the number of positive examples for a label ranges from 3 to 476 instances.

HICO Results. On the HICO dataset, we compare the networks described in the previous section with VGG-16 networks trained on just the person bounding boxes and just the full image, as well as with R*CNN and Scene-RCNN. For the latter two, we use the authors' implementation [27]. For all the networks, except the R*CNN, we use a learning rate of 10^{-5}, decayed by a factor of 0.1 every 30000 iterations. For the R*CNN, we use the recommended setting from [27] of a learning rate of 10^{-4}, with a lower and upper intersection over union (IoU) bound for secondary regions of 0.2 and 0.75 and sample 10 secondary regions per person bounding box during a single training pass. We train all networks for 60000 iterations with a momentum of 0.9. Further, all networks are finetuned till the *conv3* layer as in previous work [27,30]. We use a batch size of 10 images, resize images to a maximum size of 640 pixels, and sample a maximum of 6 person bounding boxes per image in order to fit the network in the GPU memory during training with MIL. Consistent with [28,33,34], we initialize our models with weights from the ImageNet-trained VGG-16.

Table 1 presents our comparison. As HICO is fairly new, the only published baseline [16] uses the AlexNet [35] (Table 1a). Using the VGG-16 network improves upon AlexNet by 10 mAP (first line of Table 1b). The VGG-16 network that uses just the person bounding box to make predictions with MIL performs

Table 1. Performance of various networks on the HICO person-activity dataset. Note that usage of the Bounding Box (Bbox) necessitates the usage of Multiple Instance Learning (MIL).

	Method	Full Im.	Bbox	MIL	Wtd. loss	mAP
(a)	AlexNet+SVM [16]	✓				19.4
(b)	VGG-16, full image	✓				29.4
	VGG-16, bounding box		✓	✓		14.6
	VGG-16, R*CNN		✓	✓		28.5
	VGG-16, Scene-RCNN	✓	✓	✓		29.0
(c)	Fusion-1	✓	✓	✓		33.6
	Fusion-1, weighted loss	✓	✓	✓	✓	36.0
	Fusion-2	✓	✓	✓		33.8
	Fusion-2, weighted loss	✓	✓	✓	✓	**36.1**

poorly with only 14.6 mAP (second line of Table 1b). This is not entirely surprising since the object that the person is interacting with is often not inside that person's bounding box. More surprisingly, the R*CNN architecture, which tries to find secondary boxes to support the person box, performs slightly worse than the full-image VGG network. One possible reason for this is that R*CNN has to use MIL twice during training: once for finding the secondary box for an instance, and then again while aggregating over the multiple person instances in the image. Since R*CNN samples only 10 boxes per person instance during each pass of training (same as in [27]), finding the right box for each of the 600 actions might be difficult. The Scene-RCNN, which uses the entire image as the secondary box, needs to do MIL just once, and performs marginally better than R*CNN. Another possible reason why both R*CNN and Scene-RCNN cannot outperform a full-image network is that they attempt to predict action scores independently from the person box and the secondary box before summing them. As we can see from the poor results of our bounding-box-only model (second line of Table 1b), such prediction is hard.

With our fusion networks, we immediately see improvements over the full-image network (Table 1c). The weighted loss, which penalizes mistakes on positive examples more heavily as described in Sect. 3.2, helps push the mAP higher by about 2.5 mAP for both our networks. The Fusion-2 network, which performs dimensionality reduction before local and global feature concatenation, has a slight edge probably due to lower number of parameters (Fusion-1 has 1024×512 parameters for dimensionality reduction and Fusion-2 has $2 \times 512 \times 256$, lesser by a factor of 2).

MPII Results. On the MPII dataset, we compare our networks with previously published baselines from Pischulin *et al.* [17] and Gkioxari *et al.* [27]. Our networks are trained with a learning rate of 10^{-4} with a decay of 0.1 every 12000 iterations, for 40000 iterations. We only finetune till the $fc6$ layer due to the

Table 2. Results on the MPII test set (obtained by submitting our output files by email to the authors of [17]).

Method	mAP
Dense Trajectory + Pose [17]	5.5
VGG-16, R*CNN [27]	26.7
Fusion-1, label per ground truth person instance	32.06
Fusion-2, label per ground truth person instance	**32.24**
Fusion-1, MIL over ground truth person instances	31.68
Fusion-2, MIL over ground truth person instances	31.89
Fusion-2, label per detected person instance	32.02
Fusion-2, MIL over detected person instances	31.81

smaller amount of training data than in HICO. We do not use the weighted loss on this dataset, as we did not find it to make a difference.

Table 2 shows the MPII results. The trend is similar to that in Table 1: our fusion networks outperform previous methods, with Fusion-2 having a lead over Fusion-1. Recall that the MPII training set comes with ground truth person instances, which gives us a chance to examine the effect of MIL. If we assume that the assignment of labels to the people in the image is unknown and use the MIL framework, we see a small dip in performance as opposed to assuming that the label applies to each person in the image (last two rows of Table 2). The latter gives us more training data along with full supervision and improves over MIL by around 0.4 mAP. We also tried training the network with detected person bounding boxes instead of groundtruth boxes and found that the performance was very similar, indicating that groundtruth boxes may not be necessary if there is no ambiguity in assignment of labels.

Qualitative Results. Figure 3 displays some of the predictions of our best-performing network on the HICO dataset. In spite of the lack of explicit supervision of which labels map onto a specific person instance, the network learns to reasonably assign labels to the correct person instance. It is interesting to note a few minor mistakes made by the network: in the top left example, the network confuses the tower in the background for a clock tower, and assigns the label 'no_interaction-clock' to one of the people. In the middle example of the second row, there is a false person detection (marked in red) due to the reflection in the glass, but it does not get an activity prediction since the highest-scoring label has confidence less than 0.5.

Figure 4 shows some of the failures of our system on the HICO dataset. Unusual use-cases of an object such as swinging around a backpack can confuse the deep network into misclassifying the object as in the leftmost image. Since our system relies on detected people, we can either miss or produce false positives, or label the wrong instances as shown in the middle image. Lastly, one drawback of the weakly supervised MIL framework is that it is unable to distinguish labels

blue: carry, wear-backpack
green: no_interaction-clock

blue: no label
green: hold, wield-knife

blue: no label
green: wear, carry-backpack

blue: straddle, ride, hold, sit_on-bicycle
green: no_interaction-bicycle

green: carry, hold, drag-suitcase
blue, red: no label

blue: hold, carry, hug-person, hold, carry-backpack
cyan: hold, carry-person, carry-backpack
red: carry-backpack   green: hold-person

Fig. 3. Predictions of our Fusion-2 model on the HICO test set. Detected person instances are marked in different colors and corresponding action labels are given underneath. (Color figure online)

blue: fly, pull-kite   blue, green: read, hold-laptop, carry-keyboard   almost all boxes: hold, wield, swing-baseball bat

Fig. 4. Failure examples on HICO. Incorrect classification of objects/actions, wrong interacting person detection, and inability to assign labels to correct person instances due to weak supervision and sampling are common issues.

in a crowded scenario, especially when the crowd occurs only in specific settings such as sports games (right image).

5   Visual Question Answering Results

Dataset and Tasks. In this section, we evaluate the performance of features extracted by our networks on two types of questions from the Madlibs dataset [3] that specifically target people's activities and their interactions with objects. The first type, 'Person's Activity,' asks us to choose an option that best describes the activity of the indicated person/people, while the second type, 'Pair's Relationship,' asks us to describe the relationship between the indicated person and object(s). The indicated people and objects come from ground truth annotations on the MS COCO dataset [21], from which MadLibs is derived, so there is no need to perform any automatic detection. The prompt is fixed for all questions of a particular type: 'The person/people is/are ____' and 'The person/people is/are ____ the object(s)'.

The training data for MadLibs consists of questions paired with correct answers. There are 26528 and 30640 training examples for the activity and relationship questions, respectively (the total number of distinct images is only about 10 K, but a single image can give rise to multiple questions centered on different person and object instances). In the test data, each question contains four possible answer choices, of which one is the correct answer (or best answer, in case of confusing options). Depending on the way the distractor options are selected, test questions are divided into two categories, Easy and Hard. The test sets for the activity and relationship types have 6501 and 7595 questions respectively, and each comes with Easy and Hard distractor options. Hard options are often quite confusing, with even humans disagreeing on the correct answer. Thus, the performance on filtered hard questions, on which human annotators agree with the 'correct' answer at least 50 % of the times, is also measured. Since MadLibs does not provide a set of multiple choice questions for validation, we created our own validation set of Easy questions by taking 10 % of the training images and following the distractor generation procedure of [3].

Models and Baselines. Similarly to [3], we use normalized Canonical Correlation Analysis (nCCA) [36] to learn a joint embedding space to which the image and the choice features are mapped. Given a question, we select the choice that has the highest cosine similarity with the image features in the joint embedding space as the predicted answer.

On the text side, we represent each of the choices by the average of the 300-dimensional word2vec features [37] of the words in the choice. In the case that a word is out of the vocabulary provided by [38], we represent it with all zeros.

On the image side, we compare performance obtained with three types of features. The first is obtained by passing the entire image, resized to 224×224 pixels, through the vanilla (ImageNet-trained) VGG-16 network and extracting the $fc7$ activations. This serves as the baseline, similar to the original work of Yu *et al.* [3]. The second type of feature is obtained by passing the entire image through our activity prediction network that uses full image inputs. We compare both the $fc7$ activations (of length 4096) and the class label activations (of length 600). The third type of feature is extracted by our Fusion-2 architecture (as detailed in Sect. 3). As our MadLibs question types target one or more specific people in the image, we feed in the person bounding boxes as ROIs to our network (for the relationship questions, we ignore the object bounding box). In the case that a particular question targets multiple people, we perform max pooling over the class label activations of the distinct people to obtain a single feature vector. Note that we found it necessary to use the class label activations before passing them through the logistic sigmoid/softmax as the squashing saturated the scores too close to 0 or 1.

Table 3. Performance of different visual features on Activity and Relationship MadLibs questions (Fil. H. ≡ Filtered Hard). See text for discussion.

Dataset:Network	-	Feature	Person's activity			Pair's relationship		
			Easy	Hard	Fil. H.	Easy	Hard	Fil. H.
ImageNet:VGG-19 [3]	-	fc7	80.7	65.4	68.8	63.0	54.3	57.6
ImageNet:VGG-16	-	fc7	80.79	65.14	67.73	71.45	51.47	56.28
HICO:VGG-16, Full Im.	-	cls_score	86.03	68.74	72.06	77.25	54.10	59.77
HICO:VGG-16, Full Im.	-	fc7	86.54	69.14	72.39	77.96	55.76	61.03
HICO:Fusion-2	-	cls_score	86.66	70.05	73.46	78.29	55.52	61.39
MPII:Fusion-2	-	cls_score	83.23	68.11	70.89	72.81	52.75	57.68
HICO+MPII:Fusion-2	-	cls_score	**87.57**	**71.13**	**74.45**	**78.50**	**56.17**	**62.06**

To train the nCCA model, we used the toolbox of Klein et al. [39]. We set the CCA regularization parameter using the validation sets we created, resulting in values of 0.01 and 0.001 for the $fc7$ and class score features respectively. Our learned nCCA embedding space has dimensionality of 300 (same as the dimensionality of word2vec).

Question Answering Performance. The first two rows of Table 3 contain the accuracies from the vanilla VGG baseline of Yu et al. [3] and our reproduction. Some of our numbers deviate from those of [3], probably owing to the different features used (VGG-16 v/s VGG-19), CCA toolboxes, and hyperparameter selection procedures. From the second row of Table 3, using the vanilla VGG features gives an accuracy of 80.79 % and 71.45 % on the Easy Person Activity and Easy Pair Relationship questions respectively. By extracting features from our full-image network trained on the HICO dataset, we obtain gains of around 6–7 % on the Easy questions (rows 3–4). It is interesting to note that the 600-dimensional class label features give performance comparable to the 4096-dimensional $fc7$ features. Next, features from our Fusion-2 network trained on HICO (row 5) help improve the performance further. The Fusion-2 network trained on the smaller MPII dataset (row 6) gives considerably weaker performance. Nevertheless, we obtain our best performance by concatenating class label predictions from both HICO and MPII (last row of Table 3), since some of the MPII categories are complementary to those of HICO, especially in the cases when a person is not interacting with any object. Compared to our baseline (row 2), we obtain an improvement of 6.8 % on the Easy Activity task, and 7.5 % on the Easy Relationship task. For the Hard Activity task, our improvements are 6 % and 6.7 % on the unfiltered and filtered questions, and for the Hard Relationship task, our improvements are 4.7 % and 5.8 % on the unfiltered and filtered questions respectively.

Qualitative Results. Figure 5 shows a range of correctly answered multiple choice questions using our best-performing features. By examining top labels predicted by our network, we can gain intuition into the choices of our model as these are easily interpretable unlike $fc7$ features of the VGG-16 network.

Fig. 5. Correctly answered questions of the person activity type (first two rows) and person-object relationship type (last row). The subjects of the questions are highlighted in each image. The left column below each image shows the answer choices, with the correct choice marked in red. The right column shows the activity labels and scores predicted by our best network. (Color figure online)

In fact, our top predicted labels often align very closely to the correct answer choice. In the top left image of Fig. 5, the question targets multiple people and the label scores max pooled over the people correctly predict the activity of sitting at and eating at the dining table. In the middle image of the first row, the question targets the skateboarder. Accordingly, our network gives a high score for skateboard-related activities, and a much lower score for the bicyclist in the background. In the rightmost image in the first row, our network also correctly predicts the labels for 'ride, straddle-horse' along with 'wear, carry-backpack' (which is not one of the choices). The middle and right images in the middle row show that our predictions change depending on the target bounding

  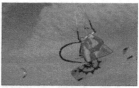

The person is _____ ?		The person is _____ the dog?		The person is _____ ?	
holding a picture	1.00, no_interaction-clock	feeding	0.99, no_interaction-microwave	parasurfing	0.84, hold-surfboard
drinking	0.73, no_interaction-vase	sitting near	0.98, no_interaction-refrigerator	walking	0.81, hold-kite
looking	0.38, wear-tie	riding with	0.96, no_interaction-oven	holding board	0.77, carry-surfboard
standing	0.12, sit_on-chair	laying with	0.93, hold-refrigerator	talking	0.22, fly-kite

Fig. 6. Failure examples. The correct choice is marked in red, and the predicted answer in blue. Failure modes mainly belong to three classes as illustrated (left to right): correct predictions but unfamiliar object ('picture'); incorrect predictions ('dog' missed); and a mix of the first two, i.e., partly correct predictions and unfamiliar setting. (Color figure online)

box: the 'hold-book' label has a much higher probability for the boy on the right, even though the network was trained using weak supervision and MIL, as detailed in Sect. 3.

Figure 6 displays some of the common failure modes of our system. In the leftmost image, even though the predicted activity labels are correct, the target object of the question ('picture') is absent from the HICO and MPII datasets so the labels offer no useful information for answering the question. The network can also make wrong predictions, as in the middle image. In the rightmost image, the choices are rather hard and confusing as the person is indeed holding onto a kite as well as a surfboard in an activity best described as 'parasurfing' or 'windsurfing'.

6 Conclusion

In this paper, we developed effective models exploiting local and global context to make person-centric activity predictions and showed how Multiple Instance Learning could be used to train these models with weak supervision. Even though we used a simple global contextual representation, we obtained state-of-the-art performance on two different datasets, outperforming more complex models like R*CNN. In future work, we hope to further explore more sophisticated contextual models and find better ways to train them on our target datasets, which feature hundreds of class labels with highly unbalanced label distributions.

We have also shown how transferring the knowledge from models trained on specialized activity datasets can improve performance on VQA tasks. While we demonstrated this on fairly narrow question types, we envision a more general-purpose system that would have access to many more input features such as person attributes, detected objects, scene information, etc. and appropriately combine them based on the question and image provided.

Acknowledgments. This material is based upon work supported by the National Science Foundation under grants CIF-1302438, IIS-1563727, Xerox UAC, and the Sloan Foundation. We would to thank Licheng Yu for his help with the MadLibs dataset.

References

1. Malinowski, M., Fritz, M.: A multi-world approach to question answering about real-world scenes based on uncertain input. In: NIPS (2014)
2. Antol, S., Agrawal, A., Lu, J., Mitchell, M., Batra, D., Zitnick, C.L., Parikh, D.: VQA: Visual Question Answering. In: ICCV (2015)
3. Yu, L., Park, E., Berg, A.C., Berg, T.L.: Visual Madlibs: fill in the blank image generation and question answering. In: ICCV (2015)
4. Xu, H., Saenko, K.: Ask, attend and answer: exploring question-guided spatial attention for visual question answering. arXiv preprint arXiv:1511.05234 (2015)
5. Zhou, B., Tian, Y., Sukhbaatar, S., Szlam, A., Fergus, R.: Simple baseline for visual question answering. arXiv preprint arXiv:1512.02167 (2015)
6. Gao, H., Mao, J., Zhou, J., Huang, Z., Wang, L., Xu, W.: Are you talking to a machine? Dataset and methods for multilingual image question answering. arXiv preprint arXiv:1505.05612 (2015)
7. Shih, K.J., Singh, S., Hoiem, D.: Where to look: focus regions for visual question answering (2016)
8. Andreas, J., Rohrbach, M., Darrell, T., Klein, D.: Deep compositional question answering with neural module networks. CoRR abs/1511.02799 (2015)
9. Fukui, A., Park, D.H., Yang, D., Rohrbach, A., Darrell, T., Rohrbach, M.: Multimodal compact bilinear pooling for visual question answering and visual grounding. CoRR abs/1606.01847 (2016)
10. Jabri, A., Joulin, A., van der Maaten, L.: Revisiting visual question answering baselines. CoRR abs/1606.08390 (2016)
11. Russakovsky, O., Deng, J., Su, H., Krause, J., Satheesh, S., Ma, S., Huang, Z., Karpathy, A., Khosla, A., Bernstein, M., Berg, A.C., Fei-Fei, L.: ImageNet large scale visual recognition challenge. IJCV **115**(3), 211–252 (2015)
12. Zhou, B., Lapedriza, A., Xiao, J., Torralba, A., Oliva, A.: Learning deep features for scene recognition using places database. In: NIPS (2014)
13. Levi, G., Hassner, T.: Age and gender classification using convolutional neural networks. In: CVPR Workshop (2015)
14. Levi, G., Hassner, T.: Emotion recognition in the wild via convolutional neural networks and mapped binary patterns. In: ACM ICMI (2015)
15. Maji, S., Bourdev, L., Malik, J.: Action recognition from a distributed representation of pose and appearance. In: CVPR (2011)
16. Chao, Y.W., Wang, Z., He, Y., Wang, J., Deng, J.: Hico: A benchmark for recognizing human-object interactions in images. In: ICCV (2015)
17. Pishchulin, L., Andriluka, M., Schiele, B.: Fine-grained activity recognition with holistic and pose based features. In: Jiang, X., Hornegger, J., Koch, R. (eds.) GCPR 2014. LNCS, vol. 8753, pp. 678–689. Springer, Heidelberg (2014). doi:10.1007/978-3-319-11752-2_56
18. Everingham, M., Van Gool, L., Williams, C.K., Winn, J., Zisserman, A.: The Pascal Visual Object Classes (VOC) challenge. IJCV **88**, 303–338 (2010)
19. Yao, B., Jiang, X., Khosla, A., Lin, A.L., Guibas, L., Fei-Fei, L.: Human action recognition by learning bases of action attributes and parts. In: ICCV (2011)

20. Ronchi, M.R., Perona, P.: Describing common human visual actions in images. In: BMVC (2015)
21. Lin, T.-Y., Maire, M., Belongie, S., Hays, J., Perona, P., Ramanan, D., Dollár, P., Zitnick, C.L.: Microsoft COCO: common objects in context. In: Fleet, D., Pajdla, T., Schiele, B., Tuytelaars, T. (eds.) ECCV 2014. LNCS, vol. 8693, pp. 740–755. Springer, Heidelberg (2014). doi:10.1007/978-3-319-10602-1_48
22. Maron, O., Lozano-Pérez, T.: A framework for multiple-instance learning. In: NIPS (1998)
23. Zhang, C., Platt, J.C., Viola, P.A.: Multiple instance boosting for object detection. In: NIPS (2005)
24. Hoffman, J., Pathak, D., Darrell, T., Saenko, K.: Detector discovery in the wild: joint multiple instance and representation learning. In: CVPR (2015)
25. Vezhnevets, A., Buhmann, J.M.: Towards weakly supervised semantic segmentation by means of multiple instance and multitask learning. In: CVPR (2010)
26. Pinheiro, P.O., Collobert, R.: From image-level to pixel-level labeling with convolutional networks. In: CVPR (2015)
27. Gkioxari, G., Girshick, R., Malik, J.: Contextual action recognition with R* CNN. In: ICCV (2015)
28. Bell, S., Zitnick, C.L., Bala, K., Girshick, R.B.: Inside-outside net: detecting objects in context with skip pooling and recurrent neural networks. CoRR abs/1512.04143 (2015)
29. Mostajabi, M., Yadollahpour, P., Shakhnarovich, G.: Feedforward semantic segmentation with zoom-out features. In: CVPR (2015)
30. Girshick, R.: Fast R-CNN. In: ICCV (2015)
31. Simonyan, K., Zisserman, A.: Very deep convolutional networks for large-scale image recognition. CoRR abs/1409.1556 (2014)
32. Ren, S., He, K., Girshick, R., Sun, J.: Faster R-CNN: towards real-time object detection with region proposal networks. In: NIPS (2015)
33. Girshick, R., Donahue, J., Darrell, T., Malik, J.: Rich feature hierarchies for accurate object detection and semantic segmentation. In: CVPR (2014)
34. Agrawal, P., Girshick, R., Malik, J.: Analyzing the performance of multilayer neural networks for object recognition. In: Fleet, D., Pajdla, T., Schiele, B., Tuytelaars, T. (eds.) ECCV 2014. LNCS, vol. 8695, pp. 329–344. Springer, Heidelberg (2014). doi:10.1007/978-3-319-10584-0_22
35. Krizhevsky, A., Sutskever, I., Hinton, G.E.: ImageNet classification with deep convolutional neural networks. In: Advances in Neural Information Processing Systems, pp. 1097–1105 (2012)
36. Gong, Y., Ke, Q., Isard, M., Lazebnik, S.: A multi-view embedding space for modeling internet images, tags, and their semantics. IJCV **106**, 210–233 (2014)
37. Mikolov, T., Sutskever, I., Chen, K., Corrado, G.S., Dean, J.: Distributed representations of words and phrases and their compositionality. In: NIPS (2013)
38. Google: Word2vec trained model. https://code.google.com/archive/p/word2vec/. Accessed 8 Mar 2016
39. Klein, B., Lev, G., Sadeh, G., Wolf, L.: Associating neural word embeddings with deep image representations using fisher vectors. In: CVPR (2015)

A Software Platform for Manipulating the Camera Imaging Pipeline

Hakki Can Karaimer$^{(\boxtimes)}$ and Michael S. Brown

Department of Electrical Engineering and Computer Science,
Lassonde School of Engineering, York University, Toronto, Canada
karaimer@yorku.ca, mbrown@eecs.yorku.ca

Abstract. There are a number of processing steps applied onboard a digital camera that collectively make up the camera imaging pipeline. Unfortunately, the imaging pipeline is typically embedded in a camera's hardware making it difficult for researchers working on individual components to do so within the proper context of the full pipeline. This not only hinders research, it makes evaluating the effects from modifying an individual pipeline component on the final camera output challenging, if not impossible. This paper presents a new software platform that allows easy access to each stage of the camera imaging pipeline. The platform allows modification of the parameters for individual components as well as the ability to access and manipulate the intermediate images as they pass through different stages. We detail our platform design and demonstrate its usefulness on a number of examples.

Keywords: Camera processing pipeline · Computational photography · Color processing

1 Introduction

Digital cameras are the cornerstone for virtually all computer vision applications as they provide the image input to our algorithms. While camera images are often modeled as simple light-measuring devices that directly convert incoming radiance to numerical values, the reality is that there are a number of processing routines onboard digital cameras that are applied to obtain the final RGB output. These processing steps are generally performed in sequence and collectively make up the camera imaging pipeline. Examples of these processing steps include Bayer pattern demosaicing, white-balance, color space mapping, noise reduction, tone-mapping and color manipulation. Many of these processing steps are well-known research topics in their own right, e.g. white-balance, color space mapping (colorimetry), and noise reduction.

Although cameras are the most prominent hardware tools in computer vision, it is surprisingly difficult to get access to the underlying imaging pipeline. This is because these routines are embedded in the camera's hardware and may involve proprietary image manipulation that is unique to individual camera manufacturers. This is a significant drawback to the research community. In particular,

© Springer International Publishing AG 2016
B. Leibe et al. (Eds.): ECCV 2016, Part I, LNCS 9905, pp. 429–444, 2016.
DOI: 10.1007/978-3-319-46448-0_26

it forces many researchers to work on topics outside the proper context of the full imaging pipeline. For example, much of the work targeting white-balance and color constancy is performed directly on the camera-specific raw images without the ability to demonstrate how it would affect the final output on the camera. Another example includes noise reduction (NR) targeting sensor noise. On a camera, NR is applied before many of the non-linear photo-finishing routines (e.g. tone-curve manipulation), however, researchers are generally forced to apply NR on the final non-linear sRGB image due to a lack of access to the camera pipeline. This presents a significant mismatch between assumptions made in the academic literature and real industry practice.

Contribution. We present a software platform to allow easy access to each stage of the imaging pipeline. Our approach operates on images saved in DNG raw image format which represents the unprocessed sensor response from the camera and the starting point for the camera processing pipeline. Our platform allows images to be opened and run through a software rendering API that parallels the onboard processing steps, including the individual processing components and their associated parameters. More specifically, our platform provides API calls that allow the modification of processing components' parameters and full access to the intermediate images at each processing stage. Such intermediate images can be modified and inserted back into the pipeline to see the effect on the final output. The proposed software platform is easily integrable with other softwares such as Matlab and provides a much needed environment for improving camera imaging, or performing experiments within the proper context of the full camera imaging pipeline.

The remainder of this paper is organized as follows: Sect. 2 discusses related work; Sect. 3 overviews our platform and the ways the pipeline can be accessed and manipulated; Sect. 4 provides a number of examples that use the platform on various routines. The paper is concluded with a short discussion and summary in Sect. 5.

2   Related Work

The basic steps comprising the camera processing pipeline are illustrated in Fig. 1 and may vary among different cameras' make and model. Full details to each component are outside the scope of this paper and readers are referred to [22]

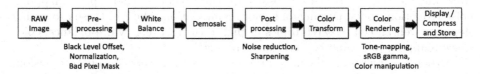

Fig. 1. This figure (adapted from [22]) overviews the common steps applied onboard a camera. Different camera hardware implementations can vary, however, most of these components will be included and in a similar processing order.

for an excellent overview. As mentioned in Sect. 1, many of the components in the pipeline (e.g. white-balance, noise reduction) are stand alone research topics in the computer vision and image processing community. Unfortunately, the hardware implementation of the camera pipeline and closed nature of proprietary cameras makes it difficult for most researchers to directly access the individual components.

To address this issue, open hardware platforms have been proposed. Early work included the CMU-camera [23] targeting robotic vision. While individual components (e.g. white-balance) were not accessible, the camera provided low-level image access and subsequent hardware releases allowed capture of the raw sensor response. A more recent and comprehensive hardware platform was the FrakenCamera introduced by Adams et al. [1]. The FrankenCamera was designed as a fully operational camera that provided full access to the underlying hardware components, including control of the flash and shutter, as well as the underlying imaging pipeline. The FrankenCamera platform targeted computational photography applications, however, the platform was suitable for modifying individual components in the imaging pipeline. While the FrankenCamera project has officially stopped, much of the platform's functionality has been incorporated into the recent Android's Camera2 API [15] that is available on devices running Android OS. The proposed work in this paper is heavily inspired by the FrankenCamera open design and aims to provide similar functionality via a software-based platform. The benefits of a software framework over a hardware solution is that it can work on images saved from a variety of different cameras and in an off-line manner. Moreover, a software platform allows greater flexibility in processing the image at intermediate stages than possible on fixed hardware implementations.

There have been a number of works that have targeted modeling the camera processing pipeline beyond simple tone-curves for radiometric calibration (e.g. [10, 18–20, 30]). These methods use input pairs of raw and sRGB images to derive a mapping to convert an sRGB image back to the raw linearized sensor response. In some cases, this mapping closely follows the underlying imaging pipeline [10, 18, 20, 30], however, in other cases the mapping is approximated by a 3D look up table [19]. Another noteworthy example is the work by Baek et al. [4] that incorporated a fast approximation of the camera pipeline for displaying raw images in the camera's view finder. While this work focused on translating sparse user interaction applied on the view finder to control the final photo-finished image, it elucidated the need to incorporate the non-linear processing steps to give a more realistic representation of the final output to the user. While these methods are useful for simulating the onboard camera imaging process, they only provide a proxy for a real camera pipeline.

The benefits of considering the full camera pipeline in various computer vision and image processing tasks have been demonstrated in prior works. For example, Bianco et al. [6,7] showed that the overall color rendition of an image can be improved by considering white-balancing and color space conversion together in the pipeline. Work by Tai et al. [25] showed that the non-linear mapping applied onboard cameras had a significant impact on image deblurring results. Recent works by Nam et al. [21] and Wong and Milanfar [27] demonstrated improvements in image denoising when the non-linear processing steps in the camera pipeline are considered in the noise model. These prior works often have to motivate their arguments via synthetic imagery generated using relatively simple camera processing models. This lack of access to a complete software platform that is able to emulate the full camera imaging pipeline is the impetus for our work.

3   Platform Overview

Our platform uses images that are saved in the Adobe Digital Negative (DNG) format. While this format is not yet supported by many of the DSLR cameras, it is currently being supported by the newer Android phones that implement the Camera 2 API. With Android's adoption of DNG, the number of raw images captured by mobile devices are expected to increase significantly. However, in the event that images are not captured in DNG, camera-specific raw formats can be converted to DNG using the Adobe DNG conversion software tool [3]. The DNG image format not only contains the raw image data but also contains meta-data that specifies parameters (e.g. scalar values or a 1D or 3D look up table (LUT)) intended to be used by different stages in the processing pipeline.

Our platform is made possible by rewriting the interface of the open source Adobe DNG SDK software [2] that provides a full software implementation of a camera pipeline to convert the DNG raw image to its final sRGB output. While this is an engineering feat, the implementation is non-trivial. The stand alone Adobe DNG SDK is not designed to allow changes to the parameters of the individual stages, instead the SDK uses the values in the DNG files meta-data directly. Thus the processing pipeline had to be decomposed into its individual stages and API calls designed to access and modify the underlying parameters. In addition, the unmodified SDK uses a multi-threaded design that breaks the image into a number of small tiles and processes them separately. This makes it difficult to access coherent intermediate images in the pipeline using the native SDK. Our modification changes this tiling structure to allow access to the intermediate image at each stage. We have also added API calls to allow customized demosaicing and noise reduction which is not supported in the native SDK.

Figure 2-(A) overviews the processing steps that are available in the proposed camera imaging platform. The top shows the steps with the associated parameters used by each of the components while Fig. 2-(B) shows the intermediate images at each stage in the pipeline. In the following, we detail each stage and its associated parameters that can be modified. The type of parameters used by the individual stages are also discussed. In the case of a 1D LUT, the same LUT is applied to each color channel individually.

Stage 1: Reading the raw image (**Params:** *None*). The unmodified raw image is read from the DNG image file. This is the unprocessed image produced by the sensor that is still in its mosaiced Bayer pattern format.

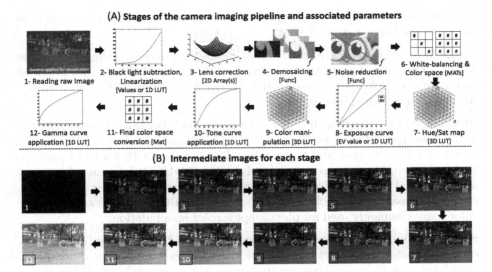

Fig. 2. The camera processing pipeline routines accessible by our software platform are shown in (A). Each component is denoted by the type of parameters it takes, e.g. scalar values, 2D Arrays, 3×3 matrices [MAT], function calls [func], or 1D or 3D Look up tables [LUT]. In addition, the software platform API supports direct access and manipulation to the intermediate images at each stage as shown in (B). (Color figure online)

Stage 2: Black light subtraction and linearization (`Params`: *Level values* or *1D LUT*). The unmodified raw image is linearized such that its values range from [0-1] in the processing pipeline. Many cameras provide a *BlackLevel* parameter that represents the black level of the sensor that deviates from 0 due to sensor noise. This is often image specific and related to other camera settings, including ISO, gain, etc. An additional *WhiteLevel* (maximum value) can also be specified. If nothing is provided, the `min` and `max` value of all intensities in the image is used to normalize the image. Another alternative is to provide a 1D LUT to perform the linearization. The 1D LUT shown in the Fig. 2-(A) is from an Nikon D40.

Stage 3: Lens/Flat Field correction (`Params`: $4 \times \text{Array}_{N \times M}$). Many cameras provide a spatially varying correction that compensates for lens distortion and uneven light fall. For example, the Motorola Nexus 6 provides four (one for each Bayer pattern pixel where G is repeated twice) scene dependent 13×17 2D arrays that are used to provide this flat field correction. These arrays are scaled and bilinearly interpolated to the image size, then multiplied to the mosaiced image.

Stage 4: Demosaicing (`Params`: func). The demosaicing step converts the single channel raw image to three full-size R/G/B color channels by interpolating the missing values in the Bayer pattern. We denote this operation as an arbitrary function, func. The default interpolation is a standard bilinear interpolation based on the Bayer pattern layout.

Stage 5: Noise reduction (`Params`: func). Similar to the demosaicing stage, noise reduction is denoted as an arbitrary function, func. This function (not provided in the Adobe SDK) has access to the intermediate image and returns back a filtered image to the pipeline.

Stage 6: White-balancing and color space conversion (`Params`:. Two 3×3 matrices). This stage performs the necessary color space conversion between the camera specific RGB color space and a standard color space (e.g. CIE XYZ or ProPhoto RGB). This colorimetric procedure involves a 3×3 white-balance matrix (generally a diagonal matrix) and a 3×3 color space transformation matrix. The default color space used by the Adobe SDK is the ProPhoto RGB, which is a wide gamut color space commonly used for photographic color manipulation.

Stage 7: Hue/Sat map application (`Params`: 3D LUT). This optional procedure is intended to be part of the color space conversion to allow a non-linear transformation to be incorporated to improve the color rendition. While this is referred to as a 'hue' and 'saturation' modification, it is implemented as a 3D LUT applied directly to the RGB values obtained in Stage 6. For example, when saving a DNG file using the X-Rite camera calibration software [28], X-Rite adds a $6 \times 6 \times 3$ LUT to the DNG meta-data. From our experience, most cameras DNG files do not include this step.

Stage 8: Exposure compensation (`Params`: *EV value*, 1D LUT). The exposure compensation is a digital exposure adjustment. While the input is given as an exposure value (EV) that is used to control shutter and aperture settings on a camera, in the digital case, this simply applies a linear gain (either up or down) to the intensities values. The EV value passed as a parameter will generate a 1D LUT with 4096 values. Alternatively, a 1D LUT can be provided directly.

Stage 9: Color manipulation (`Params`: 3D LUT). Cameras often apply their own proprietary color manipulation that is linked to different picture styles on the camera [18]. Like the Hue/Sat map, this is applied as a 3D LUT where RGB values are interpolated based on the table's entries. The size of this table can be arbitrary, for example, images saved using Nikon D40's Camera Vivid setting have a $36 \times 16 \times 16$ LUT added in the DNG meta-data.

Stage 10: Tone-curve application (`Params`: 1D LUT). A camera-specific tone-map can be specified. This is part of the photo-finishing process on board the camera. For example, the Nikon D40's Camera Vivid profile includes a LUT with 248 entries. If no tone-curve is specified, the Adobe DNG has a default tone-curve that is shown in Fig. 2).

Stage 11: Final color space conversion (`Params`: 3×3 Matrix). This color space conversion converts the internal camera working color space into the final output-referred color space. This is done using a $3{\times}3$ matrix and is assumed to be related to color space used at stage 6. The most common color space for cameras is the standard RGB (sRGB) and Adobe RGB. In this paper, the sRGB color space is used for all examples.

Stage 12: Gamma curve application (**Params**: 1D LUT). The final stage is a gamma curve that is applied as a 1D LUT with 4096 entries. This is intended to represent the sRGB gamma correction that is part of the sRGB specification, however, it can also be used for additional color modification and photo-finishing.

These twelve steps make up the collective stages that can be controlled via API calls or direct image modification to intermediate images. Access to this suite of components provides a comprehensive means for manipulating the image from the input raw to its final sRGB output. Note that it is not necessary that all steps be applied. For example, exposure compensation, noise reduction, hue/sat map modification, etc., can be skipped as necessary.

4 Results

We have developed a fully functioning software platform for use on a Windows-based PC. The software framework is developed in C++, however, it has also been modified such that API calls can be made directly from Matlab. In this section, we demonstrate several examples that serve to illustrate the various benefits our platform. The examples are divided loosely into three categories: (1) basic functionality; (2) evaluating stages at certain points in the pipeline; and (3) evaluating stages within the proper context of the full pipeline. Specifically, Sect. 4.1 demonstrates several examples that show the basic ability to manipulate the pipeline components (e.g. EV levels, tone-curve modification, and demosaicing). Section 4.2 provides an example to evaluate the color conversion stage, a task that is currently difficult to do with existing tools. Section 4.3 provides examples targeting white-balance, image denoising and image blurring that show the benefits of considering these tasks within the full pipeline.

4.1 Basic Processing

Exposure Compensation and Tone-mapping. Figure 3 starts with a simple example showing the effects of manipulating parameters for the exposure compensation and tone-mapping stages. Figure 3-(A) shows a number of EV values that are passed directly to our platform's API which generates the 1D LUT shown. In the case of the tone-mapping, the 1D LUTs are directly passed to the API as shown in Fig. 3-(B). The images shown represent the final sRGB output obtained using these parameters in the full camera pipeline.

Demosaicing. Figure 4-(A, B) demonstrates examples of two different demosaicing procedures applied to an image. In particular, we use the default bilinear interpolation and the work by Gunturk et al. [16] that uses alternating projections. Interestingly, in the work by [16], the results were demonstrated by simulating a mosaiced image by using an sRGB image and arranging its colors into a Bayer pattern structure. In our example, their approach is applied directly to a real mosaiced raw image and then returned back to the pipeline to produce a realistic result.

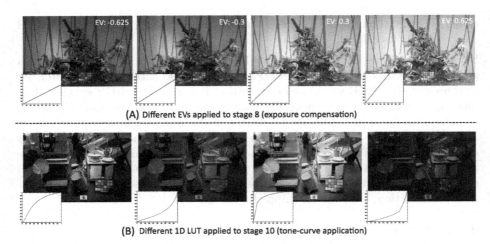

Fig. 3. (A) Examples of applying different EV and 1D LUTs for exposure compensation (stage 8) and (B) tone-mapping (stage 10).

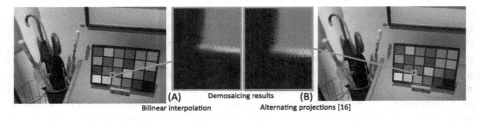

Fig. 4. Demonstrating the results of two different demosaicing algorithms, in particular (A) bilinear interpolation and (B) [16]. In this example, the intermediate image passed to stage 4 (demosaicing) is modified using [16] and inserted back into the imaging pipeline to obtain the final sRGB output. (Color figure online)

4.2 Evaluation of Components

Colorimetry Example. One challenge for existing computer vision and image processing research is the ability to obtain intermediate images in the camera pipeline to evaluate the effectiveness at individual stages. An excellent example of this is the color conversion component (stage 6). This stage is crucial in making sure that different camera-specific color spaces align to the same canonical color space after color conversion. Examining this stage in the camera pipeline is essentially evaluating the quality of the colorimetric calibration of the camera.

To demonstrate our platforms ability to assist with this task, we captured standard color rendition charts with four different mobile cameras (LG-G4, Motorola Nexus 6, Samsung S6-Edge, and an HTC One M9) under different illuminations. These mobile device cameras all support the DNG file format and have embedded in their DNG meta-data the camera's onboard parameters for this color conversion. This allows us to compare the results of the native camera's colorimetric ability with two other approaches: (1) the widely used X-Rite calibration software [28], and (2) a recent method by Bastani and Funt [5].

We use the 24 patch color rendition chart to calibrate the color space conversion parameters using the X-Rite software and the method by [5]. In this case, the color space conversion is computed from the camera raw color space to the ProPhoto color space. For all methods, including the camera native, the white-balance matrix is estimated using the neutral colors on the color chart under a specific illumination. In order to compare these three methods, we need to apply the 3 × 3 color conversion matrices to stage 6. In the case of X-Rite, we also apply the additional hue/sat map (stage 7) that is used by X-Rite to provide a further non-linear correction for the color space mapping. The color pipeline is stopped at the appropriate location for each method and the intermediate image is obtained and the color patches' average chromaticity values are compared.

The results are shown in Fig. 5-(A) for color rendition charts captured under two different illuminations. The plots show the average chromaticity of the 24

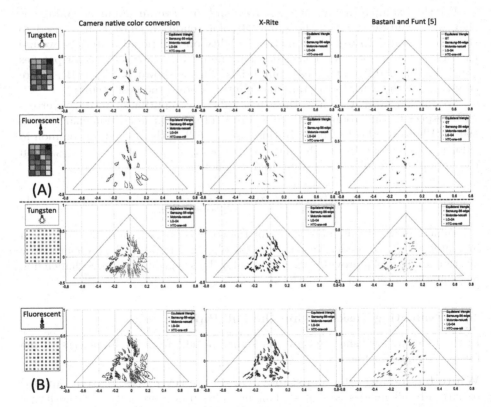

Fig. 5. This figure demonstrates the ability to evaluate different color space conversion (stage 6) methods applied to four cameras. See Sect. 4.2 for details. (Color figure online)

Table 1. The table shows the comparisons of error between native cameras, X-Rite's, and [5] color calibration (CC: color chart, AM: additional materials).

Error	Incandescent			Fluorescent			Outdoor		
	CC	AM#1	AM#2	CC	AM#1	AM#2	CC	AM#1	AM#2
Camera	0.84	1.67	3.43	0.97	2.37	4.49	0.68	1.80	3.01
X-Rite	0.33	1.06	1.57	0.48	1.68	2.72	0.15	0.74	0.95
Bastani and Funt [5]	**0.14**	**0.75**	**1.07**	**0.25**	**1.16**	**1.38**	**0.12**	**0.70**	**0.70**

color patches from the four different cameras. Under ideal colorimetric mapping, the chromaticity values should all lie at the exact same location in the chromaticity plot, however, due to errors in the color conversion matrices, they are not the same. To help with the visualization, we fit a Gaussian ellipsoid to show the spread for each color patch among the four cameras. Our experiment shows that the method by Bastani and Funt [5] provides the most consistent color space mapping.

For the example in Fig. 5-(A), X-Rite and [5] have an unfair advantage as they were calibrated using the same 24 color rendition chart that is used to show the results. To test these methods ability on additional materials, we use their estimated color space conversion parameters on a new set of color patches consisting of 81 different types of materials. This is shown in Fig. 5-(B), where again we see the work by Bastani and Funt [5] obtain the best results.

We further evaluated these three methods by computing quantitative errors with respect to the ground truth color values of the color rendition chart [29] in the ProPhoto RGB color space. In this case, we follow the procedure common in color research and consider the angular error $\epsilon_{angle}(e_{color})$ of a color e_{color} from the ground truth color e_{gt} is computed as follows:

$$\epsilon_{angle}(e_{color}) = cos^{-1}\left(\frac{e_{color} \cdot e_{gt}}{||e_{color}|| \ ||e_{gt}||}\right). \tag{1}$$

Table 1 shows the angular errors for the color chart (CC) and the additional 81 materials (AM). As demonstrated in the plots in Fig. 5-(A, B), the method by Bastani and Funt [5] provides the best results. This type of analysis is challenging without the support of our platform.

4.3   Evaluating Tasks Within the Full Pipeline

In the following, we show several tasks that benefit from having access to the full processing pipeline.

White-balancing/color constancy. One of the key processing steps applied to virtually all images is white-balancing. This procedure falls into the larger research of color constancy that mimics our human perceptual ability to perceive materials under different illuminations as the same color. White-balance approximates this ability by attempting to ensure that at least the neutral scene

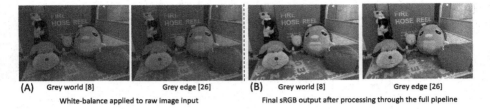

(A) Grey world [8]   Grey edge [26]   (B)   Grey world [8]   Grey edge [26]
         White-balance applied to raw image input   Final sRGB output after processing through the full pipeline

Fig. 6. (A) White-balancing algorithms applied on raw images. (B) sRGB output of white-balanced images.

materials appear achromatic in the camera color space. White-balance is applied directly to the camera raw image while the image values are still in the camera's RGB color space.

A number of research papers on this topic (e.g. [9,12]) provide subjective results of their white-balance result directly on the camera raw images. Such results, however, have little visual meaning as they provide a visual comparison in an non-standard camera-specific color space. A more appropriate way to subjectively evaluate the results would be to run the white-balanced result through the full camera pipeline to produce a realistic output that would be produced by the camera. Figure 6 shows the difference in these two approaches. In particular, two well known white-balance methods, Grey world [8] and Grey edge [26] are applied to an input image. Figure 6-(A) shows the results on the raw image and Fig. 6-(B) shows the sRGB outputs. The sRGB output provides a much more realistic comparisons of the two algorithms.

Noise Reduction. Similar to white-balancing, another research area that is at a disadvantage by not having access to the full camera pipeline is image denoising. Noise reduction is a well-suited research topic and interested readers are referred to [11] for an excellent overview. One of the major sources of image noise is what is collectively referred to as sensor noise and is attributed to underlying imaging sensor (CMOS or CCD). Because this noise is present on the sensor, it is present in the raw image at the start of the pipeline. As such, noise reduction is often applied before the non-linear stages in the camera pipeline. However, since few researchers have access to the camera pipeline, noise reduction methods, e.g. the popular BM3D method by Dabov et al. [13], are typically applied and evaluated on the sRGB output. Figure 7 demonstrates the disadvantages of applying image denoising outside the proper context of the full imaging pipeline. Our example works from a synthetic image to provide a ground truth input to compute the peak signal to noise ratio (PNSR). Figure 7-(A) shows a raw image that has been corrupted with zero-mean Gaussian noise. The noise profile for three different homogenous patches with increasing intensity values are shown. We can see that this Gaussian noise profile appears uniform over the different patches in the raw image, with only a shift by the mean intensity. Below this, we show the corresponding noisy raw image that has been processed through the whole imaging pipeline, including the non-linear stages (e.g. stage 9, 10, 12). We can

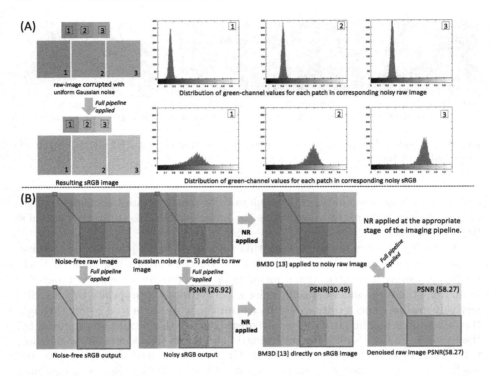

Fig. 7. (A) Noise profiles for three color patches for a raw image and corresponding sRGB image. (B) PSNR comparison of application of BM3D [13] on the raw image at stage 5 and on the final sRGB output. (Color figure online)

see that the noise distribution for different patch is significantly affected by the non-linear processing stages. In fact, it is not possible to make a uniform noise assumption for the sRGB image as the non-linear process has changed this property of the noise.

Figure 7-(B) demonstrates BM3D applied at two different places in the pipeline. The top shows BM3D applied to the raw image. The filtered result is then processed through the remaining pipeline. This represents the proper application of NR. The bottom shows BM3D applied directly to the noisy sRGB image as done in most academic literature. The PSNR for both results in the sRGB final output is computed against the ground truth (noise free) sRGB image. The PSNRs are drastically different, where the denoising applied at the right place in the pipeline is 58.27, while the application on the final non-linear sRGB stage is only 30.49.

This example serves to motivate the need for having access to the full camera pipeline when examining image denoising. Even in the inevitable case that noise reduction must be applied to the non-linear sRGB image, our software platform provides an excellent means to study sensor noise and how it is affected by the camera processing steps as done in Fig. 7-(A).

(A) raw image with 1-D motion blur | sRGB output of the blurred image | (B) Wiener [14] filtered raw image | sRGB output of de-blurred raw image | Wiener [14] filtered sRGB image

Fig. 8. (A) Motion blur is applied on the raw image and then run through the full pipeline to obtain the sRGB output. (B) Deblurring applied to the raw image and then its output using the camera pipeline, and the results obtained by directly deblurring the blurred sRGB image.

Deblurring. We conclude with a final example that was mentioned in Sect. 2 as a motivating factor for developing this software platform. In particular, the work by Tai et al. [25] demonstrated that the non-linear processes on the camera have a negative impact on image deblurring. Similar to the denoising example, [25] showed that the non-linear tone-mapping function (stage 10 and/or 12) changes the distortion profile, in this case the blur's point-spread-function (PSF), such that the PSF was no longer spatially uniform over the image. Tai et al. used this to argue that deblurring should be applied either directly to the raw image, or that care must be taken to undo any non-linear processing applied to the image before deblurring is applied. In that work, Tai et al. used a very simple camera model that applied a single 1D LUT to the raw images. This is equivalent to only applying stage 1 and 10 in our software platform.

With our platform, we are able to provide a much more realistic demonstration of Tai et al. [25] argument. Figure 8-(A) shows a raw image that has been blurred with a PSF modeling linear motion across 50 pixels and its corresponding sRGB output. This is applied directly to a demosaiced raw image (available at stage 4 in our pipeline). We then apply deconvolution via Wiener filtering [14] in two manners as shown in Fig. 8-(B). The first, as advocated by [25], is on the raw image that is then processed through the full pipeline. In the second example, we apply Wiener filter directly to the sRGB image. As expected, the results applied on the raw image are significantly better than those applied on the sRGB image. As with the prior noise reduction experiment, this example demonstrates the benefit of being able to perform various computer vision and image processing tasks within the appropriate context of the camera pipeline.

5   Discussion and Summary

This paper has presented a new software platform that allows low-level access to the individual components in the camera imaging pipeline. Specifically, our platform leverages the Adobe Digital Negative (DNG) image file format and makes the necessary modifications to the available DNG SDK to provide an extensive API for modifying the parameters of the pipeline, as well as allowing access and modification to intermediate images that can then be inserted back into the pipeline to compute the final output that would be obtained on a camera.

The usefulness of this platform has been demonstrated on a number of examples, including white-balance, noise reduction, and colorimetry. While this work is engineering in nature, we believe this platform provides a much needed mechanism for researchers to modify individual components in the pipeline and demonstrate their results within the appropriate context of the full camera imaging pipeline. Furthermore, with the adoption of the DNG raw image format by the Android OS via the Camera 2 API, the availability of DNG files is going to significantly increase, further adding to the timeliness of this platform into the computer vision community.

One limitation of our approach is that it can only operate from the captured DNG image saved by the camera. This means camera parameters such as ISO settings that directly affect analog amplification on the sensor hardware or the image's exposure at capture time cannot be modified with our platform. This can impact work targeting tasks such as high dynamic imaging (e.g. [24]). For such cases, it will be necessary to capture a number of DNG images with varying ISO or exposure settings to simulate the manipulation on the camera.

We also note that this paper represents the current camera architecture where each stage in the pipeline is self-contained. Recent work by Heide et al. [17] demonstrated the benefits of considering a re-engineered onboard camera processing system that provides a holistic consideration to image formation that is more readily able to incorporate known priors about nature images. We also envision that in the coming years the traditional pipeline described in this paper will likely see significant changes. Once again, it will be important for researchers to have access to a software platform that allow research to be performed in the proper context of the onboard imaging system.

Acknowledgments. This study was funded in part by a Google Faculty Research Award. We would also like to thank Eric Chan from Adobe Research for his discussions on the Adobe DNG SDK.

References

1. Adams, A., Talvala, E.V., Park, S.H., Jacobs, D.E., Ajdin, B., Gelfand, N., Dolson, J., Vaquero, D., Baek, J., Tico, M., et al.: The FrankenCamera: an experimental platform for computational photography. ACM Trans. Graph. **29**(4), 29:1–29:12 (2010)
2. Adobe, Sys., Inc.: DNG Software Development Kit (SDK). https://www.adobe. com/support/downloads/detail.jsp?ftpID=5475. Accessed 16 July 2015
3. Adobe, Sys., Inc.: Adobe Camera Raw and DNG Converter for Windows. https://www.adobe.com/support/downloads/product.jsp?product=106&platform =Windows. Accessed 16 July 2016
4. Baek, J., Pajak, D., Kim, K., Pulli, K., Levoy, M.: WYSIWYG computational photography via viewfinder editing. ACM Trans. Graph. **32**(6), 198:1–198:10 (2013)
5. Bastani, P., Funt, B.: Simplifying irradiance independent color calibration. In: Color Imaging XIX: Displaying, Processing, Hardcopy, and Applications (2014)

6. Bianco, S., Bruna, A., Naccari, F., Schettini, R.: Color space transformations for digital photography exploiting information about the illuminant estimation process. J. Opt. Soc. Am. A **29**(3), 374–384 (2012)
7. Bianco, S., Bruna, A.R., Naccari, F., Schettini, R.: Color correction pipeline optimization for digital cameras. J. Electron. Imaging **22**(2), 023014:1–023014:10 (2013)
8. Buchsbaum, G.: A spatial processor model for object colour perception. J. Frankl. Inst. **310**(1), 1–26 (1980)
9. Chakrabarti, A., Hirakawa, K., Zickler, T.: Color constancy with spatio-spectral statistics. IEEE Trans. Pattern Anal. Mach. Intell. **34**(8), 1509–1519 (2012)
10. Chakrabarti, A., Scharstein, D., Zickler, T.: An empirical camera model for internet color vision. In: BMVC (2009)
11. Chatterjee, P., Milanfar, P.: Is denoising dead? IEEE Trans. Image Process. **19**(4), 895–911 (2010)
12. Cheng, D., Price, B., Cohen, S., Brown, M.S.: Effective learning-based illuminant estimation using simple features. In: CVPR (2015)
13. Dabov, K., Foi, A., Katkovnik, V., Egiazarian, K.: Image denoising by sparse 3-D transform-domain collaborative filtering. IEEE Trans. Image Process. **16**(8), 2080–2095 (2007)
14. Gonzalez, R.C., Woods, R.E.: Digital Image Processing, 3rd edn. Prentice-Hall Inc., Upper Saddle River (2006)
15. Google, Inc.: Camera2 API Package Summary. http://developer.android.com/reference/android/hardware/camera2/package-summary.html. Accessed 16 July 2016
16. Gunturk, B.K., Altunbasak, Y., Mersereau, R.M.: Color plane interpolation using alternating projections. IEEE Trans. Image Process. **11**(9), 997–1013 (2002)
17. Heide, F., Steinberger, M., Tsai, Y.T., Rouf, M., Pajak, D., Reddy, D., Gallo, O., Liu, J., Heidrich, W., Egiazarian, K., Kautz, J., Pulli, K.: FlexISP: a flexible camera image processing framework. ACM Trans. Graph. **33**(6), 231:1–231:13 (2014)
18. Kim, S.J., Lin, H.T., Lu, Z., Susstrunk, S., Lin, S., Brown, M.S.: A new in-camera imaging model for color computer vision and its application. IEEE Trans. Pattern Anal. Mach. Intell. **34**(12), 2289–2302 (2012)
19. Lin, H.T., Lu, Z., Kim, S.J., Brown, M.S.: Nonuniform lattice regression for modeling the camera imaging pipeline. In: Fitzgibbon, A., Lazebnik, S., Perona, P., Sato, Y., Schmid, C. (eds.) ECCV 2012. LNCS, vol. 7572, pp. 556–568. Springer, Heidelberg (2012). doi:10.1007/978-3-642-33718-5_40
20. Lin, H., Kim, S.J., Süsstrunk, S., Brown, M.S.: Revisiting radiometric calibration for color computer vision. In: ICCV (2011)
21. Nam, S., Hwang, Y., Matsushita, Y., Kim, S.J.: A holistic approach to cross-channel image noise modeling and its application to image denoising. In: CVPR (2016)
22. Ramanath, R., Snyder, W.E., Yoo, Y., Drew, M.S.: Color image processing pipeline. IEEE Signal Process. Mag. **22**(1), 34–43 (2005)
23. Rowe, A., Goode, A., Goel, D., Nourbakhsh, I.: CMUcam3: an open programmable embedded vision sensor. Technical report CMU-RI-TR-07-13 (2007)
24. Serrano, A., Heide, F., Gutierrez, D., Wetzstein, G., Masia, B.: Convolutional sparse coding for high dynamic range imaging. Comput. Graph. Forum **35**(2), 153–163 (2016)

25. Tai, Y.W., Chen, X., Kim, S., Kim, S.J., Li, F., Yang, J., Yu, J., Matsushita, Y., Brown, M.S.: Nonlinear camera response functions and image deblurring: theoretical analysis and practice. IEEE Trans. Pattern Anal. Mach. Intell. **35**(10), 2498–2512 (2013)
26. van de Weijer, J., Gevers, T., Gijsenij, A.: Edge-based color constancy. IEEE Trans. Image Process. **16**(9), 2207–2214 (2007)
27. Wong, T.S., Milanfar, P.: Turbo denoising for mobile photographic applications. In: ICIP (2016)
28. X-Rite, Inc.: X-Rite ColorChecker Camera Calibration software. http://xritephoto. com/ph_product_overview.aspx?ID=1257&Action=Support&SoftwareID=986& catid=28. Accessed 16 July 2016
29. X-Rite, Inc.: X-Rite ColorChecker Chart. http://xritephoto.com/colorchecker-classic. Accessed 16 July 2016
30. Xiong, Y., Saenko, K., Darrell, T., Zickler, T.: From pixels to physics: probabilistic color de-rendering. In: CVPR (2012)

A Benchmark and Simulator for UAV Tracking

Matthias Mueller$^{(\boxtimes)}$, Neil Smith, and Bernard Ghanem

King Abdullah University of Science and Technology (KAUST),
Thuwal, Saudi Arabia
{matthias.mueller.2,neil.smith,bernard.ghanem}@kaust.edu.sa

Abstract. In this paper, we propose a new aerial video dataset and benchmark for low altitude UAV target tracking, as well as, a photo-realistic UAV simulator that can be coupled with tracking methods. Our benchmark provides the first evaluation of many state-of-the-art and popular trackers on 123 new and fully annotated HD video sequences captured from a low-altitude aerial perspective. Among the compared trackers, we determine which ones are the most suitable for UAV tracking both in terms of tracking accuracy and run-time. The simulator can be used to evaluate tracking algorithms in real-time scenarios before they are deployed on a UAV "in the field", as well as, generate synthetic but photo-realistic tracking datasets with automatic ground truth annotations to easily extend existing real-world datasets. Both the benchmark and simulator are made publicly available to the vision community on our website to further research in the area of object tracking from UAVs. (https://ivul.kaust.edu.sa/Pages/pub-benchmark-simulator-uav.aspx.).

Keywords: UAV tracking · UAV simulator · Aerial object tracking

1 Introduction

Visual tracking remains a challenging problem despite several decades of progress on this important topic. A broadly adopted evaluation paradigm for visual tracking algorithms is to test them on established video benchmarks such as OTB50 [42], OTB100 [41], VOT2014, VOT2015, TC128 (Temple Color) [26], and ALOV300++ [39]. Since the performance of a tracker is measured against these benchmarks, it is critical that a holistic set of real-world scenarios and a distribution of tracking nuisances (e.g. fast motion, illumination changes, scale changes, occlusion, etc.) are properly represented in the annotated dataset. The benchmark also plays a critical role in identifying future research directions in the field and how to design more robust algorithms. What is currently lacking in these well established benchmarks is a comprehensive set of annotated aerial datasets that pose many challenges introduced by unmanned airborne flight.

Empowering unmanned aerial vehicles (UAVs) with automated computer vision capabilities (e.g. tracking, object/activity recognition, etc.) is becoming

Electronic supplementary material The online version of this chapter (doi:10. 1007/978-3-319-46448-0_27) contains supplementary material, which is available to authorized users.

© Springer International Publishing AG 2016
B. Leibe et al. (Eds.): ECCV 2016, Part I, LNCS 9905, pp. 445–461, 2016.
DOI: 10.1007/978-3-319-46448-0_27

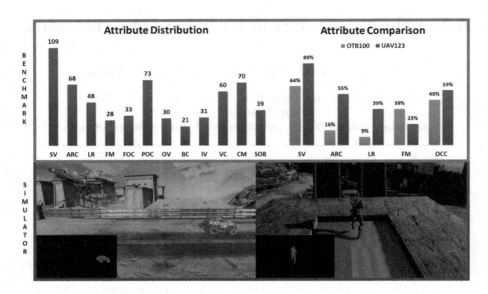

Fig. 1. *Top:* Attribute distribution across UAV123 dataset and a comparison of key attributes with OTB100. *Bottom:* Synthetic dataset generation and online tracker evaluation using the proposed simulator. For a legend of abbreviations, refer to Table 2.

a very important research direction in the field and is rapidly accelerating with the increasing availability of low-cost, commercially available UAVs. In fact, aerial tracking has enabled many new applications in computer vision (beyond those related to surveillance) including search and rescue, wild-life monitoring, crowd monitoring/management, navigation/localization, obstacle/object avoidance, and videography of extreme sports. Aerial tracking can be applied to a diverse set of objects (e.g. humans, animals, cars, boats, etc.), many of which cannot be physically or persistently tracked from the ground. In particular, real-world aerial tracking scenarios pose new challenges to the tracking problem (see Fig. 1), exposing areas for further research. This paper provides an evaluation of trackers on more than 100 new fully annotated HD videos captured from a professional grade UAV. This benchmark both complements current benchmarks establishing the aerial component of tracking and provides a more comprehensive sampling of tracking nuisances that are ubiquitous in low-altitude UAV videos. To the best of our knowledge, this is the first benchmark to address and analyze the performance of state-of-the-art trackers on a comprehensive set of annotated aerial sequences that exhibit specific tracking nuisances. We anticipate that this dataset and its tracker evaluation will provide a baseline that can be used long into the future as UAV technology advances and target trackers improve.

Visual tracking on UAVs is a very promising application, since the camera can follow the target based on visual feedback and *actively* change its orientation and position to optimize for tracking performance. This marks the defining difference compared to static tracking systems, which passively analyze a dynamic scene. Since current benchmarks are pre-recorded scenes, they cannot provide a quantifiable measure on how slower trackers would affect the performance of the UAV in *shadowing* the target. In this paper, we propose the use of a photo-realistic simulator to render real-world environments and a variety of life-like moving targets typically found in unmanned aerial recordings. The simulator uses the Unreal Engine 4 to directly feed image frames to trackers and retrieve tracking results to update UAV flight. Any tracker (e.g. written in Matlab or C++) can be tested on the simulator across a diverse set of photo-realistic simulated scenarios. Using this simulator enables the use of new quantitative methods for evaluating tracker performance in the aforementioned aerial feedback loop.

Contributions. The contributions of our work are threefold. (1) We compile a fully annotated high-resolution dataset of 123 aerial video sequences comprising more than 110 K frames. It is as large or larger than most recent, generic object tracking datasets. (2) We provide an extensive evaluation of many state-of-the-art trackers using multiple metrics [42]. By labeling the videos in the benchmark with various attributes, we can also evaluate each tracker in regards to specific aerial tracking nuisances (e.g. scale/aspect ratio change, camera motion, etc.). (3) We provide a novel approach to perform tracker evaluation by developing a high-fidelity real-time visual tracking simulator. We present first results on the performance of state-of-the-art trackers running within its environment. The combination of the simulator with an extensive aerial benchmark provides a more comprehensive evaluation toolbox for modern state-of-the-art trackers and opens new avenues for experimentation and analysis.

Related Work

UAV Datasets. A review of related work indicates that there is still a limited availability of annotated datasets specific to UAVs in which trackers can be rigorously evaluated for precision and robustness in airborne scenarios. Existing annotated video datasets include very few aerial sequences [42]. Surveillance datasets such as PETS or CAVIAR focus on static surveillance and are outdated. VIVID [6] is the only publicly available dedicated aerial dataset, but it is outdated and has many limitations due to its small size (9 sequences), very similar and low-resolution sequences (only vehicles as targets), sparse annotation (only every 10th frame), and focus on higher altitude, less dynamic fixed-wing UAVs. There are several recent benchmarks that were created to address specific deficiencies of older benchmarks and introduce new evaluation approaches [24,25,39], but they do not introduce videos with many tracking nuisances addressed in this paper and common to aerial scenarios.

Generic Object Tracking. In our proposed benchmark, we evaluate classical trackers such as OAB [11] and IVT [38] as baselines and the best-performing recent trackers according to [42]: Struck [13], CSK [17], ASLA [19], and TLD [21]. In the selection process, we reject very slow trackers despite their performance [3,4,44–47]. In addition, we include several of the latest trackers such as

MEEM [43], MUSTER [18], DSST [8] (winner VOT2014) and SRDCF [7] (winner VOT-TIR2015 and OpenCV challenge). Since current benchmarks provide no more than 1 or 2 real-world scenarios of video capture from a mobile aerial platform, it is unclear which of these new trackers would perform well in aerial scenarios where certain tracking challenges are amplified, including abrupt camera motion, significant changes in scale and aspect ratio, fast moving objects, as well as, partial and full occlusion.

UAV Tailored Tracking. Despite the lack of benchmarks that adequately address aerial tracking, the development of tracking algorithms for UAVs has become very popular in recent years. The majority of object tracking methods employed on UAVs rely on feature point detection/tracking [30,37] or color-centric object tracking [22]. Only a few works in the literature [33] exploit more accurate trackers that commonly appear in generic tracking benchmarks such as MIL [1,9], TLD [33], and STRUCK [27,28]. There are also more specialized trackers tailored to address specific problems and unique camera systems such as in wide aerial video [34,36], thermal and IR video [10,35], and RGB-D video [29].

UAV Simulation. In recent years, several UAV simulators have been created to test hardware in the loop (HIL). However, the focus is on simulating the physics of the UAV in order to train pilots or improve/tune features of a flight controller (e.g. JMAVSim [40]). The visual rendering in these simulators is often primitive and relies on off-the-shelf simulators (e.g. Realflight, Flightgear, or XPlane). They do not support advanced shading and post-processing techniques, are limited in terms of available assets and textures, and do not support MOCAP or key-frame type animation to simulate natural movement of actors or vehicles. Although simulation is popularly used in machine learning [2] and animation and motion planning [12,20], the use of synthetically generated video or simulation for tracker evaluation is a new field to explore. In computer vision, synthetic video is primarily used for training recognition systems (e.g. pedestrians [14], 3D scenes [31], and 2D/3D objects [15,32]), where a high demand for annotated data exists. The Unreal Engine 4 (UE4) has recently become fully open-source and it seems very promising for simulated visual tracking due in part to its high-quality rendering engine and realistic physics library.

2 Benchmark - Offline Evaluation

2.1 Dataset

Statistics. Video captured from low-altitude UAVs is inherently different from video in popular tracking datasets like OTB50 [42], OTB100 [41], VOT2014, VOT2015, TC128 [26], and ALOV300++ [39]. Therefore, we propose a new dataset (called UAV123) with sequences from an aerial viewpoint, a subset of which is meant for long-term aerial tracking (UAV20L). In Fig. 2, we emphasize the differences between OTB100, TC128, and UAV123. The results highlight the effect of camera viewpoint change arising from UAV motion. The variation in

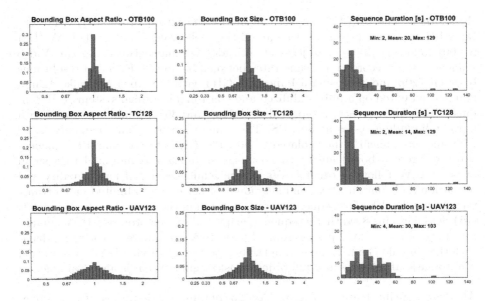

Fig. 2. *Column 1 and 2:* Proportional change of the target's aspect ratio and bounding box size (area in pixels) with respect to the first frame and across three datasets: OTB100, TC128, and UAV123 (ours). Results are compiled over all sequences in each dataset as a histogram with log scale on the x-axis. *Column 3:* Histogram of sequence duration (in seconds) across the three datasets.

Table 1. Comparison of tracking datasets in the literature. Ranking: R(1), G(2), B(3)

Dataset	UAV123	UAV20L	VIVID	OTB50	OTB100	TC128	VOT14	VOT15	ALOV300
Sequences	123	20	9	51	100	129	25	60	314
Min frames	109	1717	1301	71	71	71	171	48	19
Mean frames	915	2934	1808	578	590	429	416	365	483
Max frames	3085	5527	2571	3872	3872	3872	1217	1507	5975
Total frames	112578	58670	16274	29491	59040	55346	10389	21871	151657

bounding box size and aspect ratio with respect to the initial frame is significantly larger in UAV123. Furthermore, being mounted on the UAV, the camera is able to move with the target resulting in longer tracking sequences on average.

Our new UAV123 dataset contains a total of 123 video sequences and more than 110 K frames making it the second largest object tracking dataset after ALOV300++. The statistics of our dataset are compared to existing datasets in Table 1. Note that OTB50 is a subset of both OTB100 and TC128, so the total number of unique frames contained in all three datasets combined is only around 90 K. The datasets VOT2014 and VOT2015 are both subsets of existing datasets too. Hence, while there is a number of datasets available to the tracking community, the number of distinct sequences is smaller than expected and sequences specific to tracking from a UAV vantage point are very sparse.

Acquisition. The UAV123 dataset can be divided into 3 subsets. **(i)** Set1 contains 103 sequences captured using an off-the-shelf professional-grade UAV (DJI S1000) following different objects at altitudes varying between 5–25 m. Video sequences were recorded at frame rates between 30 and 96 FPS and resolutions between 720p and 4 K using a Panasonic GH4 with Olympus M. Zuiko 12 mm f2.0 lens mounted on a fully stabilized and controllable gimbal system (DJI Zenmuse Z15). All sequences are provided at 720p and 30 FPS and annotated with upright bounding boxes at 30 FPS. The annotation was done manually at 10 FPS and then linearly interpolated to 30 FPS. **(ii)** Set2 contains 12 sequences captured from a boardcam (with no image stabilization) mounted to a small low-cost UAV following other UAVs. These sequences are of lower quality and resolution and contain a reasonable amount of noise due to limited video transmission bandwidth. The sequences are annotated in the same manner as in Set1. **(iii)** Set3 contains 8 synthetic sequences captured by our proposed UAV simulator. Targets move along predetermined trajectories in different worlds rendered with the Unreal4 Game Engine from the perspective of a flying UAV. Annotation is automatic at 30 fps and a full object mask/segmentation is also available.

Attributes. As illustrated in Fig. 3, UAV123 contains a wide variety of scenes (e.g. urban landscape, roads, buildings, fields, beaches and a harbor/marina), targets (e.g. cars, trucks, boats, persons, groups, and aerial vehicles), and activities (e.g. walking, cycling, wakeboarding, driving, swimming, and flying). Naturally, these

Fig. 3. First frame of selected sequences from UAV123 dataset. The red bounding box indicates the ground truth annotation. (Color figure online)

Table 2. Attributes used to characterize each sequence from a tracking perspective.

Attr	Description
ARC	Aspect Ratio Change: the fraction of ground truth aspect ratio in the first frame and at least one subsequent frame is outside the range [0.5, 2]
BC	Background Clutter: the background near the target has similar appearance as the target
CM	Camera Motion: abrupt motion of the camera
FM	Fast Motion: motion of the ground truth bounding box is larger than 20 pixels between two consecutive frames
FOC	Full Occlusion: the target is fully occluded
IV	Illumination Variation: the illumination of the target changes significantly
LR	Low Resolution: at least one ground truth bounding box has less than 400 pixels
OV	Out-of-View: some portion of the target leaves the view
POC	Partial Occlusion: the target is partially occluded
SOB	Similar Object: there are objects of similar shape or same type near the target
SV	Scale Variation: the ratio of initial and at least one subsequent bounding box is outside the range [0.5, 2]
VC	Viewpoint Change: viewpoint affects target appearance significantly

sequences contain common visual tracking challenges including long-term full and partial occlusion, scale variation, illumination variation, viewpoint change, background clutter, camera motion, etc. Table 2 shows an overview of all tracking attributes present in UAV123. Figure 1 shows the distribution of these attributes over the whole dataset and a comparison to the very popular OTB100 dataset for a selection of key attributes.

Long-Term Tracking. Object tracking in an aerial surveillance setting usually requires long-term tracking, since the camera can follow the target in contrast to the static surveillance scenario. During the dataset design, some fully annotated long sequences captured in one continuous shot were split into subsequences to ensure that the difficulty of the dataset remains reasonable. For long-term tracking, we merge these subsequences and then pick the 20 longest sequences among them. Table 1 shows the statistics of the resulting dataset (UAV20L).

2.2 Evaluated Algorithms

We consider tracking algorithms for comparison on our benchmark according to their performance in OTB50 [42] and give preference to popular and reasonably fast trackers. Code for these trackers is either available online or from the authors. All selected trackers incorporate some form of model update and are discriminative, except for IVT and ASLA which use generative models. For fair

evaluation, we run all trackers with standard parameters on the same server-
grade workstation (Intel Xenon X5675 3.07 GHz, 48 GB RAM).

2.3   Evaluation Methodology

Following the evaluation strategy of OTB50 [42], all trackers are compared
using two measures: precision and success. Precision is measured as the distance
between the centers of a tracker bounding box (bb_tr) and the corresponding
ground truth bounding box (bb_gt). The precision plot shows the percentage of
tracker bounding boxes within a given threshold distance in pixels of the ground
truth. To rank the trackers, we use the conventional threshold of 20 pixels [42].
Success is measured as the intersection over union of pixels in box bb_tr and
those in bb_gt. The success plot shows the percentage of tracker bounding boxes
whose overlap score is larger than a given threshold. Moreover, we rank trackers
using the area under the curve (AUC) measure [42]. Besides one-pass evaluation
(OPE), we perform a spatial robustness evaluation (SRE) [42]. For SRE, the
initial bounding box is spatially shifted by 4 center shifts, 4 corner shifts and
scaled by 80, 90, 110 and 120 %, as done in [42].

3   Simulator - Online Evaluation

3.1   Setup and Limitations

The UE4 based simulator allows real-time tracker evaluation with the ability
to simulate the physics of aerial flight, produce realistic high-fidelity renderings
(similar to if not better than professional rendering software, e.g. 3DSMax and
Maya), and automatically generate precise ground truth annotation for offline
or real-time use cases (see Fig. 1). The UAV is modeled after the DJI S1000+,
which was used to capture the majority of the benchmark. An accurate 3D model
(same geometry/weight and thrust vectors) is subjected to game physics (UE4)
and real-world conditions (e.g. wind and gravity). The ground truth trajectory
and orientation of the target and UAV are recorded at every frame. The PID
controllers for stabilization and visual servoing (gimbal) mimic the Pixhawk FC.
For further details on the implementation, see the simulator documentation.

   UE4 allows for a large variety of post-processing rendering steps to create realistic and challenging scene images that simulate real-world UAV data.
Although not implemented for this work, motion blur, depth of field, over/under
exposure, HDR and many more features can be enabled. UE4 post-processing
rendering allows assignment of custom depth maps to any mesh in the engine.
The depth maps allows extraction of segmented annotation of the tracked target as seen through the camera viewpoint. We simulate the movement of both
a human character and a 4WD vehicle moving along set trajectories within a
detailed off-road race track with palm trees, cacti, mountains, historical buildings, lakes, and sand dunes (see Fig. 3). This is one example of many photo-
realistic UE4 worlds created by the developer community in which our UAV

Fig. 4. *Top:* Third person view of simulator environment. *Bottom:* Four UAVs are controlled by different trackers indicated by the different colors.

simulator can be used. The UAV simulator enables the integration of any tracker (MATLAB or C++) into the tracking-navigation loop; at every frame, the output bounding box of the tracker is read and used to correct the position of the UAV.

3.2   Novel Approaches for Evaluation

Our UE4 based simulator provides new possibilities for online performance measurement (see Fig. 4). Advantages include a controlled environment for isolation of specific tracking attributes, a higher degree of repeatability with rapid experiments, and generation of large annotated datasets for testing and learning. Unlike real-world scenarios where the UAV and target location are imprecisely known (e.g. error of 5–10 m), it quantitatively compares position, orientation, and velocity of the UAV at each time-step to understand the impact of the tracker on flight dynamics. For evaluation, we develop several new approaches to measure tracker performance: (1) the impact of a dynamic frame rate (trackers are fed frames at the rate of computation), (2) trajectory error between target and UAV motion, (3) accumulative distance between ground truth and tracker, and (4) long-term tracking within a controlled environment where attribute influence can be controlled and clearly measured.

3.3   Evaluation Methodology

Four trackers are selected for evaluation, namely SRDCF, MEEM, SAMF, and STRUCK. The ground truth bounding box generated from the custom depth map of the target is called GT. We first optimize the UAV visual servoing using the GT tracker (see supplementary material on our visual servoing technique). Despite absolute accuracy of the GT, the flight mechanics of the UAV limit its ability to always keep the target centered, since it must compensate for gravity, air resistance, and inertia. After evaluating the performance of the UAV with the GT, each tracker is run multiple times within the simulator provided with the same starting initialization bounding box. The target follows a pre-defined path and speed profile. The UAV tracks and follows the target for 3.5 min (ca. 6000 frames at 30 FPS). The target speed varies but is limited to 6 m/s, the UAV speed is limited to 12 m/s (similar to the real UAV). For evaluation, we measure the distance between the trajectory of the target and the UAV.

4   Experiments

4.1   Benchmark Evaluation

Overall Performance. To determine the overall performance of the different trackers on the new challenges in the UAV123 dataset, we use the evaluation paradigm proposed in [42], as outlined in Sect. 2.3. In the one-pass evaluation (OPE), each tracker processes over 110 K frames from all 123 sequences, each with a variety of attributes as shown in Table 2.

The top performing tracker on the UAV123 dataset in terms of precision and success is SRDCF [7]. This is primarily due to its high fidelity scale adaptation that is evident across every success plot. Although MEEM [43] is the top performing tracker in precision on OTB100, it cannot keep up in our dataset, primarily due to the fact that it does not have scale adaptation. SAMF [23], MUSTER [18], DSST [8], Struck [13], and ASLA [19] group into a second tier of close performing trackers, while the remaining trackers IVT [38], TLD [21], MOSSE [5], CSK [17], OAB [11], KCF [16] and DCF [16] achieve consistently lower performance. In general, with the exception of MEEM, the top five performers in terms of success exploit scale adaptation. However, since they are only adapting to scale and not aspect ratio, there is still much room for improvement. In general, the recently developed correlation based trackers perform very well in the OPE and rank in the top five in terms of precision (SRDCF, SAMF, MUSTER, DSST) and success (SRDCF, SAMF, MUSTER). Owing to their manipulation of circulant structure in the Fourier domain, these trackers require low computational cost, making them attractive for onboard UAV tracking.

In comparison with OTB100, all trackers perform much worse in OPE on the more challenging UAV123 dataset and several trackers change rankings (notably MEEM to SRDCF and MUSTER to SAMF). The difference in performance between the top trackers in OTB100 is marginal suggesting that this benchmark is getting closer to saturation. To obtain a global view of overall performance on both datasets, we plot the success results of all trackers per video in Fig. 5 as a color gradient map, where red corresponds to 0 and dark green to 1. The score of the best performing tracker per video is shown in the last row and the average across all videos per tracker is shown in the last column. In OTB100, most videos have at least one tracker that performs well; however, there exist many

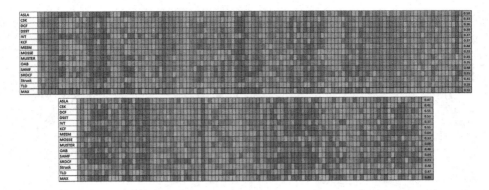

Fig. 5. *Top:* OPE success per video on UAV123. Bottom: OPE success per video for OTB100. (Color figure online)

sequences in UAV123 where none of the trackers are successful. For example, all these trackers perform poorly on low resolution videos of one UAV tracking another, an important aerial tracking scenario.

Speed Performance. In Fig. 6, most of the top performing trackers have a frame rate lower than 10 FPS and as low as 0.9 FPS (MUSTER). Note that each tracker predicts a bounding box for each frame regardless of their actual speed. Of course, this is very different when tracking is required in real-time (e.g. when tracker output is needed for persistent UAV navigation). If frames are not processed fast enough, intermediate frames are dropped resulting in larger target displacement between frames, thus, making tracking more difficult. Therefore, if the tracker has a low frame rate, its tracking performance in real-time applications is expected to degrade. In order to investigate the impact of speed on performance, we compare all trackers on the same UAV123 dataset but now temporally downsampled to 10 FPS (refer to Fig. 6). The degradation in performance ranges from 21 %–36 % for ASLA, DSST, and SAMF, and 11 %–15 % for SRDCF, STRUCK, and MUSTER. MEEM becomes the top-performing tracker in this case, although its performance degradation (7 %) is still noticeable.

Long-Term Tracking. In order to evaluate a tracker's performance in long-term tracking scenarios, we evaluate their performance on UAV20L (see Sect. 2.1). Tracking results in Fig. 6 show that all trackers perform much worse on UAV20L than on UAV123, indicating that long-term tracking remains a difficult challenge with much room for improvement. In long-term tracking cases, tracker drift is more likely to cause complete loss of the object, especially in occlusion scenarios, where the model update for the target is contaminated by the occluder. The top performer on this dataset is MUSTER, due to its short-term/long-term memory strategy that can correct past tracking mistakes.

Discussion. Throughout the evaluation, trackers perform consistently across attributes; however, we find that trackers struggle more with attributes com-

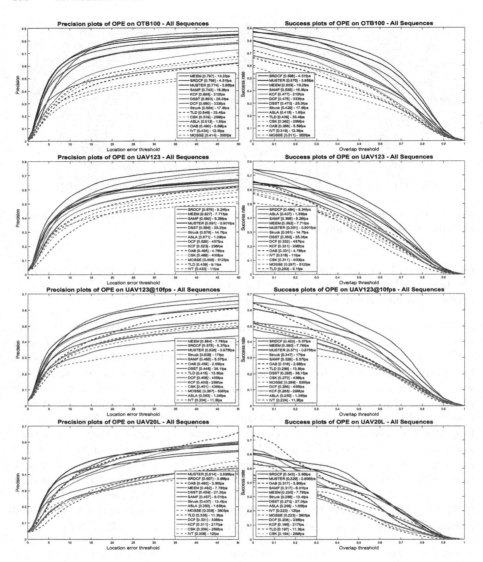

Fig. 6. From top to bottom: Precision and success plots for OPE on OTB100, UAV123, UAV123@10fps and UAV20L.

mon to aerial tracking. The most difficult attributes seem to be scale variation and aspect ratio changes but also to a lesser extent low resolution, background clutter, fast motion, and full occlusion. Scale variation is the most dominant attribute in the aerial tracking dataset, so trackers that incorporate scale adaptation are typically the top performers. There is still much room for improvement especially for attributes common in our dataset, but not very common in current datasets. Moreover, for automated tracking to be integrated on a UAV, tracking speeds must be higher, ultimately reaching real-time speeds of 30 FPS. We also observe that trackers, which have a robust update method that can help correct past mistakes (MEEM, MUSTER) or suppress background (SRDCF), perform better than those that do not. The spatial robustness evaluation which measures robustness to noise in the initialization is consistent with the OPE plots and trackers rank similarly with overall lower scores. For a detailed evaluation and discussion of all trackers for each prevalent attribute and spatial robustness, please refer to the supplementary material.

4.2   Simulator Evaluation (Quantitative and Qualitative Results)

Overall Performance. Several challenges such as significant change in scale, aspect ratio and viewpoint, illumination variation, and fast motion occur throughout the test course. Despite noticeable drift, all trackers maintain tracking at least throughout half of the course. At this point, the vehicle takes a sharp turn and accelerates down a hill; the conservative default PID setting limits the UAVs' response and most of the trackers fail (see frame 3000 in Fig. 7). However, when the PID controller is set to be more responsive, the tracking results vary significantly. SRDCF already fails at the very beginning of the course, since it is not able to handle the rapid acceleration of the object and overshoots due to the latency introduced by the tracker. The other trackers welcome the more responsive PID setting and follow the target with much more ease than before. This shows that the PID controller and tracker complement each other.

Speed Performance. The tested trackers vary in computational time with STRUCK and MEEM being the fastest. The bounding boxes of slower trackers (SCRDF and SAMF) have noticeable lag and do not remain consistently centered on the target, especially during rapid acceleration. The UAV altitude, wide vertical FOV, and PID setting can compensate for some latency, allowing the UAV to sync its speed to the vehicle. As altitude increases between the UAV and the target, the precision of the trackers improves. This is an important observation. In real-world scenarios, increasing altitude can be a UAV strategy to enhance tracking performance of slower trackers attempting to follow fast targets.

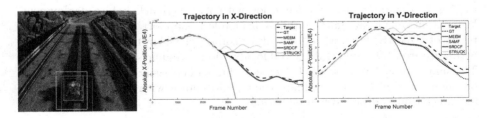

Fig. 7. Trajectory of tracker controlled UAV over the period of the simulation and multiple trackers bounding boxes layered over the tracked synthetic frame.

Long-Term Tracking. At some point, all of the trackers start to drift and usually become locked onto highly salient features of the target. Despite inaccurate bounding boxes, all trackers succeed to follow the target for more than one minute. Only SRDCF completes the course, but it only tracks a portion of the vehicle towards the end.

Discussion. Several insights can be obtained from the live tracking results within the simulator. Despite latency, trackers remain locked on the target throughout a large portion of the course. At higher altitudes latency has less impact on performance, since the UAV has more time to respond to target movement. Tracker performance is noticeably impacted by the flight dynamics and control system of the UAV. The failure of several trackers can be overcome by a more agile UAV. SRDCF's robustness and the UAV's ability to compensate for its latency make it the only tracker to complete the entire course. A major achievement however, is that all the tested state-of-the-art trackers autonomously move the UAV across a complex course. Over longer periods, the predicted center and size of the target drift primarily due to poor adaptation to scale and aspect ratio. Appearance change and partial occlusion lead to loss of the target by all trackers. The benchmark helps identify which trackers are most suitable for aerial tracking and the simulator provides insights for the best integration on a UAV. It provides many avenues to rapidly test trackers and clearly delineate their shortcomings and advantages in real-world scenarios.

5   Conclusions and Future Work

In this paper, we provide extensive empirical evidence of the shortcomings of current datasets for aerial tracking and propose a new benchmark with fully annotated sequences from the perspective of a UAV. The new dataset is similar in size to the largest available datasets for generic object tracking and the benchmark evaluates 14 state-of-the-art trackers. Extensive experiments suggest that sequences with certain tracking attributes (namely scale variation, aspect ratio change, and low resolution), which tend to be under-represented in other benchmarks and are quite common in aerial tracking scenarios, pose significant challenges to current state-of-the-art trackers. This builds the stage for further improvements in precision and speed.

Our proposed UAV simulator along with novel evaluation methods enables tracker testing in real-world scenarios with live feedback before deployment. We will make this simulator publicly available to support more progress in the realm of UAV tracking, as well as, other computer vision tasks including aerial Structure-from-Motion (SfM), aerial localization, dynamic scene monitoring, etc. The simulator is not limited to UAVs alone but can be easily extended to simulate autonomous vehicles and evaluate their performance with algorithms designed for navigation and pedestrian detection.

Acknowledgments. Research in this paper was supported by the King Abdullah University of Science and Technology (KAUST) Office of Sponsored Research.

References

1. Babenko, B., Yang, M.H., Belongie, S.: Visual tracking with online multiple instance learning. IEEE Trans. Pattern Anal. Mach. Intell. **33**(8), 1619–1632 (2010)
2. Battaglia, P.W., Hamrick, J.B., Tenenbaum, J.B.: Simulation as an engine of physical scene understanding. Proc. Natl. Acad. Sci. **110**(45), 18327–18332 (2013). http://www.pnas.org/content/110/45/18327.abstract
3. Bibi, A., Ghanem, B.: Multi-template scale-adaptive kernelized correlation filters. In: 2015 IEEE International Conference on Computer Vision Workshop (ICCVW), pp. 613–620, December 2015
4. Bibi, A., Mueller, M., Ghanem, B.: Target response adaptation for correlation filter tracking. In: Leibe, B., Matas, J., Sebe, N., Welling, M. (eds.) ECCV 2016. LNCS, vol. 9910, pp. 419–433. Springer, Switzerland (2016)
5. Bolme, D.S., Beveridge, J.R., Draper, B.A., Lui, Y.M.: Visual object tracking using adaptive correlation filters. In: 2010 IEEE Conference on Computer Vision and Pattern Recognition (CVPR), pp. 2544–2550, June 2010
6. Collins, R., Zhou, X., Teh, S.K.: An open source tracking testbed and evaluation web site. In: IEEE International Workshop on Performance Evaluation of Tracking and Surveillance (PETS 2005), January 2005
7. Danelljan, M., Hager, G., Shahbaz Khan, F., Felsberg, M.: Learning spatially regularized correlation filters for visual tracking. In: The IEEE International Conference on Computer Vision (ICCV), December 2015
8. Danelljan, M., Hger, G., Shahbaz Khan, F., Felsberg, M.: Accurate scale estimation for robust visual tracking. In: Proceedings of the British Machine Vision Conference. BMVA Press (2014)
9. Fu, C., Carrio, A., Olivares-Mendez, M., Suarez-Fernandez, R., Campoy, P.: Robust real-time vision-based aircraft tracking from unmanned aerial vehicles. In: 2014 IEEE International Conference on Robotics and Automation (ICRA), pp. 5441–5446, May 2014
10. Gaszczak, A., Breckon, T.P., Han, J.: Real-time people and vehicle detection from UAV imagery. In: Röning, J., Casasent, D.P., Hall, E.L. (eds.) IST/SPIE Electronic Imaging, vol. 7878, pp. 78780B-1–78780B-13. International Society for Optics and Photonics, January 2011
11. Grabner, H., Grabner, M., Bischof, H.: Real-time tracking via on-line boosting. In: Proceedings of the British Machine Vision Conference, pp. 6.1–6.10. BMVA Press (2006). doi:10.5244/C.20.6
12. Hamalainen, P., Eriksson, S., Tanskanen, E., Kyrki, V., Lehtinen, J.: Online motion synthesis using sequential monte carlo. ACM Trans. Graph. **33**(4), 51:1–51:12. http://doi.acm.org/10.1145/2601097.2601218
13. Hare, S., Saffari, A., Torr, P.H.S.: Struck: structured output tracking with kernels. In: 2011 International Conference on Computer Vision, pp. 263–270. IEEE, November 2011
14. Hattori, H., Naresh Boddeti, V., Kitani, K.M., Kanade, T.: Learning scene-specific pedestrian detectors without real data. In: The IEEE Conference on Computer Vision and Pattern Recognition (CVPR), June 2015
15. Hejrati, M., Ramanan, D.: Analysis by synthesis: 3D object recognition by object reconstruction. In: 2014 IEEE Conference on Computer Vision and Pattern Recognition (CVPR), pp. 2449–2456, June 2014
16. Henriques, J.F., Caseiro, R., Martins, P., Batista, J.: High-speed tracking with kernelized correlation filters. IEEE Trans. Pattern Anal. Mach. Intell. **37**(3), 583–596 (2015)

17. Henriques, J.F., Caseiro, R., Martins, P., Batista, J.: Exploiting the circulant structure of tracking-by-detection with kernels. In: Fitzgibbon, A., Lazebnik, S., Perona, P., Sato, Y., Schmid, C. (eds.) ECCV 2012. LNCS, vol. 7575, pp. 702–715. Springer, Heidelberg (2012). doi:10.1007/978-3-642-33765-9_50
18. Hong, Z., Chen, Z., Wang, C., Mei, X., Prokhorov, D., Tao, D.: Multi-store tracker (MUSTer): a cognitive psychology inspired approach to object tracking. In: 2015 IEEE Conference on Computer Vision and Pattern Recognition (CVPR), pp. 749–758, June 2015
19. Jia, X., Lu, H., Yang, M.H.: Visual tracking via adaptive structural local sparse appearance model. In: 2012 IEEE Conference on Computer Vision and Pattern Recognition (CVPR), pp. 1822–1829, June 2012
20. Ju, E., Won, J., Lee, J., Choi, B., Noh, J., Choi, M.G.: Data-driven control of flapping flight. ACM Trans. Graph. 32(5), 151:1–151:12. http://doi.acm.org/10.1145/2516971.2516976
21. Kalal, Z., Mikolajczyk, K., Matas, J.: Tracking-learning-detection. IEEE Trans. Pattern Anal. Mach. Intell. 34(7), 1409–1422 (2011)
22. Kendall, A., Salvapantula, N., Stol, K.: On-board object tracking control of a quadcopter with monocular vision. In: 2014 International Conference on Unmanned Aircraft Systems (ICUAS), pp. 404–411, May 2014
23. Kristan, M., et al.: The Visual Object Tracking VOT2014 challenge results. In: Agapito, L., Bronstein, M.M., Rother, C. (eds.) ECCV 2014. LNCS, vol. 8926, pp. 191–217. Springer, Switzerland (2015). doi:10.1007/978-3-319-16181-5_14
24. Li, A., Lin, M., Wu, Y., Yang, M.H., Yan, S.: NUS-PRO: a new visual tracking challenge. IEEE Trans. Pattern Anal. Mach. Intell. 38(2), 335–349 (2016)
25. Liang, P., Blasch, E., Ling, H.: Encoding color information for visual tracking: algorithms and benchmark. IEEE Trans. Image Process. 24(12), 5630–5644 (2015)
26. Liang, P., Blasch, E., Ling, H.: Encoding color information for visual tracking: algorithms and benchmark. IEEE Image Process. 24, 5630–5644 (2015). http://ieeexplore.ieee.org/xpls/abs_all.jsp?arnumber=7277070
27. Lim, H., Sinha, S.N.: Monocular localization of a moving person onboard a quadrotor MAV. In: 2015 IEEE International Conference on Robotics and Automation (ICRA), pp. 2182–2189, May 2015
28. Mueller, M., amd Neil Smith, G.S., Ghanem, B.: Persistent aerial tracking system for UAVs. In: 2016 IEEE/RSJ International Conference Intelligent Robots and Systems (IROS), October 2016
29. Naseer, T., Sturm, J., Cremers, D.: Followme: person following and gesture recognition with a quadrocopter. In: 2013 IEEE/RSJ International Conference on Intelligent Robots and Systems (IROS), pp. 624–630, November 2013
30. Nussberger, A., Grabner, H., Van Gool, L.: Aerial object tracking from an airborne platform. In: 2014 International Conference on Unmanned Aircraft Systems (ICUAS), pp. 1284–1293, May 2014
31. Papon, J., Schoeler, M.: Semantic pose using deep networks trained on synthetic RGB-D. CoRR abs/1508.00835 (2015). http://arxiv.org/abs/1508.00835
32. Pepik, B., Stark, M., Gehler, P., Schiele, B.: Teaching 3D geometry to deformable part models. In: 2012 IEEE Conference on Computer Vision and Pattern Recognition (CVPR), pp. 3362–3369, June 2012
33. Pestana, J., Sanchez-Lopez, J., Campoy, P., Saripalli, S.: Vision based GPS-denied object tracking and following for unmanned aerial vehicles. In: 2013 IEEE International Symposium on Safety, Security, and Rescue Robotics (SSRR), pp. 1–6, October 2013

34. Pollard, T., Antone, M.: Detecting and tracking all moving objects in wide-area aerial video. In: 2012 IEEE Computer Society Conference on Computer Vision and Pattern Recognition Workshops (CVPRW), pp. 15–22, June 2012

35. Portmann, J., Lynen, S., Chli, M., Siegwart, R.: People detection and tracking from aerial thermal views. In: 2014 IEEE International Conference on Robotics and Automation (ICRA), pp. 1794–1800, May 2014

36. Prokaj, J., Medioni, G.: Persistent tracking for wide area aerial surveillance. In: 2014 IEEE Conference on Computer Vision and Pattern Recognition (CVPR), pp. 1186–1193, June 2014

37. Qadir, A., Neubert, J., Semke, W., Schultz, R.: On-board visual tracking with Unmanned Aircraft System (UAS). In: Infotech@Aerospace Conferences. American Institute of Aeronautics and Astronautics, March 2011

38. Ross, D., Lim, J., Lin, R.S., Yang, M.H.: Incremental learning for robust visual tracking. Int. J. Comput. Vis. **77**(1–3), 125–141 (2008)

39. Smeulders, A.W.M., Chu, D.M., Cucchiara, R., Calderara, S., Dehghan, A., Shah, M.: Visual tracking: an experimental survey. IEEE Trans. Pattern Anal. Mach. Intell. **36**(7), 1442–1468 (2014)

40. Trilaksono, B.R., Triadhitama, R., Adiprawita, W., Wibowo, A., Sreenatha, A.: Hardware in the loop simulation for visual target tracking of octorotor UAV. Aircr. Eng. Aerosp. Technol. **83**(6), 407–419 (2011). http://dx.doi.org/10.1108/00022661111173289

41. Wu, Y., Lim, J., Yang, M.H.: Object tracking benchmark. IEEE Trans. Pattern Anal. Mach. Intell. **37**(9), 1834–1848 (2015)

42. Wu, Y., Lim, J., Yang, M.H.: Online object tracking: a benchmark. In: 2013 IEEE Conference on Computer Vision and Pattern Recognition, pp. 2411–2418. IEEE, June 2013

43. Zhang, J., Ma, S., Sclaroff, S.: MEEM: robust tracking via multiple experts using entropy minimization. In: Fleet, D., Pajdla, T., Schiele, B., Tuytelaars, T. (eds.) ECCV 2014. LNCS, vol. 8694, pp. 188–203. Springer, Switzerland (2014). doi:10.1007/978-3-319-10599-4_13

44. Zhang, T., Bibi, A., Ghanem, B.: In defense of sparse tracking: circulant sparse tracker. In: 2016 IEEE Conference on Computer Vision and Pattern Recognition (CVPR), June 2016

45. Zhang, T., Ghanem, B., Liu, S., Xu, C., Ahuja, N.: Robust visual tracking via exclusive context modeling. IEEE Trans. Cybern. **46**(1), 51–63 (2016)

46. Zhang, T., Ghanem, B., Xu, C., Ahuja, N.: Object tracking by occlusion detection via structured sparse learning. In: 2013 IEEE Conference on Computer Vision and Pattern Recognition Workshops, pp. 1033–1040, June 2013

47. Zhang, T., Liu, S., Xu, C., Yan, S., Ghanem, B., Ahuja, N., Yang, M.H.: Structural sparse tracking. In: 2015 IEEE Conference on Computer Vision and Pattern Recognition (CVPR), pp. 150–158, June 2015

Scene Depth Profiling Using Helmholtz Stereopsis

Hironori Mori$^{(\boxtimes)}$, Roderick Köhle, and Markus Kamm

Sony European Technology Center, Stuttgart, Germany
{Hironori.Mori,Roderick.Koehle,Markus.Kamm}@eu.sony.com

Abstract. Helmholtz stereopsis is a 3D reconstruction technique, capturing surface depth independent of the reflection properties of the material by using Helmholtz reciprocity. In this paper we are interested in studying the applicability of Helmholtz stereopsis for surface and depth profiling of objects and general scenes in the context of perspective stereo imaging. Helmholtz stereopsis captures a pair of reciprocal images by exchanging the position of light source and camera. The resulting image pair relates the image intensities and scene depth profile by a partial differential equation. The solution of this differential equation depends on the boundary conditions provided by the scene. We propose to limit the illumination angle of the light source, such that only mutually visible parts are imaged, resulting in stable boundary conditions. By simulation and experiment we show that a unique depth profile can be recovered for a large class of scenes including multiple occluding objects.

Keywords: 3D reconstruction · Depth profiling · Stereopsis · Helmholtz reciprocity

1 Introduction

Three-dimensional optical depth profiling and sensing is one of the most actively pursuit research areas in computational vision. Some of the key applications are industrial metrology, robotic vision, automotive driver assistance systems, 3D object scanning and media user interfaces. Optical depth sensing may be categorized in two groups, passive depth sensing such as stereo-vision or depth-from-defocus and active sensing technologies requiring an auxiliary light source, such as laser scanning or structured light.

Passive methods such as stereo-vision rely on the availability of scene features and require the measurement object to have diffuse reflection properties. Fringe projection methods [1] extend the applicability of stereoscopy to surfaces with homogeneous texture. The surface to be measured is illuminated by using a light projector to project a line or dot grid pattern. Since usually a repetitive pattern is used, one requirement of the fringe projection is the surface to be sufficiently smooth. For discontinuous surfaces with large height steps, phase ambiguities arise and a unique disparity assignment may not be possible. Structured light [2]

© Springer International Publishing AG 2016
B. Leibe et al. (Eds.): ECCV 2016, Part I, LNCS 9905, pp. 462–476, 2016.
DOI: 10.1007/978-3-319-46448-0_28

generalizes the concept of fringe projection and use time multiplexing to project an encoding pattern to uniquely identify surface patches.

In a recent series of publications, a novel approach to surface reconstruction was proposed by [3–5]. The idea is to use Helmholtz reciprocity to establish a relation between image intensity and the surface orientation of an observed object. Helmholtz reciprocity is a promising approach for 3D depth profiling, as it is largely independent of material reflectance and does not rely on surface texture. Our goal is to study the limitations of using Helmholtz reciprocity for general scene depth acquisition.

There have been a variety of proposals for solving the depth from Helmholtz reciprocal images. In the publication by [3,6], a multiview recovery approach is taken. It requires an initial depth estimate based on multiview-stereo correspondences and uses the surface normal estimate to refine the initial depth estimate. The approach in [7] uses a sensor fusion approach, refining the depth information obtained from a structured light scanner by utilizing the surface normal information obtained from Helmholtz reciprocity. In the publications of [4,5,8] the concept of Helmholtz stereopsis was introduced, it uses PDE integration methods to recover the depth profile along epipolar lines from a single pair of Helmholtz reciprocal images. Another interesting approach is proposed by [9], it uses variational techniques to iteratively refine an initial triangular mesh, Delaunoy showed that it is possible to recover the surface of complex scenes with multiple occluding objects.

In Helmholtz stereopsis, the scene is illuminated by a light source whereas a pair of reciprocal images is captured by exchanging the position of camera and light source. In its original conception, a point light source is used for object illumination. In our setup we use a LED pattern projector, which is commonly used for industrial laser scanning and structured light acquisition. The use of a projector for illumination allows limiting the angle of illumination. By matching the illumination aperture with the field aperture of the camera, only mutually visible parts of the scene are illuminated.

This report is organized as follows, first we will review the Helmholtz condition and formulate it in the context of perspective imaging. As we will see, this leads to an integral representation which allows solving for the surface profile in the case of multiple occluded objects. By using a light projector with a matched aperture we ensure stable boundary conditions for arbitrary scenes. For validation, we will provide simulation and experimental results of object and scene measurements.

2   Preliminaries

2.1   Perspective Surface Representation

Assuming a pinhole camera model, the image position (x, y) is related to the angular direction of an incident ray (u, v) by the focal length f. Given a discrete representation of the sensor image, the relation between the pixel index (i, j) and the angular image coordinates (u, v) is $u = \frac{\Delta x}{f}(i - i_0), v = -\frac{\Delta y}{f}(j - j_0),$

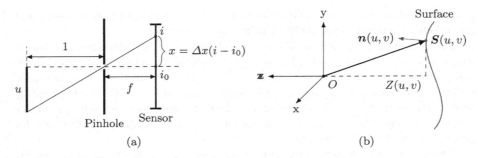

Fig. 1. (a) Illustration of the relation between the pixel index (i, j) and the angular image coordinates (u, v). (b) Illustration of surface vector description by a given scalar depth map $Z(u, v)$ at a given angular image coordinate (u, v).

whereas $\Delta x, \Delta y$ is the pixel resolution of the image sensor and (i_0, j_0) is the pixel position of the principle point (See Fig. 1a).

The surface height is described by a positive valued profile function $Z(u, v)$. As illustrated in Fig. 1b, we assume a fixed coordinate system, where the entrance pupil of the camera is located at the origin and the viewing direction of the camera is oriented along the negative z-axis. The spatial coordinates of the surface $\boldsymbol{S}(u, v)$ are then described by the perspective projection relation,

$$\boldsymbol{S}(u, v) = \begin{bmatrix} u \\ v \\ -1 \end{bmatrix} Z(u, v). \tag{1}$$

With the surface parameterized as a vector function of the image coordinates (u, v), the normal field is obtained by the cross product of the partial derivatives of the surface,

$$\boldsymbol{N}(u, v) = \frac{\partial S}{\partial u} \times \frac{\partial S}{\partial v} = \begin{vmatrix} i & j & k \\ Z + uZ_u & vZ_u & -Z_u \\ uZ_v & Z + vZ_v & -Z_v \end{vmatrix} = Z^2 \begin{bmatrix} Z_u/Z \\ Z_v/Z \\ 1 + uZ_u/Z + vZ_v/Z \end{bmatrix},$$

where Z_u, Z_v are partial derivatives of $Z(u, v)$ with respect to the variable u, v respectively.

2.2   Helmholtz Image Formation

For the measurement of a Helmholtz reciprocal image pair, the surface reflection is modeled by the radiance equations. Given a point on the surface of observation, the projected image coordinates are given by (u, v) and (u_2, v_2) for both views. The distance between the light source and the point on the surface is measured by the euclidean distances r_1, r_2. The angle between the incident ray from the light source and the surface normal is given by θ_{in} as illustrated in Fig. 2a.

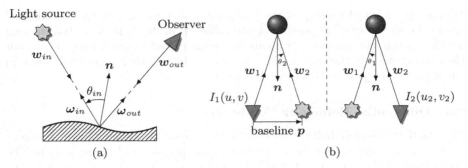

Fig. 2. (a) Reflection of light of an incident light ray at w_{in} to the reflected ray w_{out} by bidirectional reflection distribution function $f_r(\omega_{in}, \omega_{out})$. A pair of Helmholtz reciprocal images is taken, by exchanging the position of light source and observer. (b) Capturing of a pair of Helmholtz reciprocal images $I_1(u, v)$ and $I_2(u_2, v_2)$ by exchanging the position of light source and observer. The angular image coordinates of the left view are given by (u, v) and of the right view by (u_2, v_2).

The reflection of an object point at a surface is given by the radiance,

$$I_1(u, v) = \alpha f_r(\omega_2, \omega_1) cos\theta_2 / r_2^2, \tag{2}$$

by exchanging the position of camera and light source as shown in Fig. 2b, the radiance of the reciprocal image is,

$$I_2(u_2, v_2) = \alpha f_r(\omega_1, \omega_2) cos\theta_1 / r_1^2, \tag{3}$$

where $f_r(\omega_i, \omega_o)$ is the bidirectional reflectance distribution at the observed surface point with ω_i and ω_o being the unit directions of the incident and reflected ray. The factor α is a constant scaling factor incorporating the illumination intensity and the camera gain.

For physical materials the BRDF satisfies Helmholtz reciprocity. Helmholtz reciprocity states that the reflection coefficient is the same if the path of light travel is reversed $f_r(\omega_1, \omega_2) = f_r(\omega_2, \omega_1)$ with $\omega_1 = -w_1/r_1$ and $\omega_2 = -w_2/r_2$ being the normalized directions of the observation and illumination vector. By measuring a pair of Helmholtz reciprocal images, the reflection function can be eliminated resulting in the Helmholtz reciprocity condition,

$$I_1(u, v) cos\theta_1 / r_1^2 = I_2(u_2, v_2) cos\theta_2 / r_2^2. \tag{4}$$

Using this notation, the Helmholtz reciprocity condition is given by the scalar product as stated in [3–6],

$$n^T \tau = 0 \tag{5}$$

whereas the vector τ is the tangent vector to the observed surface,

$$\tau = \frac{I_1(u, v)}{r_1^3} w_1 - \frac{I_2(u_2, v_2)}{r_2^3} w_2. \tag{6}$$

We may geometrically interpret the Helmholtz condition as a vector tangent field spanned over the space of possible depth values. If in this field, an initial starting depth is given, the surface depth can be reconstructed by path integration over the tangent field. In the next section, we restate the Helmholtz partial differential equation for the perspective imaging case.

2.3   Differential Helmholtz Condition

To formulate the Helmholtz condition for the perspective imaging case, consider a camera and light source being aligned in a common focal plane at z=0. The orientation of the camera is towards the negative z-axis. The camera and light source are located in a common focal plane and separated by a baseline vector $p = [p_x\ p_y\ 0]^T$. The object surface is parameterized by a positive depth profile $Z(u,v)$ in terms of the image coordinates (u,v) of the left view. The Helmholtz reciprocal image pair is given by the image functions $I_1(u,v)$ for the left and $I_2(u_2,v_2)$ for the reciprocal right view. The perspective projection of surface point $S(u,v)$ in both reciprocal views is given by the relation,

$$S(u,v) = \begin{bmatrix} u \\ v \\ -1 \end{bmatrix} Z(u,v) = \begin{bmatrix} p_x \\ p_y \\ 0 \end{bmatrix} + \begin{bmatrix} u_2 \\ v_2 \\ -1 \end{bmatrix} Z(u,v). \tag{7}$$

From above perspective projection, the angular disparity of a point between two views is given by,

$$\begin{bmatrix} u - u_2 \\ v - v_2 \end{bmatrix} = \begin{bmatrix} p_x \\ p_y \end{bmatrix} \frac{1}{Z(u,v)}. \tag{8}$$

The observation vector for both reciprocal views is,

$$w_1 = \begin{bmatrix} u \\ v \\ -1 \end{bmatrix} Z(u,v), \quad w_2 = \begin{bmatrix} u_2 \\ v_2 \\ -1 \end{bmatrix} Z(u,v). \tag{9}$$

When capturing the image of the left view $I_1(u,v)$, the vector w_1 is the observation vector starting from the focal position of the camera located at the left position pointing to a surface point and the vector w_2 is the illumination vector starting from the position of the light source and pointing to the observed surface point. When capturing the reciprocal image, the vector w_1 becomes the illumination vector and w_2 is the observation vector for the right image.

We may now simplify the Helmholtz reciprocal condition, by substituting the scalar product between the normal and observation vector. The scalar product of illumination vector and surface normal is,

$$|n|\ r_1 cos\theta_1 = -n^T w_1 = Z^3, \tag{10}$$

$$|n|\ r_2 cos\theta_2 = -n^T w_2 = Z^3(1 + (u - u_2)Z_u/Z + (v - v_2)Z_v/Z). \tag{11}$$

By using the disparity relation 8, the scalar product 11 simplifies to,

$$-n^T w_2 = Z^3(1 + p_x Z_u/Z^2 + p_y Z_v/Z^2). \tag{12}$$

The distance between focal points and object point is given by $r_1 = |w_1| = Z\sqrt{u^2 + v^2 + 1}$, $r_2 = |w_2| = Z\sqrt{u_2^2 + v_2^2 + 1}$. Inserting the scalar products 10, 11 for perspective projection into the Helmholtz condition 4, the perspective Helmholtz condition becomes,

$$I_1(u,v)\frac{Z^3}{r_1^3} = I_2(u_2,v_2)\frac{Z^3}{r_2^3}(1 + p_x Z_u/Z^2 + p_y Z_v/Z^2). \tag{13}$$

By introducing the following changes in notation, we eliminate the explicit dependency on the depth $Z(u,v)$ and above expression becomes more concise. For a Helmholtz reciprocal pair of images, the measured intensities are normalized by a radial weight function,

$$J_1(u,v) = \frac{I_1(u,v)}{\hat{r}_1^3}, \qquad\qquad \hat{r}_1 = \sqrt{u^2 + v^2 + 1}, \tag{14}$$

$$J_2(u_2,v_2) = \frac{I_2(u_2,v_2)}{\hat{r}_2^3}, \qquad\qquad \hat{r}_2 = \sqrt{u_2^2 + v_2^2 + 1}. \tag{15}$$

The explicit dependency on $Z(u,v)$ is eliminated by introducing the reciprocal depth $D(u,v) = 1/Z(u,v)$. With the partial gradients of $D_u(u,v)$, which are $D_u(u,v) = -Z_u/Z^2$ and $D_v(u,v) = -Z_v/Z^2$, the Helmholtz condition for rectified, perspective imaging becomes

$$J_1(u,v) = J_2(u_2,v_2)(1 - p_x D_u - p_y D_v). \tag{16}$$

For a point on the surface being mutually visible in both views, the cosine term $cos\theta_2$ must be positive. For a continuous surface the weighting term in 16 satisfies the visibility constraint $(1 - p_x D_u - p_y D_v) >= 0$.

2.4   Integral Helmholtz Condition

The Helmholtz condition for perspective imaging suggests the image pairs being related by a perspective image transform by a perspective coordinate transform. Suppose, the object under observation is an arbitrarily oriented plane placed in front of camera and light source. A rectangular element in the coordinate system (u,v) of the left view, is mapped into a parallelogram in the reciprocal image coordinate system (u_2, v_2) of the right view. The change of area due to a perspective view transformation is given by the Jacobian determinant,

$$det\frac{\partial(u_2,v_2)}{\partial(u,v)} = \begin{vmatrix} \frac{\partial u_2}{\partial u} & \frac{\partial u_2}{\partial v} \\ \frac{\partial v_2}{\partial u} & \frac{\partial v_2}{\partial v} \end{vmatrix} = 1 - p_x D_u - p_y D_v. \tag{17}$$

We may express the Helmholtz reciprocity condition using the more general notation,

$$J_1(u,v)\partial(u,v) = J_2(u_2,v_2)\partial(u_2,v_2). \tag{18}$$

The intensities, normalized according to Eq. 14, of a pair of reciprocal images are related by a perspective view transform. The differential terms $\partial(u,v)$ are the size of an area patch projected into the respective coordinate system.

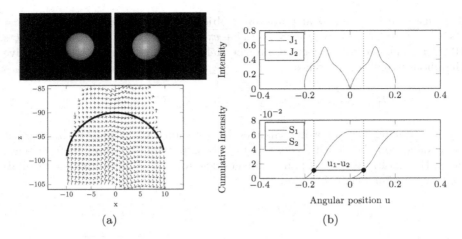

Fig. 3. (a) Raytracing of a Helmholtz image pair of a spherical object and geometric interpretation of the Helmholtz condition in terms of a surface tangent field from the figure above. (b) Intensity graph and cumulative intensity of the Helmholtz reciprocal images of the spherical object in Fig. 3a. The cumulative intensity forms a hysteresis curve. The disparity is determined by measuring the lag between both curves.

By integration, we obtain another interpretation of the Helmholtz condition. Consider an surface patch Ω mutually visible in both reciprocal images and let its projected areas be Ω_1 and Ω_2, then the area integral of the normalized intensities is identical.

$$\iint\limits_{\Omega_1} J_1(u,v)\, \mathrm{d}\Omega_1 = \iint\limits_{\Omega_2} J_2(u_2,v_2)\, \mathrm{d}\Omega_2 \tag{19}$$

If we further assume a rectified stereo configuration with a baseline vector of $p_x > 0$ and $p_y = 0$, the epipolar lines of the image pairs are parallel to the x-axis. If the object is of finite size and the background is black or sufficiently far away such that the object is mutually visible in both images, then the intensity sum along each epipolar line is expected to be equal.

In the case of rectified stereo, the identity in Eq. 19 suggests a reconstruction rule which measures the disparity from the sum of intensities along epipolar lines. For the simulated example of the spherical object in Fig. 3a, the measurement of the disparity is illustrated in Fig. 3b. At a given intensity sum level, the measured disparity is the difference of the abscissa at which the intensity sum is equal for both image pairs. By measuring the disparity for each level of the intensity sum, we may recover a disparity map, which is a valid but not necessarily unique solution to the differential equation formulated by the Helmholtz condition.

2.5   Simulation Examples

For the existence of a solution, the object to be measured is required to have sufficient reflectance and to be close to the light source such that the image signal has a sufficiently high signal noise ratio. Occluded and non-visible surface areas in one image will be located in the shadow regions of the corresponding reciprocal image. For complex geometrical scenes, the software Blender in combination with LuxRender is a suitable modeling and rendering environment. The LuxRender implementation is based on the physically based rendering engine by Pharr and Humphreys [10], it correctly models point illumination and provides a physically correct specular model (Cook-Torrance model [11]).

Boundary Conditions: For uniqueness, we need suitable boundary conditions for the Helmholtz condition. In case the object is of finite size and has a continuous surface, we may recover a unique disparity map by capturing the object such that it is mutually visible in both images. If the object is extended beyond the viewing cone of the camera, the intensity sum will have an offset compared to the intensity sum of the reciprocal image. In this case, it will be necessary to use other boundary constraints, e.g. by using stereo correspondences to determine this offset.

In case of general scenes, the object may not be bounded and we may have multiple occluding objects. One approach to relief the uniqueness problem is to introduce an aperture to the light source. By limiting the angular extend of the light source, the illumination aperture will cast a shadow into the scene. If the aperture of the camera of the reciprocal image is matched to size and shape of the light source, only those parts of the scene are illuminated which are mutually visible in the reciprocal pair of images. Figure 4a shows a Helmholtz reciprocal image pair of a sphere placed in front of an extended, untextured plane. In the figure, the illumination cone and the camera viewing cone are bounded by a circular aperture. Figure 4b compares the resulting disparity map with the ground truth. Except of the tips of the spherical object, the disparity is accurately recovered including the occluding sphere.

Occlusion and Visibility Order: The recovery artifacts at the top of the sphere are caused by a change of the order of visibility for occluding objects which have a small width compared to the distance to the background object. In this case, the shadow cast on the background object becomes detached from the occluding front object. Figure 5 illustrates the occlusion artifacts, suppose a front object of width W is placed in front of a background plane at a distance H_1 and the distance between the common focal plane of the Helmholtz setup with baseline P and the background object is H_0. If the ratio W/H_1 is less than P/H_0, the shadow S cast by the frontal object is separated from its projected image F by a visible patch of background object B. By computing the intensity sum starting at the left image boundary, the sequence of visible object patches differs for the left and right view. Measuring disparity from the intensity sum results in a feature correspondence mismatch.

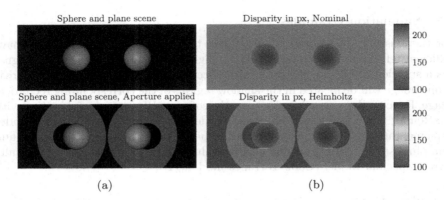

Fig. 4. (a) Top: Spherical object in front of an extended plane. Bottom: The scene is rendered with a circular illumination and camera aperture. By matching the aperture of camera and light source, boundary conditions are well defined for reconstruction. (b) Comparison of nominal versus estimated disparity.

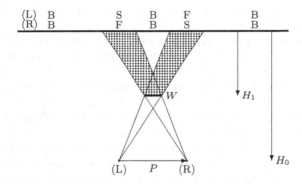

Fig. 5. Illustration of visibility order for a thin planar object in front of a background plane. The order of visibility of background and foreground object segments is reversed between left (L) and right view (R).

Noise Propagation: Since Helmholtz stereopsis estimates the disparity by integrating the intensity, an error in the input signal will not only affect the disparity estimation at the current pixel position, but also propagate to the neighboring pixel in the direction of integration. For Gaussian image noise, the error propagation of the disparity will result in a random walk. Close to the starting boundary condition, the disparity error will be small and grow continuously with the distance to the starting position. When repeating the procedure for all epipolar rows in a rectified image, the disparity will diverge randomly for each row. To reduce error propagation due to image noise, one option is to match the cumulative intensity at the left and right boundary. This is best illustrated with a planar rectangular patch, as we have in most cases two boundaries.

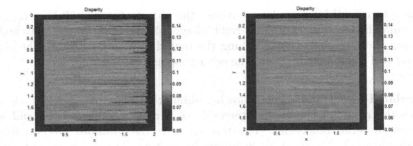

Fig. 6. In both test scenes, the baseline of the camera positions is 20 cm and the approximate working distance 1m. In the MATLAB test scene, a sphere of 10 cm radius is placed at the origin and viewed from a camera at a distance of 1m. A background plane is located 50 cm behind the sphere. Left: Disparity map initialized at the left boundary. Right: Disparity map of matched boundaries.

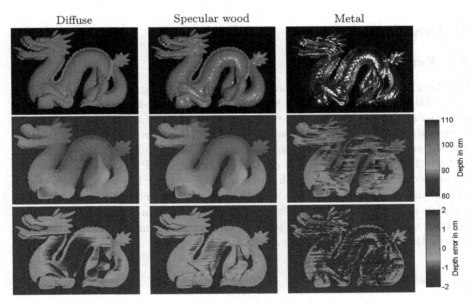

Fig. 7. Depth estimation for material simulations - (1) Diffuse, (2) Specular wood, and (3) Metal. The distance to the simulated object is approx. 100 cm at a baseline of 20 cm, a sensor width = 32 mm and f = 35 mm.

If we have multiple boundaries e.g. at the left/right aperture, we may scale the intensities in order to ensure the propagated depth matches at each boundary. The impact of error propagation in images is illustrated in Fig. 6. Since each row of the image has uncorrelated noise, each row of the disparity results in a different random walk. In the left image, the disparity is measured starting from the left of the scanline. Not only the error of the disparity will increase with the distance to the initial boundary, but also the object contour will be scraggy at the unmatched boundary. In the right image, the boundaries are matched by rescaling the intensities. By matching the boundaries on both sides, the object contour will remain smooth and the error propagation is reduced.

Specular Reflections: The following simulation example in Fig. 7 demonstrates the result of Helmholtz stereopsis to a more complex shape and with different material reflections. The test scene is the Stanford Dragon model, available from the Stanford 3D Scanning Repository. The distance between the dragon and the camera is approximately 1m. The result of depth estimation and the difference from ground truth are shown in the middle row and in the bottom row, respectively. For diffuse and specular materials the estimated depth agree very well with the ground truth. The metallic surface has too strong reflections resulting in image saturation.

3   Evaluation

3.1   Experimental Setup

For the measurements we used an industrial USB camera (IDS UI-1480-C-SE) with 5 MP image resolution and 8 bit color depth. To reduce noise and increase dynamic range, an exposure series of 5 images are captured and an HDR image is reconstructed. Ambient light subtraction is done by capturing a pair of HDR images, and subtracting the images with the respective light source turned on and off. The light source used is an LED projector (LTPR, Opto Engineering). The objective lens used for both camera and projector has a focal length f = 12 mm and aperture F/2.8. The camera and two projectors are mounted with parallel orientation on a sliding stage whereas the camera is placed in the center between the two projectors at a baseline of approx. 20 cm. By sliding the stage, the position of light source and camera is exchanged.

3.2   Calibration

For geometric calibration we used standard photogrammetric techniques using a planar rectangular grid for the estimation of the camera model. The estimated camera model is used for stereo image rectification.

In a physical setup the pinhole/spotlight assumptions used in deriving Eqs. 14 and 15 are not valid, the apodization function depends on the vignetting of the devices. For symmetry, we use the same lens type for camera and projector and make the assumption that the apodization function is radially symmetric. The intensity apodization is calibrated using a target board, instead of measuring the vignetting of the individual optical components. A more detailed discussion about Helmholtz calibration is given in [12].

For radiometric calibration, we used a target with an inverted dot pattern which white dots locate on black background. Image normalization is done by assuming radial symmetry and using a parabolic approximation. With the rectified image radiance pair given by $\hat{I}_{1,2}(u,v)$, the normalized Helmholtz image pair is given by $\hat{J}_{1,2}(u,v) = \mu(u,v)\hat{I}_{1,2}(u,v)$ with the apodization function $\mu(u,v) = 1 - \frac{1}{2}\alpha r^2$, $r^2 = u^2 + v^2$ and α being a radiometric correction parameter. By matching the cumulative intensity sum for each dot pattern of the target pattern, we may adjust the radiometric calibration parameter α.

3.3   Measurement Results

Black Background Scene: As a first measurement consider the rectified and normalized Helmholtz image of a Phythagoras statue, made of white plaster, in Fig. 8a. The statue is placed in front of a black background to have defined boundary conditions. The points which are mutually visible are identified by applying a hard threshold. The first valid point along an epipolar line can be starting point and the last valid point can be an end point. The mismatch between the intensity sum between both images is about 4 %. Figure 8a shows the estimated angular disparity map and Fig. 8b the mesh reconstruction in the coordinate space of the left camera.

Combination with Stereo Matching: If the object has sufficient texture or a corner, a starting condition can be found by using conventional stereo matching. In that case, it can be used for the references to define corresponding initial points between left and right views. Once a reliable disparity is found for one view, the corresponding point in the other view can be easily derived from the disparity. Since reliable disparities tend to be on edges or textured areas, edge detection results are predisposed to be used as a reliability map. Regarding left view, scanning disparity and reliability map starting from the left boundary to up to the right boundary, the first pixel, where the pixel which fulfills a valid disparity and a certain texture level is located, is defined as a starting point. The last point of the same condition is defined as an end point (shown in left hand images of Fig. 8c). For right view, the starting-/end points are both derived by the disparity (shown in the higher right image of Fig. 8c). The estimated disparity map using this method is shown in the lower right of Fig. 8c.

Illumination Reticles: To support arbitrary scenes, one idea is to modify the Helmholtz stereoscopic setup and introduce an aperture to the light source. By matching the size and shape of sensor and illumination aperture, both camera and illumination have same field of view which can be a definition of boundary for generic scenes. Figure 8d shows the rectangular reticle pattern installed in between an object lens, and images with projected vertical lines. Subsidiary, a pseudo camera aperture pattern is overlying by a dotted line. Illumination reticle and camera aperture clarify the boundary condition for integration in each line. A projected light for left view defines a boundary condition on the left-hand, and corresponding boundary on the right-hand is defined by pseudo camera aperture pattern. For the right view, it is the other way around. The disparity of

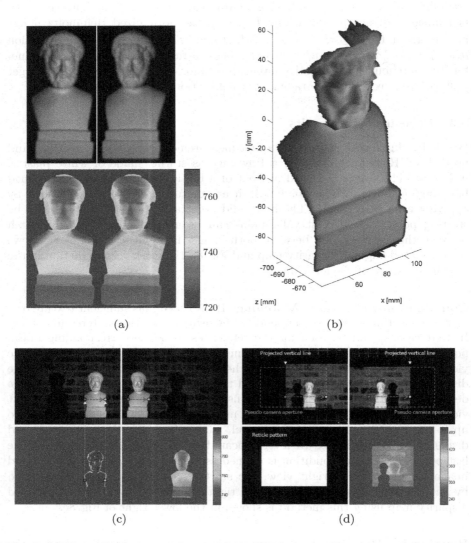

Fig. 8. (a) Normalized reciprocal image pair of Pythagoras plaster statue (above) and estimated pixel disparities of Pythagoras statue (below). The distance to the object is approx. 70 cm at a baseline of 19 cm, a pixel size of 4.4 um and f = 12 mm. (b) Surface mesh reconstruction of Pythagoras statue. (c) Combination with stereo matching, initial condition is determined by disparity map of left view (lower left). Estimated disparity map is on the below right. The distance to the object is approx. 70 cm at a baseline of 21 cm. (d) Rectangular pattern projected by a reticle on light source. Initial condition is defined by pseudo camera aperture and projected reticle patterns. Estimated disparity map is on the below right. The distance to the object and that to the background at a baseline of 21 cm are approx. 130 cm and 190 cm respectively.

background and foreground can be estimated together, however, some artifacts are visible in the disparity map (shown in the lower right of Fig. 8d.). The reason for the occlusion artifacts is explained in Sect. 2.5.

4   Conclusion

In this paper, our interest is to discuss the limits and principal problems of perspective Helmholtz stereopsis, in particular for challenging border cases such as no-texture, occlusion and stable boundary conditions for general scenes, e.g. a plain white unbounded wall or surface with specular reflections. As Helmholtz stereopsis is based on a PDE, boundary condition and noise propagation are fundamental key issues. We have extended Helmholtz stereopsis to the perspective imaging case and proposed a solution approach of the resulting differential equation based on energy conservation. By introducing an illumination aperture we are able to provide stable boundary conditions for unbounded surfaces to capture the depth profile of the scene.

The disparity estimation is robust with respect to depth discontinuities and object occlusion. However, an open problem is the visibility ordering problem in case of occlusion. The shadow cast by a occluding object may cause a change of object order between reciprocal image pairs. Without additional assumptions to match corresponding object segments, this leads to disparity mismatches. The fusion with stereo matching is one possible approach to obtain stable boundary conditions.

In the shown examples we only utilized the Helmholtz conditions and did not impose any regularizing constraints on the surface. When texture is present and smoothness assumptions can be imposed on the surface, fusion approaches such as proposed by Zickler [4] are preferable. Regularization may also help to solve issues with respect to occlusion order.

Helmholtz stereopsis is well suited for combination with structured light or fringe projection methods. Error propagation due to imaging noise and calibration errors may be reduced by using an illumination grating for scene segmentation and using partial integration for depth recovery. While structured light provides a high level of depth accuracy, its depth resolution is limited by the resolution capabilities of the pattern projector. Combining Helmholtz stereopsis with structured light allows to maintain a defined depth accuracy at a depth resolution close to the resolution limit of the imaging device.

References

1. Gorthi, S.S., Rastogi, P.: Fringe projection techniques: whither we are? Optics Lasers Eng. **48**(IMAC-REVIEW-2009-001), pp. 133–140 (2010)
2. Geng, J.: Structured-light 3D surface imaging: a tutorial. Adv. Optics Photonics **3**(2), 128–160 (2011)

3. Magda, S., Kriegman, D., Zickler, T., Belhumeur, P.N.: Beyond lambert: reconstructing surfaces with arbitrary BRDFS. In: Proceedings Eighth IEEE International Conference on Computer Vision, ICCV 2001, vol. 2, pp. 391–398. IEEE (2001)

4. Zickler, T.E., Ho, J., Kriegman, D., Ponce, J., Belhumeur, P.N.: Binocular Helmholtz stereopsis. In: Proceedings Ninth IEEE International Conference on Computer Vision,pp. 1411–1417. IEEE (2003)

5. Tu, P., Mendonça, P.R.: Surface reconstruction via Helmholtz reciprocity with a single image pair. In: Proceedings 2003 IEEE Computer Society Conference on Computer Vision and Pattern Recognition, vol. 1, pp. I-541. IEEE (2003)

6. Guillemaut, J.Y., Drbohlav, O., Sara, R., Illingworth, J.: Helmholtz stereopsis on rough and strongly textured surfaces. In: Proceedings 2nd International Symposium on 3D Data Processing, Visualization and Transmission, 3DPVT 2004, pp. 10–17. IEEE (2004)

7. Weinmann, M., Ruiters, R., Osep, A., Schwartz, C., Klein, R.: Fusing structured light consistency and Helmholtz normals for 3D reconstruction. ACM Trans. Graph. 24, 536–543 (2005)

8. Tu, P., Mendonça, P.R., Ross, J., Miller, J.: Surface registration with a Helmholtz reciprocity image pair. In: IEEE Workshop on Color and Photometric Methods in Computer Vision, vol. 7. Citeseer (2003)

9. Delaunoy, A., Prados, E., Belhumeur, P.N.: Towards full 3D Helmholtz stereovision algorithms. In: Kimmel, R., Klette, R., Sugimoto, A. (eds.) ACCV 2010. LNCS, vol. 6492, pp. 39–52. Springer, Heidelberg (2011). doi:10.1007/978-3-642-19315-6_4

10. Pharr, M., Humphreys, G.: Physically Based Rendering: From Theory to Implementation. Morgan Kaufmann, San Francisco (2010)

11. Cook, R.L., Torrance, K.E.: A reflectance model for computer graphics. ACM Trans. Graph. 1(1), 7–24 (1982)

12. Jankó, Z., Drbohlav, O., Sara, R.: Radiometric calibration of a Helmholtz stereo rig. In: Proceedings of the 2004 IEEE Computer Society Conference on Computer Vision and Pattern Recognition, CVPR 2004, vol. 1, pp. 166–171. IEEE (2004)

Projective Bundle Adjustment from Arbitrary Initialization Using the Variable Projection Method

Je Hyeong Hong[1(✉)], Christopher Zach[2], Andrew Fitzgibbon[3],
and Roberto Cipolla[1]

[1] University of Cambridge, Cambridge, UK
{jhh37,rc10001}@cam.ac.uk
[2] Toshiba Research Europe, Cambridge, UK
christopher.m.zach@gmail.com
[3] Microsoft, Cambridge, UK
awf@microsoft.com

Abstract. Bundle adjustment is used in structure-from-motion pipelines as final refinement stage requiring a sufficiently good initialization to reach a useful local mininum. Starting from an arbitrary initialization almost always gets trapped in a poor minimum. In this work we aim to obtain an initialization-free approach which returns global minima from a large proportion of purely random starting points. Our key inspiration lies in the success of the Variable Projection (VarPro) method for affine factorization problems, which have close to 100 % chance of reaching a global minimum from random initialization. We find empirically that this desirable behaviour does not directly carry over to the projective case, and we consequently design and evaluate strategies to overcome this limitation. Also, by unifying the affine and the projective camera settings, we obtain numerically better conditioned reformulations of original bundle adjustment algorithms.

Keywords: Projective bundle adjustment · Variable Projection · Nonlinear least squares

1 Introduction

Standard structure from motion (SfM) approaches are typically multi-stage pipelines comprising of feature matching or tracking, initial structure and camera estimation, and final nonlinear refinement stages. While feature matching and tracking and the nonlinear refinement stage have well-established gold standard implementations (most notably matching using SIFT features, tracking via Lucas-Kanade and nonlinear refinement via Levenberg-Marquardt), no elegant

---

J.H. Hong and R. Cipolla—Much of the work was done while the first author was an intern at Toshiba Research Europe.

B. Leibe et al. (Eds.): ECCV 2016, Part I, LNCS 9905, pp. 477–493, 2016.
DOI: 10.1007/978-3-319-46448-0_29

 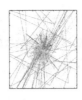 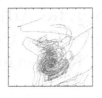

(a) Observed tracks   (b) Initial (377.29)   (c) Best affine (9.38)   (d) Best proj. (0.84)

Fig. 1. Visualization of the Di2 (see Table 7) tracks recovered using our two-stage meta-algorithms. In each run, each meta-algorithm is initialized from random camera poses and points (Fig. 1b). In the first stage, it performs affine bundle adjustment using either a Linear or Nonlinear VarPro-based algorithms, reaching the best affine optimum (Fig. 1c) in 91 % of all runs. The outputs are then used to initialize projective bundle adjustment. Although Di2 has strong perspective effects, our recommended meta-algorithms (TSMA1 and TSMA2) both reach the best projective optimum (Fig. 1d) in 90–98 % of all runs.

and generally accepted framework for estimating the initial poses and 3D structure from feature tracks is known. Even when one has a sensible starting point (initial 3D reconstruction) available, accumulated drift, undetected loop closures, etc., require a large basin of convergence for bundle adjustment to succeed. The essence of this work is widening the convergence basin of bundle adjustment thereby improving SfM systems.

If an affine or weak perspective camera model is given (or assumed), determining pose and 3D structure amounts to solving a matrix factorization problem, which is an easy task if all points are visible in every image. If the visibility pattern is sparse and structured as induced by feature tracking, matrix factorization algorithms employing the Variable Projection (VarPro) method are highly successful (i.e. return a global optimum in a large fraction of runs) even when the poses and the 3D structure are initialized arbitrarily [10,17]. Thus, the initial SfM computation can be entirely bypassed in the affine case. One obvious question is whether this is also true when using a pinhole camera model. This the main motivation of this work.

Formally, we are interested in finding global minimizers of the following nonlinear least squares projective bundle adjustment problem

$$\min_{\{P_i\}\{\tilde{\mathbf{x}}_j\}} \sum_{\{i,j\}\in\Omega} \|\boldsymbol{\pi}\left(P_i\tilde{\mathbf{x}}_j\right) - \tilde{\mathbf{m}}_{ij}\|_2^2 \tag{1}$$

without requiring good initial values for the unknowns. In (1) the unknowns are as follows: $P_i \in \mathbb{R}^{3\times4}$ is the projective camera matrix for frame i and $\tilde{\mathbf{x}}_j \in \mathbb{R}^4$ is the homogeneous vector of coordinates of point j. $\tilde{\mathbf{m}}_{ij} \in \mathbb{R}^2$ is the observed projection of point j in frame i. Ω denotes a set of visible observations and $\boldsymbol{\pi}\left(\cdot\right)$ is the perspective division such that $\boldsymbol{\pi}([x,y,z]^\top) := [x/z, y/z]^\top$. This division introduces nonlinearity to the objective, and thus we can interpret (1) as a nonlinear matrix factorization problem.

Our quest to solve (1) directly without the help of an initial structure and motion estimation step leads to the following contributions:

- **Extension of Ruhe and Wedin algorithms:** we extend the separable non-linear least squares algorithms in [19] to apply to nonseparable problems such as (1).
- **Unification of affine and projective cases:** we unify affine and projective bundle adjustment as special cases of a more general problem class. As a byproduct we obtain numerically better conditioned formulations for each of the special cases.
- **Simple two-stage meta-algorithms:** we provide numerical experiments to identify the method yielding the highest success rate overall on real and synthetic datasets. We conclude that each of two winning methods is a Variable Projection (VarPro) method-based two-stage approach, which uses either a traditional or proposed numerically stable affine bundle adjustment algorithm followed by the proposed projective bundle adjustment algorithm.

Conversely, there are limitations of this work: the scope is confined to the L^2-norm projective formulation, and consequently we may encounter new challenges when incoporating robust kernel techniques and/or extending this work to the calibrated case, which is more frequently used in practice. We discuss the iteration complexity of our proposed algorithms but do not include timing measurements as we believe meaningful run-time figures require comparable implementations (and our code in [11] is inefficient as it has not incorporated the speed-up tricks mentioned in [2,4,10]).

1.1   Related Work

In this section we briefly summarize relevant literature. The first seminal work dates back to Wiberg [24], who investigated the task of matrix factorization under missing data and whose name is today associated with the most successful method to solve this problem. The method is based on the principle of Variable Projection, which rewrites the objective in terms of a reduced set of unknowns by "minimizing out" the remaining ones. This approach is in particular promising, when the dependencies between unknowns forms a bipartite graph (which is the case in the structure from motion setting). In several works it has been experimentally verified that the Wiberg/VarPro method is far superior to naive joint optimization for matrix factorization problems (e.g. [5,10,17]), which explains the interest in the more difficult to implement VarPro methods.

In computer vision the connection between matrix factorization and affine structure from motion—but without missing data—was explored in [22]. Solving projective structure from motion via matrix factorization is more difficult, and it requires iterative methods even in the fully observed case (e.g. [21]). One step towards the application of VarPro methods in projective problems is the Nonlinear VarPro extension explored by Strelow [20], which we take as a starting point for our implementation.

All methods mentioned so far are ideally designed not to require a careful initialization for the unknown cameras and 3D structure (or matrix factors in the general case), and VarPro-derived methods work well for matrix factorization tasks even with random values as initializer. In SfM applications strong geometric constraints (we refer to [9] for a comprehensive treatment) can be used to determine sensible initial cameras and 3D structure. This initialization is subsequently used as starting point for nonlinear least-squares optimization (termed bundle adjustment) over all unknowns (see [23] for a review). Determining a good starting point for bundle adjustment is a non-trivial problem and expensive to solve in the general case. Compared to two-view and three-view geometry and to full-scale bundle adjustment this step of finding a good initializer also lacks in theoretical understanding. Hence, it is beneficial to bypass this stage altogether and investigate initialization-free methods for bundle adjustment.

2   Known Methods for Bivariate Least-Squares Optimization

Bivariate least-squares solves

$$\min_{\mathbf{u},\mathbf{v}} \|\boldsymbol{\varepsilon}(\mathbf{u},\mathbf{v})\|_2^2 \tag{2}$$

where $\mathbf{u}$ and $\mathbf{v}$ are sets of model parameters and $\boldsymbol{\varepsilon}$ is the residual vector. We can solve this by using various methods, namely Joint optimization, Variable Projection (Linear [6] and Nonlinear VarPro [20]) and Alternating least-squares (ALS), which is equivalent to RW3 (see Sects. 2.2 and 3).

The key to implementing all these methods is the use of the Levenberg-Marquardt (LM) algorithm [13,15], which is a widely used trust-region strategy.

The Levenberg-Marquardt algorithm (LM)

LM [13,15] is an extension of the Gauss-Newton algorithm, which minimizes $\|\boldsymbol{\varepsilon}(\mathbf{x})\|_2^2$ by iteratively solving its linearization and updating $\mathbf{x}$ accordingly. At each iteration, the Gauss-Newton update $\boldsymbol{\Delta}\mathbf{x}$ is the solution of the linearized problem

$$\arg\min_{\boldsymbol{\Delta}\mathbf{x}} \|\boldsymbol{\varepsilon}(\mathbf{x}) + \mathbf{J}(\mathbf{x})\boldsymbol{\Delta}\mathbf{x}\|_2^2 \tag{3}$$

where $\mathbf{x}$ denotes the parameter values from the previous iteration and $\mathbf{J}(\mathbf{x}) := \partial\boldsymbol{\varepsilon}(\mathbf{x})/\partial\mathbf{x}$. This step is likely to lead to a lower objective if the local cost surface about $\mathbf{x}$ resembles a quadratic model, but otherwise may lead to a higher objective. To overcome this, LM incorporates a regularizer to control the step size and find the augmented solution

$$\arg\min_{\boldsymbol{\Delta}\mathbf{x}} \|\boldsymbol{\varepsilon}(\mathbf{x}) + \mathbf{J}(\mathbf{x})\boldsymbol{\Delta}\mathbf{x}\|_2^2 + \lambda\|\boldsymbol{\Delta}\mathbf{x}\|_2^2 \tag{4}$$

where λ is known as the damping factor which we tune to decrease the cost. This parameter indicates the size of the trust region — the smaller the value of λ, the larger the region that can be "trusted" as quadratic.

2.1   Joint Optimization

Joint optimization solves for all parameters simultaneously. This is achieved by stacking into the vector $\mathbf{x} = [\mathbf{u}; \mathbf{v}]$ and using a Newton-like solver such as LM. In general, the update at iteration k is

$$[\mathbf{u}_{k+1}; \mathbf{v}_{k+1}] = \mathbf{x}_{k+1} = \mathbf{x}_k - (\mathtt{H}(\mathbf{x}_k) + \lambda \mathtt{I})^{-1} \mathbf{g}(\mathbf{x}_k) \tag{5}$$

where $\mathtt{H}(\mathbf{x}_k)$ is the Hessian (or its approximation) of $\|\varepsilon(\mathbf{x})\|_2^2$ at $\mathbf{x}_k$, $\mathbf{g}(\mathbf{x}_k)$ is the gradient $\nabla_\mathbf{x}\|\varepsilon(\mathbf{x}_k)\|_2^2$ and λ is the damping factor. A widely used Hessian approximation, which is also used by LM (and throughout this paper), is the Gauss-Newton matrix $2\mathtt{J}(\mathbf{x}_k)^\top \mathtt{J}(\mathbf{x}_k)$ where $\mathtt{J}(\mathbf{x}_k) := \partial \varepsilon(\mathbf{x}_k)/\partial \mathbf{x}$.

2.2   Linear Variable Projection (Linear VarPro)

Linear VarPro [6] is an approach for solving separable nonlinear least-squares [19], which is a subset of bivariate optimization problems and has a property that the residual vector is linear in at least one of two variables, e.g.

$$\min_{\mathbf{u},\mathbf{v}} \|\varepsilon(\mathbf{u}, \mathbf{v})\|_2^2 = \min_{\mathbf{u},\mathbf{v}} \|\mathtt{A}(\mathbf{u})\mathbf{v} - \mathbf{b}\|_2^2 \tag{6}$$

where $\mathbf{u}$ and $\mathbf{v}$ are sets of model parameters, ε is the residual vector, $\mathtt{A}(\mathbf{u})$ is a linear operator which depends on $\mathbf{u}$ and $\mathbf{b}$ is a constant vector. Since ε is linear in $\mathbf{v}$, we have a direct solution for $\mathbf{v}$ that minimizes (6) given $\mathbf{u}$ which we call

$$\mathbf{v}^*(\mathbf{u}) := \arg\min_{\mathbf{v}} \|\mathtt{A}(\mathbf{u})\mathbf{v} - \mathbf{b}\|_2^2 = \mathtt{A}^\dagger(\mathbf{u})\mathbf{b}. \tag{7}$$

Substituting $\mathbf{v}^*(\mathbf{u})$ for $\mathbf{v}$ in (6) yields

$$\min_{\mathbf{u}} \|\varepsilon^*(\mathbf{u})\|_2^2 := \min_{\mathbf{u}} \|\mathtt{A}(\mathbf{u})\mathbf{v}^*(\mathbf{u}) - \mathbf{b}\|_2^2 = \min_{\mathbf{u},\mathbf{v}} \| \left(\mathtt{A}(\mathbf{u})\mathtt{A}^\dagger(\mathbf{u}) - \mathtt{I}\right) \mathbf{b}\|_2^2 \tag{8}$$

which is a nonlinear reduced problem in $\mathbf{u}$ that can be solved using LM.

In [7], the authors claim that this reduced objective is almost always better conditioned than the original one. Although no formal proof is provided, we can find empirical evidence in matrix factorization [10].

Deriving the Jacobian of the Reduced Problem. First, we write the Jacobian of the original problem (6) as

$$\mathtt{J}(\mathbf{u}, \mathbf{v}) := \left[\frac{\partial \varepsilon(\mathbf{u}, \mathbf{v})}{\partial \mathbf{u}} \; \frac{\partial \varepsilon(\mathbf{u}, \mathbf{v})}{\partial \mathbf{v}} \right] = \left[\frac{\partial \varepsilon(\mathbf{u}, \mathbf{v})}{\partial \mathbf{u}} \; \mathtt{A}(\mathbf{u}) \right] =: \left[\mathtt{J}_\mathbf{u}(\mathbf{u}, \mathbf{v}) \; \mathtt{J}_\mathbf{v}(\mathbf{u}) \right]. \tag{9}$$

We then express (using the chain rule) the Jacobian of the reduced problem (8) as

$$\mathtt{J}^*(\mathbf{u}) := \frac{d\varepsilon^*(\mathbf{u})}{d\mathbf{u}} = \frac{d\varepsilon(\mathbf{u}, \mathbf{v}^*(\mathbf{u}))}{d\mathbf{u}} = \frac{\partial \varepsilon(\mathbf{u}, \mathbf{v}^*(\mathbf{u}))}{\partial \mathbf{u}} + \frac{\partial \varepsilon(\mathbf{u}, \mathbf{v}^*(\mathbf{u}))}{\partial \mathbf{v}} \frac{d\mathbf{v}^*(\mathbf{u})}{d\mathbf{u}} \tag{10}$$

$$= \mathtt{J}_\mathbf{u}(\mathbf{u}, \mathbf{v}^*(\mathbf{u})) + \mathtt{J}_\mathbf{v}(\mathbf{u})\frac{d}{d\mathbf{u}} \left[\mathtt{A}(\mathbf{u})^\dagger \mathbf{b}\right] \tag{11}$$

$$= \mathtt{J}_\mathbf{u}(\mathbf{u}, \mathbf{v}^*(\mathbf{u})) + \mathtt{J}_\mathbf{v}(\mathbf{u})\frac{d}{d\mathbf{u}} \left[\mathtt{J}_\mathbf{v}(\mathbf{u})^\dagger\right] \mathbf{b}. \tag{12}$$

If $\mathbf{v}^*(\mathbf{u})$ is differentiable, (12) is analytically tractable. (see [11].)

Ruhe and Wedin Algorithms for Linear VarPro. In [19], Ruhe and Wedin proposed three Newton-like algorithms each of which uses an approximation to the Hessian. The first algorithm, RW1, simply uses Gauss-Newton ($2J^\top J$). The second algorithm, RW2, approximates $d\mathbf{v}^*(\mathbf{u})/d\mathbf{u}$ in the Jacobian such that the approximated Gauss-Newton matrix is orthogonal to the column space of $J_\mathbf{v}(\mathbf{u})$. Finally, RW3 assumes independence of the two variables by setting $d\mathbf{v}^*(\mathbf{u})/d\mathbf{u} = 0$, leading to alternation.

Although Ruhe and Wedin did not associate any trust region strategy with the above algorithms, we can easily incorporate this by using LM.

2.3   Nonlinear Variable Projection (Nonlinear VarPro)

The approach in Sect. 2.2 can be applied only to separable nonlinear least-squares, where the objective is bivariate and linear in at least one of two variables. Strelow [20] extended this to apply to nonseparable problems, which can be expressed as

$$\min_{\mathbf{u},\mathbf{v}} \|\boldsymbol{\varepsilon}(\mathbf{u},\mathbf{v})\|_2^2 = \min_{\mathbf{u},\mathbf{v}} \|\mathbf{f}(\mathbf{u},\mathbf{v}) - \mathbf{b}\|_2^2. \tag{13}$$

Similar to Sect. 2.2, we wish to find $\mathbf{v}^*(\mathbf{u}) := \arg\min_\mathbf{v} \|\boldsymbol{\varepsilon}(\mathbf{u},\mathbf{v})\|_2^2$ and solve

$$\min_{\mathbf{u}} \|\boldsymbol{\varepsilon}^*(\mathbf{u})\|_2^2 := \min_{\mathbf{u}} \|\boldsymbol{\varepsilon}(\mathbf{u},\mathbf{v}^*(\mathbf{u}))\|_2^2. \tag{14}$$

In this case, $\mathbf{v}^*(\mathbf{u})$ may not have a closed form solution as the residual vector is nonlinear in both $\mathbf{u}$ and $\mathbf{v}$. Instead, we apply a second-order iterative solver (e.g. LM) to approximately solve $\arg\min_\mathbf{v} \|\boldsymbol{\varepsilon}(\mathbf{u},\mathbf{v})\|_2^2$ and store the final solution in $\hat{\mathbf{v}}_0^*$.

Now, assuming that $\hat{\mathbf{v}}_0^*$ has converged, we define $\hat{\mathbf{v}}^*(\mathbf{u})$ as the quantity obtained by performing one additional Gauss-Newton iteration over $\mathbf{v}$ from $(\mathbf{u}, \hat{\mathbf{v}}_0^*)$. i.e.

$$\hat{\mathbf{v}}^*(\mathbf{u}) := \hat{\mathbf{v}}_0^* + \underbrace{\arg\min_{\boldsymbol{\Delta}\mathbf{v}} \|\boldsymbol{\varepsilon}(\mathbf{u},\hat{\mathbf{v}}_0^*) + J_\mathbf{v}(\mathbf{u},\hat{\mathbf{v}}_0^*)\boldsymbol{\Delta}\mathbf{v}\|_2^2}_{\text{Additional Gauss-Newton step}} = \hat{\mathbf{v}}_0^* - J_\mathbf{v}(\mathbf{u},\hat{\mathbf{v}}_0^*)^\dagger \boldsymbol{\varepsilon}(\mathbf{u},\hat{\mathbf{v}}_0^*).$$

$$\tag{15}$$

Above expression implicitly assumes that $\boldsymbol{\varepsilon}(\mathbf{u},\mathbf{v})$ is locally linear in $\mathbf{v}$ about $\boldsymbol{\varepsilon}(\mathbf{u},\hat{\mathbf{v}}_0^*)$. This approximation allows us to estimate $d\mathbf{v}^*(\mathbf{u})/d\mathbf{u}$ by computing $d\hat{\mathbf{v}}^*(\mathbf{u})/d\mathbf{u}$:

$$\frac{d\mathbf{v}^*(\mathbf{u})}{d\mathbf{u}} \approx \frac{d\hat{\mathbf{v}}^*(\mathbf{u})}{d\mathbf{u}} = -\frac{\partial}{\partial\mathbf{u}}[J_\mathbf{v}(\mathbf{u},\hat{\mathbf{v}}_0^*)^\dagger \boldsymbol{\varepsilon}(\mathbf{u},\hat{\mathbf{v}}_0^*)]. \tag{16}$$

Combining the results of (10) and (16) yields

$$\tilde{J}^*(\mathbf{u}) := J_\mathbf{u}(\mathbf{u},\hat{\mathbf{v}}_0^*) - J_\mathbf{v}(\mathbf{u},\hat{\mathbf{v}}_0^*)\frac{\partial}{\partial\mathbf{u}}\left[J_\mathbf{v}(\mathbf{u},\hat{\mathbf{v}}_0^*)^\dagger \boldsymbol{\varepsilon}(\mathbf{u},\hat{\mathbf{v}}_0^*)\right] \tag{17}$$

$$= \left(I - J_\mathbf{v}(\mathbf{u},\hat{\mathbf{v}}_0^*)J_\mathbf{v}(\mathbf{u},\hat{\mathbf{v}}_0^*)^\dagger\right) J_\mathbf{u}(\mathbf{u},\hat{\mathbf{v}}_0^*)$$

$$- J_\mathbf{v}(\mathbf{u},\hat{\mathbf{v}}_0^*)\frac{\partial}{\partial\mathbf{u}}\left[J_\mathbf{v}(\mathbf{u},\hat{\mathbf{v}}_0^*)^\dagger\right] \boldsymbol{\varepsilon}(\mathbf{u},\hat{\mathbf{v}}_0^*) \tag{18}$$

where $\tilde{J}^*(\mathbf{u})$ is the approximate Jacobian used by Nonlinear VarPro. This expression can be further simplified using the differentiation rule for matrix pseudo-inverses [6].

In summary, one iteration of Nonlinear VarPro amounts to solving one inner minimization over $\mathbf{v}$ given $\mathbf{u}$, which outputs $\hat{\mathbf{v}}_0^* \approx \mathbf{v}^*(\mathbf{u})$, followed by one outer minimization over $\mathbf{u}$, which is achieved by linearizing the residual vector in $\mathbf{v}$ about $\varepsilon(\mathbf{u}, \hat{\mathbf{v}}_0^*)$.

For separable problems, the residual vector is always linear in $\mathbf{v}$, and therefore (18) becomes the exact Jacobian.

3 Ruhe and Wedin Algorithms for Nonlinear VarPro

We acquire the nonlinear extensions of the original Ruhe and Wedin algorithms [19] as follows: since original RW1 applies the Gauss-Newton algorithm on the reduced problem (8), we propose that Nonlinear RW1 employs the Gauss-Newton algorithm using the Jacobian derived in (18) (This is essentially the same as Strelow's General Wiberg [20]). Original RW2 projects the exact Jacobian of original RW1 to the left nullspace of $J_\mathbf{v}(\mathbf{u})$, resulting in an approximated Gauss-Newton matrix. For Nonlinear RW2, we project the Jacobian of Nonlinear RW1 to the left nullspace of $J_\mathbf{v}(\mathbf{u}, \hat{\mathbf{v}}_0^*)$, which is equivalent to discarding the latter term of (18). Lastly, original RW3 assumes $\mathbf{u}$ and $\mathbf{v}$ to be independent. For the nonlinear case, this translates to $d\hat{\mathbf{v}}^*(\mathbf{u})/d\mathbf{u} = 0$, yielding $J_\mathbf{v}(\mathbf{u}, \hat{\mathbf{v}}_0^*)$ as the approximate Jacobian of Nonlinear RW3 (Table 2.3).

Table 1. A list of approximate Jacobians used by our nonlinear extension of the Ruhe and Wedin algorithms. Nonlinear RW1 applies the Gauss-Newton (GN) algorithm on the reduced problem (14), Nonlinear RW2 makes an approximation to the Jacobian as described in Sect. 3 and Nonlinear RW3 makes a further approximation which turns it into alternation. $\hat{\mathbf{v}}_0^*$ is obtained using a second-order iterative solver (see Sect. 2.3).

Algorithm	Approximate Jacobian used
Nonlinear RW3 (ALS)	$J_{RW3} := J_\mathbf{u}(\mathbf{u}, \hat{\mathbf{v}}_0^*)$
Nonlinear RW2	$J_{RW2} := J_{RW3} - J_\mathbf{v}(\mathbf{u}, \hat{\mathbf{v}}_0^*)J_\mathbf{v}(\mathbf{u}, \hat{\mathbf{v}}_0^*)^\dagger J_\mathbf{u}(\mathbf{u}, \hat{\mathbf{v}}_0^*)$
Nonlinear RW1 (GN)	$J_{RW1} := J_{RW2} - J_\mathbf{v}(\mathbf{u}, \hat{\mathbf{v}}_0^*)\frac{\partial}{\partial \mathbf{u}}\left[J_\mathbf{v}(\mathbf{u}, \hat{\mathbf{v}}_0^*)^\dagger\right]\varepsilon(\mathbf{u}, \hat{\mathbf{v}}_0^*)$

3.1 The Sparsity of the Hessian Approximations

Okatani et al. [17] and Strelow [20] pointed out structural similarity between the Schur complement reduced system for Joint optimization and Linear VarPro. Analysing the exact differences between the two methods is a research question on its own, and therefore in this paper we just confirm numerically that the Hessian approximations of both RW1 and RW2 (linear and nonlinear) have the same sparsity pattern but are not equal to the Schur complement reduced system for Gauss-Newton based Joint optimization. Furthermore, we found (through code implementation) that the iteration complexity of our proposed nonlinear extensions is similar (same for RW2, higher for RW1) to standard bundle adjustment with embedded point iterations [12]. Hence, one LM iteration of both standard bundle adjustment and our method will take roughly similar amount of time.

4   A Unified Notation for Uncalibrated Camera Models

In this section, we present a unified notation for uncalibrated (affine and projective) cameras which allows a modularized compilation of bundle adjustment algorithms.

Affine and projective cameras are widely-used uncalibrated camera models which can be expressed in the homogeneous or the inhomogeneous form. We can incorporate both models and forms into a single camera matrix by defining

$$\mathsf{P}_i := \mathsf{P}(\mathbf{p}_i, \mathbf{q}_i, s_i, \mu_i) := \begin{bmatrix} p_{i1} & p_{i2} & p_{i3} & p_{i4} \\ p_{i5} & p_{i6} & p_{i7} & p_{i8} \\ \mu_i q_{i1} & \mu_i q_{i2} & \mu_i q_{i3} & s_i \end{bmatrix} =: \begin{bmatrix} \mathbf{p}_{i1:}^\top \\ \mathbf{p}_{i2:}^\top \\ [\mu_i \mathbf{q}_i^\top \ s_i] \end{bmatrix} \tag{19}$$

where $\mathbf{p}_i = [\mathbf{p}_{i1:}^\top, \mathbf{p}_{i2:}^\top]^\top = [p_{i1}, \cdots, p_{i8}]^\top$ and $\mathbf{q}_i = [q_{i1}, q_{i2}, q_{i3}]^\top$ are the projective camera parameters for frame i, $\mu_i \in [0,1]$ indicates the degree of "projectiveness" of frame i, and s_i is the scaling factor of the i-th camera.

Now each point is typically parametrized as

$$\tilde{\mathbf{x}}_j := \tilde{\mathbf{x}}(\mathbf{x}_j, t_j) := \begin{bmatrix} \mathbf{x}_j^\top & t_j \end{bmatrix} := \begin{bmatrix} x_{j1} & x_{j2} & x_{j3} & t_j \end{bmatrix}^\top \tag{20}$$

Table 2. A summary of uncalibrated camera models using the unified notation. $\mathsf{H} \in \mathbb{R}^{4 \times 4}$ is an arbitrary invertible matrix, and $\mathsf{A} \in \mathbb{R}^{4 \times 4}$ is an arbitrary invertible matrix with the last row set to $[0, 0, 0, 1]$. $\alpha_i, \beta_j \in \mathbb{R}$ is an arbitrary scale factor.

Form	Variable	Affine model ($\mu_i = 0$)	Projective model ($\mu_i = 1$)
Homogeneous	Camera (P_i)	$\mathsf{P}(\mathbf{p}_i, 0, s_i, 0)$	$\mathsf{P}(\mathbf{p}_i, \mathbf{q}_i, s_i, 1)$
	Point ($\tilde{\mathbf{x}}_j$)	$\tilde{\mathbf{x}}(\mathbf{x}_j, t_j)$	$\tilde{\mathbf{x}}(\mathbf{x}_j, t_j)$
	Inverse depth	$s_i t_j$	$\mathbf{q}_i^\top \mathbf{x}_j + s_i t_j$
	Model property	Nonlinear in P_i and $\tilde{\mathbf{x}}_j$	
	Gauge freedom	$\mathsf{P}_i \tilde{\mathbf{x}}_j = (\mathsf{P}_i \mathsf{H})(\mathsf{H}^{-1} \tilde{\mathbf{x}}_j)$	
	Scale freedom	$\boldsymbol{\pi}(\mathsf{P}_i, \tilde{\mathbf{x}}_j) = \boldsymbol{\pi}(\alpha_i \mathsf{P}_i, \beta_j \mathbf{x}_j)$	
Inhomogeneous	Camera (P_i)	$\mathsf{P}(\mathbf{p}_i, 0, 1, 0)$	$\mathsf{P}(\mathbf{p}_i, \mathbf{q}_i, 1, 1)$
	Point ($\tilde{\mathbf{x}}_j$)	$\tilde{\mathbf{x}}(\mathbf{x}_j, 1)$	$\tilde{\mathbf{x}}(\mathbf{x}_j, 1))$
	Inverse depth	1	$\mathbf{q}_i^\top \mathbf{x}_j + 1$
	Model property	linear in P_i and $\tilde{\mathbf{x}}_j$	nonlinear in P_i and $\tilde{\mathbf{x}}_j$
	Gauge freedom	$\mathsf{P}_i \tilde{\mathbf{x}}_j = (\mathsf{P}_i \mathsf{A})(\mathsf{A}^{-1} \tilde{\mathbf{x}}_j)$	$\mathsf{P}_i \tilde{\mathbf{x}}_j = (\mathsf{P}_i \mathsf{H})(\mathsf{H}^{-1} \tilde{\mathbf{x}}_j)$
	Scale freedom	None	

where $\mathbf{x}_j = [x_{j1}, x_{j2}, x_{j3}]^\top$ is the vector of unscaled inhomogeneous coordinates of point j and and $\tilde{\mathbf{x}}_j$ is the vector of homogeneous coordinates of point j. (19) and (20) lead to a unified projection function

$$\boldsymbol{\pi}_{ij} := \boldsymbol{\pi}(\mathrm{P}_i, \tilde{\mathbf{x}}_j) = \boldsymbol{\pi}(\mathrm{P}(\mathbf{p}_i, \mathbf{q}_i, s_i, \mu_i), \tilde{\mathbf{x}}(\mathbf{x}_j, t_j)) = \frac{1}{\mu_i \mathbf{q}_i^\top \mathbf{x}_j + s_i t_j} \begin{bmatrix} \mathbf{p}_{i1:}^\top \tilde{\mathbf{x}}_j \\ \mathbf{p}_{i2:}^\top \tilde{\mathbf{x}}_j \end{bmatrix}. \quad (21)$$

We show in Table 2 that the affine and the projective models (in both homogeneous and inhomogeneous forms) are specific instances of the unified model described above.

5 Compilation of Affine/projective Bundle Adjustment Algorithms

In this section, we present the building blocks of our bundle adjustment algorithms for uncalibrated cameras which stem from Sects. 2, 3 and 4. To simplify notations, we stack the variables introduced in Sect. 4 across all cameras or points by omitting the corresponding subscript, e.g. $\mathbf{p} = [\mathbf{p}_1^\top, \cdots, \mathbf{p}_f^\top]^\top$ and $\mathbf{x} = [\mathbf{x}_1^\top, \cdots, \mathbf{x}_n^\top]^\top$, where f is the number of frames and n is the number of points in the dataset used. We also define $\tilde{\mathbf{p}}$ to be the collection of the camera parameters $\mathbf{p}$, $\mathbf{q}$ and $\mathbf{s}$. (Note that μ is not included.) We can now rewrite (1) as

$$\min_{\mathbf{p},\mathbf{q},\mathbf{s},\mathbf{x},\mathbf{t}} \|\varepsilon(\mathbf{p}, \mathbf{q}, \mathbf{s}, \mathbf{x}, \mathbf{t}, \mu)\|_2^2. \quad (22)$$

In this paper, we assume that μ (the projectiveness vector) is fixed during optimization. (Finding an optimal way to adjust μ at each iteration is future work.) Our algorithms first eliminate points ($\tilde{\mathbf{x}}$), generating a reduced problem over camera poses ($\tilde{\mathbf{p}}$), but we could reverse the order to eliminate poses first as described in Sect. 6.1 of [23].

5.1 Required Derivatives

We only need three types of derivatives to implement all the algorithms mentioned in Sect. 2 irrespective of the camera model used.

The first two derivatives are the Jacobian with respect to camera poses ($J_{\tilde{\mathbf{p}}}$) and the Jacobian with respect to feature points ($J_{\tilde{\mathbf{x}}}$) which are the first order derivatives of the original objective (1). These Jacobians are used by both Joint optimization and VarPro but are evaluated at different points in the parameter space — at each iteration, Joint optimization evaluates the Jacobians at $(\tilde{\mathbf{p}}, \tilde{\mathbf{x}})$ whereas Linear and Nonlinear VarPro evaluate them at $(\tilde{\mathbf{p}}, \tilde{\mathbf{x}}^*(\tilde{\mathbf{p}}))$, where $\tilde{\mathbf{x}}^*(\tilde{\mathbf{p}})$ denotes a set of feature points which locally minimizes (1) given the camera parameters $\tilde{\mathbf{p}}$ (Table 3).

The third derivative, which involves a second-order derivative of the objective, is only required by Linear and Nonlinear RW1.

Table 3. A list of derivatives required for implementing affine and projective bundle adjustment algorithms based on the methods illustrated in Sect. 2. The camera parameters ($\tilde{\mathbf{p}}$) consist of $\mathbf{p}$, $\mathbf{q}$ and $\mathbf{s}$, and the point parameters ($\tilde{\mathbf{x}}$) consist of $\mathbf{x}$ and $\mathbf{t}$. Note that the effective column size of these quantities will vary depending on the parameterization of the camera model used. The Jacobians are the first-order derivatives of $\varepsilon(\mathbf{p}, \mathbf{q}, \mathbf{s}, \mathbf{x}, \mathbf{t}, \boldsymbol{\mu})$ in (22).

Required derivatives	Affine		Projective	
	Hom.	Inhom.	Hom.	Inhom.
Jacobian w.r.t. cameras ($J_{\tilde{\mathbf{p}}}$)	$\left[\dfrac{\partial\varepsilon}{\partial\mathbf{p}} \dfrac{\partial\varepsilon}{\partial\mathbf{s}} \right]$	$\dfrac{\partial\varepsilon}{\partial\mathbf{p}}$	$\left[\dfrac{\partial\varepsilon}{\partial\mathbf{p}} \dfrac{\partial\varepsilon}{\partial\mathbf{q}} \dfrac{\partial\varepsilon}{\partial\mathbf{s}} \right]$	$\left[\dfrac{\partial\varepsilon}{\partial\mathbf{p}} \dfrac{\partial\varepsilon}{\partial\mathbf{q}} \right]$
Jacobian w.r.t. points ($J_{\tilde{\mathbf{x}}}$)	$\left[\dfrac{\partial\varepsilon}{\partial\mathbf{x}} \dfrac{\partial\varepsilon}{\partial\mathbf{t}} \right]$	$\dfrac{\partial\varepsilon}{\partial\mathbf{x}}$	$\left[\dfrac{\partial\varepsilon}{\partial\mathbf{x}} \dfrac{\partial\varepsilon}{\partial\mathbf{t}} \right]$	$\dfrac{\partial\varepsilon}{\partial\mathbf{x}}$
$\dfrac{\partial[J_{\tilde{\mathbf{x}}}^{\dagger}]\varepsilon}{\partial\tilde{\mathbf{p}}}$ (required by RW1)	$\left[\dfrac{\partial[J_{\tilde{\mathbf{x}}}^{\dagger}]}{\partial\mathbf{p}} \dfrac{\partial[J_{\tilde{\mathbf{x}}}^{\dagger}]}{\partial\mathbf{s}} \right]\varepsilon$	$\dfrac{\partial[J_{\tilde{\mathbf{x}}}^{\dagger}]\varepsilon}{\partial\mathbf{p}}$	$\left[\dfrac{\partial[J_{\tilde{\mathbf{x}}}^{\dagger}]}{\partial\mathbf{p}} \dfrac{\partial[J_{\tilde{\mathbf{x}}}^{\dagger}]}{\partial\mathbf{q}} \dfrac{\partial[J_{\tilde{\mathbf{x}}}^{\dagger}]}{\partial\mathbf{s}} \right]\varepsilon$	$\left[\dfrac{\partial[J_{\tilde{\mathbf{x}}}^{\dagger}]}{\partial\mathbf{p}} \dfrac{\partial[J_{\tilde{\mathbf{x}}}^{\dagger}]}{\partial\mathbf{q}} \right]\varepsilon$

5.2 Constraining Local Scale Freedoms in Homogeneous Camera Models

Homogeneous camera models have local scale freedoms for each camera and point (see Table 2). We need to constrain these scales appropriately for the second-order update to be numerically stable — manually fixing an entry in each camera and point (as in the inhomogeneous coordinate system) may lead to numerical instability if some points or cameras are located in radical positions.

To do this, we apply a Riemannian manifold optimization framework [1,14]. The intuition behind this is that scaling each point and each camera arbitrarily does not change the objective, and therefore, each point and each camera can be viewed as lying on the Grassmann manifold (which is a subset of the Riemannian manifold).

In essence, optimization on the Grassmann manifold can be achieved [14] by projecting each Jacobian to its tangent space, computing the second-order update of parameters on the tangent space then retracting back to the manifold by normalizing each camera and/or point. This is numerically stable since the parameters are always updated orthogonal to the current solution. Details of our implementation can be found in [11].

5.3 Constraining Gauge Freedoms for the VarPro-Based Algorithms

Unlike scale freedoms, gauge freedoms are present in all camera models listed in Sect. 4.

Our VarPro-based algorithms eliminate points such that the matrix of whole camera parameters lie on the Grassmann manifold. This means that any set of cameras which share the same column space as the current set does not change the objective. With the inhomogeneous affine camera model, the matrix of whole cameras lie on a more structured variant of the Grassmann manifold as the scales are fixed to 1.

Since homogeneous camera models require both scale and gauge freedoms to be removed simultaneously (and the Jacobians are already projected to get rid of the scale freedoms), we incorporate a technique introduced in [17] to penalize the matrix of whole cameras updating along the column space of the current matrix, and this constrains all 16 gauge freedoms. (This approach can be viewed [10] as a relaxed form of the manifold optimization framework described in Sect. 5.2.) With the inhomogeneous affine model, we manipulate this technique to prevent from overconstraining the problem, and this removes 9 out of 12 gauge freedoms. More details are included in [11].

We have not implemented a gauge-constraining technique for Joint optimization but [16] could be applied.

5.4   Remarks

Combining all the aforementioned techniques yield 16 algorithms which are listed in [11]. We use 4 of them (see Table 4) to synthesize two-stage meta algorithms in Sect. 6.

As mentioned in Sect. 2.3, Nonlinear VarPro requires iterative inner minimization over points given cameras at each iteration. Our algorithms initialize points from the closest algebraic solution obtained using the Direct Linear Transformation (DLT) method [9].

Table 4. A list of affine and projective bundle adjustment algorithms used for our two-stage meta-algorithms in Sect. 6. We compile these algorithms using the building blocks from Sect. 5.

ID	Camera	Form	Strategy	Algorithm	Constrained gauge
AHRW2P	Affine	Homogeneous	Nonlinear VarPro	RW2	16 / 16
AIRW2P	Affine	Inhomogeneous	Linear VarPro	RW2	9 / 12
PHRW1P	Projective	Homogeneous	Nonlinear VarPro	RW1	16 / 16
PHJP	Projective	Homogeneous	Joint optimization	LM	None

6   Two-Stage Meta-Algorithms for Projective Bundle Adjustment

Initially, we attempted to use the projective bundle adjustment algorithms compiled in Sect. 5 directly on the datasets listed in Tables 6 and 7. However, our preliminary investigation showed that none of these work out of the box as the Linear VarPro-based algorithms do for the inhomogeneous affine case.

To resolve this, we propose the following strategy: perform affine bundle adjustment first and then use the outputs to initialize projective bundle adjustment. This is inspired by the fact that some projective algorithms such as projective matrix factorization [9, 21] and trilinear projective bundle adjustment [20]

Table 5. A list of two-stage meta-algorithms used in our experiments.

ID	First-stage (affine) algorithm	Second-stage (projective) algorithm
TSMA1	AHRW2P	PHRW1P
TSMA2	AIRW2P	PHRW1P
TSMA3	AHRW2P	PHJP
TSMA4	AIRW2P	PHJP

Table 6. Synthetic tracks of 319 points randomly generated on a sphere of radius 10.0 viewed from 36 cameras. The cameras are equidistantly positioned and form a ring of radius d, looking down the sphere at $60°$ from the vertical axis. We employ structured visibility patterns with high missing rates to depict real tracks with occlusions and tracking failures. $\mathcal{N}(\mathbf{0}, \mathbf{I})$ noise is added.

Dataset	d	Loop closed	Missing (%)	Best affine cost	Best projective cost
S30L	30.0	Yes	77.56	2.993821	0.861392
S30	30.0	No	76.92	2.947244	0.842539
S20L	20.0	Yes	77.61	7.261506	0.862520
S20	20.0	No	76.92	7.157783	0.842511
S13L	13.0	Yes	77.61	25.100919	0.863871
S13	13.0	No	76.92	24.831476	0.844125
S12L	12.0	Yes	77.61	34.871149	0.863867
S12	12.0	No	76.92	34.730023	0.844817
S11L	11.0	Yes	77.61	55.782547	0.863274
S11	11.0	No	76.92	56.946272	0.845271
S10.5L	10.5	Yes	77.61	80.700734	0.862545
S10.5	10.5	No	76.92	85.970046	0.844771

initialize all camera depths to 1, which is equivalent to employing the affine camera model. The key difference between our strategy and the aforementioned methods is that our approach enforces the affine model throughout the first stage whereas other methods can switch to the projective model straight after initialization. Since our strategy essentially places a prior on the affine model, it is important to check how this performs on strong perspective scenes.

For the first (affine) stage, we choose AIRW2P (Affine Inhomogeneous RW2 with manifold Projection) and AHRW2P (Affine Homogeneous RW2 with manifold Projection). We opt for the VarPro-based algorithms, which have large convergence basins for the affine case. We drop the RW1 series as they perform substantially slower than the RW2 series with comparable success rates. (Similar phenomenon is reported in [8,10].)

For the second (projective) stage, we choose PHRW1P (Projective Homogeneous RW1 with manifold Projection) and PHJP (Projective Homogeneous Joint optimization with manifold Projection). We drop PHRW2P after observing its poor performance on some of the datasets used. None of the inhomogeneous projective algorithms are selected due to numerical stability issues (see Sect. 5.2).

7 Experiments

All experiments were carried out on a workstation with 2.2 GHz Intel Xeon E5-2660 processor and 32 GB 1600 MHz DDR3 memory. We used MATLAB R2015b in single-threaded mode to run all the experiments.

We tested on various small synthetic (Table 6) and real SfM datasets (Table 7) derived from circular motion (Din, Dio, Di2, Hou), non-circular motion (Btb), forward movement (Cor, R47, Sth, Wil) and small number of frames (Lib, Me1, Me2, Wad).

On each dataset, we ran all four two-stage meta-algorithms listed in Table 5 for 100 runs. On each run, initial camera poses and points were drawn from $\mathcal{N}(\mathbf{0}, \mathbf{I})$. The first stage of each meta-algorithm minimized the affine version of (1), and the second stage minimized the projective version of the same problem. We set the maximum number of iterations in each stage to 1000 and the function value tolerance to 10^{-9}.

We then compared how many fractions of runs each meta-algorithm converged to the best observed minimum on each dataset, defining this quantity as the success rate. The success rates of different meta-algorithms are compared in Fig. 2a and b.

Table 7. Real datasets used for the experiments. f denotes the number of frames and n denotes the number of feature points. *Di2 was generated by projecting real points from synthetic camera poses made deliberately close to the 3D structure thereby inducing strong perspective effects.

ID	Dataset	f	n	Missing (%)	Best affine	Best projective
Btb	Blue teddy bear (trimmed) (Ponce)	196	827	80.71	0.530633	0.489283
Cor	Corridor (VGG)	11	737	50.23	2.237213	0.272462
Din	Dinosaur (trimmed) [5]	36	319	76.92	1.270153	1.114493
Dio	Dinosaur (VGG)	36	4983	90.84	1.217574	1.166165
Di2*	Dinosaur (trimmed) closer cameras	36	319	76.92	9.380473	0.838414
Hou	House (VGG)	10	672	57.65	2.750877	0.441660
Lib	Oxford University Library (VGG)	3	667	29.24	4.180297	0.172830
Me1	Merton College 1 (VGG)	3	717	22.13	3.176176	0.118450
Me2	Merton College 2 (VGG)	3	475	21.61	3.995869	0.158851
R47	Road scene point tracks #47	11	150	47.09	4.402777	3.344768
Sth	Stockholm Guildhall (trimmed) [18]	43	1000	18.01	8.833195	5.619975
Wad	Wadham College (VGG)	5	1331	54.64	3.424812	0.135711
Wil	Wilshire (Ponce)	190	411	60.73	2.703663	0.423892

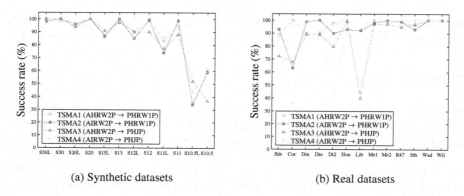

(a) Synthetic datasets   (b) Real datasets

Fig. 2. The figures show the success rates of each meta-algorithm on each dataset. (A run is counted as *successful* if and only if it reaches the best known optimum of the dataset used.) We conclude that TSMA1 and TSMA2 are winners by narrow margins.

Throughout this paper, we report the normalized cost values which can be computed as follows:

$$\sqrt{\text{Equation (1)} / (2 \times \text{Total number of visible frames over all cameras})}.$$

8 Discussions

Figure 2a and b show that TSMA1 and TSMA2 return global optimum in a large fraction of runs on most datasets. Considering that each run is initialized from arbitrary cameras and points, we believe that these are novel and valuable results.

On the synthetic datasets (Fig. 2a), all our meta-algorithms yield high success rates (74–100 %) until the ground truth cameras are moved radically close to the sphere (e.g. S10.5/L). As discussed in Sect. 6, this is somewhat expected since our strategy is inevitably biased towards affine reconstruction. However, one should bear in mind that these are extreme cases where the cameras are located only 0.5 unit away from the surface of the sphere of radius 10.0, and our strategy still succeeds with high probability on strong perspective datasets such as S11/L S12/L and S13/L. The presence of loop closure does not seem to influence success rates massively.

On the real sequences (Fig. 2b), each of TSMA1 and TSMA2 achieves 88–100 % on all datasets but one (Lib for TSMA1 and Cor for TSMA2). This demonstrates that these methods work well in practice as they provide consistent performances across different kinds of camera motions.

Regarding the first (affine) stage algorithms, we do not observe a clear boost in success rates from employing AHRW2P instead of AIRW2P. (We only observe this on the Cor dataset (see Fig. 2b), which comprises forward camera movements.) This is against our hypothesis that AHRW2P, which is a numerically-stable reformulation of AIRW2P, should perform better on strong perspective sequences.

The results imply that the potential numerical instability caused by the use of inhomogeneous coordinates is not a major issue in the affine case. (It is still an issue for the projective model.)

In addition to the main experiments, we investigated to see if our meta-algorithms could serve as an initializer for the full bundle adjustment process. We ran a projective bundle adjustment algorithm, namely PHRW1P, on the full dinosaur dataset (Dio) with the initial camera values set to those of the global optimum of the trimmed dataset (Din). This allowed PHRW1P to reach the global optimum of the full sequence within 10 iterations. Based on this observation, we believe that our meta-algorithms could be applied to a segment of large datasets to trigger incremental or full bundle adjustment.

We also tried incrementing μ (the projectiveness parameter) gradually to make the affine-projective transition smoother, but this strategy performed comparable to projective bundle adjustment without affine initialization. Implementing a fully unified algorithm still remains a challenge.

9 Conclusions

In this work we analysed if the Variable Projection (VarPro) method, which is highly successful in finding global minima in affine factorization problems without careful initialization, is equally effective in the projective scenario. Unfortunately, the answer is that the success rate of VarPro-based algorithms cannot be directly replicated in the projective setting. Thus, we proposed and evaluated several meta-algorithms to overcome this shortcoming, and each of the winning methods (TSMA1 and TSMA2) obtained success rates between 88 and 100 % on all real datasets but one. Experimentally it turns out that using an affine factorization based on VarPro to warm-start projective bundle adjustment is essential to boost the success rate.

We demonstrated that the convergence basin can be greatly enhanced using the right combination of methods. By unifying affine and projective factorization problems we also derived numerically better conditioned formulations to solve these instances.

Future work includes the followings: addressing outliers in the measurements and therefore robustness in the cost function (e.g. by incorporating robust kernel reformulation [25]) and to operate in metric instead of projective space by restricting the unknowns to the respective Lie group. A highly ambitious goal is to solve large datasets as introduced in [3] via an initialization-free approach.

Acknowledgement. The work was supported by Microsoft, Toshiba Research Europe and JNE Systech.

References

1. Absil, P.A., Mahony, R., Sepulchre, R.: Optimization Algorithms on Matrix Manifolds. Princeton University Press, New Jersey (2008)
2. Agarwal, S., Mierle, K., Others: Ceres solver (2014). http://ceres-solver.org
3. Agarwal, S., Snavely, N., Seitz, S.M., Szeliski, R.: Bundle adjustment in the large. In: Daniilidis, K., Maragos, P., Paragios, N. (eds.) ECCV 2010. LNCS, vol. 6312, pp. 29–42. Springer, Heidelberg (2010). doi:10.1007/978-3-642-15552-9_3
4. Boumal, N., Absil, P.A.: RTRMC: a Riemannian trust-region method for low-rank matrix completion. In: Proceedings of Advances in Neural Information Processing Systems 24 (NIPS 2011), pp. 406–414 (2011)
5. Buchanan, A.M., Fitzgibbon, A.W.: Damped Newton algorithms for matrix factorization with missing data. In: Proceedings of the 2005 IEEE Computer Society Conference on Computer Vision and Pattern Recognition (CVPR), vol. 2, pp. 316–322 (2005)
6. Golub, G.H., Pereyra, V.: The differentiation of pseudo-inverses and nonlinear least squares problems whose variables separate. SIAM J. Numer. Anal. (SINUM) 10(2), 413–432 (1973)
7. Golub, G.H., Pereyra, V.: Separable nonlinear least squares: the variable projection method and its applications. In: Proceedings of Inverse Problems, pp. 1–26 (2002)
8. Gotardo, P.F., Martinez, A.M.: Computing smooth time trajectories for camera and deformable shape in structure from motion with occlusion. IEEE Trans. Pattern Anal. Mach. Intell. (TPAMI) 33(10), 2051–2065 (2011)
9. Hartley, R.I., Zisserman, A.: Multiple View Geometry in Computer Vision, 2nd edn. Cambridge University Press, Cambridge (2004)
10. Hong, J.H., Fitzgibbon, A.W.: Secrets of matrix factorization: approximations, numerics, manifold optimization and random restarts. In: Proceedings of the 2015 IEEE Internatonal Conference on Computer Vision (ICCV), pp. 4130–4138 (2015)
11. Hong, J.H., Zach, C., Fitzgibbon, A.W., Cipolla, R.: Projective bundle adjustment from arbitrary initialization using the variable projection method: Supplementary document (2016). https://github.com/jhh37/projective-ba
12. Jeong, Y., Nister, D., Steedly, D., Szeliski, R., Kweon, I.S.: Pushing the envelope of modern methods for bundle adjustment. In: Proceedings of the 2010 IEEE Computer Society Conference on Computer Vision and Pattern Recognition (CVPR), pp. 1474–1481 (2010)
13. Levenberg, K.: A method for the solution of certain non-linear problems in least squares. Q. Appl. Math. 2(2), 164–168 (1944)
14. Manton, J.H., Mahony, R., Hua, Y.: The geometry of weighted low-rank approximations. IEEE Trans. Sig. Process. 51(2), 500–514 (2003)
15. Marquardt, D.: An algorithm for least-squares estimation of nonlinear parameters. J. Soc. Indus. Appl. Math. 11(2), 431–441 (1963)
16. Mishra, B., Meyer, G., Bach, F., Sepulchre, R.: Low-rank optimization with trace norm penalty. SIAM J. Optim. (SIOPT) 23(4), 2124–2149 (2013)
17. Okatani, T., Yoshida, T., Deguchi, K.: Efficient algorithm for low-rank matrix factorization with missing components and performance comparison of latest algorithms. In: Proceedings of the 2011 IEEE International Conference on Computer Vision (ICCV), pp. 842–849 (2011)
18. Olsson, C., Enqvist, O.: Stable structure from motion for unordered image collections. In: Heyden, A., Kahl, F. (eds.) SCIA 2011. LNCS, vol. 6688, pp. 524–535. Springer, Heidelberg (2011). doi:10.1007/978-3-642-21227-7_49

19. Ruhe, A., Wedin, P.Å.: Algorithms for separable nonlinear least squares problems. SIAM Rev. (SIREV) **22**(3), 318–337 (1980)
20. Strelow, D.: General and nested Wiberg minimization: L2 and maximum likelihood. In: Fitzgibbon, A., Lazebnik, S., Perona, P., Sato, Y., Schmid, C. (eds.) ECCV 2012. LNCS, vol. 7578, pp. 195–207. Springer, Heidelberg (2012). doi:10.1007/ 978-3-642-33786-4_15
21. Sturm, P., Triggs, B.: A factorization based algorithm for multi-image projective structure and motion. In: Buxton, B., Cipolla, R. (eds.) ECCV 1996. LNCS, vol. 1065, pp. 709–720. Springer, Heidelberg (1996). doi:10.1007/3-540-61123-1_183
22. Tomasi, C., Kanade, T.: Shape and motion from image streams under orthography: a factorization method. Int. J. Comput. Vis. (IJCV) **9**(2), 137–154 (1992)
23. Triggs, B., McLauchlan, P.F., Hartley, R.I., Fitzgibbon, A.W.: Bundle adjustment - a modern synthesis. In: Proceedings of the International Workshop on Vision Algorithms: Theory and Practice, ICCV 1999, pp. 298–372 (2000)
24. Wiberg, T.: Computation of principal components when data are missing. In: Proceedings of the 2nd Symposium of Computational Statistics, pp. 229–326 (1976)
25. Zach, C.: Robust bundle adjustment revisited. In: Fleet, D., Pajdla, T., Schiele, B., Tuytelaars, T. (eds.) ECCV 2014. LNCS, vol. 8693, pp. 772–787. Springer, Heidelberg (2014). doi:10.1007/978-3-319-10602-1_50

Localizing and Orienting Street Views Using Overhead Imagery

Nam N. Vo$^{(\boxtimes)}$ and James Hays

Georgia Institute of Technology, Atlanta, USA
{namvo,hays}@gatech.edu

Abstract. In this paper we aim to determine the location and orientation of a ground-level query image by matching to a reference database of overhead (e.g. satellite) images. For this task we collect a new dataset with one million pairs of street view and overhead images sampled from eleven U.S. cities. We explore several deep CNN architectures for cross-domain matching – Classification, Hybrid, Siamese, and Triplet networks. Classification and Hybrid architectures are accurate but slow since they allow only partial feature precomputation. We propose a new loss function which significantly improves the accuracy of Siamese and Triplet embedding networks while maintaining their applicability to large-scale retrieval tasks like image geolocalization. This image matching task is challenging not just because of the dramatic viewpoint difference between ground-level and overhead imagery but because the orientation (i.e. azimuth) of the street views is unknown making correspondence even more difficult. We examine several mechanisms to match in spite of this – training for rotation invariance, sampling possible rotations at query time, and explicitly predicting relative rotation of ground and overhead images with our deep networks. It turns out that explicit orientation supervision *also* improves location prediction accuracy. Our best performing architectures are roughly 2.5 times as accurate as the commonly used Siamese network baseline.

Keywords: Image geolocalization · Image matching · Deep learning · Siamese network · Triplet network

1 Introduction

In this work we propose deep learning approaches to the problem of ground to overhead image matching. Such approaches enable large scale image geolocalization techniques to use widely-available overhead/satellite imagery to estimate the location of ground level photos. This is in contrast to typical image geolocalization which relies on matching "ground-to-ground" using a reference database of geotagged photographs. It is comparatively easy (for humans and machines) to determine if two ground level photographs depict the same location, but the world is very non-uniformly sampled by tourists and street-view vehicles. On the other hand, overhead imagery densely covers the Earth thanks to satellites and other aerial surveys. Because of this widespread coverage, matching ground-level

© Springer International Publishing AG 2016
B. Leibe et al. (Eds.): ECCV 2016, Part I, LNCS 9905, pp. 494–509, 2016.
DOI: 10.1007/978-3-319-46448-0_30

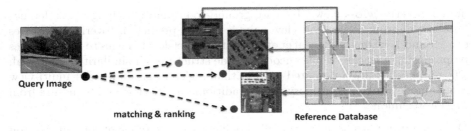

Fig. 1. Street-view to overhead-view image matching

photos to overhead imagery has become an attractive geolocalization approach [18]. However, it is a very challenging task (even for humans) because of the huge viewpoint variation and often lighting and seasonal variations, too. In this paper we try to learn how to match urban and suburban images from street-view to overhead-view imagery at fine-scale. As shown in Fig. 1, once the matching is done, the results can be ranked to generate a location estimate for a ground-level query.

To address cross-view geolocalization, the community has recently found deep learning techniques to outperform hand-crafted features [19,33]. These approaches adopt architectures from the similar task of face verification [7,28]. The method is as follows: a CNN, more specifically a Siamese architecture network [5,7], is used to learn a common low dimensional feature representation for both ground level and aerial image, where they can be compared to determine a matching score. While being superior to non-deep approaches (or pre-trained deep features), we show there is significant room for improvement.

To that end we study different deep learning approaches for matching/verification and ranking/retrieval tasks. We develop better loss functions using the novel distance based logistic (DBL) layer. To further improve the performance, we show that good representations can be learned by incorporating rotational invariance (RI) and orientation regression (OR) during training. Experiments are performed on a new large scale dataset which will be published to encourage future research. We believe the findings here generalize to similar matching and ranking problems.

1.1 Related Work

Image geolocalization uses recognition techniques from computer vision to estimate the location (at city, region, or global scale) of ordinary ground level photographs. Early work by Hays and Efros [12] studied the feasibility of this task by leveraging millions GPS-tagged images from the Internet. In [36], image localization is done efficiently by building a dataset of Google street-view images from which SIFT features are extracted, indexed and used for localization of a query image by voting. Lin et al. [18] propose the first ground-to-overhead geolocalization method. No attempt is made to learn a common feature space or match directly across views. Instead, ground-to-ground matching to a reference database of ground-overhead view pairs is used to predict the overhead features of a ground-level query. Bansal et al. [3] match street-level images to aerial images by proposing a feature which encodes facade structure self-similarity. Shan et al. [26] propose a fully automated system that registers ground-based multi-view Stereo models to aerial imagery using traditional multi-view and Structure from Motion technique.

Deep learning has been successfully applied to a wide range of computer vision tasks such as recognition of objects [16], places [37], faces [28]. Most recently, "PlaNet" [32] made use of a large amount of geo-tagged images, quantized the gps-coordinate into a number of regions and trained a CNN to classify an image's location into one of those regions. More relevant to this work is deep learning applications in cross-view images matching [19,33]. The most similar published work to ours is Lin et al. [19] which uses a Siamese network to learn a common deep representation of street-view images and 45 degree aerial or bird's eye images. This representation is shown to be better than hand-crafted or off-the-shelf CNN features for matching buildings' facades from different angles. In [33], Workman et al. show that by learning different CNNs for different scales (i.e. using aerial images at certain scales), geolocalization can be done at the local or continental level. Interestingly, they also showed that by fixing the representation of ground-level image, which is 205 categories scores learned from the Places database [37], the CNN will learn the same category scores for aerial images. Most recently, Altwaijry et al. [2] use a deep attentive architecture to match aerial images across wide baselines.

2   Dataset of Street View and Overhead Image Pairs

We study the problem of matching street-view image to overhead images for the application of image geolocalization. To that end, we collect a large scale dataset of street-view and overhead images. More specifically, we randomly queried street-view panorama images from Google Map of the US. For each panorama, we randomly made several crops and for each crop we queried Google Map for the overhead image at the finest scale, resulting in an aligned pair of street-view and overhead images. Note that we want to localize the *scene* depicted in the image and not necessarily the camera. This is possible since Google panorama images come with geo-tags and depth estimates. We performed this data collection procedure on 11 different cities in the US and produced more than 1 million pairs of images. Some example matches in Miami are shown in Fig. 2. We make this dataset available to the public.

Some similar attempts to collect a dataset for cross-view images matching task are [19,33], but neither are publicly available. We expect that the result and analysis here can be easily generalized across other datasets (or other applications like recognizing face or object instead of scene). While the technical aspects are similar, there will be qualitative differences: when training on [19], the network learns to match the facade which is visible from both views. On [33], the

Fig. 2. On the left: visualization of the positions of all Miami's panorama images that we randomly collect for further processing. On the right: examples of produced street-view and overhead pairs.

network learns to match similar categories of scenes or land cover types. And on our dataset, the network learns to recognize different fine-grained street scenes.

3   Cross-View Matching and Ranking with CNN

Before considering the ranking/retrieval task, we start with the matching/verification task formalized as following: during training phase, matched pairs of street-view and overhead images are provided as positive examples (negative examples can be easily generated by pairing up non-matched images) to learn a model. During testing, given a pair of images, the learned model is applied to classify if the pair is a match or not.

We use deep CNNs which have been shown to perform better than traditional hand-crafted features, especially for problems with significant training data available. We study 2 categories of CNNs (Fig. 3): the classification network for recognizing matches and the representation learning networks for embedding cross-view images into the same feature space. Note that the first category is not practical for the large-scale retrieval application and is used as a loose upper bound for comparison.

The second category includes the popular Siamese-like network and the triplet network. We introduce another version of Siamese and triplet networks

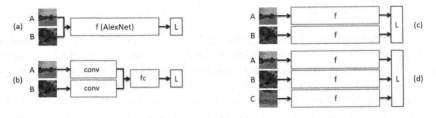

Fig. 3. Different CNN architectures: on the left is the first category: the classification network and the Siamese-classification hybrid network, on the right is the second category: the Siamese network and the triplet network

that use the *distance based logistic* layer, a novel loss function. For completeness we also include the Siamese-classification hybrid network (which will belong to the first category). In this section we will experiment with 6 networks in total.

3.1 Classification CNN for Image Matching

Since our task is basically classification, the first network we experiment with is AlexNet [16], originally demonstrated for object classification (Fig. 3(a)). It has 5 convolutional layers, followed by 3 fully-connected layers and a soft-max layer for classification. We make several modifications: (1) the input will be a 6-channel image, a concatenation of a street-view image and an overhead image, while the original AlexNet only takes 1-image input, (2) we double the number of filters in the first convolutional layer, (3) we remove the division of filters into 2 groups (this was done originally because of GPU memory limitation) and (4) the softmax layer produces 2 outputs instead of 1000 because our task is binary classification. Similar architectures have been used for comparing image patches [35].

Training the CNN is done by minimizing this loss function:

$$L(A, B, l) = LogLossSoftMax(f(I), l) \tag{1}$$

where A and B are the 2 input images, $l \in \{0, 1\}$ is the label indicating if it's a match, $I = concatenation(A, B)$ and $f(.)$ is the AlexNet that outputs class scores.

3.2 Siamese-Like CNN for Learning Image Features

The Siamese-like network, shown in Fig. 3(b), has been used for cross-view image matching [19,33] and retrieval [4,29]. It consists of 2 separate CNNs. Each sub-network takes 1 image as input and output a feature vector. Formally, given 2 images A and B, we can apply the learned network to produce the representation f(A) and f(B) that can be used for matching. This is done by computing the distance between these 2 vectors and classifying it as a match if the distance is small enough. During training, the contrastive loss is used:

$$L(A, B, l) = l * D + (1 - l) * max(0, m - D) \tag{2}$$

where D is the squared distance between f(A) and f(B), and m is the margin parameter that omits the penalization if the distance of non-matched pair is big enough. This loss function encourages the two features to be similar if the images are a match and separates them otherwise; this is visualized in Fig. 4(left).

In the original Siamese network [10], the subnetworks (f(A) and f(B)) have the same architecture and share weights. In our implementation, each subnetwork will be an AlexNet without weight sharing since the images are of different domains: one is street view and the other is overhead.

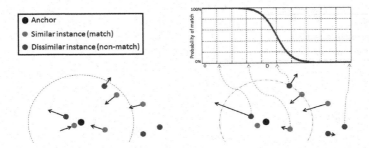

Fig. 4. Visualization of Siamese network training. We represent other instances (matches and non-matches) relative to a fixed instance (called the anchor). Left: with contrastive loss, matched instances keep being pulled closer, while non-matches are pushed away until they are out of the margin boundary, Right: log-loss with DBL: matched/nonmatched instances are pushed away from the "boundary" in the inward/outward direction.

3.3 Siamese-Classification Hybrid Network

The hybrid network is similar to the Siamese in that the input images are processed independently to produce output features and it is similar to the classification network that the features are concatenated to jointly infer the matching probability (Fig. 3(c)). Similar architectures have been used for used for cross-view matching and feature learning [1,2,11,35].

Formally let AlexNet (f) is consist of 2 parts: the set of convolutional layers (f_{conv}) and the set of fully-connected layers (f_{fc}), the loss function is:

$$L(A, B, l) = LogLossSoftMax(f_{fc}(I_{conv}), l) \tag{3}$$

Where $I_{conv} = concatenation(f_{conv}(A), f_{conv}(B))$. We expect this network to approach the accuracy of the classification network, while being slightly more efficient because intermediate features only need to be computed once per image.

3.4 Triplet Network for Learning Image Features

The fourth network that we call the triplet network or ranking network, shown in Fig. 3(c), is popular for image feature learning and retrieval [23–25,30,31,34], though its effectiveness has not been explored in cross-view image matching. More specifically it aims to learn a representation for ranking relevance between images. It consists of 3 separate CNNs instead of 2 in the Siamese network. Formally, the network takes 3 images A, B and C as inputs, where (A,B) is a match and (A,C) is not, and minimizes this hinge loss for triplet (which has been explored before its application in deep learning [6,21]):

$$L(A, B, C) = max(0, m + D(A, B) - D(A, C)) \tag{4}$$

Where D is the squared distances between the features f(A), f(B), f(C), and m is the margin parameter to omit the penalization if the gap between 2 distances

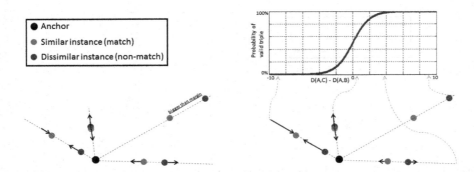

Fig. 5. Visualization of triplet network training. Each straight line originating from the anchor represents a triple. Left: with triplet/ranking loss, instances are pulled and pushed until the difference between the match distance and the non-match distance is bigger than the threshold, Right: log loss with DBL for triple. Similar to the ranking loss, but instead of relying on the threshold, the "force" depends on the current performance and confidence of the network.

is big enough. This loss layer encourages the distance of the more relevant pair to be smaller than the less relevant pair (Fig. 5(left)).

In the context of image matching, a pair of matched images (as the anchor and the match), plus a random image (as the non-match) is used as training example. With the learned representation, matching can be done by thresholding just like the Siamese network case.

3.5   Learning Image Representations with Distance-Based Logistic Loss

Despite being intuitive to understand, common loss functions based on euclidean distance might not be optimal for recognition. We instead advocate loss functions similar to the standard softmax, log-loss.

For the Siamese network, instead of the contrastive loss, we define the distance based logistic (DBL) layer for pairs of inputs as:

$$p(A, B) = \frac{1 + exp(-m)}{1 + exp(D - m)} \tag{5}$$

This outputs a value between 0 and 1, as the probability of the match given the squared distance. Then we can use the log-loss like the classification case for optimization:

$$L(A, B, l) = LogLoss(p(A, B), l) \tag{6}$$

The behavior of this loss is visualized in Fig. 4(right). Notice the difference from the traditional contrastive loss.

For the triplet network, we define the DBL for triple as following:

$$p(A, B, C) = \frac{1}{1 + exp(D(A, B) - D(A, C))} \tag{7}$$

This represents the probability that it's a valid triple: B is more relevant to A than C is to A (note that $p(A, B, C) + p(A, C, B) = 1$). Similarly the log-loss function is used, so:

$$L(A, B, C) = log(1 + exp(D(A, B) - D(A, C))) \qquad (8)$$

The behavior of this loss is visualized in Fig. 5(right).

With this novel layer, we obtain Siamese and triplet DBL-Net that allow us to optimize for the recognition accuracy more directly. As with the original loss functions, the learned feature representation can be used for efficient matching and ranking at test time (when the DBL layer is not involved).

4   Learning to Perform Rotation Invariant Matching

As we are considering the task of fine-grained street view to overhead view matching, not only spatial but also orientation alignment is important, i.e. rotating the overhead image according to the street-view's orientation instead of keeping the overhead image north oriented.

We aim to learn a rotation invariant (RI) representation of the overhead images. Similarly, Ke et al. [15] studied the problem of shape recognition without explicit alignment. In [20], nearby filters are untied to potentially allow pooling on output of different filters. This helps to learn complex representation without big filters or increasing the number of filters; however that doesn't result in an explicit RI property like we desire. Deep symmetry network [9] is capable of encoding such a property, though its advantage is not significant when training data is sufficient for traditional CNN to learn that on its own. More relevant, [8] uses data augmentation and concatenation of features from different viewpoints. However our training data comes with orientation aligned images (though not the test sets), which can potentially provide stronger supervision during training. In this section we explore techniques to take advantage of such information.

4.1   Partial Rotation Invariance by Data Augmentation

Training with multiple rotation samples: Rotation invariance (RI) can be encouraged simply by performing random rotation of overhead training images. Although invariance can help to a certain extent, there is a trade-off with discriminative ability. We propose to control the amount of rotation that the matching process will be invariant to, i.e. partial RI. Specifically this is done by adding a random amount of rotation within a certain range to the aligned overhead images. For example a 90° RI is achieved by rotating by an amount from −45° to 45°; 360° RI means fully RI.

Testing with multiple rotation samples/crops: since we don't know the correct orientation alignment at test time, if our representation is only partially rotation invariant, we have to test with multiple rotated version of the original image to find the best one. For example: with 360° RI representation, 1 sample is enough, with 180° RI representation, at least 2 rotation samples (that are 180° apart) are needed. Similar to multi-crop in classification tasks, we find that using more test time samples improves the result slightly (e.g. using 16 rotation samples at test time even if the network was trained to be 90° RI).

Multi-orientation feature averaging: as we use more rotation samples than needed, not only one but multiple of them should be good matches. For example testing with 16 rotation, we expect 16 of the them are good matches under 360° RI range, 4 under 90° RI range, etc. Therefore it makes sense to, instead of matching with a single best rotation (nearest neighbor), match with the best sequence of rotations. We propose to, depending on the degree of RI, average the features of multiple rotation samples during indexing time to obtain more stable features. This technique is especially useful in full RI case: all samples are averaged to produce a single feature, so the cost during query time is the same as using 1 sample.

4.2   Learning Better Representations with Orientation Regression

Next we propose to add an auxiliary loss function for orientation regression, where the amount of added rotation during training can be used as label for supervision. As shown in Fig. 6, the features from the last hidden layer (fc7) are concatenated, then we add 2 fully connected layers (one acting as hidden layer and one as output layer) and use Euclidean distance as our loss function for regression.

It is known that additional or 'auxiliary' losses can be very useful. For example, ranking can be improved by adding a classification layer predicting category [4,24] or attributes [13]. In [27], co-training of verification and classification is done to obtain a good representation for faces. Somewhat differently, our auxiliary loss is not directly related to the main task and its label is randomly generated by data augmentation. As the inference is done on 2 images jointly, its effect on each individual's representation can be difficult to interpret. The

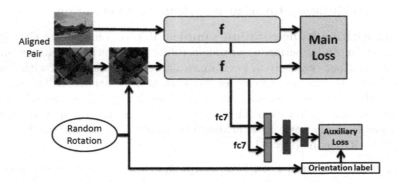

Fig. 6. Network architecture with data augmentation by random rotation and an additional branch that performs orientation regression

motivation, beyond being able to predict query orientation, is that this will make the network more orientation-aware and therefore produce a better feature representation for the localization task.

5 Experiments

Data preparation: we use our dataset of more than 1 million matched pairs of street-view and overhead-view images randomly collected from Google Maps of 11 different US cities (Sect. 2). We use all the cross-view pairs in 8 cities as training data (a total of 900k examples) and the remaining 3 cities as 3 test sets (around 70k examples per set).

We learn with mini-batch stochastic gradient descent, the standard optimization technique for training deep networks. Our batch size is 128 (64 of which are positive examples while 64 are negative examples). Training starts with a large learning rate (experimentally chosen) and get smaller as the network converges. The number of training iterations is 150k. We use Caffe framework [14].

Data augmentation: we apply random rotation of overhead images during training and use multiple rotation samples during testing (described in Sect. 4). The effect will be studied in detail in Sect. 5.2 We also apply a small amount of random cropping and random scaling.

Image Ranking and Geolocalization. While we have thus far considered location matching as a binary classification problem, our end goal is to use it for geolocalization. This application can be framed as a ranking or retrieval problem: given a query street view image and a repository of overhead images, one of which is the match, we want to rank the overhead images according to their relevance to the query so that the true match image is ranked as high as possible. The ranking task is typically approached as following: the representation learning networks are applied to the query image and the repository's images to obtain their feature vectors. Then these overhead images can be ranked by sorting the distance from their features to the query image's feature. The localization is considered successful if the true match overhead image is ranked within a certain top percentile.

Metrics: We measure both the classification and ranking performance on each test set. The classification accuracy is computed by using the best threshold on the each test set (random chance performance is 50 %). For the ranking task, we use mean recall at top K% as our measurement (the percentage of cases in which the correct overhead match of the query street view image is ranked within top K percentile, chance performance is K%). Some ranking examples are shown in Fig. 7.

5.1 Comparison of CNN Architectures

We train and compare 6 variants of CNN described in Sect. 3. All are initialized from scratch (no pretraining), trained to be 90° RI, and tested with 16 rotation samples. Quantitative comparisons are shown in the top of Table 1.

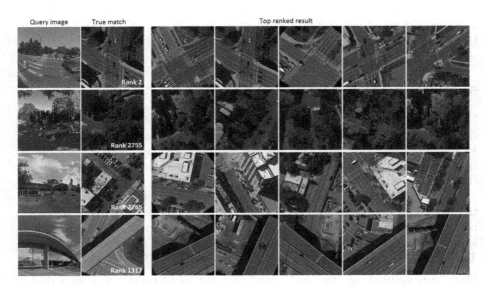

Fig. 7. Ranking result examples on the Denver test set (reference set of 70k reference images)

Table 1. Performance of different networks on different test sets

Task	Classification (accuracy)			Ranking (recall @top 1 %)		
Test set	Denver	Detroit	Seattle	Denver	Detroit	Seattle
Section 5.1 experiment (90°RI+16rots)						
Classification network	90.0	87.8	87.7	N/A	N/A	N/A
Classification hybrid	91.5	88.7	89.4	N/A	N/A	N/A
Siamese network	85.6	83.2	82.9	21.6	21.9	17.7
Triplet network	88.8	86.8	86.4	43.2	39.5	35.3
Siamese DBL-Net	90.0	88.0	**88.0**	48.4	45.0	**41.8**
Triplet DBL-Net	**90.2**	**88.4**	87.6	**49.3**	**47.1**	40.0
Section 5.2 (360°RI+OR)						
DBL-Net + 16rots	**91.5**	**90.1**	88.7	**54.8**	**52.7**	**45.5**
DBL-Net + avg16	**91.5**	90.0	**88.8**	54.0	52.2	45.3
Section 5.3						
Triplet eDBL-Net	**91.7**	**89.9**	**89.3**	**59.9**	**57.8**	**51.4**

Not surprisingly, both classification networks achieved better accuracy than the representation learning Siamese and triplet networks. This is because they jointly extract and exchange information from both input images. Somewhat unexpectedly, in our experiments the hybrid network is the better of the two. Even-though the 'pure' classification network should be capable of producing

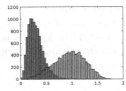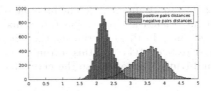

Fig. 8. Histograms of pairwise distances of features produced by the Siamese network-contrastive loss (left) and the triplet network (right). Note the crowding near zero distance for the Siamese network, which may explain poor performance for fine-grained retrieval tasks when it is important to compare small distances.

the same mapping as the hybrid, it might have trouble learning to process both images from the 1st layer.

Between the Siamese and triplet network, the triplet network outperforms the Siamese by a surprisingly large margin on both tasks. While both networks try to separate matches from non-matches, the contrastive loss function works toward a secondary objective: drive the distance between matched pair as close to 0 as possible (Fig. 8). Note that this might be a good property for the learned representation to have; but for the task of matching and ranking we found that this might compromise the main objective. One way to alleviate this problem is to add another margin to the contrastive loss function to cut the loss when the distance is small enough [17].

Analysis of Siamese and triplet network's performance has helped us develop the DBL layer. As the result, both DBL-Nets significantly outperform the original networks. While the Siamese with DBL and triplet network with DBL have comparable performances, it seems that the triplet DBL-Net is slightly better at ranking. Note that for most of the experiments we have been conducting, the performance of these two tasks strongly correlate. We use the triplet network with DBL layer for all following experiments.

5.2   Rotation Invariance

We experiment with partial rotation invariance (RI) and orientation regression (OR) (described in Sect. 4) for matching and ranking using the triplet DBL-Net. The result is shown in Table 2.

As an upper bound, we train a network where overhead images are aligned to the ground truth camera direction of the street view image (1GT). This is not a realistic usage scenario for image geolocalization since camera azimuth would typically be unknown. As expected, the network without RI performs very well when true alignment is provided during testing (1GT), but performs poorly otherwise. This baseline shows how challenging the problem has become because of orientation ambiguity. As the degree of RI during training is increased, the performance improves.

Observe that fewer numbers of test time rotated crops/samples doesn't work well if the amount of RI is limited. The full RI setting is the best when test-

Table 2. Comparisons of different amount of partial rotation invariance (RI), with and without orientation regression (OR), and different numbers of rotation samples during test time. In this experiment, the triplet network with DBL layer is tested on the Denver test set. 1GT*: in this setting, we test with 1 overhead image aligned using the ground-truth orientation (so the network doesn't have to be RI).

Task	Classification (accuracy)				Ranking (recall @top 1 %)			
Number of test rotations	1	4	16	1GT*	1	4	16	1GT*
0° RI (no RI)	63.6	68.5	87.2	95.0	11.0	18.8	37.3	76.2
45° RI	70.9	86.2	89.9	N/A	19.3	36.8	48.1	N/A
90° RI	75.8	89.5	**90.2**	N/A	24.7	44.7	**49.3**	N/A
180° RI	82.7	89.2	89.6	N/A	31.2	43.0	45.6	N/A
360° RI (full RI)	87.7	88.5	88.9	N/A	36.8	40.0	41.9	N/A
90° RI + OR	74.3	88.6	89.4	N/A	23.1	43.4	47.4	N/A
360° RI + OR	90.9	91.3	**91.5**	N/A	50.9	53.2	**54.8**	N/A
360° RI + OR + avg16	**91.5**	N/A	N/A	N/A	54.0	N/A	N/A	N/A

ing with a single sample. As the number of rotations increase, the performance improves, especially for the partially RI networks. Using 16 rotations, the 90° RI network has the highest performance. It might be the best setting for compromising between invariance and discriminate power (this might not be the case when using hundreds of samples, but we found that it's not computationally practical and the improvement is not significant).

Orientation regression's impact on the 360° RI network is surprisingly significant; its performance improves by 30 % (relatively). However OR doesn't affect 90° RI network positively, suggesting that the 2 techniques might not complement each other. It's interesting that the OR is useful even though its effect during learning is not as intuitive to understand as partial RI. As a by-product, the network can align matches. The orientation prediction has an average error of 17° for the ground truth matching overhead image and is discussed more in the supplemental document.

Finally we show the effect of applying multi-orientation feature averaging on 360° RI + OR network. By averaging the feature of 16 samples, we obtain comparable performance to exhaustively testing with 16 samples (result on all 3 test sets is shown in the 2nd part of Table 1). Though not shown here, applying this strategy to partial RI networks also slightly improve their performances.

5.3 Triplet Sampling by Exhausting Mini-batch

To speed up the training of triplet networks with the triplet hinge loss, clever triplet sampling and hard negative mining is usually applied [25,30,31]. This is because the triplet not violating the margin does not contribute to the learning. However it can skew the input distribution if not handled carefully (for instance, only mine hardest examples); different schemes were used in [25,30,31].

On the other hand, our DBL-log loss is practically a smoothed version of the hinge loss. We propose to use every possible triplet in the mini-batch. We experiment with using a mini-batch of 128 pairs of (matched) images. Since each image in our data has a single unique match only, we can generate a total of 256 * 127 triplets (256 different anchors, 1 match and 127 non-matches per anchor). This is done within our exhausting DBL log loss layer implementation (eDBL); hence the cost of processing the mini-batch is not much more expensive. In a similar spirit, recent work [22] proposes a loss function that considers the relationship between every examples in each training batch.

We train a triplet eDBL-Net+360°RI+OR+avg16. Its effect is very positive: the convergence is much faster, after around 30k iterations the network achieved similar performance as in previous experiments where each network was trained with 150k iterations using the same batch size. After 80k iterations, we achieve even better ranking performance, shown at the bottom of Table 1.

6   Conclusion

We introduce a new large scale cross-view data of street scenes from ground level and overhead. On this dataset, we have experimented with different CNN architectures extensively; the reported results and analysis can be generalized to other ranking and embedding problems. The result indicates that the Siamese network with contrastive loss is the least competitive even though it has been popular for cross-view matching. Our proposed DBL layer has significantly improved representation learning networks. Last but not least, we show how to further improve ranking performance by incorporating supervised alignment information to learn a rotational invariant representation.

Acknowledgments. Supported by the Intelligence Advanced Research Projects Activity (IARPA) via Air Force Research Laboratory, contract FA8650-12-C-7212. The U.S. Government is authorized to reproduce and distribute reprints for Governmental purposes notwithstanding any copyright annotation thereon. Disclaimer: The views and conclusions contained herein are those of the authors and should not be interpreted as necessarily representing the official policies or endorsements, either expressed or implied, of IARPA, AFRL, or the U.S. Government.

References

1. Agrawal, P., Carreira, J., Malik, J.: Learning to see by moving. In: Proceedings of the IEEE International Conference on Computer Vision, pp. 37–45 (2015)
2. Altwaijry, H., Trulls, E., Hays, J., Fua, P., Belongie, S.: Learning to match aerial images with deep attentive architectures. In: Proceedings of the IEEE Conference on Computer Vision and Pattern Recognition (2016)
3. Bansal, M., Daniilidis, K., Sawhney, H.: Ultra-wide baseline facade matching for geo-localization. In: Fusiello, A., Murino, V., Cucchiara, R. (eds.) ECCV 2012. LNCS, vol. 7583, pp. 175–186. Springer, Heidelberg (2012). doi:10.1007/978-3-642-33863-2_18

4. Bell, S., Bala, K.: Learning visual similarity for product design with convolutional neural networks. ACM Trans. Graph. (TOG) **34**(4), 98 (2015)
5. Bromley, J., Bentz, J.W., Bottou, L., Guyon, I., LeCun, Y., Moore, C., Säckinger, E., Shah, R.: Signature verification using a siamese time delay neural network. Int. J. Pattern Recogn. Artif. Intell. **7**(4), 669–688 (1993)
6. Chechik, G., Sharma, V., Shalit, U., Bengio, S.: Large scale online learning of image similarity through ranking. J. Mach. Learn. Res. **11**, 1109–1135 (2010)
7. Chopra, S., Hadsell, R., LeCun, Y.: Learning a similarity metric discriminatively, with application to face verification. In: IEEE Computer Society Conference on Computer Vision and Pattern Recognition, CVPR 2005, vol. 1, pp. 539–546. IEEE (2005)
8. Dieleman, S., Willett, K.W., Dambre, J.: Rotation-invariant convolutional neural networks for galaxy morphology prediction. Mon. Not. R. Astron. Soc. **450**(2), 1441–1459 (2015)
9. Gens, R., Domingos, P.M.: Deep symmetry networks. In: Advances in Neural Information Processing Systems, pp. 2537–2545 (2014)
10. Hadsell, R., Chopra, S., LeCun, Y.: Dimensionality reduction by learning an invariant mapping. In: 2006 IEEE Computer Society Conference on Computer Vision and Pattern Recognition, vol. 2, pp. 1735–1742. IEEE (2006)
11. Han, X., Leung, T., Jia, Y., Sukthankar, R., Berg, A.C.: MatchNet: unifying feature and metric learning for patch-based matching. In: Proceedings of the IEEE Conference on Computer Vision and Pattern Recognition, pp. 3279–3286 (2015)
12. Hays, J., Efros, A., et al.: IM2GPS: estimating geographic information from a single image. In: IEEE Conference on Computer Vision and Pattern Recognition, CVPR 2008, pp. 1–8. IEEE (2008)
13. Huang, J., Feris, R.S., Chen, Q., Yan, S.: Cross-domain image retrieval with a dual attribute-aware ranking network. In: Proceedings of the IEEE International Conference on Computer Vision, pp. 1062–1070 (2015)
14. Jia, Y., Shelhamer, E., Donahue, J., Karayev, S., Long, J., Girshick, R., Guadarrama, S., Darrell, T.: Caffe: convolutional architecture for fast feature embedding. arXiv preprint arXiv:1408.5093 (2014)
15. Ke, Q., Li, Y.: Is rotation a nuisance in shape recognition? In: Proceedings of the IEEE Conference on Computer Vision and Pattern Recognition, pp. 4146–4153 (2014)
16. Krizhevsky, A., Sutskever, I., Hinton, G.E.: ImageNet classification with deep convolutional neural networks. In: Advances in Neural Information Processing Systems, pp. 1097–1105 (2012)
17. Lin, J., Morere, O., Chandrasekhar, V., Veillard, A., Goh, H.: DeepHash: getting regularization, depth and fine-tuning right. arXiv preprint arXiv:1501.04711 (2015)
18. Lin, T.Y., Belongie, S., Hays, J.: Cross-view image geolocalization. In: 2013 IEEE Conference on Computer Vision and Pattern Recognition (CVPR), pp. 891–898. IEEE (2013)
19. Lin, T.Y., Cui, Y., Belongie, S., Hays, J.: Learning deep representations for ground-to-aerial geolocalization. In: Proceedings of the IEEE Conference on Computer Vision and Pattern Recognition, pp. 5007–5015 (2015)
20. Ngiam, J., Chen, Z., Chia, D., Koh, P.W., Le, Q.V., Ng, A.Y.: Tiled convolutional neural networks. In: Advances in Neural Information Processing Systems, pp. 1279–1287 (2010)
21. Norouzi, M., Fleet, D.J., Salakhutdinov, R.R.: Hamming distance metric learning. In: Advances in Neural Information Processing Systems, pp. 1061–1069 (2012)

22. Oh Song, H., Xiang, Y., Jegelka, S., Savarese, S.: Deep metric learning via lifted structured feature embedding. In: IEEE Conference on Computer Vision and Pattern Recognition (CVPR), June 2016

23. Parkhi, O.M., Vedaldi, A., Zisserman, A.: Deep face recognition. In: Proceedings of the British Machine Vision, vol. 1(3), p. 6 (2015)

24. Sangkloy, P., Burnell, N., Ham, C., Hays, J.: The sketchy database: learning to retrieve badly drawn bunnies. ACM Trans. Graph. (Proceedings of SIGGRAPH) (2016)

25. Schroff, F., Kalenichenko, D., Philbin, J.: FaceNet: a unified embedding for face recognition and clustering. In: Proceedings of the IEEE Conference on Computer Vision and Pattern Recognition, pp. 815–823 (2015)

26. Shan, Q., Wu, C., Curless, B., Furukawa, Y., Hernandez, C., Seitz, S.M.: Accurate geo-registration by ground-to-aerial image matching. In: 2014 2nd International Conference on 3D Vision (3DV), vol. 1, pp. 525–532. IEEE (2014)

27. Sun, Y., Chen, Y., Wang, X., Tang, X.: Deep learning face representation by joint identification-verification. In: Advances in Neural Information Processing Systems, pp. 1988–1996 (2014)

28. Taigman, Y., Yang, M., Ranzato, M., Wolf, L.: DeepFace: closing the gap to human-level performance in face verification. In: 2014 IEEE Conference on Computer Vision and Pattern Recognition (CVPR), pp. 1701–1708. IEEE (2014)

29. Wang, F., Kang, L., Li, Y.: Sketch-based 3D shape retrieval using convolutional neural networks. In: Proceedings of the IEEE Conference on Computer Vision and Pattern Recognition, pp. 1875–1883 (2015)

30. Wang, J., Song, Y., Leung, T., Rosenberg, C., Wang, J., Philbin, J., Chen, B., Wu, Y.: Learning fine-grained image similarity with deep ranking. In: 2014 IEEE Conference on Computer Vision and Pattern Recognition (CVPR), pp. 1386–1393. IEEE (2014)

31. Wang, X., Gupta, A.: Unsupervised learning of visual representations using videos. In: Proceedings of the IEEE International Conference on Computer Vision, pp. 2794–2802 (2015)

32. Weyand, T., Kostrikov, I., Philbin, J.: Planet - photo geolocation with convolutional neural networks. CoRR abs/1602.05314 (2016). http://arXiv.org/abs/1602.05314

33. Workman, S., Souvenir, R., Jacobs, N.: Wide-area image geolocalization with aerial reference imagery. In: ICCV 2015 (2015)

34. Wu, P., Hoi, S.C., Xia, H., Zhao, P., Wang, D., Miao, C.: Online multimodal deep similarity learning with application to image retrieval. In: Proceedings of the 21st ACM International Conference on Multimedia, pp. 153–162. ACM (2013)

35. Zagoruyko, S., Komodakis, N.: Learning to compare image patches via convolutional neural networks. In: Conference on Computer Vision and Pattern Recognition (CVPR) (2015)

36. Zamir, A.R., Shah, M.: Accurate Image localization based on Google maps street view. In: Daniilidis, K., Maragos, P., Paragios, N. (eds.) ECCV 2010. LNCS, vol. 6314, pp. 255–268. Springer, Heidelberg (2010). doi:10.1007/978-3-642-15561-1_19

37. Zhou, B., Lapedriza, A., Xiao, J., Torralba, A., Oliva, A.: Learning deep features for scene recognition using places database. In: Advances in Neural Information Processing Systems, pp. 487–495 (2014)

Hollywood in Homes: Crowdsourcing Data Collection for Activity Understanding

Gunnar A. Sigurdsson[1]([✉]), Gül Varol[2], Xiaolong Wang[1], Ali Farhadi[3,4], Ivan Laptev[2], and Abhinav Gupta[1,4]

[1] Carnegie Mellon University, Pittsburgh, USA
gsigurds@cs.cmu.edu
[2] Inria, Rocquencourt, France
[3] University of Washington, Seattle, USA
[4] The Allen Institute for AI, Seattle, USA
http://allenai.org/plato/charades/

Abstract. Computer vision has a great potential to help our daily lives by searching for lost keys, watering flowers or reminding us to take a pill. To succeed with such tasks, computer vision methods need to be trained from real and diverse examples of our daily dynamic scenes. While most of such scenes are not particularly exciting, they typically do not appear on YouTube, in movies or TV broadcasts. So how do we collect sufficiently many diverse but *boring* samples representing our lives? We propose a novel Hollywood in Homes approach to collect such data. Instead of shooting videos in the lab, we ensure diversity by distributing and crowdsourcing the whole process of video creation from script writing to video recording and annotation. Following this procedure we collect a new dataset, *Charades*, with hundreds of people recording videos in their own homes, acting out casual everyday activities. The dataset is composed of 9,848 annotated videos with an average length of 30 s, showing activities of 267 people from three continents. Each video is annotated by multiple free-text descriptions, action labels, action intervals and classes of interacted objects. In total, Charades provides 27,847 video descriptions, 66,500 temporally localized intervals for 157 action classes and 41,104 labels for 46 object classes. Using this rich data, we evaluate and provide baseline results for several tasks including action recognition and automatic description generation. We believe that the realism, diversity, and casual nature of this dataset will present unique challenges and new opportunities for computer vision community.

1   Introduction

Large scale visual learning fueled by huge datasets has changed the computer vision landscape [1,2]. Given the source of this data, it's not surprising that most of our current success is biased towards static scenes and objects in Internet images. As we move forward into the era of AI and robotics, however, new questions arise. How do we learn about different states of objects (*e.g.,* cut vs.

© Springer International Publishing AG 2016
B. Leibe et al. (Eds.): ECCV 2016, Part I, LNCS 9905, pp. 510–526, 2016.
DOI: 10.1007/978-3-319-46448-0_31

whole)? How do common activities affect changes of object states? In fact, it is not even yet clear if the success of the Internet pre-trained recognition models will transfer to real-world settings where robots equipped with our computer vision models should operate.

Shifting the bias from Internet images to real scenes will most likely require collection of new large-scale datasets representing activities of our boring everyday life: getting up, getting dressed, putting groceries in fridge, cutting vegetables and so on. Such datasets will allow us to develop new representations and to learn models with the right biases. But more importantly, such datasets representing people interacting with objects and performing natural action sequences in typical environments will finally allow us to learn common sense and contextual knowledge necessary for high-level reasoning and modeling.

But how do we find these boring videos of our daily lives? If we search common activities such as "drinking from a cup", "riding a bike" on video sharing websites such as YouTube, we observe a highly-biased sample of results (see Fig. 1). These results are biased towards entertainment—boring videos have no viewership and hence no reason to be uploaded on YouTube!

In this paper, we propose a novel **Hollywood in Homes** approach to collect a large-scale dataset of boring videos of daily activities. Standard approaches in the past have used videos downloaded from the Internet [3–8] gathered from movies [9–11] or recorded in controlled environments [12–17]. Instead, as the name suggests: we take the Hollywood filming process to the homes of hundreds of people on Amazon Mechanical Turk (AMT). AMT workers follow the three steps of filming process: (1) script generation; (2) video direction and acting based on scripts; and (3) video verification to create one of the largest and most diverse video dataset of daily activities.

There are threefold advantages of using the **Hollywood in Homes** approach for dataset collection: (a) Unlike datasets shot in controlled environments (*e.g.*, MPII [14]), crowdsourcing brings in diversity which is essential for generalization. In fact, our approach even allows the same script to be enacted by multiple people; (b) crowdsourcing the script writing enhances the coverage in terms of scenarios and reduces the bias introduced by generating scripts in labs; and (c) most importantly, unlike for web videos, this approach allows us to control the composition and the length of video scenes by proposing the vocabulary of scenes, objects and actions during script generation.

The Charades v1.0 Dataset. *Charades* is our large-scale dataset with a focus on common household activities collected using the Hollywood in Homes approach. The name comes from of a popular American word guessing game where one player acts out a phrase and the other players guess what phrase it is. In a similar spirit, we recruited hundreds of people from Amazon Mechanical Turk to act out a paragraph that we presented to them. The workers additionally provide action classification, localization, and video description annotations. The first publicly released version of our *Charades* dataset will contain 9,848 videos

The Charades Dataset   You Tube

Fig. 1. Comparison of actions in the Charades dataset and on YouTube: *Reading a book*, *Opening a refrigerator*, *Drinking from a cup*. YouTube returns entertaining and often atypical videos, while *Charades* contains typical everyday videos.

of daily activities 30.1 s long on average (7,985 training and 1,863 test). The dataset is collected in 15 types of indoor scenes, involves interactions with 46 object classes and has a vocabulary of 30 verbs leading to 157 action classes. It has 66,500 temporally localized actions, 12.8 s long on average, recorded by 267 people in three continents, and over 15 % of the videos have more than one person. We believe this dataset will provide a crucial stepping stone in developing action representations, learning object states, human object interactions, modeling context, object detection in videos, video captioning and many more. The dataset is publicly available at http://allenai.org/plato/charades/.

Contributions. The contributions of our work are three-fold: (1) We introduce the Hollywood in Homes approach to data collection, (2) we collect and release the first crowdsourced large-scale dataset of boring household activities, and (3) we provide extensive baseline evaluations.

The KTH action dataset [12] paved the way for algorithms that recognized human actions. However, the dataset was limited in terms of number of categories and enacted in the same background. In order to scale up the learning and the complexity of the data, recent approaches have instead tried collecting video datasets by downloading videos from Internet. Therefore, datasets such as UCF101 [8], Sports1M [6] and others [4,5,7] appeared and presented more challenges including background clutter, and scale. However, since it is impossible to find boring daily activities on Internet, the vocabulary of actions became biased towards more sports-like actions which are easy to find and download.

There have been several efforts in order to remove the bias towards sporting actions. One such commendable effort is to use movies as the source of data [18,19]. Recent papers have also used movies to focus on the video description problem leading to several datasets such as MSVD [20], M-VAD [21], and

Table 1. Comparison of Charades with other video datasets.

	Actions per video	Classes	Labelled instances	Total videos	Origin	Type	Temporal localization
Charades v1.0	6.8	157	67K	10K	267 homes	Daily activities	Yes
ActivityNet [3]	1.4	203	39K	28K	YouTube	Human activities	Yes
UCF101 [8]	1	101	13K	13K	YouTube	Sports	No
HMDB51 [7]	1	51	7K	7K	YouTube/movies	Movies	No
THUMOS'15 [5]	1–2	101	21K+	24K	YouTube	Sports	Yes
Sports 1M [6]	1	487	1.1M	1.1M	YouTube	Sports	No
MPII-cooking [14]	46	78	13K	273	30 In-house actors	Cooking	Yes
ADL [25]	22	32	436	20	20 Volunteers	Ego-centric	Yes
MPII-MD [11]	Captions	Captions	68K	94	Movies	Movies	No

MPII-MD [11]. Movies however are still exciting (and a source of entertainment) and do not capture the scenes, objects or actions of daily living. Other efforts have been to collect in-house datasets for capturing human-object interactions [22] or human-human interactions [23]. Some relevant big-scale efforts in this direction include MPII Cooking [14], TUM Breakfast [16], and the TACoS Multi-Level [17] datasets. These datasets focus on a narrow domain by collecting the data in-house with a fixed background, and therefore focus back on the activities themselves. This allows for careful control of the data distribution, but has limitations in terms of generalizability, and scalability. In contrast, PhotoCity [24] used the crowd to take pictures of landmarks, suggesting that the same could be done for other content at scale.

Another relevant effort in collection of data corresponding to daily activities and objects is in the domain of ego-centric cameras. For example, the Activities of Daily Living dataset [25] recorded 20 people performing unscripted, everyday activities in their homes in first person, and another extended that idea to animals [26]. These datasets provide a challenging task but fail to provide diversity which is crucial for generalizability. It should however be noted that these kinds of datasets could be crowdsourced similarly to our work.

The most related dataset is the recently released ActivityNet dataset [3]. It includes actions of daily living downloaded from YouTube. We believe the ActivityNet effort is complementary to ours since their dataset is uncontrolled, slightly biased towards non-boring actions and biased in the way the videos are professionally edited. On the other hand, our approach focuses more on action sequences (generated from scripts) involving interactions with objects. Our dataset, while diverse, is controlled in terms of vocabulary of objects and actions being used to generate scripts. In terms of the approach, Hollywood in Homes is also related to [27]. However, [27] only generates synthetic data. A comparison with other video datasets is presented in Table 1. To the best of our knowledge, our approach is the first to demonstrate that workers can be used to collect a vision dataset by filming themselves at such a large scale.

2   Hollywood in Homes

We now describe the approach and the process involved in a large-scale video collection effort via AMT. Similar to filming, we have a three-step process for generating a video. The first step is generating the script of the indoor video. The key here is to allow workers to generate diverse scripts yet ensure that we have enough data for each category. The second step in the process is to use the script and ask workers to record a video of that sentence being acted out. In the final step, we ask the workers to verify if the recorded video corresponds to script, followed by an annotation procedure.

2.1   Generating Scripts

In this work we focus on indoor scenes, hence, we group together rooms in residential homes (*Living Room*, *Home Office*, etc.). We found 15 types of rooms to cover most of typical homes, these rooms form the scenes in the dataset. In order to generate the *scripts* (a text given to workers to act out in a video), we use a vocabulary of objects and actions to guide the process. To understand what objects and actions to include in this vocabulary, we analyzed 549 movie scripts from popular movies in the past few decades. Using both term-frequency (TF) and TF-IDF [28] we analyzed which nouns and verbs occur in those rooms in these movies. From those we curated a list of 40 objects and 30 actions to be used as seeds for script generation, where objects and actions were chosen to be generic for different scenes.

To harness the creativity of people, and understand their bias towards activities, we crowdsourced the script generation as follows. In the AMT interface, a single scene, 5 randomly selected objects, and 5 randomly selected actions were presented to workers. Workers were asked to use two objects and two actions to compose a short paragraph about activities of one or two people performing realistic and commonplace activities in their home. We found this to be a good compromise between controlling what kind of words were used and allowing the users to impose their own human bias on the generation. Some examples of generated scripts are shown in Fig. 2. (see the website for more examples). The distribution of the words in the dataset is presented in Fig. 3.

2.2   Generating Videos

Once we have scripts, our next step is to collect videos. To maximize the diversity of scenes, objects, clothing and behaviour of people, we ask the workers themselves to record the 30 s videos by following collected scripts.

AMT is a place where people commonly do quick tasks in the convenience of their homes or during downtime at their work. AMT has been used for annotation and editing but can we do content creation via AMT? During a pilot study we asked workers to record the videos, and until we paid up to $3 per video, no worker picked up our task. (For comparison, to annotate a video [29]: 3 workers × 157 questions × 1 second per question × $8/h salary = $1.) To reduce the base cost to a more manageable $1 per video, we have used the following strategies:

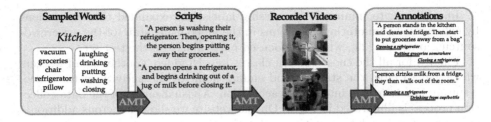

Fig. 2. An overview of the three Amazon Mechanical Turk (AMT) crowdsourcing stages in the *Hollywood in Homes* approach.

Worker Recruitment. To overcome the inconvenience threshold, worker recruitment was increased through sign-up bonuses (211 % increased new worker rate) where we awarded a $5 bonus for the first submission. This increased the total cost by 17 %. In addition, "recruit a friend" bonuses ($5 if a friend submits 15 videos) were introduced, and were claimed by 4 % of the workforce, generating indeterminate outreach to the community. US, Canada, UK, and, for a time, India were included in this study. The first three accounted for estimated 73 % of the videos, and 59 % of the peak collection rate.

Worker Retention. Worker retention was mitigated through performance bonuses every 15th video, and while only accounting for a 33 % increase in base cost, significantly increased retention (34 % increase in come-back workers), and performance (109 % increase in output per worker).

Each submission in this phase was manually verified by other workers to enforce quality control, where a worker was required to select the corresponding sentence from a line-up after watching the video. The rate of collection peaked at 1225 per day from 72 workers. The final cost distribution was: 65 % base cost per video, 21 % performance bonuses, 11 % recruitment bonuses, and 3 % verification. The code and interfaces will be made publicly available along with the dataset.

2.3 Annotations

Using the generated scripts, all (verb,proposition,noun) triplets were analyzed, and the most frequent grouped into 157 action classes (*e.g., pouring into cup, running, folding towel*, etc.). The distribution of those is presented in Fig. 3.

For each recorded video we have asked other workers to watch the video and describe what they have observed with a sentence (this will be referred to as a *description* in contrast to the previous *script* used to generate the video). We use the original script and video descriptions to automatically generate a list of interacted objects for each video. Such lists were verified by the workers. Given the list of (verified) objects, for each video we have made a short list of 4–5 actions (out of 157) involving corresponding object interactions and asked the workers to verify the presence of these actions in the video.

In addition, to minimize the missing labels, we expanded the annotations by exhaustively annotating all actions in the video using state-of-the-art crowd-sourcing practices [29], where we focused particularly on the test set.

Finally, for all the chosen action classes in each video, another set of workers was asked to label the starting and ending point of the activity in the video, resulting in a temporal interval of each action. A visualization of the data collection process is illustrated in Fig. 2. On the website we show numerous additional examples from the dataset with annotated action classes.

3   Charades v1.0 Analysis

Charades is built up by combining 40 objects and 30 actions in 15 scenes. This relatively small vocabulary, combined with open-ended writing, creates a dataset that has substantial coverage of a useful domain. Furthermore, these combinations naturally form action classes that allow for standard benchmarking. In Fig. 3 the distributions of action classes, and most common nouns/verbs/scenes in the dataset are presented. The natural world generally follows a long-tailed distribution [30,31], but we can see that the distribution of words in the dataset is relatively even. In Fig. 3 we also present a visualization of what scenes, objects, and actions occur together. By embedding the words based on their co-occurance with other words using T-SNE [32], we can get an idea of what words group together in the videos of the dataset, and it is clear that the dataset possesses real-world intuition. For example, *food*, and *cooking* are close to *Kitchen*, but note that except for *Kitchen, Home Office*, and *Bathroom*, the scene is not highly discriminative of the action, which reflects common daily activities.

Since we have control over the data acquisition process, instead of using Internet search, there are on average 6.8 relevant actions in each video. We hope that this may inspire new and interesting algorithms that try to capture this kind of context in the domain of action recognition. Some of the most common pairs of actions measured in terms of normalized pointwise mutual information (NPMI), are also presented in Fig. 3. These actions occur in various orders and context, similar to our daily lives. For example, in Fig. 4 we can see that among these five videos, there are multiple actions occurring, and some are in common. We further explore this in Fig. 5, where for a few actions, we visualize the most probable actions to precede, and most probable actions to follow that action. As the scripts for the videos are generated by people imagining a boring realistic scenario, we find that these statistics reflect human behaviour.

4   Applications

We run several state-of-the-art algorithms on Charades to provide the community with a benchmark for recognizing human activities in realistic home environments. Furthermore, the performance and failures of tested algorithms provide insights into the dataset and its properties.

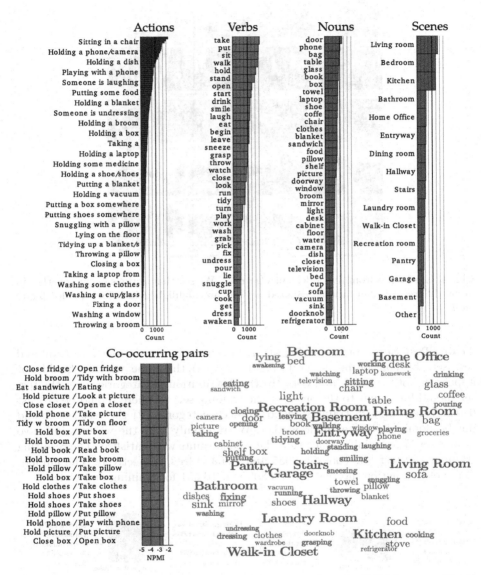

Fig. 3. Statistics for actions (gray, every fifth label shown), verbs (green), nouns (blue), scenes (red), and most co-occurring pairs of actions (cyan). Co-occurrence is measured with normalized pointwise mutual information. In addition, a T-SNE embedding of the co-occurrence matrix is presented. We can see that while there are some words that strongly associate with each other (*e.g.,* lying and bed), many of the objects and actions co-occur with many of the scenes. (Action names are abbreviated as necessary to fit space constraints.) (Color figure online)

Fig. 4. Keyframes from five videos in *Charades*. We see that actions occur together in many different configurations. (Shared actions are highlighted in color). (Color figure online)

Train/Test Set. For evaluating algorithms we split the dataset into train and test sets by considering several constraints: (a) the same worker should not appear in both training and test; (b) the distribution of categories over the test set should be similar to the one over the training set; (c) there should be at least 6 test videos and 25 training videos in each category; (d) the test set should not be dominated by a single worker. We randomly split the workers into two groups (80 % in training) such that these constraints were satisfied. The resulting training and test sets contain 7,985 and 1,863 videos, respectively. The number of annotated action intervals are 49,809 and 16,691 for training and test.

Fig. 5. Selected actions from the dataset, along with the top five most probable actions before, and after the action. For example, when *Opening a window*, it is likely that someone was *Standing up* before that, and after opening, *Looking out the window*.

4.1   Action Classification

Given a video, we would like to identify whether it contains one or several actions out of our 157 action classes. We evaluate the classification performance for several baseline methods. Action classification performance is evaluated with the standard mean average precision (mAP) measure. A single video is assigned to multiple classes and the distribution of classes over the test set is not uniform. The label precision for the data is 95.6 %, measured using an additional verification step, as well as comparing against a ground truth made from 19 iterations of annotations on a subset of 50 videos. We now describe the baselines.

Improved Trajectories. We compute improved dense trajectory features (IDT) [33] capturing local shape and motion information with MBH, HOG and HOF video descriptors. We reduce the dimensionality of each descriptor by half with PCA, and learn a separate feature vocabulary for each descriptor with GMMs of 256 components. Finally, we encode the distribution of local descriptors over the video with Fisher vectors [34]. A one-versus-rest linear SVM is used for classification. Training on untrimmed intervals gave the best performance.

Table 2. mAP (%) for action classification with various baselines.

Random	C3D	AlexNet	Two-stream-B	Two-stream	IDT	Combined
5.9	10.9	11.3	11.9	14.3	17.2	18.6

Table 3. Action classification evaluation with the state-of-the-art approach on Charades. We study different parameters for improved trajectories, by reporting for different local descriptor sets and different number of GMM clusters. Overall performance improves by combining all descriptors and using a larger descriptor vocabulary.

	HOG	HOF	MBH	HOG + MBH	HOG + HOF + MBH
K = 64	12.3	13.9	15.0	15.8	16.5
K = 128	12.7	14.3	15.4	16.2	16.9
K = 256	13.0	14.4	15.5	16.5	17.2

Static CNN Features. In order to utilize information about objects in the scene, we make use of deep neural networks pretrained on a large collection of object images. We experiment with VGG-16 [35] and AlexNet [36] to compute fc_6 features over 30 equidistant frames in the video. These features are averaged across frames, L2-normalized and classified with a one-versus-rest linear SVM. Training on untrimmed intervals gave the best performance.

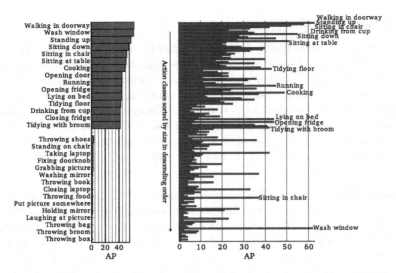

Fig. 6. On the left classification accuracy for the 15 highest and lowest actions is presented for *Combined*. On the right, the classes are sorted by their size. The top actions on the left are annotated on the right. We can see that while there is a slight trend for smaller classes to have lower accuracy, many classes do not follow that trend.

Two-Stream Networks. We use the VGG-16 model architecture [?] for both networks and follow the training procedure introduced in Simonyan et al. [37], with small modifications. For the spatial network, we applied finetuning on ImageNet pre-trained networks with different dropout rates. The best performance was with 0.5 dropout rate and finetuning on all fully connected layers. The temporal network was first pre-trained on the UCF101 dataset and then similarly finetuned on conv4, conv5, and fc layers. Training on trimmed intervals gave the best performance.

Balanced Two-Stream Networks. We adapt the previous baseline to handle class imbalance. We balanced the number of training samples through sampling, and ensured each minibatch of 256 had at least 50 unique classes (each selected uniformly at random). Training on trimmed intervals gave the best performance.

C3D Features. Following the recent approach from [38], we extract fc_6 features from a 3D convnet pretrained on the Sports-1M video dataset [6]. These features capture complex hierarchies of spatio-temporal patterns given an RGB clip of 16 frames. Similar to [38], we compute features on chunks of 16 frames by sliding 8 frames, average across chunks, and use a one-versus-rest linear SVM. Training on untrimmed intervals gave the best performance.

Action classification results are presented in Table 2, where we additionally consider **Combined** which combines all the other methods with late fusion.

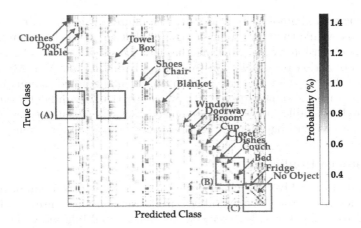

Fig. 7. Confusion matrix for the *Combined* baseline on the classification task. Actions are grouped by the object being interacted with. Most of the confusion is with other actions involving the same object (squares on the diagonal), and we highlight some prominent objects. Note: (A) High confusion between actions using *Blanket*, *Clothes*, and *Towel*; (B) High confusion between actions using *Couch* and *Bed*; (C) Little confusion among actions with no specific object of interaction (*e.g., standing up, sneezing*).

Notably, the accuracy of the tested state-of-the-art baselines is much lower than in most currently available benchmarks. Consistently with several other datasets, IDT features [33] outperform other methods by obtaining 17.2 % mAP. To analyze these results, Fig. 6(left) illustrates the results for subsets of best and worst recognized action classes. We can see that while the mAP is low, there are certain classes that have reasonable performance, for example *Washing a window* has 62.1 % AP. To understand the source of difference in performance for different classes, Fig. 6(right) illustrates AP for each action, sorted by the number of examples, together with names for the best performing classes. The number of actions in a class is primarily decided by the universality of the action (can it happen in any scene), and if it is common in typical households (writer bias). It is interesting to notice, that while there is a trend for actions with higher number of examples to have higher AP, it is not true in general, and actions such as *Sitting in chair*, and *Washing windows* have top-15 performance.

Delving even further, we investigate the confusion matrix for the *Combined* baseline in Fig. 7, where we convert the predictor scores to probabilities and accumulate them for each class. For clearer analysis, the classes are sorted by the object being interacted with. The first aspect to notice is the squares on the diagonal, which imply that the majority of the confusion is among actions that interact with the same object (*e.g., Putting on clothes*, or *Taking clothes from somewhere*), and moreover, there is confusion among objects with similar functional properties. The most prominent squares are annotated with the object being shared among those actions. The figure caption contains additional observations. While there are some categories that show no clear trend, we can observe less confusion for many actions that have no specific object of interaction. Evaluation of action recognition on this subset results in 38.9 % mAP, which is significantly higher than average. Recognition of fine-grained actions involving interactions with the same object class appears particularly difficult even for the best methods available today. We hope our dataset will encourage new methods addressing activity recognition for complex person-object interactions.

4.2   Sentence Prediction

Our final, and arguably most challenging task, concerns prediction of free-from sentences describing the video. Notably, our dataset contains sentences that have been used to create the video (*scripts*), as well as multiple video *descriptions* obtained manually for recorded videos. The scripts used to create videos are biased by the vocabulary, and due to the writer's imagination, generally describe different aspects of the video than descriptions. The description of the video by other people is generally simpler and to the point. Captions are evaluated using the CIDEr, BLEU, ROUGE, and METEOR metrics, as implemented in the COCO Caption Dataset [39]. These metrics are common for comparing machine translations to ground truth, and have varying degrees of similarity with human judgement. For comparison, human performance is presented along with the baselines where workers were similarly asked to watch the video and describe what they observed. We now describe the sentence prediction baselines in detail:

- **Random Words (RW):** Random words from the training set.
- **Random Sentence (Random):** Random sentence from the training set.
- **Nearest Neighbor (NN):** Inspired by Devlin et al. [40] we simply use a 1-Nearest Neighbor baseline computed using AlexNet fc_7 outputs averaged over frames, and use the caption from that nearest neighbor in the training set.
- **S2VT:** We use the S2VT method from Venugopalan et al. [41], which is a combination of a CNN, and a LSTM.

Table 4. Sentence Prediction. In the *script* task one sentence is used as ground truth, and in the *description* task 2.4 sentences are used as ground truth on average. We find that S2VT is the strongest baseline.

	Script					Description				
	RW	Random	NN	S2VT	Human	RW	Random	NN	S2VT	Human
CIDEr	0.03	0.08	0.11	0.17	0.51	0.04	0.05	0.07	0.14	0.53
BLEU$_4$	0.00	0.03	0.03	0.06	0.10	0.00	0.04	0.05	0.11	0.20
BLEU$_3$	0.01	0.07	0.07	0.12	0.16	0.02	0.09	0.10	0.18	0.29
BLEU$_2$	0.09	0.15	0.15	0.21	0.27	0.09	0.20	0.21	0.30	0.43
BLEU$_1$	0.37	0.29	0.29	0.36	0.43	0.38	0.40	0.40	0.49	0.62
ROUGE$_L$	0.21	0.24	0.25	0.31	0.35	0.22	0.27	0.28	0.35	0.44
METEOR	0.10	0.11	0.12	0.13	0.20	0.11	0.13	0.14	0.16	0.24

Fig. 8. Three generated captions that scored low on the CIDEr metric (red), and three that scored high (green) from the strongest baseline (S2VT). We can see that while the captions are fairly coherent, the captions lack sufficient relevance. (Color figure online)

Table 4 presents the performance of multiple baselines on the caption generation task. We both evaluate on predicting the *script*, as well as predicting the *description*. As expected, we can observe that descriptions made by people after watching the video are more similar to other descriptions, rather than the scripts used to generate the video. Table 4 also provides insight into the different evaluation metrics, and it is clear that CIDEr offers the highest resolution, and most similarity with human judgement on this task. In Fig. 8 few examples are presented for the highest scoring baseline (S2VT). We can see that while the language model is accurate (the sentences are coherent), the model struggles with providing relevant captions, and tends to slightly overfit to frequent patterns in the data (*e.g., drinking from a glass/cup*).

5   Conclusions

We proposed a new approach for building datasets. Our Hollywood in Homes approach allows not only the labeling, but the data gathering process to be crowdsourced. In addition, *Charades* offers a novel large-scale dataset with diversity and relevance to the real world. We hope that Charades and Hollywood in Homes will have the following benefits for our community:

(1) *Training data*: Charades provides a large-scale set of 66,500 annotations of actions with unique realism.
(2) *A benchmark*: Our publicly available dataset and provided baselines enable benchmarking future algorithms.
(3) *Object-action interactions*: The dataset contains significant and intricate object-action relationships which we hope will inspire the development of novel computer vision techniques targeting these settings.
(4) *A framework to explore novel domains*: We hope that many novel datasets in new domains can be collected using the Hollywood in Homes approach.

(4) *Understanding daily activities*: Charades provides data from a unique human-generated angle, and has unique attributes, such as complex co-occurrences of activities. This kind of realistic bias, may provide new insights that aid robots equipped with our computer vision models operating in the real world.

Acknowledgements. This work was partly supported by ONR MURI N00014-16-1-2007, ONR N00014-13-1-0720, NSF IIS-1338054, ERC award ACTIVIA, Allen Distinguished Investigator Award, gifts from Google, and the Allen Institute for Artificial Intelligence. The authors would like to thank: Nick Rhinehart and the anonymous reviewers for helpful feedback on the manuscript; Ishan Misra for helping in the initial experiments; and Olga Russakovsky, Mikel Rodriguez, and Rahul Sukhantakar for invaluable suggestions and advice. Finally, the authors want to extend thanks to all the workers at Amazon Mechanical Turk.

References

1. Deng, J., Dong, W., Socher, R., Li, L.J., Li, K., Fei-Fei, L.: Imagenet: a large-scale hierarchical image database. In: Computer Vision and Pattern Recognition (CVPR), pp. 248–255. IEEE (2009)
2. Zhou, B., Lapedriza, A., Xiao, J., Torralba, A., Oliva, A.: Learning deep features for scene recognition using places database. In: Neural Information Processing Systems (NIPS), pp. 487–495 (2014)
3. Caba Heilbron, F., Escorcia, V., Ghanem, B., Carlos Niebles, J.: Activitynet: a large-scale video benchmark for human activity understanding. In: Computer Vision and Pattern Recognition (CVPR), pp. 961–970. IEEE (2015)
4. Liu, J., Luo, J., Shah, M.: Recognizing realistic actions from videos in the wild. In: Computer Vision and Pattern Recognition (CVPR), pp. 1996–2003. IEEE (2009)
5. Gorban, A., Idrees, H., Jiang, Y.G., Roshan Zamir, A., Laptev, I., Shah, M., Sukthankar, R.: THUMOS challenge: action recognition with a large number of classes (2015). http://www.thumos.info/
6. Karpathy, A., Toderici, G., Shetty, S., Leung, T., Sukthankar, R., Fei-Fei, L.: Large-scale video classification with convolutional neural networks. In: Computer Vision and Pattern Recognition (CVPR), pp. 1725–1732. IEEE (2014)
7. Kuehne, H., Jhuang, H., Garrote, E., Poggio, T., Serre, T.: HMDB: a large video database for human motion recognition. In: International Conference on Computer Vision (ICCV), pp. 2556–2563. IEEE (2011)
8. Soomro, K., Roshan Zamir, A., Shah, M.: UCF101: a dataset of 101 human actions classes from videos in the wild. In: CRCV-TR-12-01 (2012)
9. Laptev, I., Marszałek, M., Schmid, C., Rozenfeld, B.: Learning realistic human actions from movies. In: Computer Vision and Pattern Recognition (CVPR), pp. 1–8. IEEE (2008)
10. Rodriguez, M.D., Ahmed, J., Shah, M.: Action mach a spatio-temporal maximum average correlation height filter for action recognition. In: Computer Vision and Pattern Recognition (CVPR), pp. 1–8. IEEE (2008)
11. Rohrbach, A., Rohrbach, M., Tandon, N., Schiele, B.: A dataset for movie description. In: Computer Vision and Pattern Recognition (CVPR). IEEE (2015)
12. Schüldt, C., Laptev, I., Caputo, B.: Recognizing human actions: a local svm approach. In: International Conference on Pattern Recognition (ICPR), vol. 3, pp. 32–36. IEEE (2004)

13. Gorelick, L., Blank, M., Shechtman, E., Irani, M., Basri, R.: Actions as space-time shapes. Trans. Pattern Anal. Mach. Intell. **29**(12), 2247–2253 (2007)
14. Rohrbach, M., Amin, S., Andriluka, M., Schiele, B.: A database for fine grained activity detection of cooking activities. In: Computer Vision and Pattern Recognition (CVPR), pp. 1194–1201. IEEE (2012)
15. Oh, S., Hoogs, A., Perera, A., Cuntoor, N., Chen, C.C., Lee, J.T., Mukherjee, S., Aggarwal, J., Lee, H., Davis, L., et al.: A large-scale benchmark dataset for event recognition in surveillance video. In: Computer Vision and Pattern Recognition (CVPR), pp. 3153–3160. IEEE (2011)
16. Kuehne, H., Arslan, A.B., Serre, T.: The language of actions: recovering the syntax and semantics of goal-directed human activities. In: Computer Vision and Pattern Recognition (CVPR). IEEE (2014)
17. Rohrbach, A., Rohrbach, M., Qiu, W., Friedrich, A., Pinkal, M., Schiele, B.: Coherent multi-sentence video description with variable level of detail. In: Jiang, X., Hornegger, J., Koch, R. (eds.) GCPR 2014. LNCS, vol. 8753, pp. 184–195. Springer, Heidelberg (2014)
18. Marszałek, M., Laptev, I., Schmid, C.: Actions in context. In: Computer Vision and Pattern Recognition (CVPR). IEEE (2009)
19. Ferrari, V., Marín-Jiménez, M., Zisserman, A.: 2D human pose estimation in TV shows. In: Cremers, D., Rosenhahn, B., Yuille, A.L., Schmidt, F.R. (eds.) Statistical and Geometrical Approaches to Visual Motion Analysis. LNCS, vol. 5604, pp. 128–147. Springer, Heidelberg (2009)
20. Chen, D.L., Dolan, W.B.: Collecting highly parallel data for paraphrase evaluation. In: Proceedings of the 49th Annual Meeting of the Association for Computational Linguistics: Human Language Technologies-Volume 1, pp. 190–200. Association for Computational Linguistics (2011)
21. Torabi, A., Pal, C., Larochelle, H., Courville, A.: Using descriptive video services to create a large data source for video annotation research. arXiv preprint arXiv:1503.01070 (2015)
22. Gupta, A., Davis, L.S.: Objects in action: an approach for combining action understanding and object perception. In: Computer Vision and Pattern Recognition (CVPR), pp. 1–8. IEEE (2007)
23. Ryoo, M.S., Aggarwal, J.K.: Spatio-temporal relationship match: video structure comparison for recognition of complex human activities. In: International Conference on Computer Vision (ICCV), pp. 1593–1600. IEEE (2009)
24. Tuite, K., Snavely, N., Hsiao, D.Y., Tabing, N., Popovic, Z.: Photocity: training experts at large-scale image acquisition through a competitive game. In: Proceedings of the SIGCHI Conference on Human Factors in Computing Systems, pp. 1383–1392. ACM (2011)
25. Pirsiavash, H., Ramanan, D.: Detecting activities of daily living in first-person camera views. In: Computer Vision and Pattern Recognition (CVPR), pp. 2847–2854. IEEE (2012)
26. Iwashita, Y., Takamine, A., Kurazume, R., Ryoo, M.S.: First-person animal activity recognition from egocentric videos. In: International Conference on Pattern Recognition (ICPR), Stockholm, Sweden, August 2014
27. Zitnick, C., Parikh, D.: Bringing semantics into focus using visual abstraction. In: Computer Vision and Pattern Recognition (CVPR), pp. 3009–3016. IEEE (2013)
28. Salton, G., Mcgill, M.J.: Introduction to Modern Information Retrieval, pp. 24–51 (1983)

29. Sigurdsson, G.A., Russakovsky, O., Farhadi, A., Laptev, I., Gupta, A.: Much ado about time: exhaustive annotation of temporal data. arXiv preprint arXiv:1607.07429 (2016)
30. Zipf, G.K.: The psycho-biology of language (1935)
31. Simoncelli, E.P., Olshausen, B.A.: Natural image statistics and neural representation. Ann. Rev. Neurosci. **24**(1), 1193–1216 (2001)
32. Van der Maaten, L., Hinton, G.: Visualizing data using t-SNE. J. Mach. Learn. Res. **9**(2579–2605), 85 (2008)
33. Wang, H., Schmid, C.: Action recognition with improved trajectories. In: International Conference on Computer Vision (ICCV) (2013)
34. Perronnin, F., Sánchez, J., Mensink, T.: Improving the Fisher kernel for large-scale image classification. In: Daniilidis, K., Maragos, P., Paragios, N. (eds.) ECCV 2010, Part IV. LNCS, vol. 6314, pp. 143–156. Springer, Heidelberg (2010)
35. Simonyan, K., Zisserman, A.: Very deep convolutional networks for large-scale image recognition. In: International Conference on Learning Representations (ICLR) (2015)
36. Krizhevsky, A., Sutskever, I., Hinton, G.E.: Imagenet classification with deep convolutional neural networks. In: Neural Information Processing Systems (NIPS) (2012)
37. Simonyan, K., Zisserman, A.: Two-stream convolutional networks for action recognition in videos. In: Neural Information Processing Systems (NIPS) (2014)
38. Tran, D., Bourdev, L., Fergus, R., Torresani, L., Paluri, M.: Learning spatiotemporal features with 3D convolutional networks. In: International Conference on Computer Vision (ICCV) (2015)
39. Chen, X., Fang, H., Lin, T., Vedantam, R., Gupta, S., Doll, P., Zitnick, C.L.: Microsoft coco captions: data collection and evaluation server. arXiv:1504.00325 (2015)
40. Devlin, J., Gupta, S., Girshick, R., Mitchell, M., Zitnick, C.L.: Exploring nearest neighbor approaches for image captioning. arXiv preprint arXiv:1505.04467 (2015)
41. Venugopalan, S., Rohrbach, M., Donahue, J., Mooney, R., Darrell, T., Saenko, K.: Sequence to sequence-video to text. In: International Conference on Computer Vision (ICCV), pp. 4534–4542 (2015)

Shuffle and Learn: Unsupervised Learning Using Temporal Order Verification

Ishan Misra[1(✉)], C. Lawrence Zitnick[2], and Martial Hebert[1]

[1] The Robotics Institute, Carnegie Mellon University, Pittsburgh, USA
{imisra,hebert}@cs.cmu.edu
[2] Facebook AI Research, Menlo Park, USA
zitnick@fb.com

Abstract. In this paper, we present an approach for learning a visual representation from the raw spatiotemporal signals in videos. Our representation is learned without supervision from semantic labels. We formulate our method as an unsupervised sequential verification task, i.e., we determine whether a sequence of frames from a video is in the correct temporal order. With this simple task and no semantic labels, we learn a powerful visual representation using a Convolutional Neural Network (CNN). The representation contains complementary information to that learned from supervised image datasets like ImageNet. Qualitative results show that our method captures information that is temporally varying, such as human pose. When used as pre-training for action recognition, our method gives significant gains over learning without external data on benchmark datasets like UCF101 and HMDB51. To demonstrate its sensitivity to human pose, we show results for pose estimation on the FLIC and MPII datasets that are competitive, or better than approaches using significantly more supervision. Our method can be combined with supervised representations to provide an additional boost in accuracy.

Keywords: Unsupervised learning · Videos · Sequence verification · Action recognition · Pose estimation · Convolutional neural networks

1 Introduction

Sequential data provides an abundant source of information in the form of auditory and visual percepts. Learning from the observation of sequential data is a natural and implicit process for humans [1–3]. It informs both low level cognitive tasks and high level abilities like decision making and problem solving [4]. For instance, answering the question "Where would the moving ball go?", requires the development of basic cognitive abilities like prediction from sequential data like video [5].

Electronic supplementary material The online version of this chapter (doi:10.1007/978-3-319-46448-0_32) contains supplementary material, which is available to authorized users.

© Springer International Publishing AG 2016
B. Leibe et al. (Eds.): ECCV 2016, Part I, LNCS 9905, pp. 527–544, 2016.
DOI: 10.1007/978-3-319-46448-0_32

In this paper, we explore the power of spatiotemporal signals, *i.e.*, videos, in the context of computer vision. To study the information available in a video signal in isolation, we ask the question: How does an agent learn from the spatiotemporal structure present in video without using supervised semantic labels? Are the representations learned using the unsupervised spatiotemporal information present in videos meaningful? And finally, are these representations complementary to those learned from strongly supervised image data? In this paper, we explore such questions by using a sequential learning approach.

Sequential learning is used in a variety of areas such as speech recognition, robotic path planning, adaptive control algorithms, *etc.* These approaches can be broadly categorized [6] into two classes: prediction and verification. In sequential prediction, the goal is to predict the signal given an input sequence. A popular application of this in Natural Language Processing (NLP) is 'word2vec' by Mikolov *et al.* [7,8] that learns distributional representations [9]. Using the continuous bag-of-words (CBOW) task, the model learns to predict a missing word given a sequence of surrounding words. The representation that results from this task has been shown to be semantically meaningful [7]. Unfortunately, extending the same technique to predict video frames is challenging. Unlike words that can be represented using limited-sized vocabularies, the space of possible video frames is extremely large [10], *eg.*, predicting pixels in a small 256×256 image leads to $256^{2 \times 3 \times 256}$ hypotheses! To avoid this complex task of predicting high-dimensional video frames, we use sequential verification.

In sequential verification, one predicts the 'validity' of the sequence, rather than individual items in the sequence. In this paper, we explore the task of determining whether a given sequence is 'temporally valid', *i.e.*, whether a sequence of video frames are in the correct temporal order, Fig. 1. We demonstrate that this binary classification problem is capable of learning useful visual representations from videos. Specifically, we explore their use in the well understood tasks of human action recognition and pose estimation. But why are these simple sequential verification tasks useful for learning? Determining the validity of a sequence requires reasoning about object transformations and relative locations through time. This in turn forces the representation to capture object appearances and deformations.

We use a Convolutional Neural Network (CNN) [11] for our underlying feature representation. The CNN is applied to each frame in the sequence and trained "end-to-end" from random initialization. The sequence verification task encourages the CNN features to be both visually and temporally grounded. We demonstrate the effectiveness of our unsupervised method on benchmark action recognition datasets UCF101 [12] and HMDB51 [13], and the FLIC [14] and MPII [15] pose estimation datasets. Using our simple unsupervised learning approach for pre-training, we show a significant boost in accuracy over learning CNNs from scratch with random initialization. In fact, our unsupervised approach even outperforms pre-training with some supervised training datasets. In action recognition, improved performance can be found by combining existing supervised image-based representations with our unsupervised representation. By training on action videos with humans, our approach learns a representation

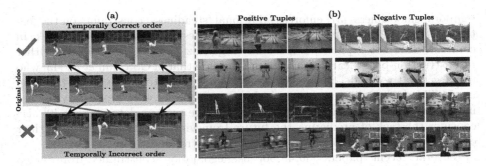

Fig. 1. (a) A video imposes a natural temporal structure for visual data. In many cases, one can easily verify whether frames are in the correct temporal order (shuffled or not). Such a simple sequential verification task captures important spatiotemporal signals in videos. We use this task for unsupervised pre-training of a Convolutional Neural Network (CNN). (b) Some examples of the automatically extracted positive and negative tuples used to formulate a classification task for a CNN.

sensitive to human pose. Remarkably, when applied to pose estimation, our representation is competitive with pre-training on significantly larger supervised training datasets [16].

2   Related Work

Our work uses unlabeled video sequences for learning representations. Since this source of supervision is 'free', our work can be viewed as a form of unsupervised learning. Unsupervised representation learning from single images is a popular area of research in computer vision. A significant body of unsupervised learning literature uses hand-crafted features and clustering based approaches to discover objects [17–19], or mid-level elements [20–24]. Deep learning methods like auto-encoders [25–27], Deep Boltzmann Machines [28], variational methods [29,30], stacked auto-encoders [31,32], and others [33,34] learn representations directly from images. These methods learn a representation by estimating latent parameters that help reconstruct the data, and may regularize the learning process by priors such as sparsity [25]. Techniques in [10,35] scale unsupervised learning to large image datasets showing its usefulness for tasks such as pedestrian detection [35] and object detection [10]. In terms of using 'context' for learning, our work is most similar to [10] which uses the spatial context in images. While these approaches are unsupervised, they do not use videos and cannot exploit the temporal structure in them. Our work is most related to work in unsupervised learning from videos [36–40]. Traditional methods in this domain utilize the spatiotemporal continuity as regularization for the learning process. Since visual appearance changes smoothly in videos, a common constraint is enforcing temporal smoothness of features [38,40–43]. Zhang and Tao [44], in particular, show how such constraints are useful for action recognition. Moving beyond just temporal smoothness, [37] enforces additional 'steadiness' constraints on the features so that the change of features across frames is meaningful. Our work, in contrast, does not explicitly impose any regularizations on the features. Other reconstruction-based learning approaches include that of Goroshin *et al.* [43] who use a generative model to predict video frames and Srivastava *et al.* [45] who use LSTMs [46]. Unlike our method, these works [38,43,45,47] explicitly predict individual frames, but do not explore large image sizes or datasets. [48,49] also consider the task of predicting the future from videos, but consider it as their end task and do not use it for unsupervised pre-training.

Several recent papers [36,48,50] use egomotion constraints from video to further constrain the learning. Jayaraman and Grauman [36] show how they can learn equivariant transforms from such constraints. Similar to our work, they use full video frames for learning with little pre-processing. Owens *et al.* [51] use audio signals from videos to learn visual representations. Another line of work [52] uses video data to mine patches which belong to the same object to learn representations useful for distinguishing objects. Typically, these approaches require significant pre-processing to create this task. While our work also uses videos, we explore them in the spirit of sequence verification for action recognition which learns from the raw video with very little pre-processing.

We demonstrate the effectiveness of our unsupervised pre-training using two extensively studied vision tasks - action recognition and pose estimation. These tasks have well established benchmark datasets [12–15]. As it is beyond the scope of this paper, we refer the reader to [53] for a survey on action recognition, and [54] for a survey on pose estimation.

3   Our Approach

Our goal is to learn a feature representation using only the raw spatiotemporal signal naturally available in videos. We learn this representation using a sequential verification task and focus on videos with human actions. Specifically, as shown in Fig. 1, we extract a tuple of frames from a video, and ask whether the frames are in the correct temporal order. In this section, we begin by motivating our use of sequential tasks and how they use the temporal structure of videos. We then describe how positive and negative tuples are sampled from videos, and describe our model.

3.1   Task Motivation

When using only raw videos as input, sequential verification tasks offer a promising approach to unsupervised learning. In addition to our approach described below, several alternative tasks are explored in Sect. 5.2. The goal of these tasks is to encourage the model to reason about the motion and appearance of the objects, and thus learn the temporal structure of videos. Example tasks may include reasoning about the ordering of frames, or determining the relative temporal proximity of frames. For tasks that ask for the verification of temporal order, how many frames are needed to determine a correct answer? If we want to determine the correct order from just two frames, the question may be ambiguous in cases where cyclical motion is present. For example, consider a short video sequence of a person picking up a coffee cup. Given two frames the temporal order is ambiguous; the person may be picking the coffee cup up, or placing it down.

To reduce such ambiguity, we propose sampling a three frame tuple, and ask whether the tuple's frames are correctly ordered. While theoretically, three frames are not sufficient to resolve cyclical ambiguity [55], we found that combining this with smart sampling (Sect. 3.2) removes a significant portion of ambiguous cases. We now formalize this problem into a classification task. Consider the set of frames $\{f_1, \ldots, f_n\}$ from an unlabeled video $\mathcal{V}$. We consider the tuple (f_b, f_c, f_d) to be in the correct temporal order (class 1, positive tuple) if the frames obey either ordering $b < c < d$ or $d < c < b$, to account for the directional ambiguity in video clips. Otherwise, if $b < d < c$ or $c < b < d$, we say that the frames are not in the correct temporal order (class 0, negative tuple).

3.2 Tuple Sampling

A critical challenge when training a network on the three-tuple ordering task is how to sample positive and negative training instances. A naive method may sample the tuples uniformly from a video. However, in temporal windows with very little motion it is hard to distinguish between a positive and a negative tuple, resulting in many ambiguous training examples. Instead, we only sample tuples from temporal windows with high motion. As Fig. 2 shows, we use coarse

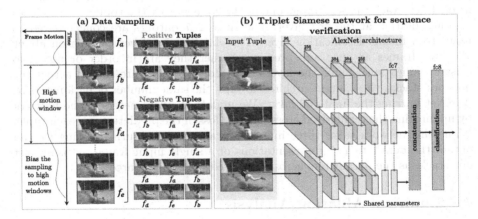

Fig. 2. (a) We sample tuples of frames from high motion windows in a video. We form positive and negative tuples based on whether the three input frames are in the correct temporal order. (b) Our triplet Siamese network architecture has three parallel network stacks with shared weights upto the fc7 layer. Each stack takes a frame as input, and produces a representation at the fc7 layer. The concatenated fc7 representations are used to predict whether the input tuple is in the correct temporal order.

frame level optical flow [56] as a proxy to measure the motion between frames. We treat the average flow magnitude per-frame as a weight for that frame, and use it to bias our sampling towards high motion windows. This ensures that the classification of the tuples is not ambiguous. Figure 1(b) shows examples of such tuples.

To create positive and negative tuples, we sample five frames $(f_a, f_b, f_c, f_d, f_e)$ from a temporal window such that $a < b < c < d < e$ (see Fig. 2(a)). Positive instances are created using (f_b, f_c, f_d), while negative instances are created using (f_b, f_a, f_d) and (f_b, f_e, f_d). Additional training examples are also created by inverting the order of all training instances, eg., (f_d, f_c, f_b) is positive. During training it is critical to use the same beginning frame f_b and ending frame f_d while only changing the middle frame for both positive and negative examples. Since only the middle frame changes between training examples, the network is encouraged to focus on this signal to learn the subtle difference between positives and negatives, rather than irrelevant features.

To avoid sampling ambiguous negative frames f_a and f_e, we enforce that the appearance of the positive f_c frame is not too similar (measured by SSD on RGB pixel values) to f_a or f_e. These simple conditions eliminated most ambiguous examples. We provide further analysis of sampling data in Sect. 4.1.

3.3 Model Parametrization and Learning

To learn a feature representation from the tuple ordering task, we use a simple triplet Siamese network. This network has three parallel stacks of layers with shared parameters (Fig. 2). Every network stack follows the standard CaffeNet [57] (a slight modification of AlexNet [58]) architecture from the conv1 to the fc7 layer. Each stack takes as input one of the frames from the tuple and produces a representation at the fc7 layer. The three fc7 outputs are concatenated as input to a linear classification layer. The classification layer can reason about all three frames at once and predict whether they are in order or not (two class classification). Since the layers from conv1 to fc7 are shared across the network stacks, the Siamese architecture has the same number of parameters as AlexNet barring the final fc8 layer. We update the parameters of the network by minimizing the regularized cross-entropy loss of the predictions on each tuple. While this network takes three inputs at training time, during testing we can obtain the conv1 to fc7 representations of a single input frame by using just one stack, as the parameters across the three stacks are shared.

4 Empirical Ablation Analysis

In this section (and in the Appendix), we present experiments to analyze the various design decisions for training our network. In Sects. 5 and 6, we provide results on both action recognition and pose estimation.

Dataset: We report all our results using split 1 of the benchmark UCF101 [12] dataset. This dataset contains videos for 101 action categories with ~9.5 k videos for training and $\sim$3.5 k videos for testing. Each video has an associated action category label. The standard performance metric for action recognition on this dataset is classification accuracy.

Details for Unsupervised Pre-training: For unsupervised pre-training, we do not use the semantic action labels. We sample about 900k tuples from the UCF101 training videos. We randomly initialize our network, and train for 100 k iterations with a fixed learning rate of 10^{-3} and mini-batch size of 128 tuples. Each tuple consists of 3 frames. Using more (4, 5) frames per tuple did not show significant improvement. We use batch normalization [59].

Details for Action Recognition: The spatial network from [60] is a well-established method of action recognition that uses only RGB appearance information. The parameters of the spatial network are initialized with our unsupervised pre-trained network. We use the provided action labels per video and follow the training and testing protocol as suggested in [60,61]. Briefly, for training we form mini-batches by sampling random frames from videos. At test time, 25 frames are uniformly sampled from each video. Each frame is used to generate 10 inputs after fixed cropping and flipping (5 crops $\times$ 2 flips), and the prediction for the video is an average of the predictions across these 25 $\times$ 10 inputs. We use the CaffeNet architecture for its speed and efficiency. We initialize the network parameters up to the `fc7` layer using the parameters from the unsupervised pre-trained network, and initialize a new `fc8` layer for the action recognition task. We finetune the network following [60] for 20k iterations with a batch size of 256, and learning rate of 10^{-2} decaying by 10 after 14k iterations, using SGD with momentum of 0.9, and dropout of 0.5. While [60] used the wider VGG-M-2048 [62] architecture, we found that their parameters transfer to CaffeNet because of the similarities in their architectures.

4.1 Sampling of Data

In this section we study the impact of sampling parameters described in Sect. 3.2 on the unsupervised pre-training task. We denote the maximum distance between frames of positive tuples by $\tau_{max} = |b-d|$. This parameter controls the 'difficulty' of positives: a very high value makes it difficult to see correspondence across the positive tuple, and a very low value gives almost identical frames and thus very easy positives. Similarly, we compute the minimum distance between the frames f_a and f_e used for negative tuples to the other frames by $\tau_{min} = \min(|a-b|, |d-e|)$. This parameter controls the difficulty of negatives with a low value making them harder, and a high value making them easier.

We compute the training and testing accuracy of these networks on the tuple prediction task on held out videos. This held out set is a union of samples using all the temporal sampling parameters. We show results in Table 1(a). We also use these networks for finetuning on the UCF101 action recognition task. Our results show that the tuple prediction accuracy and the performance on the

Table 1. We study the effect of our design choices such as temporal sampling parameters, and varying class ratios for unsupervised pre-training. We measure the tuple prediction accuracy on a held out set from UCF101. We also show action classification results after finetuning the models on the UCF101 action recognition task (split 1).

(a) Varying temporal sampling				(b) Varying class ratios			
τ_{max}	τ_{min}	Tuple Pred.	Action Recog.	Class Ratio Neg	Pos	Tuple Pred.	Action Recog.
30	15	60.2	47.2	0.5	0.5	52.1	38.1
60	15	**72.1**	**50.9**	0.65	0.35	68.5	45.5
60	60	64.3	49.1	0.75	0.25	**72.1**	**50.9**
				0.85	0.15	67.7	48.6

action recognition task are correlated. A large temporal window for positive sampling improves over a smaller temporal window (Rows 1 and 2), while a large window for negative sampling hurts performance (Rows 2 and 3).

4.2 Class Ratios in Mini-batch

Another important factor when training the model is the class ratios in each mini-batch. As has been observed empirically [63,64], a good class ratio per mini-batch ensures that the model does not overfit to one particular class, and helps the learning process. For these experiments, we choose a single temporal window for sampling and vary only the ratio of positive and negative tuples per mini-batch. We compare the accuracy of these networks on the tuple prediction task on held out videos in Table 1(b). Additionally, we report the accuracy of these networks after finetuning on the action recognition task. These results show that the class ratio used for unsupervised pre-training can significantly impact learning. It is important to have a larger percentage of negative examples.

4.3 What Does the Temporal Ordering Task Capture?

Nearest Neighbor Retrieval. We retrieve nearest neighbors using our unsupervised features on the UCF101 dataset and compare them in Fig. 3 to retrievals by the pre-trained ImageNet features, and a randomly initialized network. Additional examples are shown in the supplementary materials. We pick an input query frame from a clip and retrieve neighbors from other clips in the UCF101 dataset. Since the UCF101 dataset has clips from the same video, the first set of retrievals (after removing frames from the same input clip) are near duplicates which are not very informative (notice the random network's results). We remove these near-duplicates by computing the sum of squared distances (SSD) between the frames, and display the top results in the second row of each query. These results make two things clear: (1) the ImageNet pre-trained network focuses on

Fig. 3. We compute nearest neighbors using `fc7` features on the UCF101 dataset. We compare these results across three networks: pre-trained on ImageNet, pre-trained on our unsupervised task and a randomly initialized network. We choose a input query frame from a clip and retrieve results from other clips in the dataset. Since the dataset contains multiple clips from the same video we get near duplicate retrievals (first row). We remove these duplicates, and display results in the second row. While ImageNet focuses on the high level semantics, our network captures the human pose.

scene semantics (2) Our unsupervised pre-trained network focuses on the pose of the person. This would seem to indicate that the information captured by our unsupervised pre-training is complementary to that of ImageNet. Such behavior is not surprising, if we consider our network was trained without semantic labels, and must reason about spatiotemporal signals for the tuple verification task.

Visualizing `pool5` Unit Responses. We analyze the feature representation of the unsupervised network trained using the tuple prediction task on UCF101. Following the procedure of [65] we show the top regions for `pool5` units alongwith their receptive field in Fig. 4. This gives us insight into the network's internal feature representation and shows that many units show preference for human body parts and pose. This is not surprising given that our network is trained on videos of human action recognition, and must reason about human movements for the tuple ordering task.

Fig. 4. In each row we display the top image regions for a unit from the `pool5` layer. We follow the method in [65] and display the receptive fields (marked in red boxes) for these units. As our network is trained on human action recognition videos, many units show preference for human body parts and pose. (Color figure online)

5   Additional Experiments on Action Recognition

The previous experiments show that the unsupervised task learns a meaningful representation. In this section we compare our unsupervised method against existing baseline methods and present more quantitative results. We organize our experiments as follows: (1) Comparing our unsupervised method to learning from random initialization. (2) Exploring other unsupervised baselines and comparing our method with them. (3) Combining our unsupervised representation learning method with a supervised image representation. Additional experiments are in the supplementary material. We now describe the common experimental setup.

Datasets and Evaluation: We use the UCF101 [12] dataset which was also used for our ablation analysis in Sect. 4 and measure accuracy on the 101 action classification task. Additionally, we use the HMDB51 [13] dataset for action recognition. This dataset contains 3 splits for train/test, each with about 3.4k videos for train and 1.4k videos for testing. Each video belongs to one of 51 action categories, and performance is evaluated by measuring classification accuracy. We follow the same train/test protocols for both UCF101 and HMDB51 as described in Sect. 4. Note that the UCF101 dataset is about 2.5× larger than the HMDB51 dataset.

Implementation Details for Pre-training: We use tuples sampled using $\tau_{max} = 60$ and $\tau_{min} = 15$ as described in Sect. 4. The class ratio of positive examples per mini-batch is 25 %. The other parameters for training/finetuning are kept unchanged from Sect. 4.

Action Recognition Details: As in Sect. 4, we use the CaffeNet architecture and the parameters from [60] for both training from scratch and finetuning. We described the finetuning parameters in Sect. 4. For training from random initialization (or 'scratch'), we train for 80 k iterations with an initial learning rate of 10^{-2}, decaying by a factor of 10 at steps 50 k and 70 k. The other training parameters (momentum, batch size etc.) are kept the same as in finetuning. We use the improved data augmentation scheme (different aspect-ratio, fixed crops) from [61] for all our methods and baselines. Note that we train or finetune all the layers of the network for all methods, including ours.

5.1   Unsupervised Pre-training or Random Initialization?

In these experiments we study the advantage of unsupervised pre-training for action recognition in comparison to learning without any pre-training. We use our tuple prediction task to train a network starting from random initialization on the train split of UCF101. The unsupervised pre-trained network is finetuned on both the UCF101 and HMDB51 datasets for action recognition and compared against learning from scratch (without pre-training). We report the performance in Table 2. Our unsupervised pre-training shows a dramatic **improvement of** +12.4 % over training from scratch in UCF101 and a significant gain of +4.7 % in HMDB51. This impressive gain demonstrates the informativeness of the unsupervised tuple verification task. On HMDB51, we additionally finetune a network which was trained from scratch on UCF101 and report its performance in Table 2 indicated by 'UCF supervised'. We see that this network performs worse than our unsupervised pre-trained network. The UCF101 and HMDB51 have only 23 action classes in common [60] and we hypothesize that the poor performance is due to the scratch UCF101 network being unable to generalize to actions

Table 2. Mean classification accuracies over the 3 splits of UCF101 and HMDB51 datasets. We compare different initializations and finetune them for action recognition.

Dataset	Initialization	Mean accuracy
UCF101	Random	38.6
	(Ours) tuple verification	**50.2**
HMDB51	Random	13.3
	UCF supervised	15.2
	(Ours) Tuple verification	**18.1**

from HMDB51. For reference, a model pre-trained on the supervised ImageNet dataset [16,66] and finetuned on UCF101 gives 67.1 % accuracy, and ImageNet finetuned on HMDB51 gives an accuracy of 28.5 %.

5.2   Unsupervised Baselines

In this section, we enumerate a variety of alternative verification tasks that use only video frames and their temporal ordering. For each task, we use a similar frame sampling procedure to the one described in Sect. 4.1. We compare their performance after finetuning them on the task of action recognition. A more informative task should serve as a better task for pre-training.

Two Close: In this task two frames (f_b, f_d) (with high motion) are considered to be temporally close if $|b - d| < \tau$ for a fixed temporal window $\tau = 30$.

Two Order: Two frames (f_b, f_d) are considered to be correct if $b < d$. Otherwise they are considered incorrect. $|b - d| < 30$.

Three Order: This is the original temporal ordering task we proposed in Sect. 3.1. We consider the 3-tuple (f_b, f_c, f_d) to be correct only if the frames obey either ordering $b < c < d$ or $b > c > d$.

   We also compare against standard baselines for unsupervised learning from video.

DrLim [40]: As Eq. 1 shows, this method enforces temporal smoothness over the learned features by minimizing the l_2 distance d between representations (fc7) of nearby frames f_b, f_d (positive class or $c = 1$), while requiring frames that are not close (negative class or $c = 0$) to be separated by a margin δ. We use the same samples as in the 'Two Close' baseline, and set $\delta = 1.0$ [38].

$$L(f_b, f_d) = \mathbb{1}(c = 1)d(f_b, f_d) + \mathbb{1}(c = 0)\max(\delta - d(f_b, f_d), 0) \quad (1)$$

TempCoh [38]: Similar to the DrLim method, temporal coherence learns representations from video by using the l_1 distance for pairs of frames rather than the l_2 distance of DrLim.

Obj. Patch [52]: We use their publicly available model which was unsupervised pre-trained on videos of objects. As their patch-mining code is not available, we do not do unsupervised pre-training on UCF101 for their model.

   All these methods (except [52]) are pre-trained on training split 1 of UCF101 without action labels, and then finetuned on test split 1 of UCF101 actions and HMDB51 actions. We compare them in Table 3. Scratch performance for test split 1 of UCF101 and HMDB51 is 39.1 % and 14.8 % respectively. The tuple verification task outperforms other sequential ordering tasks, and the standard baselines by a significant margin. We attribute the low number of [52] to the fact that they focus on object detection on a very different set of videos, and thus do not perform well on action recognition.

Table 3. We compare the unsupervised methods defined in Sect. 5.2 by finetuning on the UCF101 and HMDB51 Action recognition (split 1 for both). Method with * was not pre-trained on action data.

Unsup method →	Two close	Two order	DrLim [40]	TempCoh [38]	Three Order (Ours)	Obj. Patch* [52]
Acc. UCF101	42.3	44.1	45.7	45.4	**50.9**	40.7
Acc. HMDB51	15.0	16.4	16.3	15.9	**19.8**	15.6

5.3 Combining Unsupervised and Supervised Pre-training

We have thus far seen that unsupervised pre-training gives a significant performance boost over training from random initialization. We now see if our pre-training can help improve existing image representations. Specifically, we initialize our model using the weights from the ImageNet pre-trained model and use it for the tuple-prediction task on UCF101 by finetuning for 10k iterations. We hypothesize this may add complementary information to the ImageNet representation. To test this, we finetune this model on the HMDB51 [13] action recognition task. We compare this performance to finetuning on HMDB51 without the tuple-prediction task. Table 4 shows these results.

Our results show that combining our pre-training with ImageNet helps improve the accuracy of the model (rows 3, 4). Finally, we compare against using multiple sources of supervised data: initialized using the ImageNet weights, finetuned on UCF101 action recognition and then finetuned on HMDB51 (row 5). The accuracy using all sources of supervised data is only slightly better than the performance of our model (rows 4, 5). This demonstrates the effectiveness of our simple yet powerful unsupervised pre-training.

Table 4. Results of using our unsupervised pre-training to adapt existing image representations trained on ImageNet. We use unsupervised data from training split 1 of UCF101, and show the mean accuracy (3 splits) by finetuning on HMDB51.

Initialization	Mean accuracy
Random	13.3
(Ours) tuple verification	18.1
UCF sup	15.2
ImageNet	28.5
(Ours) ImageNet + tuple verification	**29.9**
ImageNet + UCF sup	30.6

6   Pose Estimation Experiments

The qualitative results from Sect. 4.3 suggest that our network captures information about human pose. To evaluate this quantitatively, we conduct experiments on the task of pose estimation using keypoint prediction.

Datasets and Metrics: We use the FLIC (full) [14] and the MPII [15] datasets. For FLIC, we consider 7 keypoints on the torso: head, 2× (shoulders, elbows, wrists). We compute the keypoint for the head as an average of the keypoints for the eyes and nose. We evaluate the Probability of Correct Keypoints (PCK) measure [67] for the keypoints. For MPII, we use all the keypoints on the full body and report the PCKh@0.5 metric as is standard for this dataset.

Model Training: We use the CaffeNet architecture to regress to the keypoints. We follow the training procedure in [68][1]. For FLIC, we use a train/test split of 17k and 3k images respectively and finetune models for 100k iterations. For MPII, we use a train/test split of 18k and 2k images. We use a batch size of 32, learning rate of 5×10^{-4} with AdaGrad [69] and minimize the Euclidean loss (l_2 distance between ground truth and predicted keypoints). For training from scratch (Random Init.), we use a learning rate of 5×10^{-4} for 1.3M iterations.

Methods: Following the setup in Sect. 5.1, we compare against various initializations of the network. We consider two supervised initalizations - from pre-training on ImageNet and UCF101. We consider three unsupervised initializations - our tuple based method, DrLim [40] on UCF101, and the method of [52]. We also combine our unsupervised initialization with ImageNet pre-training.

Our results for pose estimation are summarized in Table 5. Our unsupervised pre-training method outperforms the fully supervised UCF network (Sect. 5.1) by +7.6 % on FLIC and +2.1 % on MPII. Our method is also competitive with ImageNet pre-training on both these datasets. Our unsupervised pre-training is complementary to ImageNet pre-training, and can improve results after being

Table 5. Pose estimation results on the FLIC and MPII datasets.

Init	PCK for FLIC						PCKh@0.5 for MPII		
	wri	elb	sho	head	Mean	AUC	Upper	Full	AUC
Random Init	53.0	75.2	86.7	91.7	74.5	36.1	76.1	72.9	34.0
Tuple Verif	**69.6**	**85.5**	**92.8**	**97.4**	**84.7**	**49.6**	<u>**87.7**</u>	85.8	**47.6**
Obj. Patch [52]	58.2	77.8	88.4	94.8	77.1	42.1	84.3	82.8	43.8
DrLim [40]	37.8	68.4	80.4	83.4	65.2	27.9	84.3	81.5	41.5
UCF Sup	61.0	78.8	89.1	93.8	78.8	42.0	86.9	84.6	45.5
ImageNet	69.6	86.7	93.6	97.9	85.8	51.3	85.1	83.5	47.2
ImageNet + Tuple	**69.7**	<u>**87.1**</u>	<u>**93.8**</u>	<u>**98.1**</u>	<u>**86.2**</u>	<u>**52.5**</u>	87.6	<u>**86.0**</u>	<u>**49.5**</u>

---

[1] Public re-implementation from https://github.com/mitmul/deeppose.

combined with it. This supports the qualitative results from Sect. 4.3 that show our method can learn human pose information from unsupervised videos.

7   Discussion

In this paper, we studied unsupervised learning from the raw spatiotemporal signal in videos. Our proposed method outperforms other existing unsupervised methods and is competitive with supervised methods. A next step to our work is to explore different types of videos and use other 'free' signals such as optical flow. Another direction is to use a combination of CNNs and RNNs, and to extend our tuple verification task to much longer sequences. We believe combining this with semi-supervised methods [70,71] is a promising future direction.

Acknowledgments. The authors thank Pushmeet Kohli, Ross Girshick, Abhinav Shrivastava and Saurabh Gupta for helpful discussions. Ed Walter for his timely help with the systems. This work was supported in part by ONR MURI N000141612007 and the US Army Research Laboratory (ARL) under the CTA program (Agreement W911NF-10-2-0016). We gratefully acknowledge the hardware donation by NVIDIA.

References

1. Cleeremans, A., McClelland, J.L.: Learning the structure of event sequences. J. Exp. Psychol. Gen. **120**(3), 235 (1991)
2. Reber, A.S.: Implicit learning and tacit knowledge. J. Exp. Psychol.: Gen. **118**(3), 219 (1989)
3. Cleeremans, A.: Mechanisms of Implicit Learning: Connectionist Models of Sequence Processing. MIT Press, Cambridge (1993)
4. Sun, R., Merrill, E., Peterson, T.: From implicit skills to explicit knowledge: a bottom-up model of skill learning. Cognit. Sci. **25**(2), 203–244 (2001)
5. Baker, R., Dexter, M., Hardwicke, T.E., Goldstone, A., Kourtzi, Z.: Learning to predict: exposure to temporal sequences facilitates prediction of future events. Vis. Res. **99**, 124–133 (2014)
6. Sun, R., Giles, C.L.: Sequence learning: from recognition and prediction to sequential decision making. IEEE Intell. Syst. **16**(4), 67–70 (2001)
7. Mikolov, T., Chen, K., Corrado, G., Dean, J.: Efficient estimation of word representations in vector space. arXiv preprint arXiv:1301.3781 (2013)
8. Mikolov, T., Sutskever, I., Chen, K., Corrado, G.S., Dean, J.: Distributed representations of words and phrases and their compositionality. In: NIPS (2013)
9. Firth, J.R.: A synopsis of linguistic theory 1930–1955 (1957)
10. Doersch, C., Gupta, A., Efros, A.A.: Unsupervised visual representation learning by context prediction. In: ICCV (2015)
11. LeCun, Y., Boser, B., Denker, J.S., Henderson, D., Howard, R.E., Hubbard, W., Jackel, L.D.: Backpropagation applied to handwritten zip code recognition. Neural Comput. **1**(4), 541–551 (1989)
12. Soomro, K., Zamir, A.R., Shah, M.: UCF101: a dataset of 101 human actions classes from videos in the wild. arXiv preprint arXiv:1212.0402 (2012)
13. Kuehne, H., Jhuang, H., Garrote, E., Poggio, T., Serre, T.: HMDB: a large video database for human motion recognition. In: ICCV (2011)

14. Sapp, B., Taskar, B.: MODEC: multimodal decomposable models for human pose estimation. In: CVPR (2013)
15. Andriluka, M., Pishchulin, L., Gehler, P., Schiele, B.: 2D human pose estimation: new benchmark and state of the art analysis. In: CVPR, June 2014
16. Deng, J., Dong, W., Socher, R., Li, L.J., Li, K., Fei-Fei, L.: Imagenet: a large-scale hierarchical image database. In: CVPR (2009)
17. Faktor, A., Irani, M.: "Clustering by Composition" – unsupervised discovery of image categories. In: Fitzgibbon, A., Lazebnik, S., Perona, P., Sato, Y., Schmid, C. (eds.) ECCV 2012, Part VII. LNCS, vol. 7578, pp. 474–487. Springer, Heidelberg (2012)
18. Sivic, J., Russell, B.C., Efros, A.A., Zisserman, A., Freeman, W.T.: Discovering objects and their location in images. In: ICCV (2005)
19. Russell, B.C., Freeman, W.T., Efros, A.A., Sivic, J., Zisserman, A.: Using multiple segmentations to discover objects and their extent in image collections. In: CVPR (2006)
20. Singh, S., Gupta, A., Efros, A.A.: Unsupervised discovery of mid-level discriminative patches. In: Fitzgibbon, A., Lazebnik, S., Perona, P., Sato, Y., Schmid, C. (eds.) ECCV 2012, Part II. LNCS, vol. 7573, pp. 73–86. Springer, Heidelberg (2012)
21. Juneja, M., Vedaldi, A., Jawahar, C., Zisserman, A.: Blocks that shout: distinctive parts for scene classification. In: CVPR (2013)
22. Doersch, C., Gupta, A., Efros, A.A.: Mid-level visual element discovery as discriminative mode seeking. In: NIPS (2013)
23. Li, Q., Wu, J., Tu, Z.: Harvesting mid-level visual concepts from large-scale internet images. In: CVPR (2013)
24. Sun, J., Ponce, J.: Learning discriminative part detectors for image classification and cosegmentation. In: ICCV (2013)
25. Olshausen, B.A., et al.: Emergence of simple-cell receptive field properties by learning a sparse code for natural images. Nature 381(6583), 607–609 (1996)
26. Bengio, Y., Thibodeau-Laufer, E., Alain, G., Yosinski, J.: Deep generative stochastic networks trainable by backprop. arXiv preprint arXiv:1306.1091 (2013)
27. Vincent, P., Larochelle, H., Bengio, Y., Manzagol, P.A.: Extracting and composing robust features with denoising autoencoders. In: ICML (2008)
28. Salakhutdinov, R., Hinton, G.E.: Deep Boltzmann machines. In: ICAIS (2009)
29. Kingma, D.P., Welling, M.: Auto-encoding variational bayes. arXiv preprint arXiv:1312.6114 (2013)
30. Rezende, D.J., Mohamed, S., Wierstra, D.: Stochastic backpropagation and approximate inference in deep generative models. arXiv preprint arXiv:1401.4082 (2014)
31. Lee, H., Battle, A., Raina, R., Ng, A.Y.: Efficient sparse coding algorithms. In: NIPS (2006)
32. Bengio, Y., Lamblin, P., Popovici, D., Larochelle, H., et al.: Greedy layer-wise training of deep networks. NIPS (2007)
33. Le, Q.V.: Building high-level features using large scale unsupervised learning. In: ICASSP (2013)
34. Wang, X., Gupta, A.: Generative image modeling using style and structure adversarial networks. In: ECCV (2016)
35. Sermanet, P., Kavukcuoglu, K., Chintala, S., LeCun, Y.: Pedestrian detection with unsupervised multi-stage feature learning. In: CVPR (2013)
36. Jayaraman, D., Grauman, K.: Learning image representations equivariant to ego-motion. In: ICCV (2015)

37. Jayaraman, D., Grauman, K.: Slow and steady feature analysis: higher order temporal coherence in video. arXiv preprint arXiv:1506.04714 (2015)
38. Mobahi, H., Collobert, R., Weston, J.: Deep learning from temporal coherence in video. In: ICML (2009)
39. Isola, P., Zoran, D., Krishnan, D., Adelson, E.H.: Learning visual groups from co-occurrences in space and time. arXiv preprint arXiv:1511.06811 (2015)
40. Hadsell, R., Chopra, S., LeCun, Y.: Dimensionality reduction by learning an invariant mapping. In: CVPR. IEEE (2006)
41. Földiák, P.: Learning invariance from transformation sequences. Neural Comput. 3(2), 194–200 (1991)
42. Wiskott, L., Sejnowski, T.J.: Slow feature analysis: unsupervised learning of invariances. Neural Comput. 14(4), 715–770 (2002)
43. Goroshin, R., Bruna, J., Tompson, J., Eigen, D., LeCun, Y.: Unsupervised learning of spatiotemporally coherent metrics. In: ICCV (2015)
44. Zhang, Z., Tao, D.: Slow feature analysis for human action recognition. TPAMI 34(3), 436–450 (2012)
45. Srivastava, N., Mansimov, E., Salakhutdinov, R.: Unsupervised learning of video representations using lstms. arXiv preprint arXiv:1502.04681 (2015)
46. Hochreiter, S., Schmidhuber, J.: Long short-term memory. Neural Comput. 9(8), 1735–1780 (1997)
47. Taylor, G.W., Fergus, R., LeCun, Y., Bregler, C.: Convolutional learning of spatiotemporal features. In: Daniilidis, K., Maragos, P., Paragios, N. (eds.) ECCV 2010, Part VI. LNCS, vol. 6316, pp. 140–153. Springer, Heidelberg (2010)
48. Zhou, Y., Berg, T.L.: Temporal perception and prediction in ego-centric video. In: ICCV (2015)
49. Vondrick, C., Pirsiavash, H., Torralba, A.: Anticipating the future by watching unlabeled video. arXiv preprint arXiv:1504.08023 (2015)
50. Agrawal, P., Carreira, J., Malik, J.: Learning to see by moving. In: ICCV (2015)
51. Owens, A., Isola, P., McDermott, J., Torralba, A., Adelson, E.H., Freeman, W.T.: Visually indicated sounds. In: CVPR (2016)
52. Wang, X., Gupta, A.: Unsupervised learning of visual representations using videos. In: ICCV (2015)
53. Poppe, R.: A survey on vision-based human action recognition. Image Vis. Comput. 28(6), 976–990 (2010)
54. Perez-Sala, X., Escalera, S., Angulo, C., Gonzalez, J.: A survey on model based approaches for 2D and 3D visual human pose recovery. Sensors 14(3), 4189–4210 (2014)
55. Shannon, C.E.: Communication in the presence of noise. Proc. IRE 37(1), 10–21 (1949)
56. Farnebäck, G.: Two-frame motion estimation based on polynomial expansion. In: Bigun, J., Gustavsson, T. (eds.) SCIA 2003. LNCS, vol. 2749, pp. 363–370. Springer, Heidelberg (2003)
57. Jia, Y., Shelhamer, E., Donahue, J., Karayev, S., Long, J., Girshick, R., Guadarrama, S., Darrell, T.: Caffe: convolutional architecture for fast feature embedding. In: ACMM (2014)
58. Krizhevsky, A., Sutskever, I., Hinton, G.E.: Imagenet classification with deep convolutional neural networks. In: NIPS (2012)
59. Ioffe, S., Szegedy, C.: Batch normalization: accelerating deep network training by reducing internal covariate shift. arXiv preprint arXiv:1502.03167 (2015)
60. Simonyan, K., Zisserman, A.: Two-stream convolutional networks for action recognition in videos. In: NIPS (2014)

61. Wang, L., Xiong, Y., Wang, Z., Qiao, Y.: Towards good practices for very deep two-stream convnets. arXiv preprint arXiv:1507.02159 (2015)
62. Chatfield, K., Simonyan, K., Vedaldi, A., Zisserman, A.: Return of the devil in the details: delving deep into convolutional nets. In: BMVC (2014)
63. Girshick, R.: Fast R-CNN. In: ICCV (2015)
64. Ren, S., He, K., Girshick, R., Sun, J.: Faster R-CNN: towards real-time object detection with region proposal networks. In: NIPS (2015)
65. Girshick, R., Donahue, J., Darrell, T., Malik, J.: Rich feature hierarchies for accurate object detection and semantic segmentation. In: CVPR (2014)
66. Russakovsky, O., Deng, J., Su, H., Krause, J., Satheesh, S., Ma, S., Huang, Z., Karpathy, A., Khosla, A., Bernstein, M., Berg, A.C., Fei-Fei, L.: ImageNet large scale visual recognition challenge. IJCV **115**(3), 211–252 (2015)
67. Yang, Y., Ramanan, D.: Articulated human detection with flexible mixtures of parts. TPAMI **35**(12), 2878–2890 (2013)
68. Toshev, A., Szegedy, C.: Deeppose: human pose estimation via deep neural networks. In: CVPR (2014)
69. Duchi, J., Hazan, E., Singer, Y.: Adaptive subgradient methods for online learning and stochastic optimization. JMLR **12**, 2121–2159 (2011)
70. Misra, I., Shrivastava, A., Hebert, M.: Watch and learn: semi-supervised learning of object detectors from videos. In: CVPR (2015)
71. Liang, X., Liu, S., Wei, Y., Liu, L., Lin, L., Yan, S.: Towards computational baby learning: a weakly-supervised approach for object detection. In: ICCV (2015)

DOC: Deep OCclusion Estimation from a Single Image

Peng Wang[1]([✉]) and Alan Yuille[1,2]

[1] University of California, Los Angeles, USA
jerryking234@gmail.com
[2] John Hopkins University, Baltimore, USA
alan.l.yuille@gmail.com

Abstract. In this paper, we propose a deep convolutional network architecture, called DOC, which detects object boundaries and estimates the occlusion relationships (i.e. which side of the boundary is foreground and which is background). Specifically, we first represent occlusion relations by a binary edge indicator, to indicate the object boundary, and an occlusion orientation variable whose direction specifies the occlusion relationships by a left-hand rule, see Fig. 1. Then, our DOC networks exploit local and non-local image cues to learn and estimate this representation and hence recover occlusion relations. To train and test DOC, we construct a large-scale instance occlusion boundary dataset using PASCAL VOC images, which we call the PASCAL instance occlusion dataset (PIOD). It contains 10,000 images and hence is two orders of magnitude larger than existing occlusion datasets for outdoor images. We test two variants of DOC on PIOD and on the BSDS ownership dataset and show they outperform state-of-the-art methods typically by more than 5AP. Finally, we perform numerous experiments investigating multiple settings of DOC and transfer between BSDS and PIOD, which provides more insights for further study of occlusion estimation.

1 Introduction

Humans are able to recover the occlusion relationships of objects from single images. This has long been recognized as an important ability for scene understanding and perception [4,15]. As shown on the left of Fig. 1, we can use occlusion relationships to deduce that the person is holding a dog, because the person's hand occludes the dog and the dog occludes the person's body. Electrophysiological [18] and fMRI [13] studies suggest that occlusion relationships are detected as early as visual area V2. Biological studies [9] also suggest that occlusion detection can require feedback from higher level cortical regions, indicating that long-range context and semantic-level knowledge may be needed. Psychophysical studies show that there are many cues for occlusion including edge convexity [23], edge-junctions, intensity gradients, and texture [35].

Electronic supplementary material The online version of this chapter (doi:10.1007/978-3-319-46448-0_33) contains supplementary material, which is available to authorized users.

© Springer International Publishing AG 2016
B. Leibe et al. (Eds.): ECCV 2016, Part I, LNCS 9905, pp. 545–561, 2016.
DOI: 10.1007/978-3-319-46448-0_33

Fig. 1. Left: Occlusion boundaries represented by orientation θ (the red arrows), which indicates occlusion relationship using the "left" rule where the left side of the arrows is foreground. Right: More examples from our Pascal instance occlusion dataset (PIOD). (Color figure online)

Computer vision researchers have also used similar cues for estimating occlusion relations. A standard strategy is to apply machine learning techniques to combine cues like convexity, triple-points, geometric context, image features like HOG, and spectral features, e.g. [5,20,37,45]. These methods, however, mostly rely on hand-crafted features and have only been trained on the small occlusion datasets currently available. But in recent years, fully convolutional deep convolutional neural networks (FCN) [29] that exploit local and non-local cues, and trained on large datasets, have been very successful for related visual tasks such as edge detection [49] and semantic segmentation [6]. In addition, visualization of deep networks [30,51] show that they can also capture and exploit the types of visual cues needed to estimate occlusion relations.

This motivates us to apply deep networks to estimate occlusion relationships, which requires constructing a large annotated occlusion dataset. This also requires making design choices such as how to represent occlusion relations and what type of deep network architecture is best able to capture the local and non-local cues required. We represent occlusion relations by a per-pixel representation with two variables: (i) a binary edge variable to indicate if a pixel in on a boundary, and (ii) a continuous-valued occlusion orientation variable (at each edge pixel) in the tangent direction of the edge whose direction indicates the occlusion relationship using the left rule (i.e. the region to the left of the edge is in front of the region to the right). Our DOC network architecture is based on recent fully convolutional networks [29] and is multi-scale so that it can take into account local and non-local image cues. More specifically, we design two versions of DOC based on [6,49] respectively.

To construct our dataset, we select PASCAL VOC images [12] where many of the object boundaries have already been annotated [7,16]. This simplifies our annotation task since we only have to label the occlusion orientation variable specifying border ownership. Our Pascal Instance Occlusion Dataset (PIOD) consists of 10,000 images and is two orders of magnitude larger than existing ones such as the BSDS border ownership [37] (200 images) and GeoContext [20] (100 images). We note that the NYU depth dataset [41] (1449 indoor images) can also be used to test occlusion relations, but restricted to indoor images.

This paper makes two main contributions: (1) We design a new representation and corresponding loss for FCN architecture showing that it performs well and is computationally efficient (0.6s/image). (2) We create a large occlusion boundary dataset over the PASCAL VOC images, which is a new resource for studying occlusion. We will release our models, code and dataset.

2   Related Work

In computer vision, studying occlusion relations has often been confined to multiview problems such as stereo and motion [2,17,42,44,48]. In these situations multiple images are available and so occlusion can be detected by finding pixels which have no correspondence between images [3,14].

Inferring occlusion relations from a single image is harder. Early work restricted to simple domains, e.g. blocks world [38] and line drawings [8] using a variety of techniques ranging from algebraic [43] to the use of markov random fields (MRF) for capturing non-local context [39,50]. The 2.1D sketch [34] is a mid-level representation of images involving occlusion relations, but it was conceptual and served to draw attention to the importance of this task.

Research on detecting occlusion relations in natural images was stimulated by the construction of the BSDS border ownership dataset [37]. Computer vision methods typically addressed this problem using a two stage approach. For example, [37] used the Pb edge detector [33] to extract edge features and then used a MRF to determine foreground and background. This was followed up [24] who used a richer set of occlusion cues. Other work by [20] introduced the use of explicit high-level cues including semantic knowledge (e.g., sky and ground) and introduced a new dataset GeoContext for this purpose. Note that in this paper we do not use explicit high-level cues although these might be implicitly captured by the deep network. Recently, [45] used multiple features (e.g., HOG) joint with structure random forest (SRF) [10] and geometric grouping cues (for non-local context) to recover the boundaries and foreground background simultaneously. Maire et al. [31,32] also designed and embed the border ownership representation into inference the segmentation depth ordering.

Occlusion relations can also be addressed using techniques which estimate 3D depth from single images. These methods typically use either MRF (to capture non-local structure) [19,26,40], deep learning [11], or combinations of both [25, 27,46]. These studies do not explicitly attempt to estimate occlusion, but it can be deduced by detecting the depth discontinuities in the estimated depth map. To train these methods, however, requires annotated 3D data which is hard to obtain for outdoor images, such as those in PASCAL VOC. Hence these methods are most suitable for indoor studies, e.g., on the NYU depth dataset [41].

Our method builds on the fully convolutional network literature and, in particular, recent work on edge detection [49] and semantic segmentation [6] which exploit multi-scale and capture local and non-local cues. We also handle network downsampling by combining the "hole" algorithm [6] and deconvolution [29].

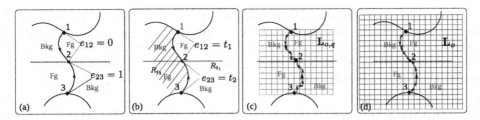

Fig. 2. Four ways to represent occlusion relations, see Sect. 3.1. Consider the boundary contour joining triple points 1 and 3 where border ownership changes at the midpoint 2. The background is to the left of the border between points 1 and 2, but it is on the right of the border between 2 and 3. The "left" rule uses the occlusion orientation on the contour, see arrow, to indicate border ownership (i.e. the left side of the arrow specifies the side of foreground). In panels (a) and (b), the triples points $1, 3$ and the junction 2 are explicitly represented. Panel (a), see [37], uses binary variables e_{12}, e_{23} to specify border ownership, while panel (b) includes explicit semantic knowledge [20] where regions are represented by their semantic types, e.g., t_1, t_2. In panels (c) and (d), the representation is pixel-based. $\mathbf{L}_{o,q}, \mathbf{L}_o$ represent occlusions in terms of a boundary indicator and an occlusion orientation variable (the dense arrows) using the "left" rule to indicate border ownership (i.e. which side is foreground). The difference is that in panel (c), see [45], $\mathbf{L}_{o,q}$ quantizes the occlusion orientation to take 8 values. In contrast, in panel (d), $\mathbf{L}_o$ allows it to take continuous values.

3   The DOC Network

This section describes our DOC deep network. Designing this network requires addressing two main issues: (1) specifying a representation for occlusion relations and a loss function, (2) a deep network architecture that captures the local and non-local cues for detecting occlusion. We now address these issues in turn (Fig. 2).

3.1   Occlusion Relations: Representation and Loss Functions

Representing Occlusion Relations. We represent occlusion relations using an edge map to represent the boundaries between objects (and background) and an orientation variable to indicate the depth ordering across the boundary. We first review existing methods for representing occlusion to motivate our choice and clarify our contribution.

Methods for representing occlusion relations can be roughly classified into four types as shown in Fig. 3. The first two types, panels (a) and (b), represent triple points and junctions explicitly (we defined junctions to be places where border ownership changes). The third and fourth types, panels (c) and (d) use a pixel-based representation with a pair of label indicating boundary and occlusion orientation. The representations in panels (a) and (b) were used in [20,37] respectively. A limitation of computer vision models which uses these types of representations is that performance is sensitive to errors in detecting triple points and junctions. The representation in panel (c) enables the use of pixel-based methods which are more robust to failures to detect triple points and junctions [45]. But it quantizes the occlusion orientation variable into 8 bins, which can be problematic because two very similar orientations can be treated as being different (if they occur in neighboring bins). Hence we propose the representation in panel (d) where the occlusion orientation variable is continuous. This pixel-based representation is well suited for deep networks using local and non-local cues and regression to estimate the continuous orientation variable.

Loss Functions for Occlusion Relations. Given an image $\mathbf{I}$ we assign a pair of labels, $\mathbf{l} = \{e, \theta\}$, to each pixel. Here $e \in \{1, 0\}$ is a binary indicator variable with $e = 1$ meaning that the pixel is located on a boundary. $\theta \in (-\pi, \pi]$ is an occlusion orientation variable defined at the boundaries, i.e. when $e = 1$, which specifies the tangent of the boundary and whose direction indicates border ownership using the "left" rule, see Figs. 3 (d) and 1 left. If $e = 0$, we set $\theta = \mathrm{nan}$ and do not use these points for the occlusion loss computation.

For training, we denote the set of training data by $\mathcal{S} = \{(\mathbf{I}_i, \mathcal{L}_i)\}_{i=1}^{N}$, where N is the number of training images, and $\mathcal{L}_i = \{\mathbf{L}_{ei}, \mathbf{L}_{oi}\}$ are the ground truth annotations, where $\mathbf{L}_{ei}$ specifies the boundary and $\mathbf{L}_{oi}$ the occlusion orientation. Our goal is to design a DCNN that can learn a mapping function parameterized by $\mathbf{W}$, i.e. $f(\mathbf{I}_i : \mathbf{W})$, that can estimate the ground truth $\mathcal{L}_i$.

To learn the parameters $\mathbf{W}$, we define a loss function:

$$l_{doc}(\mathcal{S} : \mathbf{W}) = \frac{1}{N} \left(\sum_i l_e(\mathbf{I}_i, \mathbf{L}_{ei} : \mathbf{W}) + \sum_i l_o(\mathbf{I}_i, \mathbf{L}_{oi} : \mathbf{W}) \right) \qquad (1)$$

where $l_e(\mathbf{I}, \mathbf{L}_e : \mathbf{W})$ is the loss for the boundaries, and $l_o(\mathbf{I}, \mathbf{L}_o : \mathbf{W})$ is the loss for the occlusion orientations. The boundary loss is the balanced sigmoid cross entropy loss, which is the same as the HED edge detector [49].

The occlusion orientation loss function strongly penalizes wrong directions (i.e. errors in border ownership using the "left" rule) but only weakly penalizes the tangent direction, as illustrated in Fig. 3. Let θ_j and θ_j^* respectively denote the occlusion orientation groundtruth and the estimation. Then the loss is:

$$l_o(\mathbf{I}, \mathbf{L}_o : \mathbf{W}) = -\sum_{j:e_j=1} \log P(\theta_j^* | \theta_j, \mathbf{W})$$

$$\text{where, } P(\theta_j^* | \theta_j, \mathbf{W}) = \frac{1}{Z} \begin{cases} 1 & : |\theta_j - \theta_j^*|_1 \in [0, \delta] \cup [2\pi - \delta, 2\pi + \delta] \\ \mathrm{Sigmoid}(\alpha(f(|\theta_j - \theta_j^*|_1))) & : \text{otherwise} \end{cases}$$

$$f(|\theta_j - \theta_j^*|_1) = \begin{cases} \pi/2 - |\theta_j - \theta_j^*|_1 & : |\theta_j - \theta_j^*|_1 \in [0, \pi] \\ |\theta_j - \theta_j^*|_1 - \pi & : |\theta_j - \theta_j^*|_1 \in (\pi, 2\pi] \\ 3\pi/2 - |\theta_j - \theta_j^*|_1 & : |\theta_j - \theta_j^*|_1 \in (2\pi, +\infty) \end{cases} \qquad (2)$$

where $|x|_1$ is the absolute value of x. Z is the normalizing constant. This loss function has two hyper parameters α and δ, where α is a scale factor for the sigmoid function, which controls the strength at direction inverting points. δ controls a non-penalizing range when the θ_j^* is close enough to θ_j.

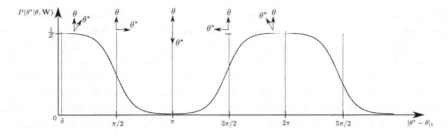

Fig. 3. The orientation probability $P(\theta_j^*|\theta_j, \mathbf{W})$ as a function of the difference between the predicted and ground truth orientation, i.e. θ^* and θ in the figure.

3.2 The Network Architecture

We experimented two DOC architectures, DOC-HED and DOC-DMLFOV, which are based respectively on the holistic-nested edge detector network (HED) [49] and the deeplab multi-scale large field of view DMLFOV network [6]. We choose these networks because: (1) Both exploit local and non-local information and have multi scale outputs (important for occlusion). (2) Both were state-of-the-art on their assigned tasks (and remain highly competitive). HED for detecting edges in the BSDS dataset [1], and DMLFOV for PASCAL semantic segmentation. Also they use different features, for edges or regions, which makes them interesting to compare. Here we refer readers to our supplementary materials or original papers for detailed network architectures.

Two Streams and up Sampling. To adapt HED and DMLFOV to estimate occlusion relations we modify them in two ways: (1) For pixel-based tasks, requiring precise localization of boundaries and estimation of occlusion orientation, we need to up sample the network outputs, to correct for low-resolution caused by max pooling (particularly important for DMLFOV which addressed the less precise task of semantic segmentation). To achieve this we combine the "hole" algorithm [7] with deconvolution up-sampling [29]. (2) To adapt HED and DMLFOV to work on the occlusion representation, see previous section, we adopt a two stream network (encouraged by prior work [47] when using deep networks to address two tasks simultaneously). For estimating the boundaries we keep the original network structure. For estimating the occlusion orientation, which requires a large range of context, we combine outputs only at higher levels of the network (experiments shown that low-level outputs were too noisy to be useful). Thus, for the DOC-HED network, we drop the side output predictions before "conv3" (as in Fig. 4), and for DOC-DMLFOV we drop the predictions (also from side outputs) before "conv3".

Training Phase. We train DOC-HED and DOC-DMLFOV using the pixel-based representations described in the previous section. They are trained on

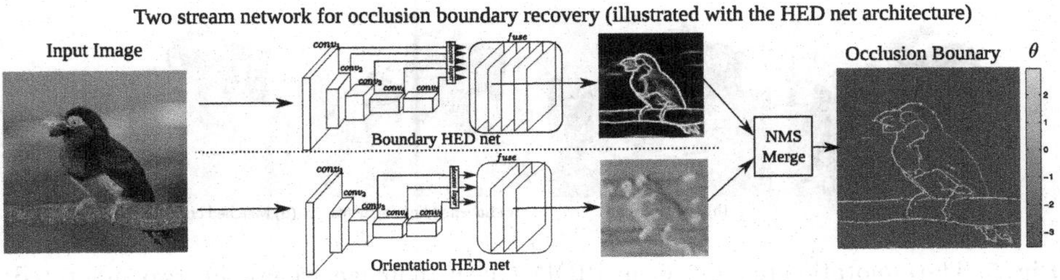

Two stream network for occlusion boundary recovery (illustrated with the HED net architecture)

Fig. 4. For inference, we first apply a two stream network (shown for HED) to predict pixel-wise boundaries and the occlusion orientations respectively. Then, we apply non-maximum suppression (NMS) to the boundaries, merge the two predictions, and recover the occlusion boundaries.

both the BSDS border ownership dataset [37] and on a new dataset, based on PASCAL VOC, which we will describe in the next section.

Testing Phase. Given an input image, DOC outputs a boundary map and an occlusion orientation map (from the two streams). To combine the results, we first perform non-maximum suppression (NMS) on the boundary map, using the method as [10]. Then we obtain the occlusion orientation for each edge pixel (i.e. pixel that we have classified as boundary) from the orientation map. Finally we adjust the orientation estimation to ensure that neighboring pixels on the curve have similar orientations. More specifically, we align the orientation to the tangent line estimated from the boundary map since we trust the accuracy of the predicted boundaries. Formally, at a pixel j, the predicted orientation and one direction of the tangent line are θ_j and θ_{tj} respectively. We set θ_j to be θ_{tj} if $|\theta_j - \theta_{tj}| \bmod 2\pi \in [0, \pi/2) \cup (3\pi/2, 2\pi]$, and to the reverse direction of θ_{tj} otherwise. Finally, motivated by the observation that the results are more reliable if the boundary and orientation predictions are consistent, we take $c_{oj} = |\cos(|\theta_j - \theta_{tj}|)|_1$ as the confidence score for the occlusion orientation prediction at pixel j. Finally, given the predicted confidence score c_{ej} from the boundary network outputs, our final confidence score for the occlusion boundary at pixel j is defined to be $c_{ej} + c_{oj}$.

4   Pascal Instance Occlusion Dataset (PIOD)

A large dataset is of critical for training and evaluating deep network models. The BSDS border ownership dataset [37] helped pioneer the study of occlusion relations on natural images but is limited because it only contains 200 images, and hence it may not be able to capture the range of occlusion relations that happen in natural images (our experiments will address how well models trained on one dataset transfer to another).

We choose to annotate occlusion on the PASCAL VOC dataset because it contains well-selected images, and other researchers have already annotated the

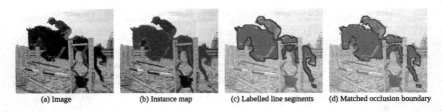

(a) Image   (b) Instance map   (c) Labelled line segments   (d) Matched occlusion boundary

Fig. 5. The annotation process of our PIOD. Given an image, we provide two annotated maps, i.e. (b) the semantic instance map and (c) the generated boundary map. An annotator needs to supplement the boundary map with directed line segments following the "left" rule. We assume the objects occlude background by default, so the annotator only needs to label the boundaries violating this rule or between adjacent instances. Finally, we match the labelled line segments to all the boundaries as shown in (d).

boundaries for 20 object instances [7,16]. These object boundary annotations are very reliable because the annotators were given clear instructions and consistency checks were performed. Hence our annotation task reduces to annotating border ownership by specifying the directions of the occlusion orientation. Our strategy is to annotate the directions of line segments to specify occlusion orientations, or boundary ownership, using the "left" rule. We do this by a two stage process, as shown in Fig. 5. The annotators are asked to label directed straight line segments which lie close to the object boundaries and whose directions specify the border ownership. The second stage is performed by an algorithm which matches the directed line segments to the annotated boundaries. The idea is that the first stage can be done quickly, since the line segments do not have to lie precisely on the edges, while the second stage gives an automated way to exploit the existing boundary annotations [7,16].

Stage 1: Annotate with Directed Line Segments. For each image, the annotator is given two annotation maps: (i) the boundary map, and (ii) the semantic instance map [7,16]. We assume the object is occluding the background, so we only annotate the boundaries between any two adjacent object instances and the boundaries where objects are occluded by background. For each boundary segment, the annotator draw a directed line segment close to the boundary whose direction indicates the occlusion orientation based on the "left" rule.

Stage 2: Matching Directed Line Segments to Object Boundaries. To associate the directed line segments to the boundary map, we developed a matching tool which maps the annotated line segments to the boundaries of all object instances. Our ground truth occlusion boundaries are then represented by a set of boundary fragments, similar to [20]. Each fragment is associated with a start and end point of a directed line segment. Finally, we convert this representation to an occlusion orientation map where each pixel on the object boundary is assigned an occlusion orientation value indicating the local occlusion direction. This process is shown in Fig. 5, where we give images with our labelled results overlaid.

Finally, we produce a frequency statistics of the object occlusion relationships and visualize it as a matrix, which we show in the supplementary materials due to space limit. It helps us to observe object interactions in PIOD.

5 Experiments

We experimented with our DOC approach on the BSDS ownership dataset [37] and our new PASCAL instance occlusion dataset (PIOD). As mentioned before, these datasets differ by size (PIOD is two orders of magnitude bigger) and boundary annotations (PIOD contains only the boundaries of the 20 PASCAL objects while BSDS includes internal and background edges).

In this section, we first propose a more reliable criteria for occlusion boundary evaluation than that used by [37,45], which was also questioned by previous work [24] (see Sect. 5.1). Then, we conduct extensive experiments with the DOC networks as described in Sect. 3.2. These show that DOC significantly outperforms the state-of-the-art [45]. Both DOC-HED and DOC-DMLFOV perform well, so we perform experiments on both PIOD and on the BSDS ownership data to gain insights about the network architectures for future research. We also study transfer between the two datasets, and other issues.

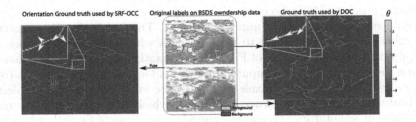

Fig. 6. Center: the two ground truth maps for each image in the BSDS ownership data. Left: limitation of the orientation map generated by SRF-OCC [45] for occlusion evaluation. In the white rectangle, the white arrows show the quantized ground truth orientation at corresponding pixels, which is not smooth or intuitively correct. Also, at bottom right, label inconsistent ground truth edges are discarded when fusing multiple maps. Right: our proposed multiple ground truth occlusion orientation maps for learning and evaluation.

Implementation Details. For the orientation loss function in Eq. (2), we set $\alpha = 4$ and $\delta = 0.05$ respectively, chosen using the validation set. For learning both networks, DOC-HED and DOC-DMLFOV, we used the deep supervision strategy [49], with the learning rate and stage-wise training the same as for HED and DMLFOV respectively. We initialized the models using versions of HED and DMLFOV released by the authors.

For learning on the BSDS ownership dataset, we followed the HED strategy and use adaptive input size for training and testing by setting the "batchsize" to 1 and "itersize" to 10. When learning on PIOD, since the number of images is very large, to save training time, we resize all the input images to 386×386 by keeping the aspect ratio and padding with zeros. We set the "batchsize" to 15 and "itersize" to 2. For both datasets, we augment each image as proposed by HED. We implement all our models based on the published parsenet [28] fork of Caffe [22], which includes both the "hole" algorithm and deconvolution. We also merge the implemented input and cross entropy loss layers from the code released by HED.

5.1 Evaluation Criteria

Specifying a criterion for evaluating occlusion relations is not easy. The problem is that it involves two tasks: detecting boundaries and specifying border ownership. One proposed criteria [37] computes the percentage of the pixels for which the occlusion relations are estimated correctly. But this criteria was criticized [24] because it depends on the selected pixel matching method (between the estimates and the groundtruth boundaries) and the choice of threshold for the edge detector. e.g., a high threshold for the edge detector will detect fewer boundaries but may label their border ownership more accurately. Another criteria was proposed by [45], who released evaluation code. But, see Fig. 6, we found two problems that may lead to unreliable results. The first is that they quantize the occlusion orientation angle to take 8 values which can lead to errors, see the white rectangle on the left of Fig. 6. This quantization problem is enhanced because the orientation was computed based on a local pixel-wise gradient (relying on a pair of neighboured pixels with 8 connections). The second problem is they evaluate on the BSDS ownership dataset which combines boundary maps from different annotators but without checking for consistency [21], which may bias the evaluation since the error cases due to label inconsistency are dropped.

To address these two problems, we first propose to compute the orientation based on a local boundary fragment of length 10 pixels, as used by [20], yielding a smoother and intuitively more reasonable ground truth orientation for evaluation, see right of Fig. 6. Secondly, for evaluating the occlusion relations, we propose a new criteria called the *Occlusion accuracy w.r.t. boundary recall Curve*, which we refer to as the *AOR curve*. This adapts edge detection and occlusion, which was similar in spirit with the PRC curve [36] for depth ordering.

Formally, given the occlusion boundary estimation result with threshold t, we find the correctly detected boundary pixels and their corresponding ground truth pixels by matching them to a ground truth map by the standard edge correspondence method [1][1]. Then for each pixel i on the estimated boundaries, its predicted occlusion orientation θ_i^* is compared to the corresponding ground truth orientation θ_i. We keep the match if $|\theta_i - \theta_i^*| \in [0, \pi/2) \cup (3\pi/2, 2\pi]$, but

---

[1] We use the toolbox from the BSDS benchmark website.

drop it as a false positive otherwise. After matching all the pixels we obtain two values: (i) the recall rate $R_e(t)$ of the ground truth boundary, and (ii) the accuracy $A_o(t)$ of occlusion orientation prediction given the recalled boundaries.

By varying the threshold t, we can summarize the relationship between $R_e(t)$ and $A_o(t)$ by a curve comparing the accuracy of border ownership as a function of the amount of boundary recalled (i.e. each point on the curve corresponds to a value of the threshold t). In our experiments, we draw the curves to uniformly sample 33 thresholds. For the AOR curve, the accuracy at high recall is most important since more test data used for evaluation yields more reliable indication for the model's ability. We will release our developed evaluation code and ground truth for reproducing all our results.

5.2   Performance Comparisons

We extensively compare our deep occlusion (DOC) approaches with different settings and configurations of the HED [49] and DMLFOV [6] networks. We also compare DOC-HED and DOC-DMLFOV to the state-of-the-art occlusion recovering algorithm [45] which we refer to as SRF-OCC (it uses structured random forests). In Fig. 7, we see almost all our models outperform SRF over both datasets over 6 %, showing the effectiveness of our approach.

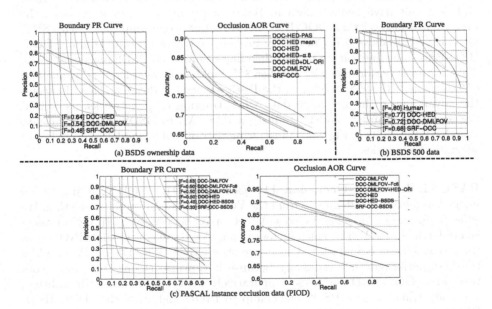

Fig. 7. Quantitative comparison on BSDS ownership data. SRF-OCC [45] is the baseline model. In (b), we show the edge detection performance on BSDS 500 testing data with models trained from the BSDS ownership data (with only 100 images). This shows the DOC-HED model we trained are comparable to those in the HED paper (best viewed in color). Details are in Sect. 5.2.

BSDS Ownership Data. The BSDS ownership dataset contains 100 training images and 100 testing images. We evaluate our deep networks on this dataset although its small size makes them challenging to train. The edge detection comparisons, see left of Fig. 7(a), show that DOC-HED performs best, DOC-DMLFOV is the runner up and SRF-OCC performs less well.

Observe that the results for DOC-HED are not as good as that reported for HED by [49] when trained and tested on the full BSDS dataset. So we evaluated our trained DOC-HED model over the standard BSDS 200 test images and give the results in Fig. 7(c), showing performance very similar to HED (Fusion-output). We think the difference is due to three reasons. Firstly, in order to give fair comparisons to SRF-OCC we train on 100 image only (unlike 300 for HED). Secondly, the images in BSDS ownership data are a non-randomly selected subset of the full BSDS dataset, where the images were chosen to study occlusion and edges inside are harder to detect. Thirdly, each image in this data only uses two ground truth annotations which might introduce labeling noise [21].

On the right of Fig. 7(a), we give results for occlusion relations using our AOR curve. Trained on just 100 images, and tested with single scale image input, the DOC-HED network (green line) performs best, outperforming SRF-OCC when the edge recall rate is higher than 0.3, and the margin goes above 4 % at high recall rate of 0.7. The relatively weak performance of the DOC-DMLFOV network (pink line) is probably because it is a more complex network than HED and does not have enough data in BSDS ownership to train it properly. Its performance is lower than DOC-HED network, but is still competitive with SRF-OCC for recall above 0.7. Finally, we investigate transfer by pre-training DOC-HED-PAS (blue line) on PIOD and then fine-tuning it on BSDS ownership data. This improves performance by another 3 %, yielding an average improvement of 6 % over the SRF-OCC model on the BSDS ownership dataset. This illustrates the advantages of having more data when training deep networks, as well as the ability to transfer models trained on PASCAL to BSDS. Finally, we give visualization results in Fig. 8(a), illustrating that our DOC model recovers better semantic boundaries.

PASCAL Instance Occlusion Dataset (PIOD). PIOD contains 10,100 images, and we take 925 images from the VOC 2012 validation set for testing. We show performance for semantic edge detection at the left of Fig. 7(c). Note there is a difference with BSDS which includes many low-level edges, while PIOD contains only object boundaries. The figure shows that DOC DMLFOV provides the best performance, presumably because it captures strong long-range context, while DOC-HED performs comparatively weaker in this case. In addition, we study transfer from BSDS ownership to PIOD and show that DOC-HED-BSDS (i.e. trained on BSDS) outperforms SRF-OCC-BSDS, but both perform much worse than the deep networks trained on PIOD.

For estimating occlusion relations, see right of Fig. 7(c), DOC-DMLFOV performs best, but only a little better than DOC-HED (i.e. by around 1.5 %) and worse than DOC-HED for recall higher than 0.78. This is because, for the boundaries which are correctly estimated, DOC-HED also gives accurate occlusion orientation estimates.

We also evaluated the ability of SRF-OCC and DOC-HED models when trained only on BSDS. As shown in the figure, DOC-HED-BSDS outperforms SRF-OCC-BSDS significantly on PIOD by a margin of 5 % and is higher at every level of recall, showing better ability of deep networks despite the small amount of training data. Some examples visualizing our results are shown in Fig. 8(b). Notice that many of the false positives in the DOC predictions are intuitively correct but were not labelled. The deep networks trained on PIOD data do much better than those trained on BSDS.

Additional Comparisons on the Two Datasets.

Tuning of α. Recall that α is the parameter controlling the sharpness of the occlusion orientation term in Eq. (2). As shown in the right of Fig. 7(a) (DOC-HED-α 8), if we set α to 8 then performance drops slightly because it only weakly penalizes the closeness between θ and θ^*, We found the optimal value to be 4, and fixed this in the experiments.

Scales of input images. On the right of Fig. 7(a) (DOC-HED mean), we show the results from averaging three images scale ($[0.5, 1.0, 1.5]$) outputs from the DOC-HED network. But multi-scale only gave marginal improvement. This suggests that for boundary detection, multi-scale networks and multi-scale input contain similar information.

Multi-scales network vs. Single scale network. We compared the final fusion output (DOC DMLFOV) vs. single side output (from the "fc8" layer) based on the DOC DMLFOV network over PIOD. As shown on the left of Fig. 7(c) (DOC DMLFOV-Fc8), single side output gives much weaker performance for boundary detection since it localizes the edges worse compared to multi-scale. On the right of Fig. 7(c), DOC DMLFOV-Fc8 performs well but is still weaker than DOC DMLFOV for occlusion recovery. This shows, as expected, that high level features contribute most to the occlusion orientation estimation.

High resolution vs. Low resolution loss. Unlike the original loss based on downsampled ground truth used by DMLFOV for training semantic segmentation [6], our loss is computed using Deconv from the label map at the original image resolution. At left of Fig. 7(c), the low resolution model (DMLFOV-LR) drops both boundary detection and occlusion orientation.

Replacing the boundary detector network stream. As the AOR curve performs a joint evaluation of boundary detection and border ownership, we must see how DOC-HED and DOC DMLFOV perform on each individual task. We already compared them for boundary detection, so we now switch the occlusion network.

In Fig. 7(a) (DOC-HED+DL-ORI), we use DOC-HED for boundary detection but DOC-DMLFOV for the occlusion orientation. This gives a performance drop of 2 % compared to DOC-HED. This shows, for dataset with internal edges like BSDS, DOC-HED also outperforms DOC-DMLFOV on occlusion prediction. In Fig. 7(c) (DOC-DMLFOV+HED-ORI), we apply the same strategy but use DOC-DMLFOV for boundaries and DOC-HED for occlusion orientation,

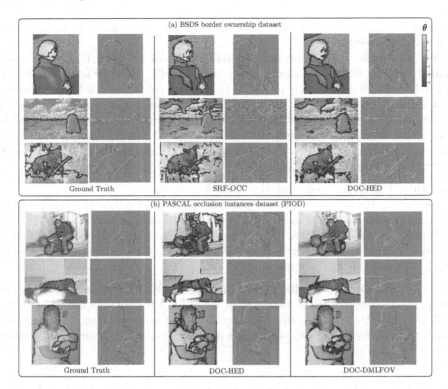

Fig. 8. Qualitative comparisons (best viewed in color). At the left side of each column, we show algorithm results compared with ground truth. The "red" pixels with arrows are correctly labelled occlusion boundaries, , the "green" pixels are correctly labeled boundaries but incorrect occlusion, and the "blue" pixels are false positive boundaries. At the right of each column, we show the occlusion boundaries by a 2.1D relief sculpture. In the figure, the foreground regions are raised (embossed). (a) Comparisons on the BSDS ownership data between SRF-OCC [45] and DOC-HED. (b) Comparisons on PIOD between DOC-HED and DOC-DMLFOV. Note for some images, some internal occlusion boundaries are recovered (although they are not labelled correct), e.g., the tire on the bike and the woman's right arm. This that DOC can generalize from boundaries to some internal edges. We give more examples in Fig. 1 of the supplementary material. (Colour figure online)

giving a result close to that from DOC-DMLFOV. This shows when training on the large dataset PIOD, DOC-HED (smaller network) can performs as well as DOC-DLMFOV for occlusion estimation. These experiments show DOC-HED performs well in general for occlusion estimation.

6   Conclusion and Future Work

In this paper, we designed an end-to-end deep occlusion network (DOC) for estimating occlusion relations. We gave two variants, DOC-HED and

DOC-DMLFOV, and show that they both give big improvements over state-of-the-art methods. We also constructed a new dataset PIOD for studying occlusion relations which is two orders of magnitude larger than comparable datasets. We show that PIOD enables better training and testing of deep networks for estimating occlusion relations. We also show good transfer from PIOD to the smaller BSDS border ownership dataset, but that methods trained on BSDS border ownership are sub-optimal on PIOD. Our results show that DOC-HED and DOC-DMLFOV have complementary strengths which can be combined in future work. We hope that our PIOD dataset will serve as a resource to stimulate research in this important research area.

Acknowledgment. This work is supported by NSF award CCF-1317376. and NSF STC award CCF-1231216. We thank Lingxi Xie, Zhou Ren for paper reading and useful advice.

References

1. Arbelaez, P., Maire, M., Fowlkes, C., Malik, J.: Contour detection and hierarchical image segmentation. IEEE Trans. Pattern Anal. Mach. Intell. **33**(5), 898–916 (2011)
2. Ayvaci, A., Raptis, M., Soatto, S.: Sparse occlusion detection with optical flow. Int. J. Comput. Vis. **97**(3), 322–338 (2012)
3. Belhumeur, P.N., Mumford, D.: A bayesian treatment of the stereo correspondence problem using half-occluded regions. In: 1992 IEEE Computer Society Conference on Proceedings of Computer Vision and Pattern Recognition, CVPR 1992, pp. 506–512. IEEE (1992)
4. Biederman, I.: On the semantics of a glance at a scene. In: Kubovy, M., Pomerantz, J.R. (Eds.) Perceptual Organization, pp. 213–263 (1981)
5. Calderero, F., Caselles, V.: Recovering relative depth from low-level features without explicit t-junction detection and interpretation. Int. J. Comput. Vis. **104**(1), 38–68 (2013)
6. Chen, L., Papandreou, G., Kokkinos, I., Murphy, K., Yuille, A.L.: Semantic image segmentation with deep convolutional nets and fully connected CRFS.In: CoRR abs/1412.7062 (2014)
7. Chen, X., Mottaghi, R., Liu, X., Fidler, S., Urtasun, R., Yuille, A.L.: Detect what you can: Detecting and representing objects using holistic models and body parts. In: CVPR, pp. 1979–1986 (2014)
8. Cooper, M.C.: Interpreting line drawings of curved objects with tangential edges and surfaces. Image Vision Comput. **15**(4), 263–276 (1997)
9. Craft, E., Schütze, H., Niebur, E., Heydt, R.: A neural model of figure-ground organization. J. Neurophysiol. **97**(6), 4310–4326 (2007)
10. Dollár, P., Zitnick, C.L.: Fast edge detection using structured forests. IEEE Trans. Pattern Anal. Mach. Intell. **37**(8), 1558–1570 (2015)
11. Eigen, D., Fergus, R.: Predicting depth, surface normals and semantic labels with a common multi-scale convolutional architecture. arXiv preprint arXiv:1411.4734 (2014)
12. Everingham, M., Gool, L., Williams, C.K.I., Winn, J., Zisserman, A.: The pascal visual object classes (VOC) Challenge. IJCV **88**(2), 303–338 (2010)

13. Fang, F., Boyaci, H., Kersten, D.: Border ownership selectivity in human early visual cortex and its modulation by attention. J. Neurosci. **29**(2), 460–465 (2009)
14. Geiger, D., Ladendorf, B., Yuille, A.: Occlusions and binocular stereo. In: Sandini, G. (ed.) ECCV 1992. LNCS, vol. 588, pp. 425–433. Springer, Heidelberg (1992)
15. Gibson, J.: The perception of surface layout: a classiffication of types. Unpublished Purple Perils essay (1968)
16. Hariharan, B., Arbelaez, P., Bourdev, L.D., Maji, S., Malik, J.: Semantic contours from inverse detectors. In: ICCV, pp. 991–998 (2011)
17. He, X., Yuille, A.: Occlusion boundary detection using pseudo-depth. In: Daniilidis, K., Maragos, P., Paragios, N. (eds.) ECCV 2010, Part IV. LNCS, vol. 6314, pp. 539–552. Springer, Heidelberg (2010)
18. Heydt, R., Macuda, T., Qiu, F.T.: Border-ownership-dependent tilt aftereffect. JOSA A **22**(10), 2222–2229 (2005)
19. Hoiem, D., Efros, A.A., Hebert, M.: Recovering surface layout from an image. IJCV **75**(1), 151–172 (2007)
20. Hoiem, D., Efros, A.A., Hebert, M.: Recovering occlusion boundaries from an image. IJCV **91**(3), 328–346 (2011)
21. Hou, X., Yuille, A., Koch, C.: Boundary detection benchmarking: beyond f-measures. In: CVPR, pp. 2123–2130 (2013)
22. Jia, Y., Shelhamer, E., Donahue, J., Karayev, S., Long, J., Girshick, R., Guadarrama, S., Darrell, T.: Caffe: convolutional architecture for fast feature embedding. arXiv preprint arXiv:1408.5093 (2014)
23. Kanizsa, G., Gerbino, W.: Convexity and symmetry in figure-ground organization. Vision and Artifact, pp. 25–32 (1976)
24. Leichter, I., Lindenbaum, M.: Boundary ownership by lifting to 2.1d. In: ICCV, pp. 9–16 (2009)
25. Li, B., Shen, C., Dai, Y., van den Hengel, A., He, M.: Depth and surface normal estimation from monocular images using regression on deep features and hierarchical crfs. In: CVPR, pp. 1119–1127 (2015)
26. Liu, B., Gould, S., Koller, D.: Single image depth estimation from predicted semantic labels. In: CVPR, pp. 1253–1260 (2010)
27. Liu, F., Shen, C., Lin, G., Reid, I.D.: Learning depth from single monocular images using deep convolutional neural fields. In: CoRR abs/1502.07411 (2015)
28. Liu, W., Rabinovich, A., Berg, A.C.: ParseNet: Looking wider to see better. In: CoRR abs/1506.04579 (2015)
29. Long, J., Shelhamer, E., Darrell, T.: Fully convolutional networks for semantic segmentation. In: CVPR, pp. 3431–3440 (2015)
30. Mahendran, A., Vedaldi, A.: Understanding deep image representations by inverting them. In: CVPR. pp. 5188–5196 (2015)
31. Maire, M.: Simultaneous segmentation and figure/ground organization using angular embedding. In: Daniilidis, K., Maragos, P., Paragios, N. (eds.) ECCV 2010, Part II. LNCS, vol. 6312, pp. 450–464. Springer, Heidelberg (2010)
32. Maire, M., Narihira, T., Yu, S.X.: Affinity CNN: Learning pixel-centric pairwise relations for figure/ground embedding. In: Computer Vision and Pattern Recognition (CVPR) (2016)
33. Martin, D.R., Fowlkes, C., Malik, J.: Learning to detect natural image boundaries using local brightness, color, and texture cues. IEEE Trans. Pattern Anal. Mach. Intell. **26**(5), 530–549 (2004)
34. Nitzberg, M., Mumford, D.: The 2.1-d sketch. In: ICCV, pp. 138–144 (1990)
35. Palmer, S.E., Ghose, T.: Extremal edge a powerful cue to depth perception and figure-ground organization. Psychol. Sci. **19**(1), 77–83 (2008)

36. Visa, G.P., Salembier, P.: Precision-recall-classification evaluation framework: application to depth estimation on single images. In: Fleet, D., Pajdla, T., Schiele, B., Tuytelaars, T. (eds.) ECCV 2014, Part I. LNCS, vol. 8689, pp. 648–662. Springer, Heidelberg (2014)

37. Ren, X., Fowlkes, C.C., Malik, J.: Figure/ground assignment in natural images. In: Leonardis, A., Bischof, H., Pinz, A. (eds.) ECCV 2006. LNCS, vol. 3952, pp. 614–627. Springer, Heidelberg (2006)

38. Roberts, L.G.: Machine Perception of Three-Dimensional Solids. Outstanding Dissertations in the Computer Sciences. Garland Publishing, New York (1963)

39. Saund, E.: Logic and MRF circuitry for labeling occluding and thinline visual contours. In: NIPS, pp. 1153–1159 (2005)

40. Saxena, A., Sun, M., Ng, A.Y.: Make3d: learning 3d scene structure from a single still image. IEEE Trans. Pattern Anal. Mach. Intell. **31**(5), 824–840 (2009)

41. Silberman, N., Hoiem, D., Kohli, P., Fergus, R.: Indoor segmentation and support inference from RGBD images. In: Fitzgibbon, A., Lazebnik, S., Perona, P., Sato, Y., Schmid, C. (eds.) ECCV 2012, Part V. LNCS, vol. 7576, pp. 746–760. Springer, Heidelberg (2012)

42. Stein, A.N., Hebert, M.: Occlusion boundaries from motion: low-level detection and mid-level reasoning. IJCV **82**(3), 325–357 (2009)

43. Sugihara, K.: An algebraic approach to shape-from-image problems. Artif. intell. **23**(1), 59–95 (1984)

44. Sundberg, P., Brox, T., Maire, M., Arbelaez, P., Malik, J.: Occlusion boundary detection and figure/ground assignment from optical flow. In: CVPR, pp. 2233–2240 (2011)

45. Teo, C.L., Fermüller, C., Aloimonos, Y.: Fast 2d border ownership assignment. In: CVPR, pp. 5117–5125 (2015)

46. Wang, P., Shen, X., Lin, Z., Cohen, S., Price, B.L., Yuille, A.L.: Towards unified depth and semantic prediction from a single image. In: CVPR, pp. 2800–2809 (2015)

47. Wang, P., Shen, X., Lin, Z.L., Cohen, S., Price, B.L., Yuille, A.L.: Joint object and part segmentation using deep learned potentials. In: CoRR abs/1505.00276 (2015)

48. Weinzaepfel, P., Revaud, J., Harchaoui, Z., Schmid, C.: Learning to detect motion boundaries. In: CVPR, pp. 2578–2586 (2015)

49. Xie, S., Tu, Z.: Holistically-nested edge detection. In: CoRR abs/1504.06375 (2015)

50. Yu, S.X., Lee, T.S., Kanade, T.: A hierarchical Markov random field model for figure-ground segregation. In: Figueiredo, M., Zerubia, J., Jain, A.K. (eds.) EMM-CVPR 2001. LNCS, vol. 2134, pp. 118–133. Springer, Heidelberg (2001)

51. Zeiler, M.D., Fergus, R.: Visualizing and understanding convolutional networks. In: Fleet, D., Pajdla, T., Schiele, B., Tuytelaars, T. (eds.) ECCV 2014, Part I. LNCS, vol. 8689, pp. 818–833. Springer, Heidelberg (2014)

RepMatch: Robust Feature Matching and Pose for Reconstructing Modern Cities

Wen-Yan Lin[1]($\boxtimes$), Siying Liu[2,3], Nianjuan Jiang[1], Minh. N. Do[3], Ping Tan[4], and Jiangbo Lu[1]($\boxtimes$)

[1] Advanced Digital Sciences Center, Singapore, Singapore
linwenyan.daniel@gmail.com, jiangbo.lu@adsc.com.sg
[2] Institute of Infocomm Research, Singapore, Singapore
[3] University of Illinois Urbana-Champagne, Champaign, USA
[4] Simon Fraser University, Burnaby, Canada

Abstract. A perennial problem in recovering 3-D models from images is repeated structures common in modern cities. The problem can be traced to the feature matcher which needs to match less distinctive features (permitting wide-baselines and avoiding broken sequences), while simultaneously avoiding incorrect matching of ambiguous repeated features. To meet this need, we develop *RepMatch*, an epipolar guided (assumes predominately camera motion) feature matcher that accommodates both wide-baselines and repeated structures. *RepMatch* is based on using *RANSAC* to guide the training of match consistency curves for differentiating true and false matches. By considering the set of all nearest-neighbor matches, *RepMatch* can procure very large numbers of matches over wide baselines. This in turn lends stability to pose estimation. *RepMatch*'s performance compares favorably on standard datasets and enables more complete reconstructions of modern architectures.

Keywords: Structure from motion · Correspondence · RANSAC

1 Introduction

Structure-from-Motion or SfM is the recovery of 3-D structure from image sets. Over the years, SfM has made remarkable progress. Current technology can create impressively large scale reconstructions, a signature achievement being the reconstruction of ancient Rome by leveraging the abundance of Internet images [1]. However, SfM systems have difficulty reconstructing modern buildings from small, user-captured datasets.

J. Lu—This study is supported by the HCCS grant at ADSC from Singapore's Agency for Science, Technology and Research.

Electronic supplementary material The online version of this chapter (doi:10. 1007/978-3-319-46448-0_34) contains supplementary material, which is available to authorized users.

B. Leibe et al. (Eds.): ECCV 2016, Part I, LNCS 9905, pp. 562–579, 2016.
DOI: 10.1007/978-3-319-46448-0_34

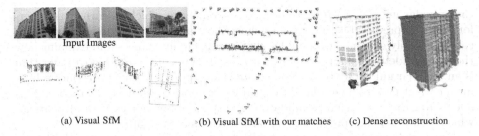

Input Images

(a) Visual SfM   (b) Visual SfM with our matches   (c) Dense reconstruction

Fig. 1. 3-D reconstruction on modern buildings. (a) Screen shot of Visual SfM [2], a classic 3-D reconstruction system which splinters the sequence into 4 segments. (b) The same reconstruction system with our matches forms a complete loop. (c) The pose estimated in (b) is sufficiently accurate for high quality dense reconstruction.

The problem stems from SfM's dependence on feature matching from which camera position (pose) and 3-D structure are inferred. Feature matching needs to procure large numbers of wide-baseline matches to prevent image sequences from splintering. Yet, it must also be robust to repetitive structures. Unfortunately, modern urban environments contain both challenges in abundance. Trees and other occluders limit available view-points, necessitating matching widely separated images. At the same time, mass production makes repeated structures ubiquitous in modern cities (e.g. rows of windows).

As matching ambiguous features inevitably results in some errors, vision researchers typically use *RANSAC* [3] for outlier rejection. By using multiple pose estimates from minimal sets of 5 to 8 matches, *RANSAC* is very effective at getting a reasonable pose estimate. However, there are practical limits on the number of wrong matches *RANSAC* can accommodate. As such, *RANSAC* is seldom applied to the set of all nearest-neighbor matches but is itself dependent on preemptive outlier removal. Typically this takes the form of a ratio test [4], which unfortunately discards a large fraction of the true matches [5]. While this framework has brought SfM much success, the quality of feature matches in modern environments is still insufficient. This manifests itself as fragmented reconstructions, with linkages around corners being especially brittle. An illustration is shown in Fig. 1(a). Thus, we propose *RepMatch*, an epipolar guided feature matcher that accommodates wide-baselines and repeated structures.

RepMatch is inspired by the highly successful guided matching framework, where an initial estimate or assumption guides the discovery of more matches. With the right guidance term, such formulations have proven remarkably stable. This is illustrated by the success of SLAM [6,7], which can reliably propagate pose given some known 3-D points. However, finding a generic guidance term applicable to general two-view pose estimation has proven challenging. Planar based guidance terms have been explored in [8,9] but are scene specific and often incur significant formulation complexity to define number of planes or demarcate planar boundaries. There are also works [10,11] which focus on epipolar geometry guidance. While this can give very accurate solutions [10], it is hard to determine the epipolar geometry without good correspondence, which in turn makes performance unpredictable. This paper shows how a core-set of guidance matches can be reliably obtained even under challenging circumstances and explains how they can guide the finding of more matches. The resultant *RepMatch* algorithm is an epipolar guided matcher which, while using pose as a cue, postpones selecting a correct pose to a very late stage (in fact a choice need never be made). This allows *RepMatch* to reliably validate the very large but noisy set of all matches which contains many previously discarded true matches [5].

RepMatch couples *BF* [5] and *RANSAC* outlier rejection schemes. *BF* computes a global match consistency function from very noisy matches. These are subsequently used to separate true and false matches. While usually accurate, *BF* is vulnerable to repeated structures which can induce large sections of consistently wrong matches. However, we observe that repetitive structures often contain micro-textures which make it possible to obtain a (often heavily shrunken) core-set of reliable matches through very strict *BF* parameters. Using *RANSAC* we can procure more local matches that are geometrically consistent with the core-set. These are used to train local *BF* curves with embedded epipolar constraints that verify geometrically consistent matches in the surrounding areas. The resultant *RepMatch* framework breaks the pose and correspondence problem into a sequence of robust steps, giving overall system stability on both wide-baselines and repetitive structures. On standard datasets, *RepMatch* tolerates up to 45° out-of-plane rotation for all scenes and has over 90° stability on some scenes. On less controlled data, *RepMatch* adds a significant stability margin to existing SfM systems, enabling complete reconstruction of modern buildings from street-level images, something difficult with previous techniques.

1.1 Related Works

RepMatch builds on *BF* [5], a wide-baseline matcher which achieves high precision and recall on challenging scenes. While *BF* recovers many previously discarded true matches, it is vulnerable to repeated structures which can induce large sections of consistently wrong matches. Our *RepMatch* framework retains *BF*'s aggressive match retrieval while avoiding its vulnerability to repeated structures. This results in an effective, general purpose wide-baseline feature matcher.

RepMatch is closely related to *RANSAC* as they are both outlier removal schemes. Many of the concepts on guidance and grouping used in this paper have also been explored within the *RANSAC* framework. However, *RANSAC* has a vulnerability as ill-conditioning of pose estimates [12] makes the minimal set estimation unstable. On the other hand, every match added to the minimal set exponentially increases the likelihood it contains an outlier [13]. Thus despite many refinements such as new sampling schemes [14], local groupings/ranking [15–17] or local pose refinements [10,18], there are practical limits on the number of outliers *RANSAC* can accommodate. In addition, because epipolar geometry is a point-to-line constraint, even if the ground-truth pose is attained, *RANSAC* often leaves some outliers which are coincident on the epipolar line. While they may not affect the two view pose estimate, such outliers are detrimental to the overall SfM system's stability. *RepMatch* addresses this problem by adding a *BF* estimator to reduce the reliance on potentially erroneous epipolar geometry while also shielding its *RANSAC* model from encountering too many outliers. This allows us to extract the true matches from the very noisy set of all nearest neighbor matches shown in Fig. 4.

Apart from *RepMatch* and *BF*, there are other preemptive outlier removal works [19–23]. Of these, the evaluation in [24] suggests *BF* provides some of the best trade-offs in computational time and match quality. In addition, *BF* has a guaranteed global minimum. Hence, we build our *RepMatch* framework on *BF*, though other match decision techniques may also be applicable.

There have also been many specialized solutions for repetitive structures, wide-baselines or urban scenes [8, 25–28]. These techniques utilize planar constraints [8] or leverage repetitions [26] to enable high quality pose and correspondence. These solutions will likely provide superior performance on specific scenes but lack generality.

Finally, we wish to acknowledge that *RepMatch* and the results achieved in this paper benefit from many years of research in supporting technologies like feature descriptor design [4, 29–31], bundle adjustment [32–35], dense reconstruction [36, 37], *RANSAC* [3, 16, 17, 38–40], geometric reasoning [41, 42] and motion coherence [43–45]. Improvements in these fields will likely benefit *RepMatch* which we hope will in turn benefit these fields.

2   Background

We approach the feature matching problem as one of reliably partitioning the set of all matching hypotheses into true and false sets. As this is not a main-stream approach, we provide some background to aid understanding.

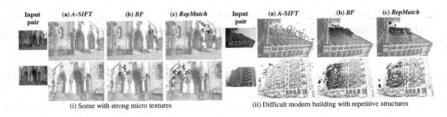

Fig. 2. Comparing three partitioning techniques with the same input matches. Match pairs are shaded with the same color across two views. Results shown are post-*RANSAC*. (a) *A-SIFT*'s ratio-test is very unstable. (b) *BF* retains many previously discarded true matches but incurs many wrong matches on modern buildings. Wrong matches appear as color inconsistencies. (c) Our proposed *RepMatch*. (Color figure online)

Using the same input match hypotheses, Fig. 2 shows the impact of different match partitioning schemes. (a) *A-SIFT* [46] uses a ratio test that requires the

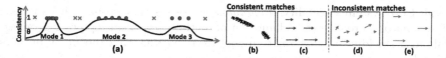

Fig. 3. Match consistency. (a) 1-D illustration of Eq. (2)'s consistency curve, $f(\mathbf{m})$. Consistency measures two basic elements, density and spatial extent, shown in Modes 1 and 2. Note: by incorporating motion into $f(\mathbf{m})$'s domain, density encapsulates motion smoothness. (b, c) show consistent matches. (b) Match is smooth and dense. (c) Match is smooth. While sparse, it has wide spatial extent. (d, e) show inconsistent matches. (d) match is not smooth. (e) Match is smooth but spatial coverage is limited.

best match score to be at least $0.6\times$ better than the second best match. (b) *BF* [5] relaxes the 0.6 threshold to attain an initial set of noisy match hypotheses from which it trains a partition function based on match consistency (a joint measure of three attributes, match density, smoothness and spatial coverage). Observe that in both (a) and (b), prior methods either retain too few matches or create too many wrong matches on repetitive structures. (c) Our *RepMatch* framework which integrates *BF* with *RANSAC* significantly enhances match stability. As our formulation makes heavy use of *BF* to estimate match consistency, we will elaborate on both *BF* and match consistency.

2.1 Bilateral Functions and Match Consistency

In *BF* [5], matches are represented on a $D = 8$ dimensional bilateral domain. Each match takes the form $\mathbf{m}_i = [\mathbf{x}_i; \mathbf{v}_i; \mathbf{o}_i]$. Here, $\mathbf{x}_i = [x_i; y_i]$ and $\mathbf{v}_i = [u_i; v_i]$ are two-dimensional vectors representing a feature point's coordinate (in the first image) and its corresponding motion vector, respectively; $\mathbf{o}_i$ is a 4×1 vector representing the relative affine feature orientation (obtained from the feature's scale and rotation parameters [5]). *BF* learns a match consistency curve (termed likelihood in [5]) from N training matches, $\{\mathbf{m}_i\}$, by minimizing the convex function:

$$\arg\min_{\mathbf{w}} \sum_{i=1}^{N} C(1 - f(\mathbf{m}_i)) + \lambda \mathbf{w}^T G \mathbf{w}, \qquad (1)$$

where $C(.)$ is a Huber function, $\mathbf{w}$ is a vector of N unknowns and G is an $N \times N$ matrix with $G(i,j) = \exp(-\|\mathbf{m}_i - \mathbf{m}_j\|^2/\sigma)$. $f(.)$ is the consistency function defined on an 8 dimensional bilateral domain. $f(.)$ is parameterized by $\mathbf{w}$ in Eq. (1) and N radial basis functions centered on the training matches:

$$f(\mathbf{m}) = \sum_{i=1}^{N} \mathbf{w}(i) \exp^{-\frac{\|\mathbf{m} - \mathbf{m}_i\|^2}{\sigma}}. \qquad (2)$$

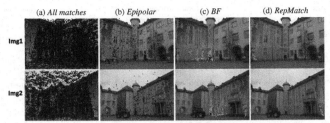

(a) *All matches*   (b) *Epipolar*   (c) *BF*   (d) *RepMatch*

Illustration on real images. Black dots in (a) & (b) indicate wrong matches.
Note: Common central tower belong to physically different parts of the building.

Fig. 4. (a) The set of all matches. (b) Thresholding with ground-truth epipolar geometry still leaves some wrong matches. (c) *BF*'s match consistency based thresholding is unstable as repetitive structures induce consistently wrong matches. (d) *RepMatch* handles such repetitive structures well.

Minimizing Eq. (1) with respect to $\mathbf{w}$ (and hence $f(.)$) provides match consistency curve $f(\mathbf{m})$. This allows a set of matches $\{\mathbf{m}_j\}$ to be partitioned into two subsets, $\mathcal{T}$ (true) and $\mathcal{F}$ (false), via thresholding:

$$\mathbf{m}_j \in \begin{cases} \mathcal{T}, \text{ if } f(\mathbf{m}_j) > \theta \\ \mathcal{F}, \text{ otherwise} \end{cases} \tag{3}$$

When minimizing Eq. (1), the local data term draws $f(.)$ to 1 while the regularization term $\mathbf{w}^T G \mathbf{w}$ pulls $f(.)$ to zero and imposes a global smoothness penalty [5]. This is illustrated in Fig. 3(a). The resultant $f(.)$ can be understood as a continuous consistency estimate, where consistency is a joint measure of two elements, (I) Density: If a region has high point density, the data term justifies a sharp spike even if it is not smooth, as shown in Mode 1 of Fig. 3(a); (II) Spatial extent: Alternatively, a large region with sparsely distributed points is also consistent as a well-rounded hump over a large extent incurs low smoothness penalty, as illustrated by Mode 2. Scattered points are considered inconsistent as their pull cannot overcome the smoothness penalty acting on them (see Mode 3 in Fig. 3(a)). As the bilateral domain encapsulates both spatial and velocity components, consistency on the bilateral domain encapsulates match density and motion smoothness. Match consistency is illustrated in Fig. 3(b–e).

Explained as match consistency, *BF*'s problem with repetitive structures is clear. Repetitive structures can induce large sections of consistent but wrong matches, creating large falsely consistent match patches shown in Fig. 4(c). Epipolar constraints can also remove many false matches as shown in Fig. 4(b), but it too leaves large numbers of wrong correspondences. This leads to our *RepMatch* framework for integrating epipolar and match consistency curves.

3   RepMatch

RepMatch is based around two innovations. First, *RepMatch* introduces a means to reliably obtain a core-set of matches even for challenging image pairs with significant repetitive structures. Second, *RepMatch* introduces a method to robustly

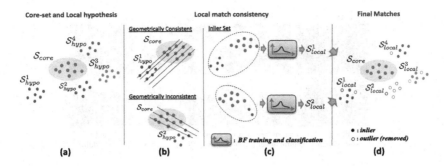

Fig. 5. Overview: *RepMatch* ensures stability by dividing the problem into three individually robust steps. (a) Core matches, S_{core} can be reliably recovered because of strict *BF* thresholds. (b) Geometric verification with epipolar lines (pose). Core matches may be quasi-degenerate and an incorrect pose estimate may discard true positives. Thus, geometric verification uses a *RANSAC* search for common geometry between core matches and each subset. This avoids discarding true positives but may retain some false positives. (c) Local *BF* curves are trained to remove the remaining false positives and discover more matches. (d) All verified matches are consolidated.

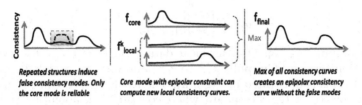

Fig. 6. *RepMatch* algorithm in Fig. 5 explained as match consistency curves.

expand this core-set by integrating *BF* with epipolar geometry. Thus, *RepMatch* divides the pose and correspondence problem into three individually robust steps, to give a robust overall system. Figure 5 gives a general overview, with a match consistency interpretation in Fig. 6.

3.1   Core-Set Discovery

Core-set discovery is based on an observation. An image of a visually perfectly repetitive pattern can be matched error-free in the absence of motion (i.e. match the image to itself). This is due to micro gray-level differences captured by descriptors. Thus, we hypothesize that the repetitive structure matching problem is not due to multiple identical descriptors but the result of subtle descriptor variations being overwhelmed by image noise (induced by motion or other sources). Due to the image's repetitive nature, many mismatches will appear "consistent", causing false modes in Fig. 6. However, even on repetitive scenes, a wrong match can be randomly assigned to many potential alternative positions, making it unlikely that false modes will be more consistent than the original

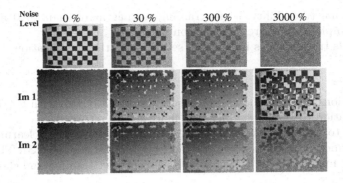

Fig. 7. Core-set recovery on a checker-board image. Image 1 is matched to a noisy version of itself with additive Gaussian noise. Noise variance is a percentage of image contrast. The smooth colors show the core-set estimation on repetitive structures is remarkably resilient to noise. (Color figure online)

true mode. The difference between true and false modes can be amplified by setting BF in Eq. (1) to a very high λ. On curves like Fig. 6 it suppresses weak modes, leaving only the strongest core-mode and its associated core-matches. These are remarkably resilient to noise as shown in Fig. 7.

3.2   Match Expansion Scheme

Once the core-set is discovered, it is theoretically possible to recover more match hypotheses from the epipolar geometry (pose) estimated from the core-set. However, pose estimation is notoriously vulnerable to degeneracies and an incorrect core-set pose may reject many true positives. Instead, core-set matches are merged with clusters of match hypotheses for joint geometric verification. This avoids rejecting true positives but will retain some false positives because of epipolar geometry's weak point-to-line relationship. However, the remaining false positives are unlikely to be consistent and can be removed by a final BF match consistency step. The resultant framework is intrinsically robust as it avoids both BF's vulnerability to false match consistencies and epipolar geometrie's vulnerability to ill conditioning and false positive rejection.

3.3   Algorithm

Training and classification operators: For later convenience, we first define training and classification operators.

BF training operator is denoted as:

$$f \leftarrow BF^t(\mathcal{S}^t, \Theta^t), \tag{4}$$

where $f(.)$ is the match consistency function defined in Eq. (2). It is learned by minimizing Eq. (1) with training matches $\mathcal{S}^t$ and BF parameters Θ^t. To maintain computational tractability, if the training set has more than 1000 matches, a random sample of 1000 are used for computation.

BF finds true matches in a match set $\mathcal{S}^c$, with the classification operator:

$$\mathcal{T} \leftarrow BF^c(f, \mathcal{S}^c, \Theta^c). \tag{5}$$

This partitions $\mathcal{S}^c$ into true and false sets through Eq. (3), with $\theta \in \Theta^c$ acting as classification parameters. Only true matches are returned.

Similar to BF, we consider $RANSAC$ with parameters α^t as learning a classification function (camera pose) trained from a set of matches, $\mathcal{S}^t$. This is used to find true matches in set $\mathcal{S}^c = \{\mathbf{m}_j\}$. The respective training and classification operators are

$$pose \leftarrow RANSAC^t(\mathcal{S}^t, \alpha^t), \tag{6}$$

$$\mathcal{T} \leftarrow RANSAC^c(pose, \mathcal{S}^c, \alpha^c), \tag{7}$$

where Eq. (7) implements epipolar thresholding:

$$\mathbf{m}_j \in \begin{cases} \mathcal{T}, \text{ if distance from epipolar line} < \alpha^c \\ \mathcal{F}, \text{ otherwise} \end{cases} \tag{8}$$

Core-set, $\mathcal{S}_{core}, f_{core}(.)$: To find the core-set of matches, we threshold the set of all matches $\mathcal{A}$, with a ratio test using threshold 0.82 (this is much weaker than the standard 0.6 to ensure sufficient matches for training [5]) to form $\mathcal{A}_{0.82}$, a set of noisy match hypotheses. BF match consistency curves, $f_{core}(.)$, are trained from $\mathcal{A}_{0.82}$ using very strict match consistency parameters. The core-set $\mathcal{S}_{core}$, is defined as all matches consistent with $f_{core}(.)$:

$$f_{core} \leftarrow BF^t(\mathcal{A}_{0.82}, \Theta^t_{strict}), \quad \mathcal{S}_{core} \leftarrow BF^c(f_{core}, \mathcal{A}, \Theta^c) \tag{9}$$

The strict parameters Θ^t_{strict} have a large λ, making $\mathcal{S}_{core}$ remarkably resistant to repeated structures.

Local hypotheses, $\mathcal{S}^k_{hypo}$: A disadvantage of BF is that it sub-samples training sets for computation efficiency. This is good for core-set estimation but hurts fine matching. Thus we cluster $\mathcal{A}_{0.82}$ into $K = 20$ disjoint subset using K-means clustering (over-segmentation is fine)

$$\mathcal{A}_{0.82} = \{\mathcal{L}^1, \mathcal{L}^2, \dots, \mathcal{L}^K\}$$

and compute a local hypothesis set through

$$f^k_{hypo} \leftarrow BF^t(\mathcal{L}^k, \Theta^t_{strict}), \quad \mathcal{S}^k_{hypo} \leftarrow BF^c(f^k_{hypo}, \mathcal{A}, \Theta^c). \tag{10}$$

Local match consistency, $\{f^k_{local}(.)\}$: We next leverage the core-set to robustly estimate local match consistency curves. Each $\mathcal{S}^k_{hypo}$ local hypothesis set is merged with the core-set $\mathcal{S}_{core}$ to form a mixed set $\mathcal{M}^k_{local}$. Core-set matches are forced to make up at least 80 % of $\mathcal{M}^k_{local}$ (if there are insufficient core-set matches, they are artificially duplicated). $RANSAC$ is performed on $\mathcal{M}_{local}^k$ and a pose hypothesis, $pose^k$ is computed

$$pose^k \leftarrow RANSAC^t(\mathcal{M}_{local}^k, \alpha^t),\tag{11}$$

This preponderance of core-set matches ensures that $RANSAC$ need not handle extremely noisy data and prevents it from inadvertently fitting local ambiguities arising from repetitive structures.

Given $pose^k$, we find matches in the local matching sets, $\mathcal{S}_{hypo}^k$ that are geometrically consistent with the core set

$$\widehat{\mathcal{S}}_{hypo}^k \leftarrow RANSAC^c(pose^k, \mathcal{S}_{hypo}^k, \alpha^c).\tag{12}$$

These are used to train locally focused BF functions which take into account geometric consistency with the core-set.

$$f_{local}^k \leftarrow BF^t(\widehat{\mathcal{S}}_{hypo}^k, \Theta^t)\tag{13}$$

Wrong local match hypotheses derived from repetitive ambiguities will have many members removed by the epipolar constraint (see Fig. 5 (b)). Correct matches will pass the epipolar constraint and the training step in Eq. (13) will create a local match consistency curve, $f_{local}^k(.)$ (see Fig. 6) that describes them, allowing subsequent procurement of more similar matches.

Final output $pose, \widehat{\mathcal{S}}_{out}$: Taking the max value of $f_{core}(.)$ and all local $f_{local}^k(.)$ curves for each point in the bilateral domain gives

$$f_{final}(\mathbf{m}) = max(\{f_{core}(\mathbf{m}), f_{local}^1(\mathbf{m}), \ldots, f_{local}^K(\mathbf{m})\}).$$

As shown in Fig. 6, this gives an epipolar-consistency curve without the false match consistency modes of BF. However, this is impractical on a continuous domain. An implementation equivalent, is to define the final match consistency derived output, $\mathcal{S}_{out}$, as the union of all matches $\mathcal{A}$, which accord any of the match consistency functions f_{core} and $\{f_{local}^k\}$

$$\mathcal{S}_{out} = BF^c(f_{core}, \mathcal{A}, \Theta^c) \cup \bigcup_{k=1}^K BF^c(f_{local}^k, \mathcal{A}, \Theta^c) = \mathcal{S}_{core} \cup \bigcup_{k=1}^K \mathcal{S}_{local}^k\tag{14}$$

A final $RANSAC$ step is performed on $\mathcal{S}_{out}$ to estimate $pose$ and the set of matches geometrically consistent with it, $\widehat{\mathcal{S}}_{out}$

$$pose \leftarrow RANSAC^t(\mathcal{S}_{out}, \alpha^t), \quad \widehat{\mathcal{S}}_{out} \leftarrow RANSAC^c(pose, \mathcal{S}_{out}, \alpha^c).\tag{15}$$

Implementation: This paper uses a basic implementation of $RANSAC$ [47] and BF (C++ re-implementation of [5] in [24]). Parameters used are detailed below. All feature coordinates are Hartley-normalized and motion vectors multiplied by 10. For core-set discovery, the training parameters $\Theta_{strict}^t = \{\lambda = 10, \sigma = 1, \epsilon = 0.1\}$, where λ and σ refer to the parameters in Eq. (1), and ϵ is the

Huber function parameter in [5]. Similarly, in training local match consistency curves, $\Theta^t = \{\lambda = 1,\ \sigma = 1,\ \epsilon = 0.1\}$. For BF classification, $\Theta^c = \{\theta = 0.6\}$. In $RANSAC$, $\alpha_t = \alpha_c = 5$ pixels is the threshold for distance to epipolar lines. On a 4-core i7 machine, our mixed MATLAB, C++ implementation of Rep-$Match$ processes a few hundred thousand feature matches in approximately 20 s. Note: when passing matches to a large-scale SfM systems, skip the final $RANSAC$ in Eq. (15). Such systems have inbuilt $RANSAC$ and pre-processing matches affects frame selection. Note: BF [5] includes a bilateral affine verification step for fine match decisions, which we retain. This verification can also be interpreted as match consistency.

4   Experiments

The experiments focus on two aspects: quantifying the performance and baseline gains of $RepMatch$ vs previous algorithms in Sect. 4.1; and integration of $RepMatch$ into an overall SfM systems in Sect. 4.2.

4.1   Quantitative Evaluation

For quantitative evaluation we use Strecha $et\ al.$'s dataset [48]. To study performance over a comprehensive range of baselines, we construct a test set by pairing all images with at least 30 % overlap from all 4 sequences in the dataset, giving a total of 619 pairs. To evaluate performance variations with baseline, we subdivide the set according to ground truth rotational baseline.[1]

As pose estimators often give wildly incorrect solutions (or crash) when they fail, average errors are less meaningful. To circumvent this, we propose to measure Success Percentage (SP):

$$\text{Success Percentage}(x) = \frac{\#\,\text{pairs with rotation (translation) error} \le x^\circ}{\text{total number of pairs}} \quad (16)$$

with error in $^\circ$. By plotting SP against x, we obtain a non-decreasing curve which gives the percentage of two view pose estimates lying below error threshold x°. The success percentage at 1° is an area of interest, as it is a commonly accepted bound for a "good" pose estimate. Finally, as the rotation and translational errors often follow identical trends, in less important cases, we plot SP against Pose Error, a consolidated statistic formed by taking the max of rotational and translational errors.

Comparisons: We begin by establishing performance baselines for a "typical" pose estimator with $RANSAC$ and non-linear re-projection error refinement step[2]. To represent $RANSAC$, we choose $USAC\ 1.0$ [13], a $RANSAC$ variant

---

[1] For fine nuances regarding experiment details and comparisons we encourage interested readers to peruse the supplementary material.

[2] We thank Chin Tat-Jun for his advice on RANSAC comparison.

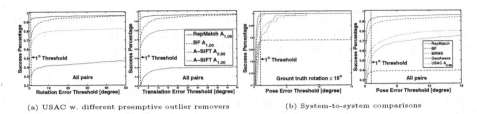

(a) USAC w. different preemptive outlier removers   (b) System-to-system comparisons

Fig. 8. Left: *RepMatch* compared against *USAC* [13] with different preemptive outlier removal schemes. Observe that *USAC*'s performance significantly improves with better preemptive outlier removal. **Right:** System to system comparison. *RepMatch*'s narrow baseline (Ground truth rotation $\leq 15°$) performance is easily comparable to the highly accurate MRMS [10] system. On All pairs, the difference is even (albeit unfairly) greater as *RepMatch* uses wide-baseline A-SIFT features while other systems use narrow baseline SIFT. This demonstrates *RepMatch*'s baseline generality.

which integrates many core *RANSAC* innovations. As it has a *PROSAC* component to take in A-SIFT match scores, *USAC* can potentially be applied to the set of all nearest neighbor matches $\mathcal{A}_{1.00}$.

Figure 8(a) compares *RepMatch* against *USAC* with bundle adjustment. *USAC* was provided with feature matches filtered by three different preemptive outlier removal schemes. The first is $\mathcal{A}_{1.00}$ with no outlier removal. As explained in the introduction, this gives expectedly low scores with a SP of only 20 % at 1°. Using a typical ratio-test $\mathcal{A}_{0.66}$ significantly improves pose estimates. Finally applying *BF* [5] match consistency curve to $\mathcal{A}_{1.00}$ and running *USAC* improves results still further. This demonstrates that preemptive outlier removal can significantly impact *RANSAC* performance and explains *RepMatch*'s excellent performance. Figure 8(b) compares *RepMatch* against other guided matching pose estimators. MRMS [10] has very high pose estimation accuracy while GeoAware [11] is designed to handle repetitive structures. As theses algorithms are tightly coupled to their feature descriptors, we perform system-to-system comparisons. At narrow baselines, with ground truth rotations less than 15°, MRMS and GeoAware have an advantage as they use SIFT [4] rather than the more ambiguous A-SIFT descriptors [46]. Despite this, *RepMatch*'s performance is easily comparable to them. The advantage of *RepMatch*'s full system is clearly evident on the set of all pairs. While the use of different descriptors means comparisons are not strictly fair, it suggests that *RepMatch* has good narrow and wide baseline capability.

Component wise evaluation: Our *RepMatch* framework integrates both *RANSAC* and *BF* outlier removal schemes. In Fig. 10 we compare the performance of *RepMatch* against its individual components. Note that as *RepMatch* shields the *RANSAC* module from outliers, we use a modified *RANSAC* with a larger minimal set of 20. All poses estimates are provided after this *RASANC* and a non-linear refinement step. For comparison to a more conventional *RANSAC* see Fig. 8(a). Figure 9 shows that *RepMatch* preemptive outlier removal provides

consistent performance gain vs both its *BF* and *RANSAC* components. This is
especially notable on the castle sequence which has many repeated structures,
resulting in *BF* under-performing *RANSAC* with a naive ratio test.

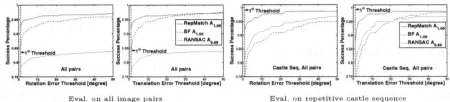

Eval. on all image pairs   Eval. on repetitive castle sequence

Fig. 9. Left: Component wise evaluation on all pairs. Observe that *RepMatch* consistently improves its *RANSAC* and *BF* components. **Right:** Castle sequence which
has significant repetition. *BF* is too aggressive and actually under-performs *RANSAC*
$\mathcal{A}_{0.66}$. *RepMatch* avoids this performance degradation.

Finally, Fig. 10 evaluates *RepMatch*'s performance at different rotational
baselines. At narrower baselines (below 45°), *RepMatch* is nearly perfect. It
also remains remarkably robust to wide-baselines and maintains a 60–70 % pass
rate at a 1° threshold for baselines exceeding 90°. Table 1 summarizes Figs. 9
and 10 and provides matching statistics. It shows *RepMatch* provides consistent
improvements over all scene types and baselines, with especially large gains at
wide-baselines and repetitive structures. While spectacularly wide-baselines are
not necessarily useful in themselves, they are an indicator of very high moderate-
baseline stability in less controlled environments, investigated in the next section.

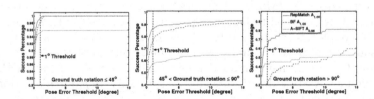

Fig. 10. Dataset divided by rotational baseline. At narrow baselines (below 45°), both
BF and *RepMatch* are nearly perfect, with close to 100 % pass at a 1° threshold. At
wider baselines, the gap between *RepMatch* and *BF* widens. Notably, *RepMatch* has a
60–70 % SP at a 1° threshold for baselines exceeding 90°.

4.2   Structure-From-Motion Systems

Here we explore *RepMatch*'s performance on less controlled modern city images
and its role in an overall SfM pipeline. Figure 11 shows reconstruction of three
modern scenes: (i) indoor; (ii) street; (iii) walking around a block. The sparse

Table 1. Evaluation on Strecha dataset [48]. We tabulate the match precision, average number of correct matches ("# matches"), Success Percentage (SP) at 1° rotation error and 1° translation error. *RepMatch* algorithm consistently improves on its individual components in terms of pose accuracy and match precision, with the difference increasing with baseline. In terms of match numbers, *RepMatch* has slightly fewer matches than *BF* but still maintains a substantial advantage over standard $\mathcal{A}_{0.66}$.

Algo.	Basline ≤ 45°				45° < Baseline ≤ 90°				Baseline ≥ 90°			
	Precision	# match	$SP(1°)$		Precision	# match	$SP(1°)$		Precision	# match	$SP(1°)$	
			Rot.	Trans.			Rot.	Trans.			Rot.	Trans.
$\mathcal{A}_{0.66}$	0.915	5845	0.953	0.939	0.556	700	0.574	0.568	0.452	293	0.429	0.452
BF	0.957	19795	0.983	0.956	0.792	5078	0.769	0.759	0.457	2185	0.214	0.287
RepMatch	0.985	17800	0.997	0.975	0.886	4612	0.876	0.870	0.709	1912	0.619	0.714

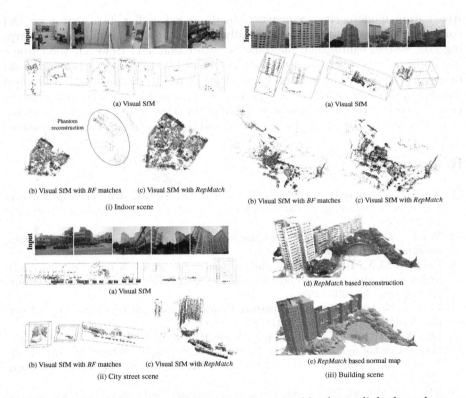

Fig. 11. Three city scenes. (i) Inside of a home. *RepMatch* can link through many weakly textured passages. *BF* also reconstructs the full flat but it creates phantom walls. (ii) A city street. Only *RepMatch* does not fragment the model. (iii) A city block. *RepMatch*'s reconstruction in (c) clearly shows the block outlines. This permits high quality dense reconstruction using [37] in (d) and (e).

reconstruction system used is *Visual SfM*, which we provide with different feature matches[3]. We show performance with *RepMatch*, *BF* and *Visual SfM*'s default matching. While none of the sequences are especially wide baselines, *Visual SfM* has multiple breaks, demonstrating the difficult nature of modern city reconstruction. Using *BF* correspondences reduces the breaks but the reconstructed point clouds show serious errors with stray frames and phantom walls. *RepMatch* permits un-fragmented, high quality reconstruction. Sequence (i) is especially interesting as *RepMatch* improves on *BF* even on indoor environments with few repetitive structures. This opens the possibility image information complementing current depth camera based floor plan recovery [49,50].

5   Discussion

Apart from modern city reconstructions discussed earlier, two view pose and correspondence estimation are potentially useful in applications like image warping [51], system calibration, photometric estimation, etc. However, the chronic instability of two view pose estimates has limited their practical usefulness and caused a gradual decline in interest. *RepMatch*'s results suggests such pessimism may be unwarranted and the basic pose estimation problem deserves more attention. Perhaps with further research, reliable two view pose and correspondence estimates will be something future vision and robotic systems take for granted.

References

1. Agarwal, S., Snavely, N., Simon, I., Seitz, S.M., Szeliski, R.: Building Rome in a day. In: Proceedings of the International Conference on Computer Vision, pp. 72–79 (2009)
2. Wu, C.: VisualSfM: a visual structure from motion system (2011). http://www.cs.washington.edu/homes/ccwu/vsfm
3. Fischler, M.A., Bolles, R.C.: Random sample consensus: a paradigm for model fitting with applications to image analysis and automated cartography. Commun. ACM **24**(6), 381–395 (1981)
4. Lowe, D.G.: Distinctive image features from scale-invariant keypoints. Int. J. Comput. Vision **60**(2), 91–110 (2004)
5. Lin, W.-Y.D., Cheng, M.-M., Lu, J., Yang, H., Do, M.N., Torr, P.: Bilateral functions for global motion modeling. In: Fleet, D., Pajdla, T., Schiele, B., Tuytelaars, T. (eds.) ECCV 2014, Part IV. LNCS, vol. 8692, pp. 341–356. Springer, Heidelberg (2014)
6. Klein, G., Murray, D.: Parallel tracking and mapping for small AR workspaces. In: IEEE and ACM International Symposium on Mixed and Augmented Reality, pp. 225–234 (2007)
7. Leonard, J.J., Durrant-Whyte, H.F.: Simultaneous map building and localization for an autonomous mobile robot. In: Proceedings of IEEE/RSJ International Workshop on Intelligent Robots and Systems, pp. 1442–1447 (1991)

---

[3] We leverage *RepMatch*'s robust pose estimate to eliminate all triplet poses with relative rotation consistency less than $2°$. *BF* was employed with the same scheme.

8. Altwaijry, H., Belongie, S.: Ultra-wide baseline aerial imagery matching in urban environments. In: Proceedings of British Machine Vision Conference (2013)
9. Kushnir, M., Shimshoni, I.: Epipolar geometry estimation for urban scenes with repetitive structures. IEEE Trans. Pattern Anal. Mach. Intell. **36**(12), 2381–2395 (2014)
10. Liu, Z., Monasse, P., Marlet, R.: Match selection and refinement for highly accurate two-view structure from motion. In: Fleet, D., Pajdla, T., Schiele, B., Tuytelaars, T. (eds.) ECCV 2014, Part II. LNCS, vol. 8690, pp. 818–833. Springer, Heidelberg (2014)
11. Shah, R., Srivastava, V., Narayanan, P.: Geometry-aware feature matching for structure from motion applications. In: Proceedings of Winter Conference on Applications of Computer Vision (WACV), pp. 278–285 (2015)
12. Xiang, T., Cheong, L.F.: Understanding the behavior of SfM algorithms: a geometric approach. Int. J. Comput. Vision **51**(2), 111–137 (2003)
13. Raguram, R., Chum, O., Pollefeys, M., Matas, J., Frahm, J.: USAC: a universal framework for random sample consensus. IEEE Trans. Pattern Anal. Mach. Intell. **35**(8), 2022–2038 (2013)
14. Goshen, L., Shimshoni, I.: Balanced exploration and exploitation model search for efficient epipolar geometry estimation. IEEE Trans. Pattern Anal. Mach. Intell. **30**(3), 1230–1242 (2008)
15. Chum, O., Matas, J.: Matching with PROSAC-progressive sample consensus. In: Proceedings of Computer Vision and Pattern Recognition, pp.220–226 (2005)
16. Ni, K., Jin, H., Dellaert, F.: GroupSAC: efficient consensus in the presence of groupings. In: Proceedings of International Conference on Computer Vision, pp. 2193–2200 (2009)
17. Sattler, T., Leibe, B., Kobbelt, L.: SCRAMSAC: improving RANSAC's efficiency with a spatial consistency filter. In: Proceedings of International Conference on Computer Vision, pp. 2090–2097 (2009)
18. Chum, O., Matas, J., Kittler, J.: Locally optimized RANSAC. In: Michaelis, B., Krell, G. (eds.) DAGM 2003. LNCS, vol. 2781, pp. 236–243. Springer, Heidelberg (2003)
19. Wang, C., Wang, L., Liu, L.: Progressive mode-seeking on graphs for sparse feature matching. In: Proceedings of European Conference on Computer Vision, pp. 788–802 (2014)
20. Wang, C., Wang, L., Liu, L.: Density maximization for improving graph matching with its applications. IEEE Trans. Image Process. **24**(7), 2110–2123 (2015)
21. Lipman, Y., Yagev, S., Poranne, R., Jacobs, D.W., Basri, R.: Feature matching with bounded distortion. ACM Trans. Graph. **33**(3), 26 (2014)
22. Pizarro, D., Bartoli, A.: Feature-based deformable surface detection with self-occlusion. Int. J. Comput. Vision **97**(1), 54–70 (2012)
23. Ok, D., Marlet, R., Audibert, J.Y.: Efficient and scalable 4-th order match propagation. In: Proceedings of Asian Conference on Computer Vision, pp. 460–473 (2012)
24. Lin, W.Y., Wang, F., Cheng, M.M., Yeung, S.K., Torr, P., Do, M., Lu, J.: CODE: Coherence based decision boundaires for feature correspondance (2016). http://www.kind-of-works.com
25. Kamiya, S., Kanazawa, Y.: Accurate image matching in scenes including repetitive patterns. In: Sommer, G., Klette, R. (eds.) RobVis 2008. LNCS, vol. 4931, pp. 165–176. Springer, Heidelberg (2008)

26. Zhang, Z., Matsushita, Y., Ma, Y.: Camera calibration with lens distortion from low-rank textures. In: Proceedings of Computer Vision and Pattern Recognition (2011)
27. Le Brese, C., Young, C., Zou, J.J.: A robust match filtering algorithm for use with repetitive patterns. In: Proceedings of Signal Processing and Communication Systems (ICSPCS) (2013)
28. Lu, X., Manduchi, R.: Wide baseline feature matching using the cross-epipolar ordering constraint. In: Proceedings of Computer Vision and Pattern Recognition (2004)
29. Mortensen, E.N., Deng, H., Shapiro, L.: A SIFT descriptor with global context. In: Proceedings of Computer Vision and Pattern Recognition (2005)
30. Bay, H., Tuytelaars, T., Van Gool, L.: SURF: speeded up robust features. In: Leonardis, A., Bischof, H., Pinz, A. (eds.) ECCV 2006, Part I. LNCS, vol. 3951, pp. 404–417. Springer, Heidelberg (2006)
31. Fan, B., Wu, F., Hu, Z.: Aggregating gradient distributions into intensity orders: a novel local image descriptor. In: Proceedings of Computer Vision and Pattern Recognition (2011)
32. Snavely, N., Seitz, S.M., Szeliski, R.: Photo tourism: exploring image collections in 3D. In: Proceedings of ACM SIGGRAPH (2006)
33. Chatterjee, A., Govindu, V.M.: Efficient and robust large-scale rotation averaging. In: Proceedings of International Conference on Computer Vision (2013)
34. Cui, Z., Tan, P.: Global structure-from-motion by similarity averaging. In: Proceedings of International Conference on Computer Vision (2015)
35. Wu, C., Agarwal, S., Curless, B., Seitz, S.M.: Multicore bundle adjustment. In: Proceedings of Computer Vision and Pattern Recognition, pp. 3057–3064 (2011)
36. Furukawa, Y., Ponce, J.: Accurate, dense, and robust multi-view stereopsis. In: Proceedings of Conference on Computer Vision and Pattern Recognition (2007)
37. Jancosek, M., Pajdla, T.: Multi-view reconstruction preserving weakly-supported surfaces. In: Proceedings of Computer Vision and Pattern Recognition, pp. 3121–3128 (2011)
38. Raguram, R., Frahm, J.M., Pollefeys, M.: Exploiting uncertainty in random sample consensus. In: Proceedings of International Conference on Computer Vision, pp. 2074–2081 (2009)
39. Torr, P.H.S., Zisserman, A.: MLESAC: a new robust estimator with application to estimating image geometry. Trans. Comput. Vision Image Underst. **78**, 138–156 (2000)
40. Chin, T.J., Purkait, P., Eriksson, A., Suter, D.: Efficient globally optimal consensus maximisation with tree search. In: Proceedings of Computer Vision and Pattern Recognition, pp. 2413–2421 (2015)
41. Cohen, A., Sattler, T., Pollefeys, M.: Merging the unmatchable: stitching visually disconnected SfM models. In: Proceedings of International Conference on Computer Vision, pp. 2129–2137 (2015)
42. Jiang, N., Tan, P., Cheong, L.F.: Seeing double without confusion: structure-from-motion in highly ambiguous scenes. In: Proceedings of Computer Vision and Pattern Recognition, pp. 1458–1465 (2012)
43. Myronenko, A., Song, X., Carreira-Perpinan, M.A.: Non-rigid point set registration: coherent point drift. In: Proceedings of Advances in Neural Information Processing Systems, pp. 1009–1016 (2006)
44. Yuille, A.L., Grzywacz, N.M.: The motion coherence theory. In: Proceedings of International Conference on Computer Vision, pp. 344–353 (1988)

45. Lin, W.Y., Cheng, M.M., Zheng, S., Lu, J., Crook, N.: Robust non-parametric data fitting for correspondence modeling. In: Proceedings of International Conference on Computer Vision, pp. 2376–2383 (2013)
46. Morel, J.M., Yu, G.: ASIFT: a new framework for fully affine invariant image comparison. SIAM J. Imaging Sci. **2**(2), 438–469 (2009)
47. Hartley, R., Zisserman, A.: Multiple View Geometry in Computer Vision. Cambridge University Press, Cambridge (2000)
48. Strecha, C., von Hansen, W., Gool, L.V., Fua, P., Thoennessen, U.: On benchmarking camera calibration and multi-view stereo for high resolution imagery. In: Proceedings of Computer Vision and Pattern Recognition, pp. 1–8 (2008)
49. Yu, L.F., Yeung, S.K., Tang, C.K., Terzopoulos, D., Chan, T.F., Osher, S.J.: Make it home: automatic optimization of furniture arrangement. ACM Trans. Graph. **30**(4), 86:1–86:12 (2011)
50. Ikehata, S., Yan, H., Furukawa, Y.: Structured indoor modeling. In: Proceedings of International Conference on Computer Vision, pp. 1323–1331 (2015)
51. Lin, W.Y., Liu, S., Matsushita, Y., Ng, T.T., Cheong, L.F.: Smoothly varying affine stitching. In: Proceedings of Computer Vision and Pattern Recognition, pp. 345–352 (2011)

Convolutional Oriented Boundaries

Kevis-Kokitsi Maninis[1][✉], Jordi Pont-Tuset[1], Pablo Arbeláez[2],
and Luc Van Gool[1,3]

[1] ETH Zürich, Zürich, Switzerland
kmaninis@vision.ee.ethz.ch
[2] Universidad de Los Andes, Bogotá, Colombia
[3] KU Leuven, Leuven, Belgium

Abstract. We present Convolutional Oriented Boundaries (COB),
which produces multiscale oriented contours and region hierarchies starting from generic image classification Convolutional Neural Networks
(CNNs). COB is computationally efficient, because it requires a single
CNN forward pass for contour detection and it uses a novel sparse boundary representation for hierarchical segmentation; it gives a significant leap
in performance over the state-of-the-art, and it generalizes very well to
unseen categories and datasets. Particularly, we show that learning to
estimate not only contour strength but also orientation provides more
accurate results. We perform extensive experiments on BSDS, PASCAL
Context, PASCAL Segmentation, and MS-COCO, showing that COB
provides state-of-the-art contours, region hierarchies, and object proposals in all datasets.

Keywords: Contour detection · Contour orientation estimation ·
Hierarchical image segmentation · Object proposals

1 Introduction

The adoption of Convolutional Neural Networks (CNNs) has caused a profound
change and a large leap forward in performance throughout the majority of fields
in computer vision. In the case of a traditionally category-agnostic field such as
contour detection, it has recently fostered the appearance of systems [1–6] that
rely on large-scale category-specific information in the form of deep architectures
pre-trained on Imagenet for image classification [7–10].

This paper proposes Convolutional Oriented Boundaries (COB), a generic
CNN architecture that allows end-to-end learning of multiscale oriented contours, and we show how it translates top performing base CNN networks into
high-quality contours; allowing to bring future improvements in base CNN architectures into semantic grouping. We then propose a sparse boundary representation for efficient construction of hierarchical regions from the contour signal.
Our overall approach is both efficient (it runs in 0.8 seconds per image) and
highly accurate (it produces state-of-the-art contours and regions on PASCAL
and on the BSDS). Figure 1 shows an overview of our system.

© Springer International Publishing AG 2016
B. Leibe et al. (Eds.): ECCV 2016, Part I, LNCS 9905, pp. 580–596, 2016.
DOI: 10.1007/978-3-319-46448-0_35

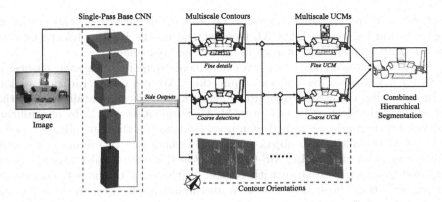

Fig. 1. Overview of COB: From a single pass of a base CNN, we obtain multiscale oriented contours. We combine them to build Ultrametric Contour Maps (UCMs) at different scales and fuse them into a single hierarchical segmentation structure.

For the last fifteen years, the Berkeley Segmentation Dataset and Benchmark (BSDS) [11] has been the experimental testbed of choice for the study of boundary detection and image segmentation. However, the current large-capacity and very accurate models have underlined the limitations of the BSDS as the primary benchmark for grouping. Its 300 train images are inadequate for training systems with tens of millions of parameters and, critically, current state-of-the-art techniques are reaching human performance for boundary detection on its 200 test images.

In terms of scale and difficulty, the next natural frontier for perceptual grouping is the PASCAL VOC dataset [12], an influential benchmark for image classification, object detection, and semantic segmentation which has a *trainval* set with more than 10 000 challenging and varied images. A first step in that direction was taken by Hariharan et al. [13], who annotated the VOC dataset for category-specific boundary detection on the foreground objects. More recently, the PASCAL Context dataset [14] extended this annotation effort to all the background categories, providing thus fully-parsed images which are a direct VOC counterpart to the human ground-truth of the BSDS. In this direction, this paper investigates the transition from the BSDS to PASCAL Context in the evaluation of image segmentation.

We derive valuable insights from studying perceptual grouping in a larger and more challenging empirical framework. Among them, we observe that COB leverages increasingly deeper state-of-the-art architectures, such as the recent Residual Networks [10], to produce improved results. This indicates that our approach is generic and can directly benefit from future advances in CNNs. We also observe that, in PASCAL, the globalization strategy of contour strength by spectral graph partitioning proposed in [15] and used in state-of-the-art methods [1,16] is unnecessary in the presence of the high-level knowledge conveyed by pre-trained CNNs and oriented contours, thus removing a significant computational bottleneck for high-quality contours. Overall, COB generates state-of-the-art contours and regions on PASCAL Context and on the BSDS while being computationally very efficient: it runs in 0.8 seconds per image.

We also conduct comprehensive experiments demonstrating the interest of COB for downstream recognition applications. We use our hierarchical regions as input to the combinatorial grouping algorithm of [16] and obtain state-of-the-art segmented object proposals on PASCAL Segmentation 2012 by a significant margin. Furthermore, we provide empirical evidence for the generalization power of COB by evaluating our object proposals without any retraining in the even larger and more challenging MS-COCO dataset, where we also report a large improvement in performance with respect to the state of the art. Our efforts on segmentation through CNNs have also found application in retinal image segmentation [17], obtaining state-of-the-art and super-human performance in vessel and optic disc segmentation, which further highlights their generality.

The COB code, pre-computed results, pre-trained models, and benchmarks are publicly available at www.vision.ee.ethz.ch/~cvlsegmentation/.

2   Related Work

The latest wave of contour detectors takes advantage of deep learning to obtain state-of-the-art results [1–6,18]. Ganin and Lempitsky [6] use a deep architecture to extract features of image patches. They approach contour detection as a multiclass classification task, by matching the extracted features to predefined ground-truth features. The authors of [3,4] make use of features generated by pre-trained CNNs to regress contours. They prove that object-level information provides powerful cues for the prediction of contours. Shen et al. [5] learn deep features using shape information. Xie and Tu [2] provide an end-to-end deep framework to boost the efficiency and accuracy of contour detection, using convolutional feature maps and a novel loss function. Kokkinos [1] builds upon [2] and improves the results by tuning the loss function, running the detector at multiple scales, and adding globalization. COB is different from this previous work in that we obtain multiscale information in a single pass of the network on the whole image, it combines the per-pixel classification with contour orientation estimation, and its output is richer than a linear combination of cues at different scales.

At the core of all these deep learning approaches, lies a *base CNN*, starting from the seminal AlexNet [7] (8 layers), through the more complex VGGNet [9] (16 layers) and inception architecture of GoogLeNet [8] (22 layers), to the very recent and very deep ResNets [10] (up to 1001 layers). Image classification results, which originally motivated these architectures, have been continuously improved by exploring deeper and more complex networks. In this work, we present results both using VGGNet and ResNet, showing that COB is modular and can incorporate and benefit from future improvements in the base CNN.

Recent work has also explored the weakly supervised or unsupervised learning of contours: Khoreva et al. [19] learn from the results of generic contour detectors coupled with object detectors; and Li et al. [20] train contour detectors from motion boundaries acquired from video sequences. Yang et al. [21] use conditional random fields to refine the inaccurately localized boundary annotations of PASCAL. Our approach uses full supervision from BSDS and PASCAL Context for contour localization and orientation.

COB exploits the duality between contour detection and segmentation hierarchies, initially studied by Najman and Schmitt [22]. Arbeláez et al. [15] showed its usefulness for jointly optimizing contours and regions. Pont-Tuset et al. [16] leveraged multi-resolution contour detection and proved its interest also for generating object proposals. We differentiate from these approaches in two aspects. First, our sparse boundary representation translates into a clean and highly efficient implementation of hierarchical segmentation. Second, by leveraging high-level knowledge from the CNNs in the estimation of contour strength and orientation, our method benefits naturally from global information, which allows bypassing the globalization step (output of normalized cuts), a bottleneck in terms of computational cost, but a cornerstone of previous aproaches.

3   Deep Multiscale Oriented Contours

CNNs are by construction multi-scale feature extractors. If one examines the standard architecture of a CNN consisting of convolutional and spatial pooling layers, it becomes clear that as we move deeper, feature maps capture more global information due to the decrease in resolution. For contour detection, this architecture implies local and fine-scale contours at shallow levels, coarser spatial resolution and larger receptive fields for the units when going deeper into the network and, consequently, more global information for predicting boundary strength and orientation. CNNs have therefore a built-in globalization strategy for contour detection, analogous to the hand-engineered globalization of contour strength through spectral graph partitioning in [15,16].

Figure 2 depicts how we make use of information provided by the intermediate layers of a CNN to detect contours and their orientations at multiple scales. Different groups of feature maps contain different, scale-specific information, which we combine to build a multiscale oriented contour detector. The remainder of this section is devoted to introducing the recent approaches to contour detection using deep learning, to presenting our CNN architecture to produce contour detection at different scales, and to explain how we estimate the orientation of the edges; all in a single CNN forward pass at the image level.

Training Deep Contour Detectors: The recent success of [2] is based on a CNN to accurately regress the contours of an image. Within this framework, the idea of employing a neural network in an image-to-image fashion without any post-processing has proven successful and serves right now as the state-of-the-art for the task of contour detection. Their network, HED, produces scale-specific contour images (side outputs) for different scales of a network, and combines their activations linearly to produce a contour probability map. Using the notation of the authors, we denote the training dataset by $S = \{(X_n, Y_n), n = 1, \ldots, N\}$,

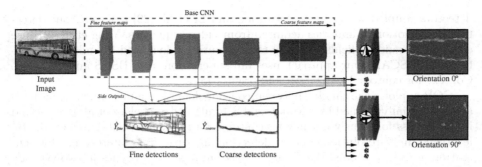

Fig. 2. Our deep learning architecture (best viewed in color). The connections show the different stages that are used to generate the multiscale contours. Orientations further require additional convolutional layers in multiple stages of the network. (Color figure online)

with X_n being the input image and $Y_n = \{y_j^{(n)}, j = 1, \ldots, |X_n|\}, y_j^{(n)} \in \{0,1\}$ the predicted pixelwise labels. For simplicity, we drop the subscript n. Each of the M side outputs minimizes the objective function:

$$\ell_{side}^{(m)}\Big(\mathbf{W}, \mathbf{w}^{(m)}\Big) = -\beta \sum_{j \in Y_+} \log P\Big(y_j = 1 | X; \mathbf{W}, \mathbf{w}^{(m)}\Big) - (1-\beta) \sum_{j \in Y_-} \log P\Big(y_j = 0 | X; \mathbf{W}, \mathbf{w}^{(m)}\Big)$$

(1)

where $\ell_{side}^{(m)}$ is the loss function for scale $m \in \{1, \ldots, M\}$, $\mathbf{W}$ denotes the standard set of parameters of the CNN, and $\{\mathbf{w}^{(m)}, m = 1, \ldots, M\}$ the corresponding weights of the the m-th side output. The multiplier β is used to handle the imbalance of the substantially greater number of background compared to contour pixels. Y_+ and Y_- denote the contour and background sets of the ground-truth Y, respectively. The probability $P(\cdot)$ is obtained by applying a sigmoid $\sigma(\cdot)$ to the activations of the side outputs $\hat{A}_{side}^{(m)} = \{a_j^{(m)}, j = 1, \ldots, |Y|\}$. The activations are finally fused linearly, as: $\hat{Y}_{fuse} = \sigma\left(\Sigma_{m=1}^M h_m \hat{A}_{side}^{(m)}\right)$ where $\mathbf{h} = \{h_m, m = 1, \ldots, M\}$ are the fusion weights. The fusion output is also trained to resemble the ground-truth applying the same loss function of Eq. 1, by optimizing the complete set of parameters, including the fusion weights $\mathbf{h}$. In the rest of the paper we use the class-balancing cross-entropy loss function of Eq. 1.

Multiscale Contours: We finetune the 50-layer ResNet [10] for the task of contour detection. The fully connected layers used for classification are removed, and so are the batch normalization layers, since we operate on one image per iteration. Therefore, the network consists mainly of convolutional layers coupled with ReLU activations, divided into 5 stages. We will refer to this architecture as the "base CNN" of our implementation. Each stage is handled as a different scale, since it contains feature maps of a similar size. At the end of a stage, there is a max pooling layer, which reduces the dimensions of the produced feature maps to a half. As discussed before, the CNN naturally contains multiscale information, which we exploit to build a multiscale contour regressor.

We separately supervise the output of the last layer of each stage (side activation), comparing it to the ground truth using the loss function of Eq. 1. This way, we enforce each side activation to produce an intermediate contour map at different resolution. The idea of supervising intermediate parts of a CNN has successfully been used in previous approaches, for a variety of tasks [2,8,23]. In the 5-scale base CNN illustrated in Fig. 2, we linearly combine the side activations of the 4 finest and 4 coarsest scales to a fine-scale and a coarse-scale output ($\hat{Y}_{fine}$ and $\hat{Y}_{coarse}$, respectively) with trainable weights. The finer scale contains better localized contours, whereas the coarse scale leads to less noisy detections. To train the two sets of weights of the linear combinations, we freeze the pre-trained weights of the base CNN.

Estimation of Contour Orientations: In order to predict accurate contour orientations, we propose an extension of the CNN that we use as multiscale contour detector. We define the task as pixel-wise image-to-image multiscale classification into K bins. We connect K different branches (sub-networks) to the base network, each of which is associated with one orientation bin, and has access to feature maps that are generated from the intermediate convolutional layers at M different scales. We assign the parts of the CNN associated with each orientation a different task than the base network: classify the pixels of the contours that match a specific orientation. In order to design these orientation-specific subtasks, we classify each pixel of the human contour annotations into K different orientations. The orientation of each contour pixel is obtained by approximating the ground-truth boundaries with polygons, and assigning each pixel the orientation of the closest polygonal segment, as shown in Fig. 5. As in the case of multiscale contours, the weights of the base network remain frozen when training these sub-networks.

Each sub-network consists of M convolutional layers, each of them appended on different scales of the base network. Thus we need $M * K$ additional layers, namely conv_scale_m_orient_k, with k= $1, \ldots, K$ and m= $1, \ldots, M$. In our setup, we use $K = 8$ and $M = 5$. All K orientations are regressed in parallel, and since they are associated with a certain angle, we post-process them to obtain the orientation map. Specifically, the orientation map is obtained as:

$$O(x,y) = \mathcal{T}\left(\arg\max_{k} B_k(x,y)\right), k = 1, \ldots, K \qquad (2)$$

where $B_k(x,y)$ denotes the response of the k-th orientation bin of the CNN at the pixels with coordinates (x,y) and $\mathcal{T}(\cdot)$ is the transformation function which associates each bin with its central angle. For the cases where two neighboring bins lead to strong responses, we compute the angle as their weighted average. At pixels where there is no response for any of the orientations, we assign random values between 0 and π, not to bias the orientations. The different orientations as well as the resulting orientation map (color-coded) are illustrated in Fig. 3.

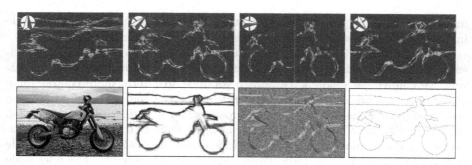

Fig. 3. Illustration of contour orientation learning. Row 1 shows the responses B_k for 4 out of the 8 orientation bins. Row 2, from left to right: original image, contour strength, learned orientation map into 8 orientations, and hierarchical boundaries.

In [15, 16, 24] the orientations are computed by means of local gradient filters. In Sect. 5 we show that our learned orientations are significantly more accurate and lead to more better region segmentations.

4   Fast Hierarchical Regions

This section is devoted to building an efficient hierarchical image segmentation algorithm from the multiscale contours and the orientations extracted in the previous section. We build on the concept of Ultrametric Contour Map (UCM) [15], which transforms a contour detection probability map into a hierarchical boundary map, which gets partitions at different granularities when thresholding at various contour strength values. Despite the success of UCMs, their low speed significantly limits their applicability.

In the remainder of this section we first describe an alternative representation of an image partition that allows us to reduce the computation time of multiscale UCMs by an order of magnitude, to less than one second. Then, we present the global algorithm to build a hierarchy of regions from the multiscale contours and the orientations presented in Sect. 3. As we will show in the experimental section, the resulting algorithm improves the state of the art significantly, at a fraction of the computational time of [16].

Sparse Boundary Representation of Hierarchies of Regions: An image partition is a clustering of the set of pixels into different sets, which we call regions. The most straightforward way of representing it in a computer is by a matrix of labels, as in the example in Fig. 4(a), with three regions on an image of size 2×3. The boundaries of this partition are the edge elements, or *edgels*, between the pixels with different labels (highlighted in red). We can assign different *strengths* to these boundaries (thicknesses of the red lines), which indicate the *confidence* of that piece of being a true boundary. By iteratively *erasing* these boundaries in order of increasing strength we obtain different partitions, which we call *hierarchy of regions*, or Ultrametric Contour Maps.

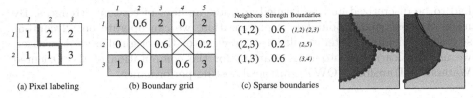

Fig. 4. Image partition representation: (a) Pixel labeling, each pixel gets assigned a region label. (b) Boundary grid, markers of the boundary positions. (c) Sparse
boundaries, lists of boundary coordinates between neighboring regions. (Color figure online)

Fig. 5. Polygon simplifi-
cation: from all boundary
points (left) to simplified
polygons (right). (Color
figure online)

These boundaries are usually stored in the *boundary grid* (Fig. 4(b)), a matrix
of double the size of the image (minus one), in which the odd coordinates represent pixels (gray areas), and the positions in between represent boundaries (red
numbers) and junctions (crossed positions).

UCMs use this representation to store their boundary *strength* values, that
is, each boundary position stores the threshold value beyond which that edgel
disappears and the two neighboring regions merge. This way, simply *binarizing*
a UCM we have a partition represented as a boundary grid.

This representation, while useful during prototyping, becomes very inefficient
at run time, where the percentage of *activated* boundaries is very sparse. Not
only are we wasting memory by storing those *empty* boundaries, but it also
makes operating on them very inefficient by having to *sweep* over the entire
matrix to perform a modification on a single boundary piece.

Inspired by how sparse matrices are handled, we designed the *sparse boundaries* representation (Fig. 4(c)). It stores a look-up table for pairs of neigbboring
regions, their boundary strength, and the list of coordinates the boundary occu-
pies. Apart from being more compact in terms of memory, this representation
enables efficient operations on specific pieces of a boundary, since one only needs
to perform a search in the look-up table and scan the activated coordinates;
instead of having to sweep the whole boundary grid.

Fast Hierarchies from Multiscale Oriented Contours: The deep CNN
presented in Sect. 3 provides different levels of detail for the image contours. A
linear combination of the layers is the straightforward way of providing a single
contour signal [2]. The approach in this work is to combine the region hierarchies
extracted from the contour signals at each layer instead of the contours directly.
We were inspired by the framework proposed in [16], in which a UCM is obtained
from contours computed at different image scales and then combined in a single
hierarchy; but instead we use the different contour outputs that are computed
in a single pass of the proposed CNN architecture.

A drawback of the original framework [16] is that the manipulation of the
hierarchies is very slow (in the order of seconds), so the operations on the UCMs

had to be discretized and performed at a low number of contour strengths. By using the fast sparse boundary representation, we can operate on all contour strengths, yielding better results at a fraction of the original cost. Moreover, we use the learned contour orientations for the computation of the Oriented Watershed Transform (OWT), further boosting performance.

5 Experiments

This section presents the empirical evidence that supports our approach. First, Sect. 5.1 explores the ablated and baseline techniques studied to isolate and quantify the improvements due to different components of our system. Then Sects. 5.2, 5.3, and 5.4 compare our results against the state-of-the-art in terms of contour orientation estimation, generic image segmentation, and the application to object proposals, respectively. In all three cases, we obtain the best results to date by a significant margin. Finally, Sect. 5.5 analyzes the gain in speed achieved mainly by the use of our sparse boundaries representation.

We extend the main BSDS benchmarks to the PASCAL Context dataset [14], which contains carefully localized pixelwise semantic annotations for the entire image on the PASCAL VOC 2010 detection trainval set. This results in 459 semantic categories across 10 103 images, which is an order of magnitude (20×) larger than the BSDS. In order to allow training and optimization of large capacity models, we split the data into train, validation, and test sets as follows: *VOC train* corresponds to the official PASCAL Context train with 4 998 images, *VOC val* corresponds to half the official PASCAL Context validation set with 2 607 images and *VOC test* corresponds to the second half with 2 498 images. In the remainder of the paper, we refer to this dataset division. Note that, in this setting, the notion of boundary is defined as separation between different semantic categories and not their parts, in contrast to the BSDS.

We used the publicly available *Caffe* [25] framework for training and testing CNNs, and all the state-of-the-art results are computed using the publicly-available code provided by the respective authors.

5.1 Control Experiments/Ablation Analysis

This section presents the control experiments and ablation analysis to assess the performance of all subsystems of our method. We train on *VOC train*, and evaluate on *VOC val* set. We report the standard F-measure at Optimal Dataset Scale (ODS) and Optimal Image Scale (OIS), as well as the Average Precision (AP), both evaluating boundaries (F_b [26]) and regions (F_{op} [27]).

Table 1 shows the evaluation results of the different variants, highlighting whether we include globalization and/or trained orientations. As a first baseline, we test the performance of MCG [16], which uses Structured Edges [24] as input contour signal, and denote it MCG [16]. We then substitute SE by the newer HED [2], trained on *VOC train* as input contours and denote it MCG-HED.

Table 1. Ablation analysis on *VOC val*: comparison of different ablated versions of our system.

Method	Global.	Orient.	Boundaries - F_b			Regions - F_{op}		
			ODS	OIS	AP	ODS	OIS	AP
MCG [16]	✓	✗	0.548	0.594	0.519	0.355	0.419	0.263
MCG-HED	✓	✗	0.691	0.727	0.693	0.459	0.520	0.374
VGGNet-Side	✓	✗	0.644	0.683	0.664	0.439	0.505	0.351
ResNet50-Side	✓	✗	0.676	0.711	0.681	0.456	0.521	0.374
Ours (VGGNet)	✗	✓	0.705	0.735	0.741	0.466	0.533	0.384
Ours (ResNet50)	✗	✗	0.734	0.767	0.757	0.475	0.545	0.405
Ours (ResNet50)	✓	✗	0.726	0.759	0.725	0.461	0.531	0.395
Ours (ResNet50)	✓	✓	0.732	0.763	0.731	0.481	**0.554**	**0.418**
Ours (ResNet50)	✗	✓	**0.737**	**0.768**	**0.758**	0.483	0.553	0.417

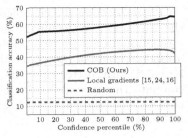

Fig. 6. Contour orientation: classification accuracy into orientations quantized in 8 bins.

Note that the aforementioned baselines require multiple passes of the contour detector (3 different scales).

In the direction of using the side outputs of the base CNN architecture as multiscale contour detections in one pass, we tested the baseline of naively taking the 5 side outputs directly as the contour detections. We trained both VGGNet [9] and ResNet50 [10] on *VOC train* and combined the 5 side outputs with our fast hierarchical regions of Sect. 4 (VGGNet-Side and ResNet50-Side).

We finally evaluate different variants of our system, as presented in Sect. 3. We first compare our system with two different base architectures: Ours(VGGNet) and Ours(ResNet50). We train the base networks for 30000 iterations, with stochastic gradient descent and a momentum of 0.9. We observe that the deeper architecture of ResNet translates into better boundaries and regions.

We then evaluate the influence of our trained orientations and globalization, by testing the four possible combinations (the orientations are further evaluated in next section). Our method using ResNet50 together with trained orientations leads to the best results both for boundaries and for regions. The experiments also show that, when coupled with trained orientations, globalization even decreases performance, so we can safely remove it and get a significant speed up. Our technique with trained orientations and without globalization is therefore selected as our final system and will be referred to in the sequel as Convolutional Oriented Boundaries (COB).

5.2 Contour Orientation

We evaluate contour orientation results by the classification accuracy into 8 different orientations, to isolate their performance from the global system. We compute the ground-truth orientations as depicted in Fig. 5 by means of the sparse boundaries representation. We then sweep all ground-truth boundary pixels and compare the estimated orientation with the ground-truth one. Since the orientations are not well-balanced classes (much more horizontal and vertical contours), we compute the classification accuracy per each of the 8 classes and then compute the mean.

Figure 6 shows the classification accuracy with respect to the confidence of the estimation. We compare our proposed technique against the local gradient estimation used in previous literature [15, 16, 24]. As a baseline, we plot the result a random guess of the orientations would get. We observe that our estimation is significantly better than the previous approach. As a summary measure, we compute the area under the curve of the accuracy (ours 58.6 %, local gradients 41.2 %, random 12.5 %), which corroborates the superior results from our technique.

5.3   Generic Image Segmentation

We present our results for contour detection and generic image segmentation on PASCAL Context [14] as well as on the BSDS500 [11], which is the most established benchmark for perceptual grouping.

PASCAL Context: We train COB in the *VOC train*, and perform hyper-parameter selection on *VOC val*. We report the final results on the unseen *VOC test* when trained on *VOC trainval*, using the previously tuned hyper-parameters. We compare our approach to several methods trained on the BSDS [2, 16, 24, 28] and we also retrain the current state-of-the-art contour detection methods HED [2] and the recent CEDN [21] on *VOC trainval* using the code provided by the respective authors.

Figure 7 presents the evaluation results of our method compared to the state-of-the-art, which show that COB outperforms all others by a considerable margin both in terms of boundaries and in terms of regions. The lower performance of the methods trained on the BSDS quantifies the difficulty of the task when moving to a larger and more challenging dataset.

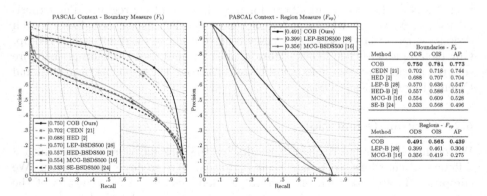

Fig. 7. PASCAL Context *VOC test* **Evaluation**: Precision-recall curves for evaluation of boundaries (F_b [26]), and regions (F_{op} [27]). Contours in dashed lines and boundaries (from segmentation) in solid lines. ODS, OIS, and AP summary measures.

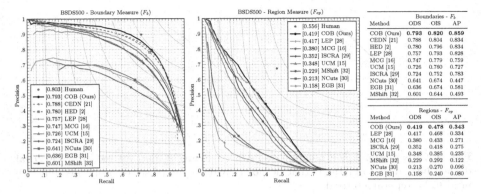

Fig. 8. BSDS500 test evaluation: precision-recall curves for evaluation of boundaries (F_b [26]), and regions (F_{op} [27]). ODS, OIS, and AP summary measures.

BSDS500: We retrain COB using only the 300 images of the *trainval* set of the BSDS, after data augmentation as suggested in [2], keeping the architecture decided in Sect. 5.1. For comparison to HED [2], we used the model that the authors provide online. We also compare with CEDN [21], by evaluating the results provided by the authors.

Figure 8 presents the evaluation results, which show that we also obtain state-of-the-art results in this dataset. The smaller margins are in all likelihood due to the fact that we almost reach human performance for the task of contour detection on the BSDS, which motivates the shift to PASCAL Context to achieve further progress in the field.

5.4 Object Proposals

Object proposals are an integral part of current object detection and semantic segmentation pipelines [33–35], as they provide a reduced search space on locations, scales, and shapes over the image. This section evaluates COB as a segmented proposal technique, when using our high-quality region hierarchies in conjunction with the combinatorial grouping framework of [16]. We compare against the more recent techniques POISE [36], MCG and SCG [16], LPO [37], GOP [38], SeSe [39], GLS [40], and RIGOR [41]. Recent thorough comparisons of object proposal generation methods can be found in [42,43].

We perform experiments on the PASCAL 2012 Segmentation dataset [12] and on the bigger and more challenging MS-COCO [44] (val set). The hierarchies and combinatorial grouping are trained on PASCAL Context. To assess the generalization capability, we evaluate on MS-COCO, which contains a large number of previously unseen categories, without further retraining.

Figure 9 shows the average recall [42] with respect to the number of object proposals. In PASCAL Segmentation, the absolute gap of improvement of COB is at least of +13 % with the second-best technique, and consistent in all the range of number of proposals. In MS-COCO, even though we did not train on any

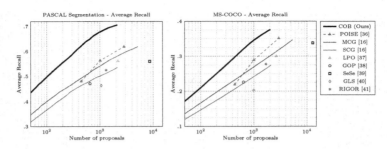

Fig. 9. Object proposals evaluation on PASCAL Segmentation val and MS-COCO val: dashed lines refer to methods that do not provide a ranked set of proposals, but they need to be reparameterized.

MS-COCO image, the percentage of absolute improvement is also consistently +13 % at least. This shows that our contours, regions, and proposals are properly learning a generic concept of object rather than some specific categories.

5.5 Efficiency Analysis

Contour detection and image segmentation, as a preprocessing step towards high-level applications, need to be computationally efficient. The previous state-of-the-art in hierarchical image segmentation [15,16] was of limited use in practice due to its computational load.

As a core in our system, the forward pass of our network to compute the contour strength and 8 orientations takes 0.28 seconds on a NVidia Titan X GPU. Table 2 shows the timing comparison between the full system COB (Ours) and some related baselines on PASCAL Context. We divide the timing into different relevant parts, namely, the contour detection step, the Oriented Watershed Transform (OWT) and Ultrametric Contour Map (UCM) computation, and the globalization (normalized cuts) step.

Column (1) shows the timing for the original MCG [16], which uses Structured Edges (SE) [24]. As a first baseline, Column (2) displays the timing of MCG if we naively substitute SE by HED [2] at the three scales (running on a GPU). By applying the sparse boundaries representation we reduce the UCM

Table 2. Timing experiments: comparing our approach to different baselines. Times computed using a GPU are marked with an asterisk.

Steps	(1) MCG [16]	(2) MCG-HED	(3) Fast UCMs	(4) COB (Ours)
Contour detection	3.08	0.39*	0.39*	0.28*
OWT and UCM	11.33	11.58	1.63	0.51
Globalization	9.96	9.97	9.92	0.00
Total time	24.37	21.94	11.94	**0.79**

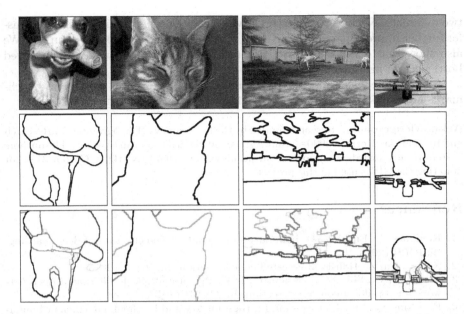

Fig. 10. Qualitative results on PASCAL - hierarchical regions. Row 1: original images, Row 2: ground-truth boundaries, Row 3: hierarchical regions with COB.

and OWT time from 11.58 to 1.63 seconds (Column (3)). Our final technique COB, in which we remove the globalization step, computes the three scales in one pass and add contour orientations, takes 0.79 seconds in mean. Overall, comparing to previous state-of-the-art, we get a significant improvement at a fraction of the computation time (24.37 to 0.79 seconds).

Qualitative Results: Fig. 10 shows some qualitative results of our hierarchical contours. Please note that COB is capable of correctly distinguishing between internal contours (e.g. cat or dog) and external, semantical, object boundaries.

6   Conclusions

In this work, we have developed an approach to detect contours at multiple scales, together with their orientations, in a single forward pass of a convolutional neural network. We provide a fast framework for generating region hierarchies by efficiently combining multiscale oriented contour detections, thanks to a new sparse boundary representation. We shift from the BSDS to PASCAL in the evaluation to unwind all the potential of data-hungry methods such as CNNs and by observing that the performance on the BSDS is close to saturation.

Our technique achieves state-of-the-art performance by a significant margin for contour detection, the estimation of their orientation, generic image segmentation, and object proposals. We show that our architecture is modular by using two different CNN base architectures, which suggests that it will be able to transfer further improvements in CNN base architectures to perceptual grouping. We also show that our method does not require globalization, which was a speed bottleneck in previous approaches.

All our code, CNN models, pre-computed results, dataset splits, and benchmarks are publicly available at www.vision.ee.ethz.ch/~cvlsegmentation/.

Acknowledgements. Research funded by the EU Framework Programme for Research and Innovation - Horizon 2020 - Grant Agreement No. 645331 - EurEyeCase. The authors gratefully acknowledge support by armasuisse, and thank NVIDIA Corporation for donating the GPUs used in this project.

References

1. Kokkinos, I.: Pushing the boundaries of boundary detection using deep learning. In: ICLR (2016)
2. Xie, S., Tu, Z.: Holistically-nested edge detection. In: ICCV (2015)
3. Bertasius, G., Shi, J., Torresani, L.: Deepedge: a multi-scale bifurcated deep network for top-down contour detection. In: CVPR (2015)
4. Bertasius, G., Shi, J., Torresani, L.: High-for-low and low-for-high: efficient boundary detection from deep object features and its applications to high-level vision. In: ICCV (2015)
5. Shen, W., Wang, X., Wang, Y., Bai, X., Zhang, Z.: Deepcontour: a deep convolutional feature learned by positive-sharing loss for contour detection. In: CVPR (2015)
6. Ganin, Y., Lempitsky, V.: N^4-Fields: Neural Network Nearest Neighbor Fields for Image Transforms. In: Cremers, D., Reid, I., Saito, H., Yang, M.-H. (eds.) ACCV 2014. LNCS, vol. 9004, pp. 536–551. Springer, Heidelberg (2015)
7. Krizhevsky, A., Sutskever, I., Hinton, G.E.: Imagenet classification with deep convolutional neural networks. In: NIPS (2012)
8. Szegedy, C., Liu, W., Jia, Y., Sermanet, P., Reed, S., Anguelov, D., Erhan, D., Vanhoucke, V., Rabinovich, A.: Going deeper with convolutions. In: CVPR (2015)
9. Simonyan, K., Zisserman, A.: Very deep convolutional networks for large-scale image recognition. In: ICLR (2015)
10. He, K., Zhang, X., Ren, S., Sun, J.: Deep residual learning for image recognition. In: CVPR (2016)
11. Martin, D., Fowlkes, C., Tal, D., Malik, J.: A database of human segmented natural images and its application to evaluating segmentation algorithms and measuring ecological statistics. In: ICCV (2001)
12. Everingham, M., Van Gool, L., Williams, C.K.I., Winn, J., Zisserman, A.: The PASCAL visual object classes challenge (VOC 2012) results (2012). http://www.pascal-network.org/challenges/VOC/voc2012/workshop/index.html
13. Hariharan, B., Arbeláez, P., Bourdev, L., Maji, S., Malik, J.: Semantic contours from inverse detectors. In: ICCV (2011)
14. Mottaghi, R., Chen, X., Liu, X., Cho, N.G., Lee, S.W., Fidler, S., Urtasun, R., Yuille, A.: The role of context for object detection and semantic segmentation in the wild. In: CVPR (2014)
15. Arbeláez, P., Maire, M., Fowlkes, C., Malik, J.: Contour detection and hierarchical image segmentation. TPAMI **33**(5), 898–916 (2011)

16. Pont-Tuset, J., Arbeláez, P., Barron, J., Marques, F., Malik, J.: Multiscale combinatorial grouping for image segmentation and object proposal generation. In: TPAMI (2016)

17. Maninis, K., Pont-Tuset, J., Arbeláez, P., Gool, L.V.: Deep retinal image understanding. In: MICCAI (2016)

18. Bertasius, G., Shi, J., Torresani, L.: Semantic segmentation with boundary neural fields. In: CVPR (2016)

19. Khoreva, A., Benenson, R., Omran, M., Hein, M., Schiele, B.: Weakly supervised object boundaries. In: CVPR (2016)

20. Li, Y., Paluri, M., Rehg, J.M., Dollár, P.: Unsupervised learning of edges. In: CVPR (2016)

21. Yang, J., Price, B., Cohen, S., Lee, H., Yang, M.H.: Object contour detection with a fully convolutional encoder-decoder network. In: CVPR (2016)

22. Najman, L., Schmitt, M.: Geodesic saliency of watershed contours and hierarchical segmentation. TPAMI 18(12), 1163–1173 (1996)

23. Lee, C.Y., Xie, S., Gallagher, P., Zhang, Z., Tu, Z.: Deeply-supervised nets (2014). arXiv preprint arXiv:1409.5185

24. Dollár, P., Zitnick, C.L.: Structured forests for fast edge detection. In: ICCV (2013)

25. Jia, Y., Shelhamer, E., Donahue, J., Karayev, S., Long, J., Girshick, R., Guadarrama, S., Darrell, T.: Caffe: Convolutional architecture for fast feature embedding (2014). arXiv preprint arXiv:1408.5093

26. Martin, D., Fowlkes, C., Malik, J.: Learning to detect natural image boundaries using local brightness, color, and texture cues. TPAMI 26(5), 530–549 (2004)

27. Pont-Tuset, J., Marques, F.: Supervised evaluation of image segmentation and object proposal techniques. TPAMI 38(7), 1465–1478 (2016)

28. Ren, Z., Shakhnarovich, G.: Image segmentation by cascaded region agglomeration. In: CVPR (2013)

29. Ren, Z., Shakhnarovich, G.: Image segmentation by cascaded region agglomeration. In: CVPR (2013)

30. Shi, J., Malik, J.: Normalized cuts and image segmentation. TPAMI 22(8), 888–905 (2000)

31. Felzenszwalb, P.F., Huttenlocher, D.P.: Efficient graph-based image segmentation. IJCV 59, 167–181 (2004)

32. Comaniciu, D., Meer, P.: Mean shift: a robust approach toward feature space analysis. TPAMI 24(5), 603–619 (2002)

33. Girshick, R., Donahue, J., Darrell, T., Malik, J.: Rich feature hierarchies for accurate object detection and semantic segmentation. In: CVPR (2014)

34. Girshick, R.: Fast R-CNN. In: ICCV. (2015)

35. Ren, S., He, K., Girshick, R., Sun, J.: Faster R-CNN: towards real-time object detection with regionproposal networks.In: NIPS (2015)

36. Humayun, A., Li, F., Rehg, J.M.: The middle child problem: revisiting parametric min-cut and seeds for object proposals. In: ICCV (2015)

37. Krähenbühl, P., Koltun, V.: Learning to propose objects. In: CVPR (2015)

38. Krähenbühl, P., Koltun, V.: Geodesic Object Proposals. In: Fleet, D., Pajdla, T., Schiele, B., Tuytelaars, T. (eds.) ECCV 2014, Part V. LNCS, vol. 8693, pp. 725–739. Springer, Heidelberg (2014)

39. Uijlings, J.R.R., Sande, K.E.A., Gevers, T., Smeulders, A.W.M.: Selective search for object recognition. IJCV 104(2), 154–171 (2013)

40. Rantalankila, P., Kannala, J., Rahtu, E.: Generating object segmentation proposals using global and local search. In: CVPR (2014)

41. Humayun, A., Li, F., Rehg, J.M.: RIGOR: Recycling Inference in Graph Cuts for generating Object Regions. In: CVPR (2014)
42. Hosang, J., Benenson, R., Dollár, P., Schiele, B.: What makes for effective detection proposals? TPAMI **38**(4), 814–830 (2016)
43. Pont-Tuset, J., Van Gool, L.: Boosting object proposals: From Pascal to COCO. In: ICCV (2015)
44. Lin, T., Maire, M., Belongie, S., Bourdev, L.D., Girshick, R.B., Hays, J., Perona, P., Ramanan, D., Dollár, P., Zitnick, C.L.: Microsoft COCO: common objects in context (2014). arXiv:1405.0312

Superpixel Convolutional Networks
Using Bilateral Inceptions

Raghudeep Gadde[1]([✉]), Varun Jampani[2], Martin Kiefel[2,3], Daniel Kappler[2], and Peter V. Gehler[2,3]

[1] Université Paris-Est, Champs-sur-Marne, LIGM (UMR 8049), CNRS, ENPC, ESIEE, UPEM, France
raghudeep.gadde@enpc.fr
[2] Max Planck Institute for Intelligent Systems, Tübingen, Germany
varun.jampani@tuebingen.mpg.de
[3] Bernstein Center for Computational Neuroscience, Tübingen, Germany

Abstract. In this paper we propose a CNN architecture for semantic image segmentation. We introduce a new "bilateral inception" module that can be inserted in existing CNN architectures and performs bilateral filtering, at multiple feature-scales, between superpixels in an image. The feature spaces for bilateral filtering and other parameters of the module are learned end-to-end using standard backpropagation techniques. The bilateral inception module addresses two issues that arise with general CNN segmentation architectures. First, this module propagates information between (super) pixels while respecting image edges, thus using the structured information of the problem for improved results. Second, the layer recovers a full resolution segmentation result from the lower resolution solution of a CNN. In the experiments, we modify several existing CNN architectures by inserting our inception module between the last CNN (1 × 1 convolution) layers. Empirical results on three different datasets show reliable improvements not only in comparison to the baseline networks, but also in comparison to several dense-pixel prediction techniques such as CRFs, while being competitive in time.

1 Introduction

In this paper we propose a CNN architecture for semantic image segmentation. Given an image $\mathcal{I} = (x_1, \ldots, x_N)$ with N pixels x_i the task of semantic segmentation is to infer a labeling $Y = (y_1, \ldots, y_N)$ with a label $y_i \in \mathcal{Y}$ for every pixel. This problem can be naturally formulated as a structured prediction problem $g : \mathcal{I} \to Y$. Empirical performance is measured by comparing Y to a human labeled Y^* via a loss function $\Delta(Y, Y^*)$, *e.g.*, with the Intersection over Union (IoU) or pixel-wise Hamming Loss.

The first two authors contribute equally to this work.

Electronic supplementary material The online version of this chapter (doi:10.1007/978-3-319-46448-0_36) contains supplementary material, which is available to authorized users.

© Springer International Publishing AG 2016
B. Leibe et al. (Eds.): ECCV 2016, Part I, LNCS 9905, pp. 597–613, 2016.
DOI: 10.1007/978-3-319-46448-0_36

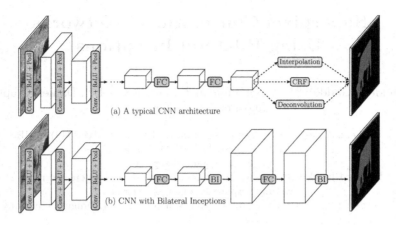

(a) A typical CNN architecture

(b) CNN with Bilateral Inceptions

Fig. 1. Illustration of CNN layout. We insert the *Bilateral Inception (BI)* modules between the *FC* (1×1 convolution) layers found in most networks thus removing the necessity of further up-scaling algorithms. Bilateral Inception modules also propagate information between distant pixels based on their spatial and color similarity and work better than other label propagation approaches.

A direct way to approach this problem would be to ignore the structure of the output variable Y and train a classifier that predicts the class membership of the center pixel of a given image patch. This procedure reduces the problem to a standard multi-class classification problem and allows the use of standard learning algorithms. The resulting classifier is then evaluated at every possible patch in a sliding window fashion (or using coarse-to-fine strategies) to yield a full segmentation of the image. With high capacity models and large amounts of training data this approach would be sufficient, given that the loss decomposes over the pixels. Such a per-pixel approach ignores the relationship between the variables $(y_1, \ldots, y_N)$, which are not i.i.d. since there is an underlying common image. Therefore, besides learning discriminative per-pixel classifiers, most segmentation approaches further encode the output relationship of Y. A dominating approach is to use Conditional Random Fields (CRF) [1], which allows an elegant and principled way to combine single pixel predictions and shared structure through unary, pairwise and higher order factors.

What relates the outputs $(y_1, \ldots, y_N)$? The common hypothesis that we use in this paper could be summarized as: *Pixels that are spatially and photometrically similar are more likely to have the same label.* Particularly if two pixels x_i, x_j are close in the image and have similar RGB values, then their corresponding labels y_i, y_j will most likely be the same. The most prominent example of spatial similarity encoded in a CRF is the Potts model (Ising model for the binary case). The work of [2] described a densely connected pairwise CRF (DenseCRF) that includes pairwise factors encoding both spatial *and* photometric similarity. The DenseCRF has been used in many recent works on image segmentation which find also empirically improved results over pure pixel-wise CNN classifiers [3–6].

In this paper, we implement the above-mentioned hypothesis of photometrically similar and near-by pixels share common labels, by designing a new "Bilateral Inception" (BI) module that can be inserted before/after the last 1×1 convolution layers (which we refer to as 'FC' layers - 'Fully-Connected' in the original image classification network) of the standard segmentation CNN architectures. The bilateral inception module does edge-aware information propagation across different spatial CNN units of the previous FC layer. Instead of using the spatial grid-layout that is common in CNNs, we incorporate the superpixel-layout for information propagation. The information propagation is performed using standard bilateral filters with Gaussian kernels, at different feature scales. This construction is inspired by [7,8]. Feature spaces and other parameters of the modules can be learned end-to-end using standard backpropagation techniques. The application of superpixels reduces the number of necessary computations and implements a long-range edge-aware inference between different superpixels. Moreover, since superpixels provides an output at the full image resolution it removes the need for any additional post-processing step.

We introduce BI modules in the CNN segmentation models of [3–5]. See Fig. 1 for an illustration. This achieves better segmentation results on all three datasets we experimented with than the proposed interpolation/inference techniques of DenseCRF [3,4] while being faster. Moreover, the results compare favorably against some recently proposed dense pixel prediction techniques. As illustrated in Fig. 1, the BI modules provides an alternative approach to commonly used up-sampling and CRF techniques.

2   Related Work

The literature on semantic segmentation is large and therefore we will limit our discussion to those works that perform segmentation with CNNs and discuss the different ways to encode the output structure.

A natural combination of CNNs and CRFs is to use the CNN as unary potential and combine it with a CRF that also includes pairwise or higher order factors. For instance [3,4] observed large improvements in pixel accuracy when combining a DenseCRF [2] with a CNN. The mean-field steps of the DenseCRF can be learned and back-propagated as noted by [9] and implemented by [5,10–12] for semantic segmentation and [13] for human pose estimation. The works of [14–16] use CNNs also in pairwise and higher order factors for more expressiveness. The recent work of [6] replaced the costly DenseCRF with a faster domain transform performing smoothing filtering while predicting the image edge maps at the same time. Our work was inspired by DenseCRF approaches but with the aim to replace the expensive mean-field inference. Instead of propagating information across unaries obtained by a CNN, we aim to do the edge-aware information propagation across *intermediate* representations of the CNN. Experiments on different datasets indicate that the proposed approach generally gives better results in comparison to DenseCRF while being faster.

A second group of works aims to inject the structural knowledge in intermediate CNN representations by using structural layers among CNN internal layers. The deconvolution layers model from [17] are being widely used for local propagation of information. They are computationally efficient and are used in segmentation networks, for *e.g.* [18]. They are however limited to small receptive fields. Another architecture proposed in [19] uses spatial pyramid pooling layers to max-pool over different spatial scales. The work of [20] proposed specialized structural layers such as normalized-cut layers with matrix back-propagation techniques. All these works have either fixed local receptive fields and/or have their complexity increasing exponentially with longer range pixel connections. Our technique allows for modeling long range (super-) pixel dependencies without compromising the computational efficiency. A very recent work [21] proposed the use of dilated convolutions for propagating multi-scale contextual information among CNN units.

A contribution of this work is to define convolutions over superpixels by defining connectivity among them. In [22], a method to use superpixels inside CNNs has been proposed by re-arranging superpixels based on their features. The technique proposed here is more generic and alleviates the need for rearranging superpixels. A method to filter irregularly sampled data has been developed in [23] which may be applicable to superpixel convolutions. The difference being that their method requires a pre-defined graph structure for every example/image separately while our approach directly works on superpixels. We experimented with Isomap embeddings [24] of superpixels but for speed reasons opted for the more efficient kernels presented in this paper. The work of [25] extracted multi-scale features at each superpixel and perform semantic segmentation by classifying each superpixel independently. In contrast, we propagate information across superpixels by using bilateral filters with learned feature spaces.

Another core contribution of this work is the end-to-end trained bilateral filtering module. Several recent works on bilateral filtering [10,26–28] back-propagate through permutohedral lattice approximation [29], to either learn the filter parameters [10,28] or do optimization in the bilateral space [26,27]. Most of the existing works on bilateral filtering use pre-defined feature spaces. In [30], the feature spaces for bilateral filtering are obtained via a non-parametric embedding into an Euclidean space. In contrast, by explicitly computing the bilateral filter kernel, we are able to back-propagate through features, thereby learning the task-specific feature spaces for bilateral filters through integration into end-to-end trainable CNNs.

3 Superpixel Convolutional Networks

We first formally introduce superpixels in Sect. 3.1 before we describe the bilateral inception modules in Sect. 3.2.

3.1 Superpixels

The term *superpixel* refers to a set of n_i pixels $S_i = \{t_1, \ldots, t_{n_i}\}$ with $t_k \in \{1, \ldots, N\}$ pixels. We use a set of M superpixels $S = \{S_1, \ldots, S_M\}$ that are disjoint $S_i \cap S_j = \emptyset, \forall i, j$ and decompose the image, $\cup_i S_i = \mathcal{I}$.

Superpixels have long been used for image segmentation in many previous works, *e.g.* [25,31–33], as they provide a reduction of the problem size. Instead of predicting a label y_i for every pixel x_i, the classifier predicts a label y_i per superpixel S_i and extends this label to all pixels within. A superpixel algorithm can pre-group pixels based on spatial and photometric similarity, reducing the number of elements and also thereby regularizing the problem in a meaningful way. The downside is that superpixels introduce a quantization error whenever pixels within one segment have different ground truth label assignments.

Figure 2 shows the superpixel quantization effect with the best achievable performance as a function in the number of superpixels, on two different segmentation datasets: PascalVOC [34] and Materials in Context [4]. We find that the quantization effect is small compared to the current best segmentation performance. Practically, we use the SLIC superpixels [35] for their runtime and [36] for their lower quantization error to decompose the image into superpixels. For details of the algorithms, please refer to the respective papers. We use publicly-available real-time GPU implementation of SLIC, called gSLICr [37], which runs at over 250 Hz per second. And the publicly available Dollar superpixels code [36] computes a superpixelization for a 400×500 image in about 300 ms using an Intel Xeon 3.33 GHz CPU.

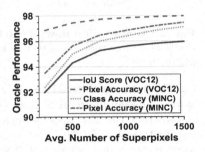

Fig. 2. Superpixel Quantization Error. Best achievable segmentation performance with a varying number of superpixels on Pascal VOC12 segmentation [34] and MINC material segmentation [4] datasets.

3.2 Bilateral Inceptions

Next, we describe the *Bilateral Inception Module* (BI) that performs Gaussian Bilateral Filtering on multiple scales of the representations within a CNN. The BI module can be inserted in between layers of existing CNN architectures.

Bilateral Filtering: We first describe the Gaussian bilateral filtering, the building block of the BI module. A visualisation of the necessary computations is shown in Fig. 3. Given the previous layer CNN activations $\mathbf{z} \in \mathbb{R}^{P \times C}$, that is P points and C filter responses. With $\mathbf{z}_c \in \mathbb{R}^P$ we denote the vector of activations of filter c. Additionally we have for every point j a feature vector $\mathbf{f}_j \in \mathbb{R}^D$. This denotes its spatial position ($D = 2$, not necessarily a grid), position and RGB color ($D = 5$), or others. Separate from the input points with features $F_{in} = \{\mathbf{f}_1, \ldots, \mathbf{f}_P\}$ we have Q output points with features F_{out}. These can be the same set of points, but also fewer ($Q < P$), equal ($Q = P$), or more ($Q > P$) points. For example we can filter a 10×10 grid ($P = 100$) and produce the result on a 50×50 grid ($Q = 2500$) or vice versa.

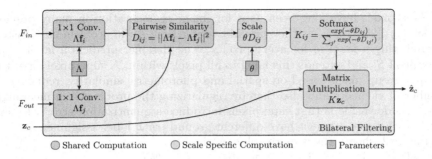

Fig. 3. Computation flow of the Gaussian Bilateral Filtering. We implemented the bilateral convolution with five separate computation blocks. Λ and θ are the free parameters.

The bilateral filtered result will be denoted as $\hat{\mathbf{z}} \in \mathbb{R}^{Q \times C}$. We apply the same Gaussian bilateral filter to every channel c separately. A filter has two free parameters: the filter specific scale $\theta \in \mathbb{R}_+$ and the global feature transformation parameters $\Lambda \in \mathbb{R}^{D \times D}$. For Λ, a more general scaling could be applied using more features or a separate CNN. Technically the bilateral filtering amounts to a matrix-vector multiplication $\forall c$:

$$\hat{\mathbf{z}}_c = K(\theta, \Lambda, F_{in}, F_{out})\mathbf{z}_c, \tag{1}$$

where $K \in \mathbb{R}^{Q \times P}$ and values for $f_i \in F_{out}, f_j \in F_{in}$:

$$K_{i,j} = \frac{\exp(-\theta \|\Lambda \mathbf{f}_i - \Lambda \mathbf{f}_j\|^2)}{\sum_{j'} \exp(-\theta \|\Lambda \mathbf{f}_i - \Lambda \mathbf{f}_{j'}\|^2)}. \tag{2}$$

From a kernel learning terminology, K is nothing but a Gaussian Gram matrix and it is symmetric if $F_{in} = F_{out}$. We implemented this filtering in Caffe [38] using different layers as depicted in Fig. 3. While approximate computations of $K\mathbf{z}_c$ exist and have improved runtime [29,39–41], we chose an explicit computation of K due to its small size. Our implementation makes use of GPU and the intermediate pairwise similarity computations are re-used across different modules. The entire runtime is only a fraction of the CNN runtime, but of course applications to larger values of P and Q would require aforementioned algorithmic speed-ups.

Bilateral Inception Module: The *bilateral inception module* (BI) is a weighted combination of different bilateral filters. We combine the output of H different filter kernels K, with different scales $\theta^1, \ldots, \theta^H$. All kernels use the same feature transformation Λ which allows for easier pre-computation of pairwise difference and avoids an over-parametrization of the filters. The outputs of different filters $\hat{\mathbf{z}}^h$ are combined linearly to produce $\bar{\mathbf{z}}$:

$$\bar{\mathbf{z}}_c = \sum_{h=1}^{H} \mathbf{w}_c^h \hat{\mathbf{z}}_c^h, \tag{3}$$

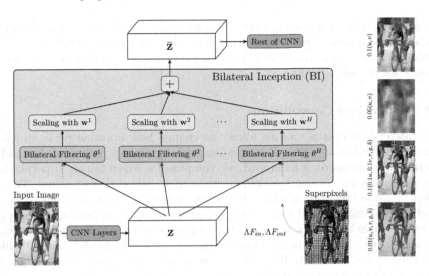

Fig. 4. Visualization of a Bilateral Inception (BI) Module. The unit activations **z** are passed through several bilateral filters defined over different feature spaces. The result is linearly combined to $\bar{\mathbf{z}}$ and passed on to the next network layer. Also shown are sample filtered superpixel images using bilateral filters defined over different example feature spaces. (u, v) correspond to position and (r, g, b) correspond to color features.

using individual weights $\mathbf{w}_c^h$ per scale θ^h and channel c. The weights $\mathbf{w} \in \mathbb{R}^{H \times C}$ are learned using error-backpropagation. The result of the inception module has C channels for every of its Q points, thus $\bar{\mathbf{z}} \in \mathbb{R}^{Q \times C}$. The inception module is schematically illustrated in Fig. 4. In short, information from CNN layers below is filtered using bilateral filters defined in transformed feature space $(\Lambda \mathbf{f})$. Most operations in the inception module are parallelizable resulting in fast runtimes on a GPU. In this work, inspired from the DenseCRF architecture from [2], we used pairs of BI modules: one with position features (u, v) and another with both position and colour features (u, v, r, g, b), each with multiple scales $\{\theta^h\}$.

Motivation and Comparison to DenseCRF: A BI module filters the activations of a CNN layer. Contrast this with the use of a DenseCRF on the CNN output. At that point the fine-grained information that intermediate CNN layers represent has been condensed already to a low-dimensional vector representing beliefs over labels. Using a mean-field update is propagating information between these beliefs. Similar behaviour is obtained using the BI modules but on different scales (using multiple different filters $K(\theta^h)$) and on the intermediate CNN activations **z**. Since in the end, the to-be-predicted pixels are not i.i.d., this blurring leads to better performance both when using a bilateral filter as an approximate message passing step of a DenseCRF as well in the system outlined here. Both attempts are encoding prior knowledge about the problem, namely that pixels close in position and color are likely to have the same label. Therefore such pixels can also have the same intermediate representation. Consider one would average CNN representations for all pixels that have the same ground truth label. This would result in an intermediate CNN representation that would be very easy to classify for the later layers.

3.3   Superpixel Convolutions

The bilateral inception module allows to change how information is stored in the higher level of a CNN. This is where the superpixels are used. Instead of storing information on a fixed grid, we compute for every image, superpixels S and use the mean color and position of their included pixels as features. We can insert bilateral inception modules to change from grid representations to super-pixel representations and vice versa. Inception modules in between superpixel layers convolve the unit activations between all superpixels depending on their distance in the feature space. This retains all properties of the bilateral filter, superpixels that are spatially close and have a similar mean color will have a stronger influence on each other.

Superpixels are not the only choice, in principle one can also sample random points from the image and use them as intermediate representations. We are using superpixels for computational reasons, since they can be used to propagate label information to the full image resolution. Other interpolation techniques are possible, including the well known bilinear interpolation, up-convolution networks [17], and DenseCRFs [2]. The quantization error mentioned in Sect. 3.1 only enters because the superpixels are used for interpolation. Also note that a fixed grid, that is independent of the image is a hard choice of where information should be stored. One could in principle evaluate the CNN densely, at all possible spatial locations, but we found that this resulted in poor performance compared to interpolation methods.

Backpropagation and Training. All free parameters of the inception module $\mathbf{w}$, $\{\theta^h\}$ and Λ are learned via backpropagation. We also backpropagate the error with respect to the module inputs thereby enabling the integration of our inception modules inside CNN frameworks without breaking the end-to-end learning paradigm. As shown in Fig. 3, the bilateral filtering can be decomposed into 5 different sub-layers. Derivatives with respect to the open parameters are obtained by the corresponding layer and standard backpropagation through the directed acyclic graph. For example, Λ is optimized by back-propagating gradients through 1×1 convolution. Derivatives for non-standard layers (pairwise similarity, matrix multiplication) are straight forward to obtain using matrix calculus. To let different filters learn the information propagation at different scales, we initialized $\{\theta^h\}$ with well separated scalar values (*e.g.* $\{1, 0.7, 0.3, ...\}$). The learning is performed using Adam stochastic optimization method [42]. The implementation is done in Caffe neural network framework [38], and the code is available online at http://segmentation.is.tuebingen.mpg.de.

4   Experiments

We study the effect of inserting and learning bilateral inception modules in various existing CNN architectures. As a testbed we perform experiments on semantic segmentation using the Pascal VOC2012 segmentation benchmark dataset [34], Cityscapes street scene dataset [43] and on material segmentation using the Materials in Context (MINC) dataset from [4]. We take different CNN architectures from the works of [3–5] and insert the inception modules before and/or after the spatial FC layers. In the supplementary, we presented some quantitative results with approximate bilateral filtering using the permutohedral lattice [29].

4.1   Semantic Segmentation

We first use the Pascal VOC12 segmentation dataset [34] with 21 object classes. For all experiments on VOC2012, we train using the extended training set of 10581 images collected by [44]. Following [5], we use a reduced validation set of 346 images for validation. We experiment on two different network architectures, (a) DeepLab model from [3] which uses CNN followed by DenseCRF and (b) CRFasRNN model from [5] which uses CNN with deconvolution layers followed by DenseCRF trained end-to-end.

DeepLab. We use the publicly available state-of-the-art pre-trained CNN models from [3]. We use the DeepLab-LargeFOV variant as a base architecture and refer to it as 'DeepLab'. The DeepLab CNN model produces a lower resolution prediction ($\frac{1}{8}\times$) which is then bilinearly interpolated to the input image resolution. The original models have been fine-tuned using both the MSCOCO [45] and the extended VOC [44] datasets. Next, we describe modifications to these models and show performance improvements in terms of both IoU and runtimes.

We add inception modules after different FC layers in the original model and remove the DenseCRF post processing. For this dataset, we use 1000 SLIC superpixels [35,37]. The inception modules after FC_6, FC_7 and FC_8 layers are referred to as $BI_6(H)$, $BI_7(H)$ and $BI_8(H)$ respectively, where H is the number of kernels. All results using the DeepLab model on Pascal VOC12 dataset are summarized in Table 1. We report the 'test' numbers without validation numbers, because the released DeepLab model that we adapted was trained using both train and validation sets. The DeepLab network achieves an IoU of 68.9 after bilinear interpolation. Experiments with $BI_6(2)$ module indicate that even only learning the inception module while keeping the remaining network fixed results in an reliable IoU improvement (+1.9). Additional joint training with FC layers significantly improved the performance. The results also show that more kernels improve performance. Next, we add multiple modules to the base DeepLab network at various stages and train them jointly. This results in further improvement of the performance. The $BI_6(2)$-$BI_7(6)$ model with two inception modules shows significant improvement in IoU by 4.7 and 0.9 in comparison to baseline model and DenseCRF application respectively. Finally, finetuning the entire network (FULL in Table 1) boosts the performance by 5.2 and 1.4 compared to the baseline and DenseCRF application.

Some visual results are shown in Fig. 5 and more are included in the supplementary. Several other variants of using BI are conceivable. During our experiments, we have observed that more kernels and more modules improve the performance, so we expect that even better results can be achieved. In Table 1, the runtime (ms) is included for several models. These numbers have been obtained using a Nvidia Tesla K80 GPU and standard Caffe time benchmarking [38]. DenseCRF timings are taken from [6]. The runtimes indicate that the overhead with BI modules is quite minimal in comparison to using Dense CRF.

In addition, we include the results of some other dense pixel prediction methods that are build on top of the same DeepLab base model. DeepLab-MSc-CRF is a multi-scale version [3] of

Table 1. Semantic Segmentation using DeepLab model IoU scores on Pascal VOC12 segmentation test dataset and average runtimes (ms) corresponding to different models. Also shown are the results corresponding to competitive dense pixel prediction techniques that used the same base DeepLab CNN. Runtimes also include superpixel computation (6 ms). In the second column, 'BI', 'FC' and 'FULL' correspond to training 'BI', 'FC' and full model layers respectively.

Model	Training	IoU	Runtime
DeepLab [3]		68.9	145 ms
With BI modules			
$BI_6(2)$	only BI	70.8	+20
$BI_6(2)$	BI+FC	71.5	+20
$BI_6(6)$	BI+FC	72.9	+45
$BI_7(6)$	BI+FC	73.1	+50
$BI_8(10)$	BI+FC	72.0	+30
$BI_6(2)$-$BI_7(6)$	BI+FC	73.6	+35
$BI_7(6)$-$BI_8(10)$	BI+FC	73.4	+55
$BI_6(2)$-$BI_7(6)$	FULL	**74.1**	+35
$BI_6(2)$-$BI_7(6)$-CRF	FULL	**75.1**	+865
DeepLab-CRF [3]		72.7	+830
DeepLab-MSc-CRF [3]		**73.6**	+880
DeepLab-EdgeNet [6]		71.7	+30
DeepLab-EdgeNet-CRF [6]		**73.6**	+860

DeepLab with DenseCRF on top. DeepLab-EdgeNet [6] is a recently proposed fast and discriminatively trained domain transform technique for propagating information across pixels. Comparison with these techniques in terms of performance and runtime indicates that our approach performs on par with latest dense pixel prediction techniques with significantly less time overhead. Several state-of-the-art CNN based systems [15,16] have achieved higher results than DeepLab on Pascal VOC12. These models are not yet publicly available and so we could not test the use of BI models in them. A close variant [26] of our work, which propose to do optimization in the bilateral space also has fast runtimes, but reported lower performance in comparison to the application of DenseCRF.

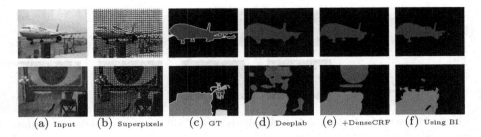

(a) Input   (b) Superpixels   (c) GT   (d) Deeplab   (e) +DenseCRF   (f) Using BI

Fig. 5. Semantic Segmentation. Example results of semantic segmentation on Pascal VOC12 dataset. (d) depicts the DeepLab CNN result, (e) CNN + 10 steps of mean-field inference, (f) result obtained with bilateral inception (BI) modules $(BI_6(2)+BI_7(6))$ between FC layers.

CRFasRNN. As a second architecture, we modified the CNN architecture trained by [5] that produces a result at an even lower resolution ($\frac{1}{16}\times$). Multiple deconvolution steps are employed to obtain the segmentation at input image resolution. This result is then passed onto the Dense-CRF recurrent neural network to obtain the final seg-

Table 2. Semantic Segmentation using CRFas-RNN model. IoU scores and runtimes corresponding to different models on Pascal VOC12 test dataset. Note that runtime also includes superpixel computation.

Model	IoU	Runtime
DeconvNet(CNN+Deconv.)	72.0	190 ms
With BI modules		
$BI_3(2)$-$BI_4(2)$-$BI_6(2)$-$BI_7(2)$	**74.9**	245
CRFasRNN (DeconvNet-CRF)	74.7	2700

mentation result. We insert BI modules after score-pool3, score-pool4, FC$_6$ and FC$_7$ layers, please see [5,18] for the network architecture details. Instead of combining outputs from the above layers with deconvolution steps, we introduce BI modules after them and linearly combined the outputs to obtain final segmentation result. Note that we entirely removed both the deconvolution and the DenseCRF parts of the original model [5]. See Table 2 for results on the DeconvNet model. Without the DenseCRF part and only evaluating the deconvolutional part of this model, one obtains an IoU score of 72.0. Ten steps of mean field inference increase the IoU to 74.7 [5]. Our model, with few additional parameters compared to the base CNN, achieves a IoU performance of 74.9, showing an improvement of 0.2 over the CRFasRNN model. The BI layers lead to better performance than deconvolution and DenseCRF combined while being much faster.

Hierarchical Clustering Analysis. We learned the network parameters using 1000 gSLIC superpixels per image, however the inception module allows to change the resolution (a non-square K). To illustrate this, we perform agglomorative clustering of the superpixels, sequentially merging the nearest two

Fig. 6. Hierarchical Clustering Analysis. From left to right: Validation performance when using different super-pixel layouts, visualization of an image with ground truth segmentation, and the $BI_6(2)$-$BI_7(6)$ result with 200, 600, and 1000 superpixels.

superpixels into a single one. We then evaluated the DeepLab-$BI_6(2)$-$BI_7(6)$ network using different levels of the resulting hierarchy re-using all the trained network parameters. Results in Fig. 6 show that the IoU score on the validation set decreases slowly with decreasing number of points and then drops for less than 200 superpixels. This validates that the network generalizes to different superpixel layouts and it is sufficient to represent larger regions of similar color by fewer points. In future, we plan to explore different strategies to allocate the representation to those regions that require more resolution and to remove the superpixelization altogether. Figure 6 shows example image with 200, 600, and 1000 superpixels and their obtained segmentation with BI modules.

4.2 Material Segmentation

We also experiment on a different pixel prediction task of material segmentation by adapting a CNN architecture finetuned for Materials in Context (MINC) [4] dataset. MINC consists of 23 material classes and is available in three different resolutions with the same aspect ratio: low (550^2), mid (1100^2) and an original higher resolution. The authors of [4] train CNNs on the mid resolution images and then combine with a DenseCRF to predict and evaluate on low resolution images. We build our work based on the Alexnet model [46] released by the authors of [4]. To obtain a per pixel labeling of a given image, there are several processing steps that [4] use for good performance. First, a CNN is applied at several scales with different strides followed by an interpolation of the predictions to reach the input image resolution and is then followed by a DenseCRF. For simplicity, we choose to run the CNN network with single scale and no-sliding. The authors used just one kernel with (u, v, L, a, b) features in the DenseCRF part. We used the same features in our

Table 3. Material Segmentation using AlexNet. Pixel accuracies and runtimes (in ms) of different models on MINC material segmentation dataset [4]. Runtimes also include the time for superpixel extraction (15 ms).

Model	Class/Total accuracy	Runtime
Alexnet CNN	55.3 / 58.9	300 ms
$BI_7(2)$-$BI_8(6)$	67.7 / 71.3	410
$BI_7(6)$-$BI_8(6)$	**69.4 / 72.8**	470
AlexNet-CRF	65.5 / 71.0	3400

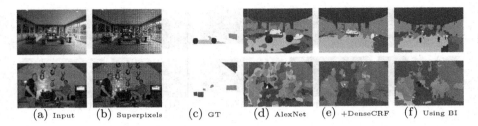

(a) Input   (b) Superpixels   (c) GT   (d) AlexNet   (e) +DenseCRF   (f) Using BI

Fig. 7. Material Segmentation. Example results of material segmentation. (d) depicts the AlexNet CNN result, (e) CNN + 10 steps of mean-field inference, (f) results obtained with bilateral inception (BI) modules ($BI_7(2)$+$BI_8(6)$) between FC layers.

inception modules. We modified the base AlexNet model by inserting BI modules after FC_7 and FC_8 layers. Again, 1000 SLIC superpixels are used for all experiments. Results on the test set are shown in Table 3. When inserting BI modules, the performance improves both in total pixel accuracy as well as in class-averaged accuracy. We observe an improvement of 12 % compared to CNN predictions and 2–4 % compared to CNN+DenseCRF results. Qualitative examples are shown in Fig. 7 and more are included in the supplementary. The weights to combine outputs in the BI layers are found by validation on the validation set. For this model we do not provide any learned setup due very limited segment training data.

4.3   Street Scene Segmentation

We further evaluate the use of BI modules on the Cityscapes dataset [43]. Cityscapes contains 20 K high-resolution (1024×2048) images of street scenes with coarse pixel annotations and another 5 K images with fine annotations, all annotations are from 19 semantic classes. The 5 K images are divided into 2975 train, 500 validation and remaining test images. Since there

Table 4. Street Scene Segmentation using DeepLab model. IoU scores and runtimes (in sec) of different models on Cityscapes segmentation dataset [43], for both half-resolution and full-resolution images. Runtime computations also include superpixel computation time (5.2 s).

Model	IoU (Half-res.)	IoU (Full-res.)	Runtime
DeepLab CNN	62.2	65.7	0.3 s
$BI_6(2)$	62.7	66.5	5.7
$BI_6(2)$-$BI_7(6)$	**63.1**	**66.9**	6.1
DeepLab-CRF	63.0	66.6	6.9

are no publicly available pre-trained models for this dataset yet, we trained a DeepLab model. We trained the base DeepLab model with half resolution images (512×1024) so that the model fits into GPU memory. The result is then interpolated to full-resolution using bilinear interpolation.

We experimented with two layouts: only a single $BI_6(2)$ and one with two inception $BI_6(2)$-$BI_7(6)$ modules. We notice that the SLIC superpixels [35] give

(a) Input   (b) Superpixels   (c) GT   (d) Deeplab   (e) Using BI

Fig. 8. Street Scene Segmentation. Example results of street scene segmentation. (d) depicts the DeepLab results, (e) result obtained by adding bilateral inception (BI) modules ($BI_6(2)+BI_7(6)$) between FC layers. More in supplementary.

higher quantization error than on VOC and thus used 6000 superpixels using [36] for our experiments. Quantitative results on the validation set are shown in Table 4. In contrast to the findings on the previous datasets, we only observe modest improvements with both DenseCRF and our inception modules in comparison to the base model. Similar to the previous experiments, the inception modules achieve better performance than DenseCRF while being faster. The majority of the computation time in our approach is due to the extraction of superpixels (5.2 s) using a CPU implementation. Some visual results with $BI_6(2)$-$BI_7(6)$ model are shown in Fig. 8 with more in supplementary.

5 Conclusion

The DenseCRF [2] with mean field inference has been used in many CNN segmentation approaches. Its main ingredient and reason for the improved performance is the use of a bilateral filter applied to the beliefs over labels. We have introduced a CNN approach that uses this key component in a novel way: filtering intermediate representations of higher levels in CNNs while jointly learning the task-specific feature spaces. This propagates information between earlier and more detailed intermediate representations of the classes instead of beliefs over labels. Further we show that image adaptive layouts in the higher levels of CNNs can be used to an advantage in the same spirit as CRF graphs have been constructed using superpixels in previous works on semantic segmentation. The computations in the 1×1 convolution layers scales in the number of superpixels which may be an advantage. Further we have shown that the same representation can be used to interpolate the coarser representations to the full image.

The use of image-adaptive convolutions in between the FC layers retains the appealing effect of producing segmentation masks with sharp edges. This is not a property of the superpixels, using them to represent information in FC layers and their use to interpolate to the full resolution are orthogonal. Different interpolation steps can be used to propagate the label information to the entire image, including bilinear interpolation, up-convolutions and DenseCRFs. We plan to investigate the effect of different sampling strategies to represent information in the higher layers of CNNs and apply similar image-adaptive ideas to videos.

We believe that the Bilateral Inception models are an interesting step that aims to directly include the model structure of CRF factors into the forward architecture of CNNs. The BI modules are easy to implement and are applicable to CNNs that perform structured output prediction.

Acknowledgements. We thank the reviewers for their valuable feedback. Raghudeep Gadde is supported by CSTB and ANR-13-CORD-0003.

References

1. Lafferty, J.D., McCallum, A., Pereira, F.C.N.: Conditional random fields: probabilistic models for segmenting and labeling sequence data. In: Proceedings of the 18th International Conference on Machine Learning, pp. 282–289 (2001)
2. Krähenbühl, P., Koltun, V.: Efficient inference in fully connected CRFs with Gaussian edge potentials. In: Advances in Neural Information Processing Systems (2011)
3. Chen, L.C., Papandreou, G., Kokkinos, I., Murphy, K., Yuille, A.L.: Semantic image segmentation with deep convolutional nets and fully connected CRFs. In: International Conference on Learning Representation (2015)
4. Bell, S., Upchurch, P., Snavely, N., Bala, K.: Material recognition in the wild with the materials in context database. In: Proceedings of the IEEE Conference on Computer Vision and Pattern Recognition, pp. 3479–3487 (2015)
5. Zheng, S., Jayasumana, S., Romera-Paredes, B., Vineet, V., Su, Z., Du, D., Huang, C., Torr, P.H.: Conditional random fields as recurrent neural networks. In: Proceedings of the IEEE International Conference on Computer Vision, pp. 1529–1537 (2015)
6. Chen, L.C., Barron, J.T., Papandreou, G., Murphy, K., Yuille, A.L.: Semantic image segmentation with task-specific edge detection using CNNs and a discriminatively trained domain transform. In: Proceedings of the IEEE Conference on Computer Vision and Pattern Recognition, pp. 4545–4554 (2016)
7. Szegedy, C., Liu, W., Jia, Y., Sermanet, P., Reed, S., Anguelov, D., Erhan, D., Vanhoucke, V., Rabinovich, A.: Going deeper with convolutions. In: Proceedings of the IEEE Conference on Computer Vision and Pattern Recognition, pp. 1–9 (2015)
8. Lin, M., Chen, Q., Yan, S.: Network in network. In: International Conference on Learning Representation (2014)
9. Domke, J.: Learning graphical model parameters with approximate marginal inference. IEEE Trans. Pattern Anal. Mach. Intell. **35**(10), 2454–2467 (2013)
10. Jampani, V., Kiefel, M., Gehler, P.V.: Learning sparse high dimensional filters: image filtering, dense CRFs and bilateral neural networks. In: Proceedings of the IEEE Conference on Computer Vision and Pattern Recognition, pp. 4452–4461 (2016)
11. Li, Y., Zemel, R.: Mean-field networks. ICML Workshop on Learning Tractable Probabilistic Models (2014)
12. Schwing, A.G., Urtasun, R.: Fully connected deep structured networks. arXiv preprint arXiv:1503.02351 (2015)
13. Kiefel, M., Gehler, P.V.: Human pose estimation with fields of parts. In: Fleet, D., Pajdla, T., Schiele, B., Tuytelaars, T. (eds.) ECCV 2014, Part V. LNCS, vol. 8693, pp. 331–346. Springer, Heidelberg (2014)

14. Chen, L.C., Schwing, A., Yuille, A., Urtasun, R.: Learning deep structured models. In: Proceedings of the 32nd International Conference on Machine Learning, pp. 1785–1794 (2015)
15. Lin, G., Shen, C., Reid, I., et al.: Efficient piecewise training of deep structured models for semantic segmentation. In: Proceedings of the IEEE Conference on Computer Vision and Pattern Recognition, pp. 3194–3203 (2016)
16. Liu, Z., Li, X., Luo, P., Loy, C.C., Tang, X.: Semantic image segmentation via deep parsing network. In: Proceedings of the IEEE International Conference on Computer Vision, pp. 1377–1385 (2015)
17. Zeiler, M.D., Krishnan, D., Taylor, G.W., Fergus, R.: Deconvolutional networks. In: Proceedings of the IEEE Conference on Computer Vision and Pattern Recognition, pp. 2528–2535 (2010)
18. Long, J., Shelhamer, E., Darrell, T.: Fully convolutional networks for semantic segmentation. In: Proceedings of the IEEE Conference on Computer Vision and Pattern Recognition, pp. 3431–3440 (2015)
19. He, K., Zhang, X., Ren, S., Sun, J.: Spatial pyramid pooling in deep convolutional networks for visual recognition. In: Fleet, D., Pajdla, T., Schiele, B., Tuytelaars, T. (eds.) ECCV 2014, Part III. LNCS, vol. 8691, pp. 346–361. Springer, Heidelberg (2014)
20. Ionescu, C., Vantzos, O., Sminchisescu, C.: Matrix backpropagation for deep networks with structured layers. In: Proceedings of the IEEE International Conference on Computer Vision, pp. 2965–2973 (2015)
21. Yu, F., Koltun, V.: Multi-scale context aggregation by dilated convolutions. In: International Conference on Learning Representation (2016)
22. He, S., Lau, R.W., Liu, W., Huang, Z., Yang, Q.: SuperCNN: a superpixelwise convolutional neural network for salient object detection. Int. J. Comput. Vis. 115, 1–15 (2015)
23. Bruna, J., Zaremba, W., Szlam, A., LeCun, Y.: Spectral networks and locally connected networks on graphs. In: International Conference on Learning Representation (2014)
24. Tenenbaum, J.B., De Silva, V., Langford, J.C.: A global geometric framework for nonlinear dimensionality reduction. Science 290(5500), 2319–2323 (2000)
25. Mostajabi, M., Yadollahpour, P., Shakhnarovich, G.: Feedforward semantic segmentation with zoom-out features. In: Proceedings of the IEEE Conference on Computer Vision and Pattern Recognition, pp. 3376–3385 (2015)
26. Barron, J.T., Poole, B.: The fast bilateral solver. In: European Conference on Computer Vision. Springer (2016)
27. Barron, J.T., Adams, A., Shih, Y., Hernández, C.: Fast bilateral-space stereo for synthetic defocus. In: Proceedings of the IEEE Conference on Computer Vision and Pattern Recognition, pp. 4466–4474 (2015)
28. Kiefel, M., Jampani, V., Gehler, P.: Permutohedral lattice CNNs. In: International Conference on Learning Representation Workshops (2015)
29. Adams, A., Baek, J., Davis, M.A.: Fast high-dimensional filtering using the permutohedral lattice. In: Computer Graphics Forum, vol. 29, pp. 753–762. Wiley Online Library (2010)
30. Campbell, N., Subr, K., Kautz, J.: Fully-connected CRFs with non-parametric pairwise potential. In: Proceedings of the IEEE Conference on Computer Vision and Pattern Recognition, pp. 1658–1665 (2013)
31. Gould, S., Zhao, J., He, X., Zhang, Y.: Superpixel graph label transfer with learned distance metric. In: Fleet, D., Pajdla, T., Schiele, B., Tuytelaars, T. (eds.) ECCV 2014, Part I. LNCS, vol. 8689, pp. 632–647. Springer, Heidelberg (2014)

32. Gonfaus, J.M., Boix, X., Van de Weijer, J., Bagdanov, A.D., Serrat, J., Gonzalez, J.: Harmony potentials for joint classification and segmentation. In: Proceedings of the IEEE Conference on Computer Vision and Pattern Recognition, pp. 3280–3287 (2010)

33. Nowozin, S., Gehler, P.V., Lampert, C.H.: On parameter learning in CRF-based approaches to object class image segmentation. In: Daniilidis, K., Maragos, P., Paragios, N. (eds.) ECCV 2010, Part VI. LNCS, vol. 6316, pp. 98–111. Springer, Heidelberg (2010)

34. Everingham, M., Gool, L.V., Williams, C., Winn, J., Zisserman, A.: The PASCAL VOC2012 challenge results (2012)

35. Achanta, R., Shaji, A., Smith, K., Lucchi, A., Fua, P., Susstrunk, S.: SLIC super-pixels compared to state-of-the-art superpixel methods. IEEE Trans. Pattern Anal. Mach. Intell. $34(11)$, 2274–2282 (2012)

36. Dollár, P., Zitnick, C.L.: Structured forests for fast edge detection. In: Proceedings of the IEEE International Conference on Computer Vision, pp. 1841–1848 (2013)

37. Ren, C.Y., Prisacariu, V.A., Reid, I.D.: gSLICr: SLIC superpixels at over 250 Hz. arXiv e-prints arXiv:1509.04232 (2015)

38. Jia, Y., Shelhamer, E., Donahue, J., Karayev, S., Long, J., Girshick, R., Guadar-rama, S., Darrell, T.: Caffe: convolutional architecture for fast feature embedding. In: Proceedings of the ACM International Conference on Multimedia, pp. 675–678. ACM (2014)

39. Paris, S., Durand, F.: A fast approximation of the bilateral filter using a signal processing approach. In: Leonardis, A., Bischof, H., Pinz, A. (eds.) ECCV 2006. LNCS, vol. 3954, pp. 568–580. Springer, Heidelberg (2006)

40. Gastal, E.S., Oliveira, M.M.: Domain transform for edge-aware image and video processing. ACM Trans. Graph. (TOG) 30, 69 (2011). ACM

41. Adams, A., Gelfand, N., Dolson, J., Levoy, M.: Gaussian KD-trees for fast high-dimensional filtering. ACM Trans. Graph. (TOG) 28, 21 (2009). ACM

42. Kingma, D., Ba, J.: Adam: a method for stochastic optimization. In: International Conference on Learning Representation (2015)

43. Cordts, M., Omran, M., Ramos, S., Scharwächter, T., Enzweiler, M., Benenson, R., Franke, U., Roth, S., Schiele, B.: The cityscapes dataset. In: CVPR Workshop on The Future of Datasets in Vision (2015)

44. Hariharan, B., Arbeláez, P., Bourdev, L., Maji, S., Malik, J.: Semantic contours from inverse detectors. In: Proceedings of the IEEE International Conference on Computer Vision, pp. 991–998 (2011)

45. Lin, T.-Y., Maire, M., Belongie, S., Hays, J., Perona, P., Ramanan, D., Dollár, P., Zitnick, C.L.: Microsoft COCO: common objects in context. In: Fleet, D., Pajdla, T., Schiele, B., Tuytelaars, T. (eds.) ECCV 2014, Part V. LNCS, vol. 8693, pp. 740–755. Springer, Heidelberg (2014)

46. Krizhevsky, A., Sutskever, I., Hinton, G.E.: Imagenet classification with deep con-volutional neural networks. In: Advances in Neural Information Processing Sys-tems, pp. 1097–1105 (2012)

Sublabel-Accurate Convex Relaxation of Vectorial Multilabel Energies

Emanuel Laude[1(✉)], Thomas Möllenhoff[1], Michael Moeller[1], Jan Lellmann[2], and Daniel Cremers[1]

[1] Technical University of Munich, Munich, Germany
emanuel.laude@in.tum.de
[2] University of Lübeck, Lübeck, Germany

Abstract. Convex relaxations of multilabel problems have been demonstrated to produce provably optimal or near-optimal solutions to a variety of computer vision problems. Yet, they are of limited practical use as they require a fine discretization of the label space, entailing a huge demand in memory and runtime. In this work, we propose the first sublabel accurate convex relaxation for vectorial multilabel problems. Our key idea is to approximate the dataterm in a piecewise convex (rather than piecewise linear) manner. As a result we have a more faithful approximation of the original cost function that provides a meaningful interpretation for fractional solutions of the relaxed convex problem.

Keywords: Convex relaxation · Optimization · Variational methods

1 Introduction

1.1 Nonconvex Vectorial Problems

In this paper, we derive a sublabel-accurate convex relaxation for vectorial optimization problems of the form

$$\min_{u:\Omega \to \Gamma} \int_\Omega \rho\big(x, u(x)\big) \, \mathrm{d}x + \lambda \, TV(u), \tag{1}$$

where $\Omega \subset \mathbb{R}^d$, $\Gamma \subset \mathbb{R}^n$ and $\rho : \Omega \times \Gamma \to \mathbb{R}$ denotes a generally nonconvex pointwise dataterm. As regularization we focus on the *total variation* defined as:

$$TV(u) = \sup_{q \in C_c^\infty(\Omega, \mathbb{R}^{n \times d}), \|q(x)\|_{S^\infty} \le 1} \int_\Omega \langle u, \operatorname{Div} q \rangle \, \mathrm{d}x, \tag{2}$$

E. Laude and T. Möllenhoff—These authors contributed equally.

Technical University of Munich—This work was supported by the ERC Starting Grant "Convex Vision".

Electronic supplementary material The online version of this chapter (doi:10.1007/978-3-319-46448-0_37) contains supplementary material, which is available to authorized users.

© Springer International Publishing AG 2016
B. Leibe et al. (Eds.): ECCV 2016, Part I, LNCS 9905, pp. 614–627, 2016.
DOI: 10.1007/978-3-319-46448-0_37

where $\| \cdot \|_{S\infty}$ is the Schatten-∞ norm on $\mathbb{R}^{n \times d}$, i.e., the largest singular value. For differentiable functions u we can integrate (2) by parts to find

$$TV(u) = \int_{\Omega} \|\nabla u(x)\|_{S^1} \, dx, \qquad (3)$$

where the dual norm $\| \cdot \|_{S^1}$ penalizes the sum of the singular values of the Jacobian, which encourages the individual components of u to jump in the same direction. This type of regularization is part of the framework of Sapiro and Ringach [19].

1.2 Related Work

Due to its nonconvexity the optimization of (1) is challenging. For the scalar case ($n = 1$), Ishikawa [9] proposed a pioneering technique to obtain globally optimal solutions in a spatially discrete setting, given by the minimum s-t-cut of a graph representing the space $\Omega \times \Gamma$. A continuous formulation was introduced by Pock et al. [15] exhibiting several advantages such as less grid bias and parallelizability.

In a series of papers [14,16], connections of the above approaches were made to the mathematical theory of *cartesian currents* [6] and the calibration method for the Mumford-Shah functional [1], leading to a generalization of the convex relaxation framework [15] to more general (in particular nonconvex) regularizers.

In the following, researchers have strived to generalize the concept of functional lifting and convex relaxation to the vectorial setting ($n > 1$). If the dataterm and the regularizer are both separable in the label dimension, one can simply apply the above convex relaxation approach in a channel-wise manner to each component separately. But when either the dataterm or the regularizer couple the label components, the situation becomes more complex [8,20].

The approach which is most closely related to our work, and which we consider as a baseline method, is the one by Lellmann et al. [11]. They consider coupled dataterms with coupled total variation regularization of the form (2).

A drawback shared by all mentioned papers is that ultimately one has to discretize the label space. While Lellmann et al. [11] propose a sublabel-accurate regularizer, we show that their dataterm leads to solutions which still have a strong bias towards the label grid. For the scalar-valued setting, continuous label spaces have been considered in the MRF community by Zach and Kohli [22] and Fix and Agarwal [5]. The paper [21] proposes a method for mixed continuous and discrete vectorial label spaces, where everything is derived in the spatially discrete MRF setting. Möllenhoff et al. [12] recently proposed a novel formulation of the scalar-valued case which retains fully continuous label spaces even after discretization. The contribution of this work is to extend [12] to vectorial label spaces, thereby complementing [11] with a sublabel-accurate dataterm.

1.3 Contribution

In this work we propose the first sublabel-accurate convex formulation of vectorial labeling problems. It generalizes the formulation for scalar-valued labeling problems [12] and thus includes important applications such as optical flow estimation or color image denoising. We show that our method, derived in a spatially continuous setting, has a variety of interesting theoretical properties as well as practical advantages over the existing labeling approaches:

- We generalize existing functional lifting approaches (see Sect. 2.2).
- We show that our method is the best convex under-approximation (in a local sense), see Propositions 1 and 2.
- Due to its sublabel-accuracy our method requires only a small amount of labels to produce good results which leads to a drastic reduction in memory. We believe that this is a vital step towards the real-time capability of lifting and convex relaxation methods. Moreover, our method eliminates the label bias, that previous lifting methods suffer from, even for many labels.
- In Sect. 2.3 we propose a regularizer that couples the different label components by enforcing a joint jump normal. This is in contrast to [8], where the components are regularized separately.
- For convex dataterms, our method is equivalent to the unlifted problem – see Proposition 4. Therefore, it allows a seamless transition between direct optimization and convex relaxation approaches.

1.4 Notation

We write $\langle x, y \rangle = \sum_i x_i y_i$ for the standard inner product on $\mathbb{R}^n$ or the Frobenius product if x, y are matrices. Similarly $\| \cdot \|$ without any subscript denotes the usual Euclidean norm, respectively the Frobenius norm for matrices.

We denote the convex conjugate of a function $f : \mathbb{R}^n \to \mathbb{R} \cup \{\infty\}$ by $f^*(y) = \sup_{x \in \mathbb{R}^n} \langle y, x \rangle - f(x)$. It is an important tool for devising convex relaxations, as the biconjugate f^{**} is the largest lower-semicontinuous (lsc.) convex function below f. For the indicator function of a set C we write δ_C, i.e., $\delta_C(x) = 0$ if $x \in C$ and ∞ otherwise. $\Delta_n^U \subset \mathbb{R}^n$ stands for the unit n-simplex.

2   Convex Formulation

2.1   Lifted Representation

Motivated by Fig. 1, we construct an equivalent representation of (1) in a higher dimensional space, before taking the convex envelope.

Let $\Gamma \subset \mathbb{R}^n$ be a compact and convex set. We partition Γ into a set $\mathcal{T}$ of n-simplices Δ_i so that Γ is a disjoint union of Δ_i up to a set of measure zero. Let t^{i_j} be the j-th vertex of Δ_i and denote by $\mathcal{V} = \{t^1, \ldots, t^{|\mathcal{V}|}\}$ the union of all vertices, referred to as labels, with $1 \leq i \leq |\mathcal{T}|$, $1 \leq j \leq n + 1$ and $1 \leq i_j \leq |\mathcal{V}|$. For $u : \Omega \to \Gamma$, we refer to $u(x)$ as a *sublabel*. Any sublabel can be written as a convex combination of the vertices of a simplex Δ_i with $1 \leq i \leq |\mathcal{T}|$ for appropriate barycentric coordinates $\alpha \in \Delta_n^U$:

$$u(x) = T_i \alpha := \sum_{j=1}^{n+1} \alpha_j t^{i_j}, \ T_i := (t^{i_1}, \ t^{i_2}, \ \ldots, \ t^{i_{n+1}}) \in \mathbb{R}^{n \times n + 1}. \tag{4}$$

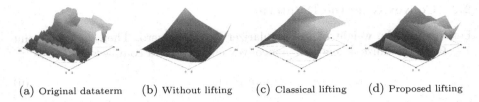

(a) Original dataterm   (b) Without lifting   (c) Classical lifting   (d) Proposed lifting

Fig. 1. In (a) we show a nonconvex dataterm. Convexification without lifting would result in the energy (b). Classical lifting methods [11] (c), approximate the energy piecewise linearly between the labels, whereas the proposed method results in an approximation that is convex on each triangle (d). Therefore, we are able to capture the structure of the nonconvex energy much more accurately.

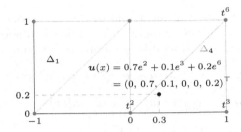

Fig. 2. This figure illustrates our notation and the one-to-one correspondence between $u(x) = (0.3, 0.2)^\top$ and the lifted $\boldsymbol{u}(x)$ containing the barycentric coordinates $\alpha = (0.7, 0.1, 0.2)^\top$ of the sublabel $u(x) \in \triangle_4 = \mathrm{conv}\{t^2, t^3, t^6\}$. The triangulation $(\mathcal{V}, \mathcal{T})$ of $\Gamma = [-1; 1] \times [0; 1]$ is visualized via the gray lines, corresponding to the triangles and the gray dots, corresponding to the vertices $\mathcal{V} = \{(-1, 0)^\top, (0, 0)^\top, \ldots, (1, 1)^\top\}$, that we refer to as the labels.

By encoding the vertices $t^k \in \mathcal{V}$ using a one-of-$|\mathcal{V}|$ representation e^k we can identify any $u(x) \in \Gamma$ with a sparse vector $\boldsymbol{u}(x)$ containing at least $|\mathcal{V}| - n$ many zeros and vice versa:

$$\boldsymbol{u}(x) = E_i \alpha := \sum_{j=1}^{n+1} \alpha_j e^{i_j}, \quad E_i := (e^{i_1}, e^{i_2}, \ldots, e^{i_{n+1}}) \in \mathbb{R}^{|\mathcal{V}| \times n+1},$$

$$u(x) = \sum_{k=1}^{|\mathcal{V}|} t^k \boldsymbol{u}_k(x), \quad \alpha \in \Delta_n^U, \ 1 \le i \le |\mathcal{T}|. \tag{5}$$

The entries of the vector e^{i_j} are zero except for the (i_j)-th entry, which is equal to one. We refer to $\boldsymbol{u} : \Omega \to \mathbb{R}^{|\mathcal{V}|}$ as the *lifted* representation of u. This one-to-one-correspondence between $u(x) = T_i \alpha$ and $\boldsymbol{u}(x) = E_i \alpha$ is shown in Fig. 2. Note that both, α and i depend on x. However, for notational convenience we drop the dependence on x whenever we consider a fixed point $x \in \Omega$.

2.2   Convexifying the Dataterm

Let for now the weight of the regularizer in (1) be zero. Then, at each point $x \in \Omega$ we minimize a generally nonconvex energy over a compact set $\Gamma \subset \mathbb{R}^n$:

$$\min_{u \in \Gamma} \rho(u). \tag{6}$$

We set up the lifted energy so that it attains finite values if and only if the argument $\boldsymbol{u}$ is a sparse representation $\boldsymbol{u} = E_i \alpha$ of a sublabel $u \in \Gamma$:

$$\boldsymbol{\rho}(\boldsymbol{u}) = \min_{1 \leq i \leq |\mathcal{T}|} \boldsymbol{\rho}_i(\boldsymbol{u}), \qquad \boldsymbol{\rho}_i(\boldsymbol{u}) = \begin{cases} \rho(T_i\alpha), & \text{if } \boldsymbol{u} = E_i\alpha, \ \alpha \in \Delta_n^U, \\ \infty, & \text{otherwise.} \end{cases} \tag{7}$$

Problems (6) and (7) are equivalent due to the one-to-one correspondence of $u = T_i\alpha$ and $\boldsymbol{u} = E_i\alpha$. However, energy (7) is finite on a nonconvex set only. In order to make optimization tractable, we minimize its convex envelope.

Proposition 1. *The convex envelope of* (7) *is given as:*

$$\boldsymbol{\rho}^{**}(\boldsymbol{u}) = \sup_{\boldsymbol{v} \in \mathbb{R}^{|\mathcal{V}|}} \langle \boldsymbol{u}, \boldsymbol{v} \rangle - \max_{1 \leq i \leq |\mathcal{T}|} \boldsymbol{\rho}_i^*(\boldsymbol{v}),$$
$$\boldsymbol{\rho}_i^*(\boldsymbol{v}) = \langle E_i b_i, \boldsymbol{v} \rangle + \rho_i^*(A_i^\top E_i^\top \boldsymbol{v}), \quad \rho_i := \rho + \delta_{\Delta_i}. \tag{8}$$

b_i *and* A_i *are given as* $b_i := M_i^{n+1}$, $A_i := \left(M_i^1, \ M_i^2, \ \ldots, \ M_i^n \right)$, *where* M_i^j *are the columns of the matrix* $M_i := (T_i^\top, \mathbf{1})^{-\top} \in \mathbb{R}^{n+1 \times n+1}$.

Proof. Follows from a calculation starting at the definition of $\boldsymbol{\rho}^{**}$. See supplementary material for a detailed derivation.

The geometric intuition of this construction is depicted in Fig. 3. Note that if one prescribes the value of $\boldsymbol{\rho}_i$ in (7) only on the *vertices* of the unit simplices Δ_n^U, i.e., $\boldsymbol{\rho}(\boldsymbol{u}) = \rho(t^k)$ if $\boldsymbol{u} = e^k$ and $+\infty$ otherwise, one obtains the linear biconjugate $\boldsymbol{\rho}^{**}(\boldsymbol{u}) = \langle \boldsymbol{u}, \boldsymbol{s} \rangle$, $\boldsymbol{s} = (\rho(t^i), \ldots, \rho(t^L))$ on the feasible set. This coincides with the standard relaxation of the dataterm used in [4,10,11,16]. In that sense, our approach can be seen as a relaxing the dataterm in a more precise way, by incorporating the true value of ρ not only on the finite set of labels $\mathcal{V}$, but also everywhere in between, i.e., on every *sublabel*.

2.3   Lifting the Vectorial Total Variation

We define the lifted vectorial total variation as

$$\boldsymbol{TV}(\boldsymbol{u}) = \int_\Omega \boldsymbol{\Psi}(D\boldsymbol{u}), \tag{9}$$

where $D\boldsymbol{u}$ denotes the distributional derivative of $\boldsymbol{u}$ and $\boldsymbol{\Psi}$ is positively one-homogeneous, i.e., $\boldsymbol{\Psi}(c\boldsymbol{u}) = c\boldsymbol{\Psi}(\boldsymbol{u}), c \geq 0$. For such functions, the meaning of

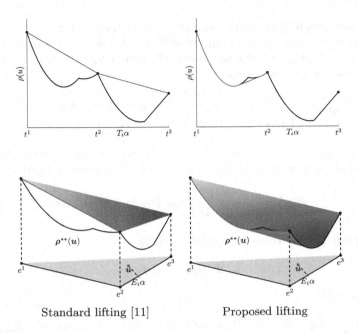

Standard lifting [11]   Proposed lifting

Fig. 3. Geometrical intuition for the proposed lifting and standard lifting [11] for the special case of 1-dimensional range $\Gamma = [a, b]$ and 3 labels $\{t^1, t^2, t^3\}$. The standard lifting correponds to a linear interpolation of the original cost in between the locations t^1, t^2, t^3, which are associated with the vertices e^1, e^2, e^3 in the lifted energy (lower left). The proposed method extends the cost to the relaxed set in a more precise way: The original cost is preserved on the connecting lines between adjacent e^i (black lines on the bottom right) up to concave parts (red graphs and lower surface on the right). This information, which may influence the exact location of the minimizer, is lost in the standard formulation. If the solution of the lifted formulation $\boldsymbol{u}$ is in the interior (gray area) an approximate solution to the original problem can still be obtained via Eq. (5). (Color figure online)

(9) can be made fully precise using the polar decomposition of the Radon measure $D\boldsymbol{u}$ [2, Corollary 1.29, Theorem 2.38]. However, in the following we restrict ourselves to an intuitive motivation for the derivation of $\boldsymbol{\Psi}$ for smooth functions.

Our goal is to find $\boldsymbol{\Psi}$ so that $\boldsymbol{TV}(\boldsymbol{u}) = TV(u)$ whenever $\boldsymbol{u} : \Omega \to \mathbb{R}^{|\mathcal{V}|}$ corresponds to some $u : \Omega \to \Gamma$, in the sense that $\boldsymbol{u}(x) = E_i\alpha$ whenever $u(x) = T_i\alpha$. In order for the equality to hold, it must in particular hold for all u that are classically differentiable, i.e., $Du = \nabla u$, and whose Jacobian $\nabla u(x)$ is of rank 1, i.e., $\nabla u(x) = (T_i\alpha - T_j\beta) \otimes \nu(x)$ for some $\nu(x) \in \mathbb{R}^d$. This rank 1 constraint enforces the different components of u to have the same jump normal, which is desirable in many applications. In that case, we observe

$$TV(u) = \int_\Omega \|T_i\alpha - T_j\beta\| \cdot \|\nu(x)\| \, \mathrm{d}x. \qquad (10)$$

For the corresponding lifted representation $\boldsymbol{u}$, we have $\nabla \boldsymbol{u}(x) = (E_i \alpha - E_j \beta) \otimes \nu(x)$. Therefore it is natural to require $\boldsymbol{\Psi}(\nabla \boldsymbol{u}(x)) = \boldsymbol{\Psi}((E_i \alpha - E_j \beta) \otimes \nu(x)) := \|T_i \alpha - T_j \beta\| \cdot \|\nu(x)\|$ in order to achieve the goal $\boldsymbol{TV}(\boldsymbol{u}) = TV(u)$. Motivated by these observations, we define

$$\boldsymbol{\Psi}(\boldsymbol{p}) := \begin{cases} \|T_i \alpha - T_j \beta\| \cdot \|\nu\| & \text{if } \boldsymbol{p} = (E_i \alpha - E_j \beta) \otimes \nu, \\ \infty & \text{otherwise,} \end{cases} \tag{11}$$

where $\alpha, \beta \in \Delta_{n+1}^U$, $\nu \in \mathbb{R}^d$ and $1 \leq i, j \leq |\mathcal{T}|$. Since the convex envelope of (9) is intractable, we derive a "locally" tight convex underapproximation:

$$\boldsymbol{R}(\boldsymbol{u}) = \sup_{\boldsymbol{q}:\Omega \to \mathbb{R}^{d \times |\mathcal{V}|}} \int_\Omega \langle \boldsymbol{u}, \text{Div } \boldsymbol{q} \rangle - \boldsymbol{\Psi}^*(\boldsymbol{q}) \, dx. \tag{12}$$

Proposition 2. *The convex conjugate of $\boldsymbol{\Psi}$ is*

$$\boldsymbol{\Psi}^*(\boldsymbol{q}) = \delta_{\mathcal{K}}(\boldsymbol{q}) \tag{13}$$

with convex set

$$\mathcal{K} = \bigcap_{1 \leq i, j \leq |\mathcal{T}|} \left\{ \boldsymbol{q} \in \mathbb{R}^{d \times |\mathcal{V}|} \mid \|Q_i \alpha - Q_j \beta\| \leq \|T_i \alpha - T_j \beta\|, \; \alpha, \beta \in \Delta_{n+1}^U \right\}, \tag{14}$$

and $Q_i = (\boldsymbol{q}^{i1}, \boldsymbol{q}^{i2}, \ldots, \boldsymbol{q}^{in+1}) \in \mathbb{R}^{d \times n+1}$. $\boldsymbol{q}^j \in \mathbb{R}^d$ are the columns of $\boldsymbol{q}$.

Proof. Follows from a calculation starting at the definition of the convex conjugate $\boldsymbol{\Psi}^*$. See supplementary material.

Interestingly, although in its original formulation (14) the set $\mathcal{K}$ has infinitely many constraints, one can equivalently represent $\mathcal{K}$ by finitely many.

Proposition 3. *The set $\mathcal{K}$ in Eq. (14) is the same as*

$$\mathcal{K} = \left\{ \boldsymbol{q} \in \mathbb{R}^{d \times |\mathcal{V}|} \mid \|D_{\boldsymbol{q}}^i\|_{S^\infty} \leq 1, \; 1 \leq i \leq |\mathcal{T}| \right\}, \quad D_{\boldsymbol{q}}^i = Q_i D \, (T_i D)^{-1}, \tag{15}$$

where the matrices $Q_i D \in \mathbb{R}^{d \times n}$ and $T_i D \in \mathbb{R}^{n \times n}$ are given as

$$Q_i D := \left(\boldsymbol{q}^{i1} - \boldsymbol{q}^{in+1}, \; \ldots, \; \boldsymbol{q}^{in} - \boldsymbol{q}^{in+1} \right), \; T_i D := \left(t^{i1} - t^{in+1}, \; \ldots, \; t^{in} - t^{in+1} \right).$$

Proof. Similar to the analysis in [11], Eq. (14) basically states the Lipschitz continuity of a piecewise linear function defined by the matrices $\boldsymbol{q} \in \mathbb{R}^{d \times |\mathcal{V}|}$. Therefore, one can expect that the Lipschitz constraint is equivalent to a bound on the derivative. For the complete proof, see supplementary material.

2.4 Lifting the Overall Optimization Problem

Combining dataterm and regularizer, the overall optimization problem is given

$$\min_{\boldsymbol{u}:\Omega\to\mathbb{R}^{|\mathcal{V}|}} \sup_{\boldsymbol{q}:\Omega\to\mathcal{K}} \int_{\Omega} \rho^{**}(\boldsymbol{u}) + \langle \boldsymbol{u}, \mathrm{Div}\,\boldsymbol{q}\rangle \,dx. \tag{16}$$

A highly desirable property is that, opposed to any other vectorial lifting app-roach from the literature, our method with just one simplex applied to a convex problem yields the same solution as the unlifted problem.

Proposition 4. *If the triangulation contains only 1 simplex, $\mathcal{T} = \{\Delta\}$, i.e., $|\mathcal{V}| = n+1$, then the proposed optimization problem* (16) *is equivalent to*

$$\min_{u:\Omega\to\Delta} \int_{\Omega} (\rho + \delta_\Delta)^{**}(x, u(x))\,dx + \lambda TV(u), \tag{17}$$

which is (1) *with a globally convexified dataterm on Δ.*

Proof. For $u = t^{n+1} + TD\tilde{u}$ the substitution $\boldsymbol{u} = \left(\tilde{u}_1, \ldots, \tilde{u}_n, 1 - \sum_{j=1}^{n} \tilde{u}_j\right)$ into ρ^{**} and $\boldsymbol{R}$ yields the result. For a complete proof, see supplementary material.

3 Numerical Optimization

3.1 Discretization

For now assume that $\Omega \subset \mathbb{R}^d$ is a d-dimensional Cartesian grid and let Div denote a finite-difference divergence operator with $\mathrm{Div}\,\boldsymbol{q} : \Omega \to \mathbb{R}^{|\mathcal{V}|}$. Then the relaxed energy minimization problem becomes

$$\min_{\boldsymbol{u}:\Omega\to\mathbb{R}^{|\mathcal{V}|}} \max_{\boldsymbol{q}:\Omega\to\mathcal{K}} \sum_{x\in\Omega} \rho^{**}(x, \boldsymbol{u}(x)) + \langle \mathrm{Div}\,\boldsymbol{q}, \boldsymbol{u}\rangle. \tag{18}$$

In order to get rid of the pointwise maximum over $\rho_i^*(\boldsymbol{v})$ in Eq. (8), we introduce additional variables $w(x) \in \mathbb{R}$ and additional constraints $(\boldsymbol{v}(x), w(x)) \in \mathcal{C}, x \in \Omega$ so that $w(x)$ attains the value of the pointwise maximum:

$$\min_{\boldsymbol{u}:\Omega\to\mathbb{R}^{|\mathcal{V}|}} \max_{\substack{(\boldsymbol{v},w):\Omega\to\mathcal{C}\\ \boldsymbol{q}:\Omega\to\mathcal{K}}} \sum_{x\in\Omega} \langle \boldsymbol{u}(x), \boldsymbol{v}(x)\rangle - w(x) + \langle \mathrm{Div}\,\boldsymbol{q}, \boldsymbol{u}\rangle, \tag{19}$$

where the set $\mathcal{C}$ is given as

$$\mathcal{C} = \bigcap_{1\leq i\leq|\mathcal{T}|} \mathcal{C}_i, \quad \mathcal{C}_i := \left\{(x,y) \in \mathbb{R}^{|\mathcal{V}|+1} \mid \rho_i^*(x) \leq y\right\}. \tag{20}$$

For numerical optimization we use a GPU-based implementation[1] of a first-order primal-dual method [14]. The algorithm requires the orthogonal projections of

---

[1] https://github.com/tum-vision/sublabel_relax.

the dual variables onto the sets $\mathcal{C}$ respectively $\mathcal{K}$ in every iteration. However, the projection onto an epigraph of dimension $|\mathcal{V}| + 1$ is difficult for large values of $|\mathcal{V}|$. We rewrite the constraints $(\boldsymbol{v}(x), w(x)) \in \mathcal{C}_i$, $1 \leq i \leq |\mathcal{T}|$, $x \in \Omega$ as $(n+1)$-dimensional epigraph constraints introducing variables $r^i(x) \in \mathbb{R}^n$, $s_i(x) \in \mathbb{R}$:

$$\rho_i^* \left(r^i(x) \right) \leq s_i(x), \quad r^i(x) = A_i^\top E_i^\top \boldsymbol{v}(x), \quad s_i(x) = w(x) - \langle E_i b_i, \boldsymbol{v}(x) \rangle. \quad (21)$$

These equality constraints can be implemented using Lagrange multipliers. For the projection onto the set $\mathcal{K}$ we use an approach similar to [7, Fig. 7].

3.2 Epigraphical Projections

Computing the Euclidean projection onto the epigraph of ρ_i^* is a central part of the numerical implementation of the presented method. However, for $n > 1$ this is nontrivial. Therefore we provide a detailed explanation of the projection methods used for different classes of ρ_i. We will consider quadratic, truncated quadratic and piecewise linear ρ.

Quadratic Case: Let ρ be of the form $\rho(u) = \frac{a}{2} u^\top u + b^\top u + c$. A direct projection onto the epigraph of $\rho_i^* = (\rho + \delta_{\Delta_i})^*$ for $n > 1$ is difficult. However, the epigraph can be decomposed into separate epigraphs for which it is easier to project onto: For proper, convex, lsc. functions f, g the epigraph of $(f + g)^*$ is the Minkowski sum of the epigraphs of f^* and g^* (cf. [17, Exercise 1.28, Theorem 11.23a]). This means that it suffices to compute the projections onto the epigraphs of a quadratic function $f^* = \rho^*$ and a convex, piecewise linear function $g^*(v) = \max_{1 \leq j \leq n+1} \langle t^{ij}, v \rangle$ by rewriting constraint (21) as

$$\rho^*(r_f) \leq s_f, \ \delta_{\Delta_i}^*(c_g) \leq d_g \ \text{ s.t. } (r, s) = (r_f, s_f) + (c_g, d_g). \quad (22)$$

For the projection onto the epigraph of a n-dimensional quadratic function we use the method described in [20, Appendix B.2]. The projection onto a piecewise linear function is described in the last paragraph of this section.

Truncated Quadratic Case: Let ρ be of the form $\rho(u) = \min \left\{ \nu, \frac{a}{2} u^\top u + b^\top u + c \right\}$ as it is the case for the nonconvex robust ROF with a truncated quadratic dataterm in Sect. 4.2. Again, a direct projection onto the epigraph of ρ_i^* is difficult. However, a decomposition of the epigraph into simpler epigraphs is possible as the epigraph of $\min\{f, g\}^*$ is the intersection of the epigraphs of f^* and g^*. Hence, one can separately project onto the epigraphs of $(\nu + \delta_{\Delta_i})^*$ and $(\frac{a}{2} u^\top u + b^\top u + c + \delta_{\Delta_i})^*$. Both of these projections can be handled using the methods from the other paragraphs.

Piecewise Linear Case: In case ρ is piecewise linear on each Δ_i, i.e., ρ attains finite values at a discrete set of sampled sublabels $\mathcal{V}_i \subset \Delta_i$ and interpolates linearly between them, we have that

$$(\rho + \delta_{\Delta_i})^*(v) = \max_{\tau \in \mathcal{V}_i} \langle \tau, v \rangle - \rho(\tau). \quad (23)$$

Again this is a convex, piecewise linear function. For the projection onto the epigraph of such a function, a quadratic program of the form

$$\min_{(x,y)\in\mathbb{R}^{n+1}} \frac{1}{2}\|x - c\|^2 + \frac{1}{2}\|y - d\|^2 \quad \text{s.t.} \ \langle\tau, x\rangle - \rho(\tau) \leq y, \forall\tau \in \mathcal{V}_i \qquad (24)$$

needs to be solved. We implemented the primal active-set method described in [13, Algorithm 16.3], and found it solves the program in a few (usually 2–10) iterations for a moderate number of constraints.

4 Experiments

4.1 Vectorial ROF Denoising

In order to validate experimentally, that our model is exact for convex dataterms, we evaluate it on the Rudin-Osher-Fatemi [18] (ROF) model with vectorial TV (2). In our model this corresponds to defining $\rho(x, u(x)) = \frac{1}{2}\|u(x) - I(x)\|^2$. As expected based on Proposition 4 the energy of the solution of the unlifted problem is equal to the energy of the projected solution of our method for $|\mathcal{V}| = 4$ up to machine precision, as can be seen in Figs. 4 and 5. We point out, that the sole purpose of this experiment is a proof of concept as our method introduces an overhead and convex problems can be solved via direct optimization. It can be seen in Figs. 4 and 5, that the baseline method [11] has a strong label bias.

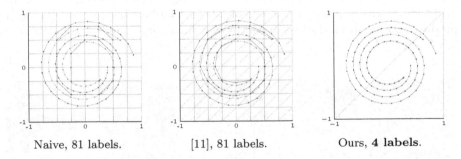

Naive, 81 labels.   [11], 81 labels.   Ours, **4 labels**.

Fig. 4. ROF denoising of a vector-valued signal $f : [0,1] \to [-1,1]^2$, discretized on 50 points (shown in red). We compare the proposed approach (right) with two alternative techniques introduced in [11] (left and middle). The labels are visualized by the gray grid. While the naive (standard) multilabel approach from [11] (left) provides solutions that are constrained to the chosen set of labels, the sublabel accurate regularizer from [11] (middle) does allow sublabel solutions, yet – due to the dataterm bias – these still exhibit a strong preference for the grid points. In contrast, the proposed approach does not exhibit any visible grid bias providing fully sublabel-accurate solutions: With only 4 labels, the computed solutions (shown in blue) coincide with the "unlifted" problem (green) (Color figure online).

| Input image | Unlifted Problem, $E = 992.50$ | Ours, $|\mathcal{T}| = 1$, $|\mathcal{V}| = 4$, $E = 992.51$ | Ours, $|\mathcal{T}| = 6$ $|\mathcal{V}| = 2 \times 2 \times 2$ $E = 993.52$ | Baseline, $|\mathcal{V}| = 4 \times 4 \times 4$, $E = 2255.81$ |

Fig. 5. Convex ROF with vectorial TV. Direct optimization and proposed method yield the same result. In contrast to the baseline method [11] the proposed approach has no discretization artefacts and yields a lower energy. The regularization parameter is chosen as $\lambda = 0.3$.

4.2   Denoising with Truncated Quadratic Dataterm

For images degraded with both, Gaussian and salt-and-pepper noise we define the dataterm as $\rho(x, u(x)) = \min\left\{\frac{1}{2}\|u(x) - I(x)\|^2, \nu\right\}$. We solve the problem using the epigraph decomposition described in the second paragraph of Sect. 3.2. It can be seen, that increasing the number of labels $|\mathcal{V}|$ leads to lower energies and at the same time to a reduced effect of the TV. This occurs as we always compute a piecewise convex underapproximation of the original nonconvex dataterm, that gets tighter with a growing number of labels. The baseline method [11] again produces strong discretization artefacts even for a large number of labels $|\mathcal{V}| = 4 \times 4 \times 4 = 64$.

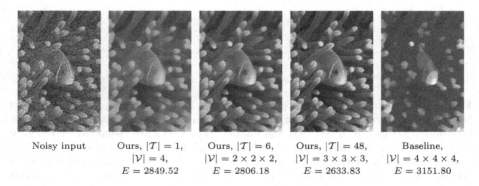

| Noisy input | Ours, $|\mathcal{T}| = 1$, $|\mathcal{V}| = 4$, $E = 2849.52$ | Ours, $|\mathcal{T}| = 6$, $|\mathcal{V}| = 2 \times 2 \times 2$, $E = 2806.18$ | Ours, $|\mathcal{T}| = 48$, $|\mathcal{V}| = 3 \times 3 \times 3$, $E = 2633.83$ | Baseline, $|\mathcal{V}| = 4 \times 4 \times 4$, $E = 3151.80$ |

Fig. 6. ROF with a truncated quadratic dataterm ($\lambda = 0.03$ and $\nu = 0.025$). Compared to the baseline method [11] the proposed approach yields much better results, already with a very small number of 4 labels.

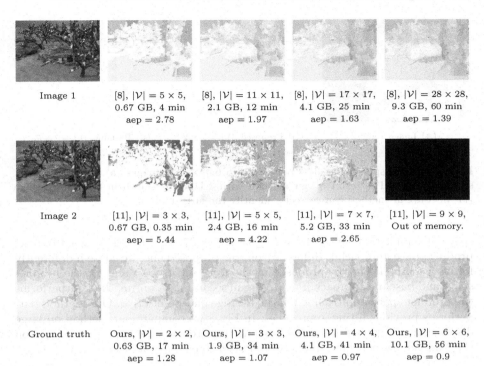

Image 1	[8], $	\mathcal{V}	= 5 \times 5$, 0.67 GB, 4 min aep = 2.78	[8], $	\mathcal{V}	= 11 \times 11$, 2.1 GB, 12 min aep = 1.97	[8], $	\mathcal{V}	= 17 \times 17$, 4.1 GB, 25 min aep = 1.63	[8], $	\mathcal{V}	= 28 \times 28$, 9.3 GB, 60 min aep = 1.39
Image 2	[11], $	\mathcal{V}	= 3 \times 3$, 0.67 GB, 0.35 min aep = 5.44	[11], $	\mathcal{V}	= 5 \times 5$, 2.4 GB, 16 min aep = 4.22	[11], $	\mathcal{V}	= 7 \times 7$, 5.2 GB, 33 min aep = 2.65	[11], $	\mathcal{V}	= 9 \times 9$, Out of memory.
Ground truth	Ours, $	\mathcal{V}	= 2 \times 2$, 0.63 GB, 17 min aep = 1.28	Ours, $	\mathcal{V}	= 3 \times 3$, 1.9 GB, 34 min aep = 1.07	Ours, $	\mathcal{V}	= 4 \times 4$, 4.1 GB, 41 min aep = 0.97	Ours, $	\mathcal{V}	= 6 \times 6$, 10.1 GB, 56 min aep = 0.9

Fig. 7. We compute the optical flow using our method, the product space approach [8] and the baseline method [11] for a varying amount of labels and compare the average endpoint error (aep). The product space method clearly outperforms the baseline, but our approach finds the overall best result already with 2×2 labels. To achieve a similarly precise result as the product space method, we require 150 times fewer labels, 10 times less memory and 3 times less time. For the same number of labels, the proposed approach requires more memory as it has to store a convex approximation of the energy instead of a linear one.

4.3   Optical Flow

We compute the optical flow $v : \Omega \to \mathbb{R}^2$ between two input images I_1, I_2. The label space $\Gamma = [-d, d]^2$ is chosen according to the estimated maximum displacement $d \in \mathbb{R}$ between the images. The dataterm is $\rho(x, v(x)) = \|I_2(x) - I_1(x + v(x))\|$, and $\lambda(x)$ is based on the norm of the image gradient $\nabla I_1(x)$.

In Fig. 7 we compare the proposed method to the product space approach [8]. Note that we implemented the product space dataterm using Lagrange multipliers, also referred to as the *global* approach in [8]. While this increases the memory consumption, it comes with lower computation time and guaranteed convergence. For our method, we sample the label space $\Gamma = [-15, 15]^2$ on 150×150 sublabels and subsequently convexify the energy on each triangle using the quickhull algorithm [3]. For the product space approach we sample the label

626   E. Laude et al.

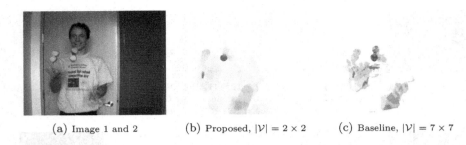

(a) Image 1 and 2   (b) Proposed, $|\mathcal{V}| = 2 \times 2$ (c) Baseline, $|\mathcal{V}| = 7 \times 7$

Fig. 8. Large displacement flow between two 640×480 images (a) using a 81×81 search window. The result of our method with 4 labels is shown in (b), the baseline [11] in (c). Our method can correctly identify the large motion.

space at equidistant labels, from 5×5 to 27×27. As the regularizer from the product space approach is different from the proposed one, we chose μ differently for each method. For the proposed method, we set $\mu = 0.5$ and for the product space and baseline approach $\mu = 3$. We can see in Fig. 7, our method outperforms the product space approach w.r.t. the average end-point error. Our method outperforms previous lifting approaches: In Fig. 8 we compare our method on large displacement optical flow to the baseline [11]. To obtain competitive results on the Middlebury benchmark, one would need to engineer a better dataterm.

5   Conclusions

We proposed the first sublabel-accurate convex relaxation of vectorial multilabel problems. To this end, we approximate the generally nonconvex dataterm in a piecewise convex manner as opposed to the piecewise linear approximation done in the traditional functional lifting approaches. This assures a more faithful approximation of the original cost function and provides a meaningful interpretation for the non-integral solutions of the relaxed convex problem. In experimental validations on large-displacement optical flow estimation and color image denoising, we show that the computed solutions have superior quality to the traditional convex relaxation methods while requiring substantially less memory and runtime.

References

1. Alberti, G., Bouchitté, G., Maso, G.D.: The calibration method for the Mumford-Shah functional and free-discontinuity problems. Calc. Var. Partial Dif. **3**(16), 299–333 (2003)
2. Ambrosio, L., Fusco, N., Pallara, D.: Functions of bounded variation and free discontinuity problems. Oxford Mathematical Monographs, The Clarendon Press, Oxford University Press, New York (2000)
3. Barber, C.B., Dobkin, D.P., Huhdanpaa, H.: The quickhull algorithm for convex hulls. ACM Trans. Math. Softw. (TOMS) **22**(4), 469–483 (1996)

4. Chambolle, A., Cremers, D., Pock, T.: A convex approach to minimal partitions. SIAM J. Imaging Sci. **5**(4), 1113–1158 (2012)
5. Fix, A., Agarwal, S.: Duality and the continuous graphical model. In: Fleet, D., Pajdla, T., Schiele, B., Tuytelaars, T. (eds.) ECCV 2014, Part III. LNCS, vol. 8691, pp. 266–281. Springer, Heidelberg (2014). doi:10.1007/978-3-319-10578-9_18
6. Giaquinta, M., Modica, G., Souček, J.: Cartesian Currents in the Calculus of Variations I, II. Ergebnisse der Mathematik und ihrer Grenzgebiete. 3, vols. 37–38. Springer, Heidelberg (1998)
7. Goldluecke, B., Strekalovskiy, E., Cremers, D.: The natural total variation which arises from geometric measure theory. SIAM J. Imaging Sci. **5**(2), 537–563 (2012)
8. Goldluecke, B., Strekalovskiy, E., Cremers, D.: Tight convex relaxations for vector-valued labeling. SIAM J. Imaging Sci. **6**(3), 1626–1664 (2013)
9. Ishikawa, H.: Exact optimization for Markov random fields with convex priors. IEEE Trans. Pattern Anal. Mach. Intell. **25**(10), 1333–1336 (2003)
10. Lellmann, J., Schnörr, C.: Continuous multiclass labeling approaches and algorithms. IEEE Trans. Pattern Anal. Mach. Intell. **4**(4), 1049–1096 (2011)
11. Lellmann, J., Strekalovskiy, E., Koetter, S., Cremers, D.: Total variation regularization for functions with values in a manifold. In: ICCV, December 2013
12. Möllenhoff, T., Laude, E., Moeller, M., Lellmann, J., Cremers, D.: Sublabel-accurate relaxation of nonconvex energies. In: CVPR (2016)
13. Nocedal, J., Wright, S.J.: Numerical Optimization, 2nd edn. Springer, New York (2006)
14. Pock, T., Cremers, D., Bischof, H., Chambolle, A.: An algorithm for minimizing the piecewise smooth Mumford-Shah functional. In: ICCV (2009)
15. Pock, T., Schoenemann, T., Graber, G., Bischof, H., Cremers, D.: A convex formulation of continuous multi-label problems. In: Forsyth, D., Torr, P., Zisserman, A. (eds.) ECCV 2008, Part III. LNCS, vol. 5304, pp. 792–805. Springer, Heidelberg (2008)
16. Pock, T., Cremers, D., Bischof, H., Chambolle, A.: Global solutions of variational models with convex regularization. IEEE Trans. Pattern Anal. Mach. Intell. **3**(4), 1122–1145 (2010)
17. Rockafellar, R., Wets, R.B.: Variational Analysis. Springer, Heidelberg (1998)
18. Rudin, L.I., Osher, S., Fatemi, E.: Nonlinear total variation based noise removal algorithms. IEEE Trans. Pattern Anal. Mach. Intell. **60**(1), 259–268 (1992)
19. Sapiro, G., Ringach, D.: Anisotropic diffusion of multivalued images with applications to color filtering. IEEE Trans. Pattern Anal. Mach. Intell. **5**(11), 1582–1586 (1996)
20. Strekalovskiy, E., Chambolle, A., Cremers, D.: Convex relaxation of vectorial problems with coupled regularization. IEEE Trans. Pattern Anal. Mach. Intell. **7**(1), 294–336 (2014)
21. Zach, C.: Dual decomposition for joint discrete-continuous optimization. In: AISTATS, pp. 632–640 (2013)
22. Zach, C., Kohli, P.: A convex discrete-continuous approach for Markov random fields. In: Fitzgibbon, A., Lazebnik, S., Perona, P., Sato, Y., Schmid, C. (eds.) ECCV 2012, Part VI. LNCS, vol. 7577, pp. 386–399. Springer, Heidelberg (2012)

Building Dual-Domain Representations
for Compression Artifacts Reduction

Jun Guo$^{(\boxtimes)}$ and Hongyang Chao

School of Data and Computer Science, and SYSU-CMU Shunde International Joint
Research Institute, Sun Yat-sen University, Guangzhou, People's Republic of China
artanis.protoss@outlook.com

Abstract. We propose a highly accurate approach to remove artifacts of
JPEG-compressed images. Our approach jointly learns a very deep convolutional network in both DCT and pixel domains. The dual-domain
representation can make full use of DCT-domain prior knowledge of
JPEG compression, which is usually lacking in traditional network-based
approaches. At the same time, it can also benefit from the prowess and
the efficiency of the deep feed-forward architecture, in comparison to
capacity-limited sparse-coding-based approaches. Two simple strategies,
i.e., Adam and residual learning, are adopted to train the very deep
network and later proved to be a success. Extensive experiments demonstrate the large improvements of our approach over the state of the arts.

Keywords: Compression artifacts reduction · Dual-domain representation · Very deep convolutional network

1 Introduction

Image restoration is a classical problem in computer vision. Among various
sources of image degradation, one of the most common causes is lossy image
compression (e.g., JPEG [34], WebP [10] and HEVC-MSP [32]). To date, as the
popularity of mobile photo apps like Instagram and rich media social networks
such as Facebook, the number of images spreading on the Internet increases
rapidly. Hence, lots of companies are forced to employ lossy compression for
saving bandwidth and storage space. Unfortunately, to meet the bit-budget constraint, lossy compression will inevitably introduce irreversible information loss,
resulting in unwanted image artifacts. Considering that performances of mis-
cellaneous visual tasks (e.g., image segmentation [27], image boundary detection [15], and image super-resolution [7]) greatly depend on the quality of inputs
images [9], how to reduce compression artifacts has attracted more and more
attentions.

Let us take JPEG as an example, as it is mostly used, to understand the compression artifacts introduced by lossy compression. As the input to the JPEG
encoder, original uncompressed images are grouped into 8×8 coding blocks,
and each block is forwarded to take the discrete cosine transform (DCT) separately. After DCT, each of the 64 DCT coefficients is uniformly quantized in

© Springer International Publishing AG 2016
B. Leibe et al. (Eds.): ECCV 2016, Part I, LNCS 9905, pp. 628–644, 2016.
DOI: 10.1007/978-3-319-46448-0_38

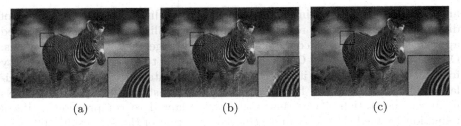

Fig. 1. (a) An uncompressed image; (b) The JPEG-compressed image of (a), where we can see multiple compression artifacts, including ringing on the boundary between the zebra and the background, blurring on the grass, and blockiness spreading on the whole image; (c) The restored image of (b) by our approach, where lots of artifacts are reduced and missing details are recovered.

conjunction with a 64-element quantization table. Note that it is this quantization step that causes a complicated combinations of numerous artifacts (see Fig. 1 for an illustration): (1) blockiness due to the individual treatment of adjacent coding blocks; (2) ringing, expressed as contours spreading along image edges, resulted from the coarse quantization of high-frequency components; and (3) blurring owing to high-frequency information loss.

Since practical lossy compression standards are not information optimal theoretically, it is possible to improve a compressed image by leveraging knowledge underused by the encoder. So far, many approaches have been proposed to deal with compression artifacts. Early works [30] tried to manually design a compression artifacts reduction procedure. Among them, pixel-domain-based approaches are rather popular. For example, Reeve and Lim [28] applied a Gaussian filter to the pixels around coding block boundaries to smooth out blocking artifacts, and Buades et al. [2] predicted pixel value by a weighted average of its surround pixels, where the weights are determined by the similarity of the corresponding image patches. Besides the pixel domain, for DCT-coded compressed images (e.g., JPEG- or HEVC-MSP-compressed images), some works tackled the problem in the DCT domain. One instance is Chen et al. [3] who applied a low pass filter to the DCT coefficients of adjacent coding blocks. Unfortunately, as aforementioned, most compression artifacts are introduced by the highly non-linear quantization step. Thus, such manually designed approaches are insufficient for modeling compression degradations and have limited restoration performances.

Nowadays, learning-based approaches are widely applied in computer vision and have achieved impressive results. The sparse coding (SC) and the convolutional neural network (CNN) are two types of the representative approaches for low-level vision tasks. For the former type [17,23,24,29], in general, input image patches are first represented by a compressed-image dictionary, and then the sparse representations (i.e., the coefficients) are passed into an uncompressed-image dictionary for reconstruction. Prior information can be naturally plugged in as constraints during the representation learning procedure. Recently, Liu et al. [24] learned sparse representations within the dual DCT-pixel domain, and achieved very promising results. However, the limited number and size of dictionaries have imposed restrictions on the capability of SC. Hence SC-based approaches tend to be accompanied with noisy edges or over-smooth regions. On the other hand, deep CNNs have been proved to possess great capability for visual tasks owing to its deep multi-layer architecture [19,31]. In particular, the SRCNN proposed by Dong et al. [7] demonstrated the power of CNNs in image restoration. Later this model was adapted to compression artifacts reduction (named ARCNN) and achieved the state-of-the-art results [6]. Nevertheless, currently CNN-based approaches just represent input images in pure pixel domain and incorporate few task-specific priors, thus there is a lot of room for improvement. Besides, as pointed out by Dong et al. [6,7], they met difficulties in training a deeper network. Transfer learning was adopted to train the four-layer ARCNN, but this technique complicates the training procedure and only obtained marginal performance gains. How to effectively train a very deep network remains to be an interesting problem.

Given the fact that JPEG images are extensive used across the world, in this paper, we still target at JPEG compression artifacts reduction. Our work tries to take advantages of both SC and CNN via a very deep architecture with JPEG-specific priors. More precisely, we build representations for input images by learning a very deep convolutional neural network in both the DCT domain and the pixel domain, namely Deep Dual-domain Convolutional neural Network (DDCN). The proposed DDCN has several appealing properties. First, learning within the dual DCT-pixel domain enables us to leverage DCT-domain prior information, so that more consistent results can be achieved, while at the same time we can still enjoy the power of traditional pixel-domain CNNs. Second, the DDCN is fully feed-forward and does not need to solve any optimization problem on usage, and hence can run much faster than most SC-based approaches like [24]. Third, with careful control of gradient updates and residual learning, the DDCN is successfully built on a much deeper architecture in comparison to previous works [6,7,24], and extensive experiments prove its superior accuracy.

2   Related Works

Our work is mainly motivated by the two state of the arts, i.e., the Dual-domain Sparse Coding (DSC) approach [24] and the ARCNN [6]. Therefore, we focus on introducing these two approaches in the following.

2.1   Dual-Domain Sparse Coding

Up to now, previous compression artifacts reduction approaches usually work either in the pixel domain [5,22,37,41,42] or in the DCT domain [8,21,39]. Unfortunately, when only operates in the pixel domain, the Inverse DCT (IDCT) is required for decompression. As a result, an isolated quantization error confined to a DCT coefficient will be propagated to all pixels of the corresponding

DCT block. What's worse, an aggressively quantized DCT coefficient can produce latent-signal-correlated structured errors in the pixel domain. Going the other way, it is extremely difficult to restore high-frequency details in pure DCT domain, since the quantization step would eliminate most high-frequency coefficients. Liu et al. [24] proposed to combine these two domains. They directly exploited residual redundancies in the DCT domain to prevent the spreading of quantization errors into the pixel domain, while at the same time a pixel-domain dictionary was learned on a large set of uncompressed images for high-frequency information recovery. In this way, the advantages of the pixel domain and the DCT domain can complement one the other. However, the DSC is overly simple (can be viewed as a two-layer network), and does not employ end-to-end training. Hence, its performance is not satisfactory, and runs extremely slow. Our work follows their dual-domain idea, but builds with a much more powerful and faster model.

2.2 Convolutional Neural Network

CNNs date back decades [20] and have recently shown explosive successes in both high-level [19,27,31] and low-level [6,7] vision tasks. Dong et al. [7] built image representations for the task of super resolution via a three-layer CNN (named SRCNN), and demonstrated impressive results. This model was further adjusted as a four-layer CNN (named ARCNN) [6] and proved to be promising in eliminating compression artifacts. However, both SRCNN and ARCNN were learned only in the pixel domain, resulting in propagation of quantization errors (as aforementioned). We will show that incorporating DCT-domain priors turns out to have great positive effect. In addition, though "deeper is better" is widely observed in high-level vision tasks, this phenomenon has not been seen in low-level ones. SRCNN and ARCNN are networks of several layers only, and they failed to obtain better performances with a deeper network. Nevertheless, we find that this problem can be somewhat mitigated by two simple tricks, i.e., gradient update restriction and residual learning.

3 Deep Dual-Domain Convolutional Network

3.1 Formulation

Consider a JPEG-compressed image $\mathbf{Y}$. Our goal is to recover from $\mathbf{Y}$ an artifact-free image $F(\mathbf{Y})$ which is as similar as possible to the original uncompressed image $\mathbf{X}$. As JPEG compression is not optimal, redundant information neglected by the JPEG encoder can still be found within a compressed image. The key issue is, how to build effective representations to automatically explore and utilize such information, so that details eliminated in the non-linear quantization step can be restored. To accomplish this task, in this paper, we develop a non-linear F as a very deep convolutional network learned in dual DCT-pixel domain, so called the Deep Dual-domain Convolutional neural Network (DDCN). Our DDCN conceptually has the following three components:

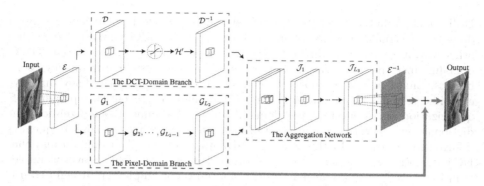

Fig. 2. An overview of the DDCN. A compressed input image is mapped to an artifact-free image via multiple non-linear layers. The DCT-domain branch tries to recover the DCT coefficients of the ground truth, while the pixel-domain branch aims to restore the pixel values directly. The aggregation network combines these two branches to produce the final output. To successfully learn a very deep model, the aggregation network predicts a residual image indeed. It is the addition of the input and the residual forms the final artifact-free output.

1. **The DCT-domain branch**: this component addresses the issue of digging DCT-domain redundancies like inter-DCT-block correlations. At the same time, DCT-domain priors such as the range of DCT coefficients are employed to improve consistency.
2. **The pixel-domain branch**: this component targets at recovering high-frequency details by leveraging spatial redundancies, e.g., similarity between image patches.
3. **The aggregation network**: this component combines the DCT-domain branch and the pixel-domain branch to generate the final artifact-free image. The prediction is expected to be similar to the uncompressed image $\mathbf{X}$.

An overview of the DDCN is depicted in Fig. 2. Without loss of generality, in the following discussions, we assume the input image $\mathbf{Y}$ is a single-channel image, i.e., a gray image. Next, we introduce each component of the DDCN in details.

3.2 The DCT-Domain Branch

To confine the quantization errors to individual DCT coefficients instead of propagating them over a wide area of pixels, we learn a non-linear mapping in the DCT domain to recover the DCT coefficients of the ground truth, namely, the DCT-domain branch. More specifically, given a JPEG-compressed image $\mathbf{Y}$, we extract a set of overlapped patches and then perform transform on them to get the corresponding DCT coefficients. Based on the resulting DCT coefficient patches, non-linear mapping modeled as a deep CNN is built, so as to automatically discover DCT-domain redundancies. This CNN is further constrained by the range of ground-truth DCT coefficients. Finally, the output is converted back

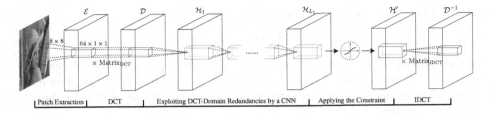

Fig. 3. A detailed illustration of the DCT-domain branch

to the pixel domain via IDCT. We detail the above operations in the following sub-sections. Figure 3 provides a summary for the DCT-domain branch.

Patch Extraction and Discrete Cosine Transform. To explore DCT-domain information of JPEG images, at first we need to extract 8×8 patches and then represent them by a set of pre-defined DCT bases, following the JPEG encoder. Both of these two operations can be implemented as convolution.

Formally, to extract patches of size $\sqrt{n} \times \sqrt{n}$ (for JPEG, $\sqrt{n}$ is set to 8), our first layer is expressed as an operation $\mathcal{E}$: $\mathcal{E}(\mathbf{Y}) = W_{\mathcal{E}} * \mathbf{Y}$, where $*$ denotes a convolution operator and the weights $W_{\mathcal{E}}$ contains n 2D filters of size $\sqrt{n} \times \sqrt{n}$. Precisely, $\mathcal{E}$ convolves an image with n "one-hot" filters, so that each convolution extracts one pixel of every $\sqrt{n} \times \sqrt{n}$ patch. As an example, to extract the top-left pixel of a patch, the corresponding filter can be designed as having 1 in its bottom right corner while leaving all the other elements to be 0s. Since all these filters are sparse, the operation $\mathcal{E}$ can run efficiently. Notice that although the JPEG standard works on non-overlapping blocks, we extract patches at arbitrary positions that misalign with DCT coding block boundaries. We emphasize that overlapping sampling is very important for removing artificial structures of JPEG compression, especially the notorious DCT blocking artifacts.

The output of $\mathcal{E}$ consists of n channels, where each patch is collapsed into a n-dimensional vector. Next, each patch is transformed into the corresponding DCT coefficient patch, by applying the $n \times n$ DCT matrix on it. This transform operation, say $\mathcal{D}$, can also be implemented as a convolutional layer $\mathcal{D}(\mathbf{Y}) = W_{\mathcal{D}} * \mathcal{E}(\mathbf{Y})$, where the weights $W_{\mathcal{D}}$ contains n 3D filters of size $n \times 1 \times 1$, initialized by the DCT matrix. The output of $\mathcal{D}$ is again composed of n channels.

Exploiting DCT-Domain Redundancies. So far we have converted image patches from the pixel domain to the DCT domain. To automatically discover and utilize redundancies in the DCT domain, we then extract non-linear representations from the output of $\mathcal{D}$. This non-linear operation can be formulated as a convolutional layer with a Parametric Rectified Linear Unit (PReLU) [12] applied on the filter response of convolution. To increase non-linearity, we repeat the above procedure. That is, to build layer i, we extract non-linear representations from the previous layer, and the output of layer i is further feed into the next layer to form another set of representations:

$$\mathcal{H}_i(\mathbf{Y}) = \text{PReLU}\left(W_{\mathcal{H}_i} * \mathcal{H}_{i-1}(\mathbf{Y}) + B_{\mathcal{H}_i}\right), \tag{1}$$

where $W_{\mathcal{H}_i}$ and $B_{\mathcal{H}_i}$ are the filters and biases of the i-th convolutional layer. By stacking a large number of non-linear layers, the capability of the DCT-domain branch can be significantly strengthen, so that more complicated redundancies may be exploited.

Now we have built highly non-linear representations for DCT-domain patches. To predict the ground-truth DCT coefficients, the final layer is implemented as a convolutional layer to project patch representations back to the DCT domain:

$$\mathcal{H}_{L_1}(\mathbf{Y}) = W_{\mathcal{H}_{L_1}} * \mathcal{H}_{L_1-1}(\mathbf{Y}) + B_{\mathcal{H}_{L_1}}. \tag{2}$$

Here $W_{\mathcal{H}_{L_1}}$ contains n filters, and L_1 is the number of convolutional layers in the DCT-domain branch disregarding $\mathcal{E}$, $\mathcal{D}$, and $\mathcal{D}^{-1}$ (introduced below).

Applying the Coefficient Range Constraint. The JPEG standard is composed of various pre-defined parameters. By wisely leveraging these parameters, pieces of side information can be sniffed out from the DCT coefficients of the compressed input image. As a result, JPEG-specific priors can be inferred and then applied to boost performance.

More specifically, the JPEG encoder performs quantization on a given uncompressed image as division of each DCT coefficient by its quantizer step size, followed by rounding to the nearest integer. The DCT coefficients of the corresponding compressed image are obtained by multiplying back the step size:

$$\mathsf{Y}(u,v) = \text{ROUND}(\mathsf{X}(u,v)/Q(u,v)) \cdot Q(u,v). \tag{3}$$

where X and Y are the DCT coefficients of the uncompressed image $\mathbf{X}$ and the compressed image $\mathbf{Y}$, respectively, u and v are indices in the DCT domain, and Q is the quantization table. Hence, given Y, the range of X is deterministic:

$$\mathsf{Y}(u,v) - Q(u,v)/2 \le \mathsf{X}(u,v) \le \mathsf{Y}(u,v) + Q(u,v)/2. \tag{4}$$

For simplicity of notation, following we denote the lower and the upper bound specified in Eq. (4) as low($\cdot$) and up($\cdot$), separately.

As discussed earlier, the DCT-domain branch tries to predict the ground-truth DCT coefficients, so the output of $\mathcal{H}_{L_1}(\mathbf{Y})$ should not exceed the corresponding DCT coefficient range. To apply this constraint, a naive thought is to add one more layer for clipping:

$$\mathcal{H}'(\mathbf{Y})_i = \begin{cases} \text{low}(\mathcal{H}_{L_1}(\mathbf{Y})_i), & \mathcal{H}_{L_1}(\mathbf{Y})_i < \text{low}(\mathcal{H}_{L_1}(\mathbf{Y})_i) \\ \mathcal{H}_{L_1}(\mathbf{Y})_i, & \text{otherwise} \\ \text{up}(\mathcal{H}_{L_1}(\mathbf{Y})_i), & \mathcal{H}_{L_1}(\mathbf{Y})_i > \text{up}(\mathcal{H}_{L_1}(\mathbf{Y})_i) \end{cases}. \tag{5}$$

Here $\mathcal{H}_{L_1}(\mathbf{Y})_i$ stands for the i-th patch in $\mathcal{H}_{L_1}(\mathbf{Y})$ (note that $\mathcal{H}_{L_1}(\mathbf{Y})$ is a set of vectors where each position is a "flattened" patch in the DCT domain), so does $\mathcal{H}'(Y)_i$. The additional layer confines the solution space and can improve the consistency and accuracy of restoration.

However, in practice the above definition of $\mathcal{H}'$ will not work. The issue, is similar to the known drawback of sigmoid in a neural network, i.e., it would make the gradients of the network become zero at almost everywhere. To overcome the vanishing gradients problem, inspired by the leaky ReLU [26], we introduce a small slope in the parts where $\mathcal{H}_{L_1}(\mathbf{Y})$ exceeds its range. As a result, Eq. (5) is rewritten as:

$$\mathcal{H}'(\mathbf{Y})_i = \begin{cases} (1-\alpha) \cdot \mathrm{low}(\mathcal{H}_{L_1}(\mathbf{Y})_i) + \alpha \cdot \mathcal{H}_{L_1}(\mathbf{Y})_i, & \mathcal{H}_{L_1}(\mathbf{Y})_i < \mathrm{low}(\mathcal{H}_{L_1}(\mathbf{Y})_i) \\ \mathcal{H}_{L_1}(\mathbf{Y})_i, & \text{otherwise} \\ (1-\alpha) \cdot \mathrm{up}(\mathcal{H}_{L_1}(\mathbf{Y})_i) + \alpha \cdot \mathcal{H}_{L_1}(\mathbf{Y})_i, & \mathcal{H}_{L_1}(\mathbf{Y})_i > \mathrm{up}(\mathcal{H}_{L_1}(\mathbf{Y})_i) \end{cases} \quad (6)$$

with $\alpha \in (0,1]^n$ being a trainable parameter like the PReLU.

Back to the Pixel Domain. To further exploit pixel-domain redundancies, the DCT-domain reconstruction, i.e., the output of $\mathcal{H}'$, need to be transformed back to the pixel domain. Hence we define another one layer $\mathcal{D}^{-1}$ on top of $\mathcal{H}'$. Intuitively, $\mathcal{D}^{-1}$ is the inverse operation of $\mathcal{D}$, which performs IDCT on each (flatten) patch. As expected, $\mathcal{D}^{-1}$ can be also implemented as a convolutional layer, whose weights are initialized by the IDCT matrix.

3.3   The Pixel-Domain Branch

The DCT coefficients mainly contain global information of an image. That is, they do not respect the spatial continuity property of normal images. Local spatial information is tangled together in the DCT coefficients. Hence, exploiting spatial redundancies and fully recovering compressed images only in the DCT domain is not an easy task. We avoid this weakness by introducing a network directly learned in the pixel domain.

Our pixel-domain branch is straight-forward. Similar to the DCT-domain branch, at first we extract image patches using the $\mathcal{E}$ layer. After that, to automatically leverage pixel-domain redundancies, the resulting patches are directly feed into a deep CNN for non-linear representation extraction. Each layer in this CNN is of the same type: a non-linear convolutional layer decorated by the PReLU. We denote these layers as $\mathcal{G}_1, \mathcal{G}_2, \ldots, \mathcal{G}_{L_2}$, where L_2 is the layer number.

3.4   The Aggregation Network

The pixel-domain branch runs in parallel with the DCT-domain branch. To better combine their capability, we concatenate their outputs and then built a non-linear aggregation network to finetune the restoration results. Within the aggregation network, the predictions coming from the DCT-domain branch and the pixel-domain branch can cross validate each other, enhancing the reconstruction quality. The aggregation network is also a deep CNN, with each layer except the last containing a convolution operation followed by a PReLU nonlinearity. These layers are named as $\mathcal{J}_1, \mathcal{J}_2, \ldots, \mathcal{J}_{L_3}$ with L_3 being the layer number.

The last layer, denoted as $\mathcal{E}^{-1}$, operates as the inverse of the patch extraction layer $\mathcal{E}$. It puts all recovered patches back to the corresponding positions in the image. This is realized via a convolutional layer, as well.

3.5 Building Very Deep Architecture

Deep learning, as indicated by its name, uses deeper architecture to achieve higher non-linearity. The increasing non-linearity enables a network to better represent input data, resulting in higher performances. However, an opposite opinion, "deeper is not better", has been pointed out recently in certain low-level vision works [6,7].

We found that, one of the core problems is still due to exploding gradients. In high-level vision task, this problem has been largely addressed by intermediate normalization like the Batch Normalization [14]. However, such solutions are not suitable for compression artifacts reduction. As a simple example, in high-level visual task such as recognition, image contrast doesn't play a significant role, so normalization is welcomed, whereas keeping the actual contrast of an input image is very important in compression artifacts reduction and thus normalization would ruin the result. As a consequence, both [7] and [6] use an extremely small learning rate for training to avoid gradient explosion. Unluckily, in this way a deeper network is difficult to train since it will require impractically long time for convergence.

We mitigate this problem by Adam [18], a newly proposed optimization technique. This technique updates model parameters $\boldsymbol{\Theta}$ as $\boldsymbol{\Theta}_t = \boldsymbol{\Theta}_{t-1} - l \cdot \widehat{\mathbf{M}}_t / (\sqrt{\widehat{\mathbf{V}}_t} + \epsilon)$, where $\widehat{\mathbf{M}}$ and $\widehat{\mathbf{V}}$ are the bias-corrected first/second moment estimates of gradient, respectively, and l is the step size. As can be seen, Adam approximately restricts gradient updates by its step size hyper-parameter, so gradient explosion can be avoided in general.

Another issue is the loss function. Given a set of m uncompressed images $\{\mathbf{X}^{(i)}\}$ and their corresponding compressed images $\{\mathbf{Y}^{(i)}\}$, the Mean Squared Error (MSE) is usually adopted to learn $\{\mathbf{X}^{(i)}\}$ directly [6,7]:

$$\text{Loss}(\boldsymbol{\Theta}) = \frac{1}{m} \sum_{i=1}^{m} \|F(\mathbf{Y}^{(i)}; \boldsymbol{\Theta}) - \mathbf{X}^{(i)}\|_2^2. \tag{7}$$

However, it can be seen that direct learning requires all information within $\mathbf{Y}$ being carried through the whole model F, though what we really care about is the difference between $\mathbf{X}$ and $\mathbf{Y}$. From another perspective, with the above loss function, F needs to have long-term memory for the input, which will easily lead to vanishing/exploding gradients, as pointed out by the famous LSTM [13]. Inspired by [11], we change the loss function to learn the residuals:

$$\text{Loss}(\boldsymbol{\Theta}) = \frac{1}{m} \sum_{i=1}^{m} \|F(\mathbf{Y}^{(i)}; \boldsymbol{\Theta}) - (\mathbf{X}^{(i)} - \mathbf{Y}^{(i)})\|_2^2. \tag{8}$$

It turns out that Eq. (8) results in faster convergence and higher accuracy (see Sect. 4.2). Note that, in residual learning, the DCT-domain branch is re-designed to learn the DCT coefficients of the residual image. Hence the lower bound and upper bound of $\mathcal{H}_{L_1}$ are updated to $-Q/2$ and $Q/2$, respectively.

4   Experiments

In this section, experimental results are presented to demonstrate the superior performance of the proposed DDCN for restoring JPEG-compressed images.

In all experiments, we use the training set (200 images) of the BSDS500 database [1] for training, and its validation set (100 images) for validation. Quantitative evaluations are conducted on its test set (200 images). Different from [6], all images are not down-scaled, as in this paper we don't evaluate the RTF [16] which has been beaten by the ARCNN [6]. In addition, for perceptual comparisons, we also perform qualitative evaluations on the Set14 [40] database. Following the protocol of other compression artifacts reduction approaches: (1) To generate JPEG-compressed images of different quality, the MATLAB JPEG encoder is applied with its "Quality" parameter set accordingly; (2) When reporting the restoration results, only the luminance channel (in YCbCr color space) is considered. Nevertheless, our approach is robust to JPEG encoders. A DDCN trained on MATLAB-encoded images still works well on images encoded by other JPEG encoders (e.g., the Python Image Library), with a negligible performance loss. Besides, our approach is not limited to single-channel inputs. RGB images can be easily handled by regarding each channel as a gray image.

4.1   Implementation Details

Preparing the Training Set. In the training phase, the training image pairs $\{\mathbf{Y}, \mathbf{X}\}$ are prepared as 55×55-pixel sub-images uniformly sampled from the training images with a stride of 21. We have attempted smaller strides but did not observe significant performance improvement. For a patch misaligned with DCT coding block boundaries, the DCT coefficient range of its most similar coding block is used. It should be emphasized again that overlapped sampling is important for destroying blocking artifacts.

Since the training set is small, to train the DDCN which has numerous layers, we consider augmenting the training data. More precisely, sub-images are also extracted from the randomly rotated and flipped version of the training images.

Network Settings. As specified in Sect. 3.2, n is set to 64 for JPEG compression artifacts reduction. Thus the patch extraction layer $\mathcal{E}$ contains 64 filters of size 8×8, and the transform layer $\mathcal{D}$ contains 64 filters of size $64 \times 1 \times 1$. Weights in these two layers are also initialized according to the discussions in Sect. 3.2. The settings of the inverse layers, $\mathcal{E}^{-1}$ and $\mathcal{D}^{-1}$, are similar to $\mathcal{E}$ and $\mathcal{D}$ respectively. These four layers are fixed during training.

The other layers are all composed of filters of the size $64 \times 3 \times 3$, i.e., each filter operators on 3×3 spatial regions across 64 channels. Every layer among $\mathcal{H}_1, \mathcal{H}_2, \ldots, \mathcal{H}_{L_1}$, $\mathcal{G}_1, \mathcal{G}_2, \ldots, \mathcal{G}_{L_2}$, and $\mathcal{J}_2, \mathcal{J}_3, \ldots, \mathcal{J}_{L_3}$ has 64 filters, while $\mathcal{J}_1$ contains 128 filters. If not specified, L_1, L_2, and L_3 are set to 10. Zero-padding is used before each of these convolutional layer to keep their output sizes equal. Filters are initialized using the He initializer [12] with values sampled from the Uniform distribution. The components of α in Eq. (6) are set to 0.1 initially.

To train the DDCN, we begin with a step size 0.001 and then decrease it by a factor of 10 when the validation error stops improving. The step size of Adam is reduced two times prior to termination. For the other hyper-parameters of Adam, we set the exponential decay rates for the first/second moment estimate to 0.9 and 0.999, respectively. We train a specific network with batch size 64 for each JPEG quality. During testing, the DDCN runs as a fully convolutional network [25] to generate full-image predictions.

4.2 Quantitative Evaluation on BSDS500

We examine our DDCN on the BSDS500 database, in comparison to the two aforementioned state-of-the-art approaches, i.e., the DSC [24] and the ARCNN [6]. We also include the latest generic image restoration framework, i.e., the Trainable Nonlinear Reaction Diffusion (TNRD) [4] for comparison. To have a comprehensive quantitative evaluation, experiments are conducted under three objective fidelity metrics: the PSNR (dB), the SSIM [35], and the PSNR-B (dB) [38]. Four JPEG quality settings are evaluated: 10, 20, 30, and 40.

The quantitative results are shown in Table 1. On the whole, our proposed DDCN outperforms all the state of the arts on all JPEG qualities and evaluation metrics by a large margin. Specifically, for the PSNR, we have achieved a gain of

Table 1. Comparisons with the State of the Arts on the BSDS500 Database.

Quality	Evaluation	JPEG	DSC	ARCNN	TNRD	DDCN	DDCN(-DCT)
10	PSNR	27.80	28.79	29.10	29.16	**29.59**	29.26
	SSIM	0.7875	0.8124	0.8198	0.8225	**0.8381**	0.8267
	PSNR-B	25.10	28.45	28.73	28.81	**29.18**	28.89
20	PSNR	30.05	30.97	31.28	31.41	**31.88**	31.55
	SSIM	0.8671	0.8804	0.8854	0.8889	**0.8996**	0.8923
	PSNR-B	27.22	30.57	30.55	30.83	**31.10**	30.84
30	PSNR	31.37	32.29	32.67	32.77	**33.26**	32.92
	SSIM	0.8994	0.9093	0.9152	0.9166	**0.9248**	0.9193
	PSNR-B	28.53	31.84	31.94	31.99	**32.31**	32.01
40	PSNR	32.30	33.23	33.55	33.73	**34.27**	33.87
	SSIM	0.9171	0.9253	0.9296	0.9316	**0.9389**	0.9336
	PSNR-B	29.49	32.71	32.78	32.79	**33.15**	32.86

more than 0.9 dB in average compared with the DSC, and have outperformed the ARCNN by about 0.6 dB in average. The TNRD was beaten by approximately 0.5 dB in average, as well. These results demonstrate the effectiveness of our task-specific dual-domain design, and the great power of the very deep architecture. Furthermore, our DDCN also produces promising results on the PSNR-B. This metric is designed specifically to measure the degree of blockiness of a given image, and thus is more sensitive to JPEG blocking artifacts. It means our DDCN is especially suitable for improving the quality of JPEG-compressed images.

Besides, our DDCN runs much faster than the DSC, thanks to the fully feed-forward computation. For the DSC, it needs more than ten minutes to process a 512×512 image on a 6-core Xeon CPU, while the DDCN only requires several seconds. In addition, when GPUs are available, our DDCN takes less than 0.3s to generate the prediction on a GeForce GTX TITAN X, whereas the DSC employs a complicated optimization procedure and is not easy to be migrated to a GPU.

Analysis on Dual-Domain Learning. To investigate the importance of dual-domain learning, we develop a variant of the DDCN which is learned in the pixel domain only (i.e., the DCT-domain branch is dropped). Table 1 also provides experimental results for this variant (denoted as "DDCN(-DCT)"). It is clear that the PSNR values are decreased, with a loss of more than 0.3 dB in average, in comparison to the DDCN. This experiment verifies the effectiveness of leveraging DCT-domain prior information. Note that the difference in performance between the DDCN and the DDCN(-DCT) is not due to their different network sizes. We have attempted to enlarge the spatial support of all trainable filters in the DDCT(-DCT) from 3×3 to 5×5, but only observe negligible improvements (less than 0.1 dB). We have also tried to increase the depth of the DDCT(-DCT), yet turn out to be unlucky. We point out that using Eq. (5) instead of Eq. (6) made the DDCN perform almost the same as the DDCN(-DCT). Thus, it is rather significant to introduce a non-zero α for avoiding the zero gradients problem.

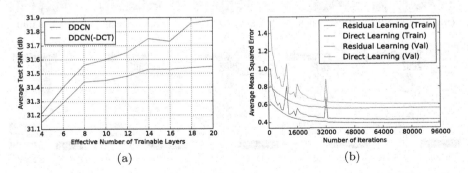

Fig. 4. (a) Average PSNR (dB) on the test set for various depths; (b) Average MSE on the training/validation set for residual learning and direct learning. Both experiments were conducted on BSDS500 with JPEG quality 20.

Analysis on Depth. We conduct another experiment to test the network sensitivity to different depths. For simplification, we keep layer numbers in the DCT-domain branch, the pixel-domain branch and the aggregation network to be the same value L, i.e., $L_1 = L_2 = L_3 = L$. Note that both two branches run in parallel, so the effective number of trainable layers in the DDCN is $\mathrm{MAX}(L_1, L_2) + L_3 = 2 \cdot L$. We evaluate the DDCN under various L ranging from 2 to 10. The average PSNR values on the test set are shown in Fig. 4(a). We can see that the performance grows as the depth increases in general. Figure 4(a) also displays the performance of the DDCN(-DCT). It can be seen that, without the help of the DCT-domain branch, the DDCN(-DCT) was always inferior to the DDCN under the same layer number, and its accuracy saturated earlier. These results proved the importance of the proposed dual-domain learning again.

Fig. 5. Qualitative comparison of various approaches under the JPEG quality 10. The corresponding PSNR values (in dB) are also shown.

Analysis on Residual Learning. Figure 4(b) illustrates the performances of residual learning and direct learning on a 20-trainable-layer DDCN (i.e., $L = 10$). The initial step size of direct learning is selected according to the best validation loss at termination. It can be observed that, in a very deep network, learning the residuals converges much faster and obtains better performance. In addition to this, we point out that Adam is indispensable. Even given 5x training time, neither residual learning nor direct learning seemed to converge without Adam.

4.3 Qualitative Evaluation on Set14

The Set14 [40] database consist of 14 widely used test images in the literature of image processing. Here we present some restored images of different approaches on this database. As can be seen in Fig. 5, the results of the DDCN are rather visually appealing. Our approach produces much sharper edges than other approaches, without any obvious blocking or ringing artifacts across the image. This experiment demonstrates that our approach is not only superior in objective fidelity metric, but also achieves better perceptual quality.

5   Conclusions and Future Work

In this paper, we systematically studied how to build effective representations for JPEG compression artifacts reduction. Based on understanding of the JPEG compression standard, we presented a very deep convolutional network learned in both the DCT domain and the pixel domain. The dual-domain learning enabled us to incorporate DCT-domain priors naturally, while we could still benefit from the great capability of traditional pixel-domain convolutional networks. Besides, we successfully built a very deep network by two simple strategies, i.e., Adam and residual learning, and observed significant performance gain with the increasing depth. Experimental results demonstrated the promise of the proposed approach.

Our DDCN is not restricted to JPEG compression. It is worth exploring whether the DDCN is able to reduce artifacts of remaining DCT-based compression standards, such as H.264/AVC [36] and HEVC-MSP [32]. In addition, by learning in other appropriate dual-domains, e.g., wavelet-pixel domain for JPEG2000 [33], the DDCN may be even extended to remove most transform-based compression artifacts. We will leave them to future work.

One limitation of our DDCN is the scalability to various JPEG qualities. Currently we need to train a separative model for each JPEG quality, which may limit its practical usage. This restriction also exists in most state of the arts, like the ARCNN. We hope to address this issue in future.

Acknowledgment. This work is partially supported by NSF of China under Grant 61173081, 61472453, U1401256, and U1501252, and the Guangzhou Science and Technology Program, China, under Grant 201510010165.

References

1. Arbelaez, P., Maire, M., Fowlkes, C., Malik, J.: Contour detection and hierarchical image segmentation. IEEE Trans. Pattern Anal. Mach. Intell. **33**(5), 898–916 (2011)
2. Buades, A., Coll, B., Morel, J.M.: A non-local algorithm for image denoising. In: IEEE Computer Society Conference on Computer Vision and Pattern Recognition, CVPR 2005, vol. 2, pp. 60–65. IEEE (2005)
3. Chen, T., Wu, H.R., Qiu, B.: Adaptive postfiltering of transform coefficients for the reduction of blocking artifacts. IEEE Trans. Circ. Syst. Video Technol. **11**(5), 594–602 (2001)
4. Chen, Y., Yu, W., Pock, T.: On learning optimized reaction diffusion processes for effective image restoration. In: Proceedings of the IEEE Conference on Computer Vision and Pattern Recognition, pp. 5261–5269 (2015)
5. Chuah, S., Dumitrescu, S., Wu, X.: l_2 optimized predictive image coding with l_∞ bound. IEEE Trans. Image Process. **22**(12), 5271–5281 (2013)
6. Dong, C., Deng, Y., Change Loy, C., Tang, X.: Compression artifacts reduction by a deep convolutional network. In: Proceedings of the IEEE International Conference on Computer Vision, pp. 576–584 (2015)
7. Dong, C., Loy, C.C., He, K., Tang, X.: Learning a deep convolutional network for image super-resolution. In: Fleet, D., Pajdla, T., Schiele, B., Tuytelaars, T. (eds.) ECCV 2014, Part IV. LNCS, vol. 8692, pp. 184–199. Springer, Heidelberg (2014)
8. Foi, A., Katkovnik, V., Egiazarian, K.: Pointwise shape-adaptive DCT for high-quality denoising and deblocking of grayscale and color images. IEEE Trans. Image Process. **16**(5), 1395–1411 (2007)
9. Gao, W., Tian, Y., Huang, T., Ma, S., Zhang, X.: The IEEE 1857 standard: empowering smart video surveillance systems. IEEE Intell. Syst. **29**(5), 30–39 (2014)
10. Google: WebP - a new image format for the web. Google Developers Website. https://developers.google.com/speed/webp/
11. He, K., Zhang, X., Ren, S., Sun, J.: Deep residual learning for image recognition (2015). arXiv preprint arXiv:1512.03385
12. He, K., Zhang, X., Ren, S., Sun, J.: Delving deep into rectifiers: surpassing human-level performance on imagenet classification. In: Proceedings of the IEEE International Conference on Computer Vision, pp. 1026–1034 (2015)
13. Hochreiter, S., Schmidhuber, J.: Long short-term memory. Neural Comput. **9**(8), 1735–1780 (1997)
14. Ioffe, S., Szegedy, C.: Batch normalization: accelerating deep network training by reducing internal covariate shift (2015). arXiv preprint arXiv:1502.03167
15. Isola, P., Zoran, D., Krishnan, D., Adelson, E.H.: Crisp boundary detection using pointwise mutual information. In: Fleet, D., Pajdla, T., Schiele, B., Tuytelaars, T. (eds.) ECCV 2014, Part III. LNCS, vol. 8691, pp. 799–814. Springer, Heidelberg (2014)
16. Jancsary, J., Nowozin, S., Rother, C.: Loss-specific training of non-parametric image restoration models: a new state of the art. In: Fitzgibbon, A., Lazebnik, S., Perona, P., Sato, Y., Schmid, C. (eds.) ECCV 2012, Part VII. LNCS, vol. 7578, pp. 112–125. Springer, Heidelberg (2012)
17. Jung, C., Jiao, L., Qi, H., Sun, T.: Image deblocking via sparse representation. Sig. Process. Image Commun. **27**(6), 663–677 (2012)
18. Kingma, D., Ba, J.: Adam: a method for stochastic optimization (2014). arXiv preprint arXiv:1412.6980

19. Krizhevsky, A., Sutskever, I., Hinton, G.E.: Imagenet classification with deep convolutional neural networks. In: Advances in Neural Information Processing Systems, pp. 1097–1105 (2012)
20. LeCun, Y., Boser, B., Denker, J.S., Henderson, D., Howard, R.E., Hubbard, W., Jackel, L.D.: Backpropagation applied to handwritten zip code recognition. Neural Comput. 1(4), 541–551 (1989)
21. Lee, K., Kim, D.S., Kim, T.: Regression-based prediction for blocking artifact reduction in JPEG-compressed images. IEEE Trans. Image Process. 14(1), 36–48 (2005)
22. List, P., Joch, A., Lainema, J., Bjontegaard, G., Karczewicz, M.: Adaptive deblocking filter. IEEE Trans. Circ. Syst. Video Technol. 13(7), 614–619 (2003)
23. Liu, X., Cheung, G., Wu, X., Zhao, D.: Inter-block consistent soft decoding of JPEG images with sparsity and graph-signal smoothness priors. In: 2015 IEEE International Conference on Image Processing (ICIP), pp. 1628–1632. IEEE (2015)
24. Liu, X., Wu, X., Zhou, J., Zhao, D.: Data-driven sparsity-based restoration of JPEG-compressed images in dual transform-pixel domain. In: Proceedings of the IEEE Conference on Computer Vision and Pattern Recognition, pp. 5171–5178 (2015)
25. Long, J., Shelhamer, E., Darrell, T.: Fully convolutional networks for semantic segmentation. In: Proceedings of the IEEE Conference on Computer Vision and Pattern Recognition, pp. 3431–3440 (2015)
26. Maas, A.L., Hannun, A.Y., Ng, A.Y.: Rectifier nonlinearities improve neural network acoustic models. Proc. ICML 30, 1 (2013)
27. Noh, H., Hong, S., Han, B.: Learning deconvolution network for semantic segmentation. In: Proceedings of the IEEE International Conference on Computer Vision, pp. 1520–1528 (2015)
28. Reeve III, H.C., Lim, J.S.: Reduction of blocking effects in image coding. Opt. Eng. 23(1), 230134–230134 (1984)
29. Rothe, R., Timofte, R., Van, L.: Efficient regression priors for reducing image compression artifacts. In: 2015 IEEE International Conference on Image Processing (ICIP), pp. 1543–1547. IEEE (2015)
30. Shen, M.Y., Kuo, C.C.J.: Review of postprocessing techniques for compression artifact removal. J. Vis. Commun. Image Represent. 9(1), 2–14 (1998)
31. Simonyan, K., Zisserman, A.: Very deep convolutional networks for large-scale image recognition (2014). arXiv preprint arXiv:1409.1556
32. Sullivan, G.J., Ohm, J.R., Han, W.J., Wiegand, T.: Overview of the high efficiency video coding (HEVC) standard. IEEE Trans. Circ. Syst. Video Technol. 22(12), 1649–1668 (2012)
33. Taubman, D.S., Marcellin, M.W.: JPEG 2000: standard for interactive imaging. Proc. IEEE 90(8), 1336–1357 (2002)
34. Wallace, G.K.: The JPEG still picture compression standard. IEEE Trans. Consum. Electron. 38(1), 18–34 (1992)
35. Wang, Z., Bovik, A.C., Sheikh, H.R., Simoncelli, E.P.: Image quality assessment: from error visibility to structural similarity. IEEE Trans. Image Process. 13(4), 600–612 (2004)
36. Wiegand, T., Sullivan, G.J., Bjøntegaard, G., Luthra, A.: Overview of the H. 264/AVC video coding standard. IEEE Trans. Circ. Syst. Video Technol. 13(7), 560–576 (2003)
37. Yang, Y., Galatsanos, N.P., Katsaggelos, A.K.: Projection-based spatially adaptive reconstruction of block-transform compressed images. IEEE Trans. Image Process. 4(7), 896–908 (1995)

38. Yim, C., Bovik, A.C.: Quality assessment of deblocked images. IEEE Trans. Image Process. **20**(1), 88–98 (2011)
39. Zakhor, A.: Iterative procedures for reduction of blocking effects in transform image coding. IEEE Trans. Circ. Syst. Video Technol. **2**(1), 91–95 (1992)
40. Zeyde, R., Elad, M., Protter, M.: On single image scale-up using sparse-representations. In: Boissonnat, J.-D., Chenin, P., Cohen, A., Gout, C., Lyche, T., Mazure, M.-L., Schumaker, L. (eds.) Curves and Surfaces 2011. LNCS, vol. 6920, pp. 711–730. Springer, Heidelberg (2012)
41. Zhai, G., Zhang, W., Yang, X., Lin, W., Xu, Y.: Efficient deblocking with coefficient regularization, shape-adaptive filtering, and quantization constraint. IEEE Trans. Multimedia **10**(5), 735–745 (2008)
42. Zhou, J., Wu, X., Zhang, L.: l_2 restoration of l_∞-decoded images via soft-decision estimation. IEEE Trans. Image Process. **21**(12), 4797–4807 (2012)

Geometric Neural Phrase Pooling: Modeling the Spatial Co-occurrence of Neurons

Lingxi Xie[1], Qi Tian[2(✉)], John Flynn[3], Jingdong Wang[4], and Alan Yuille[1]

[1] Center for Imaging Science, The Johns Hopkins University, Baltimore, MD, USA
198808xc@gmail.com, alan.l.yuille@gmail.com
[2] Department of Computer Science, University of Texas at San Antonio, San Antonio, TX, USA
qitian@cs.utsa.edu
[3] Department of Statistics, University of California, Los Angeles, CA, USA
john_flynn@mac.com
[4] Microsoft Research, Beijing, China
jingdw@microsoft.com
http://bigml.cs.tsinghua.edu.cn/~lingxi/Projects/GNPP.html

Abstract. Deep Convolutional Neural Networks (CNNs) are playing important roles in state-of-the-art visual recognition. This paper focuses on modeling the spatial co-occurrence of neuron responses, which is less studied in the previous work. For this, we consider the neurons in the hidden layer as *neural words*, and construct a set of *geometric neural phrases* on top of them. The idea that grouping neural words into neural phrases is borrowed from the Bag-of-Visual-Words (BoVW) model. Next, the **Geometric Neural Phrase Pooling** (GNPP) algorithm is proposed to efficiently encode these neural phrases. GNPP acts as a new type of hidden layer, which punishes the isolated neuron responses after convolution, and can be inserted into a CNN model with little extra computational overhead. Experimental results show that GNPP produces significant and consistent accuracy gain in image classification.

Keywords: Image classification · Convolutional Neural Networks · Spatial co-occurrence of neurons · Geometric Neural Phrase Pooling

1 Introduction

We have witnessed a significant revolution in computer vision brought by the deep Convolutional Neural Networks (CNNs). With powerful computational resources (*e.g.*, GPUs) and a large amount of labeled training data (*e.g.*, [1]), a hierarchical structure containing different levels of visual concepts is constructed and trained [2] to produce impressive performance on large-scale visual recognition tasks [3]. A pre-trained deep network is also capable of generating deep features for various tasks, such as image classification [4,5], image retrieval [6,7] and object detection [8,9].

CNN is composed of several stacked layers, each of which contains a number of neurons. We argue that modeling the co-occurrence of neuron responses is

B. Leibe et al. (Eds.): ECCV 2016, Part I, LNCS 9905, pp. 645–661, 2016.
DOI: 10.1007/978-3-319-46448-0_39

important, whereas less studied in the previous work. For this, we define a set of *geometric neural phrases* on the basis of the hidden neurons, and propose the **Geometric Neural Phrase Pooling** (GNPP) algorithm to encode them efficiently. GNPP can be regarded as a new type of layer, and inserted into a network with little computational overhead (*e.g.*, 1.29 % and 2.52 % extra time and memory costs in the experiments on **ImageNet**). We explain the behavior of GNPP by noting that it punishes the isolated neuron responses, and that the isolated responses are often less reliable than clustered ones, especially in the high-level network layers. Experimental results show that adding GNPP layers boosts image classification accuracy significantly and consistently. Later, we will discuss the benefits brought by the GNPP layer from different points of view, showing that GNPP produces better internal representation, builds latent connections, and accelerates the network training process.

The remainder of this paper is organized as follows. Section 2 briefly introduces related work. Section 3 introduces the GNPP layer, and Sect. 4 shows experimental results. We discuss the benefits brought by adding GNPP layers in Sect. 5. Finally, we conclude this work in Sect. 6.

2   Related Work

2.1   The Bag-of-Visual-Words Model

The Bag-of-Visual-Words (BoVW) model [10] represents each image as a high-dimensional vector. It typically consists of three stages, *i.e.*, descriptor extraction, feature encoding and feature aggregation.

Due to the limited descriptive ability of raw pixels, handcrafted descriptors such as SIFT [11], HOG [12] or other variants [13] are extracted. The set of local descriptors on an image is denoted as $\mathcal{D} = \{(\mathbf{d}_m, \mathbf{l}_m)\}_{m=1}^{M}$, where M is the number of descriptors, $\mathbf{d}_m$ is the description vector and $\mathbf{l}_m$ is the 2D location of the m-th word. A visual vocabulary or codebook is then built to capture the data distribution in feature space. The codebook is a set of codewords: $\mathcal{B} = \{\mathbf{c}_b\}_{b=1}^{B}$, in which B is the codebook size and each codeword has the same dimension with the descriptors. Each descriptor $\mathbf{d}_m$ is then quantized onto the codebook as a visual word $\mathbf{f}_m \in \mathbb{R}_{\geqslant 0}^{B}$. Effective feature quantization algorithms include sparse coding [14,15] and high-dimensional encoding [16–18]. $\mathcal{F} = \{(\mathbf{f}_m, \mathbf{l}_m)\}_{m=1}^{M}$ is the set of visual words. Finally, these words are aggregated as an image-level representation vector [19,20]. These Image-level vectors are then normalized and fed into machine learning algorithms [21] for training and testing, or used in some training-free image classification algorithms [7,22].

2.2   Geometric Phrase Pooling

The basic unit in the BoVW model is a *visual word*, *i.e.*, a quantized local descriptor. Dealing with individual visual words does not consider the spatial co-occurrence of visual features. To this end, researchers propose *visual phrase* [23, 24] as a mid-level data structure connecting low-level descriptors and high-level visual concepts [25]. A visual phrase is often defined as a group of neighboring visual words [25,26]. It can be used to filter out the false matches in object retrieval [24,27], or improve the descriptive ability of visual features for image classification [26,28].

Geometric Phrase Pooling (GPP) [26] is an efficient algorithm for extracting and encoding visual phrases. GPP starts from constructing, for each visual word, a *geometric visual phrase*, which is a group of visual words: $\mathcal{G}_m = (\mathbf{f}_m, \mathbf{l}_m) \cup \left\{ \left(\mathbf{f}_m^{(k)}, \mathbf{l}_m^{(k)} \right) \right\}_{k=1}^{K}$. In $\mathcal{G}_m$, $(\mathbf{f}_m, \mathbf{l}_m)$ is the *central word*, and all the other K words are *side words*, located in a small neighborhood $\mathcal{N}_m$ of the central position $\mathbf{l}_m$. GPP encodes each geometric visual phrase $\mathcal{G}_m$ by adding the maximal response of the side words to the central word: $\mathbf{p}_m = \mathbf{f}_m + \max_{k=1}^{K} \left\{ s_m^{(k)} \times \mathbf{f}_m^{(k)} \right\}$, where $\max_{k=1}^{K}\{\cdot\}$ denotes dimension-wise maximization. Note that the central word is not included in the maximization. $s_m^{(k)}$ is the smoothing weight of the k-th side word in $\mathcal{G}_m$. Most often, $s_m^{(k)}$ is determined by the Euclidean distance between $\mathbf{l}_m^{(k)}$ and $\mathbf{l}_m$, *e.g.*, $s_m^{(k)} = \exp\left\{ -\tau \times \left\| \mathbf{l}_m - \mathbf{l}_m^{(k)} \right\|_2 \right\}$, where $\tau > 0$ is the pre-defined smoothing parameter. Note that, at least in theory, the GPP algorithm can be applied to any data with a spatial attribute.

2.3 Convolutional Neural Networks

The Convolutional Neural Network (CNN) serves as a hierarchical model for large-scale visual recognition. It is based on the observation that a network with enough neurons is able to fit any complicated data distribution. In past years, neural networks were shown effective for simple recognition tasks [29]. More recently, the availability of large-scale training data (*e.g.*, ImageNet [1]) and powerful GPUs make it possible to train deep CNNs [2] which significantly outperform BoVW models. A CNN is composed of several stacked layers. In each of them, responses from the previous layer are convoluted with a filter bank and activated by a differentiable non-linearity. Hence, a CNN can be considered as a composite function, which is trained by back-propagating error signals defined by the difference between supervision and prediction at the top layer. Efficient methods were proposed to help CNNs converge faster and prevent over-fitting, such as ReLU activation [2], batch normalization [30] and regularization [31,32]. It is believed that deeper networks produce better recognition results [33–35].

The intermediate responses of CNNs, *i.e.*, the so-called deep features, serve as effective image descriptions [5], or a set of latent visual attributes [36]. They can be used for various types of vision tasks, including image classification [4,37], image retrieval [6,7] and object detection [8]. A discussion of how different CNN configurations impact deep feature performance is available in [38].

3 Geometric Neural Phrase Pooling

This section presents the Geometric Neural Phrase Pooling (GNPP) algorithm and its application to improve the CNN model.

3.1 The GNPP Layer

We start with a hidden layer $\mathbf{X}$ in the CNN model. $\mathbf{X}$ is a 3D neuron cube with $W \times H \times D$ neurons, where W, H and D are the width, height and depth of the cube. The response of each neuron corresponds to the inner-product of a local patch in the previous layer and a filter (convolutional kernel). We naturally consider the data as a set of D-dimensional *visual words* indexed over a 2D spatial domain. We denote the set as $\mathcal{X} = \{\mathbf{x}_{w,h}\}_{w=1,h=1}^{W,H}$, in which $\mathbf{x}_{w,h} \in \mathbb{R}_{\geqslant 0}^{D}$ for each w and h. The spatial domain coordinate (w, h) is not the same as the pixel coordinate (a, b) in the original image, but they are linearly corresponded.

A *geometric neural phrase* is defined as $\mathcal{G}_{w,h} = \{\mathbf{x}_{w',h'} \mid \mathbf{x}_{w',h'} \in \mathcal{N}_{w,h}\}$, where $\mathcal{N}_{w,h}$ is the neighborhood of $\mathbf{x}_{w,h}$. Given the number of side words K, we can rewrite it as $\mathcal{G}_{w,h} = \mathbf{x}_{w,h} \cup \left\{\mathbf{x}_{w,h}^{(k)}\right\}_{k=1}^{K}$, where $\mathbf{x}_{w,h}$ is the *central word*, and all the others in $\mathcal{G}_{w,h}$ are *side words*. For simplicity, we consider two fixed types of neighborhood, shown in Fig. 1. If the central word is located on the boundary of the neuron map, the side words outside the map are simply ignored.

The **Geometric Neural Phrase Pooling** (GNPP) algorithm computes an updated neural response for each geometric neural phrase $\mathcal{G}_{w,h}$ individually:

$$\mathbf{z}_{w,h} = \frac{1}{2}\left[\mathbf{x}_{w,h} + \max_{k=1}^{K}\left\{s_{w,h}^{(k)} \times \mathbf{x}_{w,h}^{(k)}\right\}\right], \tag{1}$$

where $\max_{k=1}^{K}\{\cdot\}$ is the maximization over K side words. Note that the central word is not included in the maximization. We add the coefficient $\frac{1}{2}$ to approximately preserve the average scale of neuron responses. We define a smoothing parameter $\sigma \in (0,1]$. A side word is weighted by either $s_{w,h}^{(k)} = \sigma$ or $s_{w,h}^{(k)} = \sigma^2$, according to the relative position to the central word. Of course, one can modify the definition of both neighborhood and weights, *e.g.*, using a

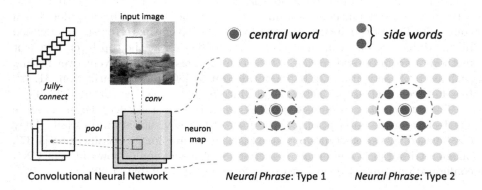

Fig. 1. Left: the architecture of a toy CNN model. A geometric neural phrase is defined on the basis of a set of neural words. Right: two types of neighborhood used in this work (best viewed in color PDF). The green side words are weighted by σ and the blue ones by σ^2, where σ is the smoothing parameter. (Color figure online)

larger neighborhood or assigning smaller weights on side words, but these minor changes do not impact much on the performance (see Sect. 4.3).

GNPP averages neuron responses over the central word and the maximal candidate among all side words. Although this looks like the behavior of a local smoother, we emphasize that GNPP is intrinsically different from other smoothers such as vanilla Gaussian blur. Gaussian blur can be formulated as convoluting the input data with a fixed kernel. Applying Gaussian blur after a convolutional layer is similar to using larger kernels, where some weights are not independent to each other. As expected, adding Gaussian blur does not obtain accuracy gain. We add a vanilla Gaussian blur layer before each pooling layer of the **LeNet**, and test it on **CIFAR10**. The baseline error rate is 17.07 % ± 0.15 %, and the network with Gaussian blur reports 17.05 % ± 0.13 %. On the other side, the network with GNPP reports 14.78 % ± 0.17 % (see Sect. 4.2). In summary, **GNPP does something that a linear smoother cannot do**.

Since GNPP does not change the dimension $(W, H$ and $D)$ of the neuron cube, we can regard GNPP as an intermediate network layer, $i.e.$, the **GNPP layer**. Although the GNPP layer can, at least in theory, appear anywhere, **we only insert it between a convolutional layer and a pooling layer**, due to the reason to be elaborated in the next subsection.

3.2   Modeling the Spatial Co-occurrence

We show that GNPP is an implicit way of punishing $isolated$ neuron responses. Therefore, GNPP works well on the assumption that $clustered$ neuron responses are more reliable than $isolated$ ones. In this subsection, we will elaborate that such an assumption is better satisfied on the high-level layers of a CNN.

To start, we note that the computation in (1) is carried out in parallel over the D channels. Without loss of generality, we only consider a single channel in a hidden layer, and our conclusion remains valid for the entire layer (containing D channels). In other words, we can simplify to the situation where we are dealing with $W \times H$ one-dimensional visual words.

In a CNN, neuron responses in one layer are generated by convolution. Convoluting data with the kernel can be regarded as template matching on different spatial locations. After ReLU activation [2], the preserved positive neuron responses correspond to those local patches with high similarity to the template. Figure 2 shows a toy example of (ReLU-activated) convolution results, in which we can find some $clustered$ high responses and some $isolated$ ones. Since GNPP averages the neuron responses over the central word and the maximal candidate of side words, the $clustered$ responses are approximately preserved, while the $isolated$ ones are punished. A toy example is shown in Fig. 2.

We explain why clustered responses are more reliable, especially on a high-level layer, where the isolated responses often correspond to unexpected random noise [39]. This is because high-level convolutional kernels are highly "specialized", $i.e.$, they often represent concrete visual concepts, $e.g.$, $car\ wheel$ or $aircraft\ nose$ [39]. Meanwhile, as the network level goes up, the receptive field of a neuron becomes larger ($e.g.$, a neuron on the $conv\text{-}5$ layer of the **AlexNet** can "see"

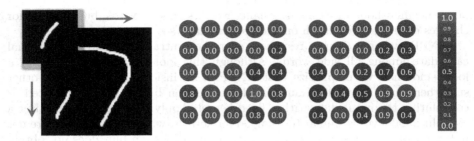

Fig. 2. A conceptual illustration of GNPP (best viewed in color PDF). Left: an image is convoluted with a template. Middle: the original one-dimensional neuron responses. Right: the responses after GNPP (type 1, $\sigma = 1.0$). The isolated high response (around the bottom-left corner) is decreased and smoothed, while the clustered high responses (around the bottom-right corner) are preserved. (Color figure online)

163×163 pixels on the input image), and neighboring neurons share more and more common visual information (*e.g.*, the overlapping rate of two neighboring neurons on the *conv-5* layer is 90.2 %). Thus, if a positive neuron response is caused by the correct match of a visual concept, its neighboring neurons are also likely to be activated, leading to a cluster of positive neuron responses. Oppositely, if it is caused by some random noise, its neighboring neurons may not be activated, and this isolated response shall be punished.

In conclusion, the core idea of GNPP is to model the spatial co-occurrence of neurons produced by a convolutional layer, or find reliable features by punishing the isolated responses which are more likely to be unexpected random noise. We note that pooling, when applied right after GNPP, is an efficient way of aggregating these rectified neuron responses. Therefore, in this work, we only insert GNPP between a convolutional layer and a pooling layer.

3.3   Comparison to Other Work

The GNPP algorithm is inspired by the GPP algorithm which originates from the BoVW model (see Sect. 2.2). GPP models the spatial context of visual words, and GNPP models the spatial co-occurrence of neural words. In the BoVW model, GPP can only be applied before a max-pooling layer, but GNPP can be inserted anywhere into the CNN model. In the **SVHN** and **CIFAR** experiments, we also show that GNPP cooperates well with the average-pooling layers.

The GNPP layer is related to the Spatial Pyramid Pooling (SPP) layer [40] and the Region-Of-Interest (ROI) pooling layer [41]. However, the motivation and working mechanism of GNPP are quite different from these two layers. The goal of GNPP is to punish isolated neuron responses and improve the descriptive power of every single neuron, while the SPP layer and the ROI pooling layer aim at summarizing local neurons into a regional description. The basic unit in the GNPP layer is a single neuron, and pooling is performed on a small set of its neighboring neurons, whereas both the SPP layer and the ROI pooling layer work on image regions. Finally, we point out that GNPP can be integrated with other network layers to further improve the recognition performance.

4   Experiments

In this section, we show the experimental results of inserting the GNPP layer into different CNN models. We first observe the performance by evaluating relatively shallow networks on small datasets, then use our conclusions to inform the application of GNPP to deeper networks and the large-scale database.

4.1   The MNIST and SVHN Datasets

MNIST [42] is one of the most popular datasets for handwritten digit recognition. It contains 60,000 training and 10,000 testing samples, uniformly distributed over 10 categories (digits 0–9). All the samples are 28×28 grayscale images. We use a modified version (2 convolutional layers) of the **LeNet** [29] as the baseline. With abbreviated notation, the network configuration is written as:

{C5(S1P0)@20-MP2(S2)}{C5(S1P0)@50-MP2(S2)}{FC500}{FC10}.

Here, C5(S1P0)@20 denotes a convolutional layer with 20 kernels of size 5×5, spatial stride 1 and padding width 0, MP2(S2) is a max-pooling layer with pooling region 2×2 and spatial stride 2, and FC500 is a fully-connected layer with 500 outputs. All the convolution results are activated by ReLU [2], and we use the softmax loss function. In the later experiments, we will directly use the same notations. We apply 20 training epochs with learning rate 10^{-3}, followed by 4 epochs with learning rate 10^{-4}, and another 1 epoch with learning rate 10^{-5}. We test each network five times individually with different initialization and report the averaged error rate and standard deviation.

The **SVHN** dataset [43] is a larger collection of 32×32 RGB images, with 73,257 training samples, 26,032 testing samples, and 531,131 extra training samples. We split the data as in the previous methods [43], *i.e.*, preserving 6,000 images for validation, and using the remainder for training. We use Local Contrast Normalization (LCN) for data preprocessing, following [44–46]. We use another version of the **LeNet** with 3 convolutional layers, abbreviated as:

{C5(S1P2)@32-MP3(S2)}{C5(S1P2)@32-AP3(S2)}{C5(S1P2)@64-AP3(S2)}{FC10}.

Here, AP indicates an average-pooling layer. We apply 12 training epochs with learning rate 10^{-3}, followed by 2 epochs with learning rate 10^{-4}, and another 1 epoch with learning rate 10^{-5}. Each network is individually tested five times.

When the GNPP layer is inserted into the network, it can appear before any subset of the pooling layers. We enumerate all the possibilities, and summarize the results in Table 1. One can observe that the use of GNPP significantly improves the recognition accuracy. The relative error rates are decreased by over 20 % on both datasets. Meanwhile, GNPP can be used with Dropout [31] (randomly discarding some neuron responses on the second pooling layer): on **MNIST**, the error rate is reduced from 0.72 % to 0.58 %.

Table 1. Classification error rates (%) on **MNIST** and **SVHN**. L1, L2 and L3 are three pooling layers, '✓' denotes that GNPP is added. T1 and T2 indicate two types of neighborhood (see Fig. 1). 1.0, 0.9 and 0.8 are σ values.

L1	L2	T1(1.0)	T1(0.9)	T1(0.8)	T2(1.0)	T2(0.9)	T2(0.8)
		$0.87 \pm .02$	$0.87 \pm .02$	$0.87 \pm .02$	$0.87 \pm .02$	$0.87 \pm .02$	$0.87 \pm .02$
✓		$0.72 \pm .04$	$0.73 \pm .03$	$0.70 \pm .05$	$0.71 \pm .06$	$0.71 \pm .06$	$0.72 \pm .04$
	✓	$0.75 \pm .03$	$0.79 \pm .02$	$0.77 \pm .05$	$0.73 \pm .04$	$0.75 \pm .04$	$0.73 \pm .05$
✓	✓	$0.72 \pm .03$	$\mathbf{0.67 \pm .04}$	$\mathbf{0.69 \pm .04}$	$\mathbf{0.63 \pm .03}$	$\mathbf{0.64 \pm .03}$	$\mathbf{0.67 \pm .03}$

(a) **MNIST**, with the 2-layer **LeNet**, no Dropout

L1	L2	T1(1.0)	T1(0.9)	T1(0.8)	T2(1.0)	T2(0.9)	T2(0.8)
		$0.72 \pm .03$	$0.72 \pm .03$	$0.72 \pm .03$	$0.72 \pm .03$	$0.72 \pm .03$	$0.72 \pm .03$
✓		$0.59 \pm .02$	$0.61 \pm .05$	$0.62 \pm .03$	$0.59 \pm .03$	$0.59 \pm .02$	$0.63 \pm .03$
	✓	$0.63 \pm .03$	$0.62 \pm .07$	$0.64 \pm .03$	$0.62 \pm .05$	$0.60 \pm .03$	$0.65 \pm .03$
✓	✓	$\mathbf{0.58 \pm .05}$	$\mathbf{0.55 \pm .02}$	$\mathbf{0.57 \pm .02}$	$\mathbf{0.54 \pm .05}$	$\mathbf{0.56 \pm .04}$	$\mathbf{0.61 \pm .05}$

(b) **MNIST**, with the 2-layer **LeNet**, Dropout ratio 0.5

L1	L2	L3	T1(1.0)	T1(0.9)	T1(0.8)	T2(1.0)	T2(0.9)	T2(0.8)
			$4.63 \pm .06$	$4.63 \pm .06$	$4.63 \pm .06$	$4.63 \pm .06$	$4.63 \pm .06$	$4.63 \pm .06$
✓			$4.46 \pm .06$	$4.47 \pm .05$	$4.42 \pm .09$	$4.42 \pm .08$	$4.42 \pm .07$	$4.43 \pm .09$
	✓		$4.15 \pm .08$	$4.18 \pm .01$	$4.17 \pm .07$	$4.08 \pm .10$	$4.19 \pm .07$	$4.20 \pm .05$
		✓	$3.76 \pm .03$	$3.72 \pm .05$	$3.77 \pm .06$	$3.53 \pm .07$	$3.64 \pm .07$	$3.65 \pm .10$
✓	✓		$4.10 \pm .05$	$4.07 \pm .03$	$4.10 \pm .05$	$4.10 \pm .07$	$4.10 \pm .03$	$4.14 \pm .07$
✓		✓	$3.55 \pm .10$	$3.60 \pm .03$	$3.67 \pm .06$	$3.47 \pm .05$	$3.47 \pm .02$	$3.55 \pm .09$
	✓	✓	$\mathbf{3.43 \pm .06}$	$3.52 \pm .07$	$\mathbf{3.55 \pm .04}$	$\mathbf{3.41 \pm .03}$	$3.42 \pm .04$	$3.51 \pm .05$
✓	✓	✓	$3.46 \pm .07$	$\mathbf{3.47 \pm .06}$	$\mathbf{3.55 \pm .06}$	$3.43 \pm .05$	$\mathbf{3.39 \pm .01}$	$\mathbf{3.46 \pm .03}$

(c) **SVHN**, with the 3-layer **LeNet**, no Dropout

4.2 The CIFAR10 and CIFAR100 Datasets

Both **CIFAR10** and **CIFAR100** datasets [47] are subsets of the 80-million tiny image database [48]. Both of them have 50,000 training and 10,000 testing samples, uniformly distributed over 10 or 100 categories. We also use the 3-layer **LeNet** as in **SVHN**, with the fully-connected layer replaced by FC100 in **CIFAR100**. We augment the training data by randomly flipping each training image with 50 % probability. We apply 120 training epochs with learning rate 10^{-3}, followed by 20 epochs with learning rate 10^{-4}, and another 10 epochs with learning rate 10^{-5}. Each network is individually tested five times.

Results with all possible GNPP settings are summarized in Table 2. Once again, GNPP improves the baseline error rate significantly: the baseline error rates on both **CIFAR10** and **CIFAR100** are reduced by more than 2 %, and the relative error rate decrease are 11.25 % and 6.56 %, respectively.

Table 2. Classification error rates (%) on the **CIFAR** datasets. We use the same notations as in Table 1. We apply Dropout on the simpler **CIFAR10** task.

L1	L2	L3	T1(1.0)	T1(0.9)	T1(0.8)	T2(1.0)	T2(0.9)	T2(0.8)
			17.07 ± .15	17.07 ± .15	17.07 ± .15	17.07 ± .15	17.07 ± .15	17.07 ± .15
✓			16.67 ± .22	16.80 ± .25	16.84 ± .12	16.65 ± .19	17.03 ± .15	17.04 ± .17
	✓		15.79 ± .22	16.09 ± .17	15.95 ± .31	15.69 ± .11	16.07 ± .27	15.90 ± .09
		✓	15.49 ± .15	15.31 ± .20	15.51 ± .25	15.27 ± .10	15.29 ± .14	15.28 ± .16
✓	✓		15.82 ± .23	15.76 ± .18	15.98 ± .14	16.05 ± .29	15.90 ± .25	15.94 ± .09
✓		✓	15.15 ± .20	15.29 ± .12	15.44 ± .19	15.29 ± .32	15.19 ± .35	15.20 ± .35
	✓	✓	**14.92 ± .18**	15.00 ± .18	15.15 ± .15	**14.83 ± .25**	14.93 ± .20	14.92 ± .16
✓	✓	✓	14.97 ± .17	**14.83 ± .23**	**14.78 ± .17**	15.22 ± .16	**14.79 ± .26**	**14.85 ± .26**

(a) **CIFAR10**, with the 3-layer **LeNet**, Dropout ratio 0.2

L1	L2	L3	T1(1.0)	T1(0.9)	T1(0.8)	T2(1.0)	T2(0.9)	T2(0.8)
			44.99 ± .19	44.99 ± .19	44.99 ± .19	44.99 ± .19	44.99 ± .19	44.99 ± .19
✓			44.62 ± .17	44.53 ± .45	44.78 ± .06	44.43 ± .29	44.58 ± .36	44.58 ± .52
	✓		43.34 ± .23	43.71 ± .19	43.37 ± .26	43.21 ± .23	43.03 ± .27	43.37 ± .30
		✓	43.11 ± .24	42.77 ± .37	42.99 ± .24	42.96 ± .32	42.81 ± .38	43.08 ± .39
✓	✓		43.99 ± .07	43.63 ± .11	43.50 ± .26	43.38 ± .37	43.34 ± .27	43.46 ± .25
✓		✓	42.85 ± .38	42.81 ± .27	42.82 ± .29	43.08 ± .27	42.79 ± .34	42.93 ± .22
	✓	✓	**42.35 ± .30**	**42.34 ± .31**	**42.04 ± .20**	**42.92 ± .33**	**42.72 ± .25**	**42.54 ± .29**
✓	✓	✓	42.97 ± .29	42.77 ± .36	42.36 ± .18	43.31 ± .34	42.85 ± .18	42.60 ± .36

(b) **CIFAR100**, with the 3-layer **LeNet**, no Dropout

4.3 Analysis on Small Experiments

Before we go into deeper networks and larger datasets, we conduct some preliminary analysis based on the results we already have.

First, although inserting GNPP before any pooling layers improves the performance, the most significant accuracy gain brought by a single GNPP layer is obtained by adding GNPP before the last pooling layer. This reinforces the conclusion drawn in Sect. 3.2, *i.e.*, GNPP works better on the high-level neuron responses. Meanwhile, on the **SVHN** and **CIFAR** datasets, adding GNPP before all three pooling layers produces inferior results to that adding GNPP before the second and third pooling layers. In the later experiments, we first add the GNPP layer before each pooling layer individually, then use the results to inform the design of the final model.

Regarding the scale of neural phrases, *i.e.*, K, we find that increasing the scale is not guaranteed to produce better recognition results. We explain this by noticing that adding a faraway side word to a neural phrase, most often, does not provide much related information but risks introducing noise to that unit. This idea can also be used to explain why a proper smoothing parameter, say, $\sigma = 0.8$, helps to reduce the contribution of faraway side words, leading to better recognition performance. One may certainly try other choices such as a large neighborhood with a very small σ, but we note that the time complexity of a GNPP layer is linear to K. In the later experiments, we will directly use the first type of neighborhood ($K = 4$) with $\sigma = 0.8$.

4.4 Deeper Networks and the State-of-the-Arts

We adopt two deeper networks on the above four small datasets to compare with the state-of-the-art results. One of them (we name it as the **BigNet**) is borrowed from [49] in the Kaggle recognition competition, and other one is the 16-layer Wide Residual Network (**WRN**) [50] with dropout. Both networks can be used in each of the four small datasets. In **CIFAR** datasets, we randomly flip the image with 50 % probability. We train the **BigNet** using 6×10^6 samples with learning rate 10^{-2}, followed by 3×10^6 samples with learning rate 10^{-3} and 1×10^6 samples with learning rate 10^{-4}, respectively. We report a 7.80 % error rate on **CIFAR10**, comparable to the original version [49], which uses a very complicated way of data preparation and augmentation to get a 6.68 % error rate. Training our model needs about 1 h, while the original version [49] requires 6 h. We train the **WRN** following the original configuration in [50].

We compare our results with the state-of-the-arts in Table 3. We add GNPP before the second and the third pooling layers for **BigNet**, and the last pooling layer for **WRN**. Although the baseline is already pretty high, GNPP still improves it by a margin: on **BigNet**, the relative error rate drops are 11.11 %, 12.62 %, 8.46 % and 4.16 % on the four datasets, respectively. Without complicated tricks, our results are very competitive among these recent works. We believe that GNPP can also be applied to other powerful networks in the future.

Table 3. Comparison of the recognition error rate (%) with the state-of-the-arts. We apply data augmentation on all these datasets, but the competitors do not use it in **CIFAR100**. Without data augmentation, we report 29.92 % and 29.17 % error rates (using **WRN**) without and with GNPP, respectively.

	MNIST	SVHN	CIFAR10	CIFAR100
Zeiler et al. [45]	0.47	2.80	15.13	42.51
Goodfellow et al. [46]	0.45	2.47	9.38	38.57
Lin et al. [51]	0.47	2.35	8.81	35.68
Lee et al. [52]	0.39	1.92	7.97	34.57
Liang et al. [53]	**0.31**	1.77	7.09	31.75
Lee et al. [54]	**0.31**	1.69	6.05	32.37
BigNet (without GNPP)	0.36	2.14	7.80	31.03
BigNet (with GNPP)	**0.32**	**1.87**	**7.14**	**29.74**
WRN (without GNPP)	0.34	1.77	5.54	25.52
WRN (with GNPP)	**0.31**	**1.67**	**5.31**	**25.01**

4.5 ImageNet Experiments

Finally, we evaluate our model on the **ImageNet** large-scale visual recognition task (the **ILSVRC2012** dataset [3] with 1000 categories). We use the **AlexNet** (provided by the **CAFFE** library [4]), abbreviated as:

```
{C11(S4)@96-MP3(S2)}{C5(S1P2)@256-MP3(S2)}{C3(S1P1)@384}{C3(S1P1)@384}
{C3(S1P1)@256-MP3(S2)}{FC4096-DO.5}{FC4096-DO.5}{FC1000}.
```

The input image is of size 227×227, randomly cropped from the original 256×256 image. Following the setting of **CAFFE**, a total of 450,000 mini-batches (approximately 90 epochs) are used for training, each of which has 256 image samples, with the initial learning rate 10^{-2}, momentum 0.9 and weight decay 5×10^{-4}. The learning rate is decreased to $1/10$ after every 100,000 mini-batches.

AlexNet contains three max-pooling layers, *i.e.*, *pool-1*, *pool-2* and *pool-5*. After individual tests, we only add GNPP before the last one (*pool-5*), since adding GNPP before either *pool-1* or *pool-2* causes accuracy drop. With the GNPP layer, the top-1 and top-5 recognition error rates are 42.16 % and 19.24 %, respectively. Comparing to the original rates (43.19 % and 19.87 %), GNPP boosts them by about 1.0 % and 0.6 %, respectively. We emphasize that the accuracy gain is not so small as it seems, especially considering that we do not introduce extra parameters and that the overall training time is only increased by 1.29 %.

Although GNPP is tested on **AlexNet**, we believe it can be applied to other models, such as **VGGNet** [33], **GoogleNet** [34] and Deep Residual Nets [35].

5 Benefits of GNPP

This section presents several discussions and diagnostic experiments that help us understand the side benefits brought by the GNPP layer.

5.1 Improving Internal Representation

Here we compare the *conv-5* layer of the standard **AlexNet** with the corresponding layers in the **GNPPNet** (defined in Sect. 4.5). That is, we compare **AlexNet**'s *conv-5* layer with **GNPPNet**'s *conv-5* layer and *GNPP-5* layer. Each layer is a $13 \times 13 \times 256$ neuron blob corresponding to 256 convolutional kernels. We average over the 256 channels and obtain a 13×13 heatmap. To allow direct comparison with the input image (227×227), we diffuse each neuron response as a Gaussian distribution over its receptive field on the input image (the same standard deviation is used on all layers). Results are shown in Fig. 3. It is observed in [39] that the activation patterns in higher convolutional layers correspond to mid-level parts. The average over filters is a crude measure that some mid-level parts are detected. Then Fig. 3 shows the spatial pattern corresponding to mid-level part detection.

First note that **AlexNet**'s *conv-5* layer and **GNPPNet**'s *GNPP-5* layer are broadly similar. This is to be expected as both of them occur at corresponding

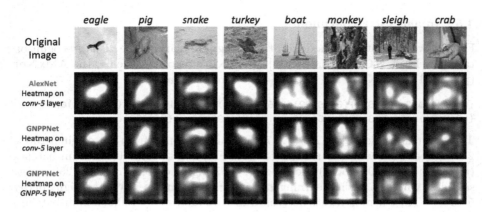

Fig. 3. Neuron response heatmaps produced by **AlexNet** and **GNPPNet**. When the background is relatively simple (*e.g.*, first two images), both methods work well. On those challenging cases, GNPP produces better saliency detection results, implying that the internal representation of CNN is improved.

places in the network architecture, *i.e.*, just before the *pool-5* layer and the fully-connected layers. We might think of the filter averages shown in Fig. 3 as spatial summaries of average scores over object parts. The higher layers in both networks combine spatial co-occurrences of parts into whole object detectors. For example, *car wheels* and *car doors* are combined into a whole *car*.

Next notice that **GNPPNet**'s *conv-5* layer is sparser and more concentrated than **AlexNet**'s *conv-5* layer. Broadly speaking the GNPP operation acts as a smoother and it is the smoothed *conv-5* layer (*i.e.*, the *GNPP-5* layer) that resembles **AlexNet**'s *conv-5* layer. The difference between **AlexNet**'s *conv-5* layer and **GNPPNet**'s *GNPP-5* layer is subtle, but we see that the *GNPP-5* layer is more diffuse corresponding to GNPP's action as local smoother.

As a result, **GNPPNet**'s *conv-5* layer produces better saliency detection results compared to **AlexNet**'s *conv-5* layer. This property can be used to extract better *deep features*. We verify our hypothesis on the **Caltech256** dataset [55]. 256-dimensional feature vectors are extracted from the *conv-5* layer by averaging over 13×13 spatial locations. The classification accuracy using the **AlexNet** is 59.36 %, and **GNPPNet** improves it to 60.56 %. This improvement is significant given that no extra time or memory is required for feature extraction.

In summary, applying GNPP to CNN produces better internal representation. The deep features extracted from the **GNPPNet** can also benefit other vision applications, such as image retrieval [6] and object detection [8,9].

5.2 Building Latent Connections

We show that GNPP builds latent connections between hidden layers in the CNN model. Consider a geometric neural phrase $\mathcal{G}_{w,h} = \mathbf{x}_{w,h} \cup \left\{ \mathbf{x}_{w,h}^{(k)} \right\}_{k=1}^{K}$. Let $\mathcal{S}_{w,h}$

be the set of neurons in the previous layer that are connected to $\mathbf{x}_{w,h}$, and $\mathcal{S}_{w,h}^{(k)}$ be the set connected to $\mathbf{x}_{w,h}^{(k)}$, $k = 1, 2, \ldots, K$. If we consider $\mathcal{G}_{w,h}$ as a *GNPP neuron*, then the set of neurons in the previous layer that are connected to it is $\mathcal{S}_{w,h} \cup \bigcup_{k=1}^{K} \mathcal{S}_{w,h}^{(k)}$. Thus, we are actually building latent neuron connections which do not exist in the original network. For example, applying GNPP (type 1) before the *pool-5* layer of the **AlexNet** increases the number of neuron connections between *conv-4* and *conv-5* from 149.5 M (million) to 348.9 M (on each neuron in *conv-5*, the number of connections to the previous layer increases from 9 to 21), meanwhile the number of learnable parameters remains unchanged.

To verify the benefits of latent connections, we train another version of **AlexNet**, referred to as **AlexNet2**, with the difference that the number of channels on the *conv-5* layer increases from 256 to 512. The number of neuron connections between *conv-4* and *conv-5* increases from 149.5 M to 299.0 $mathrmM$, comparable to 348.9 M in **GNPPNet**. **AlexNet2** requires 9.97 % extra training time and 5.58 % extra GNPP memory, while the numbers for **GNPP-Net** are 1.29 % and 2.52 %, respectively. **AlexNet2** produces 42.45 % (top-5) and 19.47 % (top-1) recognition error rates, which are higher than 43.19 % and 19.97 % reported by **AlexNet**, but lower than 42.16 % and 19.24 % reported by **GNPPNet**. To summarize, GNPP allows latent connections to be built in an efficient manner.

5.3   Accelerating Network Training

We show that adding GNPP layers accelerates the network training process, since GNPP allows visual information to propagate faster, like [56].

Let us investigate the case that training the 3-layer **LeNet** on the **SVHN** and **CIFAR** datasets. We are interested in the following question: if the input is a 32×32 image, which is the earliest layer containing a neuron able to "see" the entire image? Without GNPP, we need to wait until the *conv-3* layer. When GNPP is inserted before the second pooling layer, the receptive field of the neurons on the subsequent layers are increased. Consequently, some neurons in *pool-2* can already "see" the entire image. This allows some low-level and mid-level information (*e.g.*, object parts) be combined earlier.

As a result, GNPP helps the network training process converge faster. To verify, we plot the testing error rates and the loss function values throughout the training process. The results on the **SVHN** and **CIFAR100** datasets, using the **LeNet**, are shown in Fig. 4. One can see that GNPP causes the error rate and loss function curves drop more quickly, especially in the early epochs. For example, in the **SVHN** dataset, the network without GNPP requires about 36,000 iterations to reach 6 % error rate, while that with GNPP only needs about 15,000 iterations to get the same rate. Meanwhile, the training process reaches plateau sooner in the GNPP-equipped networks (see the error rate curve between 6–12 epochs in **SVHN**, and that between 60–120 epochs in **CIFAR100**).

With the help of GNPP, we can even train a network faster and obtain better performance. The baseline error rates on **SVHN** and **CIFAR100**, using

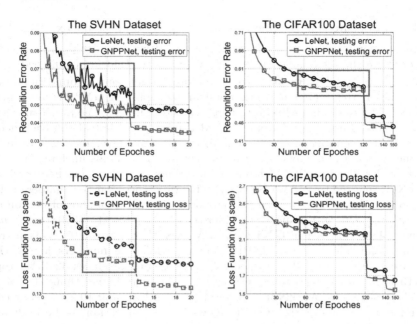

Fig. 4. Error rate and loss function curves on the **SVHN** and **CIFAR100** datasets. **GNPPNet** refers to the **LeNet** with two GNPP layers inserted before the second and third pooling layers. The curves in red frames indicate that **GNPPNet** enjoys better convergence, *i.e.*, it reaches the plateau sooner. (Color figure online)

the **LeNet**, are 4.63 % and 44.99 %, respectively. We train a GNPP-equipped **LeNet** with half training epochs under each learning rate, and obtain 3.78 % and 43.35 % error rates (the full training reports 3.55 % and 42.04 %).

6   Conclusions

In this paper, we demonstrate that constructing and encoding *neural phrases* boost the performance of state-of-the-art CNNs. We insert Geometric Neural Phrase Pooling (GNPP) as an intermediate layer into the network, and show that it improves the performance of deep networks without requiring much more computational resources. GNPP can be explained as an implicit way of modeling the spatial co-occurrence of neurons. We also show that GNPP enjoys the advantage of improving the internal representation of CNN, building latent connections, and speeding up the network training process.

We learn from GNPP that the isolated neuron responses are less reliable than the clustered ones. We hope that other kinds of prior knowledge can also be incorporated into the CNN architecture. Meanwhile, other visual tasks, including detection, segmentation, *etc.*, may also benefit from the GNPP algorithm. The exploration of these topics is left for future work.

Acknowledgements. This paper is supported by iARPA MICrONS contract D16PC00007, ONR N00014-12-1-0883, ARO grants W911NF-15-1-0290, Faculty Research Gift Awards by NEC Labs of America and Blippar, and NSFC 61429201. We thank Junhua Mao, Cihang Xie and Zhuotun Zhu for discussion.

References

1. Deng, J., Dong, W., Socher, R., Li, L., Li, K., Fei-Fei, L.: ImageNet: a large-scale hierarchical image database. In: Proceedings of Computer Vision and Pattern Recognition (2009)
2. Krizhevsky, A., Sutskever, I., Hinton, G.: ImageNet classification with deep convolutional neural networks. In: Proceedings of Advances in Neural Information Processing Systems (2012)
3. Russakovsky, O., Deng, J., Su, H., Krause, J., Satheesh, S., Ma, S., Huang, Z., Karpathy, A., Khosla, A., Bernstein, M., et al.: ImageNet large scale visual recognition challenge. Int. J. Comput. Vis., 1–42 (2015)
4. Jia, Y., Shelhamer, E., Donahue, J., Karayev, S., Long, J., Girshick, R., Guadarrama, S., Darrell, T.: CAFFE: convolutional architecture for fast feature embedding. In: ACM International Conference on Multimedia (2014)
5. Donahue, J., Jia, Y., Vinyals, O., Hoffman, J., Zhang, N., Tzeng, E., Darrell, T.: DeCAF: a deep convolutional activation feature for generic visual recognition. In: International Conference on Machine Learning (2014)
6. Razavian, A., Azizpour, H., Sullivan, J., Carlsson, S.: CNN features off-the-shelf: an astounding baseline for recognition. In: Proceedings of Computer Vision and Pattern Recognition (2014)
7. Xie, L., Hong, R., Zhang, B., Tian, Q.: Image classification and retrieval are ONE. In: International Conference on Multimedia Retrieval (2015)
8. Girshick, R., Donahue, J., Darrell, T., Malik, J.: Rich feature hierarchies for accurate object detection and semantic segmentation. In: Proceedings of Computer Vision and Pattern Recognition (2014)
9. Girshick, R.: Fast R-CNN. In: International Conference on Computer Vision (2015)
10. Csurka, G., Dance, C., Fan, L., Willamowski, J., Bray, C.: Visual categorization with bags of keypoints. In: European Conference on Computer Vision Workshop on Statistical Learning in Computer Vision, vol. 1, No. 22, pp. 1–2 (2004)
11. Lowe, D.: Distinctive image features from scale-invariant keypoints. Int. J. Comput. Vis. **60**(2), 91–110 (2004)
12. Dalal, N., Triggs, B.: Histograms of oriented gradients for human detection. In: Proceedings of Computer Vision and Pattern Recognition, pp. 886–893 (2005)
13. Xie, L., Wang, J., Lin, W., Zhang, B., Tian, Q.: RIDE: reversal invariant descriptor enhancement. In: International Conference on Computer Vision (2015)
14. Yang, J., Yu, K., Gong, Y., Huang, T.: Linear spatial pyramid matching using sparse coding for image classification. In: Proceedings of Computer Vision and Pattern Recognition, pp. 1794–1801 (2009)
15. Wang, J., Yang, J., Yu, K., Lv, F., Huang, T., Gong, Y.: Locality-constrained linear coding for image classification. In: Proceedings of Computer Vision and Pattern Recognition (2010)
16. Perronnin, F., Sánchez, J., Mensink, T.: Improving the Fisher kernel for large-scale image classification. In: Daniilidis, K., Maragos, P., Paragios, N. (eds.) ECCV 2010. LNCS, vol. 6314, pp. 143–156. Springer, Heidelberg (2010). doi:10.1007/978-3-642-15561-1_11

17. Zhou, X., Yu, K., Zhang, T., Huang, T.S.: Image classification using super-vector coding of local image descriptors. In: Daniilidis, K., Maragos, P., Paragios, N. (eds.) ECCV 2010. LNCS, vol. 6315, pp. 141–154. Springer, Heidelberg (2010). doi:10. 1007/978-3-642-15555-0_11

18. Kobayashi, T.: Dirichlet-based histogram feature transform for image classification. In: Proceedings of Computer Vision and Pattern Recognition (2014)

19. Lazebnik, S., Schmid, C., Ponce, J.: Beyond bags of features: spatial pyramid matching for recognizing natural scene categories. In: Proceedings of Computer Vision and Pattern Recognition (2006)

20. Feng, J., Ni, B., Tian, Q., Yan, S.: Geometric LP-norm feature pooling for image classification. In: Proceedings of Computer Vision and Pattern Recognition (2011)

21. Fan, R., Chang, K., Hsieh, C., Wang, X., Lin, C.: LIBLINEAR: a library for large linear classification. J. Mach. Learn. Res. 9, 1871–1874 (2008)

22. Boiman, O., Shechtman, E., Irani, M.: In defense of nearest-neighbor based image classification. In: Proceedings of Computer Vision and Pattern Recognition (2008)

23. Yuan, J., Wu, Y., Yang, M.: Discovery of collocation patterns: from visual words to visual phrases. In: Proceedings of Computer Vision and Pattern Recognition (2007)

24. Zhang, Y., Jia, Z., Chen, T.: Image retrieval with geometry-preserving visual phrases. In: Proceedings of Computer Vision and Pattern Recognition (2011)

25. Zhang, S., Tian, Q., Hua, G., Huang, Q., Li, S.: Descriptive visual words and visual phrases for image applications. In: Proceedings of ACM Multimedia (2009)

26. Xie, L., Tian, Q., Wang, M., Zhang, B.: Spatial pooling of heterogeneous features for image classification. IEEE Trans. Image Process. 23(5), 1994–2008 (2014)

27. Jiang, Y., Meng, J., Yuan, J.: Randomized visual phrases for object search. In: Proceedings of Computer Vision and Pattern Recognition (2012)

28. Xie, L., Tian, Q., Hong, R., Yan, S., Zhang, B.: Hierarchical part matching for fine-grained visual categorization. In: IEEE International Conference on Computer Vision (2013)

29. LeCun, Y., Denker, J., Henderson, D., Howard, R., Hubbard, W., Jackel, L.: Handwritten digit recognition with a back-propagation network. In: Proceedings of Advances in Neural Information Processing Systems (1990)

30. Ioffe, S., Szegedy, C.: Batch normalization: accelerating deep network training by reducing internal covariate shift. In: International Conference on Machine Learning (2015)

31. Hinton, G., Srivastava, N., Krizhevsky, A., Sutskever, I., Salakhutdinov, R.: Improving neural networks by preventing co-adaptation of feature detectors. arXiv preprint arXiv:1207.0580 (2012)

32. Xie, L., Wang, J., Wei, Z., Wang, M., Tian, Q.: DisturbLabel: regularizing CNN on the loss layer. In: Proceedings of Computer Vision and Patter Recognition (2016)

33. Simonyan, K., Zisserman, A.: Very Deep convolutional networks for large-scale image recognition. In: International Conference on Learning Representations (2015)

34. Szegedy, C., Liu, W., Jia, Y., Sermanet, P., Reed, S., Anguelov, D., Erhan, D., Vanhoucke, V., Rabinovich, A.: Going deeper with convolutions. In: Proceedings of Computer Vision and Pattern Recognition (2015)

35. He, K., Zhang, X., Ren, S., Sun, J.: Deep residual learning for image recognition. arXiv preprint arXiv:1512.03385 (2015)

36. Zhang, N., Paluri, M., Ranzato, M., Darrell, T., Bourdev, L.: PANDA: pose aligned networks for deep attribute modeling. In: Proceedings of Computer Vision and Pattern Recognition (2014)

37. Xie, L., Zheng, L., Wang, J., Yuille, A., Tian, Q.: InterActive: inter-layer activeness propagation. In: Proceedings of Computer Vision and Patter Recognition (2016)
38. Chatfield, K., Simonyan, K., Vedaldi, A., Zisserman, A.: Return of the devil in the details: delving deep into convolutional nets. In: British Machine Vision Conference (2014)
39. Wang, J., Zhang, Z., Premachandran, V., Yuille, A.: Discovering internal representations from object-CNNs using population encoding. arXiv preprint arXiv:1511.06855 (2015)
40. He, K., Zhang, X., Ren, S., Sun, J.: Spatial pyramid pooling in deep convolutional networks for visual recognition. In: Fleet, D., Pajdla, T., Schiele, B., Tuytelaars, T. (eds.) ECCV 2014. LNCS, vol. 8691, pp. 346–361. Springer, Heidelberg (2014). doi:10.1007/978-3-319-10578-9_23
41. Ren, S., He, K., Girshick, R., Sun, J.: Faster R-CNN: towards real-time object detection with region proposal networks. In: Proceedings of Advances in Neural Information Processing Systems (2015)
42. LeCun, Y., Bottou, L., Bengio, Y., Haffner, P.: Gradient-based Learning Applied to Document Recognition. Proc. IEEE **86**(11), 2278–2324 (1998)
43. Netzer, Y., Wang, T., Coates, A., Bissacco, A., Wu, B., Ng, A.: Reading digits in natural images with unsupervised feature learning. In: NIPS Workshop on Deep Learning and Unsupervised Feature Learning (2011)
44. Sermanet, P., Chintala, S., LeCun, Y.: Convolutional neural networks applied to house numbers digit classification. In: International Conference on Pattern Recognition (2012)
45. Zeiler, M., Fergus, R.: Stochastic pooling for regularization of deep convolutional neural networks. In: International Conference on Learning Representations (2013)
46. Goodfellow, I., Warde-Farley, D., Mirza, M., Courville, A., Bengio, Y.: Maxout networks. In: International Conference on Machine Learning (2013)
47. Krizhevsky, A., Hinton, G.: Learning multiple layers of features from tiny images. Technical report, University of Toronto (2009)
48. Torralba, A., Fergus, R., Freeman, W.: 80 Million tiny images: a large data set for nonparametric object and scene recognition. IEEE Trans. Pattern Anal. Mach. Intell. **30**(11), 1958–1970 (2008)
49. Nagadomi: the kaggle CIFAR10 network (2014). https://github.com/nagadomi/kaggle-cifar10-torch7/
50. Zagoruyko, S., Komodakis, N.: Wide residual networks. arXiv preprint arXiv:1605.07146 (2016)
51. Lin, M., Chen, Q., Yan, S.: Network in network. In: International Conference on Learning Representations (2014)
52. Lee, C., Xie, S., Gallagher, P., Zhang, Z., Tu, Z.: Deeply-supervised nets. In: International Conference on Artificial Intelligence and Statistics (2015)
53. Liang, M., Hu, X.: Recurrent convolutional neural network for object recognition. In: Proceedings of Computer Vision and Pattern Recognition (2015)
54. Lee, C., Gallagher, P., Tu, Z.: Generalizing pooling functions in convolutional neural networks: mixed, gated, and tree. In: International Conference on Artificial Intelligence and Statistics (2016)
55. Griffin, G., Holub, A., Perona, P.: Caltech-256 object category dataset. Technical report: CNS-TR-2007-001, Caltech (2007)
56. Srivastava, R., Greff, K., Schmidhuber, J.: Training very deep networks. In: Proceedings of Advances in Neural Information Processing Systems (2015)

Photo Aesthetics Ranking Network
with Attributes and Content Adaptation

Shu Kong[1]([✉]), Xiaohui Shen[2], Zhe Lin[2], Radomir Mech[2],
and Charless Fowlkes[1]

[1] UC Irvine, Irvine, USA
{skong2,fowlkes}@ics.uci.edu
[2] Adobe Research, San Jose, USA
{xshen,zlin,rmech}@adobe.com

Abstract. Real-world applications could benefit from the ability to automatically generate a fine-grained ranking of photo aesthetics. However, previous methods for image aesthetics analysis have primarily focused on the coarse, binary categorization of images into high- or low-aesthetic categories. In this work, we propose to learn a deep convolutional neural network to rank photo aesthetics in which the relative ranking of photo aesthetics are directly modeled in the loss function. Our model incorporates joint learning of meaningful photographic attributes and image content information which can help regularize the complicated photo aesthetics rating problem.

To train and analyze this model, we have assembled a new aesthetics and attributes database (AADB) which contains aesthetic scores and meaningful attributes assigned to each image by multiple human raters. Anonymized rater identities are recorded across images allowing us to exploit intra-rater consistency using a novel sampling strategy when computing the ranking loss of training image pairs. We show the proposed sampling strategy is very effective and robust in face of subjective judgement of image aesthetics by individuals with different aesthetic tastes. Experiments demonstrate that our unified model can generate aesthetic rankings that are more consistent with human ratings. To further validate our model, we show that by simply thresholding the estimated aesthetic scores, we are able to achieve state-or-the-art classification performance on the existing AVA dataset benchmark.

Keywords: Convolutional neural network · Image aesthetics rating · Rank loss · Attribute learning

1 Introduction

Automatically assessing image aesthetics is increasingly important for a variety of applications [1,2], including personal photo album management, automatic photo editing, and image retrieval. While judging image aesthetics is a subjective task, it has been an area of active study in recent years and substantial progress has been made in identifying and quantifying those image features that are predictive of favorable aesthetic judgements by most individuals [1–5].

© Springer International Publishing AG 2016
B. Leibe et al. (Eds.): ECCV 2016, Part I, LNCS 9905, pp. 662–679, 2016.
DOI: 10.1007/978-3-319-46448-0_40

Fig. 1. Classification-based methods for aesthetic analysis can distinguish high- and low-quality images shown in the leftmost and rightmost columns, but fail to provide useful insights about borderline images displayed in the middle column. This observation motivates us to consider rating and ranking images w.r.t aesthetics rather than simply assigning binary labels. We observe that the contribution of particular photographic attributes to making an image aesthetically pleasing depends on the thematic content (shown in different rows), so we develop a model for rating that incorporates joint attributes and content. The attributes and ratings of aesthetics on a scale 1 to 5 are predicted by our model (displayed on top and right of each image, respectively).

Early works formulate aesthetic analysis as a classification or a regression problem of mapping images to aesthetic ratings provided by human raters [4–8]. Some approaches have focused on designing hand-crafted features that encapsulate standard photographic practice and rules of visual design, utilizing both low-level statistics (*e.g.* color histogram and wavelet analysis) and high-level cues based on traditional photographic rules (*e.g.* region composition and rule of thirds). Others have adopted generic image content features, which are originally designed for recognition (*e.g.* SIFT [9] and Fisher Vector [10,11]), that have been found to outperform methods using rule-based features [12]. With the advance of deep Convolutional Neural Network (CNN) [13], recent works propose to train end-to-end models for image aesthetics classification [2,3,14], yielding state-of-the-art performance on a recently released Aesthetics Visual Analysis dataset (AVA) [15].

Despite notable recent progress towards computational image aesthetics classification (*e.g.* [1–3]), judging image aesthetics is still a subjective task, and it is difficult to learn a universal scoring mechanism for various kinds of images. For example, as demonstrated in Fig. 1, images with obviously visible high- or low-aesthetics are relatively easy to classify, but existing methods cannot generate reliable labels for borderline images. Therefore, instead of formulating image aesthetics analysis as an overall binary classification or regression problem, we argue that it is far more practical and useful to predict relative aesthetic rankings among images with similar visual content along with generating richer descriptions in terms of aesthetic attributes [16,17].

To this end, we propose to train a model through a Siamese network [18] that takes a pair of images as input and directly predicts relative ranking of their aesthetics in addition to their overall aesthetic scores. Such a structure allows us to deploy different sampling strategies of image pairs and leverage auxiliary side-information to regularize the training, including aesthetic attributes [1,3,7] and photo content [4,15,19]. For example, Fig. 1 demonstrates that photos with different contents convey different attributes to make them aesthetically pleasing. While such side information has been individually adopted to improve aesthetics classification [1,3], it remains one open problem to systematically incorporate all the needed components in a single end-to-end framework with fine-grained aesthetics ranking. Our model and training procedure naturally incorporates both attributes and content information by sampling image pairs with similar content to learn the specific relations of attributes and aesthetics for different content sub-categories. As we show, this results in more comparable and consistent aesthetics estimation results.

Moreover, as individuals have different aesthetics tastes, we argue that it is important to compare ratings assigned by an individual across multiple images in order to provide a more consistent training signal. To this end, we have collected and will publicly release a new dataset in which each image is associated with a detailed score distribution, meaningful attributes annotation and (anonymized) raters' identities. We refer to this dataset as the "Aesthetics with Attributes Database", or AADB for short. AADB not only contains a much more balanced distribution of professional and consumer photos and a more diverse range of photo qualities than available in the exiting AVA dataset, but also identifies ratings made by the same users across multiple images. This enables us to develop novel sampling strategies for training our model which focuses on relative rankings by individual raters. Interestingly, this rater-related information also enables us to compare the trained model to each individual's rating results by computing the ranking correlation over test images rated by that individual. Our experiments show the effectiveness of the proposed model in rating image aesthetics compared to human individuals. We also show that, by simply thresholding rated aesthetics scores, our model achieves state-of-the-art classification performance on the AVA dataset, even though we do not explicitly train or tune the model for the aesthetic classification task.

In summary, our main contributions are three-fold:

1. We release a new dataset containing not only score distributions, but also informative attributes and anonymized rater identities. These annotations enable us to study the use of individuals' aesthetics ratings for training our model and analyze how the trained model performs compared to individual human raters.
2. We propose a new CNN architecture that unifies aesthetics attributes and photo content for image aesthetics rating and achieves state-of-the-art performance on existing aesthetics classification benchmark.
3. We propose a novel sampling strategy that utilizes mixed within- and cross-rater image pairs for training models. We show this strategy, in combination with pair-wise ranking loss, substantially improves the performance $w.r.t.$ the ranking correlation metric.

2   Related Work

CNN for Aesthetics Classification: In [2,3,14], CNN-based methods are proposed for classifying images into high- or low-aesthetic categories. The authors also show that using patches from the original high-resolution images largely improves the performance. In contrast, our approach formulates aesthetic prediction as a combined regression and ranking problem. Rather than using patches, our architecture warps the whole input image in order to minimize the overall network size and computational workload while retaining compositional elements in the image, *e.g.* rule of thirds, which are lost in patch-based approaches.

Attribute-Adaptive Models: Some recent works have explored the use of high-level describable attributes [1,3,7] for image aesthetics classification. In early work, these attributes were modeled using hand-crafted features [7]. This introduces some intrinsic problems, since (1) engineering features that capture high-level semantic attributes is a difficult task, and (2) the choice of describable attributes may ignore some aspects of the image which are relevant to the overall image aesthetics. For these reasons, Marchesotti *et al.* propose to automatically select a large number of useful attributes based on textual comments from raters [20] and model these attributes using generic features [12]. Despite good performance, many of the discovered textual attributes (*e.g.* so_cute, those_eyes, so_close, very_busy, nice_try) do not correspond to well defined visual characteristics which hinders their detectability and utility in applications. Perhaps the closest work to our approach is that of Lu *et al.*, who propose to learn several meaningful style attributes [3] in a CNN framework and use the hidden features to regularize aesthetics classification network training.

Content-Adaptive Models: To make use of image content information such as scene categories or choice of photographic subject, Luo *et al.* propose to segment regions and extract visual features based on the categorization of photo content [4]. Other work, such as [15,19], has also demonstrated that image content is useful for aesthetics analysis. However, it has been assumed that the category labels are provided both during training and testing. To our knowledge, there is only one paper [21] that attempts to jointly predict content semantics and aesthetics labels. In [21], Murray *et al.* propose to rank images w.r.t aesthetics in a three-way classification problem (high-, medium- and low-aesthetics quality). However, their work has some limitations because (1) deciding the thresholds between nearby classes is non-trivial, and (2) the final classification model outputs a hard label which is less useful than a continuous rating.

Our work is thus unique in presenting a unified framework that is trained by jointly incorporating the photo content, the meaningful attributes and the aesthetics rating in a single CNN model. We train a category-level classification layer on top of our aesthetics rating network to generate soft weights of category labels, which are used to combine scores predicted by multiple content-adaptive branches. This allows category-specific subnets to complement each other in rating image aesthetics with shared visual content information while efficiently re-using front-end feature computations. While our primary focus is

Table 1. Comparison of the properties of current image aesthetics datasets. In addition to score distribution and meaningful style attributes, AADB also tracks raters' identities across images which we exploit in training to improve aesthetic ranking models.

	AADB	AVA [15]	PN [5]	CUHKPQ [6,22]
Rater's ID	Y	N	N	N
All real photo	Y	N	Y	Y
Attribute label	Y	Y	N	N
Score dist	Y	Y	Y	N

Fig. 2. Our AADB dataset consists of a wide variety of photographic imagery of real scenes collected from Flickr. This differs from AVA which contains significant numbers of professional images that have been highly manipulated, overlayed with advertising text, etc.

on aesthetic rating prediction, we believe that the content and attribute predictions (as displayed on the right side of images in Fig. 1) represented in hidden layers of our architecture could also be surfaced for use in other applications such as automatic image enhancement and image retrieval.

3   Aesthetics and Attributes Database

To collect a large and varied set of photographic images, we download images from the Flickr website[1] which carry a Creative Commons license and manually curate the data set to remove non-photographic images (*e.g.* cartoons, drawings, paintings, ads images, adult-content images, etc.). We have five different workers then independently annotate each image with an overall aesthetic score and a fixed set of eleven meaningful attributes using Amazon Mechanical Turk (AMT)[2]. The AMT raters work on batches, each of which contains ten images. For each image, we average the ratings of five raters as the ground-truth aesthetic score. The number of images rated by a particular worker follows long tail distribution, as shown later in Fig. 6 in the experiment.

After consulting professional photographers, we selected eleven attributes that are closely related to image aesthetic judgements: *interesting_content*,

---

[1] www.flickr.com.

[2] www.mturk.com.

object_emphasis, *good_lighting*, *color_harmony*, *vivid_color*, *shallow_depth_of_field*, *motion_blur*, *rule_of_thirds*, *balancing_element*, *repetition*, and *symmetry*. These attributes span traditional photographic principals of color, lighting, focus and composition, and provide a natural vocabulary for use in applications, such as auto photo editing and image retrieval. The final AADB dataset contains 10,000 images in total, each of which have aesthetic quality ratings and attribute assignments provided by five different individual raters. Aggregating multiple raters allows us to assign a confidence score to each attribute, unlike, e.g., AVA where attributes are binary. Similar to previous rating datasets [15], we find that average ratings are well fit by a Gaussian distribution. For evaluation purposes, we randomly split the dataset into validation (500), testing (1,000) and training sets (the rest). The supplemental material provides additional details about dataset collection and statistics of the resulting data.

Table 1 provides a summary comparison of AADB to other related public databases for image aesthetics analysis. Except for our AADB and the existing AVA dataset, many existing datasets have two intrinsic problems (as discussed in [15]), (1) they do not provide full score distributions or style attribute annotation, and (2) images in these datasets are either biased or consist of examples which are particularly easy for binary aesthetics classification. Datasets such as CUHKPQ [6,22] only provide binary labels (low or high aesthetics) which cannot easily be used for rating prediction. A key difference between our dataset and AVA is that many images in AVA are heavily edited or synthetic (see Fig. 2) while AADB contains a much more balanced distribution of professional and consumer photos. More importantly, AVA does not provide any way to identify ratings provided by the same individual for multiple images. We report results of experiments, showing that rater identity on training data provides useful side information for training improved aesthetic predictors.

Consistency Analysis of the Annotation: One concern is that the annotations provided by five AMT workers for each image may not be reliable given the subjective nature of the task. Therefore, we conduct consistency analysis on the annotations. Since the same five workers annotate a batch of ten images, we study the consistency at batch level. We use Spearman's rank correlation ρ between pairs of workers to measure consistency within a batch and estimate p-values to evaluate statistical significance of the correlation relative to a null hypothesis of uncorrelated responses. We use the Benjamini-Hochberg procedure to control the false discovery rate (FDR) for multiple comparisons [23]. At an FDR level of 0.05, we find 98.45 % batches have significant agreement among raters. This shows that the annotations are reliable for scientific research. Further consistency analysis of the dataset can be found in the supplementary material.

4   Fusing Attributes and Content for Aesthetics Ranking

Inspired by [2,24], we start by fine-tuning AlexNet [13] using regression loss to predict aesthetic ratings. We then fine-tune a Siamese network [18] which takes image pairs as input and is trained with a joint Euclidean and ranking loss (Sect. 4.2). We then append attribute (Sect. 4.3) and content category classification layers (Sect. 4.4) and perform joint optimization.

4.1   Regression Network for Aesthetics Rating

The network used in our image aesthetics rating is fine-tuned from AlexNet [13] which is used for image classification. Since our initial model predicts a continuous aesthetic score other than category labels, we replace the softmax loss with the Euclidean loss given by $loss_{reg} = \frac{1}{2N} \sum_{i=1}^{N} \|\hat{y}_i - y_i\|_2^2$, where y_i is the average ground-truth rating for image-i, and $\hat{y}_i$ is the estimated score by the CNN model. Throughout our work, we re-scale all the ground-truth ratings to be in the range of $[0, 1]$ when preparing the data. Consistent with observations in [2], we find that fine-tuning the pre-trained AlexNet [13] model performs better than that training the network from scratch.

4.2   Pairwise Training and Sampling Strategies

A model trained solely to minimize the Euclidean loss may still make mistakes in the relative rankings of images that have similar average aesthetic scores. However, more accurate fine-grained ranking of image aesthetics is quite important in applications (e.g. in automating photo album management [25]). Therefore, based on the Siamese network [18], we adopt a pairwise ranking loss to explicitly exploit relative rankings of image pairs available in the AADB data (see Fig. 3(a)). The ranking loss is given by:

$$loss_{rank} = \frac{1}{2N} \sum_{i,j} \max\left(0, \alpha - \delta(y_i \geq y_j)(\hat{y}_i - \hat{y}_j)\right) \tag{1}$$

where $\delta(y_i \geq y_j) = \begin{cases} 1, & \text{if } y_i \geq y_j \\ -1, & \text{if } y_i < y_j \end{cases}$, and α is a specified margin parameter.

By adjusting this margin and the sampling of image pairs, we can avoid the

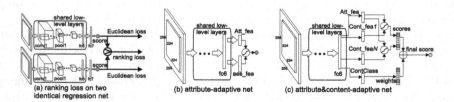

Fig. 3. Architectures for our different models. All models utilize the AlexNet front-end architecture which we augment by (a) replacing the top softmax layer with a regression net and adopting ranking loss in addition to Euclidean loss for training, (b) adding an attribute predictor branch which is then fused with the aesthetic branch to produce a final attribute-adapted rating and (c) incorporating image content scores that act as weights to gate the combination of predictions from multiple content-specific branches.

need to sample triplets as done in previous work on learning domain-specific similarity metrics [18,26,27]. Note that the regression alone focuses the capacity of the network on predicting the commonly occurring range of scores, while ranking penalizes mistakes for extreme scores more heavily.

In order to anchor the scores output by the ranker to the same scale as user ratings, we utilize a joint loss function that includes both ranking and regression:

$$loss_{reg+rank} = loss_{reg} + \omega_r loss_{rank}, \qquad (2)$$

where the parameter ω_r controls the relative importance of the ranking loss and is set based on validation data. The network structure is shown in Fig. 3(a).

Such a structure allows us to utilize different pair-sampling strategies to narrow the scope of learning and provide more consistent training. In our work, we investigate two strategies for selecting pairs of images used in computing the ranking loss. First, we can bias sampling towards pairs of images with a relatively large difference in their average aesthetic scores. For these pairs, the ground-truth rank order is likely to be stable (agreed upon by most raters). Second, as we have raters' identities across images, we can sample image pairs that have been scored by the same individual. While different raters may have different aesthetics tastes which erode differences in the average aesthetic score, we expect a given individual should have more consistent aesthetic judgements across multiple images. We show the empirical effectiveness of these sampling strategies in Sect. 5.

4.3   Attribute-Adaptive Model

Previous work on aesthetic prediction has investigated the use of attribute labels as input features for aesthetics classification (*e.g.* [7]). Rather than independently training attribute classifiers, we propose to include additional activation layers in our ranking network that are trained to encode informative attributes. We accomplish this by including an additional term in the loss function that encourages the appropriate attribute activations. In practice, annotating attributes for each training image is expensive and time consuming. This approach has the advantage that it can be used even when only a subset of training data comes with attribute annotations. Our approach is inspired by [3] which also integrates attribute classifiers, but differs in that the attribute-related layer shares the same front-end feature extraction with the aesthetic score predictor (see Fig. 3(b)). The attribute prediction task can thus be viewed as a source of side-information or "deep supervision" [28] that serves to regularize the weights learned during training even though it is not part of the test-time prediction, though could be enabled when needed.

We add an attribute prediction branch on top of the second fully-connected layer in the aesthetics-rating network described previously. The attribute predictions from this layer are concatenated with the base model to predict the final aesthetic score. When attribute annotations are available, we utilize a K-way softmax loss or Euclidean loss, denoted by $loss_{att}$, for the attribute activations and combine it with the rating and ranking losses

$$loss = loss_{reg} + \omega_r loss_{rank} + \omega_a loss_{att} \tag{3}$$

where ω_a controls relative importance of attribute fine-tuning. If we do not have enough data with attribute annotations, we can freeze the attribute layer and only fine-tune through the other half of the concatenation layer.

4.4   Content-Adaptive Model

The importance of particular photographic attributes depends strongly on image content [4]. For example, as demonstrated by Fig. 1, vivid color and rule of thirds are highly relevant in rating landscapes but not for closeup portraits. In [15,19], contents at the category level are assumed to be given in both training and testing stages, and category-specific models are then trained or fine-tuned. Here we propose to incorporate the category information into our model for joint optimization and prediction, so that the model can also work on those images with unknown category labels.

We fine-tune the top two layers of AlexNet [13] with softmax loss to train a content-specific branch to predict category labels[3] (as shown by ContClass layer in Fig. 3(c)). Rather than making a hard category selection, we use the softmax output as a weighting vector for combining the scores produced by the category specific branches, each of which is a concatenation of attribute feature and content-specific features (denoted by Att_fea and Cont_fea respectively in Fig. 3(c)). This allows for content categories to be non-exclusive (*e.g.* a photo of an individual in a nature scene can utilize attributes for either portrait and scenery photos). During training, When fine-tuning the whole net as in Fig. 3(c), we freeze the content-classification branch and fine-tune the rest network.

4.5   Implementation Details

We warp images to 256×256 and randomly crop out a 227×227 window to feed into the network. The initial learning rate is set at 0.0001 for all layers, and periodically annealed by 0.1. We set weight decay $1e-5$ and momentum 0.9. We use Caffe toolbox [29] extended with our ranking loss for training all the models.

To train attribute-adaptive layers, we use softmax loss on AVA dataset which only has binary labels for attributes, and the Euclidean loss on the AADB dataset which has finer-level attribute scores. We notice that, on the AVA dataset, our attribute-adaptive branch yields 59.11 % AP and 58.73 % mAP for attribute

---

[3] Even though category classification uses different features from those in aesthetics rating, we assume the low-level features can be shared across aesthetics and category levels.

prediction, which are comparable to the reported results of style-classification model fine-tuned from AlexNet [2]. When learning content-adaptive layers on the AVA dataset for classifying eight categories, we find the content branch yields 59 % content classification accuracy on the testing set. If we fine-tune the whole AlexNet, we obtain 62 % classification accuracy. Note that we are not pursuing the best classification performance on either attributes or categories. Rather, our aim is to train reasonable branches that perform well enough to help with image aesthetics rating.

5   Experimental Results

To validate our model for rating image aesthetics, we first compare against several baselines including the intermediate models presented in Sect. 4, then analyze the dependence of model performance on the model parameters and structure, and finally compare performance of our model with human annotation in rating image aesthetics.

5.1   Benchmark Datasets

AADB dataset contains 10,000 images in total, with detailed aesthetics and attribute ratings, and anonymized raters' identity for specific images. We split the dataset into training (8,500), validation (500) and testing (1,000) sets. Since our dataset does not include ground-truth image content tags, we use clustering to find semantic content groups prior to training content adaptive models. Specifically, we represent each image using the fc7 features, normalize the feature vector to be unit Euclidean length, and use unsupervised k-means for clustering. In our experimental comparison, we cluster training images into $k = 10$ content groups, and transform the distances between a testing image and the centroids into prediction weights using a softmax. The value of k was chosen using validation data (see Sect. 5.3). Figure 4 shows samples from four of these clusters, from which we observe consistencies within each cluster and distinctions across clusters.

AVA dataset contains approximately 250,000 images, each of which has about 200 aesthetic ratings ranging on a one-to-ten scale. For fair comparison, we follow the experimental practices and train/test split used in literature [2,3,15] which results in about 230,000 training and 20,000 test images. When fine-tuning AlexNet for binary aesthetics classification, we divide the training set into two categories (low- and high-aesthetic category), with a score threshold of 5 as used in [2,3,15]. We use the subset of images which contain style attributes and content tags for training and testing the attribute-adaptive and content-adaptive branches.

5.2   Performance Evaluation

To evaluate the aesthetic scores predicted by our model, we report the ranking correlation measured by Spearman's ρ between the estimated aesthetics scores and the ground-truth scores in the test set [30]. Let r_i indicate the rank of the ith item when we sort the list by scores $\{y_i\}$ and $\hat{r}_i$ indicate the rank when ordered by $\{\hat{y}_i\}$. We can compute the disagreement in the two rankings of a particular element i as $d_i = r_i - \hat{r}_i$. The Spearman's ρ rank correlation statistic is calculated as $\rho = 1 - \frac{6 \sum d_i^2}{N^3 - N}$, where N is the total number of images ranked. This correlation coefficient lies in the range of $[-1, 1]$, with larger values corresponding to higher correlation in the rankings. The ranking correlation is particularly useful since it is invariant to monotonic transformations of the aesthetic score predictions and hence avoids the need to precisely calibrate output scores against human ratings. For purposes of comparing to existing classification accuracy results reported on the AVA dataset, we simply threshold the estimated scores $[\hat{y}_i > \tau]$ to produce a binary prediction where the threshold τ is determined on the validation set.

5.3   Results

For comparison, we also train a model for binary aesthetics classification by fine-tuning AlexNet (AlexNet_FT_Conf). This has previously been shown to be a strong baseline for aesthetic classification [2]. We use the softmax confidence score corresponding of the high-aesthetics class as the predicted aesthetic rating. As described in Sect. 4, we consider variants of our architecture including the regression network alone (Reg), along with the addition of the pairwise ranking loss (Reg + Rank), attribute-constraint branches (Reg+Rank+Att) $and content-adaptive branches$ (Reg + Rank + Cont). We also evaluate different pair-sampling strategies including within- and cross-rater sampling.

Model Architecture and Loss Functions: Tables 2 and 3 list the performance on AADB and AVA datasets, respectively. From these tables, we notice several interesting observations. First, AlexNet_FT_Conf model yields good ranking results measured by ρ. This indicates that the confidence score in softmax

Fig. 4. Example images from four content clusters found in the training set. These clusters capture thematic categories of image content present in AADB without requiring additional manual labeling of training data.

Table 2. Performance comparison of different models on AADB dataset.

Methods	ρ
AlexNet_FT_Conf	0.5923
Reg	0.6239
Reg + Rank (cross-rater)	0.6308
Reg + Rank (within-rater)	0.6450
Reg + Rank (within- & cross-)	0.6515
Reg + Rank + Att	0.6656
Reg + Rank + Cont	0.6737
Reg+Rank+Att+Cont	**0.6782**

Table 3. Performance comparison of different models on AVA dataset.

Methods	ρ	ACC (%)
Murray et al. [15]	-	68.00
SPP [31]	-	72.85
AlexNet_FT_Conf	0.4807	71.52
DCNN [3]	-	73.25
RDCNN [3]	-	74.46
RDCNN_semantic [19]	-	75.42
DMA [2]	-	74.46
DMA_AlexNet_FT [2]	-	75.41
Reg	0.4995	72.04
Reg + Rank	0.5126	71.50
Reg + Att	0.5331	75.32
Reg + Rank + Att	0.5445	75.48
Reg + Rank + Cont	0.5412	73.37
Reg+Rank+Att+Cont	**0.5581**	**77.33**

can provide information about relative rankings. Second, the regression net outperforms the AlexNet_FT_Conf model, and ranking loss further improves the ranking performance on both datasets. This shows the effectiveness of our ranking loss which considers relative aesthetics ranking of image pairs in training the model. More specifically, we can see from Table 2 that, by sampling image pairs according to the the averaged ground-truth scores, i.e. cross-rater sampling only, Reg + Rank (cross-rater) achieves the ranking coefficient $\rho = 0.6308$; whereas if only sampling image pairs within each raters, we have $\rho = 0.6450$ by by Reg + Rank (within-rater). This demonstrates the effectiveness of sampling image pairs within the same raters, and validates our idea that the same individual has consistent aesthetics ratings. When using both strategies to sample image pairs, the performance is even better by Reg + Rank (within- & cross-), leading to $\rho = 0.6515$. This is possibly due to richer information contained in more training pairs. By comparing the results in Table 3 between "Reg" (0.4995) and "Reg+Rank" (0.5126), and between "Reg+Att" (0.5331) and "Reg+Rank+Att" (0.5445), we clearly observe that the ranking loss improves the ranking correlation. In this case, we can only exploit the cross-rater sampling strategy since rater's identities are not available in AVA for the stronger within-rater sampling approach. We note that for values of ρ near 0.5 computed over 20000 test images on AVA dataset, differences in rank correlation of 0.01 are highly statistically significant. These results clearly show that the ranking loss helps enforce overall ranking consistency.

To show that improved performance is due to the side information (e.g. attributes) other than a wider architecture, we first train an ensemble of eight rating networks (Reg) and average the results, leading to a rho = 0.5336 (c.f. Reg + Rank + Att which yields rho = 0.5445). Second, we try directly training

Table 4. Ranking performance ρ vs. rank loss weighting ω_r in Eq. 2.

ω_r	0.0	0.1	1	2
AADB	0.6382	0.6442	0.6515	0.6276
AVA	0.4995	0.5126	0.4988	0.4672

Table 5. Ranking performance (ρ) of "Reg + Rank" with different numbers of sampled image pairs on AADB dataset.

#ImgPairs	2 million	5 million
cross-rater	0.6346	0.6286
within-rater	0.6450	0.6448
within- & cross-rater	0.6487	0.6515

the model with a single Euclidean loss using a wider intermediate layer with eight times more parameters. In this case we observed severe overfitting. This suggests for now that the side-supervision is necessary to effectively train such an architecture.

Third, when comparing Reg + Rank with Reg + Rank + Att, and Reg + Rank with Reg + Rank + Cont, we can see that both attributes and content further improve ranking performance. While image content is not annotated on the AADB dataset, our content-adaptive model based on unsupervised K-means clustering still outperforms the model trained without content information. The performance benefit of adding attributes is substantially larger for AVA than AADB. We expect this is due to (1) differences in the definitions of attributes between the two datasets, and (2) the within-rater sampling for AADB, which already provides a significant boost making further improvement using attributes more difficult. The model trained with ranking loss, attribute-constraint and content-adaptive branches naturally performs the best among all models. It is worth noting that, although we focus on aesthetics ranking during training, we also achieve the state-of-the-art binary classification accuracy in AVA. This further validates our emphasis on relative ranking, showing that learning to rank photo aesthetics can naturally lead to good classification performance.

Model Hyperparameters: In training our content-adaptive model on the AADB dataset which lacks supervised content labels, the choice of cluster number is an important parameter. Figure 5 plots the ρ on validation data as a function of the number of clusters K for the Reg + Cont model (without ranking loss). We can see the finer clustering improves performance as each content specific model can adapt to a sub-category of images. However, because the total dataset is fixed, performance eventually drops as the amount of training data available for tuning each individual content-adaptive branch decreases. We thus fixed $K = 10$ for training our unified network on AADB.

The relative weightings of the loss terms (specified by ω_r in Eq. 2) is another important parameter. Table 4 shows the ranking correlation test performance on both datasets w.r.t. different choices of ω_r. We observe that larger ω_r is favored in AADB than that in AVA, possibly due to the contribution from the within-rater image pair sampling strategy. We set ω_a (in Eq. 3) to 0.1 for jointly fine-tuning attribute regression and aesthetic rating. For the rank loss, we used validation performance to set the margin α to 0.15 and 0.02 on AVA and AADB respectively.

Number of Sampled Image Pairs: Is it possible that better performance can be obtained through more sampled pairs instead of leveraging rater's information? To test this, we sample 2 and 5 million image pairs given the fixed training images on the AADB dataset, and report in Table 5 the performance of model "Reg + Rank" using different sampling strategies, *i.e.* within-rater only, cross-rater only and within-&cross-rater sampling. It should be noted the training image set remains the same, we just sample more pairs from them. We can see that adding more training pairs yields little differences in the final results, and even declines slightly when using higher cross-rater sampling rates. These results clearly emphasize the effectiveness of our proposed sampling strategy which (perhaps surprisingly) yields much bigger gains than simply increasing the number of training pairs by 2.5x.

Classification Benchmark Performance: Our model achieves state-of-the-art classification performance on the AVA dataset simply by thresholding the estimated score (Table 3). It is worth noting that our model uses only the whole warped down-sampled images for both training and testing, without using any high-resolution patches from original images. Considering the fact that the fine-grained information conveyed by high-resolution image patches is especially useful for image quality assessment and aesthetics analysis [2,3,14], it is quite promising to see our model performing so well. The best reported results [2] for models that use low resolution warped images for aesthetics classification are based on Spatial Pyramid Pooling Networks (SPP) [31] and achieves an accuracy of 72.85 %. Compared to SPP, our model achieves 77.33 %, a gain of 4.48 %, even though our model is not tuned for classification. Previous work [2,3,14] has shown that leveraging the high-resolution patches could lead to additional 5 % potential accuracy improvement. We expect a further accuracy boost would be possible by applying this strategy with our model.

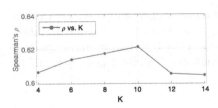 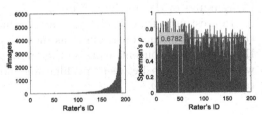

Fig. 5. Dependence of model performance by varying the number of content clusters. We select $K = 10$ clusters in our experiments on AADB.

Fig. 6. Panels show (left) the number of images labeled by each worker, and the performance of each individual rater w.r.t Spearman's ρ (Right). Red line shows our model's performance. (Color figure online)

Table 6. Human perf. on the AADB dataset.

#Images	#Workers	ρ
>0	190	0.6738
>100	65	0.7013
>200	42	0.7112
Our best	–	0.6782

Table 7. Cross dataset train/test evaluation.

Spearman's ρ	Test	
	AADB	AVA
Train AADB	0.6782	0.1566
AVA	0.3191	0.5154

5.4 Further Comparison with Human Rating Consistency

We have shown that our model achieves a high level of agreement with average aesthetic ratings and outperforms many existing models. The raters' identities and ratings for the images in our AADB dataset enable us to further analyze agreement between our model each individual as well as intra-rater consistency. While human raters produce rankings which are similar with high statistical significance, as evaluated in Sect. 3, there is variance in the numerical ratings between them.

To this end, we calculate ranking correlation ρ between each individual's ratings and the ground-truth average score. When comparing an individual to the ground-truth, we do not exclude that individual's rating from the ground-truth average for the sake of comparable evaluations across all raters. Figure 6 shows the number of images each rater has rated and their corresponding performance with respect to other raters. Interestingly, we find that the hard workers tend to provide more consistent ratings. In Table 6, we summarize the individuals' performance by choosing a subset raters based on the number of images they have rated. This clearly indicates that the different human raters annotate the images consistently, and when labeling more images, raters contribute more stable rankings of the aesthetic scores.

Interestingly, from Table 6, we can see that our model actually performs above the level of human consistency (as measured by ρ) averaged across all workers. However, when concentrating on the "power raters" who annotate more images, we still see a gap between machine and human level performance in terms of rank correlation ρ.

5.5 Cross-Dataset Evaluation

As discussed in Sect. 3, AVA contains professional images downloaded from a community based rating website; while our AADB contains a much more balanced distribution of consumer photos and professional photos rated by AMT workers, so has better generalizability to wide range of real-world photos.

To quantify the differences between these datasets, we evaluate whether models trained on one dataset perform well on the other. Table 7 provides a comparison of the cross-dataset performance. Interestingly, we find the models trained on either dataset have very limited "transferability". We conjecture there are two reasons. First, different groups of raters have different aesthetics tastes. This can be verified that, when looking at the DPChallenge website where images and ratings in the AVA dataset were taken from. DPChallenge provides a breakdown of scores which shows notable differences between the average scores among commenters, participants and non-participants. Second, the two datasets contain photos with different distributions of visual characteristics. For example, many AVA photos are professionally photographed or heavily edited; while AADB contains many daily photos from casual users. This observation motivates the need for further exploration into mechanisms for learning aesthetic scoring that is adapted to the tastes of specific user groups or photo collections [32].

6 Conclusion

We have proposed a CNN-based method that unifies photo style attributes and content information to rate image aesthetics. In training this architecture, we leverage individual aesthetic rankings which are provided by a novel dataset that includes aesthetic and attribute scores of multiple images by individual users. We have shown that our model is also effective on existing classification benchmarks for aesthetic judgement. Despite not using high-resolution image patches, the model achieves state-of-the-art classification performance on the AVA benchmark by simple thresholding. Comparison to individual raters suggests that our model performs as well as the "average" mechanical turk worker but still lags behind more consistent workers who label large batches of images. All these observations motivate us to study individual-oriented mechanism for aesthetics rating, as an example of subjective problem study.

References

1. Marchesotti, L., Murray, N., Perronnin, F.: Discovering beautiful attributes for aesthetic image analysis. Int. J. Comput. Vis. **2**, 1–21 (2014)
2. Lu, X., Lin, Z., Shen, X., Mech, R., Wang, J.Z.: Deep multi-patch aggregation network for image style, aesthetics, and quality estimation. In: ICCV (2015)
3. Lu, X., Lin, Z., Jin, H., Yang, J., Wang, J.Z.: Rapid: rating pictorial aesthetics using deep learning. In: Proceedings of the ACM International Conference on Multimedia, pp. 457–466. ACM (2014)
4. Luo, W., Wang, X., Tang, X.: Content-based photo quality assessment. In: 2011 IEEE International Conference on Computer Vision (ICCV), pp. 2206–2213. IEEE (2011)
5. Datta, R., Joshi, D., Li, J., Wang, J.Z.: Studying aesthetics in photographic images using a computational approach. In: Leonardis, A., Bischof, H., Pinz, A. (eds.) ECCV 2006. LNCS, vol. 3953, pp. 288–301. Springer, Heidelberg (2006). doi:10. 1007/11744078_23
6. Ke, Y., Tang, X., Jing, F.: The design of high-level features for photo quality assessment. In: 2006 IEEE Computer Society Conference on Computer Vision and Pattern Recognition, vol. 1, pp. 419–426. IEEE (2006)

7. Dhar, S., Ordonez, V., Berg, T.L.: High level describable attributes for predicting aesthetics and interestingness. In: 2011 IEEE Conference on Computer Vision and Pattern Recognition (CVPR), pp. 1657–1664. IEEE (2011)

8. Nishiyama, M., Okabe, T., Sato, I., Sato, Y.: Aesthetic quality classification of photographs based on color harmony. In: 2011 IEEE Conference on Computer Vision and Pattern Recognition (CVPR), pp. 33–40. IEEE (2011)

9. Lowe, D.G.: Distinctive image features from scale-invariant keypoints. Int. J. Comput. Vis. **60**(2), 91–110 (2004)

10. Perronnin, F., Sánchez, J., Mensink, T.: Improving the fisher kernel for large-scale image classification. In: Daniilidis, K., Maragos, P., Paragios, N. (eds.) ECCV 2010. LNCS, vol. 6314, pp. 143–156. Springer, Heidelberg (2010). doi:10.1007/978-3-642-15561-1_11

11. Perronnin, F., Dance, C.: Fisher kernels on visual vocabularies for image categorization. In: IEEE Conference on Computer Vision and Pattern Recognition, CVPR 2007, pp. 1–8. IEEE (2007)

12. Marchesotti, L., Perronnin, F., Larlus, D., Csurka, G.: Assessing the aesthetic quality of photographs using generic image descriptors. In: ICCV, pp. 1784–1791. IEEE (2011)

13. Krizhevsky, A., Sutskever, I., Hinton, G.E.: Imagenet classification with deep convolutional neural networks. In: Advances in Neural Information Processing Systems, pp. 1097–1105 (2012)

14. Kang, L., Ye, P., Li, Y., Doermann, D.: Convolutional neural networks for no-reference image quality assessment. In: 2014 IEEE Conference on Computer Vision and Pattern Recognition (CVPR), pp. 1733–1740. IEEE (2014)

15. Murray, N., Marchesotti, L., Perronnin, F.: Ava: a large-scale database for aesthetic visual analysis. In: 2012 IEEE Conference on Computer Vision and Pattern Recognition (CVPR), pp. 2408–2415. IEEE (2012)

16. Geng, B., Yang, L., Xu, C., Hua, X.S., Li, S.: The role of attractiveness in web image search. In: Proceedings of the 19th ACM International Conference on Multimedia, pp. 63–72. ACM (2011)

17. San Pedro, J., Yeh, T., Oliver, N.: Leveraging user comments for aesthetic aware image search reranking. In: Proceedings of the 21st International Conference on World Wide Web, pp. 439–448. ACM (2012)

18. Chopra, S., Hadsell, R., LeCun, Y.: Learning a similarity metric discriminatively, with application to face verification. In: IEEE Computer Society Conference on Computer Vision and Pattern Recognition, CVPR 2005, vol. 1, pp. 539–546. IEEE (2005)

19. Lu, X., Lin, Z., Jin, H., Yang, J., Wang, J.: Rating pictorial aesthetics using deep learning. IEEE Trans. Multimedia **17**(11), 1 (2015)

20. Marchesotti, L., Perronnin, F., Meylan, F.: Learning beautiful (and ugly) attributes. In: BMVC (2013)

21. Murray, N., Marchesotti, L., Perronnin, F., Meylan, F.: Learning to rank images using semantic and aesthetic labels. In: BMVC, pp. 1–10 (2012)

22. Luo, Y., Tang, X.: Photo and video quality evaluation: focusing on the subject. In: Forsyth, D., Torr, P., Zisserman, A. (eds.) ECCV 2008. LNCS, vol. 5304, pp. 386–399. Springer, Heidelberg (2008). doi:10.1007/978-3-540-88690-7_29

23. Benjamini, Y., Yekutieli, D.: The control of the false discovery rate in multiple testing under dependency. Ann. Stat. **29**, 1165–1188 (2001)

24. Simonyan, K., Zisserman, A.: Very deep convolutional networks for large-scale image recognition (2014). arXiv preprint arXiv:1409.1556

25. Cui, J., Wen, F., Xiao, R., Tian, Y., Tang, X.: Easyalbum: an interactive photo annotation system based on face clustering and re-ranking. In: Proceedings of the SIGCHI Conference on Human Factors in Computing Systems, pp. 367–376. ACM (2007)

26. Wang, J., Song, Y., Leung, T., Rosenberg, C., Wang, J., Philbin, J., Chen, B., Wu, Y.: Learning fine-grained image similarity with deep ranking. In: 2014 IEEE Conference on Computer Vision and Pattern Recognition (CVPR), pp. 1386–1393. IEEE (2014)

27. Schroff, F., Kalenichenko, D., Philbin, J.: Facenet: a unified embedding for face recognition and clustering. In: CVPR, pp. 815–823 (2015)

28. Lee, C., Xie, S., Gallagher, P.W., Zhang, Z., Tu, Z.: Deeply-supervised nets. In: AISTATS (2015)

29. Jia, Y., Shelhamer, E., Donahue, J., Karayev, S., Long, J., Girshick, R., Guadarrama, S., Darrell, T.: Caffe: convolutional architecture for fast feature embedding (2014). arXiv preprint arXiv:1408.5093

30. Myers, J.L., Well, A., Lorch, R.F.: Research Design and Statistical Analysis. Routledge, New York (2010)

31. He, K., Zhang, X., Ren, S., Sun, J.: Spatial pyramid pooling in deep convolutional networks for visual recognition. In: Fleet, D., Pajdla, T., Schiele, B., Tuytelaars, T. (eds.) ECCV 2014, Part III. LNCS, vol. 8691, pp. 346–361. Springer, Heidelberg (2014). doi:10.1007/978-3-319-10578-9_23

32. Caicedo, J.C., Kapoor, A., Kang, S.B.: Collaborative personalization of image enhancement. In: 2011 IEEE Conference on Computer Vision and Pattern Recognition (CVPR), pp. 249–256. IEEE (2011)

SDF-2-SDF: Highly Accurate 3D Object Reconstruction

Miroslava Slavcheva[1,2]([⊠]), Wadim Kehl[1], Nassir Navab[1], and Slobodan Ilic[1,2]

[1] Technische Universität München, Munich, Germany
{mira.slavcheva,nassir.navab}@tum.de, {kehl,slobodan.ilic}@in.tum.de
[2] Siemens AG, Munich, Germany

Abstract. This paper addresses the problem of 3D object reconstruction using RGB-D sensors. Our main contribution is a novel implicit-to-implicit surface registration scheme between signed distance fields (SDFs), utilized both for the real-time frame-to-frame camera tracking and for the subsequent global optimization. SDF-2-SDF registration circumvents expensive correspondence search and allows for incorporation of multiple geometric constraints without any dependence on texture, yielding highly accurate 3D models. An extensive quantitative evaluation on real and synthetic data demonstrates improved tracking and higher fidelity reconstructions than a variety of state-of-the-art methods. We make our data publicly available, creating the first object reconstruction dataset to include ground-truth CAD models and RGB-D sequences from sensors of various quality.

Keywords: Object reconstruction · Signed distance field · RGB-D sensors

1 Introduction

The persistent progress in RGB-D sensor technology has prompted exceptional focus on 3D object reconstruction. A key research goal is recovering the geometry of a static target from a moving depth camera. This entails estimating the device motion and fusing the acquired range images into consistent 3D models. Depending on the particular task, methods differ in their speed, accuracy and generality. Most existing solutions are SLAM-like, thus their applications lie in the field of robotic navigation where precise reconstructions are of secondary importance. In contrast, the growing markets of 3D printing, reverse engineering, industrial design, and object inspection require rapid prototyping of high quality models, which is the aim of our system.

One of the most influential works capable of real-time reconstruction is KinectFusion [12,24]. It conveniently stores the recovered geometry in an incrementally built signed distance field (SDF). However, its frame-to-model camera tracking via iterative closest points (ICP [1,6]) limits it to objects with distinct

Electronic supplementary material The online version of this chapter (doi:10.1007/978-3-319-46448-0_41) contains supplementary material, which is available to authorized users.

© Springer International Publishing AG 2016
B. Leibe et al. (Eds.): ECCV 2016, Part I, LNCS 9905, pp. 680–696, 2016.
DOI: 10.1007/978-3-319-46448-0_41

Synthetic data

Industrial sensor

Kinect

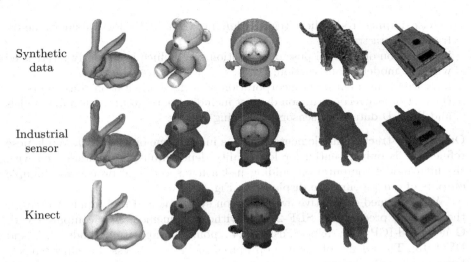

Fig. 1. SDF-2-SDF reconstructions of the proposed dataset objects. Colors vary due to difference between synthetic rendering and 3D-printed models, and camera radiometrics (Color figure online)

appearance and to uniform scanning trajectories. Other techniques use a point-to-implicit scheme [3,5] that avoids explicit correspondence search by directly aligning the point clouds of incoming depth frames with the growing SDF. Such registration has proven to be more robust than ICP, but becomes unreliable when range data is sparse or once the global model starts accumulating errors. Dense visual odometry (DVO) [15] is a SLAM approach that combines image intensities with depth information for warping between RGB-D frames in a Lucas-Kanade-like fashion [20]. Although it is susceptible to drift on poorly textured scenes, DVO achieves impressive accuracy in real time and has been incorporated as the tracking component of the object reconstruction pipeline of Kehl *et al.* [13]. The final step of the latter is a g^2o pose graph optimization [17] to ensure optimal alignment between all views. While it leads to improved model geometry, it might become prohibitively expensive for a larger amount of keyframes.

Addressing these limitations, we present SDF-2-SDF, a highly accurate 3D object reconstruction system. It comprises online frame-to-frame camera tracking, followed by swift multi-view pose optimization during the generation of the output reconstruction. These two stages can be used as completely standalone tools. Both of them employ the SDF-2-SDF registration method, which directly minimizes the difference between pairs of SDFs. Moreover, its formulation allows for integration of surface normal information for better alignment. In addition to handling larger motion and no dependence on texture, our frame-to-frame tracking strategy avoids drift caused by errors in the global model. Finally, our global refinement is faster than the pose graph optimization used in other pipelines [10,13,17]. Tackling the lack of a dataset combining ground-truth CAD models and RGB-D sequences with known camera trajectories, we have created a 3D-printed object dataset, which we make publicly available (*cf.* Sect. 5.1 for details). We highlight our contributions below:

- precise implicit-to-implicit registration between SDFs for online frame-to-frame camera tracking,
- introduction of a global pose optimization step, which is elegantly interleaved with the model reconstruction,
- improved convergence via incorporation of surface orientation constraints,
- the first object reconstruction dataset including both ground-truth 3D models and RGB-D data from sensors of varying quality.

Our parallel tracking implementation runs in real-time on the CPU. While pose refinement is only essential for low-quality depth input, it is interleaved with the final model computation, adding just a few seconds of processing. Sample outputs of our pipeline are displayed in Fig. 1.

We performed exhaustive evaluation on synthetic and real input. Moreover, the tracking precision of SDF-2-SDF without refinement was compared with Generalized-ICP [33], KinectFusion [24], point-to-implicit methods [3,5] and DVO [15]. The fidelity of the non-optimized model was assessed against Kinect-Fusion, while the refined reconstruction was compared to that of Kehl et al.'s pipeline [13] that includes posterior optimization.

2   Related Work

Fully automatic object reconstruction requires knowing the precise 6 degrees-of-freedom camera poses from which the RGB-D views were obtained. Arguably, the most widespread strategy for aligning depth data is ICP [1,6,31]. Although it is simple and generic, the method performs poorly in the presence of gross statistical outliers and large motion. Moreover, it is rather costly because it involves recomputing point correspondences in every iteration.

KinectFusion [12,24] employs an implicit surface representation (an SDF) for the continuously incremented reconstruction, but ray traces it into a point cloud on which a multi-scale point-to-plane ICP is used for frame-to-model registration. Thus, it suffers from the related drawbacks. Through a comparison to PCL's implementations of GICP [33] and KinFu [27], we show that SDF-2-SDF can handle cases where ICP fails.

Several authors [3,5,7,16,22,26,30,40] report superior registration using implicit surface representations. Notably, Bylow et al. [3] and Canelhas et al. [5] directly project the points of a tracked frame onto a global cumulative SDF and reduce the registration problem to solving an inexpensive 6×6 equation system in every iteration. Similar to [37] who leverage point-to-NDT (normal distribution transform) to NDT-to-NDT, we extend the point-to-implicit strategy to aligning pairs of SDFs. Comparisons indicate higher precision of SDF-2-SDF thanks to reduced effect of the noise inherent to explicit point coordinates.

A fast and powerful tracking system that works well on textured scenes is DVO [15,36]. It employs a photo-consistency constraint to find the best alignment between two RGB-D frames. Despite requiring a polychromatic support for the object of interest, visual odometry is used in the reconstruction pipelines of Dimashova et al. [10] and Kehl et al. [13]. These two works then execute a g^2o pose graph optimization [17], which undoubtedly yields higher quality meshes, but is rather costly. When used in dense scene reconstruction applications, graph-based optimization may last hours to days [44]. We propose improving the estimated trajectory via global implicit-to-implicit optimization. Selected keyframes are re-registered to a global SDF weighted average, which can be readily used as output reconstruction, making our refinement significantly faster.

Industrial scanning scenarios often do not permit augmenting the scene with textured components that aid tracking. Therefore we have designed an entirely photometry-independent system. Nevertheless, our energy formulation allows for combining a multitude of geometric constraints. Masuda [22] uses the difference between normal vectors to robustify SDF registration. Instead, we take the dot product as a more accurate measure of surface orientation similarity. While our approach works well without these additional constraints, they are straightforward to integrate into the SDF-2-SDF framework and lead to faster convergence.

A thorough evaluation of our system requires both ground-truth trajectories and object models. The TUM RGB-D benchmark [38] includes an ample set of sequences with associated poses, while the ICL-NUIM dataset [11] provides the synthetic model of one scene. However, both are intended for SLAM applications and feature large spaces rather than smaller-scale objects. Similarly, point cloud benchmarks [28,29] cannot be used directly by methods designed for range image registration. Existing RGB-D collections of household items, such as that of Washington University [18] and Berkeley's BigBIRD [34], either lack noiseless meshes or complete 6 DoF poses [23]. Therefore we 3D-printed a selection of objects with different geometry, size and colors, and contribute the first, to the best of our knowledge, object dataset with original CAD models and RGB-D data from various quality sensors, acquired from externally measured trajectories.

3   Geometric Preliminaries

This section describes the specifics of the SDF generation approach we used.

3.1   Mathematical Notation

An RGB-D sensor delivers a pair consisting of a depth map $D : \mathbb{N}^2 \rightarrow \mathbb{R}$ and a corresponding color image $I : \mathbb{N}^2 \rightarrow \mathbb{R}^3$. Given a calibrated device, the projection $\pi : \mathbf{x} = \pi(\mathbf{X})$ maps a 3D point $\mathbf{X} = (X, Y, Z)^\top \in \mathbb{R}^3$ onto the image location $\mathbf{x} = (x, y)^\top \in \mathbb{N}^2$. The inverse relation π^{-1} determines the 3D coordinates $\mathbf{X}$ from a pixel $\mathbf{x}$ with depth value $D(\mathbf{x})$ in a range image: $\mathbf{X} = \pi^{-1}(\mathbf{x}, D(\mathbf{x}))$.

The registration problem requires determining the rigid body transformation between the camera poses from which a pair of images were acquired. This 6 degree-of-freedom motion consists of a rotation $\mathbf{R} \in SO(3)$ and a translation $\mathbf{t} \in \mathbb{R}^3$. We use twist coordinates from the Lie algebra $se(3)$ of the special Euclidean group $SE(3)$, as they provide a minimal representation of the motion [21]:

$$\xi = (\mathbf{u} \quad \boldsymbol{\omega})^\top = (u_1, u_2, u_3, \omega_1, \omega_2, \omega_3)^\top , \tag{1}$$

where $\boldsymbol{\omega} \in \mathbb{R}^3$ corresponds to the rotational component and $\mathbf{u} \in \mathbb{R}^3$ stands for the translation. We denote the motion of any 3D point $\mathbf{X}$ in terms of ξ as $\mathbf{X}(\xi)$.

3.2   Signed Distance Fields

An SDF in 3D space is an implicit function $\phi \colon \Omega \subseteq \mathbb{R}^3 \to \mathbb{R}$ that associates each point $\mathbf{X} \in \mathbb{R}^3$ with the signed distance to its closest surface location [25]. Points within the object bounds have negative signed distance values, while points outside have positive values. Their interface is the object surface, which can be extracted as the zeroth level-set crossing via marching cubes or ray tracing. As implicit functions, SDFs have smoothing properties that make them superior to explicit 3D coordinates in many applications, as we will see in the comparison between point-to-implicit and implicit-to-implicit registration.

Registration is done by aligning projective truncated SDFs. First, the bounding volume is discretized into cubic voxels of predefined side length l.

A point $\mathbf{X}$ belongs to the voxel with index $vox \colon \mathbb{R}^3 \to \mathbb{N}^3$:

$$vox(\mathbf{X}) = int\left(1/l(\mathbf{X} - \mathbf{C}) - (1/2, 1/2, 1/2)^\top\right) ,\qquad(2)$$

where int rounds to integers, and $\mathbf{C}$ is the lower-left corner of the volume. All points within the same voxel are assigned the properties of its center

$$\mathbf{V}(\mathbf{X}) = l(vox(\mathbf{X}) + (1/2, 1/2, 1/2)^\top) + \mathbf{C} ,\qquad(3)$$

so we use $\mathbf{V}$ to denote the entire voxel. As a range image only contains measurements of surface points, the signed distance is the difference of sensor reading for the voxel center projection $\pi(\mathbf{V})$ and its depth $\mathbf{V}_Z$:

$$\phi_{true}(\mathbf{V}) = D(\pi(\mathbf{V})) - \mathbf{V}_Z \qquad(4)$$

$$\phi(\mathbf{V}) = \begin{cases} sgn(\phi_{true}(\mathbf{V})) & , \text{ if } |\phi_{true}(\mathbf{V})| \geq \delta \\ \phi_{true}(\mathbf{V})/\delta & , \text{ otherwise} \end{cases} \qquad(5)$$

$$\omega(\mathbf{V}) = \begin{cases} 1 & , \text{ if } \phi_{true}(\mathbf{V}) > -\eta \\ 0 & , \text{ otherwise} \end{cases} \qquad(6)$$

$$\zeta(\mathbf{V}) = I(\pi(\mathbf{V})) . \qquad(7)$$

The true signed distance value ϕ_{true} is usually scaled by a factor δ (related to the sensor error; we used 2 mm) and truncated into the interval $[-1, 1]$ (Eq. 5).

Binary weights ω are associated to the voxels in order to discard unseen areas from computations. All visible locations and a region of size η behind the surface (reflecting the expected object thickness) are assigned weight one (Eq. 6).

Finally, in order to be able to assign colors to the output mesh, we store a corresponding RGB triple for every voxel in an additional grid ζ of the same dimensions as ϕ (Eq. 7).

This approach of SDF generation from a single frame creates *beams* on the *interface* formed by the camera ray through the surface silhouette: voxels outside the object have signed distance 1 and neighbour with voxels behind the surface with value -1 (*cf.* Fig. 2). Beams cancel out when SDFs from multiple viewpoints are fused, and are easily omitted from calculations on projective SDFs, since

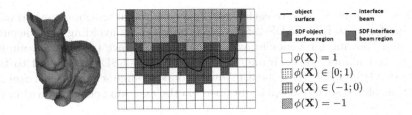

Fig. 2. Single-frame projective truncated SDF: marching cubes rendering, exhibiting viewpoint-dependent interface beams (left); cross-section along the x-y plane of the TSDF volume, identifying specialized regions (middle, right)

all voxels behind the surface have not been observed and have weight zero. However, beam voxels have faulty gradient values, but are easily excluded as well: a gradient computed via central differences will have at least one component with absolute value 1. We will often use SDF gradients, since the normalized 3D spatial gradient $\nabla_{\mathbf{X}}\phi$ equals the normals $\bar{\mathbf{n}}$ at surface locations [25].

An important Jacobian that will be needed in the numeric schemes is obtained when deriving point coordinates $\mathbf{X} \in \mathbb{R}^3$ with respect to a pose ξ. After applying the chain rule $\nabla_\xi \phi(\mathbf{X}(\xi)) = \nabla_{\mathbf{X}}\phi(\mathbf{X})\frac{\partial \mathbf{X}}{\partial \xi}$, the following holds:

$$\nabla_\xi \phi(\mathbf{X}) = \nabla_{\mathbf{X}}\phi(\mathbf{X})\left(\mathbf{I}_{3\times 3} \mid -(\mathbf{X}(\xi^{-1}))_\times\right) \in \mathbb{R}^{1\times 6} . \tag{8}$$

Once the camera poses have been determined, their SDFs can be fused into a common model Φ via the weighted averaging scheme of Curless and Levoy [9]:

$$\Phi_{t+1}(\mathbf{V}) = \frac{W_t(\mathbf{V})\Phi_t(\mathbf{V}) + \omega_{t+1}(\mathbf{V})\phi_{t+1}(\mathbf{V})}{W_t(\mathbf{V}) + \omega_{t+1}(\mathbf{V})} ,$$

$$W_{t+1}(\mathbf{V}) = W_t(\mathbf{V}) + \omega_{t+1}(\mathbf{V}) . \tag{9}$$

Each color grid channel is averaged similarly. The color weights at every voxel equal the product of ω and the cosine of the viewing ray angle, so that points whose normal is oriented towards the camera have stronger influence [3].

Note that color and normals are only valid at surface locations, defined as the ca. 1–5 voxel-wide narrow band of non-truncated voxels (*cf.* Fig. 2). This is an apt surface approximation permitting fast binary checks: $|\phi(\mathbf{V})| < 1$.

4   SDF-2-SDF Registration

Our system takes a stream of RGB-D data and pre-processes it by masking the object of interest as done in [13,32] and optionally de-noising the depth images via anisotropic diffusion [41] or bilateral filtering [39]. The frame bounding volume is automatically estimated by back-projection of all depth map pixels, as opposed to model-based methods that require manual volume selection. The volume is then slightly padded and used for the generation of both SDFs that are currently being aligned.

These steps are applied to each input image fed to our tracking method which performs frame-to-frame SDF-2-SDF registration, thus avoiding error accumulation and allowing for a moving volume of interest. Once tracking is complete, a predefined number of keyframes are globally SDF-2-SDF-registered to their weighted average. This refinement follows a coarse-to-fine scheme over voxel size. Finally, a colored surface mesh is obtained via the marching cubes algorithm [19].

4.1   Objective Function

We propose a simple scheme for implicit-to-implicit registration, whereby the direct difference of two SDFs is iteratively minimized. To achieve best alignment between frames, their per-voxel difference has to be minimal: truncated voxels have the same values, while the near-surface non-truncated voxels from both grids steer convergence towards surface overlap. Registration is facilitated by the fact that both SDFs encode the distance to the common surface. In the experimental evaluation we will demonstrate that this leads to more accurate results than when one frame is explicitly represented by its 3D cloud.

In the following ϕ_{ref} is the reference, while $\phi_{cur}(\xi)$ is the SDF of the current frame, whose pose ξ^* we are seeking. Since all voxels $\mathbf{V}$ are affected by the same transformation, their contributions can be straightforwardly added up. To ease notation, when summing over all voxels, we will omit the coordinates, e.g. we will write ϕ_{ref} instead of $\phi_{ref}(\mathbf{V})$ in sums. The main signed distance energy component is E_{geom}, to which surface normal constraints E_{norm} can be added, yielding the SDF-2-SDF objective function E_{SDF}:

$$E_{SDF}(\xi) = E_{geom}(\xi) + \alpha_{norm} E_{norm}(\xi) \, , \tag{10}$$

$$E_{geom}(\xi) = \frac{1}{2} \sum_{voxels} \left(\phi_{ref}\omega_{ref} - \phi_{cur}(\xi)\omega_{cur}(\xi) \right)^2 \, , \tag{11}$$

$$E_{norm}(\xi) = \sum_{surface\,voxels} \left(1 - \overline{\mathbf{n}}_{ref} \cdot (\overline{\mathbf{n}}_{cur}(\xi)) \right) . \tag{12}$$

The influence of E_{norm} is adjusted through its weight. By default it is not used in order to ensure optimal speed. For the tests with curvature constraints, we empirically found values in the range $(0, 1]$ to be reliable for α_{norm}.

4.2   Camera Tracking

Frame-to-model tracking can be detrimental in object reconstruction, since errors in pose estimation can introduce incorrect geometry when fused into the global model and adversely affect the subsequent tracking. Therefore we favor frame-to-frame camera tracking on single-frame SDFs.

We determine the relative transformation between two RGB-D frames by setting the pose of the first one to identity and incrementally updating the other one. The tracking minimization scheme for the geometry term is based on a first-order Taylor approximation around the current pose estimate ξ^k (Eqs. 13–15).

Like several related approaches, it leads to an inexpensive 6×6 linear system (Eq. 16). Weighting terms have been omitted from formulas for clarity. In order to avoid numerical instability, we take a step of size β towards the optimal solution (Eq. 17). In each iteration ϕ_{cur} is generated from the current pose estimate. We terminate when the translational update falls below a threshold [38].

$$\mathbf{A} = \sum_{voxels} \nabla_\xi^\top \phi_{cur}\left(\xi^k\right) \nabla_\xi \phi_{cur}\left(\xi^k\right) \tag{13}$$

$$\mathbf{b} = \sum_{voxels} \left(\phi_{ref} - \phi_{cur}\left(\xi^k\right) + \nabla_\xi \phi_{cur}\left(\xi^k\right)\xi^k\right)\nabla_\xi^\top \phi_{cur}\left(\xi^k\right) \tag{14}$$

$$\frac{\mathrm{d}E_{geom}}{\mathrm{d}\xi} = \mathbf{A}\xi - \mathbf{b} \tag{15}$$

$$\xi^* = \mathbf{A}^{-1}\mathbf{b} \tag{16}$$

$$\xi^{k+1} = \xi^k + \beta\left(\xi^* - \xi^k\right) \tag{17}$$

As stated in the preliminary section, the normals of the SDF equal its spatial gradient. Therefore, the surface orientation term imposes curvature constraints, whose derivation is mathematically equivalent to a second-order Taylor approximation of E_{geom}. Thus the objective remains the same, but convergence is speeded up. We obtain the following formula for the derivative of E_{norm} with respect to each component j of the twist coordinates:

$$\frac{\mathrm{d}E_{norm}}{\mathrm{d}\xi_j} = \sum_{surface\ voxels} -\bar{\mathbf{n}}_{ref} \cdot \left(\left(\nabla_{\mathbf{x}}\bar{\mathbf{n}}_{cur}(\xi)\right)\left(\mathbf{I}_{3\times3} \mid -(\mathbf{V}(\xi^{-1}))_\times\right)\delta_j\right),$$
$$\tag{18}$$

where δ_j is a 6-element vector of zeros with j-th component 1.

4.3 Global Pose Optimization

After tracking, a predefined number of regularly spaced keyframes are taken for generation of the final reconstruction. The weighted averaging provides a convenient way to incorporate the information from all of their viewpoints into a global model. However, when using noisy data the estimated trajectory might have accumulated drift, so the keyframes' poses need to be refined to ensure optimal geometry. For this task we propose a frame-to-model scheme based on the SDF-2-SDF registration energy, in which each pose ξ_p is better aligned with the global weighted average model. In effect, the optimization is interleaved with the computation of the final reconstruction, and only takes less than half a minute. The linearization of the energy follows a gradient descent minimization:

$$\frac{\mathrm{d}E_{geom}}{\mathrm{d}\xi} = \sum_{voxels} \left(\phi_{cur}\left(\xi\right) - \phi_{avg}\right)\nabla_\xi \phi_{cur}(\xi), \tag{19}$$

$$\xi_p^{k+1} = \xi_p^k - \alpha\frac{\mathrm{d}E_{geom}(\xi_p^k)}{\mathrm{d}\xi}. \tag{20}$$

The pose of the first camera is used as a reference and is fixed to identity throughout the whole optimization. In each iteration, the pose updates of all others are determined relative to the global model, after which they are simultaneously applied. The weighted average is recomputed every couple of iterations (10 in our case), so that the objective does not change in the meantime. Furthermore, this is done in a coarse-to-fine scheme over the voxel size to ensure that larger pose deviations can also be recovered.

5   Experimental Evaluation

In the following we compare our method to state-of-the-art approaches on data acquired with different RGB-D sensors. In all scenarios we assume a single rigid object of interest. Since the two stages of our pipeline can be used stand-alone, we assess tracking and reconstruction separately. The presented results employ solely the geometric component of the objective function, unless stated otherwise.

5.1   Test Set-up and Dataset

In order to thoroughly assess our system, we selected a set of **5 CAD models** of objects exhibiting various richness of geometry and texture (shown in Fig. 1): uni-colored (*bunny*), colored in patches (*teddy, Kenny*), densely colored (*leopard, tank*); thin (*leopard*), very small (*Kenny*), very large (*teddy*), with spherical components (*teddy, Kenny*).[1] They were 3D printed in color with a *3D Systems ZPrinter 650*, which reproduces details of resolution 0.1 mm [43]. In this way we ensure that the textured *groundtruth models* are at our disposal for evaluation, and eliminate dependence on the precision of a stitching method or system calibration that existing datasets entail.

We acquired **3 levels of RGB-D data accuracy** for each of these models: noise-free synthetic rendering in *Blender* [2], industrial phase shift sensor of resolution 0.13 mm, and a Kinect v1. We followed **2 scanning modes: turntable and handheld** for synthetic and Kinect data. Each of the synthetically generated trajectories has radius 50 cm and includes 120 poses, the handheld one is a sine wave with frequency 5 and amplitude 15 cm. The *camera poses* for the Kinect are known through a markerboard placed below the object of interest. The industrial sensor takes 4 s to acquire an RGB-D pair, permitting us to only record turntable sequences. Due to its limited field of view, we could not place a sufficiently large markerboard, so we will only use it for evaluation of model accuracy. In all cases the object of interest is put on a textured support that ensures optimal conditions for visual odometry.

Summing up, we aimed to cover a wide range of object scanning scenarios with this evaluation setup. The used RGB-D sequences for every object, sensor and mode, together with the respective ground-truth CAD models and camera trajectories are available at http://campar.in.tum.de/personal/slavcheva/3d-printed-dataset/index.html.

---

[1] The *bunny* is from The Stanford Repository [35], all other models are freely available at http://archive3d.net/. Object sizes are listed in the supplementary material.

5.2   Trajectory Accuracy

SDF-2-SDF tracking was compared with the following:

- **ICP-based approaches:** PCL's [27] frame-to-frame generalized ICP [33] (*GICP*) and frame-to-model KinectFusion [24] (*KinFu*);
- **point-to-implicit methods:** frame-to-model [5] (*FM-pt-SDF*, available as a ROS package [4]) and our frame-to-frame modification (*FF-pt-SDF*);
- **visual odometry:** DVO [15] (available online [14]) only on the object (*DVO-object*) and on the object and its richly textured background (*DVO-full*).

We evaluate the **relative** pose error (RPE) [38] per frame transformation and take the root-mean-squared, average, minimum and maximum:

$$RPE_{i \to i+1} = (\mathbf{P_i}^{-1}\mathbf{P_{i+1}})^{-1}(\mathbf{Q_i}^{-1}\mathbf{Q_{i+1}}), \qquad (21)$$

where i is the frame number, $\{\mathbf{Q_{1...n}}\}$ is the groundtruth trajectory and $\{\mathbf{P_{1...n}}\}$ is the estimated one. It evaluates the difference between the groundtruth and estimated *transformations*, and equals identity when they are perfectly aligned.

In addition, we report the average, minimum and maximum angular error per transformation. All errors are also evaluated for the **absolute** poses. Note that while our relative metric is equal to the RGB-D benchmark RPE per frame, our absolute metric is, in general, more severe than its absolute trajectory error [38]. This is because the ATE targets SLAM and first finds the best alignment between trajectories, while we use the same initial reference pose for both trajectories, since this directly influences the way frames are fused into meshes. To economize on space, we plot only the average errors, which we found to be most conclusive, and refer the reader to the supplementary material for a full tabular overview.

Synthetic data. As a proof of concept, we run tests on synthetic data, the details of which can be found in the supplementary material. SDF-2-SDF clearly outperforms the other methods with an average relative drift below 0.4 mm and angular error below 0.06°. The average absolute pose error of 2 mm corresponds to the used voxel size and suggests that given good data, only the grid resolution limits our tracking accuracy. Notably, it performs equally well regardless of object geometry and yields a negligible error with respect to the trajectory size.

Kinect sequences. Figure 3 indicates that GICP and DVO using only the object perform worst, while DVO using the object and its background performs best. SDF-2-SDF outperforms the remaining methods and is even more precise than DVO-full on turntable *bunny*, *teddy*, *tank* and handheld *teddy*, despite using only geometric constraints on the object of interest. KinFu and the two pt-SDF strategies perform similar to each other. In most cases KinFu is more accurate than pt-SDF, while frame-to-frame is slightly better than the frame-to-model pt-SDF variant. A notable failure case for FM-pt-SDF was the turntable *teddy*, where symmetry on the back caused drift from the middle of the sequence onwards, which lead to unrepairable errors in the global model and consequently flawed tracking. Similarly, FM-pt-SDF performed poorly on the turntable *Kenny* due

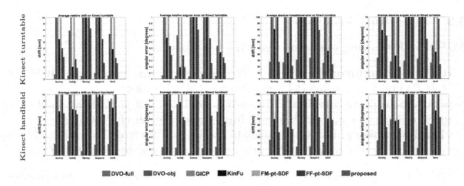

Fig. 3. Comparison of tracking errors on Kinect data

to its fine structures, while FF-pt-SDF did not suffer from error build-up and
was most accurate. These observations lead to the conclusion that a frame-to-
frame strategy is better for object reconstruction scenarios, where, as opposed
to SLAM, there is no repeated scanning of large areas that could aid tracking.
Thus, we also chose a frame-to-frame tracking mode for SDF-2-SDF, and achieve
higher precision than pt-SDF due to the denser formulation of our error function.

In the presence of severe Kinect-like noise, the sparse point clouds of objects
in the scene tend to become too corrupted and degrade registration accuracy. On
the contrary, SDF-2-SDF is more precise than cloud-based KinFu and pt-SDF
because the inherent smoothing properties of volumetric representations handle
noise better. Moreover, SDF-2-SDF relies on a denser set of correspondences:
on average, the used clouds consist of $8 \cdot 10^3$ data points, while the SDFs have
$386 \cdot 10^3$ voxels. Thus the problem is constrained more strongly, making our
proposed registration strategy more suitable for object reconstruction.

Contribution of surface orientation constraints. As E_{norm} is a second-order
energy term, it does not significantly influence accuracy, but rather convergence
speed. With $\alpha_{norm} = 0.1$ registration is 3–6 % more precise and takes 1.5–2.2
times less iterations. However, processing normals increases the time per iteration by 30–45 %. Thus E_{norm} is beneficial for objects of distinct geometry, where
normals can be reliably estimated, or when a low-noise sensor is used. For consistency and real-time speed, elsewhere in the paper we evaluate only on E_{geom}.

Convergence Analysis. We empirically analyzed the convergence basin of the
available registration methods. To mimic initial conditions where the global minimum is further away, we tested by skipping frames from the Kinect turntable
sequences. Figure 4(left) contains the averaged results. The error of SDF-2-SDF
grows at the slowest rate, indicating that thanks to its denser set of correspondences, it can determine an accurate pose from a much larger initial deviation
(up to ca. 15°), i.e. it can cope with smaller overlap. Notably, when taking every
third frame or fewer, SDF-2-SDF is considerably more precise than DVO-full.

 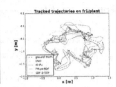 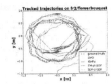 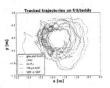

Fig. 4. Convergence analysis of registration methods with respect to frame distance (left). Estimated trajectories on the TUM RGB-D benchmark [38] (right)

Other Public Data. While our goal is object reconstruction rather than SLAM, we also evaluated the tracking component of our system on several sequences of the *3D Object Reconstruction* category of the TUM RGB-D benchmark [38]. They contain moderately cluttered scenes, unconstrained camera motion and occasionally missing depth data due to close proximity to the sensor. The whole images were used for DVO and GICP, while all other methods tracked solely using the bounding volume of the object of interest. Nevertheless, our SDF-2-SDF was the most precise method on *fr1/plant* and *fr3/teddy*, and was only slightly less accurate than FM-pt-SDF on *fr2/flowerbouquet*. The reason is that its leaves have no effective thickness, therefore the SDFs lose their power in discerning inside from outside and, depending on parameters, might oversmooth and become inferior to point cloud registration. This effect can be mitigated by a finer voxel size, at the cost of slower processing. Figure 4(right) summarizes the results, while numerical details can be found in the supplementary material.

5.3   3D Model Accuracy

As our ultimate goal is highly accurate 3D reconstruction, we assess the fidelity of output meshes against their CAD models. We report the cloud-to-model absolute distance mean and standard deviation, measured in *CloudCompare* [8].

First, the mesh obtained at the end of tracking is compared with that of *KinFu*, juxtaposing two real-time methods that do not employ posterior pose optimization (blue rows in Table 1).

Next, the mesh yielded after global refinement is compared to the method of Kehl *et al.* [13], which tracks by DVO [15], detects loop closure, optimizes the poses of 30 keyframes via g^{2}o [17], and integrates them via Zach *et al.* [42]'s TV-L^1 scheme. The code was kindly provided to us by the authors. To highlight the dependence of odometry on texture, we evaluated both on the object with its textured support (Kehl *et al.* full) and on the object only (Kehl *et al.* object).

The results in Table 1 indicate that SDF-2-SDF reconstructions are the best for high quality data, regardless whether refinement is carried out. In fact, for most objects the global optimization brings just a small improvement and is therefore not necessary on data with little noise. The mean errors of below 0.3 mm on synthetic and sub-millimeter on industrial are evidence for the high accuracy of SDF-2-SDF meshes. On the contrary, the posterior refinement leads to a considerable (up to 2.5 times) decrease in model error on Kinect data, yielding sub-millimeter

Table 1. *CloudCompare* evaluation of the absolute cloud-to-model reconstruction error.

object	method	error [mm] synth. circle		synth. wave		industr. turntab.		Kinect turntable		Kinect handheld	
		mean	std.dev.	mean	std.dev.	mean	std.dev.	mean	std.dev.	mean	std.dev.
bunny	KinFu	0.544	0.677	0.787	0.988	0.664	0.654	3.800	2.840	4.101	3.716
	ours (no refinement)	0.135	0.139	0.133	0.134	0.656	0.438	2.586	1.869	1.770	1.733
	Kehl *et al.* object	1.459	1.220	4.885	3.732	2.149	2.869	5.156	4.115	8.274	6.013
	Kehl *et al.* full	—	—	—	—	0.838	0.860	1.134	1.243	1.124	1.095
	ours (with refin.)	**0.130**	**0.137**	**0.131**	**0.133**	**0.541**	**0.436**	**0.953**	**0.843**	**0.996**	**0.853**
teddy	KinFu	0.370	0.275	0.418	0.285	0.998	0.807	1.271	1.045	2.355	1.447
	ours (no refinement)	0.161	0.179	0.146	0.142	0.930	0.588	1.078	0.890	1.589	1.537
	Kehl *et al.* object	0.358	0.303	0.257	0.193	1.028	0.892	2.306	1.862	2.287	1.826
	Kehl *et al.* full	—	—	—	—	4.828	4.215	1.221	0.858	3.066	2.380
	ours (with refin.)	**0.157**	**0.166**	**0.146**	**0.142**	**0.910**	**0.436**	**0.722**	**0.542**	**0.990**	**0.841**
Kenny	KinFu	0.418	0.311	0.440	0.359	1.650	1.451	1.511	1.387	2.874	2.727
	ours (no refinement)	0.154	0.151	0.147	0.154	0.363	0.391	1.295	1.311	2.415	2.051
	Kehl *et al.* object	0.948	0.736	1.931	1.965	1.816	1.710	3.181	3.238	*failed*	*failed*
	Kehl *et al.* full	—	—	—	—	2.553	2.644	1.263	0.850	2.282	1.381
	ours (with refin.)	**0.152**	**0.146**	**0.146**	**0.150**	**0.315**	**0.336**	**1.276**	**1.128**	2.358	1.960
leopard	KinFu	0.525	0.758	0.540	0.734	1.785	1.299	4.445	2.430	1.886	3.292
	ours (no refinement)	0.226	0.264	0.237	0.268	0.760	0.830	2.692	1.882	1.321	1.220
	Kehl *et al.* object	0.330	0.324	0.260	0.268	1.018	1.378	5.693	5.050	*failed*	*failed*
	Kehl *et al.* full	—	—	—	—	3.626	3.705	1.907	1.218	1.281	1.218
	ours (with refin.)	**0.225**	**0.263**	**0.233**	**0.266**	**0.652**	**0.614**	**1.308**	**1.154**	**1.263**	**1.111**
tank	KinFu	0.900	0.708	1.274	0.911	1.390	1.315	1.561	1.453	2.579	2.265
	ours (no refinement)	0.270	0.204	0.289	0.263	0.953	0.740	1.336	1.188	2.042	2.404
	Kehl *et al.* object	0.384	0.506	3.929	3.961	1.573	2.250	1.192	1.009	2.340	2.062
	Kehl *et al.* full	—	—	—	—	2.617	2.571	1.064	0.872	**0.946**	**0.806**
	ours (with refin.)	**0.267**	**0.199**	**0.285**	**0.263**	**0.466**	**0.416**	**0.911**	**0.745**	1.508	1.760

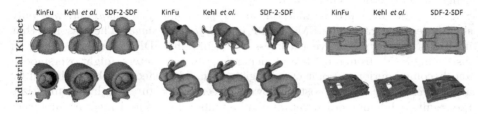

Fig. 5. Qualitative comparisons: Kinect data (top) and industrial sensor (bottom). Symmetry (*teddy*'s and *Kenny*'s backs) and thin structures (*tank*'s gun, *leopard*'s tail and legs) degrade the performance of cloud registration, causing misalignment artifacts (red ellipses), while SDF-2-SDF succeeds (see supplementary for magnified figures) (Color figure online)

precision for many of the objects. Moreover, the error is always below 2 mm, corresponding to the device uncertainty, once again indicating that our method is only limited by the sensor resolution and the chosen voxel size.

Further, the results on Kinect data demonstrate odometry's heavy dependence on texture. Kehl *et al.*'s pipeline even fails for smaller objects such as *leopard* and *Kenny* in the absence of textured surroundings. Not all tests with the industrial sensor followed the same trend, because the provided implementation required resizing the original 2040 × 1080 images to VGA resolution, leading to increased error when processing areas near the image border, where the textured table is located. The results of KinFu and SDF-2-SDF did not change for VGA and the original size, indicating lower sensitivity of volumetric approaches to such issues. Moreover, the speed of SDF-2-SDF remained unaffected, as it only depends on the voxel resolution, and not on image or point cloud size. Thus our system generalizes well not only for various object geometry, but also for any device. Figure 5 shows examples where our denser SDF-2-SDF succeeds, while other methods suffer, both on Kinect and on high-quality data.

Table 2. SDF-2-SDF runtime: average/fastest/slowest

tracking [milliseconds per frame]			refinement [total seconds]		
pre-process	reference SDF generation	minimization iterations	weighted averages	optimizing poses	marching cubes
1.7/ 1.6/ 1.8	2.6/ 1.7/ 3.8	45.3/ 41.4/ 54.9	1.9/ 0.4/ 6.8	6.1/ 0.3/ 20.2	0.6/ 0.2/ 1.3
total 49.6/ 44.7/ 60.5 ms = 20/ 22/ 17 FPS			total 8.6/ 0.9/ 28.3 s		

5.4 Implementation Details

We carried out our experiments on an 8-core Intel i7-4900MQ CPU at 2.80 GHz. As tracking at a voxel size finer than the sensor resolution is futile, we used 2 mm for all tests. SSE instructions aid efficient SDF generation, leaving the computation of each voxel's contribution to the 6×6 system as the bottleneck. To speed it up, we do not process voxels which would not have a significant influence, similar to a narrow-band technique: locations with zero weight in either volume and voxels with the same signed distance are disregarded. Thus runtime is not linear in object size, but depends on its geometry. The SDF of an object with bounding cube of side 50 cm requires only 61 MB, so memory is not an issue.

We execute the computations in parallel on the CPU, thereby achieving real-time performance between 17 and 22 FPS. Table 2 lists the time taken for each major step of our pipeline as average over all sequences, as well as the fastest (achieved on *synthetic Kenny*) and slowest (on *Kinect leopard*) runs.

On the other hand, the pose refinement has a simpler mathematical formulation, whereby only a 6-element vector is calculated in every gradient descent step. It requires at most 40 iterations on each voxel resolution level (4 mm, 2 mm, optionally 1 mm), taking up to 30 s to deliver the reconstruction, which is generated via marching cubes from the final field. In comparison, Kehl *et al.*'s pose graph optimization took 196.4 s on average (min 53 s, max 902 s) for the same amount of keyframes. Table 2 shows that our refinement is much faster.

6 Conclusions

We have developed a complete pipeline that starts with raw sensor data and delivers a highly precise 3D model without any user interaction. The underlying novel implicit-to-implicit registration method is dense and direct, whereby it avoids explicit correspondence search. The global refinement is an elegant and inexpensive way to jointly optimize the poses of several views and the reconstructed model. Experimental evaluation has shown that our reconstructions are of higher quality than those of related state-of-the-art systems.

Acknowledgements. We thank Siemens AG for funding the creation of the 3D printed dataset. We are also grateful to Patrick Wissmann for providing access to the phase shift sensor and to Tolga Birdal for his invaluable help in the image acquisition.

References

1. Besl, P.J., McKay, N.D.: A method for registration of 3-D shapes. IEEE Trans. Pattern Anal. Mach. Intell. (PAMI) **14**(2), 239–256 (1992)
2. Blender Project: Free and open 3D creation software. https://www.blender.org/. Accessed 9 Mar 2016
3. Bylow, E., Sturm, J., Kerl, C., Kahl, F., Cremers, D.: Real-time camera tracking and 3D reconstruction using signed distance functions. In: Robotics: Science and Systems Conference (RSS) (2013)
4. Canelhas, D.: sdf_tracker - ROS Wiki. http://wiki.ros.org/sdf_tracker. Accessed 9 Mar 2016
5. Canelhas, D.R., Stoyanov, T., Lilienthal, A.J.: SDF tracker: a parallel algorithm for on-line pose estimation and scene reconstruction from depth images. In: IEEE/RSJ International Conference on Intelligent Robots and Systems (IROS) (2013)
6. Chen, Y., Medioni, G.: Object modeling by registration of multiple range images. In: Proceedings of the 1991 IEEE International Conference on Robotics and Automation (ICRA), vol. 3, pp. 2724–2729 (1991)
7. Claes, P., Vandermeulen, D., Van Gool, L., Suetens, P.: Robust and accurate partial surface registration based on variational implicit surfaces for automatic 3D model building. In: Fifth International Conference on 3-D Digital Imaging and Modeling (3DIM) (2005)
8. CloudCompare: 3D point cloud and mesh processing software. http://www.daniel gm.net/cc/. Accessed 9 Mar 2016
9. Curless, B., Levoy, M.: A volumetric method for building complex models from range images. In: Proceedings of the 23rd Annual Conference on Computer Graphics and Interactive Techniques, SIGGRAPH 1996, pp. 303–312 (1996)
10. Dimashova, M., Lysenkov, I., Rabaud, V., Eruhimov, V.: Tabletop object scanning with an RGB-D sensor. In: Third Workshop on Semantic Perception, Mapping and Exploration (SPME) at the 2013 IEEE International Conference on Robotics and Automation (ICRA) (2013)
11. Handa, A., Whelan, T., McDonald, J., Davison, A.J.: A benchmark for RGB-D visual odometry, 3D reconstruction and SLAM. In: IEEE International Conference on Robotics and Automation (ICRA) (2014)
12. Izadi, S., Kim, D., Hilliges, O., Molyneaux, D., Newcombe, R., Kohli, P., Shotton, J., Hodges, S., Freeman, D., Davison, A., Fitzgibbon, A.: KinectFusion: real-time 3D reconstruction and interaction using a moving depth camera. In: ACM Symposium on User Interface Software and Technology (UIST) (2011)
13. Kehl, W., Navab, N., Ilic, S.: Coloured signed distance fields for full 3D object reconstruction. In: Proceedings of the British Machine Vision Conference (BMVC) (2014)
14. Kerl, C.: GitHub - tum-vision/dvo: dense visual odometry. https://github.com/tum-vision/dvo. Accessed 9 Mar 2016
15. Kerl, C., Sturm, J., Cremers, D.: Robust odometry estimation for RGB-D cameras. In: Proceedings of the IEEE International Conference on Robotics and Automation (ICRA) (2013)
16. Kubacki, D.B., Bui, H.Q., Babacan, S.D., Do, M.N.: Registration and integration of multiple depth images using signed distance function. In: SPIE Proceedings, vol. 8296 (2012)
17. Kümmerle, R., Grisetti, G., Strasdat, H., Konolige, K., Burgard, W.: g^{2}o: a general framework for graph optimization. In: Proceedings of the IEEE International Conference on Robotics and Automation (ICRA), pp. 3607–3613, May 2011

18. Lai, K., Bo, L., Ren, X., Fox, D.: A large-scale hierarchical multi-view RGB-D object dataset. In: IEEE International Conference on Robotics and Automation (ICRA) (2011)
19. Lorensen, W.E., Cline, H.E.: Marching cubes: a high resolution 3D surface construction algorithm. In: Proceedings of the 14th Annual Conference on Computer Graphics and Interactive Techniques, SIGGRAPH 1987, pp. 163–169 (1987)
20. Lucas, B., Kanade, T.: An iterative image registration technique with an application to stereo vision. In: Proceedings of the 7th International Joint Conference on Artificial Intelligence, IJCAI 1981, vol. 2, pp. 674–679 (1981)
21. Ma, Y., Soatto, S., Košecká, J., Sastry, S.S.: An Invitation to 3-D Vision: From Images to Geometric Models. Springer, New York (2003)
22. Masuda, T.: Registration and integration of multiple range images by matching signed distance fields for object shape modeling. Comput. Vis. Image Underst. (CVIU) 87(1–3), 51–65 (2002)
23. Narayan, K.S., Sha, J., Singh, A., Abbeel, P.: Range sensor and silhouette fusion for high-quality 3D scanning. In: IEEE International Conference on Robotics and Automation (ICRA) (2015)
24. Newcombe, R.A., Izadi, S., Hilliges, O., Molyneaux, D., Kim, D., Davison, A.J., Kohli, P., Shotton, J., Hodges, S., Fitzgibbon, A.: KinectFusion: real-time dense surface mapping and tracking. In: 10th International Symposium on Mixed and Augmented Reality (ISMAR) (2011)
25. Osher, S., Fedkiw, R.: Level Set Methods and Dynamic Implicit Surfaces. Applied Mathematical Science, vol. 153. Springer, New York (2003)
26. Paragios, N., Rousson, M., Ramesh, V.: Non-rigid registration using distance functions. Comput. Vis. Image Underst. 89(2–3), 142–165 (2003)
27. PCL: Point cloud library. http://pointclouds.org/. Accessed 9 Mar 2016
28. Pomerleau, F., Colas, F., Siegwart, R., Magnenat, S.: Comparing ICP variants on real-world data sets - open-source library and experimental protocol. Auton. Robots 34(3), 133–148 (2013)
29. Pomerleau, F., Liu, M., Colas, F., Siegwart, R.: Challenging data sets for point cloud registration algorithms. Int. J. Robot. Res. (IJRR) 31(14), 1705–1711 (2012)
30. Rouhani, M., Sappa, A.D.: The richer representation the better registration. IEEE Trans. Image Proc. 22(12), 5036–5049 (2013)
31. Rusinkiewicz, S., Levoy, M.: Efficient variants of the ICP algorithm. In: 3rd International Conference on 3D Digital Imaging and Modeling (3DIM) (2001)
32. Rusu, R.B., Holzbach, A., Blodow, N., Beetz, M.: Fast geometric point labeling using conditional random fields. In: IEEE/RSJ International Conference on Intelligent Robots and Systems (IROS) (2009)
33. Segal, A., Haehnel, D., Thrun, S.: Generalized-ICP. In: Proceesings of Robotics: Science and Systems (RSS) (2009)
34. Singh, A., Sha, J., Narayan, K., Achim, T., Abbeel, P.: BigBIRD: a large-scale 3D database of object instances. In: IEEE International Conference on Robotics and Automation (ICRA) (2014)
35. Stanford University: The Stanford 3D scanning repository. http://graphics. stanford.edu/data/3Dscanrep/. Accessed 9 Mar 2016
36. Steinbrücker, F., Sturm, J., Cremers, D.: Real-time visual odometry from dense RGB-D images. In: 2011 IEEE International Conference on Computer Vision Workshops (ICCV Workshops) (2011)
37. Stoyanov, T., Magnusson, M., Lilienthal, A.: Point set registration through minimization of the L_2 distance between 3D-NDT models. In: IEEE International Conference on Robotics and Automation (ICRA) (2012)

38. Sturm, J., Engelhard, N., Endres, F., Burgard, W., Cremers, D.: A benchmark for the evaluation of RGB-D SLAM systems. In: Proceedings of the International Conference on Intelligent Robot Systems (IROS) (2012)
39. Tomasi, C., Manduchi, R.: Bilateral filtering for Gray and color images. In: Sixth IEEE International Conference on Computer Vision (ICCV), pp. 839–846 (1998)
40. Tubic, D., Hébert, P., Laurendeau, D.: A volumetric approach for interactive 3D modeling. Comput. Vis. Image Underst. (CVIU) **92**(1), 56–77 (2003)
41. Vijayanagar, K.R., Loghman, M., Kim, J.: Real-time refinement of Kinect depth maps using multi-resolution anisotropic diffusion. Mobile Netw. Appl. **19**(3), 414–425 (2014)
42. Zach, C., Pock, T., Bischof, H.: A globally optimal algorithm for robust TV-L^1 range image integration. In: Proceedings of the 11th IEEE International Conference on Computer Vision (ICCV), pp. 1–8 (2007)
43. ZCorporation: ZPrinter 650. Hardware manual (2008)
44. Zhou, Q., Koltun, V.: Dense scene reconstruction with points of interest. ACM Trans. Graph. **32**(4), 112:1–112:8 (2013)

Knowledge Transfer for Scene-Specific Motion Prediction

Lamberto Ballan[1]([✉]), Francesco Castaldo[2], Alexandre Alahi[1],
Francesco Palmieri[2], and Silvio Savarese[1]

[1] Computer Science Department, Stanford University, Stanford, USA
lballan@cs.stanford.edu
[2] Department of Industrial and Information Engineering,
Seconda Università di Napoli, Caserta, Italy

Abstract. When given a single frame of the video, humans can not only interpret the content of the scene, but also they are able to forecast the near future. This ability is mostly driven by their rich prior knowledge about the visual world, both in terms of (*i*) the dynamics of moving agents, as well as (*ii*) the semantic of the scene. In this work we exploit the interplay between these two key elements to predict scene-specific motion patterns. First, we extract patch descriptors encoding the probability of moving to the adjacent patches, and the probability of being in that particular patch or changing behavior. Then, we introduce a Dynamic Bayesian Network which exploits this scene specific knowledge for trajectory prediction. Experimental results demonstrate that our method is able to accurately predict trajectories and transfer predictions to a novel scene characterized by similar elements.

1 Introduction

Humans glance at an image and grasp what objects and regions are present in the scene, where they are, and how they interact with each other. But they can do even more. Humans are not only able to infer what is happening at the present instant, but also predict and visualize what can happen next. This ability to forecast the near future is mostly driven by the rich prior knowledge about the visual world. Although many ingredients are involved in this process, we believe two are the main sources of prior knowledge: (*i*) the *static semantic of the scene* and (*ii*) the *dynamic of agents* moving in this scenario. This is supported also by experiments showing that the human brain combines motion cues with static form cues, in order to imply motion in our natural environment [18].

Computer vision has a rich literature on analysing human trajectories and scenes, but most of the previous work addresses these problems separately. Kitani *et al.* [16] have recently shown that by modeling the effect of the physical scene on the choice of human actions, it is possible to infer the future activity of people from visual data. Similarly, Walker *et al.* [37] forecast not only the possible motion in the scene but also predict visual appearances in the future. Although these works show very interesting results, they considered only a few selected

© Springer International Publishing AG 2016
B. Leibe et al. (Eds.): ECCV 2016, Part I, LNCS 9905, pp. 697–713, 2016.
DOI: 10.1007/978-3-319-46448-0_42

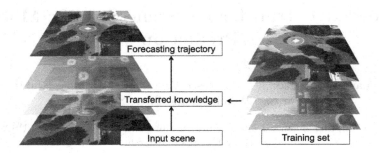

Fig. 1. Given the input scene shown in the bottom, we exploit the similarity between its semantic elements and those from a collection of training scenes, to enable activity forecasting (top image). This is achieved by transferring functional properties of a *navigation map* that is learned from the training set. Such properties include local dynamic properties of the target, as well as typical route choices (middle).

classes such as pedestrians and cars in a limited scenario. This paper aims to take a step toward the goal of a generalized visual prediction paradigm, focusing on human-space (agent-scene) interaction. Our main purpose is to take advantage of the interplay between the functional properties of the scene (instead of just semantic labels, such as grass, street, sidewalks) and the prior knowledge of moving agents, to forecast plausible paths from a new video scene.

We present a prediction model based on a Dynamic Bayesian Network formulation in which the target state is updated by using the statistics encoded in a *navigation map* of the scene. In training, the navigation map is formed as a collection of patch features, which encode the information about how previously observed agents of the same semantic class (*e.g.*, pedestrian or cyclist) have moved from that particular patch to adjacent patches. The class of the target is used to build different prediction models, since a pedestrian and a cyclist will probably navigate the same space in different manners. We consider statistics that capture different properties: (*i*) information about the direction and speed of the targets; (*ii*) a score measuring how frequently that patch has been crossed; (*iii*) identification of routing points, i.e. those patches in which the target is likely to turn or change behavior. We call all these statistics *functional properties* since they influence how an agent navigate the scene. In testing, scene semantics are used to transfer functional properties from the training set to the test image, in order to build a navigation map on a novel scene. In turn, our model exploits the information encoded in the navigation map to drive the prediction. Figure 1 illustrates our pipeline.

The contributions of this paper are three-fold: (1) Our approach is able to infer the most likely future motion by taking into account how the targets interact with the surroundings. In contrast to the previous work, our navigation map allows the model to predict rich navigation patterns by exploiting intermediate route points which lead to a more realistic path toward the final destination. (2) The information encoded in our navigation map can be transferred to a novel scene that has never been seen before. (3) We show extensive results on path forecasting and knowledge transfer on multiple classes and a large set of scenes.

2 Related Work

Activity recognition and trajectory analysis. In activity recognition [4,38, 46] the main aim is to discover and label the actions of the agents observed in the scene. Depending on the level of granularity, we could be interested in atomic actions such as pedestrians walking in the scene, or in activities involving a group of people [2,7,19,31,32]. Trajectory-based activity analysis is a traditional way of modeling human activities [24,38], which leverages motion statistics to recognize different activities. In this context, some recent work has shown that by directly modeling the impact of the environment, like trajectories of nearby pedestrians, can lead to better recognition models. To this end, social forces and contextual relationships have been effectively used to model human-human interactions in crowded environments [1,3,20,23,27,43]. Some other works show also that prior knowledge of goals yields better human-activity recognition and tracking [11,14,40]. From a complementary perspective, [34,39] take advantage of trajectories to infer the semantic of the elements of the scene, such as road and sidewalk.

Our work falls in this broad area, but we focus on the interplay between the functional properties of the scene and the dynamic of agents observed in the scene. Moreover we are interested in using this joint observation of the scene to predict the future motion of our targets.

Activity and trajectory forecasting. Some recent work [10,16,41] has put emphasis on *predicting* unobserved future actions or, more generally, path forecasting [15,30,37]. Activity prediction greatly differs from recognition as in this case we do not have complete observations of the targets. In their seminal work, Kitani *et al.* [16] have proposed an unified algorithm that learns the preferences of pedestrians navigating into the physical space. Their algorithm learns patterns such as a pedestrian prefers walking on the sidewalk avoiding obstacles (*e.g.*, cars). However, a limitation of this model is that it can only model simple trajectories where the target goes from the initial point to a final destination, without considering any local intermediate goal. More recently, Walker *et al.* [37] presented a data-driven approach which exploits a large collection of videos to predict and visualize the most likely future frames. The main novelty of their approach is that it also yields a visual "hallucination" of probable events on top of the scene. However, their framework is strongly focused on predicting the visual appearance of the target and the results are mostly related to the single car-road scenario. Similarly, [35,45] apply data-driven learning to leverage scene or video similarities to forecast the visual appearance of the near future frames. In our work we aim to make a step further by encoding agent-space interactions in our path prediction model. A key novelty of our approach is that the navigation map explicitly captures the functional interactions between the elements of the scene, and we show how this information is transferable to novel scenes.

Exploiting objects functionalities. The elements constituting our environments have a strong impact in what kind of actions we usually do in these places. Object functionalities, also known as affordances, describe the possible interactions between an agent and an object (*e.g.*, a chair is "sittable", an apple is "eatable", etc.). Recently there has been growing interest in recognizing object and scene affordances in computer vision and human-robot interaction [12,17,47]. A good example is given in [36], where action-scene correlations have been used for action prediction from static images. Functional objects are regarded as "dark matter" in [41], emanating "dark energy" that can both attract (*e.g.*, food-buses or vending machines) or repulse (*e.g.*, buildings) humans during their activities. This work is closely related to ours; however, they only study action-scene correlations, and the parameters learned on a specific scene are not transferable. In contrast, our model exploits the interconnection between the functional properties of the scene and the dynamic of agents moving in a particular context, to predict trajectories and transfer predictions to a novel scene.

Knowledge transfer. Several works have shown that when a large training set is available, it is possible to use a simple approach based on data-driven visual similarity for retrieving and transferring knowledge to new queries in both image [13,22,33] and video [5,42,45] domains. We build on this idea for transferring the knowledge encoded in our navigation map, relying on patch level similarities between our input scene and a training set of previously observed visual scenes.

3   Path Prediction

Figure 1 gives an overview of our approach. Given a scene and a moving target, we aim at generating one (or more) likely trajectory of the target by using some prior information, namely the initial state of the target itself (position and velocity) and our knowledge of the scene. The prediction is driven by what we call a *navigation map*, which is described in detail in the following subsection and shown in Fig. 2. The navigation map is a discrete representation of the space containing a rich set of information about navigation behaviors of targets that have been observed in training. By integrating these statistics and the dynamics of targets, our prediction model allows the target to change its speed (if needed) and maneuver in the scene. The class of the target is used to build different prediction models, since, for example, a pedestrian and a cyclist will navigate the same space in different manners. We achieve this goal in a probabilistic fashion, i.e. each predicted path is yielded by a underlying stochastic process, and has its own probability of being the "real" path. It is important to note that our model relies on the functional properties of the scene. This is different from [16] in that they directly model the effect of the scene semantic on the human actions. In contrast, in our model scene semantics are used only to transfer the navigation map features from a training set to a novel scene (see Sect. 4).

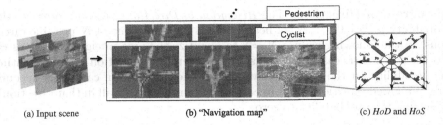

(a) Input scene   (b) "Navigation map"   (c) *HoD* and *HoS*

Fig. 2. We learn rich navigation patterns for each class of targets, and we leverage them to drive predictions. Given a scene (a), and a class label (*e.g.*, cyclist, pedestrian), we collect a navigation map which captures the interactions between the target and the scene. (b) Shows, from left to right, popularity and routing scores, and Histograms of Directions and Speeds. (c) Visualizes HoD and HoS for a particular patch. (Color figure online)

3.1 Navigation Map

Given an input scene, we overlay an uniform grid on it and build a map $\mathcal{M}$ which collects the navigation statistics. Given a class of targets, for each patch of the navigation map we consider four types of information, as described below.

Popularity Score. The score $\rho \in [0, 1]$ is related to the *popularity* of each patch of the scene. This score measures how many times a patch has been explored with respect to the others. The popularity score can be used to pick the more likely paths, among all the solutions generated by our prediction model. The criteria is to favor paths crossing the highest number of popular patches.

Figure 2b (left) shows a heatmap of possible locations where a cyclist can be seen. It is quite easy to visualize the most common bike paths on the street.

Routing Score. The score $\xi \in [0, 1]$ is related to the probability of that patch of being a *routing point*, that is a region in which the target is likely to turn or change its behavior, for instance near a turn or a wall (see the center image in Fig. 2b). Those points can be viewed as the intermediate local goals the target crosses before heading to the final destination, and any path can be approximated to different linear sub-paths between such local goals.

The routing scores are calculated by evaluating the curvature values of the training paths over the map, i.e. by discovering in which patches the target significantly changes his behavior. The curvature $\mathcal{K}$ of a parametric curve in Cartesian coordinates $c(t) = (x(t), y(t))$ is

$$\mathcal{K} = \frac{|\dot{x}\ddot{y} - \dot{y}\ddot{x}|}{(\dot{x}^2 + \dot{y}^2)^{3/2}}, \tag{1}$$

where dots refer to first and second order derivatives with respect to t. The routing values ξ are then obtained by averaging the curvature values of each training trajectory, sampled at each patch.

Histogram of Directions. The *Histogram of Directions (HoD)* represents the probability p_i, $i = 0, \ldots, N$, of heading from there into one of N possible directions. In the following we use $N = 8$ to quantize the area in eight directions Θ_i (north, north-east, east, etc.), plus another fictitious direction Θ_0 representing the possibility for the target to stop there. The distribution can easily account for not allowed directions (*e.g.*, in cases in which there is a wall in that direction), by setting that probability to zero.

Histograms of Speeds. We compute N *Histograms of Speeds (HoS)*, each of them representing the expected velocity magnitude of targets leaving that patch (the velocity direction is already given in the *HoS*). We represent the histograms by using N Gamma distributions $\Gamma(\mu_i, \sigma_i)$, because the data we are fitting are always positive and the support of the Gamma distribution is $(0, +\infty)$. Figure 2(c) shows an example of *HoD* (in *red*) and *HoS* (in *blue*).

3.2 Prediction Model

The target state variable is defined as $\mathbf{X}_k = (\mathbf{P}_k, \mathbf{V}_k)^T$, at kth discrete time step, with $\mathbf{P}_k = (X_k, Y_k)^T$ (Cartesian position) and $\mathbf{V}_k = (\Omega_k, \Theta_k)^T$ (velocity magnitude and angle). The target interacts with the navigation map $\mathcal{M}$, from which he extracts the navigation values (*HoD, HoS*, ρ and ξ) for the patch he is occupying at each time (Fig. 3). Starting from a given initial condition $\mathbf{X}_0$, our goal is to generate T_p future states $\mathbf{X}_1, .. \mathbf{X}_{T_p}$. A *path* Ψ_{T_p} is defined as a collection $\{\mathbf{X}_1, .., \mathbf{X}_{T_p}\}$ of target states.

The dynamic process describing the target motion is defined by the equations:

$$\mathbf{P}_{k+1} = \mathbf{P}_k + \begin{pmatrix} \Omega_k \cos \Theta_k \\ \Omega_k \sin \Theta_k \end{pmatrix} \Delta_k + \mathbf{w}_k, \tag{2}$$

$$\mathbf{V}_{k+1} = \Phi(\mathbf{P}_k, \mathbf{V}_k; \mathcal{M}), \tag{3}$$

where Δ_k is the sampling time (we assume $\Delta_k = 1$) and $\mathbf{w}_k \sim \mathcal{N}(\mathbf{0}, \sigma I_2)$ is a white-Gaussian process noise. Equation 2 is a nearly-constant velocity model [21], while Eq. 3 represents the function which calculates the next speed vector $\mathbf{V}_{k+1}$, assuming we know the map $\mathcal{M}$ and the current state $\mathbf{X}_k$. Although the nearly-constant velocity might seem a strong assumption (*e.g.*, the agent may have a large acceleration at an intersection), we highlight that Eq. 3 and the learned expected values in $\mathcal{M}$ allows our model to generate non-linear behaviors.

Instead of trying to write a closed-form solution for $\Phi(\cdot)$, we resort to handling the process in probabilistic terms by means of a Dynamic Bayesian Network (DBN), where the target is modeled with a Gaussian distribution over its state. The DBN is defined by the following conditional probability distributions:

$$p(\mathbf{P}_{k+1}|\mathbf{P}_k, \mathbf{V}_k) = \mathcal{N}(\begin{pmatrix} X_k + \Omega_k cos\Theta_k \\ Y_k + \Omega_k sin\Theta_k \end{pmatrix}, \sigma I_2), \tag{4}$$

$$p(\mathbf{V}_{k+1}|\mathbf{P}_k, \mathbf{V}_k; \mathcal{M}) = \begin{cases} p(\Omega_k|\mathbf{P}_k, \mathbf{V}_k; \mathcal{M}), \\ p(\Theta_k|\mathbf{P}_k, \mathbf{V}_k; \mathcal{M}), \end{cases} \tag{5}$$

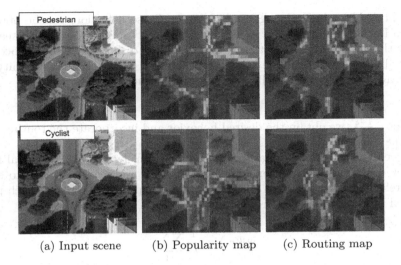

(a) Input scene   (b) Popularity map   (c) Routing map

Fig. 3. Qualitative examples for two classes. Column (a) visualizes the most common paths for both classes on the same input scene. Columns (b) and (c) show the corresponding popularity and routing heatmaps. The cyclist map is particularly informative; it shows that the routing points are located in proximity of final destinations (*e.g.*, the red area on top corresponds to bike racks) or areas where the agent may decide to turn. (Color figure online)

with

$$p(\Omega_k|\mathbf{P}_k,\mathbf{V}_k;\mathcal{M}) = \sum_{i=0}^{N} \Gamma(\mu_i,\sigma_i)p_{f_i}, \tag{6}$$

$$p(\Theta_k|\mathbf{P}_k,\mathbf{V}_k;\mathcal{M}) = p_{f_i}, \tag{7}$$

where $\Gamma(\mu_i,\sigma_i)$ is the Gamma distribution which defines the N speeds of the patch (we have chosen Gamma distribution as it is not defined for negative values and has a single peak). The probability p_{f_i} is written as

$$p_{f_i} = \frac{p_i e^{-\lambda d(\Theta_k,\Theta_i)}}{\sum_{j=0}^{N} p_j e^{-\lambda d(\Theta_k,\Theta_j)}}, \tag{8}$$

where $d(\cdot)$ is a distance metric (here we use L2 norm) and λ is a smoothing factor (the exponential is used to turn distances into probabilities). Equation 8 means that we consider the similarity between the direction of the current speed vector Θ_k and all the other possible directions Θ_i, weighted with the probability that the map assigns to that direction p_i.

We need to modify the discrete values p_{f_i} (which form a discrete distribution) described in Eq. 8 in order to incorporate the routing score $\xi \in [0,1]$. Ideally, we want our distribution to be more "randomic" (i.e. more uniform) when the routing score ξ is close to one, and more "deterministic" (i.e. always picking the most probable value) when ξ tends to zero. These behaviors can be obtained with a Beta distribution $B(x; \alpha, \beta) \propto x^{\alpha-1}(1-x)^{\beta-1}$, with $\alpha = \beta$. It is easy to verify that the Beta distribution is uniform when α tends to zero and becomes a distribution peaking at the most probable value when α tends to infinity. For this reason by writing the following transformation of random variable

$$\tilde{p}_{f_i} \propto p_{f_i}^{\alpha}(1 - p_{f_i})^{\alpha}, \tag{9}$$

with $\alpha = \frac{1-\xi}{\xi}$, we obtain the desired behavior and incorporate the routing score into the model.

Given the probabilistic nature of the algorithm, by running it several times we get different paths. As explained in Sect. 3.1, we need a criteria to select the preferred path. We do so by leveraging the popularity score ρ of each patch crossed by the target. The probability of the path Ψ_{T_g} is calculated as

$$p(\Psi_{T_g}) = \frac{1}{T_g}\sum_{i=1}^{T_g} \rho_i, \tag{10}$$

where ρ_i are the scores of the patches crossed by the target. In our experimental section we report results using different strategies to generate the preferred path.

4   Knowledge Transfer

The activities of an agent, such as a pedestrian or a cyclist, are dependent on the semantic of the scene and the surroundings in which that particular agent appears. The elements of the scene define a *semantic context*, and they might determine similar behaviours in scenes characterized by a similar context. So we design a simple retrieval-based approach which takes advantage of the similarity of the scene to transfer the functional properties (such as routing and popularity scores) that have been learned on the training set, to a new scene. This is inspired by the success of previous nonparametric approaches for scene parsing [22,33,44], but our goal is different since the local similarity of the scene is used to transfer the information required to build our navigation map. This idea is also justified by the fact that we do not have a large dataset of scenes with both pixel-level labeling and trajectory annotations. Therefore, alternative approaches which requires intensive learning are not applicable in this scenario (*e.g.*, end-to-end learning [9] or transferring mid-level representations [26]).

Scene parsing. The scene labeling is obtained using the scene parsing method presented in [44]. For each image we extract several local and global features (SIFT + LLC encoding, GIST and color histograms). The algorithm first retrieves a set of image neighbors from the training set, then superpixel classification and MRF inference are used to refine the labeling[1]. In order to evaluate how the quality of the scene labeling influences the performance of our model, we will present results using also the ground-truth image labeling.

---

[1] We built on the code provided in [44]. The parameters to be set are the number of k-NN images (9 in our experiments) and of superpixels used to classify a segment (we used 5). We used an intersection kernel and set the MRF pairwise term to 6.

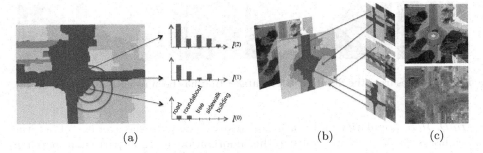

(a)   (b)   (c)

Fig. 4. (a) Computing local context descriptors (three-levels). (b) Patch matching between an input scene and the training set; similarity is computed over the semantic patches. (c) Shows the input (top) and the *hallucinated* scene (bottom) obtained by substituting each patch with its nearest-neighbors in the training set.

Semantic context descriptors. First, given a patch i, we define its *global context*. The global context descriptor is represented with a C-dimensional vector $\mathbf{g}_i$, where C is the number of labels in the ground-truth. This is obtained by computing the Euclidean distance between the centroid of the patch and the closest point in the full image labeled as c, for each $c \in C$ (*e.g.*, c can be the class *road*). The role of the global context descriptor is to account for the relative distance between each patch, and all the other semantic elements of the scene.

Then, we define the *local context* of i by looking at its contiguous local patches. We take inspiration from "shape-context representations" [6,29], and we define the local context $\mathbf{l}_i$ by encoding the spatial configuration of nearby patches at multiple levels (similarly to spatial pyramid). We use a multilevel scheme, as illustrated in Fig. 4(a). The space surrounding the current patch i is partitioned into concentric shells, considering patches at distance 0, 1 and 2, in the grid. For each patch, the local histograms are formed by counting the number of pixels labeled as c in that shell. Thus we have multiple C-dimensional histograms (three in our example), computed at different levels. These histograms are then averaged, providing the final $\mathbf{l}_i$. Note that this partitioning ignores absolute and relative orientations. We did some experiments considering also larger descriptors and a scheme with both sectors and bands, but this had a negative effect on performance. The role of the local context descriptor is to account for the local "arrangement" of the scene, and it aims to capture the local similarities which might influence the agent's behaviours toward the intermediate goals.

The final patch descriptor $\mathbf{p}_i$ is a weighted concatenation of the global and local semantic context: $\mathbf{p}_i = w\mathbf{g}_i + (1-w)\mathbf{l}_i$, where $\mathbf{g}_i$ and $\mathbf{l}_i$ are L1 normalized. The parameter w is used to weight the contribution of the two components. Section 5.3 shows how the performance is slightly influenced by this parameter.

Descriptor matching. For each patch descriptor $\mathbf{p}_i$ in the query image, we rank all patches from training images using L2 distance and keep the set $\mathcal{N}_i$ of K nearest-neighbors. Then, for each of the information collected for that patch

Fig. 5. Scenes from the Stanford-UAV dataset that has been recently presented in [28].

(*HoD*, *HoS*, popularity and routing scores) we compute the average among the neighbors in $\mathcal{N}_i$ and we transfer this information to that particular patch i. Intuitively, a good retrieval set contains semantic patches of similar scenes to the test image, in terms of both scene elements and spatial layouts. Figure 4(b) illustrates the matching procedure, while Fig. 4(c) shows a visualization of the "hallucinated" scene, obtained by substituting the original patches with their corresponding nearest-neighbors from the training set.

5   Experiments

5.1   Dataset and Evaluation Protocol

Previous works on visual prediction usually report results on a small number of videos with limited scene diversity (*e.g.*, a subset of the VIRAT dataset [25]). Moreover, these datasets have been mostly used for video-surveillance applications and are limited to human activities or human-human interactions. In this work we use the UCLA dataset [4], along with a new challenging dataset that has been recently collected on Stanford campus from a UAV [28].

UCLA-courtyard dataset. The UCLA dataset [4] consists of six annotated videos taken from two viewpoints of a courtyard at the UCLA campus. Different human activities can be spotted in these videos (people moving back and forth, entering and exiting the scene, ordering food at the food bus, talking with each other, etc.). Although the dataset has been originally collected for recognizing group activities, the semantic of the scene is quite rich. In order to allow the computation of our navigation map and the approach presented in [16], we have manually labelled the scene with 8 semantic classes: *road, sidewalk, pedestrian, car, building, grass, food bus, stairs, bench.*

Stanford-UAV dataset. This new dataset [28] provides many urban scenes (intersections, roundabouts, etc.) and several distinct classes of agents (pedestrians, cars, cyclists, skateboarders, baby carriages). The data have been collected from UAV. All videos are stabilized by registering each video frame onto a reference plane. In total we use 21 videos from 6 large physical areas (approx. $900 \, \mathrm{m}^2/\text{scene}$), corresponding to 15 different scenes. In our experiments we consider only two target classes, namely *pedestrian* and *cyclist*, because for other classes the number of trajectories available in the dataset is too scarce. We provide also the scene labeling of each scene for 10 semantic classes: *road, roundabout, sidewalk, grass, tree, bench, building, bike rack, parking lot, background.*

Fig. 6. Qualitative results on the UCLA dataset. The *blue* trajectory is ground-truth; *cyan* is the linear-prediction (LP) baseline; *yellow* is IOC [16]; *red* is our model (Color figure online).

Evaluation metric. We use the Modified Hausdorff Distance (MHD) [8] to measure the pixel distance between ground-truth trajectories and estimated paths (as in previous work [16,37]). In our evaluation, a path is assumed over when the target goes out of the scene, or when it reaches its final destination.

5.2 Path Forecasting

First, we test the performance of our framework on path forecasting on both UCLA-courtyard and Stanford-UAV dataset. We compare with Kitani *et al.* [16], which is based on inverse optimal control, and with a simple linear constant-velocity prediction baseline (similarly to [15,30]). The latter is the simplest version of our model when it does not leverage the information encoded in the navigation map. Additionally, on the Stanford-UAV dataset we also run a social-force model (similarly to [43]) and a linear prediction baseline with collision avoidance. Each method will generate a collection of likely predicted paths. In both datasets, we use 70 % of the data for training and the rest for testing; results are reported with 5-fold cross validation. In the rest of this section we often refer to the linear prediction baseline as LP, and to Kitani *et al.* [16] as IOC.

Qualitative results. Figure 6 shows some qualitative results. We observe that the trajectories predicted by our algorithm (in red) are usually very close to the ground truth paths (in blue). With respect to IOC [16] (yellow paths), we can observe that our algorithm is better in capturing the human preference in the navigation of the scene. This is particularly evident in the example shown in the middle, where the path predicted by our algorithm is significantly closer to the ground truth trajectory. This example highlights the main properties of our model. While IOC [16] aims to directly optimize the path leading to the final destination, our model tends to describe complex patterns in which the target stops to intermediate goals before heading to its final destination.

Quantitative results. We report results on path forecasting in Table 1. All the results in (a) are obtained providing both initial point and final destination, and refer to UCLA and Stanford-UAV dataset. Our model significantly outperforms the linear prediction baseline (LP), and also IOC [16]. Additionally, we report results on the Stanford-UAV dataset using a linear prediction baseline

Table 1. (a) Path forecasting results on both datasets; we report the mean MHD error of the closest path for a given final destination. (b) Shows the results of our method on the Stanford-UAV dataset, obtained using different path generation strategies.

	MHD error	
	UCLA-courtyard	*Stanford-UAV*
LP	$41.36_{\pm 0.98}$	$31.29_{\pm 1.25}$
LP$_{CA}$	-	$21.30_{\pm 0.80}$
IOC [16]	$14.47_{\pm 0.77}$	$14.02_{\pm 1.13}$
SFM [43]	-	$12.10_{\pm 0.60}$
Ours	$\mathbf{10.32}_{\pm 0.51}$	$\mathbf{8.44}_{\pm 0.72}$

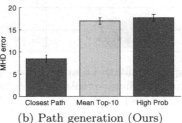

(a) Path forecasting   (b) Path generation (Ours)

with collision avoidance (LP$_{CA}$), and the social force model [43] (referred as to SFM) which models both human-space and human-human interactions. These results confirm the effectiveness of our approach even when it is compared to other methods which take advantage of the interactions between agents.

In Table 1(b) we show some results in which we investigate different path generation strategies. In other words, this is the strategy we use in our model to predict the final path among the most likely ones (see Eq. 10). We obtained the best results when we privilege a path in which the final point is closest to the goal, but significant improvements can be obtained also if we peak the path with the highest popularity scores, or the mean of the top-10 most probable paths.

5.3   Knowledge Transfer

Here we evaluate the ability of our model to generalize and make predictions on novel scenes. This generalization property is very important since it is hard and expensive to collect large statistics of agents moving in different scenes.

Some preliminary experiments on knowledge transfer have been presented also in [16], but they limited their study to a few different scenes, while we conduct an extensive analysis on the Stanford-UAV dataset. By looking at the examples in Fig. 5, we see that many elements in the scene, such as roundabouts

(a) Original image   (b) K=5   (c) K=10   (d) K=50

Fig. 7. (a) Input scene. (b, c, d) Show the "hallucinated" scene computed using our patch matching approach. The images are formed by average patches obtained with an increasing number of neighbors K. We varied the parameter K in the interval $[1, 200]$.

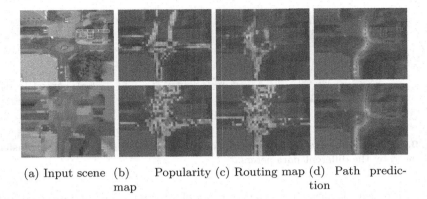

(a) Input scene (b)   Popularity (c) Routing map (d) Path predic-
                 map   tion

Fig. 8. The first row shows the results obtained in a standard path forecasting setting, while the second row shows results obtained after knowledge transfer. (a) Input scenes; (b,c) popularity and routing heatmaps; (c) demonstrates the predicted trajectory.

or grass areas between road intersections, may often appear in similar configurations. Those regularities across the scenes are detected by our semantic context descriptors, and transferred by our retrieval and patch matching procedure.

Qualitative results. Figure 7 shows a qualitative example of an "hallucinated" scene, obtained substituting each patch of the new scene with the most similar ones from the training set. Increasing the number of nearest-neighbors K, we can observe more coherent structures. The actual knowledge transfer is done by computing popularity score, routing score, HoD and HoF, for each transferred patch (as previously described in Sect. 4). In Fig. 8, we also show a qualitative example of the results obtained with or without knowledge transfer.

Quantitative results. Here we quantitatively evaluate the knowledge transfer capability of our framework. Therefore we ignore the training trajectories and functional properties encoded in the navigation map of the target scene, and we make predictions using data transferred from K nearest-neighbors retrieved from

Table 2. (a) Knowledge transfer results on the Stanford-UAV dataset (per-class and overall error). (b) How performance is influenced by the number of trajectories.

	MHD error		
	Pedestrian	*Cyclist*	Overall
LP	34.48	28.09	$31.29_{\pm 1.25}$
PM	22.75	20.58	$21.67_{\pm 1.19}$
IOC [16]	17.99	18.84	$18.42_{\pm 0.97}$
Ours	12.36	16.22	$\mathbf{14.29}_{\pm 0.84}$

(a) Path forecasting

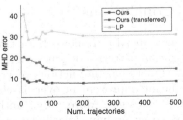

(b) Impact of training data

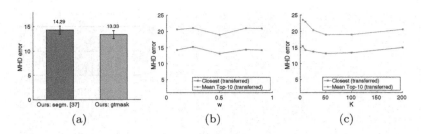

Fig. 9. This figure shows how the performance obtained with knowledge transfer is influenced by the different parameters.

the training set. Table 2 shows that our model after knowledge transfer performs well. As expected, the predictions obtained starting from the transferred maps are not good as the ones that can be obtained by training from the same scene (i.e. 14.29 ± 0.84 *vs* 8.44 ± 0.72). However, we still outperform significantly both the LP baseline and IOC [16]. We also run an additional baseline based on a simple patch matching scheme (PM), to test the efficacy of our context descriptors. Here each patch is represented with the same visual features used for image parsing, and then these features are used to find the nearest-neighbors. Finally, it is interesting to note that our performance is significantly better especially for the class *pedestrian*. We believe this is mainly due to the fact that, in the Stanford-UAV dataset, pedestrians show more non-linear behaviours (while a cyclist on the road has less route choices and so the gain *vs* the simple linear prediction model is less pronounced).

Impact of the parameters. The results reported in Table 2 has been obtained using 200 trajectories for training (the plot on the right shows how this number influences performance). We also evaluate what is the gain that can be achieved using ground-truth segmentation masks, instead of the scene parsing obtained with [44]. Interestingly enough, Fig. 9(a) shows that ground-truth segmentation gives a very slight improvement. Then the overall robustness of our framework is demonstrated by Fig. 9(b, c). The main parameters of our transfer procedure are w (i.e. the weight of the local and global context features) and K, the number of nearest-neighbors used in the retrieval stage. Our best results are obtained with $w = 0.5$ and $K = 50$.

6   Conclusions

We introduced a framework for trajectory prediction that is able to model rich navigation patterns for generic agents, by encoding prior knowledge about agent-scene functional interactions of previously observed targets. Our results show significant improvement over baselines on a large variety of scenes and different classes of target. More importantly, we show that predictions can be reliably obtained by applying knowledge transfer between scenes sharing similar semantic properties. Our future work will be focused on modeling simultaneously human-space and human-human interactions to allow predictions in crowded scenes.

Acknowledgments. We thank A. Robicquet for sharing the baseline model of [28, 43], and H.O. Song for helpful comments. This work is partially supported by Toyota (1186781-31-UDARO), ONR (1165419-10-TDAUZ), and MURI (1186514-1-TBCJE). L. Ballan is supported by an EU Marie Curie Fellowship (No. 623930).

References

1. Alahi, A., Ramanathan, V., Fei-Fei, L.: Socially-aware large-scale crowd forecasting. In: CVPR (2014)
2. Alahi, A., Boursier, Y., Jacques, L., Vandergheynst, P.: A sparsity constrained inverse problem to locate people in a network of cameras. In: DSP (2009)
3. Alahi, A., Goel, K., Ramanathan, V., Robicquet, A., Fei-Fei, L., Savarese, S.: Social LSTM: human trajectory prediction in crowded spaces. In: CVPR (2016)
4. Amer, M.R., Xie, D., Zhao, M., Todorovic, S., Zhu, S.-C.: Cost-sensitive top-down/bottom-up inference for multiscale activity recognition. In: Fitzgibbon, A., Lazebnik, S., Perona, P., Sato, Y., Schmid, C. (eds.) ECCV 2012, Part IV. LNCS, vol. 7575, pp. 187–200. Springer, Heidelberg (2012)
5. Ballan, L., Bertini, M., Serra, G., Del Bimbo, A.: A data-driven approach for tag refinement and localization in web videos. Comput. Vis. Image Underst. **140**, 58–67 (2015)
6. Belongie, S., Malik, J., Puzicha, J.: Shape matching and object recognition using shape contexts. IEEE Trans. Pattern Anal. Mach. Intell. **24**(4), 509–522 (2002)
7. Choi, W., Savarese, S.: A unified framework for multi-target tracking and collective activity recognition. In: Fitzgibbon, A., Lazebnik, S., Perona, P., Sato, Y., Schmid, C. (eds.) ECCV 2012, Part IV. LNCS, vol. 7575, pp. 215–230. Springer, Heidelberg (2012)
8. Dubuisson, M.P., Jain, A.K.: A modified Hausdorff distance for object matching. In: ICPR (1994)
9. Farabet, C., Couprie, C., Najman, L., LeCun, Y.: Learning hierarchical features for scene labeling. IEEE Trans. Pattern Anal. Mach. Intell. **35**(8), 1915–1929 (2013)
10. Fouhey, D.F., Zitnick, C.L.: Predicting object dynamics in scenes. In: CVPR (2014)
11. Gong, H., Sim, J., Likhachev, M., Shi, J.: Multi-hypothesis motion planning for visual object tracking. In: ICCV (2011)
12. Gupta, A., Kembhavi, A., Davis, L.: Observing human-object interactions: using spatial and functional compatibility for recognition. IEEE Trans. Pattern Anal. Mach. Intell. **31**(10), 1775–1789 (2009)
13. Hays, J., Efros, A.: Scene completion using millions of photographs. ACM Trans. Graph. **26**(3), 4 (2007)
14. Huang, C., Wu, B., Nevatia, R.: Robust object tracking by hierarchical association of detection responses. In: Forsyth, D., Torr, P., Zisserman, A. (eds.) ECCV 2008, Part II. LNCS, vol. 5303, pp. 788–801. Springer, Heidelberg (2008)
15. Karasev, V., Ayvaci, A., Heisele, B., Soatto, S.: Intent-aware long-term prediction of pedestrian motion. In: ICRA (2016)
16. Kitani, K.M., Ziebart, B.D., Bagnell, J.A., Hebert, M.: Activity forecasting. In: Fitzgibbon, A., Lazebnik, S., Perona, P., Sato, Y., Schmid, C. (eds.) ECCV 2012, Part IV. LNCS, vol. 7575, pp. 201–214. Springer, Heidelberg (2012)
17. Koppula, H.S., Saxena, A.: Anticipating human activities using object affordances for reactive robotic response. In: RSS (2013)
18. Krekelberg, B., Dannenberg, S., Hoffmann, K.P., Bremmer, F., Ross, J.: Neural correlates of implied motion. Nature **424**, 674–677 (2003)

712   L. Ballan et al.

19. Lan, T., Yang, W., Wang, Y., Mori, G.: Beyond actions: discriminative models for contextual group activities. In: NIPS (2010)
20. Leal-Taixe, L., Fenzi, M., Kuznetsova, A., Rosenhahn, B., Savarese, S.: Learning an image-based motion context for multiple people tracking. In: CVPR (2014)
21. Li, X.R., Jilkov, V.P.: Survey of maneuvering target tracking. Part I. Dynamic models. IEEE Trans. Aerosp. Electron. Syst. **39**(4), 1333–1364 (2003)
22. Liu, C., Yuen, J., Torralba, A.: Nonparametric scene parsing: label transfer via dense scene alignment. In: CVPR (2009)
23. Mehran, R., Oyama, A., Shah, M.: Abnormal crowd behavior detection using social force model. In: CVPR (2009)
24. Morris, B., Trivedi, M.: A survey of vision-based trajectory learning and analysis for surveillance. IEEE Trans. Circuits Syst. Video Technol. **18**, 1114–1127 (2008)
25. Oh, S., et al.: A large-scale benchmark dataset for event recognition in surveillance video. In: CVPR (2011)
26. Oquab, M., Bottou, L., Laptev, I., Sivic, J.: Learning and transferring mid-level image representations using convolutional neural networks. In: CVPR (2014)
27. Pellegrini, S., Ess, A., Schindler, K., van Gool, L.: You'll never walk alone: modeling social behavior for multi-target tracking. In: ICCV (2009)
28. Robicquet, A., Alahi, A., Sadeghian, A., Anenberg, B., Doherty, J., Wu, E., Savarese, S.: Forecasting social navigation in crowded complex scenes (2016). arXiv:1601.00998
29. Sahbi, H., Ballan, L., Serra, G., Del Bimbo, A.: Context-dependent logo matching and recognition. IEEE Trans. Image Process. **22**(3), 1018–1031 (2013)
30. Schneider, N., Gavrila, D.M.: Pedestrian path prediction with recursive Bayesian filters: a comparative study. In: Weickert, J., Hein, M., Schiele, B. (eds.) GCPR 2013. LNCS, vol. 8142, pp. 174–183. Springer, Heidelberg (2013)
31. Shu, T., Xie, D., Rothrock, B., Todorovic, S., Zhu, S.C.: Joint inference of groups, events and human roles in aerial videos. In: CVPR (2015)
32. Solera, F., Calderara, S., Cucchiara, R.: Learning to divide and conquer for online multi-target tracking. In: ICCV (2015)
33. Tighe, J., Lazebnik, S.: SuperParsing: scalable nonparametric image parsing with superpixels. In: Daniilidis, K., Maragos, P., Paragios, N. (eds.) ECCV 2010, Part V. LNCS, vol. 6315, pp. 352–365. Springer, Heidelberg (2010)
34. Turek, M.W., Hoogs, A., Collins, R.: Unsupervised learning of functional categories in video scenes. In: Daniilidis, K., Maragos, P., Paragios, N. (eds.) ECCV 2010, Part II. LNCS, vol. 6312, pp. 664–677. Springer, Heidelberg (2010)
35. Vondrick, C., Pirsiavash, H., Torralba, A.: Anticipating visual representations from unlabeled video. In: CVPR (2016)
36. Vu, T.-H., Olsson, C., Laptev, I., Oliva, A., Sivic, J.: Predicting actions from static scenes. In: Fleet, D., Pajdla, T., Schiele, B., Tuytelaars, T. (eds.) ECCV 2014, Part V. LNCS, vol. 8693, pp. 421–436. Springer, Heidelberg (2014)
37. Walker, J., Gupta, A., Hebert, M.: Patch to the future: unsupervised visual prediction. In: CVPR (2014)
38. Wang, X., Ma, K.T., Ng, G.W., Grimson, E.: Trajectory analysis and semantic region modeling using a nonparametric Bayesian model. In: CVPR (2008)
39. Wang, X., Tieu, K., Grimson, W.E.L.: Learning semantic scene models by trajectory analysis. In: Leonardis, A., Bischof, H., Pinz, A. (eds.) ECCV 2006. LNCS, vol. 3953, pp. 110–123. Springer, Heidelberg (2006)
40. Xiang, Y., Alahi, A., Savarese, S.: Learning to track: online multi-object tracking by decision making. In: ICCV (2015)

41. Xie, D., Todorovic, S., Zhu, S.C.: Inferring "dark matter" and "dark energy" from videos. In: ICCV (2013)
42. Xu, X., Hospedales, T., Gong, S.: Discovery of shared semantic spaces for multi-scene video query and summarization. IEEE Trans. Circuits Syst. Video Technol. (2016, in press)
43. Yamaguchi, K., Berg, A.C., Ortiz, L.E., Berg, T.L.: Who are you with and where are you going? In: CVPR (2011)
44. Yang, J., Price, B., Cohen, S., Yang, M.H.: Context driven scene parsing with attention to rare classes. In: CVPR (2014)
45. Yuen, J., Torralba, A.: A data-driven approach for event prediction. In: Daniilidis, K., Maragos, P., Paragios, N. (eds.) ECCV 2010, Part II. LNCS, vol. 6312, pp. 707–720. Springer, Heidelberg (2010)
46. Zen, G., Ricci, E.: Earth mover's prototypes: a convex learning approach for discovering activity patterns in dynamic scenes. In: CVPR (2011)
47. Zhu, Y., Fathi, A., Fei-Fei, L.: Reasoning about object affordances in a knowledge base representation. In: Fleet, D., Pajdla, T., Schiele, B., Tuytelaars, T. (eds.) ECCV 2014, Part II. LNCS, vol. 8690, pp. 408–424. Springer, Heidelberg (2014)

Weakly Supervised Localization Using Deep Feature Maps

Archith John Bency[1]([⊠]), Heesung Kwon[2], Hyungtae Lee[2,3], S. Karthikeyan[1], and B.S. Manjunath[1]

[1] University of California, Santa Barbara, CA, USA
{archith,karthikeyan,manj}@ece.ucsb.edu
[2] Army Research Laboratory, Adelphi, MD, USA
heesung.kwon.civ@mail.mil, htlee@umiacs.umd.edu
[3] Booz Allen Hamilton Inc., McLean, VA, USA

Abstract. Object localization is an important computer vision problem with a variety of applications. The lack of large scale object-level annotations and the relative abundance of image-level labels makes a compelling case for weak supervision in the object localization task. Deep Convolutional Neural Networks are a class of state-of-the-art methods for the related problem of object recognition. In this paper, we describe a novel object localization algorithm which uses classification networks trained on only image labels. This weakly supervised method leverages local spatial and semantic patterns captured in the convolutional layers of classification networks. We propose an efficient beam search based approach to detect and localize multiple objects in images. The proposed method significantly outperforms the state-of-the-art in standard object localization data-sets.

Keywords: Weakly supervised methods · Object localization · Deep convolutional networks

1 Introduction

Given an image, an object localization method aims to recognize and locate interesting objects within the image. The ability to localize objects in images and videos efficiently and accurately opens up a lot of applications like automated vehicular systems, searching online shopping catalogues, home and health-care automation among others. Objects can occur in images in varying conditions of occlusion, illumination, scale, pose and context. These variations make object detection a challenging problems in the field of computer vision.

The current state of the art in object detection includes methods which involve 'strong' supervision. In the context of object detection, strong supervision entails annotating localization and pose information about present objects of interest. Generating such rich annotations is a time-consuming process and is

---

© Springer International Publishing AG 2016 (outside the US)
B. Leibe et al. (Eds.): ECCV 2016, Part I, LNCS 9905, pp. 714–731, 2016.
DOI: 10.1007/978-3-319-46448-0_43

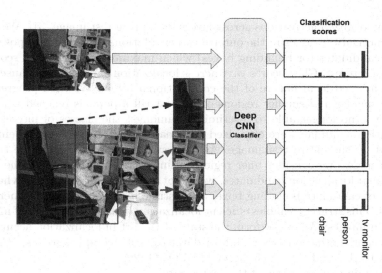

Fig. 1. When localizations centered around objects of interest are classified by Deep CNNs, the corresponding object classes are assigned high scores (Color figure online)

expensive to perform over large data-sets. Weak supervision lends itself to large-scale object detection for data-sets where only image-level labels are available. Effective localization under weak supervision enables extensions to new object classes and modalities without human-generated object bounding box annotations. Also, such methods enable generation of inexpensive training data for training object detectors with strong supervision.

Deep Convolutional Neural Networks (CNNs) [28,46] have created new benchmarks in the object recognition challenge [11]. CNNs for object recognition are trained using image-level labels to predict the presence of objects of interest in new test images. A common paradigm in analyzing CNNs has emerged where the convolutional layers are considered as data-driven feature extractors and the subsequent fully-connected layers constitute hyperplanes which delineate object categories in the learnt feature space. Non-linearities through Rectified Linear Units (ReLU) and sigmoidal transfer functions have helped to learn complex mapping functions which relate images to labels. The convolutional layers encode both semantic and spatial information extracted from training data. This information is represented by activations from the convolutional units in the network which are commonly termed as Feature Maps.

In this paper, we present a method that exploits correlation between semantic information present in Feature Maps and localization of an object of interest within an image. An example of such correlation can be seen in Fig. 1. Note that crudely localized image-patches with the objects of classes, 'chair', 'person' and 'tv monitor', generate high classification scores for the corresponding classes. This suggests that one can coarsely localize objects solely by image classification scores in this context.

CNN based classifiers are trained for the task of image recognition on large image classification data-sets [11,14,15]. The learnt convolutional filters compute spatially localized activations across layers for a given test image [31]. We examine the activation values in the outermost convolutional layer and propose localization candidates (or bounding boxes) which maximize classification scores for a class of interest. Class scores vary across localization candidates because of the aforementioned local nature of the convolutional filters. We then progressively explore smaller and smaller regions of interest till a point is reached where the classifier is no longer able to discriminate amongst the classes of interest. The localization candidates are organized in a search tree, the root node being represented by the entire test image. As we traverse from the root node towards the leaf nodes, we consider finer regions of interest. To approximate the search for optimal localization candidates, we adopt a beam search strategy where the number of candidate bounding boxes are restricted as we progress to finer localizations. This strategy enables efficient localization of multiple objects of multiple classes in images. We outperform the state-of-the-art in localization accuracy by a significant margin on two standard data-sets with complex scenes, PASCAL VOC 2012 [15] and the much larger MS COCO [29].

The main contributions of this paper are:

- We present a method that tackles the problem of object localization for images in a weakly supervised setting using deep convolutional neural networks trained for the simpler task of image-level classification.
- We propose a method where the correlation between spatial and semantic information in the convolutional layers and localization of objects in images is used explicitly for the localization problem.

2   Related Work

The task of object detection is one of the fundamental problems in computer vision with wide applicability. Variability of object appearance in images makes object detection and localization a very challenging task and thus has attracted a large body of work. Surveys of the state-of-the-art are provided in [39,50].

A large selection of relevant work are trained in the strong supervision paradigm with detailed annotated ground truth in the form of bounding boxes [16,48], object masks [4,21,27] and 3D object appearance cues [20,44]. The requirement of rich annotations curb the application of these methods in data-sets and modalities where training data is limited to weaker forms of labeling. Weak supervision for object detection tries to work around this limitation by learning localization cues from large collection of data with in-expensive annotations.

Large data-sets like Imagenet [11] and MS COCO are available with image-level labels. There has been significant work in this direction for object localization and segmentation [3,7,12,17,23,38]. Apart from image-level labels, other kinds of weak supervision include using eye-tracking data [37,43].

Deep convolutional neural networks (CNN) have seen a surge of attention from the computer vision community in the recent years. New benchmarks have been created in diverse tasks such as image classification and recognition

[5, 28, 45, 46], object detection [19, 36, 42, 51, 53] and object segmentation [6, 30, 33] among others by methods building on deep convolutional network architectures. These networks perform tasks using feature representations learnt from training data instead of traditional hand-engineered features [10, 16, 32]. Typical algorithms of this paradigm perform inference over the last layer of the network. There have been recent works [9, 22, 24] which exploit semantic information encoded in convolutional feature map activations for semantic segmentation and object detection. A prerequisite for these CNN-based algorithms is strong supervision with systems focused on detection requiring location masks or object bounding boxes for training. [52] studies the presence of object detector characteristics in image-classification CNNs, but does not provide a computational method to carry out object detection.

Oquab et al. [35] has proposed a weakly supervised object localization system which learns from training samples with objects in composite scenes by explicitly searching over candidate object locations and scales during the training phase. While this method performs well on data-sets with complex scenes, the extent of localization is limited with respect to estimating one point in the test image. The extent of the object is not estimated and detecting multiple instances of the same object class is not considered. In our proposed approach, we estimate both the location and extent of objects and are capable of estimating multiple instances of objects in the test image. Also, we use pre-existing classification networks for localization where as [35] proposes training custom adaptation layers.

3 Weakly Supervised Object Localization

3.1 Overview of the Method

We aim to localize and recognize objects in images using CNNs trained for classification. There are two distinct phases. The first phase consists of learning image-level recognition from training image sets using existing Deep CNN architectures. We use the popular Alexnet [28] and VGG-16 [45] networks for our experiments. The next phase involves generating localization candidates in the form of bounding boxes for object classes of interest. These candidates are generated from a spatial grid corresponding to the final convolutional layer of the network and are organized in a search tree. We carry out a beam-search based exploration of these candidates with the image classifier scoring the candidates and reach at a set of final localization candidates for each class of interest.

3.2 Network Architecture and Training

The Alexnet network has five convolutional layers with associated rectification and pooling layers $C_1, C_2, \ldots, C_5$, along with three fully connected layers F_6, F_7, F_8 with $M_6 = \sigma(W_6 M_5 + B_6)$, $M_7 = \sigma(W_7 M_6 + B_7)$ and $M_8 = \gamma(W_8 M_7 + B_8)$. W_n, B_n are learn-able parameters for the n-th layer, M_n is the output of the n-th layer. $\sigma(\mathbf{X}) = \max(\mathbf{0}, \mathbf{X})$ is the rectification function and $\gamma(\mathbf{X}) = [e^{\mathbf{X}[i]}/\Sigma_j e^{\mathbf{X}[j]}]$

is the softmax function. Of particular interest to us is the output of the last convolutional layer C_5, M_5 which we will refer to subsequent sections.

We learn the network parameters through stochastic gradient descent and back-propagation of learning loss error [41] from the classification layer back through the fully connected and convolutional layers. Keeping in mind that objects of multiple classes can be present in the same training image, we use the cross entropy loss function to model error loss J between ground truth class probabilities $\{p_k\}$ and predicted class probabilities $\{\hat{p}_k\}$, where $k \in \{0, 1, ..., K - 1\}$ indexes the class labels.

$$J = -\frac{1}{K} \sum_{k=0}^{K-1} [p_k \log \hat{p}_k + (1 - p_k) \log(1 - \hat{p}_k)] \tag{1}$$

As specified in [34], we remove F_8 and add two additional fully connected adaptation layers F_a, F_b. Similar to the Alexnet network, the output of these layers are computed as $M_a = \sigma(W_a M_7 + B_a)$ and $M_b = \gamma(W_b M_a + B_b)$. In order to assess the effectiveness of the proposed method for localization, these additional layers are added to facilitate re-training of the network from the Imagenet data-set to the Pascal VOC or MS COCO object detection data-sets. We initialize network parameters to values trained on the Imagenet data-set and fine-tune them [26] to adapt onto a target data-set. This is achieved by setting the learning rate parameter for the last layer weights to a higher value relative to earlier layer weights. An illustration of the network architecture is presented in Fig. 2 of [34].

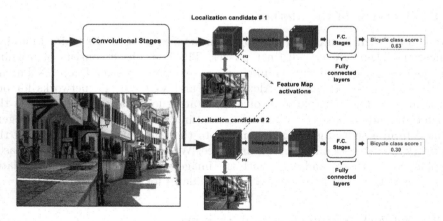

Fig. 2. An illustration of how two different localization candidates are compared in the localization process. Candidate #1 scores higher for the bicycle class than candidate #2. The first candidate is further iterated upon to achieve finer localization. The green box in the left image denotes ground-truth location of the bicycle object (Color figure online)

We train the augmented network on labeled samples from the target data-set. The trained network produces class scores at the final layer which are treated as probability estimates of the presence of a class in the test image.

The VGG-16 network, being similar to the Alexnet network, has thirteen convolutional layers $C_1, C_2, C_3, ...C_{13}$ with associated rectification and pooling layers, along with three fully connected layers F_6, F_7, F_8. Similar to the Alexnet network, the feature map M_{13} is of special interest to us. The increased number of layers and associated learnable parameters provides an improved image recognition performance when compared to the Alexnet network. The improvement however comes at the cost of increased GPU memory (442 MB vs 735 MB) and computations (6 ms vs 26 ms for classifying an image).

In addition to using image-labels to train the deep CNNs, we also use label co-occurrence information to improve classification. Some classes tend to occur together frequently. For example, people and motorbikes or people and chairs tend to share training samples. We treat the class scores from the classifier as unary scores and combine them with the likelihood of co-existence of multiple objects of different classes in the same object. We model the co-existence likelihood by building a co-occurrence matrix for class labels from the training data-set. For the class b_i,

$$s_{comb}(b_i) = s_{unary}(b_i) + \alpha \sum_{i \neq j} s_{pair}(b_i|b_j) \tag{2}$$

$$s_{pair}(b_i|b_j) = p_{pair}(b_i|b_j)s_{unary}(b_j) \tag{3}$$

$$p_{pair}(b_i|b_j) = \frac{|b_i \cap b_j|}{|b_j|} \tag{4}$$

where s_{unary} is the initial classification score for the test image, s_{pair} is the pairwise score, $|b_i \cap b_j|$ denotes the number of training samples containing the labels b_i and b_j and s_{comb} is the combined score which we use to re-score the classes for the test image. The parameter α denotes the importance given for pair-wise information in re-scoring. An optimal value is derived by testing over a randomly sampled validation sub-set from the training set.

3.3   Localization

In deep CNNs trained for classification, feature map activation values are the result of repeated localized convolutions, rectification (or other non-linear operations) and spatial pooling. Hence the structure of the network inherently provides a receptive field for each activation on the input image. The foot-print region becomes progressively coarser as we go deeper in the layers towards the fully connected layers. In a first attempt, we explore ways to exploit the spatial information encoded in the last convolutional layer for object localization.

Also, standard state-of-the-art object recognition data-sets (for e.g. Imagenet) typically have the object of interest represented in the middle of training samples. This gives rise to a bias in the classifier performance where more centered an object is in the input image, higher the corresponding class score becomes. An example is illustrated in Fig. 1. The correlation between the location of objects and class scores has been observed in other works [19, 34].

A naive approach to exploit the correlation would be to carry out a multi-scale sliding window sampling of sub-images from the test sample and spatially pool the classifier scores to generate a heat map of possible object locations for a given object class C. The number of sub-images required for effective localization can be in the order of thousands. Although powerful hardware like GPUs have brought image recognition CNNs into the domain of real-time methods, processing a large number of windows for every test sample is prohibitively expensive. A class of object detection methods [19] try to reduce the number of candidate windows by using object region proposal methods [1, 47]. Time taken to detect objects in each image using these methods still range in tens of seconds when using powerful GPUs.

For a more computationally efficient approach, we take advantage of the spatial and semantic information encoded in the final convolutional feature maps to guide the search process. We refer to the maps as M_5 for Alexnet and M_{13} for VGG-16 in the Sect. 3.2. For a general CNN network, the final convolutional layer is of size $L \times L \times T$ which means there are T feature maps of size $L \times L$. For the Alexnet and VGG-16 networks, the feature maps are of size $6 \times 6 \times 256$ and $7 \times 7 \times 512$ respectively.

Given a test image I, we forward propagate the layer responses for the image up-to the final convolutional layer C_{last} and generate the feature map activations M_{last}. We generate localization candidates which are sub-grids of the $L \times L$ grid. In concrete terms, these candidates are parametrised as boxes $b_i = [x_i, y_i, w_i, h_i]$ for $i = 1, 2, \ldots, B$ where x, y, w and h represent the coordinates of the upper-left corner, width and height and B is the total number of possible sub-grids. For each localization candidate, we sample the feature map activations contained within the corresponding boxes and interpolate them over the entire $L \times L$ grid. This is done independently over all T feature maps. For the box b_i,

$$\hat{M}_{last}^t(x, y) = f(M_{last}^t(x', y'))$$
$$\forall\, x_i \leq x' \leq x_i + w_i - 1,$$
$$y_i \leq y' \leq y_i + h_i - 1,$$
$$t \in 0, 1, \ldots, T - 1$$

where $f(.)$ is an interpolation function which resizes the activation subset of size $w_i \times h_i$ to the size $L \times L$. In the above equation, $x, y \in \{0, \ldots, L-1\}$ and bi-linear interpolation is used. After obtaining the reconstructed feature maps $\hat{M}_{last}$, we forward propagate the activations into the fully connected layers and obtain the class scores. An illustration of this step is presented in Fig. 2.

A limitation of the above approach is related to the fact that interpolating from a smaller subset to the larger grid will introduce interpolation artifacts into the reconstructed feature maps. In order to mitigate the effects of the artifacts, we limit the localization candidates to boxes with $L - 1 \leq w_i \leq L$ and $L - 1 \leq h_i \leq L$. From this limited corpus of localization candidates, we generate the

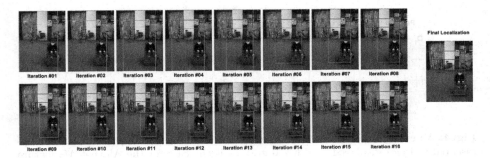

Fig. 3. A visual result of the proposed localization strategy on an image. The class scores for 'person' category are used to progressively localize the object of interest. Blue rectangles represent localization candidates considered in previous iterations and red rectangles represent current candidates (Color figure online)

corresponding $\hat{M}_{last}$ and consequently the object class scores, and choose the candidate with the highest class score. With the resultant localization candidate box b_r, we backproject onto the image space by cropping:

$$x_{crop} = \frac{x_r}{L}W, \ y_{crop} = \frac{y_r}{L}H$$
$$w_{crop} = \frac{w_r}{L}W, \ h_{crop} = \frac{h_r}{L}H \tag{5}$$

$$I_{crop}(x,y) = I(x + x_{crop}, y + y_{crop}) \ \forall \ 0 \leq x < w_{crop}$$
$$0 \leq y < h_{crop}$$

where x, y indicate pixel locations, and W and H are width and height of the test image respectively. We then repeat the above described localization process on I_{crop} till a predetermined number of iterations. A visual example of progress in the iterative process is shown in Fig. 3.

3.4 Search Strategy

The localization strategy can be visualized as traversing down a search-tree where each node corresponds to a localization candidate b_i. The root node of such a tree would be $b_0 = [0, 0, L, L]$. The children of a node b_i in the tree would be the candidates $\{b_j\}$ which lie within sub-grid corresponding to b_i and whose parameters $\{w_j\}$ and $\{h_j\}$ satisfy the below conditions:

$$w_i - 1 \leq w_j \leq w_i, \ h_i - 1 \leq h_j \leq h_i \tag{6}$$

We consider children nodes whose width or height values, but not both of them differ from the parent node by 1. This restriction is put in place so that we are minimally modifying the feature map activations for discriminating amongst

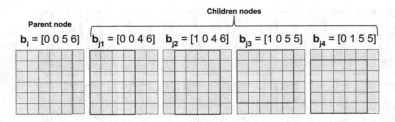

Fig. 4. An example of a parent node (represented in red) and it's children nodes (represented in blue) displayed on a 6 × 6 grid, as is the case for the Alexnet M_5 feature maps (Color figure online)

candidates. An example of a parent node b_i and the corresponding children node set $\{b_j\}$ is shown in Fig. 4.

During traversal, the child candidate with the highest score for the class C is selected. This approach is a greedy search strategy where we follow one path from the root node to a leaf node which represents the finest localization, and is susceptible to arrival at a locally optimal solution. Alternatively, we could evaluate all the nodes in the entire search-tree and could come up with the localization candidate with the highest score for class C. However, this would be computationally prohibitive.

To address this, we use the widely known beam-search [40] strategy. At each level of the search-tree we generate sets of children nodes from the current set of localization candidates using Eq. (6). We then rank them according to the scores for class C. Only the top M candidates are pursued for further evaluation. An illustration is presented in Fig. 5. In the Figure, we show an example where the two highest candidates are chosen at each level. The children nodes of these candidates are evaluated and ranked. We traverse a total of H levels. This approach helps us achieve a balance between keeping the number of computations to be tractable and avoiding greedy decisions. An additional advantage is the ability to localize multiple instances of the same class as the beam-search increases the set of localization candidates that are evaluated when compared to the greedy search strategy. Regions in the image corresponding to top-ranked candidates from each level are spatially sum-pooled using candidates scores to generate a heat-map. The heat-map is then thresholded. Bounding rectangles for the resulting binary blobs are extracted. The bounding rectangles are presented as detection results of our method. The average value of the heat-map values enclosed within detection boxes are assigned as the score of the boxes. In our experiments, we have set the value of M as 8 and H in the search tree as 10 for all data-sets. Heat-map thresholds for each class were determined by evaluation on a small validation sub-set from the training set.

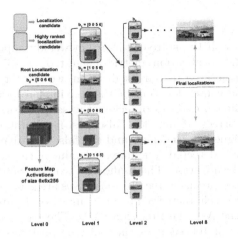

Fig. 5. A visual example of beam-search strategy to navigate the search tree amongst localization candidates. In this specific case, the class C is 'car', M is set to 2 and L is 6 (Color figure online)

4   Experiments

4.1   Data-Sets and Network Training

We evaluate our localization method on two large image data-sets, the PASCAL VOC 2007 [14], 2012 and the MS COCO. The VOC 2012 data-set has labels for 20 object categories and contains 5717 training images, 5823 validation images and 10991 test images. VOC 2007 shares the same class-labels with 2501 training images, 2510 validation images and 4952 test images. For the MS COCO data-set, there are 80000 images for training and 40504 images for validation with 80 object classes being present. These data-sets contain both image-level labels and object location annotations. For weak supervision we use the image-level labels from the training set to train classification networks and use the location annotations in the test and validation sets for evaluation.

We fine-tune the original VGG-16 and Alexnet networks (trained on Imagenet) by re-training the final fully connected layer for the VOC 2007, 2012 and MS COCO data-sets. We set the learning rate parameter to 0.001 which we decrease by a factor 10 for every 20000 training batches. Each training batch consists of 50 samples and the network was trained with 400000 batches. In order to balance the data-sets with respect to number of samples per class, we oversampled training samples from under-represented classes. We generate additional samples by a combination of adding white Gaussian noise and random rotations in the $\pm30°$ range. We use Caffe [25] as our software platform for training and deploying classification networks on an NVIDIA TITAN X Desktop GPU.

4.2   Metrics

To compare results with the state-of-the-art in weakly supervised localization methods, we use the localization metric suggested by [35]. From the class-specific heat-maps generated by our localization, we extract the region of maximal response. If the center location of the maximal response lies within the ground-truth bounding box of an object of the same class, we label the location prediction as correct. If not, the false positive count is increased as the background was assigned to the class, and the false negative count is increased because object was not detected. The maximal value of the heat-map is assigned as confidence of the localization. The confidence score is then used to rank localizations and associated precision-recall (p-r) curves are generated for each object class. The p-r curves are characterized by an estimate of the area under the curve, which is termed as the Average Precision (AP). The AP score can vary from 0 to 100. An *AP* score of 100 signifies that all true positives were localized and no false positives were assigned scores. The *AP* scores for all classes are averaged to derive the Mean Average Precision (mAP), which presents a summarized score for the entire test set. This evaluation metric differs from the traditional Intersection-over-Union (IoU) measures to determine bounding box quality w.r.t the ground-truth, as the extent of the localization is not captured.

In addition to the above metric, we are interested in measuring how effective our method is in capturing the extent of the object of interest. We calculate the standard average precision for our detection results, where true positives are determined when intersection over union (IoU) between the predicted bounding boxes and the corresponding ground-truth box of the same class exceeds 0.5. We also utilize the CorLoc [13] metric which measures the percentage of samples containing the class of interest where the IoU between detected bounding box and ground-truth box exceeds 0.5.

4.3   Results

For obtaining localization results, we fine-tuned the networks using training samples from the *train* set of PASCAL VOC 2012 data-set and tested the trained networks on the *validation* set. As we use the class-scores from the classifiers to drive our localization strategy, good classification performance is essential for robust object localization. We present the classification performance on the PASCAL VOC 2012 *validation* set in Table 1. The VGG-16 network provides improved classification with respect to Alexnet and a consequent improvement can be seen in the localization scores as well.

In Table 1, we also compare the localization results of our method with respect to recent state-of-the-art weakly supervised localization methods on the PASCAL VOC 2012 *validation* set. We achieve a significant improvement of 5 mAP over the localization performance of Oquab et al. [35]. We also compare against the RCNN [19] and Fast RCNN [18] detectors which are trained with object-level bounding boxes. Similar to the way [35] evaluates [19], we select the most confident bounding box proposal per class per image for evaluation. Since

Table 1. Comparison of image classification and object localization scores on the PASCAL VOC 2012 *validation* set. For computing localization scores, responses are labeled as correct when the maximal responses fall within a ground-truth bounding box of the same class. False negatives are counted when no responses overlap with the ground-truth annotations. The class scores of the associated image-level classification are used to rank the responses and generate average precision scores. * RCNN and Fast-RCNN are trained for object detection with object-level bounding box data. We use the most confident bounding box per class in every image for evaluation

	Image classification		Localization				
	Proposed method + VGG-16	Proposed method + Alexnet	Proposed method + VGG-16	Proposed method + Alexnet	Oquab et al. [35]	RCNN* [19]	Fast-RCNN* [18]
airplane	93.0	92.0	90.1	90.0	90.3	92.0	79.2
bike	89.7	82.9	86.4	81.2	77.4	80.8	74.7
bird	91.4	87.2	86.4	81.2	77.4	80.8	74.7
boat	89.6	83.8	77.6	82.2	79.2	73.0	65.8
bottle	69.5	54.1	56.8	47.5	41.1	49.9	39.4
bus	90.9	87.3	90.3	86.7	87.8	86.8	82.3
car	81.6	74.5	68.3	64.9	66.4	77.7	64.8
cat	92.0	87.0	89.9	85.7	91.0	87.6	85.7
chair	69.3	56.4	54.7	53.9	47.3	50.4	54.5
cow	88.9	76.7	86.8	75.8	83.7	72.1	77.2
dining table	80.2	71.1	66.4	67.9	55.1	57.6	58.8
dog	90.4	83.5	88.5	82.2	88.8	82.9	85.1
horse	90.0	85.5	89.0	84.1	93.6	79.1	86.1
motorbike	90.0	84.3	88.1	83.4	85.2	89.8	80.5
person	91.6	88.1	78.5	83.9	87.4	88.1	76.6
plant	85.5	80.1	64.1	71.7	43.5	56.1	46.7
sheep	90.4	83.5	90.0	83.1	86.2	83.5	79.5
sofa	75.5	64.5	67.0	63.7	50.8	50.1	68.3
train	91.4	90.8	89.9	89.4	86.8	82.0	85.0
tv	89.6	81.4	82.6	78.2	66.5	76.6	60.0
mAP	86.5	79.8	**79.7**	**77.1**	74.5	74.8	71.3

deep neural networks are the state-of-the-art in object detection and localization tasks, we have compared with CNN-based methods.

We summarize the localization results for the much larger MS COCO *validation* data-set in Table 2. In-spite of having weaker classification performance (54.1 mAP vs 62.8 mAP) than the network used by [35], we are able to produce stronger localization performance by a margin of 2.5 mAP with the Alexnet network and a larger margin of 8 mAP with the VGG-16 network. This is a

A.J. Bency et al.

Table 2. Comparison of localization and classification mAP scores for the MS COCO *validation* set

Method	Localization score (mAP)
Oquab et al. [35]	41.2
Proposed method + Alexnet	**43.7**
Proposed method + VGG-16	**49.2**

Table 3. Comparison of detection mean average precision scores and mean Correct Localization (CorLoc) scores on the PASCAL VOC 2007 *test* set

Method	Mean detection mAP	Mean CorLoc
Multi-fold MIL [8]	22.4	38.8
Bilen et al. [2]	27.7	43.7
LCL-pLSA [49]	**30.9**	**48.5**
Proposed method + VGG-16	25.7	46.8

significant improvement in performance over the state-of-the-art method. This is mainly because the proposed method actively seeks out image regions triggering higher classification scores for the class of interest. This form of active learning, where the localizing algorithm is the weak learner and the classifier is the strong teacher, lends us an advantage when trying to localize objects in complex scenes where multiple objects can exist in varying mutual configurations. This is also observed for the PASCAL VOC 2012 data-set. The fine-tuned VGG-16 and Alexnet networks produce classification performance scores of 74.3 mAP and 82.4 mAP respectively on the *test* set, where as the network used by [35] is scored at 86.3 mAP. As noted before, the proposed method outperforms competing methods on the localization task.

We have provided results on object bounding box detection and CorLoc for the PASCAL VOC 2007 *test* set in Table 3. We fine-tuned our network on the VOC 2007 *train* and the *validation* set, where 10 % of this joint group of images was set aside for parameter tuning, and provide test results on the *test* set. We are comparable in performance with respect to other state-of-the-art weakly supervised methods [2,8,49]. Examples of visual results for object detection are provided in Fig. 6.

Re-scoring the class likelihood scores using co-occurrence information referenced in Eq. (3) contributes to an improvement of 1.2 with the VGG-16 network in classification mAP score and 0.8 localization mAP score from Table 1.

Fig. 6. Visual sample results from the proposed method for Pascal VOC 2007 test set. Yellow rectangles overlaid on the images represent location and extent predictions. The locations of objects in the shown images are accurately estimated. Considering that only image-level labels are used for training, extent estimations are a challenging problem in this setting (Color figure online)

5   Discussion and Conclusions

The proposed method requires 2.6 s to localize an object on an image on machine with a 2.3 GHz CPU with a NVIDIA TITAN X desktop GPU. Compared to region proposal-based detection methods like RCNN which take around 20 s to detect objects, we achieve a significant reduction in localization time.

As can be seen from Table 1, an improvement in the classification performance (e.g. from Alexnet to VGG-16) directly leads to an improvement in the localization performance. As the state-of-the-art of the classification CNNs improves, we can expect a similar improvement in localization performance from our proposed method.

In summary, this method directly leverages feature map activations for object localization. This work uses the spatial and semantic information encoded in the convolutional layers and we have explored methods to utilize activations in the last convolutional layer. It would be interesting to see the improvements that could be derived by combining coarser semantic and finer localization information in earlier convolutional layers as well. Another direction to explore would be combining fast super-pixel segmentation and localization candidates from proposed method to improve detection performance.

The proposed method relies on weak supervision, with networks trained for image classification being used for localizing objects in test images with complex scenes and hence opens up possibilities for extending object localization to new object categories and image modalities without requiring expensive object-level annotations.

Acknowledgments. Research was sponsored by the Army Research Laboratory and was accomplished under Cooperative Agreement Number W911NF-09-2-0053 (the ARL Network Science CTA). The views and conclusions contained in this document are those of the authors and should not be interpreted as representing the official policies, either expressed or implied, of the Army Research Laboratory or the U.S. Government. The U.S. Government is authorized to reproduce and distribute reprints for Government purposes notwithstanding any copyright notation here on.

References

1. Alexe, B., Deselaers, T., Ferrari, V.: Measuring the objectness of image windows. IEEE Trans. Pattern Anal. Mach. Intell. **34**(11), 2189–2202 (2012)
2. Bilen, H., Pedersoli, M., Tuytelaars, T.: Weakly supervised object detection with convex clustering. In: Proceedings of the IEEE Conference on Computer Vision and Pattern Recognition, pp. 1081–1089 (2015)
3. Blaschko, M., Vedaldi, A., Zisserman, A.: Simultaneous object detection and ranking with weak supervision. In: Advances in Neural Information Processing Systems, pp. 235–243 (2010)
4. Brox, T., Bourdev, L., Maji, S., Malik, J.: Object segmentation by alignment of poselet activations to image contours. In: 2011 IEEE Conference on Computer Vision and Pattern Recognition (CVPR), pp. 2225–2232. IEEE (2011)
5. Chatfield, K., Simonyan, K., Vedaldi, A., Zisserman, A.: Return of the devil in the details: delving deep into convolutional nets. In: British Machine Vision Conference (2014)
6. Chen, L.C., Papandreou, G., Kokkinos, I., Murphy, K., Yuille, A.L.: Semantic image segmentation with deep convolutional nets and fully connected CRFs. In: ICLR (2015)
7. Chum, O., Zisserman, A.: An exemplar model for learning object classes. In: IEEE Conference on Computer Vision and Pattern Recognition, 2007. CVPR 2007, pp. 1–8. IEEE (2007)
8. Cinbis, R.G., Verbeek, J., Schmid, C.: Multi-fold MIL training for weakly supervised object localization. In: 2014 IEEE Conference on Computer Vision and Pattern Recognition (CVPR), pp. 2409–2416. IEEE (2014)
9. Dai, J., He, K., Sun, J.: Convolutional feature masking for joint object and stuff segmentation. In: Proceedings of the IEEE Conference on Computer Vision and Pattern Recognition, pp. 3992–4000 (2015)
10. Dalal, N., Triggs, B.: Histograms of oriented gradients for human detection. In: IEEE Computer Society Conference on Computer Vision and Pattern Recognition, 2005. CVpPR 2005, vol. 1, pp. 886–893. IEEE (2005)
11. Deng, J., Dong, W., Socher, R., Li, L.J., Li, K., Fei-Fei, L.: ImageNet: a large-scale hierarchical image database. In: IEEE Conference on Computer Vision and Pattern Recognition, 2009. CVpPR 2009, pp. 248–255. IEEE (2009)
12. Deselaers, T., Alexe, B., Ferrari, V.: Localizing objects while learning their appearance. In: Daniilidis, K., Maragos, P., Paragios, N. (eds.) ECCV 2010, Part IV. LNCS, vol. 6314, pp. 452–466. Springer, Heidelberg (2010)
13. Deselaers, T., Alexe, B., Ferrari, V.: Weakly supervised localization and learning with generic knowledge. Int. J. Comput. Vis. **100**(3), 275–293 (2012)
14. Everingham, M., Van Gool, L., Williams, C.K.I., Winn, J., Zisserman, A.: The PASCAL Visual Object Classes Challenge 2007 (VOC 2007) Results (2007). http://www.pascal-network.org/challenges/VOC/voc2007/workshop/index.html

15. Everingham, M., Van Gool, L., Williams, C.K.I., Winn, J., Zisserman, A.: The PASCAL Visual Object Classes Challenge 2012 (VOC 2012) Results (2012). http://www.pascal-network.org/challenges/VOC/voc2012/workshop/index.html
16. Felzenszwalb, P.F., Girshick, R.B., McAllester, D., Ramanan, D.: Object detection with discriminatively trained part-based models. IEEE Trans. Pattern Anal. Mach. Intell. **32**(9), 1627–1645 (2010)
17. Galleguillos, C., Babenko, B., Rabinovich, A., Belongie, S.: Weakly supervised object localization with stable segmentations. In: Forsyth, D., Torr, P., Zisserman, A. (eds.) ECCV 2008, Part I. LNCS, vol. 5302, pp. 193–207. Springer, Heidelberg (2008)
18. Girshick, R.: Fast R-CNN. In: International Conference on Computer Vision (ICCV) (2015)
19. Girshick, R., Donahue, J., Darrell, T., Malik, J.: Rich feature hierarchies for accurate object detection and semantic segmentation. In: 2014 IEEE Conference on Computer Vision and Pattern Recognition (CVPR), pp. 580–587. IEEE (2014)
20. Glasner, D., Galun, M., Alpert, S., Basri, R., Shakhnarovich, G.: Viewpoint-aware object detection and pose estimation. In: 2011 IEEE International Conference on Computer Vision (ICCV), pp. 1275–1282. IEEE (2011)
21. Hariharan, B., Arbeláez, P., Girshick, R., Malik, J.: Simultaneous Detection and Segmentation. In: Fleet, D., Pajdla, T., Schiele, B., Tuytelaars, T. (eds.) ECCV 2014, Part VII. LNCS, vol. 8695, pp. 297–312. Springer, Heidelberg (2014)
22. Hariharan, B., Arbelaez, P., Girshick, R., Malik, J.: Hypercolumns for object segmentation and fine-grained localization. In: The IEEE Conference on Computer Vision and Pattern Recognition (CVPR), June 2015
23. Hartmann, G., et al.: Weakly supervised learning of object segmentations from web-scale video. In: Fusiello, A., Murino, V., Cucchiara, R. (eds.) ECCV 2012. LNCS, vol. 7583, pp. 198–208. Springer, Heidelberg (2012). doi:10.1007/978-3-642-33863-2_20
24. He, K., Zhang, X., Ren, S., Sun, J.: Spatial pyramid pooling in deep convolutional networks for visual recognition. IEEE Trans. Pattern Anal. Mach. Intell. **37**(9), 1904–1916 (2015)
25. Jia, Y., Shelhamer, E., Donahue, J., Karayev, S., Long, J., Girshick, R., Guadarrama, S., Darrell, T.: Caffe: convolutional architecture for fast feature embedding. In: Proceedings of the ACM International Conference on Multimedia, pp. 675–678. ACM (2014)
26. Karayev, S., Trentacoste, M., Han, H., Agarwala, A., Darrell, T., Hertzmann, A., Winnemoeller, H.: Recognizing image style. In: Proceedings of the British Machine Vision Conference. BMVA Press (2014)
27. Kim, J., Grauman, K.: Shape sharing for object segmentation. In: Fitzgibbon, A., Lazebnik, S., Perona, P., Sato, Y., Schmid, C. (eds.) ECCV 2012, Part VII. LNCS, vol. 7578, pp. 444–458. Springer, Heidelberg (2012)
28. Krizhevsky, A., Sutskever, I., Hinton, G.E.: ImageNet classification with deep convolutional neural networks. In: Advances in Neural Information Processing Systems, pp. 1097–1105 (2012)
29. Lin, T.-Y., Maire, M., Belongie, S., Hays, J., Perona, P., Ramanan, D., Dollár, P., Zitnick, C.L.: Microsoft COCO: common objects in context. In: Fleet, D., Pajdla, T., Schiele, B., Tuytelaars, T. (eds.) ECCV 2014, Part V. LNCS, vol. 8693, pp. 740–755. Springer, Heidelberg (2014)
30. Long, J., Shelhamer, E., Darrell, T.: Fully convolutional networks for semantic segmentation. In: Proceedings of the IEEE Conference on Computer Vision and Pattern Recognition, pp. 3431–3440 (2015)

31. Mahendran, A., Vedaldi, A.: Understanding deep image representations by inverting them. In: The IEEE Conference on Computer Vision and Pattern Recognition (CVPR), June 2015
32. Murphy, K., Torralba, A., Eaton, D., Freeman, W.T.: Object detection and localization using local and global features. In: Ponce, J., Hebert, M., Schmid, C., Zisserman, A. (eds.) Toward Category-Level Object Recognition. LNCS, vol. 4170, pp. 382–400. Springer, Heidelberg (2006)
33. Noh, H., Hong, S., Han, B.: Learning deconvolution network for semantic segmentation. In: 2015 IEEE International Conference on Computer Vision (ICCV) (2015)
34. Oquab, M., Bottou, L., Laptev, I., Sivic, J.: Learning and transferring mid-level image representations using convolutional neural networks. In: CVPR (2014)
35. Oquab, M., Bottou, L., Laptev, I., Sivic, J.: Is object localization for free? weakly-supervised learning with convolutional neural networks. In: Proceedings of the IEEE Conference on Computer Vision and Pattern Recognition (2015)
36. Ouyang, W., Wang, X., Zeng, X., Qiu, S., Luo, P., Tian, Y., Li, H., Yang, S., Wang, Z., Loy, C.C., Tang, X.: DeepID-Net: deformable deep convolutional neural networks for object detection. In: The IEEE Conference on Computer Vision and Pattern Recognition (CVPR), June 2015
37. Papadopoulos, D.P., Clarke, A.D.F., Keller, F., Ferrari, V.: Training object class detectors from eye tracking data. In: Fleet, D., Pajdla, T., Schiele, B., Tuytelaars, T. (eds.) ECCV 2014, Part V. LNCS, vol. 8693, pp. 361–376. Springer, Heidelberg (2014)
38. Pourian, N., Vadivel, K.S., Manjunath, B.: Weakly supervised graph based semantic segmentation by learning communities of image-parts. In: 2015 IEEE International Conference on Computer Vision (ICCV). IEEE (2015)
39. Roth, P.S., Winter, M.: Survey of appearance-based methods for object recognition, iCG01/08 (2008)
40. Rubin, S.M., Reddy, R.: The locus model of search and its use in image interpretation. IJCAI **2**, 590–595 (1977)
41. Rumelhart, D.E., Hinton, G.E., Williams, R.J.: Learning representations by back-propagating errors. Cogn. Model. **5**, 3 (1988)
42. Sermanet, P., Eigen, D., Zhang, X., Mathieu, M., Fergus, R., LeCun, Y.: OverFeat: integrated recognition, localization and detection using convolutional networks. In: International Conference on Learning Representations (ICLR 2014). CBLS, April 2014. http://openreview.net/document/d332e77d-459a-4af8-b3ed-55ba
43. Shanmuga Vadivel, K., Ngo, T., Eckstein, M., Manjunath, B.: Eye tracking assisted extraction of attentionally important objects from videos. In: The IEEE Conference on Computer Vision and Pattern Recognition (CVPR), June 2015
44. Shrivastava, A., Gupta, A.: Building part-based object detectors via 3D geometry. In: Proceedings of the IEEE International Conference on Computer Vision, pp. 1745–1752 (2013)
45. Simonyan, K., Zisserman, A.: Very deep convolutional networks for large-scale image recognition. In: International Conference on Learning Representations (2015)
46. Szegedy, C., Liu, W., Jia, Y., Sermanet, P., Reed, S., Anguelov, D., Erhan, D., Vanhoucke, V., Rabinovich, A.: Going deeper with convolutions. In: Proceedings of the IEEE Conference on Computer Vision and Pattern Recognition, pp. 1–9 (2015)
47. Uijlings, J.R., van de Sande, K.E., Gevers, T., Smeulders, A.W.: Selective search for object recognition. Int. J. Comput. Vis. **104**(2), 154–171 (2013)

48. Viola, P., Jones, M.: Rapid object detection using a boosted cascade of simple features. In: Proceedings of the 2001 IEEE Computer Society Conference on Computer Vision and Pattern Recognition, 2001. CVpPR 2001, vol. 1, pp. I-511. IEEE (2001)
49. Wang, C., Ren, W., Huang, K., Tan, T.: Weakly supervised object localization with latent category learning. In: Fleet, D., Pajdla, T., Schiele, B., Tuytelaars, T. (eds.) ECCV 2014, Part VI. LNCS, vol. 8694, pp. 431–445. Springer, Heidelberg (2014)
50. Zhang, X., Yang, Y.H., Han, Z., Wang, H., Gao, C.: Object class detection: a survey. ACM Comput. Surv. **46**(1), 10:1–10:53 (2013). http://doi.acm.org/10.1145/2522968.2522978
51. Zhang, Y., Sohn, K., Villegas, R., Pan, G., Lee, H.: Improving object detection with deep convolutional networks via Bayesian optimization and structured prediction. In: The IEEE Conference on Computer Vision and Pattern Recognition (CVPR), June 2015
52. Zhou, B., Khosla, A., Lapedriza, A., Oliva, A., Torralba, A.: Object detectors emerge in deep scene CNNs. In: International Conference on Learning Representations (ICLR) (2015)
53. Zhu, Y., Urtasun, R., Salakhutdinov, R., Fidler, S.: segDeepM: exploiting segmentation and context in deep neural networks for object detection. In: The IEEE Conference on Computer Vision and Pattern Recognition (CVPR), June 2015

Embedding Deep Metric for Person Re-identification: A Study Against Large Variations

Hailin Shi[1,2], Yang Yang[1,2], Xiangyu Zhu[1,2], Shengcai Liao[1,2], Zhen Lei[1,2(✉)], Weishi Zheng[3], and Stan Z. Li[1,2]

[1] National Laboratory of Pattern Recognition and Center for Biometrics and Security Research, Institute of Automation, Chinese Academy of Sciences, Beijing, China
{hailin.shi,yang.yang,xiangyu.zhu,scliao,zlei,szli}@nlpr.ia.ac.cn
[2] University of Chinese Academy of Sciences, Beijing, China
[3] School of Data and Computer Science, Sun Yat-sen University, Guangzhou, China

Abstract. Person re-identification is challenging due to the large variations of pose, illumination, occlusion and camera view. Owing to these variations, the pedestrian data is distributed as highly-curved manifolds in the feature space, despite the current convolutional neural networks (CNN)'s capability of feature extraction. However, the distribution is unknown, so it is difficult to use the geodesic distance when comparing two samples. In practice, the current deep embedding methods use the Euclidean distance for the training and test. On the other hand, the manifold learning methods suggest to use the Euclidean distance in the local range, combining with the graphical relationship between samples, for approximating the geodesic distance. From this point of view, selecting suitable positive (*i.e.* intra-class) training samples within a local range is critical for training the CNN embedding, especially when the data has large intra-class variations. In this paper, we propose a novel moderate positive sample mining method to train robust CNN for person re-identification, dealing with the problem of large variation. In addition, we improve the learning by a metric weight constraint, so that the learned metric has a better generalization ability. Experiments show that these two strategies are effective in learning robust deep metrics for person re-identification, and accordingly our deep model significantly outperforms the state-of-the-art methods on several benchmarks of person re-identification. Therefore, the study presented in this paper may be useful in inspiring new designs of deep models for person re-identification.

Keywords: Person re-identification · Deep learning · CNN

1 Introduction

Given a set of pedestrian images, person re-identification aims to identify the probe image that generally captured by different cameras. Nowadays, person re-identification becomes increasingly important for surveillance and security

© Springer International Publishing AG 2016
B. Leibe et al. (Eds.): ECCV 2016, Part I, LNCS 9905, pp. 732–748, 2016.
DOI: 10.1007/978-3-319-46448-0_44

system, *e.g.* replacing manual video screening and other heavy loads. Person re-identification is a challenging task due to large variations of body pose, lighting, view angles, scenarios across time and cameras.

The framework of existing methods usually consists of two parts: (1) extracting discriminative features from pedestrian images; (2) computing the distance of samples by feature comparison. There are many works focus on these two aspects. The traditional methods work at improving suitable hand-crafted features [34,41], or good metric for comparison [13,15,18,23,26,36,38,39], or both of them [12,19,33,37]. The first aspect considers to find features that are robust to challenging factors (lighting, pose *etc.*) while preserving the identity information. The second aspect comes to the metric learning problem which generally minimizes the intra-class distance while maximizing the inter-class distance.

More recently, the deep learning methods gradually gain the popularity in person re-identification. The re-identification methods by deep learning [1,6,17,35] incorporate the two above-mentioned aspects (feature extraction and metric learning) of person re-identification into an integrated framework. The feature extraction and the metric learning are fulfilled respectively by two components in a deep neural network: the CNN part which extracts features from images, and the following metric learning part which compares the features with the metric. The FPNN [17] algorithm introduced a patch matching layer for the CNN part for the first time. Ahmed *et al.* [1] proposed an improved deep learning architecture (IDLA) with cross-input neighborhood differences and patch summary features. These two methods are both dedicated to improve the CNN architecture. Their purpose is to evaluate the pair similarity early in the CNN stage, so that it could make use of spatial correspondence of feature maps. As for the metric learning part, DML [35] adopted the cosine similarity and Binomial deviance. DeepFeature [6] adopted the Euclidean distance and triplet loss. Some others [1,17] used the logistic loss to directly form a binary classification problem of whether the input image pair belongs to the same identity.

The following are our contributions.

- For training the CNN, the hard negative mining strategy has been used in [1,27,30]. Considering the large intra-class variations in pedestrian data, we argue that, in person re-identification, the positive training pairs should also be sampled carefully since the pedestrian data is distributed as the manifold that are highly curved in the feature space. As argued in some manifold learning methods [4,29,31], it is effective to use the local Euclidean distance, combining with the graphical relationship between samples, to approximate the geodesic distance. Thus, selecting the moderate positive pairs in the local range is critical for training the network. This is an important issue but has been seldom noticed. In this paper, we propose a new training strategy, named **moderate positive mining**[1], to adaptively search the moderate positives for training. This novel training method significantly improves the identification accuracy.

---

[1] The source codes is available at http://www.cbsr.ia.ac.cn/users/hailinshi.

– In addition, we improve the network by the **weight constraint** for the metric layers. The weight constraint regularizes the metric learning part and alleviates the over-fitting problem.

2   Related Work

Positive Sample Mining. The hard negative mining strategy [30] has been used for face recognition. In person re-identification, IDLA [1] also adopted hard negative mining for the training. By forcing the model to focus on the hard negatives near the decision boundary, hard negative mining improves the training efficiency and the model performance. In this paper, we find that how to select moderate positive samples is also an essential issue for learning person re-identification model. The moderate positives are as critical as hard negatives for training the network, especially when the data has large intra-class variations. However, there are barely any previous attempt in this aspect for learning the deep embedding. In our approach, we propose the novel strategy of moderate positive mining to address the problem. We sample the moderate positives for training, and avoid using the hard ones from extreme intra-class variations of pedestrian data. We empirically find that this strategy effectively improves the identification accuracy (see Sect. 4.2).

Weight Constraint for Metric Learning. A commonly used metric by deep learning methods is the Euclidean distance [6, 27, 30]. However, the Euclidean distance is sensitive to the scale, and is blind to the correlation across dimensions. In practice, we cannot guarantee the CNN-learned features have similar scales and the de-correlation across dimensions. Therefore, using the Mahalanobis distance is a better choice for multivariate metric [22]. In the area of face recognition, DDML [11] implemented the Mahalanobis metric in their network, but without any constraint. Our metric is learned in a similar way and improved by the proposed weight constraint which helps to gain a better generalization ability.

3   Proposed Method

In this section, we firstly introduce the moderate positive mining method. Then, we revisit DDML and introduce the weight constraint.

3.1   Moderate Positive Mining

Large Intra-class Variations. There are many factors lead to the large intra-class variations in pedestrian data, such as illumination, background, misalignment, occlusion, co-occurrence of people, appearance changing, *etc.* Many of them are specific with pedestrian data. Figure 1(a) shows some hard positive cases in the data set of CUHK03 [17]. Some of them are even difficult for human to recognize.

Although CNN has a strong ability to extract features, pedestrian data follows the very irregular distribution in the feature space due to the large variations, such as the example of highly-curved manifold illustrated in Fig. 1(b). This is reflected by the fact the state-of-the-art performances on several person re-identification benchmarks are relatively poor comparing with the human face recognition task which is easier due to less intra-class variations.

Moderate Positive Mining Method. Considering the distribution in Fig. 1(b) is unknown, it is difficult to apply the geodesic distance for comparing two samples. The usual way is to use the Mahalanobis distance (or the special case Euclidean) [6,11,30] which is a suitable metric in the ideal condition (Fig. 1(c)).

On the other hand, the manifold learning methods [4,29,31] suggest to use the Euclidean distance (or heat kernel) in the local range, combining with the graphical relationship between samples, for approximating the geodesic distance. This is a feasible way to minimize the intra-class variance along the manifold for the supervised learning. However, when training the deep CNN with contrastive or triplet loss for embedding, the existing deep embedding methods use the Euclidean distance undiscriminatingly with all the positive samples.

Here, we argue that selecting positive samples in the local range (pairing by the yellow line in Fig. 1(b)) is critical for training the network; training with the positive samples of large distance (the yellow line with cross) may distort the manifold and harm the manifold learning.

The basic idea is that we reduce the intra-class variance while preserving the intrinsic graphical structure of pedestrian data via mining the moderate positive pairs in the local range.

We introduce the moderate positive mining method as follows: we select the moderate positive pairs in the range of the same subject at one time. For example, suppose a subject having 6 images, of which 3 from a camera and 3 from another. We can totally match 9 positive pairs from this subject. If we use the easiest positive pair of the nine, the convergence will be very slow; if we use

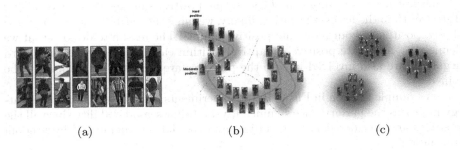

(a)   (b)   (c)

Fig. 1. (a) Some hard positive cases in CUHK03. (b) Illustration of the highly-curved manifold of 3 identities. (c) Gaussian distribution is suitable to perform Mahalanobis metric. Best viewed in color. (Color figure online)

the hardest, the learning will be damaged. Thus, we pick the moderate positive pairs that are between the two extreme cases.

Given two sets of pedestrian images $\mathcal{I}_1$ and $\mathcal{I}_2$ come from two disjoint cameras. Denote $\mathbf{I}_1 \in \mathcal{I}_1$ and $\mathbf{I}_2^p \in \mathcal{I}_2$ as a positive pair (from the same identity), and $\mathbf{I}_1 \in \mathcal{I}_1$ and $\mathbf{I}_2^n \in \mathcal{I}_2$ as a negative pair (from different identities). Denote $\boldsymbol{\Psi}(\cdot)$ as the CNN, $d(\cdot, \cdot)$ is the Mahalanobis or Euclidean distance. The mining method is described as follows:

Algorithm 1. Moderate Positive Mining

Input: randomly select an anchor sample $\mathbf{I}_1$, its positive samples $\{\mathbf{I}_2^{p_1}, \ldots, \mathbf{I}_2^{p_k}\}$ and negative samples $\{\mathbf{I}_2^{n_1}, \ldots, \mathbf{I}_2^{n_k}\}$ to form a mini-batch.

Step 1 Input the images into the network for obtaining the features, and compute their distances $\{d(\boldsymbol{\Psi}(\mathbf{I}_1), \boldsymbol{\Psi}(\mathbf{I}_2^{p_1})), \ldots, d(\boldsymbol{\Psi}(\mathbf{I}_1), \boldsymbol{\Psi}(\mathbf{I}_2^{p_k}))\}$ and $\{d(\boldsymbol{\Psi}(\mathbf{I}_1), \boldsymbol{\Psi}(\mathbf{I}_2^{n_1})), \ldots, d(\boldsymbol{\Psi}(\mathbf{I}_1), \boldsymbol{\Psi}(\mathbf{I}_2^{n_k}))\}$;

Step 2 mine the hardest negative sample

$$\hat{\mathbf{I}}_2^n = argmin_{j=1\ldots k}\{d(\boldsymbol{\Psi}(\mathbf{I}_1), \boldsymbol{\Psi}(\mathbf{I}_2^{n_j}))\};$$

Step 3 from the positive samples, choose those $\tilde{\mathbf{I}}_2^{p_m}$ satisfying

$$d(\boldsymbol{\Psi}(\mathbf{I}_1), \boldsymbol{\Psi}(\tilde{\mathbf{I}}_2^{p_m})) \leq d(\boldsymbol{\Psi}(\mathbf{I}_1), \boldsymbol{\Psi}(\hat{\mathbf{I}}_2^n));$$

Step 4 mine the hardest one among these chosen positives as our moderate positive sample

$$\hat{\mathbf{I}}_2^p = argmax_{\tilde{\mathbf{I}}_2^{p_m}}\{d(\boldsymbol{\Psi}(\mathbf{I}_1), \boldsymbol{\Psi}(\tilde{\mathbf{I}}_2^{p_m}))\}.$$

If none of the positives satisfies the condition in **Step 3**, choose the positive with the smallest distance as the moderate positive sample.

Output: The moderate positive sample $\hat{\mathbf{I}}_2^p$.

Firstly, we randomly select an anchor sample and its positive samples and negative samples (with equal number) to form a mini-batch; then, we mine the hardest negative sample, and choose the positive samples that have smaller distances than the hardest negative; finally, we mine the hardest one among these chosen positives as our moderate positive sample. The reason to do so is that we define the "moderate positive" adaptively within each subject while their hard negatives are also involved in case the positives are too easy or too hard to be mined.

An example is given in Fig. 2. In the experiments, this dynamic mining strategy improves the performance significantly, and shows good stability since all the positives are considered in each subject and the data is augmented by random translation.

Fig. 2. An example of the moderate positive mining in learning.

3.2 Weight Constraint for Deep Metric Learning

Once the CNN extract the features from a pair of images, the metric layers are performed subsequently to calculate the distance, as shown in Fig. 3. The metric learning layer is like the structure proposed in DDML [11], and its learning is improved via a weight constraint.

Recalling the two sets of pedestrian images $\mathcal{I}_1$ and $\mathcal{I}_2$ mentioned above, denote $\mathcal{X}_1$ and $\mathcal{X}_2$ are the corresponding feature sets extracted by the CNN. $\mathbf{x}_1 = \mathbf{\Psi}(\mathbf{I}_1)$, $\mathbf{x}_2^p = \mathbf{\Psi}(\mathbf{I}_2^p)$ and $\mathbf{x}_2^n = \mathbf{\Psi}(\mathbf{I}_2^n)$ are the corresponding features of the anchor, positive and negative samples.

Revisiting DDML. The Mahalanobis distance is formulated as

$$d(\mathbf{x}_1, \mathbf{x}_2) = \sqrt{(\mathbf{x}_1 - \mathbf{x}_2)^T \mathbf{M}(\mathbf{x}_1 - \mathbf{x}_2)}, \tag{1}$$

where $\mathbf{x}_2 \in \{\mathbf{x}_2^p, \mathbf{x}_2^n\}$, $\mathbf{M}$ is a symmetric positive semi-definite matrix. Learning $\mathbf{M}$ under the constraint of positive semi-definite is difficult. We make use of its decomposition $\mathbf{M} = \mathbf{W}\mathbf{W}^T$. Learning $\mathbf{W}$ is much easier, and $\mathbf{W}\mathbf{W}^T$ is always positive semi-definite. We develop the distance as follows

$$\begin{aligned} d(\mathbf{x}_1, \mathbf{x}_2) &= \sqrt{(\mathbf{x}_1 - \mathbf{x}_2)^T \mathbf{W}\mathbf{W}^T (\mathbf{x}_1 - \mathbf{x}_2)} \\ &= \sqrt{(\mathbf{W}^T(\mathbf{x}_1 - \mathbf{x}_2))^T (\mathbf{W}^T(\mathbf{x}_1 - \mathbf{x}_2))} \\ &= \|\mathbf{W}^T(\mathbf{x}_1 - \mathbf{x}_2)\|_2. \end{aligned} \tag{2}$$

The inner product $\mathbf{W}^T(\mathbf{x}_1 - \mathbf{x}_2)$ can be implemented by a linear fully-connected (FC) layer in which the weight matrix is defined by $\mathbf{W}^T$. The output of the FC layer is calculated by

$$\mathbf{y} = f(\mathbf{W}^T\mathbf{x} + \mathbf{b}), \tag{3}$$

where $\mathbf{b}$ is the bias term. The identity function is used as the activation $f(\cdot)$ for the linear FC layer. As shown in Fig. 3, the feature vectors $\mathbf{x}_1$ and $\mathbf{x}_2$ are fed into the subtraction layer. Then, the difference is transformed by the linear FC layer with the weight matrix $\mathbf{W}^T$. For the symmetry of the distance, we fix the bias term $\mathbf{b}$ to zero throughout the training and test. Finally, the L2 norm is computed as the output distance $d(\mathbf{x}_1, \mathbf{x}_2)$. This structure remains equivalent when switching the position of the subtraction layer and the FC layer.

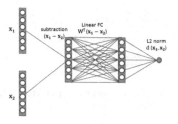

Fig. 3. The metric learning layers compute the distance of two samples. $\mathbf{x}_1$ and $\mathbf{x}_2$ are the feature vectors extracted by the CNN from the images. The weight $\mathbf{W}$ is regularized by the proposed constraint in the learning.

Weight Constraint. The objective is to minimize the intra-class distance and maximize the inter-class distance. The training loss is defined as

$$L = d(\mathbf{\Psi}(\mathbf{I}_1), \mathbf{\Psi}(\mathbf{I}_2^p)) + [m - d(\mathbf{\Psi}(\mathbf{I}_1), \mathbf{\Psi}(\mathbf{I}_2^n))]_+, \tag{4}$$

where $\mathbf{I}_1$, $\mathbf{I}_2^p$ and $\mathbf{I}_2^n$ are the input images corresponding to the features $\mathbf{x}_1$, $\mathbf{x}_2^p$ and $\mathbf{x}_2^n$, and m is the margin which is set to 2 in the implementation. In each time of the forward propagation, either the first term or the second term of Eq. 4 is computed. Then the loss is obtained by combining the two terms, and we compute the gradient.

Compared with the Mahalanobis distance, the Euclidean distance has less discriminability but better generalization ability, because it does not take account of the scales and the correlation across dimensions [22]. Here, we impose a constraint that keep the matrix $\mathbf{M}$ having large values at the diagonal and small entries elsewhere, so we can achieve a balance between the unconstrained Mahalanobis distance and the Euclidean distance. The constraint is formulated as the Frobenius norm of the difference between $\mathbf{W}\mathbf{W}^T$ and identity matrix $\mathbf{I}$,

$$L = d(\mathbf{\Psi}(\mathbf{I}_1), \mathbf{\Psi}(\mathbf{I}_2^p)) + [m - d(\mathbf{\Psi}(\mathbf{I}_1), \mathbf{\Psi}(\mathbf{I}_2^n))]_+$$
$$s.t. \quad \|\mathbf{W}\mathbf{W}^T - \mathbf{I}\|_F^2 \leq C, \tag{5}$$

where C is a constant. We further combine the constraint into the loss function as a regularization term:

$$\hat{L} = L + \frac{\lambda}{2}\|\mathbf{W}\mathbf{W}^T - \mathbf{I}\|_F^2, \tag{6}$$

where λ is the relative weight of regularization, $\hat{L}$ is the new loss function. For updating the weight matrix $\mathbf{W}$, the gradient w.r.t. $\mathbf{W}$ is computed by

$$\frac{\partial \hat{L}}{\partial \mathbf{W}} = \frac{\partial L}{\partial \mathbf{W}} + \lambda(\mathbf{W}\mathbf{W}^T - \mathbf{I})\mathbf{W}. \tag{7}$$

When λ is small, the Mahalanobis distance takes into account the correlations across dimensions. However, it may overfit to the training set, since the metric matrix (*i.e.* WW^T) is learnt from the training set which is usually small in person re-identification. On the other hand, when λ is large, the matrix WW^T becomes close to the identity matrix. In the extreme case, WW^T equals to the identity matrix, and the distance reduces to the Euclidean distance. In this situation, the Euclidean distance does not consider the correlation, but may generalize robustly to unseen test sets. So, we incorporate the advantage of the Mahalanobis and Euclidean distances and balance the matching accuracy and generalization performance via the constraint.

4 Experiments

Our method is implemented via remodifying the CUDA-Convnet [14] framework. We report the evaluation with the one-shot standard protocol on three common benchmarks of person re-identification, *i.e.* CUHK03 [17], CUHK01 [16] and VIPeR [9].

We begin with the description of CNN architecture we used for extracting features. Then we report the evaluation on the validation set of CUHK03 for analyzing the effects of the moderate positive mining (Sect. 4.2), the weight constraint (Sect. 4.3), and the CNN architecture (Sect. 4.4). Then, we compare our performance with the state-of-the-art methods on CUHK03 and CUHK01 (Sects. 4.5 and 4.6). Finally, we show the proposed method also performs well on the small data-set of VIPeR [9] and gains competitive results (Sect. 4.7).

4.1 CNN Architecture

The CNN is built by 3 branches with the details shown in Fig. 4. The input image is normalized to 128×64 RGB. Then, it is split into three 64×64 overlapping color patches, each of which is charged by a branch. Each branch is constituted of 3 convolutional layers and 2 pooling layers. No parameter sharing is performed between branches. Then, the 3 branches are concluded by a FC layer with the ReLU activation. Finally, the output feature vector $\mathbf{x}$ is computed by another FC layer with linear activation. For the computational stability, the features are normalized before sending to the metric learning layers. The CNN and the metric layers are learned jointly via backward propagation.

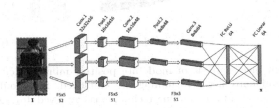

Fig. 4. The CNN architecture. Top: layer type and output size. Bottom: convolution parameters with "F" and "S" denoting the filter size and stride, respectively.

Our network has much lighter weights (0.84M parameters) compared with the previous best methods on CUHK03&01 (IDLA [1], 2.32M) and VIPeR (Deep-Feature [6], 26M). The reason that we build the CNN architecture in branches is to learn specific features from the different human body parts of pedestrian image; meanwhile, the morphological information is preserved from each part of human body. DML [35] adopted a similar architecture but with tied weights between branches. In Sect. 4.4, the experiments show the advantage of our untied architecture.

4.2   Analysis of Moderate Positive Mining

CUHK03 contains 1,369 subjects, each of which has around 10 images. The default protocol randomly selects 1,169 subjects for training, 100 for validation, and 100 for test. We pre-train the CNN with a softmax classification on the training set as the baseline. The outputs of softmax correspond to the identities.

To demonstrate the advantage of moderate positive mining, we compare the performances on the validation set with and without the moderate positive mining. The cumulative matching characteristic (CMC) curves and the rank-1 identification rates are shown in Fig. 5(a). We can find that the collaboration of moderate positive mining and hard negative mining achieves the best result (red line). The absence of moderate positive mining leads to a significant derogation of performance (blue). This reflects that the manifold is badly learned if all the positive pairs are used undiscriminatingly.

If both of the two mining methods are not used (magenta), the network gives very low identification rate at low ranks, even worse than the baseline (black). This indicates that moderate positive mining and hard negative mining are both crucial for training.

The CMC curves of the 3 trained networks tend to be saturated after the rank exceeds 20, whereas the baseline network remains at a relatively low identification

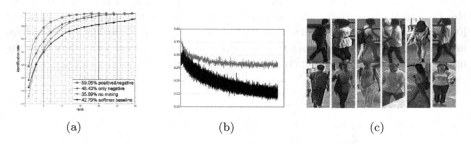

(a)   (b)   (c)

Fig. 5. (a) Performance analysis of moderate positive mining. Red: both moderate positive mining and hard negative mining are employed. Blue: only hard negative mining is employed. Magenta: no mining technique is employed during training. Black: the softmax baseline. (b) The loss curves along training iterations. Black: training set. Red: validation set. (c) Some positives mined by the moderate positive mining method. (Color figure online)

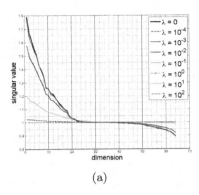
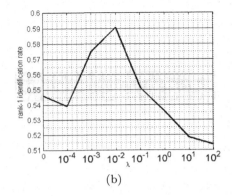

(a)   (b)

Fig. 6. (a) The spectrums of the matrix **M**. The spectrums with $\lambda = 10^1, 10^0$ are very close; those with $\lambda = 10^{-3}, 10^{-4}, 0$ are also very close. Best viewed in color. (b) The rank-1 identification rates with different λ of the weight constraint.

rate. This indicates that the training with the metric layers is the basic contributor of the improvement.

The training of network converges well as the loss value descending with respect to the iterations (shown in Fig. 5(b)). Some positives, which are mined by moderate positive mining during training, are shown in Fig. 5(c). These positives are with moderate extent of difficulty compared with those hard ones in Fig. 1(a).

4.3 Analysis of Weight Constraint

We inspect the metric matrices learned with different relative weights (λ) of the regularization. In Fig. 6(a), we show the spectrums of the matrix **M**. We also show the corresponding rank-1 identification rates in Fig. 6(b).

When $\lambda = 10^2$, the singular values are almost constant at 1, which means the metric layers almost give the Euclidean distance. This leads to the low variance and high bias. As λ increases, the matrix has varying singular values across dimensions. This implies that the learned metric suits the training data well, but is more likely to have over-fitting. Therefore, a moderate value of λ gives a trade-off between the variance and bias, which is an appropriate choice for good performance (Fig. 6(b)).

4.4 Analysis of Untied Branches

We show the learned filters of untied branches in Fig. 7(a). The network has learned remarkable color representations, which is coherent with the results of IDLA [1]. Since we apply untied weights between branches, each branch learns different filters from their own part. As shown in Fig. 7(a) where each row demonstrates a filter set from one branch, we can find each branch has its own emphasis in color. For example, the middle branch inclines to violet and blue, whereas

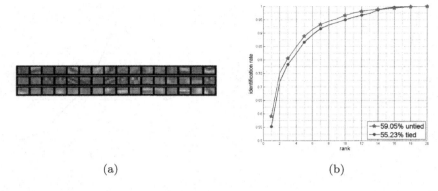

(a)   (b)

Fig. 7. (a) The learned filters of the first convolutional layer. The top, middle and bottom lines correspond to the 3 branches in the proposed CNN. Best viewed in color. (b) The performances with and without tied weights between branches. (Color figure online)

the bottom branch has learned filters of obviously lighter colors than the other two. The reason is that pedestrian images have regular appearance of human body. Each part has its own color distribution. Therefore, the branches learn the part-specific filters, the morphological information is taken into account for the features.

We compare the performances with and without tied weights between branches in Fig. 7(b). We augment the filter number in the tied-branches network so to make roughly equal parameter number with the untied-branch. The untied-branch network gains a better performance than that of tied branches. It reflects that, when the network has a certain complexity, the neural structure (*i.e.* tied vs untied) becomes very important. How to organize the network structure is a critical issue for good performance.

4.5   Performance on CUHK03

We adopt a random translation for the training data augmentation. The images are randomly cropped (0–5 pixels) in horizon and vertical, and stretched to recover the size. According to the validation results (Sect. 4.3), we set the parameter $\lambda = 10^{-2}$ in all the following experiments. The moderate positive mining and hard negative mining are employed.

CUHK03 has 2 versions, one has manually labeled images, and the other has detected images. We evaluate our method on the test set of both versions. We compare our performance with the traditional methods and deep learning methods. The traditional methods include LOMO-XQDA [19], KISSME [13], LDM [10], RANK [24], eSDC [40], SDALF [7], LMNN [32], ITML [5], Euclid [40]. The deep learning methods include FPNN [17] and IDLA [1]. IDLA and LOMO-XQDA gained the previously best performance on CUHK03. The CMC curves and the rank-1 identification rates are shown in Fig. 8. Our method achieves

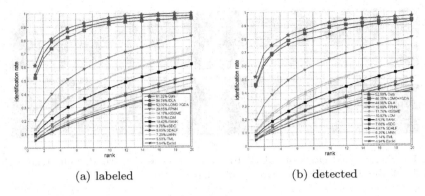

(a) labeled   (b) detected

Fig. 8. CMC curves and rank-1 identification rates on the CUHK03 data set. Our method outperforms the previous methods on both labeled (a) and detected (b) versions.

better performance than the previous state-of-the-art methods on not only the labeled version but also the detected version. This indicates that our method achieves good robustness to the misalignment of detection.

4.6   Performance on CUHK01

The CUHK01 data set contains 971 subjects, each of which has 4 images under 2 camera views. According to the protocol in [16], the data set is divided into a training set of 871 subjects and a test set of 100. We train the network on CUHK03, and further fine-tune it on CUHK01, as the same setting with the state-of-the-art method IDLA [1]. We compare our approach with the previously mentioned methods. The CMC curves and rank-1 identification rates are shown in Fig. 9(a). Our approach gains the best result (the red line) with 69 % rank-1 identification rate.

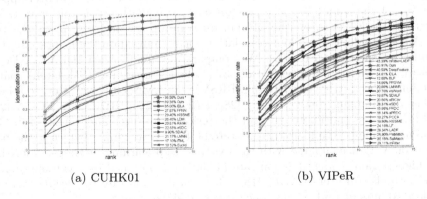

(a) CUHK01   (b) VIPeR

Fig. 9. CMC curves and rank-1 identification rates on CUHK01 (a) and VIPeR (b). (Color figure online)

Fig. 10. Some failed cases on CUHK01 by the proposed method. Left: true gallery. Middle: probe. Right: false positive. (Color figure online)

Besides, to inspect the limitation of the data set CUHK01, we involve the recently released Market1501 [42] into the training. As the training data increases, our network gives a better performance (the red dash line marked as "*Ours **") with 87% rank-1 identification rate. We show certain failed cases in Fig. 10. In each block, we give the true gallery, probe and false positive image from left to right. We find that most failed cases come from the dark color images or the negative pairs with significant color correspondence. This phenomenon is in line with the fact [1] that the learned filters in network mainly focus on image colors (as shown in Fig. 7(a)). The re-identification problem becomes extremely difficult when the true positive pairs have inconsistent colors in view while the negative pairs have similar colors (due to the lighting, camera setting *etc.*).

4.7   Performance on VIPeR

The VIPeR [9] data set includes 632 subjects, each of which has 2 images from two different cameras. Although VIPeR is a small data set which is not suitable for training CNN, we are still interested in the performance on this challenging task. The data set is randomly split into two subsets, each has non-overlapping subjects of the same size. The two subsets are for either training or test. We fine-tune the network on the 316-person training set and test it on the test set. We also adopt a random translation for training data augmentation. The results are shown in Fig. 9(b). We compare our model with IDLA [1], Deep-Feature [6], visual word (visWord) [37], saliency matching (SalMatch), patch matching (PatMatch) [39], ELF [8], PRSVM [3], LMNNR [2], eBiCov [21], local Fisher discriminant analysis (LF) [28], PRDC [43], aPRDC [20], PCCA [25], mid-level filters (mFilter) [41] and the fusion of mFilter and LADF [18]. Our approach achieves the identification rate of 40.91% at rank 1, which is the best result on VIPeR compared with the existing deep learning methods. Note that the highest rank-1 identification rate (43.39%) is obtained by a combination of two methods (mFilter+LADF) [18]. The identification rate by DeepFeature [6] is close to ours at rank 1, but much lower at higher ranks.

5   Conclusion

The large variations of pedestrian data is a challenging point for the person re-identification methods. Although CNN has a strong ability to extract features, pedestrian data follows the very irregular distribution in the feature space due to the large variations. In order to cope with the problem and train the robust deep embedding, the positive training samples should be selected deliberately. In this paper, we propose a novel moderate positive mining method to embed robust deep metric for person re-identification. We find that mining the moderate positive samples is crucial for training deep networks, especially when it comes to the difficult data with large intra-class variations (*e.g.* pedestrian). The moderate positive mining method dynamically select the suitable positive pairs for learning robust embedding adaptive to the data manifold. Moreover, we propose the weight constraint for gaining the good robustness to the over-fitting problem in person re-identification.

Due to these improvements, our method achieves state-of-the-art performances on CUHK03 and CUHK01, and competitive results on VIPeR. By mining the moderate positive samples for the training, we can reduce the intra-class variance while preserving the intrinsic graphical structure of pedestrian data; the metric weight constraint helps to improve the generalization ability of the network, especially when the most parameters are in the metric layers.

Acknowledgement. This work was supported by the National Key Research and Development Plan (Grant No. 2016YFC0801003), the Chinese National Natural Science Foundation Projects #61473291, #61572501, #61502491, #61572536, NVIDIA GPU donation program and AuthenMetric R&D Funds.

References

1. Ahmed, E., Jones, M., Marks, T.K.: An improved deep learning architecture for person re-identification. In: 2015 IEEE Conference on Computer Vision and Pattern Recognition (CVPR). IEEE (2015)
2. Bak, S., Corvee, E., Bremond, F., Thonnat, M.: Multiple-shot human re-identification by mean Riemannian covariance grid. In: 2011 8th IEEE International Conference on Advanced Video and Signal-Based Surveillance (AVSS), pp. 179–184. IEEE (2011)
3. Bazzani, L., Cristani, M., Perina, A., Murino, V.: Multiple-shot person re-identification by chromatic and epitomic analyses. Pattern Recognit. Lett. **33**(7), 898–903 (2012)
4. Belkin, M., Niyogi, P.: Laplacian eigenmaps for dimensionality reduction and data representation. Neural Computat. **15**(6), 1373–1396 (2003)
5. Davis, J.V., Kulis, B., Jain, P., Sra, S., Dhillon, I.S.: Information-theoretic metric learning. In: Proceedings of the 24th International Conference on Machine Learning, pp. 209–216. ACM (2007)
6. Ding, S., Lin, L., Wang, G., Chao, H.: Deep feature learning with relative distance comparison for person re-identification. Pattern Recognit. **48**(10), 2993–3003 (2015)

7. Farenzena, M., Bazzani, L., Perina, A., Murino, V., Cristani, M.: Person re-identification by symmetry-driven accumulation of local features. In: 2010 IEEE Conference on Computer Vision and Pattern Recognition (CVPR), pp. 2360–2367. IEEE (2010)
8. Gheissari, N., Sebastian, T.B., Hartley, R.: Person reidentification using spatiotemporal appearance. In: 2006 IEEE Computer Society Conference on Computer Vision and Pattern Recognition, vol. 2, pp. 1528–1535. IEEE (2006)
9. Gray, D., Brennan, S., Tao, H.: Evaluating appearance models for recognition, reacquisition, and tracking. In: Proceedings of IEEE International Workshop on Performance Evaluation for Tracking and Surveillance (PETS), vol. 3. Citeseer (2007)
10. Guillaumin, M., Verbeek, J., Schmid, C.: Is that you? Metric learning approaches for face identification. In: 2009 IEEE 12th International Conference on Computer Vision, pp. 498–505. IEEE (2009)
11. Hu, J., Lu, J., Tan, Y.P.: Discriminative deep metric learning for face verification in the wild. In: 2014 IEEE Conference on Computer Vision and Pattern Recognition (CVPR), pp. 1875–1882. IEEE (2014)
12. Khamis, S., Kuo, C.-H., Singh, V.K., Shet, V.D., Davis, L.S.: Joint learning for attribute-consistent person re-identification. In: Agapito, L., Bronstein, M.M., Rother, C. (eds.) ECCV 2014. LNCS, vol. 8927, pp. 134–146. Springer, Heidelberg (2015). doi:10.1007/978-3-319-16199-0_10
13. Koestinger, M., Hirzer, M., Wohlhart, P., Roth, P.M., Bischof, H.: Large scale metric learning from equivalence constraints. In: 2012 IEEE Conference on Computer Vision and Pattern Recognition (CVPR), pp. 2288–2295. IEEE (2012)
14. Krizhevsky, A., Sutskever, I., Hinton, G.E.: ImageNet classification with deep convolutional neural networks. In: Advances in Neural Information Processing Systems, pp. 1097–1105 (2012)
15. Li, W., Wang, X.: Locally aligned feature transforms across views. In: 2013 IEEE Conference on Computer Vision and Pattern Recognition (CVPR), pp. 3594–3601. IEEE (2013)
16. Li, W., Zhao, R., Wang, X.: Human reidentification with transferred metric learning. In: Lee, K.M., Matsushita, Y., Rehg, J.M., Hu, Z. (eds.) ACCV 2012, Part I. LNCS, vol. 7724, pp. 31–44. Springer, Heidelberg (2013)
17. Li, W., Zhao, R., Xiao, T., Wang, X.: DeepReID: Deep filter pairing neural network for person re-identification. In: 2014 IEEE Conference on Computer Vision and Pattern Recognition (CVPR), pp. 152–159. IEEE (2014)
18. Li, Z., Chang, S., Liang, F., Huang, T.S., Cao, L., Smith, J.R.: Learning locally-adaptive decision functions for person verification. In: 2013 IEEE Conference on Computer Vision and Pattern Recognition (CVPR), pp. 3610–3617. IEEE (2013)
19. Liao, S., Hu, Y., Zhu, X., Li, S.Z.: Person re-identification by local maximal occurrence representation and metric learning. In: Proceedings of the IEEE Conference on Computer Vision and Pattern Recognition, pp. 2197–2206 (2015)
20. Liu, C., Gong, S., Loy, C.C., Lin, X.: Person re-identification: what features are important? In: Fusiello, A., Murino, V., Cucchiara, R. (eds.) ECCV 2012. LNCS, vol. 7583, pp. 391–401. Springer, Heidelberg (2012). doi:10.1007/978-3-642-33863-2_39
21. Ma, B., Su, Y., Jurie, F.: BiCov: a novel image representation for person re-identification and face verification. In: British Machive Vision Conference, 11 pages (2012)
22. Manly, B.F.: Multivariate Statistical Methods: A Primer. CRC Press, Boca Raton (2004)

23. Martinel, N., Micheloni, C., Foresti, G.L.: Saliency weighted features for person re-identification. In: Agapito, L., Bronstein, M.M., Rother, C. (eds.) ECCV 2014. LNCS, vol. 8927, pp. 191–208. Springer, Heidelberg (2015). doi:10.1007/978-3-319-16199-0_14
24. McFee, B., Lanckriet, G.R.: Metric learning to rank. In: Proceedings of the 27th International Conference on Machine Learning (ICML-2010), pp. 775–782 (2010)
25. Mignon, A., Jurie, F.: Pcca: A new approach for distance learning from sparse pairwise constraints. In: 2012 IEEE Conference on Computer Vision and Pattern Recognition (CVPR), pp. 2666–2672. IEEE (2012)
26. Paisitkriangkrai, S., Shen, C., van den Hengel, A.: Learning to rank in person re-identification with metric ensembles. In: Proceedings of the IEEE Conference on Computer Vision and Pattern Recognition, pp. 1846–1855 (2015)
27. Parkhi, O.M., Vedaldi, A., Zisserman, A.: Deep face recognition. In: Proceedings of the British Machine Vision (2015)
28. Pedagadi, S., Orwell, J., Velastin, S., Boghossian, B.: Local fisher discriminant analysis for pedestrian re-identification. In: 2013 IEEE Conference on Computer Vision and Pattern Recognition (CVPR), pp. 3318–3325. IEEE (2013)
29. Roweis, S.T., Saul, L.K.: Nonlinear dimensionality reduction by locally linear embedding. Science 290(5500), 2323–2326 (2000)
30. Schroff, F., Kalenichenko, D., Philbin, J.: FaceNet: A unified embedding for face recognition and clustering. In: Proceedings of the IEEE Conference on Computer Vision and Pattern Recognition (2015)
31. Tenenbaum, J.B., De Silva, V., Langford, J.C.: A global geometric framework for nonlinear dimensionality reduction. science 290(5500), 2319–2323 (2000)
32. Weinberger, K.Q., Blitzer, J., Saul, L.K.: Distance metric learning for large margin nearest neighbor classification. In: Advances in Neural Information Processing Systems, pp. 1473–1480 (2005)
33. Xiong, F., Gou, M., Camps, O., Sznaier, M.: Person re-identification using kernel-based metric learning methods. In: Fleet, D., Pajdla, T., Schiele, B., Tuytelaars, T. (eds.) ECCV 2014, Part VII. LNCS, vol. 8695, pp. 1–16. Springer, Heidelberg (2014)
34. Yang, Y., Yang, J., Yan, J., Liao, S., Yi, D., Li, S.Z.: Salient color names for person re-identification. In: Fleet, D., Pajdla, T., Schiele, B., Tuytelaars, T. (eds.) ECCV 2014, Part I. LNCS, vol. 8689, pp. 536–551. Springer, Heidelberg (2014)
35. Yi, D., Lei, Z., Li, S.Z.: Deep metric learning for practical person re-identification (2014). arXiv preprint arXiv:1407.4979
36. Zhang, Z., Saligrama, V.: Prism: person re-identification via structured matching (2014). arXiv preprint arXiv:1406.4444
37. Zhang, Z., Chen, Y., Saligrama, V.: A novel visual word co-occurrence model for person re-identification. In: Agapito, L., Bronstein, M.M., Rother, C. (eds.) ECCV 2014. LNCS, vol. 8927, pp. 122–133. Springer, Heidelberg (2015). doi:10.1007/978-3-319-16199-0_9
38. Zhang, Z., Chen, Y., Saligrama, V.: Group membership prediction. In: 2015 IEEE International Conference on Computer Vision (ICCV). IEEE (2015)
39. Zhao, R., Ouyang, W., Wang, X.: Person re-identification by salience matching. In: 2013 IEEE International Conference on Computer Vision (ICCV), pp. 2528–2535. IEEE (2013)
40. Zhao, R., Ouyang, W., Wang, X.: Unsupervised salience learning for person re-identification. In: 2013 IEEE Conference on Computer Vision and Pattern Recognition (CVPR), pp. 3586–3593. IEEE (2013)

41. Zhao, R., Ouyang, W., Wang, X.: Learning mid-level filters for person re-identification. In: 2014 IEEE Conference on Computer Vision and Pattern Recognition (CVPR), pp. 144–151. IEEE (2014)
42. Zheng, L., Shen, L., Tian, L., Wang, S., Wang, J., Tian, Q.: Scalable person re-identification: a benchmark. In: IEEE International Conference on Computer Vision (2015)
43. Zheng, W.S., Gong, S., Xiang, T.: Person re-identification by probabilistic relative distance comparison. In: 2011 IEEE Conference on Computer Vision and Pattern Recognition (CVPR), pp. 649–656. IEEE (2011)

Learning to Track at 100 FPS with Deep Regression Networks

David Held$^{(\boxtimes)}$, Sebastian Thrun, and Silvio Savarese

Department of Computer Science, Stanford University, Stanford, USA
{davheld,thrun,ssilvio}@cs.stanford.edu

Abstract. Machine learning techniques are often used in computer vision due to their ability to leverage large amounts of training data to improve performance. Unfortunately, most generic object trackers are still trained from scratch online and do not benefit from the large number of videos that are readily available for offline training. We propose a method for offline training of neural networks that can track novel objects at test-time at 100 fps. Our tracker is significantly faster than previous methods that use neural networks for tracking, which are typically very slow to run and not practical for real-time applications. Our tracker uses a simple feed-forward network with no online training required. The tracker learns a generic relationship between object motion and appearance and can be used to track novel objects that do not appear in the training set. We test our network on a standard tracking benchmark to demonstrate our tracker's state-of-the-art performance. Further, our performance improves as we add more videos to our offline training set. To the best of our knowledge, our tracker (Our tracker is available at http://davheld.github.io/GOTURN/GOTURN.html) is the first neural-network tracker that learns to track generic objects at 100 fps.

Keywords: Tracking · Deep learning · Neural networks · Machine learning

1 Introduction

Given some object of interest marked in one frame of a video, the goal of "single-target tracking" is to locate this object in subsequent video frames, despite object motion, changes in viewpoint, lighting changes, or other variations. Single-target tracking is an important component of many systems. For person-following applications, a robot must track a person as they move through their environment. For autonomous driving, a robot must track dynamic obstacles in order to estimate where they are moving and predict how they will move in the future.

Electronic supplementary material The online version of this chapter (doi:10.1007/978-3-319-46448-0_45) contains supplementary material, which is available to authorized users.

B. Leibe et al. (Eds.): ECCV 2016, Part I, LNCS 9905, pp. 749–765, 2016.
DOI: 10.1007/978-3-319-46448-0_45

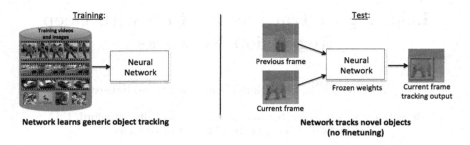

Fig. 1. Using a collection of videos and images with bounding box labels (but no class information), we train a neural network to track generic objects. At test time, the network is able to track novel objects without any fine-tuning. By avoiding fine-tuning, our network is able to track at 100 fps

Generic object trackers (trackers that are not specialized for specific classes of objects) are traditionally trained entirely from scratch online (i.e. during test time) [3,15,19,36], with no offline training being performed. Such trackers suffer in performance because they cannot take advantage of the large number of videos that are readily available to improve their performance. Offline training videos can be used to teach the tracker to handle rotations, changes in viewpoint, lighting changes, and other complex challenges.

In many other areas of computer vision, such as image classification, object detection, segmentation, or activity recognition, machine learning has allowed vision algorithms to train from offline data and learn about the world [5,9,13, 23,25,28]. In each of these cases, the performance of the algorithm improves as it iterates through the training set of images. Such models benefit from the ability of neural networks to learn complex functions from large amounts of data.

In this work, we show that it is possible to learn to track generic objects in real-time by watching videos offline of objects moving in the world. To achieve this goal, we introduce *GOTURN*, Generic Object Tracking Using Regression Networks. We train a neural network for tracking in an entirely offline manner. At test time, when tracking novel objects, the network weights are frozen, and no online fine-tuning required (as shown in Fig. 1). Through the offline training procedure, the tracker learns to track novel objects in a fast, robust, and accurate manner.

Although some initial work has been done in using neural networks for tracking, these efforts have produced neural-network trackers that are too slow for practical use. In contrast, our tracker is able to track objects at 100 fps, making it, to the best of our knowledge, the fastest neural-network tracker to-date. Our real-time speed is due to two factors. First, most previous neural network trackers are trained online [7,24,26,27,30,34,35,37,39]; however, training neural networks is a slow process, leading to slow tracking. In contrast, our tracker is trained offline to learn a generic relationship between appearance and motion, so no online training is required. Second, most trackers take a classification-based approach, classifying many image patches to find the target object [24,26,27,30,33,37,39]. In contrast, our tracker uses a regression-based approach, requiring just a single feed-forward pass through the network to regresses directly to the location of the target object. The combination of offline training and one-pass regression leads to a significant speed-up compared to previous approaches and allows us to track objects at real-time speeds.

GOTURN is the first generic object neural-network tracker that is able to run at 100 fps. We use a standard tracking benchmark to demonstrate that our tracker outperforms state-of-the-art trackers. Our tracker trains from a set of labeled training videos and images, but we do not require any class-level labeling or information about the types of objects being tracked. GOTURN establishes a new framework for tracking in which the relationship between appearance and motion is learned offline in a generic manner. Our code and additional experiments can be found at http://davheld.github.io/GOTURN/GOTURN.html.

2   Related Work

Online training for tracking. Trackers for generic object tracking are typically trained entirely online, starting from the first frame of a video [3,15,19,36]. A typical tracker will sample patches near the target object, which are considered as "foreground" [3]. Some patches farther from the target object are also sampled, and these are considered as "background." These patches are then used to train a foreground-background classifier, and this classifier is used to score patches from the next frame to estimate the new location of the target object [19,36]. Unfortunately, since these trackers are trained entirely online, they cannot take advantage of the large amount of videos that are readily available for offline training that can potentially be used to improve their performance.

Some researchers have also attempted to use neural networks for tracking within the traditional online training framework [7,16,24,26,27,30,34,35,37,39], showing state-of-the-art results [7,21,30]. Unfortunately, neural networks are very slow to train, and if online training is required, then the resulting tracker will be very slow at test time. Such trackers range from 0.8 fps [26] to 15 fps [37], with the top performing neural-network trackers running at 1 fps on a GPU [7,21,30]. Hence, these trackers are not usable for most practical applications. Because our tracker is trained offline in a generic manner, no online training of our tracker is required, enabling us to track at 100 fps.

Model-based trackers. A separate class of trackers are the model-based trackers which are designed to track a specific class of objects [1,11,12]. For example, if one is only interested in tracking pedestrians, then one can train a pedestrian detector. During test-time, these detections can be linked together using temporal information. These trackers are trained offline, but they are limited because they can only track a specific class of objects. Our tracker is trained offline in a generic fashion and can be used to track novel objects at test time.

Other neural network tracking frameworks. A related area of research is patch matching [14,38], which was recently used for tracking in [33], running at 4 fps. In such an approach, many candidate patches are passed through the network, and the patch with the highest matching score is selected as the tracking output. In contrast, our network only passes two images through the network, and the network regresses directly to the bounding box location of the target object. By avoiding the need to score many candidate patches, we are able to track objects at 100 fps.

Prior attempts have been made to use neural networks for tracking in various other ways [18], including visual attention models [4,29]. However, these approaches are not competitive with other state-of-the-art trackers when evaluated on difficult tracker datasets.

3   Method

3.1   Method Overview

At a high level, we feed frames of a video into a neural network, and the network successively outputs the location of the tracked object in each frame. We train the tracker entirely offline with video sequences and images. Through our offline training procedure, our tracker learns a generic relationship between appearance and motion that can be used to track novel objects at test time with no online training required.

3.2   Input/Output Format

What to track. In case there are multiple objects in the video, the network must receive some information about which object in the video is being tracked. To achieve this, we input an image of the target object into the network. We crop and scale the previous frame to be centered on the target object, as shown in Fig. 2. This input allows our network to track novel objects that it has not seen before; the network will track whatever object is being input in this crop. We pad this crop to allow the network to receive some contextual information about the surroundings of the target object.

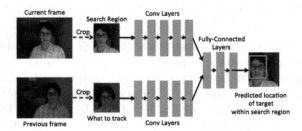

Fig. 2. Our network architecture for tracking. We input to the network a search region from the current frame and a target from the previous frame. The network learns to compare these crops to find the target object in the current image

In more detail, suppose that in frame $t - 1$, our tracker previously predicted that the target was located in a bounding box centered at $c = (c_x, c_y)$ with a width of w and a height of h. At time t, we take a crop of frame $t - 1$ centered at (c_x, c_y) with a width and height of $k_1 w$ and $k_1 h$, respectively. This crop tells the network which object is being tracked. The value of k_1 determines how much context the network will receive about the target object from the previous frame.

Where to look. To find the target object in the current frame, the tracker should know where the object was previously located. Since objects tend to move smoothly through space, the previous location of the object will provide a good guess of where the network should expect to currently find the object. We achieve this by choosing a search region in our current frame based on the object's previous location. We crop the current frame using the search region and input this crop into our network, as shown in Fig. 2. The goal of the network is then to regress to the location of the target object within the search region.

In more detail, the crop of the current frame t is centered at $c' = (c'_x, c'_y)$, where c' is the expected mean location of the target object. We set $c' = c$, which is equivalent to a constant position motion model, although more sophisticated motion models can be used as well. The crop of the current frame has a width and height of $k_2 w$ and $k_2 h$, respectively, where w and h are the width and height of the predicted bounding box in the previous frame, and k_2 defines our search radius for the target object. In practice, we use $k_1 = k_2 = 2$.

As long as the target object does not become occluded and is not moving too quickly, the target will be located within this region. For fast-moving objects, the size of the search region could be increased, at a cost of increasing the complexity of the network. Alternatively, to handle long-term occlusions or large movements, our tracker can be combined with another approach such as an online-trained object detector, as in the TLD framework [19], or a visual attention model [2, 4, 29]; we leave this for future work.

Network output. The network outputs the coordinates of the object in the current frame, relative to the search region. The network's output consists of the coordinates of the top left and bottom right corners of the bounding box.

3.3 Network Architecture

For single-target tracking, we define a novel image-comparison tracking architecture, shown in Fig. 2 (note that related "two-frame" architectures have also been used for other tasks [10, 20]). In this model, we input the target object as well as the search region each into a sequence of convolutional layers. The output of these convolutional layers is a set of features that capture a high-level representation of the image.

The outputs of these convolutional layers are then fed through a number of fully connected layers. The role of the fully connected layers is to compare the features from the target object to the features in the current frame to find where the target object has moved. Between these frames, the object may have undergone a translation, rotation, lighting change, occlusion, or deformation.

The function learned by the fully connected layers is thus a complex feature comparison which is learned through many examples to be robust to these various factors while outputting the relative motion of the tracked object.

In more detail, the convolutional layers in our model are taken from the first five convolutional layers of the CaffeNet architecture [17,23]. We concatenate the output of these convolutional layers (i.e. the pool5 features) into a single vector. This vector is input to 3 fully connected layers, each with 4096 nodes. Finally, we connect the last fully connected layer to an output layer that contains 4 nodes which represent the output bounding box. We scale the output by a factor of 10, chosen using our validation set (as with all of our hyperparameters). Network hyperparameters are taken from the defaults for CaffeNet, and between each fully-connected layer we use dropout and ReLU non-linearities as in CaffeNet. Our neural network is implemented using Caffe [17].

3.4 Tracking

During test time, we initialize the tracker with a ground-truth bounding box from the first frame, as is standard practice for single-target tracking. At each subsequent frame t, we input crops from frame $t-1$ and frame t into the network (as described in Sect. 3.2) to predict where the object is located in frame t. We continue to re-crop and feed pairs of frames into our network for the remainder of the video, and our network will track the movement of the target object throughout the entire video sequence.

4   Training

We train our network with a combination of videos and still images. The training procedure is described below. In both cases, we train the network with an L1 loss between the predicted bounding box and the ground-truth bounding box.

4.1   Training from Videos and Images

Our training set consists of a collection of videos in which a subset of frames in each video are labeled with the location of some object. For each successive pair of frames in the training set, we crop the frames as described in Sect. 3.2. During training time, we feed this pair of frames into the network and attempt to predict how the object has moved from the first frame to the second frame (shown in Fig. 3). We also augment these training examples using our motion model, as described in Sect. 4.2.

Our training procedure can also take advantage of a set of still images that are each labeled with the location of an object. This training set of images teaches our network to track a more diverse set of objects and prevents overfitting to the objects in our training videos. To train our tracker from an image, we take random crops of the image according to our motion model (see Sect. 4.2). Between these two crops, the target object has undergone an apparent translation and

Fig. 3. Examples of training videos. The goal of the network is to predict the location of the target object shown in the center of the video frame in the top row, after being shifted as in the bottom row. The ground-truth bounding box is marked in green (Color figure online)

Fig. 4. Examples of training images. The goal of the network is to predict the location of the target object shown in the center of the image crop in the top row, after being shifted as in the bottom row. The ground-truth bounding box is marked in green (Color figure online)

scale change, as shown in Fig. 4. We treat these crops as if they were taken from different frames of a video. Although the "motions" in these crops are less varied than the types of motions found in our training videos, these images are still useful to train our network to track a variety of different objects.

4.2 Learning Motion Smoothness

Objects in the real-world tend to move smoothly through space. Given an ambiguous image in which the location of the target object is uncertain, a tracker should predict that the target object is located near to the location where it was previously observed. This is especially important in videos that contain multiple nearly-identical objects, such as multiple fruit of the same type. Thus we wish to teach our network that, all else being equal, small motions are preferred to large motions.

To concretize the idea of motion smoothness, we model the center of the bounding box in the current frame (c'_x, c'_y) relative to the center of the bounding box in the previous frame (c_x, c_y) as

$$c'_x = c_x + w \cdot \Delta x \qquad (1)$$
$$c'_y = c_y + h \cdot \Delta y \qquad (2)$$

where w and h are the width and height, respectively, of the bounding box of the previous frame. The terms Δx and Δy are random variables that capture the change in position of the bounding box relative to its size. In our training set, we find that objects change their position such that Δx and Δy can each be modeled with a Laplace distribution with a mean of 0 (see Supplementary Material for details). Such a distribution places a higher probability on smaller motions than larger motions.

Similarly, we model size changes by

$$w' = w \cdot \gamma_w \tag{3}$$
$$h' = h \cdot \gamma_h \tag{4}$$

where w' and h' are the current width and height of the bounding box and w and h are the previous width and height of the bounding box. The terms γ_w and γ_h are random variables that capture the size change of the bounding box. We find in our training set that γ_w and γ_h are modeled by a Laplace distribution with a mean of 1. Such a distribution gives a higher probability on keeping the bounding box size near the same as the size from the previous frame.

To teach our network to prefer small motions to large motions, we augment our training set with random crops drawn from the Laplace distributions described above (see Figs. 3 and 4 for examples). Because these training examples are sampled from a Laplace distribution, small motions will be sampled more than large motions, and thus our network will learn to prefer small motions to large motions, all else being equal. We will show that this Laplace cropping procedure improves the performance of our tracker compared to the standard uniform cropping procedure used in classification tasks [23].

The scale parameters for the Laplace distributions are chosen via cross-validation to be $b_x = 1/5$ (for the motion of the bounding box center) and $b_s = 1/15$ (for the change in bounding box size). We constrain the random crop such that it must contain at least half of the target object in each dimension. We also limit the size changes such that $\gamma_w, \gamma_h \in (0.6, 1.4)$, to avoid overly stretching or shrinking the bounding box in a way that would be difficult for the network to learn.

4.3   Training Procedure

To train our network, each training example is alternately taken from a video or from an image. When we use a video training example, we randomly choose a video, and we randomly choose a pair of successive frames in this video. We then crop the video according to the procedure described in Sect. 3.2. We additionally take k_3 random crops of the current frame, as described in Sect. 4.2, to augment the dataset with k_3 additional examples. Next, we randomly sample an image, and we repeat the procedure described above, where the random cropping creates artificial "motions" (see Sects. 4.1 and 4.2). Each time a video or image gets sampled, new random crops are produced on-the-fly, to create additional diversity in our training procedure. In our experiments, we use $k_3 = 10$, and we use a batch size of 50.

The convolutional layers in our network are pre-trained on ImageNet [8,31]. Because of our limited training set size, we do not fine-tune these layers to prevent overfitting. We train this network with a learning rate of 1e–5, and other hyperparameters are taken from the defaults for CaffeNet [17].

5   Experimental Setup

5.1   Training Set

As described in Sect. 4, we train our network using a combination of videos and still images. Our training videos come from ALOV300++ [32], a collection of 314 video sequences. We remove 7 of these videos that overlap with our test set (see Supplementary Material for details), leaving us with 307 videos to be used for training. In this dataset, approximately every 5th frame of each video has been labeled with the location of some object being tracked. These videos are generally short, ranging from a few seconds to a few minutes in length. We split these videos into 251 for training and 56 for validation/hyper-parameter tuning. The training set consists of a total of 13,082 images of 251 different objects, or an average of 52 frames per object. The validation set consists of 2,795 images of 56 different objects. After choosing our hyperparameters, we retrain our model using our entire training set (training + validation). After removing the 7 overlapping videos, there is no overlap between the videos in the training and test sets.

Our training procedure also leveraged a set of still images that were used for training, as described in Sect. 4.1. These images were taken from the training set of the ImageNet Detection Challenge [31], in which 478,807 objects were labeled with bounding boxes. We randomly crop these images during training time, as described in Sect. 4.2, to create an apparent translation or scale change between two random crops. The random cropping procedure is only useful if the labeled object does not fill the entire image; thus, we filter those images for which the bounding box fills at least 66 % of the size of the image in either dimension (chosen using our validation set). This leaves us with a total of 239,283 annotations from 134,821 images. These images help prevent overfitting by teaching our network to track objects that do not appear in the training videos.

5.2   Test Set

Our test set consists of the 25 videos from the VOT 2014 Tracking Challenge [22]. We could not test our method on the VOT 2015 challenge [21] because there would be too much overlap between the test set and our training set. However, we expect the general trends of our method to still hold.

The VOT 2014 Tracking Challenge [22] is a standard tracking benchmark that allows us to compare our tracker to a wide variety of state-of-the-art trackers. The trackers are evaluated using two standard tracking metrics: accuracy (A) and robustness (R) [6,22], which range from 0 to 1. We also compute accuracy errors $(1 - A)$, robustness errors $(1 - R)$, and overall errors $1 - (A + R)/2$.

Each frame of the video is annotated with a number of attributes: occlusion, illumination change, motion change, size change, and camera motion. The trackers are also ranked in accuracy and robustness separately for each attribute, and the rankings are then averaged across attributes to get a final average accuracy and robustness ranking for each tracker. The accuracy and robustness rankings are averaged to get an overall average ranking.

6 Results

6.1 Overall Performance

The performance of our tracker is shown in Fig. 5, which demonstrates that our tracker has good robustness and performs near the top in accuracy. Further, our overall ranking (computed as the average of accuracy and robustness) outperforms all previous trackers on this benchmark. We have thus demonstrated the value of offline training for improving tracking performance. Moreover, these results were obtained after training on only 307 short videos. Figure 5 as well as analysis in the supplement suggests that further gains could be achieved if the training set size were increased by labeling more videos. Qualitative results, as well as failure cases, can be seen in the Supplementary Video; currently, the tracker can fail due to occlusions or overfitting to objects in the training set.

On an Nvidia GeForce GTX Titan X GPU with cuDNN acceleration, our tracker runs at 6.05 ms per frame (not including the 1 ms to load each image in OpenCV), or 165 fps. On a GTX 680 GPU, our tracker runs at an average of

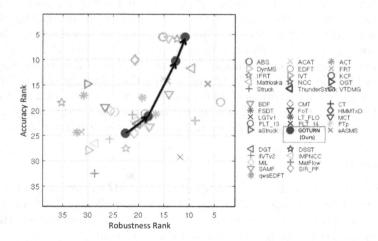

Fig. 5. Tracking results from the VOT 2014 tracking challenge. Our tracker's performance is indicated with a blue circle, outperforming all previous methods on the overall rank (average of accuracy and robustness ranks). The points shown along the black line represent training from 14, 37, 157, and 307 videos, with the same number of training images used in each case (Color figure online)

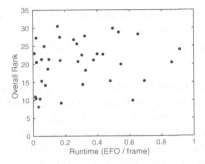

Fig. 6. Rank vs runtime of our tracker (red) compared to the 38 baseline methods from the VOT 2014 Tracking Challenge (blue). Each blue dot represents the performance of a separate baseline method (best viewed in color). Accuracy and robustness metrics are shown in the supplement (Color figure online)

9.98 ms per frame, or 100 fps. If only a CPU is available, the tracker runs at 2.7 fps. Because our tracker is able to perform all of its training offline, during test time the tracker requires only a single feed-forward pass through the network, and thus the tracker is able to run at real-time speeds.

We compare the speed and rank of our tracker compared to the 38 other trackers submitted to the VOT 2014 Tracking Challenge [22] in Fig. 6, using the overall rank score described in Sect. 5.2. We show the runtime of the tracker in EFO units (Equivalent Filter Operations), which normalizes for the type of hardware that the tracker was tested on [22]. Figure 6 demonstrates that ours was one of the fastest trackers compared to the 38 other baselines, while outperforming all other methods in the overall rank (computed as the average of the accuracy and robustness ranks). Note that some of these other trackers, such as ThunderStruck [22], also use a GPU.

Our tracker is able to track objects in real-time due to two aspects of our model: First, we learn a generic tracking model offline, so no online training is required. Online training of neural networks tends to be very slow, preventing real-time performance. Online-trained neural network trackers range from 0.8 fps [26] to 15 fps [37], with the top performing trackers running at 1 fps on a GPU [7,21,30]. Second, most trackers evaluate a finite number of samples and choose the highest scoring one as the tracking output [24,26,27,30,33,37,39]. With a sampling approach, the accuracy is limited by the number of samples, but increasing the number of samples also increases the computational complexity. On the other hand, our tracker regresses directly to the output bounding box, so GOTURN achieves accurate tracking with no extra computational cost, enabling it to track objects at 100 fps.

6.2   How Does It Work?

How does our neural-network tracker work? There are two hypotheses that one might propose:

1. The network compares the previous frame to the current frame to find the target object in the current frame.
2. The network acts as a local generic "object detector" and simply locates the nearest "object."

We differentiate between these hypotheses by comparing the performance of our network (shown in Fig. 2) to the performance of a network which does not receive the previous frame as input (i.e. the network only receives the current frame as input). For this experiment, we train each of these networks separately. If the network does not receive the previous frame as input, then the tracker can only act as a local generic object detector (hypothesis 2).

Figure 7 shows the degree to which each of the hypotheses holds true for different tracking conditions. For example, when there is an occlusion or a large camera motion, the tracker benefits greatly from using the previous frame, which enables the tracker to "remember" which object is being tracked. Figure 7 shows that the tracker performs much worse in these cases when the previous frame is not included. In such cases, hypothesis 1 plays a large role, i.e. the tracker is comparing the previous frame to the current frame to find the target object.

On the other hand, when there is a size change or no variation, the tracker performs slightly worse when using the previous frame (or approximately the same). Under a large size change, the corresponding appearance change is too drastic for our network to perform an accurate comparison between the previous frame and the current frame. Thus the tracker is acting as a local generic object detector in such a case and hypothesis 2 is dominant. Each hypothesis holds true in varying degrees for different tracking conditions, as shown in Fig. 7.

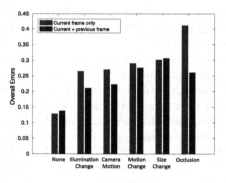

Fig. 7. Overall tracking errors for our network which receives as input both the current and previous frame, compared to a network which receives as input only the current frame (lower is better). This comparison allows us to disambiguate between two hypotheses that can explain how our neural-network tracker works (see Sect. 6.2). Accuracy and robustness metrics are shown in the supplement

6.3 Generality vs Specificity

How well can our tracker generalize to novel objects not found in our training set? For this analysis, we separate our test set into objects for which at least 25 videos of the same class appear in our training set and objects for which fewer than 25 videos of that class appear in our training set. Figure 8 shows that, even for test objects that do not have any (or very few) similar objects in our training set, our tracker performs well. The performance continues to improve even as videos of unrelated objects are added to our training set, since our tracker is able to learn a generic relationship between an object's appearance change and its motion that can generalize to novel objects.

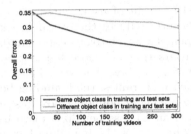

Fig. 8. Overall tracking errors for different types of objects in our test set as a function of the number of videos in our training set (lower is better). Class labels are not used by our tracker; these labels were obtained only for the purpose of this analysis. Accuracy and robustness metrics are shown in the supplement

Additionally, our tracker can also be specialized to track certain objects particularly well. Figure 8 shows that, for test objects for which at least 25 videos of the same class appear in the training set, we obtain a large improvement as more training videos of those types of objects are added. This allows the user to specialize the tracker for particular applications. For example, if the tracker is being used for autonomous driving, then the user can add more objects of people, bikes, and cars into the training set, and the tracker will learn to track those objects particularly well. At the same time, Fig. 8 also demonstrates that our tracker can track novel objects that do not appear in our training set, which is important when tracking objects in uncontrolled environments.

6.4 Ablative Analysis

In Table 1, we show which components of our system contribute the most to our performance. We train our network with random cropping from a Laplace distribution to teach our tracker to prefer small motions to large motions (e.g. motion smoothness), as explained in Sect. 4.2. Table 1 shows the benefit of this approach compared to the baseline of uniformly sampling random crops ("No motion smoothness"), as is typically done for classification [23]. As shown, we reduce errors by 20 % by drawing our random crops from a Laplace distribution.

Table 1. Comparing our full GOTURN tracking method to various modified versions of our method to analyze the effect of different components of the system

GOTURN variant	Overall errors	Accuracy errors	Robustness errors
L2 loss	0.43	0.69	0.17
No motion smoothness	0.30	0.48	0.13
Image training only	0.35	0.54	0.16
Video training only	0.29	0.44	0.13
Full method (Ours)	**0.24**	**0.39**	**0.10**

Table 1 also shows the benefit of using an L1 loss compared to an L2 loss. Using an L1 loss significantly reduces the overall tracking errors from 0.43 to 0.24. Because the L2 penalty is relatively flat near 0, the network does not sufficiently penalize outputs that are close but not correct, and the network would often output a bounding box that was slightly too large or too small. When applied to a sequence of frames, the bounding box would grow or shrink without bound until the predicted bounding box was just a single point or the entire image. In contrast, an L1 loss penalizes more harshly answers that are only slightly incorrect, which keeps the bounding box size closer to the correct size and prevents the bounding box from shrinking or growing without bound.

We train our tracker using a combination of images and videos. Table 1 shows that, given the choice between images and videos, training on only videos gives a much bigger improvement to our tracker performance. At the same time, training on both videos and images gives the maximum performance for our tracker. Training on a small number of labeled videos has taught our tracker to be invariant to background motion, out-of-plane rotations, deformations, lighting changes, and minor occlusions. Training from a large number of labeled images has taught our network how to track a wide variety of different types of objects. By training on both videos and images, our tracker learns to track a variety of object types under different conditions, achieving maximum performance.

7 Conclusions

We have demonstrated that we can train a generic object tracker offline such that its performance improves by watching more training videos. During test time, we run the network in a purely feed-forward manner with no online fine-tuning required, allowing the tracker to run at 100 fps. Our tracker learns offline a generic relationship between an object's appearance and its motion, allowing our network to track novel objects at real-time speeds.

Acknowledgments. We acknowledge the support of Toyota grant 1186781-31-UDARO and ONR grant 1165419-10-TDAUZ.

References

1. Andriluka, M., Roth, S., Schiele, B.: People-tracking-by-detection and people-detection-by-tracking. In: IEEE Conference on Computer Vision and Pattern Recognition, 2008. CVpPR 2008, pp. 1–8. IEEE (2008)
2. Ba, J., Mnih, V., Kavukcuoglu, K.: Multiple object recognition with visual attention. arXiv preprint arXiv:1412.7755 (2014)
3. Babenko, B., Yang, M.H., Belongie, S.: Visual tracking with online multiple instance learning. In: IEEE Conference on Computer Vision and Pattern Recognition, 2009. CVPPR 2009, pp. 983–990. IEEE (2009)
4. Bazzani, L., Larochelle, H., Murino, V.,Ting, J.a., Freitas, N.D.: Learning attentional policies for tracking and recognition in video with deep networks. In: Proceedings of the 28th International Conference on Machine Learning (ICML-2011), pp. 937–944 (2011)
5. Bo, L., Ren, X., Fox, D.: Multipath sparse coding using hierarchical matching pursuit. In: 2013 IEEE Conference on Computer Vision and Pattern Recognition (CVPR), pp. 660–667. IEEE (2013)
6. Cehovin, L., Kristan, M., Leonardis, A.: Is my new tracker really better than yours? In: 2014 IEEE Winter Conference on Applications of Computer Vision (WACV), pp. 540–547. IEEE (2014)
7. Danelljan, M., Hager, G., Shahbaz Khan, F., Felsberg, M.: Learning spatially regularized correlation filters for visual tracking. In: Proceedings of the IEEE International Conference on Computer Vision (ICCV), pp. 4310–4318 (2015)
8. Deng, J., Dong, W., Socher, R., Li, L.J., Li, K., Fei-Fei, L.: ImageNet: a large-scale hierarchical image database. In: IEEE Conference on Computer Vision and Pattern Recognition, 2009. CVPPR 2009, pp. 248–255. IEEE (2009)
9. Donahue, J., Hendricks, L.A., Guadarrama, S., Rohrbach, M., Venugopalan, S., Saenko, K., Darrell, T.: Long-term recurrent convolutional networks for visual recognition and description. arXiv preprint arXiv:1411.4389 (2014)
10. Dosovitskiy, A., Fischery, P., Ilg, E., Hazirbas, C., Golkov, V., van der Smagt, P., Cremers, D., Brox, T., et al.: FlowNet: learning optical flow with convolutional networks. In: 2015 IEEE International Conference on Computer Vision (ICCV), pp. 2758–2766. IEEE (2015)
11. Fan, J., Xu, W., Wu, Y., Gong, Y.: Human tracking using convolutional neural networks. IEEE Trans. Neural Netw. 21(10), 1610–1623 (2010)
12. Geiger, A.: Probabilistic models for 3D urban scene understanding from movable platforms. Ph.D. thesis, KIT (2013)
13. Girshick, R., Donahue, J., Darrell, T., Malik, J.: Rich feature hierarchies for accurate object detection and semantic segmentation. In: 2014 IEEE Conference on Computer Vision and Pattern Recognition (CVPR), pp. 580–587. IEEE (2014)
14. Han, X., Leung, T., Jia, Y., Sukthankar, R., Berg, A.C.: MatchNet: unifying feature and metric learning for patch-based matching. In: Proceedings of the IEEE Conference on Computer Vision and Pattern Recognition, pp. 3279–3286 (2015)
15. Hare, S., Saffari, A., Torr, P.H.: Struck: structured output tracking with kernels. In: 2011 IEEE International Conference on Computer Vision (ICCV), pp. 263–270. IEEE (2011)
16. Hong, S., You, T., Kwak, S., Han, B.: Online tracking by learning discriminative saliency map with convolutional neural network. In: Proceedings of the 32nd International Conference on Machine Learning, 6–11 July 2015, Lille (2015)

17. Jia, Y., Shelhamer, E., Donahue, J., Karayev, S., Long, J., Girshick, R., Guadarrama, S., Darrell, T.: Caffe: Convolutional architecture for fast feature embedding. arXiv preprint arXiv:1408.5093 (2014)
18. Jin, J., Dundar, A., Bates, J., Farabet, C., Culurciello, E.: Tracking with deep neural networks. In: 2013 47th Annual Conference on Information Sciences and Systems (CISS), pp. 1–5. IEEE (2013)
19. Kalal, Z., Mikolajczyk, K., Matas, J.: Tracking-learning-detection. IEEE Trans. Pattern Anal. Mach. Intell. **34**(7), 1409–1422 (2012)
20. Karpathy, A., Toderici, G., Shetty, S., Leung, T., Sukthankar, R., Fei-Fei, L.: Large-scale video classification with convolutional neural networks. In: Proceedings of the IEEE Conference on Computer Vision and Pattern Recognition, pp. 1725–1732 (2014)
21. Kristan, M., Matas, J., Leonardis, A., Felsberg, M., Cehovin, L., Fernandez, G., Vojir, T., Hager, G., Nebehay, G., Pflugfelder, R.: The visual object tracking vot2015 challenge results. In: Proceedings of the IEEE International Conference on Computer Vision (ICCV) Workshops, pp. 1–23 (2015)
22. Kristan, M., et al.: The visual object tracking VOT2014 challenge results. In: Agapito, L., Bronstein, M.M., Rother, C. (eds.) ECCV 2014. LNCS, vol. 8926, pp. 191–217. Springer, Heidelberg (2015). doi:10.1007/978-3-319-16181-5_14
23. Krizhevsky, A., Sutskever, I., Hinton, G.E.: ImageNet classification with deep convolutional neural networks. In: Advances in Neural Information Processing Systems, pp. 1097–1105 (2012)
24. Kuen, J., Lim, K.M., Lee, C.P.: Self-taught learning of a deep invariant representation for visual tracking via temporal slowness principle. Pattern Recognit. **48**(10), 2964–2982 (2015)
25. Levi, G., Hassner, T.: Age and gender classification using convolutional neural networks. In: 2015 IEEE Conference on Computer Vision and Pattern Recognition Workshop (CVPRW) (2015)
26. Li, H., Li, Y., Porikli, F.: DeepTrack: learning discriminative feature representations by convolutional neural networks for visual tracking. In: Proceedings of the British Machine Vision Conference. BMVA Press (2014)
27. Li, H., Li, Y., Porikli, F.: DeepTrack: learning discriminative feature representations online for robust visual tracking. arXiv preprint arXiv:1503.00072 (2015)
28. Long, J., Shelhamer, E., Darrell, T.: Fully convolutional networks for semantic segmentation. In: Proceedings of the IEEE Conference on Computer Vision and Pattern Recognition, pp. 3431–3440 (2015)
29. Mnih, V., Heess, N., Graves, A., et al.: Recurrent models of visual attention. In: Advances in Neural Information Processing Systems, pp. 2204–2212 (2014)
30. Nam, H., Han, B.: Learning multi-domain convolutional neural networks for visual tracking. arXiv preprint arXiv:1510.07945 (2015)
31. Russakovsky, O., Deng, J., Su, H., Krause, J., Satheesh, S., Ma, S., Huang, Z., Karpathy, A., Khosla, A., Bernstein, M., et al.: ImageNet large scale visual recognition challenge. Int. J. Comput. Vis. 1–42 (2014)
32. Smeulders, A.W., Chu, D.M., Cucchiara, R., Calderara, S., Dehghan, A., Shah, M.: Visual tracking: an experimental survey. IEEE Trans. Pattern Anal. Mach. Intell. **36**(7), 1442–1468 (2014)
33. Tao, R., Gavves, E., Smeulders, A.W.M.: Siamese instance search for tracking. In: Proceedings of the IEEE Conference on Computer Vision and Pattern Recognition (2016)

34. Wang, L., Ouyang, W., Wang, X., Lu, H.: Visual tracking with fully convolutional networks. In: Proceedings of the IEEE International Conference on Computer Vision (ICCV), pp. 3119–3127 (2015)
35. Wang, N., Li, S., Gupta, A., Yeung, D.Y.: Transferring rich feature hierarchies for robust visual tracking. arXiv preprint arXiv:1501.04587 (2015)
36. Wang, N., Shi, J., Yeung, D.Y., Jia, J.: Understanding and diagnosing visual tracking systems. arXiv preprint arXiv:1504.06055 (2015)
37. Wang, N., Yeung, D.Y.: Learning a deep compact image representation for visual tracking. In: Advances in Neural Information Processing Systems, pp. 809–817 (2013)
38. Zagoruyko, S., Komodakis, N.: Learning to compare image patches via convolutional neural networks. In: Proceedings of the IEEE Conference on Computer Vision and Pattern Recognition, pp. 4353–4361 (2015)
39. Zhang, K., Liu, Q., Wu, Y., Yang, M.H.: Robust visual tracking via convolutional networks. arXiv preprint arXiv:1501.04505 (2015)

Matching Handwritten Document Images

Praveen Krishnan[(✉)] and C.V. Jawahar

CVIT, IIIT, Hyderabad, India
praveen.krishnan@research.iiit.ac.in, jawahar@iiit.ac.in

Abstract. We address the problem of predicting similarity between a pair of handwritten document images written by potentially different individuals. This has applications related to matching and mining in image collections containing handwritten content. A similarity score is computed by detecting patterns of text re-usages between document images irrespective of the minor variations in word morphology, word ordering, layout and paraphrasing of the content. Our method does not depend on an accurate segmentation of words and lines. We formulate the document matching problem as a structured comparison of the word distributions across two document images. To match two word images, we propose a convolutional neural network (CNN) based feature descriptor. Performance of this representation surpasses the state-of-the-art on handwritten word spotting. Finally, we demonstrate the applicability of our method on a practical problem of matching handwritten assignments.

Keywords: Handwritten word spotting · CNN features, plagiarism detection

1 Introduction

Matching two document images has several applications related to information retrieval like spotting keywords in historical documents [8], accessing personal notes [22], camera based interface for querying [45], retrieving from video databases [27], automatic scoring of answer sheets [40], and mining and recommending in health care documents [25]. Since OCRs do not reliably work for all types of documents, one resorts to image based methods for comparing textual content. This problem is even more complex when considering unconstrained handwritten documents due to the high variations across the writers. Moreover, variable placement of the words across the documents makes a rigid geometric matching ineffective. In this work, we design a scheme for matching two handwritten document images. The problem is illustrated in Fig. 1(a). We validate the effectiveness of our method on an application, named as measure of document similarity (MODS).[1] MODS compares two handwritten document images and provides a normalized score as a measure of similarity between two images.

---

[1] In parallel to measure of software similarity (MOSS) [36], which has emerged as the de facto standard across the universities to compare software solutions from students.

© Springer International Publishing AG 2016
B. Leibe et al. (Eds.): ECCV 2016, Part I, LNCS 9905, pp. 766–782, 2016.
DOI: 10.1007/978-3-319-46448-0_46

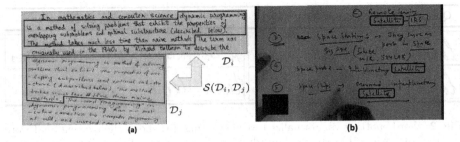

Fig. 1. (a) Given two document images $\mathcal{D}_i$ and $\mathcal{D}_j$, we are interested in computing a similarity score $\mathcal{S}(\mathcal{D}_i, \mathcal{D}_j)$ which is invariant to (i) writers, (ii) word flow across lines, (iii) spatial shifts, and (iv) paraphrasing. In this example, the highlighted lines from $\mathcal{D}_i$ and $\mathcal{D}_j$ have almost the same content but they widely differ in terms of spatial arrangement of words. (b) Query-by-text results on searching with "satellite" on an instructional video. The spotted results are highlighted in the frame.

Text is now appreciated as a critical information in understanding natural images [14,26,48]. Attempts for wordspotting in natural images [48] have now matured to end-to-end frameworks for recognition and retrieval [14,16,47]. Natural scene text is often seen as an isolated character image sequence in arbitrary view points or font styles. Recognition in this space is now becoming reliable, especially with the recent attempts that use CNNs and RNNs [14,42]. However, handwritten text understanding is still lacking in many aspects. For example, the best performance on the word spotting (or retrieval) on the popular IAM data set [24] is an mAP of 0.55 [3]. In this work, we improve this to 0.80. We achieve this with the help of synthetic handwritten data that now enables the exploitation of deep learnt representations for handwritten data.

Word Spotting. Initial attempts for matching handwritten words were based on DTW [32] and HMM [9,34] over variable length feature representations. Although these models were flexible, they were not really scalable. Many approaches such as [2,29,35] demonstrated word spotting using fixed length representation based on local features such as SIFT and HOG in a bag of words (BOW) framework. Most of these works employed better feature representations such as Fisher vectors [2,29], latent semantic indexing [35] and techniques such as query expansion and re-ranking for enhancing the performance. However, the applicability of these methods are still limited for multi-writer scenarios. Recently, Almazán *et al.* [3] proposed a label embedding and attributes learning framework where both word images and text strings are embedded into a common subspace with an associated metric to compare both modalities.

Matching documents. Matching textual documents is a well studied problem in text processing [23] with applications in plagiarism detection in electronic documents [31]. For softwares, MOSS [36] provides a solution to compare two programs and is robust against a set of alterations e.g., formatting and changes in variable names. However, when the documents are scanned images, these meth-

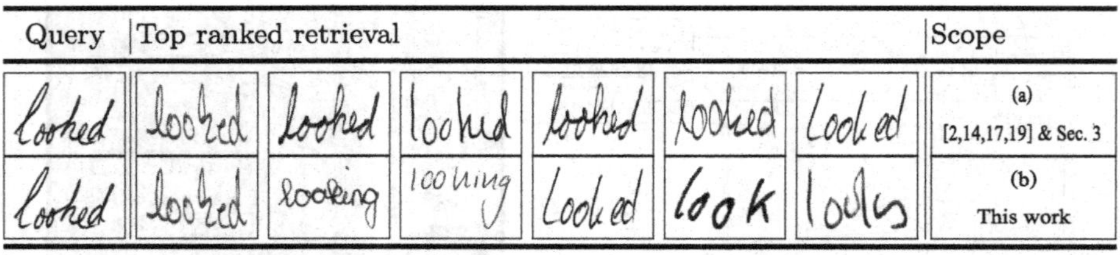

Query	Top ranked retrieval							Scope
looked	*looked*	*looked*	*looked*	*looked*	*looked*	*Looked*		(a) [2,14,17,19] & Sec. 3
looked	*looked*	*looking*	*looking*	*Looked*	*look*	*looks*		(b) This work

Fig. 2. Word spotting vs. normalized word spotting. (a) shows the conventional word spotting task while (b) extends the task to retrieve semantically similar words using a normalized representation. Here we deal with popular inflectional ending present due to agglutinative property of a language.

ods can not be directly applied. There have been some attempts [4,17] to find duplicate and near duplicates in multimedia databases. However, they are not directly applicable to documents where the objective is to compare images based on the textual content. For printed documents, matching based on geometry or organization of a set of keypoints has been successful [10,44,46]. This works well for duplicate as well as cut-and-paste detection in printed documents. However, due to unique set of challenges in handwritten documents such as wide variation of word styles, the extraction of reliable keypoints with geometric matching is not very successful. Other major challenges include paraphrasing of the textual content, non-rigidity of word ordering which leads to word overflows across lines. In our proposed method, we uses locality constraints to achieve invariance to such variations. We also extend the word spotting to take care of the popular word morphological variations in the image space as shown in Fig. 2(b). The proposed features can associate similarity between word images irrespective of word morphological variations due to changes in tense and voice of the sentence construction. In the context of retrieval systems it improves overall recall and helps in matching documents in a semantic space.

Contributions. In this work, we compute a similarity score by detecting patterns of text re-usages across documents written by different individuals irrespective of the minor variations in word forms, word ordering, layout or paraphrasing of the content. In the process of comparing two document images, we design a module that compares two handwritten words using CNN features and report a 56 % error reduction in word spotting task on the challenging dataset of IAM [24] and pages from George Washington (GW) collection [9]. We also propose a normalized feature representation for word images which is invariant to different inflectional endings or suffixes present in words. The advantage of our matching scheme is that it does not require an accurate segmentation of the documents. To calibrate the similarity score with that of human perception, we conduct a human experiment where a set of individuals are advised to create similar documents with natural variations. Our solution reports a score that match the human evaluation with a mean normalized discounted cumulative gain ($nDCG$) of 0.89. Finally, we demonstrate two immediate applications (i) search-

Fig. 3. (a) The top two rows show the variations in handwritten images, the bottom two rows demonstrate the challenges of intra class variability in images across writers. (b) Sample images from the IIIT-HWS dataset created as part of this work to address the lack of training data for for learning complex CNN networks

ing handwritten text from instructional videos, and (ii) comparing handwritten assignments. Figure 1(a,b) shows a sample result from these applications.

2   CNN Features for Handwritten Word Images

The proposed document image matching scheme employs a discriminative representation for comparing two word images. Such a representation needs to be invariant to (i) both inter and intra class variability across writers, (ii) presence of skew, (iii) quality of ink, and (iv) quality and resolution of the scanned image. Figure 3(a) demonstrates the challenges in matching across writers and documents. The top two rows show the variations across images in which some are even hard for humans to read without enough context of nearby words. The bottom two rows show different instances of same word written by different writers, e.g., "inheritance" and "Fourier" where one can clearly notice the variability in shape for each character in the word image. In this work we use convolutional neural networks (CNN) motivated by the recent success of deep neural networks [6,15,18,39,43] and the availability of better learning schemes [12,13]. Even though CNN architectures such as [19,38] were among the first to show high performing classifier for MNIST handwritten digits, application of such ideas for unconstrained continuous handwritten words or documents has not been demonstrated possibly due to the lack of data, and also the lack of appropriate training schemes.

2.1   IIIT-HWS Dataset

To address the lack of data for training handwritten word images, we build a synthetic handwritten dataset of 1 million word images. We call this dataset as IIIT-HWS. Some of the sample images from this dataset are shown in Fig. 3(b). Note that these images are very similar to natural handwriting. IIIT-HWS dataset is formed out of 750 publicly available handwritten fonts. We use a subset of Hunspell dictionary and pick a unique set of 10 K words for this purpose. For each word, we randomly sample 100 fonts and render its corresponding image. During this process, we vary the following parameters: (i) kerning level (inter character space), (ii) stroke width, and (iii) mean foreground and background pixel distributions. We also perform Gaussian filtering to smooth the final rendered image. Moreover, we prefer to learn a case insensitive model for each word category, hence we perform three types of rendering, namely, all letters capitalized, all letters lower and only the first letter in caps.[2]

2.2   HWNet Architecture and Transfer Learning

The underlying architecture of our CNN model (HWNet) is inspired from [15]. We use a CNN with five convolutional layers with 64, 128, 256, 512 and 512 square filters with dimensions: 5, 5, 3, 3 and 3 respectively. The next two layers are fully connected ones with 2048 neurons each. The last layer uses a fully connected (FC) layer with dimension equal to number of classes, 10K in our case, and is further connected to the softmax layer to compute the class specific probabilities. Rectified linear units are used as the non-linear activation units after each weight layer except the last one, and 2×2 max pooling is applied after first, second, and fourth convolutional layers. We use a stride of one and padding is done to preserve the spatial dimensionality. We empirically observed that the recent approach using batch normalization [13] for reducing the generalization error, performed better as compared to dropouts. The weights are initialized randomly from normal distribution, and during training the learning rate is reduced on a log space starting from 0.1. The input to the network is a gray scale word image of fixed size 48×128. HWNet is trained on the IIIT-HWS dataset with 75-15-10 % train-validation-test split using a multinomial logistic regression loss function to predict the class labels, and the weights are updated using mini batch gradient descent algorithm with momentum.

Transfer learning. It is well-known that off-the-shelf CNNs [7,33] trained for a related task could be adapted or fine-tuned to obtain reasonable and even state-of-the-art performance for new tasks. In our case we prefer to perform a transfer learning from synthetic domain (IIIT-HWS) to real world setting. Here we use popular handwritten labeled corpora such as IAM and GW to perform the transfer learning. It is important to keep the learning rates low in such setting, else the network quickly unlearns the generic weights learned in the initial layers. In this work, we extract the features computed from the last FC layer to represent each handwritten word image.

3   Normalized Word Spotting

Word spotting [3,22] has emerged as a popular framework for search and retrieval of text in images with applications in retrieving text from historical manuscripts, handwritten documents where the performance of optical character recognition

---

[2] More details on dataset, codes and trained CNN models are available at:- http://cvit. iiit.ac.in/research/projects/cvit-projects/matchdocimgs.

(OCR) is still limited. It is typically formulated as a retrieval problem where the query is an exemplar image (query-by-example) and the task is to retrieve all word images with similar content. It uses holistic word image representation [2,22] which does not demand character level segmentation and the retrieval is performed using nearest neighbor search. Figure 2(a) shows a word spotting result which retrieves similar word images for the query "looked". In this work, our interest lies in finding the document similarity between a pair of handwritten documents written by different writers in an unconstrained setting. We observe that such a problem can be addressed in a word spotting framework where the task would be to match similar words between a pair of documents using the proposed CNN features for handwritten word images.

HWNet provides a generic representation for word spotting by retrieving word images with the exact content written. While addressing the larger problem of document retrieval, on similar lines of a text based information retrieval pipeline, we relax this constraint and prefer to retrieve not just similar or exact words but also their common variations. These variations are observed in languages due to morphology. In English, we observe such variations in the form of inflectional endings (suffixes) such as "-s (plural), -ed (past tense), -ess (adjective), -ing (continuous form)" etc. These suffixes are added to the root word, and thereby resulting in a semantically related word. A stemmer, such as the Porter stemmer [30] can strip out common suffixes which generates a normalized representation of words with common roots. We imitate the process of stemming in the visual domain by labeling the training data in terms of root words given by the Porter stemmer, and use the HWNet architecture to learn a normalized representation which captures the visual representation of word images along with the invariance to its inflectional endings. We observe that such a network learns to give less weights to popular word suffixes and gives a normalized representation which is better suited for document image retrieval tasks. Figure 2(b) shows the normalized word spotting results obtained using the proposed features that includes both "similar" and "semantically-similar" results, e.g., "look", "looks", "looking" and "looked".

4   Measure of Document Similarity (MODS)

Matching printed documents for retrieving the original documents and detecting cut-and-paste for finding plagiarism were attempted in the past by computing interest points in word images and their corresponding matches [10,44]. However, handwritten documents have large intra class variability to reliably detect interest points. In addition, the problem of word-overflow in which words from the right end of the document overflow and appear on the left end of the next line make the matching based on rigid geometry infeasible. We state our problem as follows: *given a pair of document images, compute a similarity score by detecting patterns of text re-usages between documents irrespective of the minor variations in word morphology, word ordering, layout and paraphrasing of the content.* Our matching scheme is broadly split into two stages. The first stage involves segmentation of document into multiple possible word bounding boxes while the later stage computes a structured document similarity score which obeys loose word ordering and its content.

4.1 Document Segmentation

A document image contains structured objects. The objects here are the words and structure is the order in which words are presented. Segmentation of a handwritten document image into constituent words is a challenging task because of the unconstrained nature of documents such as variable placements of page elements (figures, graphs and equations), presence of skewed lines, and irregular kerning. Most of the methods such as [11,41] are bottom-up approaches with tunable parameters to arrive at a unique segmentation of words and lines. Considering the complexity of handwritten documents, we argue that a reasonably practical system, should work with multiple possible lines and word segmentation proposals with a high recall. We use a simple multi-stage bottom-up approach similar to [20] by forming three sets of connected components (CCs) on the binarized image based on its sizes. CCs in s_1 set contains area less than 0.1μ, s_3 set contains CCs having area large than $\mu + 2\sigma$ while remaining CCs are categorized as s_2. Here μ, σ is mean and standard deviation respectively. The small (s_1), medium (s_2) and large (s_3) CC sets are assumed to be punctuation, actual characters and high probable line merge respectively. We associate each component in s_2 with its adjacent component if the cost given by:- $Cost(i,j) = OL(i,j) + D(i,j) + \theta(i,j)$, is above a certain threshold. Here i, j are two components, OL is the amount of overlap in y-axis which is given by intersection over union, D is the normalized distance between the centroids of the ith and j^{th} component, and $\theta(i,j)$ gives the angle between the centroids of the components. After the initial assignment, we now associate the s_3 components by checking whether these components intersects in the path of detected lines. In such a case, we slice the component horizontally and join it to the top and the bottom line respectively. Finally the components present in s_1 are associated with nearest detected lines. Given the bounding boxes of a set of CCs and its line associations, we analyse the inter CC spacing and derive multiple thresholds to group it into words. This results in multiple word bounding box hypotheses with a high recall. Minor reduction in the precision at this stage is taken care by our matching scheme.

4.2 SWM Matching

We first define a similarity score between a pair of documents as the sum of word matches (SWM). We use l_2 normalized CNN descriptors of the corresponding words images w_k and w_l and compute the l_2 distance d_{kl}. We define the document similarity as the symmetric distance between the best word matches across the documents as follows:-

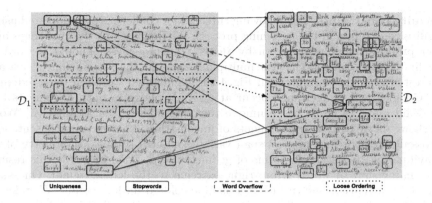

Fig. 4. A few major challenges of the matching process between a pair of documents $\mathcal{D}_1$ and $\mathcal{D}_2$. (i) Finding a unique match of each potential word, (ii) removal of stopwords, (iii) invariance to word overflow problems, and (iv) exploiting the loose ordering of words in matching.

$$\mathcal{S}_N(\mathcal{D}_i, \mathcal{D}_j) = \frac{1}{|\mathcal{D}_i| + |\mathcal{D}_j|} \left(\sum_{w_k \in \mathcal{D}_i} \min_{w_l \in \mathcal{D}_j} d_{kl} + \sum_{w_l \in \mathcal{D}_j} \min_{w_k \in \mathcal{D}_i} d_{lk} \right). \quad (1)$$

This is a normalized symmetric distance where $|\mathcal{D}_i|$ is the number of words in the document $\mathcal{D}_i$. In order to reduce the exhaustive matches, we use an approximate nearest neighbor search using KD trees.

4.3   MODS Matching

The problem of document matching and devising a scheme to compute similarity score is a challenging task. This problem along with the challenges is illustrated in Fig. 4. We address these problems along with their solution at two levels: (i) individual word matches, and (ii) bringing locality constraints.

Word matches. (i) Alternations: In general, the pair of documents of interest need not have the same content and hence, not all words need to have a correspondence in the second image. We enforce this with a simple threshold γ on the distance used for matching. (ii) Stopwords: The presence of stopwords in documents acts as a noise which corrupts the matching process for any IR system due their high frequency. In Fig. 4 we show some of these words in dark green boxes. We observed that the trained HWNet is reasonably robust in classifying stopwords due to their limited number and increased presence in training data. Therefore, we could take the softmax scores (probabilities) from last layer of HWNet and classify a word image as a stopword if the scores of one of stopword classes is above a certain threshold.

Locality constraints. The following three major challenges are addressed using locality constraints in the matching process. We first list out the challenges and later propose the solution given by MODS. (i) Uniqueness: Though a word in the first image can match with multiple images in the second image, we are interested in a unique match. In Fig. 4 the highlighted words in dark red such as "Google" and "PageRank" occur at multiple places in both documents but the valid matches needs to be unique that obeys the given locality. (ii) Word overflow: As we deal with documents of unconstrained nature, similar sentences across different documents can span variable number of lines, a property of an individual writing style. In terms of geometry of position of words this results in a major shift of words (from right extreme to the left extreme). One such pair of occurrence is shown in Fig. 4 as blue colored dashed region. We refer to this problem as word overflow. (iii) Loose ordering: Paraphrasing of the words as shown in the Fig. 4 as black dashed rectangle, is a common technique to conceal the act of copying where one changes the order of the words keeping the semantics intact.

We observe that the most informative matching words are the ones which preserve the consistency within a locality. We enforce locality constraints by splitting the document into multiple overlapping rectangular regions. The idea is to find out the best matching pairs of regions within two documents and associate them with individual word matches. For finding the cost of associating two rectangular regions, we formulate the problem as a weighted bipartite graph matching where the weights are the cosine distances of word images in feature space. We use the popular Hungarian algorithm to compute the cost of word assignments, which leads to a one to one mapping of word images between a pair of regions. The score computed between a pair of rectangular regions denoted as p and q from documents $\mathcal{D}_i$ and $\mathcal{D}_j$ respectively is given by:

$$Score(p) = \max_{q \in R(\mathcal{D}_j)} \left(\frac{\sum_{(k,l) \in Matches(p,q)} (1 - d_{kl})}{max(|p|, |q|)} \right), \forall p \in R(\mathcal{D}_i), \qquad (2)$$

where, $R(\mathcal{D}_j)$ denotes the set of all rectangular regions in a document image and $|.|$ denotes number of words in the region. The function $Matches(p, q)$ returns the assignments given by the Hungarian algorithm. Finally, the normalized MODS score for a pair of documents is defined as follows:

$$\mathcal{S}_M(\mathcal{D}_i, \mathcal{D}_j) = \frac{\sum_{p \in R(\mathcal{D}_i)} Score(p)}{max(|\mathcal{D}_i|, |\mathcal{D}_j|)}. \qquad (3)$$

5   Experiments

In this section, we empirically evaluate the proposed CNN representation for the task of word spotting on standard datasets. We validate the effectiveness of these features on newer tasks such as retrieving semantically similar words, searching keywords from instructional videos and finally demonstrate the performance of the MODS algorithm for finding similarity between documents on annotated datasets created for this purpose.

Table 1. Quantitative results on word spotting using the proposed CNN features along with comparisons with various existing hand designed features on IAM and GW dataset.

Dataset	DTW[3]	SC-HMM[34]	FV[3]	EX-SVM[2]	KCCA[1]	KCSR[3]	Ours
GW	0.6063	0.5300	0.6272	0.5913	0.8563	0.9290	**0.9484**
IAM	0.1230	-	0.1566	-	0.5478	0.5573	**0.8061**

5.1 Word-Spotting

We perform word spotting in a *query-by-example* setting. We use IAM [24] and George Washington [9] (GW) dataset, popularly used in handwritten word spotting and recognition tasks. In case of the IAM dataset, we use the standard partition for training, testing, and validation provided along with the corpus. For GW dataset, we use a random set of 75 % for training and validation, and the remaining 25 % for testing. Each word image except the stop words in the test corpus is taken as the query to be ranked across all other images from the test corpus including stop-words acting as distractions. The performance is measured using the standard evaluation measure namely, mean Average Precision (mAP). HWNet architecture is fine-tuned using the respective standard training set for each test scenario. Table 1 compares the proposed features from state-of-the-art methods on these datasets. The results are evaluated in a case-insensitive manner as used in previous works [2,3]. The proposed CNN features clearly surpasses the current state-of-the-art method [3] on IAM and GW, reducing the error rates by ∼ 56 % and ∼ 27 % respectively. This demonstrates the invariance of features for both multi-writer scenario (IAM) and historical documents (GW). Some of the qualitative results are shown in the top three rows of Fig. 6(a). One can observe the variability of each retrieved result which demonstrates the robustness the proposed features.

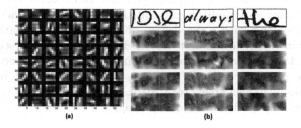

Fig. 5. Visualization: (a) The weights of first layer of HWNet. (b) Four possible reconstructions [21] of three sample word images shown in columns. These are re-constructed from the representation of final layer of HWNet.

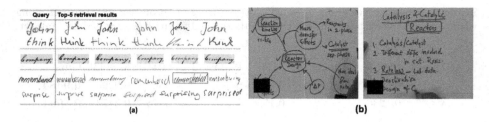

(a)   (b)

Fig. 6. Qualitative results: (a) Query-by-example results for the task of word spotting results on IAM and GW dataset. The bottom two rows shows results from normalized feature representation where one can observe we are also able to retrieve words with related meanings. (b) Query-by-text results on searching with "reactor" on an instructional video. The top two results are shown along with the spotted words which are highlighted in the frame.

Table 2. Word spotting results using normalized features and its comparisons with exact features.

Evaluation	CNN	CNN_{Norm}
Exact	**0.8061**	0.7955
Inexact	0.7170	**0.7443**

Visualizations. Figure 5 shows the visualization of the trained HWNet architecture using popular schemes demonstrated in [18,21]. Figure 5(a) visualizes the weights of the first layer which bears a resemblance to Gabor filters and detects edges in different orientations. Figure 5(b) demonstrates the visualization from a recent method [21] which inverts the CNN encoding back to image space and arrives at possibles images which have high degree of probability for that encoding. This gives a better intuition of the learned layers and helps in understanding the invariances of the network. Here, we show the query images on the first row and its reconstruction in the following rows. One can observe that in almost all reconstructions there are multiple translated copies of the characters present in the word image along with some degree of orientations. Similarly, we can see the network is invariant to the first letter being in capital case (see Label: "the" at Col:3, Row:4) which was part of the training process. The reconstruction of the first image (see Label: "rose" at Col:1, Row:1) shows that possible reconstruction images includes Label: "rose" (Col:1, Row:2) and "jose" (Col:1, Row:3) since there is an ambiguity in the query image.

5.2   Enhancements and Applications

We now analyse the performance of the normalized features for retrieving semantically similar words which has not been yet attempted in handwritten domain and plays an important role in matching similar documents. We also demonstrate an application of MODS framework in a collection of instructional videos by retrieving relevant frames corresponding to user queries.

Normalized Word Spotting. Table 2 shows the quantitative results of the normalized (CNN_{Norm}) features which are invariant to common word inflectional endings and thereby learn features for stem or the root part of the word image. For this experiment, we update the evaluation scheme (ref. as inexact) to include not only similar word images but also the word images having common stem. We use Porter stemmer [30] for calculating the stem of a word. Table 2 also compares the performance of CNN features used in Sect. 5.1 and validate it over inexact evaluation. Here we obtain a reduced mAP of 0.7170 whereas using the normalized features, we improve the mAP to 0.7443. We also observe that using normalized features for exact evaluation results in a comparable performance (0.7955) which motivates us to use them in document similarity problems. In Fig. 6(a), the bottom two rows shows qualitative results using these normalized features. The retrieval results for query "surprise" contains the word "surprised", "surprising" along with the keyword "surprise".

Searching in Instructional Videos. To demonstrate the effectiveness and generalization ability of the proposed CNN features we performed an interesting task of searching inside instructional videos where the tutor write handwritten text to aid students in the class. We conducted the experiment in a query-by-text scenario where the query text is synthesized into a word image using one of the fonts used in the IIIT-HWS dataset. We took five popular online course videos from NPTEL [28] on different topics from YouTube and manually extracted frames containing textual regions. For each frame, we obtained multiple segmentation output from the proposed segmentation method. For evaluation, we handpicked 20 important queries and labeled the frames containing them. We obtained a frame level mAP of 0.9369 on this task. Figure 6(b) shows the top-2 matching frames for the query "reactor" along with the spotted words. One can observe that along with retrieving exact matches, we also retrieve similar keywords such as "Reactors", and "Reaction".

5.3   HW-DocSim Dataset and Evaluations

We start with the textual corpus presented in [5] for plagiarism detection. The corpus contains plagiarized short answers to five unique questions given to 19 participants. Hence the corpus contains around 100 documents of which 95 were created in a controlled setting while five were the original answers (source document) which were given to participants to refer to and copy. There are four types or degree of plagiarism introduced in this collection: (i) *near copy*, where the content is an exact copy from different parts from the source; (ii) *light revision*, where the content is taken from source but with slight revisions such as replacing words with synonyms, (iii) *heavy revision*, which includes heavy modification such as paraphrasing, combining or splitting sentences and changing the

Table 3. Quantitative evaluation of various matching schemes on HW-DocSim dataset. We compare the performance of proposed MODS framework using CNN features over baseline methods such as NN, BOW, and embedded attributes proposed in [3].

Method	NN	BOW	SWM	MODS	SWM	MODS
Feature	Profile	SIFT	KCSR [3]		CNN	
$nDCG$@99	0.5856	0.6128	0.7968	0.8444	0.8569	**0.8993**
AUC		0.5377	0.4516	0.8231	0.8302	0.9465	**0.9720**

order; and (iv) *non-plagiarized*, where the content is prepared independently on the same topic. For the task of generating handwritten document images, we included a total of 24 students and asked them to write on plain white sheets of paper. For each document we use a separate student to avoid any biases in writing styles. To keep the content close to its natural form, we did not mention any requirements on spacing between words, and lines, and did not put any constraints on the formatting of text in the form of line breaks and paragraphs. In case of mistakes, the written word was striked out and writing was continued.

Evaluation Methodology. To evaluate the performance, we took all source-candidate document pairs and computed their similarity scores. Here we only verify whether the document is similar (plagiarized) or not while discarding the amount of plagiarism. The performance is measured using area under the ROC curve (AUC) by sorting the scores of all pairs. In another experiment, we compute graded similarity measure in accordance to each source document posed as a query which expects the ranking according to the degree of copying. Here we use normalized discounted cumulative gain ($nDCG$), a measure used frequently in information retrieval when grading is needed. Here the query is presented as the *source* document and the target documents are all documents present in the corpus. The discounted cumulative gain (DCG) at position p is given as $DCG_p = \sum_{i=1}^{p}(2^{rel_i} - 1)/(log_2(i + 1))$ where rel_i is the ground truth relevance for the document at rank i. In our case, the relevance measures are represented as: 3 - *near copy*, 2 - *light revision*, 1 - *heavy revision*, and 0 - *not copied*. The normalized measure $nDCG$ is defined as $DCG_p/IDCG_p$, where $IDCG$ is the DCG measure for ideal ranking. $nDCG$ values scale between $0.0 - 1.0$ with 1.0 for ideal ranking.

Results. We now establish two baselines for comparison. Our first approach uses a classical visual bag of words (BOW) approach computed at the interest points. The BOW representation has been successfully used in many image retrieval tasks including the document images [37,49]. We use SIFT descriptors, quantized using LLC and represented using a spatial pyramid of size 1×3. Our second baseline (NN) uses the classical word spotting scheme based on profile features similar to [32]. While the first one is scalable for large datasets, the second one is not really appropriate due to the time complexity of classical DTW.

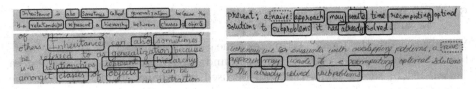

Fig. 7. Qualitative results of the MODS matching algorithm from HW-DocSim dataset. Here we show two sample matching pairs in two columns. The top region is taken from source and bottom one is plagiarized. The highlighted words in rectangle have been correctly matched along with few words which remain undetected.

In both these methods, the best match is identified as the document which has most number of word/patch matches. Table 3 reports the quantitative evaluation for various matching schemes along with the baselines. The proposed MODS framework along with CNN features performs better in both evaluation measures consistently. Using SWM word matching scheme over the proposed CNN features, we achieve an $nDCG$ score of 0.8569 and AUC of 0.9465. This is further improved in the MODS, which incorporates loose ordering and is invariant to word overflow problems. Note that in both cases (SWM and MODS), the stopwords are removed as preprocessing. We also evaluate our framework with the state-of-the-art features proposed in [3] and observe a similar trend which validates the effectiveness of MODS. Figure 7 shows some qualitative results of matching pairs from HW-DocSim dataset.

5.4   Human Evaluations

To validate the performance of the system on an unrestricted collection, we introduce HW-1K dataset which is collected from the real assignments of a class as part of an active course. The dataset contains nearly 1 K handwritten pages from more than 100 students. The content in these documents varied from text, figures, plots and mathematical symbols. Most of the documents follow a complex layout with misalignment in paragraphs, huge variations in line and word spacing and a high degree of skewness over the content.

We perform a human evaluation where we picked a set of 50 assignment images written by different students, and gathered the top-1 similar document image present in the corpus using MODS. We then ask five humans evaluators to give a score to the top-1 retrieval on a likert scale of $0-3$ where 0 is *"very dissimilar"*, 1 is *"similar only for few word matches"*, 2 is *"partially similar"* and 3 is *"totally similar"*. Here, the scale-1 refers to the case where the document pair refers to the same topic. Thus there could be individual word matches but the text is not plagiarized. The average agreement to the human judgments as evaluated for the top-1 similar document is reported at 2.356 with 3 as the best score.

6 Discussions

We propose a method which estimates a measure of similarity for two handwritten documents. Given a set of digitized handwritten documents, we estimate a ranked list of similar pairs that can be used for manual validation, as in the case of MOSS and deciding the amount of plagiarism. Our document similarity score is computed using a CNN feature descriptor at the word level which surpasses the state-of-the-art results for the task of word spotting in multi-writer scenarios. We believe that with an annotated, larger set of natural handwritten word images, the performance can be further improved. We plan to use weakly supervised learning techniques for this purpose in the future.

Throughout this work, we characterize the document images with textual content alone. Many of the document images also have graphics. Our method fails to compare them reliably. On a qualitative analyses of the failures, we also find that the performance of matching mathematical expressions e.g., equations and symbols is inferior to the textual content. We believe identifying regions with graphics and applying separate scheme for matching such regions can further enhance the performance of our system.

Acknowledgments. Praveen Krishnan is supported by TCS Research Scholar Fellowship.

References

1. Almazán, J., Gordo, A., Fornés, A., Valveny, E.: Handwritten word spotting with corrected attributes. In: ICCV (2013)
2. Almazán, J., Gordo, A., Fornés, A., Valveny, E.: Segmentation-free word spotting with exemplar SVMs. PR **47**(12), 3967–3978 (2014)
3. Almazán, J., Gordo, A., Fornés, A., Valveny, E.: Word spotting and recognition with embedded attributes. PAMI **36**(12), 2552–2566 (2014)
4. Chum, O., Philbin, J., Zisserman, A.: Near duplicate image detection: min-hash and tf-idf weighting. In: BMVC (2008)
5. Clough, P.D., Stevenson, M.: Developing a corpus of plagiarised short answers. LREC **45**(1), 5–24 (2011)
6. Deng, J., Dong, W., Socher, R., Li, L.J., Li, K., Fei-Fei, L.: ImageNet: a large-scale hierarchical image database. In: CVPR (2009)
7. Donahue, J., Jia, Y., Vinyals, O., Hoffman, J., Zhang, N., Tzeng, E., Darrell, T.: Decaf: a deep convolutional activation feature for generic visual recognition. In: ICML (2014)
8. Fernández-Mota, D., Manmatha, R., Fornés, A., Llados, J.: Sequential word spotting in historical handwritten documents. In: DAS (2014)
9. Fischer, A., Keller, A., Frinken, V., Bunke, H.: Lexicon-free handwritten word spotting using character HMMs. PRL **33**(7), 934–942 (2012)
10. Gandhi, A., Jawahar, C.V.: Detection of cut-and-paste in document images. In: ICDAR (2013)
11. Gatos, B., Stamatopoulos, N., Louloudis, G.: ICDAR2009 handwriting segmentation contest. IJDAR **14**(1), 25–33 (2011)

12. Hinton, G.E., Srivastava, N., Krizhevsky, A., Sutskever, I., Salakhutdinov, R.R.: Improving neural networks by preventing co-adaptation of feature detectors. CoRR (2012)
13. Ioffe, S., Szegedy, C.: Batch normalization: accelerating deep network training by reducing internal covariate shift. CoRR (2015)
14. Jaderberg, M., Simonyan, K., Vedaldi, A., Zisserman, A.: Reading text in the wild with convolutional neural networks. IJCV **116**(1), 1–20 (2014)
15. Jaderberg, M., Simonyan, K., Vedaldi, A., Zisserman, A.: Synthetic data and artificial neural networks for natural scene text recognition. CoRR (2014)
16. Jaderberg, M., Vedaldi, A., Zisserman, A.: Deep features for text spotting. In: Fleet, D., Pajdla, T., Schiele, B., Tuytelaars, T. (eds.) ECCV 2014, Part IV. LNCS, vol. 8692, pp. 512–528. Springer, Heidelberg (2014)
17. Ke, Y., Sukthankar, R., Huston, L.: An efficient parts-based near-duplicate and sub-image retrieval system. In: ACM Multimedia (2004)
18. Krizhevsky, A., Sutskever, I., Hinton, G.E.: Imagenet classification with deep convolutional neural networks. In: NIPS (2012)
19. Lecun, Y., Bottou, L., Bengio, Y., Haffner, P.: Gradient-based learning applied to document recognition. Proc. IEEE **86**(11), 2278–2324 (1998)
20. Louloudis, G., Gatos, B., Pratikakis, I., Halatsis, C.: Text line and word segmentation of handwritten documents. PR **42**(12), 3169–3183 (2009)
21. Mahendran, A., Vedaldi, A.: Understanding deep image representations by inverting them. In: CVPR (2015)
22. Manmatha, R., Han, C., Riseman, E.M.: Word spotting: a new approach to indexing handwriting. In: CVPR (1996)
23. Manning, C.D., Raghavan, P., Schütze, H.: Introduction to Information Retrieval. Cambridge University Press, Cambridge (2008)
24. Marti, U., Bunke, H.: The IAM-database: an English sentence database for offline handwriting recognition. IJDAR **5**(1), 39–46 (2002)
25. Milewski, R., Govindaraju, V.: Handwriting analysis of pre-hospital care reports. In: CBMS (2004)
26. Mishra, A., Alahari, K., Jawahar, C.V.: Top-down and bottom-up cues for scene text recognition. In: CVPR (2012)
27. Mishra, A., Alahari, K., Jawahar, C.V.: Image retrieval using textual cues. In: ICCV (2013)
28. NPTEL: http://nptel.ac.in/ (2016). Accessed 10 Mar 2016
29. Perronnin, F., Rodríguez-Serrano, J.A.: Fisher kernels for handwritten word-spotting. In: ICDAR (2009)
30. Porter, M.F.: An algorithm for suffix stripping. Program **14**(3), 130–137 (1980)
31. Potthast, M., Hagen, M., Beyer, A., Busse, M., Tippmann, M., Rosso, P., Stein, B.: Overview of the 6th international competition on plagiarism detection. In: CLEF (2014)
32. Rath, T.M., Manmatha, R.: Word spotting for historical documents. IJDAR **9**(2–4), 139–152 (2007)
33. Razavian, A.S., Azizpour, H., Sullivan, J., Carlsson, S.: CNN features off-the-shelf: an astounding baseline for recognition. In: CVPR (2014)
34. Rodríguez-Serrano, J.A., Perronnin, F.: A model-based sequence similarity with application to handwritten word spotting. PAMI **34**(11), 2108–2120 (2012)
35. Rusiñol, M., Aldavert, D., Toledo, R., Lladós, J.: Efficient segmentation-free keyword spotting in historical document collections. PR **48**(2), 545–555 (2015)
36. Schleimer, S., Wilkerson, D.S., Aiken, A.: Winnowing: local algorithms for document fingerprinting. In: SIGMOD (2003)

37. Shekhar, R., Jawahar, C.V.: Document specific sparse coding for word retrieval. In: ICDAR (2013)
38. Simard, P.Y., Steinkraus, D., Platt, J.C.: Best practices for convolutional neural networks applied to visual document analysis. In: ICDAR (2003)
39. Simonyan, K., Zisserman, A.: Very deep convolutional networks for large-scale image recognition. In: ICLR (2015)
40. Srihari, S.N., Collins, J., Srihari, R.K., Srinivasan, H., Shetty, S., Brutt-Griffler, J.: Automatic scoring of short handwritten essays in reading comprehension tests. Artif. Intell. **172**(2), 300–324 (2008)
41. Stamatopoulos, N., Gatos, B., Louloudis, G., Pal, U., Alaei, A.: ICDAR 2013 handwriting segmentation contest. In: ICDAR (2013)
42. Su, B., Lu, S.: Accurate scene text recognition based on recurrent neural network. In: Cremers, D., Reid, I., Saito, H., Yang, M.-H. (eds.) ACCV 2014. LNCS, vol. 9003, pp. 35–48. Springer, Heidelberg (2015)
43. Szegedy, C., Liu, W., Jia, Y., Sermanet, P., Reed, S., Anguelov, D., Erhan, D., Vanhoucke, V., Rabinovich, A.: Going deeper with convolutions. In: CVPR (2015)
44. Takeda, K., Kise, K., Iwamura, M.: Real-time document image retrieval for a 10 million pages database with a memory efficient and stability improved LLAH. In: ICDAR (2011)
45. Takeda, K., Kise, K., Iwamura, M.: Real-time document image retrieval on a smartphone. In: DAS (2012)
46. Vitaladevuni, S.N.P., Choi, F., Prasad, R., Natarajan, P.: Detecting near-duplicate document images using interest point matching. In: ICPR (2012)
47. Wang, K., Babenko, B., Belongie, S.J.: End-to-end scene text recognition. In: ICCV (2011)
48. Wang, K., Belongie, S.: Word spotting in the wild. In: Daniilidis, K., Maragos, P., Paragios, N. (eds.) ECCV 2010, Part I. LNCS, vol. 6311, pp. 591–604. Springer, Heidelberg (2010)
49. Yalniz, I.Z., Manmatha, R.: An efficient framework for searching text in noisy document images. In: DAS (2012)

Semantic Clustering for Robust Fine-Grained Scene Recognition

Marian George[1][(✉)], Mandar Dixit[2], Gábor Zogg[1], and Nuno Vasconcelos[2]

[1] Department of Computer Science, ETH Zurich, Zurich, Switzerland
`mageorge@inf.ethz.ch, gzogg@student.ethz.ch`
[2] Statistical and Visual Computing Lab, UCSD, San Diego, CA, USA
`{mdixit,nvasconcelos}@ucsd.edu`

Abstract. In domain generalization, the knowledge learnt from one or multiple source domains is transferred to an unseen target domain. In this work, we propose a novel domain generalization approach for fine-grained scene recognition. We first propose a semantic scene descriptor that jointly captures the subtle differences between fine-grained scenes, while being robust to varying object configurations across domains. We model the occurrence patterns of objects in scenes, capturing the informativeness and discriminability of each object for each scene. We then transform such occurrences into scene probabilities for each scene image. Second, we argue that scene images belong to hidden semantic topics that can be discovered by clustering our semantic descriptors. To evaluate the proposed method, we propose a new fine-grained scene dataset in cross-domain settings. Extensive experiments on the proposed dataset and three benchmark scene datasets show the effectiveness of the proposed approach for fine-grained scene transfer, where we outperform state-of-the-art scene recognition and domain generalization methods.

1 Introduction

Scene classification is an important problem for computer vision. Discovering the discriminative aspects of a scene in terms of its global representation, constituent objects and parts, or their spatial layout remains a challenging endeavor. Indoor scenes [1] are particularly important for applications such as robotics. They are also particularly challenging, due to the need to understand images at multiple levels of the continuum between things and stuff [2]. Some scenes, such as a garage or corridor, have a distinctive holistic layout. Others, such as a bathroom, contain unique objects. All of these challenges are aggravated in the context of fine-grained indoor scene classification. Fine-grained recognition targets the problem of sub-ordinate categorization. While it has been studied in the realm of objects, e.g. classes of birds [3], or flowers [4], it has not been studied for scenes.

In real-world applications, vision systems are frequently faced with the need to process images taken under very different imaging conditions than those in

Electronic supplementary material The online version of this chapter (doi:10.1007/978-3-319-46448-0_47) contains supplementary material, which is available to authorized users.

© Springer International Publishing AG 2016
B. Leibe et al. (Eds.): ECCV 2016, Part I, LNCS 9905, pp. 783–798, 2016.
DOI: 10.1007/978-3-319-46448-0_47

their training sets. This is frequently called the cross-domain setting, since the domain of test images is different from that of training. For example, store images taken with a smartphone can differ significantly from those found on the web, where most image datasets are collected. The variation can be in terms of the objects displayed (e.g. the latest clothing collection), their poses, the lighting conditions, camera characteristics, or proximity between camera and scene items. It is well known that the performance of vision models can degrade significantly due to these variations, which is known as the dataset bias problem [5,6].

To address the dataset bias problem, many domain adaptation [7] approaches have been proposed [8–11] to reduce the mismatch between the data distributions of the training samples, referred to as source domain, and the test samples, referred to as the target domain. In domain adaptation, target domain data is available during the training process, and the adaptation process needs to be repeated for every new target domain. A related problem is *domain generalization*, in which the target domain data is unavailable during training [12–16]. Such problem is important in real-world applications where different target domains may correspond to images of different users with different cameras.

In this work, we study the problem of domain generalization for fine-grained scene recognition by considering store scenes. As shown in Fig. 2, store classification frequently requires the discrimination between classes of very similar visual appearance, such as a drug store vs. a grocery store. Yet, there are also classes of widely varying appearance, such as clothing stores. This makes the store domain suitable to test the robustness of models for scene classification.

To this end, we make the following contributions. We first propose a semantic scene descriptor that jointly captures the subtle differences between fine-grained scenes, while being robust to the different object configurations across domains. We compute the occurrence statistics of objects in scenes, capturing the informativeness of each detected object for each scene. We then transform such occurrences into scene probabilities. This is complemented by a new measure of the

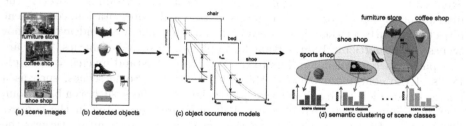

Fig. 1. Overview of our semantic clustering approach. (a) scene images from all scene classes are first projected into (b) a common space, namely object space. (c) Object occurrence models are computed to describe conditional scene probabilities given each object. The maximal vertical distance between two neighboring curves at a threshold θ is the discriminability of the object at θ. (d) Scene images are represented by semantic scene descriptors (bottom), and clustering these descriptors exploit the semantic topics in fine-grained scene classes (top). (Color figure online)

discriminability of an object category, which is used to derive a discriminant dimensionality reduction procedure for object-based semantic representations. Second, we argue that scene images belong to multiple hidden semantic topics that can be automatically discovered by clustering our semantic descriptors. By learning a separate classifier for each discovered domain, the learnt classifiers are more discriminant. An overview of the proposed approach is shown in Fig. 1.

The third contribution is the introduction of the *SnapStore* dataset, which addresses fine-grained scene classification with an emphasis on robustness across imaging domains. It covers 18 visually-similar store categories, with training images downloaded from Google image search and test images collected with smartphones. To the best of our knowledge, SnapStore is the first dataset with these properties. It will be made publicly available from the author web-pages.

Finally, we compare the performance of the proposed method to state-of-the-art scene recognition and domain generalization methods. These show the effectiveness of the proposed scene transfer approach.

2   Related Work

Recent approaches have been proposed to target domain generalization for vision tasks. They can be roughly grouped into classifier based [13,14] approaches and feature-based [12,15] approaches. In [13], a support vector machine approach is proposed that learns a set of dataset-specific models and a visual-world model that is common to all datasets. An exemplar-SVM approach is proposed in [14] that exploits the structure of positive samples in the source domain. In feature-based approaches, the goal is to learn invariant features that generalize across domains. In [12], a kernel-based method is proposed that learns a shared subspace. A feature-learning approach is proposed in [15] that extends denoising autoeconders with naturally-occurring variability in object appearance. While the previous approaches yield good results in object recognition, their performance was not investigated for scene transfer. Also, to the best of our knowledge, there is no prior work that exploits a semantic approach to domain generalization.

Many approaches have been proposed for scene classification. A popular approach is to represent a scene in terms of its semantics [17,18], using a pre-defined vocabulary of visual concepts and a bank of detectors for those concepts [19–23]. A second class of approaches relies on the automatic discovery of mid-level patches in scene images [24–27]. While all these methods have been shown able to classify scenes, there are no previous studies of their performance for fine-grained classification. Our method is most related to object-based approaches that are more suitable for fine-grained scenes than holistic representation methods, such as the scene gist [28]. Our proposed method is more invariant than previous attempts, such as objectBank [19] and the semantic FV [21]. These methods provide an encoding based on raw (CNN-based) detection scores, which vary widely across domains. In contrast, we quantize the detection scores into scene probabilities for each object. Such probabilities are adaptive to the varying detection scores through considering a range of thresholds. The process of quantization imparts invariance to the CNN-based semantics, thus improves the generalization ability. We compare with both representations in Sect. 6.

A Convolutional Neural Network [29,30], is another example of a classifier that has the ability to discover "semantic" entities in higher levels of its feature hierarchy [31,32]. The scene CNN of [30] was shown to detect objects that are discriminative for the scene classes [32]. Our proposed method investigates scene transfer using a network trained on objects only, namely imageNET [33]. This is achieved without the need to train a network on millions of scene images, which is the goal of transfer. We compare the performance of the two in Sect. 6.

3   SnapStore Dataset

In order to study the performance of different methods for domain generalization for fine-grained scene recognition, we have assembled the SnapStore dataset. This covers 18 fine-grained *store* categories, shown in Fig. 2. Stores are a challenging scene classification domain for several reasons. First, many store categories have similar gist, i.e. similar global visual appearance and spatial layout. For example, grocery stores, drug stores, and office supply stores all tend to contain long rows of shelves organized in a symmetric manner, with similar floor and ceiling types. Second, store categories (e.g., clothing) that deviate from this norm, tend to exhibit a wide variation in visual appearance. This implies that image models applicable to store classification must be detailed enough to differentiate among different classes of very similar visual appearance and invariant enough to accommodate the wide variability of some store classes.

SnapStore contains 6132 training images, gathered with Google image search. The number of training images per category varies from 127 to 892, with an average of 341. Training images were scaled to a maximum of 600 pixels per axis. Testing images were taken in local stores, using smartphones. This results in images that are very different from those in the training set, which tend to be

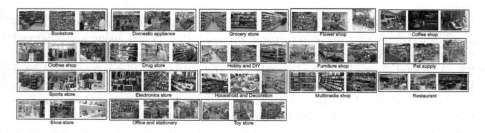

Fig. 2. An overview of the proposed fine-grained scene *SnapStore* dataset. The dataset contains 18 store categories that are closely related to each other. For each category, 3 training images are shown. Some categories are significantly visually similar with very confusing spatial layout and objects. Other store classes have widely varying visual features, which is difficult to model.

more stylized. The test set consists of 502 images with ground truth annotations for store class, store location type (shopping mall, street mall, industrial area), GPS coordinates, and store name. Images have a fixed size of 960×720 pixels. Test images differ from training images in geographical location, lighting conditions, zoom levels, and blurriness. This makes SnapStore a good dataset in which to test the robustness of scene classification to wide domain variations.

While datasets such as Places [30] or SUN [34] contain some store categories, the proposed dataset is better suited for domain generalization of fine-grained scenes; first, SnapStore contains store classes that are more confusing, e.g., Drug store, DIY store, Office supplies store, and Multimedia store. Also, large datasets favor the use of machine learning methods that use data from the target domain to adapt to it. In contrast, the images of SnapStore are explicitly chosen to stress robustness. This is the reason why the test set includes images shot with cellphones, while the training set does not. Overall, SnapStore is tailored for the evaluation of representations and enables the study of their robustness at a deeper level than Places or SUN. We compare the three datasets in Sect. 6.

4   Discriminative Objects in Scenes

There is a wide array of scenes that can benefit from object recognition, even if object cues are not sufficient for high recognition accuracy. For example, we expect to see flowers in a flower shop, shoes and shoe boxes in a shoe shop, and chairs and tables in a furniture shop. Nevertheless, it remains challenging to learn models that capture the discriminative power of objects for scene classification. First, objects can have different degrees of importance for different scene types (e.g., chairs are expected in furniture stores, but also appear in shoe stores). Rather than simply accounting for the presence of an object in a scene, there is a need to model how informative the object is of that scene. Second, object detection scores can vary widely across images, especially when these are from different domains. In our experience, fixing the detection threshold to a value with good training performance frequently harms recognition accuracy on test images where the object appears in different poses, different lighting, or occluded.

4.1   Object Detection and Recognition

An object recognizer $\rho : \mathcal{X} \to \mathcal{O}$ is a mapping from some feature space $\mathcal{X}$ to a set of object class labels $\mathcal{O}$, usually implemented as $o = \arg\max_k f_k(x)$, where $f_k(x)$ is a confidence score for the assignment of a feature vector $x \in \mathcal{X}$ to the kth label in $\mathcal{O}$. An object detector is a special case, where $\mathcal{O} = \{-1, 1\}$ and $f_1(x) = -f_{-1}(x)$. In this case, $f_1(x)$ is simply denoted as $f(x)$ and the decision rule of (Sect. 4.1) reduces to $o = sgn[f(x)]$.

The function $f(x) = (f_1(x), \ldots, f_O(x))$, where O is the number of object classes is usually denoted as the predictor of the recognizer or detector. Component $f_k(x)$ is a *confidence score* for the assignment of the object to the kth class. This is usually the probability $P(o|x)$ or an invertible transformation of it.

Given an object recognizer, or a set of object detectors, it is possible to detect the presence of object o in an image x at *confidence level* θ by thresholding the prediction $f_o(x)$ according to

$$\delta(x|o; \theta) = h[f_o(x) - \theta] \tag{1}$$

where $h(x) = 1, x \geq 0$ and $h(x) = 0$ otherwise. Thus, $\delta(x|o; \theta)$ is an indicator for the assignment of image x to object class o at confidence level θ.

4.2   Learning an Object Occurrence Model

Our Object Occurrence Model (OOM) answers the following question on a threshold bandwidth of $[\theta_{min}; \theta_{max}]$ with a resolution of $\Delta\theta$: *"how many images from each category contain the object at least once above a threshold θ?"*. We do not fix the threshold of object detection θ at a unique value as this threshold would be different across domains. Formally, given a set $\mathcal{I}_c$ of images from a scene class c, the maximum likelihood estimate of the probability of occurrence of object o on class c, at confidence level θ, is

$$p(o|c; \theta) = \frac{1}{|\mathcal{I}_c|} \sum_{x_i \in I_c} \delta(x_i|o; \theta). \tag{2}$$

We refer to these probabilities, for a set of scene classes $\mathcal{C}$, as the object occurrence model (OOM) of $\mathcal{C}$ at threshold θ. This model summarizes the likelihood of appearance of all objects in all scene classes, at this level of detection confidence.

4.3   Discriminant Object Selection

Natural scenes contain many objects, whose discriminative power varies greatly. For example, the "wall" and "floor" objects are much less discriminant than the objects "pot," "price tag," or "flower" for the recognition of "flower shop" images. To first order, an object is discriminant for a particular scene class if it appears frequently in that class and is uncommon in all others. In general, an object can be discriminant for more than one class. For example, the "flower" object is discriminant for the "flower shop" and "garden" classes.

We propose a procedure for discriminant object selection, based on the OOM of the previous section. This relies on a measure of the *discriminant power* $\phi_\theta(o)$ of object o with respect to a set of scene classes $\mathcal{C}$ at confidence level θ. The computation of $\phi_\theta(o)$ is performed in two steps. First, given object o, the classes $c \in \mathcal{C}$ are ranked according to the posterior probabilities of (4). Let $\gamma(c)$ be the ranking function, i.e. $\gamma(c) = 1$ for the class of largest probability and $\gamma(c) = |\mathcal{C}|$ for the class of lowest probability. The class of rank r is then $\gamma^{-1}(r)$. The second step computes the discriminant power of object o as

$$\phi_\theta(o) = \max_{r \in \{1,...,|\mathcal{C}|-1\}} p(\gamma^{-1}(r)|o; \theta) - p(\gamma^{-1}(r+1)|o; \theta). \tag{3}$$

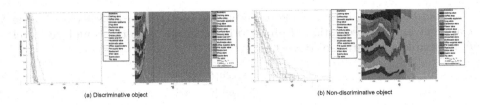

(a) Discriminative object   (b) Non-discriminative object

Fig. 3. An example of (a) a discriminative object (book) and (b) a non-discriminative object (bottle). In each case, the left plot is identical to the plot of Fig. 1c. The discriminative object (*book*) occurs frequently in few categories at a given confidence level. However, for the same confidence level, the *bottle* object, occurs in many categories. The plot on the right of (a) and (b) shows the occurrence normalized in 1-norm for each θ. The region above the maximal θ for any occurrence is interpreted as 1 for the category with the highest probability.

The procedure is illustrated in Fig. 1c, where each curve shows the probability $p(c|o;\theta)$ of class c as a function of the confidence level. At confidence level θ, the red, green, yellow, and blue classes have rank 1 to 4 respectively. In this example, the largest difference between probabilities occurs between the green and yellow classes, capturing the fact that the object o is informative of the red and green classes but not of the yellow and blues ones.

Figure 3 shows examples of a discriminative and a non-discriminative object in the SnapStore dataset. The discriminative object, *book*, occurs in very few scene classes (mainly bookstore) with high confidence level. On the other hand, the non-discriminant *bottle* object appears in several classes (grocery store, drug store, and household store) with the same confidence level.

5   Semantic Latent Scene Topics

In this section, we describe our approach of representing a scene image as scene probabilities, followed by discovering hidden semantic topics in scene classes.

5.1   Semantic Scene Descriptor

In this work, we propose to represent an image x by a descriptor based on the $\mathcal{O} \times \mathcal{C}$ matrix M of posterior probabilities $p(c|o)$ of classes given objects detected in the image. Object detectors or recognizers produce multiple object detections in x, which are usually obtained by applying the recognizer or detector to image patches. Object detectors are usually implemented in a 1-vs-rest manner and return the score of a binary decision. We refer to these as hard detections. On the other hand, object recognizers return a score vector, which summarizes the probabilities of presence of each object in the patch. We refer to these as soft detections. Different types of descriptors are suitable for soft vs. hard detections. In this work, we consider both, proposing two descriptors that are conceptually identical but tuned to the traits of the different detection approaches.

From the OOM, it is possible to derive the posterior probability of a scene class c given the observation of object o in an image x, at the confidence level θ, by simple application of Bayes rule

$$p(c|o;\theta) = \frac{p(o|c;\theta)p(c)}{\sum_i p(o|i;\theta)p(i)}, \tag{4}$$

where $p(o|c;\theta)$ are the probabilities of occurrence of (2) and $p(c)$ is a prior scene class probability. The range of thresholds $[\theta_{min}, \theta_{max}]$ over which θ is defined is denoted the *threshold bandwidth* of the model.

Hard Detections. Given the image x, we apply to it the ith object detector, producing a set of n_i bounding boxes, corresponding to image patches $\mathcal{X}_i = \{z_1^{(i)}, \ldots, z_{n_i}^{(i)}\}$, and a set of associated detection scores $\mathcal{S}_i = \{s_1^{(i)}, \ldots, s_{n_i}^{(i)}\}$. To estimate the posterior probabilities $p(c|o_i)$, we adopt a Bayesian averaging procedure, assuming that these scores are samples from a probability distribution $p(\theta)$ over confidence scores. This leads to $p(c|o_i) = \sum_k p(c|o_i, \theta = s_k^{(i)})p(\theta = s_k^{(i)})$. Assuming a uniform prior over scores, we then use $p(\theta = s_k^{(i)}) = 1/n_i$ to obtain

$$p(c|o_i) = \frac{1}{n_i}\sum_k p(c|o_i, \theta = s_k^{(i)}). \tag{5}$$

In summary, the vector of posterior probabilities is estimated by averaging the OOM posteriors of (4), at the confidence levels associated with the object detections in x. This procedure is repeated for all objects, filling one row of M at a time. The rows associated with undetected objects are set to zero.

The proposed semantic descriptor is obtained by stacking M into a vector and performing *discriminant* dimensionality reduction. We start by finding an object subset $\mathcal{R} \subset \mathcal{O}$ which is discriminant for scene classification. This reduces dimensionality from $|\mathcal{O}| \times |\mathcal{C}|$ to $|\mathcal{R}| \times |\mathcal{C}|$ as discussed in Sect. 4.3. This procedure is repeated using a spatial pyramid structure of three levels (1×1, 2×2, and 3×1), which are finally concatenated into a 21 K dimensional feature vector.

Soft Detections. A set of n patches $\mathcal{X} = \{z_1, \ldots, z_n\}$ are sampled from the image and fed to an object recognizer, e.g. a CNN. This produces a set $\mathcal{S} = \{s_1, \ldots, s_n\}$ of vectors s_k of confidence scores. The vector s_k includes the scores for the presence of all $|\mathcal{O}|$ objects in patch z_k. Using the OOM posteriors of (4), each s_k can be converted into a matrix M^k of class probabilities given scores. Namely the matrix whose i^{th} row is given by $M_i^K = p(c|o_i, s_{k,i})$, which is the vector of class probabilities given the detection of object o_i at confidence $s_{k,i}$.

The image x is then represented as a bag of descriptors $\mathcal{X} = \{M^1, M^2, \ldots M^n\}$ generated from its patches. This is mapped into the soft-VLAD [23,35] representation using the following steps. First, the dimensionality of the matrices M^k is reduced by selecting the most discriminant objects $\mathcal{R} \subset \mathcal{O}$, as discussed in Sect. 4.3. Second, each matrix is stacked into a $\mathcal{R} \times \mathcal{C}$ vector, and dimensionality reduced to 500 dimensions, using PCA. The descriptors are then encoded with the soft-kmeans assignment weighted first order residuals, as suggested in [23].

5.2   Semantic Clustering

When learning knowledge from web data or multiple datasets, it is usually assumed that training images may come from several hidden topics [14,16] that may correspond to different viewing angles, or imaging conditions. While previous works rely on image features like DeCaF fc6 [20] to discover latent topics in *object* datasets, we instead propose to discover *semantic* topics that provide a higher level of abstraction, which generalizes better than lower-level features especially for *scene* datasets. Each of the hidden topics can contain an arbitrary number of images from an arbitrary number of scene classes. For example, furniture store images can be semantically divided into different groups, as shown in Fig. 1, including (1) images of dining furniture that are semantically related to some images in 'Coffee Shop' and 'Restaurant' classes, (2) images of seating furniture, like sofas and ottomans, that are related to waiting areas in 'Shoe shop' class, and (3) images of bedroom furniture that are more unique to furniture stores. By exploiting such underlying semantic structure of fine-grained classes, we achieve better discriminability by learning a separate multi-class classifier for each latent topic. Furthermore, improved generalization ability is achieved through integrating the decisions from all the learnt classifiers at test time [36]. This is especially useful when the test image does not fall uniquely into one of the topics as is usually common in cross-domain settings. We note that our goal is to project the training images into a semantic space that can yield informative groups when clustered using any clustering method, not necessarily k-means.

In practice, we first partition the training data into D semantic latent topics using k-means clustering over our semantic descriptors (Sect. 5.1) from all training images. Note that we do not assume any underlying distribution in the data and we do not utilize scene labels in discovering the latent topics. We then learn a classifier $f_{c,d}(\mathbf{x})$ for each class c in each latent topic d using only the training samples in that domain. The classifier models of each latent topic are learnt using 1-vs-rest SVM with linear kernel, using the JSGD library [37]. The regularization parameter and learning rate were determined by 5-fold cross validation. At test time, we predict the scene class of an image x as the class with the highest decision value after average pooling the classifier decisions from all topics, by using $y = arg\max_c \sum_{d=1}^{D} f_{c,d}(\mathbf{x})$. We also experimented with max pooling over classifier decisions, which yielded inferior results.

6   Experiments

A number of experiments were designed to evaluate the performance of the proposed method. All datasets are weakly labeled - scene class labels, no object bounding boxes - and we report average classification accuracy over scene classes.

In all experiments, hard object detections were obtained with the RCNN of [38] and soft detections with the CNN of [29]. We empirically fix $k = 5$ for k-means clustering (Sec. 5.2), however the results are insensitive to the exact value of k.

6.1   Analysis of the Object Occurrence Model (OOM)

In this experiment, we used the new SnapStore dataset, which addresses fine-grained classification, and MIT67 [1], which addresses coarse-grained indoor scenes. The latter includes 67 indoor scene categories. We used the train/test split proposed by the authors, using 80 training and 20 test images per class.

Figure 4a shows the matrix of posterior class probabilities learned by the OOM, for hard detections on SnapStore. A similar plot is shown in the supplement for detections on MIT67. The figure shows a heatmap of the probabilities $p(c|o_i; \theta)$ of (4) at the confidence level $\theta = 0.9$. Note that the OOM captures the informative objects for each scene class, e.g., bookshelf is highly discriminant for the bookstore class. Furthermore, when an object is discriminant for multiple

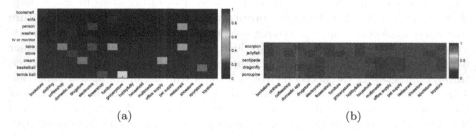

(a)   (b)

Fig. 4. Scene likelihoods for all scene classes for (a) the top 10 discriminative objects and (b) the least discriminative objects using RCNN-200 on SnapStore

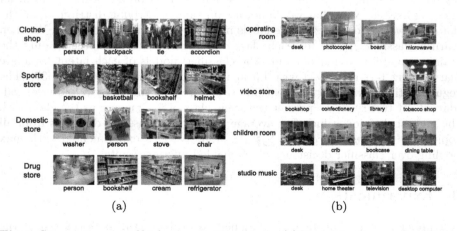

(a)   (b)

Fig. 5. Scene categories of higher recognition rate for (a) hard detections on SnapStore, and (b) soft detections on MIT67.

Table 1. Classification accuracy as a function of the number of discriminant objects for SnapStore and MIT67

Dataset	OOM [CNN-1000]	OOM [CNN-500]	OOM [CNN-300]
SnapStore	43.1	44.6	**45.4**
MIT67	68.0	**68.2**	66.4

classes, the class probabilities reflect the relative importance of the object, e.g., table is discriminant for coffee shops, furniture stores, and restaurants but more important for the coffee shop class. While nearly all coffee shop images contain tables, furniture store images sometimes depict beds, sofas or other objects, and some pictures of fast-food restaurant lack tables. Figure 4b shows the same heatmap for the least discriminant objects. The scene probabilities are now identical for all objects, which are hardly detected in any of the scenes.

Figure 5 shows the top four correctly-classified scene classes on SnapStore and MIT67. Scene classes are sorted from top to bottom by decreasing classification accuracy. For each scene, we show the most probable objects (most common object on the left) along with the bounding box of highest detection score. While there are noisy detections in each class, e.g. accordion in clothes shop, as a whole the detections are quite informative of the scene class. Failure cases on SnapStore include multimedia store, office supply store, and toy store.

We investigated the performance as a function of the number of selected discriminant objects (Sect. 4.3). Table 1 summarizes the performance of soft-detections (CNN) without semantic clustering, when using different numbers of objects. For both datasets, the selection of discriminant objects is beneficial, although the gains are larger in SnapStore. Using a reduced object vocabulary also reduces the dimensionality of the descriptors, leading to more efficient classification. For hard detections on SnapStore, we observed a similar improvement of performance for reduction from the 200 object vocabulary of the RCNN to 140 objects. On MIT67, the 200 object vocabulary proved inadequate to cover the diversity of objects in the 67 scene classes. Given these results, we fixed the number of objects at 140 for hard-detections (RCNN) and 300 for soft detections (CNN) on SnapStore. On MIT67, we used 200 and 500 objects, respectively.

6.2   Cross Recognition Performance on SnapStore Dataset

We performed a comparison to state-of-the-art scene recognition and transfer methods on the **18** classes of SnapStore in Table 2. We additionally compare with ObjectBank [19] when using RCNN and CNN detections as our method in exactly the same settings, to perform a fair comparison with it. We cannot compare with Undo-Bias [13] as it requires the source domains to be explicitly associated with multiple datasets. We compare with their method in Sect. 6.3.

OOM with RCNN outperformed all other methods, including a finetuned Places CNN. Semantic clustering further improves the recognition by $\approx 2\,\%$. Note

Table 2. Comparison of classification accuracies on SnapStore. *-Indicates results for a single scale of 128×128 patches

Method	Accuracy (%)
GIST [28]	22.8
DiscrimPatches [25]	25.0
ObjectBank [19]	32.6
ImageNET finetune	38.6
ImagetNET fc7 + SVM (DeCaF) [20]	40.2
Places finetune	42.4
Places fc7	44.2
ObjectBank [CNN]*	34.8
ObjectBank [RCNN]	36.3
fc8-VLAD (semantic FV) [21]*	43.8
DICA [12]	24.2
OOM [CNN]* (Ours)	45.4
OOM [RCNN] (Ours)	45.7
OOM-semanticClusters [RCNN] (Ours)	**47.9**

that Places fc7 is trained on scenes, while we use a network trained on objects only, which shows successful scene transfer. Places fine-tune surprisingly yielded worse performance than Places fc7. This is because Places fine-tune overfits to training views, performing better on images from the training domain, but worse on the new domain. Our method improves over ObjectBank by $\approx 9\,\%$, when using CNN detectors and recognizers. This is attributed to our invariant representation that does not rely on raw detection scores, which are different across domains. The small dimensionality of the DICA descriptor limits its discriminative ability.

6.3   Cross Recognition Performance on Multiple Datasets

Here, we evaluate the effectiveness of the proposed algorithm when using multiple fine-grained scene datasets. We also study the bias in each dataset, showing the benefits of using SnapStore to test the robustness of recognition methods.

Datasets. We used images from the **9** fine-grained store scene classes that are common among SnapStore, SUN [34], and Places [30] datasets. Effectively, we have 4 datasets, each divided into training and validation sets. The class names and detailed training-test configuration are provided in the supplement.

Baselines. We compared two variants of our method, namely OOM on RCNN (**OOM**) and OOM on RCNN + semantic clustering (**OOM-SC**), with 6 baselines: **DeCaF**, DeCaF + k-means clustering (**DeCaF-C**), Undo-Bias [13] (**U-B**), **DICA** [12], ObjectBank on RCNN (**OB**), and ObjectBank on RCNN + our proposed semantic clustering (**OB-SC**). For DeCaF-C, we set $k = 2$, which yielded the best results for this method. Note that we cannot compare with Places CNN in this experiment as it was trained using millions of images from Places dataset, thus violating the conditions of domain generalization on *unseen* datasets.

Results. To show the dataset bias and evaluate the ground truth performance, we first measured the cross-recognition performance of a linear SVM on DeCaF fc7 features when using the training set of one dataset and the test set of another dataset. We summarize the results in Table 3. Results show a significant bias in datasets gathered from the web (SnapWeb, SUN, Places). This is shown by the significant drop in performance by $> 12\%$ when using SnapPhone dataset, which is gathered in real settings using a smartphone, as the testing set. In contrast, the cross-recognition performance when using SUN and Places datasets as train/test sets is much better, with only 3% drop in performance when compared to ground truth (same-domain) recognition. This emphasizes the benefits of using the proposed SnapStore dataset in evaluating scene transfer methods.

We then evaluated the cross-recognition performance of the proposed method and the baselines, as summarized in Table 4. Our method outperforms other methods on five out of seven cross-domain scenarios and on average. The improvement of the proposed approach over DeCaF is more significant in the experiment in Sect. 6.2. This is due to the similarity of images in SUN, Places, and SnW, all collected on the web, which benefits the DeCaF baseline. When testing on SnP even OOM beats DeCaF on 3 of 4 cases with an average of 58% vs. 57%. Clustering DeCaF features (DeCaF-C) yielded worse performance than

Table 3. Ground truth and cross-recognition accuracy (%) of DeCaF+SVM baseline on multiple fine-grained scene datasets

Training/Test	SUN	SnapWeb	Places	SnapPhone
SUN	**68.7**	57.1	65.7	56.5
SnapWeb	62.7	**71.9**	60.9	58.2
Places	64.2	59.2	**67.6**	53.8

Table 4. Cross-recognition accuracy (%) on SnapStore training set (SnW), SnapStore test set (SnP), SUN, and Places (Pla) datasets

Train	Test	DeCaF	DeCaF-C	U-B	DICA	OB	OB-SC	OOM	OOM-SC
SnW	SnP	58.2	56.3	N/A	42.1	30.0	37.4	61.1	**62.0**
SUN	SnP	56.5	53.9	N/A	45.5	39.2	35.9	54.4	**56.9**
Pla	SnP	53.8	49.1	N/A	37.7	27.6	28.3	**54.8**	54.6
SnW, SnP	Pla, SUN	59.1	59.9	52.3	49.2	22.7	25.7	57.3	**60.6**
SnW, SUN	SnP, Pla	60.6	58.5	50.3	52.2	37.4	37.7	61.0	**63.2**
SUN, Pla, SnW	SnP	59.7	57.2	47.8	53.5	36.3	39.1	61.6	**62.5**
SUN, SnP, SnW	Pla	**63.8**	62.2	33.8	50.8	27.4	30.2	59.8	63.3
Average		58.8	56.7	46.0	47.2	32.9	33.4	58.5	**60.4**

Table 5. Comparison of classification accuracies on MIT67. *-Indicates results for a single scale of 128 × 128 patches.

Method	Accuracy (%)
IFV [24]	60.7
MLrep [26]	64.0
DeCaF [20]	58.4
ImageNET finetune	63.9
OverFeat + SVM [22]	69
fc6 + SC [40]	68.2
fc7-VLAD [23] [4 scales/1 scale*]	68.8/65.1
ObjectBank [RCNN/CNN*]	41.5/48.5
fc8-FV [21] [4 scales/1 scale*]	72.8/68.5
OOM [RCNN] (Ours)	49.4
OOM [CNN]* (Ours)	68.2
OOM-semClusters (Ours)	68.6

the DeCaF baseline. This is because DeCaF features are spatial maps that discriminate between parts of objects or at most individual objects. Thus, clustering them produces clusters of visually similar object parts, limiting invariance against varying object poses and shapes across domains. Recent work [39] made similar observations about DeCaF clusters for object datasets. One interesting observation is the inferior performance of domain generalization methods. While such methods yielded impressive performance on object datasets, they are unsuitable for fine-grained scenes; Undo-Bias associates a source domain to each source dataset, which does not capture the semantic topics across the scene classes, while the small dimensionality of the DICA descriptor limits its discriminability.

6.4 Scene Recognition on Coarse-Grained and Same Domain Dataset

Finally, we compared the performance to state-of-the-art scene recognition methods on the coarse-grained MIT67 dataset in Table 5. Soft detections achieved the best performance. The performance of hard-detections was rather weak, due to the limited vocabulary of the RCNN. We achieve comparable performance to state-of-the-art scene recognition algorithms, which shows that the effectiveness of the proposed method is more pronounced in cross-domain settings.

7   Conclusion

In this work, we proposed a new approach for domain generalization for fine-grained scene recognition. To achieve robustness against varying object configurations in scenes across domains, we quantize object occurrences into conditional scene probabilities. We then exploit the underlying semantic structure of our representation to discover hidden semantic topics. We learn a disriminant classifier for each domain that captures the subtle differences between fine-grained scenes. SnapStore, a new dataset of fine-grained scenes in cross-dataset settings was introduced. Extensive experiments have shown the effectiveness of the proposed approach and the benefits of SnapStore for fine-grained scene transfer.

References

1. Quattoni, A., Torralba, A.: Recognizing indoor scenes. In: CVPR (2009)
2. Adelson, E.H.: On seeing stuff: the perception of materials by humans and machines. In: Proceedings of SPIE, vol. 4299, pp. 1–12 (2001)
3. Welinder, P., Branson, S., Mita, T., Wah, C., Schroff, F., Belongie, S., Perona, P.: Caltech-UCSD birds 200. Technical report CNS-TR-201, Caltech (2010)
4. Nilsback, M.E., Zisserman, A.: Automated flower classification over a large number of classes. In: ICVGIP (2008)
5. Torralba, A., Efros, A.: Unbiased look at dataset bias. In: CVPR (2011)
6. Perronnin, F., Senchez, J., Liu, Y.: Large-scale image categorization with explicit data embedding. In: CVPR (2010)
7. Patel, V.M., Gopalan, R., Li, R., Chellappa, R.: Visual domain adaptation: a survey of recent advances. IEEE Signal Process. Mag. **32**, 53–69 (2014)
8. Bruzzone, L., Marconcini, M.: Domain adaptation problems: a DASVM classification technique and a circular validation strategy. PAMI **32**, 770–787 (2010)
9. Duan, L., Tsang, I.W., Xu, D.: Domain transfer multiple kernel learning. PAMI **34**, 465–479 (2012)
10. Baktashmotlagh, M., Harandi, M., Lovell, M.S.B.: Unsupervised domain adaptation by domain invariant projection. In: ICCV (2013)
11. Fernando, B., Habrard, A., Sebban, M., Tuytelaars, T.: Unsupervised visual domain adaptation using subspace alignment. In: ICCV (2013)
12. Muandet, K., Balduzzi, D., Scholkopf, B.: Domain generalization via invariant feature representation. In: ICML (2013)
13. Khosla, A., Zhou, T., Malisiewicz, T., Efros, A.A., Torralba, A.: Undoing the damage of dataset bias. In: Fitzgibbon, A., Lazebnik, S., Perona, P., Sato, Y., Schmid, C. (eds.) ECCV 2012, Part I. LNCS, vol. 7572, pp. 158–171. Springer, Heidelberg (2012). doi:10.1007/978-3-642-33718-5_12
14. Xu, Z., Li, W., Niu, L., Xu, D.: Exploiting low-rank structure from latent domains for domain generalization. In: Fleet, D., Pajdla, T., Schiele, B., Tuytelaars, T. (eds.) ECCV 2014, Part III. LNCS, vol. 8691, pp. 628–643. Springer, Heidelberg (2014)
15. Ghifary, M., Kleijn, W.B., Zhang, M., Balduzzi, D.: Domain generalization for object recognition with multi-task autoencoders. In: ICCV (2015)
16. Niu, L., Li, W., Xu, D.: Visual recognition by learning from web data: a weakly supervised domain generalization approach. In: CVPR (2015)
17. Rasiwasia, N., Vasconcelos, N.: Scene classification with low-dimensional semantic spaces and weak supervision. In: CVPR (2008)
18. Kwitt, R., Vasconcelos, N., Rasiwasia, N.: Scene recognition on the semantic manifold. In: Fitzgibbon, A., Lazebnik, S., Perona, P., Sato, Y., Schmid, C. (eds.) ECCV 2012, Part IV. LNCS, vol. 7575, pp. 359–372. Springer, Heidelberg (2012)

19. Li, L.J., Su, H., Xing, E.P., Fei-Fei, L.: Object bank: a high-level image representation for scene classification and semantic feature sparsification. In: NIPS (2010)

20. Donahue, J., Jia, Y., Vinyals, O., Hoffman, J., Zhang, N., Tzeng, E., Darrell, T.: DeCaF: a deep convolutional activation feature for generic visual recognition. In: ICML (2014)

21. Dixit, M., Chen, S., Gao, D., Rasiwasia, N., Vasconcelos, N.: Scene classification with semantic fisher vectors. In: CVPR (2015)

22. Razavian, A.S., Azizpour, H., Sullivan, J., Carlsson, S.: CNN features off-the-shelf: an astounding baseline for recognition. In: CVPR Workshops (2014)

23. Gong, Y., Wang, L., Guo, R., Lazebnik, S.: Multi-scale orderless pooling of deep convolutional activation features. In: Fleet, D., Pajdla, T., Schiele, B., Tuytelaars, T. (eds.) ECCV 2014, Part VII. LNCS, vol. 8695, pp. 392–407. Springer, Heidelberg (2014)

24. Juneja, M., Vedaldi, A., Jawahar, C.V., Zisserman, A.: Blocks that shout: distinctive parts for scene classification. In: CVPR (2013)

25. Singh, S., Gupta, A., Efros, A.A.: Unsupervised discovery of mid-level discriminative patches. In: Fitzgibbon, A., Lazebnik, S., Perona, P., Sato, Y., Schmid, C. (eds.) ECCV 2012, Part II. LNCS, vol. 7573, pp. 73–86. Springer, Heidelberg (2012)

26. Doersch, C., Gupta, A., Efros, A.: Mid-level visual element discovery as discriminative mode seeking. In: NIPS (2013)

27. Sun, J., Ponce, J.: Learning discriminative part detectors for image classification and cosegmentation. In: ICCV (2013)

28. Oliva, A., Torralba, A.: Modeling the shape of the scene: a holistic representation of the spatial envelope. IJCV **42**(3), 145–175 (2001)

29. Krizhevsky, A., Sutskever, I., Hinton, G.E.: ImageNet classification with deep convolutional neural networks. In: NIPS (2012)

30. Zhou, B., Lapedriza, A., Xiao, J., Torralba, A., Oliva, A.: Learning deep features for scene recognition using places database. In: NIPS (2014)

31. Zeiler, M.D., Fergus, R.: Visualizing and understanding convolutional networks. In: Fleet, D., Pajdla, T., Schiele, B., Tuytelaars, T. (eds.) ECCV 2014, Part I. LNCS, vol. 8689, pp. 818–833. Springer, Heidelberg (2014)

32. Zhou, B., Khosla, A., Lapedriza, À., Oliva, A., Torralba, A.: Object detectors emerge in deep scene CNNS. CoRR, abs/1412.6856 (2014)

33. Deng, J., Dong, W., Socher, R., Li, L.J., Li, K., Fei-Fei, L.: Imagenet: a large-scale hierarchical image database. In: CVPR (2009)

34. Xiao, J., Hays, J., Ehinger, K., Oliva, A., Torralba, A.: SUN database: large-scale scene recognition from abbey to zoo. In: CVPR (2010)

35. Jégou, H., Douze, M., Schmid, C., Pérez, P.: Aggregating local descriptors into a compact image representation. In: CVPR (2010)

36. Kittler, J., Hatef, M., Duin, R.P.W., Matas, J.: On combining classifiers. PAMI **20**(3), 226–239 (1998)

37. Akata, Z., Perronnin, F., Harchaoui, Z., Schmid, C.: Good practice in largescale learning for image classification. PAMI **36**(3), 507–520 (2013)

38. Girshick, R., Donahue, J., Darrell, T., Malik, J.: Rich feature hierarchies for accurate object detection and semantic segmentation. In: CVPR (2014)

39. Tzeng, E., Hoffman, J., Zhang, N., Saenko, K., Darrell, T.: Deep domain confusion: maximizing for domain invariance. CoRR, abs/1412.3474 (2014)

40. Liu, L., Shen, C., Wang, L., van den Hengel, A., Wang, C.: Encoding high dimensional local features by sparse coding based Fisher vectors. In: NIPS (2014)

Scene Understanding

Ambient Sound Provides Supervision for Visual Learning

Andrew Owens[1(✉)], Jiajun Wu[1], Josh H. McDermott[1], William T. Freeman[1,2], and Antonio Torralba[1]

[1] Massachusetts Institute of Technology, Cambridge, USA
andrewo@mit.edu
[2] Google Research, Cambridge, USA

Abstract. The sound of crashing waves, the roar of fast-moving cars – sound conveys important information about the objects in our surroundings. In this work, we show that ambient sounds can be used as a supervisory signal for learning visual models. To demonstrate this, we train a convolutional neural network to predict a statistical summary of the sound associated with a video frame. We show that, through this process, the network learns a representation that conveys information about objects and scenes. We evaluate this representation on several recognition tasks, finding that its performance is comparable to that of other state-of-the-art unsupervised learning methods. Finally, we show through visualizations that the network learns units that are selective to objects that are often associated with characteristic sounds.

Keywords: Sound · Convolutional networks · Unsupervised learning

1 Introduction

Sound conveys important information about the world around us – the bustle of a café tells us that there are many people nearby, while the low-pitched roar of engine noise tells us to watch for fast-moving cars [10]. Although sound is in some cases complementary to visual information, such as when we listen to something out of view, vision and hearing are often informative about the same structures in the world. Here we propose that as a consequence of these correlations, concurrent visual and sound information provide a rich training signal that we can use to learn useful representations of the visual world.

In particular, an algorithm trained to predict the sounds that occur within a visual scene might be expected to learn objects and scene elements that are associated with salient and distinctive noises, such as people, cars, and flowing water. Such an algorithm might also learn to associate visual scenes with the ambient sound textures [25] that occur within them. It might, for example, associate the sound of wind with outdoor scenes, and the buzz of refrigerators with indoor scenes.

Although human annotations are indisputably useful for learning, they are expensive to collect. The correspondence between ambient sounds and video is,

© Springer International Publishing AG 2016
B. Leibe et al. (Eds.): ECCV 2016, Part I, LNCS 9905, pp. 801–816, 2016.
DOI: 10.1007/978-3-319-46448-0_48

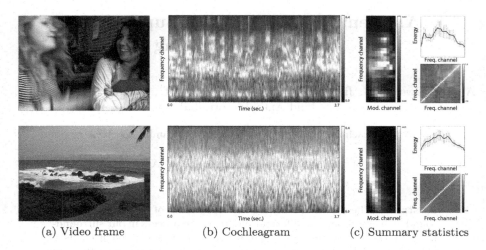

(a) Video frame   (b) Cochleagram   (c) Summary statistics

Fig. 1. Visual scenes are associated with characteristic sounds. Our goal is to take an image (a) and predict time-averaged summary statistics (c) of a cochleagram (b). The statistics we use are (clockwise): the response to a bank of band-pass modulation filters; the mean and standard deviation of each frequency band; and the correlation between bands. We show two frames from the Flickr video dataset [34]. The first contains the sound of human speech; the second contains the sound of wind and crashing waves. The differences between these sounds are reflected in their summary statistics: e.g., the water/wind sound, which is similar to white noise, contains fewer correlations between cochlear channels.

by contrast, ubiquitous and free. While there has been much work on learning from unlabeled image data [4,22,35], an audio signal may provide information that that is largely orthogonal to that available in images alone – information about semantics, events, and mechanics are all readily available from sound [10].

One challenge in utilizing audio-visual input is that the sounds that we hear are only loosely associated with what we see. Sound-producing objects often lie outside of our visual field, and objects that are capable of producing character-istic sounds – barking dogs, ringing phones – do not always do so. A priori it is thus not obvious what might be achieved by predicting sound from images.

In this work, we show that a model trained to predict held-out sound from video frames learns a visual representation that conveys semantically meaningful information. We formulate our sound-prediction task as a classification problem, in which we train a convolutional neural network (CNN) to predict a statistical summary of the sound that occurred at the time a video frame was recorded. We then validate that the learned representation contains significant information about objects and scenes.

We do this in two ways: first, we show that the image features that we learn through our sound-prediction task can be used for object and scene recognition. On these tasks, our features obtain similar performance to state-of-the-art unsupervised and self-supervised learning methods. Second, we show that the intermediate layers of our CNN are highly selective for objects. This augments recent work [38] showing that object detectors "emerge" in a CNN's internal representation when it is trained to recognize scenes. As in the scene recognition task, object detectors emerge inside of our sound-prediction network. However, our model learns these detectors from an unlabeled audio-visual signal, without any explicit human annotation.

In this paper, we: (1) present a model based on visual CNNs and sound textures [25] that predicts a video frame's held-out sound; (2) demonstrate that the CNN learns units in its convolutional layers that are selective for objects, extending the methodology of Zhou et al. [38]; (3) validate the effectiveness of sound-based supervision by using the learned representation for object- and scene-recognition tasks. These results suggest that sound data, which is available in abundance from consumer videos, provides a useful training signal for visual learning.

2 Related Work

We take inspiration from work in psychology, such as Gaver's Everyday Listening [10], that studies the ways that humans learn about objects and events using sound. In this spirit, we would like to study the situations where sound tells us about visual objects and scenes. Work in auditory scene analysis [6,7,23] meanwhile has provided computational methods for recognizing structures in audio streams. Following this work, we use a sound representation [25] that has been applied to sound recognition [6] and synthesis tasks [25].

Recently, researchers have proposed many unsupervised learning methods that learn visual representations by solving prediction tasks (sometimes known as *pretext* tasks) for which the held-out prediction target is derived from a natural signal in the world, rather than from human annotations. This style of learning has been called "self supervision" [4] or "natural supervision" [30]. With these methods, the supervisory signal may come from video, for example by having the algorithm estimate camera motion [1,17] or track content across frames [12,27,35]. There are also methods that learn from static images, for example by predicting the relative location of image patches [4,16], or by learning invariance to simple geometric and photometric transformations [5]. The assumption behind these methods is that, in order to solve the pretext task, the model has to implicitly learn about semantics and, through this process, develop image features that are broadly useful.

While we share with this work the high-level goal of learning image representations, and we use a similar technical approach, our work differs in significant ways. In contrast to methods whose supervisory signal comes entirely from the imagery itself, ours comes from a modality (sound) that is complementary to vision. This is advantageous because sound is known to be a rich source of information about objects and scenes [6,10], and it is largely invariant to visual transformations, such as lighting, scene composition, and viewing angle. Predicting sound from images thus requires some degree of generalization to visual

(a) Images grouped by audio cluster   (b) Clustered audio stats. (c) CNN model

Fig. 2. Visualization of some of the audio clusters used in one of our models (5 of 30 clusters). For each cluster, we show (a) the images in the test set whose sound textures were closest to the centroid (no more than one frame per video), and (b) we visualize aspects of the sound texture used to define the cluster centroid – specifically, the mean and standard deviation of the frequency channels. We also include a representative cochleagram (that of the leftmost image). Although the clusters were defined using audio, there are common objects and scene attributes in many of the images. We train a CNN to predict a video frame's auditory cluster assignment (c).

transformations. Moreover, our supervision task is based on solving a straight-forward classification problem, which allows us to use a network design that closely resembles those used in object and scene recognition (rather than, for example, the siamese-style networks used in video methods).

Our approach is closely related to recent audio-visual work [30] that predicts soundtracks for videos that show a person striking objects with a drumstick. A key feature of this work is that the sounds are "visually indicated" by actions in video – a situation that has also been considered in other contexts, such as in the task of visually localizing a sound source [9,13,19] or in evaluating the synchronization between the two modalities [32]. In the natural videos that we use, however, the sound sources are frequently out of frame. Also, in contrast to other recent work in multi-modal representation learning [2,28,33], our technical approach is based on solving a self-supervised classification problem (rather than a generative model or autoencoder), and our goal is to learn visual representations that are generally useful for object recognition tasks.

3   Learning to Predict Ambient Audio

We would like to train a model that, when given a frame of video, can predict its corresponding sound – a task that implicitly requires knowledge of objects and scenes.

3.1 Statistical Sound Summaries

A natural question, then, is how our model should represent sound. Perhaps the first approach that comes to mind would be to estimate a frequency spectrum at the moment in which the picture was taken, similar to [30]. However, this is potentially suboptimal because in natural scenes it is difficult to predict the precise timing of a sound from visual information. Upon seeing a crowd of people, for instance, we might expect to hear the sound of speech, but the precise timing and content of that speech might not be directly indicated by the video frames.

To be closer to the time scale of visual objects, we estimate a statistical summary of the sound, averaged over a few seconds. We do this using the sound texture model of McDermott and Simoncelli [25], which assumes that sound is stationary within a temporal window (we use 3.75 s). More specifically, we closely follow [25] and filter the audio waveform with a bank of 32 band-pass filters intended to mimic human cochlear frequency selectivity. We then take the Hilbert envelope of each channel, raise each sample of the envelope to the 0.3 power (to mimic cochlear amplitude compression), and resample the compressed envelope to 400 Hz. Finally, we compute time-averaged statistics of these subband envelopes: we compute the mean and standard deviation of each frequency channel, the mean squared response of each of a bank of modulation filters applied to each channel, and the Pearson correlation between pairs of channels. For the modulation filters, we use a bank of 10 band-pass filters with center frequencies ranging from 0.5 to 200 Hz, equally spaced on a logarithmic scale.

To make the sound features more invariant to gain (e.g., from the microphone), we divide the envelopes by the median energy (median vector norm) over all timesteps, and include this energy as a feature. As in [25], we normalize the standard deviation of each cochlear channel by its mean, and each modulation power by its standard deviation. We then rescale each kind of texture feature (i.e. marginal moments, correlations, modulation power, energy) inversely with the number of dimensions. The sound texture for each image is a 502-dimensional vector. In Fig. 1, we give examples of these summary statistics for two audio clips. We provide more details about our audio representation in the supplementary material.

3.2 Predicting Sound from Images

We would like to predict sound textures from images – a task that we hypothesize leads to learning useful visual representations. Although multiple frames are available, we predict sound from a single frame, so that the learned image features will be more likely to transfer to single-image recognition tasks. Furthermore, since the actions that produce the sounds may not appear on-screen, motion information may not always be applicable.

While one option would be to regress the sound texture v_j directly from the corresponding image I_j, we choose instead to define explicit sound categories and formulate this visual recognition problem as a classification task. This also makes it easier to analyze the network, because it allows us to compare the

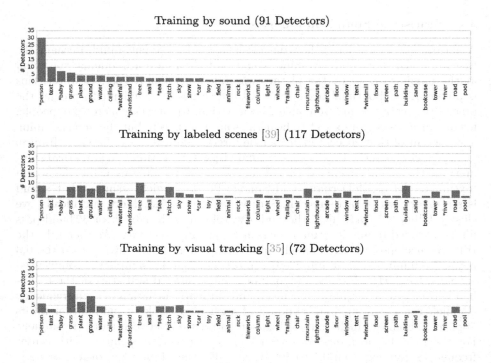

Fig. 3. Histogram of object-selective units in networks trained with different styles of supervision. From top to bottom: training to predict ambient sound (our Clustering model); training to predict scene category using the Places dataset [39]; and training to do visual tracking [35]. Compared to the tracking model, which was also trained without semantic labels, our network learns more high-level object detectors. It also has more detectors for objects that make characteristic sounds, such as *person*, *baby*, and *waterfall*, in comparison to the one trained on Places [39]. Categories marked with * are those that we consider to make characteristic sounds.

internal representation of our model to object- and scene-classification models with similar network architecture (Sect. 4.1). We consider two labeling models: one based on a vector quantization, the other based on a binary coding scheme.

Clustering audio features. In the *Clustering* model, the sound textures $\{v_j\}$ in the training set are clustered using k-means. These clusters define image categories: we label each sound texture with the index of the closest centroid, and train our CNN to label images with their corresponding labels.

We found that audio clips that belong to a cluster often contain common objects. In Fig. 2, we show examples of such clusters, and in the supplementary material we provide their corresponding audio. We can see that there is a cluster that contains indoor scenes with children in them – these are relatively quiet scenes punctuated with speech sounds. Another cluster contains the sounds of many people speaking at once (often large crowds); another contains many water scenes (usually containing loud wind sounds). Several clusters capture general scene attributes, such as outdoor scenes with light wind sounds. During training, we remove examples that are far from the centroid of their cluster (more than the median distance to the vector, amongst all examples in the dataset).

Binary coding model. For the other variation of our model (which we call the *Binary* model), we use a binary coding scheme [14,31,36] equivalent to a multi-label classification problem. We project each sound texture v_j onto the top principal components (we use 30 projections), and convert these projections into a binary code by thresholding them. We predict this binary code using a sigmoid layer, and during training we measure error using cross-entropy loss.

For comparison, we trained a model (which we call the *Spectrum* model) to approximately predict the frequency spectrum at the time that the photo was taken, in lieu of a full sound texture. Specifically, for our sound vectors v_j in this model, we used the mean value of each cochlear channel within a 33.3-millisecond interval centered on the input frame (approximately one frame of a 30 Hz video). For training, we used the projection scheme from the Binary model.

Training. We trained our models to predict audio on a 360,000-video subset of the Flickr video dataset [34]. Most of the videos in the dataset are personal video recordings containing natural audio, though many were post-processed, e.g. with added subtitles, title screens, and music. We divided our videos into training and test sets, and we randomly sampled 10 frames per video (1.8 million training images total). For our network architecture, we used the CaffeNet architecture [18] (a variation of Krizhevsky et al. [21]) with batch normalization [15]. We trained our model with Caffe [18], using a batch size of 256, for 320,000 iterations of stochastic gradient descent.

4   Results

We evaluate the image representation that our model learned in multiple ways. First, we demonstrate that the internal representation of our model contains convolutional units (neurons) that are selective to particular objects, and we analyze those objects' distribution. We then empirically evaluate the quality of the learned representation for several image recognition tasks, finding that it achieves performance comparable to other feature-learning methods that were trained without human annotations.

4.1   What Does the Network Learn to Detect?

Previous work [38] has shown that a CNN trained to predict scene categories will learn convolutional units that are selective for objects – a result that follows naturally from the fact that scenes are often defined by the objects that compose them. We ask whether a model trained to predict ambient sound, rather than explicit human labels, would learn object-selective units as well. For these experiments, we used our Clustering model, because its network structure is similar to that of the scene-recognition model used in [38].

Fig. 4. Top 5 responses for neurons of various networks, tested on the Flickr dataset. Please see the supplementary material for more visualizations.

Quantifying object-selective units. Similar to the method in [38], we visualized the images that each neuron in the top convolutional layer (conv5) responded most strongly to. To do this, we sampled a pool of 200,000 images from our Flickr video test set. We then collected, for each convolutional unit, the 60 images in this set that gave the unit the largest activation. Next, we applied the so-called synthetic visualization technique of [38] to approximately superimpose the unit's receptive field onto the image. Specifically, we found all of the spatial locations in the layer for which the unit's activation strength was at least half that of its maximum response. We then masked out the parts of the image that were not covered by the receptive field of one of these high-responding spatial units. We assumed a circle-shaped receptive field, obtaining the radius from [38]. To examine the effect of the data used in the evaluation, we also applied this visualization technique to other datasets (please see the supplementary material).

Next, for each neuron we showed its masked images to three human annotators on Amazon Mechanical Turk, and asked them: (1) whether an object is present in many of these regions, and if so, what it is; (2) to mark the images whose activations contain these objects. Unlike [38], we only considered units that were selective to objects, ignoring units that were selective to textures. For each unit, if at least 60 % of its top 60 activations contained the object, we considered it to be selective for the object (or following [38], we say that it is a *detector* for that object). We then manually labeled the unit with an object category, using the category names provided by the SUN database [37]. We found that 91 of the 256 units in our model were object-selective in this way, and we show a selection of them in Fig. 4.

We compared the number of these units to those of a CNN trained to recognize human-labeled scene categories on Places [38]. As expected, this model – having been trained with explicit human annotations – contained more object-selective units (117 units). We also asked whether object-selective neurons appear in the convolutional layers when a CNN is trained on other tasks that do not use human labels. As a simple comparison, we applied the same methodology to the egomotion-based model of Agrawal et al. [1] and to the tracking-based method of Wang and Gupta [35]. We applied these networks to whole images in all cases resizing the input image to 256 × 256 pixels and taking the center 227 × 227 crop), though we note that they were originally trained on cropped image regions.

We found that the tracking-based method also learned object-selective units, but that the objects that it detected were often textural "stuff," such as grass, ground, and water, and that there were fewer of these detection units in total (72 of 256). The results were similar for the egomotion-based model, which had 26 such units. In Fig. 3 and in the supplementary material, we provide the distribution of the objects that the units were selective to. We also visualized neurons from the method of Doersch et al. [4] (as before, applying the network to whole images, rather than to patches). We found a significant number of the units were selective for position, rather than to objects. For example, one convolutional unit

Table 1. Row 1: the number of detectors (i.e. units that are selective to a particular object); row 2: the number of detectors for objects with characteristic sounds; row 3: fraction of videos in which an object's sound is audible (computed only for object classes with characteristic sounds); row 4: given that an activation corresponds to an object with a characteristic sound, the probability that its sound is audible. There are 256 units in total for each method.

Method	Sound	Places
# Detectors	91	117
# Detectors for objects with characteristic sounds	49	26
Videos with object sound	43.7 %	16.9 %
Characteristic sound rate	81.2 %	75.9 %

responded most highly to the upper-left corner of an image – a unit that may be useful for the training task, which involves predicting the relative position of image patches. In Fig. 4, we show visualizations of a selection of object-detecting neurons for all of these methods.

The differences between the objects detected by these methods and our own may have to do with the requirements of the tasks being solved. The other unsupervised methods, for example, all involve comparing multiple input images or sub-images in a relatively fine-grained way. This may correspondingly change the representation that the network learns in its last convolutional layer – requiring its the units to encode, say, color and geometric transformations rather than object identities. Moreover, these networks may represent semantic information in other (more distributed) ways that would not necessarily be revealed through this visualization method.

Analyzing the types of objects that were detected. Next, we asked what kinds of objects our network learned to detect. We hypothesized that the object-selective neurons were more likely to respond to objects that produce (or are closely associated with) characteristic sounds. To evaluate this, we (an author) labeled the SUN object categories according to whether they were closely associated with a characteristic sound. We denote these categories with a ∗ in Fig. 3. Next, we counted the number of units that were selective to these objects, finding that our model contained significantly more such units than a scene-recognition network trained on the Places dataset, both in total number and as a proportion (Table 1). A significant fraction of these units were selective to people (adults, babies, and crowds).

Finally, we asked whether the sounds that these objects make were actually present in the videos that these video frames were sampled from. To do this, we listened to the sound of the top 30 video clips for each unit, and recorded whether the sound was made by the object that the neuron was selective to (e.g. , human speech for the *person* category). We found that 43.7 % of these videos contained the objects' sounds (Table 1).

4.2   Evaluating the Image Representation

We have seen through visualizations that a CNN trained to predict sound from an image learns units that are highly selective for objects. Now we evaluate, experimentally, how well the CNN's internal representation conveys information that is useful for recognizing objects and scenes.

Since our goal is to measure the amount of semantic information provided by the learned representation, rather than to seek absolute performance, we used a simple evaluation scheme. In most experiments, we computed image features using our CNN and trained a linear SVM to predict object or scene category using the activations in the top layers.

Object recognition. First, we used our CNN features for object recognition on the PASCAL VOC 2007 dataset [8]. We trained a one-vs.-rest linear SVM to detect the presence of each of the 20 object categories in the dataset, using the activations of the upper layers of the network as the feature set (pool5, fc6, and fc7). To help understand whether the convolutional units considered in Sect. 4.1 directly convey semantics, we also created a global max-pooling feature (similar to [29]), where we applied max pooling over the entire convolutional layer. This produces a 256-dimensional vector that contains the maximum response of each convolutional unit (we call it *max5*). Following common practice, we evaluated the network on a center 227×227 crop of each image (after resizing the image to 256×256), and we evaluated the results using mean average precision (mAP). We chose the SVM regularization parameter for each method by maximizing mAP on the validation set using grid search (we used $\{0.5^k \mid 4 \leq k < 20\}$).

The other unsupervised (or self-supervised) models in our comparison [1,4, 35] use different network designs. In particular, [4] was trained on image patches, so following their experiments we resized its convolutional layers for 227×227 images and removed the model's fully connected layers[1]. Also, since the model of Agrawal et al. [1] did not have a pool5 layer, we added one to it. We also considered CNNs that were trained with human annotations: object recognition on ImageNet [3] and scene categories on Places [39]. Finally, we considered using the k-means weight initialization method of [20] to set the weights of a CNN model (we call this the *K-means* model).

We found that our best-performing of our model (the binary-coding method) obtained comparable performance to other unsupervised learning methods, such as [4]. Both models based on sound textures (Clustering and Binary) outperformed the model that predicted only the frequency spectrum. This suggests that the additional time-averaged statistics from sound textures are helpful. For these models, we used 30 clusters (or PCA projections): in the supplementary material, we consider varying the number of clusters, finding that there is a small improvement from increasing it, and a substantial decrease in performance when using just two clusters. The sound-based models significantly outperformed other

---

[1] As a result, this model has a larger pool5 layer than the other methods: 7×7 vs. 6×6. Likewise, the fc6 layer of [35] is smaller (1,024 dims. vs. 4,096 dims.).

methods when we globally pooled the conv5 features, suggesting that the convolutional units contain a significant amount of semantic information (and are well suited to being used at this spatial scale).

Scene recognition. We also evaluated our model on a scene recognition task using the SUN dataset [37], a large classification benchmark that involves recognizing 397 scene categories with 7,940 training and test images provided in multiple splits. Following [1], we averaged our classification accuracy across 3 splits, with 20 examples per scene category. We chose the linear SVM's regularization parameter for each model using 3-fold cross-validation.

We again found that our features' performance was comparable to other models. In particular, we found that the difference between our models was smaller than in the object-recognition case, with both the Clustering and Binary models obtaining performance comparable to the patch-based method with pool5 features.

Pretraining for object detection. Following recent work [4,20,35], we used our model to initialize the weights of a CNN-based object detection system (Fast R-CNN [11]), verifying that the results improved over random initialization. We followed the training procedure of Krähenbühl et al. [20], using 150,000 iterations of backpropagation with an initial learning rate of 0.002, and we compared our model with other published results (we report the numbers provided by [20]).

Our best-performing model (the Clustering model) obtains similar performance to that of Wang and Gupta's tracking-based model [35], while the overall best results were from variations of Doersch et al.'s patch-based model [4,20]. We note that the network changes substantially during fine-tuning, and thus the performance is fairly dependent on the parameters used in the training procedure. Moreover all models, when fine-tuned in this way, achieve results that are close to those of a well-chosen random initialization (within 6 % mAP). Recent work [20,26] has addressed these optimization issues by rescaling the weights of a pretrained network using a data-driven procedure. The unsupervised method with the best performance combines the rescaling method of [20] with the patch-based pretraining of [4].

Sound prediction. We also asked how well our model learned to solve its sound prediction task. We found that on our test set, the clustering-based model (with 30 clusters) chose the correct sound label 15.8 % of the time. Pure chance in this case is 3.3 %, while the baseline of choosing the most commonly occurring label is 6.6 %.

Audio supervision. It is natural to ask what role audio plays in the learning process. Perhaps, for example, our training procedure would produce equally good features if we replaced the hand-crafted sound features with hand-crafted *visual* features, computed from the images themselves. To study this, we replaced our sound texture features with (512-dimensional) visual texton histograms [24], using the parameters from [37], and we used them to train a variation of our Clustering model.

Table 2. (a) Mean average precision for PASCAL VOC 2007 classification, and accuracy on SUN397. Here we trained a linear SVM using the top layers of different networks. We note in Sect. 4.2 that the shape of these layers varies between networks. (b) Mean average precision on PASCAL VOC 2007 using Fast-RCNN [11]. We initialized the CNN weights using those of our learned sound models. (c) Per-class AP scores for the VOC 2007 classification task with pool5 features (corresponds to mAP in (a)).

Method	VOC Cls. (%mAP)				SUN397 (%acc.)			
	max5	pool5	fc6	fc7	max5	pool5	fc6	fc7
Sound (cluster)	36.7	45.8	44.8	44.3	**17.3**	**22.9**	20.7	14.9
Sound (binary)	**39.4**	**46.7**	47.1	47.4	17.1	22.5	**21.3**	**21.4**
Sound (spect.)	35.8	44.0	44.4	44.4	14.6	19.5	18.6	17.7
Texton-CNN	28.9	37.5	35.3	32.5	10.7	15.2	11.4	7.6
K-means [20]	27.5	34.8	33.9	32.1	11.6	14.9	12.8	12.4
Tracking [35]	33.5	42.2	42.4	40.2	14.1	18.7	16.2	15.1
Patch pos. [4]	26.8	46.1	-	-	9.8	22.2	-	-
Egomotion [1]	22.7	31.1	-	-	9.1	11.3	-	-
ImageNet [21]	**63.6**	**65.6**	69.6	73.6	29.8	34.0	37.8	37.8
Places [39]	59.0	63.2	65.3	66.2	**39.4**	**42.1**	**46.1**	**48.8**

Method	(%mAP)
Random init. [20]	41.3
Sound (cluster)	44.1
Sound (binary)	43.3
Motion [35,20]	44.0
Egomotion [1,20]	41.8
Patch pos. [4,20]	46.6
Calib. + Patch [4,20]	**51.1**
ImageNet [21]	**57.1**
Places [39]	52.8

(a) Image classification with linear SVM   (b) Finetuning detection

Method	aer	bk	brd	bt	btl	bus	car	cat	chr	cow	din	dog	hrs	mbk	prs	pot	shp	sfa	trn	tv
Sound (cluster)	68	**47**	38	54	15	45	**66**	45	42	23	37	28	73	58	**85**	25	26	32	67	42
Sound (binary)	69	45	38	56	**16**	**47**	65	45	41	**25**	37	28	**74**	**61**	**85**	26	**39**	32	**69**	38
Sound (spect.)	65	40	35	54	14	42	63	41	39	24	32	25	72	56	81	**27**	33	28	65	40
Texton-CNN	65	35	28	46	11	31	63	30	41	17	28	23	64	51	74	9	19	33	54	30
K-means	61	31	27	49	9	27	58	34	36	12	25	21	64	38	70	18	14	25	51	25
Motion [35]	67	35	41	54	11	35	62	35	39	21	30	26	70	53	78	22	32	37	61	34
Patches [4]	**70**	44	**43**	**60**	12	44	**66**	**52**	44	24	**45**	**31**	73	48	78	14	28	**39**	62	**43**
Egomotion [1]	60	24	21	35	10	19	57	24	27	11	22	18	61	40	69	13	12	24	48	28
ImageNet [21]	79	**71**	**73**	75	**25**	60	80	**75**	51	**45**	60	**70**	**80**	**72**	**91**	42	**62**	56	82	62
Places [39]	**83**	60	56	**80**	23	**66**	**84**	54	**57**	40	**74**	41	**80**	68	90	**50**	45	**61**	**88**	**63**

(c) Per class mAP for image classification on PASCAL VOC 2007

As expected, the images that belong to each cluster are visually coherent, and share common objects. However, we found that the network performed significantly worse than the audio-based method on the object- and scene-recognition metrics (Table 2a). Moreover, we found that its convolutional units rarely were selective for objects (generally they responded responded to "stuff" such as grass and water). Likely this is because the network simply learned to approximate the texton features, obtaining low labeling error without high-level generalization. In contrast, the audio-based labels – despite also being based on another form of hand-crafted feature – are largely invariant to visual transformations, such as lighting and scale, and therefore predicting them requires some degree of generalization (one benefit of training with multiple, complementary modalities).

5 Discussion

Sound has many properties that make it useful as a supervisory training signal: it is abundantly available without human annotations, and it is known to convey information about objects and scenes. It is also complementary to visual information, and may therefore convey information not easily obtainable from unlabeled image analysis.

In this work, we proposed using ambient sound to learn visual representations. We introduced a model, based on convolutional neural networks, that predicts a statistical sound summary from a video frame. We then showed, with visualizations and experiments on recognition tasks, that the resulting image representation contains information about objects and scenes.

Here we considered one audio representation, based on sound textures, but it is natural to ask whether other audio representations would lead the model to learn about additional types of objects. To help answer this question, we would like to more systematically study the situations when sound does (and does not) tell us about objects in the visual world. Ultimately, we would like to know what object and scene structures are detectable through sound-based training, and we see our work as a step in this direction.

Acknowledgments. This work was supported by NSF grants #1524817 to A.T; NSF grants #1447476 and #1212849 to W.F.; a McDonnell Scholar Award to J.H.M.; and a Microsoft Ph.D. Fellowship to A.O. It was also supported by Shell Research, and by a donation of GPUs from NVIDIA. We thank Phillip Isola and Carl Vondrick for the helpful discussions, and the anonymous reviewers for their comments (in particular, for suggesting the comparison with texton features in Sect. 4.2).

References

1. Agrawal, P., Carreira, J., Malik, J.: Learning to see by moving. In: ICCV (2015)
2. Andrew, G., Arora, R., Bilmes, J.A., Livescu, K.: Deep canonical correlation analysis. In: ICML (2013)
3. Deng, J., Dong, W., Socher, R., Li, L.J., Li, K., Fei-Fei, L.: Imagenet: a large-scale hierarchical image database. In: CVPR (2009)
4. Doersch, C., Gupta, A., Efros, A.A.: Unsupervised visual representation learning by context prediction. In: ICCV (2015)
5. Dosovitskiy, A., Springenberg, J.T., Riedmiller, M., Brox, T.: Discriminative unsupervised feature learning with convolutional neural networks. In: NIPS (2014)
6. Ellis, D.P., Zeng, X., McDermott, J.H.: Classifying soundtracks with audio texture features. In: ICASSP (2011)
7. Eronen, A.J., Peltonen, V.T., Tuomi, J.T., Klapuri, A.P., Fagerlund, S., Sorsa, T., Lorho, G., Huopaniemi, J.: Audio-based context recognition. In: IEEE TASLP (2006)
8. Everingham, M., Van Gool, L., Williams, C.K., Winn, J., Zisserman, A.: The Pascal Visual Object Classes (VOC) challenge. IJCV **88**(2), 303–338 (2010)
9. Fisher III, J.W., Darrell, T., Freeman, W.T., Viola, P.A.: Learning joint statistical models for audio-visual fusion and segregation. In: NIPS (2000)
10. Gaver, W.W.: What in the world do we hear?: an ecological approach to auditory event perception. Ecol. Psychol. **5**(1), 1–29 (1993)
11. Girshick, R.: Fast R-CNN. In: ICCV (2015)
12. Goroshin, R., Bruna, J., Tompson, J., Eigen, D., LeCun, Y.: Unsupervised feature learning from temporal data. arXiv preprint arXiv:1504.02518 (2015)

13. Hershey, J.R., Movellan, J.R.: Audio vision: using audio-visual synchrony to locate sounds. In: NIPS (1999)
14. Indyk, P., Motwani, R.: Approximate nearest neighbors: towards removing the curse of dimensionality. In: STOC (1998)
15. Ioffe, S., Szegedy, C.: Batch normalization: accelerating deep network training by reducing internal covariate shift. In: ICML (2015)
16. Isola, P., Zoran, D., Krishnan, D., Adelson, E.H.: Learning visual groups from co-occurrences in space and time. In: ICLR Workshop (2016)
17. Jayaraman, D., Grauman, K.: Learning image representations tied to ego-motion. In: ICCV (2015)
18. Jia, Y., Shelhamer, E., Donahue, J., Karayev, S., Long, J., Girshick, R., Guadarrama, S., Darrell, T.: Caffe: convolutional architecture for fast feature embedding. In: MM (2014)
19. Kidron, E., Schechner, Y.Y., Elad, M.: Pixels that sound. In: CVPR (2005)
20. Krähenbühl, P., Doersch, C., Donahue, J., Darrell, T.: Data-dependent initializations of convolutional neural networks. In: ICLR (2016)
21. Krizhevsky, A., Sutskever, I., Hinton, G.E.: Imagenet classification with deep convolutional neural networks. In: NIPS (2012)
22. Le, Q.V., Ranzato, M.A., Monga, R., Devin, M., Chen, K., Corrado, G.S., Dean, J., Ng, A.Y.: Building high-level features using large scale unsupervised learning. In: ICML (2012)
23. Lee, K., Ellis, D.P., Loui, A.C.: Detecting local semantic concepts in environmental sounds using Markov model based clustering. In: ICASSP (2010)
24. Leung, T., Malik, J.: Representing and recognizing the visual appearance of materials using three-dimensional textons. IJCV 43(1), 29–44 (2001)
25. McDermott, J.H., Simoncelli, E.P.: Sound texture perception via statistics of the auditory periphery: evidence from sound synthesis. Neuron 71(5), 926–940 (2011)
26. Mishkin, D., Matas, J.: All you need is a good init. arXiv preprint arXiv:1511.06422 (2015)
27. Mobahi, H., Collobert, R., Weston, J.: Deep learning from temporal coherence in video. In: ICML (2009)
28. Ngiam, J., Khosla, A., Kim, M., Nam, J., Lee, H., Ng, A.Y.: Multimodal deep learning. In: ICML (2011)
29. Oquab, M., Bottou, L., Laptev, I., Sivic, J.: Is object localization for free?-weakly-supervised learning with convolutional neural networks. In: Proceedings of the IEEE Conference on Computer Vision and Pattern Recognition (2015)
30. Owens, A., Isola, P., McDermott, J., Torralba, A., Adelson, E.H., Freeman, W.T.: Visually indicated sounds. In: CVPR (2016)
31. Salakhutdinov, R., Hinton, G.: Semantic hashing. Int. J. Approx. Reason. 50(7), 969–978 (2009)
32. Slaney, M., Covell, M.: Facesync: A linear operator for measuring synchronization of video facial images and audio tracks. In: NIPS (2000)
33. Srivastava, N., Salakhutdinov, R.R.: Multimodal learning with deep Boltzmann machines. In: NIPS (2012)
34. Thomee, B., Shamma, D.A., Friedland, G., Elizalde, B., Ni, K., Poland, D., Borth, D., Li, L.J.: The new data and new challenges in multimedia research. arXiv preprint arXiv:1503.01817 (2015)
35. Wang, X., Gupta, A.: Unsupervised learning of visual representations using videos. In: ICCV (2015)
36. Weiss, Y., Torralba, A., Fergus, R.: Spectral hashing. In: NIPS (2009)

37. Xiao, J., Hays, J., Ehinger, K.A., Oliva, A., Torralba, A.: Sun database: large-scale scene recognition from abbey to zoo. In: CVPR (2010)
38. Zhou, B., Khosla, A., Lapedriza, A., Oliva, A., Torralba, A.: Object detectors emerge in deep scene CNNs. In: ICLR 2015 (2014)
39. Zhou, B., Lapedriza, A., Xiao, J., Torralba, A., Oliva, A.: Learning deep features for scene recognition using places database. In: NIPS (2014)

Grounding of Textual Phrases in Images by Reconstruction

Anna Rohrbach[1]([✉]), Marcus Rohrbach[2,3], Ronghang Hu[2], Trevor Darrell[2], and Bernt Schiele[1]

[1] Max Planck Institute for Informatics, Saarbrücken, Germany
{arohrbach,schiele}@mpi-inf.mpg.des
[2] UC Berkeley EECS, Berkeley, CA, USA
{rohrbach,ronghang,trevor}@eecs.berkeley.edu
[3] ICSI, Berkeley, CA, USA

Abstract. Grounding (i.e. localizing) arbitrary, free-form textual phrases in visual content is a challenging problem with many applications for human-computer interaction and image-text reference resolution. Few datasets provide the ground truth spatial localization of phrases, thus it is desirable to learn from data with no or little grounding supervision. We propose a novel approach which learns grounding by reconstructing a given phrase using an attention mechanism, which can be either latent or optimized directly. During training our approach encodes the phrase using a recurrent network language model and then learns to attend to the relevant image region in order to reconstruct the input phrase. At test time, the correct attention, i.e., the grounding, is evaluated. If grounding supervision is available it can be directly applied via a loss over the attention mechanism. We demonstrate the effectiveness of our approach on the Flickr30k Entities and ReferItGame datasets with different levels of supervision, ranging from no supervision over partial supervision to full supervision. Our supervised variant improves by a large margin over the state-of-the-art on both datasets.

1 Introduction

Language grounding in visual data is an interesting problem studied both in computer vision [18,24,25,28,35] and natural language processing [29,34] communities. Such grounding can be done on different levels of granularity: from coarse, e.g. associating a paragraph of text to a scene in a movie [41,52], to fine, e.g. localizing a word or phrase in a given image [18,35]. In this work we focus on the latter scenario. Many prior efforts in this area have focused on rather constrained settings with a small number of nouns to ground [28,31]. On the contrary, we want to tackle the problem of grounding arbitrary natural language phrases in images. Most parallel corpora of sentence/visual data do not provide localization annotations (e.g. bounding boxes) and the annotation process is costly. We propose an approach which can learn to localize phrases relying only on phrases associated with images without bounding box annotations but

© Springer International Publishing AG 2016
B. Leibe et al. (Eds.): ECCV 2016, Part I, LNCS 9905, pp. 817–834, 2016.
DOI: 10.1007/978-3-319-46448-0_49

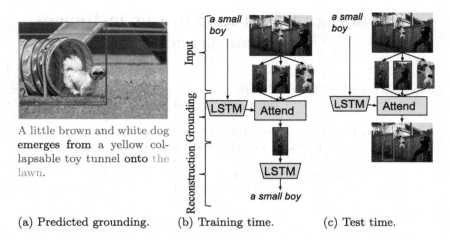

(a) Predicted grounding.   (b) Training time.   (c) Test time.

Fig. 1. (a) Without bounding box annotations at training time our approach GroundeR can ground free-form natural language phrases in images. (b) During training our latent attention approach reconstructs phrases by learning to attend to the correct box. (c) At test time, the attention model infers the grounding for each phrase. For semi-supervised and fully supervised variants see Fig. 2.

which is also able to incorporate phrases with bounding box supervision when available (see Fig. 1).

The main idea of our approach is shown in Fig. 1(b, c). Let us first consider the scenario where no localization supervision is available. Given images paired with natural language phrases we want to localize these phrases with a bounding box in the image (Fig. 1c). To do this we propose a model (Fig. 1b) which learns to attend to a bounding box proposal and, based on the selected bounding box, reconstructs the phrase. As the second part of the model (Fig. 1b, bottom) is able to predict the correct phrase only if the first part of the model attended correctly (Fig. 1b, top), this can be learned without additional bounding box supervision. Our method is based on *Ground*ing with a *R*econstruction loss and hence named *GroundeR*. Additional supervision is integrated in our model by adding a loss function which directly penalizes incorrect attention before the reconstruction step. At test time we evaluate whether the model attends to the correct bounding box.

We propose a novel approach to grounding of textual phrases in images which can operate in all supervision modes: with no, a few, or all grounding annotations available. We evaluate our GroundeR approach on the Flickr30k Entities [35] and ReferItGame [26] datasets and show that our unsupervised variant is better than prior work and our supervised approach significantly outperforms state-of-the-art on both datasets. Interestingly, our semi-supervised approach can effectively exploit small amounts of labeled data and surpasses the supervised variant by exploiting multiple losses.

2   Related Work

Grounding Natural Language in Images and Video. For grounding language in images, the approach of [28] is based on a Markov Random Field which aligns 3D cuboids to words. However it is limited to nouns of 21 object classes relevant to indoor scenes. [22] uses a Conditional Random Field to ground the specifically designed scene graph query in the image. [25] grounds dependency-tree relations to image regions using Multiple Instance Learning and a ranking objective. [24] simplifies this objective to just the maximum score and replaces the dependency tree with a learned recurrent network. Both works have not been evaluated for grounding, but we discuss a quantitative comparison in Sect. 4. Recently, [35] presented a new dataset, Flickr30k Entities, which augments the Flickr30k dataset [49] with bounding boxes for all noun phrases present in textual descriptions. [35] report the localization performance of their proposed CCA embedding [14] approach. [45] proposes Deep Structure-Preserving Embedding for image-sentence retrieval and also applies it to phrase localization, formulated as ranking problem. The Spatial Context Recurrent ConvNet (SCRC) [18] and the approach of [33] use a caption generation framework to score the phrase on the set of proposal boxes, to select the box with highest probability. One advantage of our approach over [18,33] is its applicability to un- and semi-supervised training regimes. We believe that our approach of encoding the phrase optimizes the better objective for grounding than scoring the phrase with a text generation pipeline as in [18,33]. As for the fully-supervised regime we empirically show our advantage over [18]. [36] attempts to localize relation phases of type Subject-Verb-Object at a large scale in order to verify their correctness, while relying on detectors from [8].

In the video domain some of the representative works on spatial-temporal language grounding are [31] and [50]. These are limited to small set of nouns.

Object co-localization focuses on discovering and detecting an object in images or videos without any bounding box annotation, but only from image/video level labels [3,6,23,30,38,40,51]. These works are similar to ours with respect to the amount of supervision, but they focus on a few discrete classes, while our approach can handle arbitrary phrases and allows for localization of novel phrases. There are also works that propose to train detectors for a wide range of concepts using image-level annotated data from web image search, e.g. [4,8]. These approaches are complementary to ours in the sense of obtaining large scale concept detectors with little supervision, however they do not tackle complex phrases e.g. "a blond boy on the left" which is the focus of our work.

Attention in Vision Tasks. Recently, different attention mechanisms have been applied to a range of computer vision tasks. The general idea is that given a visual input, e.g. set of features, at any given moment we might want to focus only on part of it, e.g. attend to a specific subset of features [2]. [46] integrates spatial attention into their image captioning pipeline. They consider two variants: "soft" and "hard" attention, meaning that in the latter case the model is only allowed to pick a single location, while in the first one the attention "weights" can be distributed over multiple locations. [21] adapts the soft-attention mechanism and attends to bounding box proposals, one word at a time, while generating an image captioning. [47] relies on a similar mechanism to perform temporal attention for selecting frames in video description task. [48] uses attention mechanism to densely label actions in a video sequence. Our approach relies on soft-attention mechanism, similar to the one of [46]. We apply it to the language grounding task where attention helps us to select a bounding box proposal for a given phrase.

Bi-directional Mapping. In our model, a phrase is first mapped to a image region through attention, and then the image region is mapped back to phrase during reconstruction. There is conceptual similarity between previous work and ours on the idea of bi-directional mapping from one domain to another. In autoencoders [43], input data is first mapped to a compressed vector during encoding, and then reconstructed during decoding. [5] uses a bi-directional mapping from visual features to words and from words to visual features in a recurrent neural network model. The idea is to generate descriptions from visual features and then to reconstruct visual features given a description. Similar to [5], our model can also learn to associate input text with visual features, but through attending to an image region rather than reconstructing directly from words. In the linguistic community, [1] proposed a CRF Autoencoder, which generates latent structures for the given language input and then reconstructs the input from these latent structures, with the application to e.g. part-of-speech tagging.

3   GroundeR : *Ground*ing by *R*econstruction

The goal of our approach is to ground natural language phrases in images. More specifically, to ground a phrase p in an image I means to find a region r_j in the image which corresponds to this phrase. r_j can be any subset of I, e.g. a segment or a bounding box. The core insight of our method is that there is a bi-directional correspondence between an image region and the phrase describing it. As a correct grounding of a textual phrase should result in an image region which a human would describe using this phrase, i.e. it is possible to reconstruct the phrase based on the grounded image region. Thus, the key idea of our approach is to learn to ground a phrase by reconstructing this phrase from an automatically localized region. Figure 1 gives an overview of our approach.

In this work, we utilize a set of automatically generated bounding box proposals $\{r_i\}_{i \in N}$ for the image I. Given a phrase p, during training our model works in two parts: the first part aims to attend to the most relevant region r_j (or potentially also multiple regions) based on the phrase p, and then the second part tries to reconstruct the same phrase p from region(s) r_j it attended to in the first phase. Therefore, by training to reconstruct the text phrase, the model learns to first ground the phrase in the image, and then generate the phrase from that region. Figure 2a visualizes the network structure. At test time, we

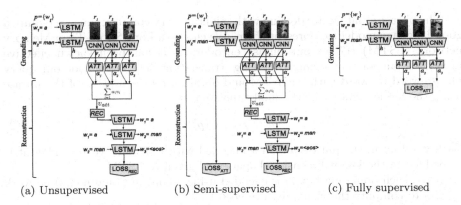

(a) Unsupervised   (b) Semi-supervised   (c) Fully supervised

Fig. 2. Our model learns grounding of textual phrases in images with (a) no, (b) little (c) or full supervision of localization, through a grounding part and a reconstruction part. During training, the model distributes its attention to a single or several boxes, and learns to reconstruct the input phrase based on the boxes it attends to. At test time, only the grounding part is used.

remove the phrase reconstruction part, and use the first part for phrase grounding. The described pipeline can be extended to accommodate partial supervision, i.e. ground-truth phrase localization. For that we integrate an additional loss into the model, which directly optimizes for correct attention prediction, see Fig. 2b. Finally, we can adapt our model to the fully supervised scenario by removing the reconstruction phase, see Fig. 2c.

In the following we present the details of the two parts in our approach: learning to attend to the correct region for a given phrase and learning to reconstruct the phrase from the attended region. For simplicity, but without loss of generality, we will refer to r_j as a single bounding box.

3.1   Learning to Ground

We frame the problem of grounding a phrase p in image I as selecting a bounding box r_j from a set of image region proposals $\{r_i\}_{i=1,\cdots,N}$. To select the correct bounding box, we define an attention function f_{ATT} and select the box j which receives the maximum attention:

$$j = \arg\max_i f_{ATT}(p, r_i) \tag{1}$$

In the following we describe the details of how we model the attention in f_{ATT}. The attention mechanism used in our model is inspired by and similar to the soft attention formulations of [21, 46]. However, our inputs to the attention predictor are not single words but rather multi-word phrases, and consequently we also do not have a "doubly stochastic attention" which is used in [46] to normalize the attention across words.

The phrases that we are dealing with might be very complex thus we require a good language model to represent them. We choose a Long Short-Term Memory network (LSTM) [17] as our phrase encoder, as it has been shown effective in various language modeling tasks, e.g. translation [39]. We encode our query phrase word by word with an LSTM and obtain a representation of the phrase using the hidden state h at the final time step as:

$$h = f_{LSTM}(p) \qquad (2)$$

Each word w_t in the phrase p is first encoded with a one-hot-vector. Then it is embedded in the lower dimensional space and given to LSTM.

Next, each bounding box r_i is encoded using a convolutional neural network (CNN) to compute the visual feature vector v_i:

$$v_i = f_{CNN}(r_i) \qquad (3)$$

Based on the encoded phrase and feature representation of each proposal, we use a two layer perceptron to compute the attention on the proposal r_i:

$$\bar{\alpha}_i = f_{ATT}(p, r_i) = W_2\phi(W_h h + W_v v_i + b_1) + b_2 \qquad (4)$$

where ϕ is the rectified linear unit (ReLU): $\phi(x) = max(0, x)$. We found that this architecture performs better than e.g. a single layer perceptron with a hyperbolic tangent nonlinearity used in [2].

We get normalized attention weights α_i by using softmax, which can be interpreted as probability of region r_i being the correct region $r_{\hat{j}}$:

$$\alpha_i = P(i = \hat{j}|\bar{\alpha}) = \frac{\exp(\bar{\alpha}_i)}{\sum_{k=1}^{N} \exp(\bar{\alpha}_k)} \qquad (5)$$

If at training time we have ground truth information, i.e. that $r_{\hat{j}}$ is the correct proposal box, then we can compute the loss L_{att} based on our prediction as:

$$L_{att} = -\frac{1}{B}\sum_{b=1}^{B} \log(P(\hat{j}|\bar{\alpha})), \qquad (6)$$

where B is the number of phrases per batch. This loss activates only if the training sample has the ground-truth attention value, otherwise, it is zero. If we do not have ground truth annotations then we have to define a loss function to learn the parameters of f_{ATT} in a weakly supervised manner. In the next section we describe how we define this loss by aiming to reconstruct the phrase based on the boxes that are attended to. At test time, we calculate the IOU (intersection over union) value between the selected box r_j and the ground truth box $r_{\hat{j}}$.

3.2   Learning to Reconstruct

The key idea of our phrase reconstruction model is to learn to reconstruct the phrase only from the attended boxes. Given an attention distribution over the boxes, we compute a weighted sum over the visual features and the attention weights α_i:

$$v_{att} = \sum_{i=1}^{N} \alpha_i v_i, \tag{7}$$

which aggregates the visual features from the attended boxes. Then, the visual features v_{att} are further encoded into v'_{att} using a non-linear encoding layer:

$$v'_{att} = f_{REC}(v_{att}) = \phi(W_a v_{att} + b_a) \tag{8}$$

We reconstruct the input phrase based on this encoded visual feature v'_{att} over attended regions. During reconstruction, we use an image description LSTM that takes v'_{att} as input to generate a distribution over phrases p:

$$P(p|v'_{att}) = f_{LSTM}(v'_{att}) \tag{9}$$

where $P(p|v'_{att})$ is a distribution over the phrases conditioned on the input visual feature. Our approach for phrase generation is inspired by [9,44] who have effectively used LSTM for generating image descriptions based on visual features. Given a visual feature, it learns to predict a word sequence $\{w_t\}$. At each time step t, the model predicts a distribution over the next word w_{t+1} conditioned on the input visual feature v'_{att} and all the previous words. We use a single LSTM layer and we feed the visual input only at the first time step. We use LSTM as our phrase encoder as well as decoder. Although one could potentially use other approaches to map phrases into a lower dimensional semantic space, it is not clear how one would do the reconstruction without the recurrent network, given that we have to train encoding and decoding end-to-end.

Importantly, the entire grounding+reconstruction model is trained as a single deep network through back-propagation by maximizing the likelihood of the ground truth phrase $\hat{p}$ generated during reconstruction, where we define the training loss for batch size B:

$$L_{rec} = -\frac{1}{B} \sum_{b=1}^{B} \log(P(\hat{p}|v'_{att})) \tag{10}$$

Finally, in the semi-supervised model we have both losses L_{att} and L_{rec}, which are combined as follows:

$$L = \lambda L_{att} + L_{rec} \tag{11}$$

where parameter λ regulates the importance of the attention loss.

4   Experiments

We first discuss the experimental setup and design choices of our implementation and then present quantitative results on the test sets of Flickr30k Entities (Tables 1 and 2) and ReferItGame (Table 3) datasets. We find our best results to outperform state-of-the-art on both datasets by a significant margin. Figures 3 and 4 show qualitatively how well we can ground phrases in images.

4.1   Experimental Setup

We evaluate GroundeR on the datasets Flickr30k Entities [35] and ReferItGame [26]. Flickr30k Entities [35] contains over 275K bounding boxes from 31K images associated with natural language phrases. Some phrases in the dataset correspond to multiple boxes, e.g. "two men". For consistency with [35], in such cases we consider the union of the boxes as ground truth. We use 1,000 images for validation, 1,000 for testing and 29,783 for training. The ReferItGame [26] dataset contains over 99K regions from 20K images. Regions are associated with natural language expressions, constructed to disambiguate the described objects. We use the bounding boxes provided by [18] and the same test split, namely 10K images for testing; the rest we split in 9K training and 1K validation images.

We obtain 100 bounding box proposals for each image using Selective Search [42] for Flickr30k Entities and Edge Boxes [53] for ReferItGame dataset. For our semi-supervised and fully supervised models we obtain the ground-truth attention by selecting the proposal box which overlaps most with the ground-truth box, while the overlap IOU (intersection over union) is above 0.5. Thus, our fully supervised model is not trained with all available training phrase-box pairs, but only with those where such proposal boxes exist.

On the Flickr30k Entities for the visual representation we rely on the VGG16 network [37] trained on ImageNet [7]. For each box we extract a 4,096 dimensional feature from the fully connected fc7 layer. We also consider a VGG16 network fine-tuned for object detection on PASCAL [10], trained using Fast R-CNN [12]. In the following we refer to both features as VGG-CLS and VGG-DET, respectively. We do not fine-tune the VGG representation for our task to reduce computational and memory load, however, our model trivially allows back-propagation into the image representation which likely would lead to further improvements. For the ReferItGame dataset we use the VGG-CLS features and additional spatial features provided by [18]. We concatenate both and refer to the obtained feature as VGG+SPAT. For the language encoding and decoding we rely on the LSTM variant implemented in Caffe [20] which we initialize randomly and jointly train with the grounding task.

At test time we compute the accuracy as the ratio of phrases for which the attended box overlaps with the ground-truth box by more than 0.5 IOU.

4.2   Design Choices and Findings

In all experiments we use the Adam solver [27], which adaptively changes the learning rate during training. We train our models for about 20/50 epochs for the Flickr30k Entities/ReferItGame dataset, respectively, and pick the best iteration on the validation set.

Next, we report our results for optimizing hyperparameters on the validation set of Flickr30k Entities while using the VGG-CLS features.

Regularization. Applying L2 regularization to parameters (weight decay) is important for the best performance of our unsupervised model. By introducing the weight decay of 0.0005 we improve the accuracy from 20.33 % to 22.96 %. In contrast, when supervision is available, we introduce batch normalization [19] for the phrase encoding LSTM and visual feature, which leads to a performance improvement, in particular from 37.42 % to 40.93 % in the supervised scenario.

Layer Initialization. We experiment with different ways to initialize the layer parameters. The configuration which works best for us is using uniform initialization for LSTM, MSRA [16] for convolutional layers, and Xavier [13] for all other layers. Switching from Xavier to MSRA initialization for the convolutional layers improves the accuracy of the unsupervised model from 21.04 % to 22.96 %.

4.3   Experiments on Flickr30k Entities Dataset

We report the performance of our approach with multiple levels of supervision in Table 1. In the last line of the table we report the proposal upper-bound accuracy, namely the presence of the correct box among the proposals (which overlaps with the ground-truth box with $IOU > 0.5$).

Unsupervised Training. We start with the unsupervised scenario, i.e. no phrase localization ground-truth is used at training time. Our approach, which relies on VGG-CLS features, is able to achieve 24.66 % accuracy. Note that the

Table 1. Phrase localization performance on Flickr30k Entities with different levels of bounding box supervision, accuracy in %.

Approach	Accuracy		
	Other	VGG-CLS	VGG-DET
Unsupervised training			
Deep fragments [6]	21.78	–	–
GroundeR	–	24.66	28.94
Supervised training			
CCA [35]	–	27.42	–
SCRC [18]	–	27.80	–
DSPE [45]	–	–	43.89
GroundeR	–	41.56	47.81
Semi-supervised training			
GroundeR 3.12 % annot.	–	33.02	42.32
GroundeR 6.25 % annot.	–	37.10	44.02
GroundeR 12.5 % annot.	–	38.67	44.96
GroundeR 25.0 % annot.	–	39.31	45.32
GroundeR 50.0 % annot.	–	40.72	46.65
GroundeR 100.0 % annot.	–	42.43	48.38
Proposal upperbound	77.90	77.90	77.90

VGG network trained on ImageNet has not seen any bounding box annotations at training time. VGG-DET, which was fine-tuned for detection, performs better and achieves 28.94 % accuracy. We can further improve this by taking a sentence constraint into account. Namely, it is unlikely that two different phrases from one sentence are grounded to the same box. Thus we post-process the attended boxes: we jointly process the phrases from one sentence and greedily select the highest scoring box for each phrase, while the same box cannot be selected twice. This allows us to reach the accuracy of 25.01 % for VGG-CLS and 29.02 % for VGG-DET. While we currently only use a sentence constraint as a simple post processing step at test time, it would be interesting to include a sentence level constraint during training as part of future work. We compare to the unsupervised Deep Fragments approach of [25]. Note, that [25] does not report the grounding performance and does not allow for direct comparison with our work. With our best case evaluation[1] of Deep Fragments [25], which also relies on detection boxes and features, we achieve an accuracy of 21.78 %. Overall, the ranking objective in [25] can be seen complimentary to our reconstruction objective. It might be possible, as part of future work, to combine both objectives to learn even better models without grounding supervision.

Supervised Training. Next we look at the fully supervised scenario. The accuracy achieved by [35] is 27.42 %[2] and by SCRC [18] is 27.80 %. Recent approach of [45] achieves 43.89 % with VGG-DET features. Our approach, when using VGG-CLS features achieves an accuracy of 41.56 %, significantly improving over prior works that use VGG-CLS. We further improve our result to impressive 47.81 % when using VGG-DET features.

Semi-supervised Training. Finally, we move to the semi-supervised scenario. The notation "x % annot." means that x % of the annotated data (where ground-truth attention is available) is used. As described in Sect. 3.2 we have a parameter λ which controls the weight of the attention loss L_{att} vs. the reconstruction loss L_{rec}. We estimate the value of λ on validation set and fix it for all iterations. We found that we need higher weight on L_{att} when little supervision is available. E.g. for 3.12 % of supervision $\lambda = 200$ and for 12.5 % supervision $\lambda = 50$. This is due to the fact that in these cases only 3.12 %/12.5 % of labeled instances contribute to L_{att}, while all instances contribute to L_{rec}.

---

[1] We train the Deep Fragments model [25] on the Flickr30k dataset and evaluate with the Flickr30k Entities ground truth phrases and boxes. Our trained Deep Fragments model achieves 11.2 %/16.5 % recall@1 for image annotation/search compared to 10.3 %/16.4 % reported in [25]. As there is a large number of dependency tree fragments per sentence (on average 9.5) which are matched to proposal boxes, rather than on average 3.0 noun phrases per sentence in Flickr30k Entities, we make a best case study in favor of [25]. For each ground-truth phrase we take the maximum overlapping dependency tree fragments (w.r.t. word overlap), compute the IOU between their matched boxes and the ground truth, and take the highest IOU.

[2] The number was provided by the authors of [35], while in [35] they report 25.30 % for phrases automatically extracted with a parser.

Table 2. Detailed phrase localization, Flickr30k Entities, accuracy in %.

Phrase type	People	Clothing	Body parts	Animals	Vehicles	Instruments	Scene	Other	Novel
Number of instances	5,656	2,306	523	518	400	162	1,619	3,374	2,214
Unsupervised training									
Grounde𝑅 (VGG-DET)	44.32	9.02	0.96	46.91	46.00	19.14	28.23	16.98	25.43
Supervised training									
CCA embedding [35]	29.58	24.20	10.52	33.40	34.75	35.80	20.20	20.75	n/a
Grounde𝑅 (VGG-CLS)	53.80	34.04	7.27	49.23	58.75	22.84	52.07	24.13	34.28
Grounde𝑅 (VGG-DET)	61.00	38.12	10.33	62.55	68.75	36.42	58.18	29.08	40.83
Semi-supervised training									
Grounde𝑅 (VGG-DET) 3.12 % annot.	56.51	29.84	9.18	57.34	59.75	28.40	50.71	24.48	34.28
Grounde𝑅 (VGG-DET) 100.0 % annot.	60.24	39.16	14.34	64.48	67.50	38.27	59.17	30.56	42.37
Proposal upperbound	85.93	66.70	41.30	84.94	89.00	70.99	91.17	69.29	79.90

When integrating 3.12 % of the available annotated data into the model we significantly improve the accuracy from 24.66 % to 33.02 % (VGG-CLS) and from 28.94 % to 42.32 % (VGG-DET). The accuracy further increases when providing more annotations, reaching 42.43 % for VGG-CLS and 48.38 % for VGG-DET when using all annotations. As ablation of our semi-supervised model we evaluated the supervised model while only using the respective x % of annotated data. We observed consistent improvement of our semi-supervised model over the supervised model. Interestingly, when using all available supervision, L_{rec} still helps to improve performance over the supervised model (42.43 % vs. 41.56 %, 48.38 % vs. 47.81 %). Our intuition for this is that L_{att} only has a single correct bounding box (which overlaps most with the ground truth), while L_{rec} can also learn from overlapping boxes with high but not best overlap.

Results per Phrase Type. Flickr30k Entities dataset provides a "type of phrase" annotation for each phrase, which we analyze in Table 2. Our unsupervised approach does well on phrases like "people", "animals", "vehicles" and worse on "clothing" and "body parts". This could be due to confusion between people and their clothing or body parts. To address this, one could jointly model the phrases and add spatial relations between them in the model. Body parts are also the most challenging type to detect, with the proposal upper-bound of only 41.3 %. The supervised model with VGG-CLS features outperforms [35] in all types except "body parts" and "instruments", while with VGG-DET it is better or similar in all types. Semi-supervised model brings further significant performance improvements, in particular for "body parts". In the last column we report the accuracy for novel phrases, i.e. the ones which did not appear in the training data. On these phrases our approach maintains high performance, although it is lower than the overall accuracy. This shows that learned language representation is effective and allows transfer to unseen phrases.

Summary Flickr30k Entities. Our unsupervised approach performs similar (VGG-CLS) or better (VGG-DET) than the fully supervised methods of [18,35] (Table 1). Incorporating a small amount of supervision (e.g. 3.12 % of annotated data) allows us to outperform [18,35] also when VGG-CLS features are used. Our best supervised model achieves 47.81 %, surpassing all the previously reported results, including [45]. Our semi-supervised model efficiently exploits the reconstruction loss L_{rec} which allows it to outperform the supervised model.

4.4   Experiments on ReferItGame Dataset

Table 3 summarizes results on the ReferItGame dataset. We compare our approach to the previously introduced fully supervised method SCRC [18], as well as provide reference numbers for two other baselines: LRCN [9] and CAFFE-7K [15] reported in [18]. The LRCN baseline of [18] is using the image captioning model LRCN [9] trained on MSCOCO [32] to score how likely the query phrase is to be generated for the proposal box. CAFFE-7K is a large scale object classifier trained on ImageNet [7] to distinguish 7K classes. [15] predicts a class for each proposal box and constructs a word bag with all the synonyms of the class-name based on WordNet [11]. The obtained word bag is then compared to the query phrase after both are projected to a joint vector space. Both approaches are unsupervised w.r.t. the phrase bounding box annotations. Table 3 reports the results of our approach with VGG, as well as VGG+SPAT features of [18].

Table 3. Phrase localization performance on ReferItGame with different levels of bounding box supervision, accuracy in %.

Approach	Accuracy		
	Other	VGG	VGG+SPAT
Unsupervised training			
LRCN [9] (reported in [18])	8.59	–	–
CAFFE-7K [15] (reported in [18])	10.38	–	–
GroundeR	–	10.69	10.70
Supervised training			
SCRC [18]	–	–	17.93
GroundeR	–	23.44	26.93
Semi-supervised training			
GroundeR 3.12 % annot.	–	13.70	15.03
GroundeR 6.25 % annot.	–	16.19	19.53
GroundeR 12.5 % annot.	–	19.02	21.65
GroundeR 25.0 % annot.	–	21.43	24.55
GroundeR 50.0 % annot.	–	22.67	25.51
GroundeR 100.0 % annot.	–	24.18	28.51
Proposal upperbound	59.38	59.38	59.38

Unsupervised Training. In the unsupervised scenario our GroundeR performs competitive with the LRCN and CAFFE-7K baselines, achieving 10.7 % accuracy. We note that in this case VGG and VGG+SPAT perform similarly.

Supervised Training. In the supervised scenario we compare to the best prior work on this dataset, SCRC [18], which reaches 17.93 % accuracy. Our supervised approach, which uses identical visual features, significantly improves this performance to 26.93 %.

Semi-supervised Training. Moving to the semi-supervised scenario again demonstrates performance improvements, similar to the ones observed on Flickr30k Entities dataset. Even the small amount of supervision (3.12 %) significantly improves performance to 15.03 % (VGG+SPAT), while with 100 % of annotations we achieve 28.51 %, outperforming the supervised model.

Summary ReferItGame Dsataset. While the unsupervised model only slightly improves over prior work, the semi-supervised version can effectively learn from few labeled training instances, and with all supervision it achieves 28.51 %, improving over [18] by a large margin of 10.6 %. Overall the performance on ReferItGame dataset is significantly lower than on Flickr30k Entities. We attribute this to two facts. First, the training set of ReferItGame is rather small compared to Flickr30k (9k vs. 29k images). Second, the proposal upperbound on ReferItGame is significantly lower than on Flickr30k Entities (59.38 % vs 77.90 %) due to the complex nature of the described objects and "stuff" image regions.

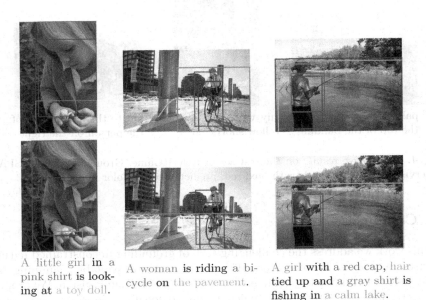

A little girl in a pink shirt is looking at a toy doll.

A woman is riding a bicycle on the pavement.

A girl with a red cap, hair tied up and a gray shirt is fishing in a calm lake.

Fig. 3. Qualitative results on the test set of Flickr30k Entities. Top: GroundeR (VGG-DET) unsupervised, bottom: GroundeR (VGG-DET) supervised.

4.5   Qualitative Results

We provide qualitative results on Flickr30K Entities dataset in Fig. 3. We compare our unsupervised and supervised approaches, both with VGG-DET features. The supervised approach visibly improves the localization quality over the unsupervised approach, which nevertheless is able to localize many phrases correctly. Figure 4 presents qualitative results on ReferItGame dataset. We show the predictions of our supervised approach, as well as the ground-truth boxes. One can see the difficulty of the task from the presented examples, including two failures in the bottom row. One requires good language understanding in order to correctly ground such complex phrases. In order to ground expressions like "hut to the nearest left of the person on the right" we would need to additionally model relations between objects, an interesting direction for future work.

two people on right   picture of a bird flying above sand   dat alpaca up in front, total coffeelate swag

palm tree coming out of the top of the building   guy with blue shirt and yellow shorts   hut to the nearest left of the person on the right

Fig. 4. Qualitative results on the test set of ReferItGame: GroundeR (VGG+SPAT) supervised. Green: ground-truth box, red: predicted box. (Color figure online)

5   Conclusion

In this work we address the challenging task of grounding unconstrained natural phrases in images. We consider different scenarios of available bounding box supervision at training time, namely none, little, and full supervision. We propose a novel approach, GroundeR, which learns to localize phrases in images by attending to the correct box proposal and reconstructing the phrase and is able to operate in all of these supervision scenarios. In the unsupervised scenario we are competitive or better than related work. Our semi-supervised approach works well with a small portion of available annotated data and takes advantage of the unsupervised data to outperform purely supervised training using the same amount of labeled data. It outperforms state-of-the-art, both on Flickr30k Entities and ReferItGame dataset, by 4.5 % and 10.6 %, respectively.

Our approach is rather general and it could be applied to other regions such as segmentation proposals instead of bounding box proposals. Possible extensions are to include constraints within sentences at training time, jointly reason about multiple phrases, and to take into account spatial relations between them.

Acknowledgements. Marcus Rohrbach was supported by a fellowship within the FITweltweit-Program of the German Academic Exchange Service (DAAD). This work was supported by DARPA, AFRL, DoD MURI award N000141110688, NSF awards IIS-1427425 and IIS-1212798, and the Berkeley Artificial Intelligence Research (BAIR) Lab.

References

1. Ammar, W., Dyer, C., Smith, N.A.: Conditional random field autoencoders for unsupervised structured prediction. In: Advances in Neural Information Processing Systems (NIPS) (2014)
2. Bahdanau, D., Cho, K., Bengio, Y.: Neural machine translation by jointly learning to align and translate. In: International Conference on Learning Representations (ICLR) (2015)
3. Blaschko, M., Vedaldi, A., Zisserman, A.: Simultaneous object detection and ranking with weak supervision. In: Advances in Neural Information Processing Systems (NIPS), pp. 235–243 (2010)
4. Chen, X., Gupta, A.: Webly supervised learning of convolutional networks. In: Proceedings of the IEEE International Conference on Computer Vision (ICCV) (2015)
5. Chen, X., Zitnick, C.L.: Mind's eye: a recurrent visual representation for image caption generation. Proceedings of the IEEE Conference on Computer Vision and Pattern Recognition (CVPR) (2015)
6. Cinbis, R.G., Verbeek, J., Schmid, C.: Multi-fold MIL training for weakly supervised object localization. In: Proceedings of the IEEE Conference on Computer Vision and Pattern Recognition (CVPR) (2014)
7. Deng, J., Dong, W., Socher, R., Li, L.J., Li, K., Fei-Fei, L.: Imagenet: a large-scale hierarchical image database. In: Proceedings of the IEEE Conference on Computer Vision and Pattern Recognition (CVPR) (2009)
8. Divvala, S., Farhadi, A., Guestrin, C.: Learning everything about anything: Webly-supervised visual concept learning. In: Proceedings of the IEEE Conference on Computer Vision and Pattern Recognition (CVPR) (2014)
9. Donahue, J., Hendricks, L.A., Guadarrama, S., Rohrbach, M., Venugopalan, S., Saenko, K., Darrell, T.: Long-term recurrent convolutional networks for visual recognition and description. In: Proceedings of the IEEE Conference on Computer Vision and Pattern Recognition (CVPR) (2015)
10. Everingham, M., Van Gool, L., Williams, C.K., Winn, J., Zisserman, A.: The Pascal Visual Object Classes (VOC) challenge. Int. J. Comput. Vis. (IJCV) **88**(2), 303–338 (2010)

11. Fellbaum, C.: WordNet: An Electronical Lexical Database. The MIT Press, Cambridge (1998)
12. Girshick, R.: Fast R-CNN. In: Proceedings of the IEEE International Conference on Computer Vision (ICCV) (2015)
13. Glorot, X., Bengio, Y.: Understanding the difficulty of training deep feedforward neural networks. In: International Conference on Artificial Intelligence and Statistics, pp. 249–256 (2010)
14. Gong, Y., Wang, L., Hodosh, M., Hockenmaier, J., Lazebnik, S.: Improving image-sentence embeddings using large weakly annotated photo collections. In: Fleet, D., Pajdla, T., Schiele, B., Tuytelaars, T. (eds.) ECCV 2014, Part IV. LNCS, vol. 8692, pp. 529–545. Springer, Switzerland (2014)
15. Guadarrama, S., Rodner, E., Saenko, K., Zhang, N., Farrell, R., Donahue, J., Darrell, T.: Open-vocabulary object retrieval. In: Robotics: Science and Systems (2014)
16. He, K., Zhang, X., Ren, S., Sun, J.: Delving deep into rectifiers: surpassing human-level performance on imagenet classification. In: Proceedings of the IEEE Conference on Computer Vision and Pattern Recognition (CVPR) (2015)
17. Hochreiter, S., Schmidhuber, J.: Long short-term memory. Neural Comput. 9(8), 1735–1780 (1997)
18. Hu, R., Xu, H., Rohrbach, M., Feng, J., Saenko, K., Darrell, T.: Natural language object retrieval. In: Proceedings of the IEEE Conference on Computer Vision and Pattern Recognition (CVPR) (2016)
19. Ioffe, S., Szegedy, C.: Batch normalization: accelerating deep network training by reducing internal covariate shift. arXiv:1502.03167 (2015)
20. Jia, Y., Shelhamer, E., Donahue, J., Karayev, S., Long, J., Girshick, R., Guadarrama, S., Darrell, T.: Caffe: convolutional architecture for fast feature embedding. In: Proceedings of the ACM International Conference on Multimedia, pp. 675–678. ACM (2014)
21. Jin, J., Fu, K., Cui, R., Sha, F., Zhang, C.: Aligning where to see and what to tell: image caption with region-based attention and scene factorization. arXiv:1506.06272 (2015)
22. Johnson, J., Krishna, R., Stark, M., Li, L.J., Shamma, D., Bernstein, M., Fei-Fei, L.: Image retrieval using scene graphs. In: Proceedings of the IEEE Conference on Computer Vision and Pattern Recognition (CVPR), pp. 3668–3678 (2015)
23. Joulin, A., Tang, K., Fei-Fei, L.: Efficient image and video co-localization with Frank-Wolfe algorithm. In: Fleet, D., Pajdla, T., Schiele, B., Tuytelaars, T. (eds.) ECCV 2014, Part VI. LNCS, vol. 8694, pp. 253–268. Springer, Heidelberg (2014)
24. Karpathy, A., Fei-Fei, L.: Deep visual-semantic alignments for generating image descriptions. In: Proceedings of the IEEE Conference on Computer Vision and Pattern Recognition (CVPR) (2015)
25. Karpathy, A., Joulin, A., Fei-Fei, L.: Deep fragment embeddings for bidirectional image sentence mapping. In: Advances in Neural Information Processing Systems (NIPS) (2014)
26. Kazemzadeh, S., Ordonez, V., Matten, M., Berg, T.L.: Referit game: referring to objects in photographs of natural scenes. In: Proceedings of the Conference on Empirical Methods in Natural Language Processing (EMNLP) (2014)
27. Kingma, D., Ba, J.: Adam: a method for stochastic optimization. arXiv:1412.6980 (2014)
28. Kong, C., Lin, D., Bansal, M., Urtasun, R., Fidler, S.: What are you talking about? Text-to-image coreference. In: Proceedings of the IEEE Conference on Computer Vision and Pattern Recognition (CVPR), pp. 3558–3565. IEEE (2014)

29. Krishnamurthy, J., Kollar, T.: Jointly learning to parse and perceive: connecting natural language to the physical world. Trans. Assoc. Comput. Linguist. (TACL) **1**, 193–206 (2013)

30. Kwak, S., Cho, M., Laptev, I., Ponce, J., Schmid, C.: Unsupervised object discovery and tracking in video collections. In: Proceedings of the IEEE International Conference on Computer Vision (ICCV) (2015)

31. Lin, D., Fidler, S., Kong, C., Urtasun, R.: Visual semantic search: retrieving videos via complex textual queries. In: Proceedings of the IEEE Conference on Computer Vision and Pattern Recognition (CVPR), pp. 2657–2664. IEEE (2014)

32. Lin, T.-Y., et al.: Microsoft COCO: common objects in context. In: Fleet, D., Pajdla, T., Schiele, B., Tuytelaars, T. (eds.) ECCV 2014, Part V. LNCS, vol. 8693, pp. 740–755. Springer, Switzerland (2014)

33. Mao, J., Huang, J., Toshev, A., Camburu, O., Yuille, A., Murphy, K.: Generation and comprehension of unambiguous object descriptions. In: Proceedings of the IEEE Conference on Computer Vision and Pattern Recognition (CVPR) (2016)

34. Matuszek, C., Fitzgerald, N., Zettlemoyer, L., Bo, L., Fox, D.: A joint model of language and perception for grounded attribute learning. In: Proceedings of the International Conference on Machine Learning (ICML) (2012)

35. Plummer, B., Wang, L., Cervantes, C., Caicedo, J., Hockenmaier, J., Lazebnik, S.: Flickr30k entities: collecting region-to-phrase correspondences for richer image-to-sentence models. In: Proceedings of the IEEE International Conference on Computer Vision (ICCV) (2015)

36. Sadeghi, F., Divvala, S.K., Farhadi, A.: Viske: visual knowledge extraction and question answering by visual verification of relation phrases. In: Proceedings of the IEEE Conference on Computer Vision and Pattern Recognition (CVPR) (2015)

37. Simonyan, K., Zisserman, A.: Very deep convolutional networks for large-scale image recognition. In: International Conference on Learning Representations (ICLR) (2015)

38. Song, H.O., Girshick, R., Jegelka, S., Mairal, J., Harchaoui, Z., Darrell, T.: On learning to localize objects with minimal supervision. arXiv:1403.1024 (2014)

39. Sutskever, I., Vinyals, O., Le, Q.V.: Sequence to sequence learning with neural networks. In: Advances in Neural Information Processing Systems (NIPS), pp. 3104–3112 (2014)

40. Tang, K., Joulin, A., Li, L.J., Fei-Fei, L.: Co-localization in real-world images. In: Proceedings of the IEEE Conference on Computer Vision and Pattern Recognition (CVPR). IEEE (2014)

41. Tapaswi, M., Bäuml, M., Stiefelhagen, R.: Book2movie: aligning video scenes with book chapters. In: Proceedings of the IEEE Conference on Computer Vision and Pattern Recognition (CVPR), pp. 1827–1835 (2015)

42. Uijlings, J.R., van de Sande, K.E., Gevers, T., Smeulders, A.W.: Selective search for object recognition. Int. J. Comput. Vis. (IJCV) **104**(2), 154–171 (2013)

43. Vincent, P., Larochelle, H., Bengio, Y., Manzagol, P.A.: Extracting and composing robust features with denoising autoencoders. In: Proceedings of the International Conference on Machine Learning (ICML) (2008)

44. Vinyals, O., Toshev, A., Bengio, S., Erhan, D.: Show and tell: a neural image caption generator. In: Proceedings of the IEEE Conference on Computer Vision and Pattern Recognition (CVPR) (2015)

45. Wang, L., Li, Y., Lazebnik, S.: Learning deep structure-preserving image-text embeddings. In: Proceedings of the IEEE Conference on Computer Vision and Pattern Recognition (CVPR) (2016)

46. Xu, K., Ba, J., Kiros, R., Courville, A., Salakhutdinov, R., Zemel, R., Bengio, Y.: Show, attend and tell: neural image caption generation with visual attention. In: Proceedings of the International Conference on Machine Learning (ICML) (2015)
47. Yao, L., Torabi, A., Cho, K., Ballas, N., Pal, C., Larochelle, H., Courville, A.: Describing videos by exploiting temporal structure. In: Proceedings of the IEEE International Conference on Computer Vision (ICCV) (2015)
48. Yeung, S., Russakovsky, O., Jin, N., Andriluka, M., Mori, G., Fei-Fei, L.: Every moment counts: dense detailed labeling of actions in complex videos. arXiv:1507.05738 (2015)
49. Young, P., Lai, A., Hodosh, M., Hockenmaier, J.: From image descriptions to visual denotations: new similarity metrics for semantic inference over event descriptions. Trans. Assoc. Comput. Linguist. 2, 67–78 (2014)
50. Yu, H., Siskind, J.M.: Grounded language learning from video described with sentences. In: Proceedings of the Annual Meeting of the Association for Computational Linguistics (ACL), pp. 53–63 (2013)
51. Yu, H., Siskind, J.M.: Sentence directed video object codetection. arXiv:1506.02059 (2015)
52. Zhu, Y., Kiros, R., Zemel, R., Salakhutdinov, R., Urtasun, R., Torralba, A., Fidler, S.: Aligning books and movies: towards story-like visual explanations by watching movies and reading books. In: Proceedings of the IEEE International Conference on Computer Vision (ICCV) (2015)
53. Zitnick, C.L., Dollár, P.: Edge boxes: locating object proposals from edges. In: Fleet, D., Pajdla, T., Schiele, B., Tuytelaars, T. (eds.) ECCV 2014, Part V. LNCS, vol. 8693, pp. 391–405. Springer, Switzerland (2014)

Improving Multi-label Learning with Missing Labels by Structured Semantic Correlations

Hao Yang[1(✉)], Joey Tianyi Zhou[2], and Jianfei Cai[3]

[1] Rolls-Royce@NTU Corp Lab, Singapore, Singapore
lancelot365@gmail.com
[2] IHPC, A*STAR, Singapore, Singapore
zhouty@ihpc.a-star.edu.sg
[3] School of Computer Science and Engineering, NTU, Singapore, Singapore
ASJFCai@ntu.edu.sg

Abstract. Multi-label learning has attracted significant interests in computer vision recently, finding applications in many vision tasks such as multiple object recognition and automatic image annotation. Associating multiple labels to a complex image is very difficult, not only due to the intricacy of describing the image, but also because of the incompleteness nature of the observed labels. Existing works on the problem either ignore the label-label and instance-instance correlations or just assume these correlations are linear and unstructured. Considering that semantic correlations between images are actually structured, in this paper we propose to incorporate structured semantic correlations to solve the missing label problem of multi-label learning. Specifically, we project images to the semantic space with an effective semantic descriptor. A semantic graph is then constructed on these images to capture the structured correlations between them. We utilize the semantic graph Laplacian as a smooth term in the multi-label learning formulation to incorporate the structured semantic correlations. Experimental results demonstrate the effectiveness of the proposed semantic descriptor and the usefulness of incorporating the structured semantic correlations. We achieve better results than state-of-the-art multi-label learning methods on four benchmark datasets.

1 Introduction

Multi-label learning has been an important research topic in machine learning [1–3] and data mining [4,5]. Unlike conventional classification problems, in multi-label learning each instance can be associated with multiple labels simultaneously. During recent years, multi-label learning has been applied on many computer vision tasks, especially on visual object recognition [6–8] and automatic image annotation [9–11]. In addition to the difficulty of assigning multiple labels/tags to complex images, multi-label learning often encounters the problem of incomplete labels. In real world scenarios, since the number of possible labels/tags is often very large (could be as large as the whole vocabulary set) and there often exist ambiguities among labels (e.g., "car" vs "SUV"), it is very

© Springer International Publishing AG 2016
B. Leibe et al. (Eds.): ECCV 2016, Part I, LNCS 9905, pp. 835–851, 2016.
DOI: 10.1007/978-3-319-46448-0_50

difficult to obtain a perfectly labeled training set. Figure 1 shows some examples of annotations from FLICKR25K dataset. We can see that many possible labels are missing as it is impossible for labelers to go through the entire vocabulary set to extract all proper tags.

animal, **clouds**, *grass*, *green*, **lake**, *landscape*, **plantlife**, *reindeer*, **sky**, **water**

Audi, **car**, **structures**, *racing*, *road*, *track*, **transport**

Fig. 1. Example labels from FLICKR25K dataset. The bold face labels are original annotations from the users. The italic labels are other possible labels. These examples illustrate the missing labels problem of multi-label learning.

Due to the incompleteness nature of multi-label learning, many methods have been proposed to solve the problem of multi-label learning with missing labels. Most existing works focus on exploiting the correlations between features and labels (feature-label correlations) [12], the correlations between labels (label-label correlations) and the correlations between instances (instance-instance correlations) [1,3,9,13]. Binary relevance (BR) [12] is a popular baseline for multi-label classification, which simply treats each class as a separate binary classification and makes use of feature-label correlations to solve the problem. However, its performance can be subpar as it ignores the correlations between labels and between instances. Several matrix completion based methods [3,5,14] handle the missing labels problem by implicitly exploiting label label correlations and instance-instance correlations with low-rank regularization on the label matrix. FastTag [13] also implicitly utilizes label-label correlations by learning an extra linear transformation on the label matrix to recover possible missing labels. On the other hand, LCML [1] explicitly handles missing labels with a probabilistic model.

Although these existing works exploit the correlations for learning classifiers and recovering missing labels, they generally (implicitly) assume that those correlations are linear and unstructured. However, in real world applications, especially image recognition, the label-label correlations and instance-instance correlations are actually structured. For example, label "landscape" is likely to co-exist with labels like "sky", "mountain", "river", etc., but it is not likely to co-exist with "desk", "computer", "office", etc. Deng et al. [15] already shows that the structured *label* correlations can benefit *multi-class classification*. In this work, we focus on exploiting the structured correlations between *instances* to improve *multi-label learning*. Given proper prior knowledge, our framework can also incorporate structured label correlations easily.

The key to utilize structured instance-instance correlations is to make use of semantic correlations between images, as *semantically similar images should share similar labels*. If we can effectively extract good semantic representations from images, we should be able to capture the structured correlations between instances.

A semantic representation of an image is a high level description of the image. One popular semantic representation is based on the score vectors of the classifier outputs. Many works have discussed the potential of such representations [16–20]. For example, Su and Jurie [20] proposed to use bag of semantics (BoS) to improve the image classification accuracy. Lampert et al. [19] employed semantics representations to describe objects by their attributes. Dixit et al. [17] combined CNN (*convolutional neural networks*) activations, semantic representations and Fisher vectors to improve scene classification. Kwitt et al. [18] also proposed to apply semantic representations on manifold for scene classification.

In this paper, we propose a new semantic representation, which is the concatenation of a global semantic descriptor and a local semantic descriptor. The global part of our semantic representation is similar to [17], which is the object-class posterior probability vector extracted from CNN trained with ILSVRC 2012 dataset. The global semantic descriptor describes "what is the image in general" according to a large number of concepts developed in the general large-scale dataset. We also introduce a local semantic descriptor extracted by averagely pooling the labels/tags of visual neighbors of each image in the specific target domain. The local semantic descriptor describes "what does the image specifically look like". By combining the global and the local semantic descriptors, we achieve more accurate semantic representation.

With the accurate semantic descriptions of images, we propose to incorporate semantic instance-instance correlations to the multi-label learning problem by adding structures via graph. To be specific, after projecting the images into semantic space, we consider each semantic representation as a node and the whole image set as an undirected graph. Each edge of the graph connects two semantic image representations, and its weight represents the similarity between the node pair. We introduce the semantic graph Laplacian as a smooth term in the multi-label learning formulation to incorporate structured instance-instance correlations captured by the semantic graph. Experiments on four benchmark datasets demonstrate that by incorporating structured instance-instance semantic correlations, our proposed method significantly outperforms the state-of-the-art multi-label learning methods, especially at low observed rates of training labels (e.g. only observing 10 % of the given training labels). The major contributions of this paper lie in the proposed semantic representation and the proposed method to incorporate structured semantic correlations into multi-label learning.

2 Related Works on Multi-label Learning

Binary Relevance (BR) [12] is a standard baseline for multi-label learning, which treats each label as an independent binary classification. Linear or kernel classification tools such as LIBLINEAR [21] can then be applied to solve each binary classification subproblem. Although in general BR can achieve certain accuracy for multi-label learning tasks, it has two drawbacks. First of all, BR ignores the correlations between labels and between instances, which could be helpful for recognition. Secondly, as the label set size grows, the computational cost for BR in both training and testing becomes infeasible. To solve the first problem, some researchers proposed to estimate the label correlations from the training data. In particular, Hariharan et al. [22] and Petterson and Caetano [23] represent label dependencies by pairwise correlations computed from the training set, but such representations could be crude and inaccurate if the distribution of the training data is biased. LCML [1] uses a probability model to explicitly handle the label correlations. In multi-class classification, [15] exploits external label relation graph to model the correlations between labels. There also exist some works [4,5,14] that use the idea of matrix completion to implicitly deal with label correlations by imposing a nuclear norm to the formulation. To solve the second problem of BR, PLST [24] and CPLST [25] reduce the dimension of the label set by PCA related methods. Hsu et al. [26] employs a compressed sensing based approach to reduct the label set size. In addition to reducing label set size, these methods also decorrelate the labels, thus solving the first problem to a certain degree.

Nearest neighbors (NN) related methods are also commonly utilized in multi-label related applications. For label propagation, Kang et al. [27] proposed the Correlated label propagation (CLP) framework that propagates multiple labels jointly based on kNN methods. Yang et al. [28] utilized NN relationships as the label view in a multi-view multi-instance framework for multi-label object recognition. TagProp [29] combines metric learning and kNN to propagate labels. For tag refinement, Zhu et al. [30] proposed to use low-rank matrix completion formula with several graph constraints as the objective function to refine noisy or incomplete labels. For tag ranking, several methods [31–33] have been proposed to learn a ranking function utilizing the correlations between tags.

3 Problem Formulation

In the context of multi-label learning, let matrix $Y \in \mathbb{R}^{n \times c}$ refer to the true label (tag) matrix with rank r, where n is the number of instances and c is the size of label set. As Y is generally not full-rank, without loosing generality, we can assume $n \geq c \geq r$ and $Y_{i,j} \in \{0, 1\}$. Given the data set $X \in \mathbb{R}^{n \times d}$, $n \geq d$, where d is the feature dimension of an instance. We make the following assumption:

Assumption 1. *The column vectors in Y lie in the subspace spanned by the column vectors in X.*

Assumption 1 essentially means the label matrix Y can be accurately predicted by the linear combinations of the features of data set X, which is the assumption generally used in linear classification [3,14,21]. Therefore, the goal of multi-label learning is to learn the linear projection $M \in \mathbb{R}^{d \times c}$ such that it minimizes the reconstruction error:

$$\min_{M} \|XM - Y\|_F^2,\qquad(1)$$

where $\|\cdot\|_F$ is the Frobenius norm.

Since the label matrix is generally incomplete in the real world applications, we assume $\tilde{Y} \in \mathbb{R}^{n \times c}$ to be the observed label matrix, where many entries are unknown. Let $\Omega \subseteq \{1,\ldots,n\} \times \{1,\ldots,c\}$ denote the set of the indices of the observed entries in Y, we can define a linear operator $\mathcal{R}_\Omega(Y) : \mathbb{R}^{n \times c} \mapsto \mathbb{R}^{n \times c}$ as

$$\tilde{Y}_{i,j} = [\mathcal{R}_\Omega(Y)]_{i,j} = \begin{cases} Y_{i,j} & (i,j) \in \Omega \\ 0 & (i,j) \notin \Omega \end{cases}\qquad(2)$$

Then, the multi-label learning problem becomes: given $\tilde{Y}$ and X, how to find the optimal M so that the estimated label matrix XM can be as close to the ground-truth label matrix Y as possible.

Similar to [3,14], we can make use of the low-rank property of Y and optimize the following objective function:

$$\min_{M} \lambda\|XM\|_* + \frac{1}{2}\|\mathcal{R}_\Omega(XM) - \tilde{Y}\|_F^2,\qquad(3)$$

where $\|\cdot\|_*$ is the nuclear norm and λ is the tradeoff parameter. (3) is quintessentially the same as the matrix completion problem in [34].

Minimizing $\|XM\|_*$ could be intractable for large-scale problems. If we assume that X is orthogonal, which can be easily fulfilled by applying PCA to the original data set X if it is not already orthogonal, we can reformulate (3) to

$$\min_{M} \lambda\|M\|_* + \frac{1}{2}\|\mathcal{R}_\Omega(XM) - \tilde{Y}\|_F^2\qquad(4)$$

so that the problem can be solved much more efficiently [14].

The problem with (4) is that by employing the low rank condition, it implicitly assumes that rows/columns of label matrix Y is linearly dependent, i.e., the instance-instance correlations and label-label correlations are linear and unstructured. However, in real world applications, these correlations are actually structured. For example, [15] has already demonstrated that structured label-label correlations can benefit multi-class classification. In this work, we mainly consider the structured correlations among instances, but our framework can easily incorporate label-label correlations, if proper prior knowledge is available (such as the label relation graph in [15]).

To incorporate structured instance-instance correlations, we make one additional assumption:

Assumption 2. *Semantically similar images should have similar labels.*

It is reasonable to make this assumption as labels in multi-label image recognition problem can be viewed as a kind of semantic description of images. However, due to the limited label set size and missing labels problem, the observed labels are generally not precise enough. We will discussed this problem in detail in Sect. 4.

Assuming that we are able to accurately to project images to the semantic space, we can then incorporate structured instance-instance correlations based on Assumption 2. Specifically, an undirected weighted graph $G_s = (V_s, E_s, W_s)$ can be constructed with vertices $V_s = \{1, \ldots, n\}$ (each vertex corresponds to the semantic representation of one image instance), edges $E_s \subseteq V_s \times V_s$, and the $n \times n$ edge weight matrix W_s that describes the similarity among image instances in semantic space. According to Assumption 2, the learned label matrix XM on the semantic graph G_s should be smooth. To be specific, for any two instances $x_i, x_j \in X$, if they are semantically similar, i.e. the weight $w_{i,j}^s$ of edge $e_{i,j}^s$ on the semantic graph is large, their labels should also be similar, i.e., the distance between the learned labels of these two instances should be small. Thus, we define another regularization, aiming to minimize the distance between the learned labels of any two semantically similar instances:

$$\sum_{i,j} w_{i,j}^s \|(x_i - x_j)M\|_2^2, \qquad (5)$$

where $w_{i,j}^s$ is the $\{i, j\}$-th entry of the weight matrix W_s.

(5) is equivalent to

$$\|M\|_{L_s} \triangleq \mathrm{tr}(M^T X^T L_s X M), \qquad (6)$$

where $L_s = D_s - W_s$ is the Laplacian of graph G_s and $D_s = \mathrm{Diag}(\sum_{j=1}^n w_{ij}^s)$. (6) is often referred as the Laplacian regularization term [35]. For simplicity, We use $\|\cdot\|_{L_s}$ to represent to the Laplacian regularization on M with respect to L_s. We add this regularization term to the multi-label learning formulation to incorporate structured instance-instance correlations to the problem. In this way, the objective function of our multi-label learning with structured instance-instance correlations becomes:

$$\min_M F(M) = \lambda \|M\|_* + \gamma_s \|M\|_{L_s} + \frac{1}{2} \|\mathcal{R}_\Omega(XM) - \tilde{Y}\|_F^2, \qquad (7)$$

where γ_s is the trade-off parameter.

If proper structured label-label correlations are available, we can also incorporate the information by adding another Laplacian regularization term on M with the label correlation graph. Specifically, assuming we have an undirected graph $G_t = (V_t, E_t, W_t)$ with the $c \times c$ weight matrix W_t that captures the structured label-label correlations, we can similarly define the corresponding Laplacian regularization as

$$\|M\|_{L_t} \triangleq \mathrm{tr}(XML_t M^T X^T), \qquad (8)$$

where L_t is the Laplacian of the label correlation graph. However, unlike the label relation graph used in [15] for multi-class classification, the label correlations for multi-label learning are much more complicated and currently there is no such information available for multi-label learning, to the best of our knowledge. Therefore, in this paper, we stick to (7) as our optimization objective function.

The formulation of Zhu et al. [30] is closely related to ours, but with two key differences. Firstly, they focus on solving the tag refinement problem rather than classification. More importantly, our graph construction process is based on relationships in the semantic space with the proposed semantic descriptor rather than in the feature space, which we will describe in the following sections.

4   Semantic Descriptor Extraction

As we have discussed, if we are able to represent the image set with a semantic graph G_s, we can incorporate structured instance-instance correlations to the multi-label learning problem. The problem now is: how to effectively project the images to the semantic space and build an appropriate semantic correlation graph.

For a multi-label learning problem, the labels of images can be viewed as semantic descriptions. However, since the size of the label set for many real-world applications is limited and more importantly the observed labels could be largely incomplete, using just the available labels as semantic descriptors would not be sufficient.

Previous works [16,17,19] make use of the posterior probabilities of the classifications on some general large-scale datasets such as ILSVRC 2012 [36] and PLACE database [37] with large number of classes as the semantic descriptors. In this paper, we also adopt such approach and utilize the score vector from CNN trained on ILSVRC 2012 as our global semantic descriptor. To better adapt the global descriptor to the target domain, we further develop feature selection to select most relevant semantic concepts. Moreover, we also propose to pool labels from visual neighbors of each instance in the target domain as the local semantic descriptor. The resulting overall semantic descriptor is empirically shown to have better discriminative power and stability over its individual components. In the following, we describe the details of the developed global and local semantic descriptors.

4.1   Global Semantic Descriptor

Given a vocabulary $\mathcal{D} = \{d_1, \ldots, d_s\}$ of s semantic concepts, a semantic descriptor of image x_i can be seen as the combination of these concepts, denoted as $g_i \in \mathbb{R}^s$, $g_i(j) \in \{0, 1\}$. As the precise concept combination is not available, naturally we exploit the score vector extracted from the classifiers to describe the semantics of an image. Considering such semantic descriptor is essentially posterior class probabilities of a given image, we call it *global* semantic descriptor. Specifically, similar to [17], we apply CNN trained with ILSVRC 2012 and

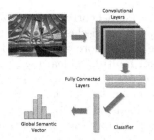

Fig. 2. The extraction of the global semantic descriptor using CNN trained with ILSVRC 2012. Each image is projected to the semantic space through the convolutional and fully connected layers of CNN.

use the resulting posterior class probabilities as the global semantic vector. The process is illustrate in Fig. 2. The problem with such global semantic vectors is that many semantic concepts in the source dataset might not be relevant to the target dataset. For example, if images from the target dataset are mainly related to animals, the responses of these images on some concepts such as man-made objects are generally not helpful and could even cause confusions. To eliminate such irrelevant or noisy concepts, we propose a simple feature selection method. Specifically, let's denote the global semantic descriptions of a set of n images with respect to concepts $\mathcal{D}$ as $\tilde{\mathcal{D}} = \left\{ \tilde{d}_i \in \mathbb{R}^n, i = 1 \ldots, s \right\}$, and their observed labels $\tilde{Y} = \{ \tilde{y}_i^c \in \mathbb{R}^n, i = 1 \ldots, c \}$. We measure the relevance between semantic concept i and the given label set as:

$$R_i = \sum_{j=1}^{c} I(\tilde{d}_i, \tilde{y}_j^c), \tag{9}$$

where $I(a, b)$ evaluates the mutual information between a and b. R_i essentially measures the accumulated linear dependency between concept i and the given labels. After obtaining R_i for all concepts, $\tilde{s}$ concepts are selected based on descending order of R_i to preserve the most relevant $\tilde{s}$ concepts for the target dataset. The resulting global semantic descriptors for the target dataset is then denoted as $\mathcal{G} = \left\{ g_i \in \mathbb{R}^{\tilde{s}}, i = 1 \ldots, n \right\}$.

4.2   Local Semantic Descriptor

In addition to global semantic descriptor, we propose to extract local semantic descriptor to enhance the stability of the semantic descriptor and its relevance to target labels. Motivated by kNN classification, our basic idea is to utilize visual neighbors to generate local semantic descriptor. As illustrated in Fig. 3, the visual neighbors of an image are likely to share similar labels. If some labels of a particular image are missing, it is reasonable to assume that the observed labels of its visual neighbors can be helpful to approximate the semantic description

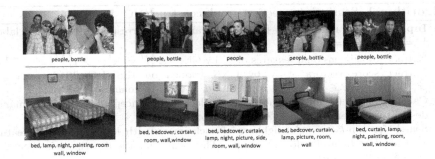

people, bottle   people, bottle   people   people, bottle   people, bottle

bed, lamp, night, painting, room   bed, bedcover, curtain,   bed, bedcover, curtain,   bed, bedcover, curtain,   bed, curtain, lamp,
wall, window   room, wall,window   lamp, night, picture, side,   lamp, picture, room,   night, painting, room,
                                     room, wall, window   wall   wall, window

Fig. 3. Examples of label relevance between visual neighbors. The images on the right are the top-4 visual neighbors of the images on the left. The upper images are from VOC 2007 and the bottom images are from IAPRTC-12. As shown here, visual neighbors are likely to share similar labels.

of the image. Therefore, we include labels of visual neighbors as part of our proposed semantic descriptor.

To be specific, for an image x_i, we search for its top-k_v visual neighbors, which have observed labels $\tilde{y}_j^r \in \mathbb{R}^c, j = 1, \ldots, k_v$. The local semantic descriptor of x_i is defined as

$$l_i = \frac{1}{k_v} \sum_{j=1}^{k_v} \tilde{y}_j^r. \tag{10}$$

(10) is essentially an average pooling of labels y_j, which tells "what does the image look like". By find l_i for all images, we can form a set of local semantic descriptors $\mathcal{L} = \{l_i \in \mathbb{R}^c, i = 1 \ldots, n\}$ for the target dataset. The final semantic descriptor set $\mathcal{S}$ is the direct concatenation of $\mathcal{G}$ and $\mathcal{L}$, denoted as $\mathcal{S} = \{s_i \in \mathbb{R}^{\tilde{s}+c}, i = 1 \ldots, n\}$ and $s_i^T = [g_i^T, l_i^T]$.

Note that in order to find accurate visual neighbors, we extract a low dimensional CNN feature from each image for distance measurements (see Sect. 6.1 for details). We discuss the effectiveness of the proposed semantic descriptors empirically in Sect. 6.2.

4.3 Graph Construction

After extracting the semantic descriptor set $\mathcal{S}$, we can now construct the semantic correlation graph based on $\mathcal{S}$. In particular, we treat each semantic representation s_i as a node v_i^s of the undirected graph G_s in the semantic space. To effectively construct the edges $e_{i,j}^s$ between node v_i and other nodes, following the general idea of [38], we first search for k_s neighbors in the semantic space of v_i, which we refer as semantic neighbors. Note that the number of semantic neighbors k_s can be different from the number of visual neighbors k_v that we use for building local semantic descriptors. We then connect v_i and its k_s semantic neighbors to form the edges from v_i. The weight of an edge is defined as the

Algorithm 1. Semantic correction graph construction

1: **Input**: A set of images $X = \{x_1, \ldots, x_n\}$ and their corresponding observed labels $\tilde{Y} = \{\tilde{y}_i \in \mathbb{R}^n, i = 1 \ldots, c\}$.
2: Extract low-dimensional features of X by CNN as $X^l = \left[x_1^l; \ldots; x_n^l\right]^T$, $x^l \in \mathbb{R}^{d_l}$.
3: Extract score vectors of X by CNN trained on ILSVRC 2012 as $X^s = \left[x_1^s; \ldots; x_n^s\right]^T$, $x^s \in \mathbb{R}^s$. Let $\tilde{\mathcal{D}} = X^s$ and $\tilde{d}_i$ is the i-th column vector of X^s
4: Calculate R_i in (9) for all concepts and select top $\tilde{s}$ concepts. The global semantic descriptor is then $\mathcal{G} = \left\{g_i \in \mathbb{R}^{\tilde{s}}, i = 1 \ldots, n\right\}$, $g_i = x_i^{\tilde{s}}$.
5: Search for top-k_v visual neighbors of each image with low dimensional feature x_i^l. Calculate l_i in (10) for all images. The local semantic descriptor is then $\mathcal{L} = \{l_i \in \mathbb{R}^c, i = 1 \ldots, n\}$.
6: Concatenate $\mathcal{G}$ and $\mathcal{L}$ for $\mathcal{S}$, where $s_i^T = \left[g_i^T, l_i^T\right]$.
7: Search for top-k_s semantic neighbors of each image s_i. Connect neighbor nodes as edges. Calculate the weight $w_{i,j}^s$ of edge $e_{i,j}^s$ using (11).

dot-product between its two nodes, i.e.,

$$w_{i,j}^s = s_i^T s_j. \tag{11}$$

The complete process for constructing the semantic correlation graph is summarized in Algorithm 1.

5   Proximal Gradient Descent Based Solver

Solving our objective function (7) is not straightforward, although it is convex, the nuclear norm $\|\cdot\|_*$ is non-smooth. Following [14,39], we employ an *accelerated proximal gradient* (APG) method to solve the problem.

We first consider minimizing the smooth loss function without the nuclear norm regularization:

$$\min_M \; f(M) = \gamma_s \|M\|_{L_s} + \frac{1}{2}\|\mathcal{R}_\Omega(XM) - \tilde{Y}\|_F^2, \tag{12}$$

A well-known fact [40] is that the gradient step

$$M_k = M_{k-1} - \mu_k \bigtriangledown f(M_{k-1}) \tag{13}$$

for solving the smooth problem can be formulated as a proximal regularization of the linearized function $f(M)$ at M_{k-1} as

$$M_k = \arg\min_M P_{\mu_k}(M, M_{k-1}) \tag{14}$$

where

$$P_{\mu_k}(M, M_{k-1}) = f(M_{k-1}) + \langle M - M_{k-1}, \bigtriangledown f(M_{k-1})\rangle + \frac{1}{2\mu_k}\|M - M_{k-1}\|_F^2,$$

Algorithm 2. APG-Graph

1: **Initialization:** $\theta_1 = \theta_2 \in (0,1]$, $M_1 = M_2$, $\mu = A$, $\rho > 1$, and stopping criterion ϵ

2: $k = 2$;

3: **while** $F(M_{k+1}) \leq (1 - \epsilon)F(M_k)$ **do**

4:    $V_k = M_k + \theta_k(\theta_{k-1}^{-1} - 1)(M_k - M_{k-1})$

5:    $M_{k+1} = \arg\min_M Q_\mu(M, V_k)$

6:    **while** $F(M_{k+1}) > Q_\mu(M_{k+1}, V_k)$ **do**

7:       $\mu = \mu * \rho$

8:       $M_{k+1} = \arg\min_M Q_\mu(M, V_k)$

9:    **end while**

10:    $\theta_{k+1} = (\sqrt{\theta_k^4 + 4\theta_k^2} - \theta_k^2)/2$

11:    $k = k + 1$

12: **end while**

$\langle A, B \rangle = tr(A^T B)$ denotes the matrix inner product, and μ_k is the step size of iteration k.

Based on the above derivation, following [39], (7) is then solved by the following iterative optimization:

$$M_k = \arg\min_M Q_{\mu_k}(M, M_{k-1}) \triangleq P_{\mu_k}(M, M_{k-1}) + \lambda \|M\|_* . \qquad (15)$$

Further ignoring the terms that do not dependent on M, we simplify (15) into minimizing

$$\frac{1}{2\mu_k} \|M - (M_{k-1} - \mu_k \bigtriangledown f(M_{k-1}))\|_F^2 + \lambda \|M\|_* , \qquad (16)$$

which can be solved by singular value thresholding (SVT) techniques [41].

Algorithm 2 shows the APG method we used for solving (7). Similar to [14], we introduce an auxiliary variable V (line 4) to accelerate the convergence. At each step, by utilizing the Lipschitz continuity of the gradient of $f(\cdot)$, the step size μ_k can be found in iterative fashion. Specifically, we start from a constant $\mu_1 = A$ and iteratively increase μ_k until the following condition is met:

$$F(M_k) \leq Q_{\mu_k}(M_k, M_{k-1}) \qquad (17)$$

which is equivalent to line 6 in Algorithm 2.

6   Experimental Results

In this section, we compare our proposed APG-Graph algorithm with several state-of-the-art methods on four widely used multi-label learning benchmark datasets. The details of the benchmark datasets can be found in Table 1. We follow the pre-defined split of TRAIN and TEST[1]. To mimic the effect of missing

---

[1] http://lear.inrialpes.fr/people/guillaumin/data.php.

Table 1. Dataset information

Dataset	#Train	#Test	#Labels	#Avg labels
VOC 2007	5011	4952	20	1.4
ESP GAME	18689	2081	268	4.5
FLICKR 25K	12500	12500	38	4.7
IAPRTC-12	17665	1962	291	5.7

labels, we uniformly sample $\omega\%$ of labels from each class of the TRAIN set, where $\omega \in \{10, 20, 30, 40, 50\}$. It means we only use $10 - 50\%$ of the training labels. We use mean average precision (mAP) as our evaluation metric, which is the mean of average precision across all labels/tags of the TEST set and is widely used in multi-label learning.

NUS-WIDE is also widely used as multi-label classification benchmark dataset. Unfortunately, we cannot obtain all the images from NUS-WIDE dataset. Since we are unable to extract the semantic descriptors without original images, we cannot perform experiments in this dataset.

6.1 Experiment Setup

Feature representation for input data X: For all the image instances (TRAIN and TEST), we need to find their effective feature representations as the input data X. Note that for simplicity, we abuse the notation X for both the input image set and the corresponding image description set. In particular, we employ the 16-layer very deep CNN model in [42]. We apply the CNN pre-trained on ILSVRC 2012 dataset to each image and use the activations of the 16-th layer as the visual descriptor (4096-dimensional) of the image. We then concatenate the semantic descriptor s_i developed in Algorithm 1 with this 4096-dimensional visual descriptor as the overall feature representation for image x_i. To satisfy our Assumption 2, we further apply PCA to the overall feature representations to decorrelate the features. The dimension of PCA features is set to preserve 90 % energy of the original features, which results in the final descriptor of dimensions around 700.

Finding visual neighbors: To find accurate visual neighbors for local semantic descriptor, we extract a low-dimensional CNN descriptor for each image. We use the same 16-layer very deep CNN structure, except that the activations of the 16-th fully connected layer is of 128 dimensions instead of 4096. The 128-d descriptors denoted as X^l are used to find visual neighbors as described in Sect. 4.2.

Baselines: We compare our method with the following baselines.

- MAXIDE [14]: A matrix completion based multi-label learning method using training data as side information to speed up the training process. Although the formulation of MAXIDE incorporate a label correlation matrix, while in experiments MAXIDE actually sets it as identity matrix. MAXIDE outperforms other matrix completion based methods like MC-1 and MC-b [4,9]. The formulation of MAXIDE is similar to our formulation without the Laplacian regularization term.

- FASTTAG [13]: A fast image tagging algorithm based on the assumption of uniformly corrupted labels. FASTTAG learns an extra transformation on the label matrix to recover its missing entries. It achieves state-of-the-art performances on several benchmark datasets.
- BINARY RELEVANCE [12]: BR is a popular baseline for multi-label classification. It treats each class as a separate binary classification to solve the problem. Here we consider linear binary relevance and use LIBLINEAR [21] to train a binary classifier for each class.
- LEAST SQUARES: LS is a a ridge regression model which uses the partial subset of labels to learn the decision parameter M.

We cross-validate the parameters of these methods on smaller subsets of benchmark datasets to ensure best performance.

Our parameters: The learning part of our method has two parameters γ_s and λ as shown in (7). Similar to other methods, we cross-validate on a small subset of benchmark datasets to get the best parameters. The parameters for the semantic correlation graph construction are decided empirically. Specifically, the number of semantic concepts $\tilde{s}$ used in global semantic descriptors is set to be $0.5\,c$. The number of visual neighbors k_v is set to be 50 and the number of semantic neighbors k_s is set to be 10.

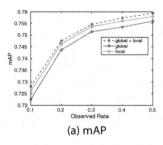

(a) mAP

Fig. 4. Validation experiments of the three semantic descriptors on Flickr25K dataset. We can see from the mAP that the proposed global + local semantic descriptor achieves the best performance

6.2 Validation of Semantic Descriptor

We validate the effectiveness of the proposed semantic descriptor on Flickr25K dataset by demonstrating the classification accuracy. As shown in Fig. 4, for the recognition rate on the test set, our proposed global + local descriptor has the

highest mAP consistently. The gain over just using local semantic descriptor is
not so large though. We suspect that since the global semantic descriptors are
extracted from ILSVRC dataset, which is an object dataset, and the tags of
Flickr25K are mostly *not* related to objects, the global semantic descriptor is
not so helpful in this case. If we use other sources of global semantic vocabulary
more related to scene, e.g., PLACE database, we could potentially have even
better performance.

6.3 Comparison with Other Methods

Figure 5 shows the mAP results of our proposed method and the four baselines on the four benchmark datasets. It can be seen that our method (APG-
GRAPH) constantly outperforms other methods, especially when the observed
rate is small. The performance gain validates the effectiveness of our proposed
semantic descriptors and the usage of structured instance-instance correlation.
On the other hand, MAXIDE generally achieves similar recognition rate as BR for
observed rates ranging from 0.2 to 0.5 while it outperforms BR at an observed
rate of 0.1, which suggests that the unstructured correlation enforced by the
low-rank constraint (nuclear norm) is helpful at small observed rates, but the
effect is similar to the L2 norm used in SVM classification at large observed label
rates. We use the code provided by [13] for FASTTAG. It seems that FASTTAG
is not very effective in our experiments, especially for datasets with fewer labels
(VOC2007 and FLICKR25K). We suspect that the hyper-parameter tuning in
FASTTAG is not stable when the labels are fewer. We also show some examples of

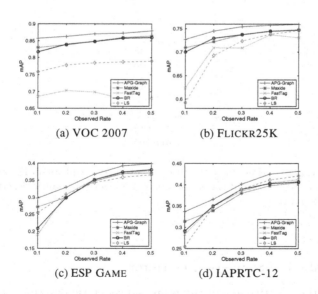

(a) VOC 2007   (b) FLICKR25K

(c) ESP GAME   (d) IAPRTC-12

Fig. 5. The mAP Results (in %) of different methods on the four benchmark datasets
with observed label rates ranging from 0.1 to 0.5.

Fig. 6. Examples of generated labels using our proposed APG-Graph method. We only observe 10 % of the given labels in the training set. The upper images are randomly selected from the test set of VOC 2007 with top-2 labels shown. The bottom images are randomly selected from the test set of ESP GAME with top-5 labels shown. As we can see, the labels accurately match the images.

recognized images in Fig. 6. Note that other methods such as TagProp [29] and TagRelevance [43] are not designed for our problem setting and cannot handle missing labels properly, thus in our preliminary experiments their results are bad and we choose not to report them.

7   Conclusion

In this paper, we have incorporated structured semantic correlations to solve the missing label problem of multi-label learning. Specifically, we project images to the semantic space with an effective semantic descriptor. A semantic graph is then constructed on these images to capture the structured correlations between images. We utilize the semantic graph Laplacian as a smooth term in the multi-label learning formulation to incorporate these correlations. Experimental results demonstrate the effectiveness of our proposed multi-label learning framework as well as our proposed semantic representation. Future works could include utilizing other large scale datasets such as PLACE as another source of global semantic concepts and incorporating structured label correlations.

Acknowledgments. This research is supported by Singapore MoE AcRF Tier-1 Grant RG138/14 and also partially by Rolls-Royce@NTU Corportate Lab Project C-RT3.5. The Tesla K40 used for this re-search was donated by the NVIDIA Corporation.

References

1. Bi, W., Kwok, J.T.: Multilabel classification with label correlations and missing labels. In: AAAI, pp. 1680–1686 (2014)
2. Liu, M., Luo, Y., Tao, D., Xu, C., Wen, Y.: Low-rank multi-view learning in matrix completion for multi-label image classification. In: AAAI, pp. 2778–2784 (2015)
3. Yu, H., Jain, P., Kar, P., Dhillon, I.S.: Large-scale multi-label learning with missing labels. In: ICML, pp. 593–601 (2014)

4. Kong, X., Ng, M.K., Zhou, Z.: Transductive multilabel learning via label set propagation. IEEE TKDE **25**(3), 704–719 (2013)

5. Kong, X., Wu, Z., Li, L., Zhang, R., Yu, P.S., Wu, H., Fan, W.: Large-scale multilabel learning with incomplete label assignments. In: SDM, pp. 920–928 (2014)

6. Everingham, M., Gool, L., Williams, C.K., Winn, J., Zisserman, A.: The PASCAL visual object Classes (VOC) challenge. IJCV **88**(2), 303–338 (2010)

7. Gong, Y., Jia, Y., Leung, T., Toshev, A., Ioffe, S.: Deep convolutional ranking for multilabel image annotation. CoRR abs/1312.4894 (2013)

8. Oquab, M., Bottou, L., Laptev, I., Sivic, J.: Learning and transferring mid-level image representations using convolutional neural networks. In: CVPR, pp. 1717–1724 (2014)

9. Cabral, R.S., la Torre, F.D., Costeira, J.P., Bernardino, A.: Matrix completion for multi-label image classification. In: NIPS, pp. 190–198 (2011)

10. Tariq, A., Foroosh, H.: Feature-independent context estimation for automatic image annotation. In: CVPR, pp. 1958–1965 (2015)

11. Wang, Q., Shen, B., Wang, S., Li, L., Si, L.: Binary codes embedding for fast image tagging with incomplete labels. In: Fleet, D., Pajdla, T., Schiele, B., Tuytelaars, T. (eds.) ECCV 2014, Part II. LNCS, vol. 8690, pp. 425–439. Springer, Heidelberg (2014)

12. Tsoumakas, G., Katakis, I.: Multi-label classification: an overview. IJDWM **3**(3), 1–13 (2007)

13. Chen, M., Zheng, A.X., Weinberger, K.Q.: Fast image tagging. In: ICML, pp. 1274–1282 (2013)

14. Xu, M., Jin, R., Zhou, Z.: Speedup matrix completion with side information: application to multi-label learning. In: NIPS, pp. 2301–2309 (2013)

15. Deng, J., Ding, N., Jia, Y., Frome, A., Murphy, K., Bengio, S., Li, Y., Neven, H., Adam, H.: Large-scale object classification using label relation graphs. In: Fleet, D., Pajdla, T., Schiele, B., Tuytelaars, T. (eds.) ECCV 2014, Part I. LNCS, vol. 8689, pp. 48–64. Springer, Heidelberg (2014)

16. Bergamo, A., Torresani, L.: Classemes and other classifier-based features for efficient object categorization. IEEE TPAMI **36**(10), 1988–2001 (2014)

17. Dixit, M., Chen, S., Gao, D., Rasiwasia, N., Vasconcelos, N.: Scene classification with semantic Fisher vectors. In: CVPR, pp. 2974–2983 (2015)

18. Kwitt, R., Vasconcelos, N., Rasiwasia, N.: Scene recognition on the semantic manifold. In: Fitzgibbon, A., Lazebnik, S., Perona, P., Sato, Y., Schmid, C. (eds.) ECCV 2012, Part IV. LNCS, vol. 7575, pp. 359–372. Springer, Heidelberg (2012)

19. Lampert, C.H., Nickisch, H., Harmeling, S.: Attribute-based classification for zero-shot visual object categorization. IEEE TPAMI **36**(3), 453–465 (2014)

20. Su, Y., Jurie, F.: Improving image classification using semantic attributes. IJCV **100**(1), 59–77 (2012)

21. Fan, R., Chang, K., Hsieh, C., Wang, X., Lin, C.: LIBLINEAR: a library for large linear classification. JMLR **9**, 1871–1874 (2008)

22. Hariharan, B., Zelnik-Manor, L., Vishwanathan, S.V.N., Varma, M.: Large scale max-margin multi-label classification with priors. In: ICML, pp. 423–430 (2010)

23. Petterson, J., Caetano, T.S.: Submodular multi-label learning. In: NIPS, pp. 1512–1520 (2011)

24. Tai, F., Lin, H.: Multilabel classification with principal label space transformation. Neural Comput. **24**(9), 2508–2542 (2012)

25. Chen, Y., Lin, H.: Feature-aware label space dimension reduction for multi-label classification. In: NIPS, pp. 1538–1546 (2012)

26. Hsu, D., Kakade, S., Langford, J., Zhang, T.: Multi-label prediction via compressed sensing. In: NIPS, pp. 772–780 (2009)
27. Kang, F., Jin, R., Sukthankar, R.: Correlated label propagation with application to multi-label learning. In: CVPR, pp. 1719–1726 (2006)
28. Yang, H., Zhou, J.T., Zhang, Y., bin Gao, B., Wu, J., Cai, J.: Exploit bounding box annotations for multi-label object recognition. In: CVPR, pp. 280–288 (2016)
29. Guillaumin, M., Mensink, T., Verbeek, J.J., Schmid, C.: Tagprop: discriminative metric learning in nearest neighbor models for image auto-annotation. In: IEEE 12th International Conference on Computer Vision, ICCV 2009, 27 September - 4 October 2009, Kyoto, Japan, pp. 309–316 (2009)
30. Zhu, G., Yan, S., Ma, Y.: Image tag refinement towards low-rank, content-tag prior and error sparsity. In: Proceedings of the 18th International Conference on Multimedia 2010, 25–29 October 2010, Firenze, Italy, pp. 461–470 (2010)
31. Liu, D., Hua, X., Yang, L., Wang, M., Zhang, H.: Tag ranking. In: Proceedings of the 18th International Conference on World Wide Web, WWW 2009, 20–24 April 2009, Madrid, Spain, pp. 351–360 (2009)
32. Jeong, J., Hong, H., Lee, D.: ikang2006-tagranker: an efficient tag ranking system for image sharing and retrieval using the semantic relationships between tags. Multimedia Tools Appl. **62**(2), 451–478 (2013)
33. Zhuang, J., Hoi, S.C.H.: A two-view learning approach for image tag ranking. In: Proceedings of the Forth International Conference on Web Search and Web Data Mining, WSDM 2011, Hong Kong, China, 9–12 February 2011, pp. 625–634 (2011)
34. Candès, E.J., Recht, B.: Exact matrix completion via convex optimization. Found. Comput. Math. **9**(6), 717–772 (2009)
35. Ando, R.K., Zhang, T.: Learning on graph with Laplacian regularization. In: NIPS, pp. 25–32 (2006)
36. Russakovsky, O., Deng, J., Su, H., Krause, J., Satheesh, S., Ma, S., Huang, Z., Karpathy, A., Khosla, A., Bernstein, M., Berg, A.C., Fei-Fei, L.: ImageNet large scale visual recognition challenge. IJCV **115**, 211–252 (2015)
37. Zhou, B., Lapedriza, À., Xiao, J., Torralba, A., Oliva, A.: Learning deep features for scene recognition using places database. In: NIPS, pp. 487–495 (2014)
38. Belkin, M., Niyogi, P., Sindhwani, V.: Manifold regularization: a geometric framework for learning from labeled and unlabeled examples. JMLR **7**, 2399–2434 (2006)
39. Ji, S., Ye, J.: An accelerated gradient method for trace norm minimization. In: ICML, pp. 457–464 (2009)
40. Bertsekas, D.P.: Nonlinear Programming. Athena Scientific, Belmont (1999)
41. Cai, J.F., Candès, E.J., Shen, Z.: A singular value thresholding algorithm for matrix completion. SIAM J. Optim. **20**(4), 1956–1982 (2010)
42. Simonyan, K., Zisserman, A.: Very deep convolutional networks for large-scale image recognition. CoRR abs/1409.1556 (2014)
43. Li, X., Snoek, C.G.M., Worring, M.: Learning social tag relevance by neighbor voting. IEEE Trans. Multimedia **11**(7), 1310–1322 (2009)

Visual Relationship Detection
with Language Priors

Cewu Lu$^{(\boxtimes)}$, Ranjay Krishna$^{(\boxtimes)}$, Michael Bernstein, and Li Fei-Fei

Stanford University, Stanford, USA
{cwlu,ranjaykrishna,msb,feifeili}@cs.stanford.edu

Abstract. Visual relationships capture a wide variety of interactions between pairs of objects in images (e.g. "man riding bicycle" and "man pushing bicycle"). Consequently, the set of possible relationships is extremely large and it is difficult to obtain sufficient training examples for all possible relationships. Because of this limitation, previous work on visual relationship detection has concentrated on predicting only a handful of relationships. Though most relationships are infrequent, their objects (e.g. "man" and "bicycle") and predicates (e.g. "riding" and "pushing") independently occur more frequently. We propose a model that uses this insight to train visual models for objects and predicates individually and later combines them together to predict multiple relationships per image. We improve on prior work by leveraging language priors from semantic word embeddings to finetune the likelihood of a predicted relationship. Our model can scale to predict thousands of types of relationships from a few examples. Additionally, we localize the objects in the predicted relationships as bounding boxes in the image. We further demonstrate that understanding relationships can improve content based image retrieval.

1 Introduction

While objects are the core building blocks of an image, it is often the relationships between objects that determine the holistic interpretation. For example, an image with a `person` and a `bicycle` might involve the man `riding`, `pushing`, or even `falling off` of the bicycle (Fig. 1). Understanding this diversity of relationships is central to accurate image retrieval and to a richer semantic understanding of our visual world.

Visual relationships are a pair of localized objects connected via a predicate (Fig. 2). We represent relationships as $\langle$object$_1$-predicate-object$_2\rangle^1$. Visual relationship detection involves detecting and localizing pairs of objects in an

---

[1] In natural language processing [2–5], relationships are defined as $\langle$subject-predicate-object$\rangle$. In this paper, we define them as $\langle$object$_1$-predicate-object$_2\rangle$ for simplicity.

Electronic supplementary material The online version of this chapter (doi:10.1007/978-3-319-46448-0_51) contains supplementary material, which is available to authorized users.

© Springer International Publishing AG 2016
B. Leibe et al. (Eds.): ECCV 2016, Part I, LNCS 9905, pp. 852–869, 2016.
DOI: 10.1007/978-3-319-46448-0_51

| riding | falling off | pushing | next to | carrying |

Fig. 1. Even though all the images contain the same objects (a `person` and a `bicycle`), it is the relationship between the objects that determine the holistic interpretation of the image.

Fig. 2. Visual Relationship Detection: Given an image as input, we detect multiple relationships in the form of ⟨object₁-relationship-object₂⟩. Both the objects are localized in the image as bounding boxes. In this example, we detect the following relationships: ⟨`person - on - motorcycle`⟩, ⟨`person - wear - helmet`⟩ and ⟨`motorcycle - has - wheel`⟩.

image and also classifying the predicate or interaction between each pair (Fig. 2). While it poses similar challenges as object detection [1], one critical difference is that the size of the semantic space of possible relationships is much larger than that of objects. Since relationships are composed of two objects, there is a greater skew of rare relationships as object co-occurrence is infrequent in images. So, a fundamental challenge in visual relationship detection is learning from very few examples.

Visual Phrases [6] studied visual relationship detection using a small set of 13 common relationships. Their model requires enough training examples for every possible ⟨object₁-predicate-object₂⟩ combination, which is difficult to collect owing to the infrequency of relationships. If we have N objects and K predicates, Visual Phrases [6] would need to train $\mathcal{O}(N^2K)$ unique detectors separately. We use the insight that while relationships (e.g. "person jumping over a fire hydrant") might occur rarely in images, its objects (e.g. `person` and `fire hydrant`) and predicate (e.g. `jumping over`) independently appear more frequently. We propose a **visual appearance module** that learns the appearance of objects and predicates and fuses them together to jointly predict relationships. We show that our model only needs $\mathcal{O}(N + K)$ detectors to detect $\mathcal{O}(N^2K)$ relationships.

Another key observation is that relationships are semantically related to each other. For example, a "person riding a horse" and a "person riding an elephant" are semantically similar because both `elephant` and `horse` are animals. Even if we haven't seen many examples of "person riding an elephant", we might be able to infer it from a "person riding a horse". Word vector embeddings [7] naturally lend themselves in linking such relationships because they capture semantic similarity in language (e.g. `elephant` and `horse` are cast close together in a word vector space). Therefore, we also propose a **language module** that uses pretrained word vectors [7] to cast relationships into a vector space where similar relationships are optimized to be close to each other. Using this embedding space, we can finetune the prediction scores of our relationships and even enable zero shot relationship detection.

In this paper, we propose a model that can learn to detect visual relationships by (1) (1) learning visual appearance models for its objects and predicates and (2) using the relationship embedding space learnt from language. We train our model by optimizing a bi-convex function. To benchmark the task of visual relationship detection, we introduce a new dataset that contains 5000 images with 37, 993 relationships. Existing datasets that contain relationships were designed for improving object detection [6] or image retrieval [8] and hence, don't contain sufficient variety of relationships or predicate diversity per object category. Our model outperforms all previous models in visual relationship detection. We further study how our model can be used to perform zero shot visual relationship detection. Finally, we demonstrate that understanding relationships can improve image-based retrieval.

2   Related Work

Visual relationship prediction involves detecting the objects that occur in an image as well as understanding the interactions between them. There has been a series of work related to improving object detection by leveraging **object co-occurrence** statistics [9–14]. Structured learning approaches have improved scene classification along with object detection using hierarchial contextual data from co-occurring objects [15–18]. Unlike these methods, we study the *context* or *relationships* in which these objects co-occur.

Some previous work has attempted to learn **spatial relationships** between objects [13,19] to improve segmentation [19]. They attempted to learn four spatial relationships: "above", "below", "inside", and "around" [13]. While we believe that that learning spatial relationships is important, we also study non-spatial relationships such as `pull` (actions), `taller than` (comparative), etc.

There have been numerous efforts in **human-object interaction** [20–22] and action recognition [23] to learn discriminative models that distinguish between relationships where $object_1$ is a human (e.g. "playing violin" [24]). Visual relationship prediction is more general as $object_1$ is not constrained to be a human and the `predicate` doesn't have to be a verb.

Visual relationships are not a new concept. Some papers explicitly collected relationships in images [25–29] and videos [27,30,31] and helped models map these relationships from images to language. Relationships have also improved object localization [6,32–34]. A meaning space of relationships have aided the cognitive task of mapping images to captions [35–38]. Finally, they have been used to generate indoor images from sentences [39] and to improve image search [8,40]. In this paper, we formalize visual relationship prediction as a task onto itself and demonstrate further improvements in image retrieval.

The most recent attempt at relationship prediction has been in the form of **visual phrases**. Learning appearance models for visual phrases has shown to improve individual object detection, i.e. detecting "a person riding a horse" improves the detection and localization of "person" and "horse" [6,41]. Unlike our model, all previous work has attempted to detect only a handful of visual relationships and do not scale because most relationships are infrequent. We propose a model that manages to scale and detect millions of types of relationships. Additionally, our model is able to detect unseen relationships.

3   Visual Relationship Dataset

Visual relationships put objects in context; they capture the different interactions between pairs of objects. These interactions (shown in Fig. 3) might be verbs (e.g. wear), spatial (e.g. on top of), prepositions (e.g. with), comparative (e.g. taller than), actions (e.g. kick) or a preposition phrase (e.g. drive on). A dataset for visual relationship prediction is fundamentally different from a dataset for object detection. A relationship dataset should contain more than just objects localized in images; it should capture the rich variety of interactions between pairs of objects (predicates per object category). For example, a person can be associated with predicates such as ride, wear, kick etc. Additionally, the dataset should contain a large number of possible relationships types.

Existing datasets that contain relationships were designed to improve object detection [6] or image retrieval [8]. The Visual Phrases [6] dataset focuses on 17 common relationship types. But, our goal is to understand the rich variety of infrequent relationships. On the other hand, even though the Scene Graph

Fig. 3. (left) A log scale distribution of the number of instances to the number of relationships in our dataset. Only a few relationships occur frequently and there is a long tail of infrequent relationships. (right) Relationships in our dataset can be divided into many categories, 5 of which are shown here: verb, spatial, preposition, comparative and action.

Table 1. Comparison between our visual relationship benchmarking dataset with existing datasets that contain relationships. Relationships and Objects are abbreviated to Rel. and Obj. because of space constraints.

	Images	Rel. types	Rel. instances	# Predicates per Obj. category
Visual phrases [6]	2,769	13	2,040	120
Scene graph [8]	5,000	23,190	109,535	2.3
Ours	5,000	6,672	37,993	24.25

dataset [8] has 23,190 relationship types[2], it only has 2.3 predicates per object category. Detecting relationships on the Scene Graph dataset [8] essentially boils down to object detection. Therefore, we designed a dataset specifically for benchmarking visual relationship prediction.

Our dataset (Table 1) contains 5000 images with 100 object categories and 70 predicates. In total, the dataset contains 37,993 relationships with 6,672 relationship types and 24.25 predicates per object category. Some example relationships are shown in Fig. 3. The distribution of relationships in our dataset highlights the long tail of infrequent relationships (Fig. 3(left)). We use 4000 images in our training set and test on the remaining 1000 images. 1,877 relationships occur in the test set but never occur in the training set.

4 Visual Relationship Prediction Model

The goal of our model is to detect visual relationships from an image. During training (Sect. 4.1), the input to our model is a fully supervised set of images with relationship annotations where the objects are localized as bounding boxes and labelled as ⟨object₁-predicate-object₂⟩. At test time (Sect. 4.2), our input is an image with no annotations. We predict multiple relationships and localize the objects in the image. Figure 4 illustrates a high level overview of our detection pipeline.

4.1 Training Approach

In this section, we describe how we train our visual appearance and language modules. Both the modules are combined together in our objective function.

---

[2] Note that the Scene Graph dataset [8] was collected using unconstrained language, resulting in multiple annotations for the same relationship (e.g. ⟨man - kick - ball⟩ and ⟨person - is kicking - soccer ball⟩). Therefore, 23,190 is an inaccurate estimate of the number of unique relationship types in their dataset. We do not compare with the Visual Genome dataset [42] because their relationships had not been released at the time this paper was written.

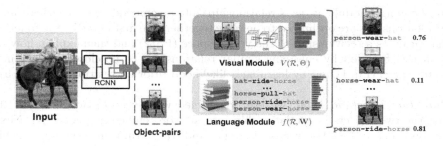

Fig. 4. A overview of our visual relationship detection pipeline. Given an image as input, RCNN [43] generates a set of object proposals. Each pair of object proposals is then scored using a (1) visual appearance module and a (2) language module. These scores are then thresholded to output a set of relationship labels (e.g. ⟨person - riding - horse⟩). Both objects in a relationship (e.g. person and horse) are localized as bounding boxes. The parameters of those two modules (W and Θ) are iteratively learnt in Sect. 4.1.

Visual Appearance Module. While Visual Phrases [6] learned a separate detector for every single relationship, we model the appearance of visual relationships $V()$ by learning the individual appearances of its comprising objects and predicate. While relationships are infrequent in real world images, the objects and predicates can be learnt as they independently occur more frequently. Furthermore, we demonstrate that our model outperforms Visual Phrases' detectors, showing that learning individual detectors outperforms learning detectors for relationships together (Table 2).

First, we train a convolutional neural network (CNN) (VGG net [44]) to classify each of our $N = 100$ objects. Similarly, we train a second CNN (VGG net [44]) to classify each of our $K = 70$ predicates using the union of the bounding boxes of the two participating objects in that relationship. Now, for each ground truth relationship $R_{\langle i,k,j \rangle}$ where i and j are the object classes (with bounding boxes O_1 and O_2) and k is the predicate class, we model V (Fig. 4) as:

$$V(R_{\langle i,k,j \rangle}, \Theta | \langle O_1, O_2 \rangle) = P_i(O_1)(\mathbf{z}_k^T \text{CNN}(O_1, O_2) + s_k)P_j(O_2) \qquad (1)$$

where Θ is the parameter set of $\{\mathbf{z}_k, s_k\}$. $\mathbf{z}_k$ and s_k are the parameters learnt to convert our CNN features to relationship likelihoods. $k = 1, \ldots, K$ represent the K predicates in our dataset. $P_i(O_1)$ and $P_j(O_2)$ are the CNN likelihoods of categorizing box O_1 as object category i and box O_2 as category j. $\text{CNN}(O_1, O_2)$ is the predicate CNN features extracted from the union of the O_1 and O_2 boxes.

Language Module. One of our key observations is that relationships are semantically related to one another. For example, ⟨person - ride - horse⟩ is semantically similar to ⟨person - ride - elephant⟩. Even if we have not seen any examples of ⟨person - ride - elephant⟩, we should be able to infer it from similar relationships that occur more frequently (e.g. ⟨person - ride - horse⟩).

Our language module projects relationships into an embedding space where similar relationships are optimized to be close together. We first describe the function that projects a relationship to the vector space (Eq. 2) and then explain how we train this function by enforcing similar relationships to be close together in a vector space (Eq. 4) and by learning a likelihood prior on relationships (Eq. 5).

Projection Function. First, we use pre-trained word vectors (word2vec) [7] to cast the two objects in a relationship into an word embedding space [7]. Next, we concatenate these two vectors together and transform it into the relationship vector space using a projection parameterized by $\mathbf{W}$, which we learn. This projection presents how two objects interact with each other. We denote *word2vec()* as the function that converts a word to its 300 *dim.* vector. The relationship projection function (shown in Fig. 4) is defined as:

$$f(\mathcal{R}_{\langle i,k,j \rangle}, \mathbf{W}) = \mathbf{w}_k^T [word2vec(t_i), word2vec(t_j)] + b_k \tag{2}$$

where t_j is the word (in text) of the jth object category. $\mathbf{w}_k$ is a 600 *dim.* vector and b_k is a bias term. $\mathbf{W}$ is the set of $\{\{\mathbf{w}_1, b_1\}, \dots, \{\mathbf{w}_k, b_k\}\}$, where each row presents one of our K predicates.

Training Projection Function. We want to optimize the projection function $f()$ such that it projects similar relationships closer to one another. For example, we want the distance between ⟨man - riding - horse⟩ to be close to ⟨man - riding - cow⟩ but farther from ⟨car - has - wheel⟩. We formulate this by using a heuristic where the distance between two relationships is proportional to the word2vec distance between its component objects and predicate:

$$\frac{[f(\mathcal{R}, \mathbf{W}) - f(\mathcal{R}', \mathbf{W})]^2}{d(\mathcal{R}, \mathcal{R}')} = constant, \quad \forall \mathcal{R}, \mathcal{R}' \tag{3}$$

where $d(\mathcal{R}, \mathcal{R}')$ is the sum of the cosine distances (in word2vec space [7]) between of the two objects and the predicates of the two relationships $\mathcal{R}$ and $\mathcal{R}'$. Now, to satisfy Eq. 3, we randomly sample pairs of relationships ($\langle \mathcal{R}, \mathcal{R}' \rangle$) and minimize their variance:

$$K(\mathbf{W}) = var(\{\frac{[f(\mathcal{R}, \mathbf{W}) - f(\mathcal{R}', \mathbf{W})]^2}{d(\mathcal{R}, \mathcal{R}')} \quad \forall \mathcal{R}, \mathcal{R}'\}) \tag{4}$$

where $var()$ is a variance function. The sample number we use is 500K.

Likelihood of a Relationship. The output of our projection function should ideally indicate the likelihood of a visual relationship. For example, our model should not assign a high likelihood score to a relationship like ⟨dog - drive - car⟩, which is unlikely to occur. We model this by enforcing that if $\mathcal{R}$ occurs more frequently than $\mathcal{R}'$ in our training data, then it should have a higher likelihood of occurring again. We formulate this as a rank loss function:

$$L(\mathbf{W}) = \sum_{\{\mathcal{R},\mathcal{R}'\}} \max\{f(\mathcal{R}',\mathbf{W}) - f(\mathcal{R},\mathbf{W}) + 1, 0\} \qquad (5)$$

While we only enforce this likelihood prior for the relationships that occur in our training data, the projection function $f()$ generalizes it for all $\langle$object$_1$-predicate-object$_2\rangle$ combinations, even if they are not present in our training data. The max operator here is to encourage correct ranking (with margin) $f(\mathcal{R},\mathbf{W}) - f(\mathcal{R}',\mathbf{W}) \geq 1$. Minimizing this objective enforces that a relationship with a lower likelihood of occurring has a lower $f()$ score.

Objective Function. So far we have presented our visual appearance module ($V()$) and the language module ($f()$). We combine them to maximize the rank of the ground truth relationship $\mathcal{R}$ with bounding boxes O_1 and O_2 using the following rank loss function:

$$C(\Theta,\mathbf{W}) = \sum_{\langle O_1,O_2\rangle,\mathcal{R}} \max\{1 - V(\mathcal{R},\Theta|\langle O_1,O_2\rangle)f(\mathcal{R},\mathbf{W})$$
$$+ \max_{\langle O_1',O_2'\rangle \neq \langle O_1,O_2\rangle, \mathcal{R}'\neq\mathcal{R}} V(\mathcal{R}',\Theta|\langle O_1',O_2'\rangle)f(\mathcal{R}',\mathbf{W}), 0\} \qquad (6)$$

We use a ranking loss function to make it more likely for our model to choose the correct relationship. Given the large number of possible relationships, we find that a classification loss performs worse. Therefore, our final objective function combines Eq. 6 with Eqs. 4 and 5 as:

$$\min_{\Theta,\mathbf{W}}\{C(\Theta,\mathbf{W}) + \lambda_1 L(\mathbf{W}) + \lambda_2 K(\mathbf{W})\} \qquad (7)$$

where $\lambda_1 = 0.05$ and $\lambda_2 = 0.002$ are hyper-parameters that were obtained though grid search to maximize performance on the validation set. Note that both Eqs. 6 and 5 are convex functions. Equation 4 is a biquadratic function with respect to $\mathbf{W}$. So our objective function Eq. 7 has a quadratic closed form. We perform stochastic gradient descent iteratively on Eqs. 6 and 5. It converges in $20 \sim 25$ iterations.

4.2 Testing

At test time, we use RCNN [43] to produce a set of candidate object proposals for every test image. Next, we use the parameters learnt from the visual appearance model (Θ) and the language module ($\mathbf{W}$) to predict visual relationships ($\mathcal{R}^*_{\langle i,k,j\rangle}$) for every pair of RCNN object proposals $\langle O_1,O_2\rangle$ using:

$$\mathcal{R}^* = \arg\max_{\mathcal{R}} V(\mathcal{R},\Theta|\langle O_1,O_2\rangle)f(\mathcal{R},\mathbf{W}) \qquad (8)$$

5   Experiments

We evaluate our model by detecting visual relationships from images. We show that our proposed method outperforms previous state-of-the-art methods on our dataset (Sect. 5.1) as well as on previous datasets (Sect. 5.3). We also measure how our model performs in zero-shot learning of visual relationships (Sect. 5.2). Finally, we demonstrate that understanding visual relationship can improve common computer vision tasks like content based image retrieval (Sect. 5.4).

5.1   Visual Relationship Detection

Setup. Given an input image, our task is to extract a set of visual relationships $\langle$object$_1$-predicate-object$_2\rangle$ and localize the objects as bounding boxes in the image. We train our model using the 4000 training images and perform visual relationship prediction on the 1000 test images.

The evaluation metrics we report is **recall @ 100** and **recall @ 50** [45]. **Recall @ x** computes the fraction of times the correct relationship is predicted in the top **x** confident relationship predictions. Since we have 70 predicates and an average of 18 objects per image, the total possible number of relationship predictions is $100 \times 70 \times 100$, which implies that the random guess will result in a recall @ 100 of 0.00014. We notice that mean average precision (mAP) is another widely used metric. However, mAP is a pessimistic evaluation metric because we can not exhaustively annotate all possible relationships in an image. Consider the case where our model predicts $\langle$person - taller than - person$\rangle$. Even if the prediction is correct, mAP would penalize the prediction if we do not have that particular ground truth annotation.

Detecting a visual relationship involves classifying both the objects, predicting the predicate and localization both the objects. To study how our model performs on each of these tasks, we measure visual relationship prediction under the following conditions:

1. In **predicate detection** (Fig. 5(left)), our input is an image and set of localized objects. The task is to predict a set of possible predicates between pairs of objects. This condition allows us to study how difficult it is to predict relationships without the limitations of object detection [43].
2. In **phrase detection** (Fig. 5(middle)), our input is an image and our task is to output a label $\langle$object$_1$-predicate-object$_2\rangle$ and localize the entire relationship as *one* bounding box having at least 0.5 overlap with ground truth box. This is the evaluation used in Visual Phrases [6].
3. In **relationship detection** (Fig. 5(right)), our input is an image and our task is to output a set of $\langle$object$_1$-predicate-object$_2\rangle$ and localize *both* object$_1$ and object$_2$ in the image having at least 0.5 overlap with their ground truth boxes simultaneously.

Comparison Models. We compare our method with some state-of-that-art approaches [6,44]. We further perform ablation studies on our model, considering

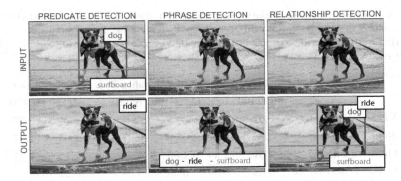

Fig. 5. We evaluate visual relationship detection using three conditions: predicate detection (where we only predict the predicate given the object classes and boxes), phrase detection (where we label a region of an image with a relationship) and relationship detection (where we detect the objects and label the predicate between them).

just the visual appearance and the language module, including the likelihood term (Eq. 4) and embedding term (Eq. 5) to study their contributions.

- **Visual phrases.** Similar to Visual Phrases [6], we train deformable parts models for each of the 6,672 relationships (e.g. "chair under table") in our training set.
- **Joint CNN.** We train a CNN model [44] to predict the three components of a relationship together. Specifically, we train a 270 (100 + 100 + 70) way classification model that learns to score the two objects (100 categories each) and predicate (70 categories). This model represents the Visual phrases
- **Visual appearance (Ours - V only).** We only use the visual appearance module of our model described in Eq. 6 by optimizing $V()$.
- **Likelihood of a relationship (Ours - L only).** We only use the likelihood of a relationship described in Eq. 5 by optimizing $L()$.
- **Visual appearance + naive frequency (Ours - V + naive FC).** One of the contributions of our model is the ability to use a language prior via our semantic projection function $f()$ (Eq. 2). Here, we replace $f()$ with a function that maps a relationship to its frequency in our training data. Using this naive function, we hope to test the effectiveness of $f()$.
- **Visual appearance + Likelihood (Ours - V + L only).** We use both the visual appearance module (Eq. 6) and the likelihood term (Eq. 5) by optimizing both $V()$ and $L()$. The only part of our model missing is $K()$ Eq. 4, which projects similar relationships closer.
- **Visual appearance + likelihood + regularizer (Ours - V + L + Reg.).** We use the visual appearance module and the likelihood term and add an L_2 regularizer on W.
- **Full Model (Ours - V + L + K).** This is our full model. It contains the visual appearance module (Eq. 6), the likelihood term (Eq. 5) and the embedding term (Eq. 4) from similar relationships.

Table 2. Results for visual relationship detection (Sect. 5.1). R@100 and R@50 are abbreviations of Recall @ 100 and Recall @ 50. Note that in predicate det., we are predicting multiple predicates per image (one between every pair of objects) and hence R@100 is less than 1.

	Phrase Det.		Relationship Det.		Predicate Det.	
	R@100	R@50	R@100	R@50	R@100	R@50
Visual phrases [6]	0.07	0.04	-	-	1.91	0.97
Joint CNN [44]	0.09	0.07	0.09	0.07	2.03	1.47
Ours - V only	2.61	2.24	1.85	1.58	7.11	7.11
Ours - L only	0.08	0.08	0.08	0.08	18.22	18.22
Ours - V + naive FC	6.39	6.65	5.47	5.27	28.87	28.87
Ours - V + L only	8.59	9.13	9.18	9.04	35.20	35.20
Ours - V + L + Reg.	8.91	9.60	9.63	9.71	36.31	36.31
Ours - V + L + K	**17.03**	**16.17**	**14.70**	**13.86**	**47.87**	**47.87**

Results. Visual Phrases [6] and Joint CNN [44] train an individual detector for every relationship. Since the space of all possible relationships is large (we have 6,672 relationship types in the training set), there is a shortage of training examples for infrequent relationships, causing both models to perform poorly on predicate, phrase and relationship detection (Table 2). (Ours - V only) can't discriminative between similar relationships by itself resulting in 1.85 R@100 for relationship detection. Similarly, (Ours - L only) always predicts the most frequent relationship ⟨person - wear - shirt⟩ and results in 0.08 R@100, which is the percentage of the most frequent relationship in our testing data. These problems are remedied when both V and L are combined in (Ours - V + L only) with an increase of 3% R@100 in on both phrase and relationship detection and more than 10% increase in predicate detection. (V + Naive FC) is missing our relationship projection function $f()$, which learns the likelihood of a predicted relationship and performs worse than (Ours - V + L only) and (Ours - V + L + K). Also, we observe that (Ours - V + L + K) has an 11% improvement in comparison to (Ours - V + L only) in predicate detection, demonstrating that the language module from similar relationships significantly helps improve visual relationship detection. Finally, (Ours - V + L + K) outperforms (Ours - V + L + Reg.) showcasing the $K()$ is acting not only as a regularizer but is learning to preserve the distances between similar relationships.

By comparing the performance of all the models between relationship and predicate detection, we notice a 30% drop in R@100. This drop in recall is largely because we have to localize two objects simultaneously, amplifying the object detection errors. Note that even when we have ground truth object proposals (in predicate detection), R@100 is still 47.87.

Qualitative Results. In Fig. 6(a), (b) and (c), Visual Phrase and Joint CNN incorrectly predict a common relationship: ⟨person - drive - car⟩ and

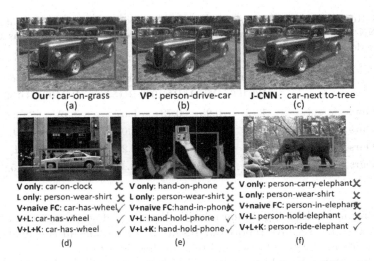

Fig. 6. (a), (b) and (c) show results from our model, Visual Phrases [6] and Joint CNN [44] on the same image. All ablation studies results for (d), (e) and (f) are reported below the corresponding image. Ticks and crosses mark the correct and incorrect results respectively. Phrase, object$_1$ and object$_2$ boxes are in blue, red and green respectively. (Color figure online)

⟨car - next to - tree⟩. These models tend to predict the most common relationship as they see a lot of them during training. In comparison, our model correctly predicts and localizes the objects in the image. Figure 6(d), (e) and (f) compares the various components of our model. Without the relationship likelihood score, (Ours - V only) incorrectly classifies a wheel as a clock in (d) and mislabels the predicate in (e) and (f). Without any visual priors, (Ours - L only) always reports the most frequent relationship ⟨person - wear - shirt⟩. (Ours - V + L) fixes (d) by correcting the visual model's misclassification of the wheel as a clock. But it still does not predict the correct predicate for (e) and (f) because ⟨person - ride - elephant⟩ and ⟨hand - hold - phone⟩ rarely occur in our training set. However, our full model (Ours - V + L + K) leverages similar relationships it has seen before and is able to correctly detect the relationships in (e) and (f).

5.2   Zero-shot Learning

Owing to the long tail of relationships in real world images, it is difficult to build a dataset with every possible relationship. Therefore, a model that detects visual relationships should also be able to perform zero-shot prediction of relationships it has never seen before. Our model is able to leverage similar relationships it has already seen to detect unseen ones.

Setup. Our test set contains 1,877 relationships that never occur in our training set (e.g. ⟨elephant - stand on - street⟩). These unseen relationships can be

Table 3. Results for zero-shot visual relationship detection (Sect. 5.2). Visual Phrases, Joint CNN and Ours - V + naive FC are omitted from this experiment as they are unable to do zero-shot learning.

	Phrase Det.		Relationship Det.		Predicate Det.	
	R@100	R@50	R@100	R@50	R@100	R@50
Ours - V only	1.12	0.95	0.78	0.67	3.52	3.52
Ours - L only	0.01	0.00	0.01	0.00	5.09	5.09
Ours - V + L only	2.56	2.43	2.66	2.27	6.11	6.11
Ours - V + L + K	**3.75**	**3.36**	**3.52**	**3.13**	**8.45**	**8.45**

inferred by our model using similar relationships (e.g. ⟨dog - stand on - street⟩) from our training set. We report our results for detecting unseen relationships in Table 3 for predicate, phrase, and relationship detection.

Results. (Ours - V) achieves a low 3.52 R@100 in predicate detection because visual appearances are not discriminative enough to predict unseen relationships. (Ours - L only) performs poorly in predicate detection (5.09 R@100) because it automatically returns the most common predicate. By comparing (Ours - V + L+ K) and (Ours - V + L only), we find the use of K gains an improvement of 30% since it utilizes similar relationships to enable zero shot predictions.

5.3 Visual Relationship Detection on Existing Dataset

Our goal in this paper is to understand the rich variety of infrequent relationships. Our comparisons in Sect. 3 show that existing datasets either do not have enough diveristy of predicates per object category or enough relationship types. Therefore, we introduced a new dataset (in Sect. 3) and tested our visual relationship detection model in Sects. 5.1 and 5.2. In this section, we run additional experiments on the existing visual phrases dataset [6] to provide further benchmarks.

Setup. The visual phrase dataset contains 17 phrases (e.g. "dog jumping"). We evaluate the models (introduced in Sect. 5.1) for visual relationship detection on 12 of these phrases that can be represented as a ⟨object₁-predicate-object₂⟩ relationship. To study zero-shot learning, we remove two phrases ("person lying on sofa" and "person lying on beach") from the training set, and attempt to recognize them in the testing set. We report mAP, R@50 and R@100.

Results. In Table 4 we see that our method is able to perform better than the existing Visual Phrases' model even though the dataset is small and contains only 12 relationships. We get a mAP of 0.59 using our entire model as compared to a mAP of 0.38 using Visual Phrases' model. We also outperform the Joint CNN baseline, which achieves a mAP of 0.54. Considering that (Ours - V only) model performs similarly to the baselines, we believe that our full model's improvements on this dataset are heavily influenced by the language priors. By learning to

Table 4. Visual phrase detection results on Visual Phrases dataset [6].

	Phrase detection			Zero-shot phrase detection		
	R@100	R@50	mAP	R@100	R@50	mAP
Visual phrase [6]	52.7	49.3	38.0	-	-	-
Joint CNN	75.3	71.5	54.1	-	-	-
Ours V only	72.0	68.6	53.4	13.5	11.3	5.3
Ours V + naive FC	77.8	73.4	55.8	-	-	-
Ours V + L only	79.3	76.7	57.3	17.8	15.1	8.8
Ours V + L + K	**82.7**	**78.1**	**59.2**	**11.4**	**23.9**	**18.5**

embed similar relationships close to each other, the language model's aid can be thought of as being synonymous to the improvements achieved through training set augmentation. Finally, we see a similar improvements in zero shot learning.

5.4 Image based Retrieval

An important task in computer vision is image retrieval. An improved retrieval model should be able to infer the relationships between objects in images. We will demonstrate that the use of visual relationships can improve retrieval quality.

Setup. Recall that our test set contains 1000 images. Every query uses 1 of these 1000 images and ranks the remaining 999. We use 54 query images in our experiments. Two annotators were asked to rank image results for each of the 54 queries. To avoid bias, we consider the results for a particular query as ground truth only if it was selected by both annotators. We evaluate performance using R@1, R@5 and R@10 and median rank [8]. For comparison, we use three image descriptors that are commonly used in image retrieval: CNN [44], GIST [46] and SIFT [47]. We rank results for a query using the L_2 distance from the query image. Given a query image, our model predicts a set of visual relationships $\{R_1, \ldots, R_n\}$ with a probability of $\{P_1^q, \ldots, P_n^q\}$ respectively. Next, for every

Fig. 7. Examples retrieval results using an image as the query.

Table 5. Example image retrieval using a image of a ⟨`person - ride - horse`⟩ (Sect. 5.4). Note that a *higher* recall and *lower* median rank indicates better performance.

	Recall @ 1	Recall @ 5	Recall @ 10	Median rank
GIST [46]	0.00	5.60	8.70	68
SIFT [47]	0.70	6.10	10.3	54
CNN [44]	3.15	7.70	11.5	20
Visual phrases [6]	8.72	18.12	28.04	12
Our model	**10.82**	**30.02**	**47.00**	**4**

image I_i in our test set, it predicts $R_1, \ldots, R_n$ with a confidence of $\{P_1^i, \ldots, P_n^i\}$. We calculate a matching score between an image with the query as $\sum_{j=1}^{n} P_j^q * P_j^i$. We also compare our model with Visual Phrases' detectors [6].

Results. SIFT [47] and GIST [46] descriptors perform poorly with a median rank of 54 and 68 (Table 5) because they simply measure structural similarity between images. CNN [44] descriptors capture object-level information and performs better with a median rank of 20. Our method captures the visual relationships present in the query image, which is important for high quality image retrieval, improving with a median rank of 4. When queried using an image of a "person riding a horse" (Fig. 7), SIFT returns images that are visually similar but are not semantically relevant. CNN retrieves one image that contains a horse and one that contains both a man and a horse but neither of them capture the relationship: "person riding a horse". Visual Phrases and our model are able to detect the relationship ⟨`person - ride - horse`⟩ and perform better.

6   Conclusion

We proposed a model to detect multiple visual relationships in a single image. Our model learned to detect thousands of relationships even when there were very few training examples. We learned the visual appearance of objects and predicates and combined them to predict relationships. To finetune our predictions, we utilized a language prior that mapped similar relationships together – outperforming previous state of the art [6] on the visual phrases dataset [6] as well as our dataset. We also demonstrated that our model can be used for zero shot learning of visual relationships. We introduced a new dataset with 37, 993 relationships that can be used for further benchmarking. Finally, by understanding visual relationships, our model improved content based image retrieval.

Acknowledgements. Our work is partially funded by an ONR MURI grant.

References

1. Everingham, M., Gool, L., Williams, C.K., Winn, J., Zisserman, A.: The pascal visual object classes (voc) challenge. Int. J. Comput. Vis. **88**(2), 303–338 (2010)
2. Zhou, G., Zhang, M., Ji, D.H., Zhu, Q.: Tree kernel-based relation extraction with context-sensitive structured parse tree information. EMNLP-CoNLL **2007**, 728 (2007)
3. GuoDong, Z., Jian, S., Jie, Z., Min, Z.: Exploring various knowledge in relation extraction. In: Proceedings of the 43rd Annual Meeting on Association for Computational Linguistics, Association for Computational Linguistics, pp. 427–434 (2005)
4. Culotta, A., Sorensen, J.: Dependency tree kernels for relation extraction. In: Proceedings of the 42nd Annual Meeting on Association for Computational Linguistics, Association for Computational Linguistics, p. 423 (2004)
5. Socher, R., Huval, B., Manning, C.D., Ng, A.Y.: Semantic compositionality through recursive matrix-vector spaces. In: Proceedings of the 2012 Joint Conference on Empirical Methods in Natural Language Processing and Computational Natural Language Learning, Association for Computational Linguistics, pp. 1201–1211 (2012)
6. Sadeghi, M.A., Farhadi, A.: Recognition using visual phrases. In: 2011 IEEE Conference on Computer Vision and Pattern Recognition (CVPR), pp. 1745–1752. IEEE (2011)
7. Mikolov, T., Chen, K., Corrado, G., Dean, J.: Efficient estimation of word representations in vector space. arXiv preprint arXiv:1301.3781 (2013)
8. Johnson, J., Krishna, R., Stark, M., Li, L.J., Shamma, D.A., Bernstein, M., Fei-Fei, L.: Image retrieval using scene graphs. In: IEEE Conference on Computer Vision and Pattern Recognition (CVPR) (2015)
9. Mensink, T., Gavves, E., Snoek, C.G.: Costa: Co-occurrence statistics for zero-shot classification. In: 2014 IEEE Conference on Computer Vision and Pattern Recognition (CVPR), pp. 2441–2448. IEEE (2014)
10. Salakhutdinov, R., Torralba, A., Tenenbaum, J.: Learning to share visual appearance for multiclass object detection. In: 2011 IEEE Conference on Computer Vision and Pattern Recognition (CVPR), pp. 1481–1488. IEEE (2011)
11. Ladicky, L., Russell, C., Kohli, P., Torr, P.H.S.: Graph cut based inference with co-occurrence statistics. In: Daniilidis, K., Maragos, P., Paragios, N. (eds.) ECCV 2010, Part V. LNCS, vol. 6315, pp. 239–253. Springer, Heidelberg (2010)
12. Rabinovich, A., Vedaldi, A., Galleguillos, C., Wiewiora, E., Belongie, S.: Objects in context. In: IEEE 11th International Conference on Computer vision, ICCV 2007, pp. 1–8. IEEE (2007)
13. Galleguillos, C., Rabinovich, A., Belongie, S.: Object categorization using co-occurrence, location and appearance. In: IEEE Conference on Computer Vision and Pattern Recognition, CVPR 2008, pp. 1–8. IEEE (2008)
14. Galleguillos, C., Belongie, S.: Context based object categorization: a critical survey. Comput. Vis. Image Underst. **114**(6), 712–722 (2010)
15. Choi, M.J., Lim, J.J., Torralba, A., Willsky, A.S.: Exploiting hierarchical context on a large database of object categories. In: 2010 IEEE Conference on Computer vision and Pattern Recognition (CVPR), pp. 129–136. IEEE (2010)
16. Izadinia, H., Sadeghi, F., Farhadi, A.: Incorporating scene context and object layout into appearance modeling. In: 2014 IEEE Conference on Computer Vision and Pattern Recognition (CVPR), pp. 232–239. IEEE (2014)

17. Fidler, S., Leonardis, A.: Towards scalable representations of object categories: learning a hierarchy of parts. In: IEEE Conference on Computer Vision and Pattern Recognition, CVPR 2007, pp. 1–8. IEEE (2007)
18. Sivic, J., Russell, B.C., Efros, A., Zisserman, A., Freeman, W.T., et al.: Discovering objects and their location in images. In: Tenth IEEE International Conference on Computer Vision, ICCV 2005, vol. 1, pp. 370–377. IEEE (2005)
19. Gould, S., Rodgers, J., Cohen, D., Elidan, G., Koller, D.: Multi-class segmentation with relative location prior. Int. J. Comput. Vis. **80**(3), 300–316 (2008)
20. Rohrbach, M., Qiu, W., Titov, I., Thater, S., Pinkal, M., Schiele, B.: Translating video content to natural language descriptions. In: 2013 IEEE International Conference on Computer Vision (ICCV), pp. 433–440. IEEE (2013)
21. Yao, B., Fei-Fei, L.: Modeling mutual context of object and human pose in human-object interaction activities. In: 2010 IEEE Conference on Computer Vision and Pattern Recognition (CVPR), pp. 17–24. IEEE (2010)
22. Maji, S., Bourdev, L., Malik, J.: Action recognition from a distributed representation of pose and appearance. In: 2011 IEEE Conference on Computer Vision and Pattern Recognition (CVPR), pp. 3177–3184. IEEE (2011)
23. Gupta, A., Kembhavi, A., Davis, L.S.: Observing human-object interactions: using spatial and functional compatibility for recognition. IEEE Trans. Pattern Anal. Mach. Intell. **31**(10), 1775–1789 (2009)
24. Yao, B., Fei-Fei, L.: Grouplet: a structured image representation for recognizing human and object interactions. In: 2010 IEEE Conference on Computer Vision and Pattern Recognition (CVPR), pp. 9–16. IEEE (2010)
25. Ramanathan, V., Li, C., Deng, J., Han, W., Li, Z., Gu, K., Song, Y., Bengio, S., Rossenberg, C., Fei-Fei, L.: Learning semantic relationships for better action retrieval in images. In: Proceedings of the IEEE Conference on Computer Vision and Pattern Recognition, pp. 1100–1109 (2015)
26. Guadarrama, S., Krishnamoorthy, N., Malkarnenkar, G., Venugopalan, S., Mooney, R., Darrell, T., Saenko, K.: Youtube2text: recognizing and describing arbitrary activities using semantic hierarchies and zero-shot recognition. In: 2013 IEEE International Conference on Computer Vision (ICCV), pp. 2712–2719. IEEE (2013)
27. Regneri, M., Rohrbach, M., Wetzel, D., Thater, S., Schiele, B., Pinkal, M.: Grounding action descriptions in videos. Trans. Assoc. Comput. Linguist. **1**, 25–36 (2013)
28. Thomason, J., Venugopalan, S., Guadarrama, S., Saenko, K., Mooney, R.: Integrating language and vision to generate natural language descriptions of videos in the wild. In: Proceedings of the 25th International Conference on Computational Linguistics (COLING), August 2014
29. Yao, J., Fidler, S., Urtasun, R.: Describing the scene as a whole: joint object detection, scene classification and semantic segmentation. In: 2012 IEEE Conference on Computer Vision and Pattern Recognition (CVPR), pp. 702–709. IEEE (2012)
30. Kulkarni, G., Premraj, V., Dhar, S., Li, S., Choi, Y., Berg, A.C., Berg, T.L.: Baby talk: understanding and generating image descriptions. In: Proceedings of the 24th CVPR. Citeseer (2011)
31. Zitnick, C.L., Parikh, D., Vanderwende, L.: Learning the visual interpretation of sentences. In: 2013 IEEE International Conference on Computer Vision (ICCV), pp. 1681–1688. IEEE (2013)
32. Gupta, A., Davis, L.S.: Beyond nouns: exploiting prepositions and comparative adjectives for learning visual classifiers. In: Forsyth, D., Torr, P., Zisserman, A. (eds.) ECCV 2008, Part I. LNCS, vol. 5302, pp. 16–29. Springer, Heidelberg (2008)

33. Kumar, M.P., Koller, D.: Efficiently selecting regions for scene understanding. In: 2010 IEEE Conference on Computer Vision and Pattern Recognition (CVPR), pp. 3217–3224. IEEE (2010)

34. Russell, B.C., Freeman, W.T., Efros, A., Sivic, J., Zisserman, A., et al.: Using multiple segmentations to discover objects and their extent in image collections. In: 2006 IEEE Computer Society Conference on Computer Vision and Pattern Recognition, vol. 2, pp. 1605–1614. IEEE (2006)

35. Farhadi, A., Hejrati, M., Sadeghi, M.A., Young, P., Rashtchian, C., Hockenmaier, J., Forsyth, D.: Every picture tells a story: generating sentences from images. In: Daniilidis, K., Maragos, P., Paragios, N. (eds.) ECCV 2010, Part IV. LNCS, vol. 6314, pp. 15–29. Springer, Heidelberg (2010)

36. Berg, A.C., Berg, T.L., Daume III, H., Dodge, J., Goyal, A., Han, X., Mensch, A., Mitchell, M., Sood, A., Stratos, K., et al.: Understanding and predicting importance in images. In: 2012 IEEE Conference on Computer Vision and Pattern Recognition (CVPR), pp. 3562–3569. IEEE (2012)

37. Hoiem, D., Efros, A.A., Hebert, M.: Putting objects in perspective. Int. J. Comput. Vis. **80**(1), 3–15 (2008)

38. Fang, H., Gupta, S., Iandola, F., Srivastava, R., Deng, L., Dollár, P., Gao, J., He, X., Mitchell, M., Platt, J., et al.: From captions to visual concepts and back. arXiv preprint arXiv:1411.4952 (2014)

39. Chang, A.X., Savva, M., Manning, C.D.: Semantic parsing for text to 3d scene generation. ACL **2014**, 17 (2014)

40. Schuster, S., Krishna, R., Chang, A., Fei-Fei, L., Manning, C.D.: Generating semantically precise scene graphs from textual descriptions for improved image retrieval. In: Proceedings of the Fourth Workshop on Vision and Language (VL 2015) (2015)

41. Choi, W., Chao, Y.W., Pantofaru, C., Savarese, S.: Understanding indoor scenes using 3d geometric phrases. In: 2013 IEEE Conference on Computer Vision and Pattern Recognition (CVPR), pp. 33–40. IEEE (2013)

42. Krishna, R., Zhu, Y., Groth, O., Johnson, J., Hata, K., Kravitz, J., Chen, S., Kalantidis, Y., Li, L.J., Shamma, D.A., Bernstein, M., Fei-Fei, L.: Visual genome: connecting language and vision using crowdsourced dense image annotations. Int. J. Comput. Vis. (2016)

43. Girshick, R., Donahue, J., Darrell, T., Malik, J.: Rich feature hierarchies for accurate object detection and semantic segmentation. In: Computer Vision and Pattern Recognition (2014)

44. Simonyan, K., Zisserman, A.: Very deep convolutional networks for large-scale image recognition. arXiv preprint arXiv:1409.1556 (2014)

45. Alexe, B., Deselaers, T., Ferrari, V.: Measuring the objectness of image windows. IEEE Trans. Pattern Anal. Mach. Intell. **34**(11), 2189–2202 (2012)

46. Oliva, A., Torralba, A.: Modeling the shape of the scene: a holistic representation of the spatial envelope. Int. J. Comput. Vis. **42**(3), 145–175 (2001)

47. Lowe, D.G.: Distinctive image features from scale-invariant keypoints. Int. J. Comput. Vis. **60**(2), 91–110 (2004)

Author Index